M000310117

$100

West's Law School
Advisory Board

JESSE H. CHOPER
Professor of Law,
University of California, Berkeley

DAVID P. CURRIE
Professor of Law, University of Chicago

YALE KAMISAR
Professor of Law, University of San Diego
Professor of Law, University of Michigan

MARY KAY KANE
Chancellor, Dean and Distinguished Professor of Law,
University of California,
Hastings College of the Law

LARRY D. KRAMER
Dean and Professor of Law, Stanford Law School

WAYNE R. LaFAVE
Professor of Law, University of Illinois

JONATHAN R. MACEY
Professor of Law, Yale Law School

ARTHUR R. MILLER
Professor of Law, Harvard University

GRANT S. NELSON
Professor of Law,
University of California, Los Angeles

JAMES J. WHITE
Professor of Law, University of Michigan

PROPERTY LAW

CASES, MATERIALS AND PROBLEMS

Third Edition

By

Sandra H. Johnson

Professor of Law
Tenet Endowed Chair in Health Law and Ethics
Saint Louis University, School of Law

Peter W. Salsich, Jr.

McDonnell Professor of Justice in American Society
Saint Louis University, School of Law

Thomas L. Shaffer

Robert E. & Marion D. Short Professor of Law Emeritus
Notre Dame Law School

Michael Braunstein

Professor of Law
Moritz College of Law
The Ohio State University

Alan M. Weinberger

Associate Dean for Faculty and Professor of Law
Saint Louis University, School of Law

AMERICAN CASEBOOK SERIES®

THOMSON
™
WEST

Mat #40356579

Thomson/West have created this publication to provide you with accurate and authoritative information concerning the subject matter covered. However, this publication was not necessarily prepared by persons licensed to practice law in a particular jurisdiction. Thomson/West are not engaged in rendering legal or other professional advice, and this publication is not a substitute for the advice of an attorney. If you require legal or other expert advice, you should seek the services of a competent attorney or other professional.

American Casebook Series and West Group are trademarks registered in the U.S. Patent and Trademark Office.

COPYRIGHT © 1992 WEST PUBLISHING CO.
© West, a Thomson business, 1998
© 2006 Thomson/West
      610 Opperman Drive
      P.O. Box 64526
      St. Paul, MN 55164–0526
      1–800–328–9352

Printed in the United States of America

ISBN–13: 978-0-314-16011-9
ISBN–10: 0-314-16011-6

 TEXT IS PRINTED ON 10% POST CONSUMER RECYCLED PAPER

To
Anne and Emily
In memory of Professor William Dewey Rollison
In memory of Peter W. Salsich, Sr.
Robin and Noah and Lee
Colin Sprung

*

Preface to the Third Edition

This book is designed for regular first year property law courses, whether they be one-semester, four-hour courses, or two-semester five-or-six hour courses. Basic doctrinal and policy issues respecting property are covered, although some topics are treated in greater detail than others. The topics are arranged in a rather standard order, reflecting the general consensus that possessory and ownership concepts should be mastered before exposure to the common law system of estates in land, the property transfer system, and the rules respecting private and public restrictions on use.

The major innovation of the book is an extensive integration of three related topics, not normally covered in "substantive" first year courses: 1) counseling and planning, 2) legal ethics, and 3) non-adversarial, as well as adversarial, approaches to dispute resolution.

Background material and exercises are provided to introduce students to the planning aspect of property law, including the counseling skill of evaluating the strengths and weaknesses of a range of alternative courses of action for acquiring and disposing of property, and the procedure for planning the process for resolving disputes, e.g., through leases, arrangements for homeowners' associations, co-operative and condominium boards, and collective approaches to land use covenants.

The first year property course provides an ideal vehicle for the introduction of students to ethical and moral issues facing lawyers. Decisions regarding acquisition or disposition of property have lasting consequences for a variety of reasons, including the long term nature of most property transactions, the fact that property transactions, particularly the purchase of a home, often represent the largest investment by a family, and the emphasis on private ownership of property in our legal system. Lawyers have struggled to describe their place in the process, but have had difficulty in doing so. Property transactions tend to produce the largest number of lawyer malpractice complaints, as well as potential for conflicts of interest because of dual representation of buyer and seller or parents and children. Such issues are explored throughout the book as the relevant legal doctrine is covered.

The inclusion of dispute resolution serves a number of purposes. It acquaints students, during their first year of law study, both with techniques of dispute resolution not ordinarily presented in the casebook method of law teaching, and with an expanded, more realistic view of the role of the lawyer outside of litigation. In addition, the students' consideration of dispute avoidance and dispute resolution can lead them to a more sophisticated tolerance for ambiguity in the law as they see the limits of rules in resolving disputes.

In many areas of property law, particularly the acquisition, development, and transfer of land, the lawyer's role is to guide individuals so that their goals can be achieved. In a system that relies so heavily on voluntary transactions, resort to litigation usually is an admission of failure to accomplish a desired result.

Property law presents few legal theories that allow for compromise of claims by the courts. There is no comparative negligence concept, no contributory negligence theory. In part, this is due to the subject matter of the dispute. Rarely are judges or juries in property cases allowed to play Solomon and divide the *res* between the parties. Ownership of property must be clear and undiluted in order to enhance its transferability and productivity. Physical division of property often destroys its value.

In considering how to resolve property disputes, students are exposed to the limits of rules on property relationships. Perhaps because of the doctrinal or rule-oriented nature of property law, students tend to believe that "punching the right buttons" will produce an answer to every property dispute. Problems and questions following the cases are designed to contradict this perception. For example, litigating adverse possession disputes over boundary lines in a residential neighborhood may produce a property winner, but destroy the neighborly relationship in the process.

Exercises in dispute resolution are included to introduce students to skills and methods of dispute resolution and also to reinforce property doctrine by application of that doctrine to the solution of particular problems. For example, landlord-tenant problems provide excellent vehicles for comparing adversarial (arbitration, litigation) techniques for resolving disputes with non-adversarial techniques (mediation, negotiation). Students generally have some familiarity with the emotional and physical settings of landlord-tenant disputes. Parties to a landlord-tenant dispute often desire to maintain their relationship of landlord and tenant after the dispute is resolved. The revolution in landlord-tenant law has changed dramatically the relative bargaining positions of landlord and tenant. Comparative exercises in arbitration and mediation can illustrate these points, as well as provide a useful means of reinforcing the process of learning the law.

The attorney-client relationship is explored in a number of settings, particularly in the acquisition and disposition of property. Questions concerning the lawyer's obligation to be loyal to her clients and to serve the public are raised. Opportunities are presented to discuss the relationship of morality to law, and the concept of law practice as a profession.

The book is shorter than many first year law books for a reason. We wanted the book to serve as a teaching resource rather than as a research tool or a law treatise. Our experience with first year classes persuades us that 10 to 15 pages per 50 minute class is about all that can realistically be covered because of the emphasis placed in the first year on the development of analytical skills. We have edited cases as much as possible and have oriented the notes toward teaching rather than research.

Brackets indicate that only a citation has been omitted. Deletions are noted by ellipses at the point of deletion and by centered ellipses where a paragraph or more has been omitted. Most footnotes have been omitted. Those that are retained have been renumbered consecutively by chapter.

The co-authors are pleased to welcome Professor Alan Weinberger as co-author of this edition. He has made an invaluable contribution to the revision of the book.

We are also grateful to our superb research assistants Zach Best, David Pfeffer and Melanie Rankin. We received excellent staff support from Stephanie Haley, Mary Ann Jauer and Lori Owens. Linda Harrington continued her valuable support for Professor Shaffer's work. Professor Braunstein thanks Pat Schirtzinger, without whose assistance with typing, proofing and administration, this project would never have been completed, and George Hoskins, who has an uncanny ability to find cases with interesting facts, is a great proofreader, and all in all is the most gifted research assistant with whom he has had the good fortune to work.

We hope you will enjoy the study of Property law as much as we do. Property law is a fascinating blend of economics, history, philosophy, and politics. It mirrors society and the tensions among individuals and groups as we struggle to allocate fairly the resources of our planet and to provide opportunities for people to develop their individual talents and interests. Property law is about things, but more importantly, it is about people—with all their accomplishments, foibles, quirks, energy, and spirit.

S.H.J.
P.W.S.
T.L.S.
M.B.
A.M.W.

May, 2006

*

Acknowledgements

Permission to reprint from the following material is gratefully acknowledged.

American Bar Association, Model Rules of Professional Conduct. Copyright © 1983 by the American Bar Association. All rights reserved. Permission to reprint granted by the American Bar Association.

American Land Title Association, Owner's Policy Form from the Understanding the ALTA Title Insurance Policy Forms Handbook. Reprinted with the permission of the American Land Title Association.

Berger, Hard Leases Made Bad Law, Colum.L.Rev. Vol. 74 pp. 814–815 (1974). Copyright © 1974 by the Directors of the Columbia Law Review Association. All Rights Reserved. This article originally appeared at 74 Colum.L.Rev. 791 (1974). Reprinted by permission.

Blanchard and Meehan, Mediation from a Law Student Perspective. Reprinted by permission of the authors.

Boatmen's Residential Note and Mortgage Forms. Reprinted with permission of Boatman's National Bank.

Alexander A. Bove, Jr., The Boston Globe, May 19, 1988. Reprinted with permission of Mr. Bove.

Boyer, Hovenkamp and Kurtz, The Law of Property, Problem 4.8 (1991). Reprinted with permission of West Publishing Co.

Braunstein, Structural Change and Inter-Professional Competitive Advantage: An Example Drawn from Residential Real Estate Conveyancing, 62 Mo.L.Rev. 241–242, 248–250, 259–270 (1997). Copyright 1997 by the Curators of the University of Missouri. Reprinted with permission from the Missouri Law Review.

Brokerage Listing Agreement. Reprinted by permission of the Columbus, Ohio, Board of Realtors.

Brown and Shaffer, Toward a Jurisprudence for the Law Office, 17 American Journal of Jurisprudence 125 (1972).

Cohen, Selections from The Ethicist, a regular column in the New York Times Magazine that is reprinted in the South Bend Tribune.

Dagan & Heller, The Liberal Commons, 110 Yale L.J. 549, 602–610 (2001). Reprinted by permission of the Yale Law Journal Company and William S. Hein Company.

Ellickson, Suburban Growth Controls: An Economic and Legal Analysis. Reprinted from The Yale Law Journal, Vol. 86, pp. 385, 490 (1977) by permission of the Yale Law Journal Company, Fred B. Rothman & Company and the author.

Epstein, Notice and Freedom of Contract in the Law of Servitudes, 55 S.Cal.L.Rev. 1353–1368 (1982), reprinted with the permission of the Southern California Law Review and the author.

Fletcher, "Courthouse Heirs," Va. Lawyers Weekly, July 25, 1988. Reprinted with permission of Paul E. Fletcher and Virginia Lawyers Weekly.

French, Servitudes Reform and the New Restatement of Property, 73 Cornell L.Rev. 928 (1988). Copyright © 1988 by Cornell University. All Rights Reserved. Reprinted by permission of the Cornell Law Review, Fred B. Rothman & Co. and the author.

L. Glantz, Mike Ahab problem. Reprinted with permission of Professor Leonard Glantz, Boston University.

Halper, Can You Find a Fair Lease? 14 Real Est.L.J. 99, 100–101, 121 (1985). Reprinted by permission of the Publisher from the Real Estate Law Journal, volume number 14, "Can You Find a Fair Lease?" © Warren, Gorham & Lamont 1985.

Kmiec, Inserting the Last Remaining Pieces into The Takings Puzzle, 38 Wm. & Mary L.Rev. 995, 1044–1046 (1997). Reprinted with the permission of the William and Mary Law Review and the author.

Kurtz, Moynihan's Introduction to the Law of Real Property 81–82, 89–90, 92–96 (4th Ed. 2005). Reprinted by permission of West Publishing Company.

Malloy & Smith, Real Estate Transactions: Problems, Cases and Materials, 2d Ed., 524–531, 539–545 (2002). Reprinted with the permission of Aspen Publishers, Inc.

Morgan, "The Evolving Concept of Professional Responsibility", 90 Harvard Law Review 702. Copyright © (1977) by the Harvard Law Review Association. Reprinted by permission of the Harvard Law Review Association and the author.

G. Nelson & D. Whitman, Real Estate Finance Law 505–506, 534–538, 776–780 (2d Ed.1985). Reprinted by permission of West Publishing Company.

North Shore Woods Lease, South Bend, Indiana. Reprinted with permission of Joel Bullard, General Partner.

Off Campus Rental Agreement, University of Notre Dame (1988). Reprinted with permission of the University of Notre Dame.

O. Phipps, Titles in a Nutshell 216 (1968). Reprinted with permission of West Publishing Co.

Preble & Cartwright, Convertible and Shared Appreciation Loans: Unclogging The Equity of Redemption, originally published in: 20 Real Prop., Prob. & T.J. 821, 823–824 (1985). Reprinted by permission of the American Bar Association and the authors.

Probate, Trust and Real Property Section, Indiana State Bar, "Uniform Marital Property Act," Res Gestae, November, 1984, p. 237. Reprinted with permission of the Indiana State Bar Association.

Rait, Lollipop Condominiums: Air Rights, The Takings Clause, and Disclosure Under New York's New Guidelines, 17 Real Estate Law Journal 335, 337–340 (1989). Reprinted with permission of Warren Gorham, & Lamont, Inc.

Reichman, Toward a Unified Concept of Servitudes, 55 S.Cal.L.Rev. 1177–1260 (1982), reprinted with the permission of the Southern California Law Review, and the author.

Restatement (Second) of Property §§ 5.4, 6.1 Comment (d), 450, 476, 535, 547. Copyright by the American Law Institute. Reprinted with the permission of the American Law Institute.

Restatement (Third) of Property §§ 1.2(1), 1.4, 2.4, 2.6(e), 2.12, 2.14–15, 3.4–.5, 4.10, 5.3–.4, 7.3–7.8. Copyright by The American Law Institute. Reprinted with the permission of The American Law Institute.

Riskin, Mediation and Lawyers, 43 Ohio State L.J. 29–30, 34–36 (1982). Originally published at 43 Ohio St.L.J. 29 (1982). Reprinted by permission of the Ohio State Law Journal and the author.

Riskin & Westbrook, Instructor's Manual, Dispute Resolution and Lawyers, 277–286, 398, 402–404, 544–556 (1987). Reprinted by permission of West Publishing Company.

Salsich, Keystone Bituminous Coal, First English and Nollan: A Framework for Accommodation? 34 J.Urb. & Contemp.L. 173, 187–190 (1988).

Salsich, Life After The Takings Trilogy—A Hierarchy of Property Interests? 19 Stetson L.Rev. 795, 811 (1990). Reprinted with permission from Stetson Law Review.

Salsich and Fitzgerald, Mediation of Landlord-Tenant Disputes, 19 Creighton L.Rev. 791–95, 809–15 (1986). Reprinted from Creighton Law Review by permission. Copyright © 1986 by Creighton University School of Law.

Salsich & Tryniecki, Land Use Regulation, 245–247, 352–353 (2nd Ed. 2003). Reprinted by permission © 2003 by the American Bar Association.

Shaffer, The Ethics of Estate Planning, Probate Notes, American College of Probate Counsel, Spring, 1979, p. 19. Reprinted with permission of The American College of Probate Counsel.

Shaffer, American Legal Ethics 453–455 (1985). Copyright © 1985 by Matthew Bender & Company, Inc. Reprinted with permission.

Shaffer, Using the Pervasive Method of Teaching Legal Ethics in a Property Course, 46 St. Louis U.L.J. 656, 661–664 (2002). Reprinted with permission of Saint Louis University Law Journal.

Shaffer and Cochran, Lawyers, Clients, And Moral Responsibility, 113–134 (© 1994, West Publishing Co.). Reprinted with permission of West Publishing Company.

Shaffer and Mooney, The Planning and Drafting of Wills and Trusts 173–179 (3d ed. 1991). Reprinted with permission of the Foundation Press, Inc.

Sterk, "Freedom from Freedom of Contract," 70 Iowa L.Rev. 615 (1985) (reprinted with permission).

Stoebuck & Whitman, The Law of Property, 3d Ed., 367–370 (2000). Reprinted by permission of West Publishing Company.

Thompson, Crisis in Rural America: The Genesis of Farmer-Lender Mediation, Nat. Inst. for Dispute Rev., FORUM, p. 4 (Fall 1990).

Underkuffler, On Property: An Essay, 100 Yale L.J. 127, 130–131, 143 (1990). Reprinted with permission from Yale Law Journal.

Uniform Residential Landlord and Tenant Act, 7B Uniform Laws Annotated 460–461, 474–477 (1985). Reprinted by permission of West Publishing Company. This Act has been reprinted through the permission of the National Conference of Commissioners on Uniform State Laws, and copies of the Act may be ordered from them at a nominal cost at 676 North St. Clair Street, Suite 1700, Chicago, Illinois 60611, (312) 915–0195.

Uniform Vendor and Purchaser Risk Act. This Act has been reprinted through the permission of the National Conference of Commissioners on Uniform State Laws, and copies of the Act may be ordered from them at a nominal cost at 676 North St. Clair Street, Suite 1700, Chicago, Illinois 60611, (312) 915–0195.

Summary of Contents

Table of Contents

Page

*

Table of Cases

The principal cases are in bold type. Cases cited or discussed in the text are roman type. References are to pages. Cases cited in principal cases and within other quoted materials are not included.

PROPERTY LAW

CASES, MATERIALS AND PROBLEMS

Third Edition

*

Chapter One

BASIC PROPERTY CONCEPTS: POSSESSION AND OWNERSHIP

When we think of "property," we often think of things like "my house," "your car," "our land," "her iPod." This instinctive notion of property, however, doesn't really serve us well when we study property law. It is much too limited in a number of ways.

First, U.S. property law does not refer only to tangible things we can hold in our hands or sit on or walk upon. Property also consists of things that we cannot see or touch, but which are protected as property in our system. One of the major forms of intangible property in the U.S. system is intellectual property—the fruits or expressions of creative work. "Her iPod" provides us with many examples. The creative work expressed in the melody, arrangement, and lyrics of the music she listens to is protected *as property* through copyright laws. The engineering creativity and expertise required to write the software or design the hardware that makes the iPod work is protected *as property* either through copyright or through patent laws or both. Just as one can break the law by stealing an iPod, one who steals, or copies, the creative work of another can be in violation of the inventor's or creator's property rights. Many high-profile cases currently bear witness to the centrality of intellectual property in 21st century commerce, whether it is the battle over the Google Library, or over the Blackberry, or over the control of DNA sequences. Concepts of property are used as well to protect such intangibles as a lawyer's, doctor's or horse trainer's interest in her professional license or a celebrity's interest in the use of his identity or fame.

Second, we often operate as well with the assumption that the owner of property is either obvious or is simply a question of investigation—even where ownership might be confused in the mists of time or the movement of natural boundaries. Our common experience is that we can discover who the true owner is simply by getting the records straight. Instead, as you will see, identifying the owner can be a political and philosophical challenge. If you have been around children, you know that they often have an intense awareness of "ownership." It is not uncommon to overhear wails of "It's mine!" "No, it's mine!" How have you as a parent, a teacher, or just an adult bystander resolved those disputes? If you believe those who are displeased with your decision, you simply chose the one you liked the best. You may have chosen on the basis of merit, whatever that meant in the particular situation. Or, you may have chosen the oldest or the youngest; the one who needed it the most; the one who could make the best use of the thing; the one who had expended the most effort to get the thing; or the one who had it first.

New property is being created at breakneck speed. Whether it is an item that has been presumed valueless (such as waste now convertible to fuel, or the nuisance that is now valuable crude oil or the detritus of surgically removed tissue) or an item that is newly "discovered" (such as the "New World," or DNA sequences, or mineral nodules on the deep sea floor) or an item that seems to have been orphaned (such as a Barry Bonds home run ball flying to the outfield or a sapphire broach in the safe on the Titanic), conflicts over ownership are likely to follow the increase in value.

Third, property law does not so much focus on the thing, but rather upon the relationship among persons as to a thing. The property is not only the thing itself—the house, the car, the land, the iPod—but rather the rights that the owner holds in relation to these goods. U.S. law operates primarily out of a concept that property is a "bundle of sticks," an aggregation of rights, including the right to transfer, the right to possess, the right to use, and the right to exclude. These rights can be divided among individuals, just as land can be physically divided into parcels.

Each case in this first chapter provides responses to each one of the following questions in different contexts: Should the subject or object in dispute be treated as "property?" Who is the owner? What does it mean to be the owner of this property? To facilitate your study of each question, however, the cases are organized under the question that is the particular emphasis of that case.

These cases also provide an opportunity for examining the role that the concept of property plays in our system and the variety of competing ideas concerning property and the allocation of ownership rights. You may develop a sense in this chapter that property law is extraordinarily malleable and that the concept of property is infinitely elastic. Reserve judgment. In the chapters that follow this introduction, you will see some strong counterweights to flexibility and change in property law. These opposing forces are stability and predictability, and they tend to take a stronger hand in some property controversies than in others.

I. IS IT PROPERTY?

MOORE v. REGENTS OF THE UNIVERSITY OF CALIFORNIA

Court of Appeal, Second District, Division 4, California, 1988.
249 Cal.Rptr. 494.

Ed. note: We have provided edited versions from both the California Court of Appeals decision and the California Supreme Court opinion in this case. You decide which is the more persuasive.

* * *

In 1976, plaintiff and appellant sought medical treatment at the Medical Center of the University of California, Los Angeles (UCLA), * * * for a condition known as hairy-cell leukemia. He was seen by Dr. David W. Golde, who confirmed the diagnosis. As a necessary part of the treatment for this disease, plaintiff's spleen was removed at UCLA in October of 1976.

Without plaintiff's knowledge or consent, Dr. Golde and Shirley G. Quan, a UCLA employee, * * * developed a cell-line from plaintiff's cells which is capable of producing pharmaceutical products of enormous therapeutic and commercial value. * * * The Regents, Golde and Quan patented the cell-line along with methods of producing many products therefrom. In addition, these defendants entered into a series of commercial agreements for rights to the cell-line and its products * * *. The market potential of products from plaintiff's cell-line was predicted to be approximately three billion dollars by 1990. Hundreds of thousands of dollars have already been paid under these agreements to the developers. Without informing plaintiff, and in pursuit of their research efforts, Golde and UCLA continued to monitor him and take tissue samples from him for almost seven years following the removal of his spleen.

* * *

Plaintiff alleges that his Blood and Bodily Substances, including but not limited to his blood, blood components, by-products, bodily tissues, lymphokines, genetic material, genetic sequences, conditioned medium, spleen, sperm, bone marrow aspirate, and other substances derived from his Blood and Bodily Substances, are his tangible personal property, and the activities of the defendants as set forth herein constitute a substantial interference with plaintiff's possession or right thereto, as well as defendants' wrongful exercise of dominion over plaintiff's personal property rights in his Blood and Bodily Substances.

According to the complaint, plaintiff's cell-line and the products from it were not developed through any extraordinary scientific methodology invented or employed by defendants, nor created by defendants. The cell-line and products were obtained exclusively through live specimens and samples of plaintiff's blood and bodily substances. Plaintiff alleged damages, including lost profits, and punitive damages.

* * *

In deciding whether plaintiff can state a cause of action for conversion on the facts set forth in his complaint, it is necessary to review the requirements of conversion.

Conversion is "a distinct act of dominion wrongfully exerted over another's personal property in denial of or inconsistent with his title or rights therein, ... without the owner's consent and without lawful justification." [   ] It is " 'an act of wilful interference with a chattel, done without lawful justification, by which any person entitled thereto is deprived of use and possession.' " [   ]

For conversion, a plaintiff need only allege: "(1) plaintiffs' ownership or right to possession of the property at the time of the conversion; (2) defendants' conversion by a wrongful act or disposition of plaintiffs' property rights; and (3) damages. [   ]"

* * *

The foundation for the action of conversion rests neither in the knowledge nor the intent of the defendant. It rests upon the unwarranted interference by defendant with the dominion over the property of the plaintiff from which injury to the latter results. [   ]

* * *

As the ensuing analysis will establish, we have concluded that plaintiff's allegation of a property right in his own tissue is sufficient as a matter of law. We have been cited to no legal authority, public policy, nor universally known facts of biological science concerning the particular tissues referred to in this pleading [   ] which compel a conclusion that this plaintiff cannot have a sufficient legal interest in his own bodily tissues amounting to personal property. Absent plaintiff's consent to defendants' disposition of the tissues, or lawful justification, such as abandonment, * * * the complaint adequately pleads all the elements of a cause of action for conversion.

We have approached this issue with caution. The evolution of civilization from slavery to freedom, from regarding people as chattels to recognition of the individual dignity of each person, necessitates prudence in attributing the qualities of property to human tissue. There is, however, a dramatic difference between having property rights in one's own body and being the property of another. To our knowledge, no public policy has ever been articulated, nor is there any statutory authority, against a property interest in one's own body. * * *

Until recently, the physical human body, as distinguished from the mental and spiritual, was believed to have little value, other than as a source of labor. In recent history, we have seen the human body assume astonishing aspects of value. Taking the facts of this case, for instance, we are told that John Moore's mere cells could become the foundation of a multi-billion dollar industry from which patent holders could reap fortunes. For better or worse, we have irretrievably entered an age that requires examination of our understanding of the legal rights and relationships in the human body and the human cell.

* * *

"As a matter of legal definition, 'property' refers not to a particular material object but to the right and interest or domination rightfully obtained over such object, with the unrestricted right to its use, enjoyment and disposition. In other words, [in] its strict legal sense 'property' signifies that dominion or indefinite right of use, control, and disposition which one may lawfully exercise over particular things or objects; thus 'property' is nothing more than a collection of rights." [   ]

The definitions of property are not restrictive and exclusive. "In legal usage, the word 'property' is a term of broad and extensive application, and it is also a term of large import, with the very broadest and most extensive signification." [   ]

[California] Civil Code section 654 defines property as follows: "The ownership of a thing is the right of one or more persons to possess and use it to the exclusion of others. In this Code, the thing of which there may be ownership is called property." Civil Code section 14, subdivision (3) provides: "The words 'personal property' include money, goods, chattels, things in action, and evidences of debt...." * * * These sections have been interpreted to mean that "the word 'property' is a generic term which includes anything subject to ownership...." [   ]

Property is " 'every species of right and interest capable of being enjoyed as such upon which it is practicable to place a money value.' " [   ]

The rights of dominion over one's own body, and the interests one has therein, are recognized in many cases. These rights and interests are so akin to property interests that it would be a subterfuge to call them something else.

Venner v. State [   ] involved determination of whether police illegally seized narcotics filled balloons found with defendant's feces in a hospital bedpan. The court dealt with the question of whether the balloons were abandoned. In discussing this point, the court noted: "It could not be said that a person has no property right in wastes or other materials which were once a part of or contained within his body, but which normally are discarded after their separation from the body. It is not unknown for a person to assert a continuing right of ownership, dominion, or control, for good reason or for no reason, over such things as excrement, fluid waste, secretions, hair, fingernails, toenails, blood, and organs or other parts of the body, whether their separation from the body is intentional, accidental, or merely the result of normal body functions." [   ]

Although the subject matter here does not equate with or have the dignity of the human cell, the legal significance of this reference is the court's statement that it *cannot* be said that a person has no property right in materials which were once part of his body.

In *Bouvia v. Superior Court* [   ] the court confirmed the long established rule that: " '[A] person of adult years and in sound mind has the right, in the exercise of control over his own body, to determine whether or not to submit to lawful medical treatment.' It follows that such a patient has the right to refuse *any* medical treatment, even that which may save or prolong her life. [   ] The court reiterated Judge Cardozo's statement in *Schloendorff v. Society of New York Hospital* [   ] that: 'Every human being of adult years and sound mind has a right to determine what shall be done with his own body....' " [   ] This control of one's own body is certainly an incident of interest in property.

* * *

The essence of a property interest—the ultimate right of control—therefore exists with regard to one's own human body.

Even though the rights and interests one has over one's own body may be subject to important limitations because of public health concerns, the absence of unlimited or unrestricted dominion and control does not negate the existence of a property right for the purpose of a conversion action. [   ]

Defendants' position that plaintiff cannot own his tissue, but that they can, is fraught with irony. Apparently, defendants see nothing abnormal in their exclusive control of plaintiff's excised spleen, nor in their patenting of a living organism derived therefrom. We cannot reconcile defendant's assertion of what appears to be their property interest in removed tissue and the resulting cell-line with their contention that the source of the material has no rights therein.

Defendants also claim that plaintiff cannot have an interest in the cell-line derived from his tissues since he is only the source of the thing studied. "Thus, the cells involved have no inherent value until a cell line is derived and created to produce useful products. Plaintiff tries to obscure this unassailable fact by creating the impression his cells *themselves* have miraculous curative powers...." (Emphasis in original.)

Defendants contend that plaintiff has no property right in the knowledge gained or the new things made in the course of the study of his cells. This is an inaccurate characterization of this case. Plaintiff's complaint does not allege a conversion of ideas gained from study of his cells, but conversion of the cells, and their progeny, themselves. Plaintiff was not simply the object of study to increase knowledge. His spleen and cells were taken by defendants to their laboratory, where they extracted his genetic material, placed it in a growth medium, and, by cell division, created an "immortal" cell-line—one that could forever produce products of enormous commercial value to defendants. * * *

Human cells were essential to the creation of the cell-line. * * * Without these small indispensable pieces of plaintiff, there could have been no three billion dollar cell-line.

The fact that defendants' skill and efforts modified the tissue and enhanced its value does not negate the existence of a conversion. Any questions as to defendants' alteration of plaintiff's tissue go to what damages, if any, he might be entitled if successful at trial. * * *

Defendants further contend that plaintiff's spleen could not be converted because, being diseased, it was a thing of no value. The allegations in the complaint, however, indicate the opposite is true. While removal of plaintiff's spleen may have been necessary to the treatment of his disease, the cells it contained became the foundation of a multi-billion dollar industry. The extraordinary lengths to which defendants went to obtain a specimen for their work shows their belief in its value. This belief has proven correct. The fact the spleen was at one time of little utility to plaintiff does not mean its value was so minimal it could not be converted.

[Defendants also contended that the plaintiff did not have a property interest in his DNA. In responding, the court referred to state law recognizing the right of publicity at issue in the *Midler* case, *infra*.] Plaintiff's cells and genes are part of his person. * * * If the courts have found a sufficient proprietary interest in one's persona, how could one not have a right in one's own genetic material, something far more profoundly the essence of one's human uniqueness than a name or a face?

A patient must have the ultimate power to control what becomes of his or her tissues. To hold otherwise would open the door to a massive invasion of human privacy and dignity in the name of medical progress.

* * *

[The defendants also claimed that Moore had "abandoned" his spleen when it was surgically removed. Because abandonment of property requires intent to do so, the court concludes that Moore did not abandon his property.]

The judgments of dismissal are reversed with directions to the trial court to take proceedings consistent with the views set forth in the foregoing opinion.

MOORE v. REGENTS OF THE UNIVERSITY OF CALIFORNIA

Supreme Court of California, 1992.
51 Cal.3d 120, 271 Cal.Rptr. 146, 793 P.2d 479.

* * *

* * * [Early on in the course of treating Moore] all defendants, including Golde, were aware that "certain blood products and blood components were of great value in a number of commercial and scientific efforts" and that access to a patient whose blood contained these substances would provide "competitive, commercial, and scientific advantages." [Dr. Golde told Moore only that his spleen needed to be removed to slow the course of his disease.]

Before the operation, Golde and Quan "formed the intent and made arrangements to obtain portions of [Moore's] spleen following its removal'' and to take them to a separate research unit. Golde gave written instructions to this effect on October 18 and 19, 1976. These research activities "were not intended to have * * * any relation to [Moore's] medical * * * care." However, neither Golde nor Quan informed Moore of their plans to conduct this research or requested his permission. * * *

Moore returned to the UCLA Medical Center several times between November 1976 and September 1983. He did so at Golde's direction and based upon representations "that such visits were necessary and required for his health and well-being, and based upon the trust inherent in and by virtue of the physician-patient relationship. * * * " On each of these visits Golde withdrew additional samples of "blood, blood serum, skin, bone marrow aspirate, and sperm." On each occasion Moore traveled to the UCLA Medical Center from his home in Seattle because he had been told that the procedures were to be performed only there and only under Golde's direction.

"In fact, [however,] throughout the period of time that [Moore] was under [Golde's] care and treatment, * * * the defendants were actively involved in a number of activities which they concealed from [Moore] * * *." Specifically, defendants were conducting research on Moore's cells and planned to "benefit financially and competitively * * * [by exploiting the cells] and [their] exclusive access to [the cells] by virtue of [Golde's] on-going physician-patient relationship. * * * "

Sometime before August 1979, Golde established a cell line from Moore's T-lymphocytes. On January 30, 1981, the Regents applied for a patent on the cell line, listing Golde and Quan as inventors. "[B]y virtue of an established policy * * *, [the] Regents, Golde, and Quan would share in any royalties or profits * * * arising out of [the] patent." The patent issued on March 20, 1984, naming Golde and Quan as the inventors of the cell line and the Regents as the assignee of the patent. * * *

* * *

Based upon these allegations, Moore attempted to state 13 causes of action. * * *

* * *

[Editor's note: The Supreme Court holds that Moore did state a claim for breach of fiduciary duty and lack of informed consent based on the defendant physicians' failure to disclose their intended use of his body fluids and tissue. Only the portion of the opinion that concerns conversion is reproduced here.]

1. MOORE'S CLAIM UNDER EXISTING LAW

"To establish a conversion, plaintiff must establish an actual interference with his *ownership or right of possession.* * * * Where plaintiff neither has title to the property alleged to have been converted, nor possession thereof, he cannot maintain an action for conversion." [   ]

Since Moore clearly did not expect to retain possession of his cells following their removal, to sue for their conversion he must have retained an ownership interest in them. But there are several reasons to doubt that he did retain any such interest. First, no reported judicial decision supports Moore's claim, either directly or by close analogy. Second, California statutory law drastically limits any continuing interest of a patient in excised cells. Third, the subject matters of the Regents' patent—the patented cell line and the products derived from it—cannot be Moore's property.

Neither the Court of Appeal's opinion, the parties' briefs, nor our research discloses a case holding that a person retains a sufficient interest in excised cells to support a cause of action for conversion. We do not find this surprising, since the laws governing such things as human tissues, transplantable organs, blood, fetuses, pituitary glands, corneal tissue, and dead bodies deal with human biological materials as objects sui generis, regulating their disposition to achieve policy goals rather than abandoning them to the general law of personal property. It is these specialized statutes, not the law of conversion, to which courts ordinarily should and do look for guidance on the disposition of human biological materials.

* * *

The next consideration that makes Moore's claim of ownership problematic is California statutory law, which drastically limits a patient's control over excised cells. Pursuant to Health and Safety Code section 7054.4, "[n]otwithstanding any other provision of law, recognizable anatomical parts, human tissues, anatomical human remains, or infectious waste following conclusion of scientific use shall be disposed of by interment, incineration, or any other method determined by the state department [of health services] to protect the public health and safety." Clearly the Legislature did not specifically intend this statute to resolve the question of whether a patient is entitled to compensation for the nonconsensual use of excised cells. A primary object of the statute is to ensure the safe handling of potentially hazardous biological waste materials. Yet one cannot escape the conclusion that the statute's practical effect is to limit, drastically, a patient's control over excised cells. By restricting how excised cells may be used and requiring their eventual destruction, the statute eliminates so many of the rights ordinarily attached to property that one cannot simply assume that what is left amounts to "property" or "ownership" for purposes of conversion law.

It may be that some limited right to control the use of excised cells does survive the operation of this statute. There is, for example, no need to read the statute to permit "scientific use" contrary to the patient's expressed wish. A fully informed patient may always withhold consent to treatment by a physician whose research plans the patient does not approve. That right, however, * * * is protected by the fiduciary-duty and informed-consent theories.

Finally, the subject matter of the Regents' patent—the patented cell line and the products derived from it—cannot be Moore's property. This is because the patented cell line is both factually and legally distinct from the cells taken from Moore's body.[1] Federal law permits the patenting of organisms that represent the product of "human ingenuity," but not naturally occurring organisms. [ ] * * * It is this *inventive effort* that patent law rewards, not the discovery of naturally occurring raw materials. Thus, Moore's allegations that he owns the cell line and the products derived from it are inconsistent with the patent, which constitutes an authoritative determination that the cell line is the product of invention. * * *

2.   SHOULD CONVERSION LIABILITY BE EXTENDED?

* * *

There are three reasons why it is inappropriate to impose liability for conversion based upon the allegations of Moore's complaint. First, a fair balancing of the relevant policy considerations counsels against extending the tort. Second, problems in this area are better suited to legislative resolution. Third, the tort of conversion is not necessary to protect patients' rights. For these reasons, we conclude that the use of excised human cells in medical research does not amount to a conversion.

Of the relevant policy considerations, two are of overriding importance. The first is protection of a competent patient's right to make autonomous medical decisions. That right * * * is grounded in well-recognized and long-standing principles of fiduciary duty and informed consent. [ ] This policy weighs in favor of providing a remedy to patients when physicians act with undisclosed motives that may affect their professional judgment. The second important policy consideration is that we not threaten with disabling civil liability innocent parties who are engaged in socially useful activities, such as researchers who have no reason to believe that their use of a particular cell sample is, or may be, against a donor's wishes.

* * *

[A]n examination of the relevant policy considerations suggests an appropriate balance: Liability based upon existing disclosure obligations,

---

1. The distinction between primary cells (cells taken directly from the body) and patented cell lines is not purely a legal one. Cells change while being developed into a cell line and continue to change over time. [ ] * * * The cell line in this case, for example, after many replications began to generate defective and rearranged forms of the HTLV–II virus. A published research paper to which defendants contributed suggests that "the defective forms of virus were probably gen-

erated during the passage [or replication] of the cells rather than being present in the original tumor cells of the patient." Possibly because of these changes in the virus, the cell line has developed new abilities to grow in different media. (Chen, McLaughlin, Gasson, Clark & Golde, Molecular Characterization of Genome of a Novel Human T-cell Leukaemia Virus, Nature (Oct. 6, 1983) vol. 305, p. 505.)

* * *

rather than an unprecedented extension of the conversion theory protects patients' rights of privacy and autonomy without unnecessarily hindering research.

To be sure, the threat of liability for conversion might help to enforce patients' rights indirectly. This is because physicians might be able to avoid liability by obtaining patients' consent, in the broadest possible terms, to any conceivable subsequent research use of excised cells. Unfortunately, to extend the conversion theory would utterly sacrifice the other goal of protecting innocent parties. Since conversion is a strict liability tort, it would impose liability on all those into whose hands the cells come, whether or not the particular defendant participated in, or knew of, the inadequate disclosures that violated the patient's right to make an informed decision. In contrast to the conversion theory, the fiduciary-duty and informed-consent theories protect the patient directly, without punishing innocent parties or creating disincentives to the conduct of socially beneficial research.

* * *

* * * Since the patent office requires the holders of patents on cell lines to make samples available to anyone, many patent holders place their cell lines in repositories to avoid the administrative burden of responding to requests. At present, human cell lines are routinely copied and distributed to other researchers for experimental purposes, usually free of charge. This exchange of scientific materials, which still is relatively free and efficient, will surely be compromised if each cell sample becomes the potential subject matter of a lawsuit. [   ]²

* * * So long as a physician discloses research and economic interests that may affect his judgment, the patient is protected from conflicts of interest. Aware of any conflicts, the patient can make an informed decision to consent to treatment, or to withhold consent and look elsewhere for medical assistance. As already discussed, enforcement of physicians' disclosure obligations protects patients directly, without hindering the socially useful activities of innocent researchers.

For these reasons, we hold that the allegations of Moore's third amended complaint state a cause of action for breach of fiduciary duty or lack of informed consent, but not conversion.

* * *

ARABIAN, JUSTICE, concurring.

2. * * * The availability of patent protection for cell lines actually *increases* the availability of research materials, since the Patent Office requires patent holders to make patented microorganisms available to researchers immediately after a patent issues. [   ] Generally available cell lines are of substantial importance not just to academic research, but to commercial research as well. Indeed, some biotechnology companies "do not use any original human tissue in research, concentrating their efforts on established cell lines instead. These companies obtain and manipulate generally available cell lines, resulting in new, unique, or improved cell lines." [   ]

Plaintiff has asked us to recognize and enforce a right to sell one's own body tissue *for profit*. He entreats us to regard the human vessel—the single most venerated and protected subject in any civilized society—as equal with the basest commercial commodity. He urges us to commingle the sacred with the profane. He asks much.

* * *

MOSK, JUSTICE, dissenting.

* * *

The concepts of property and ownership in our law are extremely broad. [   ]* * *

Being broad, the concept of property is also abstract: rather than referring directly to a material object such as a parcel of land or the tractor that cultivates it, the concept of property is often said to refer to a "bundle of rights" that may be exercised with respect to that object—principally the rights to possess the property, to use the property, to exclude others from the property, and to dispose of the property by sale or by gift. * * * But the same bundle of rights does not attach to all forms of property. For a variety of policy reasons, the law limits or even forbids the exercise of certain rights over certain forms of property. For example, both law and contract may limit the right of an owner of real property to use his parcel as he sees fit [citing zoning, nuisance and real covenants]. Owners of various forms of personal property may likewise be subject to restrictions on the time, place, and manner of their use [citing public health and safety regulations]. Limitations on the disposition of real property, while less common, may also be imposed [citing condominium agreements]. Finally, some types of personal property may be sold but not given away, [citing property in bankruptcy] while others may be given away but not sold, [citing wild fish and game captured by sports people] and still others may neither be given away nor sold [citing professional licenses].

In each of the foregoing instances, the limitation or prohibition diminishes the bundle of rights that would otherwise attach to the property, yet what remains is still deemed in law to be a protectible property interest. * * * The same rule applies to Moore's interest in his own body tissue: even if we assume that section 7054.4 limited the use and disposition of his excised tissue in the manner claimed by the majority, Moore nevertheless retained valuable rights in that tissue. Above all, at the time of its excision he at least had *the right to do with his own tissue whatever the defendants did with it:* i.e., he could have contracted with researchers and pharmaceutical companies to develop and exploit the vast commercial potential of his tissue and its products. Defendants certainly believe that *their* right to do the foregoing is not barred by section 7054.4 and is a significant property right, as they have demonstrated by their deliberate concealment from Moore of the true value of his tissue, their efforts to obtain a patent on the Mo cell line, their contractual agreements to exploit this material, their exclusion of

Moore from any participation in the profits, and their vigorous defense of this lawsuit.

* * *

In any event, in my view whatever merit the majority's single policy consideration may have is outweighed by two contrary considerations, i.e., policies that are promoted by recognizing that every individual has a legally protectible property interest in his own body and its products. First, our society acknowledges a profound ethical imperative to respect the human body as the physical and temporal expression of the unique human persona. One manifestation of that respect is our prohibition against direct abuse of the body by torture or other forms of cruel or unusual punishment. Another is our prohibition against indirect abuse of the body by its economic exploitation for the sole benefit of another person. The most abhorrent form of such exploitation, of course, was the institution of slavery. Lesser forms, such as indentured servitude or even debtor's prison, have also disappeared. Yet their specter haunts the laboratories and boardrooms of today's biotechnological research-industrial complex. It arises wherever scientists or industrialists claim, as defendants claim here, the right to appropriate and exploit a patient's tissue for their sole economic benefit.

Notes and Questions

1. Both the appellate court and the supreme court agreed that there was no case or statute directly on point for this case. In the absence of prior law, a metaphorical legal fork in the road confronted these courts. Each took a different road—one finding in the absence of controlling precedent or statute that a property right should be found; and the other, holding the opposite in part because there was no authoritative statute or case law. As a matter of legal process, which is the better approach?

2. What property did John Moore claim? Was it the same property that the defendants claimed? What relief does Moore claim? Does he want his spleen back, in terms of its value when it was removed? Or, is he claiming that he is an owner of the cell line developed from his tissue and is entitled to its current value? What's the difference between giving Moore damages for failure of informed consent and giving him a partial or total ownership interest in the cell line? What did the scientists do to the excised tissue to be entitled to ownership of the cell line, even to the exclusion of Moore? How does their effort support a claim of ownership?

3. What is the holding of the California Supreme Court in this case? Does Moore have any legally enforceable right to transfer or sell his tissue? Consider the following scenarios:

    (a) Assume that John Moore, David Golde, and UCLA had actually entered into an agreement concerning the use of Moore's body fluids and tissues that provided that John Moore was to get a small percentage of payments received by Golde or UCLA for products developed from his cells. If UCLA and Golde had refused to pay the amount agreed upon, do you think that the California Supreme Court would refuse to enforce the agreement?

(b) Assume that David Golde and UCLA meet another patient with the potential of John Moore. How should they handle the situation? The majority opinion in *Moore* holds that they must disclose to the patient Dr. Golde's participation in research. If university counsel drafts a disclosure document that is accurate and understandable and the patient understands the situation and signs the document giving the researchers the right to the desired tissue, both the treatment and the research can proceed. What if the patient refuses to consent unless he is compensated? Can the university pay him? Would you treat this situation any differently than the previous one?

(c) The California Court of Appeals held that Moore had a property interest, and the Supreme Court held that he didn't. Did it really matter which result the courts reached in terms of future relationships between researchers and patients as long as they established a clear rule?

4. Although we refer to the interests protected by copyright, patents, trademarks, and the right to publicity as property in our discussion here, the propertization of "intellectual *property*" is not necessarily a given. While the property concept is widely and deeply embedded in the intellectual property field at this point, it is a development that is receiving mixed reviews. See, generally, Michael Carrier, Cabining Intellectual Property Through a Property Paradigm, 54 Duke L. J. 1 (2004).

5. *Moore* is often viewed as presenting the question of whether human tissue or body parts can be "property." This concern is evident in Justice Arabian's concurring opinion to the Supreme Court decision, for example. In fact, California law does recognize that human tissue can be property. See, for example, Hecht v. Superior Court, 16 Cal.App.4th 836, 20 Cal.Rptr.2d 275 (1993), in which the court distinguished *Moore* to hold that, because of its ability to produce life, sperm is unique property. In *Hecht*, the donor deposited his sperm in a sperm bank before committing suicide. In his will, he specified that the sperm should be released to the woman with whom he had been living in the event that she decided to bear his child. The administrator of the estate and the donor's two adult children sought an order for the sperm to be destroyed. They argued that, according to *Moore*, the donor had no property interest in his sperm once it left his body, so he did not have the right to mandate how it was used. The court held that men who use sperm banks to store sperm for their own future use maintain property rights in the sperm, so the donor retained decision making authority as to the use of the sperm for reproduction.

The issue of property rights in the body also arises in the removal of tissue or organs from deceased persons. In Newman v. Sathyavaglswaran, 287 F.3d 786 (9th Cir. 2002), the federal court concluded that California law does recognize "quasi property" rights in the human body and held that the family of a deceased man whose corneas were taken without his or their permission had a cause of action for the deprivation of property without due process. Should this situation be treated differently from other claims that the human body is property? For discussion, see Note, "She's Got Bette Davis['s] Eyes:" Assessing the Nonconsensual Removal of Cadaver Organs under the Takings and Due Process Clauses, 90 Colum.L.Rev. 528 (1990). Because the supply of transplantable human organs still falls far short of the numbers required, there have been some proposals that human organs should be viewed as property subject to sale. Federal law currently prohibits the sale of organs for transplant. 42 U.S.C. § 274(e). At the same time, neither federal nor state law prohibits the sale of blood, semen or ova. Should the prohibitions on the sale of organs for transplant be continued? Should it be extended to other tissue or body fluids? For discussion see, David Kasserman, Markets for Organs: Myths and Misconceptions, 18 J. Contemp. Health L. & Pol'y 567 (2002); David J. Rothman, Ethical and Social Consequences of Selling a Kidney, 288 J.A.M.A. 1640 (2002).

The purpose of the property claim in cases such as *Newman* and the opinion of the Court of Appeals in *Moore* is to protect the integrity of the body. Do property rights protect bodily integrity and liberty, or devalue them? On the "commodification" of the human body see, Margaret Jane Radin, Contested Commodities (1996) and Peter Halewood, Law's Bodies: Disembodiment and the Structure of Liberal Property Rights, 81 Iowa L. Rev. 1331 (1996). Would a rule that prohibited all commercial use of human bodies be workable? Where would you expect lines to be drawn? Does *Moore* identify any boundaries?

6. One significant concern in the opinions of the California courts in *Moore* is whether the recognition of property rights for John Moore would depress scientific research by stimulating litigation and giving Moore the right to veto the development of the cell line. In fact, most protection for intangible property, including intellectual property as a subset and the scientists' claim in *Moore* specifically, is founded on the view that recognition of property rights will encourage investment and trade by providing protection for the one identified as the owner. Another justification is related and is evident in the Supreme Court's majority opinion in *Moore*: recognition of property in the expressions of such effort rightly follows the investment of labor expended in the creative process. One can acquire property by creating it. The federal patent, trademark, and copyright systems frame the property scheme for intellectual property in the U.S. In classic economic theory, patent and copyright law encourage innovation, investment, and trade. In the biomedical field, however, there is a debate over whether the scope of patents has expanded so much that patent law is having the opposite effect— in fact, the effect that the majority in the Supreme Court decision in *Moore* feared would occur if Moore were recognized to hold property rights in his tissue.

Are these concerns, about the impact of property law on innovation appropriate concerns for judges in cases like *Moore*? Should judges decide what is property and who the owner is by speculating on the economic effect of their decision? Should they instead try to define the essence of property ownership in relation to human rights or morality?

7. The ultimate result in *Moore* has been influential and well accepted in the particular context of the relationship between researchers and patients/donors/sources. For example, in *Greenberg v. Miami Children's Hospital Research Institute, Inc.*, 264 F.Supp.2d 1064 (S.D. Fla. 2003), the court relied on *Moore* to hold that donors of tissue and family medical histories did

not have a property interest in body tissue and genetic information they voluntarily gave to researchers. In this case, Greenberg had approached a medical researcher with the idea of developing a screening test for Canavan disease, a rare but devastating, invariably fatal genetic illness in young children. Families at risk for Canavan disease provided tissue samples, medical histories, and funding. Without the families' knowledge, the researcher received a patent on the resultant medical screening test and entered into licensing agreements through which he and the Institute would receive royalty payments. The plaintiffs filed an action for conversion, arguing that they expected that the test would be made available for free. The court refused to recognize a property interest, but did allow a claim of unjust enrichment. The parties settled after the decision.

Disputes over the ownership of cell lines that occur between a researcher and parties other than the "donor" (as in *Moore*) may be resolved differently. See U.S. v. Arora, 860 F.Supp. 1091 (D.Md.1994), affirmed *per curiam* 56 F.3d 62 (4th Cir. 1995) in which the court recognized a conversion claim for compensatory and punitive damages against a researcher who caused the "death" of a cell line and distinguished and questioned the decision in *Moore*. But see Miles v. Scripps Clinic, 810 F.Supp. 1091 (1993), holding that a claim of conversion for "the right to commercialize" a cell line would not be recognized in California because of state law limitations on the use of conversion for intangible property rights.

8. The majority opinion invites legislative action. Consider what your role as an attorney might be in participating in such action. How does that role work when the lawyer is an advocate—for example, representing the Regents in their quest for "competitive, commercial, and scientific advantage"? Does it make a difference that the lawyer is "just" a citizen, serving without retainer or fee? What if you were appearing as just a member of a nonprofit health care support group for persons affected by a genetically based illness? The Model Rules of Professional Conduct, Rule 3.9, invoke litigation rules for such a "nonadjudicative" case *if* the lawyer is "representing a client," but not, apparently, if the lawyer is merely being a citizen. The rules for being only a citizen are not clear. When the lawyer is an advocate, Rule 3.9 requires that she "disclose that the appearance is in a representative capacity" and conform to rules on candor (3.3), fairness (3.4), and decorum (3.5). That might or might not include a friendly appearance; it apparently would not include a mere-citizen appearance. The issues were perhaps not as clear when the law practice of Louis D. Brandeis was subjected to Senate-committee autopsy after President Wilson nominated him to a seat on the U.S. Supreme Court. The issues of disclosing capacity and compensation were vividly threshed out there. See John Frank, The Legal Ethics of Louis D. Brandeis, 17 Stanford Law Review 707 (1965).

MIDLER v. FORD MOTOR CO.

United States Court of Appeals, Ninth Circuit, 1988.
849 F.2d 460.

NOONAN, CIRCUIT JUDGE:

This case centers on the protectibility of the voice of a celebrated chanteuse from commercial exploitation without her consent. Ford Motor Company and its advertising agency, Young & Rubicam, Inc., in 1985 advertised the Ford Lincoln Mercury with a series of nineteen 30 or 60 second television commercials in what the agency called "The Yuppie Campaign." The aim was to make an emotional connection with Yuppies, bringing back memories of when they were in college. Different popular songs of the seventies were sung on each commercial. The agency tried to get "the original people," that is, the singers who had popularized the songs, to sing them. Failing in that endeavor in ten cases the agency had the songs sung by "sound alikes." Bette Midler, the plaintiff and appellant here, was done by a sound alike.

Midler is a nationally known actress and singer. She won a Grammy as early as 1973 as the Best New Artist of that year. Records made by her since then have gone Platinum and Gold. She was nominated in 1979 for an Academy award for Best Female Actress in The Rose, in which she portrayed a pop singer. Newsweek in its June 30, 1986 issue described her as an "outrageously original singer/comedian." Time hailed her in its March 2, 1987 issue as "a legend" and "the most dynamic and poignant singer-actress of her time."

When Young & Rubicam was preparing the Yuppie Campaign it presented the commercial to its client by playing an edited version of Midler singing "Do You Want To Dance," taken from the 1973 Midler album, "The Divine Miss M." After the client accepted the idea and form of the commercial, the agency contacted Midler's manager, Jerry Edelstein. The conversation went as follows: "Hello, I am Craig Hazen from Young and Rubicam. I am calling you to find out if Bette Midler would be interested in doing ... ?" Edelstein: "Is it a commercial?" "Yes." "We are not interested."

Undeterred, Young & Rubicam sought out Ula Hedwig whom it knew to have been one of "the Harlettes" a backup singer for Midler for ten years. Hedwig was told by Young & Rubicam that "they wanted someone who could sound like Bette Midler's recording of [Do You Want To Dance]." She was asked to make a "demo" tape of the song if she was interested. She made an a capella demo and got the job.

At the direction of Young & Rubicam, Hedwig then made a record for the commercial. The Midler record of "Do You Want To Dance" was first played to her. She was told to "sound as much as possible like the Bette Midler record," leaving out only a few "aahs" unsuitable for the commercial. Hedwig imitated Midler to the best of her ability.

After the commercial was aired Midler was told by "a number of people" that it "sounded exactly" like her record of "Do You Want To Dance." Hedwig was told by "many personal friends" that they thought it was Midler singing the commercial. Ken Fritz, a personal manager in the entertainment business not associated with Midler, declares by affidavit that he heard the commercial on more than one occasion and thought Midler was doing the singing.

Neither the name nor the picture of Midler was used in the commercial; Young & Rubicam had a license from the copyright holder to use the song. At issue in this case is only the protection of Midler's voice. The district court described the defendants' conduct as that "of the average thief." They decided, "If we can't buy it, we'll take it." The court nonetheless believed there was no legal principle preventing imitation of Midler's voice and so gave summary judgment for the defendants. Midler appeals.

* * *

California Civil Code section 3344 is . . . of no aid to Midler. The statute affords damages to a person injured by another who uses the person's "name, voice, signature, photograph or likeness, in any manner." The defendants did not use Midler's name or anything else whose use is prohibited by the statute. The voice they used was Hedwig's, not hers. The term "likeness" refers to a visual image not a vocal imitation. The statute, however, does not preclude Midler from pursuing any cause of action she may have at common law; the statute itself implies that such common law causes of action do exist because it says its remedies are merely "cumulative." [ ]

The companion statute protecting the use of a deceased person's name, voice, signature, photograph or likeness states that the rights it recognizes are "property rights." [ ] By analogy the common law rights are also property rights. . . .

. . . California will recognize an injury from "an appropriation of the attributes of one's identity." [ ] . . .

Why did the defendants ask Midler to sing if her voice was not of value to them? Why did they studiously acquire the services of a soundalike and instruct her to imitate Midler if Midler's voice was not of value to them? What they sought was an attribute of Midler's identity. Its value was what the market would have paid for Midler to have sung the commercial in person.

. . . A voice is as distinctive and personal as a face. The human voice is one of the most palpable ways identity is manifested. We are all aware that a friend is at once known by a few words on the phone. At a philosophical level it has been observed that with the sound of a voice, "the other stands before me." D. Ihde, Listening and Voice 77 (1976). A fortiori, these observations hold true of singing, especially singing by a singer of renown. The singer manifests herself in the song. To impersonate her voice is to pirate her identity. [ ]

We need not and do not go so far as to hold that every imitation of a voice to advertise merchandise is actionable. We hold only that when a distinctive voice of a professional singer is widely known and is deliberately imitated in order to sell a product, the sellers have appropriated what is not theirs. . . . Midler has made a showing, sufficient to defeat summary judgment, that the defendants here for their own profit in selling their product did appropriate part of her identity.

Notes and Questions

1. Of what was Midler claiming ownership? Herself? Her voice? The fruits of her creative work? Her fame? What was Ford appropriating? Was it the "personhood" of Bette Midler or a "commercial opportunity"?

2. In Parks v. LaFace Records, 329 F.3d 437 (6th Cir. 2003), the court considered a claim by Rosa Parks, the civil rights leader who triggered the watershed Montgomery bus boycott in 1955, against the music duo OutKast. OutKast had named one of their raps "Rosa Parks" and prominently identified "Rosa Parks" as a hit single on its 1998 CD Aquemini. Although the lyrics of the piece did not otherwise mention Rosa Parks by name, Mrs. Parks claimed that OutKast had violated her property rights. The legal basis of her claim was that the use of her name had violated both her "right of publicity" under Michigan state law and a federal prohibition on false advertising relating to the use of trademarks. The Sixth Circuit held that Mrs. Parks held a property right in her name and could exclude OutKast from using her name in the manner used in the CD:

> Rosa Parks clearly has a property interest in her name.... It is beyond question that Parks is a celebrity.... We find that Parks' prior commercial activities [including her authorization of the use of her name on a CD of gospel music identified as a tribute to her] and her international recognition as a symbol of the civil rights movement endow her with a trademark interest in her name the same as if she were a famous actor or musician.... [Referring to Parks' claim of a right of publicity, the court quotes the opinion in Carson v. Here's Johnny Portable Toilets, Inc., 698 F.3d 831 (6th Cir. 1983):] "The theory of the right is that a celebrity's identity can be valuable in the promotion of products, and the celebrity has an interest that may be protected from unauthorized commercial exploitation of that identity." [   ] As such the common law right of publicity forms a species of property right.

Despite holding that Parks held a property right in the use of her name, the court struggled mightily with the issue of whether OutKast's First Amendment rights would outweigh Parks' interest. The court holding unequivocally that music is "firmly ensconsed within the protections of the First Amendment," notes that "the First Amendment cannot permit anyone who cries 'artist' to have *carte blanche* when it comes to naming and advertising his or her works, art though it may be." The court, noting that "intellectual property rights are not free; they're imposed at the expense of future creators and the public at large," considered several possible tests for balancing the interests at stake before remanding the case to the trial court for decision as to whether the title "Rosa Parks" had any artistic relevance to the song with the result that OutKast's First Amendment rights would prevail.

3. The courts in *Parks* and *Midler* both reference the plaintiff's character as a celebrity or well-known personality, or in the Divine Miss M.'s case, "a professional singer" with a "distinctive voice," in upholding their rights to protect their identity from nonconsensual appropriation. The court in *Midler* specifically notes that its holding does not extend far enough to protect just anyone's voice. Should you and I have the same rights as Rosa

Parks and Bette Midler in preventing the commercial use of our identities? Is it an appropriation of personal identity to have our voices or our images used without our consent? Would it matter whether the advertisement is for something that results in a positive association as compared to a negative association? Se Mark P. McKenna, The Right of Publicity and Autonomous Self-Definition, 67 U. Pitt. L. Rev. 225 (2005), arguing that neither the right to privacy nor labor theories of property adequately explain or define the right of publicity.

4.   Trademark and right to publicity cases such as this give a window into pop culture. Among the cases considered by the Sixth Circuit were: *New Kids on the Block v. News Am. Publ'g, Inc.,* 971 F.2d 302, 306 (9th Cir.1992) (rejecting the group's challenge to the use of its name by newspapers conducting fan polls); Rogers v. Grimaldi, 875 F.2d 994 (2d Cir. 1989) (rejecting Ginger Rogers' claim against Fellini's use of her name in the title of the movie "Fred and Ginger," in which the plot revolved around the reunion of two former cabaret dancers whose fans nicknamed them after the more famous pair); Mattel, Inc. v. MCA Records, 296 F.3d 894 (9th Cir. 2002), holding that Aqua's First Amendment rights in the song "Barbie Girl" trumped Mattel's trademark in a case that the court called "Speech–Zilla Meets Trademark Kong."

5.   About half of the states have created a "right of publicity" that allows individuals to control the use of their likenesses during the course of their lifetimes. Although this right of publicity typically expires at the death of the individual, in some states the right survives death. The Elvis Presley estate, for example, is thriving on its ability to use, to transfer and to exclude others from the right to use The King's likeness. See, State ex rel. Elvis Presley International Memorial Foundation v. Crowell, 733 S.W.2d 89 (Tenn.App.1987). For the continuing Elvis property saga, see Julie Bosman, *The King's Legacy All Shook Up: He Bought Elvis, and Plans to Cash In,* N.Y. Times, March 5, 2006, at 31, reporting on events subsequent to the 2005 $100–million purchase of "Elvis's name and likeness—but not his music."

6.   Of course, these intellectual property rights are transferable, and in many cases the courts have held that performance contracts transferred these rights. See, e.g., Muller v. Walt Disney Productions, 871 F.Supp. 678 (S.D.N.Y.1994) (holding that the Fantasia conductor had transferred all rights to his performance to Walt Disney Productions, including rights to release Fantasia on video); Rooney v. Columbia Pictures Industries, Inc., 538 F.Supp. 211 (S.D.N.Y.1982) (holding that Mickey Rooney transferred his property rights in his movie contracts and so was not entitled to payments for releases to television.)

PROBLEM: CREATING THE TREASURE TROVE

On January 21, 2003, the Governor of Utah announced a new joint venture originally called GenData—a not-for-profit corporation formed by the state, the University of Utah, and the Huntsman Cancer Foundation.

The project combines databases now held by the three partners and creates a database or a "biobank" that will form the foundation for medical research. The joint public-private project also will allow researchers to link to state databases such as the state's cancer registry. The Governor said that the project is enriched in Utah because of the wealth of genealogical information maintained in that state. In fact, in 2005, GenData changed its name to LineaData to emphasize this strength. See its website at http://www.lineagen.org.

The database at the University was begun approximately 20 years ago with the support and cooperation of members of the Church of Jesus Christ of Latter-day Saints, who provided family medical history for the good of research. One news article reported that some DNA samples are included in the database, but that it consists primarily of family medical histories, genealogy records, the state's vital statistics records, driver's licenses and so on. The executive director of the Huntsman Cancer Foundation said that "knowing the genetic cause of disease is important, but also knowing the interaction of environment and other population factors could play a huge role in improved science."

The leaders of the project said the information is entirely confidential. In his State of the State address, the Governor asked the legislature to "build into law an impenetrable wall of privacy protection." The legislature had already appropriated more than $3 million for the project.

The Governor also stated that the project will attract venture capital and pharmaceutical and medical research organizations "from all over the world" to the state of Utah. The Governor declared that the project would create a "scientific treasure." Joe Bauman and Amy Joi Bryson, "Leavitt Announces Utah Genetics Project," Deseret News B03 (1/22/03); Troy Goodman, "State Invests in Database for Biotech," Salt Lake Trib. A1 (1/22/03); "GenData Announces Collaboration for Undisclosed Disorders" Drug Week 144 (2/4/05).

There are many other examples of these new biobanks. For example, Iceland has entered into a joint venture with deCode for a biobank consisting of tissue samples and the health records of the citizenry of Iceland. The joint venture anticipates the development of commercial products, and the government and the company will share in the profits. See Jamaica Potts, At Least Give the Natives Glass Beads: An Examination of the Bargain Made Between Iceland and deCode Genetics with Implications for Global Prospecting, 7 Va. J. Law & Tech. 8 (2002). See also Special Issue on Regulation of Biobanks, 33 J. of Law, Med. & Ethics (Spring 2005).

What are the property issues embedded in Utah's enterprise? Who may claim ownership interests and of what?

(A version of this problem appears in Furrow, Greaney, Johnson, Jost and Schwartz, Health Law—Materials, Cases and Problems 1313–1314 (5th ed. Thomson West 2004)).

II. WHO IS THE OWNER?

The *Moore* case addressed the question of whether human tissue can be property, but it also addressed the question we consider in more detail in this section: who is the owner of property? In the *Moore* case, this issue was presented in Moore's challenge to the ownership of the cell line developed by the scientists from his tissue.

In this section, we examine cases in which courts have resolved disputes between two or more persons claiming ownership of the same property. Like your decision to grant the desired object to a particular child in the story that begins this chapter, the courts need a rationale for their choice of the owner among the disputants. In the cases that follow, you will see the courts using some form of the theory that "possession" is a legally recognized method of acquiring property rights. In fact, some argue that possession holds a preferred position as a foundation of a claim of ownership:

> Any chain of ownership or title must have a first link ... [The maxim of the common law is that] possession is the root of title. Merely to state the proposition is to raise two critical questions: what counts as possession, and why is it the basis for a claim to title. In exploring the quaint old cases' answers to these questions, we hit on some fundamental views about the nature and purpose of the property regime. Carol M. Rose, Possession As the Origin of Property, 52 U.Chi.L.Rev. 73 (1985).

Of course, if possession alone resulted in title or ownership, we would have a system that created great incentives for theft (and terrific inefficiencies in the protection of our things). The common law maxim might be understood as *first* possession is the root of title. Test that concept in the cases below.

A. DISCOVERY AND OCCUPANCY

JOHNSON AND GRAHAM'S LESSEE v. McINTOSH

United States Supreme Court, 1823.
21 U.S. (8 Wheat.) 543, 5 L.Ed. 681.

Mr. Chief Justice Marshall delivered the opinion of the Court.

[This was an action in ejectment, by which the plaintiff sought to recover possession of a large tract of the land north of the Ohio river in southern Illinois and Indiana. The plaintiff claimed the land through grants to predecessors in title from the Illinois and Piankeshaw (Wabash) Indians in 1773, several years after the conclusion of the French and Indian Wars. Because of the hostilities of the Revolutionary War and the War of 1812, plaintiff's predecessors never took possession of the land. The defendant received title to the land through a patent (grant) issued by the United States in 1818 as part of a program to reward veterans for their service in the military and to encourage settlement of the Northwest territory.]

* * * The facts, as stated in the case agreed, show the authority of the chiefs who executed this conveyance, so far as it could be given by their own people; and likewise show, that the particular tribes for whom these chiefs acted were in rightful possession of the land they sold. The inquiry, therefore, is, in a great measure, confined to the power of Indians to give, and of private individuals to receive, a title, which can be sustained in the courts of this country.

As the right of society to prescribe those rules by which property may be acquired and preserved is not, and cannot, be drawn into question; as the title to lands, especially, is, and must be, admitted, to depend entirely on the law of the nation in which they lie; it will be necessary, in pursuing this inquiry, to examine, not simply those principles of abstract justice, which the Creator of all things has impressed on the mind of his creature man, and which are admitted to regulate, in a great degree, the rights of civilized nations, whose perfect independence is acknowledged; but those principles also which our own government has adopted in the particular case, and given us as the rule for our decision.

On the discovery of this immense continent, the great nations of Europe were eager to appropriate to themselves so much of it as they could respectively acquire. Its vast extent offered an ample field to the ambition and enterprise of all; and the character and religion of its inhabitants afforded an apology for considering them as a people over whom the superior genius of Europe might claim an ascendency. The potentates of the old world found no difficulty in convincing themselves, that they made ample compensation to the inhabitants of the new, by bestowing on them civilization and Christianity, in exchange for unlimited independence. But as they were all in pursuit of nearly the same object, it was necessary, in order to avoid conflicting settlements, and consequent war with each other, to establish a principle, which all should acknowledge as the law by which the right of acquisition, which they all asserted, should be regulated, as between themselves. This principle was, that discovery gave title to the government by whose subjects, or by whose authority, it was made, against all other European governments, which title might be consummated by possession. The exclusion of all other Europeans, necessarily gave to the nation making the discovery the sole right of acquiring the soil from the natives, and establishing settlements upon it. It was a right with which no Europeans could interfere. It was a right which all asserted for themselves, and to the assertion of which, by others, all assented. Those relations which were to exist between the discoverer and the natives, were to be regulated by themselves. The rights thus acquired being exclusive, no other power could interpose between them.

In the establishment of these relations, the rights of the original inhabitants were, in no instance, entirely disregarded; but were, necessarily, to a considerable extent, impaired. They were admitted to be the rightful occupants of the soil, with a legal as well as just claim to retain possession of it, and to use it according to their own discretion; but their rights to complete sovereignty, as independent nations, were necessarily diminished, and their power to dispose of the soil, at their own will, to whomsoever they pleased, was denied by the original fundamental principle, that discovery gave exclusive title to those who made it. While the different nations of Europe respected the right of the natives, as occupants, they asserted the ultimate dominion to be in themselves; and claimed and exercised, as a consequence of this ultimate dominion, a power to grant the soil, while yet in possession of the natives. These grants have been understood by all, to convey a title to the grantees, subject only to the Indian right of occupancy.

The history of America, from its discovery to the present day, proves, we think, the universal recognition of these principles. Spain did not rest her title solely on the grant of the Pope. Her discussions respecting boundary, with France, with Great Britain, and with the United States, all show that she placed it on the rights given by discovery. Portugal sustained her claim to the Brazils by the same title. France, also, founded her title to the vast territories she claimed in America on discovery. However conciliatory her conduct to the natives may have been, she still asserted her right of dominion over a great extent of country, not actually settled by Frenchmen, and her exclusive right to acquire and dispose of the soil which remained in the occupation of Indians. Her monarch claimed all Canada and Acadie, as colonies of France, at a time when the French population was very inconsiderable, and the Indians occupied almost the whole country. He also claimed Louisiana, comprehending the immense territories watered by the Mississippi, and the rivers which empty into it, by the title of discovery. The letters-patent granted to the Sieur Demonts, in 1603, constitute him Lieutenant–General, and the representative of the king, in Acadie, which is described as stretching from the 40th to the 46th degree of north latitude; with authority to extend the power of the French over that country, and its inhabitants, to give laws to the people, to treat with the natives, and enforce the observance of treaties, and to parcel out, and give title to lands, according to his own judgment. The States of Holland also made acquisitions in America, and sustained their right on the common principle adopted by all Europe. * * * The claim of the Dutch was always contested by the English; not because they questioned the title given by discovery, but because they insisted on being themselves the rightful claimants under that title. Their pretensions were finally decided by the sword.

* * * Thus, all the nations of Europe, who have acquired territory on this continent, have asserted in themselves, and have recognized in others, the exclusive right of the discoverer to appropriate the lands occupied by the Indians. Have the American states rejected or adopted this principle?

By the treaty which concluded the war of our revolution, Great Britain relinquished all claim, not only to the government, but to the "propriety and territorial rights of the United States," whose boundaries were fixed in the second article. By this treaty, the powers of government, and the right to soil, which had previously been in Great Britain, passed definitively to these states. We had before taken possession of them, by declaring independence; but neither the declaration of independence, nor the treaty confirming it, could give us more than that which we before possessed, or to which Great Britain was before entitled. It has never been doubted, that either the United States, or the several states, had a clear title to all the lands within the boundary lines described in the treaty, subject only to the Indian right of occupancy, and that the exclusive power to extinguish that right, was vested in that government which might constitutionally exercise it.

* * *

The states, having within their chartered limits different portions of territory covered by Indians, ceded that territory, generally, to the United States, on conditions expressed in their deeds of cession, which demonstrate the opinion, that they ceded the soil as well as jurisdiction, and that in doing so, they granted a productive fund to the government of the Union. The lands in controversy lay within the chartered limits of Virginia, and were ceded with the whole country north-west of the river Ohio. This grant contained reservations and stipulations, which could only be made by the owners of the soil; and concluded with a stipulation, that "all the lands in the ceded territory, not reserved, should be considered as a common fund, for the use and benefit of such of the United States as have become, or shall become, members of the confederation," & c., "according to their usual respective proportions in the general charge and expenditure, and shall be faithfully and *bonâ fide* disposed of for that purpose, and for no other use or purpose whatsoever." The ceded territory was occupied by numerous and warlike tribes of Indians; but the exclusive right of the United States to extinguish their title, and to grant the soil, has never, we believe, been doubted.

* * *

The United States, then, have unequivocally acceded to that great and broad rule by which its civilized inhabitants now hold this country. They hold, and assert in themselves, the title by which it was acquired. They maintain, as all others have maintained, that discovery gave an exclusive right to extinguish the Indian title of occupancy, either by purchase or by conquest; and gave also a right to such a degree of sovereignty, as the circumstances of the people would allow them to exercise. The power now possessed by the government of the United States to grant lands, resided, while we were colonies, in the crown or its grantees. The validity of the titles given by either has never been questioned in our courts. It has been exercised uniformly over territory in possession of the Indians. The existence of this power must negative the existence of any right which may conflict with and control it. An absolute title to lands cannot exist, at the same time, in different persons, or in different governments. An absolute must be an exclusive title, or at least a title which excludes all others not compatible with it. All our institutions recognise the absolute title of the crown, subject only to the Indian right of occupancy, and recognise the absolute title of the crown to extinguish that right. This is incompatible with an absolute and complete title in the Indians.

We will not enter into the controversy, whether agriculturists, merchants and manufacturers, have a right, on abstract principles, to expel hunters from the territory they possess, or to contract their limits. Conquest gives a title which the courts of the conqueror cannot deny, whatever the private and speculative opinions of individuals may be, respecting the original justice of the claim which has been successfully asserted. * * *

Although we do not mean to engage in the defence of those principles which Europeans have applied to Indian title, they may, we think, find some excuse, if not justification, in the character and habits of the people whose rights have been wrested from them. The title by conquest is acquired and maintained by force. The conqueror prescribes its limits. Humanity, however, acting on public opinion, has established, as a general rule, that the conquered shall not be wantonly oppressed, and that their condition shall remain as eligible as is compatible with the objects of the conquest. Most usually, they are incorporated with the victorious nation, and become subjects or citizens of the government with which they are connected. The new and old members of the society mingle with each other; the distinction between them is gradually lost, and they make one people. Where this incorporation is practicable, humanity demands, and a wise policy requires, that the rights of the conquered to property should remain unimpaired; that the new subjects should be governed as equitably as the old, and that confidence in their security should gradually banish the painful sense of being separated from their ancient connections, and united by force to strangers. When the conquest is complete, and the conquered inhabitants can be blended with the conquerors, or safely governed as a distinct people, public opinion, which not even the conqueror can disregard, imposes these restraints upon him; and he cannot neglect them, without injury to his fame, and hazard to his power.

But the tribes of Indians inhabiting this country were fierce savages, whose occupation was war, and whose subsistence was drawn chiefly from the forest. To leave them in possession of their country, was to leave the country a wilderness; to govern them as a distinct people, was impossible, because they were as brave and as high-spirited as they were fierce, and were ready to repel by arms every attempt on their independence. What was the inevitable consequence of this state of things? The Europeans were under the necessity either of abandoning the country, and relinquishing their pompous claims to it, or of enforcing those claims by the sword, and by the adoption of principles adapted to the condition of a people with whom it was impossible to mix, and who could not be governed as a distinct society, or of remaining in their neighborhood, and exposing themselves and their families to the perpetual hazard of being massacred. Frequent and bloody wars, in which the whites were not always the aggressors, unavoidably ensued. European policy, numbers and skill prevailed; as the white population advanced, that of the Indians necessarily receded; the country in the immediate neighborhood of agriculturists became unfit for them; the game fled into thicker and more unbroken forests, and the Indians followed. The soil, to which the crown originally claimed title, being no longer occupied by its ancient inhabitants, was parcelled out according to the will of the sovereign power, and taken possession of by persons who claimed immediately from the crown, or mediately, through its grantees or deputies.

That law which regulates, and ought to regulate in general, the relations between the conqueror and conquered, was incapable of application to a people under such circumstances. The resort to some new and different rule, better adapted to the actual state of things, was unavoidable. Every rule which can be suggested will be found to be attended with great difficulty. However extravagant the pretension of converting the discovery of an inhabited country into conquest may appear; if the principle has been asserted in the first instance, and afterwards sustained; if a country has been acquired and held under it; if the property of the great mass of the community originates in it, it becomes the law of the land, and cannot be questioned. So too, with respect to the concomitant principle, that the Indian inhabitants are to be considered merely as occupants, to be protected, indeed, while in peace, in the possession of their lands, but to be deemed incapable of transferring the absolute title to others. However this restriction may be opposed to natural right, and to the usages of civilized nations, yet, if it be indispensable to that system under which the country has been settled, and be adapted to the actual condition of the two people, it may, perhaps, be supported by reason, and certainly cannot be rejected by courts of justice.

* * *

Another view has been taken of this question, which deserves to be considered. The title of the crown, whatever it might be, could be acquired only by a conveyance from the crown. If an individual might extinguish the Indian title, for his own benefit, or, in other words, might purchase it, still he could acquire only that title. Admitting their power to change their laws or usages, so far as to allow an individual to separate a portion of their lands from the common stock, and hold it in severalty, still it is a part of their territory, and is held under them, by a title dependent on their laws. The grant derives its efficacy from their will; and, if they choose to resume it, and make a different disposition of the land, the court of the United States cannot interpose for the protection of the title. The person who purchases lands from the Indians, within their territory, incorporates himself with them, so far as respects the property purchased; holds their title under their protection, and subject to their laws. If they annul the grant, we know of no tribunal which can revise and set aside the proceeding. We know of no principle which can distinguish this case from a grant made to a native Indian, authorizing him to hold a particular tract of land in severalty. As such a grant could not separate the Indian from his nation, nor give a title which our courts could distinguish from the title of his tribe, as it might still be conquered from, or ceded by his tribe, we can perceive no legal principle which will authorize a court to say, that different consequences are attached to this purchase, because it was made by a stranger. By the treaties concluded between the United States and the Indian nations, whose title the plaintiffs claim, the country comprehending the lands in controversy has been ceded to the United States, without any reservation of their title. These nations had been at war with the United States, and had an unquestionable right to annul any grant they had made to American citizens. Their cession of the country, without a reservation of this land, affords a fair presumption, that they considered it as of no validity. They ceded to the United States this very property, after having used it in common with other lands, as their own, from the date of their deeds to the time of cession; and the attempt now made, is to set up their title against that of the United States.

The proclamation issued by the king of Great Britain, in 1763, has been considered, and we think, with reason, as constituting an additional objection to the title of the plaintiffs. By that proclamation, the crown reserved under its own dominion and protection, for the use of the Indians, "all the land and territories lying to the westward of the sources of the rivers which fall into the sea from the west and north-west," and strictly forbade all British subjects from making any purchases or settlements whatever, or taking possession of the reserved lands. * * * It is supposed to be a principle of universal law, that, if an uninhabited country be discovered by a number of individuals, who acknowledge no connection with, and owe no allegiance to, any government whatever, the country becomes the property of the discoverers, so far at least as they can use it. They acquire a title in common. The title of the whole land is in the whole society. It is to be divided and parcelled out according to the will of the society, expressed by the whole body, or by that organ which is authorized by the whole to express it. If the discovery be made, and possession of the country be taken, under the authority of an existing government, which is acknowledged by the emigrants, it is supposed to be equally well settled, that the discovery is made for the whole nation, that the country becomes a part of the nation, and that the vacant soil is to be disposed of by that organ of the government which has the constitutional power to dispose of the national domains, by that organ in which all vacant territory is vested by law.

* * * So far as respected the authority of the crown, no distinction was taken between vacant lands and lands occupied by the Indians. The title, subject only to the right of occupancy by the Indians, was admitted to be in the king, as was his right to grant that title. The lands, then, to which this proclamation referred, were lands which the king had a right to grant, or to reserve for the Indians.

* * *

Much reliance is also placed on the fact, that many tracts are now held in the United States, under the Indian title, the validity of which is not questioned. Before the importance attached to this fact is conceded, the circumstances under which such grants were obtained, and such titles are supported, ought to be considered. These lands lie chiefly in the eastern states. It is known that the Plymouth Company made many extensive grants, which, from their ignorance of the country, interfered with each other. It is also known, that Mason, to whom New Hampshire, and Gorges, to whom Maine was granted, found great difficulty in managing such unwieldy property. The country was settled by emigrants, some from Europe, but chiefly from Massachusetts, who took possession of lands they found unoccupied, and secured themselves in that possession by the best means in their power. The disturbances in England, and the civil war and revolution which followed those disturbances, prevented any interference on the part of the mother country, and the proprietors were unable to maintain their title. In the meantime, Massachusetts claimed the country and governed it. As her claim was adversary to that of the proprietors, she encouraged the settlement of persons made under her authority, and encouraged, likewise, their securing themselves in possession, by purchasing the acquiescence and forbearance of the Indians.

After the restoration of Charles II., Gorges and Mason, when they attempted to establish their title, found themselves opposed by men, who held under Massachusetts, and under the Indians. The title of the proprietors was resisted; and though, in some cases compromises were made, and in some, the opinion of a court was given ultimately in their favor, the juries found uniformly against them. They became wearied with the struggle, and sold their property. The titles held under the Indians, were sanctioned by length of possession; but there is no case, so far as we are informed, of a judicial decision in their favor.

* * *

It has never been contended, that the Indian title amounted to nothing. Their right of possession has never been questioned. The claim of government extends to the complete ultimate title, charged with this right of possession, and to the exclusive power of acquiring that right. The object of the crown was, to settle the sea-coast of America; and when a portion of it was settled, without violating the rights of others, by persons professing their loyalty, and soliciting the royal sanction of an act, the consequences of which were ascertained to be beneficial, it would have been as unwise as ungracious, to expel them from their habitations, because they had obtained the Indian title, otherwise than through the agency of government. The very grant of a charter is an assertion of the title of the crown, and its words convey the same idea. * * *

[The] charter, and [the] letter [to Rhode Island], certainly sanction a previous unauthorized purchase from Indians, under the circumstances attending that particular purchase, but are far from supporting the general proposition, that a title acquired from the Indians would be valid against a title acquired from the crown, or without the confirmation of the crown.

The acts of the several colonial assemblies, prohibiting purchases from the Indians, have also been relied on, as proving, that, independent of such prohibitions, Indian deeds would be valid. But, we think, this fact, at most, equivocal. While the existence of such purchases would justify their prohibition, even by colonies which considered Indian deeds as previously invalid, the fact that such acts have been generally passed, is strong evidence of the general opinion, that such purchases are opposed by the soundest principles of wisdom and national policy.

After bestowing on this subject a degree of attention which was more required by the magnitude of the interest in litigation, and the able and elaborate arguments of the bar, than by its intrinsic difficulty, the court is decidedly of opinion, that the plaintiffs do not exhibit a title which can be sustained in the courts of the United States; and that there is no error in the judgment which was rendered against them in the district court of Illinois.

Judgment affirmed, with costs.

Notes and Questions

1.   The plaintiffs, Joshua Johnson and Thomas Graham, claimed the disputed land as devisees under the will of Thomas Johnson, one of the original grantees in a 1773 conveyance from the Indian tribes. Thomas Johnson died in 1819. Why was the Indians' right to transfer relevant nearly fifty years after the original conveyance?

2.   How did Justice Marshall frame the issue of the case? What alternatives exist for identifying the issues in this case? Can this case be reconciled with Rose's statement that "possession is the root of title" in our common-law system? Is this a case about what counts as possession?

3.   *Johnson v. McIntosh* illustrates competing views of the nature and source of property ownership. The following excerpts elaborate on that question.

John Quincy Adams, Oration at the Anniversary of the Sons of the Pilgrims (December 22, 1802):

> There are moralists who have questioned the right of Europeans to intrude upon the possessions of the aborigines in any case and under any limitations whatsoever. But have they maturely considered the whole subject? The Indian right of possession itself stands, with regard to the greatest part of the country, upon a questionable foundation. Their cultivated fields, their constructed habitations, a space of ample sufficiency for their subsistence, and whatever they had annexed to themselves by personal labor, was undoubtedly by the laws of nature theirs. But what is the right of a huntsman to the forest of a thousand miles over which he has accidentally ranged in quest of prey? Shall the liberal bounties of Providence to the race of man be monopolized by one of ten thousand for whom they were created? * * * Shall he forbid the wilderness to blossom like the rose? Shall he forbid the oaks of the forest to fall before the ax of industry and rise again transformed into

the habitations of ease and elegance? * * * Shall the mighty rivers, poured out by the hands of nature as channels of communication between numerous nations, roll their waters in sullen silence and eternal solitude to the deep? Have hundreds of commodious harbors, a thousand leagues of coast, and a boundless ocean been spread in the front of this land, and shall every purpose of utility to which they could be applied be prohibited by the tenant of the woods? No, generous philanthropists!

In a letter, generally, though perhaps not accurately, attributed to Chief Seattle of the Duwanish Indians in Washington State, responding to the President Franklin Pierce's expression of interest in buying the tribe's land:

> The Great Chief in Washington sends word that he wishes to buy our land. How can you buy or sell the sky—the warmth of the land? The idea is strange to us. Yet we do not own the freshness of the air or the sparkle of the water. How can you buy them from us? Every part of this earth is sacred to my people. * * *

> We know that white man does not understand our ways. One portion of the land is the same to him as the next, for he is a stranger who comes in the night and takes from the land whatever he needs. The earth is not his brother but his enemy, and when he has conquered it he moves on. * * *

How would you describe the concept of possession that Adams holds? How does it differ from the concept held by Chief Seattle? Or, does Chief Seattle have no concept of possession? Of course, one cannot generalize the comments attributed to Chief Seattle to all Native American cultures. See, for example, Kenneth H. Bobroff, Retelling Allotment: Indian Property Rights and the Myth of Common Ownership, 54 Vand. L. Rev. 1559 (2001).

4.   One way to evaluate legal reasoning in an area of law is to examine the cultural myths that underlie the analysis. According to William Bassett, the property law of sixteenth and seventeenth-century England, which formed the foundation of the property relationships of the colonists with the Native Americans, was informed by the "myth of the nomad." The characterization of Native Americans as nomadic people is quite clear in John Quincy Adams' oration, as is the proposed relation of this characterization to the allocation of property rights. Bassett argues that the roots of the nomad myth in North America had been set in the justifications of the dispossession of the Irish by the English "colonization" of Ireland in the sixteenth century. Bassett distinguishes this colonization from earlier invasions of Ireland in that this effort included dispossessing the majority of the inhabitants of their property rather than ousting only the ruling class. Because the English viewed the Gaelic Irish as barbarians, according to Bassett, they were able to justify war and expropriation of the Irish lands. Quoting a variety of sources, Bassett finds that the English viewed the Irish as pagans ["They are all Papists by their profession, but in the same so blindly and brutishly informed for the most part as that you would rather think them atheists or infidels."] The Gaelic Irish were viewed as barbarians because they "neither possessed any grounds, nor had any seats or houses to dwell in, but wandered through wilderness and desert places driving their flocks

and herds of beasts before them.'' The self-stated mission of the English was ''to inhabit and reforme so barbarous a nation.''

The relationship of the nomadic myth to the allocation of property rights emerged from the work of natural-law theorists and social theorists of the eighteenth century who, according to Bassett, viewed economic and social development as occurring in stages. Adam Smith, for example, identified the following four stages: ''first, the Age of Hunters; second, the Age of Shepherds; third, the Age of Agriculture; and fourth, the Age of Commerce.'' According to this view, private property does not arise until agriculture takes hold. Bassett, The Myth of the Nomad in Property Law, 4 J. of Law and Religion 133 (1986).

Robert Williams traces the rule of conquest to the Crusades. He relates the European history of the crusades to *Johnson v. McIntosh*, which, according to Williams, incorporates ''[t]he Christian European legal tradition of cultural racism and discrimination against non-Christian peoples, first brought to the new World by Columbus, and translated and adopted by English Protestant monarchs in North America.'' Columbus's Legacy: The Rehnquist Court's Perpetuation of European Cultural Racism Against American Indian Tribes, 39 Fed. B. News & J. 6 (1992). See also Robert A. Williams, Jr., The American Indian in Western Legal Thought: The Discourses of Conquest (1990).

Susan Williams, in a response to Bassett, argues that ''it is not possible, nor would it be desirable, to 'demythologize' the law. * * * The effort to eliminate those myths would produce legal concepts that were far less human, and probably no more humane.'' Williams, The Uses of Myth: A Response to Professor Bassett, 4 J. of L. and Religion 153 (1986). See also, Peter H. Russell, Recognizing Aboriginal Title (University of Toronto Press, 2004), in which the author analyzes the roots of the European doctrine of discovery, its application in Australia, and the recognition of the survival of native land rights after discovery and settlement.

One contemporary area of property law in which one might say a ''myth'' has operated is landlord-tenant law. Margaret Radin, in her article, Property and Personhood, 34 Stan. L. Rev. 957 (1982), observes that ''[c]ourts frequently picture the residential lease transaction as taking place between a poor or middle-class tenant acquiring a home and a business enterprise owning and leasing residential property. This is one basis for the revolution in tenants' rights. Courts began to view the rights in question as more closely related to the personhood of the tenant than to that of the landlord, and accordingly moved to protect the leasehold as the tenant's home.'' Radin does not call these characterizations mythology. She uses them, instead, to illustrate a sense of the interrelationship of certain types of property and one's personhood. (Bassett lists the landlord-tenant law reform cases among cases revealing a mythology in property law.)

Does identifying an assumption or generalization or observation as a ''myth'' add anything to the critique of a case or a specific set of legal norms? On what basis would you find a myth useful, if ever? Destructive?

5. Is the treatment of the Native American claims in *Johnson* based on a categorization that favors Europeans as a matter of racial identity? How

do, or can, property rights become racialized? Consider Cheryl Harris's analysis of the matter:

> The racialization of identity and the racial subordination of Blacks and Native Americans provided the ideological basis for slavery and conquest. Although the systems of oppression of Blacks and Native Americans differed in form—the former involving the seizure and appropriation of labor, the latter entailing the seizure and appropriation of land—undergirding both was a racialized conception of property implemented by force and ratified by law.
>
> The origins of property rights in the United States are rooted in racial domination. Even in the early years of the country, it was not the concept of race alone that operated to oppress Blacks and Indians; rather, it was the interaction between conceptions of race and property that played a critical role in establishing and maintaining racial and economic subordination.
>
> The hyper-exploitation of Black labor was accomplished by treating Black people themselves as objects of property. Race and property were thus conflated by establishing a form of property contingent on race—only Blacks were subjugated as slaves and treated as property. Similarly, the conquest, removal, and extermination of Native American life and culture were ratified by conferring and acknowledging the property rights of whites in Native American land.

Cheryl I. Harris, Whiteness as Property, 106 Harv. L. Rev. 1707, 1715–1716 (1993).

6. Discussing the mythology adopted in an opinion resolving a legal question of property ownership, and analyzing the costs and benefits of a particular allocation, are different ways of raising the question of who *ought* to be called "owner," using "ought" in a moral, political, or economic context rather than simply as a way of asking who the rules determine should be the owner. These issues are neatly raised in questions concerning "original owners" or "first owners." A nearly endless variety of answers have been proposed for the question of who ought to be the owner. The labor theory argues that the one who applies labor to a thing and *transforms* it deserves to be the owner; the social contract theory argues that the owner is the one who received title through the consent of humanity or society; the natural law theory argues that the identification of the owner is to be found in natural principles of human ordering; utilitarianism argues that ownership is placed where it achieves the greatest aggregate good (i.e., the greatest good for the greatest number). Which of these theories, if any, are evident in *Johnson v. McIntosh*? In *Moore*? Recall these theories as you read the cases in the following sections as well.

7. In policymaking, decisions concerning conflicting claims or positions are often examined through a cost-benefit analysis. In this analysis, the costs (disadvantages quantified and weighted by severity and probability) are identified and compared to the benefits (similarly quantified and weighted) of the proposed result. Describe the cost-benefit analysis that might be performed by Adams and Chief Seattle in considering a potential resolution of the dispute in *Johnson*. What counts, for each of them, as a cost or a benefit?

Do these cases and *Johnson v. McIntosh* indicate that we have a legal norm that the most productive user gets title? Or do the claims that government should take away the property of one individual for the benefit of another or of the community indicate that we do not actually value property rights very highly? You will return to both of these questions in the materials on adverse possession in this chapter and later in the materials on eminent domain.

8. A new history of *Johnson v. McIntosh* explains some of the story behind the chain of title at issue in the case. In Conquest by Law (Oxford University Press, 2005), Lindsay Robertson describes the backstory drawn from documents of the time held by the United Illinois and Wabash Land Companies, the real plaintiffs in interest, according to Robertson:

> *Johnson* was a collusive case, an attempt by speculators in Indian lands to take advantage of since-closed loopholes in the early federal judicial system to win a judgment from the Supreme Court recognizing their claim to millions of acres. To achieve this, the speculators brought onto their payroll many of the leading figures of the early republic, including ... Daniel Webster ... and General William Winder, the lawyer who represented William M'Intosh, the Companies' *Johnson* opponent, before the Supreme Court. Their efforts might well have succeeded had not Chief Justice John Marshall been guided by his own interests at the time the case finally came before him. Marshall saw *Johnson* as a vehicle for removing an obstacle standing between his former colleagues in the Virginia's Revolutionary War militia and bounty lands promised them in western Kentucky. To resolve an ongoing dispute over title to these lands, Marshall incorporated the discovery doctrine into his opinion in the *Johnson* case, converting what might have been a one-paragraph decision into one comprising more than thirty-three pages.

Robertson goes on to describe the political environment when the facts supporting the claim originally occurred, 50 years before the case was litigated. Calling it "a time of almost mind-numbing jurisdictional confusion," Robertson describes how the regime for Indian land titles disintegrated as the British Empire in North America was beginning to break apart. While the French, the Indian nations, and then the British Crown originally confined the colonists' acquisition of Indian land titles to the area east of the Allegheny Mountains, the ability of the Crown to enforce that limit was undermined by the decline of its power in the Colonies and by land speculators using "fraudulent" legal documents that appeared to give them authority to acquire the previously segregated and unobtainable land. Because the authority of the Crown was weakened by turmoil and distance, the fraudulent documents persuaded local authorities that the transactions were legitimate, thus creating conflicting claims of title.

9. Marshall notes that Indian lands could be acquired by the discoverer through purchase or, failing that, conquest. After the Revolutionary War, George Washington communicated his desires concerning tribes who had sided with Great Britain in the war.

Washington recommended the establishment of a boundary between U.S. and Indian lands and the purchase of Indian lands held east of that line: "[T]here is nothing to be obtained by an Indian War but the soil they live on and this can be had by purchase at less expense, and without that bloodshed . . . ." Documents of United States Indian Policy 102 (1990 2d. ed.). As quoted in Getches, Wilkinson and Williams, Federal Indian Law (1992 3d. ed.) at p. 96.

The idea of separating the Indian nations from the states continued unabated. Although first pursued primarily through purchase, the federal policy changed drastically with the presidency of Andrew Jackson. During that administration, the state of Georgia extended state sovereignty over the resident Indian nations, including the Cherokee Nation, with the support of Jackson. The forced removal of the Cherokees and others from Georgia and other states to areas west of the Mississippi caused terrific conflict in Congress. That conflict moved to the Supreme Court.

Chief Justice Marshall, throughout his tenure on the Supreme Court, was engaged in a political struggle for the life of the Court. The "Marshall Trilogy," which includes *Johnson*, Cherokee Nation v. Georgia, 30 U.S. (5 Pet.) 1, 8 L.Ed. 25 (1831), and Worcester v. Georgia, 31 U.S. (6 Pet.) 515, 8 L.Ed. 483 (1832) reflected that struggle. It was clear that neither Jackson nor the state of Georgia would comply with an order that Georgia stop its extension of state law over the Cherokees. Just a few months before issuing the opinions in *Cherokee Nation*, Marshall had granted a writ of habeas corpus to a Cherokee man who had been convicted of murdering another Cherokee on Cherokee land. The state of Georgia defied the writ and hanged the man. Getches, Wilkinson, & Williams at page 130.

In *Cherokee Nation*, Marshall held that the Supreme Court had no original jurisdiction over the Cherokee Nation claim (that the extension of state control over Cherokee lands was illegal). The opinion did allow for appellate review to the Supreme Court rather than only original jurisdiction, however, and it iterated major principles of judicial review. The case is viewed as similar in significance to the case of Marbury v. Madison, 5 U.S. (1 Cranch) 137, 2 L.Ed. 60 (1803), which first established the authority of the Supreme Court. In *Worcester*, which also involved Georgia's extension of jurisdiction over the Cherokee Nation, Marshall confirmed his view of the Indian tribes as sovereign nations, though limited by the exclusive control exercised by the U.S. federal government as conqueror. In so doing, Marshall held that the individual states did not have jurisdiction over the tribes.

Marshall's trilogy of decisions "incited a constitutional crisis that remains one of the most severe and acrimonious in our history." David H. Getches, Conquering the Cultural Frontier: The New Subjectivism of the Supreme Court in Indian Law, 84 Calif. L. Rev. 1573, 1583 (1996). See also, Burke, The Cherokee Cases: A Study in Law, Politics and Morality, 21 Stan. L. Rev. 500 (1969). Although a direct confrontation was avoided in the aftermath of *Worcester*, the Cherokee Nation ultimately won on its legal claim of protection from control by the state, but lost the war as the Cherokees were forcibly moved through the infamous Trail of Tears to the western territories. Peter Russell, in Recognizing Aboriginal Title, argues instead that the failure of Marshall's opinion in *Worcester* to turn the tide illustrates that "decisions of high courts upholding Aboriginal rights in settler democracies will be ineffective if they go against the tide of opinion and outlook in the dominant society." Perhaps especially so if the President disagrees with the court.

10. How do we reconcile Marshall's adoption of a rule of law originating in monarchy for our new democracy and his use of the legal framework of colonialism for a legal system that had just thrown off colonial rule? Peter Russell, in Recognizing Aboriginal Title (2004) (a study of the development of the law of aboriginal rights in Canada and Australia), argues that:

> Not only was Marshall's jurisprudence as good as it could get for his own time, but, for nearly a century and a half, it set a higher standard of justice than was obtainable through the colonizers' courts anywhere else on earth.... Given the tendency of colonial authority to be less liberal to Indigenous people the closer its locus of power is to them, [Marshall's limitation of the power of the states could have been significant.]

Philip Frickey, in (Native) American Exceptionalism in Federal Public Law, 119 Harv. L. Rev. 431 (2005), argues that current U.S. federal law relating to Native Americans and tribal sovereignty is marked by incoherence and subjectivism. He argues that:

> [The United States] is a constitutional democracy built through the legalized coercion of colonialism. [The] commitment to liberty, egalitarianism, individualism, populism, and laissez-faire made America exceptional. These values are largely consistent with the constitutional democracy that was built on top of the colonial process, but patently incongruent with the colonization buried underneath.... [T]he rule of law serves remarkably divergent purposes, justifying colonialism in the pursuit of constitutionalism. It should come as no surprise, therefore, that the rule of law cannot be easily harmonized across the colonial-constitutional divide.

In U.S. v. Lara, 541 U.S. 193, 124 S.Ct. 1628, 158 L.Ed.2d 420 (2004), concerning Constitutional and tribal criminal procedure, Justice Thomas stated: "[U]ntil we begin to analyze these questions honestly and rigorously, the confusion ... will continue to haunt our cases."

11. According to Marshall, what activities of the European settlers gained for them property rights in the land claimed by the Indians? Is there any evidence in *Johnson* that the successful claimants or their predecessors had themselves engaged in any activity on the disputed land? What did the property rights gained by the Europeans entitle them to do in relation to the land? Did the Indians have any property rights remaining? What was the source and nature of those rights? In his thorough analysis of the Marshall cases and in comparison with Supreme Court jurisprudence on tribal sovereignty as against state regulation, Getches notes that the Marshall cases established that the Indian tribes were sovereigns, that their sovereignty did not include authority in external or foreign affairs but was complete internally in terms of self-government, and could be limited only by the congressional authority of the United States. Under these principles, Indian tribal law operated on Indian-owned lands separately and independently of the law of the state within which the tribal lands were located. Getches argues that the Marshall Trilogy and the allocation of exclusive authority to the federal

government, rather than to the state governments, was pivotal in creating the necessary legal space for the beginnings of substantial economic development on tribal lands, although he argues that the Supreme Court did not hold a steady course on the economic independence of the Indian nations and encroached on their sovereignty in a series of cases in the 1980s.

12.   Can it be said that two or more people can hold property interests in the same piece of land at the same time? One of the characteristics of the modern Anglo–American concept of property is that property can be divided into numerous separate interests on several levels of abstraction, including space, time, and function. The trust concept, discussed in greater detail in Chapter Two, is one example of this conceptualization. In a trust, the managerial rights and responsibilities associated with property are separated from the rights to enjoy the fruits of the property. The manager (trustee) has strict obligations (a fiduciary responsibility) to account to the beneficiary of the trust. The trust concept is a central pillar of federal Indian law as it eventually developed, with the federal government viewed as a trustee.

If you have been in the Field Museum of Natural History in Chicago, you saw a prominent example of the trust concept established in *Johnson*. The U.S. government, a private landowner, and a research institute were among those fighting over ownership of the Tyrannosaurus rex skeleton named Sue. A Native American landowner, Williams, sold rights to unearth a recently discovered dinosaur fossil to the Black Hills Institute of Geological Research. The federal government subsequently seized the fossil, claiming that Williams was not entitled to sell the fossil because the U.S. government actually held the title to Williams' land in trust. The Eighth Circuit Court of Appeals, in *Black Hills Institute of Geological Research v. Williams*, 88 F.3d 614 (8th Cir. 1996), based its holding, in part, on the distinction between real and personal property:

> The ownership issue depends on our construction of several statutes governing Indian trust land. Sue Hendrickson discovered the fossil on land to which the United States holds legal title in trust for Williams, an individual Indian. Under the trust instrument, the United States will hold the land "in trust for the sole use and benefit of" Williams until the trust relationship expires on September 23, 1994.... Until the trust expires in 1994, Williams is a beneficial owner of the land, retaining certain judicially-recognized rights but lacking the absolute right to dispose of the land as he pleases.

* * *

> These statutes and regulations establish a scheme by which beneficial owners of Indian land such as Williams may alienate all or part of their interest before their trust instruments expire. Outside of the permitted transactions not applicable here, the only way such owners may alienate an interest in their trust land is by securing the prior approval of the Secretary. An attempted sale of an interest in Indian trust land in violation of this requirement is void and does not transfer title.

* * *

> Thus, the relevant inquiry for purposes of assessing the validity of the transaction is whether the fossil was personal property or land before

Black Hills excavated it. If it was land within the meaning of the relevant statutes and regulations, the transaction between Williams and Black Hills is void and the United States holds Sue in trust for Williams because the trust continued in Sue when she became personalty. [   ]

The court held that the fossil was land, or real property, before the excavation; and that Williams' sale to Black Hills (at a price of $5,000) was void. Once Sue was excavated and no longer was part of the land, she became personal property that Williams was entitled to sell. Eventually, the Field Museum of Chicago bought Sue at an auction for $8.4 million, of which Williams received $7.6 million, and the auction company received the balance.

B. CAPTURE

PIERSON v. POST

Supreme Court of New York, 1805.
3 Cai. R. 175.

TOMPKINS, J. delivered the opinion of the court.

This was an action of trespass on the case commenced in a justice's court, by the present defendant against the now plaintiff.

The declaration stated that Post, being in possession of certain dogs and hounds under his command, did, "upon a certain wild and uninhabited, unpossessed and waste land, called the beach, find and start one of those noxious beasts called a fox," and whilst there hunting, chasing and pursuing the same with his dogs and hounds, and when in view thereof, Pierson, well knowing the fox was so hunted and pursued, did, in the sight of Post, to prevent his catching the same, kill and carry it off. A verdict having been rendered for the plaintiff below, the defendant there sued out a *certiorari,* and now assigned for error, that the declaration and the matters therein contained were not sufficient in law to maintain an action.

* * *

The question submitted by the counsel in this cause for our determination is, whether Lodowick Post, by the pursuit with his hounds in the manner alleged in his declaration, acquired such a right to, or property in, the fox as will sustain an action against Pierson for killing and taking him away?

The cause was argued with much ability by the counsel on both sides, and presents for our decision a novel and nice question. It is admitted that a fox is an animal *feræ naturæ,* and that property in such animals is acquired by occupancy only. These admissions narrow the discussion to the simple question of what acts amount to occupancy, applied to acquiring right to wild animals.

If we have recourse to the ancient writers upon general principles of law, the judgment below is obviously erroneous. Justinian's Institutes (lib. 2, tit. 1, sec. 13), and Fleta (lib. 3, ch. 2, p. 175), adopt the principle, that pursuit alone vests no property or right in the huntsman; and that even pursuit, accompanied with wounding, is equally ineffectual for that purpose, unless the animal be actually taken. The same principle is recognized by Breton (lib. 2, ch. 1, p. 8).

Puffendorf (lib. 4, ch. 6, sec. 2 and 10) defines occupancy of beasts *feræ naturæ,* to be the actual corporeal possession of them, and Bynkershock is cited as coinciding in this definition. It is indeed with hesitation that Puffendorf affirms that a wild beast mortally wounded or greatly maimed, cannot be fairly intercepted by another, whilst the pursuit of the person inflicting the wound continues. The foregoing authorities are decisive to show that mere pursuit gave Post no legal right to the fox, but that he became the property of Pierson, who intercepted and killed him.

It, therefore, only remains to inquire whether there are any contrary principles or authorities, to be found in other books, which ought to induce a different decision. Most of the cases which have occurred in England, relating to property in wild animals, have either been discussed and decided upon the principles of their positive statute regulations, or have arisen between the huntsman and the owner of the land upon which beasts *feræ naturæ* have been apprehended; the former claiming them by title of occupancy, and the latter *ratione soli.* Little satisfactory aid can, therefore, be derived from the English reporters.

Barbeyrac, in his notes on Puffendorf, does not accede to the definition of occupancy by the latter, but, on the contrary, affirms that actual bodily seizure is not, in all cases, necessary to constitute possession of wild animals. He does not, however, describe the acts which, according to his ideas, will amount to an appropriation of such animals to private use, so as to exclude the claims of all other persons, by title of occupancy, to the same animals; and he is far from averring that pursuit alone is sufficient for that purpose. To a certain extent, and as far as Barbeyrac appears to me to go, his objections to Puffendorf's definition of occupancy are reasonable and correct. That is to say, that actual bodily seizure is not indispensable to acquire right to, or possession of, wild beasts; but that, on the contrary, the mortal wounding of such beasts, by one not abandoning his pursuit, may, with the utmost propriety, be deemed possession of him; since thereby the pursuer manifests an unequivocal intention of appropriating the animal to his individual use, has deprived him of his natural liberty, and brought him within his certain control. So, also, encompassing and securing such animals with nets and toils, or otherwise intercepting them in such a manner as to deprive them of their natural liberty, and render escape impossible, may justly be deemed to give possession of them to those persons who, by their industry and labor, have used such means of apprehending them. * * *

We are the more readily inclined to confine possession or occupancy of beasts *feræ naturæ,* within the limits prescribed by the learned authors above cited, for the sake of certainty, and preserving peace and order in society. If the first seeing, starting or pursuing such animals, without having so wounded, circumvented or ensnared them, so as to deprive them of their natural liberty, and subject them to the control of their pursuer, should afford the basis of actions against others for intercepting and killing them, it would prove a fertile source of quarrels and litigation.

However uncourteous or unkind the conduct of Pierson towards Post, in this instance, may have been, yet this act was productive of no injury or damage for which a legal remedy can be applied. We are of opinion the judgment below was erroneous, and ought to be reversed.

LIVINGSTON, J. My opinion differs from that of the court.

[The question of this case is:] Whether a person who, with his own hounds, starts and hunts a fox on waste and uninhabited ground, and is on the point of seizing his prey, acquires such an interest in the animal as to have a right of action against another, who in view of the huntsman and his dogs in full pursuit, and with knowledge of the chase, shall kill and carry him away.

This is a knotty point, and should have been submitted to the arbitration of sportsmen, without poring over Justinian, Fleta, Bracton, Puffendorf, Locke, Barbeyrac, or Blackstone, all of whom have been cited; they would have had no difficulty in coming to a prompt and correct conclusion. In a court thus constituted, the skin and carcass of poor Reynard would have been properly disposed of, and a precedent set, interfering with no usage or custom which the experience of ages has sanctioned, and which must be so well known to every votary of Diana. But the parties have referred the question to our judgment, and we must dispose of it as well as we can, from the partial lights we possess, leaving to a higher tribunal the correction of any mistake which we may be so unfortunate as to make. By the pleadings it is admitted that a fox is a "wild and noxious beast." Both parties have regarded him, as the law of nations does a pirate, *"hostem humani generis,"* and although *"de mortuis nil nisi bonum"* be a maxim of our profession, the memory of the deceased has not been spared. His depredations on farmers and on barnyards, have not been forgotten; and to put him to death wherever found, is allowed to be meritorious, and of public benefit. Hence it follows, that our decision should have in view the greatest possible encouragement to the destruction of an animal, so cunning and ruthless in his career. But who would keep a pack of hounds; or what gentleman, at the sound of the horn, and at peep of day, would mount his steed, and for hours together, *"sub jove frigido,"* or a vertical sun, pursue the windings of this wily quadruped, if, just as night came on, and his stratagems and strength were nearly exhausted, a saucy intruder, who had not shared in the honors or labors of the chase, were permitted to come in at the death, and bear away in triumph the object of pursuit? Whatever Justinian may have thought of the matter, it must be recollected that his code was compiled many hundred years ago, and it would be very hard indeed, at the distance of so many centuries, not to have a right to establish a rule for ourselves. In his day, we read of no order of men who made it a business, in the language of the declaration in this cause, "with hounds and dogs to find, start, pursue, hunt, and chase," these animals, and that, too, without any other motive than the preservation of Roman poultry; if this diversion had been then in fashion, the lawyers who composed his institutes, would have taken care not to pass it by, without suitable encouragement. If anything, therefore, in the digests or pandects shall appear to militate against the defendant in error, who, on this occasion, was the fox hunter, we have only to say *tempora mutantur;* and if men themselves change with the times, why should not laws also undergo an alteration?

It may be expected, however, by the learned counsel, that more particular notice be taken of their authorities. I have examined them all, and feel great difficulty in determining, whether to acquire dominion over a thing, before in common, it be sufficient that we barely see it, or know where it is, or wish for it, or make a declaration of our will respecting it; or whether, in the case of wild beasts, setting a trap, or lying in wait, or starting, or pursuing, be enough; or if an actual wounding, or killing, or bodily tact and occupation be necessary. Writers on general law, who have favored us with their speculations on these points, differ on them all; but, great as is the diversity of sentiment among them, some conclusion must be adopted on the question immediately before us. After mature deliberation, I embrace that of Barbeyrac as the most rational and least liable to objection. If at liberty, we might imitate the courtesy of a certain emperor, who, to avoid giving offense to the advocates of any of these different doctrines, adopted a middle course, and by ingenious distinctions, rendered it difficult to say (as often happens after a fierce and angry contest) to whom the palm of victory belonged. He ordained, that if a beast be followed with large dogs and hounds, he shall belong to the hunter, not to the chance occupant; and in like manner, if he be killed or wounded with a lance or sword; but if chased with beagles only, then he passed to the captor, not to the first pursuer. If slain with a dart, a sling, or a bow, he fell to the hunter, if still in chase, and not to him who might afterwards find and seize him.

Now, as we are without any municipal regulations of our own, and the pursuit here, for aught that appears on the case, being with dogs and hounds of imperial stature, we are at liberty to adopt one of the provisions just cited, which comports also with the learned conclusion of Barbeyrac, that property in animals *feræ naturæ* may be acquired without bodily touch or manucaption, provided the pursuer be within reach, or have a reasonable prospect (which certainly existed here) of taking what he has thus discovered an intention of converting to his own use.

When we reflect also that the interest of our husbandmen, the most useful of men in any community, will be advanced by the destruction of a beast so pernicious and incorrigible, we cannot greatly err in saying that a pursuit like the present, through waste and unoccupied lands, and which must inevitably and speedily have terminated in corporeal possession, or bodily seisin, confers such a right to the object of it, as to make any one a wrong-doer who shall interfere and shoulder the spoil. The justice's judgment ought, therefore, in my opinion, to be affirmed.

Judgment of reversal.

Notes and Questions

1. When you read the case, how did you imagine that Post, the gentleman with the hounds, appeared? How was he dressed, for example? Pierson? The case refers to the fact that the events took place on "wild and uninhabited, unpossessed and waste land." This is legally significant because the landowner would have rights in this case that may have trumped those of both Post and Pierson, or at least would have set boundaries on those rights. At least one history of the case, however, argues that more was involved. Bethany Berger, in It's Not About the Fox: The Untold History of Pierson v. Post, ___ Duke L. J. ___ (2006), argues that "the heart of the conflict was a contest over which community would control the shared resources of the town and how those resources would be used." According to Berger, Pierson was a "proprietor," one who had inherited special rights to the commons from the town's founders. Post was nouveau riche, with wealth inherited from his father's trade in the West Indies. Post's fox hunt "would have been perceived as [a] display of conspicuous wealth" while Pierson's less elaborate hunting method "followed the town's traditions of puritan thrift." Thus, the dispute, in Berger's view, was about who would control the resources of the town that were held in common and "whether agricultural traditions or commerce and wealth would define its social organization."

2. Livingston recommends referring the case to the "arbitration of sportsmen" for resolution of the case. Courts often look to the "custom of the trade" for standards of behavior. What is the advantage of doing so? Has Livingston, however, selected a partisan in this case? And when he concludes that favoring the fox-and-hounds man in this case also benefits the farmer, is he trying to smooth over the deeper community conflict that Berger has identified?

3. The rule governing the case before the Supreme Court of New York in *Pierson* was clear to the majority: "a fox is an animal *feræ naturæ,* and . . . property in such animals is acquired by occupancy only." In deciding the case before them, did the court simply follow the rule or did it do something else? On what basis did the majority find that mere pursuit was not sufficient to establish a property right? With what policies was the court concerned? The majority opinion discusses situations of "mortal wounding." What relevance did an action of "mortal wounding" have to this case?

4. An article in Wisconsin Natural Resources (Nov./Dec. 1986) describes a conflict among sportsmen. A hunter named Preuss writes to the magazine: "I have had an experience that is giving me mixed feelings on deer hunting, human nature and doing what is right." Preuss reports that he was standing in the middle of his woodlot, heard five shots to the west, and then saw deer running down a wooded hill. Preuss shot the deer, which dropped immediately, though the bullet hit the deer only in the back. Preuss administered the "killing shot" to the neck and then went back to his stand

for a cup of coffee before dressing the deer. When he returned to the deer, another hunter was there and claimed that he had "gutshot" the buck only 75 yards from that spot. This second hunter claimed ownership under an "unwritten law" that the "first hunter to put a killing shot into a deer owns a deer." Preuss, who had reluctantly let the second hunter have the deer, asked readers of the magazine: "Whose deer was it?" Many readers responded. One wrote: "Hunter ethics and common sense dictate that the person who administers the killing shot should be the legal claimant. Since it is common knowledge, among those who know, that a gutshot deer does not die for at least a couple of days or longer, the stranger's argument is totally ridiculous." Another hunter wrote that he had shot an eight-point buck, trailed it, "but didn't find it until the next morning—dead from a gutshot, bloated and spoiled. How I wish another hunter had 'finished off' that fine deer. He could have had the venison, and the animal wouldn't have suffered a slow death." Another hunter disagrees: "A gutshot deer is a dead deer." And another says, "[I]t belongs to the hunter who first wounded the animal and was sportsman enough to follow up his shot. Only greed . . . would make a hunter tag another person's cripple. The owner of the deer is the one who drew first blood."

The article reports that, according to an attorney with the state's Department of Natural Resources, the Wisconsin Supreme Court in 1914 ruled that a wounded animal belongs to the person who brings it under control in a way to make actual possession practically inevitable. This gives the hunter a property right that cannot be divested by someone who intervenes and kills the animal. The attorney also reported that under Wisconsin statute, however, "a deer must be tagged immediately upon taking it. Failure to tag a deer as required by statute relieves the hunter of any vested property right in the animal. Therefore, it appears that in this instance, the hunter who ultimately tagged the deer has ownership." What is the purpose of the statute requiring that deer be tagged in order to preserve the ownership of the hunter?

5. Did Post suffer harm from Pierson? If you conclude that Pierson harmed Post, would you have a better chance of success by focusing the attention of the court on Pierson's wrongful acts rather than on property rights that Post may have acquired? Is the engagement in a lawful activity enough to give Post the right to continue that lawful activity without interference? See, e.g., Keeble v. Hickeringill, 103 Eng.Rep. (Q.B. 1707) (shots fired at flying ducks to scare them away from decoys that plaintiff put on his duck pond held to be an unlawful interference with plaintiff's right to use his property in a lawful manner). Suppose that instead of firing shots, the defendant had used a mechanical duck that was a more effective attraction than the plaintiff's decoys? Suppose that Pierson used a mechanical rabbit to entice the fox to him and away from Post? Would you apply *Keeble* to Greenpeace efforts to disrupt seal and whale hunting?

6. One way to analyze property rules is to examine the consequences a rule would have for human behavior. The "law and economics" school of thought is one form of analysis that focuses attention on the consequences of legal rules. See Bruce Ackerman, Economic Foundations of Property Law (1975), for a good collection of some of the classic articles using a law and economics approach to analyze property law issues.

The rule of capture established in *Pierson* illustrates one of the paradigms of the economic analysis of property law. You will recall that Livingston's opinion in *Pierson* based its result in part on its view that killing of foxes was to be encouraged and that the court's holding would encourage that behavior. The rule of capture establishes a race for first possession of the resource itself, whether it be foxes, oil and gas, or fish. Several economists have described the impact of this race on the overconsumption of the resource itself. For example: "The blade of grass that the manorial cow herd leaves behind is valueless to him, for tomorrow it may be eaten by another's animal; the oil left under the earth is valueless to the driller, for another may legally take it; the fish left in the sea are valueless to the fisherman, because there is no assurance that they will be there for him tomorrow if they are left behind today." Gordon, The Economic Theory of a Common Property Resource: The Fishery, Journal of Political Economy (1954) at 124. Other consequences include the overinvestment in the means of production; for example, better and more lobster traps to maximize the catch during a legally-limited season. See also, David Haddock, First Possession versus Optimal Timing: Limiting the Dissipation of Economic Value, 64 Wash. U.L.Q. 775 (1986). Federal management plans have been developed to rebuild and conserve declining fish stocks due to the overfishing incentive of *Pierson v. Post*. The illustration of the inefficiencies of the rule of capture is also used by Garrett Hardin in his classic article, The Tragedy of the Commons, 162 Science 1243 (1968), to justify private ownership of property.

PROBLEM: AHAB, OLIVE, AND THE WHALE

Relying only on *Pierson*, how would you resolve the following problem?

Mike "Captain" Ahab, a whaler, located a whale and harpooned it. His harpoon was attached to his boat by a super strong rope. However, following a long and exhausting struggle, the rope broke and the whale swam free. Ahab was somewhat upset, but comforted himself in the knowledge that his harpoon had been engraved with the following words:

IF FOUND, PLEASE NOTIFY MIKE AHAB OF ROCKPORT, MAINE, WHO IS THE OWNER OF THIS HARPOON AND ANY WHALE IN WHICH IT MAY BE FOUND.

The following day Olive Holmes, a law student, found the whale on the beach in front of her summer home. She thought to herself, "I read the case of *Pierson v. Post,* and it is clear to me that Ahab does not own this whale." She accordingly sold the whale to a whale processor and used the money to pay part of her tuition.

Olive returned the harpoon to Ahab but refused to turn over the proceeds of the sale. You are a lawyer. Ahab comes to you with this story and is extremely upset. He thinks the whale is his and that the money Olive Holmes got for the whale should be returned to him. He wants to know if he can win a lawsuit against Ms. Holmes for the value of the whale. On the basis of *Pierson v. Post* alone, what would you tell him and why? (This problem was developed by Professor Leonard Glantz, Boston University.)

C. THE CAPTURE ANALOGY

Argument by analogy is a common tool of legal analysis. The rule of *feræ naturæ* used in *Pierson* has been extended by analogy beyond property rights in wild animals to property rights in "migratory resources" such as oil and gas. In the case below, the Supreme Court of Kentucky modifies case law that relied on the rule of capture for oil and gas and that had stated the law of Kentucky for the previous fifty years.

TEXAS AMERICAN ENERGY CORPORATION v. CITIZENS FIDELITY BANK & TRUST COMPANY

Supreme Court of Kentucky, 1987.
736 S.W.2d 25.

[Ed. note: Texas American purchased Western Kentucky Gas Company (Western), a natural gas retailer. Western purchases gas from fields in Texas and Louisiana, and pipes the gas through its distribution pipeline and into underground storage fields in Kentucky. The natural gas is retrieved during peak demand mid-winter months for distribution to customers. In order for Western to purchase these gas reserves, Texas American entered into a loan agreement with Citizens Fidelity. This dispute arose when Texas American sought to use these gas reserves as security for the loan. Texas American considered the reserves to be personal property; therefore, only a "security interest" was required. Citizens Fidelity, however, considered the gas to be part of the real estate since it had been injected back into the land. If the natural gas is considered part of the real estate, a "mortgage interest" is required to secure the loan. The differences between a security and mortgage interest are not important for our discussion. Consider how the principles in *Pierson v. Post* are used to resolve the property status of natural gas.]

OPINION OF THE COURT

This court having granted discretionary review from an opinion of the Court of Appeals and being of the opinion that the Amended Opinion of the Hopkins Circuit Court by Honorable Thomas B. Spain, judge of said court, is correct, hereby adopts that opinion as the opinion of this court, as follows:

"With these facts in mind, we now move to the first question to be answered, namely whether natural gas, removed from its original 'home' and injected into a foreign location with confinement integrity, remains personal property as it is uniformly held to be upon its original production, or whether it reverts to an interest in real estate.

"The parties agree that until now the case law in Kentucky has considered such injected or extraneous gas not to be personal property when it is not confined. This is because of an opinion of the late revered Commissioner Osso Stanley of the former Court of Appeals in the now fifty-year-old case of *Hammonds v. Central Kentucky Natural Gas Co.,* 255 Ky. 685, 75 S.W.2d 204 (1934).

"In that case Della Hammonds owned 54 unleased acres located within the boundary of the gas company's 15,000 acre gas storage field. It was undisputed that the reservoir underlay her tract. She sued alleging trespass because the gas company's injected gas had 'invaded' the formation under her land without her consent. The trial Court found against her [and] Kentucky's highest Court [affirmed], holding that once the foreign gas was injected back into the earth, (into an uncontrolled gas storage formation), it ceased being the property of the gas company, and would only become personal property again when and if it was produced or reduced to actual possession by extraction a second time.

"In reaching this conclusion, Commissioner Stanley traced the evolution of judicial thought with regard to oil and gas as distinguished from the 'solid minerals.' He adopted the then popular theory that because of their fugacious nature, oil and gas were 'wild and migratory in nature,' and hence similar to animals *feræ naturæ* (i.e. wild by nature). This being so, he reasoned, the law as applied to wild animals ought to be applicable by analogy to oil and gas—minerals *feræ naturæ.* Consequently, since a fox until his capture in the forest belonged to all mankind, and if trapped and released in another forest reverted to common property, shouldn't the same logic apply to 'captured' and injected natural gas? Commissioner Stanley also quoted from Thornton's Work on Oil and Gas, Sect. 1264, wherein Judge Willis equated injected gas in storage with timber. 'Standing in the woods, timber is a part of the land. When severed it becomes personal property. If made into lumber and used to construct a building it becomes again a part of the land to which it is attached. When gas is stored in the natural reservoir it is subject to all the properties that inhered in it originally. A neighbor could take it with impunity through adjacent wells, if he owned land within the radius of the reservoir. Hence it should be taxed only as part of the land in which it is placed, and in such circumstances could not be treated as personal property."

"Texas American calls this Court's attention to the cases of *White v. New York State Natural Gas Corporation,* 190 F.Supp. 342 (W.D.Pa. 1960) and *Lone Star Gas Company v. Murchison,* 353 S.W.2d 870; 94 A.L.R.2d 529 (Tex.1962). In both these cases *Hammonds* is referred to and rejected, along with the 'wild animal' analogy as applied to injected stored gas. The following portion of the opinion in *White* is particularly succinct:

> Generally stated, the law relating to ownership of wild animals is based on possessory concepts, with title being acquired only by reduction of the animal *feræ naturæ* to possession and being divested by loss of possession through escape and return of the animal to its natural and ferocious state. [   ]

It becomes readily apparent, however, that a strict application of this analogy to the present facts is of no benefit to the plaintiff's cause. To begin with, the storage gas in question has not escaped from its owners. On the contrary, it is yet very much in the possession of the storage companies, being within a well-defined storage field, the Hebron–Ellisburg Field, and being subject to the control of the storage companies through the same wells by which the gas originally had been injected into the storage pool. [   ]

Moreover, there has been no return of storage gas to its 'natural habitat' since Southwest gas, differing materially in chemical and physical properties from native Oriskany gas, is not native to the Oriskany Sands underlying the Hebron–Ellisburg Field. Deferring to the analogy of animals *feræ naturæ* under the circumstances of this case would no more divest a storage company of title to stored gas than a zookeeper in Pittsburgh to title to an escaped elephant. [   ]

"In *Lone Star* the Court comments that our *Hammonds* case 'in its application of *feræ naturæ* doctrine, has been the subject of violent adverse criticism by many authors and law review writers' [   ]

* * * The analogy of wild animals upon which Hammonds is founded fails to undergird the ultimate decision of that case. Gas has no similarity to wild animals. Gas is an inanimate, diminishing non-reproductive substance lacking any will of its own, and instead of running wild and roaming at large as animals do, is subject to be moved solely by pressure or mechanical means. It cannot be logically regarded as personal property of the human race as are wild animals, instead of being turned loose in the woods as the fanciful fox or placed in the streams as the fictitious fish, gas, a privately owned commodity, has been stored for use, as required by the consuming public being, as alleged by appellant, subject to its control and withdrawal at any time. Logic and reason dictates the application of the White decision rather than Hammonds, to the end, that in Texas, the owner of gas does not lose title thereof by storing the same in a well-defined underground reservoir.

"For the same 'sound and logical reason, especially in the light of advanced knowledge and scientific achievement in the oil and gas industry * * *' this Court is of the opinion that it is time to limit *Hammonds* and to now hold that natural gas once converted to personal property by extraction remains personal property notwithstanding its subsequent storage in underground reservoirs with confinement integrity.

"*Hammonds* should be narrowly construed or limited as it applies to the instant case, for the reason that the fact situations in the two are distinguishable. In *Hammonds* there was a known 'leak' in the gas storage reservoir inasmuch as Mrs. Hammonds' land was, in fact, a part of the natural reservoir, though not controlled by the storage company. In the case at hand, however, it has been stipulated that the gas reservoir has total integrity, and the gas cannot escape nor can it be extracted by anyone except Western. Using the *feræ naturæ* analogy,

Western has captured the wild fox, hence reducing it to personal property. The fox has not been released in another forest, permitting it to revert to the common property of mankind; but rather, the fox has only been released in a private confinement zoo. The fox is no less under the control of Western than if it were on a leash.

"Accordingly, the Court is of the opinion that *Hammonds* does not control in the instant case and that under the stipulated facts, the injected gas remains the personal property of Western.

"This being so, there is no more reason to require that it can only be hypothecated or encumbered by a real estate mortgage than there would be to require such of a recreational vehicle temporarily parked at a campground or of coal stockpiled at a tipple."

It is therefore the opinion of this court that, in those instances when previously extracted oil or gas is subsequently stored in underground reservoirs capable of being defined with certainty and the integrity of said reservoirs is capable of being maintained, title to such oil or gas is not lost and said minerals do not become subject to the rights of the owners of the surface above the storage fields. * * *

STEPHENS, C.J., and GANT, LAMBERT, LEIBSON, VANCE and WINTERSHEIMER, JJ., concur.

STEPHENSON, J., dissents and files a separate dissenting opinion.

Notes and Questions

1. What is left of *Hammonds* after the *Texas American* case?

2. How do you assess whether an analogy is persuasive? The *Hammonds* case, quoted in *Texas American,* found that gas was like a wild animal and so applied rules that were developed for resolving ownership claims to wild animals to the issue before them. How is the wild animal analogy a good analogy for gas? A bad analogy? Why would lawyers argue legal questions by using analogies? Does your answer depend on how accurately the analogy describes the actual "behavior" of oil and gas? Does it depend on the consequences of the application of the analogy, i.e., who wins or loses in the case or who has title? Does it depend on how the analogy affects productivity, security, conservation, predictability? Would you apply the concept of capture to underground water, for example when it is being removed to fill millions of plastic bottles of spring water? (See, e.g. Michigan Citizens for Water Conservation v. Nestle, 269 Mich.App. 25, 709 N.W.2d 174 (2005)).

3. When the valuable commercial potential of oil and gas was discovered in the United States, considerable litigation ensued over ownership rights in these natural resources. Courts established ownership interests in oil and gas by analogizing these substances to other forms of property, and applying the property rules associated with those forms of property. In *Texas American,* for example, you saw an application of the rule of capture. Other alternatives also existed.

Under traditional common law, *cujus est solum, ejus est usque ad coelum et ad inferos*: To whomever the soil belongs, he owns also to the sky and to the depths. In other words, the surface owner was also considered the owner of the column of air directly above his surface, extending to the heavens, and a column of dirt directly below his surface, extending to the center of the earth. This ownership included any thing that might be found within this column of air and dirt. (Air rights can be very valuable, for example, even though there is "nothing" there. Bagli, "$430 a Square Foot, for Air? Only in New York Real Estate,)" N.Y.Times 11/30/05 (A1).

Courts analogized oil and gas to other solid minerals that were part of the land. Thus, whoever owned the surface over an oil or gas reservoir, also owned the oil and gas. However, unlike solid minerals, oil and gas have physical properties that allow these substances to migrate within connected underground caverns or within rock that can act like a sponge for these materials. This migration is caused by changes in pressure that result from extracting the oil and gas. Thus, if oil is extracted from reservoir 1, oil from reservoir 2 may migrate into reservoir 1, replacing the oil that has been extracted. If oil from your reservoir migrates into your neighbor's reservoir because he has been drilling, do you have a cause of action against your neighbor under *ad coelum*? Under the rule of capture? Which allocation rule furthers the goal of productive use of property? Is productivity an appropriate goal? The only goal?

For a creative analysis of both the historical rationale for and the positive and negative consequences of the application of the rule of capture both to oil and gas and to wildlife, see, Rance L. Craft, Of Reservoir Hogs and Pelt Fiction: Defending the Ferae Naturae Analogy Between Petroleum and Wildlife, 44 Emory L.J. 697 (1995).

POPOV v. HAYASHI

Superior Court, San Francisco County, California.
2002 WL 31833731.

McCarthy, J.

In 1927, Babe Ruth hit sixty home runs. That record stood for thirty four years until Roger Maris broke it in 1961 with sixty one home runs. Mark McGwire hit seventy in 1998. On October 7, 2001, at PacBell Park in San Francisco, Barry Bonds hit number seventy three. That accomplishment set a record which, in all probability, will remain unbroken for years into the future.

The event was widely anticipated and received a great deal of attention.

The ball that found itself at the receiving end of Mr. Bond's bat garnered some of that attention. Baseball fans in general, and especially people at the game, understood the importance of the ball. It was worth a great deal of money and whoever caught it would bask, for a brief period of time, in the reflected fame of Mr. Bonds.

With that in mind, many people who attended the game came prepared for the possibility that a record setting ball would be hit in their direction. Among this group were plaintiff Alex Popov and defendant Patrick Hayashi. They were unacquainted at the time. Both men brought baseball gloves, which they anticipated using if the ball came within their reach.

They, along with a number of others, positioned themselves in the arcade section of the ballpark. This is a standing room only area located near right field. It is in this general area that Barry Bonds hits the greatest number of home runs. The area was crowded with people on October 7, 2001 and access was restricted to those who held tickets for that section.

Barry Bonds came to bat in the first inning. With nobody on base and a full count, Bonds swung at a slow knuckleball. He connected. The ball sailed over the right-field fence and into the arcade.

Josh Keppel, a cameraman who was positioned in the arcade, captured the event on videotape. Keppel filmed much of what occurred from the time Bonds hit the ball until the commotion in the arcade had subsided. He was standing very near the spot where the ball landed and he recorded a significant amount of information critical to the disposition of this case.

In addition to the Keppel tape, seventeen percipient witnesses testified as to what they saw after the ball came into the stands. The testimony of these witnesses varied on many important points. Some of the witnesses had a good vantage point and some did not. Some appeared disinterested in the outcome of the litigation and others had a clear bias. Some remembered the events well and others did not. Some were encumbered by prior inconsistent statements which diminished their credibility.

The factual findings in this case are the result of an analysis of the testimony of all the witnesses as well as a detailed review of the Keppel tape. Those findings are as follows:

When the seventy-third home run ball went into the arcade, it landed in the upper portion of the webbing of a softball glove worn by Alex Popov. While the glove stopped the trajectory of the ball, it is not at all clear that the ball was secure. Popov had to reach for the ball and in doing so, may have lost his balance.

Even as the ball was going into his glove, a crowd of people began to engulf Mr. Popov. He was tackled and thrown to the ground while still in the process of attempting to complete the catch. Some people intentionally descended on him for the purpose of taking the ball away, while others were involuntarily forced to the ground by the momentum of the crowd.

Eventually, Mr. Popov was buried face down on the ground under several layers of people. At one point he had trouble breathing. Mr. Popov was grabbed, hit and kicked. People reached underneath him in the area of his glove. Neither the tape nor the testimony is sufficient to establish which individual members of the crowd were responsible for the assaults on Mr. Popov.

* * *

Mr. Popov intended at all times to establish and maintain possession of the ball. At some point the ball left his glove and ended up on the ground. It is impossible to establish the exact point in time that this occurred or what caused it to occur.

Mr. Hayashi was standing near Mr. Popov when the ball came into the stands. He, like Mr. Popov, was involuntarily forced to the ground. He committed no wrongful act. While on the ground he saw the loose ball. He picked it up, rose to his feet and put it in his pocket.

Although the crowd was still on top of Mr. Popov, security guards had begun the process of physically pulling people off. Some people resisted those efforts. One person argued with an official and another had to be pulled off by his hair.

Mr. Hayashi kept the ball hidden. He asked Mr. Keppel to point the camera at him. At first, Mr. Keppel did not comply and Mr. Hayashi continued to hide the ball. Finally after someone else in the crowd asked Mr. Keppel to point the camera at Mr. Hayashi, Mr. Keppel complied. It was only at that point that Mr. Hayashi held the ball in the air for others to see. Someone made a motion for the ball and Mr. Hayashi put it back in his glove. It is clear that Mr. Hayashi was concerned that someone would take the ball away from him and that he was unwilling to show it until he was on videotape. Although he testified to the contrary, that portion of his testimony is unconvincing.

Mr. Popov eventually got up from the ground. He made several statements while he was on the ground and shortly after he got up which are consistent with his claim that he had achieved some level of control over the ball and that he intended to keep it. Those statements can be heard on the audio portion of the tape. When he saw that Mr. Hayashi had the ball he expressed relief and grabbed for it. Mr. Hayashi pulled the ball away. Security guards then took Mr. Hayashi to a secure area of the stadium.

It is important to point out what the evidence did not and could not show. Neither the camera nor the percipient witnesses were able to establish whether Mr. Popov retained control of the ball as he descended into the crowd. Mr. Popov's testimony on this question is inconsistent on several important points, ambiguous on others and, on the whole, unconvincing. We do not know when or how Mr. Popov lost the ball.

Perhaps the most critical factual finding of all is one that cannot be made. We will never know if Mr. Popov would have been able to retain control of the ball had the crowd not interfered with his efforts to do so. Resolution of that question is the work of a psychic, not a judge

LEGAL ANALYSIS

* * *

In the case at bar, Mr. Popov is not claiming that Mr. Hayashi damaged the ball or that he interfered with Mr. Popov's use and enjoyment of the ball. He claims instead that Mr. Hayashi intentionally took it from him and refused to give it back. * * *

[Mr. Popov's claim of conversion cannot succeed], however, unless the baseball rightfully belongs to Mr. Popov. One who has neither title nor possession, nor any right to possession, cannot sue for conversion. The deciding question in this case then, is whether Mr. Popov achieved possession or the right to possession as he attempted to catch and hold on to the ball.

The parties have agreed to a starting point for the legal analysis. Prior to the time the ball was hit, it was possessed and owned by Major League Baseball. At the time it was hit it became intentionally abandoned property. The first person who came in possession of the ball became its new owner.

The parties fundamentally disagree about the definition of possession. In order to assist the court in resolving this disagreement, four distinguished law professors participated in a forum to discuss the legal definition of possession. The professors also disagreed.

The disagreement is understandable. Although the term possession appears repeatedly throughout the law, its definition varies depending on the context in which it is used. Various courts have condemned the term as vague and meaningless.

This level of criticism is probably unwarranted.

While there is a degree of ambiguity built into the term possession, that ambiguity exists for a purpose. Courts are often called upon to resolve conflicting claims of possession in the context of commercial disputes. A stable economic environment requires rules of conduct which are understandable and consistent with the fundamental customs and practices of the industry they regulate. Without that, rules will be difficult to enforce and economic instability will result. Because each industry has different customs and practices, a single definition of possession cannot be applied to different industries without creating havoc.

This does not mean that there are no central principles governing the law of possession. It is possible to identify certain fundamental concepts that are common to every definition of possession.

* * *

The task of this court is to use these principles as a starting point to craft a definition of possession that applies to the unique circumstances of this case.

We start with the observation that possession is a process which culminates in an event. The event is the moment in time that possession is achieved. The process includes the acts and thoughts of the would be possessor which lead up to the moment of possession.

The focus of the analysis in this case is not on the thoughts or intent of the actor. Mr. Popov has clearly evidenced an intent to possess the baseball and has communicated that intent to the world. The question is whether he did enough to reduce the ball to his exclusive dominion and control. Were his acts sufficient to create a legally cognizable interest in the ball?

Mr. Hayashi argues that possession does not occur until the fan has complete control of the ball. . . .

Mr. Popov argues that this definition requires that a person seeking to establish possession must show unequivocal dominion and control, a standard rejected by several leading cases. [The court cites *Pierson*, among other cases.] Instead, he . . . suggest[s] that possession occurs when an individual intends to take control of a ball and manifests that intent by stopping the forward momentum of the ball whether or not complete control is achieved.

* * *

The degree of control necessary to establish possession varies from circumstance to circumstance. "The law . . . does not always require that one who discovers lost or abandoned property must actually have it in hand before he is vested with a legally protected interest. The law protects not only the title acquired by one who finds lost or abandoned property but also the right of the person who discovers such property, and is actively and ably engaged in reducing it to possession, to complete this process without interference from another. The courts have recognized that in order to acquire a legally cognizable interest in lost or abandoned property a finder need not always have manual possession of the thing. Rather, a finder may be protected by taking such constructive possession of the property as its nature and situation permit." [ ]

This rule is applied in cases involving the hunting or fishing of wild animals or the salvage of sunken vessels. The hunting and fishing cases recognize that a mortally wounded animal may run for a distance before falling. The hunter acquires possession upon the act of wounding the animal not the eventual capture. Similarly, whalers acquire possession by landing a harpoon, not by subduing the animal.

* * *

These rules are contextual in nature. The are crafted in response to the unique nature of the conduct they seek to regulate. Moreover, they are influenced by the custom and practice of each industry. The reason that absolute dominion and control is not required to establish possession in the cases cited by Mr. Popov is that such a rule would be unworkable and unreasonable. The "nature and situation" of the property at issue does not immediately lend itself to unequivocal dominion and control. It is impossible to wrap ones arms around a whale, a fleeing fox or a sunken ship.

The opposite is true of a baseball hit into the stands of a stadium. Not only is it physically possible for a person to acquire unequivocal dominion and control of an abandoned baseball, but fans generally expect a claimant to have accomplished as much. The custom and practice of the stands creates a reasonable expectation that a person will achieve full control of a ball before claiming possession. There is no reason for the legal rule to be inconsistent with that expectation. . . .

Mr. Popov has not established by a preponderance of the evidence that he would have retained control of the ball after all momentum ceased and after any incidental contact with people or objects. Consequently, he did not achieve full possession. That finding, however, does not resolve the case. The reason we do not know whether Mr. Popov would have retained control of the ball is not because of incidental contact. It is because he was attacked. His efforts to establish possession were interrupted by the collective assault of a band of wrongdoers.

A decision which ignored that fact would endorse the actions of the crowd by not repudiating them. Judicial rulings, particularly in cases that receive media attention, affect the way people conduct themselves. This case demands vindication of an important principle. We are a nation governed by law, not by brute force.

As a matter of fundamental fairness, Mr. Popov should have had the opportunity to try to complete his catch unimpeded by unlawful activity. To hold otherwise would be to allow the result in this case to be dictated by violence. That will not happen. For these reasons, the analysis cannot stop with the valid observation that Mr. Popov has not proved full possession.

The legal question presented at this point is whether an action for conversion can proceed where the plaintiff has failed to establish possession or title. It can. An action for conversion may be brought where the plaintiff has title, possession or the right to possession.

Here Mr. Popov seeks, in effect, a declaratory judgment that he has either possession or the right to possession. . . .

Consistent with this principle, the court adopts the following rule. Where an actor undertakes significant but incomplete steps to achieve possession of a piece of abandoned personal property and the effort is interrupted by the unlawful acts of others, the actor has a legally cognizable pre-possessory interest in the property. That pre-possessory interest constitutes a qualified right to possession which can support a cause of action for conversion.

Possession can be likened to a journey down a path. Mr. Popov began his journey unimpeded. He was fast approaching a fork in the road. A turn in one direction would lead to possession of the ball—he would complete the catch. A turn in the other direction would result in a failure to achieve possession—he would drop the ball. Our problem is that before Mr. Popov got to the point where the road forked, he was set upon by a gang of bandits, who dislodged the ball from his grasp.

Recognition of a legally protected pre-possessory interest, vests Mr. Popov with a qualified right to possession and enables him to advance a legitimate claim to the baseball based on a conversion theory. Moreover it addresses the harm done by the unlawful actions of the crowd.

It does not, however, address the interests of Mr. Hayashi. The court is required to balance the interests of all parties.

Mr. Hayashi was not a wrongdoer. He was a victim of the same bandits that attacked Mr. Popov. The difference is that he was able to extract himself from their assault and move to the side of the road. It was there that he discovered the loose ball. When he picked up and put it in his pocket he attained unequivocal dominion and control.

If Mr. Popov had achieved complete possession before Mr. Hayashi got the ball, those actions would not have divested Mr. Popov of any rights, nor would they have created any rights to which Mr. Hayashi could lay claim. Mr. Popov, however, was able to establish only a qualified pre-possessory interest in the ball. That interest does not establish a full right to possession that is protected from a subsequent legitimate claim. On the other hand, while Mr. Hayashi appears on the surface to have done everything necessary to claim full possession of the ball, the ball itself is encumbered by the qualified pre-possessory interest of Mr. Popov. At the time Mr. Hayashi came into possession of the ball, it had, in effect, a cloud on its title.

An award of the ball to Mr. Popov would be unfair to Mr. Hayashi. It would be premised on the assumption that Mr. Popov would have caught the ball. That assumption is not supported by the facts. An award of the ball to Mr. Hayashi would unfairly penalize Mr. Popov. It would be based on the assumption that Mr. Popov would have dropped the ball. That conclusion is also unsupported by the facts. Both men have a superior claim to the ball as against all the world. Each man has a claim of equal dignity as to the other. We are, therefore, left with something of a dilemma.

Thankfully, there is a middle ground.

[The court decides to split the ball (actually, the ownership of the ball) between both parties as an exercise of its power in equity!]

Notes and Questions

1.   Did Judge McCarthy adopt a particular definition of possession? Did he identify who possessed the ball first? This is a situation that is likely to repeat itself in the future. Is Judge McCarthy's rule one that will lead to certainty, or will it encourage contests over home run balls? Is there a rule that would have made the identification of the possessor/owner easier in future cases?

2. Judge McCarthy argues that the concept of possession requires both intent and action on the part of the claimant. He further argues that the criteria for what action is required of the claimant depends on the circumstances. What criteria did he use in this case? Did he conclude that a home run baseball on the fly is like a wild animal? Does the analogy work?

3. Baseball fans may be interested in further discussion of their rights to baseballs hit into the stands. Judge McCarthy relied on Paul Finkelman, Fugitive Baseballs and Abandoned Property: Who Owns the Home Run Ball?, 23 Cardozo L. Rev. 1609 (2002). Steven Semeraro disagrees with Professor Finkelman in An Essay on Property Rights in Milestone Home Run Baseballs, 56 SMU L. Rev. 2281 (2003).

4. Arguments concerning possession come into play in resolving disputes concerning sunken treasure. The Columbus–America Discovery Group (based in Columbus, Ohio) won exclusive salvage rights in 1987 by successfully arguing "tele-possession" of the wreck of the Central America (and its gold cargo worth up to $1 billion), which lay under 8,000 feet of water. Columbus–America based their claim on retrieving one piece of coal using a deep-water robot they named Nemo. The judge allowed the salvage claim despite the failure to meet the customary standard requiring a diver to physically visit the site. Yet to be decided was the ownership of the cargo itself.

Columbus–America Discovery Group claimed ownership. Columbus–America spent 13 years and $12 million in finding the ship, which, incidentally, was not located on the spot identified in the earlier court case concerning the wreck. Some competitors of Columbus–America claimed that it misrepresented the location of the wreck in order to decoy the real site. Columbus–America claims it discovered the wreck as it was heading toward the earlier identified location. According to the president of Columbus–America, "no one was there," and his team "exercised exclusive control over the shipwreck site." They went on to recover a good deal of the approximately three tons of cargo.

Contenders for the gold also included ten insurance companies that claimed they paid off on the loss when the ship was sunk in 1857. Columbus–America claimed that the insurance companies could not prove they paid for the loss; and even if they could, that they abandoned the wreck and made no effort to recover it. The insurance companies responded that they simply don't abandon property and, furthermore, that the gold was simply "in storage."

Columbia University also made a claim. The University stated that Columbus–America relied on sonar studies that the University had produced. The University also claimed that a vessel it owned discovered the shipwreck in 1984 but had not realized it at the time.

Finally, preservationists were upset that Columbus–America was destroying the wreck by retrieving the cargo. The gold already recovered was on display briefly before it was moved to an undisclosed location. Preservationists claim that the wreck could be a valuable resource to historians, oceanographers, and archaeologists. (Taken from a series of news articles reported April 3–6, 1990.)

What do you think of the utility of a rule of tele-possession in granting salvage rights? How would you resolve this dispute? Would any of the theories of property ownership we discussed earlier influence your result?

Judge Donald Russell begins his opinion, one of many judicial opinions on the Columbus–America case, in this way:

> When Erasmus mused that '[a] common shipwreck is a source of consolation to all,' [   ], he quite likely did not foresee inconcinnate free-for-alls among self-styled salvors. [   ] Without doubt the Dutch scholar also could not imagine legal brawls involving self-styled "finders" from Ohio, British and American insurance underwriters, an heir to the Miller Brewing fortune, a Texas oil millionaire, an Ivy League university, and an Order of Catholic monks. Yet that is what this case involves, with the prize being up to one billion dollars in gold.

Columbus–America Discovery Group v. Atlantic Mutual Insurance Co., 974 F.2d 450 (4th Cir.1992). (His was not the last appellate decision in this case. In 1995, the Fourth Circuit again considered the claims of the investors, the salvor and others and held that the district court's award of 90% of the salvage to Columbus–America was not excessive. Columbus–America Discovery Group v. Atlantic Mutual Insurance Co., 56 F.3d 556 (4th Cir.1995), cert. denied, 516 U.S. 938, 116 S.Ct. 352, 133 L.Ed.2d 248 and 516 U.S. 990, 116 S.Ct. 521, 133 L.Ed.2d 429.)

One of the issues in the litigation was whether the law of finders or the law of salvage should apply. The results of any particular case could be quite different depending on which doctrine would apply, as finders law would recognize a claim of abandonment of the wreck by the title holder, while salvage would maintain title in the original owners but allow the salvors a generous "salvage award" against the value of the wreck and its cargo.

Does it make sense to have a specific legal doctrine for wrecked ships? Is this another illustration of Judge Livingston's desire to submit the dispute over the fox in *Pierson* to the arbitration of sportsmen?

NOTE ON WATER LAW

> If water were our chief symbol for property, we might think of property rights—and perhaps other rights—in a quite different way. We might think of rights literally and figuratively as more fluid and less fenced-in; we might think of property as entailing less of the awesome Blackstonian power of exclusion and more of the qualities of flexibility, reasonableness and moderation, attentiveness to others, and cooperative solutions to common problems. Carol M. Rose, Property as the Keystone Right? 71 Notre Dame L.Rev. 329 (1996).

Through most of your study of property law in this course, you will be focused on land as the paradigm of property, though you will in this chapter have limited encounters with chattels (personal property) and with intangibles (intellectual property). Property law concepts also govern resources, such as oil and gas, which do not conform to the characteristics of land. The major resource of this sort is water.

Water is the subject of intense battles, especially although not only in the western states. Water is a most critical resource, absolutely necessary for life, for agriculture, for development, for most beneficial uses of land. Competing uses of water are often in dire conflict: upstream uses may make downstream uses totally impossible. Although residents of urban areas may be aware of and sensitive to pollution of water sources they use or the rivers and streams in their surrounding area, they often cannot appreciate the concerns of the residents of western, more arid, and more agricultural states over diversion and control of water.

Battles over water have been played out between states. For example, Maryland and Virginia litigated a dispute over access to water in the Potomac River in Virginia v. Maryland, 540 U.S. 56, 124 S.Ct. 598, 157 L.Ed.2d 461 (2003) (interpreting a 1785 compact regulating relations between the states as to the withdrawal of water from the River). The nature of water, and the nature of the rights framework applicable to this resource, unavoidably makes neighbors interdependent. For example, in Brady v. Abbott Laboratories, 433 F.3d 679 (9th Cir. 2005), Abbott Laboratories pumped ground water out of the ground to allow it to construct a foundation for a new building. Its pumping of the water lowered the level of the water table, however, with the effect that Brady's pecan orchard died for lack of water. (Pecan trees apparently have shallow roots, and the reduction in the water table put the water out of reach.) Environmental concerns are a central issue as well. The next time you buy a bottle of spring water, you may want to keep Michigan Citizens for Water Conservation v. Nestle, 269 Mich.App. 25, 709 N.W.2d 174 (2005) in mind. In this case, the plaintiff argued that Nestle's pumping of 400 gallons of water per minute violated plaintiff's riparian rights.

The property law applicable to water in general differs mightily from the rules applicable to land. Water law must account for the fact that water is critical to the activities of many, many users; that the uses can be in conflict; and that, in many or most of its forms, water is moving. Touch the river twice and you have not touched the same water.

Because of these characteristics, water law has borne a much broader claim of public rights and governmental administration than has land law. Beyond shared characteristics, water law varies by the form of the water (whether a navigable waterway, a lake, surface water, or flowing water, for example) and among the states. For example, the doctrine of correlative rights allocates rights to underground water. Under this system, all surface owners above a common aquifer have a right to take water from the reservoir. Along with this right, however, are corresponding duties not to injure the reservoir, take an undue portion, or waste the water that was taken. Similarly, under the doctrine of riparian rights, all surface owners adjacent to a flowing stream have a right to use the water. This right also carries with it a duty not to use the water in a way that would diminish the quantity or quality of water reaching downstream riparian owners. Several western states use a concept of "prior appropriation," now usually only with a required governmental permit, to allow access to flowing water by persons who do not own the land adjacent to the water. Can you see why many of the western states, including Nevada, New Mexico, and Arizona, might have chosen "prior appropriation" over riparian rights? Prior appropriation gives the party who first puts water to a beneficial use the right to use that water to the exclusion of others. Can you see why almost all of the prior appropriation states have put a governmental permit system in place to regulate the uses made of the water?

D. FINDERS (AND, INCIDENTALLY, "CONSTRUCTIVE" POSSESSION)

Every so often you read in the newspaper of some lucky person who has found a significant sum of money or jewels. Most states have statutes governing the law of finders. Some of these statutes codify common-law rules that distinguished among "lost" items, "mislaid" items, "abandoned" items, and "treasure trove." It is interesting to examine the historical roots of such distinctions and their current utility, if any; but that is not the purpose of including finders cases here. The cases on finders illustrate some important points concerning the legal concept of possession, building on possession as capture in *Pierson* and including the flexible concept of "constructive possession." Many of the property rules that you will study later, especially adverse possession of land, rely on possession as a determining factor. In addition to developing a sense of the legal definition of possession, you should focus on what has been called the "relativity of title."

ARMORY v. DELAMIRIE

King's Bench, 1722.
1 Strange 525.

The plaintiff being a chimney sweeper's boy found a jewel and carried it to the defendant's shop (who was a goldsmith) to know what it was, and delivered it into the hands of the apprentice, who under pretence of weighing it, took out the stones, and calling to the master to let him know it came to three halfpence, the master offered the boy the money, who refused to take it, and insisted to have the thing again; whereupon the apprentice delivered him back the socket without the stones. And now in trover against the master these points were ruled:

1. That the finder of a jewel, though he does not by such finding acquire an absolute property or ownership, yet he has such a property as will enable him to keep it against all but the rightful owner, and consequently may maintain trover.

* * *

3. As to the value of the jewel several of the trade were examined to prove what a jewel of the finest water that would fit the socket would be worth; and the Chief Justice directed the jury, that unless the

defendant did produce the jewel, and shew it not to be of the finest water, they should presume the strongest against him, and make the value of the best jewels the measure of their damages: which they accordingly did.

Notes and Questions

1. How does *Armory* illustrate the proposition that possession is the root of title if the possessor (the jeweler's apprentice) is not held to have title?

2. If the chimney sweep's boy had lost the jewel on the way to the jeweler and the jeweler's apprentice had simply found it on the street, would the chimney sweep's boy still win in a suit to recover the jewel? Your answer to that question will illustrate the relativity of title. The concept of relativity of title contributes to the modern legal notion that property is not a thing—a car, land, a book—but the legal relationships of persons as to a thing. This definition of property as relationship will be further explored in the discussion of property rights in body parts and the right to exclude later in this chapter.

NOTE ON BAILMENTS

The legal relationship between the chimney sweep's boy and the jeweler in *Armory* is called a bailment. Bailments are common relationships in commerce and in friendships. Bailments occur frequently and are very familiar to anyone who has released possession of a chattel to another with the understanding, either express or implied, that the thing is to be returned to his or her possession at some time in the future. For example, you take your shoes to a shop for repair or your clothes for cleaning. Or you lend a book or your notes to a classmate. Or at semester's end, you store furniture with a storage company. In each of these situations you have released possession of your property with the expectation that this thing is to be returned to you later.

In analyzing a claim based on bailment, the first question to consider is whether a bailment exists. A bailment requires that the bailee "take possession" of the thing and have the intent to possess or control the item.

The bailment can be either expressed or implied. In an expressed bailment, the bailor and bailee have discussed the critical terms of the bailment. For example, the bailor and bailee explicitly agree that the bailor's furniture will be deposited in the bailee's warehouse for a period of six months and that the bailee will then return the furniture. In an implied bailment, the parties may have failed to discuss the terms of the bailment. Your friend says "May I have your car?" and you toss her the keys. This can be an implied bailment in which the law fills in the missing terms. A second type of implied bailment occurs when the parties had not specifically intended a bailment, but the law places their relationship in that legal framework nonetheless. An example of this type of implied bailment is the relationship between the finder and the loser of a thing. (Did you wonder whether the chimney sweep's boy received a windfall in *Armory* by getting the full value of the jewel rather than the value of the jewel adjusted by the odds that the "true owner" would return and demand the jewel from the boy? Part of the rationale for awarding the finder the full value is that he is a bailee to the loser and has the general duty to return the thing found.)

Once the relationship is characterized as a bailment, the second issue is to identify the type of bailment. There are three choices at this point: (i) bailment for the sole benefit of the bailee (e.g., as when A borrows B's car); (ii) bailment for the sole benefit of the bailor (e.g., in a situation in which A stores B's stereo during summer vacation as a favor to B); and (iii) bailment for the mutual benefit of bailor and bailee (e.g., the deposit of an item with a shop for repair).

The characterization of the bailment purportedly defines the liability of the bailee for bailed goods that are lost, damaged, or stolen due to the bailee's negligence. The bailment for the sole benefit of the bailee results in the bailee's liability for even slight negligence; the bailment for the sole benefit of bailor results in the bailee's liability only for gross negligence; and the bailment for mutual benefit results in the bailee's liability for ordinary negligence. Whether a particular failing of a bailee is grossly negligent, slightly negligent, or simply negligent is determined in light of the particular circumstances.

Develop arguments for *both* the bailee and bailor in the following case:

(A) Diana Lewis and Irene Preston both work for the same company downtown and have offices in the same building. In August, Diana, who has all her personal mail delivered to her office, took a two-week vacation to the Rocky Mountains. Before she left, she asked Irene to take all her mail to Irene's house for the duration of her vacation. Diana had done the same for Irene earlier in the summer.

The mail at the company was distributed by a company letter carrier who simply placed the day's mail on each person's desk. Each day, Irene picked up Diana's mail at Diana's desk.

When Diana arrived home from her vacation, she went to Irene's house and retrieved her mail. She then noticed that two items that she had expected to receive were missing.

(1) First, a small box containing a necklace valued at approximately $200 was not among the mail. Upon investigation, Diana discovered that the box had been delivered to the company and had been placed by the company letter carrier on Diana's desk. Evidently, a fellow office worker had picked up Diana's mail that day and placed it, including the box, on Irene's desk while Irene was out to lunch. The box apparently was quickly stolen by a still-unknown thief who thus had quite a successful day at the office.

(2) Second, Diana was missing a $1,000 negotiable bond sent to her by her father. Irene did recall Diana's receiving a "certified-return receipt requested" letter from her father; however, Irene can't find it now. Irene had left the mail on her desk while she briefly left her office. Although she made every effort to recover the letter, she was unsuccessful.

(B) Would your arguments be different if Diana had paid Irene for her services? What if she had brought her a thank-you gift?

HANNAH v. PEEL

King's Bench, 1945.
1 K.B. 509.

Action tried by BIRKETT, J.

On December 13, 1938, the freehold of Gwernhaylod House, Overton-on-Dee, Shropshire, was conveyed to the defendant, Major Hugh Edward Ethelston Peel, who from that time to the end of 1940 never himself occupied the house and it remained unoccupied until October 5, 1939, when it was requisitioned, but after some months was released from requisition. Thereafter it remained unoccupied until July 18, 1940, when it was again requisitioned, the defendant being compensated by a payment at the rate of 250*l.* a year. In August, 1940, the plaintiff, Duncan Hannah, a lance-corporal, serving in a battery of the Royal Artillery, was stationed at the house and on the 21st of that month, when in a bedroom, used as a sick-bay, he was adjusting the black-out curtains when his hand touched something on the top of a window-frame, loose in a crevice, which he thought was a piece of dirt or plaster. The plaintiff grasped it and dropped it on the outside window ledge. On the following morning he saw that it was a brooch covered with cobwebs and dirt. Later, he took it with him when he went home on leave and his wife having told him it might be of value, at the end of October, 1940, he informed his commanding officer of his find and, on his advice, handed it over to the police, receiving a receipt for it. In August, 1942, the owner not having been found the police handed the brooch to the defendant, who sold it in October, 1942, for 66*l.*, to Messrs. Spink & Son, Ltd., of London, who resold it in the following month for 88*l.* There was no evidence that the defendant had any knowledge of the existence of the brooch before it was found by the plaintiff. The defendant had offered the plaintiff a reward for the brooch, but the plaintiff refused to accept this and maintained throughout his right to the possession of the brooch as against all persons other than the owner, who was unknown. By a letter, dated October 5, 1942, the plaintiff's solicitors demanded the return of the brooch from the defendant, but it was not returned and on October 21, 1943, the plaintiff issued his writ claiming the return of the brooch, or its value, and damages for its detention. By his defence, the defendant claimed the brooch on the ground that he was the owner of Gwernhaylod House and in possession thereof.

BIRKETT, J. There is no issue of fact in this case between the parties. As to the issue in law, the rival claims of the parties can be stated in this way: The plaintiff says: "I claim the brooch as its finder and I have a good title against all the world, save only the true owner." The defendant says: "My claim is superior to yours inasmuch as I am the freeholder. The brooch was found on my property, although I was never in occupation, and my title, therefore, ousts yours and in the absence of the true owner I am entitled to the brooch or its value." Unhappily the law on this issue is in a very uncertain state and there is need of an authoritative decision of a higher court. Obviously if it could be said with certainty that this is the law, that the finder of a lost article, wherever found, has a good title against all the world save the true owner, then, of course, all my difficulties would be resolved; or again, if it could be said with equal certainty that this is the law, that the possessor of land is entitled as against the finder to all chattels found on the land, again my difficulties would be resolved. But, unfortunately, the authorities give some support to each of these conflicting propositions.

In the famous case of *Armory v. Delamirie,* the plaintiff, who was a chimney sweeper's boy, found a jewel and carried it to the defendant's shop, who was a goldsmith, in order to know what it was, and he delivered it into the hands of the apprentice in the goldsmith's shop, who made a pretence of weighing it and took out the stones and called to the master to let him know that it came to three-halfpence. The master offered the boy the money who refused to take it and insisted on having the jewel again. Whereupon the apprentice handed him back the socket of the jewel without the stones, and an action was brought in trover against the master, and it was ruled "that the finder of a jewel, though he does not by such finding acquire an absolute property or ownership, yet he has such a property as will enable him to keep it against all but the rightful owner, and consequently may maintain trover." The case of *Bridges v. Hawkesworth* is in process of becoming almost equally as famous because of the disputation which has raged around it. The headnote in the Jurist is as follows: "The place in which a lost article is found does not constitute any exception to the general rule of law, that the finder is entitled to it as against all persons except the owner." The case was in fact an appeal against a decision of the county court judge at Westminster. The facts appear to have been that in the year 1847 the plaintiff, who was a commercial traveler, called on a firm named Byfield & Hawkesworth on business, as he was in the habit of doing, and as he was leaving the shop he picked up a small parcel which was lying on the floor. He immediately showed it to the shopman, and opened it in his presence, when it was found to consist of a quantity of Bank of England notes, to the amount of 65*l.* The defendant, who was a partner in the firm of Byfield & Hawkesworth, was then called, and the plaintiff told him he had found the notes, and asked the defendant to keep them until the owner appeared to claim them. Then various advertisements were put in the papers asking for the owner, but the true owner was never found. No person having appeared to claim them, and three years having elapsed since they were found, the plaintiff applied to the defendant to have the notes returned to him, and offered to pay the expenses of the advertisements, and to give an indemnity. The defendant refused to deliver them up to the plaintiff, and an action was brought in the county court of Westminster in consequence of that refusal. The county court judge decided that the defendant, the shopkeeper, was entitled to the custody of the notes as against the plaintiff, and gave judgment for the defendant. Thereupon the appeal was brought which came before the court composed of Patteson J. and Wightman J. Patteson J. said: "The notes which are the subject of this action were incidentally dropped, by mere accident, in the shop of the defendant, by the owner of them. The facts do not warrant the supposition that they had been deposited there intentionally, nor has the case been put at all upon that ground. The plaintiff found them on the floor, they being manifestly lost by someone. The general right of the finder to any article which has been lost, as against all the world, except the true owner, was established in the case of *Armory v. Delamirie* which has never been disputed. This right would clearly have accrued to the plaintiff had the notes been picked up by him outside the shop of the defendant and if he once had the right, the case finds that he did not intend, by delivering the notes to the defendant, to waive the title (if any) which he had to them, but they were handed to the defendant merely for the purpose of delivering them to the owner should he appear." Then a little later: "The case, therefore, resolves itself into the single point on which it appears that the learned judge decided it, namely, whether the circumstance of the notes being found inside the defendant's shop gives him, the defendant, the right to have them as against the plaintiff, who found them." After discussing the cases, and the argument, the learned judge said: "If the discovery had never been communicated to the defendant, could the real owner have had any cause of action against him because they were found in his house? Certainly not. The notes never were in the custody of the defendant, nor within the protection of his house, before they were found, as they would have been had they been intentionally deposited there; and the defendant has come under no responsibility, except from the communication made to him by the plaintiff, the finder, and the steps taken by way of advertisement. * * * We find, therefore, no circumstances in this case to take it out of the general rule of law, that the finder of a lost article is entitled to it as against all persons except the real owner, and we think that that rule must prevail, and that the learned judge was mistaken in holding that the place in which they were found makes any legal difference. Our judgment, therefore, is that the plaintiff is entitled to these notes as against the defendant."

It is to be observed that in *Bridges v. Hawkesworth* which has been the subject of immense disputation, neither counsel put forward any argument on the fact that the notes were found in a shop. Counsel for the appellant assumed throughout that the position was the same as if the parcel had been found in a private house, and the learned judge spoke of "the protection of his (the shopkeeper's) house." The case for the appellant was that the shopkeeper never knew of the notes. Again, what is curious is that there was no suggestion that the place where the notes were found was in any way material; indeed, the judge in giving the judgment of the court expressly repudiates this * * *. It is, there-fore, a little remarkable that in *South Staffordshire Water Co. v. Shar-man,* Lord Russell of Killowen C.J. said: "The case of *Bridges v. Hawkesworth* stands by itself, and on special grounds; and on those grounds it seems to me that the decision in that case was right. Someone had accidentally dropped a bundle of banknotes in a public shop. The shopkeeper did not know they had been dropped, and did not in any sense exercise control over them. The shop was open to the public, and they were invited to come there." That might be a matter of some doubt. Customers were invited there, but whether the public at large was, might be open to some question. * * * Patteson J. [in *Bridges*] never made any reference to the public part of the shop and, indeed, went out of his way to say that the learned county court judge was wrong in holding that the place where they were found made any legal difference.

Bridges v. Hawkesworth has been the subject of considerable com-ment by text-book writers and, amongst others, by Mr. Justice Oliver Wendell Holmes, Sir Frederick Pollock and Sir John Salmond.... Mr. Justice Oliver Wendell Holmes wrote: "Common law judges and civilians would agree that the finder got possession first and so could keep it as against the shopkeeper. For the shopkeeper, not knowing of the thing, could not have the intent to appropriate it, and, having invited the public to his shop, he could not have the intent to exclude them from it." So he introduces the matter of two intents which are not referred to by the judges who heard the case. [The court describes the positions of other commentators on *Bridges* who all agree that the premises owner did not have custody of the notes because he did not know they were there and could not, therefore, claim title.]

* * * The facts [in *South Staffordshire*] were that the defendant Sharman, while cleaning out, under the orders of the plaintiffs, the South Staffordshire Water Company, a pool of water on their land, found two rings embedded in the mud at the bottom of the pool. He declined to deliver them to the plaintiffs, but failed to discover the real owner. In an action brought by the company against Sharman in detinue it was held that the company were entitled to the rings. Lord Russell of Killowen C.J. said: "The plaintiffs are the freeholders of the locus in quo, and as such they have the right to forbid anybody coming on their land or in any way interfering with it. They had the right to say that their pool should be cleaned out in any way that they thought fit, and to direct what should be done with anything found in the pool in the course of such cleaning out. It is no doubt right, as the counsel for the defendant contended, to say that the plaintiffs must show that they had actual control over the locus in quo and the things in it; but under the circumstances, can it be said that the Minster Pool and whatever might be in that pool were not under the control of the plaintiffs? In my opinion they were. * * * The principle on which this case must be

decided, and the distinction which must be drawn between this case and that of *Bridges v. Hawkesworth,* is to be found in a passage in Pollock and Wright's 'Essay on Possession in the Common Law,' [   ]. 'The possession of land carries with it in general, by our law, possession of everything which is attached to or under that land, and, in the absence of a better title elsewhere, the right to possess it also'." If that is right, it would clearly cover the case of the rings embedded in the mud of the pool * * *. Lord Russell continued: "And it makes no difference that the possessor is not aware of the thing's existence * * *. [W]here a person has possession of house or land, with a manifest intention to exercise control over it and the things which may be upon or in it, then, if something is found on that land, whether by an employee of the owner or by a stranger, the presumption is that the possession of that thing is in the owner of the locus in quo." *South Staffordshire Water Co. v. Sharman* which was relied on by counsel for the defendant, has also been the subject of some discussion. It has been said that it establishes that if a man finds a thing as the servant or agent of another, he finds it not for himself, but for that other, and indeed that seems to afford a sufficient explanation of the case. The rings found at the bottom of the pool were not in the possession of the company, but it seems that though Sharman was the first to obtain possession of them, he obtained them for his employers and could claim no title for himself.

* * *

* * * It is fairly clear from the authorities that a man possesses everything which is attached to or under his land. Secondly, it would appear to be the law from the authorities I have cited, and particularly from *Bridges v. Hawkesworth* that a man does not necessarily possess a thing which is lying unattached on the surface of his land even though the thing is not possessed by someone else. A difficulty however, arises, because the rule which governs things an occupier possesses as against those which he does not, has never been very clearly formulated in our law. * * *

There is no doubt that in this case the brooch was lost in the ordinary meaning of that term, and I should imagine it had been lost for a very considerable time. Indeed, from this correspondence it appears that at one time the predecessors in title of the defendant were considering making some claim. But the moment the plaintiff discovered that the brooch might be of some value, he took the advice of his commanding officer and handed it to the police. His conduct was commendable and meritorious. The defendant was never physically in possession of these premises at any time. It is clear that the brooch was never his, in the ordinary acceptation of the term, in that he had the prior possession. He had no knowledge of it, until it was brought to his notice by the finder. * * * In those circumstances I propose to follow the decision in *Bridges v. Hawkesworth,* and to give judgment in this case for the plaintiff for 66*l.*

Judgment for plaintiff.

Notes and Questions

1. Major Peel lost, but why? Do you think the result would have been different had Peel actually lived in the house himself? Why or why not? The Gospel written by St. Matthew includes the following advice to finders:

> [T]he kingdom of heaven is like a treasure hid in a field; which when a man has found it, he hides it, and for joy thereof goes and sells all that he has, and buys the field.

Does this scriptural advice imply that Hannah is law in the Kingdom?

2. How does the court handle the *South Staffordshire* case? Do you think that the holdings in *Bridges* and *South Staffordshire* are reconcilable? Contradictory? The court deciding *Bridges* relied on bailment law to support its holding against the shopowner. How?

3. After having read *Hannah,* and the facts and results of *Bridges* and *South Staffordshire* as discussed in *Hannah, Armory v. Delamirie* appears to be a very simple case. Assume now that in addition to the chimney sweep's boy and the jeweler's apprentice, the owner of a tavern, where the chimney sweep's boy found the jewel lying on a brick in the fireplace, also claimed the jewel. If this dispute were in court, what should the arguments be and who should win? If instead, both the chimney sweep's boy and the tavern owner show up at the jeweler's claiming the jewel, what should the jeweler do?

4. As evidenced in *Armory v. Delamirie* and *Hannah v. Peel,* courts sometimes base the ownership of "found" property on whether the property is characterized as "lost," "mislaid," "abandoned," or "treasure trove." When the true owner has been unintentionally dispossessed of the property, it is considered lost. At common law, the finder of lost property is entitled to possess the lost property against everyone but the true owner. Mislaid property is that which is intentionally put in a certain place, to be retrieved at a later date, but which is subsequently forgotten. The finder of mislaid property acquires no rights in the property, and the owner of the site where the property is found has a right against all but the true owner. When an owner intends to relinquish all rights in the property and leaves it so that it may be appropriated by another, the property is deemed abandoned. The finder of abandoned property has an unqualified right to the property. Treasure trove is money, coins, gold, or silver hidden either under or above the ground, which has been hidden for a length of time so that it is not reasonably possible to determine the true owner. Treasure trove is usually awarded to the finder so long as the finder is not trespassing. However, some states do not recognize the category of treasure trove and classify the property under lost or mislaid, depending upon all the circumstances.

The courts use these categories to resolve conflicting claims. See, for example, the following cases. $6325 found on seat of chair in safe deposit vault, finder claiming cash was lost and bank claiming it was mislaid: Paset v. Old Orchard Bank and Trust Co., 62 Ill.App.3d 534, 19 Ill.Dec. 389, 378 N.E.2d 1264 (1978), (holding that cash was lost); family donated bags of old clothing to thrift shop where employee discovered a wallet and sterling silver in the bags, purchased the bags, and claimed the property was "abandoned": Kahr v. Markland, 187 Ill.App.3d 603, 135 Ill.Dec. 196, 543 N.E.2d 579 (1989) (holding that items were lost and must be returned to true owner).

5.   States typically have enacted statutes to codify or alter common law principles applying to lost, mislaid, or abandoned property. What purpose, if any, does the distinction between lost and mislaid serve? Based on your study of *Armory* and *Hannah*, why did the courts develop these distinctions? Should statutes continue or eliminate these legal distinctions?

N.Y. Personal Property Law §§ 251–256 (McKinney's):

§ 251.   Definitions

1.   The term "property" as used in this article means money, instruments payable, drawn or issued to bearer or to cash, goods, chattels and tangible personal property other than (a) "instruments" as defined in subdivision two of this section, (b) animals, (c) wrecks governed by the provisions of the navigation law, (d) logs and other property governed by section three hundred twenty-three of the town law and (e) vehicles governed by the vehicle and traffic law.

* * *

3.   The term "lost property" as used in this article includes lost or mislaid property. Abandoned property, waifs and treasure trove, and other property which is found, shall be presumed to be lost property and such presumption shall be conclusive unless it is established in an action or proceeding commenced within six months after the date of the finding that the property is not lost property.

4.   The term "owner" as used in this article means any person entitled to possession of the lost property as against the finder and against any other person who has made a claim.

5.   The term "finder" as used in this article means the person who first takes possession of lost property.

§ 252.   Found property ... to be deposited with police ...

1.   [A]ny person who finds lost property of the value of twenty dollars or more or comes into possession of property of the value of twenty dollars or more with knowledge that it is lost property or found property shall, within ten days after the finding or acquisition of possession thereof, either return it to the owner or report such finding or acquisition of possession and deposit such property in a police station or police headquarters of the city where the finding occurred or possession was acquired. . . .

3.   Except as provided in subdivision four of this section, any person who shall refuse or wilfully neglect to comply with ... this section shall be guilty of a misdemeanor and upon conviction thereof shall be punished by a fine of not more than one hundred dollars or imprisonment not exceeding six months or both.

4.   A person shall not be subject to criminal prosecution for failure to report a finding or acquisition of possession of found property ... if, in lieu thereof, he delivers the property or instrument to the person in possession of the premises where the property or instrument was found, provided he had no reason to believe that such person would not comply with ... this section.

A person who delivers found property or a found instrument to the person in possession of the premises where the property or instrument was found is not liable to the owner or person entitled thereto for such delivery if he had no reason to believe that such person in possession of the premises would not comply with . . . this section.

§ 254. Disposition of lost property

* * *

2. If at the end of the period specified in [this statute] the owner has not claimed the property, it shall be delivered to the finder, or person entitled to assert the rights of the finder . . . upon his demand therefor, and upon payment of all reasonable expenses incurred in connection therewith.

§ 256. Exceptions

1. If a finder takes possession of lost property while he is upon premises with respect to which his presence is a crime, the person in possession of the premises where the lost property was found shall have the rights of the finder . . . if, before the property is delivered to the finder by the police, he files with the police having custody of the property a written notice asserting his rights.

2. If the finder is an officer or employee of the state or of a public corporation and takes possession of the property in the course of his official duty, the state or public corporation shall be deemed to be the finder. . . .

3. If either lost property deposited with the police or an instrument deposited with the police was discovered upon the enclosed safe deposit premises of a safe deposit company or safe deposit department of a bank, the police shall return it to the safe deposit company or bank at the expiration of six months from the date of deposit. Upon receipt thereof the safe deposit company or bank shall hold the property or instrument as bailee for the person entitled thereto. If such person has not claimed it at the expiration of fifteen years from the date it was returned by the police . . . the safe deposit company or bank shall pay that portion of such property which consists of money to the comptroller as unclaimed property. . . .

For an interpretation of the history and effect of this statute, see *Hurley v. City of Niagara Falls*, 30 A.D.2d 89, 289 N.Y.S.2d 889 (1968), concerning a bundle of bills amounting to $4,990 that was found behind a wooden block on the floor of a cabinet by a contractor doing work for the owner of the building:

At common law the principle was early (1722) established that the finder acquires a right in a found chattel good against the whole world except the true owner (Armory v. Delamirie, 1 Strange 505, 93 E.R. 664). Among the many subtleties that developed in this area of the law one was presented by the conflicting claims of the finder and the owner of the premises where the finding occurred. In answering this question the decisions through the years developed two further refinements.

First, whether the finding occurred in a place open to the public or in a private place. [   ] Second, whether the chattels had been lost or mislaid.
. . .

The general common law rule is that the finder of mislaid property on premises of another acquires no special property in it and that the right of possession as against all except the true owners is in the owner or occupant of the premises where the property is discovered. This rule is based on the legal fiction that mislaid property is presumed to have been left in the custody of the owner or occupier of the premises upon which it is found. [   ]

A further exception, however, to the common law doctrine of mislaid property (and one here pertinent) is the rule that treasure trove which by modern definition includes paper money and not only buried treasure but money hidden in places above the ground [   ] belongs to the finder and not to the owner of the locus. [   ]

[Sections 251 and 256 reproduced above were] added to the Personal Property Law as the result of recommendations, studies and hearings of the Law Revision Commission in successive years. [   ] . . . [E]xhaustive studies of the law of lost property were made at the direction of the Commission. . . .

* * *

The statute . . . abolished the distinction between "lost" and "mislaid" property. There is no indication that the Legislature intended the former "public place—private place" distinction to survive. This view is fortified by other provisions of the enactment (§ 256, subds. 3 and 4) which establish differing procedures where property is found in certain public places (safe deposit premises, banks and transportation facilities).

We conclude that plaintiff, as the person who first took possession of the money, was the finder thereof. The statutory period for the retention by the police having expired it should be delivered to him at which time title thereto shall vest in him.

Could the owner of the building have any other claim against the finder in this case?

6.   Major Peel argued that he was entitled to the brooch because it was in his house. Major Peel's claim would not satisfy the requirements of actual possession; however, it may fit within a claim of constructive possession. Black's Law Dictionary defines the word "constructive" as "that which is established by the mind of the law in its act of construing facts, conduct, circumstances, or instruments; that which has not the character assigned to it in its own essential nature, but acquires such character in consequence of the way in which it is regarded by a rule or policy of law; * * * inferred, implied, made out of legal interpretation." In defining "constructive possession," Black's states that constructive possession is "not actual but [is] assumed to exist."

Are there any limits to constructive possession? Or is it simply a method for courts to reach the result that they want? How did you use constructive possession in your arguments on Diana's and Irene's bailment problem? You will come back to constructive possession when you study adverse possession.

E. ADVERSE POSSESSION

Adverse possession is a combination of statutory and common law. The statutory foundation for adverse possession is the statute of limitations on an action for ejectment of trespassers. Statutes of limitations limit the amount of time an aggrieved party has to bring suit against a wrongdoer. The statutes govern all common-law actions including actions for breach of contract, negligence, and professional malpractice, as well as ejectment of trespassers. The Missouri statute of limitations, which governs the case that follows, provides:

> 516.010 Actions for recovery of lands commenced, when.—No action for the recovery of any lands, tenements or hereditaments, or for the recovery of the possession thereof, shall be commenced, had or maintained by any person, whether citizen, denizen, alien, resident or non-resident of this state, unless it appear that the plaintiff, his ancestor, predecessor, grantor or other person under whom he claims was seized or possessed of the premises in question, within ten years before the commencement of such action.

The primary purpose of a statute of limitations is to assure that lawsuits are brought within a reasonable amount of time. The doctrine of adverse possession triggers another result as well. Under this doctrine, a trespasser who meets the requirements of adverse possession over the required period of time (usually the statutory limit for an action in ejectment) may not only bar a suit by the owner, but actually may take title to the property himself.

Trespass is not ordinarily viewed as a good thing. Why is it rewarded in adverse possession? Are trespassers sometimes good? In most adverse-possession cases, however, the relative goodness or badness of the claimants is not directly addressed. Instead, possession is rewarded for some of the same reasons discussed in the material following *Johnson v. McIntosh*. As you might expect, however, good and bad are not totally ignored. The extent to which concerns over "good" and "bad" trespassers enter adverse possession cases is discussed after the following case.

TESON v. VASQUEZ

Court of Appeals of Missouri, 1977.
561 S.W.2d 119.

GUNN, PRESIDING JUDGE.

This is a consolidated cross appeal from judgments of the circuit court, sitting without a jury, quieting title to certain tracts of land located in St. Louis County in claimants, Teson, Sommers, Keeven and Behle, by adverse possession and quieting title to other tracts in defendants Vasquez under their quitclaim deed. Defendants argue on appeal that the elements of adverse possession were not established by the claimants in whom title was quieted. Claimants, Klaus and Teson, who were found not to have established title by adverse possession, appeal from the court's finding, arguing that they proved their title under that theory.

We affirm in part and reverse in part.

Claimant, Lawrence Teson, commenced this suit on August 25, 1969, by filing a petition in the circuit court seeking to have title to certain lands near his home quieted in favor of himself and his wife. Defendants, Leo and Velma Vasquez, then filed a motion to make more definite and certain. No further action was taken until December 8, 1972, when Teson, with leave of court, filed a first amended petition seeking to quiet title to the same tract of land by adverse possession. Claimants, Keeven, Behle, Klaus and Sommers, who claimed title to nearby and adjoining lands by adverse possession, were added as parties plaintiff. Defendant's answer, filed March 30, 1973, was a general denial. In their counterclaim, defendants alleged that they were conveyed good title to the entire property in question by a quitclaim deed from Hugo and Alvina Essen on October 2, 1950 and prayed that title be quieted in them on the basis of this recorded deed.[3] Prior to trial defendants' motion to separate was sustained, and each claimant's suit was ordered to be tried separately but seriatim. The Teson and Sommers cases were so tried. Because of the confusion and repetition of evidence encountered in those cases, the Keeven–Behle and Klaus cases were tried together.

The property in controversy consists of approximately 208 acres of rich river bottom land in northeast St. Louis County. It is bounded on the north by the Missouri River and on the south by Aubuchon Road. The eastern and western boundaries are not marked by any distinct landmarks but are merely prolongations of United States survey lines from their endpoint at Aubuchon Road extending to the Missouri River. The four parcels claimed by adverse possession are shaped roughly as rectangles, and each is bounded by Aubuchon Road, the river and the prolongations of the United States survey lines. Title to a 92 acre parcel situated between the Teson and Klaus tracts was quieted in defendants in *Baxter v. Vasquez,* 501 S.W.2d 201 (Mo.App.1973). This suit concerns the title to the remaining 208 acres purportedly conveyed to defendants by the Essens under the 1950 quitclaim deed. The following generally depicts the location of the property involved:

3. In their counterclaim, defendants disclaimed ownership to certain property lying between Aubuchon Road and Cowmire Creek, even though it was within the tract described by the deed from the Essens because it was found to have been erroneously included.

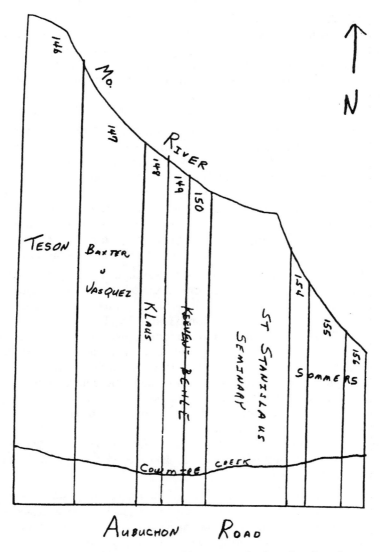

The land in controversy, though it is rich farmland today, was not always so. In the mid 1800's when the area was first surveyed and platted this land was an island in the middle of the Missouri River. The St. Louis County bank of the river was located at what is now called Cowmire Creek near Aubuchon Road. Over the last century and one half, the river channel slowly shifted northward until the former island became attached to the St. Louis County riverbank. Even after it became part of the mainland early in this century, almost none of the land was suitable for farming because of the low-lying swampy character of the land, the dense growth of timber, brush and vines and the frequent flooding. In 1950 when the Essens conveyed this property to defendants, it remained largely a vast wasteland of little value. Since that time many improvements have taken place increasing the worth of the land. One or more levees have been constructed which have lessened, though not eliminated, the flooding problems, and which have decreased the acreage covered by swamps. Additionally, the land was cleared of floodplain vegetation. This clearing occurred slowly and sporadically in the 1950's, but its pace quickened appreciably in the early 1960's and has continued until the present. Today the vast majority of the land is suitable for farming. There remain, however, a number of low-lying sloughs criss-crossing the property as well as the free-flowing Cowmire Creek.

Before detailing and examining claimant's acts of possession which allegedly vested title in them to the land in controversy, we indite the well settled precepts of the law of adverse possession. The claimant has the burden of proving by the preponderance of the evidence the existence for the entire statutory period of each and every element of adverse possession. He must show actual, hostile, i.e., under a claim of right, open and notorious, exclusive and continuous possession of the property for ten years [the statutory period in Missouri.] Failure to prove any one element prevents the ripening of title by adverse possession. [   ]

In dealing with a case of adverse possession, it must be remembered that we are presented with mixed questions of law and fact in which the application of the facts to the law presents the major issues of controversy. Moreover, our task is further complicated by the fact that every piece of property is unique. Thus, in determining whether the facts in evidence authorize a finding that the elements of adverse possession have been satisfied, each case must be decided in light of its own unique circumstances. Much depends on the location, the character and the use to which the land in question may reasonably be put. [   ] Those specific manifestations of possession and ownership exhibited by a claimant which would support a finding of title by adverse possession in a populous and highly developed area are not the same as those which would support such a finding where, as here, the property is sparsely populated farm and waste land. * * *

The first element is actual possession. Two concepts are relevant in determining whether a claimant has established his actual possession of the land claimed. They are his present ability to control the land and his intent to exclude others from such control. Where the claimant occupies land without color of title, in order to prevail, he must show physical possession of the entire area claimed. A mere mental enclosure of land does not constitute the requisite actual possession. Rather, there must be continual acts of occupying, clearing, cultivating, pasturing, erecting fences or other improvements and paying taxes on the land. The performance of all or any combination of these acts of occupancy serves as evidence of actual possession but is not conclusive. [   ] Each case must be decided on its own peculiar facts.

Where the claimant occupies land under color of title the requirement of actual possession of the entire area claimed is relaxed. By statute, one who occupies land under color of title is required only to physically possess a part of the tract claimed in the name of the whole, if during the period of possession he exercises the usual acts of ownership over the whole. Thus, color of title is not an element of adverse possession, but it serves to extend actual possession of some portion of the land claimed to constructive possession of the whole tract described in the instrument providing the basis for color of title.[4] The instrument relied upon as color of title must be bona fide and must purport on its face to convey title to the land. [   ] It need not actually convey legal title so long as it pretends to make the claimant the apparent owner. Even a void deed is sufficient to constitute color of title if it includes within its description the land claimed. [   ]

In addition to describing the land claimed, it is also required that the true owner have actual or constructive notice of the instrument and its contents. Thus, he must be advised not only of the claimant's actual possession, which must be open and notorious to satisfy the requirements of adverse possession, but also the constructive extent and boundary of the land claimed. [   ] This can only be known by being actually apprised of the contents or having the opportunity to be so apprised by the fact of recordation of the instrument bestowing color of title. Once color of title is established, less weight of evidence is required to support an adverse entry under its apparent authority than for a bare entry by one without a claim of right. [   ]

The second element which must be proved to establish adverse possession is that the possession be hostile or under a claim of right. Naked possession asserted for any period of time, no matter how lengthy, is insufficient to ripen into adverse possession. For possession to be hostile it is neither required that the true owner have knowledge of the hostile claim of right or that the claimant intend to deprive him of title. The possession must be opposed and antagonistic to the claims of all others, i.e., the claimant must occupy the land with the intent to possess it as his own and not in subservience to a recognized, superior claim of another. Furthermore, the claim of right or ownership must be unequivocal.

The third element of adverse possession is that the possession be open and notorious. To satisfy this element it is necessary to prove that the claimant's occupancy was conspicuous, widely recognized and commonly known. One may not acquire title by adverse possession if his occupancy has been so covert that it is unknown to the persons who deal regularly with and around the land claimed. The reason the law requires open and notorious possession for title to ripen by adverse possession is to give the owner cause to know of the adverse claim of ownership by another. Thus, if the true owner has actual knowledge that another claims in defiance of and in opposition to his title, the openness and notoriety requirement is satisfied. It is not the mere knowledge of occupation of his land by another which will prejudice the true owner's

---

4. There has been some confusion over the distinction between color of title and claim of right. The former relates to the existence of a deed or proceeding which apparently vests the title to the land in question in the claimant. The latter is part of the element of hostile possession and requires that claimant enter and remain on the land with a belief that his right to do so is superior to that of the alleged owner. [   ]

rights under his title. Rather, it is the adverse and hostile character of the occupation which must be known. If actual knowledge is not proved then the claimant must show an occupancy so obvious and well recognized as to be inconsistent with and injurious to the real owner's rights that the law will authorize a presumption from the facts that he had such knowledge.

The fourth element of adverse possession, that of exclusivity of possession, only requires that the claimant occupy the land for his own use and not for that of another. Generally, one may not be vicariously vested with title by adverse possession as a result of possession by another, though where there is the requisite relationship between the parties, tacking of possession is allowed. [Tacking is discussed later in this case.] * * *

The final element of adverse possession is that the occupancy be continuous, *i.e.,* without lapse, for the entire statutory period. Temporary absence from the land without an intention to abandon possession will not break the continuity of possession; intermittent and sporadic occupancy will. In judging the continuity of possession, the character and use to which the land is adaptable must be taken into account. For instance, under the facts of this case, the periodic flooding which made access to and use of the property impossible for entire growing seasons would not interrupt the continuity of possession unless there was an intent to abandon possession after the waters receded.

One overriding requirement to establish adverse possession to a particular piece of property is that the precise location of the land claimed be identified in such a way that the boundaries may be ascertained and recognized. Absent proof by claimant of the exact location of lands claimed, any judgment would be void, because it would rest entirely on speculation and conjecture. * * *

[W]e review both the law and the evidence giving due recognition to the superior position of the trial court to judge the credibility of the witnesses. The judgment must be sustained unless it is without substantial evidentiary support, unless it is against the weight of the evidence or unless it erroneously declares or applies the law.

The land claimed by Lawrence Teson is a fertile 75 acre strip contained within the prolongation of the United States survey 146 extending north of Aubuchon Road to the Missouri River. It lies within the river's floodplain with the result that the low-lying areas are often covered by back water from the several sloughs which traverse the land. In 1950 when the Essens conveyed this land to defendants, it was almost totally overgrown with timber, brush and vines. Only a negligible portion was suitable for farming. The only commercial activity on the land at that time was intermittent timber and pulp wood removal by various persons.

In 1925, Teson was conveyed title by quit-claim deed to 23 11/100 acres lying within United States survey 146 immediately adjacent to Aubuchon Road. There was no mention in this deed of land lying north of Aubuchon Road or of any right to accretions. Nevertheless, Teson testified that it was his understanding that the deed conveyed not only the land lying south of Aubuchon Road but also accretions on the north to the river. It is uncontested that Teson did in fact farm a parcel of the land claimed immediately north of Aubuchon Road continuously since 1941 when the elements permitted. So much of this parcel as lies between Aubuchon Road and Cowmire Creek is not in controversy, because defendant has disclaimed any rights of ownership to land south of Cowmire Creek. Whether the parcel farmed by Teson near Aubuchon Road included land north of Cowmire Creek was in dispute.

In addition to farming the southern parcel Teson claims that he and his sons began clearing and farming small "spots" (4–5 acres each) on the north near the river sometime in the late 1950's. Exactly where these "spots" were located and whether they were kept continuously cleared in the wake of the periodic floods which inundated the land is not clear from the evidence. These early instances of clearing were accomplished by man and horse power alone, without the aid of modern equipment. In the early 1960's the pace of clearing was accelerated and larger sections of land within the strip claimed by Teson were made tillable and were farmed. By 1962 twelve acres, 1500–2000 feet south of the river's bank, were suitable for farming. In 1964, Teson hired a heavy equipment operator for a few days to help clear more land. This clearing activity has continued so that at the time of trial approximately 50 acres were cleared and used as farmland. Though Teson, who was 81 years of age at the time of trial, testified that he continuously farmed lands on the northern end of the property near the river prior to 1960, he admitted in his deposition that he only began farming this tract a few years prior to trial, because before that time it was all timber.

Teson testified that the boundary of the land he claimed was marked by cedar and iron posts from Aubuchon Road back to the river. He admitted that the iron posts were implanted after a survey he had conducted five to seven years prior to the trial. Teson claimed that at one time fences existed in places along his claimed boundary but that they were washed out by floods. At the time of trial no fences existed marking any boundaries on this property.

In addition to cutting timber, clearing brush and farming the reclaimed areas, Teson claimed to have paid taxes on the property from 1925 to 1965. He introduced receipts for those years showing that he paid taxes on 75 acres of accretions, but the receipts did not specify where those 75 acres were located. Further, in 1968, Teson paid over $1400 for repair to a levee crossing the parcel claimed. He also claims to have ejected various hunters and other intruders from the land over the years. He contends that at one time in the 1950's, he personally warned defendant not to intrude on the property he claimed.

Defendant relies solely on the 1950 quit-claim deed from the Essens as the basis for his claim of title. Defendant rarely visited this property. He averaged only ten visits per year over the entire 300 acre tract, and these were primarily for recreational purposes. 1953 was the only year defendant farmed any part of the land claimed, and he planted only a few acres near the river. Defendant, who owned an excavating business, directed his employees to enter the property with heavy equipment in 1964 to clear approximately ten acres to be used for farming by his relatives. Also, defendant paid real estate taxes on the property from 1948 to the time of trial. He carried liability insurance on the property from 1959.

Defendant testified that he never saw Teson on the contested property prior to 1964. Several witnesses, adjoining landowners and former farm laborers, testified that they observed no farm activity on the tract claimed by Teson prior to the early 1960's when small patches of land near the river were cleared of underbrush.

The trial court held that Teson's 1925 deed did not constitute color of title. Nevertheless, it held that Teson had established the elements of adverse possession to a tract of approximately twenty acres adjacent to Aubuchon Road extending north of Cowmire Creek to a small tarn known as "Round Pond." Title to a second parcel of almost forty acres near the river was also vested in Teson. Title to the land between these two parcels was quieted in defendant.

Under the foregoing facts we affirm the trial court's judgment as to the parcel near Aubuchon Road and reverse as to the parcel near the river. The trial court correctly concluded that Teson could claim no color of title to the property north of Aubuchon Road under his 1925 deed. As such, he could acquire title by adverse possession only to the lands he had actually physically possessed for the statutory period. Teson's proof failed to establish that he had continuously and actually possessed any specific portion of the property near the river. There was testimony of sporadic clearing and cultivation of land somewhere near the river over the years by various persons, including defendant and his relatives. There was little credible evidence of any sustained and permanent clearing until the mid 1960's. Teson admitted in his deposition that he had not farmed the northern portion of the land claimed until the last few years before the trial, because it was covered with timber. Though there is sufficient proof that Teson and his sons did engage in some farming activities on the land near the river, the evidence completely failed to establish the precise boundaries of any tract Teson used for the statutory period. As such, the trial court had no basis to conclude that Teson actually and continuously possessed the 40 acre tract it awarded him.

Furthermore, title by adverse possession to land near the river could not vest in Teson, because his possession was not open and notorious for the entire statutory period. There is no evidence that defendant had actual knowledge of Teson's possession. Nor does the record reveal sufficient facts from which we could presume constructive knowledge on the part of defendant. Teson's presence on the land was only sporadic and until the mid 1960's was confined to small areas which he could clear with hand equipment. The land was densely thicketed with trees, brush and vines which served to obscure any progress made. Moreover, there were no fences or other readily observable boundaries. Thus, the trial court's finding of title by adverse possession to the northern 40 acres in Teson was in error, because actual, open and notorious possession was not proved. Nor were exact boundaries established to any smaller parcel for which the elements of adverse possession may have been satisfied. Therefore, the trial court's designation of title to the northern 40 acres in Teson was speculative and conjectural and cannot stand.

As to the southern portion near Aubuchon Road, it cannot be said that the trial court erred in finding title by adverse possession in Teson. It is clear that Teson had acquired title to the tract between Aubuchon Road and Cowmire Creek by adverse possession. Defendant disclaimed any interest in this property, and its ownership was not in controversy. The land in question is only that which lies between Cowmire Creek and Round Pond.

The testimony was conflicting, but there was competent evidence that Teson had farmed the 20 acres between Aubuchon Road and Round Pond continuously for a time well beyond the statutory period. This parcel, unlike that near the river, was in plain sight from Aubuchon Road. The cultivation must have been clearly visible from the public thoroughfare and open and notorious.

The trial court's finding of title in defendant to the center portion of the tract claimed by Teson was correct. Defendant introduced a recorded quitclaim deed clearly encompassing this area. For the purpose of conveying title, a quitclaim is as effective as any other deed. Teson, on the other hand, relied entirely on an adverse possession theory which he failed to prove. He had no basis on which to claim this center portion as the trial court correctly concluded.

The land claimed by Sommers is that included within the prolongation of United States survey 154 lying north of Old Charbonnier Road to the Missouri River. Sommers contends that the land was conveyed to him and his wife on October 3, 1952, by a warranty deed from John Little and wife. The deed described the land as consisting of 3 ½ acres in the western portion of survey 154 but further recited that the land was bounded by the Missouri River with all accretions.

Defendant Vasquez claims title to the property in question north of Cowmire Creek under the 1950 quitclaim deed from the Essens. He disclaims any title to land within the prolongation of survey 154 lying south of Cowmire Creek.

Shortly after Mr. Sommers took possession of the property in 1952, he erected fences along the entire prolongation of survey 154 to the Missouri River. He maintained those fences until the early 1960's. During this period he also constructed a barn just north of Cowmire Creek. His agricultural activities included raising a small number of Brahman cattle and up to 80 horses on the property. Although about

80% of the property was already cleared in 1952, Sommers continued the clearing operations so that almost the entire area was cleared by the time of the trial.

Sometime between 1960 and 1967 Sommers traded the use of land claimed by him north of Cowmire Creek to St. Stanislaus Seminary, an adjacent landowner, for the use of other seminary property. The seminary then removed the fences north of the creek and farmed the land as its own until 1971 when another party purchased the seminary property. Sommers testified, however, that he continued to use the barn north of Cowmire Creek until 1965. Both Vasquez and Sommers claimed to have paid real estate taxes on the property.

Defendant testified that at the time he was conveyed the property in 1950 it was used for crop and pasture land and that fences were on the eastern and western boundaries. He acknowledged that he never made use of the property but stated that it was he who gave permission to St. Stanislaus Seminary to use the land in 1960 or 1961. Defendant admitted that as early as 1954 he was aware that a barn had been constructed and that livestock was being raised on the property.

The trial court correctly concluded that the recorded deed from the previous owners, the Littles, to the Sommers gave the latter color of title to the land claimed. Though ambiguous because of the reference to the 3 ½ acre plot, the deed clearly purports on its face to convey title in Sommers to land bounded on the north by the Missouri River with all accretions. The only real challenge to the court's finding that Sommers established title by adverse possession relates to whether his possession was continuous for the requisite period. The evidence shows that Sommers entered into possession of the property in 1952 and exercised sufficient dominion over it until the trade so that title could be vested in him by adverse possession. The evidence does not clearly and unambiguously establish the date of the trade with the seminary. Sommers, an elderly gentleman who had suffered a stroke just prior to trial, testified as to various dates between 1960 and 1964. Other witnesses, who lived or worked nearby stated that the trade occurred in 1967. No one from the seminary testified as to the date of the trade.

No question of law is presented under these facts. We are faced squarely with a question of the credibility and accuracy of the various witnesses. We defer to the superior opportunity of the trial court to judge the credibility of the witnesses and to resolve the inconsistencies in testimony. The judgment quieting title in claimant Sommers must be affirmed.

The property claimed by Keeven and Behle consists of 76 acres lying within the prolongations of United States surveys 149 and 150 between Cowmire Creek and the Missouri River. They rest their claim of ownership on adverse possession but argue they have at least color of title by virtue of a 1963 warranty deed from Mary Hagen. The Hagens were purportedly conveyed title to this property in 1954. At that time, little of the property had been cleared for farming. But Hagen initiated clearing operations so that by 1962, 20 acres near the river and 15–20 acres near Cowmire Creek were cleared and farmed. Hagen used the uncleared middle section to raise hogs. Hagen's farming operations continued until the fall of 1961 when he failed to harvest his soybean crop. He died in early 1962.

After Mrs. Hagen gave Keeven and Behle the deed in April of 1963, they immediately began to fence the eastern and western boundaries of the land from Cowmire Creek to the river. Once the fencing project was completed in October, 1963, cattle were placed on the property. Simultaneously with the fencing, claimants began clearing the land of its dense overgrowth of floodplain vegetation. By 1965 they had cleared over 30 acres for farming. They planted this acreage in bluegrass for use in their commercial sod business and installed a portable irrigation system. After a few years the cattle were removed and about 500 head of hogs were placed on the property. From 1963 until the time of trial claimants paid taxes on this property.

Defendant claims the property under the 1950 Essen deed. He rarely visited this property, though he admitted seeing some small areas farmed and noticed a few stray hogs on the property in the mid 1950's. Defendant first learned that Keeven and Behle claimed the land in the prolongation of surveys 149 and 150 at a wedding the parties attended in 1963. At that time defendant told them that he had prior deed to the same property and that Keeven and Behle had better check their title. Defendant maintains that he told them that they could go ahead and use the property until "the deeds were straightened out." Obviously, the disputed claims of ownership were not reconciled though defendant, and Keeven had several telephone conversations on the subject subsequent to their meeting at the wedding. In addition to Keeven and Behle, defendant maintained that he had given permission to Donald Teson, Louis Tebeau and the priests at St. Stanislaus Seminary to farm his bottom land including the surveys 149 and 150 parcels. He neither charged nor received rent from any of the parties. The trial court held that Keeven and Behle had established their title by adverse possession to the entire parcel claimed.

* * *

Defendant's challenge to Keeven and Behle's claim of title by adverse possession goes solely to the continuity of possession. In order to prevail, claimants must be able to tack their possession to that of their grantors, the Hagens. When the Hagens took possession of this property in 1954, they were presented with a deed from the prior owner which set the northern boundary of their property at the Missouri River. Therefore, they occupied the land under color of title. As such, the Hagens needed only to have actual possession of a part of the property with the intent to possess the whole. This they did. Mr. Hagen cleared and farmed sections near the river and Cowmire Creek in addition to raising hogs on the property. It is true that Mr. Hagen failed to harvest his soybean crop in the fall of 1961, but in light of the fact that he died in early 1962 the trial court could reasonably conclude that he had not abandoned the property. The finding of continuous possession for the statutory period by tacking the possessions of the Hagens and Keeven and Behle has support in the record. The trial court's judgment quieting title by adverse possession in them is supported by substantial evidence and is affirmed.

* * *

* * * The judgment of the trial court quieting title in defendant to the tract claimed by Klaus and the tract claimed by Teson north of Round Pond must be affirmed.

KELLY and WEIER, JJ., concur.

Notes and Questions

1. Adverse possession apparently is a very common claim in litigation over the ownership of property. More than 450 judicial opinions concerning or referencing adverse possession claims were issued in 2005 alone.

2. The court states that one claiming title through adverse possession must satisfy all of the requirements for the required period of time. When do you begin counting for each of the claimants in *Teson*? For successful claims, the adverse possessors actually become the owners of the property on the date on which the ten-year period is satisfied. When was this for each of the successful claimants in this case? Why might you want to know the exact date upon which title transferred to the trespassor?

3. In order for the adverse claimant to succeed, the elements of adverse possession must exist throughout the entire statutory period. Thus, any significant interruption in the claimant's possession will defeat the continuity requirement. After such a break in possession, reentry by the claimant begins the statutory period anew. Interruptions may occur due to the claimant's voluntary absence, conditions of the property, or ouster by the true owner or another. But what constitutes a significant interruption? The same considerations used to determine actual possession are also used to determine whether a given interruption is substantial enough to break the chain of continuity; i.e., the nature of the property, its suitability for the use, and the totality of circumstances. For example, in Weiss v. Meyer, 208 Neb. 429, 303 N.W.2d 765 (1981), several years of drought that prevented the cultivation of hay did not create a disruption in the continuity of possession.

4. The title holder can interrupt the statutory period by filing suit for ejectment. The time for adverse possession stops on the date of the filing. In *Teson,* Vasquez claimed that he learned of Keeven's and Behle's claim at a wedding reception in 1963. Vasquez claimed that he told Keeven and Behle to "go ahead and use the property" until things were resolved. How could Vazquez have argued that this conversation interrupted Keeven's and Behle's claim?

5. The common law requirements for adverse possession can be modified by legislation. States may establish varying statutory times for acquiring title by adverse possession dependent upon the wild or uncultivated nature

of the land. See, e.g., N.J.Rev.Stat. § 2A:14–30; Ark. Code Ann. S 18–11–103. Other states adjust the statutory period where the claim is under "color of title," diminishing the period necessary to acquire valid title. Payment of taxes may create a presumption of "color of title." See, e.g., Ark.Code Ann. § 18–11–102. Frequently, adverse claims require payment of taxes during the statutory period before title can be vested in the possessor. See, e.g., Ind.Code Ann. § 32–1–20–1. Also, some states have specified what acts are considered possessory, such as establishing boundaries by a substantial enclosure or cultivating the land. See, e.g., Fla.Stat. § 95.16. Finally, some states limit the amount of land that may be claimed and how frequently any person may make adverse possession claims. See, e.g., Haw.Rev.Stat. § 669–1(c).

Consider the following specific provisions as examples of those cited above. Which best balance the competing interests and justifications for adverse possession?

(a) A statute doubling the amount of time required for adverse possession if the land is wild or uncultivated.

(b) A statute that requires proof of payment of taxes by the adverse possessor.

(c) A statute that limits any individual adverse possessor to no more than one claim for title by virtue of adverse possession in a 20–year period.

(d) A statute of limitations setting the period for adverse possession of 10 years (Missouri)? 7 years (Arkansas)? 30 years (New Jersey)?

6.   All state statutes of limitations contain provisions to toll or extend the period for persons under specific disabilities when the cause of action accrues. Insanity, minority of age, imprisonment, and absences due to military duty are typical disabilities. See, e.g., Mings v. Mings, 782 S.W.2d 165 (Mo.App.1990); Barstow v. State of Texas, 742 S.W.2d 495 (Tex.App. 1987); Hillman v. Stults, 263 Cal.App.2d 848, 70 Cal.Rptr. 295 (1968). Disabilities that arise after the statute of limitations begins to run will not stop the running of the clock.

The Arkansas statute of limitations for ejectment includes the following provision on disabilities:

> If any person who is, or shall be, entitled to commence and prosecute a suit or action in law or equity is, or shall be, at the time the right or title first accrued come or fallen within the age of twenty-one (21) years or non compos mentis, the person or his heirs, shall and may, notwith-standing the seven (7) years may have expired, bring his suit or action if the infant or non compos mentis, or his heirs, shall bring it within three (3) years next after full age or coming of sound mind.

Ark.Code.Ann. § 18–61–101(b). Assume that Jones owned land currently possessed by Parker and that Jones wants to bring an action for ejectment under Arkansas law where the statute of limitations for this action is seven years. You find that Parker has been in possession for ten years. Is the action barred if (1) Jones was 10 years old when P took possession? (2) Jones was 15 years old when Parker took possession? (3) Jones was mentally ill and incompetent when Parker took possession?

7. When an individual adverse possessor cannot meet the statutory period for possession, he may still acquire title by tacking periods of a prior possessor who has met the requirements of adverse possession. Thus, a series of adverse possessors may sequentially tack their possessory times, until the statutory period is fulfilled. The combined possessions, however, must create a continuous chain of adverse possession. Tacking is only allowed where privity exists between the prior and current adverse possessor. Any voluntary transfer or surrender of the property is sufficient to establish privity. Similarly, when the true owner transfers his title to the property, the statutory time that has run against him is tacked to the new owner of record title. Thus, the new owner has only the remaining statutory time to seek ejectment of the adverse possessor. For example, assuming a ten-year statutory period, if the possessor has established the elements for adverse possession for seven years, and the true owner transfers his title, the subsequent title holder only has three years in which to seek ejectment of the possessor.

The following problem to test the requirements of tacking is provided in Hovenkamp and Kurtz, Principles of Property Law (6th ed. 2005):

> O owned Blackacre. In a jurisdiction where the statutory period to recover the possession of real property was 20 years, A went into adverse possession of Blackacre and remained in possession for 5 years. A then died intestate. H was A's sole heir. H took possession of Blackacre, remained in possession for the next 3 years and then conveyed Blackacre to M. M remained in possession of Blackacre for 2 years and then died. Under M's will Blackacre was bequeathed to P who took possession of Blackacre for 5 years and then orally conveyed the premises to X. X possessed the premises for 3 years and leased it to L for one year. When the lease was terminated, X re-possessed Blackacre. Two weeks later X joined the United States Army. Before leaving for military service, X called D and advised [her] to take over Blackacre and make the most of it and that X would make no further claim to it. D took possession at X's suggestion and remained in possession for 2 months when D was called to another state on account of her father's serious illness. She went and stayed with her father for 3 months and then returned to Blackacre and remained in possession for more than 3 years. D then called O and said to him: "O, I have decided to abandon Blackacre. It is yours if you want it." D then moved off Blackacre with no intent to return. Who owns Blackacre?

8. What should be the result in circumstances where the true owner has actual knowledge of the claimant's possession and use? Can the true owner's lack of action ever count as implied permission negating a claim of adverse possession? For example, in Deatherage v. Lewis, 131 Ill.App.3d 685, 86 Ill.Dec. 797, 475 N.E.2d 1364 (1985), the claimant attempted to tack his father's prior possession of the land onto his possession. The father, however, had been a good friend of the true owner, leading the court to believe that the father's possession was not hostile. What criteria should the courts use to determine hostility in such cases? Should the courts require more possessory acts than might otherwise be required? What purpose would such a requirement serve? For more on the hostility element, see *Charlton v. Crocker* below.

9.   You may have noticed in reading the case and notes in this section on adverse possession that there is great significance attached to whether the person claiming adverse possession fenced in the area. Why do you suppose that is? You might consider that fencing is the most common way of exerting control over land. Or you might conclude that fencing land that is not your own is the most visible way of giving notice to the owner that you are exerting control. Some of the discussion in *Teson* concerning activities that constitute actual possession is reminiscent of the discussion of acquisition of property in *Johnson v. McIntosh*.

Not surprisingly, some scholars have attributed other broader meanings to the significance of fencing. Professor Alexander identifies four unspoken premises of "Fortress America" signified by the importance of fences: "insecurity of our own existence and hunger for order; the sense that self is protected from ambiguity by boundaries and distance from others; an insistence that freedom lies in personal choice; and frustration that accompanies a sense of incompleteness." Alexander, Demythologizing Law, 3 J. of Law and Religion 167 (1985). Professor Shaffer responds to these views by arguing that good fences make good neighbors. He describes a strip of land between his yard and that of his neighbor: "I do not know where people in the county court house would say my side lawn ends and my neighbor's begins; my neighbor doesn't know either. We each fertilize and cut two or three mower widths past where the line probably is; the broad strip of lawn over which we communicate—over which we do justice—is the best nourished and best cut part of either lawn." He notes that if they have to someday find a boundary, they are both at risk, but states that "lawyers provide moral leadership in such enterprises, more often than we think." Shaffer, Slippered Feet Aboard the African Queen, 3 J. of Law and Religion 193 (1985).

10.   Should a lawyer ever take into account the relative righteousness of a client's claim? Rule 2.1, A.B.A. Model Rules of Professional Conduct (2002): "In representing a client, a lawyer shall exercise independent professional judgment and render candid advice. In rendering advice, a lawyer may refer not only to law but to other considerations such as moral, economic, social and political factors...." The comment says, "[T]he lawyer's responsibility as advisor may include indicating that more may be involved than strictly legal considerations." Why do the rule-makers use "may" three times rather than a commanding imperious word?

Does adverse possession present a moral, social or political issue? If a client comes to you to ask what he needs to gain title to a neighbor's land by adverse possession, what do you plan to tell him? Will you tell him to trespass?

11.   The doctrine of agreed boundaries has developed to lend stability to agreements made by neighboring landowners to fix a disputed or uncertain boundary. An actual transfer of land does not take place; rather, the boundary is redefined by an expressed agreement of the parties. The agreement does not need to be in writing in order to be binding, but the subsequent conduct of the parties must demonstrate that the agreement exists. Boundaries by agreement require: (a) uncertainty or dispute as to the true boundary; (b) an express or implied agreement that designates what the

parties will consider to be the boundary; and (c) acceptance of, or acquiescence to, the agreed upon boundary for a period of time, frequently equal to the statute of limitations for adverse possession. See Annot. 7 A.L.R. 4th 53 (1981). Would this resolve Professor Shaffer's situation with his neighbor? A threshold determination is whether there is an unknown, uncertain or disputed boundary. See, Gameson v. Remer, 96 Idaho 789, 537 P.2d 631 (1975), holding that since the subdivision plat was recorded, the true boundaries were known and the doctrine of agreed boundaries was inapplicable.

A common source of disputes is whether there has been an agreement to set a boundary. It is generally stated that mere acquiescence to a barrier or monument is not sufficient to establish title. See Townsend v. Koukol, 148 Mont. 1, 416 P.2d 532 (1966), holding that there was no evidence of an agreement and that mere acquiescence to a fence as a barrier did not establish boundary by acquiescence. See also Mesnick v. Caton, 183 Cal. App.3d 1248, 228 Cal.Rptr. 779 (1986), in which the court held that there was no evidence of an express agreement, and an implied agreement was negated by the unkempt condition and the irregular shape and contour of a grapestick fence. An implied agreement was found in Herrmann v. Woodell, 107 Idaho 916, 693 P.2d 1118 (App.1985). The plaintiffs sought title up to a fence, which was erected within the legal description of the defendant's land. The court held that where there is no proof of an express agreement, erection of a fence and long-term acquiescence to the fence as a boundary establishes a *rebuttable* presumption of an implied agreement. Finally, the agreement must establish a certain and defined boundary. See DeClerk v. Johnson, 268 Ark. 868, 596 S.W.2d 359 (App.1980), where the court held that when the evidence only indicated that the agreement was to an approximate boundary, and not to a definite and certain line, there was no boundary by agreement.

CHARLTON v. CROCKER

Court of Appeals of Missouri, 1984.
665 S.W.2d 56.

TITUS, JUDGE.

This is a suit involving ownership and possessory rights to three contiguous lots in a platted subdivision situate in Camden County, Missouri. The case was tried to the court sitting without a jury and judgment was rendered for defendants. From this judgment, vesting title to the property in defendants, plaintiffs have appealed.

Plaintiffs, husband and wife, base their claim to the disputed land on three warranty deeds executed on July 31, 1981, each of which conveyed one of the three constituent lots. Defendants, husband and wife, base their claim upon title acquired by adverse possession of the land for the ten-year period prescribed. * * *

The land in question consists of lots 9, 10, and 11 in Revelation Subdivision, dedicated and developed by Frank and Bertha Heise. In April of 1971 defendants Tommie and Ruth Crocker purchased and moved onto adjacent lots 7 and 8, where they established their residence in a two-bedroom house. Within that month a number of fires broke out in the subdivision, posing a threat to but never actually harming the Crocker home.[5] As their trial testimony reflects, defendants considered the brush-covered condition of lots 9, 10, and 11 a danger to their property and desired that the neighboring lots be cleared sufficiently to minimize the risk of fire.[6]

To that end they contacted Mrs. Heise as well as the attorney for the subdivision and the Camden County prosecutor. According to Mr. Crocker, both Mrs. Heise and the subdivision's attorney acknowledged that the condition of lots 9, 10, and 11 presented a fire hazard and opined that it would be all right if defendant cleared them himself. The prosecutor was said to have advised that defendant could not get into any trouble for clearing the lots and that, "if [the record owners] don't pay you for your labor, after ten years you could claim [the property]." The prosecutor also informed Mr. Crocker of the availability of the mechanic's lien as a device to secure payment for labor done on the lots. Before commencing work on the property defendants again consulted Mrs. Heise, who reiterated her previous "authorization" to do so.

Defendants initiated clearing in April, 1971, with what Mr. Crocker described as "a chopping axe and a grubbing hoe." Sometime later that year—the rather underdeveloped record does not indicate specifically when—Mr. Crocker began to remove vegetation with the aid of a "brush hog" and a tractor. He testified that his son, grandson, sister-in-law, and brother-in-law assisted in the clearing effort at various times (not subject to specific recollection by defendant) by removing brush, raking leaves, picking up rocks, etc. Further, defendant hired one Carl Coffee to "brush hog" the lots on a number of occasions. The record is not as complete as it might be with respect to this activity but it appears that brush-hogging was done "every year" over the six years next preceding trial.[7] Mr. Crocker testified to having done some brush-hogging himself— "three or four times"—over the years. Additional acts of clearing by defendants included the extraction of tree stumps, the removal in 1972 of seven pick-up truckloads of trash, and the removal of what defendant estimated to be 35 to 40 tons of rock. Defendants also installed a water line across the property sometime in 1974 or 1975; seeded, fertilized, and limed the property in the fall of 1980; and constructed a fence along the north and south sides of the property in early 1981.

Aside from defendants' clearing activity, their ostensible exercise of dominion over the property included the placement thereon of certain

---

5. On one occasion some neighbors of defendants fought a fire to keep it from defendants' house and that of another resident of the vicinity.

6. Mr. Crocker testified that at the time he and his wife moved onto their lots the vegetation on lots 9, 10, and 11 ranged in height from one and a half to eleven feet.

The lots were also covered with debris, including piled brush and leaves, discarded beverage cans and bottles, and assorted other refuse.

7. The date of trial, which served as a reference point for much of the testimony, was September 27, 1982.

items of personalty. Among these were a flat-bed trailer, left on the property for approximately one year (the year immediately prior to trial); a bulldozer used to remove stumps, left for a time during 1981; axles and wheels, left somewhere on the lots for three months in 1981; and three 55–gallon drums used as trash barrels, placed on the property at the inception of defendants' "occupancy" and still there as of the time of trial.

The foregoing catalog of acts performed on the property by defendants does not include such evidence as would indicate what defendants regarded to be the legal significance of those acts. Inasmuch as this issue is the focal point of our discussion, infra, testimony adduced in regard thereto is here presented at some length.

Mr. Crocker testified that since 1971 whenever he had been asked about ownership of the disputed lots and whether they were for sale he had responded by saying they were his and were not for sale. He did not, however, allude to any specific occasions on which such communications took place. He further testified to having once told Carl Coffee that plaintiff Mr. Charlton tried to buy the lots "out from under me" and to having told Mr. Charlton that he, defendant, was claiming the lots and would build a house on them someday.

As mentioned, supra, the record indicates that the *sine qua non* to defendants' commencement of activity on the property was that it presented a fire hazard to their lots 7 and 8. On four disparate occasions during trial defendants testified to this effect, stating that their original purpose in clearing the disputed property was to protect their home from fire.

Also relevant to Mr. Crocker's "attitude" toward his performance of work on the property is the following exchange, excerpted from his testimony on cross-examination:

Q: [by Mr. Foster]: And you expected to get paid for that [the work on lots 9–11], didn't you? You mowed someone else—

A: To claim title to the land.

Q: Answer my question.—You expected to get paid for it?

A: Paid for it by title to the land.

* * *

Q: And you expected to get paid for that, didn't you? For the work that you did on that property?

A: From someone, or the title.

Mr. Crocker testified that he tried to get the Adamses, the record owners until July 31, 1981, to clean up the lots, to "let somebody else do it, hire them or let me do it or sell me the lots" and that he sent a letter to them—the record is silent as to whom specifically—requesting as much. Asked when he sent this letter defendant responded, "It started in April of '71."

On or about April 19, 1982, Mr. Crocker filed a mechanic's lien against lots 9–11 which stated as the basis for the $4275 "debt" secured the various items of labor performed by defendants on the property since 1971. The lien also recited the following:

This [i.e., the assertion of a lien] is the result of the advice of the prosecuting attorney's office in April, 1971 when I could not get an answer from the Adams's (sic) on the condition of the property or what they would do about cleaning it up. Wilbur Adams promised to come and talk to me and he never did.

Mr. Crocker could not recall exactly when Adams made this promise, only that he did so "before five years ago," i.e., before September of 1977. Sometime prior to filing the lien, Mr. Crocker sent the Adamses a handwritten statement dated September 23, 1981, which set forth the specific acts of labor performed by defendants on lots 9–11 and requested payment of $4275. Plaintiffs received such a bill on or about April 19, 1982.

On redirect examination defendants' attorney sought to clarify what Mr. Crocker's intention had been in filing the lien. Defendant stated his aim had been "[t]o get paid for the work that I had done on the lots or get title to it (sic)." When asked on cross-examination why for the five years between the date the letter was sent to Adams and the date the lien was filed he had done nothing to obtain payment for his work, Mr. Crocker responded: "because [Adams] said he would come and see me and he never did."

Mr. Crocker testified that he paid no taxes on lots 9–11 for any of the ten years during which he purports to have asserted his claim. He stated that instead of paying the taxes he "went to see if they were paid." Mr. Charlton testified that he paid taxes on the lots for 1981, the first year of his record ownership.

Defendant Ruth Crocker's testimony also includes statements which reflect upon the nature of defendants' claim to the lots. It appears therefrom that in 1971 defendants bought a mobile home which they placed on their lots 7 and 8 and which they used as a residence. When asked on direct examination why defendants sold this mobile home in the fall of 1978, Mrs. Crocker responded, "we had to delete [it] because it was sitting so close to the property line that we could not build or add onto the back of it because it was only about six feet from the property line of lot 9." Twice during cross-examination of Mrs. Crocker inquiry was made as to defendants' reason for selling their mobile home and on both occasions she stated that they could not build onto the back of it because it was too close to the property line. * * *

Plaintiffs contend ... that the trial court's finding of adverse possession was against the weight of the evidence in that it included a determination that defendants in fact asserted the requisite claim of right to lots 9–11. Specifically, plaintiffs point to three distinct and affirmative actions of defendants, each of which is said to have evinced a recognition on their part that, despite their dominion over and "affect-ed" claim to the property, title thereto was actually held by others. * * *

The first of the three actions alluded to, supra, occurred in April of 1971 at the inception of the relevant ten-year period, when defendants requested permission from the subdivision owner to work on lots 9–11. We recount that such a request was made on more than one occasion, the most recent immediately prior to defendants' commencement of activity on the property. That defendants sought permission to work on the lots—even from someone arguably without such interest in them as would confer upon her authority to grant permission—strongly suggests that, as of that time, defendants were not asserting the unequivocal claim of ownership required in order for title by adverse possession to ripen. * * *

Inasmuch as defendants' request for permission to work on the lots was made of someone other than the record owner, we feel obliged to explain that it is not necessary, in order for an adverse possession claim to fail for want of hostility, that the claimant believe title to be held by the record owner as such. It is enough that he be doubtful as to his own right to the property. This much is evident from those cases holding that possession of land in recognition of a lack of title is insufficient to ripen into title by adverse possession [   ]: "It is not necessary that [the claimant] intend to take away from the true owner something which he knows belongs to another, or even that he be indifferent as to the facts of the legal title. It is the intent to possess, and not the intent to take irrespective of his right, which governs."

One other observation must be made concerning defendants' re-quests for permission to clear the lots. While it is true that such requests, as evidence of an absence of hostility, may be rendered irrele-vant by a subsequent categorical assertion of right on the part of the adverse claimant,[8] such a situation did not obtain in this case. Defen-dants had the burden of establishing the existence for the statutory period of all the elements of adverse possession. The evidence allows for no other conclusion than that such period extended from 1971 to 1981. There appears no evidence, save defendants' references at trial to their subjective claim to the property as of 1971, of such a positive, unequivo-cal act as would counter the inference to be drawn from their requests for permission that they did not actually believe themselves to have a right to the property.

The second significant intent-probative action of defendants was the sale of their mobile home in the fall of 1978. Mrs. Crocker thrice testified

---

8. "An adverse claim must be hostile at its inception. The phrase 'hostile in its in-ception' does not relate to the original entry of the disseisor, but to the act by which the possession became adverse; in other words, the possession must have been hostile for the statutory period. Thus the original en-try need not always be of a hostile character .... [W]here the original entry is not ad-verse, it does not become so and the statute does not begin to run as against the rightful owner until the adverse claimant disavows the idea of holding for, or in subserviency to, another and actually sets up an exclu-sive right in himself by some clear, positive, and unequivocal act brought home to the owner." 3 Am.Jur.2d, Adverse Possession § 33, pp. 117–118.

that she and her husband sold their mobile home when it became apparent that they could not build or otherwise add onto it because it was positioned too close to the property line of lot 9. Defendants' fear of encroachment upon that property presupposed a belief on their part that they were without right to do so. Such is the essence of the kind of equivocal claim that courts of this state have refused to recognize as sufficient for purposes of adverse possession. * * *

That Mrs. Crocker's candid revelation ... may very well have been inadvertent only lends strength to its character as a window on the minds of defendants, as claimants. * * *

The last of defendants' three displays of tergiversation occurred in April of 1982 when Mr. Crocker filed a mechanic's lien against the disputed property to secure payment for the work he and his wife had done thereon. The trial court determined that the assertion of this lien was not prejudicial to defendants' adverse possession claim inasmuch as such action is within the ambit of the following principle, enunciated in *Mather v. Walsh,* 107 Mo. 121, 131, 17 S.W. 755, 757 (1891), and relied upon more recently in *Feinstein v. McGuire,* 297 S.W.2d 513, 517[7] (Mo.1957), and *Jurgensmeyer v. Yoest,* 647 S.W.2d 808, 810[3] (Mo.App. 1982): "A direct purchase of any ostensible *title* by one in possession has no * * * force as an admission. A party in possession of land may *fortify* his right *thereto* by acquiring any outstanding interest *therein,* without thereby weakening the force or effect of his possession." (Emphasis supplied.)

With due respect to the court below, we think that *Mather* is inapposite. The assertion of a lien against property does not constitute the acquisition of an outstanding interest in that property. On the contrary, the effectiveness of a lien as a security device depends upon its nature as a *charge upon* property *of another,* i.e., the debtor. [ ] The defendants may have filed the lien merely to "cover themselves" in the event their adverse possession claim failed simply underscores the provisional and contingent nature of their posture vis-a-vis the property in question. The numerous cases requiring an *unequivocal* claim of right on the part of an adverse possessor make it clear that such mugwumpery is fatal to an adverse possession claim.

It may be urged that, as defendants did not file the mechanic's lien until after the ten-year period in question, hence, after title to the property would have ripened, such action is irrelevant to the issue of whether defendants' possession was of a hostile character. The answer to this contention may be found in *Bridle Trail Assoc. v. O'Shanick,* 290 S.W.2d 401, 407[10] (Mo.App.1956), wherein the court noted that "a request [for permission to use the property of another], made even after the expiration of the period of limitation, has been characterized as 'important,' 'strong,' 'very powerful' evidence tending to show that the prior possession was not adverse." * * *

Our review of this case has left us with the suspicion that defendants, informed of a wonderful land acquisition device called "adverse possession'', were purposely attempting to establish its elements with respect to the disputed property. While it is true, owing to the absence of a good faith requirement, that one may acquire property of another by means of a knowing and deliberate satisfaction of all the requirements of adverse possession, one of those requirements is that the adverse possession be under an *unequivocal* claim of right. In that connection, the three actions discussed, supra, are collectively something of a Pinocchio's nose on the otherwise ingenuous countenance of defendants' claim. * * * The judgment is reversed and the cause remanded with directions to the trial court to enter judgment for plaintiffs, awarding them possession of the property in question and quieting in them title to same.

FLANIGAN, P.J., GREENE, C.J., and CROW, J., concur.

Notes and Questions

1. Why did the Crockers lose? Do you think that the appellate court simply viewed them as people who behaved badly and lied about it? Why do you think the trial court judge awarded the land to the Crockers?

2. On the question of hostility, consider the transcript of the cross-examination of a claimed adverse possessor who had built a fence enclosing some land that he did not own:

Q. In the building of that fence, you were not going to try to get or you were not claiming property that you did not have a deed for, were you?

A. I was merely building a fence where—

Q. You were not trying to claim property that you did not have a deed for, were you?

A. I was only—are you saying that I—

Q. I asked you a question.

A. I don't know what you want me to say.

Q. Mr. Norman, I am just asking you a question. You did not intend to claim some property that you did not have a deed for but you were just going to build a fence, is that right?

A. Yes, I guess that would be right.

Why did the adverse possessor hesitate in responding to these questions? Was he under the mistaken belief that he was being accused of theft? Was he concerned that if he admitted that he knew the land was not his when he built the fence, his claim would be rejected? The trial court had denied the adverse possessor's claim because he had not made a "claim of right" to the property. The appellate court agreed with the trial court's result but not with its reasoning:

The intent with which a claimant must possess real property to establish title by adverse possession is an elusive, somewhat ethereal, element. The requirement varies between the states. [ ] It has been the subject of numerous texts and articles. [ ] Statements concerning the required intent are contained in appellate decisions in this state from its early history to date. Such statements are often dictum. Frequently they are recitations from a prior decision. They vary in their thrust and often are cursorily inconsistent. The cases do contain statements indicating the nature of the claim under which one possesses land is of little consequence. The following is an example. " ... It is the intent to possess, and not the intent to take irrespective of his right, which governs...." [   ]

The sufficiency of the claim by one in possession is not to be measured by the morality of that claim or the legal efficacy of an instrument under which the claim is made. Nonetheless, it must be an intent to claim to possess the land as the owner.

* * *

[E]ach claim of adverse possession must be decided upon the basis of its own unique circumstances. [   ] [T]he appellant acknowledged that he had asked permission to build the road. In light of these circumstances, the appellant's admission he was "merely building a fence" has greater significance. It is "positive proof" to support the judgment of the circuit court. ...

Norman v. Allison, 775 S.W.2d 568 (Mo.App.1989). Does the court imply that the result would have been different if the claimant had not asked for permission to build the road over the owner's land sometime prior to building the fence?

Compare the testimony in *Norman* with the following:

Q. At the time you measured the land you intended to possess only the land that you had title to?

A. Yes.

Q. In building the fence you were not intending to acquire title to property that you didn't own?

A. No. I was fencing what I believed I owned.

Q. At the time you constructed the fence you did not intend to claim property for which you had no deed?

A. That's right.

Q. You didn't expect to have more acreage in actuality than your deed represented that you had?

A. Oh no.

In *Underwood v. Hash*, 67 S.W.3d 770 (Mo. App. 2002), the court specifically distinguished this testimony from that in *Norman* because this possessor had not asked permission from the title owners of the land. The court said the claimant had "made it clear that he had fenced and possessed land that he believed he owned and was entitled to," and that this alone distinguishes the case from *Norman*.

3. The Crockers apparently relied on the advice of the prosecuting attorney. Was the attorney representing Mr. and Mrs. Crocker? Was the advice legally sound? How will you handle similar requests for information or your opinion? Although the authorities are in some confusion, the best

learning is that an attorney-client relationship is formed at the moment the client or potential client relies on the lawyer's advice. If, as here, the lawyer's other commitments preclude having the person who consults him as a client, the lawyer should give no advice (except perhaps the advice to consult another lawyer). If the lawyer is "merely" answering "just one question" at a party, or on the telephone or street corner, she should understand that, for purposes of professional discipline (touching on such duties as confidentiality, avoiding conflicts of interest, and competence), she is being a lawyer and that person is her client. Many lawyers refuse to give casual legal advice in these situations for these reasons; their refusal is, of course, often misunderstood.

4. If adverse possession requires proof of the state of mind of the claimant, how would you, as an attorney, handle the preparation for trial of a client claiming adverse possession? Assume, for example, that the Crockers have come to you for help in gaining title to the disputed land. Would you tell them that adverse possession requires an unequivocal intent to claim the land as their own? Or would you ask them first what they had intended over the years; i.e., to claim title or not? What would you have advised if they came to you ten years or so earlier? (Recall that the court in *Charlton v. Crocker* specifically quoted several passages from the testimony of the Crockers.)

Ethical Consideration 7–6 of the ABA Model Code of Professional Responsibility provides:

> Whether the proposed action of a lawyer is within the bounds of the law may be a perplexing question when his client is contemplating a course of conduct having legal consequences that vary according to the client's intent, motive, or desires at the time of the action. Often a lawyer is asked to assist his client in developing evidence relevant to the state of mind of the client at a particular time. He may properly assist his client in the development and preservation of evidence of existing motive, intent, or desire; obviously he may not do anything furthering the creation or preservation of false evidence. In many cases a lawyer may not be certain as to the state of mind of his client, and in those situations he should resolve reasonable doubts in favor of his client.

The more recent ABA Model Rules of Professional Conduct provide in Rule 3.4 that a lawyer shall not "falsify evidence, counsel or assist a witness to testify falsely."

The ABA Model Code Ethical Consideration 7–3 addresses the role of the lawyer as counselor: "In asserting a position on behalf of his client, an advocate for the most part deals with past conduct and must take the facts as he finds them. By contrast, a lawyer serving as adviser primarily assists his client in determining the course of future conduct and relationships. While serving as advocate, a lawyer should resolve in favor of his client doubts as to the bounds of the law. In serving a client as adviser, a lawyer in appropriate circumstances should give his professional opinion as to what the ultimate decisions of the courts would likely be as to the applicable law."

A commentator on the role of standards governing the lawyer as adviser stated that "such standards should require a greater recognition and protec-tion for the interest of the public generally than is presently expressed in the canons. Also, the counselor's obligation should extend to requiring him to inform and to impress upon the client a just solution of the problem, considering all the interests involved." Thode, The Ethical Standard for the Advocate, 39 Texas L.Rev. 575, 578–579 (1961). See also, Thomas D. Morgan and Ronald D. Rotunda, Professional Responsibility, "Limits on the Advice a Lawyer May Give," at 280–283 (8th ed. 2003). What implications would this approach have for advising clients concerning adverse possession claims?

When the judicial inquiry is serious about imposing a good faith requirement, the inquiry involves something like the plea Jimmy Stewart set up for his client in "Anatomy of a Murder." Or like the subjective attitude of the donor of property under the old Section 2035 of the Internal Revenue Code, which imposed the federal estate tax on "gifts in contemplation of death." Stewart, playing the role of a criminal-defense lawyer in the wilds of the Upper Peninsula of Michigan, was hoping to use as a theory the way his state defined "irresistible impulse" in the defense of insanity: He visited the jail, stopped his new client from telling him what had happened, and presented a little lecture on what the law recognized as the state of mind for the insanity defense. Then he left the jail. He returned later and asked his client (Ben Gazzara), "What happened?" The tax cases construed "contemplation of death" literally, so that a transfer was taxable if made as if in a will, or to avoid estate taxes, but it was not taxable if made so that someone could get the crops in or continue the business. See T. Shaffer, Death, Property, and Lawyers, Ch. 6 (1970).

In Ponder v. Ponder, 275 Ga. 616, 571 S.E.2d 343 (2002), a second wife claimed and obtained by probate decree title in her late husband's real estate, and then conveyed the real estate to her children, after her husband died without a will. She did not recognize (or, apparently, even report to the court) that her husband had been married before and left a child and heir by his first marriage. Eighteen years later, the child by the first marriage claimed his share as one of his late father's heirs. His step-siblings, who had taken possession, claimed adverse possession and moved for summary judgment, which the trial judge granted. The Georgia Supreme Court reversed, finding (among other things) that one issue in the case was the stepmother's good faith in claiming heirship and (perhaps by mistake, perhaps not) leaving her stepson out; that issue was a question of fact precluding summary judgment. Suppose you were advising the widow in that case and the question became what was in her mind when she opened the estate without mentioning her stepson. The question might have been whether she did not include him because she did not know he needed to be included. Perhaps she thought—or will say she thought—that a widow was sole heir. (One alternative explanation would be that she left him out because she knew he was an heir and meant to cheat him.) You and your client have to come up with an explanation for the trial judge, who has the case and the fact issue on remand: You need first to explain to your client what the question is. Do you (as Jimmy Stewart's character would have done) tell her what the law is before you ask her why she left out her stepson?

5. Traditional hornbook presentation of the law of adverse possession holds that the doctrine does not require the claimant to prove his subjective intent, but rather examines only the claimant's acts of possession. Under this view, the "good faith" or "bad faith" of the claimant is irrelevant.

There has been an ongoing scholarly debate over whether or not recent judicial decisions in adverse possession cases have favored claimants who occupied property with a subjective good faith belief, though mistaken, that they actually owned the property they claim, and disfavored claimants who occupied property in bad faith by occupying land that they knew belonged to someone else. See Helmholz, Adverse Possession and Subjective Intent, 61 Wash.U.L.Q. 331 (1983); Cunningham, Adverse Possession and Subjective Intent: A Reply to Professor Helmholz, 64 Wash.U.L.Q. 65 (1986); Cunningham, More On Adverse Possession: A Rejoinder to Professor Helmholz, 64 Wash.U.L.Q. 1167 (1986).

Professor Helmholz argues that while judicial decisions have not explicitly required good faith, the subjective good faith and bad faith of the claimants have influenced the courts' application of the doctrinal requirements of adverse possession, especially in relation to the requirement of hostility. On the other hand, Professor Cunningham believes that the existence of good faith or bad faith has not influenced judicial opinions, and that the decisions that Helmholz categorizes as turning on good faith or bad faith actually are based purely on an application of the requirements of adverse possession. Cunningham questions why courts would not openly state that ethical considerations are a factor if in fact these concerns are important in their decisions. Do you think that courts are influenced by factors that are not specifically relevant to the applicable rules in a case? If so, is this appropriate?

6. Two cases directly addressing the issue of a "good faith" requirement for adverse possession reached opposing conclusions. In Halpern v. Lacy Investment Corporation, 259 Ga. 264, 379 S.E.2d 519, 521 (1989), the court held that only a good faith trespass could ripen into title by adverse possession: "To enter upon the land without any honest claim of right to do so is but a trespass." In contrast, the Washington Supreme Court affirmed an appellate court decision denying title to the claimant for his failure to prove exclusivity, but discussed the issue of intentional trespass: "The doctrine of adverse possession ... protect[s] both those who knowingly appropriated the land of others and those who honestly held the property in the belief that it was their own." ITT Rayonier v. Bell, 112 Wash.2d 754, 774 P.2d 6, 9 (1989). Which do you think is the better rule?

THE GOOD NEIGHBOR PROBLEM

The Andersons and Sullivans both purchased their homes in 1978, when the Woodlands subdivision was first developed. The Andersons live on a corner lot; their house faces Briarwood Lane; and their backyard abuts the Sullivans' side yard. The Sullivans' home faces Clovercrest Lane. A drainage ditch borders these two lots, but veers inward into the Andersons' yard as it approaches Clovercrest Lane. This creates a triangular-shaped, partially-wooded area that is included in the Andersons' deed. Although the two families have been friends for the past 11 years, they have never discussed who owns this area.

Mr. Sullivan has always mowed the cleared area of the triangle. Both the Anderson and Sullivan children have played together in the triangle, setting up a lemonade stand in the summers and using the cleared area as part of a playing field for football and soccer games. In 1982, Mr. Sullivan helped the children build a tree house on the area, but it has since been dismantled. In 1987, Mr. Anderson built a bridge over the ditch, leading to the triangle, and since then Mrs. Anderson has cultivated various wild flowers and plants in the wooded areas. Since the bridge has been built, Mr. Anderson has also mowed the cleared areas of the triangle.

The Andersons have planned to build a gazebo in this triangle, and a 1989 survey confirmed that it was part of their property. Recently, at the annual Woodlands picnic, the Sullivans learned of the gazebo plans and are outraged. They think the gazebo will be unsightly, and in plain view from their living room window. Furthermore, the triangle looks like it belongs to them, and they have been caring for it since they moved into their home. Can the Sullivans prevent the Andersons from building the gazebo? What claims can they make? What defenses will the Andersons raise? (Assume a ten-year statute of limitations.) Would you advise the Sullivans to sue the Andersons?

MEDIATION: THE PATIO PROBLEM

This problem is based on a case handled by a dispute resolution center in St. Louis. In reviewing this case, assume that you are an attorney employed by a neighborhood dispute resolution center that offers non-adversarial dispute resolution services, including mediation. You have been asked to help the parties attempt to reach a resolution of this dispute.

This case concerns two adjacent property owners, Mr. and Mrs. Miller and Mr. and Mrs. Aimes. The parties live in a 20–year–old subdivision. Eight months ago, Mr. and Mrs. Aimes had a concrete patio poured in their backyard. About a week after the work was completed, Mr. and Mrs. Miller, who had been on vacation while the work was done, advised Mr. and Mrs. Aimes of the fact that the new patio was one foot over the property line and so extended onto the Miller property.

Fifteen years ago, a fence had been erected by the predecessor in title to Mrs. and Mr. Aimes on what was mistakenly believed to be the boundary line. The fence was actually placed three feet beyond the property line so that it rested on the Miller property. Mrs. and Mr. Miller purchased the property five years ago; and Mrs. and Mr. Aimes purchased their property eight years ago. Mrs. and Mr. Aimes have always mowed the lawn up to the fence and had planted two trees near the fence. Mr. and Mrs. Miller first discovered that the fence was actually on their property rather than on the boundary line when a survey was taken recently as part of an application for a home equity loan.

What would your strategy be in helping these parties to resolve their dispute? What do you think the chances are that some resolution can be worked out? If Mr. and Mrs. Miller had come to you for legal advice and raised the possibility of working through the dispute resolution center, how would you have advised them? How would you have advised Mrs. and Mr. Aimes?

III. WHAT DOES IT MEAN TO BE THE OWNER?

Mine As Against All Others?

You already have seen claims of title "as against the whole world" in *Armory*. The rule of capture and the actual and exclusive possession requirements of adverse possession embody apparent preferences for exclusive control as an indication of ownership. How essential is exclusion to our notion of property? When it is said, as it was in the notes following *Armory* and by Professor Grey above, that modern thought views property rights as a relationship among persons as to a thing, what are the boundaries of that relationship? Consider the following viewpoints:

> In a developed society a man's property is not merely something which he controls and enjoys, which he can make the basis of his labour and the scene of his ordered activities but something whereby he can control another man and make it the basis of that man's labour and the scene of activities ordered by himself. ... Now these two functions of property, the control of things, which gives freedom and security, and the control of persons through things, which gives power to the owner, are very different. In some respects they are radically opposed. Hobhouse, The Historical Evolution of Property, in Fact and in Idea, *in* Property: Its Duties and Rights 3, 9–11 (ed. 1922).

> God the Lord and Father of all, has given no one of his Children such a Property, in his peculiar Portion of the things of this World, but that he has given his needy Brother a Right to the Surplusage of his Goods; so that it cannot justly be denied him, when his pressing Wants call for it. And therefore no Man could ever have a just Power over the Life of another, by Right of property in Land or Possessions. John Locke, Two Treatises on Government at 205 (P. Laslett rev. ed. 1963) (3d ed. 1968).

A Bundle of Sticks?

In American property law, we often refer to property ownership as comprised of a "bundle of sticks;" i.e., a collection of rights associated with property. Some of the sticks in the bundle—or some of the rights associated with the ownership of property—include the right to exclude, the right to transfer, the right to use, and the right to possess. This concept was introduced in the notes following *Johnson v. McIntosh* when you were asked to consider what property rights remained in the Native

Americans, if any, and what property rights lodged in the European discoverers and later conquerors.

This concept of property as divisible by rights or functions is as real *legally* as the concept that land is divisible geographically. It remains a metaphor, however, though a powerful one. This metaphor of the bundle of sticks well represents the texture of property ownership. It explains how one person can be the owner of property (the landlord) while another has the right to possess the property (the tenant). It describes how one individual (the holder of the option to purchase the property) can prohibit another from transferring property to which she holds title. It creates a picture of a situation in which the landowner (of the servient estate) may be subject to the right of another (the owner of the easement) to use his property, to drive through it, to harvest from it, and so on. It explains why the holder of a patent on a DNA sequence can license another to use the sequence in developing a drug or screening test.

The "bundle of sticks" maximizes the value of property. While the right to possess and the right to exclude are valued quite highly, the other property rights are equally important:

> If we stopped with possession, we would have a system of property rights that worked up to a grand blockade. The world would remain a tundra, in which I could keep my own place on the barren square of the checkerboard. It is with the right to use and the right to transfer that production and economically advantageous transfers are possible. Richard Epstein, Property and Necessity, 13 Harv.J. of Law & Publ.Pol. 2 (1990).

Thomas Grey, in contrast, attributes the disintegration of property rights to the bundle-of-sticks metaphor. According to Grey, the bundle-of-sticks concept abstracts property and is responsible for shifting the focus from the relationship between a person and a thing to a relationship among persons with respect to a thing. With that shift, the concept of property became largely irrelevant, in his view, in legal and economic analysis of the allocation of resources. Thomas Grey, The Disintegration of Property, 22 Nomos: Property (1980).

The bundle-of-sticks concept dominates modern thought in the United States about what property is. Some of the sticks in the bundle—the right to use, the right to transfer, the right to possess—are discussed throughout this text, as you will see and have seen already. We look now at the right to exclude through a case that raises questions concerning both the rights and obligations of landowners. Some view the right to exclude as the quintessential element of property ownership in part because it is the source of the right to say "No, you can't use my property; and no, I won't sell, either."

STATE v. SHACK

Supreme Court of New Jersey, 1971.
58 N.J. 297, 277 A.2d 369.

WEINTRAUB, C.J.

Defendants entered upon private property to aid migrant farmworkers employed and housed there. Having refused to depart upon the demand of the owner, defendants were charged with violating N.J.S.A. 2A:170–31 which provides that "[a]ny person who trespasses on any lands * * * after being forbidden so to trespass by the owner * * * is a disorderly person and shall be punished by a fine of not more than $50." Defendants were convicted in the Municipal Court of Deerfield Township and again on appeal in the County Court of Cumberland County on a trial *de novo*. We certified their further appeal before argument in the Appellate Division.

Before us, no one seeks to sustain these convictions. The complaints were prosecuted in the Municipal Court and in the County Court by counsel engaged by the complaining landowner, Tedesco. However Tedesco did not respond to this appeal, and the county prosecutor, while defending abstractly the constitutionality of the trespass statute, expressly disclaimed any position as to whether the statute reached the activity of these defendants.

Complainant, Tedesco, a farmer, employs migrant workers for his seasonal needs. As part of their compensation, these workers are housed at a camp on his property.

Defendant Tejeras is a field worker for the Farm Workers Division of the Southwest Citizens Organization for Poverty Elimination, known by the acronym SCOPE, a nonprofit corporation funded by the Office of Economic Opportunity pursuant to an act of Congress, 42 U.S.C.A. §§ 2861–2864. The role of SCOPE includes providing for the "health services of the migrant farm worker."

Defendant Shack is a staff attorney with the Farm Workers Division of Camden Regional Legal Services, Inc., known as "CRLS," also a nonprofit corporation funded by the Office of Economic Opportunity pursuant to an act of Congress, 42 U.S.C.A. § 2809(a)(3). The mission of CRLS includes legal advice and representation for these workers.

Differences had developed between Tedesco and these defendants prior to the events which led to the trespass charges now before us. Hence when defendant Tejeras wanted to go upon Tedesco's farm to find a migrant worker who needed medical aid for the removal of 28 sutures, he called upon defendant Shack for his help with respect to the legalities involved. Shack, too, had a mission to perform on Tedesco's farm; he wanted to discuss a legal problem with another migrant worker there employed and housed. Defendants arranged to go to the farm together. Shack carried literature to inform the migrant farmworkers of the assistance available to them under federal statutes, but no mention seems to have been made of that literature when Shack was later confronted by Tedesco.

Defendants entered upon Tedesco's property and as they neared the camp site where the farmworkers were housed, they were confronted by Tedesco who inquired of their purpose. Tejeras and Shack stated their missions. In response, Tedesco offered to find the injured worker, and as to the worker who needed legal advice, Tedesco also offered to locate the man but insisted that the consultation would have to take place in Tedesco's office and in his presence. Defendants declined, saying they had the right to see the men in the privacy of their living quarters and without Tedesco's supervision. Tedesco thereupon summoned a State Trooper who, however, refused to remove defendants except upon Tedesco's written complaint. Tedesco then executed the formal complaints charging violations of the trespass statute.

I.

The constitutionality of the trespass statute, as applied here, is challenged on several scores. * * *

These constitutional claims are not established by any definitive holding. We think it unnecessary to explore their validity. The reason is that we are satisfied that under our State law the ownership of real property does not include the right to bar access to governmental services available to migrant workers and hence there was no trespass within the meaning of the penal statute. The policy considerations which underlie that conclusion may be much the same as those which would be weighed with respect to one or more of the constitutional challenges, but a decision in nonconstitutional terms is more satisfactory, because the interests of migrant workers are more expansively served in that way than they would be if they had no more freedom than these constitutional concepts could be found to mandate if indeed they apply at all.

II.

Property rights serve human values. They are recognized to that end, and are limited by it. Title to real property cannot include dominion over the destiny of persons the owner permits to come upon the premises. Their well-being must remain the paramount concern of a system of law. Indeed the needs of the occupants may be so imperative and their strength so weak, that the law will deny the occupants the power to contract away what is deemed essential to their health, welfare, or dignity.

Here we are concerned with a highly disadvantaged segment of our society. We are told that every year farmworkers and their families numbering more than one million leave their home areas to fill the seasonal demand for farm labor in the United States. The Migratory Farm Labor Problem in the United States (1969 Report of Subcommittee on Migratory Labor of the United States Senate Committee on Labor and Public Welfare), p. 1. The migrant farmworkers come to New Jersey in substantial numbers. The report just cited places at 55,700 the number of man-months of such employment in our State in 1968 (p. 7). The numbers of workers so employed here in that year are estimated at 1,300 in April; 6,500 in May; 9,800 in June; 10,600 in July; 12,100 in August; 9,600 in September; and 5,500 in October (p. 9).

The migrant farmworkers are a community within but apart from the local scene. They are rootless and isolated. Although the need for their labors is evident, they are unorganized and without economic or political power. It is their plight alone that summoned government to their aid. In response, Congress provided under Title III–B of the Economic Opportunity Act of 1964 (42 U.S.C.A. § 2701 et seq.) for "assistance for migrant and other seasonally employed farmworkers and their families." Section 2861 states "the purpose of this part is to assist migrant and seasonal farmworkers and their families to improve their living conditions and develop skills necessary for a productive and self-sufficient life in an increasingly complex and technological society." Section 2862(b)(1) provides for funding of programs "to meet the immediate needs of migrant and seasonal farmworkers and their families, such as day care for children, education, health services, improved housing and sanitation (including the provision and maintenance of emergency and temporary housing and sanitation facilities), legal advice and representation, and consumer training and counseling." As we have said, SCOPE is engaged in a program funded under this section, and CRLS also pursues the objectives of this section although, we gather, it is funded under § 2809(a)(3), which is not limited in its concern to the migrant and other seasonally employed farmworkers and seeks "to further the cause of justice among persons living in poverty by mobilizing the assistance of lawyers and legal institutions and by providing legal advice, legal representation, counseling, education, and other appropriate services."

These ends would not be gained if the intended beneficiaries could be insulated from efforts to reach them. It is in this framework that we must decide whether the camp operator's rights in his lands may stand between the migrant workers and those who would aid them. The key to that aid is communication. Since the migrant workers are outside the mainstream of the communities in which they are housed and are unaware of their rights and opportunities and of the services available to them, they can be reached only by positive efforts tailored to that end. *The Report of the Governor's Task Force on Migrant Farm Labor* (1968) noted that "One of the major problems related to seasonal farm labor is the lack of adequate direct information with regard to the availability of public services," and that "there is a dire need to provide the workers with basic educational and informational material in a language and style that can be readily understood by the migrant" (pp. 101–102). The report stressed the problem of access and deplored the notion that property rights may stand as a barrier, saying "In our judgment, 'no trespass' signs represent the last dying remnants of paternalistic behavior" (p. 63).

A man's right in his real property of course is not absolute. It was a maxim of the common law that one should so use his property as not to injure the rights of others. Broom, Legal Maxims (10th ed. Kersley 1939), p. 238; 39 Words and Phrases, "Sic Utere Tuo ut Alienum Non Laedas," p. 335. Although hardly a precise solvent of actual controversies, the maxim does express the inevitable proposition that rights are relative and there must be an accommodation when they meet. Hence it has long been true that necessity, private or public, may justify entry upon the lands of another.

The subject is not static. As pointed out in 5 Powell, Real Property (Rohan 1970) § 745, pp. 493–494, while society will protect the owner in his permissible interests in land, yet

" * * * [S]uch an owner must expect to find the absoluteness of his property rights curtailed by the organs of society, for the promotion of the best interests of others for whom these organs also operate as protective agencies. The necessity for such curtailments is greater in a modern industrialized and urbanized society than it was in the relatively simple American society of fifty, 100, or 200 years ago. The current balance between individualism and dominance of the social interest depends not only upon political and social ideologies, but also upon the physical and social facts of the time and place under discussion."

Professor Powell added in § 746, pp. 494–496:

"As one looks back along the historic road traversed by the law of land in England and in America, one sees a change from the viewpoint that he who owns may do as he pleases with what he owns, to a position which hesitatingly embodies an ingredient of stewardship; which grudgingly, but steadily, broadens the recognized scope of social interests in the utilization of things. * * *

"To one seeing history through the glasses of religion, these changes may seem to evidence increasing embodiments of the golden rule. To one thinking in terms of political and economic ideologies, they are likely to be labeled evidences of 'social enlightenment,' or of 'creeping socialism' or even of 'communistic infiltration,' according to the individual's assumed definitions and retained or acquired prejudices. With slight attention to words or labels, time marches on toward new adjustments between individualism and the social interests."

This process involves not only the accommodation between the right of the owner and the interests of the general public in his use of his property, but involves also an accommodation between the right of the owner and the right of individuals who are parties with him in consensual transactions relating to the use of the property. * * *

The argument in this case understandably included the question whether the migrant worker should be deemed to be a tenant and thus entitled to the tenant's right to receive visitors, [ ], or whether his residence on the employer's property should be deemed to be merely incidental and in aid of his employment, and hence to involve no possessory interest in the realty. [ ] These cases did not reach employment situations at all comparable with the one before us. Nor did they involve the question whether an employee who is not a tenant may have visitors notwithstanding the employer's prohibition. Rather they were concerned with whether notice must be given to end the employee's right to remain upon the premises, with whether the employer may remove the discharged employee without court order, and with the availability of a particular judicial remedy to achieve his removal by process. We of course are not concerned here with the right of a migrant worker to remain on the employer's property after the employment is ended.

We see no profit in trying to decide upon a conventional category and then forcing the present subject into it. That approach would be artificial and distorting. The quest is for a fair adjustment of the competing needs of the parties, in the light of the realities of the relationship between the migrant worker and the operator of the housing facility.

Thus approaching the case, we find it unthinkable that the farmer-employer can assert a right to isolate the migrant worker in any respect significant for the worker's well-being. The farmer, of course, is entitled to pursue his farming activities without interference, and this defendants readily concede. But we see no legitimate need for a right in the farmer to deny the worker the opportunity for aid available from federal, State, or local services, or from recognized charitable groups seeking to assist him. Hence representatives of these agencies and organizations may enter upon the premises to seek out the worker at his living quarters. So, too, the migrant worker must be allowed to receive visitors there of his own choice, so long as there is no behavior hurtful to others, and members of the press may not be denied reasonable access to workers who do not object to seeing them.

It is not our purpose to open the employer's premises to the general public if in fact the employer himself has not done so. We do not say, for example, that solicitors or peddlers of all kinds may enter on their own; we may assume for the present that the employer may regulate their entry or bar them, at least if the employer's purpose is not to gain a commercial advantage for himself or if the regulation does not deprive the migrant worker of practical access to things he needs.

And we are mindful of the employer's interest in his own and in his employees' security. Hence he may reasonably require a visitor to identify himself, and also to state his general purpose if the migrant worker has not already informed him that the visitor is expected. But the employer may not deny the worker his privacy or interfere with his opportunity to live with dignity and to enjoy associations customary among our citizens. These rights are too fundamental to be denied on the basis of an interest in real property and too fragile to be left to the unequal bargaining strength of the parties. [ ]

It follows that defendants here invaded no possessory right of the farmer-employer. Their conduct was therefore beyond the reach of the trespass statute. The judgments are accordingly reversed and the matters remanded to the County Court with directions to enter judgments of acquittal.

For reversal and remandment: CHIEF JUSTICE WEINTRAUB and JUSTICES JACOBS, FRANCIS, PROCTOR, HALL and SCHETTINO—6.

For affirmance: None.

CROSS v. TEXAS

Court of Appeals of Texas, El Paso, 2004.
2004 WL 1535606.

LARSEN, JUSTICE.

In April 2000, Michael Cross attempted to collect signatures at an El Paso shopping mall to have Pat Buchanan added to the ballot for the 2000 presidential election. Mall officials asked Cross to leave, and when he refused to do so, they called the police. Cross was subsequently arrested and convicted for criminal trespass and was assessed a $500 fine. Cross appeals, contending that the application of the criminal trespass statute in this case violates his right to free speech under the United States and Texas Constitutions. We conclude that Cross's federal constitutional claim has been foreclosed by decisions of the United States Supreme Court and that Cross has not demonstrated why we should interpret the Texas Constitution more broadly than the Unites States Constitution in this regard. Accordingly, we will affirm the judgment of the trial court.

FACTUAL AND PROCEDURAL BACKGROUND

The facts in this case are essentially undisputed. Sunland Park Mall is a 950,000–square-foot enclosed shopping center with movie theaters and over one-hundred stores grouped around a common area and surrounded by a large parking lot. There are only three large malls in El Paso, and Sunland Park is the only one on the west side of town. Some department stores have their only west-side location at Sunland Park. The Mall and its parking lot are open to the general public during business hours. But the Mall does not allow people to put handbills on vehicles parked in the lot. The Mall allows a number of noncommercial activities on the premises and it does not require those who enter the Mall to shop. For example, people may sit in the food court without purchasing food, walk the common area for exercise, or attend free organ concerts. The Mall also allows various organizations to use the common area. To take advantage of this opportunity, an organization must complete a common-area application and obtain approval from Mall management. The application form states that the Mall retains sole discretion to permit or not permit any person or organization to use the common area. The Mall's marketing director, Sylvia Hernandez, testified that the purpose of the Mall is to "make money." Therefore, in considering whether to grant an application, the Mall considers whether the proposed activity will increase traffic flow into the Mall, whether it will enhance the image of the Mall, and whether it will offend the Mall's customers or tenants. Based upon these considerations, the Mall does not grant common-area applications for partisan political activities. For example, the Mall refused an application by the El Paso Jaycees to solicit signatures regarding a bond issue because the Mall did not want to give the appearance of having "taken a side" on the issue. But the Mall granted an application to set up early voting booths in the common area because that activity was not partisan and because the Mall hoped that some of the voters would stay to shop after voting.

Before the day that he was arrested, Cross attempted to solicit signatures for his petition at the Mall. When he was stopped by the Mall's security guards, he went to the Mall office and was told that he had to complete a common-area application before conducting his activities at the Mall. Cross refused to complete and submit an application. Hernandez and the Mall's manager, Connie Warner, testified that even if Cross had submitted an application, it would have been turned down because of the political nature of his activities.

The following Saturday, Cross positioned himself at one of the Mall's main entrances and approached shoppers as they entered the Mall. Warner testified that some Mall patrons were offended by Cross and reported his activities to the Mall's management; others simply ignored him. Hernandez and a Mall security guard informed Cross that he did not have permission to conduct his activities at the Mall and that he would have to leave. When Cross refused to leave, Hernandez called the police. Upon their arrival, the police again asked Cross to leave the Mall premises, and he again refused. At that point, he was placed under arrest for criminal trespass.

* * *

United States Constitution

In his first issue, Cross asserts that the criminal trespass statute, as applied in this case, violates the First Amendment to the United States Constitution. Specifically, he argues that he was entitled to exercise his right to free speech at Sunland Park Mall because the Mall is the functional equivalent of a town square.

The First Amendment generally forbids content-based restrictions on free speech. [   ] But it is also axiomatic that the First Amendment only forbids abridgment of speech by the government. [   ]. The United States Supreme Court recognized a narrow exception to this second axiom in *Marsh v. Alabama* [(1946).]

In *Marsh,* a Jehovah's Witness was convicted of criminal trespass for distributing religious literature on a sidewalk in a town that was wholly owned by a private corporation. The town had all the characteristics of an ordinary town, including residences, a business block, sewers, and a post office. The Court noted that distribution of the literature on a public sidewalk would obviously have been protected by the First Amendment. The Court then held that "the circumstance that the property rights to the premises where the deprivation of liberty . . . took place, were held by others than the public, is not sufficient to justify the State's permitting a corporation to govern a community of citizens so as to restrict their fundamental liberties. . . ." Furthermore, the State's enforcement of that restriction through its criminal trespass statute could not stand.

The Court extended *Marsh* in *Amalgamated Food Employees Union Local 590 v. Logan Valley Plaza, Inc.,* [(1968)]. In that case, a state court issued an injunction prohibiting union members from picketing a store at a shopping center. [   ] As in *Marsh,* the Court noted that the picketing would have been protected by the First Amendment if it had occurred on a public sidewalk.[   ]. The Court also believed that the shopping center was the "functional equivalent of the business district . . . involved in *Marsh.*" [   ]The Court concluded that "because the shopping center serves as the community business block 'and is freely accessible and open to the people in the area and those passing through,' . . . the State may not delegate the power, through the use of its trespass laws, wholly to exclude those members of the public wishing to exercise their First Amendment rights on the premises in a manner and for a purpose generally consonant with the use to which the property is actually put." [   ]

Four years later, the Court retreated from *Logan Valley* in *Lloyd Corp. v. Tanner,* [(1972)], a case we will discuss in some detail because of its factual similarities to this case. *Lloyd* involved an attempt by anti-war protesters to distribute handbills at a mall that covered approximately fifty acres and had sixty tenants, including several department stores. [   ] The mall was generally open to the public and made a "considerable effort" to attract shoppers and to create community goodwill. [   ] To this end, some civic and charitable organizations were permitted, "by invitation and advance arrangement," to use mall facilities. [   ] The mall did not allow organizations to use the mall for political purposes, except that presidential candidates of both parties were allowed to speak in the hope that people who came to hear the candidates would shop before leaving the mall. [   ] The mall also prohibited the distribution of handbills because that activity might annoy customers and was incompatible with the mall's purpose. [   ] The mall employed security guards, who were commissioned by the city, had police authority within the mall, wore uniforms similar to those worn by city police, and were licensed to carry handguns. [   ]

Under these facts, the Court held that the protesters did not have a First Amendment right to distribute their handbills at the mall. [   ] The Court distinguished *Logan Valley* on two grounds. First, the free-speech activities in *Logan Valley* were targeted at a store in the shopping center, rather than at the public at large. Second, the targeted store in

Logan Valley was located within a large private enclave, leaving the picketers with no other reasonable opportunities to convey their message to its intended audience, whereas the *Lloyd* mall was crossed by public streets and sidewalks. [   ] The Court distinguished *Marsh* on the ground that it involved "the assumption by a private enterprise of all of the attributes of a state-created municipality and the exercise by that enterprise of semiofficial municipal functions as a delegate of the State. In effect, the owner of the company town was performing the full spectrum of municipal powers and stood in the shoes of the State." [   ]

The Court acknowledged that the mall was generally open to the public and that it had been used for various noncommercial activities. But the mall was open to the public for the purpose of doing business and the noncommercial activities were allowed for the purpose of bringing in potential shoppers. [   ] The Court also emphasized:

> [T]he First and Fourteenth Amendments safeguard the rights of free speech and assembly by limitations on state action, not on action by the owner of private property used nondiscriminatorily for private purposes only . . . . . Although . . . the courts properly have shown a special solicitude for the guarantees of the First Amendment, this Court has never held that a trespasser or an uninvited guest may exercise general rights of free speech on property privately owned and used nondiscriminatorily for private purposes only. [   ]

Although the *Lloyd* Court attempted to distinguish, rather than overrule, *Logan Valley,* the Court later made plain that *Logan Valley* is no longer good law. In *Hudgens,* the Court stated that "the reasoning . . . in *Lloyd* cannot be squared with the reasoning . . . in *Logan Valley* "and that "the rationale of *Logan Valley* did not survive the Court's decision in the *Lloyd* case." [   ] *Hudgens* involved an attempt by striking union members to picket in an enclosed mall. [   ] The Court held that since the anti-war protesters in *Lloyd* did not have a First Amendment right to distribute their handbills in a mall, the picketers likewise did not have a First Amendment right to advertise their strike in the mall. [   ]

From reviewing these decisions, it is apparent that the First Amendment guarantee of free speech does not apply in a privately owned shopping mall. . . .

Given the Supreme Court's pronouncements in *Lloyd* and *Hudgens,* and *Lloyd's* factual similarities to this case, it would appear that Cross had no First Amendment right to solicit signatures at Sunland Park Mall.

* * *

TEXAS CONSTITUTION

In his second and third issues, Cross asserts that the criminal trespass statute, as applied in this case, violates the Texas Constitution's guarantees of free speech and assembly. [   ]

After the United States Supreme Court's decisions in *Lloyd* and *Hudgens,* the California Supreme Court held that the solicitation of petition signatures at a shopping center is an activity protected by the California Constitution. [   ] The United States Supreme Court affirmed the California Supreme Court's decision, stating, *"Lloyd* . . . does not . . . limit the authority of the State to exercise its police power or its sovereign right to adopt in its own Constitution individual liberties more expansive than those conferred by the Federal Constitution." [   ]

Following California's lead, a few states have concluded that the free-speech provisions in their own constitutions protect speech at shopping centers. *See, e.g., Bock v. Westminster Mall Co.,* 819 P.2d 55, 56 (Colo.1991); *New Jersey Coalition Against War v. J.M.B. Realty Corp.,* 138 N.J. 326, 650 A.2d 757, 760 (N.J.1994). But most courts that have considered the question have declined the Supreme Court's invitation to interpret their state constitutions more broadly in this regard. [   ].

There is no reported case addressing whether the free-speech provision of the Texas Constitution protects speech at a shopping mall. [   ]

* * *

The Texas Constitution provides:

> Every person shall be at liberty to speak, write or publish his opinions on any subject, being responsible for the abuse of that privilege; and no law shall ever be passed curtailing the liberty of speech or of the press. . . .

Cross argues that the language of article I, section 8 is broader than the First Amendment. He also points out that the language of this provision is similar to the free-speech provision in the California Constitution, which the California Supreme Court has construed to protect the type of activity at issue in this case. [   ] Additionally, Cross argues that public policy supports the result he seeks.

The Texas Supreme Court has indicated that in some ways article I, section 8 provides a broader guarantee of free speech than the First Amendment. [   ] This determination is based on section 8's first clause, which is phrased as an affirmative grant of the right to speak rather than as a restriction on governmental interference with speech. [   ]

Although Cross relies on the first sentence of section 8, he does not articulate how or why the language and history of that sentence demonstrate an intent to protect speech on private property. Moreover, the Texas Supreme Court has held that state action is required before a person may maintain a claim for violation of article I, section 8. [   ] Generally, state action is only present for otherwise private conduct when the conduct can be fairly attributed to the government. *Id.* There is no evidence to show that the operations of Sunland Park Mall could be fairly attributed to the government. *But see Golden Gateway Ctr. v. Golden Gateway Tenants Ass'n,* 26 Cal.4th 1013, 111 Cal.Rptr.2d 336, 29 P.3d 797, 810 (Cal.2001) (holding that the actions of a private property owner constitute state action if the property is freely and openly accessible to the public). And, as we have already noted, judicial enforcement of neutral trespass laws generally does not amount to state action. [   ]

The California Supreme Court's decision in *Robins v. PruneYard* does not convince us that article I, section 8 protects speech at a shopping mall. Although the California free-speech provision is similar to that of Texas, the California Supreme Court did not rest its decision on an examination of the text or history of the provision. [   ] * * * Furthermore, as the California Supreme Court has acknowledged, most states with similar constitutional provisions have declined to follow *Robins.* [   ]

Finally, Cross relies on "demographic and sociological changes." He points out that when *Lloyd* was written—over thirty years ago—the Court considered large shopping malls to be a relatively new concept in shopping center design. [   ] Now, according to Cross, "it is widely accepted that the downtown areas of many large urban cities are functionally dead and the suburban or outlying shopping mall fulfills many of the purposes and is used by citizens for pursuits which formerly would have been carried on in the town square or downtown."

The record contains no evidence to support Cross's assertion that the downtowns of the United States or Texas in general, or of El Paso in particular, are functionally dead. Nor is there any evidence to suggest an absence of public spaces where Cross could have solicited signatures. In dismissing Cross's habeas appeal, we stated:

> [T]he gravamen of Cross's ... argument [is] that the Mall has become the functional equivalent of the town square such that his First Amendment right to free political speech is protected on otherwise private property. In both his briefing and at oral argument, Cross attempted to support this conclusion by arguing that sociological changes to the nature of public space in American society have occurred. However there was no testimonial or documentary evidence to substantiate this contention....

DISSENTING OPINION

CHEW, JUSTICE.

I disagree with several conclusions reached in the majority's opinion, therefore I respectfully dissent.

* * *

While it is evident that the Supreme Court's decision in *Lloyd Corp. v. Tanner* effectively forecloses any federal guarantee of free speech in a privately-owned shopping mall, the Texas Constitution's affirmative grant of free speech should be interpreted to afford its citizens broader protections than its federal counterpart under these circumstances....

In *Davenport v. Garcia,* the Texas Supreme Court recognized that over the course of our constitutional history, Texas has specifically guaranteed an affirmative right to speak and included its expansive freedom of expression clause in its 1836, 1861, 1866, 1869 and 1876 constitutions. [ ] The *Davenport* Court also acknowledged that Texas' free speech provision is broader than the First Amendment in some aspects. [ ] Even though there is nothing in our constitutional text that explicitly limits the free speech protection to violations by state actors, the Texas Supreme Court has held state action is required to trigger protection of our guaranteed expressional rights. [ ]

While our free speech provision has been interpreted in such a way as not to reach any private action, the quasi-public character of large shopping malls in modern America raises a serious concern that expressional rights are being denied in locales that private owners have intentionally transformed into the functional equivalent or replacement of traditional public squares or gathering places. [ ] See New Jersey Coalition Against the War in the Middle East v. J.M. B. Realty, [ ] (mall owners who have so transformed the life of society for their profit should not be permitted to claim a theoretically-important right of silence from the multitudes they have invited). Sunland Park is a 950,000 square-foot facility, containing over one hundred stores. Sunland Park permits a number of noncommercial activities on its premises and implicitly invites the public to enter and use its space—without requiring them to shop. However, it refuses to permit partisan political activities. After appropriating the characteristics and purposes of a traditional public forum by inviting the general public to make use of its space for noncommercial activities, owners of large shopping malls like Sunland Park should not be permitted to later deny the full consequences of their open invitation. Free expression of political ideas and political discourse is a central component to the traditional public forum and should remain so, despite its change of location to the mall.

Notes and Questions

1.   Why did Justice Weintraub believe that the interests of the migrants in *State v. Shack* would receive greater protection under common law property rules than under the constitutional rights asserted? Justice Larsen's opinion holds that state action is required as a prerequisite for the state and federal constitutional rights asserted by the defendant in *Cross*. Would Cross have done better to assert a common law rather than constitutional claim?

2.   Did Justice Weintraub decide that migrant farm workers and their lawyers and caseworkers had property rights in Tedesco's land? In their place of residence? If not, what was the basis of his decision?

3.   Was Justice Weintraub saying that there was no good reason not to permit the lawyer and the caseworker to talk to the migrant farm workers in private on the owner's property? What does this do to the power to exclude? Would Justice Weintraub permit the landowner to exclude the lawyer and the caseworker under other circumstances? If so, what might those circumstances be?

4.   The court in *Cross* emphasizes that the First Amendment does not limit action "by the owner of private property used nondiscriminatorily for

private purposes only," quoting the U.S. Supreme Court. What does "non-discriminatorily" mean? If the First Amendment's protection requires that the claimant prove that there was "state action" involved, why these limitations on private owners? Did the mall owners in El Paso act nondiscriminatorily? In fact, weren't they quite discriminating in deciding who would be allowed on the premises? What are the boundaries between acceptable selectivity and impermissible discrimination? In *Cross*, the shopping mall excluded an individual petitioning on behalf of Pat Buchanan. What if the mall had earlier allowed petitioning on behalf of Governor Bush? What if the mall had allowed petitioning for a legislative initiative to repeal a sales tax?

5. Suppose a privately-owned shopping mall with a "no solicitation" policy is the beneficiary of considerable financial assistance from public authorities, including the purchase by the city of $2 million in improvements that the mall owner made to adjacent streets and drainage systems. The mall also provides rent-free space in the mall to the city for a police substation from which police respond to complaints throughout the city as well as in the mall. In addition, the Army, Navy, and Marine Corps have recruiting stations in the mall, and the county clerk maintains a temporary office for voter registration in the mall. Would these facts tip the balance in favor of the "public forum" characterization? See Bock v. Westminster Mall Co., 819 P.2d 55, (Colo.1991) (mall "effectively functions as a latter-day public forum" and thus may not prohibit distribution of political pamphlets and solicitation of signatures for petitions regarding governmental policies). Is there any set of facts under which the *Cross* court would find that a shopping mall was being used for public purposes?

PROBLEMS: BRUCE WAYNE AND WESTGATE

Both *Shack* and *Cross* may be viewed as cases in which the owner's use of the property had an impact on the scope of the owner's right to exclude. What were the pivotal facts in these cases? What do you think the result would be if these two courts were faced with the following situations?

(a) Bruce Wayne owns an estate that is coveted by not-for-profit and political organizations for fundraising events. Mr. Wayne frequently lends his estate to organizations such as the Arts Council, the local chapter of the United Nations Association, state and local political campaigns, and a number of other organizations. There is at least one event each month on his grounds. Many of these fundraisers include speeches by nationally prominent individuals associated with the particular cause. Most often these events are open to the general public who pay the suggested or required contribution for admission. Mr. Wayne rarely attends these events, as he is frequently out of town.

This weekend, an organization called Freedom for the Arts is holding a fundraiser. This event has been listed in the calendar section of the newspaper and in its society column. Admission requires that you reserve a ticket in advance by calling Freedom for the Arts. The tickets are free. They intend to raise money through pledges and an auction during the event. Mr. Wayne's personal assistant has heard that a number of persons who have reserved tickets intend to circulate leaflets opposing government funding of several performance artists, including the person who will perform as the major attraction for the fundraiser. They also intend to stand with their backs turned to the stage during the performance and all speeches. Does Mr. Wayne have a right to prevent these people from attending?

(b) Westgate Manor is a private assisted-living center for elderly individuals who are too physically or mentally impaired to live alone, but who do not need skilled nursing care. Residents rent their own apartment at Westgate and pay a monthly service fee. Westgate provides a full range of services including a dining hall, doctors' house calls, recreation, housekeeping, and seasonal shopping. It also provides transportation to shopping areas and entertainment for those able to take advantage of the service. The management of Westgate has established a set of rules that govern the usual concerns. Some of these rules govern access to Westgate by visitors. Children are allowed to visit only between 9:00 a.m. and 5:00 p.m., for example. All guests must check in at the front gate, and only guests who have an invitation by a resident and whose names are recorded at the gate are allowed access. Certain groups are welcomed for particular purposes. For example, a choir attends Sunday services, and groups of school children visit to perform on certain holidays.

Several groups have asked permission to talk with the residents of Westgate. Some of these groups are political. (Like most groups of older citizens, a very large percentage of residents of Westgate vote.) Other groups want to inform residents of services available from local hospitals, support groups and other sources. All of these requests have been denied. Does the owner-operator of Westgate have a right to exclude these groups?

COMPLEX NEGOTIATION PROBLEM: THE SCHOOL AND THE SHELTER

One of the questions raised by the "power to exclude" cases is whether litigation is the ideal way to resolve such disputes. In fact, property lawyers spend a small fraction of their time in courts and use other techniques, particularly negotiation, in helping clients work through a process of accommodation similar to the process of analysis used in *State v. Shack*.

Property lawyers who work on land-use and development problems resort to negotiation in two different types of situations: (1) "deal making"—where the client is seeking to develop property in some particular manner and needs to acquire sufficient control over the property, or seeks to raise money for the project; and (2) "dispute resolution"—where the client is seeking to resolve a dispute concerning the use of the property with neighbors, public officials, or partners. In both situations, the client's interests may require a greater degree of flexibility in approaching the matter than the "winner take all" outcome with which litigation may be concerned. This is particularly true if the client has a relationship with her potential adversaries that she wishes to maintain after the matter at hand is resolved.

Property rights questions, such as those raised in *Shack* and *Cross,* may be amenable to negotiated or mediated settlements outside of court. Offered the opportunity to negotiate a resolution of issues with Tedesco in *State v. Shack,* should the attorneys for the farm workers negotiate or litigate? If offered terms that would satisfy the needs of the farm workers on Tedesco's farm, should the attorneys recommend that their clients accept the offer or litigate? Under the holding of *Cross,* is it advisable for the shopping mall to broaden access to the premises?

You might try a simulated negotiation of the following problem:

Representatives of Vo-tech University have come to your city to offer the homeless the opportunity to enroll in vocational training courses. The courses can be financed with federally-subsidized loans. University recruiters offer to help applicants complete the necessary paperwork for the loans as part of the application process. Typical courses meet for three hours one night a week for 12 weeks. Tuition for most courses is $750. Students can enroll in as many as three courses at a time.

The Shining Light Shelter is a private, not-for-profit, church-affiliated corporation that provides beds for 85 homeless individuals each night, and a day center, where homeless individuals can receive a meal, take a shower, and get some medical care. The Shelter has refused to give school recruiters access to the shelter to talk to the residents each night. Officials of the shelter have said that they refused access because "homeless people are being set up for failure"; job prospects are uncertain; and homeless people have no realistic possibility of being able to repay the loans. Also, the visits might be disruptive, and persons who are "psychiatrically impaired" might be exploited. A negotiation session has been scheduled for two hours from now. Representatives of the shelter, the school, and the homeless will participate. A press conference is scheduled for later that day.

Chapter Two

COMMON LAW ESTATES

I. INTRODUCTION

When you think of owning a piece of land, you might think of your ownership as defined by the physical boundaries of that land. You own "203 Main Street." Or, you own "lot number 12, block 25, plat 18." We describe the ownership of land quite differently in this chapter, however, when we speak of common law estates and future interests. Change the picture of land ownership in your mind at this point. Don't focus on the physical boundaries for now; instead, focus on characteristics of time and conditions relating to use; the possession and the transferability of the land; and to the use of a conveyance of property to control another's behavior.

It is quite likely that your professor at this point will change the picture used to represent land ownership. She or he will not be drawing a square or rectangle, but will use an arrow pointing from left to right indicating a change in ownership, a conveyance. This change in symbol represents the change in our focus.

From this point on, the word "estate" will not signify a particular parcel of land but will signify these attributes of land ownership. We are less concerned with what the square or rectangle communicates in terms of physical boundaries and more concerned with the other properties that define ownership. The very meaning of "estate" changes from a physical thing to a creature of the mind defined by time and by conditions.

Time and condition boundaries on ownership are driven by very human desires. People want to control the disposition and use of their property, sometimes long after their own death. If they are making a gift of their property, they often want to attach strings to the gift. Landed individuals sometimes want to control others' lives using their land as a tool to do this. For example, a spouse might want to bequeath land to the surviving spouse only so long as he or she does not remarry. Parents might want to encourage their son or daughter to graduate from law school by giving their child valuable property to take effect upon gradua-

115

tion, while other parents might want (for whatever reason) to give their child property only so long as that child does not enroll in law school. Similarly, a parent might want to condition a gift of land on their child's marrying within their faith, or abstaining from alcohol, or learning a trade. Grandparents might want to transfer land to a favorite charity, but want to make sure that their favorite grandchild has the benefit of that property during his or her lifetime. A donor may donate land to a university but only if the university is bound to follow the donor's intent that the land be used only for a law school, or for a hospital, or for a library, or more generally for university purposes. Most of the devices you will study in this chapter are most commonly used in intra-family and donative transfers.

As a lawyer designing property conveyances to achieve these desires, you could advise your client simply to tell the grantee of his or her wishes and hope for the best. Or, you could have the receiving party sign a contract. Or, you could use property law; i.e., common law estates and future interests. The tools of the trade that you will learn in this chapter are devices that have their origins in the archaic and that have developed incrementally over time. Lawyers use devices that are centuries old to create thoroughly modern relationships.

The origins of United States conveyancing law begin several hundred years ago in England. Much of the history is a history of evasion—working around limits on property ownership and transfer set by the ruling powers or trying to avoid paying taxes wherever legally possible. To that extent, the history of common law estates has much in common with modern-day property transactions.

A BRIEF HISTORY OF THE ENGLISH FEUDAL SYSTEM

Current Anglo–American property law has its roots in the Norman Settlement of England in 1066. Although American property law of estates draws most directly from English law (which itself drew from Roman law), other civilizations, more ancient than medieval England, also had developed forms similar to those you are studying in this chapter. See Robert C. Ellickson and Charles DiA. Thorland, Ancient Land Law: Mesopotamia, Egypt, Israel, 71 Chicago–Kent Law Review 321, 368–369 (1995) for a description of Mesopotamian life estates, for example.

As William the Conqueror took over the English throne, he established an aristocracy by redistributing the land to his faithful kinsmen and associates. Each took the land with the same rights and privileges as his English predecessor in title. In exchange for the land granted by the Conqueror, the landholder had to supply a certain number of knights to serve in the Conqueror's military. This was an ongoing obligation for the privilege of holding land "under" the king. This system allowed the king to control England and to protect it from military invasion.

In order to meet the service requirements, the tenant-in-chief, holding the land directly under the king, began to create sub-tenures. In exchange for military service, the tenants in chief gave land to their knights. In addition, the smaller landholders surrendered their land to more powerful landholders in exchange for protection. As a result, the tenurial system expanded exponentially. Twenty years after the invasion of England, the Conqueror, in response to the more complex system, arranged for a comprehensive and detailed survey of the land of England which was compiled in the Domesday Book. The Conqueror used the book to determine taxes and to monitor the results of this post-conquest redistribution process.

The lord of the land had a legal relationship with the tenant. The lord owed protection and warranty to the tenant in exchange for services. The service due to the lord ran with the land no matter how many sub-tenures were created. However, the lord of the sub-tenure could contract with the tenant of the sub-tenure to shift the responsibility of providing the service to the tenant of the sub-tenure.

At first, the service required was a matter strictly between the lord and tenant, but the king eventually had to limit the variety of tenures to a manageable amount. There were two general categories of tenure. A free tenure required a definite and certain service which was worthy of a free man (as compared to a serf). An unfree tenure meant service was dependent on the will of the lord and was of a servile nature. In addition, a free-tenure tenant was protected by the king's court while the unfree-tenure tenant had only the lord's court.

Land retained by the lord for his own use was called a manor, which was an agricultural, governmental and fiscal unit. The lord would allow serfs, called villeins, to hold portions of the land in return for labor. Under these unfree tenures, the villeins had no rights against the lord except for protection, and the service requirement as well as the land held was at the will of the lord. However, as agricultural labor grew scarce due to the plague of the Black Death, most lords began to accept money rent rather than labor service.

Eventually, the service requirement became fixed and definite. The unfree tenures became known as copyhold tenures. The tenants could transfer their land, but only by surrender and admittance. The tenant had to surrender the land to the lord for use of a person chosen by the tenant, and the lord had to admit that person as a tenant. The new tenant was given a copy of the transaction as recorded on the rolls of the manorial court as evidence of his title. At first, this unfree tenant was only given protection in the manorial courts, but later the courts of equity and common law courts provided the tenant with protection against the lord and others. Unfree tenure was abolished in England in 1926.

In addition to the service requirements imposed on free tenures, there were other obligations to the lord, known as incidents of tenure, which resulted from the feudal relationship. For example, "homage" was a ceremony that required the tenant to kneel before the lord and solemnly acknowledge himself to be the man of the lord. "Fealty" was an oath taken by the tenant in which he swore to be faithful to the lord. A "relief" was a monetary payment to the lord for the privilege of succeeding to the tenant's ancestor's lands. This entitled the heir to immediate possession, but when the tenant-in-chief died, the king had first seisin (*primer seisin*) of all land held under the tenant-in-chief. A showing of hardship, homage and relief payment were required for the heir to reacquire possession. "Escheat" occurred when a tenant died without heirs or committed a felony. Escheat caused the land to remit to the lord. The best and most accessible source on the history of feudal land ownership and common law estates and future interests is Kurtz, Moynihan's Introduction to the Law of Real Property (4th ed. 2005). Our introduction here is but a brief summary of the background provided in that "little gem."

Feudal land systems were not transplanted from England to the United States, although you will remember from *Johnson v. McIntosh* in Chapter 1 that title in the U.S. still generally proceeds in the first instance from the sovereign. In Hawaii, however, feudal land tenure was not abolished until 1967. Part of the story of the feudal land system and its abolition is told in Hawaii Housing Authority v. Midkiff, 467 U.S. 229, 104 S.Ct. 2321, 81 L.Ed.2d 186 (1984), which is discussed in Chapter 7. During the course of the transition from the tenurial system in that state, one of the authors had the good fortune of visiting Oahu and, looking out over beautiful land to the shore, saw a billboard advertising: "FOR SALE 50 fee simple acres + one waterfall." Keep reading to learn what "fee simple" means on that billboard. As you will learn below, the fee simple absolute is the perfect estate, and there couldn't be a more perfect place for it.

Although the U.S. did not incorporate a feudal tenurial system of land titles, we did keep the more visible and incidental manifestations of the system. The estates and future interests you study in this chapter crossed the pond without essential conceptual change.

II. FEE SIMPLE ABSOLUTE AND LIFE ESTATE

The essence of all of the tools of common law estates and future interests is the precise use of language. The use of the correct words was critically important in earlier times and remains important today. Ambiguity is the archenemy of the property lawyer in conveyancing as much as it can be an assist to the contract lawyer in facilitating a workable agreement in the face of areas of disagreement that may or may not develop into performance problems. In conveying property by deed or gift or will, the client will not be pleased if judicial interpretation is required for an ambiguity that could have been avoided in the first place. In property conveyancing, a "win" in court is a costly victory and may reveal the inadequate skills of the lawyer who was responsible for drafting the conveyance.

The most notable example of the symbolic and precise use of words in estates is the phrase required to create the estate called the "fee simple absolute." The fee simple absolute is the highest or most complete estate that can be owned. The estate is of potentially infinite duration: even though the owner of the estate surely will die, the estate itself need not. There is no limitation on use inherent to the fee simple absolute. Any limitations on use would have to be imposed externally through zoning laws or subdivision agreements or nuisance law or similar sources. There is no limitation on alienability, devisability or inheritability in a fee simple absolute.

To convey a fee simple absolute, you are required under common law to use a particular "magic" or symbolic phrase or mantra. That phrase is "and his [or her or their] heirs." So, if the grantor[1] wants to convey a fee simple absolute to Mary, he does so by using the following phrase in the deed or will through which he will be conveying the property: "to Mary and her heirs."

"To Mary" are considered "words of purchase;" i.e., the words that identify the person or entity to whom the land is transferred. "And her heirs" are considered "words of limitation;" i.e., the words that describe the quality of estate that Mary receives—in this case a fee simple absolute. Mary's heirs actually receive nothing at all in this conveyance because the word "heirs" is being used in its symbolic form only. As "words of limitation," the phrase "and her heirs" conveys no property interest to the heirs.

This is certainly counterintuitive. Make sure you understand this point now, or it will plague you later. In the conveyance "to Mary and her heirs," Mary's heirs receive no interest whatsoever. The words "and her heirs" are to be understood as purely symbolic.

If the conveyance transfers the land "to Mary and her heirs," with no other qualification, you know that Mary has received a fee simple absolute. You might be wondering why you wouldn't just say "to Mary in fee simple absolute," which would be simpler. The short answer is: because we've always used "and her heirs" to designate fee simple absolute. A conveyance "to Mary in fee simple absolute" would indeed convey to Mary a fee simple absolute, but you still need to know the significance of "to Mary and her heirs" because that is still the most common way lawyers draft the fee simple absolute.

A conveyance that stated "to Mary," rather than "to Mary and her heirs," did not convey a fee simple absolute in common law. Instead, "to Mary" conveyed only a life estate. The conveyance of a life estate does not require magic words, words with solely symbolic meaning. It is

---

1. In the conveyances you will study in this text, including in the next few paragraphs, you are to assume that the grantor (traditionally identified as "O" if not specifically named) owns a fee simple absolute before the first transaction is made unless a lesser estate is specified in the facts. Thus, in the conveyance "O to Mary" you are to assume that O owned a fee simple absolute prior to the conveyance to Mary.

effective for you to convey a life estate by being more explicit, for example by conveying the property:

to Mary for life,

to Mary for her lifetime, or

to Mary, a life estate.

A life estate is quite limited, in comparison to a fee simple absolute. Unlike the fee simple absolute, the life estate is not potentially infinite in duration; it does not survive the death of the owner. The life estate instead terminates upon the death of the life tenant, the person by whose lifetime the life estate is measured.

So, if Mary is given a life estate by the conveyance "O to Mary for life," upon Mary's death, the life estate expires automatically. In contrast, if Mary is given a fee simple absolute by the conveyance "O to Mary and her heirs," upon Mary's death, the fee simple absolute remains in her estate to be distributed according to her will or according to the state's statute of intestate succession if she dies without a will.

The life estate is transferable, just as a fee simple absolute is transferable. If Mary owns a life estate and transfers her property to Joe, Joe receives a life estate *pur autre vie*. Joe's life estate is measured by the lifetime of a person other than the owner of the estate: it is measured *pur autre vie*, by the life of another. Joe's life estate *pur autre vie* lasts so long as Mary lives. Upon Mary's death, Joe's life estate *pur autre vie* expires. (We will return to the life estate *pur autre vie* a little later to explore some of the "what if" questions you are probably considering already.)

While a fee simple absolute does not have any inherent limitations on the use of the land, use of the land by the owner of a life estate is inherently limited. The use of a life estate is limited by the doctrine of waste. This doctrine is discussed in *Woodrick v. Wood*, which appears below.

Apparently, modern lawyers and do-it-yourselfers are somewhat less inclined to attend to the precision in language (or to the prestidigitation) required by the common law estates system. Many state legislatures, therefore, have relaxed the requirement that conveyances use the phrase "and his heirs" as magic words for the conveyance of a fee simple absolute. For example, many states have statutes that provide that

the term "heirs," or other words of inheritance, shall not be necessary to create or convey an estate in fee simple, and every conveyance of real estate shall pass all the estate of the grantor therein, unless the intent to pass a less estate shall expressly appear, or be necessarily implied in the terms of the grant. Mo. Stat. § 442.460.

This statute, and the many that are similar, tells you that the conveyance "to Mary" is to be presumed to convey a fee simple absolute unless you have evidence that the grantor intended to give less. This overturns the older common law rule and is compatible with the general modern preference for more marketable, less restricted title. Still, note the ambiguity inherent in this statute. Fee simple absolute is presumed in the absence of the phrase "and her heirs" *only* if there is no evidence of a grantor's intent to convey a lesser estate. What might constitute evidence that a grantor transferring land "to Mary" and not "to Mary and her heirs" intended to give her only a life estate?

There is one last piece you need before you can test your understanding so far on the problems below. Conveyancing follows a principle analogous to the physics principle of conservation of energy in which it is posited that energy is never consumed, it just changes form. "Conservation of estates" requires that all "parts" of the perfect fee simple absolute estate be accounted for at all times. A life estate is "less" than a fee simple absolute because some part of the fee simple absolute is missing: the fee simple absolute's potentially infinite duration. Because a "piece" of the fee simple absolute is missing, the principle of conservation of estates requires that we account for that piece when a life estate is carved out.

If Mary receives a life estate rather than a fee simple absolute from the grantor, someone has to be holding the missing piece. In terms of a time line, we need to account for the ownership of the property at Mary's death. Her will does not govern the disposition of ownership because her life estate has expired with her death.

If the grantor retains the missing piece, that interest is called a reversion. If another person (*i.e.*, a third party, and not Mary and not the grantor) is granted the missing piece at the point that Mary receives her life estate, that interest is called a remainder. (There are several types of remainders but we save discussion at that level of detail for later. We will also give you more information later on the operation of "future interests," the generic category in which remainders and reversions fall.) If the grantor retained the reversion at the time of his transfer to Mary but later transfers his interest to someone other than Mary, that piece is still called a reversion. The same is true for remainders. You might remember this by remembering that for reversions and remainders "the name stays the same" through subsequent transfers. Or: "Once a reversion, always a reversion."

You can see how a life estate plus a remainder or reversion spreads ownership "on the plane of time." It divides ownership chronologically by creating both a present possession in property (an "estate") that will end at a future event (the death of Mary) and an interest (the remainder or reversion) that will determine possession upon Mary's death.

The most common use of the life estate has been to provide ownership (and therefore material support) for a relative until that relative dies and then to give full ownership to another relative, often one in the next generation. It has also been used in commercial land transactions where a small piece of land is needed for a larger long-term development but the owner (usually very elderly) does not want to sell because his or her home sits on the land. Can you see how a life estate might work in the latter situation?

PRACTICE PROBLEMS

Property may be transferred by sale, by gift, or by bequest. If the property is sold or given away, the transfer is effective upon delivery of the deed. For purposes of this chapter, always assume that the deed has been delivered at the same moment it was executed. If a landowner provides for the transfer of his property in his will, that transfer is effective only upon his (the testator's) death. This allows a person to change his mind (and his will) over and over again. Only at death, is the will effective to actually transfer property.

Identify the fees simple absolute, life estates, reversions and remainders in these conveyances:

1.   Oswald grants Blackacre "to Mary and her heirs."

2.   Oswald sells Goldacre "to Mary for life."

3.   Oswald sells Greenacre "to Mary."

4.   Assume that Oswald died after selling Goldacre "to Mary for life." At his death, Oswald's will devises all of his property "to my grandchild Julio and his heirs."

5.   Oswald sells Blackacre "to Mary, and then to John and his heirs."

6.   Oswald transfers Goldacre "to Mary in fee simple absolute."

7.   Oswald transfers Brownacre "to Mary for life." Mary sells Brownacre "to John and his heirs."

8.   Oswald sells Blackacre "to Mary and her heirs." Mary then sells Blackacre "to John and his heirs," but Mary's son and daughter try to block the sale claiming that they have an ownership interest in Blackacre. Will the children succeed?

9.   Oswald dies owning Greenacre. In his will, he devised Greenacre "to Mary, and then to my children and their heirs."

10.   Oswald transfers Goldacre "to Mary for life." Oswald then sells Goldacre "to John."

11.   Oswald gives Blackacre "to Mary for life." Mary dies leaving a will that devises Blackacre "to my son Paul." Does Paul own Blackacre?

BLACK v. BLACK

Supreme Court of Appeals of West Virginia, 1982.
171 W.Va. 307, 298 S.E.2d 843.

McHugh, Justice.

E.E. Black and Minnie Black, both of whom are now deceased, had a farm near Seneca Rocks, Pendleton County. That farm contained approximately 460 acres. Their children, Claude Black, I.D. Black and the appellant [Jessie Black], became joint owners of the farm.

By a document dated January 3, 1950, and referred to in the complaint as a "written joint survivorship and partnership agreement," Claude Black, I.D. Black and the appellant agreed as follows:

WHEREAS the parties hereto are the joint owners of the E.E. Black home farm * * * and they having mutually agreed among themselves that in the event of the death of any one or more of said parties the survivor or survivors shall receive their interest therein.

NOW, THEREFORE, THIS AGREEMENT WITNESSETH, that in the event of the death of any of the parties to this agreement the other parties hereto shall receive the interest of said deceased party, and

WHEREAS we, the said parties hereto, being the joint owners of said farm and operate the same jointly and are the joint owners of the personal property used in connection of said farm, it is agreed between us that all personal property owned by either of us shall go to the survivor or survivors upon the death of each or any of us.

That agreement was recorded in the office of the Clerk of the County Commission of Pendleton County.

Subsequently, Claude Black, I.D. Black and the appellant executed a joint will. That will named Paul Black and James Paul Geary as executors and was dated August 11, 1969. That will provided, in part, as follows:

FIRST: It is the desire of each of us that all of our property, both real and personal, shall remain and continue in the family, and to carry into effect that intention, it is the will of each of us, to-wit: I.D. Black, Claude Black and Jessie Black, that upon the death of any one of us, all the property, both real and personal, belonging to him or her, shall go to the survivors of that one; and upon the death of either of said survivors, all of the property of that one shall go to the remaining survivor, this being the joint and several will of each and all of us.

SECOND: Providing, further, however, that upon the death of the last survivor of I.D. Black, Claude Black, and Jessie Black, all of the estate, both real and personal, then remaining, shall go to and become the property in fee of the following named nieces and nephews and in the share and interest so shown.

There were seven nieces and nephews named in the will and each was to receive a one-seventh interest in the estate "then remaining." Those nieces and nephews and the executors are appellees in this action.

Neither Claude Black nor I.D. Black ever married. They died without issue. Claude Black died on April 30, 1971, and I.D. Black died on March 14, 1976. The joint will was recorded in both instances in

Pendleton County during probate proceedings. Appraisement and final settlement reports were recorded. * * *

In July, 1979, [Jessie Black] filed a complaint in circuit court in which she asserted that having survived the deaths of Claude Black and I.D. Black, both the 1950 agreement and the joint will vested her with fee simple title to the 460 acre farm and 36 acre tract and all the personal property located upon that real estate. Specifically, the appellant alleged that inasmuch as she owned all the property in question, she could sell or dispose of it in fee simple, and none of the appellees had any interest in the property. * * *

The appellees filed an answer in which they denied the essential allegations of the complaint. They also filed a counterclaim in which they asserted that * * * the two deeds dated February 17, 1979 [from Jessie Black to others], were null and void.

With respect to the issue of the appellant's interest in the property in question, the circuit court resolved the matter upon the record without a jury and without taking evidence. By order dated March 10, 1981, the circuit court held that pursuant to the joint will, the appellant had a life estate only in the 460 acre farm and the 36 acre tract, and a life interest only in the personal property, with the right to consume that personal property through normal use. The circuit court declared that the interests in the remainder of both the real and the personal property were held by the seven nieces and nephews or their heirs. Furthermore, the circuit court held the deeds dated February 17, 1979, to be null and void to the extent those deeds purported to convey more than the appellant's life interest in the property. * * *

The reasons for the ruling of the circuit court against the appellant were stated in the circuit court's memorandum of opinion dated January 7, 1981. The circuit court concluded as follows concerning the joint will:

> There is no intent by the three Testators to vest the survivor with the assets of the estate absolutely, but the intent is clearly expressed that the survivor shall have a lifetime interest only, then the assets shall vest in the third parties, nieces and nephews, named in the will.

> The * * * agreement dated January 3, 1950, entered into by the parties was completely modified and superseded by their subsequent agreement as set forth and contained in their joint will.

[Jessie Black] contends that, having survived Claude Black and I.D. Black, she acquired fee simple title to the real property and personal property in question, because (1) the language of the will so indicates, and (2) the will does not contain phrases such as "life estate" limiting her interest. * * *

The [nephews and nieces] contend, however, that the will clearly provides them with a remainder in fee to the property in question. In this regard, the appellees contend that the appellant is bound by the provisions of the will because Claude Black, I.D. Black and [Jessie Black] mutually agreed upon the will's provisions, one of which provisions allegedly provides the appellees with a remainder in fee to the property in question. * * *

W.Va.Code, 36–1–16 [1931] provides as follows:

If any interest in or claim to real or personal property be given by sale or gift inter vivos or by will to one, with a limitation over either by way of remainder or of executory devise or any other limitation, and by the same conveyance or will there be conferred, expressly or by implication, a power upon the first taker in his lifetime or by will to use or dispose absolutely of such property, the limitation over shall not fail or be defeated except to the extent that the first taker shall have lawfully exercised such power of disposal. The proceeds of a disposal under such power shall be held subject to the same limitations and the same power of use or disposal as the original property, unless a contrary intent shall appear from the conveyance or will.

The effect of that statute is to preserve the initial validity of the limitation over, subject to the first taker's power of disposal. * * *

The common law rule * * * was as follows:

Where there is a devise or bequest to one in *general terms* and there is a subsequent limitation over of what remains at the first taker's death, if there is also given to the first taker an unlimited and unrestricted power of absolute disposal, express or implied, the devise or bequest to the first taker is construed to pass a fee [simple], and the limitation over is invalid. * * *

The joint will in the action before this Court * * * does not expressly confer upon the appellant an estate "during the term of her natural life." Nevertheless, from a reading of the entire will, this Court concludes, as did the circuit court, that the appellant received under the will a life estate only in the property in question and that the named nieces and nephews received a remainder in fee simple.

That conclusion is clearly mandated by the provisions of the joint will, and, as the appellees assert, reference to extrinsic evidence is not appropriate. As indicated by the provisions of W.Va.Code, 36–1–16 [1931], the remainder or gift over to the named nieces and nephews does not fail but, rather, is subject to the appellant's power of disposal, if any, conferred by the will. No such power of disposal, either by express provision or by implication, was conferred upon the appellant by this particular will. Rather, the will, after stating the desire of the testators to keep the property in the family, directs that upon the death of the appellant, the property shall "become the property in fee" of the named nieces and nephews.

Although the joint will provides that the nieces and nephews shall receive the property "then remaining," we do not believe that the phrase "then remaining" is sufficient in this action to defeat the remainder or gift over to the named nieces and nephews. We agree with the circuit court that the phrase "then remaining" refers to the ordinary use and consumption of property by a life tenant during the course of a life estate. * * *

Notes and Questions

1. Could a grantee own a reversion? Yes. See if you can guess how that might have come about in *Black v. Black*. Remember the principle for remainders and reversions that "the name stays the same." Could a grantor own a remainder? Yes. See if you can imagine how that might have come about in *Black v. Black*. Could someone own a life estate that was not measured by his own life? Yes. See if you can imagine how that might have come about in *Black v. Black*.

2. Many family situations—and the Black family is perhaps an example—are such that a division into life estates and remainders is too rigid to be workable. More exacting tools are needed. It is possible to put residential, or farm, or business property in one generation, with future interests in the next generation, but it may become necessary to sell some of the property during the life of the life tenant, or to use it in the present in a way that is not consistent with life ownership. For example, a spouse may choose to devise to the surviving spouse a life estate with remainders to the deceased spouse's children anticipating that the life estate will support the surviving spouse for his or her lifetime. But should the property not provide adequate support in its current form, the devising spouse may want to assure that the children cannot block the sale of the property at its optimal price. Assume, for example, that the land is a small farm that is no longer profitable but that the surrounding countryside has become very desirable for suburban residential and commercial development. It is likely that developers would not be interested in acquiring a life estate only. Can you see why? Of course, the surviving spouse and all of the children could sell all of their interests to the developer in which case the developer would have all the pieces of a fee simple absolute and would, in fact, have a fee simple absolute in the land. Do you see how that happens? But if one child refused to sell, or has already lost his remainder to the owners of the local casino who refuse to sell, the sale would not be able to go forward. The developer would no longer be interested. The argued-for power of disposal in the *Black* case might be a way to make the life estate more flexible and answer this problem. What are the risks and benefits of using such a device? (You should assume, of course, that the lawyer using the device drafts the document so that it is clear that the device is being used.)

3. Even with the power of disposal, the life estate places very serious restrictions on the life tenant and may make it impossible to sell the land or to make productive use of it. An alternative is to use a trust in which the land is transferred to a trustee and where the trustee is charged with satisfying the grantor's intent concerning the distribution of income and the use of the land. The trust is discussed later in this chapter, and at great length in courses on trusts and estates.

PIGG v. HALEY

Supreme Court of Virginia, 1982.
224 Va. 113, 294 S.E.2d 851.

COMPTON, JUSTICE.

The focus of this appeal is upon the validity of an agreement, executed to settle uncertainties arising from the doubtful meaning of provisions in a will.

Edward F. Haley, a resident of Charlotte County, died testate on July 13, 1977, survived by his wife, appellee Eva F. Haley. The testator's one-page holograph, duly probated shortly after his death, provides in part:

"Third: Whatever land I may own, including buildings, furniture, farming equipment of all kinds, livestock of every description, automobiles, money in hand, or in banks, or owing to me, shall immediately upon my decease become the property of my wife, Eva F. Haley, to be used for her decent support during her natural life.

"Fourth: It is my will and desire that upon the death of my said wife whatever residue of my estate either real or personal which she has not consumed or disposed of shall become the property of Garland D. Pigg."

Appellant Pigg, a resident of Fairfax County, was a distant cousin of the testator.

At his death, Haley owned certain personal property and an undivided one-half interest in approximately 152 acres of land in Charlotte County; his wife owned the remaining one-half interest in the realty.

Because of doubt as to the meaning of the foregoing language in the will, the agreement in dispute was executed about two weeks after Haley's death by the widow and Pigg. Drafted by an attorney, the operative portions of the agreement provide:

"1. That all personal property, both tangible and intangible, in the Estate of Edward F. Haley, shall be the sole and exclusive property of Eva F. Haley, with complete right to dispose of the same in any manner that she might deem fit, and the party of the second part relinquishes any interest that he might acquire under the will of Edward F. Haley, in this regard.

"2. That the interest in any real estate that Edward F. Haley died seized and possessed of in Charlotte County, Virginia, shall be construed as to give his wife, Eva F. Haley, a life estate therein exclusively, with the remainder over to Garland D. Pigg, upon her death, in fee simple and absolutely."

Subsequently, the widow and appellees Donald F. Haley and Betty R. Haley, his wife, executed a real estate contract in May of 1979 for the sale by the widow to the Haleys of 30 acres from the 152-acre tract.

Within a month, the present suit was filed by the widow and the Haleys against Pigg. By virtue of the contract, the Haleys claim "an equitable fee interest" in the 30 acres. * * *

Following an October 1979 ore tenus hearing, the trial judge ruled from the bench in favor of the plaintiffs, declaring the agreement [between Eva Haley and Garland Pigg] void. The court found the agreement lacked adequate consideration.* In the January 1980 final decree, from which we awarded Pigg an appeal, the court decided that the effect of the will "was to vest in [the widow] the right to consume and dispose of, by sale, gift, or otherwise, the property of" the testator. Thus, the court implicitly held that Pigg received nothing under the will which he could relinquish in the agreement.

Upon appeal, as in the court below, the validity of the agreement depends upon the interpretation of the will. Our analysis, of necessity, will be in two steps. Initially, we must interpret the will. Because the words of the will are of doubtful meaning and the uncertainty is not resolved by reading the will as a whole, we will consider admissible extrinsic evidence to establish the relevant facts and circumstances that surrounded the testator at the time the will was executed. * * * Next, we must address the issue of consideration and, in so doing, we will consider all the relevant circumstances disclosed by the record. * * *

The decedent [Edward F. Haley] and his wife [Eva] married in 1937. He taught in an Alabama high school for a period of time and, because he was a native of Virginia, the couple moved to Charlotte County where both husband and wife worked. He farmed, taught, and sold life insurance; she was a registered nurse. During the 1940s, with their joint funds, the couple purchased the 152–acre "farm" in question, deeded to them "jointly" and without "a survivorship clause," and later built a residence on the property. They worked on the farm together, and actually participated in the construction of their home.

As a hobby, the decedent engaged in genealogical research. During the 1940s, when he was teaching at Hargrave Military Academy, the decedent "discovered" Pigg, a fourth cousin, while searching records in Chatham. Pigg, about seven or eight years old at the time, lived near Chatham with his parents. Thereafter, a close personal relationship developed between the decedent, who had no children, and Pigg, whose father died when he was a young person. Calling the decedent "Uncle Frank," young Pigg regularly visited the decedent and his wife on their farm, staying for periods of time during the summer months.

After Pigg completed high school, the decedent helped Pigg during the 1950s obtain entry to Ferrum College, the decedent's alma mater, and "arranged" for Pigg to have a scholarship there. Later, Pigg lived

---

* Editor's note: In order for there to be consideration for the agreement, both Pigg and Haley had to bring something of value to the table. A "bargained for exchange" is required. If Pigg received nothing of value under the will to exchange for widow Haley's agreement, the agreement lacked "consideration" and would not be enforceable.

with the decedent and his wife while he attended one semester at Longwood College, where Mrs. Haley was employed as a nurse.

After finishing college, Pigg taught for a period of time at Staunton Military Academy. He married in 1962. Subsequently, Pigg, his wife, who was also a teacher, and their children spent a part of all the regular holidays—Thanksgiving, Christmas, Easter, and the summer—with the Haleys. The Piggs had possession of a key to the Haleys' home so they could enter if no one was there when they arrived for a visit. When asked to describe the relationship existing between her husband and Pigg in 1964, when the will in question was written, the widow testified they were "friends" and "[r]easonably close." Pigg stated he and Haley had a "close" relationship.

After 1964, the decedent advanced Pigg $10,000 to purchase a 130–acre tract adjacent to the property in question. The loan subsequently was repaid. According to the evidence, the regular visits and the personal relationship between the Piggs and the Haleys continued into the 1970s and past 1972 when Mrs. Haley retired from her employment at Longwood College.

During the decedent's final illness, while he was hospitalized in Farmville, the Piggs came from their home in Fairfax, having been called by Mrs. Haley. When Haley died, the Piggs assisted with the funeral arrangements.

Within a week of the death, an unwitnessed typewritten will dated in 1963 was found in Haley's desk at home. When the widow was advised the writing could not be admitted to probate, a further search among Haley's effects was made with the assistance of the Piggs. Finally, Mrs. Pigg discovered the will in question among Haley's voluminous genealogical notes.

On the day the will was probated, Lelia Hoy, a Charlotte County attorney who had reviewed the will, told the widow she had only a life interest in her husband's estate, observing: "You own nothing; you have the use of the property, the use of the farm; the proceeds of the farm until you die; and you have the interest from the money until you die."

The widow testified that this news was "overwhelming" because she had no knowledge of a will; in fact, Haley told his wife during his last illness "that he had no will." The widow testified she felt she had been "sabotaged" because in 1964, when the will was written, the couple "did not have any money;" they had recently finished making large, regular payments over a ten-year period on a joint annuity.

The widow, accompanied by the Piggs, then went to Farmville to consult R.A. Wilmouth, the proprietor of "a bookkeeping tax service." Wilmouth had prepared income tax returns for the testator for a number of years. In discussing the tax aspects of the estate, he said to the widow: " 'You will receive the interest from the money, and you will have the proceeds from the farm.' "Upon Wilmouth's recommendation, the widow, still accompanied by the Piggs, then consulted E. Preston Lancaster, Jr., a Farmville attorney.

Lancaster, noting the ambiguity in the will, mentioned that a court interpretation should be sought. But "the main thing on [the widow's] mind," according to Pigg, was that an agreement be prepared to fix the interests of the respective parties.

According to Pigg, the widow stated to him repeatedly, after realizing that the meaning of the will was uncertain: " 'Uncle Frank and I always wanted you to have the farm, and we didn't intend for you to have the money.' "The widow testified that she suggested the agreement in an effort to "salvage some property for myself." When asked whether the testator before his death mentioned "the possibility of leaving an interest in the farm" to Pigg, the widow said: "I did not recall that he said that." The widow previously had stated in a deposition in responding to a similar question: " 'Well, he might have mentioned it vaguely.' "

The record shows that the widow suggested the terms of the agreement to Lancaster who, on the date it was executed, dictated the language of the document to his secretary in the presence of the widow and the Piggs. According to Lancaster, the widow said to him that the agreement reflected "what her husband would have wanted." At the time the agreement was executed, Lancaster asked both parties whether they understood the document and whether "these were the terms that [they] wanted"; the widow responded "yes" and Pigg said: " 'If that's what she wants, that's okay with me.' "

Even though the agreement recites "in consideration of the sum of TEN DOLLARS ($10.00), and other good and valuable consideration, the receipt of which is hereby acknowledged, and the love and affection that exists between the parties," no money actually passed between the parties.

Before construing the will, Code § 55–11, the doctrine of *May v. Joynes,* 61 Va. (20 Gratt.) 692 (1871), and Code § 55–7 should be reviewed. Code § 55–11 provides:

> "When any real estate is conveyed, devised or granted to any person without any words of limitation such devise, conveyance or grant shall be construed to pass the fee simple or other whole estate or interest which the testator or grantor has power to dispose of in such real estate, unless a contrary intention shall appear by the will, conveyance or grant."

Under *May v. Joynes,* "where a life estate is given to the first taker coupled with the absolute power of disposition, the added power raises the life estate to a fee in real property and absolute ownership of personalty, and any limitations in the remainder over are void for repugnancy and uncertainty. * * * "But the foregoing rule has been modified by statute.

Code § 55–7 provides, in part:

"A. If any interest in or claim to real estate or personal property be disposed of by deed or will for life, with a limitation in remainder over, and in the same instrument there be conferred expressly or by implication a power upon the life tenant in his lifetime or by will to dispose absolutely of such property, the limitation in remainder over shall not fail, or be defeated, except to the extent that the life tenant shall have lawfully exercised such power of disposal."

The effect of the statute is to validate the gift over "where the first taker is given an *express estate for life,* coupled with the absolute power of disposition" * * *.

It is against this background that the competing parties debate the meaning of the will. The widow says she acquired either an absolute fee simple interest, in which case § 55–7 would not apply, or she acquired "a life estate coupled with an absolute power of disposition during her life," in which case the savings provisions of § 55–7 would apply. But, the argument continues, under the latter alternative, the second taker must prove what property, if any, remains at the death of the first taker, and it is doubtful that Pigg will be able to prove at the widow's death that she did not dispose of all the testator's property. Thus, in either event, says the widow, Pigg received under the will nothing which he could surrender in the agreement.

Pigg contends that the will created an express life estate in the testator's property in Eva Haley, coupled with an absolute inter vivos power of disposition, and a remainder over to Pigg. He argues the widow took less than a fee simple interest in the realty and less than an absolute interest in the personalty. Consequently, Pigg urges, his interest acquired under the will was such as to constitute sufficient consideration for the agreement. We concur.

The extrinsic facts show the circumstances surrounding the testator in 1964 when he wrote the will. A strong bond existed between the Haleys who, at that time, had been married 27 years. They had labored together in operating their farm and in building their home, pooling their financial resources acquired from their respective occupations. There was also a close, avuncular relationship between the testator and Pigg, a tie based on mutual respect and affection that, at the time, had existed for over 20 years. Consequently, the parol evidence established that the objects of the testator's affection were, principally, his wife and, secondarily, Pigg. * * *

Against this background, we turn to the language of the clauses in issue. The testator provided in the Third clause that whatever land he owned, "including" items of personal property, should immediately upon his decease "become the property" of his wife, "to be used for her decent support during her natural life." Then, he wrote in clause Fourth: "It is my will and desire that upon the death of my said wife whatever residue of my estate either real or personal which she has not consumed or disposed of shall become the property of Garland D. Pigg."

We conclude, contrary to the widow's contention, that the words "shall immediately upon my decease become the property of my wife * * * to be used for her decent support during her natural life," created an express life estate in the testator's property. * * * Here * * * we believe the language points to the intention of the testator to provide for the support and comfort of his wife during her life, but, upon her death, such of the property which she had not consumed would pass to Pigg, his esteemed kinsman. Such a plan, under these facts and circumstances, would benefit both objects of the testator's affection.

The question then becomes whether Code § 55–7 is applicable to clauses Third and Fourth. We think it is. An express life estate was created, fulfilling the first requirement of the statute. The Fourth clause confers expressly a power upon the life tenant in her lifetime, as she agrees on brief, to dispose absolutely of the property, thus satisfying the second requirement. In addition, the language of the Fourth clause manifestly is a limitation in remainder over, thus fulfilling the third statutory requirement. Finally, there is a corpus; property remains undisposed of by the life tenant on which the "limitation in remainder over" can operate. * * *

And, as we have said, the interest Pigg acquired under the will affords the basis for adequate consideration in the agreement. * * * Pigg acquired a remainder interest under the will in the realty and personalty. In order to make certain that which the will rendered ambiguous and vague, the parties entered into this agreement, in which Pigg relinquished his interest in all of the decedent's personalty and acquired a "remainder * * * in fee simple" in the realty. While it is true, as the widow argues, that under our interpretation of the will eventually there may have been no property remaining undisposed of by the life tenant at the time of her death, nonetheless, Pigg in 1977 suffered a detriment by agreeing to surrender his interest in the personalty, at a time when the property had not been dissipated.

Finally, the widow argues the agreement is void because, as the trial judge found, there was a mutual mistake of fact. She contends that the parties entered into the agreement upon the mistaken assumption that she acquired under the will a life estate only, when "at a minimum" she was given "a life estate in her husband's property and, without any dispute, the unfettered right to dispose of it."

Generally, equity, while relieving mistakes of fact, will not give relief from a mistake of law, except in extraordinary cases. * * * But that rule has been confined to mistakes of the general rules of law, and does not apply to the mistakes made by individuals as to their own private legal rights and interests, such as to the ownership of property. Those private rights are treated as matters of fact, albeit the result of matters of law. * * * However, the latter rule has no application to cases of compromise, when doubts have arisen as to the rights of parties, and they have intentionally entered into an agreement to compromise and settle those doubts. * * * This is such a case.

Manifestly, the record shows that the parties to the agreement both were in doubt as to their respective interests under the will, that they intentionally made a sincere effort to settle their respective claims, and that they endeavored to avoid the litigation suggested by Lancaster. Consequently, and the transaction being devoid of overreaching or unfair dealing on either side, we will not annul the agreement on the ground of mutual mistake.

For the foregoing reasons, we conclude that the trial court erred in declaring the agreement of July 26, 1977 void and in removing the cloud on the title to the 30–acre tract. Accordingly, we will declare such agreement valid and enforceable, reverse the judgment appealed from, and enter final judgment dismissing the bill of complaint.

Notes and Questions

1. Mr. Haley directed the disposition of his property upon his death by will. The individuals who take property under a will are called the "beneficiaries," the "devisees" or the "legatees." In colloquial language, we may call them "heirs," but that is a term we reserve in law to identify a different class. You will recall that the term "heirs" has a purely symbolic meaning in a conveyance "to Mary and her heirs." It does not identify a class of persons; nor does it transfer property to those persons: the words "and her heirs" are used there only as words of limitation.

In other contexts, however, the term "heirs" does describe a class of persons—those individuals to whom the property of a deceased individual is transferred if the decedent dies without a legally effective will. Such a person dies "intestate," and his or her property is distributed according to the state's statute of intestate succession. Although we commonly refer to individuals such as the spouse and children as "heirs" of a living person, it is an inaccurate characterization. No one has any heirs until he has died. Only at the point of his death can a person's heirs be identified. In particular, the children of a living parent are not that parent's heirs. They may become so upon the parents' deaths, but not before. Until then, they may be said to have a "naked expectancy;" however, with the number of early retirees among baby boomers, their children may simply be said to have false hopes of any inheritance.

A typical statute of intestate succession distributes a share of the property to the surviving spouse and the rest (or the entire estate if there is no surviving spouse) to the decedent's children or their descendants. If there are no surviving spouse or children (or grandchildren), the estate is distributed to other family members (such as grandparents, siblings, aunts and uncles) in order of priority established in the statute. If the word "heirs" is used to identify a particular class of persons, if "her heirs" are used as words of purchase instead of words of limitation (a situation we analyze later), it describes those individuals who would have taken the property under the statute of intestate succession. Try these problems:

(a) Ophelia sells Greenacre "to Mark and his heirs." Assume that Mark is alive and has two children. Do the children have any ownership interest in Greenacre while Mark is alive?

(b) Assume now that Mark has died without a will and is survived by his two children. Who owns Greenacre?

(c) Assume instead that Mark has died with a will, is survived by his two children, but left all of his property, including Greenacre, to his best friend. Who owns Greenacre?

2. Mr. Haley's 1963 will was not used to distribute his property probably because it lacked witnesses and so was invalid under state law. The 1977 will that was used to distribute his property was valid in Virginia even though it was holographic; i.e., handwritten and unwitnessed. Why would a state have a law that would make an unwitnessed typewritten will invalid and an unwitnessed handwritten will valid, as many states do? Is there any argument against enforcing a holographic will as in *Pigg*? Could Haley's handwritten "will" have been a rough draft about which he later changed his mind? A threat? Where was the holographic will found? Does this indicate Haley intended it to be his will?

3. The question considered by the court is whether the agreement between Pigg and Haley was supported by consideration and so was a legally enforceable contract. How did the dispute over whether Mr. Haley's will gave his widow a life estate with power of disposition or a fee simple absolute relate to the question of consideration for the agreement?

4. The Uniform Probate Code, § 3–912 provides: "[S]uccessors may agree among themselves to alter the interests, shares, or amounts to which they are entitled under the will of the decedent * * * in any way that they provide in a written contract. * * * The [executor] shall abide by the terms of the agreement. * * * "The policy behind § 3–912, and the policy behind similar statutes or case-law doctrines in states that have not adopted the Uniform Probate Code, is the preservation of family concord, even when the agreement of the successors departs radically from the pattern the testator put in the will. The question in a case such as *Pigg v. Haley* is why the agreement (and the statute or case-law policy that encouraged the parties to make an agreement) failed of its purpose—so that the matter had to be resolved by judges:

(a) Both Mrs. Haley and the Piggs visited the lawyer's office in Farmville and were together, in fact, and perhaps in spirit, for the making of an agreement that would conform their ownership either to what Mr. Haley seemed to have had in mind, or to Mrs. Haley's needs, or to both. Is there something: (i) in the express agreement itself; or (ii) in the way the agreement was made, that gives a hint as to why the harmony did not last?

(b) The lawyer first strongly advised taking the will to court, so that a judge could tell the parties what Mr. Haley's will meant. But the policy of law such as U.P.C. § 3–912 is that Mrs. Haley and Mr. and Mrs. Pigg could decide for themselves what effect the will was to have on their property ownership, and on their relationship(s) with one another. They could have made their own law and have been their own judges. And here, apparently, they were willing to do that, at least for a moment. What are the advantages and disadvantages of agreement versus litigation in such a situation?

(c) Drafting a will that is clear in terms of the property interests it purports to create is a matter of law-office skill. Could this rather tragic family quarrel have been avoided if Mr. Haley had had a lawyer draft his will? How would you have done the job?

(d) Drafting an agreement that settles a dispute, or makes clear what is otherwise unclear, also involves skill. Could this *agreement* have been drafted in such a way as to have avoided a lawsuit over its validity?

(e) Obtaining commitment from each party to a contract is another matter that involves skill. Here, commitment was related to skill at resolving the dispute in an effective, lasting, mutually understood way. That, in turn, involved skill at locating and describing the human conflict that a dispute involves—getting it out into the open, where it could have been dealt with. How might have the lawyer tried to get these parties to a more stable agreement? Is that part of a lawyer's job? What skill set would be needed to accomplish this?

(f) Could the agreement that Mr. Lancaster dictated to his secretary as Mrs. Haley and Mr. Pigg looked on have failed because the parties were not separately represented? Or, would separate representation for each party have thwarted any effort to reach agreement?

Mr. Lancaster's role, in dealing with both Mrs. Haley and Mr. Pigg, is one our regulators have come to call "the lawyer as intermediary." Its most famous example was in the law office of Louis D. Brandeis, in Boston, 1907. ("The Lennox Case," discussed in John P. Frank, The Legal Ethics of Louis D. Brandeis, 17 Stanford L. Rev. 683 (1965)). In comes a father and son team who run a tannery business. The tannery business is heads over heels in debt. The owners bring with them a D.C. lawyer and two of his clients, both of them creditors, among many, of the tannery business. It is more of a mess than the one in Mr. Lancaster's office in Farmville, but all present think Mr. Brandeis can do something about it. The tannery owners, and the creditors, and the creditors' lawyer, and Mr. Brandeis, talk together. All together. Mr. Brandeis listens and then proposes an assignment for the benefit of creditors, a state-law alternative to bankruptcy (which is federal law). Everybody agrees. And everybody agrees that Mr. Brandeis is to be the trustee over assets assigned for creditors.

Mr. Brandeis then does a thorough and open job as trustee; he does what he said he would do before they chose him to be trustee, which was to "get a square deal for everyone." The assignment does not avoid bankruptcy, but when the business is finally liquidated the assets pay creditors forty cents on the dollar, which, in the annals of corporate bankruptcy, is pretty good. Still, nobody was happy. The tannery owners got a new lawyer, a bankruptcy lawyer, who at one point turned to Mr. Brandeis and asked him, "Whom did you represent when you advised an assignment for the benefit of creditors?" Mr. Brandeis's answer was a dramatic and seminal moment in American legal ethics. Mr. Brandeis, who met with and advised the owners of a bankrupt business, its officers, its principal creditors, and a lawyer for creditors, said of his work that day: *"I should say I was counsel for the situation."*

Mr. Brandeis went on to the bench—all the way up, while he was at it—to the U.S. Supreme Court. He barely made it through confirmation by the Senate after he was nominated by President Wilson, but the opposition was not because of his law practice; it was because he was Jewish. Every living ex-president of the American Bar Association (seven of them) opposed him. His opponents of course dredged up reasons other than their opposition to a Jew being on the federal supreme court. The most prominent was that the way he practiced law was not ethical in that he disregarded conflicts of interest. One piece of evidence was what he said in the tannery case—his claim that he had been counsel for the situation.

Written two generations after that, long after Justice Brandeis's death, John Frank's Stanford article is generally a pro-Brandeis piece, but along the way Judge Frank wrote that Brandeis's answer when he was asked whom he represented in the tannery case—"I should say I was counsel for the situation"—was "one of the most unfortunate phrases he ever uttered." "Lawyers," Judge Frank decided, "are not retained by situations." (Not even, one supposes, Mr. Lancaster in Farmville.)

Fifteen years after the Frank article on Brandeis, Professor Geoffrey Hazard published Ethics in the Practice of Law (1979). That book was a prelude to the Model Rules of Professional Conduct (R.P.C.), which became in due course the official regulatory source for most American lawyers. Geoffrey Hazard was the principal architect of those Rules. In his book, he told the tannery story and approved of what Brandeis said there. Eventually Hazard proposed to the American Bar Association a new ethics rule to express endorsement of what Brandeis said, Judge Frank to the contrary notwithstanding. Rule 2.2 of the R.P.C. refers to "the lawyer as intermediary." Hazard might have called it "the lawyer for the situation."

There is something to be said for retaining Brandeis's word "situation." The theologian Joseph Fletcher called his controversial book Situation Ethics. The associate pastor of the parish church one of us belongs to phoned and said he needed to talk to a lawyer about "a situation." "I don't have problems," he said. "I have situations." He is Irish and not long back from long service as a missionary in Africa. Lots of vocabulary is available to him, but he says he has "situations." It is a rich word.

A commission of the A.B.A. surveyed the Rules four years ago and recommended changes, some of which the A.B.A. House of Delegates approved in 2002. Most of the noise about those recommendations, and most of the A.B.A. debate since then, has been about confidentiality, securities fraud, Enron, the Sarbanes–Oxley Act, and so forth. Less prominent among the 2002 changes are a new rule for lawyer-mediators and the "deletion" of Rule 2.2. The A.B.A. "model" now has "lawyer as mediator," but it no longer has "lawyer as intermediary." Judge Frank's grumble about situations was vindicated in a latter-day A.B.A. committee; one can hear Judge Frank's words echoing through the report: "Lawyers are not retained by situations." (Some state courts have deleted the former R.P.C. 2.2 from the rules for lawyers, and some have not.) Mr. Lancaster might say, to the contrary, that lawyers *are* retained by situations. He might want to take the Brandeis–Hazard side of this subtle historic tension.

The stated A.B.A. reason for deleting R.P.C. 2.2 is that the subject is adequately covered by Rule 1.7, which deals with conflicts of interest in general. Rule 1.7 covers "concurrent conflicts of interest." Rule 2.2 was mostly intended to cover *potential* conflicts of interest—two examples being the businessmen in the Brandeis law office, those who made up the "situation" that day, and such ordinary daily events as a couple making wills or a landlord and tenant who want a written lease or business colleagues who want to form a partnership. The point about a potential conflict is that the parties are together, want to be together, banking on the possibility that they will not get into a conflict or, if they do, that they will be able to work it out.

Rule 1.7 has been and is a super-structure for all of the traditional edifice on lawyer conflicts of interest. The original comments show that it was meant to deal with interests that are "directly adverse," with representation that carries "material limitations" on a lawyer's work, and with client interests that would "foreclose courses of action" the lawyer ought to take for some of the clients. (Some comments to Rule 1.7 are helpful on intermediary practice, but they are more useful with reference to Rule 2.2 than with reference to conflicts of interest.)

Here is a prosaic, law-office example of how Rule 2.2 works in practice, and one reason why many lawyers think the A.B.A. should have left it alone: One of us (Shaffer) supervises law students in a clinic for low-income people who come to a university legal-aid clinic to have their wills done. Many of these clients are among the working poor, and many are married. Those who are married and want wills done usually come in together, and when they come in together both spouses say they want wills. One of the things an aging male supervisor points out to the student-lawyers who undertake such work is that, based on vast experience, married people do not always agree with each other. He suggests that, before the student-lawyer gets very far into the particulars of one of these jobs, she get her two clients to notice

— that they do not always agree with one another;

— that perhaps their lawyer can help them in some of their coming disagreements; and

— that we propose, right at the beginning of the job, that they ask their lawyer to be a lawyer not for either of them alone but for what Brandeis would call the situation.

The student-lawyer gives her clients a letter, signed eventually by the lawyer and by each spouse. The letter says:

— that the student thinks she can represent both spouses;

— that she has explained "the risks and advantages" of her representing both of them;

— that she believes she can represent the situation (which really means "represent the family," but we don't say that in the letter; maybe we should); and

— that she can do the job in a "manner that is compatible with the best interests of each of you."

Our letter says "best interests of *each* of you" because the rule takes clients one at a time. But it is better to say "best interests of *both* of you," because we think of this as family practice, and we think that the interests of a family, in this work, are a single set of interests. At least, they are until we know better. (Anyway, "best interests of both of you" is what Brandeis meant by "situation," isn't it?))

Our student-lawyer promises to be impartial; she promises to explain alternatives thoroughly; she writes in the letter that she thinks "there is little risk of prejudice to either of your interests," but that she will withdraw from representing *both* spouses if *either* spouse wants her to, or if she comes to believe she cannot do the job as she has just said she plans to do it. Her letter tracks Rule 2.2. It exploits the arcane word "intermediary," which was not Brandeis's word; he said "counsel for the situation." As things have turned out, "intermediary" may have been an unfortunate word, because it sounds like "mediator." The lawyer for the situation is not a mediator. Both an intermediary and a mediator work with people who have or may have disagreements, but a mediator does not represent either of them. An intermediary represents *both* of them. (Compare new (2002) R.P.C. 2.4, "Lawyer Serving as Third–Party Neutral.")

WOODRICK v. WOOD

Court of Appeals of Ohio, Eighth Dist., 1994.
1994 WL 236287.

BLACKMON, JUDGE.

This is an appeal from a judgment of the Cuyahoga County Court of Common Pleas denying a request by Patricia Woodrick, plaintiff-appellant, for an injunction prohibiting Catherine Wood, defendant-appellee, from removing a barn that partially rests on a parcel of land in which Woodrick has a remainder interest. . . .

Catherine Wood and her husband, George Wood, owned several parcels of land including parcel number 105. George Wood died in 1987. In his will, he made the following bequests with respect to his property: I devise and bequeath to my beloved wife, Catherine Dorothy Wood, a life estate in my marital property located at 6207 Dora Blvd., Independence, Ohio, and all my other real estate. Upon the death of my wife, Catherine Dorothy Wood, I direct that the property * * * be bequeathed one-half (50%) to my son, Sheridan George Wood, and one-half (50%) to my daughter, Patricia C. Woodrick.

* * *

For over 25 years, a barn has been situated on the land. The barn was initially used as a stable but has not housed any horses for many years. Some of the wood in the structure has begun to rot. . . .

Catherine Wood and Sheridan Wood sought to raze the barn located on Lots 105 and 106. Woodrick filed a complaint against Catherine and Sheridan Wood seeking to enjoin them from razing the barn.

* * *

The issue raised by this appeal is whether the holder of a remainder interest in a parcel of land may prohibit the life tenant of such property from destroying structures on the land. Woodrick alleges that the destruction of the barn would amount to waste since the barn has a value of $3200. Wood argues that the barn is in a state of disrepair and that the destruction of the barn would enhance the value of the property as residential property. She also claims that, due to changes in local zoning ordinances, the barn could no longer be used for its original purpose (a horse stable).

An injunction is an available remedy to prevent an act of waste. [ ] Consequently, our review of the trial court's decision to deny the injunction requires a mixed standard of review. The trial court's findings of fact must be accepted as long as they are supported by competent and credible evidence. In the case *sub judice*, the operative facts were stipulated to by the parties. Therefore, our review is limited to whether the trial court correctly applied the law of waste to the facts. In determining whether the trial court correctly decided that the destruction of the barn would not constitute waste, we must conduct a plenary review of that decision. [ ]

Waste is defined as an abuse or destructive use of property by one in rightful possession. Blacks' Law Dictionary 5th ed. 1979. Wood was rightfully in possession of the land as a life tenant. . . .

At common law, anything which in any way altered the identity of leased premises was waste, regardless of whether the act happened to be beneficial or detrimental to the remainder interest. However, the common law rule has never been recognized in Ohio. . . . In the case sub judice, the life tenant sought to remove the barn in order to improve the value of the property. The preservation of the barn would require the property owner to forego the making of an improvement which would add to the value of the property. [Ohio caselaw holds] that a life tenant had the right to make beneficial use of the property even though she would be altering the land in order to do so.

In Bellows Co. v. Covell (1927), 28 Ohio App. 277, 280, the court stated that acts which would technically constitute waste as defined under the common law would not be enjoined when they resulted in improving rather than injuring the property.

> "[F]or actionable waste, substantial pecuniary damage to the reversion should be required and . . . the mere alteration of the demised premises which renders them unfit for their former use without decreasing their general value, is not enough." Id. at 281.

Woodrick claims that, since the barn itself has a monetary value of $3200, its destruction would diminish the value of the property by $3200 and would, therefore, constitute waste. This argument is refuted by the evidence submitted by [Wood] which indicates that the removal of the barn would actually increase the value of the property. The trial court recognized the value of the barn by ordering [Wood] to pay Woodrick $3200 if [she] destroyed the barn. This order adequately assured that Woodrick would be adequately compensated for the removal of the barn. The removal of the barn would increase the value of the property in which Woodrick had a remainder interest. The destruction of the barn, though objectionable to Woodrick, does not constitute waste to the property.

Woodrick also argues that the trial court's decision to award her the monetary value of the barn authorizes Wood as life tenant to commit waste as long as a proper price is paid. We find this argument unpersuasive. As discussed above, the removal of the barn does not constitute waste to the property since the value of the property will not be diminished by the barn's destruction. Woodrick presented evidence that the barn itself has value and that she has personal property stored there but has not shown that the presence of the barn on the property adds any value to the property. The relevant inquiry is always whether the contemplated act of the life tenant would result in diminution of the value of the property. The evidence in the record indicates that destroying the barn would increase the value of the property. Since the act of destroying the barn would not result in diminution of the value of the property, it would not constitute waste. The trial court's decision to award Woodrick the value of the barn was not a payment to justify waste but was, instead, indicative of the trial court's intent to protect the rights of both parties and to reach a fair resolution of their dispute according to the law.

Notes and Questions

1. The Ohio court rejects the common law definition of waste which would prohibit the life tenant from altering the property in any substantial way, even if the alteration would increase the financial value of the property. If the common law rule were applied in *Woodrick*, the life tenant would have been prohibited from razing the barn. Instead, the Ohio court counted as waste only those alterations that reduced the value of the land. Which is the better rule, and why? What possible value could Woodrick attach to the barn if its razing would increase the value of the property?

2. *Woodrick* involved an affirmative act (the razing of the barn) as waste. Waste by affirmative act is considered "voluntary waste." A life tenant is also prohibited from committing "permissive waste" commonly defined as failure to meet a limited duty to make repairs on the property as well as a duty to pay property taxes, assessments and mortgage payments due on the property. Recall your study of adverse possession. Would it be waste for a life tenant to fail to eject a long-term trespasser?

3. Remedies for waste vary considerably among the states. Some states allow for forfeiture of the life estate if egregious waste is committed. Others provide by statute for multiplied damages (e.g., treble damages). Most courts will grant an injunction where the plaintiff proves that the planned act (e.g., razing the barn) would constitute waste. In *Woodrick*, however, the court

denied the injunction, concluding that the razing of the barn would not constitute waste. What is the basis, then, for the award of damages? For an extensive discussion of waste and available remedies, see Stoebuck and Whitman, The Law of Property (3d ed. 2000) §§ 4.1 to 4.5.

4. Woodrick is able to sue Wood for waste because Woodrick owns a property interest in the land even though she did not currently have the right to possess the land. Her interest is called a remainder. Even without the right to possess the land now, a remainder is a valuable interest. As illustrated in this case, a person owning a remainder (as well as a person owning a reversion) can block some uses by the life tenant. Remainders and reversions can be and often are sold. How much would you pay for a remainder if, for example, the land were currently valued at $500,000 and the life tenant was 99 years old? You will read more about remainders in the following section.

5. Why does the doctrine of waste apply to life estates but not to the fee simple absolute? Should property owners, even owners of fee simple absolute, be able to destroy their own property? For an interesting discussion advocating the right to destroy one's own property, see Lior Jacob Strahilevitz, The Right to Destroy, 114 Yale L. J. 781 (2005).

III. AN INTRODUCTION TO FUTURE INTERESTS: REMAINDERS AND REVERSIONS

Present Possessory Estates

The fee simple absolute, life estate and life estate *pur autre vie* are three types of "present possessory estates" or "present possessory interests." These estates are called "present possessory" because they entitle the holder of the estate to possession of the land now. So the owner of a fee simple absolute, the owner of a life estate and the owner of a life estate *pur autre vie* have the right to possess the land by virtue of their ownership of the present possessory estate.

Future Interests

You will recall that the principle of conservation of estates requires that all parts of the fee simple absolute, the perfect or most complete estate, be accounted for when a lesser estate is transferred. So, the life estate requires a reversion or remainder. If Oswald transfers a life estate to Mary, either Oswald will retain the reversion or Oswald will (in the same document transferring the life estate to Mary) transfer a remainder to someone else. A deed conveying property from Oswald "to Mary for life" transfers a life estate to Mary while Oswald retains a reversion, while a deed transferring property from Oswald "to Mary for life and then to John and his heirs" gives Mary a life estate and John a remainder. If there is a life estate, there must be a remainder or reversion created at the same time.

These interests—the remainder and reversion and others like them—are called "future interests." They are called "future" interests because the holder does not have the right to possess the property now even though he or she will either certainly or probably or possibly have a right to take possession later. The "future" in future interests refers only to this right to possession. The ownership of the future interest is present; that is, an individual who owns a future interest owns an interest *now* even though the possession will occur, if at all, only in the future. Future interests have value *now*. They are not only a chance at something; they *are* something.

Imagine that you own a remainder in a piece of real estate that has attracted the attention of developers. As we have discussed previously, developers (of shopping centers, subdivisions, factories, airports and so on) would not be satisfied with acquiring only a life estate in the land they need. So it is likely in such a case that either the developer or the owner of the life estate will approach you to buy your future interest, your remainder. Can you see that the future interest has value now even though it does not carry the current right to possess the land, even though it is not a present possessory estate? Under the doctrine of waste, as described in *Woodrick,* the individual holding the future interest had a right to block action by the owner of the present possessory estate.

The late Dean Oval Phipps of the University of South Dakota School of Law and Saint Louis University School of Law provided these short definitions in his work on Titles in a Nutshell (1968). Some students find this approach useful, and in service to them we offer five of Dean Phipps' "Twelve Rules and Definitions:"

(1) Interest: An aggregate of rights, privileges, powers, and immunities appertaining to some person the exclusive enjoyment of which constitutes him owner or part owner of a particular property asset.

(2) Possessory Interest: A present interest which entitles the holder thereof to present possession of the asset.

(3) Future Interest: A present interest which does not entitle the holder thereof to present possession of the asset, but which will or may later entitle him to such possession.

(4) Reversion: A future interest, that part of his legal estate still retained by the grantor when he conveys away an estate smaller than he has.

(5) Remainder: A future interest in someone other than the grantor which according to its terms may become possessory upon the normal termination of some particular estate of freehold.

Reversions and Remainders

You have already encountered the reversion and the remainder. Both are future interests. There are several kinds of remainders. The distinctions among the types of remainders made an immense difference in medieval property practice and in nineteenth-century American practice. Although the significance of the differences among remainders is much less in modern American property law, there are still important consequences that follow from the category in which the remainder falls. You will see this especially, for example, when you study the Rule Against Perpetuities later in this chapter.

Remainders fall within two general groups—contingent remainders and vested remainders. One approach to understanding the distinction between vested and contingent remainders is to work with the definitions of the two. A contingent remainder is one that is subject to a condition precedent, or is owned by an "unascertained" party, or both. For example:

1. "To Alice for life, then to Bart and his heirs if Bart marries Charlotte" creates a life estate in Alice and a contingent remainder in Bart because of the condition precedent to Bart's taking possession of the estate. (The conveyance also includes a reversion in the grantor to account for a "missing piece." Do you see why?)

2. "To Alice for life, then to the heirs of Bart" creates a life estate in Alice and a contingent remainder in the heirs of Bart. In this conveyance, "heirs of Bart" are words of purchase and describe who owns the remainder. Conveying property "to Bart and his heirs" (the phraseology you studied earlier) has a different result from conveying property "to the heirs of Bart," as you now see. The remainder held by the heirs of Bart is a contingent remainder because so long as Bart is alive there is not one individual who can now be identified as an heir of Bart. No living person has heirs even though lay people often colloquially refer to someone as an heir to a living person. Thus, the owners of the future interest in this conveyance are "unascertained." A similar situation is created when the land is conveyed "to Alice for life, then to Alice's children" if Alice has no children at the time of the conveyance. When the future interest holder is "unascertained;" as in these examples, that unascertained person owns a contingent remainder. Because the remainder is contingent, the grantor still also holds a reversion. We have already drawn your attention to the point that in each of these two illustrations "to the heirs of Bart" and "to the children of Alice" the terms "heirs" and "children" are words of purchase, not words of limitation. (Remember our earlier discussion: "heirs" and "children" do not describe the same group of people. These words are not synonymous, despite their common colloquial use.)

Whether the remainder is a contingent remainder because of the presence of a condition precedent or because the person(s) owning the remainder is or are unascertained, the remainder is called simply a contingent remainder. There is only one name for both situations.

There are, in contrast, three kinds of vested remainders. These are: (a) vested remainder; (b) vested remainder subject to open; and (c) vested remainder subject to divestment.

A remainder is a "vested remainder" if there are both no conditions precedent to possession (other than the natural expiration of the preceding estate) *and* the party owning the remainder is "ascertained." For example, "to Ambrose for life, then to Barbara and her heirs" creates a life estate in Ambrose and a "vested remainder" in Barbara. The fact that Ambrose must die for Barbara to take possession requires only the "natural expiration of the preceding estate" and so does not make Barbara's interest contingent. When Ambrose dies, Barbara takes a fee simple absolute. If Barbara dies before Ambrose, her future interest (i.e., her vested remainder) passes to her estate. From there, it is distributed according to her will, or if she dies without a will, by the state's statute of intestate succession (which you know distributes the property of the deceased individual along prescribed family lines).

A "vested remainder subject to open" is one that is held by a group of people where one or more members of that group is in existence while others are unascertained. So, as in our earlier example of contingent remainders, a transfer "to Alice for life, and then to Alice's children" creates a life estate in Alice, a contingent remainder in Alice's children while Alice has no children, and a reversion in the grantor. But, if Alice has at least one child at the time of the transfer, that same language creates a life estate in Alice and a "vested remainder subject to open" in Alice's only child. (It has been customary to say that the grantor still has a reversion in this conveyance for reasons that will become apparent only at the end of this chapter in the discussion of the Rule Against Perpetuities). So if the grantor transfers the property "to Alice for life, and then to Alice's children" and Alice has no children at the time of the conveyance, the future interest in the unascertained children is a contingent remainder. If Alice has at least one child at the time of the conveyance, the future interest in that child is a vested remainder subject to open. The name of the remainder adjusts to changes over time. So, if at the time of the conveyance Alice had no children but subsequently has a child, the contingent remainder created at the time of the conveyance is transformed into a vested remainder subject to open.

You might think of the vested remainder subject to open as being "open" to additional children should Alice have any other children in the future. So, if Alice has a second, third or fourth child, they will also have a vested remainder subject to open. If you have observed that the proportionate share of Alice's first child is reduced by each additional child (from the whole, to a half, to a third, and so on), you are correct. This is why the vested remainder subject to open is also known as "vested remainder subject to partial divestment" although we won't be using that term in this text. In the world of common law estates, you must assume that people can have children no matter what their age or physical condition. In our example, if Alice is 89 and has two children, the interest held by those children is still called a vested remainder subject to open.

Consider these scenarios:

Grace transfers her land "to Analee for life, and then to Brad's children." Assume that Analee and Grace are still living when the following events occur:

(a) Brad is living and currently has no children. The future interest following the life estate is a contingent remainder, even though *and* because there are no children yet in existence. Can you see why it is a contingent remainder? (Also, Grace retains a reversion.)

(b) Brad is living and currently has at least one child. The future interest following the life estate is a vested remainder subject to open. Can you see why? (Grace still has a reversion.)

(c) Brad has died and is survived by two children. The future interest following the life estate is now a vested remainder. Why? (Grace has no reversion.)

(d) Brad has died without ever having children. The remainder disappears forever at Brad's death. Who owns the land?

The third type of remainder is the "vested remainder subject to divestment." This vested remainder looks very much like a contingent remainder because the vested remainder subject to divestment actually includes a condition. The distinction between the vested remainder subject to divestment and the contingent remainder lies in the difference between conditions subsequent and conditions precedent, a distinction you may have studied in your Contracts course. Any condition can be written as either a condition precedent or a condition subsequent. It often does not help to ask whether the condition itself must be met "before" the remainderperson takes possession or "after." For example: "to Alice for life, then to Bart and his heirs so long as Bart marries Charlotte before Alice dies" creates a contingent remainder in Bart. But if we write the conveyance as "to Alice for life, then to Bart and his heirs but if Bart does not marry Charlotte before Alice dies, then to the grantor," we have used the same condition but have given Bart a vested remainder subject to divestment. (The grantor has a reversion in both conveyances.)

We will look at the operation of conditions more closely in a later section, but you can see at this point that the language used to describe the condition makes a critical difference in distinguishing a vested remainder subject to divestment from a contingent remainder. Substantively, the distinction between these two remainders is important to the operation of the Rule Against Perpetuities which will be discussed later in this chapter. Try your hand naming the estate and future interests in these conveyances:

(a) Ozzie to Adrian for life, then to Beverly and her heirs so long as Beverly moves to California before Adrian's death.

(b) Ozzie to Adrian for life, then to Beverly and her heirs, but if Beverly does not move to California before Adrian's death, then to Ozzie.

The first conveyance conveys a life estate to Adrian, and a contingent remainder to Beverly because the condition is written as a condition precedent. Ozzie holds a reversion. The second conveyance conveys a life estate to Adrian, a vested remainder subject to divestment in Beverly, and a reversion to Ozzie. Same condition, but two different results.

There is one final permutation in this area of contingent remainders and vested remainders subject to divestment. This occurs when the future interest following the contingent remainder or the vested remainder subject to divestment is transferred in the original conveyance to someone other than the grantor. For example:

(a) Ozzie to Adrian for life, then to Beverly and her heirs so long as Beverly moves to California before Adrian's death; but if she doesn't, then to Colin and his heirs.

(b) Ozzie to Adrian for life, then to Beverly and her heirs, but if Beverly does not move to California before Adrian's death, then to Colin and his heirs.

In the first conveyance Colin owns an alternative contingent remainder. In the second conveyance Colin's interest also has a specific name and specific characteristics, which we will discuss later in the section on "executory interests." Once again, the distinction in form is simply the language chosen to describe the condition. Because Beverly's interest in the first conveyance is a contingent remainder, Colin's interest is a contingent remainder, alternative to Beverly's because only one or the other and not both will take possession. Because Beverly's interest in the second conveyance is a vested remainder subject to divestment, Colin's interest is an "executory interest."

Remainders and reversions are transferable. If they are transferred, they will keep the name first given them unless other relevant circumstances have changed as well. For example, the conveyance from Oswald "to Mary for life" gave a life estate to Mary while Oswald retained a reversion. If Oswald later transfers his remaining interest in the land to someone else (e.g., Oswald "to Bob"), that person receives a reversion not a remainder. (Remember: "once a reversion, always a reversion.")

You were already introduced to a situation where the remainder changes its own name because of changes in relevant facts. Recall how the remainder changed as Brad had children in our earlier exercise. If in our conveyance above concerning whether Bart married Charlotte, if Bart marries Charlotte before Alice dies his remainder becomes a vested remainder.

Finally, there is one more piece of information to add. When you identify a future interest, you should also add the present possessory estate that the future interest holder will have if and when he takes possession. So, for example, "Oona to Mary for life, then to Bob and his heirs" grants Mary a life estate and Bob a vested remainder *in fee simple absolute*. The "in" signifies that Bob will take the property in fee simple absolute when he comes into possession. When Bob takes possession, he will own the land in fee simple absolute. A future interest holder may be given less. So, for example, "Oona to Mary for life, then to Bob for life, then to Sue and her heirs" grants Mary a life estate, Bob a vested remainder *in* life estate or a vested remainder *for* life, and Sue a vested remainder *in* fee simple absolute.

PRACTICE PROBLEMS

Identify the present possessory estate and future interests created in these conveyances. Assume that each party with a given name is alive unless specifically indicated otherwise.

1.   Omar to Andrew for life.

2.   Omar to Agatha for life, then to Bill and his heirs.

3.   Omar to Agatha for life, then to Bill and his heirs. After the conveyance, Bill has died leaving a will giving all of his property to his wife Carrie. Agatha is still alive.

4.   Omar to Alice for life, then to Beatrice and her heirs if Beatrice survives Alice.

5.   Omar to Andrew for life. After this conveyance, Omar dies and wills all of his property "to Blake and his heirs."

6.   Omar to Andre for life, then to Andre's children and their heirs.

   a) Assume that Andre has one child, Beverly.

   b) Assume that Andre has no children.

7.   Omar to Alex for life, then to Belinda and her heirs if Belinda graduates from law school. Assume that Belinda has graduated from law school.

8.   Omar to Alex for life, then to Belinda and her heirs, but if Belinda does not graduate from law school, the land goes to Omar and his heirs.

   a) Assume that Belinda has graduated from law school.

   b) Assume that Belinda has not graduated from law school.

9.   Omar to Annabelle for life, then to Byron and his heirs if Byron marries before Annabelle dies, and to Casanova and his heirs if Byron does not marry before Annabelle's death.

A DIVERSION: THE FEE TAIL

U.S. law has never provided a form of property ownership in which a family, as a legal person, is owner (although it provides for ownership by corporations as legal persons). There are forms of ownership for married couples, but these do not reach the principal goal family ownership would attempt to reach. This is the desire that is usually put in terms of the property owner wanting to keep property "in the family." You can imagine that this desire may arise with farmland or with family homesteads or manors.

English law and custom did deal with family ownership, though, by putting legal ownership of a deceased family member's property in the oldest surviving male in the family. "Heir" meant *one person,* the oldest son or a circumstantial substitute where the oldest son could not take ownership or where there were no sons. Ownership in any generation was, typically, in one person; and even after this form of inheritance (primogeniture) was no longer imposed by law (after 1540), law-office practice preserved it as the conventional form in England until the twentieth century. Notice, for example, the substantial suffering that falls on families of women in the novels of Jane Austen (or their movie versions including the mother and daughters in Sense and Sensibility), or the thousands of pages of plot that Anthony Trollope develops from the fact that one person among a dozen is in line to take all of a family's wealth.

The Extinction of the Fee Simple Conditional

Early in the thirteenth century, English common law provided that an owner of property could convey in such a way that descent in ownership could be confined to descent within the grantor's family. What English common law allowed was the creation of a particular present possessory estate that would allow an owner to set the lineal intra-family descent of land in motion—legally, enforceably and over the generations.

In order to invoke that present possessory estate with this form of lineal descent, the grantor of the property would convey the property "to Sam and the heirs *of his body.*" These three words are used only for this estate. The result was that Sam was not able to convey the property; the idea was that he would use and hold the property during his life, and the transfer of ownership at his death would be a transition within the family. The common way of referring to this estate, and a reference that is still used today, is to say that the property is "entailed." This estate in land was originally known as the *fee simple conditional.* This estate was abolished in 1285. Except in one or two states, the fee simple conditional is not a modern form of ownership in the U.S.

Note the difference between this estate and the fee simple absolute. The words are different: "to Sam and the heirs of his body" are not the same as "to Sam and his heirs." And the estates are radically different. In the latter conveyance, which creates a fee simple absolute, Sam may sell to whomever he wishes during his lifetime and, if he dies owning the fee simple absolute, he may devise the estate to anyone he chooses. In contrast, with the entailed fee Sam could only transfer the equivalent of a life estate *pur autre vie.* At Sam's death, the land would descend to the "heirs of his body." Sam could not devise the estate to his widow, to a charity, or to anyone.

The persons owning these fees simple conditional often wanted to sell the land themselves. Over generations of time, lawyers figured out ways for Sam to convey property that he held in fee simple conditional. The common law had come eventually to say that, if a child were born to Sam and his spouse, Sam could convey a fee simple absolute (*i.e.,* full ownership): He still *owned* a fee simple conditional, but he could sell someone else full ownership, a *fee simple absolute.*

This meant that property eventually could rather easily be taken out of the fee simple conditional. The great English landowners were not happy with that result: If your daughter was about to marry Sam, and you were about to give the happy couple a thousand acres of England, you wanted to see to it that the property descended to your grandchildren and not to Sam's race-course companions, or, even worse, to members of *his* family rather than yours. The law had at one time assured that result with the fee simple conditional; the lawyers had ruined the fee simple conditional; the cure was legislation. The barons got their legislation in 1285, in the statute *De Donis Conditionalibus.*

The Rise of the Fee Tail

Under *De Donis,* after the common-law judges construed it, a new form of ownership was created: *the fee tail.* A grant to Sam created this form of ownership in Sam with the same words that had been used to create the fee simple conditional: "to Sam and the heirs of his body." The statute abolished the fee simple conditional. The new estate, the fee tail, could not be "disentailed"; that is, the "tenant in tail" (Sam) could not convey any more than he had. Sam's heir took the estate Sam had, whether Sam had conveyed to a third person or not. Sam's heir took, after Sam's death, as heir. The words of the deed, "heirs of his body" were words of limitation, not of purchase. If the family ran out of "issue" (that is, lineal descendants of Sam), and whenever it did—even if that were 200 years away—the property reverted to the grantor (or the grantor's heirs, as the grantor himself was likely to be deceased). Ownership in Sam's family ended, by the terms of the original deed. The power to possess the land returned to the original grantor. The original grantor had owned this reversion all along; it had value, in him, all along. It was an interest he had because he did not give it away when he gave Sam the fee-tail deed. The original grantor retained this interest. There were four possibilities when Sam's line of lineal descendants ran out (in five years, or ten, or five hundred) and possession shifted out of Sam's family.

(i) The grantor might be living; possession would revert to him.

(ii) The grantor might not be living; possession would "revert" to the grantor's heir(s) who, for property-law purposes, *is* the grantor.

(iii) The grantor might, at the time of the deed to Sam, have given the grantor's reversion to someone else ("to Sam and the heirs of his body, then to Elmer and his heirs"), in which case Elmer or his heir could claim possession. Elmer held a remainder while Sam or one of his descendants held the fee tail. Elmer's remainder in this case was in fee simple absolute. It could have been a remainder in fee tail ("to Sam and the heirs of his body, then to Elmer and the heirs of his body"), in which case the grantor had a reversion.

(iv) The grantor might have conveyed to Sam in fee tail without creating a remainder at that time ("to Sam and the heirs of his body"), and then, at a later time, have given his reversion to Elmer ("all of my interest in the land to Elmer and his heirs"), in which case:

(a) Sam would at first have had a fee tail with reversion in the grantor; and then

(b) Sam would have had a fee tail with reversion in Elmer in fee simple absolute.

Just to make sure you understand this so far, what are the interests created in the following deeds, all after the creation of the fee tail by statute in 1285?

(a) Henry conveys "to Sam and the heirs of his body." Sam and his wife have a son Eric.

(b) Henry conveys "to Sam and the heirs of his body, and then to Dorothy and her heirs." Sam and his wife have no children (yet).

(c) Henry conveys "to Sam and the heirs of his body and then to Dorothy and her heirs." Sam and his wife have no children (yet). Henry dies; Henry's heir is Elmer.

(d) Henry conveys "to Sam and the heirs of his body." Sam and his wife have no children (yet). Henry dies; Henry's heir is Elmer.

The fee tail arrangement for keeping property in the family appears to have worked for about two centuries. No doubt lawyers for people like Sam kept chipping away at it though. And no doubt, in the long run, government was going to side with people like Sam, rather than with the original grantors, which is where the land came from, for three reasons: (i) government generally wants to force transactions in land, especially transactions to transfer ownership between generations, as occasions for imposing transfer taxes; (ii) government ordinarily does not favor family ownership of large amounts of land because land is power, especially in an agrarian society; and (iii) as the sustaining economy of England became a trading economy, concentrations of wealth in land were undesirable because wealth tied up in land did not circulate and stimulate the economy.

In any event, by the end of the fifteenth century, the common-law courts had recognized a form of *disentailment,* through which people in Sam's situation could do what they had been able to do before 1285. They could, as the county-seat lawyers in America came to say later, *dock the entail.* The fifteenth-century procedure for docking entails was devious, complex, and expensive. The eventual form was a piece of paper that the tenant in tail signed and recorded in the land records. After 1500, the fee tail was not a dependable way to keep property in the family.

The fee tail was used, from the sixteenth century on, as part of an extensive scheme invented by family solicitors, called the strict settlement. The key to the strict settlement was not the fee tail, though; the key was to bring the heir before his (male) elders, and the family solicitor, as soon as he was of age, and bribe him into surrendering his ability to disentail the family estates. In itself, the fee tail began to fade from its medieval prominence and become a quaint old tool in the property lawyer's tool box.

The Fee Tail in the United States

For some reason, the disentailable fee tail was widely used in property practice in the United States in the nineteenth and early twentieth centuries. It is still used in some places. It was available, and was disentailable, and still is in some places, because most states accepted the statute *De Donis* and the fifteenth-century case law on disentailment, as part of American common law. The fact that the fee tail was, when used, vulnerable to disentailment would seem to indicate that its main value in county-seat practice was as a will substitute: If I take title to my farm in tail, the farm will, at my death, go to my children. If that is what I want to happen, I won't have to make a will saying so. "Heirs of his body" in a fee-tail deed meant, in American practice, all of the grantee's children rather than only the eldest male child. The grantor could, however, specify a "fee tail male" ("to Sam and the male heirs of his body") or a "fee tail female" ("to Sam and the female heirs of his body").

In any case, the fee tail has now been abolished in most American states, and one or two never recognized it in the first place, holding that *De Donis* was not part of their common law. The legal question in most places, when a lawyer comes across a fee-tail deed, is what ownership it creates, since, by statute in most jurisdictions, it cannot create a common-law fee tail. There are four common statutory possibilities:

(i) The tenant in tail (Sam) may have, by statute, a life estate, with remainder in fee simple absolute to his issue. If Sam has no issue, ownership will revert to the grantor. Sam never has more than a life estate.

(ii) The tenant in tail may have a fee simple absolute.

(iii) The tenant in tail may have in effect what he would have had before *De Donis:* an estate for life that becomes a fee simple absolute upon the birth of issue. ("Issue" means lineal descendants). It is not limited to children but includes as many future generations as are in existence when the word is applied. It excludes collateral descendents (*e.g.*, nephews and nieces).

(iv) In one or two states he will have a common law fee tail and will have available a simple form of disentailment.

For a fascinating (yes, really) history of the fee tail, see Jeffrey Stake, Evolution of Rules in a Common Law System: Differential Litigation of the Fee Tail and Other Perpetuities, 32 Fla. St. U. L. Rev. 401

(2005). Professor Stake also suggests that the demise of the fee tail should be reconsidered.

IV. THE DEFEASIBLE FEES: PRESENT POSSESSORY ESTATES SUBJECT TO CONDITIONS

You have seen how an estate can be combined with a future interest to provide for ownership over time. A grantor, in effect, determines at the moment of the conveyance both the current ownership of the present possessory estate in the land and its ownership in the future. By combining life estates, remainders and reversions, the grantor can set a path for the ownership of a plot of land over the course of several lifetimes.

Ownership can also be subject to conditions. The use of conditions allows a grantor to plan for the future by providing for changes in ownership based on foreseeable events. Subjecting ownership to conditions also allows the transferor to control the behavior of the owners or the use of the land.

Drafting conditions without ambiguity is an art. In fact, it is such an art that there are many, many cases in which the conditions are not entirely clear. Can you see the ambiguity in the following conditions?

A donor wants to give land to a school so long as the land is used "for school purposes."

An elderly couple is willing to transfer their home to a favorite grandchild so long as the grandchild "cares for us in our old age."

An individual is willing to sell a beautiful piece of land to another only if the buyer will "keep the land in its natural state."

A buyer is willing to allow an elderly seller to keep a life estate in the land as long as the seller "resides in the house."

A seller is willing to sell a building formerly used as a church if the buyer will avoid uses that are "inconsistent with the building's character as a former church."

A donor who is concerned about the ravages of alcohol upon college-age students wants to provide that the university may keep the building he is giving them only if "no liquor is sold on the premises." Or, is he better off specifying that no liquor be "served?" Or, "consumed?"

Of course, not every eventuality can be anticipated, but it is the goal of the law-office property lawyer to do her or his best on that score. By far, the most difficult questions arising in disputes over conditions on ownership are ones of deciding what the condition actually means.

You have already seen such conditions as they relate to remainders. Recall that a remainder that is subject to a condition precedent is a contingent remainder and that a remainder that is subject to a condition subsequent is a vested remainder subject to divestment. The conveyance "to Able for life, then to Blake and his heirs if Blake survives Able" gives Blake a contingent remainder in fee simple absolute; but the conveyance "to Able for life, then to Blake and his heirs, but if Blake does not survive Able, to grantor and his heirs" gives Blake a vested remainder subject to divestment in fee simple absolute. The grantor has a reversion in fee simple absolute in each conveyance. The condition in the first conveyance is a condition precedent; and the condition in the second, a condition subsequent. In these examples, the difference between condition precedent and condition subsequent is determined only by the words used to connect the condition to the future interest. Contingent remainders and vested remainders subject to divestment are future interests, as you know.

Present possessory estates can also be subject to conditions. There are three present possessory estates that *by definition* include conditions. As a group these are known as the "defeasible fees."

There are three types of defeasible fees. They are:

    (a) fee simple determinable;

    (b) fee simple subject to condition subsequent; and

    (c) fee simple subject to executory limitation.

Each of these estates involves ownership subject to a condition. They are known as defeasible fees—fees because they are fees simple, but defeasible because (unlike the fee simple absolute) these estates can be terminated by the operation of a condition. Here, the "fee simple" is only *potentially* infinite because of the operation of the condition.

Two of the defeasible fees—the fee simple determinable and the fee simple subject to a condition subsequent—are distinguished from each other on exactly the same basis as are contingent remainders and vested remainders subject to divestment. The fee simple determinable includes a condition that is a condition precedent; and the fee simple subject to a condition subsequent, a condition that is a condition subsequent (just as it says). So, a conveyance from Ophelia "to Arthur and his heirs so long as the land is farmed" grants Arthur a "fee simple determinable;" but a conveyance from Ophelia "to Arthur and his heirs provided the land is farmed" grants Arthur "a fee simple subject to a condition subsequent."

If you are creating one of these estates, it will be important to use the correct language. Historically, phrases containing express durational language have come to be accepted as indicative of conditions precedent (and so, fee simple determinable). These include "while," "during," "until" and "so long as." Others have been accepted as indicating condition subsequent (and so, fee simple subject to condition subsequent). These are "provided that," "but if," and "upon condition that."

Language that specifically indicates automatic or immediate termination upon breach of the condition is also influential in distinguishing these estates. The fee simple determinable terminates "automatically" upon breach of the condition while the fee simple subject to a condition subsequent requires an action by the holder of the future interest for termination. This characteristic of these estates is discussed more in the cases that follow. In addition, some use a rule of thumb that the right of re-entry must be expressed or the general preference will be to interpret the conveyance as creating a fee simple determinable.

When the question is not one of drafting a conveyance in order to create one estate rather than another, but rather is whether an already transferred estate is either a fee simple determinable or a fee simple subject to a condition subsequent, the language used by the drafter can give you important clues. The words used to describe the condition (e.g., "so long as;" "while;" "provided;" or "but if") can determine whether the condition is precedent (creating a fee simple determinable) or a condition subsequent (creating a fee simple subject to a condition subsequent). Or, the language can leave you clueless, in which case the task is to divine the grantor's intent or to exercise certain set preferences. See *Ocean City* and *Higbee* which follow.

You can see that a defeasible fee is not as "complete" as the fee simple absolute. The fee simple absolute by definition has no conditions on the use of the land or the behavior of the owner. The fee simple absolute does not terminate upon the happening of an event. But the defeasible fees have these conditions, and so the defeasible fees are "less" than the fee simple absolute.

The principle of conservation of estates tells us that we must complete the conveyances and account for the missing piece. And so the defeasible fees must be accompanied by a future interest. Look again at the examples of the fee simple determinable and the fee simple subject to a condition subsequent provided in the previous paragraph. Who owns the future interest in those conveyances? No one is specified, and so the owner of the future interest, by default, is Ophelia, the grantor. In fact, both the fee simple determinable and the fee simple subject to condition subsequent *must* be followed by a future interest held by the *grantor*.

A defeasible fee may indeed be followed by a future interest held by another party, however. For example: Ophelia "to Abelaird and his heirs so long as the land is farmed; but if the land is not farmed, then to Billings and his heirs." Because both the fee simple determinable and fee simple subject to condition subsequent *must* be followed by a future interest held by the grantor, this conveyance can create neither of those defeasible fees. Instead, a defeasible fee with the future interest held by a party other than the grantor creates the third type of defeasible fee—a "fee simple subject to executory limitation." In a case of disturbing asymmetry in the common law, it does not matter whether the condition in the fee simple subject to executory limitation is a condition precedent or a condition subsequent. This defeasible fee occurs *whenever* the future interest in a defeasible fee is held in the first instance by one other than the grantor.

As you would expect, each of the future interests that accompanies the defeasible fees has a name. The name of the future interest that always accompanies the fee simple determinable is "possibility of reverter.'' The future interest that accompanies the fee simple subject to a condition subsequent is ''right of entry,'' also known as ''power of termination.'' If you understood the information provided in the previous paragraph, you know that these future interests are retained by the grantor at the time of the conveyance. The future interest that accompanies the fee simple subject to executory limitation is called an ''executory interest.'' (Another acceptable name for the fee simple subject to executory limitation is ''fee simple subject to executory interest.'') Once again, if you understood the previous paragraph, you know that the executory interest here must be held by someone other than the grantor at the time of the conveyance.

The defeasible fees and their accompanying future interests pair up like this:

Defeasible Fee——Future Interest

Fee simple determinable——Possibility of reverter

Fee simple subject to condition subsequent——Right of Entry

Fee simple subject to executory limitation——Executory Interest

PRACTICE PROBLEMS

1. Greg to Anna and her heirs so long as no liquor is served on the premises.

2. Grace to Alex and his heirs provided that the land is used for residential purposes.

3. Greg to Abel and his heirs so long as no hunting is allowed on the property; if hunting is allowed, then the land is to go to PETA for an animal sanctuary.

4. Grace to Alice and her heirs; but if gambling is allowed on the premises, then to Blanche and her heirs.

5. Now assume that the condition is broken in each of the conveyances. Who would then own the property?

MAYOR AND CITY COUNCIL OF OCEAN CITY v. TABER

Court of Appeals of Maryland, 1977.
279 Md. 115, 367 A.2d 1233.*

ORTH, JUDGE.

This appeal concerns the ownership of an improved lot of ground at the northwest corner of Atlantic Avenue and Caroline Street in Ocean

* Editor's note: This opinion is difficult to read. We realize that you will be reading it to find something that fits our outline (i.e., ownership that is subject in some way to a condition). But you will be rewarded here, we think, by spending some extra time to locate the broader property law context in it.

For instance, the four or five deeds and the local judicial decree the court identifies in the county land records show how ''record title'' to land is established by a search in the public records in the county courthouse. In times past (and still in some communities), you could almost always find two or three lawyers in the county record-

City, Maryland, which was occupied and used by the United States of America as a Life Saving Station for almost a hundred years. At the hub of the controversy is whether the United States acquired title in fee simple absolute through adverse possession or lost all its right, title, interest and estate in the property by realization of a possibility of reverter.

I

The relevant record title to the property devolves through three conveyances: 1) a deed dated 28 July 1876 from Stephen Taber and wife to Hillary R. Pitts, Benjamin Jones Taylor and George W. Purnell, Trustees (the Trustees), recorded among the Land Records of Worcester County in Liber I.T.M. No. 4, folios 536–537 (the 1876 deed); 2) a deed dated 11 September 1878 from the Trustees to the United States of America, recorded among the aforesaid Land Records in Liber I.T.M. No. 6, folios 400–402 (the 1878 deed); 3) a deed dated 23 June 1967 from the United States of America to the Mayor and City Council of Ocean City, recorded among the aforesaid Land Records in Liber F.W.H. No. 220, folios 449–451 (the 1967 deed). * * *

II

On 15 January 1869 Stephen Taber and Hepburn S. Benson obtained a patent from the State of Maryland. The patent, preserved in the Hall of Records in Liber W.L. & W.S. No. 2, folios 326–327, gave Taber and Benson "The Lady's Resort to the Ocean," a 280 acre tract of land along the Atlantic Ocean in Worcester County. Taber acquired Benson's interest by deed dated 9 October 1871 and recorded among the aforesaid Land Records in Liber I.T.M. No. 1, folios 591–592.

er's office, hauling down and looking through the massive tomes the court here identifies by number. In most cases the search was to back up a lawyer's opinion that her client, or someone her client proposed to deal with, owned the land in question. Here, the "chain of title" is part of the evidence in a lawsuit. In all jurisdictions the presence of the documents in the office gives "constructive" notice to the world of the owner's claim, and in that way controls the assertion, by injured parties, of the claim that they were purchasers without notice of prior conflicting claims to the land.

Another instance of broader context here is the presence of mistakes in documents and the use of devices such as the statute of limitations on property claims to overcome the effect of mistakes: The recorder does not inspect or validate documents; they go into the land records warts and all. And, of course, people go into possession of land thinking that the document with the mistakes in it establishes their titles. Lawyers seeking to protect their clients' title have to take steps to correct mistakes, which steps include quitclaim deeds and the assertion of the statute of limitations (adverse possession). Both devices appear in this story.

Finally, the facts of this case show how property fits into a community with civic purposes and leaders who are out to serve the common good. A town gets started and grows through control of large tracts of real estate. Planners of towns, one way or another, have to provide for essential public services, such as a public life-saving station by the ocean and space for streets and parks. The lawyers for the government of Ocean City failed in this case to gain control of land they thought belonged within these public purposes; but, as you can see by the court's last footnote, they had other cards to play.

Stephen Taber created Ocean City, "desirous," as he explained in the 1876 deed, "of conforming to the views and general public sentiment of the people of Worcester and the adjacent counties in their desire to establish a place as a seaside Summer Resort and the promotion of the growth of the same." Fifty acres of "The Lady's Resort to the Sea," with his acquiescence and approval, were "laid off into a town, with lots, streets and avenues, as is called and known as Ocean City," and he granted the fifty acres to the Trustees by the deed of 1876, appending a plat of the proposed town.[1] The terms of the trust were set out in the habendum clause. The Trustees were to hold the property

> upon trust, that they or their successors shall convey the same, with as little delay as practicable, at the expense of the grantee or grantees named in the deeds in lots as they are described on said plat and according to their numbers; to such persons as draw the same at a distribution of said lots, made by the Stockholders of the Atlantic Hotel Company at the Atlantic Hotel at Ocean City on the thirty first day of August Eighteen Hundred and Seventy Five. And if there are any lots remaining which are not drawn at the aforesaid distribution, then and in that event, the said trustees or their successors are hereby authorized and empowered to sell and convey the same to such persons as they think proper or to make any other disposition of said lots they think proper and appropriate the proceeds thereof in such manner as they shall deem most advantageous to the interest of said Ocean City.

Lot no. 3, as laid out on the plat, was at the northwest corner of Atlantic Avenue and Caroline Street. Its exact size is not shown, for the plat reflects neither lot dimensions nor a scale. It was, however, much larger than the size of the other lots except that of the Atlantic Hotel. It was bounded by the west side of Atlantic Avenue on the east, the north side of Caroline Street on the south and the east side of Baltimore Avenue on the west and was of irregular width.

The deed of 1878 conveyed a part of lot no. 3 to the United States of America. The part conveyed was described as "beginning at the northwest corner of Atlantic Avenue and Caroline Street thence running westerly by and with the north side of Caroline Street one hundred feet thence northerly by a line parallel with Atlantic Avenue fifty feet then easterly by a line parallel to Caroline Street one hundred feet to Atlantic Avenue, hence by and with the west side of Atlantic Avenue fifty feet to the place of beginning, all in Ocean City, County of Worcester and State

---

1. The conveyance excepted and reserved from the fifty acres "so much thereof as has been by deed bearing even date herewith, conveyed to the Atlantic Hotel Company of Berlin, and also so much thereof as has been by deed bearing even date herewith granted to Wiscomico and Pocomoke Rail Road Company, together with the right of said Rail Road Company to occupy not to exceed sixteen feet in width for the construction, maintenance and operation of a rail road through and along Baltimore Avenue its entire length." The grant was also subject to streets and avenues (except Caroline Street) as laid down on the plat. There were 205 lots laid out between Atlantic Avenue on the east, Synepuxent Bay on the west, past Caroline Street on the north and to Division Street on the south.

of Maryland." The deed declared that lot no. 3 had not been drawn in the distribution and that a part thereof had been sold to the United States by the Trustees for the sum of one dollar. The deed recited that the Secretary of the Treasury of the United States had been authorized by Act of Congress of 3 March 1875 "whenever he shall deem it advisable, to acquire, by donation or purchase in behalf of the United States, the right to use and occupy sites for life saving, or life boat stations * * * "and that the Secretary of the Treasury deemed "it advisable to acquire on behalf of the United States the right to use and occupy, the hereinafter described lot of land, as a site for Life Saving Station, as is indicated by his signature hereto. * * * "The Part of lot no. 3 granted by the deed was "for the purpose of a Life Saving Station, and also the right to erect such structures, upon the said land, as the United States may see fit, and to remove any and all such structures and appliances at any time, the said premises to be used and occupied, for the purpose named in said act of March 3, 1875. * * * "The habendum clause read:

> to have and to hold the said lot of land and privileges, unto the United States from this date for the purpose aforesaid. And it is further stipulated, that when the United States shall fail to use the said Life Saving Station, the land hereby conveyed for the purpose aforesaid, shall, without any legal proceedings, suit or otherwise, revert to the said Trustees, their successors and assigns, absolutely, and they shall be entitled to re-enter upon and take possession thereof free from all encumbrances of every nature or kind.

The deed was signed and acknowledged by the Trustees and signed by the Secretary of the Treasury.

The 1967 deed was designated a "quitclaim Deed." The United States of America was "Grantor", and the Mayor and City Council of Ocean City, Maryland, was "Grantee." It witnessed that "the Grantor has remised, released and forever quitclaimed, and by these presents does remise, release and forever quitclaim any and all right, title and interest which [the United States] may have, on an 'as is, where is' basis" to two parcels of land and designated improvements thereon. The first parcel described was the lot conveyed by the 1878 deed.[2] The habendum clause read: "TO HAVE AND TO HOLD the premises herein granted unto the Grantee, its successors and assigns forever." The deed expressly declared that it was "executed and delivered to the Grantee

---

2. The description of the first parcel in the 1967 deed is the same as the description in the 1878 deed except that the beginning point in the 1967 deed is given as "the northeast corner of Atlantic Avenue and Caroline Street." This is an obvious error, probably arising in the deciphering of the handwriting in the 1878 deed.

The second parcel as described in the 1967 deed was a lot fifty feet wide and one hundred feet deep immediately adjoining the rear of the first parcel. The deed did not contain a "being" clause, and the source of the title to the second parcel was not disclosed therein and does not appear in the record before us. It follows that the resolution of the case *sub judice* does not affect this second parcel.

without representations, warranties or covenants, either express or implied."

III

On 17 July 1973 an equity action for a declaratory judgment was instituted in the Circuit Court for Worcester County by Thomas T. Taber, Jr., et alii (appellees) against the Mayor and City Council of Ocean City (appellant), et alii. Motions for Summary Judgment filed by appellees and by appellant were determined without hearing or argument by agreement. The motions were denied on 4 December 1975 with the suggestion that the parties "submit the entire proceeding to the Court upon the pleadings and exhibits in the file." The suggestion was followed. On 17 December all parties, through their counsel, requested that the court "render an Opinion and Order based upon the pleadings and exhibits presently on file herein, after giving due consideration to the memoranda of the various parties filed herein, and render its decision hereon at its earliest convenience without a hearing or taking of testimony on this matter." The court honored the request, and its order came forth on 8 April 1976. Only the Mayor and City Council of Ocean City noted an appeal therefrom to the Court of Special Appeals. We granted a writ of certiorari before decision by that Court.

Appellant would have the 1878 deed be ineffective. Thus, it reasons, the United States, and appellant through privity of estate * * * would have acquired legal title to the property by adverse possession. * * *

The 1878 deed conveyed an estate in fee simple determinable. Such an estate has long been recognized in Maryland. * * * The estate is discussed in 1 H.T. Tiffany, The Law of Real Property § 220 (3rd ed. B. Jones 1939):

> An estate in fee simple determinable, sometimes referred to as a base or a qualified fee, is created by any limitation which, in an otherwise effective conveyance of land, creates an estate in fee simple and provides that the estate shall automatically expire upon the occurrence of a stated event.

> * * *

> No set formula is necessary for the creation of the limitation, any words expressive of the grantor's intent that the estate shall terminate on the occurrence of the event being sufficient. * * * So, when land is granted for certain purposes, as for a schoolhouse, a church, a public building, or the like, and it is evidently the grantor's intention that it shall be used for such purpose only, and that, on the cessation of such use, the estate shall end, without any re-entry by the grantor, an estate of the kind now under consideration is created.

> * * *

> If one who has an estate in fee simple creates a determinable fee in favor of another, he has thereafter merely a possibility of re-

acquiring the land by reason of the occurrence of the contingency named or indicated, this possibility being known as a possibility of reverter.

See Restatement of Property § 44 (1936). We described a possibility of reverter in *Ringgold v. Carvel* * * * (1950):

> A possibility of reverter is any reversionary interest which is subject to a condition precedent. * * * When the owner of an estate in fee simple absolute transfers an estate in fee simple determinable, the transferor has a possibility of reverter. In other words, if one who has an estate in fee simple creates a determinable fee in another, he has thereafter merely a possibility of reobtaining the land by reason of the occurrence of the indicated contingency. Thus, where land is devised for a certain purpose, and it is the testator's intention that it shall be used for that purpose only, and that on the cessation of such use, the estate shall end without re-entry by the grantor, a possibility of reverter arises. * * * In case of a diversion of the land from the purpose for which it was devised, the heirs of the testator may be entitled to have the land again by reverter.[5]

What the United States acquired in the property was a determinable fee and nothing more. Of course, the United States had the power to convey what it owned. "The owner of a determinable fee has all the rights of an owner in fee simple * * *; conveyance of the property does not necessarily terminate the fee, but the grantee takes it subject to the same liability to termination as existed before the grant." 1 H.T. Tiffany, The Law of Real Property, § 220 (3rd ed. B. Jones 1939). Thus, having validly acquired a determinable fee, the United States could convey it. This it did by the 1967 deed, which remised, released and forever quitclaimed any and all right, title and interest which it had and on an "as, where is" basis. The United States expressly made no warranties or covenants with reference to the property. The most that appellant acquired from the United States as to the first parcel described in the 1967 deed was a determinable fee, subject to the liability to termination set out in the 1878 deed. The trial judge "specifically" found that the 1967 deed established "the fact that the United States of America, as of that date, did 'fail to use the said Life Saving Station.' "This finding was not clearly erroneous. Maryland Rule 886. It is ironic that evidence of the occurrence of the event terminating the estate was supplied by delivery of the 1967 deed conveying the determinable fee. The estate in fee simple determinable having terminated, the property reverted, and appellant was left with no right, title, interest or estate whatsoever. * * *

---

5. A reversion, on the other hand, is "any reversionary interest which is not subject to a condition precedent. * * * It is the residue of an estate left in the testator to commence in possession after the determination of some particular estate devised by him. Hence, a reversion arises whenever the owner of real estate devises or conveys an interest in it less than his own. The logical conception of it in the common law is that it is a return by operation of law to the owner of a portion of that which he owned before and in reality had never lost."

We note that, as the 1878 deed was in full force and effect, the statutory period for adverse possession would not start to run until 23 June 1967, the date of the occurrence of the event terminating the estate of fee simple determinable as found by the trial judge. Code (1957, 1973 Repl.Vol.) Art. 21, § 6–103 (now Real Property Art. § 6–103) provides:

> Possession of land * * * after termination of an estate of fee simple determinable shall be deemed adverse and hostile * * * from the occurrence of the event terminating an estate of fee simple determinable.

The trial judge correctly found that appellant had not acquired title by virtue of adverse possession.

Appellant asks if the appellees are "estopped from asserting a claim to the premises under the theories of estoppel, waiver or laches?" In the circumstances, it is patent that they are not. The 1878 deed divided the fee simple absolute estate in the property into the fee simple determinable estate conveyed by the Trustees and a possibility of reverter which remained in the hands of the Trustees. As we have observed, when the United States stopped using the property for a Life Saving Station, there was a diversion of the land from the purpose for which it was conveyed, the estate held by the United States was determined, and automatically a fee simple absolute estate was reestablished in those entitled under the original grantors. * * * It was not necessary for appellees to assert a claim to the fee simple absolute estate or to take any other positive action. They acquired a fee simple absolute estate by the realization of the possibility of reverter. * * *

[O]ur holding here goes only to the first parcel and does not determine any rights with respect to the second parcel.[7]

Judgment Affirmed; Costs To Be Paid By Appellant.

HIGBEE CORPORATION v. KENNEDY, EXECUTOR

Superior Court of Pennsylvania, 1981.
286 Pa.Super. 101, 428 A.2d 592.

PRICE, JUDGE.

* * * [A]ppellant, James J. Kennedy * * * contends that the trial court erred in determining that his interest in the disputed tract of land was a fee simple determinable. For the following reasons we agree with appellant and, therefore, reverse the order and remand for further proceedings consistent with this opinion. * * *

[T]he pleadings in this case disclose the following facts. Appellee, the Higbee Corporation [hereinafter Higbee], owns approximately nine acres

---

7. In a trial memorandum submitted by appellees and included in the joint record extract, it is averred that by ordinance dated 3 December 1968 appellant enacted legislation to condemn "the land which is the subject matter hereof." Pursuant to the or-dinance, appellant instituted a condemnation action in the Circuit Court for Worcester County. We do not know whether this action covered both parcels of land. The outcome of the action is not disclosed in the record before us.

of property in Bethel Park, Allegheny County, Pennsylvania. Kennedy and Higbee both claim under color of title a narrow strip of land that passes through Higbee's property.[1] Seeking to acquire clear title to the entire tract Higbee filed an action to quiet title and a complaint in equity against Kennedy. Higbee subsequently filed an action to quiet title against all possible claimants. These actions were consolidated for trial in May of 1979. Higbee raised preliminary objections in the nature of a demurrer to Kennedy's answer and new matter.

The trial court relied upon the following provision contained in the original grant to Kennedy's property in reaching its determination.

> To have and to hold the said piece of land above-described the hereditaments and premises hereby granted or mentioned and intended so to be with the appurtenances unto the said party of the second part his heirs and assigns to and for the only proper use and behoof of the said party of the second part his heirs and assigns forever provided the party of the second part his heirs and assigns wishes to make use of it for the purpose of a road. The party of the second part agrees to keep a good fence around the above-mentioned lot, failing to do so forfeits his claim, whenever the party of the second part wishes to give up his claim to said lot he is to have full privilege to remove all fencing materials whenever the party of the second part his heirs and assigns fails to fulfill this agreement the land is to revert to the party of the first part. * * *

The sole issue for our consideration is whether the estate created by the deed was a fee simple determinable or a fee simple subject to a condition subsequent. A fee simple determinable is an estate in fee that automatically reverts to the grantor upon the occurrence of a specified event. * * * The interest held by the grantor is termed a possibility of reverter. * * * Words of indubitable limitation, such as "so long as," "during," "while" and "until," are generally used to create the fee simple determinable. * * *

"If, on the other hand, the deed conveyed a fee simple subject to a condition subsequent, then upon the noncompliance with the stated condition the grantor or his successor in interest would have the power to terminate the preceding estate. Thus, the grantors would have a right of re-entry." *Stolarick v. Stolarick* [1976]. * * * At common law conditional language in conjunction with a clause granting the grantor or his successors the right to re-enter and terminate the estate upon breach of condition was required to create the fee simple subject to a condition subsequent. * * * "The principal distinction between the two estates is that a right of re-entry requires some action to perfect title by the

1. On March 24, 1868, James Higbee recorded a deed conveying the tract now in dispute to John Lafferty. John Lafferty subsequently conveyed the tract to Henry Kuckert, who in turn, conveyed the tract to George Acker, Jr. On December 2, 1909, George Acker, Jr.'s widow, Amanda Acker, made a conveyance of the property to Mary Kennedy. Appellant claims to have acquired title to the tract as an heir of Mary Kennedy. We note, however, that the trial court had not determined whether appellant does, in fact, have standing to assert title to the tract.

grantor or his successor, while a reverter vests automatically." Restatement of Property § 57 (1936). * * *

A grantor and his successor are capable of transmitting both a possibility of reverter and a right of re-entry by inheritance, conveyance, assignment or lease. * * **5** The grantor is characterized as retaining these interests because when he creates a fee simple determinable or a fee simple subject to a condition subsequent he does not dispose of his entire interest in the land. Therefore, the interests are deemed vested at the time of their creation. * * *

We first examine the effect of the following clause: "forever *provided* the [grantee] his heirs and assigns wishes to make use of it for the purpose of a road." (Emphasis added.) We concur with the parties' consensus that the portions of the deed preceding this phrase create a fee simple. However, we cannot agree with appellee's contention that this conditional language limits the estate to a fee simple determinable. Words such as "provided," "if," or "upon the condition that" express condition and, therefore, indicate the existence of a fee simple subject to a condition subsequent. In *Stolarick v. Stolarick* * * * we held that when conditional language is followed by reverter clause, absent a showing of contrary intent, we will find a fee simple subject to a condition subsequent. * * **6**

The term "wishes" refers to the state of mind of the grantee. Thus, it is evident that mere nonuse of the property as a road does not establish that the condition has been broken. The estate can be deemed forfeited only upon a showing that the grantee has no inclination to use the property as a road. Since the record does not contain any evidence maintaining that appellant had no desire to use the property as a road, we cannot agree that this provision has been breached.

We find the following clause more perplexing: the [grantee] agrees to keep a good fence around the above-mentioned lot, failing to do so *forfeits* his claim, whenever the [grantee] wishes to give up his claim to said lot he is to have full privilege to remove all fencing materials

---

5. At common law a possibility of reverter was generally viewed as "a mere possibility that a right, or an estate in land, might arise in the future upon the happening of a contingency." *London v. Kingsley* * * * (1951). It could be disposed only by release since it was not categorized as an actual estate in land. * * * However, Pennsylvania has long recognized that the power to alienate a possibility of reverter is in accordance with the public policy favoring the alienability of land, and thus permits the disposition of all reversionary interests, including the possibility of reverter, by devise, grant, assignment or release. * * *

6. In reaching our decision in * * * we cited with approval the following provision of the Restatement of Property [Sec. 45]:

When an otherwise effective conveyance contains a clause which provides that "if," or "upon the condition that," or "provided that" a stated event occurs, then the estate created "shall be null and void" or "shall revert back," a problem in construction is presented as to whether such conveyance creates an estate in fee simple subject to a condition subsequent or an estate in fee simple determinable. Such a conveyance more commonly manifests an intent to create an estate in fee simple subject to a condition subsequent. * * *

whenever the [grantee] his heirs and assigns fail to fulfill this agreement the land is to revert to the [grantor]

(Emphasis added). The term "forfeits" is conditional language and, coupled with the absence of words of incontestable limitation, indicates the existence of a fee simple subject to a condition subsequent. The provision of reverter to the grantor, on the other hand, infers that the estate is a fee simple determinable. Since a fee simple determinable automatically divests a grantee of his interest in an estate, without regard to the current status of a grantor or his successors in interest, it is more cumbersome upon the alienability of land than a fee simple subject to a condition subsequent.[7] It is our opinion that the grantor, as draftsman of the deed, bears the heavy burden of using clear and unambiguous language to make explicit his intent to create this type of onerous limitation to an estate in land. * * * Therefore, only in the absence of ambiguity will we find in favor of a fee simple determinable. * * * Accordingly, in absence of contrary intent, we view the conflicting terminology herein as creating a fee simple subject to a condition subsequent.

The order of the court of common pleas is reversed and this action is remanded for further proceedings consistent with this opinion.

Notes and Questions

1. As the *Higbee* court's second footnote indicates, historically the grantor's retained future interest after either of these defeasible estates was inalienable. The grantor could not separately convey the future interest; he could not one day give a deed that said, "to the bishop so long as the property is used as a cemetery" and then, the next day, give a deed that said, "my possibility of reverter in the cemetery to John." (The reason for this had to do with the common law's horror of assigning causes of action.) But grantors do not live forever, and these grantor future interests have to survive the deaths of the grantors or the defeasible estate is not, after all, a useful tool for clients. Even where possibilities of reverter and rights of entry are inalienable, as they are in some jurisdictions, they are descendible; they pass to the grantor's heirs upon the grantor's death.

In most American states, possibilities of reverter and rights of entry are now both alienable and descendible. In some states, they (or one or the other of these interests) cannot be alienated by deed but can be given in the grantor's will (devisable even though not otherwise alienable).

2. Neither *Ocean City* nor *Higbee* involved controversy over whether the event foreseen by the words of condition had occurred. That can be a question of fact, a question of local politics, and a question of public policy as well. The Appellate Court of Illinois has dealt with several phrases in such a case, in a series of opinions that span the decade of the 1980s. It involves a

---

7. Indeed, since a possibility of reverter is not subject to the rule against perpetuities, it can work to divest a party of property centuries after both the grantor and the reason for the condition have ceased to exist. [Editor's note: The Rule Against Perpetuities is discussed near the end of this chapter.]

gift made in 1941 by Mr. and Mrs. W.E. Hutton to the trustees of a school in Allison, Illinois, "for school purposes only." A school was built on the property, and students studied there until 1973. After that time, the school authorities used the school building for storage.

The Huttons' heirs, a family named Mahrenholz, argued that the use of the school building for storage caused the "automatic" reversion of possession of the land to them as holders of a possibility of reverter. In a series of opinions in the 1980s, the Appellate Court decided ambiguous language in the deed created a fee simple determinable, which vindicated the Mahrenholz's property theory of automatic termination upon breach. As they found out when they went back to court, however, the categorization of the school's estate as a fee simple determinable did not establish that a reversion of possession had taken place in 1973.

In Mahrenholz v. County Board, 188 Ill.App.3d 260, 135 Ill.Dec. 771, 544 N.E.2d 128 (1989), the court had to consider what "school purposes" means (or meant in the 1941 Hutton conveyance). That appears to be a question of fact; but, as the court treated it, it is more fundamentally a question:

—(a) of judicial policy (deference to the finder of fact, in this case the trial judge, who "conducted a personal inspection and examination of the school and its contents");

—(b) of politics, and politics of a familiar local and often virulent sort, between people who run the public schools and people who disapprove of the way the schools are being run; and

—(c) of political theory, that is, of the appropriate deference higher government should, in sound philosophical theory, accord to lower government. It was possible to say that, since "school purposes" were words in a deed, the appellate judges should have asked what those words meant to Mr. and Mrs. Hutton. But the court can be taken to have treated the grant of land here as if it had come from a higher level of government.

The court addresses the issue:

The question ... becomes whether storage of school property constitutes a legitimate "school purpose." We believe that, in general, the answer is yes. School populations are not static. They change from year to year.... In order to accommodate such changes, storage facilities are necessary.... Clearly, having such equipment and supplies on hand furthers the ultimate goal of educating students.... [P]laintiffs contend defendants are using the building for nothing more than a "dumping ground" ... while allowing the building to deteriorate.... The evidence at trial, however ... [shows the Board] spent substantial amounts of money to maintain the structure.... We ... will not substitute our judgment for that of the trial court when faced with conflicts in the evidence and issues of the credibility of witnesses.... We agree with plaintiffs that defendants could have found more convenient storage facilities, which were less expensive to maintain. It is not for us, however, to determine whether defendants' use of the premises is in the best economic interest of the district and its taxpayers.

What has sound economy in local government to do with the meaning of "school purposes" in a deed? Why is the "legitimacy" of the purpose relevant, if the school is actually using the building? Should the court instead look only at what the grantor intended by the term? If so, how do you find out what the grantor meant? What interests are favored if we entertain the individualized inquiry of what *this* grantor meant as opposed to developing a more generalizable definition of this term?

3. One problem with defeasible fees is that the condition may be broken many years after the conveyance, with the results described in the true report below:

James Cocke was a man who planned ahead. Some 237 years ahead.

Cocke deeded a half-acre of land to Henrico County in 1751, stipulating that the property be used for a courthouse. In the handwritten deed, Cocke inserted language providing that if the county ever moved the courthouse, "then the said lot shall revert and be the property of James Cocke and his heirs forever."

The following year, Henrico built a courthouse on the corner of what is now 22nd and Main Streets in Richmond. There it stayed until 1840, when it was moved slightly because part of the building was in Main Street. In 1896, the county built the current brick structure, replacing a building burned during the Civil War. At all times, the county courthouse remained on the Cocke property.

Then, in 1975, Henrico moved its courthouse to a new government center in the suburbs of Richmond. The Cocke clan, led by Richmond real estate lawyer Richard Cocke, filed a chancery suit in 1984 [and successfully reclaimed] the property.

[Now the owners have to be found. Who are the heirs, in 1988, of James Cocke?] A thick, two-volume family history entitled "Cockes and Cousins" may * * * prove helpful. Cocke originally filed one volume of the genealogy with his initial suit papers.

Locating all owners may be time-consuming. When asked how long the process might take, Richard Cocke said, "I hope I'm not pipedreaming to say a couple years."

Cocke said he will request that the property be sold, saying it is "unrealistic and impractical" to keep the property in the hands of so many people. * * *

Richard Cocke, the great-great-great-great-grandson of James Cocke, said his "conservative estimate" is that potentially 1,000 heirs might have an interest. * * *

Cocke declined to specify exactly what steps will be taken to locate the heirs, because, he said, he had not met with the commissioner.

However, he thought they would set up some kind of guidelines to insure that reasonable notice is given to potential heirs. "We expect to use the services of a professional genealogist," he said. [Paul Fletcher, "Courthouse Heirs," Virginia Lawyers Weekly (July 25, 1988) p. 1.]

4. Conditions that require illegal acts or otherwise violate public policy are unenforceable. The standard remedy is judicial elimination of the condi-

tion on ownership. This may result in reversion of the land to the grantor. In some cases, however, the courts have revised conditions to bring them in line with current law and policy. See Kevin A. Bowman, The Short Term Versus The Dead Hand: Litigating Our Dedicated Public Parks, 65 U. Cinn. L. Rev. 595 (1997). Conditions that violate public policy include conditions that operate as a total restraint on marriage, although it is generally held that estates terminable upon marriage may be upheld if the restraint is only partial. Direct restraints on alienation are usually not enforceable; but if the restraint is very narrowly drawn in time and scope an exception may be made judicially. State law varies as to whether any direct restrictions on transferability of land are enforceable. See also the treatment of restraints on alienation in trusts, *infra*. For an interesting discussion of the use of defeasible fees in the early development of suburbia see Timothy Jost, The Defeasible Fee and the Birth of the Modern Residential Subdivision, 49 Mo. L. Rev. 695 (1984).

5. Life estates can also be subject to conditions. For example: "Oscar to Abigail for life so long as she remains unmarried" gives Abigail a life estate subject to a condition, sometimes called a life estate determinable. Oscar retains a reversion. Contrast this with "Oscar to Abigail and her heirs so long as she remains unmarried." In this conveyance, Abigail receives a fee simple determinable and Oscar retains a possibility of reverter. Do you see the difference in the language of the conveyance? And, what would you say Abigail receives in "Oscar to Abigail so long as she remains unmarried?"

REVIEW PROBLEMS

These review problems test what you have learned concerning the identification of estates and future interests to this point. Identify the present possessory estate and all of the future interests in these conveyances.

1. Oglethorpe to Alice and her heirs.

2. Oglethorpe to Alexia and the heirs of her body.

3. Oglethorpe to Able and his heirs so long as the property is used for residential purposes.

4. Oglethorpe to Anne and her heirs, but if the property is not used for residential purposes, to Beardsley and his heirs.

5. Oglethorpe to Albert for life.

6. Oglethorpe to Annalee for life, then to Boone and his heirs.

7. Oglethorpe to Axl Rose for life, then to Brandy and her heirs if Brandy survives Axl Rose.

8. Oglethorpe to Alec and his heirs provided the land is used for residential purposes.

9. Oglethorpe to Adele and her heirs. Adele promises that the land will be used for residential purposes.

10. Oglethorpe to Adelaide and her heirs. Adelaide contracts, in consideration of the transfer, that the property will be used only for residential purposes.

11. Oglethorpe to Ariel for life, then to Brant and his heirs. Brant dies before Ariel. His will devises all of his property to your law school. Ariel then dies.

12. Oglethorpe to Ava for life. Before either he or Ava dies, Oglethorpe conveys all of his property to Happy Hearts Lifecare Center.

13. Oglethorpe to Alonzo for life. Alonzo dies with a will leaving all of his property to his wife.

14. Oglethorpe to Antonio so long as he remains in Missouri.

15. Oglethorpe to Antonio and his heirs so long as he remains in Missouri.

16. Oglethorpe to Abner for life, then to Belinda, then to Charlotte and her heirs.

17. Oglethorpe to Anya for life, then to Booker and his heirs if Booker survives Anya, but if Booker does not survive Anya, then to Oglethorpe.

18. Oglethorpe to Antoinette and her heirs so long as the land is farmed. After this conveyance, Oglethorpe transfers all of his property to his son Bob. Oglethorpe then dies leaving a will that transfers all of his property to the Humane Society. Oglethorpe is survived by his son Bob and his wife Corabeth. Antoinette reads of Oglethorpe's death in the newspaper and stops farming. A week later, a troop of Girl Scouts camping on the land suffers severe but nonfatal injuries due to a landslide. They want to know who owns the land so that they can file suit.

V. EXECUTORY INTERESTS: THE LAST OF THE FUTURE INTERESTS

You now have a repertoire of present possessory estates and their companion future interests: fee simple absolute; life estate and life estate *pur autre vie* (paired with remainders and reversions); fee simple determinable (paired with the possibility of reverter); fee simple subject to condition subsequent (paired with the right of entry); and the fee simple subject to executory limitation (paired with the executory interest).

Executory Interests in Contemporary Law

The last piece you have to fill in to complete your toolbox of freehold estates and future interests is the executory interest. Executory interests are defined by Dean Phipps, who was quoted earlier, as "a future interest in someone other than the grantor which according to its terms if it becomes possessory must do so otherwise than as would a remainder." An executory interest can only be created in a grantee.

You have already seen one situation in which an executory interest exists—as a companion to the fee simple subject to executory limitation. So, in "Opie to Anastasia and her heirs so long as the land is farmed; but if it is not farmed, to Bailey and his heirs,'' Anastasia has a fee simple subject to executory limitation and Bailey has an executory interest in fee simple absolute. This type of executory interest is called a "shifting" executory interest because the future interest shifts from one grantee to another.

An executory interest is created as well when a vested remainder subject to divestment is followed by a future interest in a grantee. So, "Odell to Amos for life, then to Billy and his heirs, but if Billy does not survive Amos, to Calhoun and his heirs" grants Amos a life estate; Billy a vested remainder subject to divestment in fee simple absolute; and Calhoun an executory interest in fee simple absolute. This, too, is a "shifting" executory interest. (Note for comparison: that "Odell to Amos for life, then to Billy and his heirs if Billy survives Amos, but if Billy does not survive Amos, to Calhoun and his heirs" grants Amos a life estate, Billy and Calhoun alternative contingent remainders in fee simple absolute, and Odell a reversion. And "Odell to Amos for life, then to Bill and his heirs, but if Billy does not survive Amos, to Odell and his heirs" grants Amos a life estate; Billy a vested remainder subject to divestment in fee simple absolute; and Odell a reversion.)

With this new information, try your hand at identifying the estate and future interests in each of the following conveyances:

(a) Lorenz to Patricia and her heirs provided the wetlands on the property are left in their natural state, but if they are not, then to the Nature Conservatory and its heirs and assigns.

(b) Beulah to Caleb and his heirs so long as a chapel is maintained on the property; but if it is not, to the First Church of the Resurrection and its heirs and assigns.

(c) Delia to Edward for life, then to his daughter Fernanda and her heirs if she is living at the time of Edward's death; if she is not, to his son Gordo and his heirs.

(d) Harold to Ichabod for life, and then to June and her heirs; but if June does not survive Ichabod, then to Kerry and her heirs.

There is one more instance where an executory interest is created. A springing executory interest exists where there is an *unavoidable* "lapse in seisin" or gap in ownership of a present possessory estate in the land. For example, "Oswald to Amil for life, and one day after Amil's death, to Barry and his heirs" creates a life estate for Amil and a springing executory interest in fee simple absolute for Barry. There is an unavoidable one-day delay between the expiration of Amil's life estate (at Amil's death) and Barry's fee simple absolute. Note that the gap in seisin must be *unavoidable*. So, for example, "Oswald to Alicia for life, then to Brandon and his heirs if Brandon marries Suellen" grants Alicia a life estate and Brandon a contingent remainder in fee simple absolute even though it could happen that Alicia will die before Brandon marries Suellen and while Brandon may still marry Suellen (i.e., while Brandon is alive). The potential gap here is not unavoidable; indeed, it may not occur at all. (And did you catch that Oswald retained a reversion in each of these conveyances?)

Another way to distinguish shifting and springing executory interests, if you care to, is to imagine that a shifting executory interest shifts an interest from one grantee to another while a springing executory interest springs the interest from the grantor to a grantee.

Executory Interests in the Sixteenth Century

Under the common law as it existed prior to 1536, a shifting executory interest was not enforceable. The Statute of Uses in 1536 recognized and made it possible to create executory interests in common law.

While the common law courts held that a shifting executory interest was not legally effective prior to the statute, the Chancellor's equity courts would uphold this future interest.* Triggering the Chancellor's jurisdiction required drafting the future interest in a particular manner. It required medieval lawyers to "raise a use." The lawyer "raised a use" by conveying legal title to a person called a "feoffee to uses" who held the property for "the use of" the grantees. Such a conveyance would read: Grantor "to T and his heirs for the use of A and his heirs so long as the land is used for pasture, then to B and his heirs." T would be the feoffee to uses. The feoffee to uses was a real person, who holds legal title, but his office was fictional. He didn't *do* anything. The grantees are in possession and for all practical purposes responsible as owners.

By the end of the fifteenth century the use of uses by property lawyers had proliferated to the point where it had become a major concern to the common law bar and to the King. The King (Henry VIII) was interested in reducing uses because uses were devices for avoiding death taxes payable to the crown. The common law bar was interested in reducing uses because the chancery bar threatened to dominate property law practice, since it could better accommodate grantee's desires.

---

* During all of the most formative period of English property law, which became the basis of Anglo–American property law, two systems of courts competed with one another for judicial business. The first was the system of the common law and the common law courts, which trace their origin to the dispatching of royal judges to the English countryside by King Henry II. The other system of law was equity and the chancery courts which operated closer to the throne. The Chancellor was, at least until the 16th century, a priest, perhaps the confessor to the King.

Each of these systems offered advantages and disadvantages to property owners. Their sources of law were different: equity tended to look to moral impulses and to continental or canon (church) law while the common law courts tended to look at the customs and practices of the people it judged. The judges in the two systems were different, with different educations and different political and professional loyalties. A lawyer would practice either in the equity courts or in the common law courts, and they competed for business as well. The two courts developed quite different rules of property law with the effect that an arrangement may not be enforceable in the law courts, but may be enforceable in the equity courts. Even in our current system, we have rules of "equity" and rules of "law," and we have "equitable remedies" and "legal remedies," although we do not maintain separate courts or separate systems of law.

The most enduring result of this property law alliance was the Statute of Uses of 1536. The novel device invented in that statute to cut down the influence of the Chancellor's property rules was to *execute uses*. This device left the property tools intact but changed the courts in which the tools were employed. It moved equity's business to the common law courts. The Statute of Uses eliminated the jurisdictional distinction between common law and the Chancellor's rules by making executory interests common law devices. Executory interests after the Statute were legal interests, not equitable interests. The Statute of Uses did not eliminate the executory interest; what it did was to put the executory interest at the disposal of a different set of lawyers and judges. These were new *common law* interests, but they were not new property interests. Until modern times (and even in modern times, by force of professional habit) executory interests were (are) set up the same way the old equitable interests had been set up by the chancery lawyers, prior to Henry VIII.*

Another way to look at this is to say that the Statute of Uses eliminated the feoffee to uses but not the conveyance to him. You still raised a use by a transfer to the feoffee to uses, but the Statute then "executed" the use by making the beneficial owner's equitable interest a common law legal interest instead. Whatever equitable ownership the real owner had held in use he now held in common law. Consider "to T and his heirs for the use of A and his heirs so long as the land is farmed, then to B and his heirs."

Before the Statute, A held an equitable fee simple determinable; after the Statute, A held a legal fee simple determinable. Before the Statute, B held an executory interest under the Chancellor's rules (no interest under common law rules); after the Statute, B held a legal executory interest. B's interest was still not a remainder; it would not be today. Before the Statute T held the legal fee simple; after the Statute he still got a legal fee simple but it disappeared as soon as he got it.

---

* Does that mean you still raise a use? Maybe. You do not need these days to use "magic words" in creating shifting and springing executory interests. One way to explain that is to say that you still have to raise a use and that the law has dispensed with the magic words. The value of thinking of it that way is that it helps you to remember that it was necessary until fairly recently to use the magic words. In some places in 19th century America, for example, if the drafter wrote, "To A for life and one day later to B and her heirs," the attempt to create an interest (a common law springing executory interest) in B would fail. You had to say "To T and his heirs for the use of A for life and one day later to B and her heirs," or in some other way define the interest in a way that, prior to 1536, would have made it equitable. It is not now necessary to convey to the "feoffee to uses" (or to use one of the other ways 16th century English lawyers used to raise a use), but you could argue, if you like metaphysics, that the use is still raised— raised by the necessity to use an executory interest rather than a remainder. One could also argue that such a position is sterile historicism. Take your pick—but remember: (1) If you are asked about the situation in, say, 1700, lawyers then were still using magic words to raise uses; and (2) there remains in modern law a distinction between the remainder and the executory interest, and the distinction makes a difference.

PRACTICE PROBLEMS

Relying on modern post–1536 law, identify the estates and future interests created by these conveyances.

1.   Otis to Amelia and her heirs provided the land is farmed, but if it is not farmed, to Ballard and his heirs.

2.   Otis to Ava for life, and then to Barbara and her heirs so long as Barbara survives Ava; but if Barbara does not survive Ava, to Clarice and her heirs.

3.   Otis to Asa and her heirs upon her graduation from law school. Assume that Asa is a member of your law school class.

4.   Otis to Aleisha for life, then to Boland and his heirs, but if Aleisha is survived by children, then to those children and their heirs.

5.   Otis to Anna for life, then to Bill and his heirs, but if Bill has divorced Anna, to Charlie and his heirs.

6.   Otis to Alex, so long as the property issued for residential purposes; if it is not, to Bond and his heirs.

NOTE ON TRUSTS

A trust is a fiduciary relationship in which one person (trustee) is the holder of the title to property (trust property) subject to an equitable obligation to keep or use the property for the benefit of another (beneficiary). The trust is created when a person (settlor) intentionally causes the trust to come into existence, sometimes orally, but generally through a written document called the trust instrument. The fiduciary relationship that a trust creates between the trustee and the beneficiary means that the trustee has a significant amount of control over the trust property and has a duty to act in the interest of the beneficiary. (You recall the reference to the federal-tribal trust in the notes following *Johnson v. McIntosh,* and you can see that the "feoffee to uses" would be viewed as a trustee.)

Setting up and administering a trust can be very expensive. Nevertheless, a trust provides two distinct advantages over a common law conveyance. First, the trustee will act as a "gatekeeper," protecting the corpus of the trust from the beneficiary in order to ensure the wealth is available for a longer period of time. Second, the trustee often has the power to sell and convert the corpus of the trust into more lucrative forms of wealth spread out over the plane of time. These features protect the corpus of the trust from depletion while allowing the beneficiary to enjoy the benefits of the trust. Because of the expense of establishing and maintaining a trust and because of persistent desires to avoid the intervention of lawyers, common law conveyancing is still common despite the wealth-maximization and control properties of the trust.

The trust has been, for a century and a half, a principal device for gathering together borrowed capital for American business purposes. It is also a principal device for pooled investments; many "mutual funds" that are marketed to the public are trusts. And the trust is the basic tool used by property lawyers in arranging property ownership for members of families. Here are some examples.

A trust may be useful where clients need to find ways to separate management of the business from enjoyment of business profits and to do this in reference to a range of people that may include both an ailing 90–year–old founder of the firm who still "comes in to the office every morning" and to child who will one day win the Nobel Prize for her poetry and will never come into the office at all. The trust can provide fiduciary management for disabled clients. The trust may be the only device that will work well for the client who has business to do or investment to see to but who fears her own disability—especially mental disability—from age or poor health, and who needs a device that will be available to provide as much substitute management as the occasion requires, from no management of her property to a substitute for guardianship. A trust may be useful in minimizing liability for estate taxes.

Parents in young families want (or, after they talk to their lawyers, come to want) "estate planning" devices to protect their minor children from some of the material effects of the unlikely but disastrous death of both parents before the children "come of age." A trust allows parents (or grandparents or aunts or uncles) to continue management to an age chosen by the settlor (grantor) of the trust; clients have been known to choose the age of 50; many choose ages between 25 and 30. A trust can avoid using any age and instead define "coming of age" in terms of an event (such as graduation from college or marriage), or it can leave the matter to a trustee's judgment.*

A trust can also be used to restrain the transfer of property even where the same restraint would be unenforceable as an illegal restraint on alienation if done otherwise. A series of 19th–century American cases held that a restraint on alienation—even a restraint on the alienation of a fee simple—is possible when the interest being restrained is an *equitable* interest. This rule—which is now followed in all but a couple of the states—was justified with the arguments: (i) that the property had not been removed from the market (since the trustee held an unrestrained legal fee simple); or, if it had, (ii) that such removal had been the will of the settlor of the trust, who held an unrestrained legal fee simple and should have been able to do what he wanted with his own property. For example:

> to Manon and her heirs, in trust for Monique and her heirs, and Monique shall not alienate her interest, voluntarily or involuntarily.

"Involuntary" alienation occurs when the property is taken by Monique's creditors. Such a restraint on alienation is particularly useful in protecting property from creditors and so from the excesses of spend-

---

* See T. Shaffer and C. Mooney, and A. Boettcher, The Planning and Drafting of   Wills and Trusts, ch. 3, 10 (4th ed. 2001).

thrifts. The protection of spendthrifts from themselves is a special function of trusts.

The modern trust grew out of a little open space—a loophole, if you like—in the Statute of Uses. The statute by its terms executed all uses, which meant: (i) ownership in equity became ownership in law; and (ii) the feoffee to uses (the person we would today call a trustee) remained necessary, but only for a moment. That worked as it was supposed to work for the cases in which the use was a fiction and the feoffee to uses (trustee) had nothing to do. It did not work, though, for cases in which the grantor of the use (whom we would today call the settlor or a trustor) wanted the property to be managed for the equitable owner (whom we today call the beneficiary or the *cestui que trust*). This is the case of the "active" use (trust), as distinguished from the "passive" or "dry" use (trust). The judges, as you will by now have no doubt guessed, construed the Statute of Uses not to reach active trusts. The way you tell which is which is to ask if the feoffee to uses (trustee) has duties. If the trustee has duties, the trust survives the Statute of Uses. The trustee has legal title and fiduciary duties to the beneficiary. The beneficiary has equitable title.

Not all states have pervasive rules forbidding dry trusts. It is possible in some states to separate legal and equitable ownership without imposing duties on the trustee. One dubious advantage this device offers, where it is available, is that land ownership can be concealed from the public and even from local government. An owner who does not want it known that he is an owner transfers title to (or, more likely, takes title in) a trust. The deed conveying title is recorded in the public land records, but it shows only the name of the trustee. If there is a written agreement between the trustee and the equitable owner, it is not recorded. Standard Statute-of-Uses (common) law would hold the trust executed—that is, no trust at all. A few states permit such dry trusts; some of these justify the device by construction of the Statute of Uses; in some states it is provided for by statute.

VI. RULES FURTHERING MARKETABILITY: DESTRUCTIBILITY, SHELLEY'S CASE, WORTHIER TITLE, AND PERPETUITIES

It may be natural for landowners to try to control the use and disposition of property far into the future, but it is equally natural for the government to resist that attempt. Government generally has acted in favor of assuring that events that allow for taxation of the value of the property occur. One of the principal ways to tax wealth is to tax it at the death of the current owner. One of the principal means of avoiding such a tax is to spread ownership on the plane of time, so that the death of a possessor is not a transition in ownership. Furthermore, a market economy requires circulating wealth rather than concentration over many generations in particular family groups, although whether law is successful in resisting this human drive is open to question. Of course, current efforts to repeal or eviscerate the federal estate tax, called the "death tax" in the repeal effort, follow a different theory entirely.

Division of property between possessory estates and vested future interests complicates the sale of property. After the conveyance "to Alicia for life, then to Bartolomeo and his heirs," a buyer can obtain a possessory fee simple by getting deeds from both Alicia and Bartolomeo. Transaction costs are somewhat higher than in the fee simple and the conveyance gives two parties instead of one, veto power over the sale, but these are not insurmountable obstacles. The division of property ownership between possessory estates and *contingent* future interests, however, tends to keep property out of the market. For example, "to Alicia for life, then to the heirs of Bartolomeo and their heirs" creates a contingent remainder in persons who cannot be ascertained until after Bartolomeo's death. A conveyance "to my children for life, then to my grandchildren who survive them" puts a condition of survival on the grandchildren's future interests and similarly makes ultimate ownership of the fee uncertain. Forces most affected by the inefficiencies that such conveyances create will pressure for change in the rules, for example, through legislation or through case law. Those interested in controlling their property while conveying it—for example, through defeasible fees setting conditions on the use of the property in the context of family, or charity, or even environmental conservation—will find new and creative ways to make that happen despite efforts to the contrary.

We look at three historic ways the common law resisted forms of ownership that keep property in the family; that avoid taxation upon death; that make transfer difficult because of uncertainty in the identity of the owners; or that dissipate ownership over many parties. These three rules are:

(A) the *destructibility of contingent remainders*;

(B) the *Rule in Shelley's Case* and the *Doctrine of Worthier Title* (considered together because they are a lot alike); and

(C) the *Rule Against Perpetuities*.

A. THE DESTRUCTIBILITY OF CONTINGENT REMAINDERS

This doctrine is no longer important for law practice, but the dynamic that made destructibility possible still is. For that reason, and for historical interest, we need to pause briefly over this first category.

Consider a couple of examples. In this first example, the contingent remainder is destroyed if it does not vest before the termination of the preceding estate.

(1) Grandma, by deed, gave the family property "to my son Saul for life, then, if she reaches the age of 21, to his daughter, my beloved granddaughter, Leah and her heirs." Leah was then 12. Grandma's deed made a valid transfer under common law rules: Saul had a possessory life estate; Leah had a contingent remainder in fee simple (contingent on her

reaching her 21st birthday). If Leah had reached her 21st birthday during Saul's life, her remainder would have become a vested remainder in fee simple. But suppose she did not; suppose that Leah was only 18 when Saul died. In that case, Leah's remainder failed. To give it effect in such circumstances would be to allow the ownership to lapse (i.e., revert to Grandma) between Saul's death and Leah's 21st birthday, and then to spring up again when Leah had her birthday party. The old common law lawyers spoke of this as a lapse in seisin, meaning a lapse in "freehold" possession of the sort Grandma and Saul had. This would allow a springing interest and, under common law rules, a remainder cannot spring; it must take effect at the expiration of the prior estate—or fail. In this case it failed. The contingent remainder was destroyed. At Saul's death the fee ownership reverted to Grandma.

This aspect of destructibility of contingent remainders is no longer in effect. Instead, at Saul's death, Leah's interest becomes a springing executory interest and she can still take possession when she reaches 21. Grandma would own the possessory estate until then.

In this next example, the contingent remainder is destroyed through the operation of merger:

(2) Same facts as in the first illustration except that Saul does not die when Leah is 18. Assume, though, that Saul fears what will happen if his daughter should get the property. Perhaps she is a spendthrift. Saul goes to see his lawyer; the lawyer still has in his tool box an antique destructibility tool—a tool modern reform has taken away from us. By using this old tool, the lawyer could have destroyed Leah's contingent remainder. It works this way:

(i) Grandma is still living.

(ii) There is a reversion after Leah's contingent remainder. There is always a reversion after a contingent remainder; in this case there is a realistic, non-fictional reversion, because Leah may not be 21 when poor Saul dies, which, in view of the way Leah is treating him, could be any day now. Possession may revert to Grandma between Saul's death and Leah's 21st birthday.

(iii) Saul holds the life estate and is in possession.

(iv) Grandma agrees with Saul that something must be done about Leah.

(v) Grandma conveys her reversion to Saul.

The result of this last conveyance was to put both the possessory life estate and the reversion in the same person. The doctrine was that the two then merged to become a fee simple absolute, and any intervening *contingent* remainders were destroyed:

(i) This would not be the case if Leah's remainder had been vested (e.g., she had already become 21). In that case the reversion would have disappeared when Leah became 21, and there would be no future interest to merge with Saul's life estate.

(ii) But it would have been possible even if, logically, there could be no return of possession to the grantor under the terms of the deed ("Saul for life, then, if she reaches her 21st birthday, to Leah and her heirs, and if not, to Rachel and her heirs"). There is always a reversion after contingent remainders. The fiction is essential to the doctrine. The doctrine is that both remainders are destructible.

As with most of these old doctrines, lawyers found a way to make such contingent remainders indestructible. By the year 1700 they had successfully argued to the common law courts that executory interests should not be destructible, so that all Grandma had to do, if she wanted Leah's future interest to be indestructible, was to—what?

B. THE RULE IN SHELLEY'S CASE AND THE DOCTRINE OF WORTHIER TITLE

The Rule in Shelley's Case

SEYMOUR v. HEUBAUM

Appellate Court of Illinois, 1965.
65 Ill.App.2d 89, 211 N.E.2d 897.

DAVIS, JUSTICE.

This is a suit seeking construction of a will and a declaratory judgment that plaintiff is owner in fee simple absolute of certain real estate. The issue before the Court is the applicability of the rule in Shelley's case to a certain devise contained in the will of Effie Seymour, who died in 1939. If the rule is applicable * * * its abrogation by statute in 1953 * * * will not affect the determination here as the statute has no retroactive application. * * *

After making certain specific bequests, Effie Seymour provided. * * *

* * * I give, devise and bequeath all the rest and residue of my estate real or personal, wherever situate, including all my right, title and interest in and to the real estate known as * * * to J. Harter Kirkpatrick * * * as trustee, to be held in trust for the benefit of my son William H. Seymour during his lifetime and upon his death to be paid to his lawful heirs. * * * "

[W]illiam died in 1960 leaving a will in which he devised all of his property to his wife, the plaintiff, who brought this suit seeking a construction of Effie Seymour's will and a judgment declaring that her husband took a fee interest under his mother's will, capable of being devised to her. This contention is premised upon the applicability of the rule in Shelley's case to the mother's will, converting the remainder to William's lawful heirs into a remainder in fee in William. The trial court held that the rule in Shelley's case was applicable and that William thus took the remainder as well as the life estate, which constituted the fee;

and that, therefore, he had the power to dispose of the same by will. The defendants, the heirs of William other than his widow, prosecuted this appeal.

Stated simply, the rule in Shelley's case is that whenever, in the same instrument, an estate of freehold is limited to the ancestor, and a remainder to his heirs, either mediately or immediately, in fee, or in tail, the word "heirs" is one of limitation of the estate, and not of purchase, and the ancestor takes the fee. * * * Whenever the grants of the freehold and remainder are contained in the same instrument, there are three requisites for application of the rule: First, a freehold estate must be granted to the ancestor; second, a remainder must be limited to "his heirs," general or special, as such—that is, by the name of heirs and without explanation as meaning sons, children, etc.; and third, the two estates, freehold and the remainder, must both be of the same quality,— that is, both must be either legal or equitable. * * *

[I]t matters not that the creator of the instrument in question manifested an intent that the property pass in a manner different than that resulting from the application of the rule. That is, in fact, the necessary result of the rule. It operates on the remainder alone, taking it from the heirs and vesting it in the ancestor; and although the preceding estate of freehold is a circumstance necessary to its application, such estate is not directly affected by it. The ordinary rules of construction are applicable only in first determining if there is a "freehold";[8] if there is a remainder in the "heirs," and if the two estates are of the same quality. These determinations are made wholly independently of the rule in Shelley's case itself. * * *

It is not disputed that the will of Effie Seymour granted an equitable life estate, and thus a freehold, to her son, William. The defendants contend, however, that the second and third requisites for the application of the rule are not present. They argue that the second requisite is absent because the word "heirs" was intended to designate certain persons other than those ordinarily encompassed within the meaning of the word, and it was thus used as a "word of purchase" not of "limitation"; and that the third requisite is missing in that the life estate was equitable and the remainder was legal. Hence, they urge that the two estates were not of the same quality. Lastly, they contend that the plaintiff is guilty of laches and is further estopped from asserting the application of the rule in Shelley's case.

Defendants contend that since Effie Seymour's will contained two specific bequests of $100.00 each to her two step-daughters, described as "my daughters," she thus evidenced an intent that the two named step-daughters were to take under her will as her own son's "heirs," although not technically such. If this intention were clearly manifested, we concede that the word "heirs" would not have been used in its

---

8. A freehold is a fee simple, a fee tail, or a life estate. For purposes of this rule a   freehold is a fee tail or a life estate. (Eds.)

technical and legal sense and the rule in Shelley's case could not be applied. However, it is not readily apparent to us how the two specific bequests of $100.00 each to her respective step-daughters, designated as "daughters," manifests an intent that they are to be included in the devise of the entire residue of her estate to the "lawful heirs" of her son upon his death. We think rather, that such bequests to each of her step-daughters would indicate an intent to exclude them from the residuary estate; and that the designation of her son's "lawful heirs" as the ones to ultimately take upon his death indicated that Effie Seymour had exhausted her specific wishes by prior bequests and when disposing of her residuary estate, she was content to let the law then take its course. * * *

That the word "heirs" is preceded by the word "lawful" does not affect its ordinary or technical meaning. * * * The word "heirs" as used by Effie Seymour in her will, was used as a word of limitation and not of purchase, and the second requisite for the application of the rule in Shelly's case is present.

Whether the remainder interest is legal or equitable must depend upon the character of the trust created by Effie Seymour's will. If the trustee was vested with the fee simple title under the trust created by the will, coupled with the power to sell, convey, rent, mortgage, etc., it follows that the life estate limited to William H. Seymour was equitable and the remainder interest given to his "lawful heirs," was likewise equitable—the same as the life estate. * * *

The quantity of the estate taken by the trustee is not determined from the particular form of the devise to the trustee, but, rather, from the intention manifested by the testator in defining the scope, extent and purpose of the trust and the duties of the trustee thereunder. The trustee will take whatever legal estate is necessary for him to carry out the purpose of the trust and his duties thereunder. If a fee is required, a fee will be taken; if a lesser estate will suffice, then only such an estate will vest. * * *

Our courts have long held that a devise to a trustee in which there is a power in the trust to sell, necessarily vests the fee in the trustee. * * *

While we do not deem it crucial to our determination, two other provisions of the will are consistent with the apparent intent to convey a fee to the trustee. The trustee was directed to pay for a proper burial for the life tenant. The fact that the trustee has duties to perform after the death of the life tenant suggests a legal fee in the trustee, rather than life estate coupled with powers. * * *

If the legal estate continued in the trustee after the death of the life tenant, no matter how short the period, there cannot during that same period be a legal vested remainder in the heirs of the life tenant. The remainder interest given to the heirs must then, of necessity, be equitable in nature. * * *

The will further provided that upon the death of William Seymour, the rest and residue of the estate that was devised and bequeathed in trust, was then "to be paid" to his lawful heirs. The defendants urge that the word "paid" cannot be interpreted to mean "convey" and suggest that it might be construed to mean "descend," in which case, they argue, the trust became passive immediately upon the death of the life tenant, and was executed by the Statute of Uses, and the remainder interest was then legal. * * * This argument, however, is more ingenious than persuasive. The wording of the fifth paragraph of the will does not suggest or require the liquidation of the trust estate. Nor do the words "to be paid" lend themselves to the interpretation of being synonymous with "descend". * * *

As to whether the Statute of Uses may ever operate to execute a trust in which the trustee has obtained full legal title or whether, in such cases, the trustee retains the active duty of conveying the legal title upon the termination of all other active duties, it appears that our courts have not always reached consistent conclusions. * * * Insofar as the application of the rule in Shelley's case is concerned, however, the determination of whether or not the Statute of Uses becomes operative, is irrelevant. For if we concede the operation of the Statute of Uses which would convert the remainder from an equitable into a legal interest, even then the statute may not execute the trust until all of the active duties of the trustee have been performed and nothing remains to be done. * * * The inquiry to be made regarding the applicability of the rule in Shelley's case is as to the effect of the instrument creating the freehold and remainder estates on the date such an instrument becomes effective. In the case of a will, it is as of the date of the testator's death. Thus, if a trust is created in a will, with the result that the freehold is equitable, the inquiry to be made in determining the quality or nature of the remainder must be as to the quantum or size of the trustee's estate at the inception of the trust. If it is a fee interest, then the freehold and remainder must be equitable in nature. * * * If both estates—the freehold and remainder—are of the same quality at the time the trustee takes title, it matters not that the quality or nature of one of the estates might, or might not, be altered at some later time. * * *

All of the requisites for the application of the rule in Shelley's case are here present, with the result that the life tenant, William Seymour, was given the fee to the real estate in question under the will of Effie Seymour. The application of the rule in Shelley's case to a particular case depends, not upon the quantity of the estate intended to be given to the ancestor, but upon the estate devised to his heirs. It conclusively expresses the intention of the testator, and governs and controls in determining the estate devised, notwithstanding the expression of an intention on the part of the testator that the ancestor shall take a less estate than the fee. It changes the remainder to the heirs of the devisee, into a remainder to the ancestor, so that he has a life estate with the remainder in fee to himself. * * *

Notes and Questions

1.   Arkansas abolished the Rule in Shelley's Case by statute in 2003. Ark. Code Ann. § 18–12–303. The Rule in Shelley's Case has been abolished in Illinois and virtually everywhere else. There may be as many as four states where it is still in force, but generalizations on the point are not to be trusted. In Indiana, for example, the issue has not been presented in the appellate courts for more than a century. The last time it was presented, the Supreme Court condemned the Rule but refused to abolish it judicially. The Indiana Trust Code has abolished it, but only as to trusts. Some writers say the Rule may still obtain in Colorado, Delaware, and perhaps elsewhere. Does it surprise you that such a thing as whether the Rule in Shelley's Case is in force in a particular jurisdiction could be so unclear? If you are practicing in a state that has abolished the Rule, you may still not be free to ignore it as it may continue to apply to conveyances that occurred before the date on which the Rule was abolished. See, e.g., National Turpentine & Pulpwood Corp. v. Mills, 57 So.2d 838 (Fla. 1952).

2.   The Rule in Shelley's Case applies where one instrument is used to convey a life estate in an individual and a remainder in that person's heirs (or the heirs of his body) and where the life estate and remainder are both legal or both equitable. For example: "Orvis to Atwater for life, then to Atwater's heirs," or "Orvis to Atwater for life, then to the heirs of Atwater's body." Under the Rule in Shelley's Case, the remainder in each becomes a remainder in Atwater. If there is no intervening interest, Atwater owns a fee simple absolute (in the first) or fee tail (in the second) through merger.

3.   Look at the statement of the Rule in Shelley's Case in note 2. If you wanted to create a remainder in a grantee's heirs as in the conveyances in that note, how could you do it and entirely avoid the application of the Rule?

4.   For an interesting telling of the history of the Rule in Shelley's Case in a modern context, see Julia Belian, Medicaid, Elective Shares, and the Ghosts of Tenures Past, 38 Creighton L. Rev. 1111 (2005). See also, Richard Davis and Stanley Kent, The Impact of the Uniform Trust Code on Special Needs Trusts, 1 NEALA Journal 235 (2005), for a modern application of the rule:

> In determining, a special needs trust beneficiary's eligibility for SSI, the Social Security Administration looks to state law to determine whether the trust is irrevocable. In a few states, including Ohio, the SSA takes the position that a trust, which by its terms is irrevocable, is treated as being revocable if it fails to name a remainder beneficiary, or if the remainder beneficiaries are the settlor's heirs.... Using the Doctrine of Worthier Title or the Rule in Shelley's case, the SSA sometimes takes the position that such a trust is revocable, even if its terms state that it is irrevocable.

The Doctrine of Worthier Title

The Doctrine of Worthier Title is similar to the Rule in Shelley's Case because it, too, operates on a remainder held by heirs. The Doctrine of Worthier Title operates where there is an inter vivos transfer of an estate to a grantee and a remainder or executory interest in the grantor's heirs. For example: "Oscar to Azalea for life, then to my heirs."

Worthier Title would take the contingent remainder held by Oscar's heirs and make it a reversion in Oscar. So the conveyance to Azalea becomes, under the operation of Worthier Title, Oscar "to Azalea for life, and then to Oscar and his heirs." Make sure you understand the difference.

Worthier Title should be considered a tax rule because it created a taxable event where the grantor had avoided it. After the operation of the Doctrine upon a contingent remainder or executory interest in the grantor's heirs, the heirs of the grantor took by inheritance, not under the deed, and their title was "worthier"—which seems to have meant that it was taxable. "A purported devise of an estate to heirs is inoperative if it is the identical estate that they are entitled to take in case of intestacy. . . . The doctrine is [also] . . . applicable if an *inter vivos* gift is followed by a gift to the [grantor's] 'heirs' or 'next of kin'. . . ." Burby, Real Property 336–337 (3d ed. 1965), tracking Coke on Littleton.

The Doctrine of Worthier Title has not been abolished clearly, mostly because Judge Benjamin Nathan Cardozo, in Doctor v. Hughes, 225 N.Y. 305, 122 N.E. 221 (1919), turned it into a rule of construction— so judges don't have to abolish it; they can keep it around in case it might come in handy some time. A dozen states, including Cardozo's New York, have abolished it by legislation.

C. THE RULE AGAINST PERPETUITIES

NOTE: THE MODERN RULE AGAINST PERPETUITIES

It's about the money. The Rule Against Perpetuities was first established in 1285, but even in the 21st Century, the Rule is very much in play. The Rule has always been viewed as difficult, but it may be even more so now as the individual states of the Union make distinctive alterations in the Rule that vary from state to state. One of the more significant changes in recent years is the trend among the states to abolish the Rule as it applies to trusts:

> To attract trust business and the lawyers' fees and trustees' com-missions that come with it, twenty-one states have abolished the Rule as applied to interests in trust. . . . Real money is at stake. [T]hrough 2003, roughly $100 billion in trust assets have poured into the abolishing states. Robert H. Sitkoff, The Lurking Rule Against Accumulations of Income, 100 Northwestern U. L. Rev. 501 (2006)

Sitkoff and a co-author in an earlier study reported that states abolish-ing the rule had on average experienced an increase of $6 billion (a 20% increase) in trust assets located in that state, although states that taxed trusts did not capture such gains. Robert Sitkoff and Max Schanzenbach, Jurisdictional Competition for Trust Funds: An Empirical Analysis of Perpetuities and Taxes, 115 Yale L. J. 356 (2005). So, the Rule Against Perpetuities has become a point of competition among the states for investment and job creation.

When we study the Rule Against Perpetuities, we approach it from three directions. First, we study the traditional common law Rule so that we understand the baseline against which changes such as those described are taking place. David Becker's article will provide you encouragement in your efforts to understand the traditional form of the Rule. (If You Think You No Longer Need to Know Anything About the Rule Against Perpetuities, Then Read This, 74 Wash. U. L.Q. 713 (1996)). Second, we study the several ways that the states are adjusting the Rule so that we are familiar with the most influential models. Abolishing the Rule *as it applies to trusts* while allowing it to continue to apply to real estate is one example of state law change. Others include, for example, setting a specific time limit for expiration of conditions and allowing an appointed fiduciary or a judge to reform the conveyance to avoid violation of the rule. Third, throughout our study, we want to be aware of the competing policies that motivate judges and state legislatures to take action in this area and that might supply a counterweight to the competitive abolition taking place in regard to trusts. Why the willingness to abandon a Rule with a centuries' old life span? Or, maybe you would ask why it took so long? Why the special treatment for trusts? What interests are served and disserved in the change?

One further note: Although we will limit our consideration to the application of the Rule to freehold estates and future interests, it has much broader implications. As you can see above, the common law rule (even still in a good number of states) applies to trusts, for example. In addition, it has applied to interests such as options to purchase and rights of first refusal. We draw your attention to its reach at this point just in case you still needed to be convinced of the Rule's importance beyond the bar exam.

NORTH CAROLINA NATIONAL BANK v. NORRIS

Court of Appeals of North Carolina, 1974.
21 N.C.App. 178, 203 S.E.2d 657.

Action for a declaratory judgment to determine whether certain provisions of the last will of B.F. Montague violated the rule against perpetuities. * * *

B.F. Montague died a resident of Wake County on or about 1 April 1928, leaving a will dated 19 November 1927. At the time of his death, he left surviving a widow, three daughters who were then 38, 40 and 43 years of age, and one grandchild, Thomas A. Norris, Jr., who was then six years of age; there were no children or grandchildren born subsequent to the death of B.F. Montague. Montague's widow, daughters, and only grandchild have successively deceased. Thomas A. Norris, Jr., the grandchild, died 10 January 1973, leaving surviving four children, who are the defendants herein, and a last will naming plaintiff herein as the Executor.

The pertinent provisions of the will of B.F. Montague are the following:

"FOURTH: I give, devise and bequeath to my three daughters, May M. Allison and Annie M. Hunter and Marjorie M. Norris, all of my estate, below described, during their natural lives and at the death of either of my said daughters, I give, devise and bequeath all of said property to the survivor or survivors alike, and at the death of the last survivor, I give, devise and bequeath all of my estate below described to the child or children of my said daughters for and during the natural life or lives of such child or children (my grandchild or grandchildren) with remainder over to the lawful issue of such grandchild or grandchildren forever. In default of such issue from such grandchild or grandchildren, the remainder shall go to Peace Institute of Raleigh, N.C., absolutely and forever. First of all, however, I give, devise and bequeath to my wife, Bettie L. Montague, a life estate in and to all the property below described in this section (Section FOURTH), and at her death, the same shall descend to my said daughters in the manner and form above specified in this section (Section FOURTH)."

There then follows a description of certain tracts of real property in Raleigh, N.C.

If the rule against perpetuities was violated by the foregoing provisions of Montague's will, title to the real property in question would have been vested in his grandchild, Thomas A. Norris, Jr., immediately prior to Norris's death and would now be vested in plaintiff by virtue of Norris's will. If the rule was not violated, title to such property would now be vested in defendants, Montague's great-grandchildren.

The trial court, concluding as a matter of law that the attempted devise of the remainder interest to the testator's great-grandchildren violated the rule against perpetuities, entered judgment that title to the property in question is now vested in plaintiff as Executor under the will of Thomas A. Norris, Jr., subject to the provisions of Norris's will. * * *

PARKER, JUDGE.

The common-law rule against perpetuities has been long recognized and enforced in this jurisdiction, and its application has the continuing sanction of our State Constitution. This rule, which is "not one of construction but a positive mandate of law to be obeyed irrespective of the question of intention" * * * has been stated by our Supreme Court as follows:

"No devise or grant of a future interest in property is valid unless the title thereto must vest, if at all, not later than twenty-one years, plus the period of gestation, after some life or lives in being at the time of the creation of the interest. If there is a possibility such future interest may not vest within the time prescribed, the gift or grant is void". * * *

The devise which B.F. Montague attempted to make in Item Fourth of his will to his great-grandchildren of the remainder interest after the termination of the successive life estates granted to his widow, his daughters, and his grandchildren, clearly violated the rule. As of the date of the testator's death, which in case of wills is the time at which the validity of the limitation is to be ascertained, the possibility existed, at least insofar as the law views the matter, that one or more children might thereafter be born to one or more of the Montague's three surviving daughters. Had this occurred, the life estates which he provided for his grandchildren might well have extended and postponed vesting of the remainder in his great-grand-children to a date beyond the time prescribed by the rule. It is the possibility, not the actuality, of such an occurrence which renders the grant void. As stated by the author of [an American Law Reports annotation], "it should be noted that a remainder to great-grandchildren whose vesting is not limited upon termination of a secondary life estate in a named grandchild, but upon the death of all the creator's grandchildren as a class, is invalid, since other grandchildren might be born after the creation of the future interests and postpone the vesting of the remainder beyond the permitted period."

Appellant here acknowledges the possibility that a grandchild or grandchildren might have been born after Montague's death with the result that vesting of at least portions of the remainder might have been postponed beyond the period permitted by the rule, but seeks to invoke the so-called "Doctrine of Separability" to save the devise to the great-grandchildren in the present case. That doctrine has been stated by the author of the last-cited Annotation as follows:

> "While a class gift may not be split and is either good or bad in toto, it has been held that where a creator makes a gift of remainder to his great-grandchildren following life estates successively in his children and grandchildren in such a manner as to constitute separate and distinct devises or bequests to different classes, which take effect at different times, upon the respective death of the life tenants, and the number of classes or shares is definitely fixed within the period of the rule, although not until after the creator's death, the question of remoteness is to be considered with reference to each share separately. * * * "

As we read Item Fourth of Montague's will, however, we find the doctrine of separability simply not applicable in the present case. Montague did not devise life estate[s] successively to his children and grandchildren "in such a manner as to constitute separate and distinct devises or bequests to different classes, *which take effect at different times, upon the respective death of the life tenants*." (Emphasis added.) Quite to the contrary, he devised all of the property described in Item Fourth of his will, first to his wife for life, then to his three daughters for life and at the death of any of them to the survivors or survivor for life, then, upon the death of the last to survive of his daughters, and still dealing with *all* of his estate, "to the child or children" of his daughters "for and during the natural life or lives of such child or children" (his grandchild or grandchildren), and finally, and still dealing with *one* property interest, "with remainder over to the lawful issue of such grandchild or grandchildren forever." In default of such issue, "the remainder" is devised to Peace Institute. All the way through the testator dealt with only *one* remainder to take effect at *one* time. Though he obviously contemplated the possibility that he might have more than one grandchild, he did not provide any "separate and distinct" devise of separate portions of the remainder interest to the issue of each grandchild to take effect at different times upon the respective death of each grandchild. Nothing in his will indicates any intention that each of his grandchildren should have a separate life estate in a separate share that each such separate share should vest separately at the death of such grandchild in such grandchild's issue. * * *

Notes and Questions

1. Perhaps the following approach will help you work through some of the more common Perpetuities issues. Sometimes it helps to deal from your strength. You know how to identify the present possessory estates and future interests. The Rule Against Perpetuities does not invalidate the following: present possessory estates; future interests held by the grantor; or vested remainders and vested remainders subject to divestment. It can operate to invalidate only: executory interests; contingent remainders; and vested remainders subject to open. So, first begin by identifying the present possessory estate and the future interest(s) created by the conveyance.

As to the future interests to which the Rule can apply, the Rule in its traditional form will invalidate only those interests that will not vest (if at all) within 21 years of a life in being at the time of the conveyance. In its traditional form, it is critical that the analysis stand on the date of the conveyance and look forward to what might happen or what might have happened rather than what actually did happen. How does this perspective from the date of the conveyance work out in the *Norris* case?

As you stand on the date of the conveyance, describe for yourself the event that will cause the future interest to vest or fail to ever vest. First, what will the interest be when it has vested? An executory interest must become a present possessory estate; a contingent remainder must become either a present possessory estate or a vested remainder; a vested remainder subject to open must become either a present possessory estate or a vested remainder. Second, what event will cause that transformation to happen or will mark the point at which that transformation can never happen? For example, does the grantee have to marry? Does someone have to survive the death of another? Does someone have to graduate? Does the owner of the present possessory estate have to stop farming?

The operation of the Rule requires that you identify a "life in being" on the date of the conveyance. The life in being can be anyone who is alive on the date of the conveyance, but you will save yourself time and aggravation if you try to identify only those people whose lives could have some effect on the satisfaction or failure of the condition that must be met in order for the future interest to become vested or to fail to vest forever.

And finally, you must "terminate" the relevant lives in being. Terminate each of the relevant lives in being on the effective date of the conveyance, look 21 years plus nine months forward and ask: Will the future interest at issue either: (1) have vested or (2) is it at that time impossible for that future interest to ever vest? If the future interest instead may still vest (sometime after the perpetuities period), the future interest violates the Rule and, in the Rule's common law form, would be void.

2. *Norris* is an excellent example of one of the major principles of the common law Rule. The Rule, when unadulterated by more recent statutory revisions, does not consider facts as they actually occurred after the conveyance, but rather only facts as they might have occurred. Mr. Montague's will said "grandchildren," and he left only three living children. At the time of the litigation of this case, it was clear that the only grandchild to have been born was Thomas. Looking at the family on the day that Mr. Montague's will became effective (*i.e.*, on the date of his death), however, there might have been additional grandchildren to follow, none of whom were alive on the effective date of the conveyance.

3. Could you have drafted Montague's will so that the gift to Montague's descendants in Thomas' generation would not have violated the Rule? Try this: "then to my grandchild Thomas." Perhaps this doesn't really meet Montague's desire. How about: "then to those of my grandchildren who are living at my death (or at the death of my last living daughter)." Another way to draft around the Rule is to grant a power to a fiduciary to reform the instrument if it proves invalid under the Rule. Another approach is to include a clause that states: "All interests created in this will shall vest no later than twenty-one years after the death of the last to die of me, my wife Jane, and those of my lineal descendants who are living at my death. Upon expiration of this period, all income interests shall terminate and the principal shall be distributed to the persons entitled to receive the income." A final approach is to make sure that you use future interests which are not subject to the Rule. Which are those, and how might you use them?

4. We are currently in a period when judges are likely to try to avoid applying the Rule Against Perpetuities to invalidate a property interest by stretching reasonable interpretations of the conveyance or by limiting the Rule. (More on this point below.) Many years ago, however, judges were more likely to use the Rule actively to overturn "dynastic" gifts. This approach to the Rule resulted in the establishment of some presumptions that may strike us as unrealistic. These include the "unborn widow," the "fertile octogenarian," and the "magic gravel pit." Consider the following examples:

a) To Stephen for life, then to Stephen's widow for life, then to Stephen's children who survive her and their heirs. At the time of the conveyance, Stephen has a life estate. "Stephen's widow" has a contingent remainder in life state. Can you see why this is so? At what point will we know who Stephen's widow is? Her interest does not violate the Rule. The future interest in Stephen's children, however, violates the Rule because of the unborn widow presumption: Stephen's "widow" is not a life in being at the time of the conveyance. Although Stephen may be advanced in years and married to a woman of his own age, it is presumed that he may in fact divorce or be widowed himself and marry a woman who was not yet born on the date of the conveyance. How could you draft around this presumption?

b) To my nieces and nephews for life, and then to their children and their heirs. The future interest in the children violates the Rule because of the fertile octogenarian presumption. Assume that the grantor's parents are still living and in their 80s. The grantor has two siblings, and it is their children for whom he intends the life estate, and it is their children's children who are granted the remainder. The grantor's "nieces and nephews" cannot be lives in being because the grantor's parents, even though in their 80s, are presumed to have children who will be born after the date of the conveyance. It is those children who will bear the "nieces and nephews" in the conveyance.

c) To my son, my gravel pits, to be worked until they are exhausted and then to be sold with the proceeds divided among my issue then living. The gravel pit, in fact, certainly would be exhausted within four years if worked at the current rate. Still, the future interest violates the Rule because, under the presumption of the magic gravel pit, the pit is presumed to have an infinite supply of gravel.

See, W. Barton Leach, Perpetuities in a Nutshell, 51 Harvard L. Rev. 638 (1938). Leach raged against the Rule, and named these three presumptions from application of the Rule by the courts.

PRACTICE PROBLEMS

Identify the present possessory estates and future interests in the problems below. Decide whether any interest violates the common law Rule Against Perpetuities, the Rule in Shelley's Case, or the Doctrine of Worthier Title.

1. Orville to Andy and his heirs so long as the land is farmed; but if it is not farmed to Bonnie and her heirs.

2. Orville to Annie and her heirs so long as the land is farmed.

3. Orville to Arthur and his heirs so long as the land is farmed; but if it is not farmed, to Brooke for life.

4. Orville to Adam for life, then to Adam's children for life, then to Adam's grandchildren who survive their parents.

5. Orville to Arvid for life, then to his widow, and then to his children who survive her. Assume that Arvid is 89 and is married to Bella, his wife of 65 years, and that they have three children.

6. Orville to Amanda for life, then to Amanda's children who survive her.

7. Orville to Abby for life, then to her children who reach the age of 30.

8. Orville to Andre for life, then to Andre's heirs.

9. Orville to Alan for life, then to Orville's heirs.

10. Orville to Alain for life, then to Orville and his heirs.

11.   Orville to Alana and her heirs so long as no development is allowed on the land; but if construction of any building is undertaken, then to the Nature Conservancy, a charitable organization.

NOTE: STATUTORY REFORMS OF THE RULE

The purpose of the Rule Against Perpetuities seems patently clear: it must be animated by an abhorrence of perpetual control of property. So, we think of the Rule as prohibiting "dead hand control" of property, especially land. Our concern is perhaps that an individual should not be able to restrict the use of land in perpetuity because conditions and circumstances change in ways that cannot be anticipated; and, if the restriction by the original grantor is sacrosanct, the land may become useless or at least less than optimally productive. But, then, why don't we have a rule that simply alters restrictions when they actually do become outdated or inefficient, rather than *ab initio*, as the Rule does? If a grantor includes a condition in the conveyance that prohibits the use of electricity on the property or that prohibits selling the property to women, why don't we simply allow the courts to void the condition or restate the condition in a way that better comports with current circumstances or public policy? In fact, we do have that doctrine operating under the name of *cy pres*. Why, then, does the Rule persist at all?

When we look at the Rule itself, we see that it doesn't even refer to restrictions on use or alienation, but rather it refers to the "vesting" of interests. It should perhaps be called the "Rule Against Remote Vesting." Why might we support a policy that forces earlier vesting of interests? One might grant that conditional or contingent interests generally raise the transaction costs in achieving a sale, but does the Rule Against Perpetuities actually respond to that problem?

Perhaps what the Rule Against Perpetuities is actually concerned about is restraining the concentration of wealth in the hands of a few— the so called "dynastic wealth." In an economy in which the primary source of wealth is land, as it was in England when the Rule was established, one might be concerned that landed families might be able to tie up the property in the family for generations and generations with the result that the land may not be put to its best use and, more importantly, that others cannot compete for that wealth and resource by bidding for it. Does the public policy against wealth concentration still apply in the U.S. considering the sharp reductions in the federal estate tax, for example? In addition, our estate law policies rely, in part, on the idea that allowing an owner of property to control that property even beyond death incentivizes economically useful behavior on the part of property owners.

Finally, now that you have learned how to draft around the Rule Against Perpetuities and avoid its [gravel] pitfalls, do you want the Rule abolished? Where is your economic advantage as a licensed professional with valuable, esoteric knowledge if the Rule and others like it fade away? Maybe we just don't have the respect for formality in legal thought or inaccessibility that we used to. Perhaps we have actually gotten too good at drafting around the Rule, so that it has become simply a trap for those represented by less skilled (or average) attorneys.

In any case, forces of change have attacked the Rule Against Perpetuities. We have already commented that judges have shifted from vigilance against remote vesting and dead-hand control toward protection of grantor's intent. They do this, for example, by "naming" the suspect future interest as one not subject to the Rule or by interpreting a restriction in a way that avoids violation. We have already noted that nearly half of the states by statute have abolished the Rule as to trusts by statute. The states have taken other approaches as well.

States have used several models for revision of the Rule. There is substantial variety among the states, in fact. Moreover, these models may exist alongside legislation that abolishes the Rule in the case of trusts alone. We present two approaches: "wait and see" and specific rejection of the presumptions that Professor Leach found so offensive.

The Uniform Statutory Rule Against Perpetuities (USRAP) adopts a wait-and-see approach; and its approach has been adopted by several states. See, California's statute, for example:

California Probate Code § 21205

A nonvested property interest is invalid unless one of the following conditions is satisfied:

(a) When the interest is created, it is certain to vest or terminate no later than 21 years after the death of an individual then alive.

(b) The interest either vests or terminates within 90 years after its creation.

As you can see, for challenges at the effective date of the conveyance, or perhaps as a guide when drafting conveyances, the statute retains the common law Rule. If the interest is invalid under the original Rule, the statute alters the timeframe of the Rule by broadening it to focus on events as they actually occurred. This avoids voiding future interests in cases like *Norris* where the interest would actually have vested in a timely fashion. The period of 90 years was meant to be an approximation of the actual "perpetuities period" in the common law Rule. Of course, "wait and see" creates some of its own ambiguities and problems.

In addition to the alternative 90–year period, the USRAP, and the California Probate Code, also allow for judicial reformation of the offending future interest to allow it to satisfy the ninety-year period. Reformation could include several options, including voiding the future interest, allowing the future interest to vest (including vesting to a present possessory estate) or creating a future interest in the grantor (as grantor future interests are always vested). You can see that this creates some uncertainty in who owns the property, but that uncertainty is deferred for ninety years from the date of the conveyance. The expectation is that most future interests that fail under the common-law Rule because they *might* vest too remotely will, in fact, vest within the ninety years.

A second statutory alteration of the rule goes specifically to the presumptions that appear to defy biology or appear quite unlikely to actually occur. The Illinois statute addresses these presumptions and also creates one more weapon to defeat the common law Rule:

Application of the Rule Against Perpetuities
765 ILCS 305/4

* * *

(b) The period of the rule against perpetuities shall not commence to run in connection with any disposition of property or interest therein, and no instrument shall be regarded as becoming effective for purposes of the rule against perpetuities, and no interest or power shall be deemed to be created for purposes of the rule against perpetuities as long as, by the terms of the instrument, the maker of the instrument has the power to revoke the instrument or to transfer or direct to be transferred to himself the entire legal and equitable wnership of the property or interest therein.

(c) In determining whether an interest violates the rule against perpetuities:

(1) it shall be presumed

(A) that the interest was intended to be valid,

(B) in the case of an interest conditioned upon the probate of a will, the appointment of an executor, administrator or trustee, the completion of the administration of an estate, the payment of debts, the sale or distribution of property, the determination of federal or state tax liabilities or the happening of any administrative contingency, that the contingency must occur, if at all, within the period of the rule against perpetuities, and

(C) where the instrument creates an interest in the "widow," "widower," or "spouse" of another person, that the maker of the instrument intended to refer to a person who was living at the date that the period of the rule against perpetuities commences to run;

(2) where any interest, but for this subparagraph (c)(2), would be invalid because it is made to depend upon any person attaining or failing to attain an age in excess of 21 years, the age specified shall be reduced to 21 years as to every person to whom the age contingency applies;

(3) if, notwithstanding the provisions of subparagraphs (c)(1) of this Section, the validity of any interest depends upon the possibility of the birth or adoption of a child,

(A) no person shall be deemed capable of having a child until he has attained the age of 13 years,

(B) any person who has attained the age of 65 years shall be deemed incapable of having a child,

(C) evidence shall be admissible as to the incapacity of having a child by a living person who has not attained the age of 65 years, and

(D) the possibility of having a child or more remote descendant by adoption shall be disregarded.

How would the California and Illinois statutes change your answer to the Practice Problems, above, in cases where you found that a future interest violated the common law Rule Against Perpetuities?

FINAL REVIEW PROBLEMS

Assume that the Rule in Shelley's Case, the Doctrine of Worthier Title, and the Rule Against Perpetuities apply. For the Rule Against Perpetuities, use both the common law version and the Illinois version. Identify the estate and future interests created in each conveyance first without operation of the rules furthering marketability and then, applying the rules.

1. Oswald to Adams for life, then to Adams's heirs.

2. Oswald to Andres for life, then to Boswell and his heirs, but if Andres dies without children, to Chambers and her heirs.

3. Oswald to Annie and the heirs of her body, then to Bob and his heirs.

4. Oswald to Arthur for life, then to Arthur's children for life.

5. Oswald to Alice when she graduates from veterinary school. (Alice is a first-year veterinary med student).

6. Oswald to Aloysius and his heirs as long as he remains unmarried, then to Bill and his heirs.

7. Oswald to Agatha for life, then to Barbara and her heirs if Agatha dies unmarried.

8. O'Neil to Aman for life, then to Community Hospital so long as it continues to provide charity care.

9. Oswald to Anthony for life, then to Blake and his heirs, but if Blake uses the land for commercial purposes, to Chelsea and her heirs.

10. Oswald to Agnes and her heirs so long as liquor is not served, then to Brad for life.

11. Oswald to Alana and her heirs so long as liquor is not served, then to Barclay and his heirs.

12. Otero to Annunzio and his heirs, but if Annunzio fails to graduate from law school, to Boaz and her heirs.

13. Otero to Aleisha and her heirs upon Aleisha's reaching the age of 21. Aleisha is now two.

14. Otero, in his will: "to my widow for life, then to my children alive at the time of her death and their heirs."

15. Otero, in his will: "to my son Arturo for life, then to Saint Louis University as long as the land is used for student parking. The residue of my estate to the Animal Protective Association and its successors."

16. Otero to Abner, then to Abner's children and their heirs. Abner takes possession of the land and later dies childless and testate; his will devises all of his property to his wife.

17. Otero, by deed in 1997: "My real property in St. Louis to the St. Louis Zoo and its successors, so long as it remains open to the public free of charge." Before he died in 1998, Otero deeded all of his real estate, in fee simple absolute, to the Art Institute of Chicago and its successors.

18. Ochs, in her will, gave her entire estate: "to my son Antonio so long as he lives, then to his wife if she survives him, and then to his children and their heirs."

19. Ochs to Anna for life, then to the first daughter of Anna who reaches 21 and her heirs. At the time of the deed, Anna has two daughters, Bette, who is 20; and Clara, who is 18.

20. Ochs to Alicia for life, then to Bonnie and her heirs, but if Bonnie does not survive Alicia, then to Claire and her heirs. An extra task: After you have identified the interests created by this document, draft two conveyances with the identical condition but using different future interests.

21. Oona to Alexia for life, then to her children and their heirs. Alexia wants to tear down the single-family residence that is on the deeded land and build a multi-unit condominium for well-to-do law students. Her son opposes her plan and will try to stop her. Can he succeed?

22. Onassis to Alpheus for life, then to the heirs of Onassis and their heirs. After the deed is delivered, Onassis dies testate; his will leaves all of his property to the United Way of New York City.

23. O'Brien to Avia for life, then to the children of Avia who reach 30 and their heirs. Avia has one child at the effective date of this instrument. Then, two years later, she has a second child, who dies at the age of six. Then, four years after the death of the second child, she has a third child. The first and third children reach the age of 30. Identify the interests at each event.

24. O'Brien, in his will: "to Atticus for life, then to the children of Atticus who have reached the age of 30 by the time of Atticus's death and their heirs."

25. O'Brien to Abigail for life, then to the grandchildren of Abigail who reach the age of 21 and their heirs.

26. O'Neal to Alfalfa for life, then to Braswell and his heirs if Braswell survives Alfalfa. Subsequently, Braswell loses all of his property to Craig in a poker game.

27. Odell to Ari for life. Ari sells all of his property to Colleen.

CLOSING NOTE

You have shifted between two frames throughout this chapter. One frame asked you to imagine yourself trying to understand a client's desires and carrying them out through careful drafting. The second frame asked you to examine a dispute over a conveyance that took effect before you arrived on the scene. Unlike the conveyances in the first frame, which are still malleable in terms of the language chosen, the conveyances in the second frame are frozen in time as are the events that have triggered the dispute.

Here are some excerpts from a conversation about law-office jurisprudence that relates to your experience. The participants are the late Professor Louis M. Brown, a great teacher of preventive law and founder of the national client-counseling competition, who died in 1996, and one of your authors.*

> Brown: We assume that some alternatives are legally safer than others. There is a jurisprudential foundation for this premise. It lies within a formula which can be diagrammed as FACT—LAW (or legal consequence). There can be no legal consequence save that which rests upon some factual occurrence(s). Change or alter facts and you may modify legal consequences. It does make a difference in legal consequences whether a person does or does not sign on the dotted line. One set of words, rather than another set of words, can make a legal difference in the rights and duties of the parties. Because legal consequences are constructed on facts, preventive law guidance is possible. The helping lawyer seeks to guide the client so as to maximize his rights and minimize his risks * * *.

This is to say that, in litigation, what Professor Brown calls "curative law," the law follows from the "facts of the case." These facts are established before the court is involved. The facts are a premise for the law; they are like the statement of facts in an appellate opinion. They are, to use a word Professor Brown uses in teaching preventive law, *cold*.

In law-office law, the sequence is reversed. The law is the cold premise; the facts follow from the law. *Office lawyers choose the facts* in order to locate and specify the law that will do for the client what the client wants done. Office facts are, to use Professor Brown's word, *hot*.

In another distinction about facts, Professor Brown notes that curative law, because of circumstantial limits on what the judges in the courthouse can do, takes account only of limited sets of facts. It limits

---

* Louis M. Brown and Thomas L. Shaffer, "Toward a Jurisprudence for the Law Office," 17 American Journal of Jurisprudence 125 (1972).

the facts it will consider, for example, through concepts of relevance or reliability that are embodied in the law of evidence. In that sense, the facts in litigation law are often said to be *hard* facts. Office law takes account of context, nuance, and emotion more carefully and more obviously. Office law considers *soft* facts. Professor Brown continues:

> In curative law we seek to determine and manage past facts, and attach the desired legal consequences to them. At this level legal consequences can be attached without any consideration of the client's emotional involvement. In general, the client's total emotional equipment is not usually part of the word formula in codes of law. I believe, though, that the total environment does become involved in the lawyering process. That process includes, but is not limited to, the LAW—FACT formula. An elemental translation of that formula leads to the question—what is the applicable law or legal result? But * * * the answer to that question is often insufficient for lawyering. In earthy terms, the client's questions are: What do I do? What course of action? What decisions must I make, or [what decisions] do you, as my lawyer, make?
>
> In preventive-law practice the LAW—FACT formula provides the legal consequences to a proposed course of action, but does not provide the answer to the ultimate decision, that is, for example, Should the client sign? In litigation practice the lawyer may make or decline to make a prediction of an attainable legal result if his client, or potential client, brings a lawsuit, but the lawyering (and client) decision is whether and when to bring the suit. * * *
>
> Shaffer: The irrational facts—the emotional and feeling facts—may well be the greatest distinction between office lawyering and what you call 'curative law.' In this connection, I find useful your recognition that law-office decision-making is a vastly more complex (and * * * more openly emotional) environment. Three preliminary points should be made about that distinction, though:
>
> First, litigation decisions, especially those we in retrospect regard as historic, have never been confined in conception or consequences to the facts in the record. They have always reflected what Holmes called 'the felt necessity of the time.' And, I think, good legal counselors take the emotional climate of a case into account when they act or advise in reference to probable judicial (or, for that matter, legislative) decisions in the case. * * *
>
> "Second, litigation law (law which comes from the FACT—LAW continuum) is not very useful, and is rarely dispositive, in legal counseling. Part of the reason is that good law-office decision-making comes from a preventive-law stance in the lawyer; and that 'lawyering' stance always takes broader account of human factors than [predicting what courts or legislators may do]. Another part of the reason is that the client who is making a law-office decision is being counseled toward an ability to choose as well as toward choice

itself. The legal counselor is in what our friend Robert S. Redmount calls a *facilitative* posture.*

Finally, the law-office decision depends for its soundness and survival on acceptance and validation in people and in places where factors relevant to litigation either don't count, or don't count enough. An example is a dead [person's] will which depends in its operative phase on the largely emotional consent of family members who take or fail to take under it. The factors relating to judges' law in both of these examples are usually, literally, irrelevant. * * *

Brown: In the practice of preventive law, the lawyering process can be * * * complex. Elementary preventive-law practice appears relatively simple; that is, the lawyer describes (predicts) for a client the legal consequences of a proposed course of action. The lawyer informs a client, about to sign an apartment lease already signed by the landlord, that his client's signature creates, in the usual situation, a legal obligation (to pay rent, etc.) and some legal rights (to occupy the premises, etc.). But a more extended preventive-law practice might be addressed to predictions in a different realm. The preventive-law issues can become predictions as to whether a dispute will likely arise in the future, and if a dispute arises, then a prediction as to the behavior of the parties during that dispute, and a prediction of the legal consequences of that dispute. When we think in terms of potential disputes, we are concerned with only the 'minimizing risks' aspect of preventive-law practice. The practice of 'maximizing rights' complicates the process. It is at this point that the lawyering creativity stretches one's imagination. The issue is not confined to determining which alternative course of action presented by the client for the lawyer's consideration is best calculated to maximize the client's position; but, in addition, whether there is or might be another (as yet unstated) course of action even more appropriate, and which may further improve the client's legal (and practical) position. * * *

* R. Redmount, "Humanistic Law Rev. 98 (1969).
Through Legal Counseling," 2 Conn. L.

Chapter Three

CONCURRENT OWNERSHIP

INTRODUCTION: PROPERTY IN FAMILIES

In Chapter Two our focus was on fragmenting real property ownership on the plane of time–between the present right to possession and the right to possession in the future, perhaps following the expiration of a person's life or perhaps as a result of some condition. In Chapter Three our focus will be on joint ownership by two or more persons not consecutively, but simultaneously or concurrently.

Anglo–American property law has developed forms of collective property ownership for business. It is possible for partners in a business to put the title to their property in a form that will not be affected by the death or defection of a partner. The Uniform Partnership Act provides a form of tenancy in partnership that will accomplish that. The most common form of collective ownership in business planning is ownership of business property in a business corporation, a fictional legal person who neither dies nor defects. Similar forms of ownership have been developed for voluntary and charitable organizations, such as lodges and churches, and even for ownership by communities: The equitable "ownership" of property held in a charitable trust, for example, is in theory in the community. The "ownership" interests of the community, including that the assets be used solely for the purposes established in the trust and that officers fulfill their fiduciary duties to the charitable trust, are enforced by the attorney general of the state.

But property law has not developed a form of collective property ownership for families. There is no moral or conceptual reason we can think of to explain why family ownership of property has not been accommodated in a similar way. (Of course, a family business can be put into partnership or into a "closely held" corporation, but we are thinking of family property, the family home, the family estate in the country, the family farm, as "home" as much as "business".) Our guess is that family ownership has not been so accommodated because the transition of ownership at death has been a convenient time for government to assert control over family property or to impose taxes on it. It could also be that our legal system actually views "family" somewhat skeptically—as in, every family is dysfunctional in its own way (paraphrasing Tolstoy). Attempts by the current owner of family property, to assure continued ownership in the family, have in any case been a major occasion for governmental interference in family life.

It is easier to approximate family ownership in a current generation than it is to approximate family ownership that reaches across generations (as business ownership in a corporation reaches across generations). It is possible to create collective ownership of property, in *married* partners, in the current generation: Marital ownership is the most common instance of concurrent ownership. Lawyers will, of course, try to use forms of marital ownership as a means to family ownership that reaches across generations; we will want to keep an eye on those attempts and on how they work.

It has been possible for centuries for two or more people to own a single tract of land in undivided shares (the *tenancy in common*). Such common ownership can be spread on the plane of time, divided among interests, made subject to conditions, and held in equity as well as in law. It has also been possible to own undivided shares in such a way that the surviving co-owners take the share of the co-owner who dies first (the *joint tenancy*). The common law even developed a form of this collective ownership that it limited to married partners, probably so that the husband could control the wife's interest (the *tenancy by the entirety*). Except for the third form of ownership, these devices were not exclusively for married people, but they have come in modern practice to be used by married people more than in any other personal relationship, and they have come to be the dominant form of ownership of residential and agricultural real estate in the United States. Whatever their history, the tenancy in common, the joint tenancy, and the tenancy by the entirety have become our culture's answer to the family's need to own property as a family. These concurrent, marital forms of property ownership are the subject of the first section in this chapter.

A fourth form of collective ownership, the tenancy in coparcenary, existed in England at early common law where land descended from the ancestors to two or more females in the absence of a male heir. Female heirs in this situation held title to the property jointly as coparceners. The estate in coparcenary was not generally recognized in this country, and it is now obsolete as a separate form of concurrent ownership. Shelton F. Kurtz, MOYNIHAN'S INTRODUCTION TO THE LAW OF REAL PROPERTY, 4th ed. 292–293 (2005).

The subject of the second section in this chapter is the porous nature of ownership by one member of the family: Not all family property is owned collectively. Much of it is still owned by one member of the family. Members of the family other than the owner are likely to exert pressure to have the family's interest in the property recognized despite the name that is put on the land records in the courthouse.

The family's interest is most likely to appear when the current or nominal owner of the property dies. Most likely, inheritance will be to members of the family. Most cultures force inheritance in this way. English and American property law has generally not forced inheritance.

But a disdain for forced inheritance (such as continental legal systems have) does not mean that English law had no way to recognize property claims from members of the family other than the property owner. A man's widow, for example, was not an heir of his real property, in Anglo–American law, until relatively recently. "The heir," from *De Donis* through nineteenth-century English novels, meant the oldest son, or some functional substitute for the oldest son who was in a younger generation. But the widow had a moral (and therefore, ultimately, in some way or other, legal) claim to her husband's property. Even if the culture did not regard her as a partner of her husband, it pretty much had to regard her as a dependent, and she had at least a claim to means of supporting herself during widowhood. The law's response to the claim was the widow's right to *dower*. In Professor Moynihan's definition, "a widow was entitled on the death of her husband to a life estate in one-third of the lands of which he had been seised at any time during the marriage of an estate in fee simple or in fee tail, provided that the estate was one capable of being inherited by issue of the marriage." Sheldon F. Kurtz, MOYNIHAN'S INTRODUCTION TO THE LAW OF REAL PROPERTY, 4th ed. 71 (2005).

The surviving husband was a different case with a similar result. The widower was not his wife's heir, and her family's solicitor had probably arranged things so that her property would go to her children after she and her husband were dead. But the husband, until relatively recently, controlled his wife's property during their lives together. His legal claim to his wife's property, after she died, was probably based on the fact that he had grown accustomed to controlling her property while she was alive—that and the possibility that he might have children to look after. (Of course, he often needed his wife's property in order to support himself: The young Victorian gentleman, according to the novels, had either to marry a rich woman or ruin his whole life and go to work. But a patriarchal culture was not likely to phrase the widower's claim in terms of dependence, even if he was in fact dependent, as—according to the novels—he usually was.) The law's response to his claim was the widower's right to *curtesy*. In Professor Moynihan's definition, curtesy was "a life estate to which the husband was entitled in all lands of which his wife was seised in fee simple or in fee tail at any time during the marriage provided that there was issue born alive capable of inheriting the estate." Sheldon F. Kurtz, MOYNIHAN'S INTRODUCTION TO THE LAW OF REAL PROPERTY, 4th ed. 70 (2005).

Finally, continental community-property theories found their way into American law through the French settlement of Louisiana and Spanish settlements in the Southwest and on the Pacific coast. Spanish law recognizes marriage as a community, and the community as the owner of property earned by the community. The husband controlled the community's property (as the husband in England controlled both the jointly-owned property and his wife's property), but the property was, in theory, half his wife's. A form of this collective marital ownership survives in the nine community-property states and is the basis of modern marital-property proposals in several of the common-law states.

I. FORMS OF CONCURRENT OWNERSHIP

By concurrent ownership, we mean that the holder of an estate in real property is entitled to possession of the land not alone, but simultaneously together with others. All such persons are said to hold title concurrently, or in co-ownership.

Imagine a couple, Frank and Mary Tregrear, who have located and signed a broker's form contract to buy their first home in the suburbs. They have heeded the advice of the newspaper financial columnists—as not every couple does—and have consulted a lawyer for representation in the formalities of purchase. The lawyer is talking to them and she asks: "How do you want to take title?" They looked puzzled, and the lawyer asks, "Whose names do you want on the deed?" And Mary asks: "What do you advise?"

The evident choices are: (i) Mary; (ii) Frank; (iii) Mary and Frank as tenants in common; (iv) Mary and Frank as joint tenants; and, in some (but not all) states, (v) Mary and Frank as tenants by the entirety. If one of the first two forms is chosen, the spouse not mentioned will have claims on the property of the sort we will consider in Section II of this chapter.

A. TENANCY IN COMMON

In modern law, the *basic* form of concurrent ownership is the tenancy in common. It is not the most widely used, but it is the form the law presumes where the words of the deed are not clear. For example: "Oscar to Adelaide and Beatrice and their heirs" and "Oscar to Alan, Bob, and Carl and their heirs" both create a tenancy in common in fee simple absolute. One can also have a tenancy in common in the other freehold estates you just studied in the previous chapter. People ordinarily would not voluntarily elect to take title to real property as tenants in common. They would almost surely elect to form a partnership or other entity. And yet large amounts of property come to be held in tenancy in common. If you consider the estates illustrated by the review problems in Chapter Two, you will understand how property comes to be held by tenants in common. What does it mean to hold title to property in this form of ownership?

In a tenancy in common:

— The parties own in separate undivided shares, which need not be equal fractional shares. Each tenant in common has an equal right to possess and enjoy every part of the property. There are no geographic divisions in ownership. Absent agreement to the contrary, their shares lack boundaries. If A and B are tenants in common, A has an equal right with B to possession of the whole land. Conversely, no one cotenant has the right to exclusive possession of any particular part of the property. Unity of possession, and the abstraction of undivided ownership, are the principal attributes and essential dynamic of the tenancy in common. Each cotenant has the theoretical right to possess the entire property, subject to the concurrent exercise of that same right by other cotenants.

— Each co-owner has a cause of action to have his share, as we lawyers say it, "set off by metes and bounds." That can be done, and almost always is, by agreement; but if the owners do not agree, any one of them can ask a judge to *partition* the property. The judge will appoint commissioners to go to the land and divide it up. The judge has the power to adjust unequal shares by imposing obligations of cash payment, known as *owelty*, to make the shares work out. If the property cannot be divided equally, the judge has the power to order it sold so that the money equivalent of the land can be divided.

— Each cotenant owns a separate property interest. Each cotenant is free, without the permission (and notwithstanding the express objection) of the others, to transfer her interest by deed, or by lease. Each cotenant's interest can be transferred by will or inheritance, or burdened with secured debt. The unsecured creditors of each of them can reach that cotenant's interest for the satisfaction of claims that have been reduced to judgment. If a creditor succeeds to ownership by foreclosure or execution, the creditor then owns as a tenant in common with the other cotenant(s).

— Tenants in common have been treated in the law as a group of owners. Any one of them can get out if he wants to, but, until he does, he consents to being treated as the member of a group. For example, no cotenant has a legal claim on the others for time and expense spent in making improvements. However, if one cotenant makes a profit on the land, from outsiders, the other cotenants have a claim to a share of the profits.

— Absent expression of the grantor's intention to the contrary, the tenancy in common is the presumed form of concurrent ownership in the case of a transfer to two or more unmarried grantees. If there is doubt about what form of concurrent ownership a deed has created, it is a tenancy in common. Most states have statutes to this effect because the common-law presumption favored joint tenancy. If modern owners want to own as joint tenants, or as tenants by the entirety, they probably have to make their intention explicit. If property is conveyed to two or more people, with no statement of how it is to be held, they will hold as tenants in common. (However, in states that recognize the tenancy by the entirety, identification of the concurrent owners as married to one another is probably enough to establish a tenancy by the entirety.)

CHOSAR CORPORATION v. OWENS

Supreme Court of Virginia, 1988.
235 Va. 660, 370 S.E.2d 305.

STEPHENSON, JUSTICE.

The principal questions in this appeal are (1) whether mining of coal owned by cotenants without the consent of all owners constitutes waste and the exclusion of the interests of the nonconsenting owners entitling them to injunctive relief, and (2) if such mining does constitute waste and the exclusion of the nonconsenting owners' interests, whether the consenting coal owners may permit a third party to transport coal from adjoining land through an underground passageway created by such mining, over the objection of the nonconsenting owners.

In this chancery cause, Beulah Owens and others (collectively, Owens) seek to enjoin Chosar Corporation and William H. Drake (collectively, Chosar) from mining coal in which Owens owns an undivided fractional interest and from hauling coal from the land of a third party through an underground passageway created by such mining. The trial court ruled that "the mining of coal by Chosar and its lessees * * *, without the consent of all cotenants, is the commission of waste, the exclusion by [Chosar] of [Owens] from their interest in the property, and an appropriation thereof to [Chosar]." The court also ruled that fewer than all cotenants could not permit the haulage of coal, produced from other lands, through underground passages carved out of the jointly-owned coal. Consequently, the trial court permanently enjoined Chosar from such mining and haulage, ordered an accounting, and referred the cause to a special commissioner. * * *

The relevant facts are undisputed. The coal in controversy lies within a 61–acre tract of land in Dickenson County (the Willis tract). The coal is owned by the heirs and successors in title of Andrew and Crissie Willis (collectively, Willis). At present, approximately 90 persons own undivided interests in the coal.

Approximately 85 percent of the co-owners executed leases transferring to Chosar "all their right, title and interest" in all the merchantable seams of coal on the Willis tract. The leases provided for a royalty that is the greater of two dollars per 2,000 pounds of coal or eight percent of the price obtained from the coal. The leases also granted Chosar the right to transport coal from adjoining lands through underground passageways on the leased premises.

The most valuable coal on the Willis tract is the "Splashdam seam," which is several hundred feet beneath the surface of the land. Chosar subleased the right to mine the Splashdam seam to coal operators at a royalty rate of 14 percent of the selling price.

Because the Splashdam seam does not outcrop on the Willis tract, access for underground mining had to be achieved from other lands. Consequently, Chosar obtained a lease from Pittston Resources, Inc. (Pittston), to mine coal from land owned by Pittston that adjoins the Willis tract. Thus, a portal was established at the outcropping of the Splashdam seam on the Pittston tract, approximately 200 feet from the Willis tract's boundary.

The mining operation proceeded from the portal to the Willis tract, thence through the Willis tract to Pittston's land on the opposite side. Thereafter, coal mined from Pittston's property was transported underground through the passageways on the Willis tract and thence to the surface. The passageways on the Willis tract were created by the mining operation.

Although a cotenant may transfer to another his undivided interest in the common property without the consent of his cotenants * * * nonconsenting cotenants are not bound by an agreement purporting to lease the entire property or any specific portion thereof * * *. A lessee claiming under such a lease acquires rights no greater than those of his lessor. * * * Consequently, our inquiry here necessarily focuses upon the extent of the consenting cotenants' rights in the common coal lands.

We first consider whether Chosar's mining of the coal without the consent of all owners constituted waste. Generally, waste is defined as "[a] destruction or material alteration or deterioration of the freehold, or of the improvements forming a material part thereof, by any person rightfully in possession, but who has not the fee title or the full estate." Black's Law Dictionary 1425 (5th ed. 1979). At common law, a cotenant was not liable to his cotenants for waste. * * * The common law, however, has been changed by statute: "If a tenant in common, joint tenant or parcener commit waste, he shall be liable to his cotenants, jointly or severally, for damages." Code § 55–212. Injured parties also have a remedy at law for waste committed by "any tenant of land * * * while he remains in possession." Code § 55–211.

Notwithstanding these statutory remedies, a court of equity, in a proper case, may grant an injunction to prohibit waste. * * * What constitutes waste sufficient to entitle the injured party to injunctive relief depends upon the circumstances of each particular case. * * * For example, the cutting of timber in some instances may constitute waste, while in other cases it may be a benefit. * * *

In the case of tenants in common, no tenant can change or alter the common property to the injury of his cotenants without their consent. * * * Injunctive relief against a cotenant is proper where the injury is material, continuing, and not adequately remedied in damages. * * *

In the present case, the extraction of coal from the Willis tract is a material and continuing destruction of the very substance of the mineral estate. The consenting cotenants had no right to remove coal from the common property without the consent of Owens. Consequently, the consenting cotenants could not authorize Chosar to mine coal from the property without the consent of the other cotenants. We conclude, therefore, that the trial court correctly ruled that Chosar's mining within the Willis tract constituted the commission of waste. Because continued mining would cause irreparable harm to Owens, we further conclude that the trial court properly enjoined Chosar from committing further waste.

We next consider whether Chosar's mining of the Willis tract excluded the nonconsenting cotenants from their interest in the property. At common law, one cotenant who used the common land exclusively was not required to account to the other cotenants unless his use resulted in an ouster or exclusion of his cotenants. * * * Now, however, an accounting may be had against a cotenant "for receiving more than comes to his just share or proportion." Code § 8.01–31.

In his use of the common property, a cotenant cannot appropriate to himself the entire estate * * * or unilaterally partition the property by appropriating to himself any specific portion of the property. * * * If a cotenant desires partition, he may seek relief under Code § 8.01–81. That section also authorizes courts to compel partition of "mineral rights east and south of the Clinch River."

Significantly, however, courts had no authority to partition mineral rights until 1964.[1] In that year, the General Assembly amended the predecessor to Code § 8.01–81 to permit the partition of mineral rights "east of the Blue Ridge mountains." Acts 1964, c. 167. Subsequently, the General Assembly again amended that section, empowering courts to partition mineral rights "east and south of the Clinch River." Acts 1968, c. 412.

Thus, by negative implication, Code § 8.01–81 prohibits the partitioning of mineral rights west and north of the Clinch River, which is where the mineral rights in the Willis tract are located. If a court has no authority to partition mineral rights west and north of the Clinch River, *a fortiori,* such mineral rights cannot be partitioned without the consent of all cotenants.

In the present case, however, Chosar's conduct of mining operations was such an appropriation of a specific portion of the Splashdam seam, and in effect, a unilateral partitioning of the mineral estate. Thus, we conclude that the trial court correctly ruled that Chosar's mining excluded the nonconsenting cotenants from their interests in the property.

Similarly, the transporting of coal from Pittston's adjoining land through the underground passageway created in the Willis tract by Chosar's mining constitutes an exclusion of the nonconsenting owners'

---

1. In a situation where there is no common-law partition remedy for tenants in common, and no statutes such as Justice Stephenson is about to describe, partition is nonetheless possible when all cotenants agree. Suppose a case in which they *do* agree; even there judicial partition is not available (and hardly seems necessary any-

way). How does a lawyer go about the task, though? Note that, in a case such as this, it is going to be important to show clear title in the records in the courthouse: Third parties are not going to risk investment under conveyances that might be subject to challenge—particularly not in Virginia after this case. (Eds.)

interest in the property. Moreover, the underground passageway is a product of the waste of the estate. Allowing Chosar to use the tunnel to transport coal would permit Chosar to profit from its own wrongdoing. We conclude, therefore, that the trial court properly enjoined Chosar from further haulage. * * *

Affirmed and remanded.

THOMAS, JUSTICE, dissenting.

This is an extremely important property case which, in my opinion, has been wrongly decided by the majority in a decision that could have dire adverse consequences for the Commonwealth. The basic dispute is over the mining of coal. The owners of 85% of the coal in question want to mine. The owners of the remaining 15% of the coal do not want to mine. As the majority acknowledges, because of Code § 8.01–81, the dispute between the owners cannot be resolved by a partition suit. Thus, the owners are locked in battle with no way out. The result of the majority opinion is that the rights of the 15% who do not want to mine have been made paramount to the rights of the 85% who want to mine. Indeed, the principle of the majority opinion is such that if the mineral rights here in dispute were jointly owned by 1,000,000 people and 999,999 of these co-owners wanted to mine, one solitary co-owner could enjoin all mining. The majority's decision is neither required nor justified by existing Virginia law; moreover, it is not sound in principle or logic.

Two issues were presented to the trial court. The first was whether Chosar, the 85% owner of the mineral rights in the Willis tract, committed waste by mining coal from the property. The second was whether Chosar committed a trespass by hauling coal belonging to third parties through tunnels in the Willis tract which had been created by the mining that was claimed to be waste. The trial court ruled against Chosar on both points. * * *

* * *

Chosar has never claimed exclusive right to all the coal from the mine in question. Chosar has always acknowledged the ownership interest of its co-owners. Further, Chosar attempted to leave unmined sufficient coal to represent the interest of the 15% who did not want to mine and Chosar also set up a fund into which it made royalty payments for the benefit of those who had refused to mine. * * * Chosar never contended that it had a right to all the coal and all the proceeds from the sale of the coal. * * *

I would treat the present problem as a case of first impression in the commonwealth and establish a rule that protects the property rights of both the minority and the majority. * * *

* * *

With regard to the issue of trespass and waste, I would consider the totality of the circumstances, including the fact that coal can be enjoyed only through extraction and is valuable only as a result of extraction. * * * Moreover, I would consider the fact that an overwhelming majority of the interest holders want to mine yet are prohibited from partitioning the property. Then I would adopt a rule such as that which is said to be the majority rule regarding extraction of oil and gas: "Under the rule which is applied in the majority of states which have decisions on the point, a cotenant in the fee may enter to explore for and produce oil and gas without consent of his cotenants. *He must, however, account to his cotenants for their proportionate share of production*" (emphasis added). By such rule, in the special class of cases represented by the instant appeal, I would undertake to prevent a tyranny of the minority interest holders. Without such a rule, the majority's interest in otherwise valuable mineral rights could be absolutely destroyed on the whim of one recalcitrant co-owner.

The portion of the majority opinion which concerns the haulage issue does not even address the issue which was presented to this Court. That issue is whether Chosar trespassed upon its own property when it transported a third party's coal through passageways located in the Willis tract. The facts are that the haulage does nothing to damage the mineral estate.

I cannot understand, and the majority does not explain, how a co-owner of property can trespass on his own property simply by moving through that property. The haulage issue does not involve a question of entering the property to commit waste. Hauling coal through tunnels is not the same as removing coal from the property. The theory of trespass in the context of waste is that not even a co-owner of property will be permitted to enter the property to commit waste. In that limited situation, the law says that even the co-owner has no right to be on the property. But where no act of waste is being committed, the co-owner's original rights to enter his property will obtain.

The majority has, by brute force, simply declared that because it was waste to extract coal in the first instance, it is trespass to move through the tunnels created by the original extraction even if no more extraction is being done. I disagree with the first proposition. But even if it were true, the second proposition does not follow from the first. I would reverse the judgment of the trial court on both issues.

Notes and Questions

1. Justice Thomas's moral argument in his dissent depends on the disproportionate power of "one recalcitrant co-owner." Perhaps his argument is that such an arrangement is anti-democratic; if so, it is an argument that might be raised in many property situations. In one sense all of property law is anti-democratic: Property is power and, generally, the more you own the more power you have. Perhaps Justice Thomas only wants to bring the law governing co-ownership of coal fields within that sort of regime.

It is more likely, though, that his argument is that mining coal is a progressive thing to do in southwestern Virginia—that development of this natural resource in that part of the Commonwealth is for the common good. We will evade that interesting issue, to the dismay of both capitalists and environmentalists among our readers, by turning from the appellate reports to the law office.

2.   In law-office property law, the governing morality is not the morality of judges; it is almost always the morality of one's client. For example: Assume our client, Ms. Elizabeth Lupton, owns 500 acres in a more opulent part of Virginia—in the horse country not far from Washington, D.C. She is talking to us about her will; and it is clear that what she wants, more than anything, is to leave our office with the assurance that her horse farm will not be turned into a bedroom subdivision for bureaucrats from the nation's capital. The "objects of her bounty," as we lawyers put it, are five nephews and nieces. They are also her only heirs. All of them except one are urban people who don't have much interest in horses or where horses live.

One niece, Lucy, is different and is of one mind with Ms. Lupton on the preservation of horses in Northern Virginia. If Ms. Lupton's will said "my horse farm to my nephews and nieces," they would hold, after her death, as tenants in common. Development of the land might end up being impeded by Lucy, that "one recalcitrant co-owner," but not for long, since in this case, unlike *Chosar,* partition would be available and four-fifths of the farm could be partitioned, then developed (and the remaining one-fifth would not be much of a horse farm). Tenancy in common will not get what our client wants. Make some alternative suggestions for her, please. In doing so, review in your mind some of the devices we discussed in Chapter Two.

B.   JOINT TENANCY AND TENANCY BY THE ENTIRETY

1.   *Joint Tenancy*

At early common law, rules of construction favored the joint tenancy, because operation of the right of survivorship led eventually and inevitably to the vesting of title in a single person. But courts of equity, in the interests of justice, would reverse the constructional preference to favor tenancy in common. The joint tenancy form of concurrent ownership features a unity of ownership among the joint tenants. Professor Moynihan attributes to Blackstone the traditional notion that joint tenancies must have four unities. They must be created: (1) at the same time, (2) by the same title, (3) with the same possession; and (4) with the same interests. Sheldon F. Kurtz, MOYNIHAN'S, INTRODUCTION TO THE LAW OF REAL PROPERTY, 4th ed. 274 (2005). For example, Owen conveys in one deed the family home to his two daughters, "Ann and Beth, and their heirs." The interest was created 1) at the same time by the use of one deed, 2) by the same title, as both are named in the deed as equal holders, 3) with the same possession, as each has an equal right to possession, and 4) with the same interests, as both have fee simple title.

Modern courts are not often fussy about the law of unities. The unities are invoked, when they are noticed at all, to explain a result the judges reach on other grounds. In any case, shares in joint tenancy are equal:

— The right of survivorship, or *jus accrescendi*, is a major characteristic of joint tenancy and an important distinction from tenancy in common. Upon the death of one joint tenant, the property passes automatically to the other joint tenant(s). Joint tenancy prevails over descent by will and inheritance. That makes it attractive as a will substitute. It is, in American rural legal folklore, the poor man's will. Wife and husband own homes as joint tenants so that when he dies, it will be hers—period. Without her going to a probate judge, or a lawyer, or even to the courthouse. All she needs to establish her ownership are: (i) the deed, which is already recorded in the courthouse, or bank records creating a joint account, or transfer-agent records showing joint ownership of securities; and (ii) evidence of her husband's death, which will also be a matter of public record.

— The other side of that feature is that neither spouse's will disposes of the joint-tenancy house, account, or securities unless the spouse of the testator dies first (in which case the property is not held in joint tenancy when the testator dies).

— Each joint tenant can, though, convey his interest during life. Suppose Ann in our imaginary couple above makes a deed to her friend Carol of her interests in the house. Will Carol have exactly what Ann had (undivided possession with Beth, while both Ann and Beth are both alive, with a chance for full ownership if Ann survives Beth, or nothing if she doesn't)? Answer: No. Ann's deed will *sever* the joint tenancy—that is, convert it into a tenancy in common between Beth and Carol.

Illustration

1) "Owen—Ann & Beth and their heirs as joint tenants and not as tenants in common".

2) "Ann—Carol and her heirs."

Beth & Carol now share as tenants in common. Either can then seek partition and get her interest out by metes and bounds or by sale and division of the proceeds.

At common law, it was not necessary to specify joint tenancy so long as the four unities were present. Modern law, however, requires specific identification of the joint tenancy. Today, while a few states have abolished the survivorship element of joint tenancy, most states have enacted statutes that reverse the common law presumption from joint tenancy to tenancy in common "unless a contrary intention is expressed." Iowa Code Ann. § 557.15, cited in 4 Thompson on Real Property, Thomas Edition (David A. Thomas, ed., 1994). Under the statutes, the grantor must state that joint tenancy is the intended result of a conveyance of concurrent ownership. For example, Owen's deed of the family home to his two daughters should read "Ann and Beth, and their heirs. as joint tenants and not as tenants in common."

The possibility of secret severance is one of the main disadvantages of joint tenancy. Harms v. Sprague, 105 Ill.2d 215, 85 Ill.Dec. 331, 473 N.E.2d 930 (1984) [reproduced in Chapter Five], tells a story about secret severance that illustrates the disadvantage. The case puts us in mind of Garrison Keillor, of "Prairie Home Companion," and the Norwegian bachelor farmers of Lake Woebegone, Minnesota. John and William held their farm as joint tenants. They fell out and John fell in with their neighbor Charlie Sprague. Charlie needed some money but no lender would loan it to him without a guarantor. John said he would be the guarantor for Charlie's loan. But the lenders said they needed collateral from John as guarantor, and John put up the farm: He mortgaged his and William's farm to secure Charlie Sprague's note. Then he moved off the farm and moved in with Charlie. Then he died. Then William found out about the mortgage and went to a lawyer, who brought a quiet-title action joining as defendants both Charlie and the lenders.

The circuit judge said that the mortgage severed the joint tenancy—which pleased the lenders (we trust you understand why). The appellate court reversed and held that the mortgage did not sever the joint tenancy—which pleased William. Why was William pleased?

The Supreme Court of Illinois affirmed and took a firm line on what causes a severance. A mortgage does not. A mortgage is not like a grant of "title." But if John had secretly *deeded* his interest to Charlie Sprague, the joint tenancy would clearly have been severed and Charlie and William would hold the farm as tenants in common.

Unilateral severance by self-conveyance has long been a source of confusion. For example, could John have severed the joint tenancy by deeding his interest to himself? The safer practice and, in some jurisdictions the only effective method, would be for John to have deeded the property first to a strawman, or nominee, who would immediately reconvey the property back to John. Recent decisions have allowed severance of a joint tenancy by unilateral self-conveyance without the need for an intermediary strawman. See, e.g., Taylor v. Canterbury, 92 P.3d 961 (Colo. 2004).

On the question of what constitutes a severance, see also Estate of Phillips v. Nyhus, 124 Wash.2d 80, 874 P.2d 154 (1994), holding that an enforceable contract to sell land by *all* joint tenants did not constitute a severance. Thus, upon the death of one joint tenant, all proceeds of the sale went to the surviving joint tenants. The Supreme Court of Washington observed that jurisdictions with reported cases are almost evenly divided on the question of whether a contract of sale by all joint tenants automatically severs a joint tenancy. In joining the states that find no severance, the Washington court noted that a contract to sell executed by all joint tenants is not inconsistent with the right of survivorship.

While an enforceable contract to sell by *one* joint tenant severs a joint tenant, mere execution of a contract by all joint tenants without evidence of an intent to destroy the right of survivorship does not sever a joint tenancy, the court concluded. Real estate contracts are discussed *infra* in Chapter Five.

In order to prevent the gross injustice of a killer acquiring title to joint tenancy property through right of survivorship, a number of states have "slayer statutes" providing for severance in the event one joint tenant is convicted of the murder of another. See e.g., Cal. Prob. Code § 251 (2005); 755 ILCS 5/2–6 (2005); Iowa Code § 633.535 (2004); MCLA 700.2803(2)(a)(ii)(b) (2005). See also Uniform Probate Code § 2–803(c)(2) (1993).

In the absence of such a statute, courts have invoked their equity power to deny the right of survivorship when one joint tenant murders another. See, e.g., *Lakatos v. Estate of Billotti*, 203 W.Va. 553, 509 S.E.2d 594 (1998):

> "Even in the complex and sophisticated world of modern law, we still treasure and revere our ancient equitable maxims. These principles of law became equitable maxims because the simple, immutable truths which they contain are so basically and universally fair that they are without dispute obvious to all.... [T]he old equitable maxim *nemo ex suo delicto meliorem suam conditionem facere potest*, which we commonly state as no man should profit from his own wrong, but which literally means no one can make his condition better by his own misdeed, supports the conclusion we reach today."

For a description of the approaches used by courts in other states, see *Duncan v. Vassaur*, 550 P.2d 929, 932 (Okl. 1976). In view of the extent of joint tenancy property held by married couples, the amount of attention paid by courts and legislators to the joint tenant as killer is a tragic commentary.

WILLIAMS v. STUDSTILL

Supreme Court of Georgia, 1983.
251 Ga. 466, 306 S.E.2d 633.

HILL, CHIEF JUSTICE.

From revolutionary times until 1976, the law was that joint tenancy as it existed at common law[3] was abolished in this state. * * *[4] This case

---

3. At common law an estate in joint tenancy, with right of survivorship, was created in any case where land was granted to two or more persons. The creation of the estate in two or more persons, without more, carried with it the right of survivorship. * * * If a joint tenant conveyed his interest to another, the joint tenancy was severed and converted to a tenancy in common and the right of survivorship was defeated by the severance. * * *

4. In 1976, the General Assembly provided that a true joint tenancy could exist in Georgia: "(a) Deeds and other instruments of title, including any instrument in which one person conveys to himself and one or more other persons, any instrument in which two or more persons convey to themselves or to themselves and another or others, and wills taking effect after January 1, 1977, may create a joint interest with involves an attempt to create a joint tenancy by will in 1970. The trial court held that a joint tenancy was created, but was destroyed by severance. This appeal followed.

Alice C. Studstill died in 1970, possessed of 750 acres of land in Dodge County, Georgia, which she devised as follows: "I give, bequeath and devise that track of land known as the Daniel Mill Pond Place * * * containing approximately 750 acres, to my children, James H. Studstill and Mary Ella S. Studstill [now Williams], *as joint tenants and not as tenants in common and to the survivor of them in fee simple.*" (Emphasis supplied.) * * *

In 1980, Mary Ella S. Studstill Williams conveyed her interest to her nephew, James Arthur Williams, reserving a life estate and timber rights to herself. In June, 1982, James H. Studstill died testate leaving his widow, Louise, as his executrix and sole heir. In her suit against Mary Ella and James A. Williams, Louise claims a one-half interest in the property.

Louise contends that under the case law, a joint tenancy could be expressly created before the 1976 statute, that Mary Ella's deed to James severed the four unities required of a joint tenancy and created a tenancy in common, and that thereafter upon her husband's death, she inherited his interest in the tenancy in common. Mary Ella and James contend that the case law prior to the 1976 statute clearly establishes that although joint tenancies, as such, were abolished, the creation of a right of survivorship is not prohibited, and that the right of survivorship is enforceable where expressly created and is not destroyed by severance. The trial court found that the joint tenancy was converted into a tenancy in common by virtue of severance and found in favor of Louise. * * *

[W]herever an instrument creates an estate which at common law would be held to be a joint tenancy, in this State the instrument would be held to take effect as to all its terms, except so far as it provided by implication for survivorship among the tenants, and such tenants would be held to occupy to each other, so far as this question is concerned, the relation of tenants in common. While the doctrine of survivorship as applied to joint tenancies has been distinctly abolished and does not exist in this State, there is no law of this State that we are aware of which prevents parties to a contract, or a testator in his will, from expressly providing that an interest in property shall be dependent upon survivorship. Of course all presumptions are against such an intention; but where the contract or will provides, either in express terms or by necessary implication, that the doctrine of survivorship shall be recog-

survivorship in two or more persons. Any instrument of title in favor of two or more persons shall be construed to create interests in common without survivorship between or among the owners unless the instrument expressly refers to the takers as 'joint tenants,' 'joint tenants and not as tenants in common,' or 'joint tenants with survivorship' or as taking 'jointly with sur-

vivorship.' *Any instrument using one of the forms of expression referred to in the preceding sentence or language essentially the same as one of these forms of expression shall create a joint tenancy estate or interest that may be severed as to the interest of any owner by his lifetime transfer of all or a part of his interest."* * * *

nized, we know of no reason why a provision in the contract or will dependent upon such doctrine may not become operative under the laws of this State. * * * At common law an estate in joint tenancy, with the incident of survivorship, was created in any case where lands or tenements were granted to two or more persons, to be held in fee simple, fee tail, for life, for years, or at will. The mere creation of the estate in two or more persons, without more, drew to it the incident of survivorship. * * * In Georgia the mere creation of the estate in two or more persons never draws to it survivorship as an incident, and the presumption is in all cases that survivorship was not intended. But where by express terms or necessary implication a survivorship is provided for, the law of Georgia allows it to exist. * * *

In his article entitled "Joint Tenancy in Georgia," 3 Ga.St.Bar J. 29 (1966), William H. Agnor * * * said * * *: "All that was suggested * * * was that a right of survivorship could be created. This meant that property, real or personal, could be transferred to A and B so that they would hold as tenants in common until one of them died and at that time the survivor would take a fee simple. They held life estates and each of them had a contingent remainder interest in fee simple. Specifically, they held cross, alternative, contingent remainders. Neither A nor B acting alone could defeat the contingent remainder held by the other." * * *

Despite the presumption to the contrary, Alice C. Studstill clearly intended by the language in her will to create a right of survivorship in her son James and her daughter Mary Ella, and we so hold. * * *

Although a right of survivorship created by contract or by will was recognized, under the Georgia law at the time this will was executed, the joint tenancy with its unity of time, title, interest and possession had long been abolished in this state. * * * Thus, the doctrine of severance also had no place in our law at the time that the interests of these parties were created. * * * As Agnor observed (above) "Neither A [Mary Ella] nor B [James Studstill] acting alone could defeat the contingent remainder held by the other." We decline to engraft the doctrine of severance into pre–1976 deeds and wills as we find the result reached here to be consistent with the testator's intent. The trial court erred in holding otherwise.

Judgment reversed.

Notes and Questions

1. The reversal of the presumption from the common law favorite (joint tenancy) to the modern favorite (tenancy in common) can cause problems for unwary conveyancers, as the *Studstill* case illustrates. Suppose instead, Alice Studstill had conveyed her land to her children "as joint tenants and not as tenants in common"? Under a Virginia statute requiring that the intent to create a right of survivorship "manifestly appears from the tenor of the instrument," would Alice's language have created a joint

tenancy? *See* Hoover v. Smith, 248 Va. 6, 444 S.E.2d 546 (Va. 1994) (this language did not clearly manifest intent to create an estate with survivorship). What language was missing?

2. Michigan case law also makes the distinction between; (i) a joint tenancy; and (ii) "a joint life estate with indestructible survivorship." In one of the 1988 Michigan bar examinations, the examiners put this problem to applicants:

> Grant, owner of Goldacre, Irons, Michigan, in 1981, deeded Goldacre to his unmarried adult daughters, Amy and Betty, by a deed which described the grantees as "my daughters Amy and Betty, jointly, with the right of survivorship." Goldacre is an apartment building, which at all relevant times has been fully rented and well-run by an on-site manager. After Grant deeded to Amy and Betty, net rental income was simply divided evenly and paid in equal shares to Amy and to Betty. This continued until 1986 when Amy deeded "my interest in Goldacre" to her favorite nephew, Norman. Thereafter, net rent distributions, which had been paid to Amy, were paid to Norman.

> In late 1987, Betty, a Michigan resident, died, willing her entire estate to Environmental Awareness, a recognized charitable organization. Amy survived. Who now owns what interest in Goldacre? Discuss and decide.

3. Another example: One of us was once asked to talk to a "Parents Without Partners" meeting, about wills. (A not infrequent request made of lawyers is to speak to meetings of clubs and church organizations about property-law matters—more often than not about making wills. Lawyers have always been generous about giving their time in the community in this way—no doubt, usually, for reasons attributable to civic virtue, although less altruistic reasons may occur to you.) After the talk, a member of the audience came up (a frequent occurrence on such occasions), possibly for some free legal advice, but, for all that appeared, in order to teach this lawyer something he had not learned in law school.

This man said he was a widower and had one child, an 18–year–old son who had recently graduated from high school. The man said he owned his house now; it had been held in a tenancy by entirety until his wife died two years before the club's meeting. And he had several thousand dollars in a bank account, which had been "held jointly" before his wife died. He had, he said, just a month before, made it unnecessary to see a lawyer about a will. How had he done that? He had "put the boy's name on everything." He had, as the conversation then showed, placed his savings in a joint bank account ("JTWROS," father and son) and filled out and signed a dime-store form deed that put the house in joint tenancy. The lawyer (one of us) nodded and asked how the son was doing. (There was no malice in this question; the lawyer was just trying to change the subject.) The father said, "Just fine. He joined the Marines. He is in basic training at Camp Pendleton [San Diego], California."

Please evaluate what this parent did.

4. Under the terms of O's will, Blackacre is devised "to A and B, and their heirs, as joint tenants with right of survivorship, but if the property is ever used for rock concerts, then to the Red Cross." One year after O's

death, A dies intestate. C is A's sole heir. One year after A's death, B dies testate. B's will leaves all of his property to the Salvation Army. One year after B's death, the property is the site of a Pink Floyd farewell concert. What is the status of title to Blackacre?

5.   Under the terms of O's will, Blackacre is devised to A, B and C, in fee simple absolute, as joint tenants with right of survivorship. One year after O's death, A conveys his interest in Blackacre to D. The following year, B dies intestate, leaving H as his sole heir. What is the status of title to Blackacre? Suppose that instead of dying intestate, B died with a will leaving all of his property to H. Would your answer be the same? Why is A's conveyance effective to sever the joint tenancy with right of survivorship, but B's will is not? Are not they both expressions of the grantor's intentions with respect to his interest in the land? Why is one entitled to be credited and the other not?

6.   Under the terms of O's will, Greenacre is devised to A, B and C, in fee simple absolute, as joint tenants with right of survivorship. One year after O's death, A conveys all of his interest in Greenacre to B. Thereafter, B dies testate, leaving all of his property to D. What is the status of title to Greenacre?

2.   *Tenancy by the Entirety*

The *tenancy by the entirety* may be understood as an unseverable joint tenancy with right of survivorship that can only be held by married persons. As with a joint tenancy, the four unities are required to create a tenancy by the entirety. Additionally, the parties must be married to one another at the time they take title. The identification of the concurrent owners as married to one another in the conveyance is generally sufficient to establish the tenancy by the entirety.

This form of concurrent ownership is not severable except by divorce. Generally, divorce settlements indicate what will become of the property, but if not, the property will, depending on the jurisdiction, become either a tenancy in common or a joint tenancy with right of survivorship so long as the parties do nothing else to destroy the four unities.

The feature of unseverability except by divorce has its advantages in those states that recognize the common-law tenancy by the entirety (and most do not): Suppose, for example, that Frank and Mary may be able to take title in an old-fashioned tenancy by the entirety. Suppose Mary is a director of a public corporation. Lawsuits against directors are beginning to proliferate: lawsuits that might leave her with million-dollar personal liabilities that could be executed on their home. How would you suggest the Tregrears take title to their house?

Would joint tenancy serve the clients as well as tenancy by the entirety?

Can the Tregrears protect themselves from liabilities to other creditors—furniture companies, for example, or plumbers and garbage collectors?

SCHWAB v. KRAUSS

Supreme Court of New York, Appellate Division, 1991.
165 A.D.2d 214, 566 N.Y.S.2d 974.

LEVINE, JUSTICE.

In July 1984, defendant obtained a judgment in the amount of $36,893 against Allen Abrahams in Supreme Court, New York County. Some three months later, that judgment was docketed in Rockland County where Abrahams and his wife, Helen Abrahams, owned real property as tenants by the entirety. Subsequently, in May 1985, the Abrahamses filed a joint petition in bankruptcy; however, Allen Abrahams' debt to defendant was not discharged during the bankruptcy proceeding.

While in bankruptcy, the Abrahamses, in December 1986, attempted to sell their Rockland County property to plaintiffs without the consent of the trustee in bankruptcy. Plaintiffs concede on this appeal that the deed they received was void. The following November Allen Abrahams died, and in March 1988 plaintiffs obtained a second deed to the Rockland County property from Helen Abrahams' trustee in bankruptcy in exchange for an additional $10,000.

In April 1988, defendant sought to execute his previously acquired judgment lien on the property purchased by plaintiffs. Plaintiffs then commenced the instant action seeking a judgment declaring that they are the lawful owners of the property free of defendant's lien. Defendant counterclaimed for dismissal of the complaint and enforcement of his judgment. Plaintiffs then moved for summary judgment. Supreme Court denied that motion and granted defendant summary judgment dismissing the complaint. Upon reargument, Supreme Court reversed its initial decision and granted summary judgment in favor of plaintiffs, concluding that the tenancy by the entirety survived the filing of the joint petition and that, upon Allen Abrahams' death, Helen Abrahams' interest in the property held by the trustee ripened into a fee absolute free from defendant's lien. This appeal by defendant followed.

Defendant's sole contention on this appeal is that the Abrahamses' filing of a joint bankruptcy petition and the resulting transfer into the bankruptcy estate of the real property held by them as tenants by the entirety effected a termination of the entireties estate. We disagree. When a husband and wife in this State take title to real property as tenants by the entirety, each spouse acquires an undivided one-half interest in the property with the right of survivorship, which right cannot be destroyed without the consent of both spouses. * * * Although either spouse may mortgage or convey his or her own interest in the tenancy, such act will not impair the nonconsenting spouse's survivorship interest. * * *

Here, upon the Abrahamses' filing of the joint bankruptcy petition pursuant to 11 USC § 302, the respective interest of each spouse was effectively transferred into his or her individual bankruptcy estate. * * * Despite defendant's assertion to the contrary, we cannot conclude that these transfers by way of the joint petition had the same effect as a joint consensual conveyance of the property, which clearly would have terminated the entireties estate. * * * The purpose of the joint bankruptcy petition is merely to ease administration and, in the absence of an order from the Bankruptcy Court consolidating the Abrahamses' estates * * * such estates existed separately in the hands of the trustee. * * * Thus, each estate contained what was essentially a survivorship interest. Following Allen Abrahams' death, the survivorship interest contained in Helen Abrahams' estate ripened into a fee interest by operation of law. * * * Consequently, defendant's lien, which was valid only as against Allen Abrahams' interest in the entireties estate, was extinguished along with his debtor's interest in the property and plaintiffs took title to the property from the trustee free and clear of that lien. Accordingly, Supreme Court was correct in granting summary judgment in favor of plaintiffs.

Order and judgment affirmed, with costs.

Notes

1. American states have varied the rigors of the common-law tenancy by the entirety. The most common reason for doing so is the effect on the estate of 19th-century statutes permitting married women to own property, make wills, enter into contracts, etc. All states adopted such legislation, commonly called married-women's property acts; but very few of these statutes addressed the effect of the reform on the tenancy by the entirety. The Supreme Court of Hawaii, in its opinion in Sawada v. Endo, 57 Hawaii 608, 561 P.2d 1291 (1977), concluded that 19 states at that time preserved the tenancy by the entirety. These included Hawaii, and in Hawaii, as is usually the case, the married-women's property act did not say what effect the statutory removal of common-law disabilities was to have on the tenancy by the entirety. In the *Sawada* case, as is typical, a creditor of one spouse was attempting to execute a judgment against that spouse on entireties property. The court divided the states into four groups on the question of whether a creditor can do that:

"In the Group I states (Massachusetts, Michigan, and North Carolina) the estate is essentially the common law tenancy by the entireties, unaffected by the Married Women's Property Acts. As at common law, the possession and profits of the estate are subject to the husband's exclusive dominion and control. * * * [A]s at common law, the *husband* may convey the entire estate subject only to the possibility that the wife may become entitled to the whole estate upon surviving him. * * * As at common law, the obverse as to the wife does not hold true. * * * In [some of the Group I states] the use and income from the estate is not subject to levy during the marriage for the separate debts of either spouse.

"In the Group II states (Alaska, Arkansas, New Jersey, New York, and Oregon) the interests of the debtor spouse in the estate may be sold or levied upon for his or her separate debts, subject to the other spouse's contingent right of survivorship. * * * Alaska, which has been added to this group, has provided by statute that the interest of a debtor spouse in any type of estate, except a homestead[5] as defined and held in tenancy by the entirety, shall be subject to his or her separate debts. * * *

"In the Group III jurisdictions (Delaware, District of Columbia, Florida, Indiana, Maryland, Missouri, Pennsylvania, Rhode Island, Vermont, Virginia, and Wyoming) an attempted conveyance by either spouse is wholly void, and the estate may not be subjected to the separate debts of one spouse only. * * *

"In Group IV, the two states of Kentucky and Tennessee hold that the contingent right of survivorship appertaining to either spouse is separately alienable by him and attachable by his creditors during the marriage. * * * The use and profits, however, may neither be alienated nor attached during coverture."

The judges in Hawaii decided to join Group III: "[T]he interest of a husband or a wife in an estate by the entireties is not subject to the claims of his or her individual creditors during the joint lives of the spouses." 561 P.2d at 1295.

In those few Group I states in which, according to the *Sawada* court's opinion, the husband has exclusive control, the equal-protection clause of the fourteenth amendment probably requires a change in state law that makes the spouses equal—so that, for example, the spouses have equal control of the property while both are alive. That will not mean, though, that the creditors of one spouse can reach the entireties property; the *Sawada* court did not address the question of control under the equal-protection clause.

2. In one of the 1986 bar examinations, the Michigan examiners put this question:

In 1978 valuable vacant lakefront land in Michigan was deeded to "Joe and Ann, husband and wife, as tenants by the entireties." The grantor thought Joe and Ann were married, but they never were, and knew they weren't. Joe and Ann lived together until 1980, then parted, unable to agree as to what to do about the land, except that each would pay half the property taxes.

This arrangement continued until 1985, and the land grew increasingly valuable. A developer, Don, approached Joe about buying it for a high price. Joe said, "I'll sell you my half, but you'll have to deal with Ann about hers." Don agreed, and paid Joe well for a deed conveying to Don "my (Joe's) interest" in the land. A few weeks later, before Don

---

5. "Homestead rights" are statutory. They make certain property, or a certain amount of property value, immune from creditors. They often require that the property be part of a family home and that the family live in it; the property interest protected is usually an interest held for a family, but is not necessarily a marital interest; the statutes do not require that the owner be married. The statutory exemption in Alaska was unusual in the way it combined the homestead concept with the tenancy by the entirety. See the next note, on similar and more recent legislation in Massachusetts. (Eds.)

had approached Ann, Joe was killed in an automobile accident. When Don soon after contacted Ann and offered to buy her half, he learned that Ann claims to own the entire interest in the land. Don, of course, insists that *he* owns an undivided half bought from Joe.

(a) What are the four possible types of tenancies which might be argued by the parties?

(b) Discuss the effects on the parties.

(c) What is the probable result under Michigan law?

3. Alexander A. Bove, Jr., a Boston lawyer who writes about property-law matters in a weekly column in the Boston Globe, compared, in one of his columns (May 19, 1988), the relative protection afforded in his state by entireties ownership and a statutory homestead right (one that resembles homestead rights in other jurisdictions):

"The declaration of homestead is relatively simple and can be made on a principal residence by anyone with a spouse and/or children. It is a simple, one-page sworn statement by either of the spouses declaring a homestead in their principal residence and recorded at the registry of deeds. The declaration protects up to $100,000 of equity in the house from a creditor's attack.

"In addition to making a homestead declaration, a couple could hold their house under a 'new' tenancy by the entirety, one where the deed creating the tenancy is dated after Feb. 10, 1980. This prevents a creditor of either spouse from having the house sold. * * *

"In 1979 Massachusetts passed a law that exempts a couple's principal residence from seizure and sale by a creditor of either spouse. The non-debtor spouse must continue to occupy the property as the principal residence and the residency held under a tenancy by the entirety created after Feb. 10, 1980.

"The creditor protection, however, does not excuse a couple from paying on their mortgage, nor does it protect them or a dependent family member against debts for 'necessaries': food, clothing, medical costs.

"The protection does not extend to creditors of both spouses for the same debt, such as where they are jointly liable for income taxes.

"The typical debt that would be protected might be where the husband made a bad business decision and was sued by a customer for damages, or where he injured someone in an auto accident and was sued for personal injuries. In either case, if the husband's house were held under a qualified tenancy by the entirety, neither the customer nor the injured party could reach the house, even though each had a valid claim.

"If the husband has no other assets, therefore, the customer and the injured party may simply be out of luck, since the statute prohibits a creditor from forcing a sale of the house.

"All of this has been relatively clear. The unanswered question was: Even though a creditor could not force a sale of the house, could he place an attachment on it, thereby preventing the couple from disposing of the house or remortgaging it without paying off the creditor? If this were so, just how protective is the law that protects the house?

"Not that protective, says the Massachusetts Supreme Judicial Court. Although a couple's house may not be sold by a creditor, it may definitely be attached.

"In the deciding case, the wife, Maureen P., was involved in an automobile accident and was sued by the injured party. In the process, the injured party's lawyer sought to attach Maureen's house. Maureen's husband objected to the attachment, pointing to the Massachusetts law that prevented a seizure and execution (sale) of their residence, which was held under a 'new' tenancy by the entirety.

"In upholding the creditor's right to attach Maureen's house, however, the court said the law was designed only to protect the couple's right to continued possession of the house, and allowing a creditor to place an attachment on it did not upset this right. Therefore, Maureen and her husband could still live in the house, even though it had been legally attached. * * *

"Although a creditor can attach your house so you won't be able to sell it or refinance it, the decision does not mean your enjoyment and occupancy will be otherwise affected: a forced sale by a creditor is still prohibited while you live there.

"Unfortunately, this is not much consolation, since the attachment can remain on the house for 20 years or more after the judgment. Aside from winning the lawsuit or settling with the creditor, therefore, it appears your only hope in such a case is to survive the debtor spouse, but this is difficult to plan, in most cases.

"Previously Massachusetts law of tenancy by the entirety followed the antiquated common law rule that the husband was entitled to sole possession of the property, plus all the rents, if any, and the wife had nothing more than a survivorship right. A creditor of the husband, therefore, could conceivably acquire the right to occupy and rent the property to satisfy the husband's debt.

"For a time there was some confusion as to whether the special protection from creditors applied to all tenancies by the entirety or just to those created on or after Feb. 11, 1980, the effective date of the new law. After all, there were many thousands of Massachusetts couples who held their house under a tenancy by the entirety created long before the law was enacted, and if the protection did not extend to them, it might be possible for a creditor of the husband to have the couple evicted from their own house. This confusion and concern lasted a few years, until February 1984, when the Massachusetts Supreme Judicial Court decided the issue.

"In that case, a homeowner engaged a contractor, who, although already paid for the job, decided not to finish it. The homeowner sued the contractor and got a judgment against him for about $6,000, yet the contractor still stubbornly refused to pay.

"It so happened the contractor and his spouse owned their house under a tenancy by the entirety, and that title was taken before enactment of the 1979 law. Donald Orkin, the attorney for the home-owner, pursued the matter in Housing Court and subsequently got a sheriff to sell the contractor's house to satisfy the judgment against the contractor/husband.

"Despite this decision, however, there was apparently still some concern on the part of the Housing Court judge as to the confusion between the old and new tenancy by the entirety. Therefore, he asked the Supreme Judicial Court to consider it.

"The court held simply that tenancies by the entirety created before Feb. 11, 1980, were governed by the old law in such cases. * * * [T]he husband had sole right to possession and rents and, therefore, a judg-ment creditor of the husband could have the property sold. A principal residence held under a tenancy by the entirety created on or after Feb. 11, 1980, would be exempt from seizure and sale. * * *

"So what do you do if you already own your house under an old tenancy by the entirety (created before Feb. 11, 1980) and you want creditor protection as a new tenancy by the entirety? You must create a new tenancy. This is done by a transfer from you and your spouse to a straw (a third party who has no true interest in the property, but who merely acts as a go-between, since spouses cannot transfer to them-selves), and the straw would immediately re-transfer the property back to the two of you as tenants by the entirety. * * * * "

UNITED STATES v. CRAFT

Supreme Court of the United States, 2002.
535 U.S. 274, 122 S.Ct. 1414, 152 L.Ed.2d 437.

JUSTICE O'CONNOR delivered the opinion of the Court.

This case raises the question whether a tenant by the entirety possesses "property" or "rights to property" to which a federal tax lien may attach. 26 U.S.C. § 6321. Relying on the state law fiction that a tenant by the entirety has no separate interest in entireties property, the United States Court of Appeals for the Sixth Circuit held that such property is exempt from the tax lien. We conclude that, despite the fiction, each tenant possesses individual rights in the estate sufficient to constitute "property" or "rights to property" for the purposes of the lien, and reverse the judgment of the Court of Appeals.

I

In 1988, the Internal Revenue Service (IRS) assessed $482,446 in unpaid income tax liabilities against Don Craft, the husband of respon-dent Sandra L. Craft, for failure to file federal income tax returns for the years 1979 through 1986. When he failed to pay, a federal tax lien attached to "all property and rights to property, whether real or person-al, belonging to" him. 26 U.S.C. § 6321.

At the time the lien attached, respondent and her husband owned a piece of real property in Grand Rapids, Michigan, as tenants by the entirety. After notice of the lien was filed, they jointly executed a quitclaim deed purporting to transfer the husband's interest in the property to respondent for one dollar. When respondent attempted to sell the property a few years later, a title search revealed the lien. The IRS agreed to release the lien and allow the sale with the stipulation that half of the net proceeds be held in escrow pending determination of the Government's interest in the property.

Respondent brought this action to quiet title to the escrowed proceeds. The Government claimed that its lien had attached to the husband's interest in the tenancy by the entirety. The District Court granted the Government's motion for summary judgment, holding that the federal tax lien attached at the moment of the transfer to respondent, which terminated the tenancy by the entirety and entitled the Government to one-half of the value of the property. Both parties appealed. The Sixth Circuit held that the tax lien did not attach to the property because under Michigan state law, the husband had no separate interest in property held as a tenant by the entirety. * * *

* * *

We granted certiorari to consider the Government's claim that respondent's husband had a separate interest in the entireties property to which the federal tax lien attached.

II

Whether the interests of respondent's husband in the property he held as a tenant by the entirety constitutes "property and rights to property" for the purposes of the federal tax lien statute, 26 U.S.C. § 6321, is ultimately a question of federal law. The answer to this federal question, however, largely depends upon state law. The federal tax lien statute itself "creates no property rights but merely attaches consequences, federally defined, to rights created under state law." [   ] Accordingly, "[w]e look initially to state law to determine what rights the taxpayer has in the property the Government seeks to reach, then to federal law to determine whether the taxpayer's state-delineated rights qualify as 'property' or 'rights to property' within the compass of the federal tax lien legislation." [   ]

A common idiom describes property as a "bundle of sticks"—a collection of individual rights which, in certain combinations, constitute property. [   ] State law determines only which sticks are in a person's bundle. Whether those sticks qualify as "property" for purposes of the federal tax lien statute is a question of federal law.

In looking to state law, we must be careful to consider the substance of the rights state law provides, not merely the labels the State gives these rights or the conclusions it draws from them. Such state law labels are irrelevant to the federal question of which bundles of rights constitute property that may be attached by a federal tax lien. In *Drye v. United States,* we considered a situation where state law allowed an heir subject to a federal tax lien to disclaim his interest in the estate. [528

U.S. 49 (1999)] The state law also provided that such a disclaimer would "creat[e] the legal fiction" that the heir had predeceased the decedent and would correspondingly be deemed to have had no property interest in the estate. Id., at 53. We unanimously held that this state law fiction did not control the federal question and looked instead to the realities of the heir's interest. We concluded that, despite the State's characterization, the heir possessed a "right to property" in the estate—the right to accept the inheritance or pass it along to another—to which the federal lien could attach. Id., at 59–61.

III

We turn first to the question of what rights respondent's husband had in the entireties property by virtue of state law. In order to understand these rights, the tenancy by the entirety must first be placed in some context.

* * *

A tenancy by the entirety is a unique sort of concurrent ownership that can only exist between married persons. * * * Because of the common-law fiction that the husband and wife were one person at law (that person, practically speaking, was the husband * * *), Blackstone did not characterize the tenancy by the entirety as a form of concurrent ownership at all. Instead, he thought that entireties property was a form of single ownership by the marital unity. * * * Neither spouse was considered to own any individual interest in the estate; rather, it belonged to the couple.

Like joint tenants, tenants by the entirety enjoy the right of survivorship. Also like a joint tenancy, unilateral alienation of a spouse's interest in entireties property is typically not possible without severance. Unlike joint tenancies, however, tenancies by the entirety cannot easily be severed unilaterally. * * * Typically, severance requires the consent of both spouses * * * or the ending of the marriage in divorce * * *. At common law, all of the other rights associated with the entireties property belonged to the husband: as the head of the household, he could control the use of the property and the exclusion of others from it and enjoy all of the income produced from it. * * *. The husband's control of the property was so extensive that, despite the rules on alienation, the common law eventually provided that he could unilaterally alienate entireties property without severance subject only to the wife's survivorship interest.

With the passage of the Married Women's Property Acts in the late 19th century granting women distinct rights with respect to marital property, most States either abolished the tenancy by the entirety or altered it significantly. * * * Michigan's version of the estate is typical of the modern tenancy by the entirety. Following Blackstone, Michigan characterizes its tenancy by the entirety as creating no individual rights whatsoever: "It is well settled under the law of this State that one tenant by the entirety has no interest separable from that of the other. . . . Each is vested with an entire title." [   ] And yet, in Michigan, each tenant by the entirety possesses the right of survivorship. * * * Each spouse—the wife as well as the husband—may also use the property, exclude third parties from it, and receive an equal share of the income produced by it. * * * Neither spouse may unilaterally alienate or encumber the property, [   ] although this may be accomplished with mutual consent. [   ] Divorce ends the tenancy by the entirety, generally giving each spouse an equal interest in the property as a tenant in common, unless the divorce decree specifies otherwise. * * *

In determining whether respondent's husband possessed "property" or "rights to property" we look to the individual rights created by these state law rules. According to Michigan law, respondent's husband had, among other rights, the following rights with respect to the entireties property: the right to use the property, the right to exclude third parties from it, the right to a share of income produced from it, the right of survivorship, the right to become a tenant in common with equal shares upon divorce, the right to sell the property with the respondent's consent and to receive half the proceeds from such a sale, the right to place an encumbrance on the property with the respondent's consent, and the right to block respondent from selling or encumbering the property unilaterally.

IV

We turn now to the federal question of whether the rights Michigan law granted to respondent's husband as a tenant by the entirety qualify as "property" or "rights to property" under [26 U.S.C. § 6321]. The statutory language authorizing the tax lien "is broad and reveals on its face that Congress meant to reach every interest in property that a taxpayer might have." "Stronger language could hardly have been selected to reveal a purpose to assure the collection of taxes." [   ] We conclude that the husband's rights in the entireties property fall within this broad statutory language.

Michigan law grants a tenant by the entirety some of the most essential property rights: the right to use the property, to receive income produced by it, and to exclude others from it. [   ] These rights alone may be sufficient to subject the husband's interest in the entireties property to the federal tax lien. They gave him a substantial degree of control over the entireties property, and, as we noted in *Drye*, "in determining whether a federal taxpayer's state-law rights constitute 'property' or 'rights to property,' [t]he important consideration is the breadth of the control the [taxpayer] could exercise over the property." 528 U.S., at 61.

The husband's rights in the estate, however, went beyond use, exclusion, and income. He also possessed the right to alienate (or otherwise encumber) the property with the consent of respondent, his wife. [   ] It is true, as respondent notes, that he lacked the right to unilaterally alienate the property, a right that is often in the bundle of property rights. * * * There is no reason to believe, however, that this one stick—the right of unilateral alienation—is essential to the category of "property."

This Court has already stated that federal tax liens may attach to property that cannot be unilaterally alienated. In *United States v. Rodgers,* 461 U.S. 677 (1983), we considered the Federal Government's power to foreclose homestead property attached by a federal tax lien. Texas law provided that " 'the owner or claimant of the property claimed as homestead [may not], if married, sell or abandon the homestead without the consent of the other spouse.' " Id., at 684–685 * * *. We nonetheless stated that "[i]n the homestead context ... , there is no doubt ... that not only do *both* spouses (rather than neither) have an independent interest in the homestead property, but that a federal tax lien can at least *attach* to each of those interests." 461 U.S., at 703, n. 31 [ ].

Excluding property from a federal tax lien simply because the taxpayer does not have the power to unilaterally alienate it would, moreover, exempt a rather large amount of what is commonly thought of as property. Accordingly, the fact that respondent's husband could not unilaterally alienate the property does not preclude him from possessing "property and rights to property" for the purposes of § 6321.

Respondent's husband also possessed the right of survivorship—the right to automatically inherit the whole of the estate should his wife predecease him. Respondent argues that this interest was merely an expectancy, which we suggested in *Drye* would not constitute "property" for the purposes of a federal tax lien. 528 U.S., at 60, n.7 * * *. *Drye* did not decide this question, however, nor do we need to do so here. As we have discussed above, a number of the sticks in respondent's husband's bundle were presently existing. It is therefore not necessary to decide whether the right to survivorship alone would qualify as "property" or "rights to property" under § 6321.

That the rights of respondent's husband in the entireties property constitute "property" or "rights to property" "belonging to" him is further underscored by the fact that, if the conclusion were otherwise, the entireties property would belong to no one for the purposes of § 6321. Respondent had no more interest in the property than her husband; if neither of them had a property interest in the entireties property, who did? This result not only seems absurd, but would also allow spouses to shield their property from federal taxation by classifying it as entireties property, facilitating abuse of the federal tax system.* * *.

Justice Scalia's and Justice Thomas' dissents claim that the conclusion that the husband possessed an interest in the entireties property to which the federal tax lien could attach is in conflict with the rules for tax liens relating to partnership property. * * *. This is not so. As the authorities cited by Justice Thomas reflect, the federal tax lien does attach to an individual partner's interest in the partnership, that is, to the fair market value of his or her share in the partnership assets. * * *. As a holder of this lien, the Federal Government is entitled to "receive . . . the profits to which the assigning partner would otherwise be entitled," including predissolution distributions and the proceeds from dissolution. * * *.

There is, however, a difference between the treatment of entireties property and partnership assets. The Federal Government may not compel the sale of partnership assets (although it may foreclose on the partner's interest). * * *. This disparity in treatment between the two forms of ownership, however, arises from our decision in *United States v. Rodgers,* [461 U.S. 677 (1983)] (holding that the Government may foreclose on property even where the coowners lack the right of unilateral alienation), and not our holding today. In this case, it is instead the dissenters' theory that departs from partnership law, as it would hold that the Federal Government's lien does not attach to the husband's interest in the entireties property at all, whereas the lien may attach to an individual's interest in partnership property.

* * *

Respondent argues that Congress could not have intended the passage of the federal tax lien statute to alter the generally accepted rule that liens could not attach to entireties property. [　] The common-law rule was not so well established with respect to the application of a federal tax lien that we must assume that Congress considered the impact of its enactment on the question now before us. There was not much of a common-law background on the question of the application of federal tax liens, as the first court of appeals cases dealing with the application of such a lien did not arise until the 1950's. [　] This background is not sufficient to overcome the broad statutory language Congress did enact, authorizing the lien to attach to "all property and rights to property" a taxpayer might have.

We therefore conclude that respondent's husband's interest in the entireties property constituted "property" or "rights to property" for the purposes of the federal tax lien statute. We recognize that Michigan makes a different choice with respect to state law creditors: "[L]and held by husband and wife as tenants by entirety is not subject to levy under execution on judgment rendered against either husband or wife alone." [　] But that by no means dictates our choice. The interpretation of 26 U.S.C. § 6321 is a federal question, and in answering that question we are in no way bound by state courts' answers to similar questions involving state law. As we elsewhere have held, " 'exempt status under state law does not bind the federal collector.' "[　].

V

The judgment of the United States Court of Appeals for the Sixth Circuit is accordingly reversed, and the case is remanded for proceedings consistent with this opinion. *It is so ordered.*

* * *

Justice Thomas, with whom Justice Stevens and Justice Scalia join, dissenting.

The Court today allows the Internal Revenue Service (IRS) to reach proceeds from the sale of real property that did not belong to the taxpayer, respondent's husband, Don Craft, * * * because, in the Court's view, he "possesse[d] individual rights in the [tenancy by the entirety] estate sufficient to constitute 'property' or 'rights to property' for the purposes of the lien" created by 26 U.S.C. § 6321. The Court does not contest that the tax liability the IRS seeks to satisfy is Mr. Craft's alone, and does not claim that, under Michigan law, real property held as a tenancy by the entirety belongs to either spouse individually. Nor does the Court suggest that the federal tax lien attaches to particular "rights to property" held individually by Mr. Craft. Rather, borrowing the metaphor of "property as a 'bundle of sticks'—a collection of individual rights which, in certain combinations constitute property," the Court proposes that so long as sufficient "sticks" in the bundle of "rights to property" "belong to" a delinquent taxpayer, the lien can attach as if the property itself belonged to the taxpayer.

This amorphous construct ignores the primacy of state law in defining property interests, eviscerates the statutory distinction between "property" and "rights to property" drawn by § 6321, and conflicts with an unbroken line of authority from this Court, the lower courts, and the IRS. Its application is all the more unsupportable in this case because, in my view, it is highly unlikely that the limited individual "rights to property" recognized in a tenancy by the entirety under Michigan law are themselves subject to lien. I would affirm the Court of Appeals and hold that Mr. Craft did not have "property" or "rights to property" to which the federal tax lien could attach.

I

Title 26 U.S.C. § 6321 provides that a federal tax lien attaches to "all property and rights to property, whether real or personal, belonging to" a delinquent taxpayer. It is uncontested that a federal tax lien itself "creates no property rights but merely attaches consequences, federally defined, to rights created under state law." [ ] Consequently, the Government's lien under § 6321 "cannot extend beyond the property interests held by the delinquent taxpayer," [ ] under state law. Before today, no one disputed that the IRS, by operation of § 6321, "steps into the taxpayer's shoes," and has the same rights as the taxpayer in property or rights to property subject to the lien. I would not expand " 'the nature of the legal interest' "the taxpayer has in the property beyond those interests recognized under state law.

A

If the Grand Rapids property "belong[ed] to" Mr. Craft under state law prior to the termination of the tenancy by the entirety, the federal tax lien would have attached to the Grand Rapids property. But that is not this case. As the Court recognizes, pursuant to Michigan law, as under English common law, property held as a tenancy by the entirety does not belong to either spouse, but to a single entity composed of the married persons. Neither spouse has "any separate interest in such an estate." Because Michigan does not recognize a separate spousal interest in the Grand Rapids property, it did not "belong" to either respondent or her husband individually when the IRS asserted its lien for Mr. Craft's individual tax liability. Thus, the property was not property to which the federal tax lien could attach for Mr. Craft's tax liability.

The Court does not dispute this characterization of Michigan's law with respect to the essential attributes of the tenancy by the entirety estate. However, relying on *Drye v. United States, 528 U.S. 49, 59 (1999),* * * * the Court suggests that Michigan's definition of the tenancy by the entirety estate should be overlooked because federal tax law is not controlled by state legal fictions concerning property ownership. But the Court misapprehends the application of *Drye* to this case.

Drye * * * was concerned not with whether state law recognized "property" as belonging to the taxpayer in the first place, but rather with whether state laws could disclaim or exempt such property from federal tax liability after the property interest was created. *Drye* held only that a state-law disclaimer could not retroactively undo a vested right in an estate that the taxpayer already held, and that a federal lien therefore attached to the taxpayer's interest in the estate. [ ] * * *

Extending this Court's "state law fiction" jurisprudence to determine whether property or rights to property *exist* under state law in the first place works a sea change in the role States have traditionally played in "creating and defining" property interests. By erasing the careful line between state laws that purport to disclaim or exempt property interests after the fact, which the federal tax lien does not respect, and state laws' definition of property and property rights, which the federal tax lien does respect, the Court does not follow *Drye,* but rather creates a new federal common law of property. This contravenes the previously settled rule that the definition and scope of property is left to the States. [ ]

B

That the Grand Rapids property does not belong to Mr. Craft under Michigan law does not end the inquiry, however, since the federal tax lien attaches not only to "property" but also to any "rights to property" belonging to the taxpayer. While the Court concludes that a laundry list of "rights to property" belonged to Mr. Craft as a tenant by the entirety, * * * it does not suggest that the tax lien attached to any of these particular rights.[3] Instead, the Court gathers these rights together and

---

3. Nor does the Court explain how such "rights to property" survived the destruction of the tenancy by the entirety, although, for all intents and purposes, it ac-

knowledges that such rights as it identifies exist by virtue of the tenancy by the entirety estate. Even Judge Ryan's concurrence in the Sixth Circuit's first ruling in this opines that there were sufficient sticks to form a bundle, so that "respondent's husband's interest in the entireties property constituted 'property' or 'rights to property' for the purposes of the federal tax lien statute." * * *

But the Court's "sticks in a bundle" metaphor collapses precisely because of the distinction expressly drawn by the statute, which distinguishes between "property" and "rights to property." The Court refrains from ever stating whether this case involves "property" or "rights to property" even though § 6321 specifically provides that the federal tax lien attaches to "property" and "rights to property" "belonging to" the delinquent taxpayer, and not to an imprecise construct of "individual rights in the estate sufficient to constitute 'property' or 'rights to property' for the purposes of the lien."

Rather than adopt the majority's approach, I would ask specifically, as the statute does, whether Mr. Craft had any particular "rights to property" to which the federal tax lien could attach. He did not. * * * Such "rights to property" that have been subject to the § 6321 lien are valuable and "pecuniary," i.e., they can be attached, and levied upon or sold by the Government. * * * [ ] With such rights subject to lien, the taxpayer's interest has "ripen [ed] into a present estate" of some form and is more than a mere expectancy, and thus the taxpayer has an apparent right "to channel that value to [another]" [ ].

In contrast, a tenant in a tenancy by the entirety not only lacks a present divisible vested interest in the property and control with respect to the sale, encumbrance, and transfer of the property, but also does not possess the ability to devise any portion of the property because it is subject to the other's indestructible right of survivorship. [ ] * * *

It is clear that some of the individual rights of a tenant in entireties property are primarily personal, dependent upon the taxpayer's status as a spouse, and similarly not susceptible to a tax lien. For example, the right to use the property in conjunction with one's spouse and to exclude all others appears particularly ill suited to being transferred to another, and to lack "exchangeable value," [ ].

Nor do other identified rights rise to the level of "rights to property" to which a § 6321 lien can attach, because they represent, at most, a contingent future interest, or an "expectancy" that has not "ripen[ed] into a present estate." [ ] By way of example, the survivorship right wholly depends upon one spouse outliving the other, at which time the survivor gains "substantial rights, in respect of the property, theretofore never enjoyed by [the] survivor." While the Court explains that it is "not necessary to decide whether the right to survivorship alone would qualify as 'property' or 'rights to property' "under § 6321, the facts of this case demonstrate that it would not. Even assuming both that the right of survivability continued after the demise of the tenancy estate and that

matter is best read as making the Federal Government's right to execute its lien dependent upon the factual finding that the conveyance was a fraudulent transaction. See 140 F.3d 638, 648–649 (C.A.6 1998).

the tax lien could attach to such a contingent future right, creating a lienable interest upon the death of the nonliable spouse, it would not help the IRS here; respondent's husband predeceased her in 1998, and there is no right of survivorship at issue in this case.

Similarly, while one spouse might escape the absolute limitations on individual action with respect to tenancy by the entirety property by obtaining the right to one-half of the property upon divorce, or by agreeing with the other spouse to sever the tenancy by the entirety, neither instance is an event of sufficient certainty to constitute a "right to property" for purposes of § 6321. Finally, while the federal tax lien could arguably have attached to a tenant's right to any "rents, products, income, or profits" of real property held as tenants by the entirety, Mich. Comp. Laws Ann. § 557.71 (West 1988), the Grand Rapids property created no rents, products, income, or profits for the tax lien to attach to.

In any event, all such rights to property, dependent as they are upon the existence of the tenancy by the entirety estate, were likely destroyed by the quitclaim deed that severed the tenancy. [ ] Unlike a lien attached to the property itself, which would survive a conveyance, a lien attached to a "right to property" falls squarely within the maxim that "the tax collector not only steps into the taxpayer's shoes but must go barefoot if the shoes wear out." [ ]

Accordingly, I conclude that Mr. Craft had neither "property" nor "rights to property" to which the federal tax lien could attach.

III

Finally, while the majority characterizes Michigan's view that the tenancy by the entirety property does not belong to the individual spouses as a "state law fiction," *ante,* at 1419, our precedents, including *Drye,* 528 U.S., at 58–60, 120 S.Ct. 474, hold that state, not federal, law defines property interests. Ownership by "the marriage" is admittedly a fiction of sorts, but so is a partnership or corporation. There is no basis for ignoring this fiction so long as federal law does not define property, particularly since the tenancy by the entirety property remains subject to lien for the tax liability of *both* tenants.

* * *

Just as I am unwilling to overturn this Court's longstanding precedent that States define and create property rights and forms of ownership, [ ] I am equally unwilling to redefine or dismiss as fictional forms of property ownership that the State has recognized in favor of an amorphous federal common-law definition of property. I respectfully dissent.

Notes

1. As mentioned earlier, the tenancy by the entirety is unseverable. *Schwab v. Krauss* provides the general rule for those states where the

tenancy by the entirety exists: land held by husband and wife in a tenancy by the entirety is unreachable by creditors of either the husband or wife. However, in *U.S. v. Craft*, the Supreme Court held that a tenancy by the entirety is subject to a federal tax lien against one of the owners, even though the state of Michigan protected the property from creditors.

2. Note that the Court used a two-step process to determine whether the federal tax lien could attach to the Crafts' property. First, the Court looked to state law to determine the rights afforded tenants by the entirety. After determining the rights provided by state law, the Court considered whether the federal tax code encompassed such property rights so as to allow the federal government to place a lien against the property. The rights of tenants by the entirety under Michigan law support the attachment of a federal tax lien against the property. Given the broad language of the tax code as interpreted in *Craft*, is it likely that property held in tenancy by the entirety in other states would be protected from attachment of federal tax liens?

3. In United States v. One Single Family Residence, 894 F.2d 1511 (11th Cir.1990), federal prosecutors attempted to seize property held by the entireties, under the extraordinary power federal drug enforcers have to bring about the forfeiture of property used in drug trafficking (21 U.S.C. Sec. 881). The property was in Florida which, with 14 other states, holds that the entireties estate is not severable. The alleged offender's wife was not involved in the alleged drug dealing; she argued that she could not be deprived of her property under the government's statutory authority. Lawyers for the couple argued (and the court held) that the government's power does not extend to what the innocent cotenant has; the government gets what she doesn't have. Here the wife had an unseverable interest in the entire property, with the result that the government was not able to seize anything. In this case the couple took title to the house before the alleged offense by the husband; the court noted that its holding would not permit a drug offender to establish entireties ownership after the offense, under the apparently well-established principle that the government's seizure takes effect at the time of the offense. A similar result was reached in U.S. v. Lee, 232 F.3d 556 (7th Cir. 2000), where the federal government attempted to seize property, co-owned in tenancy by the entirety by an innocent spouse, which had not been used for illegal activities.

Suppose that the property was held as joint tenants. Can the government seize the property? (Yes. See U.S. v. One Parcel of Real Estate, 41 F.3d 1448 (11th Cir.1995)). What if the property was held as tenants by the entirety but purchased with money from illegal drug transactions? Can the government seize the property? (See U.S. v. One Parcel of Real Estate at 298 N.W. 45th Street, Boca Raton, 804 F.Supp. 319 (S.D.Fla.1992), *aff'd per curiam*, 12 F.3d 218 (11th Cir.1993), holding that since the property was purchased after the criminal action, the government could seize the property. A drug trafficker cannot hide the proceeds of an illegal activity in another's name to avoid detection or seizure.)

A slight twist on this scenario involves the sale of property held as tenants by the entirety to pay a criminal fine. In Baldwin v. U.S., 805 F.Supp. 1026 (S.D. Fla. 1992), the husband was convicted of failing to pay taxes and was sentenced to twenty years in prison and a $100,000 fine. The government wanted to seize and sell the property, giving the wife one-half of the proceeds and keeping the other half as payment of the husband's fine. The court held that the wife has an "undivided right to possession, title, and enjoyment of the whole property." Classifying the ownership interest as a tenancy in common would constitute a "taking" because it would fundamentally change the wife's property interest, the court held.

C. MANAGEMENT AND DISPOSITION OF CONCURRENTLY–HELD PROPERTY

Concurrent owners may disagree about how to manage and dispose of their property. This may be particularly true in cases where only some of the concurrent owners occupy the property. Should the occupiers of the property pay rent to the non-occupiers? Should they share income derived from the property with non-occupiers? Should the non-occupiers share in the costs of management, such as insurance, maintenance, repairs and taxes? Can the non-occupiers force the occupiers to sell the property and divide the proceeds? Can the occupier acquire title to the entire property under the law of adverse possession?

In the absence of statutes governing concurrent ownership, courts generally answer these questions by resorting to the logic of concurrent ownership: an individual interest in the whole. All members of the community have the rights and responsibilities of ownership. All may possess the whole, regardless of the size of their fractional shares. Therefore, unless and until the occupiers have prevented the non-occupiers from taking possession (known as an "ouster") or have agreed to pay for the value of their occupation, they do not have to pay rent to the non-occupiers. However, if the property generates income, e.g., as an apartment building or a farm, the occupiers must share the income received from third parties with the non-occupiers after appropriate offsets for maintenance and other appropriate expenses. Disputes regarding amounts are resolved through court-ordered procedures called *accountings*. See, e.g., Wood v. Wood, 51 Ark.App. 47, 908 S.W.2d 96 (Ark.Ct.App.1995) (purchase by one cotenant of property at tax sale is considered a redemption of co-owned property for the benefit of all the cotenants); Martin v. Martin, 878 S.W.2d 30 (Ky.Ct.App.1994) (occupying cotenants not required to pay rent to non-occupying co-tenants). See, generally William B. Stoebuck and Dale A. Whitman, The Law of Property, 3rd ed. 203–214 (2000).

At early common law, a co-owner who incurred expenses for repairs or improvements to the property did so as a volunteer and could not recover from his fellow co-owners. This makes sense in the case of improvements on the theory that a co-owner ought not be improved out of his estate. Applied to repair, however, the doctrine was a disincentive to maintenance of real property. Today some courts allow an action for contribution to compel non-occupiers to reimburse occupiers for their fractional shares of the cost of essential repairs to the property. See

Sheldon F. Kurtz, Moynihan's Introduction to the Law of Real Property, 4th ed. 285 (2005).

Questions about disposition can and normally are resolved by agreement among the concurrent owners. However, when agreement is not reached, one or more concurrent owners may seek a court order to physically divide the property or to sell it and divide the proceeds. The procedure, called *partition*, may be governed by statute or by the court's equity powers, as the next case illustrates.

JOHNSON v. HENDRICKSON

Supreme Court of South Dakota, 1946.
71 S.D. 392, 24 N.W.2d 914.

Sickel, J.

This is an action for the partition of real property. Henry W. Bauman and Katie B. Bauman were husband and wife. Their children consisted of three, named Grace, Arthur, and Vernon. The husband died intestate in 1904, leaving an estate consisting of an improved quarter section of land in Clark County. The decree of the circuit court determined the right of inheritance to this land as follows: One-third to the widow, two-ninths to each of the three children. * * * The widow then married the defendant Karl Hendrickson. The children of this marriage consisted of twin boys named Kenneth and Karroll. Katie B. Hendrickson, widow of Henry W. Bauman, wife of Karl Hendrickson and mother of all the children, never moved from this land during her lifetime. Karl Hendrickson, her husband, lived there with her until she died, and still lives upon the land. All the children lived on this land during their minority and at various periods of time after attaining their majority. The mother died in May 1944 and left her property by will as follows: To her husband, Karl Hendrickson, one-half; to each of the children of the second marriage one-fourth; to the children of her first marriage, five dollars each. * * * Plaintiffs in this action are the three children of the first marriage of Katie B. Hendrickson. They allege in their complaint that the land is so situated that it cannot be partitioned among the various owners either individually or in groups, without prejudice to such owners, and ask that it be sold in one tract. Defendants deny that the partition in kind would be prejudicial to the owners. The circuit court determined the claims and liabilities of all the parties as to mortgages paid and improvements made, and adjudged that the land be sold. From this decree the defendants have appealed. * * *

The appellants * * * proposed that the partition in kind be made by allotting to them, as owners collectively of a one-third interest in the land, the southeast forty-acre tract with all the buildings and improvements situated thereon, and the hog house now on the southwest forty-acre tract, and by allotting to the three respondents, as owners of a two-thirds interest in the land, the other three forty-acre tracts with no buildings, but upon which is situated a forty-acre slough. The first question presented then is whether the court was justified in deciding that the land be sold. * * *

[A] sale may be ordered if it appear to the satisfaction of the court that the value of the share of each cotenant, in case of partition, would be materially less than his share of the money equivalent that could probably be obtained for the whole. * * * [A] sale is justified if it appears to the satisfaction of the court that the value of the land when divided into parcels is substantially less than its value when owned by one person. This land is now owned by six persons. The largest individual interest is two-ninths and the smallest is one-twelfth. Partition in kind would require the division of the land into not less than four parcels: Two-ninths to each of the three respondents, and one-third to appellants, collectively. It is a matter of common knowledge in this state that the division of this quarter section of land, located as it is, into four or more separate tracts would materially depreciate its value, both as to its salability and as to its use for agricultural purposes. * * *

Appellants * * * offer, as an alternative, to purchase the two-thirds interest of the three respondents in the land by paying to them the sum of $800 each. This latter proposition is an offer of settlement, not a proposed plan of partition. The law favors the compromise and settlement of disputed claims because it is the interest of the state that there should be an end to litigation, but such offer does not present a justiciable question. It is the function of the court to hear and decide questions of law and fact, not to use its influence to bring about the composition of disputes.

The widow inherited from her first husband an undivided one-third interest in the farm. After she married appellant Karl Hendrickson in 1909 she continued to occupy the farm * * * with her children, her second husband, and the children of the second marriage. During such occupancy they remodeled the house, built the barn, hog house, granary, wash house, milk house, chicken house, fences, and two wells, at a cost of over $9,000. Appellants Karl Hendrickson and the two sons of the second marriage claim in this action that as the devisees of Katie B. Hendrickson, and present owners of an undivided one-third interest in the farm, they are entitled to credit for such improvements.

The rule at common law is that a tenant in common cannot compel his cotenants to contribute to his expenditures for improvements placed by him on the common property without the consent or agreement of the cotenants. * * * It is also the general rule, with some exceptions not pertinent to this case, that a life tenant who makes permanent improvements upon real property with full knowledge of his title will be presumed to have made them for his own benefit, and that he cannot recover anything therefor from the remainderman. * * * The rule in regard to the rights of tenants in common as stated above has been modified by courts of equity in partition cases. * * *

[C]ourts generally make suitable allowance, on partition, for improvements made in good faith by a cotenant in possession, to the extent that the value of the property has been enhanced thereby. * * * This modification of the common law rule, however, does not alter the rule as to life tenants who have no interest in the remainder, or their successors in interest after the termination of the life estate.

In this case, Katie B. Hendrickson had a homestead interest in the land from the date of her first husband's death until she died in 1944. She also owned a one-third interest in it by right of inheritance from her first husband. She was, therefore a tenant in common with the children of the first marriage, and a life tenant by virtue of her homestead right. Under the rules to which we have referred she would be entitled in partition, as a tenant in common, to contribution for improvements made, but as a life tenant such contribution would be denied. Cases like this, where the person making the improvements has a life estate and is also a tenant in common, are generally decided by the court on equitable principles, that is, "according to its own notions of general justice and equity between the parties." * * *

This case does not deal with the right to offset the value of improvements against rents and profits accruing after the termination of the life estate. Such rents and profits have been accounted for in this action. Neither did the widow who made the improvements believe or understand that she was the sole owner of the remainder. Decisions of other courts dealing with such propositions are not pertinent to the facts in this case. Here the evidence shows that improvements consisting of a house, barn, granary, chicken house, and shed, all old, were situated upon this farm in 1909. In 1910 a granary was built, in 1911 a chicken house and in subsequent years the barn was torn down and a new one constructed in its place. The house was repaired and remodeled, a hog house, wash house, garage, milk house, fences, and wells were also constructed in the following years.

In the year 1909 the mortgage on the homestead was $2,500. It was increased to as much as $7,000 to pay for improvements, debts, and to buy another quarter section of land across the road. Arthur Bauman was born in 1893 and remained at home until he was twenty-seven years of age. Grace Bauman was born in 1895 and remained at home until her mother died in 1944. Vernon Bauman was born in 1898 and remained at home until he was thirty-six years of age. These three children of the first marriage worked but received no wages while at home, and none of them had separate incomes, except the daughter from some chickens and Vernon from some farming which he did on his own account. During all the time that these three children of the first marriage remained at home they and their mother occupied the homestead as such, and owned it as tenants in common. The second husband and the children of the second marriage were members of the same family. The mother was the head of this family. She owned all the personal property and managed all the family affairs. The improvements, incumbrances, and additional land were made and paid for out of the land by the combined efforts of all. The respondents made substantial contributions to the family income out of which these things were accomplished, during their minority, and also during their majority. The family had the use of the greater part of the improvements over a period of more than thirty years. These improvements and the payment of the mortgage have greatly enhanced the value of the estate. Karl Hendrickson and his two sons now own a one-third interest in the homestead, improved and free from debt, and the additional quarter section of land. The circuit court determined that under these circumstances an allowance to Karl Hendrickson and his sons for the improvements made and the indebtedness paid would be inequitable, and this conclusion is amply supported by the evidence. * * *

Finding no error in the record the judgment is affirmed.

Notes and Questions

1. Why did the court think that partition in kind would necessarily result in the division of the land into four parts? Do you agree?

2. The availability of partition as the remedy of choice for disgruntled tenants in common may explain the judicial reluctance to enforce rights of contribution in the co-ownership context. The common law of tenancy in common demonstrates "an affirmative policy of nonintervention. Indeed, the courts' attitudes towards co-ownership could best be described by the adage *if you don't like it, get out of it* (by partitioning it)." Symeon C. Symeonides and Nicole D. Martin, The New Law of Co–Ownership: A *Kommentar*, 68 TUL. L. REV. 69, 74 (1993).

The common law right of partition available to tenants in common has long been regarded as absolute and unconditional. See, e.g., Cheeks v. Herrington, 523 So.2d 1033 (Miss. 1988); Heldt v. Heldt, 29 Ill.2d 61, 193 N.E.2d 7 (1963); Davis v. Davis, 128 Ill.App.2d 427, 262 N.E.2d 788 (1970). The availability of partition is said not to yield to hardship, inconvenience, or injury to others, nor is it influenced by the motivation of the party seeking partition. 4 Thompson on Real Property, Thomas Edition (David A. Thomas, ed., 1994). However, some recent holdings suggest that partition may not be granted as a matter of right in all cases, and will not be available where rights of other cotenants would be defeated or curtailed if partition were allowed. See, e.g., Baker v. Drabik, 224 N.J.Super. 603, 541 A.2d 229 (App. Div. 1988); Redick v. Jackson 1991 WL 27298 (Conn. Super.)

While partition by public sale seems fair on its face, one party will generally be in a relatively stronger position to bid on the property. Some limitation on the right to partition would afford a measure of protection of the reliance interest on continuation of the relationship by the more vulnerable party when the more powerful party seeks to end the relationship. Joseph W. Singer, The Reliance Interest in Property, 40 STAN. L. REV. 614, 750 (1988). For example, a single-family house will not be readily capable of physical partition. Rather than forcing a party to vacate after a failed relationship of mutual dependence, the possessor might be permitted to take the entire property upon compensating the other with owelty.

For an example of a decision enforcing a waiver of the right to partition by agreement among tenants in common, see Mansour Properties v. I–85/GA. 20 Ventures, Inc., 277 Ga. 632, 592 S.E.2d 836 (2004).

3. Katie B. Hendrickson was the sort of prairie pioneer woman Willa Cather wrote about. Among modern novelists the one most likely to do justice to such a character is, no doubt, Anne Tyler (*Accidental Tourist, Breathing Lessons, Dinner at the Homesick Restaurant, The Clockwinder, Ladder of Years, Patchwork Planet, Saint Maybe, Celestial Navigation, The Tin Can Tree, Back When We Were Grown-ups*). Tyler writes about bizarre families that are held together in bizarre ways—families that are put together by resilient heroines such as Katie Hendrickson, who put together two husbands and five children. Tyler's point, like Judge Sickel's, would be that, when Katie was alive, they were one family and were at home—even into the children's middle age. How does such a story end up in a set of oral arguments, by lawyers, in the highest court of the state, arguments over whether Katie Hendrickson's farm should be sold—should be sold not because efficiency or production require it, or because the bank is foreclosing its mortgage, but because Katie Hendrickson's family, now that she is gone, cannot live together on her farm? They have turned Katie's farm, the physical thing that held them together, into a battle field.

4. Title to the farm was originally taken in the name of Henry W. Bauman, Katie's first husband. All of the forms of marital ownership were available to the person who drew up that conveyance. Did that lawyer choose the one that was best for Henry and Katie and their children?

5. Henry Bauman did not make a will; the farm went to Katie and the children by intestate succession. (Note that by that time in the development of Anglo–American inheritance, the widow was an heir.) Was that pattern of distribution and control the best one for Katie and her children?

6. Katie, as Henry's widow, had both a homestead right and a share as Henry's heir. The homestead right gave her a life estate on the property that is analogous to common-law dower (life estate in one-third of her husband's lands), which we will take up again in the next section. Might a lawyer working on Henry Bauman's will have pulled Katie's two interests together and used them as elements in a single planning scheme? (Katie could probably have waived her homestead interest.)

7. Katie did make a will. Suppose she had come to your law office for that purpose. What such a lawyer is asked to do is to contemplate the possibility that Katie will die leaving two sets of children, a husband, and this prosperous quarter section of South Dakota. The six people who live with her need, then, to have a substitute for her presence among them—and the thing available as building material for the substitute is this good farm. The will maker here is asked to fashion a substitute for Katie's presence in her family:

— It is evident why Katie left only five dollars each to her older children, but does it make sense? Was that the way to deal with the issue of equality among children? Come to that, how important is equality among children? Who do you suppose answered these questions in Katie's lawyer's office?

— Katie's lawyer has to deal with some givens, the most limiting of which was that she did not get the whole farm from her first husband. She has a life interest in her homestead and a one-third fee-simple interest. The older children, in middle age by the time of this lawsuit, own six-ninths of the farm. Katie apparently did not feel she could give them more. Is there anything else she could do to influence them to work for family harmony? Notice that the tragedy in a case like this—and there are thousands of such cases in the reports—is not that the land gets chopped up, but that the people do.

— Some facts that might be worth taking into account if we got into a time machine, one that could go to Clark County, South Dakota, and had a chance to work on Katie's will (or on Henry's, or on the original deed to Henry, or—best of all—on all three):

— The possibility and advisability of equal distribution among all of the children. Notice that it may be possible to provide a mechanism here, rather than a recipe. Notice, too, that it is unlikely that five children in one farm family will all want to be farmers when they grow up, but very likely that at least one of them will want to be a farmer.

— The possibility of providing a system for taking account of time and expense spent on improvements, and of taking into account who had a home on the farm and for how long (an alternative, that is, to the common-law rules on claims among cotenants).

— The possibility of providing not only a mechanism but also a decision maker other than the circuit judge (who apparently got so angry at these squabbling relatives that he threw up his hands and ordered the property sold).

Suppose a very clever lawyer could figure out a set of complex devices that would resolve these questions and would affect not only the ownership of this farm but also the human relationships among those Katie left behind. Drafting them involves technical language, including language that might cause Katie (who has to sign the devices and pay for the preparation of them) confusion and unnecessary concern. What do you think of a lawyer-client strategy that will explain them to Katie only in a very general and comforting way: "This will take care of the ownership question. And this will take care of the management question." And suppose, finally, that Katie is willing to sign without understanding (clients usually are). What do you think of that way of practicing law?

Comment "[5]" to Rule 2.1, Rules of Professional Conduct (2002 additions to 1983 text underlined):

"In general, a lawyer is not expected to give advice until asked by the client. However, when a lawyer knows that a client proposes a course of action that is likely to result in substantial adverse legal consequences to the client, *the lawyer's* duty to the client under Rule 1.4 may require that the lawyer ["act" deleted] *offer advice* if the client's course of action is related to the representation. *Similarly, when a matter is likely to involve litigation, it may be necessary under Rule 1.4 to inform the client of forms of dispute resolution that might constitute reasonable alternatives to litigation.* A lawyer ordinarily has no duty to initiate investigation of a client's affairs or to give advice that the client has indicated is unwanted, but a lawyer may initiate advice to a client when doing so appears to be in the client's interest."

"Offer advice" was substituted for "act" in 2002. What difference did that make?

8. If a family could own land as a corporation does, as a single, separate, legal person, and if Henry and Katie had taken ownership of their quarter section of Clark County in the name of their family, would the result in this case have been less tragic? Would it have made it easier to do the sort of planning you were asked to think about in Question 7?

9. Many farm families today incorporate their farms—home, business, and all. If Henry and Katie had done that, presumably the quarter section would have been conveyed to Bauman Farm, Inc., and common stock would have been issued as Henry and Katie directed. Would that form of ownership have made any difference in this case? Would it have made it easier to do the sort of planning you were asked to think about in Question 7?

10. Is the law incapable of doing anything about this family tragedy? Is it inevitably the case, in an orderly commonwealth, that an offer of compromise presents nothing a judge can deal with? Is it even the case that the only reason for the law to favor settlement of disputes in a family is "because it is in the interest of the state that there should be an end to litigation"?

Could the parties have agreed that the trial judge should act as an arbitrator who would pass on the purchase proposal, characterized by Judge Sickel as a nonjusticiable "offer of settlement?" See DDI Seamless Cylinder International Inc. v. General Fire Extinguisher Corp.,14 F.3d 1163, 1166 (7th Cir.1994) (Parties do not have power, under Federal magistrate statutes authorizing arbitration, to appoint judge before whom case is brought to act as arbitrator, but they may agree on simplified procedures for hearing case, including a limited waiver of the right to appeal).

11. In Wendell Berry's short story, "It Wasn't Me" (one of six stories in *The Wild Birds,* 1986), Wheeler Catlett, county-seat Kentucky property lawyer, drew a will for a farmer named Jack Beechum. Wheeler's client, a widower, had a daughter who was not interested in his farm. When Jack was forced by ill health to retire, he and Wheeler located tenant farmers, Elton and Mary Penn, to farm the place. Jack later wanted Elton and Mary to have the farm. The will Wheeler drew for him gave the farm to Jack's daughter, Clara Pettit, and the value of half the farm to Elton and Mary. (His estate would have only the farm in it, so that, in effect, and at the time he made the will, this amounted to giving Elton and Mary half the farm.) It occurred to him later that maybe Clara would not want to sell the farm to Elton and Mary, or that the value would appreciate. He left an undelivered, handwritten note to Wheeler, saying that he wanted Clara to sell the farm to Elton and Mary, at date-of-will value. The note was of no legal effect.

After Jack died, as Jack feared, Clara refused to sell to Elton and Mary and put the farm up for sale at auction. Wheeler devoted himself to seeing to it that Elton got the farm anyway. He got Elton to bid, successfully, much more than Elton thought he could afford. Wheeler then created a security fund to back Elton's debt. Why? Not only out of a sense of obligation to Jack, but also because, "Wheeler is a seer of visions—not the heavenly visions of saints and mystics, but the earthly ones of a mainly practical man who sees the good that has been possible in this world, and beyond that, the good that is desirable in it." Wheeler finally told Elton that he had to help him get the farm "because Mr. Beechum wanted it to happen, and because the farm * * * wanted it to, and because you wanted it to * * * [a]nd because what has happened has been desirable to a lot of people we never knew, who lived before us."

That solved the legal problem and probably solved the financial one, but it did not solve the human problem. The human problem was that Elton did not want to have to be grateful: "I want to make it on my own. I don't want a soul to thank." Wheeler, the lawyer for the situation, then undertakes to convert Elton to awareness of the fact that he is not alone in the world, and to the acceptance of having to thank the people he is in it with: "I don't think your old friend has left you in shape to live thankless," he says to Elton.

Wheeler Catlett's argument to his client is an argument about property. He says it is only possible to live without gratitude for property if it is "a kind of property you can put in your pocket. * * * But when you quit living in the price and start living in the place, you're in a different line of succession." There is no way Elton's debt can be paid back, Wheeler says: "We're dealing in goods and services that we didn't make, that can't exist at all except as gifts. Everything about a place that's different from its price is a gift. Everything about a man or woman that's different from their price is a gift. The life of a neighborhood is a gift. * * * Once the account is kept and the bill presented, the friendship ends, the neighborhood is finished, and you're back to where you started. The starting place doesn't have anybody in it but you." Elton is converted then. He laughs. "You're going to be my friend, it sounds pret' near like, because you can't get out of it."

PROBLEM

Mrs. Wylick is visiting your office to discuss the disposition of her estate. The visit is at the insistence of Mrs. Wylick's favorite granddaughter, Rose Jones. Both Mrs. Wylick and her granddaughter have come to the attorney's office.

Mrs. Wylick is 75 and has a slight hearing problem. Mrs. Wylick has been in the hospital for cancer twice in the last 15 years. In both cases, the cancer was surgically removed, and there has been no recurrence of the disease; however, Mrs. Wylick fears the return of the cancer. In addition, she has begun to suffer from periodic high blood pressure. Aside from the cancer, Mrs. Wylick is robust for her age and has no apparent health difficulties.

She becomes depressed frequently because she doesn't have anyone to talk with. She is also very distressed because she can't keep her house as clean as she used to because she can't see as well as she once did. Finally, she doesn't think she is eating right because she doesn't have the desire to cook only for herself.

Mrs. Wylick has three children and five grandchildren. She is not speaking to her eldest child, a son named John, and has not seen him for eight years. She has twins, Martha and George. The twins are 40 years old. Martha is married and has three children. Martha is Mrs. Wylick's favorite child, although they did not speak for a ten-year period about 20 years ago. The favorite granddaughter, Rose, is Martha's eldest child. George is single and lives with Mrs. Wylick.

Mrs. Wylick owns her own home in which both she and her son George live. She also owns a duplex from which she receives rental income, and a vacant lot on the city's south side.

Mrs. Wylick would like George to have a place to live even after she dies, but she doesn't want him to have "too much" because she considers him irresponsible. She doesn't want him to be able to sell the home, and she wants her home to go to her granddaughter after George dies.

She wants the duplex to go to Martha. In fact, because she has trouble getting around and fears that she may face a lengthy hospitalization, she would like to "add Martha's name" to the duplex now. Martha has always helped her maintain the duplex.

Mrs. Wylick's vacant lot is next to a public community college. She would like to give the lot to the community college, but she is worried that the state may take any income from the property's sale. It that would happen, she would rather have the property go to her heirs.

What steps would you suggest she take to accomplish her goals?

NOTE ON TRANSFER–ON–DEATH (TOD) STATUTES

Several states have transfer-on-death (TOD) or pay-on-death (POD) statutes. These statutes allow the owner of property to name a beneficiary of the title to property so that when the owner dies, the property transfers to the beneficiary without being subject to probate. A will is not necessary for property to transfer under a TOD or POD statute. Michigan has one of the simplest TOD statutes: "Registration in beneficiary form may be shown by the words 'transfer on death' or 'TOD', or by the words 'pay on death' or 'POD', after the name of the registered owner and before the name of a beneficiary." See M.C.L. 700.6305 (2002). See also, Tex. Prob. Code Ann. § 436 (West 2003); Fla. Stat. Ann. § 655.82 (bank accounts); §§ 711.501–711.512 (real and personal property) (West 2000).

To take title to the property the beneficiary only needs to prove the owner's death, which is a matter of public record. The owner is free to change the beneficiary at any time without notification to the beneficiary. What does this suggest about the beneficiary's present ownership interest in the property? Pay-on-death transfers are held to be non-testamentary transfers even though they do not occur until the death of the owner. See M.C.L. 700.6309 (2002); Tex. Prob. Code Ann. § 454 (West 1995); Fla. Stat. Ann. § 711.509 (West 1996). In 1991, the Uniform Law Commissioners approved for recommendation to the states the Uniform Nonprobate Transfers on Death Act. By 2005, 45 states had adopted it in whole or in part, the hold-outs being Louisiana, Missouri,

New York, North Carolina and Texas. 8B Uniform Laws Annotated, Estate, Probate and Related Laws 191 (West 1993 and Supp. 1997).

What advantages do TOD transfers have for the owner? For the beneficiary? For the courts?

DAGAN AND HELLER, THE LIBERAL COMMONS
110 Yale L.J. 549, 602–623 (2001).

IV. Tragic Choice in American Co–Ownership

* * *

The default American law of co-ownership invites tragedy: It undermines cooperation even when co-owners seek to work together, encourages distrust and misuse that may delay or even prevent use of emerging resources, and, more generally, imposes enduring losses whenever strategic behaviors or transaction costs deter people from voluntarily adopting a more tailored liberal commons form. American law currently forces people to choose between laboriously contracting for their own liberal commons or suffering under existing background rules that encourage conflict, mismanagement, and division. Property law can do better.

The decline in black rural landownership * * * forms the backdrop for our co-ownership case study. The decline in black landownership that has frequently been understood as an inevitable result of the workings of ownership and management of commons resources may instead be, in some part, the contingent result of discrete legal choices. * * *

A. The Disappearance of Black Rural Landowners

* * *

2.   The Rise and Fall of Heir Property

Consider a common tale of commons property: In 1887, John Brown, a black man, bought eighty acres of land in Rankin County, Mississippi; in 1935, he died intestate, leaving his wife and children as heirs who in turn also died intestate, leaving the land to their children and grandchildren. * * * One of these grandchildren, Willie Brown, began consolidating ownership in the land by buying the interests of five of John's nine children: Frances, Minnie, Adda, Joe, and Lizzie. By the time Willie died, he had accumulated an undivided 41/72d interest, which he left to his wife Ruth. In 1978, Ruth filed for partition in kind of the farm, asking that her interest be physically separated from the remainder held by sixty-six other Brown heirs, whose interests ranged from 1/18th down to 1/19,440th of the farm. * * * The court, however, ordered the land partitioned by sale with the proceeds divided among the heirs. * * * At the sale, a white-owned lumber company outbid Ruth. * * * Ruth got some cash—more than she was willing or able to pay, but perhaps less than she would have demanded to compensate her for the farm's subjective value in preserving her family's cohesion and traditions. Just after the Civil War, when John Brown bought his eighty acres, black landownership in America began a steep rise. Nearly a century later, Ruth Brown lost her family land, and black landownership had nearly disappeared.

The uprooting of landed heirs is an oft-repeated tale in black America, particularly in the rural South. * * * From 1920 to 1978, the number of black-operated farms in the United States dropped 94%, from almost one million to just over 57,000; by comparison, white-operated farms dropped 56%, from about 5.4 million to 2.4 million. * * * In absolute terms, there are fewer than 19,000 black farmers in America today—less than 1% of American farmers—and black Americans continue to abandon farms at a rate three times that of white Americans. * * * Why? Leave aside racial discrimination and wealth effects for the moment, factors that matter in this story and to which we return. * * * Some scholarly explanations for the precipitous decline of black landownership have focused on the role of partition sales, which are the background legal mechanism governing disposition of co-owned land in the Brown family saga. * * * Over a quarter of remaining black-owned land in the Southeast is now "heir property" averaging eight co-owners, five of whom live outside the Southeast. * * * By 1986, "more Mississippi land [was] owned by blacks in Chicago than by blacks in Mississippi." * * * As one study concludes, partition laws "are unquestionably the judicial method by which most heir property is lost." * * *

Heir property is just co-owned property arguably rendered ungovernable because of repeated rounds of intestate succession—a particular issue for Southern rural black landowners with "superstitions about making wills," * * * but no desire to have their family farmland broken up or sold. In general, when a landowner dies intestate (that is, without a will), the heirs at law receive fractional undivided interests in the land. For example, each of John Brown's nine children received a 1/9th undivided interest in the eighty acres. Often, this first generation of heirs successfully manages their parents' property, but second and third generations multiply quickly and prove less and less able collectively to cope. * * *

Over time, practical problems become unresolvable. Under the American law of co-ownership, unless fractional owners unanimously consent, the underlying land cannot be managed in any useful way; nor can it be mortgaged; nor can any discrete fraction of the land be sold. Without effective democratic self-governance mechanisms for co-owned property, "[h]eir property is rarely improved or developed, due to the threat of partition sales and the difficulty of obtaining credit on partial interests in the property. 'In fact, a third more heir than non-heir property is not being used at all.' " * * * Thus, "[t]he sale of the land, usually precipitated by an heir who is more than one generation removed from the originating source, becomes inevitable." * * *

3. Community–Destroying Exit

What are the paths that lead to the end of black landownership? First, as with the Brown example, resident heirs may bring suit to quiet title intending to acquire ownership in severalty of part of the farm. * * * By seeking a partition in kind, these heirs express their preference to stay on the land and to gain access to mortgages and other ordinary incidents of sole private ownership. * * * Despite the heirs' request, and the law's nominal preference for partition in kind, courts usually order a partition sale because the number of heirs and limited size of the property make physical division impracticable. * * * The second, more sinister, path to partition sales originates with nonresident heirs. A non-family-member may acquire a distant nonresident heir's fractional share in a family farm specifically for the purpose of forcing a partition sale at which the outsider can buy the whole tract. * * * Because heir property is very common among rural blacks, "the black community is particularly vulnerable to the unscrupulous partition sale brought about by someone buying out the interest of a single heir and then demanding that the land be sold." * * *

Partition sales, like foreclosure and tax sales, prove to be poor, often rigged markets with little information and few buyers: "[T]he purchaser[s] at these [partition and] tax sales are almost always white persons, frequently local lawyers or relatives of the local officials, who make it their business to keep abreast of what properties are going to auction and who attend the auctions prepared to buy." * * * Given wealth disparities, widespread discrimination in access to credit for rural black households, and the ordinary imperfections of these rural auctions, partition sales in practice mean the transfer of the land from resident black heirs with fractional interests to white purchasers who often pay below market value and pay nothing for the farm's intangible value in preserving family cohesion. * * *

Farming, from all reports, is a chancy business. If cashing out simply improves blacks' overall position and consolidates economically obsolete farms, * * * then the decline in black landownership may not be a serious problem, notwithstanding the congressional studies * * * and private initiatives * * * concerned with halting this trend. However, declining black landownership also can be traced in part, perhaps, to the difficulty of governing fractionated land, resulting in partition sales initiated either by resident heirs seeking to improve land management or by nonresident heirs and their purchasers seeking to acquire the whole farm at bargain prices.[229] The hostility of American law toward co-

---

229. There are incentives outside of property law that also encourage partition. For example, attorney fee structures often award lawyers 10% of the land value on partition sale, but not if the title problem is informally resolved. There are many stories of lawyers who have initiated partition suits for heirs over the objection of the heirs' families. In one case, a New York heir asked her lawyer to provide deeds to the family property, but the lawyer instead filed an action for sale and partition. When the heir fired the lawyer, the lawyer then found another heir to prosecute the suit. [Emergency Land Fund, The Impact of Heir Property on Black Rural Land Tenure in the Southeastern Region of the United States 292–93 (1980)]. Also, the tax system encourages partition sales by favoring wealthy investors who can write off certain losses in ways not available to low-or moderate-income farmers. See [U.S. Comm'n on Civil Rights, The Decline of Black Farming in America 4].

ownership appears to impose several costs, not only on individual black families, but perhaps on farm communities more broadly.

Landownership provides benefits other than just farm income. Commoners may prefer not to sell because they identify alternative economic uses or they place a high subjective value on keeping the land in the family. For example, one study of a rural North Carolina community showed how landownership provides reciprocal benefits within black families: Older owners can obligate children by allowing them to settle on the land, and the children then provide support for the elderly landowner in this residential enclave. * * * By contrast, the study notes, landless elderly people are less likely to be able to mobilize informal support and more likely to suffer lower living standards. * * * Along with simple economic reasons, there may also be cognitive framing issues for sales: A farm might stay in the family because the family would not be "willing to accept" the market price, but if forced to bid at auction, that same family might only be "willing to pay" a lower amount and would thus lose the farm. * * * Finally, when commoners do decide to sell nonviable farms, they get only distressed prices for individual share sales or at partition auctions. They could do better by marketing the property cooperatively, but if the law facilitated cooperation, then they might not want to sell in the first instance.[234]

We cannot know how much of the sharp decline of black landownership should be attributed to race and class discrimination, or to market forces that make small farms not economically viable. Encouraging and enabling black farmers to write wills and improving the integrity of partition auctions may have ameliorated the decline to an extent. It seems plausible, however, that, at least on the margin, some of this decline might have resulted from a particular default legal regime that does not support commons ownership and instead actively undermines any possibility for its success, even when the family deeply desires to continue working together, to keep land in the family, and to give family members a fair share when they leave.

B. How Law Can Dissolve Tragic Choice

The American law of co-ownership shrinks from any attempt to facilitate management of co-owned resources. Instead, by providing incentives for mismanagement, the default rules of the common law make the continuing existence of a commons a risky enterprise for commoners (technically, usually cotenants).[235] Over time and in many ways, the

---

234. Perhaps locking people together by preventing alienation, the no-exit illiberal solution, would have kept more farms within the family. But such a solution, even if it achieved community-preserving goals, would still be tragic, because it sacrifices each heir's liberty to exit. Further, we question whether preventing alienability would necessarily achieve even instrumental community-building goals. Consider the disas-

trous consequences of the federal allotment policy for Native Americans that locked people together without providing effective internal self-governance mechanisms. See [Michael A. Heller, The Boundaries of Private Property, 108 Yale L.J. 1163, 1213–17 (1999) (discussing the tragedy of the anticommons resulting from these policies)].

235. Cotenants are those who share land under the common-law regime of ten-

American law of co-ownership dilutes the value of interests in commons ownership, making them less and less usable for the commoners. Combined, the rules promote underuse, overuse, and underinvestment— anything but the actions of an ordinary sole owner managing his or her own property. Given the penalty default legal regime of the common law, the tragedy of the commons turns out to be a self-fulfilling prophecy.

Notes

1. Professors Dagan and Heller argue that law reform is necessary to address the problem of the significant decline in black rural landownership in the south as a result of forced partition sales. Their ambitious proposal involves a three-fold approach to reforming the tenancy in common under a so-called "liberal commons model."

(a) *Retaining the Right to Exit*—Noting that the freedom of alienation is a central organizing principle of American property law, the authors acknowledge that the right to exit the tenancy in common must be preserved. However, in order to encourage cooperation and provide a safety valve against forced partition sales, exit rights may be limited by exit taxes, rights of first refusal, and mandatory waiting periods before sale.

(b) *Preserving Individual Cotenants' Rights to Make Autonomous Decisions*—Because all co-tenants are free to occupy and use the land, there is a risk of overexploitation. Cotenants may also be deterred from making improvements if they are not certain they will be compensated. Both problems create divisions among cotenants, leading to the deterioration of the property and, ultimately, to a demand for partition. Accordingly, the authors recommend a mechanism for an accounting among cotenants for overuse, in addition to a cause of action for contribution for improvements. In this way, the law can encourage trust among cotenants and provide remedies other than partition in cases of abuse.

(c) *Encouraging Collective Decision–Making*—Finally, the authors recommend the creation of a democratic dispute resolution structure within the tenancy in common form of ownership, with full disclosure and open discussion of matters to be decided by cotenants. A democratic structure with limitations to protect against minority exploitation may provide a system of cooperation that fosters trust within the commons. A cotenant may seek judicial review of management decisions if the process is unfair, or if decisions are made on the basis of self-interest rather than utility.

2. Can you think of other ways to restructure the system of concurrent estates to better preserve co-ownership? For another excellent treatment of the decline in black landownership in the south, see Thomas W. Mitchell, From Reconstruction to Deconstruction: Undermining Black Landowner-

ancy in common. Each individual tenant has an interest in the same undivided piece of property. Unlike joint tenants, cotenants have no right of survivorship. See Jesse Dukeminier & James E. Krier, Property 322 (4th ed. 1998). In all states where it existed, the presumption in favor of joint tenancy has been abolished almost completely, id. at 323, so, on death and in the absence of a will, heirs hold property as tenants in common. Abolishing the presumption of joint tenancy thus may have had the unintended effect of accelerating fractionation.

ship, Political Independence, and Community Through Partition Sales of Tenancies in Common, 95 Nw. U.L.Rev. 505 (2001).

3. Consider the example described as "sinister" by Professors Dagan and Heller of the non-family-member who acquires a fractional share in a family farm owned in tenancy in common for the sole purpose of forcing partition, intending to take advantage of his superior economic power to acquire the entire property for himself. It is unlikely that such a transfer can occur without the active involvement of an attorney in its structure and implementation. Are there any ethical constraints that a lawyer should consider before deciding whether to participate in the transaction? To what extent is it proper for a lawyer, in counseling a client, to take considerations of justice, fairness and morality into account when the client engages in conduct that may have an adverse effect on others or on society?

Should traditional ethical rules emphasizing unswerving loyalty to achieving clients' goals govern a lawyer's conduct outside of the adversary context? One commentator has called for the adoption of the following professional rule for the nonadvocate:

"When acting in a professional capacity other than that of advocate, a lawyer shall not render assistance to a client when the lawyer knows or it is obvious that such assistance is intended or will be used ... to allow the client to obtain an unconscionable advantage over another person." Murray L. Schwartz, "The Professionalism and Accountability of Lawyers," 66 Cal. L. Rev. 669, 685–86 (1978). Exploitation of the underprivileged, unsophisticated and uneducated has been held to be among the various practices that may constitute unconscionability. *Williams v. Walker–Thomas Furniture Company*, 350 F.2d 445 (D.C. Cir. 1965).

FRIEDMAN, PROFESSIONALISM IN THE AMERICAN ADVERSARY SYSTEM

41 Emory Law Journal 467, 471–2 (1992).

[I]n a free society, lawyers enhance the rule of law by enhancing the autonomy of each individual. We do this by counseling our clients about their lawful choices and by helping them to achieve the lawful goals that they choose in accordance with their interests as they perceive them to be.

This does not mean that counseling with regard to moral as well as legal responsibilities is inappropriate. On the contrary, it is an essential element of the lawyer's responsibility. In the final analysis, however, the lawyer should always remember that the decision whether to forego legally available objectives or methods because of nonlegal facts is ultimately for the client and not for the lawyer.

4. Consider the possible role of the fiduciary relationship. Parties in a fiduciary relationship owe each other a duty not only to act fairly, but with the utmost good faith. Fiduciary duty may require, for example, that a party subordinate self-interest and act altruistically foregoing personal profit. Traditional fiduciary relationships include partnership, attorney-client, agent-principal, trustee-beneficiary, and familial relationships. The typical remedy for breach is the imposition of a constructive trust on the personal

profit received by a party in violation of his fiduciary duty, as well as punitive damages. Would the purchase of a fractional interest by a non-family-member in a family farm for the sole purpose of forcing partition constitute a breach of fiduciary duty if the tenancy in common was recognized as a fiduciary relationship?

5. Consider the following hypothetical situation: Cotenants A and B own Greenacre in equal undivided shares as tenants in common. A is in sole physical possession of the property; B is out of possession. While occupying the property, A discovers the existence of vast subsurface oil reserves. If A enters into an arrangement with Apex Oil Company to exploit the potential value of the oil reserves, A would be obligated to pay B half of the profit A realizes. Accordingly, it might occur to A that his industry and good fortune would better be rewarded by making an offer to buy B's interest in the property, without disclosing this knowledge. B accepts. A subsequently entertains offers to purchase Greenacre and eventually sells the land to Apex Oil Company, realizing a massive profit. Does B state a cause of action against A?

6. Each cotenant has an equal right to possess and enjoy all or any portion of the property as if he were the sole owner, but only because possession by one is deemed possession by and for the benefit of all. This has led courts in many states to recognize at least a quasi-fiduciary duty in limited circumstances between cotenants, on the basis that the tenancy in common involves an expectation of mutual trust and fairness between the parties. *In re Marriage of Mullen*, 123 Wash.App. 1007 (2004) (co-tenants who acquire another's half interest in the property have a duty to disclose third party offers); *Cooper v. Cooper*, 783 A.2d 430, 436 (Vt. 2001) ("Each cotenant has a duty to protect and secure the common interest, and neither co-tenant may assume a hostile attitude toward his other co-tenants."); *Wilson v. S.L. Rey*, 21 Cal.Rptr.2d 552, 556 (1993) (co-tenants are considered to be fiduciaries unless they do not acquire their interests at the same time in the same instrument and no "relationship of confidence and trust exists between them").

In other states, courts have held that tenants in common are not fiduciaries without either a formal agreement or contract providing that such a relationship exists or a personal relationship, such as marriage. In these jurisdictions, co-tenants owe a duty of good faith that does not rise to the level of fiduciary duty. See generally *Burk v. Demaray*, 646 N.W.2d 635, 643 (Neb. 2002); *Turkey Creek, LLC v. Rosania*, 953 P.2d 1306 (Colo. App. 1998); *Scott v. Scruggs*, 836 S.W.2d 278, 282 (Tex. App. 1992).

7. Should tenants in common owe the full range of duties imposed on parties in other fiduciary relationships, such as partners in a partnership? Like those of partners, the legal rights of concurrent property owners are so intermingled and intertwined that any exercise of rights by one co-owner has the potential to endanger or hinder others. Like members of a partnership, cotenants have the ability to inflict significant tort and environmental

liability on each other. Unlike partners, tenants in common do not always voluntarily associate. However, because the right to partition traditionally is automatic, tenants in common who remain together are engaged in a voluntary mutual undertaking not unlike that of partners. See Alan M. Weinberger, "Expanding the Fiduciary Relationship Bestiary: Does Concurrent Ownership Satisfy the Family Resemblance Test?" 24 Seton Hall L. Rev. 1776 (1994).

PROBLEM

At the beginning of their first year of law school, Carl Curtis and three of his classmates got together and purchased a two-story four-unit off-campus apartment building, taking title as tenants-in-common. They divided up the apartments among themselves, each occupying the same unit throughout their time in law school and sharing expenses equally.

Following graduation, Curtis' three classmates all took jobs out-of-town. Curtis stayed behind. For the past two years, he has been leasing out two of the three units occupied by his former classmates on a month-to-month basis. He combined the two upstairs units into one apartment where he has been living ever since.

After enduring three years together with him during law school, his former classmates were happy to be able to put some distance between themselves and Curtis. His racial prejudice had become a source of embarrassment to them. It would not be an exaggeration to describe Curtis as a bigot. Determined not to live in close proximity with non-whites, for the past two years Curtis has gone to great lengths to avoid having vacant apartments available for rent by minority applicants. By charging significantly below-market rents and relying strictly on word-of-mouth, Curtis has been able to keep the first-floor units fully occupied without having to advertise for tenants. For example, while apartments comparable to the ones in Curtis' building typically rent for $800 per month, Curtis only charges $550, out of which he pays the real estate taxes, insurance and upkeep. Sadly, Curtis' method of "complying" with the nation's fair housing laws is not unique.

Curtis' classmates have not received any money from him with respect to the property since they moved away. Explain what legal rights and remedies are available to them.

D. CONDOMINIUMS

R. MALLOY AND J. SMITH, REAL ESTATE TRANSACTIONS: PROBLEMS, CASES AND MATERIALS
524–531, 539–545 (2d ed. 2002).

As a general definition, a *condominium is* a single unit in a multiunit project together with an undivided interest in the common areas and facilities (usually called the "common elements"). The owner of a condominium generally has fee simple title to the unit and owns a percentage share of the common elements as a tenant in common with her neighbors. Common elements typically include the land, the building systems, and the project amenities ...

Property held as a condominium is a form of ownership, and it is not any particular architectural style. Many people get confused and think that a condominium is just a unit in an apartment-type building that you can own. Though it is true that many condominiums look like apartment buildings, many others do not. The condominium form of ownership can be applied to a number of physically different types of structures or property shapes. For instance, there are neighborhoods with stand-alone single-family homes with yards that are structured as condominiums.... Nor are condominiums limited to housing. There are also business offices, stores in shopping centers, boat slips at marinas, parking places at garages, and university football stadiums that are structured as condominiums and available to be bought and sold and transferred by deed. In short, merely looking at something physically or aesthetically will not tell you if it is part of a condominium project. The condominium form of ownership is purely legal and not physical.

Although condominiums are located in all parts of the United States, they are highly concentrated in a few areas. In addition to California and Florida, condominiums are quite numerous in New York, Illinois, New Jersey, and Texas.... In terms of market profile, the typical condominium owner, when compared to other homeowners, is less likely to be married, more likely to be female, more likely to be from a population group that is either older than the average or younger than the average (seniors and yuppies), and generally has a median income about 15 percent higher than the general population.

Condominiums have become an increasingly important part of the market, especially in urban areas and communities with high land costs.... Although some condominiums are luxury housing units and can cost a large amount of money, many condominiums are positioned in the marketplace as low-cost alternatives to single-family homes. The lower-cost condominium units are very marketable to young buyers under the age of 35. Another important market segment for condominiums are people over age 55. Both age groups include many persons who tend not to be as highly interested in maintaining a yard and property outside of their immediate living space. Many of the younger owners are new entrants into the workforce who are concentrating on their careers. As for the older buyers, many have sold a single-family home and opted for a condominium now that the children are all grown. They see these units as a way to continue independent housing arrangements but with little or no personal responsibility for yard work, upkeep, or maintenance.

All states have statutes that govern the creation and operation of condominiums. Although most authorities believe a condominium may be created at common law, this has not proven workable due to a number of conceptual and procedural problems. The condominium statutes establish a specific set of ownership rights that are identified by reference to legal documents prepared in accordance with statutory requirements and filed with a government entity. Consequently, the first place to look when considering this form of property is at local state statutory law that enables the creation of this form of ownership....

The extent of the common property—the "common elements"—is the distinguishing feature of the condominium form of ownership. A buyer's exclusive fee interest usually extends only to the interior space and surfaces of the unit. The common elements include all structural materials, internal wall spaces, wiring, plumbing, and other items, as well as stairways, hallways, elevators, open spaces, lawns, amenities, and exterior structural surfaces. It is the complex system of shared ownership that makes the common law ill-suited to the task of condominium ownership. There are simply too many cross-easements, use rights, and restrictions to deal with in an easy fashion under the common law. There is also the problem of the old common-law principle that a fee owner of real property owns from the center of the earth to the heights of the heavens. Rejecting this often quoted adage, the condominium form means owning a mere block of air space defined by interior walls floating somewhere between the surface of the earth and the top of the building or structure in which a unit is located. This air space might be located on the second, fifth, or thirtieth floor of a building, and over time the building may settle or shift, causing the location of the space, in common-law terms, to encroach on some other owner's rights. State condominium statutes have largely succeeded in overcoming these problems.

The primary legal document for a condominium project is the Declaration of Condominium, wherein a property owner declares the legally described property to be henceforth held in the condominium form.... The declaration must spell out all the elements required to be addressed by the statutes and must clearly define by narrative reference, and usually by drawings, the identification of each ownership unit and all common property. The declaration must also address the rights and responsibilities of all unit owners regarding both the individual ownership property and the common property. The declaration further provides for the handling of liability of a unit owner for such things as contract or tort liability concerning matters that arise with respect to either unit or common property.... Furthermore, the declaration establishes a condominium unit owners association, provides for rules and regulations to govern the orderly operation of the condominium, and authorizes assessments against each unit owner to pay for condominium expenses....

In a condominium development, there are likely to be both "common elements" and "limited common elements" associated with unit ownership. Common elements consist of all those portions of the condominium property that are not defined in the declaration as part of a unit. The common elements are owned in common by all the unit owners. Typical examples of common elements are hallways, stairways, elevators, plumbing, green areas, and swimming pools. Limited common elements are those common elements defined in the declaration as being for the limited or exclusive use of a particular unit while not in themselves being part of the described unit. Examples include unit patios, balconies, window flower boxes, and parking spaces. A unit owner is given a specified undivided share in all common elements. The share is usually stated as a fraction or a percentage based on the relationship that the unit has to the whole of the condominium.... These undivided interests cannot be severed from the unit ownership, nor can they be partitioned....

Condominium ownership provides the same benefits as other forms of home ownership, even though it tends to be more restrictive from a lifestyle point of view. The interest in a condominium unit can be bought and sold, mortgaged, assigned, devised, and leased just like the interest in any other home. Restrictions may be placed on these rights, and they can be enforceable as long as they do not act as an unreasonable restraint on alienation. The scope of reasonableness is likely to be greater in the condominium setting than with the single-family detached home, because of the codependency of the living arrangements between unit owners and because of their undivided interests in the common elements....

Although we have discussed condominiums as a form of residential housing, it should be kept in mind that the concept can be applied to a variety of properties. The University of South Carolina made a pregame tailgate parking lot into a condominium where individuals could purchase a fee interest in a parking space and use it for pregame parties. Some office buildings are structured so that lawyers and others are not merely tenants but also are fee owners of their office space as units in an office building condominium. The same concept can be applied to store space in a shopping center and to just about any other type of property, so long as the local state statute has a broad scope. The advantage to owning these interests rather than renting is that you have an equity position in the property, and the parking space, office, or store area you own may appreciate in value over time....

Cooperative housing is another form of joint ownership in which a unit owner has exclusive use of a dwelling together with rights to shared or common areas. In a cooperative, title to all of the real estate is held by a corporation, with each shareholder having the right to a dwelling unit pursuant to a long-term lease from the corporation. In some ways a housing cooperative is similar to a condominium. For either form to work, project documents must clearly designate the ownership interests and use rights. A cooperative has a unit owners association and rules and restrictions much like those used in other forms of shared housing. Just as for condominiums, the cooperative unit owners are given voting rights and are assessed fees and charges based on allocations set forth in the organizing documentation. Like the condominium, the cooperative form of ownership can be applied to a variety of real estate activities, but it is almost always used in a multiunit housing building....

In all cases, the purchase of a unit in a cooperative involves the acquisition of a stock certificate in the cooperative entity. This is treated as a personal property interest. Stock ownership carries a right to a lease for a particular unit in the cooperative. In many jurisdictions, a cooperative is, therefore, viewed as having both a personal property (stock certificate) and a real property (lease) component....

The unit owner in a cooperative ... has a bundle of property rights that are transferable subject to the limitations set forth in the cooperative documents. Thus, an owner may sell, assign, sublease, or devise her interest. The unit owner may also obtain financing using her property rights as collateral....

The continuing viability of the cooperative housing market is now driven mostly by a desire on the part of some homeowners to exercise a great deal of control over who will be their neighbors. Courts readily uphold express limitations on cooperative unit owners' transfers of ownership as long as those limits do not impose an unreasonable restraint on alienation, with *unreasonable* being understood within the unique context of the cooperative form of ownership. Buying into a cooperative requires the approval of the cooperative board....

The current owners are given a great deal of discretion with respect to whom they approve or do not approve to be fellow stockholders and unit owners. Because they are financially dependent on each other, the cooperative form of living permits even more restrictions on use, enjoyment, and transferability of an interest than other forms of communal living. The cooperative owners do not just live in close proximity and share ownership of common elements, they are financially responsible for a shared debt. This factor has traditionally allowed cooperative boards to reject ownership applications without giving a reason for denial. When reasons are given for a denial, they have typically been upheld by the courts so long as the reason does not violate an antidiscrimination statute....

Some famous people who have been rejected by cooperatives are Cher, Barbara Streisand, Gloria Vanderbilt, and Richard Nixon.... President Nixon has the honor of being rejected by two different cooperatives in New York City.... You can be rejected for having poor taste in clothing or a pet that is not pleasing to the eye, for being overweight, or for having an occupation and a lifestyle that simply do not fit in well with the image of the cooperative. Lawyers are often unwelcome because they are assumed to be litigious. Political figures and movie stars are seen as attracting too much attention. Not surprisingly, minorities also seem to have difficulty getting approved by cooperative boards.

M. MITCHELL RAIT, LOLLIPOP CONDOMINIUMS: AIR RIGHTS, THE TAKINGS CLAUSE, AND DISCLOSURE UNDER NEW YORK'S NEW GUIDELINES

17 Real Estate Law Journal 335, 337–340 (1989).

A lollipop condominium is a legally separate residence built on top of an existing condominium. Since the New York Condominium Act requires residential condominiums to be built on a piece of property (leading to fee simple absolute ownership), the upper condominium must be provided with an easement to touch the land. This is usually accomplished through an elevator shaft or a column of the building leading to the land directly beneath the shaft or column. This piece of land is then assigned to the upper condominium. The result is a tall stem with a building balanced on top, hence the name "lollipop."

A consequence of lollipop condominiums is the reduction in the share of common interests of the original owners. The new purchasers of the upper condominium cut into the portion of the shared facilities owned originally by the lower owners. This effect also occurs in "phasing," the lateral counterpart to lollipops. An obstacle is presented, however, by Section 339–i(1) of the New York Real Property Law. This section establishes a permanent character of the common interests, preventing any fluctuation of the interest shares. Similarly, New York State's attorney general requires specification of the undivided fractional interest attached to each unit for ownership.

Virginia, on the other hand, unequivocally allows a developer to reserve the right to expand. The Virginia statute merely requires three criteria: (1) the explicit reservation of an option to expand the condominium; (2) a statement of any limitations on that option; and (3) a seven-year time limitation upon which the option to expand will expire. In 1965, the Association of the Bar of the City of New York disapproved a proposed amendment to Section 339–i(1) of the New York Real Property Law that would have provided developers with the leeway found in the Virginia statute: "[T]hat the declaration may specifically provide for an increase or decrease of the common interest upon the happening of one or more of the following events: (a) the addition of units to the condominium; (b) the removal of units from the condominium." The Association * * * contended that the clause would place the unit purchaser in a position that was far too uncertain. The initial purchasers could never be certain what the extent of the finished development would be and, hence, what the unit owner's fractional interest, share of expenses, and proportionate voting strengths would be. * * *

With the restriction of Section 339–i(1) of the New York Real Property Law and without the flexibility found in the proposed amendment, sponsors have nonetheless accomplished their goal. First, the sponsor would indeed comply with the rigid requirements of the Condominium Act by setting forth with particularity the common interests of the initial offering. Second, the sponsor would contractually arrange easements, covenants, and restrictions with the offerees. Such provisions, many of them blanket retentions, would satisfy the requirement of Section 339–i(2) of the New York Real Property Law, allowing alteration of the common interest applicable to each unit via the consent of all unit owners. Unanimity would be accomplished through the agreements. It is these contractual provisions that are the target of the attorney general's new guidelines. The Real Estate Financing Bureau prohibited vague boiler-plate reservations of expansion rights unless the sponsor disclosed future plans in great detail. The result was that developers who did not have firm construction plans within four or five years, according to the Real Estate Financing Bureau, were prevented from retaining developmental rights. * * *

Notes and Questions

1. The condominium is a form of concurrent ownership that allows residents of multi-family developments to achieve an ownership interest in the units they occupy. Note how it differs from the cooperative. The fee title actually is to a cube of air. The components of the building supporting the various cubes of air are part of the common elements in which unit owners have interests as tenants in common. As the *Rait* article suggests, describing the common elements is a very important part of the paperwork creating a condominium.

2. Condominiums and co-operatives are two of four distinct ownership forms for large tract residential and commercial development. The others are fee ownership of individual lots and improvements along with easements to use common areas (discussed in Chapter Six) and fee ownership of the entire development with possessory leases granted to the occupants (discussed in Chapter Four). Compare the ownership elements of the four. How much of the property bundle of sticks is present in each one? How much control over the day-to-day management of the property does each form give the occupants?

3. The conversion of existing rental properties to condominium ownership and the resulting displacement of tenants presents a variety of legal and public policy issues, particularly in urban areas where there is a shortage of housing units and a significant elderly population. In recent years, legislation designed to forestall condominium conversion has been enacted in several larger cities, sometimes requiring approval of the conversion by majority vote of affected tenants, or granting senior citizens the right, notwithstanding the conversion of their building, to remain in their units for the balance of their lifetimes in a form of statutory tenancy, a determinable life estate in effect. See Comment, The Condominium Conversion Problem: Cases and Solutions, 1980 Duke L.J. 306.

4. While the condominium form of ownership has taken over the market for shared housing in most parts of the country, the cooperative form of ownership is a way of life for many residents of New York City. In 1995, New York Times reporters N.R. Kleinfield and Tracie Rozhon reviewed the

history of cooperatives, called co-ops, in New York, beginning with the Tenth Street Studio built in 1857 to house artists and their work. The reporters found that over 400,000 co-op units were contained in over 8,000 co-op buildings in the city. This is more than half of all co-ops in the United States. At the same time, only about 1,000 condominium complexes existed in New York. N.R. Keinfield with Tracie Rozhon, In Flat Market, Co-op Life Has Steep Ups and Downs, The New York Times, Oct. 30, 1995, at A1. Note that the property of a co-op is owned by a not-for-profit corporation, whose members are the residents of the co-ops under long term leases. Thus, members are both landlords and tenants.

Compare the condominium and cooperative. What are the relative strengths and weaknesses?

5. A variation of the condominium that has achieved considerable popularity in areas that cater to tourists and vacationers is the *time-share*. In a time-share, the possessory element of concurrent ownership is limited to a specified recurring period of time. The Model Real Estate Time–Share Act, also promulgated in 1980 by the Uniform Law Commissioners, defines a time-share estate as "a right to occupy a unit ... during [5] or more separated time periods over a period of at least [5] years ... coupled with a freehold estate or an estate for years in a time-share property.... " Model Real Estate Time–Share Act, § 1–102 (14).

6. The guidelines of the Attorney General of New York, to which Mr. Rait refers, are one approach to the problem of unconscionability. Another and more common solution is in the moral conversation between the developer and the developer's lawyer. Business lawyers exercise moral influence on their clients constantly, and law professors occasionally ask them to be even more resolute than they are. Professor Harry W. Jones, an esteemed elder in the teaching part of the profession, for example: "J.M.L., fine lawyer and truly good man * * * behind his office desk as counselor and advisor. A major corporate client * * * is concerned about possible claims from its distributors and customers and wants something put into its standard form contracts to insulate the company from possible liability, even for losses caused by the company's own negligence, default or neglect. The corporation is a big fellow in its industry; the standard form contract will be offered on a take-it-or-leave-it basis, and the smaller distributors and consumers will have no alternative but to take it. J.M.L. would never for a moment think of putting such an oppressive clause into a contract of his own. Do the accepted ethical standards of the legal profession instruct or authorize him to do for his client what he would never do for himself? Should he be troubled in conscience if he drafts the requested insulation clause with technical precision, so as to make it legally enforceable, and, by including it in the client's standard contract, imposes it on every small businessman with whom the client deals? * * *

"There must be some point, short of running over one's grandmother, at which the lawyer's own personal and social morality will rebel against his traditional allegiance to his client. My revered mentor, J.M.L., unquestionably drew the line somewhere." ("Lawyers and the Uneasy Ethics of Partisanship," 23 Villanova Law Review 957 [1978].)

II. PROPERTY CLAIMS IN MARRIAGE

The first part of this chapter considered common-law forms of concurrent property ownership. Although these have not been, either conceptually or historically, forms of family or marital ownership, they have become, in our modern American culture, popular arrangements for ownership of property by people who are married to one another. The tenancy in common and the joint tenancy (including derivative personal-property arrangements such as joint bank accounts and joint tenancies in securities and safety deposit boxes) are forms of marital property ownership by planning. The tenancy by the entirety is a form of marital property ownership, but it is less useful than the joint tenancy because it is often not available for personal property.

In this section, we consider property claims in marriage, claims under policies maintained by the state to protect spouses. These are forms of ownership and claims on ownership that have to do with marriage. In most cases these forms and claims have to do with property in families, since marriages usually involve families in which property interests, like children, are his, hers, and ours. The most interesting question, often, is how ownership works out in families. Since families do not usually consult lawyers except in crisis, this question,is: How does ownership work out when the family is put through divorce or through the death of one of its property owners?

We carefully do not say when the family is "broken up" by one of these events. What is significant for present purposes is that such events bring families into law offices. Such events do not necessarily break up families, which are resilient old things—not easy to break. A follower of Anne Tyler, winner of the Pulitzer Prize and chronicler of the modern American family, is bound to say that families can survive death and divorce. We who follow Anne Tyler are going to notice, though, that property is often involved in the question of whether a family breaks up over divorce or death—and that means that a property lawyer is involved: A property lawyer is present, in one way or another, making things better or making things worse.

As noted earlier, the common law property system was extremely patriarchal. Married women, in particular, had little ability to own or manage property in the eyes of the law. They were, legally, totally dependant on their husbands.

In the period before the Civil War, married women began to seek legal equality, particularly by claiming a property right in their household labor. While the movement was not successful, it did help spur passage of married women's property acts, which gave married women the same rights as single women to own property. The story of the unsuccessful attempts to gain legal status for household work through a joint property regime and the subsequent shift in emphasis to the ultimately successful quest for the right to vote is told eloquently by

Reva B. Siegel, Home As Work: The First Woman's Rights Claims Concerning Wives' Household Labor, 1850–1880, 103 Yale L.J. 1073 (1994).

For an argument that enactment of married women's property acts was driven by greater recognitions of women's family responsibilities rather than their entrance into the business world, see Richard H. Chused, Married Women's Property Law: 1800–1850, 71 Georgetown L.J. 1359 (1983). See also Elizabeth Bowles Warbasse, The Changing Legal Rights of Married Women, 1800–1861 (Garland Press Dissertation Series 1987); Marylynn Salmon, Women and the Law of Property in Early America (North Carolina Press 1986); Laura Padilla, Gendered Shades of Property: A Status Check on Gender, Race & Property, 5 J. GENDER RACE & JUST. 361, 362–375 (2002) (reviewing former and current laws respecting women's rights concerning property).

A. CLAIMS AGAINST THE OWNER

Imagine a visit to the law office by a brother and sister who own a junkyard—a prosperous and growing junkyard. They have, with help from our law office, incorporated their business; in form, what they own is stock in the junkyard corporation. Title to the land on which the business is conducted is in the corporation, Junkyard, Inc. Junkyard stock is all either of them owns, but it is a lot. Each is almost a millionaire.

One of them, Michelle, is married; she and her husband, Charles, have two unmarried teen-aged children. Jake, Michelle's little brother, is not married and has no children—but he is engaged and planning to be married in a couple of months, to a dermatologist named Elizabeth.

Michelle and Jake come to see their lawyer together. They tell the partner who does their legal work that they want to disinherit their spouses and children (or, in Jake's case, his fiancee). Each wants the stock in the business to go to the other—all of it.

A place to begin thinking about such a client agenda (certainly not the only place, and maybe not even the best) is in terms of what the law will let them do: The doctrinal notion to begin with is that disinheritance is something a client can usually do in our property system. Property can be given to a spouse or to children or to siblings or to friends or to a hospital:

— There has not been any significant restraint on disinheriting children or other relatives; the most that even the most modern Anglo–American system provides is support for dependent children, and that is in many places limited to support during the judicially-supervised administration of the estate.

— There had not been, for that matter, any significant restraint on *disinheriting* a spouse. Spouses had claims to life interests in the dead person's property (dower and curtesy), but the idea there was not inheritance so much as to *provide for* the spouse during widowhood. These claims were not claims of forced inheritance; they were more like debts.

In terms, then, of what the law will allow our clients to do, things look about as promising as things ever look. (Of course, the situation would not be the same in a community-property state.) Michelle wants to disinherit Charles and their children. Jake wants to disinherit Elizabeth before he marries her. We can do both jobs. They may not be simple, but we can do them. Consider our nuts and bolts:

First, it will matter *when* the siblings got or get the *property* we are depriving these families of. Then it will matter *when* we are doing this *legal work* for them. Jake, for example, is a different case from Michelle, in both respects. And the value of their stock now is a different case from the additional value their stock will have at the time a spouse's claim is made on it. It matters whether we are talking about what will happen when one of the spouses finds out about our legal work and files for divorce, or talking about what will happen when one of the siblings dies and the spouse survives.

In most American states today, as the professional descendants of the Victorian family solicitor, we would be considering Elizabeth and Charles as in the following situations:

— Neither would be, or would need to be, an heir in order to have a claim: In a narrow sense of the word, both Michelle and Jake can disinherit their spouses by making wills that give their entire estates (*i.e.*, the property each will own when he dies) to one another.

— In Victorian society (and in a few American states still) each wife (assuming Elizabeth is by then a wife) has a common-law *dower* claim to a *life estate in one third of the real property that her husband owned during their marriage.* Only real property that was an *estate of inheritance,* and was held in a *legal* (as distinguished from equitable) form of ownership was vulnerable to this claim. So, for example, if the siblings had not yet incorporated their business, they could tend to that on the eve of Jake's marriage—put the land ownership in the corporation and ownership of stock in the siblings—and thereby defeat Elizabeth's dower claim. There is no dower in shares of stock; they are not real property. The dower claim thus became limited as wealth was put in stock markets rather than farms, but dower is persistent in other ways. It attaches at marriage or when property is acquired by the husband, and once it attaches it stays attached; it is "inchoate." Although the wife cannot do anything with her dower interest so long as the husband is alive, the husband cannot get rid of it so long as the wife is alive.

— Since the junkyard was real property, owned in part by Michelle, owned when she and Charles were married, the ante-nuptial devices of Victorian lawyers are not useful for disinheriting

Charles either. The husband, at common law, had a parallel inchoate interest in the wife's property (curtesy); it did not attach unless children were born to the couple, but then it was a life interest in *all* of the wife's property. Modern American constitutional law would probably require that the interests of spouses be equal. Most American states have abolished common-law dower and curtesy.

— Most states have adopted an "elective share" system in addition to or rather than dower and curtesy. The critical elective-share time, if we are working for Michelle and Jake, will be the time of the death of one of the siblings. At that point, a surviving spouse can claim a significant share of the estate as a *statutory share*. A will giving everything to someone else—the decedent's sibling, in this case—will not prevent this claim; it is a matter, in the popular phrase, of "taking against the will." But the critical moment is death; if the decedent has disposed of property prior to death (given it to his sister say), the common elective share provided by American statutes won't reach that lifetime (or, as lawyers say, *inter-vivos*) transfer. The great disadvantage an elective-share system has over dower and curtesy (for Michelle and Jake) is that it reaches all kinds of property—real, personal, mixed, tangible and intangible—where dower and curtesy reach only real property. An elective-share statute will reach the corporate stock. The great advantage for our clients is that the elective share does not touch lifetime transfers. An elective-share claim by Elizabeth would reach Jake's junkyard stock, but not if Jake gave it to Michelle before Jake's death.

PEZZA v. PEZZA

Supreme Court of Rhode Island, 1997.
690 A.2d 345.

BOURCIER, JUSTICE.

This case comes before us on appeal from a final judgment of the Superior Court. The plaintiff below, Olga Pezza (Olga), had filed a petition seeking a declaration of her rights in four parcels of real estate that her deceased husband, Anthony Pezza (Anthony), had transferred prior to his death into an irrevocable trust for the benefit of his children by a former marriage. The trial justice found that the trust treated by Anthony was valid, constituted a completed and absolute inter vivos transfer by the time he died, and would not be declared invalid for the purpose of satisfying Olga's statutory survival interest, as codified in G.L. 1956 § 33–25–2.[1]

---

1. General laws 1956 § 33–25–2 reads as follows: "Whenever any person shall die leaving a husband or wife surviving, the real estate owned by the decedent in fee simple at his or her death shall descend and pass to the husband or wife for his or her natural life subject, however, to any encumbrances existing at death; provided that the liability, if any, of the decedent to discharge the encumbrance or encumbrances shall

Anthony owned and operated a garage door sales and installation business in Johnston, Rhode Island. His son, Michael Pezza (Michael), and his daughter, Patricia Pezza (Patricia), were both at one time or another employed in that business. Both Michael and Patricia were children of Anthony's first marriage, which ended when his first wife, Florida, died.

On February 21, 1973, Anthony married Olga, whose first marriage had ended in divorce. At some point during their marriage, Olga was listed as the joint owner of a residence in Florida that Anthony had inherited from his mother. Olga and Anthony also shared several joint bank accounts.

On December 29, 1983, Anthony created an inter vivos trust in which he named himself trustee and his son, Michael, successor trustee. Four parcels of real estate, acquired by Anthony prior to his marriage to Olga, were conveyed to that trust. Also conveyed to the trust were the shares of stock owned by Anthony in his garage door business corporation. Anthony's intent when conveying his real and personal property into the trust, as expressed to his attorney who drafted the trust documents, was to have his children own the property after his death, in satisfaction of a deathbed promise he had made to his first wife.[2] However, despite his conveyance of the property to the trust, Anthony continued to occupy one of the parcels as his marital estate. Furthermore, he continued to collect rents from the other three parcels. Additionally, as part of the trust agreement, Anthony retained the power to revoke the trust and the power to demand payment of the principal.

Anthony's will, executed simultaneously with the trust, contained a "pour-over" provision that provided that any of his remaining assets would be placed into and become part of the trust upon his death.

On June 25, 1986, following a disagreement between Anthony and Olga, Anthony resigned as trustee of the trust created on December 29, 1983, and pursuant to the provisions of the trust agreement, appointed his son, Michael, as his successor trustee. Anthony also on that same date waived his right to revoke the trust.

On November 14, 1986, Olga commenced divorce proceedings against Anthony.

On December 5, 1986, less than a month after commencement of the divorce proceedings, Anthony disclaimed his power to demand payment of the trust principal, to be effective as of June 25, 1986, that being the date when Michael was appointed successor trustee and Anthony waived his right to revoke the trust.

Anthony died testate on August 18, 1990.

---

not be impaired. The provisions of §§ 33–1–1 and 33–1–2 shall be subject to the provisions of this chapter and of § 33–1–6.''

2. Some property was not conveyed to the trust. Anthony explained to his attorney that it was his intention that Olga would retain possession of the house in Florida and would enjoy the benefit of certain monetary assets, including his individual retirement account.

In her complaint for declaratory relief filed in the Providence County Superior Court on January 17, 1991, Olga contended that Anthony's transfer of his real property into the trust for the benefit of his children from his first marriage was a fraudulent attempt on his part to deny her of her marital rights granted pursuant to § 33–25–2, which provides that a surviving spouse becomes entitled to a life estate in all of his or her deceased spouse's real estate owned in fee simple at the time of his or her death. Olga contended that the trust should be declared invalid and that she should be declared to have a life estate in the real property that Anthony had deeded to the trust.

After trial without a jury on February 14 and 17, 1994, the trial justice, in a written decision entered pursuant to Rule 52(a) of the Superior Court Rules of Civil Procedure, found that Olga had failed to prove a fraudulent transfer on the part of Anthony in creating the trust and that no legal basis had been shown for invalidating the final trust agreement executed by Anthony on December 29, 1983. The trial justice determined initially that the trust became irrevocable and nontestamentary in nature as a result of Anthony's actions taken on June 25 and December 9, 1986. The trial justice in his decision noted further that, in deciding whether to enforce the trust agreement, there existed a conflict between two competing policy concerns, namely, the right of a property owner to freely alienate his or her property interests and the right of a surviving spouse to some continuation of his or her interest in the property owned by his or her deceased spouse in fee simple at the time of his or her death, the latter right being the policy concern that was once protected by dower and curtesy prior to their abolition by § 33–25–1. Section 33–25–2, which grants a life estate to a surviving spouse, replaced dower and curtesy as the means through which a surviving spouse's rights are protected.

. . .

This Court has not yet considered the question of whether an inter vivos trust can be used to defeat a surviving spouse's statutory right to a life estate in his or her deceased spouse's real estate. Therefore, when an issue of first impression is presented to us, we generally look to other jurisdictions for guidance.

Those other jurisdictions that have previously considered the question of whether an inter vivos trust can be used to defeat a surviving spouse's statutory survival interest in real estate have used various approaches in their analyses. The two primary tests employed by the various courts examining this issue are known as the fraudulent intent test, otherwise known as the intent to defraud test, and the illusory transfer test. In the fraudulent transfer text, the court examines several case-specific factors in order to determine whether in the particular case before it the deceased spouse had at the time of the transfer of property into the trust an intent to defraud his or her spouse of his or her statutory survival interest. Those factors are "if the transfer was made without consideration; the size of the transfer in relation to the [spouse's] total assets; the time between the transfer and the [spouse's] death; relations which existed between the husband and wife at the time of the transfer; and the source from which the property came." *Sherrill v. Mallicote,* 57 Tenn. App. 241, 417 S.W.2d 798, 802 (1967). Once those factors have been considered, the court must then decide whether the transfer was made with an intent to deprive the surviving spouse of his or her statutory share, and if the court determine that such an intent to deprive was present, the court will invalidate the transfer and make the trust property available for distribution to the surviving spouse pursuant to the jurisdiction's statutory survival share statute. *See also Hanke v. Hanke,* 123 N.H. 175, 459 A.2d 246 (1983).

The illusory transfer test involves an approach different from that of the fraudulent intent test. It focuses not on the intent of the transferor-spouse but, instead, on the substance of the transfer itself, that is, whether the transfer was "real" or "illusory." In *Newman,* [v. *Dore,* 275 N.Y. 371, 9 N.E.2d 966 (1937)], the most often cited case involving the illusory transfer test, the New York court noted that most jurisdictions have declined to adopt the fraudulent intent test either because to do so would "cast doubt upon the validity of all transfers made by a married man [or woman], outside of the regular course of business" or because it was "difficult to find a satisfactory logical foundation for it." 9 N.E.2d at 968. The court opined that the fraudulent intent of the spouse making the inter vivos transfer to a trust was not relevant to the court's inquiry because the law in New York at the time *Newman* was decided gave a surviving spouse only an expectancy interest in the real property of the other spouse, an interest conditioned on the fact that the spouse would own some real property at the time of his or her death. Furthermore, the court noted that the law in New York at that time did not restrict transfers of property during the life of a spouse. Therefore, the court in *Newman,* concluded that no right of the wife had been invaded by the husband's inter vivos transfer of his property, which incidentally acted to defeat the wife's mere expectancy interest in her statutory survival share. As a result, the Newman court held that the only relevant inquiry in the factual situation before it wherein the surviving spouse had only an expectancy interest prior to the death of the other spouse was whether the spouse who had transferred the property had "in good faith divested himself [or herself] of ownership of his [or her] property or ha[d] made an illusory transfer." 9 N.E.2d at 969. The court explained that although an intent to defraud is not relevant to the court's inquiry under the illusory transfer test, the court must nonetheless still consider whether the deceased spouse, when he or she made the inter vivos transfer to the trust, had an "intent to divest himself [or herself] of the ownership of the property." *Id.*

The relevance of intent when applying the illusory transfer test was further considered later in *Johnson* v. *La Grange State Bank,* 73 Ill. 2d 342, 22 Ill. Dec. 709, 383 N.E.2d 185 (1978). In that case the Illinois court ... concluded that "an inter vivos transfer of property is valid as against the marital rights of the surviving spouse unless the transaction is tantamount to a fraud as manifested by the absence of donative intent to make a conveyance of a present interest in the property conveyed. Without such an intent the transfer would simply be a sham or merely a colorable or illusory transfer of legal title. * * * [I]f no interests passed under the trusts to the beneficiaries before the death of the settler then the trusts are testamentary and invalid." *Id.*, 22 Ill. Dec. at 718, 383 N.E.2d at 194.

In order for a transfer of real property to a trust to be real, valid, and nonillusory, the spouse transferring the property must effectuate a completed inter vivos transfer by conveyance that both divests him or her of all ownership in the property and that, also, at the time of conveyance, is made with the proper donative intent. [　]

.　.　.

Turning now to the case facts before us, we conclude, as did the court in *Newman*, that our statute, § 33–25–2, which grants a life estate to a surviving spouse in the real property owned in fee simple by his or her spouse at the time of his or her death, creates only an expectancy interest in the surviving spouse. The interest that descends and passes by § 33–25–2 does not become vested until one spouse dies while owning real property in fee simple. Until the time of death there is no means by which to determine the exact extent of the interest to which the surviving spouse is entitled, and therefore, a surviving spouse cannot possess a determinable vested interest until his or her spouse dies. Because § 33–25–2 creates only an expectancy interest, a property-owning spouse is free, while he or she is alive, to transfer his or her real property without interfering with any vested right of a surviving spouse. We believe that the illusory transfer test rule, in the context of the case facts before us in this appeal, also serves both to recognize and to give deserved deference to the policy interests once protected by our former dower and curtesy statute, § 33–25–1, and the right of surviving spouses intended by § 33–25–2. That rule mandates that any conveyance of real estate made by one spouse to any third party or trust must be real and complete and not illusory [　]. We adopt now the illusory transfer test as the proper test to be used when determining whether a now-deceased spouse's inter vivos transfer of real property is sufficient to defeat a surviving spouse's statutory share pursuant to § 33–25–2.

When that test is applied to the facts in the record before us, it is clear that Anthony's transfer of his property to the trust was real and complete as of December 5, 1986, at which time, having previously resigned as trustee and having previously appointed his son as successor trustee, he disclaimed his power to compel any reconveyance to him of the real estate subject to the trust pursuant to G.L. 1956 § 34–5–2, thus making the trust completely irrevocable and real. Anthony's intent when creating the trust, as noted earlier, was relevant only insofar as it tended to establish whether he had an intent to totally divest himself of the real estate, that is, whether he had the present donative intent that was required for the validity of his inter vivos transfer. Arguably, Anthony possessed only an intent to create a testamentary gift when he first attempted to establish the trust on December 29, 1983, evidenced by the fact that he retained the power to revoke the trust, retained the power to demand payment of the trust principal, and was the named trustee as well as the trust beneficiary. However, he certainly possessed and expressed the necessary present donative intent by June 25, 1986, when he named his son as successor trustee and totally divested himself of the right to revoke the trust. When later, on December 5, 1986, he disclaimed his right to demand any payment of the trust principal, it became absolutely clear that the trust was not then illusory. Therefore, at the time of Anthony's death on August 18, 1990, the trust was complete, valid, and real, having been made so with a then-present donative intent on Anthony's part, which completed divested him of all benefits of trust property ownership. Therefore, the trial justice's findings that the terms of the trust agreement should be enforced and that the real property conveyed to the trust by Anthony is not subject to Olga's statutory survival interest as codified in § 33–25–2 are without error. It was Olga's burden at trial to establish "by clear and satisfactory evidence" that Anthony did not intend, *in praesenti*, on December 5, 1986, to then finally and completely divest himself of all ownership and control over the trust property and to vest immediate exclusive ownership and control in the trust. [ ] She failed to so persuade the trial justice whose findings we sustain.

Accordingly, for all the foregoing reasons, Olga's appeal is denied and dismissed . . .

Notes and Questions

1.   The lawyer who seeks to set up either (i) conveyance of real property from Jake to the corporation, on the eve of his marriage; or (ii) conveyance of stock, by Jake, to Michelle, during Jake's life and after his marriage to Elizabeth, will have to proceed with some care to come to terms with the substantial body of case law having to do with eve-of-marriage transfers to frustrate dower claims or lifetime gratuitous transfers to frustrate statutory-share claims. (You can see how case law on one issue is authority on the other issue. Should it be?) Can you suggest how evidence might be assembled and preserved, at and before the time of transfer, to protect the transfers from attacks such as the one in Pezza?

2.   Some states have enacted legislation that pulls certain lifetime transfers is to seek legislation that will pull lifetime transfers back into the decedent's estate for the limited purpose of satisfying statutory-share claims. In some ways this extends the inchoate character of dower to an elective-share system and gives a surviving spouse the best of both worlds. The analogy might be (and has been) to death taxes. Those taxes, both state and federal, reach lifetime gratuitous transfers, including joint tenancies (where the decedent has placed her property in a joint tenancy with a donee),

outright gifts, trust arrangements in which the decedent reserved a life interest, and even life insurance and survivor's retirement benefits. Such lifetime transfers are not invalid, but they are vulnerable to having to be partially undone in order to pay death taxes—or the elective share to the widow or widower: New York and Pennsylvania adopted "augmented estate" statutory-share systems a generation ago. The Uniform Probate Code, adopted in 1969 and revised in 1990 and 1993, provides such a system, and several states have adopted it. Statutes of this sort typically: (i) refer to and build on the existing elective-share statute (*e.g.,* a surviving spouse may claim his intestate share of the estate "against the will"); (ii) list a range of lifetime transfers that can be set aside to "augment" the estate against which the elective share can be taken (but are not otherwise set aside); (iii) provide that the same list of transfers be applied as to the surviving spouse, so that a tenancy by the entirety or an outright gift to the surviving spouse is also brought into the augmented estate; and (iv) direct a computation of the elective-share fraction against the augmented estate, followed by reduction for amounts the surviving spouse already received. For an argument that current elective share statutes fail to fully consider what property is a product of the marriage and therefore do not always treat the surviving spouse fairly, see Angela Vallario, *Spousal Election: Suggested Equitable Reform for the Division of Property at Death*, 52 Cath. U. L. Rev. 519 (2003) (proposing an "Equitable Elective Share Statute").

NOTE: ON MORALS IN THE LAW OFFICE[6]

In my classes in wills and trusts we use Justice Holmes's bad-man theory of law when we discuss the rules * * * protecting spouses from disinheritance. * * *

[Even] in those few states which use "augmented estate" systems * * * the obstacles are surmountable. [Some] of those systems of protection, for instance, [exclude] life insurance. One way to disinherit a spouse is to reduce everything to cash and to buy life insurance with it—insurance which, in this case would be [on the life of Jake, with Morgan as beneficiary, or vice versa]. * * *

The students come to see that they are equal to a difficult bit of planning. They gather confidence in their own learning and ability. They discover that it is easier to defeat a family than it is to defeat the government.

And then I say to them: Now that you know you *can* do it, I want to know whether you *would* do it. I get three sorts of answers to this moral question: (1) Some students say that the moral question is not for a lawyer to answer; it is for the client. Our professional ideals point to doing for people what they want done, within the limits of the law. In fact, our system works best when each lawyer does his best for his client and the system itself irons out the differences. (2) Some students say

6. Thomas L. Shaffer, "The Ethics of Estate Planning," Probate Notes, American   College of Probate Counsel, Spring 1979, p. 19.

they would not, under any conditions, do this work for this client. They argue that our professional ideals point toward clients' conduct which is moral as well as legal. Professional ideals do not suspend the lawyer's conscience; lawyers still have to answer for what they do. (3) A final answer is that the lawyers should talk to the client about this question. Lawyers have moral influence on their clients; a lawyer's work should include efforts to help clients make choices that are morally sound, and this is accomplished by sharing with the client the burden of hard choices.

[Maybe] those three schools of ethical thought sum up the morality of practicing law. The first is role-determined; it says, in effect, that lawyers are like plumbers, or clerks in hardware stores. They do what their customers want done. The second is a morality of conscientious objection; it says that a lawyer cannot base her behavior on what people expect of her as a lawyer, but that she has a conscience of her own. The third is a morality of care. * * * [I]t says that the moral life is a shared life: No person is an island, it says; "and therefore never send to know for whom the bell tolls, it tolls for thee." I care for my client and have a right to expect that my client will care for me.

Each of these three orientations has its promise and its limitations; the third, the morality of care, is, I think, the most difficult, but it is the morality I urge on my students.

The morality of role depends on an idea about the function of the profession in society, and on an idea about the function of each lawyer within the profession. It offers security, as functional definitions of people always do, but it does not offer moral breadth or depth. Even so, the debate that goes on in our profession about the moral responsibility of lawyers takes place almost entirely within this limited morality of role. Those who defend the adversary system argue that lawyers should do what clients want done because the courts, or the free-enterprise economy, or Social Darwinism, will make things come out right. The more modern school of "public interest law," which argues that lawyers have a duty to see to the social usefulness of what their clients do, is morally similar in that it, like the adversary-ethic argument, bases its case on the principle that lawyers should serve the public interest.

The problem with either branch in the morality of role is that it is only as good as the system * * * the lawyer is said to serve. Professionalism does not contain within itself a basis for questioning the goodness of the system. Or, to put that thought another way, professionalism assumes that the system can provide goodness. It assumes that *power* can provide goodness. But power cannot provide goodness, and those who assume that power can provide goodness risk ending up in the service of evil. Albert Speer, or the S.S. colonel in "The Holocaust," did not set out to serve evil; they set out to serve power, on the assumption that power would provide a good society for themselves and their families. They fooled themselves, as many others did in the German establishment of their day, and the consequences were as bad as anything that has ever happened to the world.

The morality of conscientious objection depends on * * * moral isolation. It assumes that each lawyer and each client makes decisions alone, that these people in the law office do not depend upon and influence one another. That idea seems to me to be untrue. My observation, from more than 20 years [30 years now] of studying, teaching, and practicing law, is that clients are almost always influenced by lawyers, and that lawyers are influenced by clients. In fact, lawyers tend to become like their clients. Lawyers are, in a way, more influenced than influencing.

We Americans cherish a myth of rugged individualism, but our history, like the history of any people, is a history of dependence and influence. Dependence and influence are almost as pronounced in professional relationships as they are in the family. We tend to forget how dependent we are until we are stuck in an airline waiting room, wondering about a delayed flight across the country, or until we are out looking for a job. If we were capable of moral reflection at such moments, we would realize how much we depend on our clients, and they on us. In the moral life, dependence is a matter of fact and a matter of aspiration. As the great theologian Karl Barth put it:

> He who takes the risk of counseling must be prepared to be counseled in turn by his brother if there is need of it. Such mutual counseling in a concrete situation is an event. It is a part of the ethos which is realized ethics. The ethos * * * implies that he refrain from attempting too much and becoming thereby a lawgiver.

The prominent problem with the morality of conscientious objection is that it assumes a moral isolation that is not truthful. A more subtle problem is that it assumes a moral life without risk; if I set out to give moral assistance to my client, I must, as Barth says, be prepared to accept moral assistance, and that is scary. That is less secure than my students, who decide that they must do the right thing in their law offices, suppose it to be.

The morality of care is based on the dynamics of making up your mind. The most interesting examples of people making up their minds are in literature—in Trollope's novels *The Warden* and *The Duke's Children,* for two examples, or in C.P. Snow's novel about justice, *The Affair.* The process in which a strong, good person decides what to do, or decides to change her mind, is a wondrous and subtle process, but one thing that seems to be present in these literary cases is the influence of other people. I argue that the morality of care is not a matter of deciding to exert influence or to be influenced. It is a matter of admitting that we do influence and are influenced. It is a matter, in the first instance, of truthfulness. Once we tell ourselves the truth about influence, we can begin to take moral account of the influences we exert and the influences exerted on us.

If influence is admitted it is possible to work toward a morality of influences. Most lawyers would probably say that the most important principle in exerting moral influence on clients is respect for the freedom of the client. Modern philosophical ethics * * * sets down limits * * * which forbid coercion, dishonesty, and manipulation. Within the practice of respect for the moral freedom of clients, the influence lawyers choose to exert can range from acceptance of the moral choices of clients to advertent attempts at conversion. At one end of this spectrum of influence are lawyers who ask only that their clients consider moral choices seriously; at the other end are lawyers who ask their clients to pray with them. All along the spectrum is a realization that moral problems in professional relationships are shared. My concern for my client includes the concern that he become a better person. I have an investment in his goodness. It is not enough that he and I make moral choices that are right; our goal is moral choices that cause us to become better people. * * *

The morality of care also assumes skills. It requires the ability to listen and to elicit, the ability to focus on what worries the client, and not merely on the art of planning to do what the client says she wants done. In the example my students work with, the skills involved are skills for talking about the client's family and about the [client's brother and their business]. These are counseling skills, not advocacy or planning skills. * * * They are skills Carl Rogers pointed toward when he said to his client:

> To be of assistance to you I will put aside myself—the self of ordinary interaction—and enter into your world of perception as completely as I am able. I will become, in a sense, another self for you—an alter ego of your own attitudes and feelings—a safe opportunity for you to discern yourself more clearly * * * to choose more significantly.

There is no morally responsible way to limit the work of the law office to filling orders or to the naked assertion of moral choice. My client and I are in this thing together. * * *

———

In a return to the question of morals in the law office, Professors Shaffer and Cochran identified four ways that lawyers deal with clients and moral concerns in the law office:

1) the lawyer as *godfather*, one who "makes choices for someone, irrespective of harm to others, and who carries them out, often with harm to others;"

2) the lawyer as *hired gun*, whose "job is to *empower* the client, not to question the client's morality;"

3) The lawyer as *guru*, who "makes moral choices for clients and tells them what to do," and

4) The lawyer as *friend*, who "wants the client to be and to become a better person." Thomas L. Shaffer & Robert F. Cochran, Jr., Lawyers, Clients, and Moral Responsibility 7, 16, 32, 42 (1994).

Review the materials we have studied so far, particularly the disputes that resulted in litigation. Can you see these approaches reflected in the litigation strategies? Do any of them predominate? Would mediation emphasize different approaches, or are all used at one time or another?

B. COMMUNITY PROPERTY

The most coherent and consistent body of American marital-property law is the system of community property we inherited from our Spanish forebears. This system is in effect in Louisiana, Texas, New Mexico, Arizona, Nevada, California, Idaho, and Washington. The community-property system turns on the principle that earnings in a marriage belong to the marriage (the "community"). It is not determinative that record ownership of property traceable to the earnings of one spouse is in that spouse's name. Earnings and property traceable to earnings are community property and are *owned,* from the first, half and half.

The system has had its patriarchal past, as much as the common-law property system has. The old rule was that the husband controlled the community's property, so that, for all practical purposes, community ownership became an issue only at divorce or death. Legislation and judicial decisions parallel to *Pezza* in community-property states limit the old principle, where it has not been abolished entirely, so that third persons dealing with one spouse are much less able than they once were to assume that the actions will bind the other spouse . .

The system is also complicated by definitions of what is community property and what is not. Property a spouse owned at the time of marriage, inherited property, and gift property, are probably the clearest examples of "separate" (non-community) property. Paychecks, bank accounts into which earnings are deposited, and houses and automobiles bought from such accounts, are probably the clearest examples of community property. Employer-provided fringe benefits, such as life insurance and retirement pay, are a middle case. And damages recovered for torts committed on one of the spouses by a third party are a good example for discussion; such issues have not yet been dealt with everywhere by case law or statute.

The character of property is subject to the agreement of the spouses. Thus property can be "transmuted" from community to separate, or vice versa, or to a form that is functionally neither. A joint-and-survivor bank account, or joint securities ownership, are possible in community-property states, for example, as are joint tenancies in other property.

While only nine states embrace community property law, these states contain about 80 million residents who have approximately $1 trillion invested in retirement plans along with other property they may own. The interaction of state community property law and major federal legislation designed to encourage and protect retirement savings is reviewed in the following case.

BOGGS v. BOGGS

Supreme Court of the United States, 1997.
520 U.S. 833, 117 S.Ct. 1754, 138 L.Ed.2d 45.

JUSTICE KENNEDY delivered the opinion of the Court.

We consider whether the Employee Retirement Income Security Act of 1974 (ERISA), 88 Stat. 832, as amended, 29 U.S.C. § 1001 *et seq.*, preempts a state law allowing a nonparticipant spouse to transfer by testamentary instrument an interest in undistributed pension plan benefits. Given the pervasive significance of pension plans in the national economy, the congressional mandate for their uniform and comprehensive regulation, and the fundamental importance of community property law in defining the marital partnership in a number of States, the question is of undoubted importance. We hold that ERISA preempts the state law.

Isaac Boggs worked for South Central Bell from 1949 until his retirement in 1985. Isaac and Dorothy, his first wife, were married when he began working for the company, and they remained husband and wife until Dorothy's death in 1979. They had three sons. Within a year of Dorothy's death, Isaac married Sandra, and they remained married until his death in 1989.

Upon retirement, Isaac received various benefits from his employer's retirement plans. One was a lump sum distribution from the Bell System Savings Plan for Salaried Employees (Savings Plan) of $151,628.94, which he rolled over into an Individual Retirement Account (IRA). He made no withdrawals and the account was worth $180,778.05 when he died. He also received 96 shares of AT & T stock from the Bell South Employee Stock Ownership Plan (ESOP). In addition, Isaac enjoyed a monthly annuity payment during his retirement of $1,777.67 from the Bell South Service Retirement Program.

The instant dispute over ownership of the benefits is between Sandra (the surviving wife) and the sons of the first marriage. The sons' claim to a portion of the benefits is based on Dorothy's will. Dorothy bequeathed to Isaac one-third of her estate, and a lifetime usufruct in the remaining two-thirds. A lifetime usufruct is the rough equivalent of a common law life estate. She bequeathed to her sons the naked ownership in the remaining two-thirds, subject to Isaac's usufruct. All agree that, absent preemption, Louisiana law controls and that under it Dorothy's will would dispose of her community property interest in Isaac's undistributed pension plan benefits. A Louisiana state court . . . ascribed to Dorothy's estate a community property interest in Isaac's Savings Plan account valued at the time at $21,194.29.

Sandra contests the validity of Dorothy's 1980 testamentary transfer, basing her claim to those benefits on her interest under Isaac's will and 29 U.S.C. § 1055. Isaac bequeathed to Sandra outright certain real property including the family home. His will also gave Sandra a lifetime usufruct in the remainder of his estate, with the naked ownership interest being held by the sons. Sandra argues that the sons' competing claim, since it is based on Dorothy's 1980 purported testamentary transfer of her community property interest in undistributed pension plan benefits, is preempted by ERISA. The Bell South Service Retirement Program monthly annuity is now paid to Sandra as the surviving spouse.

. . .

II

. . .

This case lies at the intersection of ERISA pension law and state community property law. None can dispute the central role community property laws play in the nine community property States. It is more than a property regime. It is a commitment to the equality of husband and wife and reflects the real partnership inherent in the marital relationship. State community property laws, many of ancient lineage, "must have continued to exist through such lengths of time because of their manifold excellences and are not lightly to be abrogated or tossed aside." 1 W. de Funiak, Principles of Community Property 11 (1943). The community property regime in Louisiana dates from 1808 when the territorial legislature of Orleans drafted a civil code which adopted Spanish principles of community property. [ ] Louisiana's community property laws, and the community property regimes enacted in other states, implement policies and values lying within the traditional domain of the States. These considerations inform our preemption analysis. [ ]

The nine community property States have some 80 million residents, with perhaps $1 trillion in retirement plans. [ ] This case involves a community property claim, but our ruling will affect as well the right to make claims or assert interests based on the law of any State, whether or not it recognizes community property. Our ruling must be consistent with the congressional scheme to assure the security of plan participants and their families in every State. . . .

ERISA is an intricate, comprehensive statute. Its federal regulatory scheme governs employee benefit plans, which include both pension and welfare plans. All employee benefit plans must conform to various reporting, disclosure and fiduciary requirements, [ ] while pension plans must also comply with participation, vesting, and funding requirements [ ]. The surviving spouse annuity and QDRO (qualified domestic relations order) provisions, central to the dispute here, are part of the statute's mandatory participation and vesting requirements. These provisions provide detailed protections to spouses of plan participants which, in some cases, exceed what their rights would be were community property law the sole measure.

ERISA's express preemption clause states that the Act "shall supersede any and all State laws insofar as they may now or hereafter relate to any employee benefit plan.... § 1144(a). We can begin, and in this case end, the analysis by simply asking if state law conflicts with the provisions of ERISA or operates to frustrate its objects ... We hold that there is a conflict, which suffices to resolve the case....

We first address the survivor's annuity and then turn to the other pension benefits.

III

Sandra Boggs, as we have observed, asserts that federal law preempts and supersedes state law and requires the surviving spouse annuity to be paid to her as the sole beneficiary. We agree.

ERISA requires that every qualified joint and survivor annuity include an annuity payable to a nonparticipant surviving spouse. The survivor's annuity may not be less than 50% of the amount of the annuity which is payable during the joint lives of the participant and spouse. § 1055(d)(1). Provision of the survivor's annuity may not be waived by the participant, absent certain limited circumstances, unless the spouse consents in writing to the designation of another beneficiary, which designation also cannot be changed without a further spousal consent, witnessed by a plan representative or notary public. § 1055(c)(2). Sandra Boggs, as the surviving spouse, is entitled to a survivor's annuity under these provisions. She has not waived her right to the survivor's annuity, let alone consented to having the sons designated as the beneficiaries.

Respondents say their state law claims are consistent with these provisions. Their claims, they argue, affect only the disposition of plan proceeds after they have been disbursed by the Bell South Service Retirement Program, and thus nothing is required of the plan. ERISA's concern for securing national uniformity in the administration of employee benefit plans, in their view, is not implicated....

We disagree. The statutory object of the qualified joint and survivor annuity provisions, along with the rest of § 1055, is to ensure a stream of income to surviving spouses. Section 1055 mandates a survivor's annuity not only where a participant dies after the annuity starting date but also guarantees one if the participant dies before then. See Sections 1055(a)(2), (e). These provisions, enacted as part of the Retirement Equity Act of 1984 (REA), Pub. L. 98–397, 98 Stat. 1426, enlarged ERISA's protection of surviving spouses in significant respects. Before REA, ERISA only required that pension plans, if they provided for the payment of benefits in the form of an annuity, offer a qualified joint and survivor annuity as an option entirely within a participant's discretion [ ]. REA modified ERISA to permit participants to designate a beneficiary for the survivor's annuity, other than the nonparticipant spouse, only when the spouse agrees. § 1055(c)(2). Congress' concern for surviving spouses is also evident from the expansive coverage of § 1055, as amended by REA. Section 1055's requirements, as a general matter, apply to all "individual account plans" and "defined benefits plans." § 1055(b)(1). The terms are defined, for

§ 1055 purposes, so that all pension plans fall within those two categories. See § 1002(35). While some individual account plans escape § 1055's surviving spouse annuity requirements under certain conditions, Congress still protects the interests of the surviving spouse by requiring those plans to pay the spouse the nonforfeitable accrued benefits, reduced by certain security interests, in a lump sum payment. § 1055(b)(1)(C).

ERISA's solicitude for the economic security of surviving spouses would be undermined by allowing a predeceasing spouse's heirs and legatees to have a community property interest in the survivor's annuity. Even a plan participant cannot defeat a nonparticipant surviving spouse's statutory entitlement to an annuity. It would be odd, to say the least, if Congress permitted a predeceasing nonparticipant spouse to do so. Nothing in the language of ERISA supports concluding that Congress made such an inexplicable decision. Testamentary transfers could reduce a surviving spouse's guaranteed annuity below the minimum set by ERISA (defined as 50% of the annuity payable during the joint lives of the participant and spouse). In this case, Sandra's annuity would be reduced by approximately 20%, according to the calculations contained in the sons' state court filings. There is no reason why testamentary transfers could not reduce a survivor's annuity by an even greater amount. Perhaps even more troubling, the recipient of the testamentary transfer need not be a family member. For instance, a surviving spouse's § 1055 annuity might be substantially reduced so that funds could be diverted to support an unrelated stranger.

In the face of this direct clash between state law and the provisions and objectives of ERISA, the state law cannot stand.... It would undermine the purpose of ERISA's mandated survivor's annuity to allow Dorothy, the predeceasing spouse, by her testamentary transfer to defeat in part Sandra's entitlement to the annuity § 1055 guarantees her as the surviving spouse. This cannot be. States are not free to change ERISA's structure and balance.

Louisiana law, to the extent it provides the sons with a right to a portion of Sandra Boggs' § 1055 survivor's annuity, is preempted.

· · ·

(Discussion of monthly annuity payments and ESOP share of stock omitted)

(Dissenting opinion omitted.)

Note and Question

One question left open in *Boggs* was "whether ERISA would permit a nonparticipant spouse to obtain a divisible community property interest in benefits paid out during the existence of the community between the participant and that spouse." 520 U.S. at 845. Would a state statute authorizing prison officials to deduct 35% of all funds received by an inmate from outside sources violate ERISA? See Wright v. Riveland, 219 F.3d 905, 921 (9th Cir. 2000) (no).

C. UNIFORM MARITAL PROPERTY ACT (UMPA)

In the decades after the Second World War, another attempt was made in the common law states to redefine the relationship of married women to property based on the motion of marriage as a partnership. The Uniform Martial Property Act, (UMPA) was the expression of this effort. The following excerpt describes the basic elements of UMPA.

PROBATE, TRUST AND REAL PROPERTY SECTION, INDIANA STATE BAR ASSOCIATION, "UNIFORM MARITAL PROPERTY ACT"

Res Gestae, November 1984, p. 237.

In July of 1983, the Commissioners on Uniform State Laws approved for promulgation the Uniform Marital Property Act ("UMPA"). If adopted by Indiana, UMPA would change Indiana's present common law system of property ownership to a community property based system. This course has already been taken by Wisconsin, a former common law property state, which adopted a look-alike UMPA in the spring of 1984.

UMPA was designed to address property problems occurring as a result of increases in the incidences of divorce and the numbers of marriages in which both spouses are employed outside the home.

Moreover, it reflects increased pressures to recognize the services of the full time homemaker as a contributor to a couple's economic success. UMPA treats the property acquired during a marriage ("marital property") as "ours" rather than as "yours or mine." * * *

UMPA's *determination date* is the last to occur of (i) the parties' marriage, (ii) the date the parties move into the enacting state, or (iii) the effective date of UMPA's enactment in the state.

UMPA provides for three categories of property: "marital," "individual" and "mixed." Property owned by an individual prior to marriage is individual property, as is property acquired by gift made by, or inheritance received from, a third person to a spouse. Except as specifically provided in UMPA, the interest of a spouse in property owned immediately before UMPA's enactment is individual property.

Property acquired by a spouse through exchange for or with the proceeds of the spouse's individual property remains individual property as does appreciation of individual property. Other examples of individual property include recoveries from the other spouse for UMPA "breaches" and recoveries for personal injuries.

Except as noted above, and unless reclassified by * * * agreement * * *, all other property acquired by a couple after UMPA's determination date is "marital" property.

Earnings, income earned or accrued by a spouse on marital property, and income earned or accrued by a spouse on individual property *after* UMPA's determination date are "marital" property. Each spouse is the owner of an undivided one-half interest in all marital property.

Marital and individual property may be commingled, resulting in "mixed" property under UMPA. Mixed property (other than life insurance and deferred employment benefits) is deemed to be "marital" property unless the component of the mixed property which is not marital property can be traced. This rule is in line with UMPA's general presumption that all property owned by spouses is marital property. * * *

Mixed property can * * * result from "sweat equity"—defined as the application by one spouse of substantial labor, effort, inventiveness, physical or intellectual skill, creativity, or managerial activity with respect to the other spouse's individual property.

Marital property attributable to that application is created if reasonable compensation is not received by the spouse applying the sweat equity and if substantial appreciation results from the spouse's labor. * * *

The classification rules would introduce a new element in Indiana practice when marriages terminate either by death or dissolution. It would be necessary to determine the source of property, trace the income of individual and marital property, and trace the growth in asset value realized from appreciation of individual property. Additional problems would be presented by mixed property. * * *

[M]arried persons may, by way of a marital property agreement, agree to just about any matter relating to their property that is not illegal or immoral. Marital property agreements cannot be used to vary some provisions of UMPA, such as its good faith requirement, the provisions protecting third parties, and the provisions concerning the support of dependent children.

The fact that a marital property agreement can be revoked or amended only by a later marital property agreement provides considerable protection to spouses in probate matters. A will or trust can be altered unilaterally, while a marital property agreement alteration would require the signatures of both spouses. There are some similarities between these agreements and the antenuptial agreements effective under current Indiana law. * * *

Both spouses must act together to control marital property held in the names of both spouses. * * * Either spouse has sole management and control rights over a marital property asset which is titled in that spouse's name alone.

Thus the precise language of title may be determinative of control and will necessitate careful attention when titling real or personal property. UMPA specifically authorizes the titling of marital property.

UMPA contains rules restricting the ability of one spouse to make a gift to a third party of marital property controlled by that spouse. UMPA leaves the amount of the gift which can be made without joinder by the other spouse to the discretion of the adopting state, but sets forth $500.00 as a suggested limit.* * *

Creditors' rights are not diminished by UMPA and may, in fact, be somewhat enlarged. UMPA (1) establishes a presumption that any obligation (including one attributable to an act or omission) incurred by a spouse during marriage is incurred in the interest of the marriage or family; and (2) allows the obligation to be satisfied out of all the marital property and the incurring spouse's individual property.

Any other obligation (also including one attributable to an act or omission) incurred by a spouse is satisfied first out of that spouse's individual property and then out of his or her interest in marital property.

Thus creditors' rights are expanded through an ability to [garnish] a non-contracting spouse's wages to satisfy debts, unless it can be shown that those debts were not incurred in the interest of the marriage or family.

On the other hand, the non-contracting spouse's interest in marital property is protected against creditor's claims arising out of the purely personal obligations of the incurring spouse. * * *

In addition to creditors, UMPA provides protection to bona fide purchasers for value. This is the same bona fide purchaser that all lawyers get to know and love in law school—with one exception. A bona fide purchaser *with* notice is protected. Therefore, third party purchasers of marital property are under no duty of inquiry and may rely on record title. * * *

Survivorship Marital Property. UMPA creates a new designation of property known as "survivorship marital property." By using these words in a title, rather than the words "marital property," total ownership rights in the marital property will rest in the surviving spouse upon death. In this way, among others, probate may be avoided. * * *

Because UMPA creates vested interests in marital property while still permitting individual management and control of that property, some method is necessary to allow the noncontrolling spouse to review the activities of the controlling spouse and to remedy any injustice to the noncontrolling spouse's interests.

UMPA's method is to give the noncontrolling spouse a claim against the controlling spouse for a breach of the controlling spouse's good faith duty.

To remedy the breach, a court can order an accounting of all property and obligations of the spouses and can determine each spouse's rights of ownership in, beneficial enjoyment of, or access to, marital property. It can adjust their interests as may be necessary to remedy an injustice unless these interests fall within particular classes. * * *

[A]fter dissolution or death, each spouse would own an undivided one-half interest in the marital property. However, this result could be changed on dissolution by an agreement or court order.

The adoption of UMPA would require some rethinking of Indiana's intestate and elective share statutes. Since the surviving spouse would, under UMPA, own one-half of the marital property, this one-half share would not pass as part of a deceased spouse's probate estate (although it may be administered as part of it).

If UMPA were enacted and present Indiana law were not changed, the surviving spouse would be entitled to one-half of the couple's marital property and to an intestate or elective share of the deceased spouse's individual property and share of marital property.

Notes

1. The Indiana State Bar Association has consistently opposed enactment of UMPA in Indiana. Wisconsin remains the only state to have adopted UMPA. The Wisconsin statute is discussed in Howard S. Erlanger & June M. Weisberger, From Common Law Property to Community Property: Wisconsin's Marital Property Act Four Years Later 1990 WIS. L. REV. 769. The Oregon Law Commission began considering UMPA in 2001 but changed its focus in 2002 to the statutory elective share. http://www.willamette.edu/law/oregonlaw commission/home/work_groups3.html, last visited March 29, 2006.

2. When the marital property act became effective in Wisconsin, James Bartelt, a reporter for the Green Bay Press–Gazette, interviewed legislators from his newspaper's region, and reported their comments (November 17, 1985):

> Senator Alan Lasee, noting that couples can, by agreement, keep their property in common-law forms of ownership: "There is this concept of man and wife sitting at the kitchen table working things out. But the result is going to be going to an attorney to find out what to do to protect their property. Even attorneys who have attended seminars say, 'My God, what did you do down there?' "

> Senator Jerome Van Sistine * * * voted for the new property system "with very mixed emotions." It could cause problems for small business, and some couples with one spouse having a long and terminal illness might even consider divorce to preserve property, he said.

> Senator Lloyd Kincaid * * * said a big plus for the new system is the transfer of property when there is no will. "If there is a will, there is safety. But for the thousands of people without a will, the widow is left in trouble," he said. Kincaid said he "formulated my position on equal

opportunities for women. Women have always played a second-place role as far as pay is concerned''. * * *

Rep. Cletus Vanderperren * * * said he supported the * * * bill ''very reluctantly. I suppose now that 50 percent of marriages end in divorce it can be a good idea to divide property. It's more of an attorneys' bill,'' he said.

Rep. Sharon Metz * * * said she ''voted for marital property right down the line. Under the English common law system, men own all the property and almost own the women. This provides for sharing. When a couple prospers, each shares equally.''

3. In common-law states, when one spouse holds most or all of the couple's property, divorce-court judges often have the power to rearrange legal ownership. See, e.g., Indiana Code § 31–15–7–4, requiring the court to divide the property ''in a just and reasonable manner'' through a variety of specified ways. It is not fatal to fairness for a wife in divorce that the property is all held by the husband. (Judges will usually respect the spouses' agreement on division of property, by the way, and that also will normally involve re-arrangement of ownership.)

Most states have enacted statutes similar to the Indiana Statute noted above calling for equitable distribution of property. Spurred by promulgation of the Uniform Marriage and Divorce Act (UMDA) in 1970 and the ensuing debate over its resemblance to community property law, many states enacted an equitable distribution system similar to the one adopted by Massachusetts:

> Upon divorce ... the court may assign to either husband or wife all or any part of the estate of the other, including but not limited to all vested and nonvested benefits, rights and funds accrued during the marriage and which shall include, but not be limited to, retirement benefits, pension, profit-sharing, annuity, deferred compensation and insurance. In determining the ... nature and value of the property, if any, to be so assigned, the court ... shall consider the length of the marriage, the conduct of the parties during the marriage, the age, health, station, occupation, amount and sources of income, vocational skills, employability, estate, liabilities and needs of each of the parties and the opportunity of each for future acquisition of capital assets and income. In fixing the nature and value of the property to be so assigned, the court shall also consider the present and future needs of the dependent children of the marriage. The court may also consider the contribution of each of the parties in the acquisition, preservation or appreciation in value of their respective estates and the contribution of each of the parties as a homemaker to the family unit.... Mass.

Gen. Laws Ann. ch.208, § 34.

Proper classification of property as marital or non-marital is an essential element of an equitable distribution system. See, e.g. Moore v. Moore, S.W.3d 2006 WL 692251 (Mo. App. 2006) (husband as president of a family corporation had obligations to stockholders that prevented trial court from classifying all of company's increased stock value as marital property). A useful and detailed discussion of equitable distribution is found in Brett R.

Turner, Equitable Distribution of Property, 2d Ed. (Shepard's/McGraw–Hill, 1994).

The argument is therefore made that a marital-property act is more symbolic than anything else in changing the situation of women in divorce cases. Or, to put that point another way, opponents argue that, if the evil to be corrected is unfairness in divorce cases, the price of dual control of property during an intact marriage is too great a price to pay for reform. The counter-argument is that pooled ownership and dual control of property throughout the marriage recognizes in the law the philosophical and moral understanding of what marriage is.

Chapter Four

THE LANDLORD–TENANT RELATIONSHIP

INTRODUCTION

As we have seen, it is possible in our property system for two or more persons to hold interests in the same piece of property at the same time. Examples previously studied include Indian title, finders, the common law system of estates in land, and concurrent ownership.

In this chapter, we will study the law governing the landlord-tenant relationship, an important form of property sharing, in which possession and ownership of land are held voluntarily by two different persons. We will examine the common law concept, a non-freehold estate in which possession, or tenure, of land formed the basis for the relationship. We will also study the revolutionary changes in the law that took place in a 20–year period beginning in the mid–1960s, particularly with respect to residential landlord-tenant relationships, as well as the rules for entering into and exiting from the relationship. In addition, we will introduce the idea of mediation as a non-adversarial method of resolving disputes that may be particularly useful in a landlord-tenant setting.

I. NONADVERSARIAL RESOLUTION OF LANDLORD–TENANT DISPUTES

The following problem, which will be the focal point of our dispute resolution discussion, can also provide a useful setting for consideration of the other materials in this chapter. As you study the materials in this chapter, ask yourself what Kelly Green and Lance Lord did or did not do to provoke the controversy, what specific laws govern their relationship, and what they might have done differently to prevent the dispute from arising or to resolve it once it had arisen. A mediation exercise based on this problem is located at the end of the chapter.

In considering this problem, you may wish to consult Hyman, Swimming in the Deep End: Dealing with Justice in Mediation, 6

Cardozo J. Conflict Resol. 19 (2004) (arguing that mediators should be more willing to pay attention to justice in mediation instead of focusing solely on helping parties reach agreement) and Wexler, Practicing Law for Poor People, 79 Yale L.J. 1049 (1970), discussed in T. Shaffer, American Legal Ethics: Text, Readings, and Discussion Topics 36–39 (1985), (arguing that the client, not the lawyer, should decide objectives and tactics). Review also the materials on lawyer-client relations in the adverse possession section of Chapter One and in the estates and family property sections of Chapters Two and Three.

THE INEXPERIENCED LANDLORD: A MEDIATION EXERCISE FOR PROPERTY LAW*

Assume it is now February. Nearly two years ago, Kelly Green signed a one-year lease, renting an attractive older apartment for herself, her two-year old daughter, Susan, and her twelve-year old son, Michael. The rent was $600.00 a month, with heat furnished. There were nineteen other units in the building, which was fully rented at the time. The lease that Kelly signed contained a printed clause requiring the tenant to make all repairs. Kelly crossed out this clause and initialled the change. The lease also contained a typed clause stating that the landlord did not warrant the habitability of the premises.

At the time the lease was signed, Lance Lord, the landlord, and owner of the building promised Kelly that he would make certain repairs in the apartment and would provide screens for all the windows. Kelly asked for the screens because the apartment was on the second floor, and she was worried about her children's safety. When Kelly and the children moved in three weeks later, the screens had been placed in the windows, but other promised repairs had not been made. Moreover, the floor was wet with fresh varnish and as a result Kelly and her children had to spend the night in a motel.

During the first year that Kelly lived there, Lance's brother, Ray, lived in the building and provided some maintenance in return for a lower rent. He kept the common areas clean and made occasional minor repairs. Despite letters from Kelly, however, Lance never sent anyone to repair a malfunctioning oven and a broken kitchen cabinet door.

Believing that Lance would eventually fulfill his promises, Kelly renewed her lease the following July. The situation began to deteriorate soon thereafter. Ray moved out of the building, and Lance hired a series of incompetent maintenance men to replace him. The hall and stairways were rarely swept. The trash was not regularly carried out to the curb to be picked up, so the trash containers often overflowed. There were roaches in all the apartments.

* An earlier version appeared in L. Riskin & J. Westbrook, Instructor's Manual, Dispute Resolution and Lawyers 398, 402–404 (1987). Reprinted with permission from West Group.

Revisions were contributed by Professor Barbara Fick, Notre Dame Law School.

Kelly's son, Michael, usually was home alone after school, and often brought friends over to play ball. They fixed snacks and regularly left food out on the kitchen table. They were energetic and noisy, trampling grass in the backyard and destroying some of the flowers and bushes while chasing balls. They occasionally broke windows while batting or throwing balls.

The new maintenance men made haphazard attempts at building repairs that were beyond their capabilities. One of them tried to unclog a stopped-up drain in Kelly's kitchen by using a commercial drain cleaner. The drain had become clogged when a plastic top of a milk bottle fell into it as Michael was fixing an afternoon snack. After the drain cleaner was used, the sink continued to back-up. One day, water saturated with the powerful drain cleaner chemicals spilled onto the kitchen floor when Susan was playing while her mother was washing the dinner dishes. The overflow ruined the kitchen carpeting which Kelly had personally installed.

After Labor Day, Lance announced that he was going ahead with plans to install separate heating units in each apartment. The tenants had agreed to this contingency when they renewed their leases. (The renewed leases also provided for a twenty-dollar reduction in monthly rent as soon as the new furnaces were installed because of the expected energy efficiency of the new heating units.) Lance stated in a letter to the tenants that the work would be done in an orderly fashion and would be completed within a month.

As it turned out, the work was not completed until the middle of December because the workmen did not come every day. Each apartment was in a state of upheaval for a week or more while the new furnace was being installed. Plaster dust accumulated because the contractor did not clean up daily as he had agreed to do. The workmen were very careless— leaving dangerous tools around and leaving rings of keys to all the apartments where anyone could have taken them. They also left apartment doors standing open when they left for the day. During this time one of the apartments, rented by Gene Fitzsimmons, was burglarized and his stereo was taken.

The weather turned cold in early November before the new furnaces were working. Lance did not turn on the old boiler which was still functional, although he had promised to provide heat until the new furnaces were working. The building was without heat during all of November and the first two weeks of December, although the lease agreements expressly provided that the landlord was to furnish heat from October 1 through May 1 unless there were circumstances beyond his control.

Installation of the furnaces finally was completed by mid-December. As the weather turned colder, however, it became apparent that the new furnaces did not work very well. Most of the tenants found that their kitchens were now unheated. As a result, while Kelly was out of town during Christmas vacation, the pipes in her kitchen froze, then burst and flooded the kitchen. When Kelly returned from vacation, she walked into an apartment that smelled like a cave from the resulting dampness. Several of her kitchen appliances had suffered water damage. Lance had not repaired the pipes while she was gone. Eventually, the maintenance man made a half-hearted and unsuccessful attempt to repair the pipes. Now, whenever Kelly washes her dishes, water seeps into the apartment below which is rented by Jane Hughett. Before Hughett noticed the leak, her sofa had sustained water damage.

In January, Kelly helped organize a tenants meeting. Tenants from twelve of the twenty units attended. (Four units were vacant and four elderly tenants did not come because they were afraid Lance might not renew their leases if they did.) At this meeting, all those present voted to withhold their rent until the building was properly maintained and repaired, and to discourage prospective tenants from leasing the vacant units. They have informed Lance Lord of their decision to withhold the rent and to hire a lawyer to pursue their legal rights. Lance responded by telling them that he would begin eviction proceedings against anyone who withheld the rent.

a) Prepare a memorandum identifying the factual and legal issues for either the landlord or one of the tenants.

b) Prepare a plan, on behalf of either the landlord or one of the tenants, that could be the basis for a settlement of the dispute.

c) Use this problem to test your understanding of the legal principles. Prepare a memo discussing the legal issues (after you have studied the materials in the chapter).

Landlord-tenant disputes, particularly ones involving conditions within particular apartments or interpretations of specific lease provisions, may be better suited to nonadversarial forms of dispute resolution such as negotiation and mediation than to the traditional adversarial model of litigation. Landlords and tenants both generally want "good" counterparts and both generally want the landlord-tenant relationship to continue once established. When disputes flare up, communication between the parties, rather than communication to a judge, may allow the parties to preserve their relationship while resolving their dispute.

L. RISKIN, MEDIATION AND LAWYERS*
43 Ohio State L.J. 29–30, 34–36, 43–46 (1982).

A mediator helps disputants toward resolving their disagreement. Unlike a judge or arbitrator, however, the mediator lacks authority to impose a decision on the parties; he can only facilitate the process. Mediation has been and remains the dominant method of processing disputes in some quarters of the world. In parts of the Orient litigation is seen as a shameful last resort, the use of which signifies embarrassing failure to settle the matter amicably. Though it is unclear to what extent

* Reprinted with permission of the Ohio
State Law Journal and Professor Riskin.

philosophy influences practice, the connection between the prominence of mediation and a Confucian heritage has been noted repeatedly by scholars. In the Confucian view,

> [a] lawsuit symbolized disruption of the natural harmony that was thought to exist in human affairs. Law was backed by coercion, and therefore tainted in the eyes of Confucianists. Their view was that the optimum resolution of most disputes was to be achieved not by the exercise of sovereign force but by moral persuasion. Moreover, litigation led to litigiousness and to shameless concern for one's own interest to the detriment of the interests of society.

This idea—that the natural and desirable condition is harmony—contrasts sharply with the predominant Western perspectives which focus on freedom as an absence of restraint and on autonomy and individual liberty as the highest goal. These Western notions, crystallized in the adversary system, pervade the American legal process and the lives of most of its citizens, including its lawyers. In recent years, though, mediation as a means of dispute processing has sent vines through the adversarial fence. They differ somewhat in purpose, orientation, and direction, but share a rapid growth rate. The development of mediation promises much that is good for American society and carries significant dangers as well.

* * *

I.   Mediation in the United States

* * *

C.   Mediation and the Law

Mediation offers some clear advantages over adversary processing: it is cheaper, faster, and potentially more hospitable to unique solutions that take more fully into account nonmaterial interests of the disputants. It can educate the parties about each other's needs and those of their community. Thus, it can help them learn to work together and to see that through cooperation both can make positive gains. One reason for these advantages is that mediation is less hemmed-in by rules of procedure or substantive law and certain assumptions that dominate the adversary process. There are, of course, assumptions that affect the procedure and results achieved in mediations—assumptions about mutuality, cooperation, and fairness, and general principles that ought to govern; in some systems, rules that approximate applicable law even serve as starting points. But in mediation—as distinguished from adjudication and, usually, arbitration—the ultimate authority resides with the disputants. The conflict is seen as unique and therefore less subject to solution by application of some general principle. The case is neither to be governed by a precedent nor to set one. Thus, all sorts of facts, needs, and interests that would be excluded from consideration in an adversary, rule-oriented proceeding could become relevant in a mediation. Indeed, whatever a party deems relevant is relevant. In a divorce mediation, for instance, a spouse's continuing need for emotional support could become important, as could the other party's willingness and ability to give it. In most mediations, the emphasis is not on determining rights or interests, or who is right and who is wrong, or who wins and who loses because of which rule; these would control the typical adjudicatory proceeding. The focus, instead, is upon establishing a degree of harmony through a resolution that will work for these disputants.

A danger inheres in this alegal character: individuals who are not aware of their legal position are not encouraged by the process to develop a rights-consciousness or to establish legal rights. Thus, the risk of dominance by the stronger or more knowledgeable party is great. Accordingly, for society to maximize the benefits of mediation while controlling its dangers, it must carefully adjust the role of lawyers in the mediation process.

Though mediation agreements typically neither set nor follow legal precedent, they often have important legal consequences. Frequently, the mere making of an agreement defers legal action by one of the disputants or the government. The agreement itself may establish or avoid legally enforceable rights. To reduce the danger that less powerful persons unwittingly will give up legal rights that would be important to them, they must be afforded a way of knowing about the nature of the adversary process and the result it would likely produce. But the very presentation of the rules that would probably govern a decision if the matter were litigated may impel parties toward adopting the predicted results, rather than regarding the law as simply one factor—to be blended with a variety of economic, personal, and social considerations—in reaching a decision. At the same time, if such information is not readily available to them, they are not necessarily free from influence by the law; they may be basing their decisions to mediate and their judgments during mediation upon inaccurate assumptions about what result would follow from adversary processing.

D.   The Role of the Mediator

Nearly all mediators seek to help the disputants achieve an agreement. Most have educational objectives as well, especially where the parties will have a continuing relationship. There are, however, enormous differences in procedures and in roles that mediators adopt. Some will act merely as go-betweens, keeping open lines of communication. They may or may not give their own suggestions when the parties have deadlocked. Some mediators will separate the parties physically; others will insist on keeping them together. Some mediators will urge that the parties propose solutions; others will make their own proposals and try to persuade the parties to accept them and may even apply economic, social, or moral pressure to achieve a "voluntary" agreement.

One of the principal functions of the mediator is managing the communications process. He must intervene carefully at the correct moments. Accordingly, he must understand interpersonal relations and negotiations. He must be able to listen well and perceive the underlying emotional, psychological, and value orientations that may hold the keys to resolving more quantifiable issues. And he must arrange for these to be honored in the mediation process, the agreement, and the resulting relationship. A like sensitivity is essential for good lawyering as well, but it occupies a more prominent place on the list of skills required of a mediator.

* * *

II.   HEADWINDS: PRESSURES AGAINST LAWYERS'
PROPER INVOLVEMENT IN MEDIATION

Most lawyers neither understand nor perform mediation nor have a strong interest in doing either. At least three interrelated reasons account for this: the way most lawyers, as lawyers, look at the world; the economics and structure of contemporary law practice; and the lack of training in mediation for lawyers.

A.   *The Lawyer's Standard Philosophical Map*

E.F. Schumacher begins his *Guide for the Perplexed* with the following story:

> On a visit to Leningrad some years ago, I consulted a map * * * but I could not make it out. From where I stood, I could see several enormous churches, yet there was no trace of them on my map. When finally an interpreter came to help me, he said: "We don't show churches on our maps." Contradicting him, I pointed to one that was very clearly marked. "That is a museum," he said, "not what we call a 'living church.' It is only the 'living churches' we don't show."

> It then occurred to me that this was not the first time I had been given a map which failed to show many things I could see right in front of my eyes. All through school and university I had been given maps of life and knowledge on which there was hardly a trace of many of the things that I most cared about and that seemed to me to be of the greatest possible importance to the conduct of my life.

The philosophical map employed by most practicing lawyers and law teachers, and displayed to the law student—which I will call the lawyer's standard philosophical map—differs radically from that which a mediator must use. What appears on this map is determined largely by the power of two assumptions about matters that lawyers handle: (1) that disputants are adversaries—*i.e.*, if one wins, the others must lose—and (2) that disputes may be resolved through application, by a third party, of some general rule of law. These assumptions, plainly, are polar opposites of those which underlie mediation: (1) that all parties can benefit through a creative solution to which each agrees; and (2) that the situation is unique and therefore not to be governed by any general principle except to the extent that the parties accept it.

The two assumptions of the lawyer's philosophical map (adversariness of parties and rule-solubility of dispute), along with the real demands of the adversary system and the expectations of many clients, tend to exclude mediation from most lawyers' repertoires. They also blind lawyers to other kinds of information that are essential for a mediator to see, primarily by riveting the lawyers' attention upon things that they must see in order to carry out their functions. The mediator must, for instance, be aware of the many interconnections between and among disputants and others, and of the qualities of these connections; he must be sensitive to emotional needs of all parties and recognize the importance of yearnings for mutual respect, equality, security, and other such non-material interests as may be present.

On the lawyer's standard philosophical map, however, the client's situation is seen atomistically; many links are not printed. The duty to represent the client zealously within the bounds of the law discourages concern with both the opponents' situation and the overall social effect of a given result.

Moreover, on the lawyer's standard philosophical map, quantities are bright and large while qualities appear dimly or not at all. When one party wins, in this vision, usually the other party loses, and, most often, the victory is reduced to a money judgment. This "reduction" of nonmaterial values—such as honor, respect, dignity, security, and love—to amounts of money, can have one of two effects. In some cases, these values are excluded from the decision makers' considerations, and thus from the consciousness of the lawyers, as irrelevant. In others, they are present but transmuted into something else—a justification for money damages. Much like the church that was allowed to appear on the map of Leningrad only because it was a museum, these interests—which may in fact be the principal motivations for a lawsuit—are recognizable in the legal dispute primarily to the extent that they have monetary value or fit into a clause of a rule governing liability.

The rule orientation also determines what appears on the map. The lawyer's standard world view is based upon a cognitive and rational outlook. Lawyers are trained to put people and events into categories that are legally meaningful, to think in terms of rights and duties established by rules, to focus on acts more than persons. This view requires a strong development of cognitive capabilities, which is often attended by the under-cultivation of emotional faculties. This combination of capacities joins with the practice of either reducing most nonmaterial values to amounts of money or sweeping them under the carpet, to restrict many lawyers' abilities to recognize the value of mediation or to serve as mediators.

The lawyer's standard philosophical map is useful primarily where the assumptions upon which it is based—adversariness and amenability to solution by a general rule imposed by a third party—are valid. But when mediation is appropriate, these assumptions do not fit. The problem is that many lawyers, because of their philosophical maps, tend to suppose that these assumptions are germane in nearly any situation that they confront as lawyers. The map, and the litigation paradigm on which it is based, has a power all out of proportion to its utility. Many lawyers, therefore, tend not to recognize mediation as a viable means of reaching a solution; and worse, they see the kinds of unique solutions that mediation can produce as threatening to the best interests of their clients.

"One of the central difficulties of our legal system," says John Ayer, "is its capacity to be deaf to the counsel of ordinary good sense." A law school classroom incident shows how quickly this deafness afflicts students—usually without anyone noticing. Professor Kenney Hegland writes:

In my first year Contracts class, I wished to review various doctrines we had recently studied. I put the following:

In a long term installment contract, Seller promises Buyer to deliver widgets at the rate of 1000 a month. The first two deliveries are perfect. However, in the third month Seller delivers only 999 widgets. Buyer becomes so incensed with this that he rejects the delivery, cancels the remaining deliveries and refuses to pay for the widgets already delivered. After stating the problem, I asked "If you were Seller, what would you say?" What I was looking for was a discussion of the various common law theories which would force the buyer to pay for the widgets delivered and those which would throw buyer into breach for cancelling the remaining deliveries. In short, I wanted the class to come up with the legal doctrines which would allow Seller to crush Buyer.

After asking the question, I looked around the room for a volunteer. As is so often the case with the first year students, I found that they were all either writing in their notebooks or inspecting their shoes. There was, however, one eager face, that of an eight year old son of one of my students. It seems that he was suffering through Contracts due to his mother's sin of failing to find a sitter. Suddenly he raised his hand. Such behavior, even from an eight year old, must be rewarded.

"OK," I said, "What would you say if you were the seller?"

"I'd say 'I'm sorry'."

I do not mean to imply that all lawyers see only what is displayed on the lawyer's standard philosophical map. The chart I have drawn exaggerates certain tendencies in the way many lawyers think. Any good lawyer will be alert to a range of nonmaterial values, emotional considerations, and interconnections. Many lawyers have "empathic, conciliatory" personalities that may incline them to work often in a mediative way. And other lawyers, though they may be more competitive, would recognize the value of mediation to their clients. I do submit, however, that most lawyers, most of the time, use this chart to navigate.

Notes and Questions

1. Mediation often is described as an "alternative" method of dispute resolution. The assumption underlying this comparison is that the "normal" method of dispute resolution is litigation or its adversarial cousin, arbitration. But if only 10% of all disputes actually go to trial and receive a verdict, shouldn't mediation be compared to, and evaluated against, negotiated settlements? *See* Bush, "What Do We Need a Mediator For?": Mediation's "Value–Added" For Negotiators, 12 Ohio St. J. on Disp. Resol. 1 (1996) (arguing that mediators' most important contribution is assisting parties reduce the barriers to negotiated settlements). For an argument that mediators can help the poor and disadvantaged in a landlord-tenant context by focusing on both rights and interests, see Kurtzberg & Henikoff, 1997 J. Disp. Resol. 53 (1997).

2. The role of law and lawyers in mediation can be problematic. Mediators may discourage the presence of lawyers for the parties because they might make the process unduly formal and legalistic. Some disputants, of course, see lawyers before the mediation, and a few do bring their lawyers into the sessions. Others who want or need lawyers are given referrals by mediators.

II. THE LANDLORD–TENANT CONCEPT: SEPARATING POSSESSION FROM OWNERSHIP OF LAND

The terms, landlord and tenant, describe the relationship created when the right to exclusive possession of land is transferred but the owner ("landlord") retains a reversionary interest in the rest of the property bundle. The transferee ("tenant") gains a present possessory interest in the land in return for the payment of a bargained-for consideration called rent.

Modern landlord-tenant law is a blend of contract and property law spiked with dashes of public policy and seasoned with a heavy dose of history. Landlord-tenant relationships are created by contracts, and thus are governed by contract law. But these contracts rearrange property rights in land, and thus also are governed by property law. The lease, which is the written document evidencing the relationship, therefore is both a contract and a conveyance.

The history of landlord-tenant law is the story of a continuing struggle for domination of the landlord-tenant relationship by principles of contract law and principles of property law, set against a rich tapestry of Anglo–American social and political history. An excellent historical summary is found in Kurtz, Moynihan's Introduction to the Law of Real Property 78–127 (4th ed., 2005). More detailed discussions are found in A.W.B. Simpson, A History of the Land Law (Rev. ed. 1986), R. Schoshinski, American Law of Landlord and Tenant (1980 & Supp. 2005), and Plucknett, Concise History of the Common Law (5th ed. 1956).

For a variety of reasons, holders of leasehold interests in land did not achieve the same status in medieval English communities as did holders of fee simple, fee tail, and life estates. To distinguish leasehold interests from the freehold estates, the common law used the term "nonfreehold" estates or "tenancies." Three types of nonfreehold estates were recognized by the common law, estates for years, periodic estates, and estates at will. In addition, a tenancy at sufferance commonly was recognized along with, in recent years, what has come to be called a statutory tenancy.

A. NONFREEHOLD ESTATES

The characteristics of nonfreehold estates are discussed in the following excerpt.

S. KURTZ, MOYNIHAN'S INTRODUCTION TO THE LAW OF REAL PROPERTY

81–82, 89–90, 92–96 (4th ed., 2005).

A. THE ESTATE FOR YEARS

An estate for years is any estate having a duration for a fixed or computable period of time, usually expressed in terms of a unit of a year or of a multiple or fraction of a year. Thus, a lease for one thousand years creates an estate for years. Likewise, a lease "for two weeks commencing July 1 next year" creates an estate for years. Typically the estate for years has a fixed beginning date and a fixed ending date set forth in the lease. The requirement of definiteness of duration, however, is satisfied if the estate has a certain ending date even though its commencement in possession is stated to depend on the happening of a specified event. The stipulated event may be the completion of a building by the landlord on the land subject to the lease. But if the termination date is indefinite the estate does not meet the traditional requirement for a term of years. This requirement of certainty of duration relates to the maximum period of duration. The estate for years may, like an estate in fee simple or a life estate, be defeasible by reason of being subject to a special limitation, a condition subsequent, or an executory interest. In fact, most leases create estates for years on condition subsequent by reason of the presence in the lease of a clause giving the landlord a right of re-entry or power of termination on breach by the tenant of any of the specified conditions set out in the lease.

* * *

B. THE PERIODIC TENANCY

A periodic estate is a tenancy which continues for a year or a fraction of a year and for successive similar periods unless terminated by either party by proper notice. There are various kinds of periodic tenancies but the most common are those from year to year and from month to month. By its nature, the periodic tenancy is continuous and of indefinite duration. Thus, if the tenancy is from month to month it is a single, continuous tenancy until terminated, not a tenancy for one month which comes to an end at the expiration of the month and is renewed for the following month.

Although historically the periodic estate was derived from the tenancy at will, its general characteristics are similar to those of the estate for years. The interest of the tenant is assignable, the tenant is liable for permissive waste, and the death of either landlord or tenant does not terminate the tenancy. Unlike the estate for years which terminates without notice at the end of the specified term, the periodic estate continues until terminated by the giving of proper notice by either party. The common law required a six months' notice to terminate a tenancy from year to year, and for lesser periods a notice equal to the period. Thus for a tenancy from month to month the notice of termination must be a month's notice. In all cases the notice must terminate the estate at the end of a period, not at some intermediate day. * * *

A periodic tenancy may be created by express agreement of the parties, by a letting for an indefinite time with rent payable at periodic intervals, by holding over with the assent of the lessor after the expiration of an estate for years, or by entry into possession under an invalid lease.

A common method of creating such tenancies is by inference on a general letting when the rent is payable periodically. * * *

C. THE TENANCY AT WILL

An estate (or tenancy) at will is an estate which is terminable at the will of either landlord or tenant and has no other specified period of duration. Such a tenancy is properly an estate because the tenant has an exclusive right to possession and may maintain an action of trespass or ejectment against persons interfering with his possessory interest. Its duration is dependent on the will of both parties and, unlike the periodic estate, no formal notice of a prescribed length of time is required for its termination.

A tenancy at will may be created by an express agreement between the landlord and tenant that the tenant shall hold possession so long as both parties agree. Such explicit agreements are relatively infrequent and more often a tenancy at will is inferred in situations where the holding is indefinite and a periodic tenancy cannot be presumed. Thus, if property is let for an indefinite time and no rent is reserved, the natural inference is that the parties intended a tenancy at will. * * *

At common law a tenancy at will could be terminated by either party, without formal notice, by expressing an intention to treat the tenancy as ended. In the event of termination by the landlord, the tenant was allowed a reasonable time to remove his personal property and was entitled to emblements. Because the relation assumes the assent of both parties to a continuance of the tenancy the death of either landlord or tenant terminates the estate. Additionally, a conveyance of the reversion by the landlord ends the tenancy at will. A lease for years made by the landlord to a third person has the same effect and it is immaterial that the lease was made for the purpose of putting an immediate end to the tenancy. An assignment by the tenant terminates his estate but, according to the modern view, a sublease by the tenant is effective between the parties thereto.

Because the ability of the tenancy at will to abruptly terminate at either party's will gave economic security to neither landlord nor tenant, statutes in most states require that either party desiring to terminate shall give the other written notice of a specified length of time, usually thirty days or a period equal to the interval between rent days. These statutes have generally been construed as not prescribing an exclusive mode of termination, therefore, the estate comes to an end on the death of either party and on conveyance or lease by the landlord. The estate at will even as modified by statute may not be the precise equivalent of a periodic estate.

D.   The Tenancy at Sufferance

A tenancy at sufferance is a possessory interest in land which exists when a person who had an estate in land wrongfully continues in possession after the termination of such estate. * * *

In view of the minimal interest of the tenant at sufferance, why is that interest still included in the catalogue of estates? The main justification seems to be that it lends support to the doctrine that the landlord may at his election convert the tenancy at sufferance of the holdover tenant into a periodic tenancy, or, in some states, into a tenancy for a definite period. In a few jurisdictions the interest of the tenant at sufferance has been enlarged by statutes requiring that the landlord give written notice, usually thirty days, before commencing an action against the tenant to recover possession.

E.   Statutory Tenancies

In recent years there has developed a form of tenancy unknown to the common law. This tenancy, apart from express agreement, is terminable at will by the tenant but is terminable by the landlord but only under limited circumstances. For example, a tenant of public housing cannot be evicted except for cause and after the landlord follows a procedure prescribed in the public housing regulations. In effect the tenant has a determinable life estate. Similarly, a tenant who occupies rent control housing may have an estate that is more expansive than the traditional common-law tenancies. Some statutes give the residential tenant the right to continue occupancy despite the termination of the duration of the term specified in the lease. These anomalous modern tenancies may be conveniently grouped under the heading of "Statutory Tenancies."

The common law tenancies at will and at sufferance can have relevance for people who are homeless. Suppose a group of homeless persons occupies vacant, city-owned apartment units. Can the city use self help to evict them as squatters? Does this raise the same policy issue as adverse possession does, or is it a different question? The following case discusses these issues.

CITY OF NEW YORK v. UTSEY

Supreme Court, Appellate Term, New York, 2000.
185 Misc.2d 715, 714 N.Y.S.2d 410.

ARONIN, J.P, SCHOLNICK AND PATTERSON, JJ.

Final judgment unanimously reversed without costs, petitioner's motion for summary judgment denied and summary judgment granted in favor of occupants dismissing the petition.

The issue in this squatter proceeding is whether occupants are tenants at will or at sufferance and thus entitled to a 30–day notice pursuant to Real Property Law § 228.[1] We hold that under the circumstances of this case occupants are tenants at will and that the City's failure to serve the required 30–day notice upon them mandates dismissal of the petition.

The City commenced this squatter proceeding [ ] in the beginning of August 1997 after serving a 10–day notice to quit upon the occupants. Its petition alleges that the City took title to the premises, a house at 527 Linwood Street, Brooklyn, on June 25, 1987 by virtue of an in-rem tax foreclosure action. (It was later clarified that the City took title as the result of a Supreme Court condemnation proceeding.) The petition further alleges that occupants intruded into the premises without the City's permission on July 26, 1988. Occupants defended on the ground, among others, that they became tenants by virtue of the City's continued tolerance of their occupancy for over 8 years and that as tenants they were entitled to a 30–day notice.

Upon a motion by the City for summary judgment, the City showed that the property is slated for development as part of 172 two-family homes to be built in the area and that occupants' presence was interfering with the City's plan to build affordable housing. The City claimed that it had allowed occupants to remain from 1991 to 1998 because there had not been funding available to rehabilitate the building.

---

1. A tenancy at will or by sufferance, however created, may be terminated by a written notice of not less than thirty days given in behalf of the landlord, to the tenant, requiring him to remove from the premises; which notice must be served, either by delivering to the tenant or to a person of suitable age and discretion, residing upon the premises, or if neither the tenant nor such a person can be found, by affixing it upon a conspicuous part of the premises, where it may be conveniently read. At the expiration of thirty days after the service of such notice, the landlord may re-enter, maintain an action to recover possession, or proceed, in the manner prescribed by law, to remove the tenant, without further or other notice to quit.

In opposition, occupant Thelma Utsey showed that her family consists of herself, three of her children, ages 25, 23 and 12, and a grandchild, age 1; that before they commenced their occupancy the house was used by drug dealers and was totally uninhabitable; that after entering into occupancy in January 1989, occupants cleaned the premises and repaired it, by installing pipes, plumbing, toilets, sinks, electrical wiring, a refrigerator, and new flooring, and by repairing the roof, the walls and the ceilings at a cost of thousands of dollars and much hard work; that, in 1990, they had the premises inspected by an engineer and provided the City with his written report as well as receipts for the repairs; that they have electric, gas and telephone service in their own name; that the adults are registered to vote; that Ms. Utsey's school-age child goes to the local public school; and that they are active members of the East New York community.

Occupants further showed that, in 1990, the City brought a squatter proceeding against them, which it subsequently discontinued, and that immediately after discontinuing that proceeding, the City sought a writ of assistance in the condemnation proceeding, which application was denied in June 1991. Since that time, in reliance on the City's allowing them to remain, they have installed aluminum siding, new windows, stairways, walls and kitchen flooring. Occupants also indicated that they remain committed to purchasing the home from the City. Citing, *inter alia, Walls v. Giuliani*, 916 F. Supp. 214 [1996], occupants claimed that by virtue of the City's inaction for seven years they became tenants at sufferance or at will.

The Housing Court granted the City's motion for summary judgment, reasoning that contrary to the holding in *Walls, supra*, a tenancy at sufferance arises only when one holds over after the termination of a lawful tenancy (*Livingston v. Tanner*, 14 N.Y. 64); that occupants had failed to offer any evidence of a conscious policy by the City to acquiesce in their occupancy; and that a trespass, even of 11 years, could not deprive the City of its legal remedies "if the time frame is within that for adverse possession."

We think the Housing Court correctly declined to follow *Walls v. Giuliani supra*. In *Walls*, the court reasoned that, because a trespass can ripen (in some jurisdictions) into a peaceable actual possession and the occupant may then bring a forcible entry and detainer proceeding, it must follow that a possessory interest (a tenancy at sufferance) has been created where an owner acquiesces in a trespasser's occupancy for a substantial amount of time.

The *Walls* court's conclusion that a trespass can ripen into a tenancy at sufferance is contrary to established principles of law. "An estate at sufferance is an interest in land which exists when a person who had a possessory interest in land by virtue of an effective conveyance, wrongfully continues in possession of the land after the termination of said interest . . ." (Restatement of Property § 22; see, *Livingston v. Tanner*, 14 N.Y. 64; 1 Tiffany Real Property § 174 [ed.]). It is essential to the creation of this interest that the party previously have had a possessory interest. As the Housing Court correctly held, the occupancy by a trespasser who never had such a possessory interest cannot ripen into a tenancy at sufferance.

However, an occupancy by a squatter or trespasser can ripen into a tenancy at will as, for instance, where there is an express agreement of the parties or an acceptance of rent (*Kassover v. Gordon Family Assoc.*, 120 Misc.2d 196, 465 N.Y.S.2d 668; see, 51 C.J.S., Landlord and Tenant § 158). A tenancy at will may also arise by implication, and an obligation to pay rent is not a necessary incident of such a tenancy (*Harris v. Frink*, 49 N.Y. 24, 32). In order for a tenancy at will to arise, however, the occupancy must be subordinate, not adverse, to the title of the true owner (*Biglow v. Biglow*, 75 App.Div. 98, 77 N.Y.S. 716; In re Wilson's Estate, 349 Pa. 646, 37 A.2d 709). The Court of Appeals has stated that an owner's acquiescence in a continued occupancy (where the occupancy is subordinate to the title of the owner) may, where the facts so warrant, justify an inference that a tenancy at will has been created (*Kerrains v. People*, 60 N.Y. 221, 225).

In *Walls* the squatters' occupancy was adverse to the City's title, and the squatters were claiming title by adverse possession. In contrast, the occupancy here was at all relevant times subordinate to the interest of the City since the occupants had acknowledged the City's title.

The record shows, contrary to the findings of the Housing Court, that the City, after bringing the unsuccessful 1989 squatter proceeding and after unsuccessfully seeking a writ of assistance from the Supreme Court in 1990, made a conscious decision to allow occupants to remain in the premises for an indefinite term because the funding to proceed with the urban renewal project was not available. At the time the City made this decision, it was already clear from the preceding litigations and from occupants' submission to the City of the receipts and of the engineering report, that occupants were not claiming title and that they were interested in working with the City to purchase the property from it (*cf, Manhattan School of Music v. Solow*, 175 A.D.2d 106, 571 N.Y.S.2d 958; 2 N.Y. Jur. 2d, Adverse Possession and Prescription, § 33 [offer to purchase the property by one in possession constitutes an acknowledgment of the owner's title]). The City was also aware of the substantial improvements that occupants had made and were continuing to make to the premises and of their stabilizing influence upon the neighborhood. Under these circumstances, we hold that they remained in occupancy as tenants at will. Based upon the City's failure to serve a 30–day notice (Real Property Law § 228), the petition must be dismissed.

Notes and Questions

1. Suppose the owner of a house signed a document transferring the right to possession "for the full term of while [the grantee] shall wish to live in the city, from and after the 1st day of August, 2005." Assuming an

agreement to pay rent, has a landlord-tenant relationship been established? If so, what type of tenancy was created? See Thompson v. Baxter, 107 Minn. 122, 119 N.W. 797 (1909) (life estate, rather than nonfreehold interest, created). What about an agreement that one party may remain in possession during the pendency of a law suit brought to determine who has title to the property? See Birk v. Lane, 354 N.W.2d 594 (Minn. App. 1984) (distinguishing *Thompson* and concluding that a tenancy for a term was created). An interpretation often given is that language permitting one to stay as long as desired or wished creates only a tenancy at will on the theory that by implication the desire/wish provision is applicable to both parties. See W. Stoebuck & D. Whitman, Property 267 (3rd ed., 2000).

2. Requirements that landlords and tenants give notice of their intentions respecting renewal of tenancies are an important part of modern landlord-tenant law. The common law requirements were geared to an agricultural society and often required lengthy notice periods (e.g., six months) for decisions not to renew periodic tenancies from year to year and decisions to renew tenancies for a term of years. Modern statutes and leases typically impose a shorter notice requirement, usually based on rental payment periods, such as 30 days. Longer notice periods, such as 90 or 180 days, are commonly required for multi-year commercial leases. Examine the notice requirements in the sample leases that follow the next two cases. What do the leases provide if those notice requirements are not met? What if a tenant fails to provide the required notice of intent to renew a tenancy for a term of years, but the landlord continues to transact business with the tenant in person? See Perrotti v. Chiodo, 21 Conn.App. 288, 573 A.2d 342 (1990) (landlord's personal transaction of business with tenant constituted waiver of lease requirement for notice of intent to renew by registered mail).

3. A major feature of nonfreehold estates is the requirement that the tenant pay rent. A popular textbook of the 19th Century describes rent as follows:

> [W]e may consider rent simply as a periodical compensation, in money or otherwise, agreed to be given by the tenant to the landlord for the use of realty, the payment of which may be enforced like any other demand. I say agreed to be given, because where one occupies another's land without a lease containing a special agreement to pay a fixed rent, the compensation which may be recovered, is not in the shape of rent, but of damages in an action for *use and occupation,* or for *mesne profits.* * * * When the relation of landlord and tenant has been created, the estate of the landlord is denominated a *reversion,* to which rent is said to be incident. If therefore he conveys the reversion, the future rent passes with it, and when he dies it goes to his heirs; but it is otherwise if the rent be already due. If the tenant be evicted by a paramount title in a stranger, or actually expelled by the landlord, his obligation to pay rent ceases; but no destruction of the premises by fire, flood, or other inevitable accident, will discharge the obligation, unless the lease contains a provision to that effect. * * *

T. Walker, Introduction to American Law, Designed as a First Book for Students 305 (4th Ed.1860).

4.   Times specified in leases are often critical. This is particularly so in sellers' markets, notably so in retail-business premises in dense neighborhoods (among other places)—for example, retail premises in Manhattan, where rents accelerate all the time and possession changes quickly. A common way to encourage tenants to comply with provisions on time is to impose additional charges on tenants who fail to comply with deadlines. Late rent charges are probably the most common example. Another example is a provision for increased rent from a tenant who fails to vacate when the lease says he should. New York courts sometimes uphold, and sometimes refuse to uphold, such provisions; when they have been upheld it has been with the explanation that the lease is a contract and contracts can validly provide for liquidated damages.

With that rationale, such provisions have been upheld in New York when the hold-over rent was double or treble the rent otherwise called for in the lease. The cases distinguish between a penalty (not enforced) and an enforceable liquidated-damages contract provision. The difference, in one recent federal case, turned on whether there was "evidence that the sum was grossly disproportionate to actual damages." In re T.R. Acquisition Corp., 309 B.R. 830 (S.D.N.Y. 2003), refused to enforce the clause. Suppose you are working on a lease for a landlord client: How are you going to go about drafting a lease clause on hold-over rent that would pass muster? Suppose your client wants double rent for hold-over times, assessed on a monthly basis—i.e., if the tenant holds over one day she owes a month's rent, at the hold-over rate. (Rent under the lease is paid by the month.)

5.   John and Mary Byers signed a contract to purchase a house in St. Louis from Robert Owens. Closing, at which title was to be transferred, was to take place within 90 days. Because the Byers were moving from Chicago and needed a place to stay before the closing, Robert Owens agreed to permit them to move into the house before the closing if they signed a form lease that he had prepared with a beginning date of September 1 and ending date the following August 31. The Byers signed the form lease on August 15. However, before they could move to St. Louis, they received word that the employment opportunity which was bringing them to St. Louis had been canceled. As a result they were unable to purchase the house and remained in Chicago. Do the Byers have any legal obligations under common law landlord-tenant principles? See Arthur Treacher's Fish & Chips of Fairfax v. Chillum Terrace, 272 Md. 720, 327 A.2d 282 (1974) (tenancy for a term was conveyed as a future interest, but obligation to pay rent did not arise until tenant actually entered and took possession. Until that point, damages for breach of contract, but not back rent, are recoverable).

Suppose that you are counsel to the Byers and you discover that the lease was not properly executed and the local statute of frauds requires a writing. What advice can/should you give them? What concerns would you raise with them?

PROBLEM

Lander and Toner signed the following written memorandum:

"I, Lander, lease to Toner the property known as 'Camp Happy Trails' for the sum of $500 per year, with the option to renew the lease as long as the camp is run as a business for profit."

Have the parties established a valid landlord-tenant relationship? If so, what type of tenancy was created? See Womack v. Hyche, 503 So.2d 832 (Ala.1987) (clause permitting renewal as long as camp is run for a profit held unenforceable as "tending to create a perpetuity" without the "plain and unambiguous" language expressing such intention that courts have required when applying the non-freehold exception to the rule against perpetuity). *Accord,* Linton Coal Co. v. South Cent. Resources, 590 So.2d 911 (Ala. 1991) (clause permitting renewal "so long as there is recoverable coal remaining in the lands leased hereby" creates only a tenancy at will because, while the coal eventually will be exhausted, "the date of that occurrence is entirely uncertain," making it impossible to ascertain the term of the lease).

If you were asked to correct the legal problem created by the original memorandum, how would you redraft it? In redrafting, pay attention to the advice of Professor David Mellinkoff: "Some day someone will read what you have written, trying to find something wrong with it. This is the special burden of legal writing, and the special incentive to be as precise as you can." D. Mellinkoff, Legal Writing: Sense and Nonsense 15 (St. Paul, Minn., 1982), as quoted in Burnham, Teaching Legal Ethics in Contracts, 41 J. of Legal Educ. 105, 116 (1991).

B.   EXCHANGE OF POSSESSION FOR RENT

As the Walker excerpt indicates, the heart of the landlord-tenant transaction is an exchange of possession for a valuable consideration called rent. Under the common law, the obligation of the tenant to pay rent was considered absolute in return for which the tenant received the full possessory rights discussed in Chapter One. The following cases explore this concept.

PARADINE v. JANE

King's Bench, 1647.
82 Eng.Rep. 897.

In debt the plaintiff declares upon a lease for years rendering rent at the four usual feasts; and for rent behind for three years, ending at the Feast of the Annunciation, 21 Car. brings his action; the defendant pleads, that a certain German prince, by name Prince Rupert, an alien born, enemy to the King and kingdom, had invaded the realm with an hostile army of men; and with the same force did enter upon the defendant's possession, and him expelled, and held out of possession from the 19 of July 18 Car. till the Feast of the Annunciation, 21 Car. whereby he could not take the profits; whereupon the plaintiff demurred, and the plea was resolved insufficient.

* * *

It was resolved, that the matter of the plea was insufficient; for though the whole army had been alien enemies, yet he ought to pay his rent. And this difference was taken, that where the law creates a duty or charge, and the party is disabled to perform it without any default in him, and hath no remedy over, there the law will excuse him. As in the case of waste, if a house be destroyed by tempest, or by enemies, the lessee is excused. * * * Now the rent is a duty created by the parties upon the reservation, and had there been a covenant to pay it, there had been no question but the lessee must have made it good, notwithstanding the interruption by enemies, for the law would not protect him beyond his own agreement, no more then in the case of reparations; this reservation then being a covenant in law, and whereupon an action of covenant hath been maintained (as Roll said) it is all one as if there had been an actual covenant. Another reason was added, that as the lessee is to have the advantage of casual profits, so he must run the hazard of casual losses, and not lay the whole burthen of them upon his lessor; and Dyer 56.6. was cited for this purpose, that though the land be surrounded, or gained by the sea, or made barren by wildfire, yet the lessor shall have his whole rent: and judgment was given for the plaintiff.

SANTA FE TRAIL NEIGHBORHOOD REDEVELOPMENT CORP v. W.F. COEN & COMPANY

Mo. Court of Appeals, Western Dist., 2005.
154 S.W.3d 432.

ELLIS, JUDGE.

Appellants, Dr. Henrik A. Knudsen and his wife Rogene F. Knudsen, appeal a judgment of the Circuit Court of Jackson County in their civil action for apportionment and distribution of an award of damages which was paid into the registry of the court after certain real property they owned was condemned. The Knudsens claim the trial court erred in distributing a part of the award to Respondent, Dr. Joan R. Walker, since Dr. Walker was not entitled to any distribution whatsoever. We reverse and remand for entry of a new judgment in favor of Dr. Walker.

The underlying facts of this case are undisputed. In 1965, the Knudsens purchased real estate located at 1520 South Noland Road in Independence, Jackson County, Missouri ("the Property"). The Property, on which a building had been constructed, was used as a dental office beginning in 1967, and Dr. Knudsen practiced dentistry there until he retired in 2001. In 1977, the Knudsens built an addition onto the front of the building, connecting to the building's existing plumbing and electrical systems. The reception room for the dental offices in the building was located in the front of the building and was shared by everyone in the building. There was a parking lot in the rear of the building that was also shared by the occupants of the building, as well as by patients.

At some point prior to 1996, Appellants began renting space in the building to another dentist, Dr. Branstetter. At this time, Dr. Walker worked for Dr. Knudsen. Dr. Branstetter subsequently sold his dental practice to Dr. Walker, who, on November 15, 1996, entered into a written agreement with the Knudsens to occupy the office space that had formerly been occupied by Dr. Branstetter. Pursuant to the terms of the agreement, Dr. Walker took possession of her office space in the building on November 15, 1996. . . .

The professional office space leased to Dr. Walker pursuant to the Agreement was described as "office space consisting of 1,164 square feet, more or less," and was further described as comprising "approximately 46.6% of the total leasable space within the office building." The diagrams attached to the Agreement indicate that the leased space included a common reception area and a common area in the basement that were to be shared by all occupants. The Agreement also provided that the Knudsens would maintain the building's rear parking lot, which Dr. Walker and her patients were permitted to use.

The Agreement expressly provided that "contract shall create the relationship of Landlord and Tenant between the parties thereto" and that "Landlord gives to Tenant exclusive control of the Leased Premises." In addition, the Agreement gave Dr. Walker the right to "assign this lease or sublease all or portions of the Leased Premises to others if such operation is within the purposes for which the Leased Premises may be used," as long as she obtained the prior written consent of the Knudsens, which was not to be unreasonably withheld.

The Agreement specified an initial lease term of five years at a basic monthly rental rate of $775 per month, and required Dr. Walker to pay a $775 security deposit for the leased space. The term of the Agreement as initially executed was from November 15, 1996, to November 14, 2001.[ ] The Agreement also specified that Dr. Walker had the option to renew the lease for an additional five-year term upon giving written notice to the Knudsens of her intent to do so at any time prior to three months before the end of the original term of the lease. If renewed, the basic monthly rental rate, during each subsequent year following the end of the original five-year term of the Agreement, was to incrementally increase by an amount related to the increase in the Consumer Price Index (CPI) as computed and published by the United States Department of Labor Statistics for the area encompassing the Property.

On December 5, 2000, Dr. Walker's attorney sent a letter to the Knudsens via certified mail giving them timely notice of Dr. Walker's desire and intent to renew the Agreement for a second five-year term. [ ]

On August 30, 2001, a Petition for Condemnation was filed by the Santa Fe Trail Neighborhood Redevelopment Corporation ("Santa Fe") requesting, among other things, that all of the real property owned by the Knudsens which was situated in the Martha's Vineyard Subdivision be condemned as blighted and in need of redevelopment. This included not only the Property, but also an adjacent vacant lot owned by the Knudsens. On November 14, 2001, the trial court entered an order condemning both pieces of real estate.

[   ] Santa Fe was ordered to pay $275,000 into the court registry as damages for the takings by Santa Fe, and the trial court also ordered Santa Fe to pay "reasonable tenant moving expenses."....

[The parties disagreed on how much, if any, of the $275,000 should be paid to Dr. Walker. The trial court awarded Dr. Walker $47,000, plus interest, for the taking of her leasehold. The Knudsons appealed, claiming she had only a license revocable at will. Licenses are discussed in Chapter 6.—Eds.]

The difference between a lease and a license is a "technical distinction which is 'often difficult to determine.' " *St. Louis Southwestern Ry. Co. v. State Tax Comm'n*, 319 S.W.2d 559, 564 (Mo.1959) (quoting 51 C.J.S. *Landlord & Tenant* § 202e(2)). This distinction is critical in condemnation cases because while "a leaseholder possesses an interest in property for which he must be compensated in condemnation a mere licensee generally does not." State ex rel. *State Highway Comm'n v. Johnson*, 592 S.W.2d 854, 857 (Mo.App. E.D.1979).

In order for one to have a compensable interest in a condemnation proceeding, "[t]he interest held [in] the property for which compensation must be rendered ... must consist of some definite right of domination in and over the [property], such as the right of user, or exclusion, or disposition. A mere contractual relationship is not sufficient in itself." *Millhouse v. Drainage Dist. No. 48 of Dunklin County*, 304 S.W.2d 54, 58 (Mo. App. S.D.1957). Other than to show their express intent, it matters not what the parties themselves call their agreement....

A license is only a privilege to enter certain premises for a specific purpose. A license does not vest any title, interest or estate in the licensee and may be revoked at the will of the licensor. In contrast, a lease is "any agreement which gives rise to relationship of landlord and tenant" and "[   ] is for exclusive possession of tenements for a determinate period." A landlord-tenant relationship is created when: (1) there is reversion in the landlord; (2) creation of an estate in the tenant either at will or for a term less than that which the landlord holds; (3) transfer of exclusive possession and control of the tenant; and (4) a contract.

Kimack v. Adams, 930 S.W.2d 505, 507 (Mo.App. E.D.1996) ...

Applying the facts to this well-developed body of Missouri law, it is clear that the contractual Agreement between the Knudsens and Dr. Walker was a lease creating a landlord-tenant relationship and a leasehold estate, rather than merely a revocable license. To begin with, the technical words of a lease appear throughout the entire Agreement, which, when considered along with the circumstances under which it was made, is a very strong indication that from the outset, both parties intended it to be a lease rather than a license.

Moreover, the Knudsens held a fee simple interest in the Property, while Dr. Walker was granted a possessory interest therein for only a limited term, i.e., five years. The parties mutually agreed to a fixed rental rate for a definite amount of office space for the period of five years, and at the conclusion of this period, possession of that office space would revert to the Knudsens unless the Agreement was renewed. See *Kirk v. Mattier*, 140 Mo. 23,41 S.W. 252, 254 (1897) (noting that contract language specifying "the term of years and the fixed rent" was "inconsistent with a mere license.")

Furthermore, Dr. Walker's actions of paying the security deposit and making regular monthly rental payments to the Knudsens, along with her actual continuous possession and control of the office space for the purposes authorized by the terms of the Agreement, fulfilled the express intention of the parties that Dr. Walker enjoy exclusive possession and control thereof during the term of the Agreement. The Agreement further granted Dr. Walker the right to assign her interests under the Agreement or sublease all or any portion of the office space to a third party for similar uses upon prior written consent of the Knudsens, which consent was not to be unreasonably withheld. These factors are all inconsistent with the grant of only a license, because "of the essential characteristics [of a license] is the absence of the right to possession of the land." *Friend*, 476 S.W.2d at 138.

In addition, the Agreement nowhere states that it could be revoked at the whim or pleasure of the Knudsens. This, too, is entirely inconsistent with a mere license, because "[t]he essential attribute of a bare license is the right of the grantor to freely revoke it any time." *Kansas City Area Transp. Auth. v. Ashley*, 485 S.W.2d 641, 644 (Mo.App. W.D. 1972). To the contrary, the Agreement gave Dr. Walker the option to renew the Agreement for an additional five-year term simply by giving timely written notice to the Knudsens of her intent to do so. "The holder of an option to renew a lease has an interest in the land. The right of renewal constitutes a part of the tenant's interest in the land, and forms a substantial and integral part of the agreement . . . It is a part of the estate granted, an interest in or encumbrance on the property." *Land Clearance for Redevelopment Corp. v. Doernhoefer*, 389 S.W.2d 780, 785 (Mo. 1965) (internal citations and quotations omitted). For this reason, if no other, it can hardly be said that Dr. Walker occupied the office space as only a licensee.

Notwithstanding all this, the Knudsens cite the Agreement as providing that "no estate shall pass out of the Landlord," claiming that Dr. Walker thereby contracted away her right to claim any estate in the Property—even a leasehold. However, as noted by Dr. Walker, while those words do indeed appear in the Agreement, they have been taken out of their proper context. In its entirety, the quoted clause reads as follows:

> NO ESTATE IN LAND: This contract shall create the relationship of Landlord and Tenant between the parties thereto: no estate shall pass out of Landlord.

Taking the Agreement as a whole into consideration, as we must, we think the only reasonable reading of this clause is that the portion cited by the Knudsens is intended to clarify that the Agreement grants Dr. Walker only a temporary (*i.e.*, leasehold) interest in the Property as opposed to a permanent one (e.g., a fee simple interest). . . .

Accordingly, we hold that the Agreement between the Knudsens and Dr. Walker was not merely a revocable privilege to enter the Property for a specific purpose, but a fully executed lease which had been properly renewed, by Dr. Walker and at her option, for a new five-year term nearly nine months before Santa Fe commenced condemnation proceedings. Point denied.

[The court then went on to address the remaining points of the appeal.]

For this reason, we reverse and remand with instructions that the trial court enter a new judgment not inconsistent with this opinion. [   ] All concur.

Notes and Questions

1. As you will learn in your Contracts course, the Common Law has long since recognized an exception to the rule of *Paradine v. Jane* for contracts that are impossible to perform through no fault of the obligor. See, e.g., Albert M. Greenfield & Co. v. Kolea, 475 Pa. 351, 380 A.2d 758 (1977) (accidental destruction of building by fire excused tenant from obligation to pay rent when building was an essential part of the bargain and parties had not otherwise allocated the risk of loss); Restatement, (Second), of Property § 5.4 (1976) (landlord breaches obligation if, after entry by tenant, building is destroyed suddenly by non man-made force, landlord fails to correct situation within a reasonable time after being requested to do so by tenant, and parties have not validly agreed otherwise). But does this mean that *Paradine* is dead? Should a person who leases land near a river be excused from paying rent because the river flooded and destroyed her crops, or because a tropical storm caused severe flooding to the first floor of commercial property? See Jenson v. Haynes, 633 S.W.2d 154 (Mo.App.1982) (flooding of farmland did not excuse rent obligation because flooding was a foreseeable risk); Portnoy v. Omnicare Pharmaceutics, Inc., 2004 WL 1535780 (E.D. Pa. 2004) (flooding did not excuse payment of rent because languages of lease and purchase of flood insurance indicated the parties contemplated possibility of flood).

2. As noted in *Santa Fe Trail*, a lease transfers the right of exclusive possession and control to the tenant for the duration of the lease term in return for payment of rent and compliance with other lease covenants. This interest is a compensable interest when property is taken by eminent domain. Suppose a tenant of residential property permits a third party to enter the leased premises and film commercials promoting diet and weight loss products without requesting or obtaining permission from the landlord. May the landlord sue the third party for trespass or wrongful invasion of property? See *Merz v. Professional Health Control of Augusta, Inc. (PHC)*, 175 Ga.App. 110, 332 S.E.2d 333 (1985) (landlord, "by executing the lease, contracted away any expectations of privacy as to the leased property"). Suppose *PHC* had been trying unsuccessfully for years to get the owners'

consent to film a pool-side commercial on this property? Might the owners actually have had a stronger case if this were commercial property?

3. Licenses are discussed in Chapter 6 *infra*. The use of eminent domain to acquire property is discussed in Chapter 7 *infra*.

III. CREATION OF THE RELATIONSHIP

As the preceding materials indicate, a landlord-tenant relationship can be created orally by the voluntary transfer of possession of land. Such relationships are governed generally by the common law rules discussed in the Moynihan excerpt.

Most people, however, prefer to reduce their understanding of the relationship to writing in a document called a lease. In fact, a writing is required to create enforceable longer term landlord-tenant obligations through the application of the Statute of Frauds, a statute you will study in your Contracts course.

A. THE LEASE

The following leases are examples of residential landlord-tenant transactions. One might be said to be "landlord friendly," the other "tenant friendly." Can you see the difference?

APARTMENT LEASE

_____ hereinafter referred to as Lessor, for and in consideration of the agreements hereinafter made between it and _____, hereinafter referred to as Lessee, does hereby lease to Lessee for a private residence or dwelling only, the premises known and described as follows, to wit:

Apartment _____ in the building known as _____ in the City of _____, County of _____, State of _____

1. TERM. The term of this lease shall be twelve (12) months commencing on _____, 19_ and ending on the _____ day of _____, 19_ which term shall be automatically renewed for a like term unless notice in writing is sent by either party to this lease to the other at least thirty (30) days prior to the end of the current term.

2. RENT. As rent, Lessee hereby agrees to pay Lessor the sum of _____ Dollars ($_____) per month, for each month during the term of this lease, such rent to be paid in advance on the first day of each calendar month, without relief from valuation or appraisement laws. A late charge will be added to Lessee's account, in the amount of $10.00, if payment is not received by the 5th day of the month. A penalty of $10.00 will be added to Lessee's account for any check returned by the bank for non-payment.

3. SECURITY DEPOSIT. Lessee hereby deposits with Lessor the sum of _____ Dollars ($_____) as security for Lessee's performance of

this lease. In the event Lessee complies fully with all covenants and conditions of the lease, security deposit agreement, and rules and regulations, said sum shall be returned to Lessee within thirty (30) days following the satisfactory termination of this lease. In the event of a breach or default by Lessee in respect to any of the terms or conditions of this lease, Lessor may apply sum or any part thereof to any costs, damages, losses, or injuries caused by Lessee by such breach or default and without in any manner waiving or limiting Lessor's rights to further hold Lessee for costs, damages, losses, or injuries otherwise due. *This security deposit is not and shall not be considered the rent payment for the last or any other month of the term of this lease.*

4.   RULES AND REGULATIONS. The rules and regulations are incorporated by reference and made a part of the written lease between Lessor and Lessee, and are to be strictly followed by all residents. Lessee shall comply with all the rules and regulations now or at any time hereafter during the existence of this lease adopted by Lessor, which are brought to the notice of Lessee, both in regard to the apartment community as a whole and as to the premises herein leased. Lessee further acknowledges receiving and reading a copy of said rules and regulations and agrees to abide by them.

5.   OCCUPANCY. Lessee agrees not to assign or transfer this lease or any interest therein or sublet the premises or any part thereof without the prior written consent of Lessor. The premises shall be used and occupied in a safe, careful, and proper manner by Lessee without waste of water; that no trade, business or occupation shall be carried on therein; that premises shall not be used or permitted to be used for any unlawful purpose; nor shall premises, or any part thereof, be used for any purpose that, in the judgment of Lessor, will injure the reputation of the premises or building of which they are a part; or disturb or annoy the residents of the building or the neighborhood. No additional lock or fastening shall be placed upon any door without written permission of Lessor.

6.   CONDITION OF PREMISES. Lessee agrees that no representation as to condition or repair of the premises, and no promise to decorate, alter, repair or improve the premises, has been made, except such as is contained in the lease. Lessee agrees that he shall examine the premises prior to his occupancy thereof and that his occupancy of the premises shall be conclusive evidence of his satisfaction and approval of the premises as being in good physical condition and in good order and repair.

7.   PETS. Lessee shall not keep any pets of any kind or description in the leased unit or on the premises of which the unit forms a part without the prior written consent of Lessor. In the event consent is given to the keeping of a pet, Lessee shall pay to Lessor a one-time fee of $50.00, as set forth in the Pet Agreement.

8.   UTILITIES AND MAINTENANCE. Lessor agrees to maintain and care for the lawns, parking areas and common grounds, to provide

reasonable snow and trash removal, and to furnish janitor service at reasonable times for and to maintain the hallways and corridors of the community of which the unit is a part. Lessor shall provide heat, water and sewage facilities to the premises. Lessor shall also make available such other utility services as may be necessary to serve the leased premises, including telephone and electricity, but Lessee shall individually pay for his/her use of such utility services.

9. ALTERATIONS. Lessee shall make no alterations or additions to the premises, nor shall Lessee install or have done any painting or decoration of the unit without written consent of Lessor. Lessee shall not attach any article of a permanent character or any sign containing writing or printing to any window, floor, ceiling, door or wall, without the written consent of Lessor. Lessee shall, on termination of this lease, surrender to Lessor the quiet and peaceable possession of the premises in as good order as it was at the commencement of the term, reasonable wear and tear excepted.

10. OWNER'S OR AGENT'S RIGHT TO ENTER. Lessor shall have the right to show the premises to prospective lessees for a period of thirty (30) days prior to the termination of this lease. Lessee shall permit Lessor to enter the said premises at all reasonable times to inspect the premises or for any purpose connected with the repair, improvement, care and management of the premises in which the same are situated.

11. FIRE OR CASUALTY. In the event the leased premises are destroyed by fire, wind, or other causes beyond the control of Lessor, or are torn down by properly constituted authorities of the federal, state, county or city governments, or any other governmental authority, then in any of these events the lease shall cease and terminate as of the date of such destruction. If the leased premises are injured by fire, wind, rain, or other causes, so as to render the same partially unrentable or partly unfit for use, but are repairable within a reasonable time, then this lease shall remain in full force and effect, but Lessee's rent shall be proportionally reduced until the premises are repaired.

12. RIGHTS OF LESSOR UPON DEFAULT. Upon failure to pay any installment or rent of any part thereof when due, or if Lessee shall violate any other term, condition or covenant of this lease, or if Lessee shall fail promptly to take possession of or shall abandon the premises, Lessor shall have the right to re-enter and repossess the premises. Lessor shall have the option to change the lock on the entry door to prevent Lessee's re-entry into the unit until such defaults are corrected, and to remove all persons therefrom and to remove all property therefrom and, in such event, this lease and all rights of Lessee as resident shall terminate, but Lessee shall remain liable for the rent herein specified during the remaining term of this lease plus Lessor's cost of repossessing the premises. Lessee hereby waives notice of any failure or default and any demand of Lessor for possession of the premises. In the event Lessor shall repossess the premises, Lessor shall not be required to exercise diligence in reletting the premises in order to mitigate Lessee's

obligations hereunder, nor will it be required to accept any resident for the premises offered by Lessee. The failure on the part of Lessor to re-enter or repossess the premises, or to exercise any of its rights hereunder upon any default, shall not preclude Lessor from the exercise of any such rights during the continuance of such default or upon any of Lessor's right to terminate the lease for nonpayment of rent when due, and no notice or demand shall be required for the enforcement thereof. If Lessee shall violate or breach any term or condition of this lease, Lessee shall pay all costs and expenses, including attorney's fees, incurred by Lessor in connection with its exercising any right or remedies it may have under this lease because of such violation or breach.

13. NOTICES AND RENTS. All notices and demands authorized or required to be given Lessee hereunder may be served upon Lessee in person or by regular mail and addressed to him/her at the leased premises. All notices required to be given hereunder to Lessor, and all rent payments, shall be given or sent Lessor at this office or such other place as Lessor may designate and shall not be effective until received.

14. RIVER, PONDS AND LAGOONS. The involved unit is one of several, all of which constitute a residential project which adjoins the * * * River. In addition there [are] situated on such project ponds or lagoons. Lessor owns to the eastern water's edge of such River and has no authority or jurisdiction thereover, and accordingly cannot police same. Lessee, the members of his/her family, invitees and guests enter into or onto such River at their sole risk and responsibility, and Lessor shall not be liable for any injury or damage to person or property by reason of any such ponds or lagoons.

15. EQUIPMENT AND PERSONALTY. Lessor is furnishing equipment and other items of personalty for use by Lessee in the involved unit. Lessee shall not make any substitutions therefor or remove same without prior written consent of Lessor. None of such items, including articles substituted with the consent of Lessor, shall be removed from the leased premises at any time. Furthermore, on the yielding of possession of the involved unit, either by reason of termination or expiration of this lease, or otherwise, all of such items of equipment and personalty so furnished by Lessor (including any articles substituted by either Lessee or Lessor) shall be delivered up to Lessor along with the involved unit in the same condition as when received, ordinary wear excepted. Lessee shall be charged and shall pay for all costs of cleaning, repair, replacement and redecorating not occasioned by normal wear.

16. LESSEE YIELDING POSSESSION. At the termination of this lease, Lessee shall yield up immediate possession of the premises to Lessor and return the keys to said apartment/townhouse to Lessor at the office of the Manager, and failing to do so shall pay liquidated damages for the whole time such possession is withheld, a sum equal to twice the amount of the rent herein reserved prorated for each day of withholding. Any such holding over shall not create a new term of this lease if notice

to terminate the lease has prior thereto been given by Lessor or Lessee. It is understood, however, that the acceptance of any such liquidated damages by Lessor shall not constitute waiver by Lessor of its right of re-entry as herein set forth.

RULES AND REGULATIONS

It is our intent that _____ be the finest residential neighborhood in our area. In order to attain that objective, we shall strive at all times to render prompt and efficient service to the property. Since residents must also cooperate if the community is to be highly regarded, the following rules will be in effect. * * *

RENTAL PAYMENTS: All rents are due and payable in advance on the first day of each lease month. Rents may be paid either by mail or in person. Rents will be considered delinquent if not paid in full within five days. There will be a ten dollar ($10.00) late fee on all delinquent rents.

MAINTENANCE: PLEASE MAKE REQUESTS FOR REPAIRS BY PHONING THE OFFICE DURING NORMAL OFFICE HOURS. THE NUMBER IS _____. FOR EMERGENCY SERVICE WHEN THE OFFICE IS CLOSED, CALL _____. Your cooperation will enable the management to provide you with quick and efficient service. Emergency calls, however, will be handled immediately. No charge is made for normal repairs. Any repairs or replacements necessitated by a resident's negligence will be charged to the resident and will be due and payable with the following [month's] rent.

SOLICITING: Soliciting is strictly forbidden. It is requested that residents notify the office if a solicitor appears, and appropriate action will be taken.

NOTICE OF INTENT TO VACATE: After the first year of occupancy, residents are required to sign a new lease in order to continue living in their unit. Management will notify the resident of his lease expiration approximately thirty (30) days in advance.

SUBLETTING: According to the terms of your lease, you do not have the right to sublet without prior consent. However, under certain conditions we may permit you to do so, providing you secure another resident whose application to lease is approved by the office prior to the date on which you wish to vacate the premises under lease.

VACATING APARTMENT: After a resident has vacated his/her apartment, we will make a formal inspection of that apartment, room by room, looking for any damages such as: floors, windows, baseboards, plumbing fixtures, chips on sinks or tubs, broken tile, cabinets, dirty appliances, etc. The inspection will also include the checking of each appliance to make certain they all operate properly. After writing the inspection report, a final letter is sent to the resident returning the deposit minus any charges.

CARPET: All residents are required to have their carpet cleaned at their own expense once a year. The work must be done by a professional cleaning service. Please retain receipts for management's approval upon vacating the apartment. If carpet has not been correctly cleaned annually, a pro-rated charge will be deducted from the security deposit. * * *

TRASH: Bottles, cans, newspapers, magazines, and all garbage or trash not disposable through the disposal must be taken to the trash containers outside the building. Please use plastic bags large enough to be closed at the top.

PATIO & LAWN AREAS: When using barbecue grills, braziers or other outside means of preparing food, residents shall assume any and all liability arising from this. Absolutely no plants are to be planted in the grounds by residents.

ADDITIONS: Any additions that will be attached to the walls, floors or ceilings must be approved by management. Such additions will be considered permanent and will become the property of _____, unless otherwise specified in writing by the management. No change in color of walls will be permitted without written permission.

KEYS: Keys are the responsibility of the resident. Each resident will be given two (2) keys for the apartment door and one (1) key for the mail box at the time of occupancy. There is a $2.00 charge for each replacement. If the resident needs to be let into his/her unit at any time other than during office hours, there will be a $5.00 charge.

STORAGE: Individual storage areas have been assigned to each unit. They should not be used for storage of newspapers or other materials creating a fire hazard. Individual padlocks should be provided by the resident. The use of these rooms is entirely gratuitous, and we accept no responsibility whatsoever for the care or custody of any articles deposited therein.

PARKING: One (1) parking space is provided for each unit. Other unassigned guest parking is also available. Dead storage parking of cars as well as the parking of boats, trailers, or commercial vehicles is not permitted, and these items will be removed by the management at the owner's expense. * * *

THE UNDERSIGNED, HAVING READ THE AFORESAID RULES AND REGULATIONS, HEREBY AGREE(S) TO ABIDE BY THEM AT ALL TIMES DURING RESIDENCY AT _____.

TENANT(S) _____

LANDLORD _____

RENTAL AGREEMENT*

This lease, made this _____ day of _____, 19__, by and between _____, the landlord, and _____, the tenant(s). The landlord and tenant(s) agree to the following mutually dependent provisions:

* Off–Campus Housing Guide, University of Notre Dame (1988). Reprinted with permission.

1. The landlord has this day leased to the tenant(s) the premises known and described as _____, Number _____ in the City of _____, County of _____ to be occupied only as a residence of said tenant(s) and no more than _____ other persons upon the terms and conditions set forth in this lease. The premises, which shall be placed in actual possession of the tenant(s), are partly/fully furnished. The term of this lease shall be from _____, 19__ to _____, 19__.

2. The tenant(s) shall pay to the landlord as rent, for the term stated, $_____ per month payable on the _____ of each month. If the tenant(s) remain in the premises at the termination of the lease, they shall be considered hold over tenant(s) and the landlord shall be entitled to collect the daily rent for each day that the tenant(s) remain.

3. The tenant(s) shall:

    a. Pay all rents promptly when due.

    b. Pay for any damage to the leased premises or to the appliances and fixtures therein, caused by any act of negligence of the tenant(s) or any member of his or her family or a guest—damage due to ordinary and normal wear and tear, or loss or damage by fire excepted.

    c. Place garbage and refuse inside the containers provided by the landlord.

    d. Keep the apartment/house and grounds in a clean and sanitary condition.

    e. Abide by municipal code regulations regarding care and occupancy of the premises.

    f. Surrender possession of the premises to the landlord upon the end of the term above, and be allowed to remove any fixtures they attached, provided they repair or pay cost of repairing any damage done by such removal.

4. The landlord or his or her agent(s) shall have the right to enter the leased premises for the following purposes: inspecting the premises for damage or needed repairs or improvements only, without intruding into a tenant(s) personal effects; making necessary repairs or improvements; exhibiting the premises to prospective tenants, purchasers or mortgagees. Such entry may be made only between the hours of 10:00 a.m. and 7:00 p.m. after advance notice of at least 24 hours to the tenant(s) of the date, time, and purpose of the entry. Entry may be made without prior notice if the landlord or his or her agent reasonably believes that an emergency exists, such as a fire or broken water pipe, and requires immediate entry without notice.

5. In addition to the requirements herein understood as a binding covenant of habitability and quiet enjoyment, the landlord shall be specially responsible for the following maintenance duties.

   a. Repairs to the exterior of the premises.

   b. Repairs to sewers, heating, all appliances, wiring and plumbing facilities.

   c. Repairs to all common areas, doors, windows, and stairs.

   d. Maintaining an extermination service for the premises, providing for the elimination of all vermin and rodents prior to and throughout occupancy.

   e. Painting all interior areas of the premises with interior non-lead base paint of a grade capable of being washed without streaking.

   f. Installing and maintaining locks on all exterior windows and doors, and on the door to all common areas.

   g. Providing and installing screens, storm windows, and window shades in good condition for all windows in the premises.

   h. Maintaining the premises and common areas in accordance with city or county housing, building and zoning standards.

   i. The landlord shall be responsible not only for his own, but also any agent(s) negligent maintenance or non-maintenance of the premises and agrees to pay tenant(s) or any member of his or her household or guest for damages for personal injuries resulting from such negligence.

6. All notices to quit and evictions shall be issued in strict adherence to the laws of Indiana regarding forcible entry and detainer. Notice of any lease violations and opportunity to correct them must be given at least one week before beginning legal proceedings.

7. The tenant(s) have this day paid a security or damage deposit of $_____ to be returned within thirty (30) days of the expiration of this lease minus the cost of repairing any damage (except ordinary wear and tear) caused by the tenant(s) or anyone legally acting under tenant(s) control, the cost of putting the premises in as clean a condition as the tenant(s) found them, and any rent due. The security deposit shall be forfeited only to extent it reflects actual damages. The landlord will also be under a duty to mitigate damages.

8. If the landlord fails to perform necessary repairs within the one month following written notification, such repairs may be effected by the tenant. The cost of such repairs may then be deducted from the rent provided that a written notification of such intention precedes the repairs by a period of ten (10) days and

an itemized statement, including cost of agent, of such repairs is provided by the tenant to the landlord after completion.

9. If the premises become uninhabitable through acts of third parties, an act of God, a condemnation order, the tenant(s) may at his option elect to terminate the lease, or to remain and pay a proportional amount of the rent.

10. The tenant(s) shall, in addition to the rent, provide for the following utilities:

    water _____; oil _____; gas _____; telephone _____; electricity _____; refuse pick-up _____

11. The tenant(s) may sublet or assign the leased premises for any part of the term of this lease, upon written consent of the landlord, which consent shall not unreasonably be withheld.

12. Should any tenant(s) become unable to fulfill his obligation due to extraordinary circumstances defined exclusively as severely debilitating illness, death, suspension or expulsion from the University, all obligations of the parties to this lease shall cease on that date and the tenant shall be responsible for only the rent then owing.

13. Exhibits A and B attached hereto are made a part of this lease.

14. If at the time of initial occupancy all defects enumerated in Exhibit B have not been remedied, the lessee reserves the right of termination of this lease and all obligations contained herein within twenty (20) days. At such time, the tenant shall be entitled to recovery of all money paid.

15. The landlord hereby assures the tenant that the housing covered under this lease conforms to all appropriate local housing ordinances and codes. In the event that the tenants are advised by local administrative agencies that they must move as a result of non-conformance with housing ordinances or codes, the landlord shall allow the students to move from the premises immediately without any further obligation for lease payments and the refund of any security deposits shall also be made immediately in full subject only to deduction of any clean-up or damage problems as covered more specifically elsewhere in this lease.

16. This lease and written notations upon it constitute the entire lease agreement between landlord and tenant(s). It may be later modified only by a signed agreement between the landlord and tenant(s).

SIGNED

_____

LANDLORD

TENANT(S)

TENANT(S)

TENANT(S)

CONDITION OF PREMISES AT THE TIME OF OCCUPANCY

1. STOVE
2. REFRIGERATOR
3. WASHER
4. DRYER
5. FURNITURE
   A. LIVING ROOM
   B. DINING ROOM
   C. BEDROOMS
   D. AUXILIARY ROOMS
6. BATHROOM FACILITIES
7. WINDOWS
8. WALLS & CEILING
   A. LIVING ROOM
   B. DINING ROOM
   C. KITCHEN
   D. BEDROOMS
   E. BASEMENT
   F. ATTIC
   G. AUXILIARY ROOMS
9. DRAPES
10. CARPETS AND/OR FLOORS
11. STEPS
    A. EXTERIOR
    B. INTERIOR
12. GARAGE
13. MIRRORS & DECORA-
    TIONS
14. PAINT
    A. EXTERIOR
    B. INTERIOR
15. GUTTERS & DOWN-
    SPOUTS
16. GARBAGE CANS
17. YARD
18. ELECTRICAL FACILITIES
19. WALKWAYS & ACCESS AR-
    EAS
20. FURNACE & WATER
    HEATER
21. PLUMBING

SIGNED

LANDLORD_____

TENANT(S)_____

TENANT(S)_____

EXHIBIT A

THE FOLLOWING IS AN IN-
VENTORY OF FURNITURE
PROVIDED IN THE PREMISES:

ROOM _____
_____
_____

ROOM _____

EXHIBIT B

THE FOLLOWING IS A LIST OF
DAMAGES OR DEFECTS IN
THE PREMISES EXISTING AS
OF THE _____ day of _____
19___.

ROOM _____
_____
_____

ROOM _____

ROOM _____   ROOM _____

ROOM _____   ROOM _____

Initialed

LANDLORD _____

TENANT(S) _____

TENANT(S) _____

Notes and Questions

1.   Examine the two lease forms carefully. Do they appear to be balanced, or do they give one or the other party a more favorable position? Do the leases attempt to do more than simply create a tenancy? What about allocation of risk of loss? Responsibility for maintenance and repairs? Use of facilities? Transferability?

2.   If you or a friend of yours have ever been a landlord or a tenant, make a list of problems that you or your friend experienced in that situation. Do the leases address your experiences? Adequately? What modifications would you suggest to the lease forms based on your experiences?

3.   In studying the lease forms, identify places in each lease where common law rules appear to be relied upon, and places where such rules appear to be varied. Does the common law, for example, require that landlord-tenant relationships be in writing? Are there reasons why a landlord or a tenant would favor an oral arrangement rather than a written one?

B. ALLOCATING RISKS THROUGH LEASES—PUBLIC POLICY AND ETHICAL QUESTIONS

VERMES v. AMERICAN DISTRICT TELEPHONE CO.

Supreme Court of Minnesota, 1977.
312 Minn. 33, 251 N.W.2d 101.

Scott, Justice.

These are separate appeals by two of the defendants in an action brought by Harry Vermes, owner of a jewelry store in the Foshay Tower in Minneapolis, to recover losses sustained when his store was burglarized. Defendants were the American District Telegraph Company (ADT), which had supplied Vermes with a burglary detection system; the

Apache Corporation (Apache), which had leased the space to Vermes; and The Towle Company (Towle), which managed the Foshay Tower at the time of the burglary.

Trial was by jury in the district court. In a special verdict, the jury allocated negligence percentages among the parties and set damages at $23,000. Plaintiff's post-trial motion to increase damages to $47,185.03 was granted. Defendants' motions for judgment notwithstanding the verdict and a new trial were denied. These appeals are by ADT and Apache from the judgment below and the order denying the various post-trial motions.

In 1968 Harry Vermes leased space in the Foshay Tower's first floor for his jewelry store. A few weeks later Vermes entered into a contract with ADT for burglar alarm service. In 1970 Towle replaced Apache as building manager.

On Monday morning, August 23, 1971, Vermes discovered that his store had been burglarized. The police investigation determined that entry had been made through the ceiling of the vault area. A mechanical-equipment access room was located over the plaintiff's store and the thin floor of this room formed the ceiling of plaintiff's store. The construction design allowed easy entry into the vault from above. The wholesale value of the property taken was $47,185.03.

* * *

The liability of a landlord to a tenant is necessarily based upon different considerations than that owed a tenant by a third party with whom the tenant merely contracts for certain specific services. The lease between Vermes and Apache contained the following clause:

> "Lessee also agrees to be responsible for and to relieve Lessor from all liability by reason of any damages or injuries to any person or thing which may arise from or be due to the use, misuse or abuse of all or any of the elevators, hatches, openings, stairways, hallways of any kind whatsoever which may exist or hereafter be erected or constructed on the said premises, or from any kind of injury which may arise from any other cause whatsoever on the said premises or the building of which the demised premises are a part, whether such damage, injury, use, misuse or abuse be caused by or result from the negligence of Lessor, its servants or agents or any other person or persons whatsoever."

On appeal Apache contends that this clause is valid and applies with full force to plaintiff. Vermes responds by arguing that (1) the negligence alleged (i.e., leasing Vermes space not suitable for a jewelry store) occurred prior to the lease, and (2) the exculpatory clause may be void as against public policy, citing the following language from *Rossman v. 740 River Drive,* Minn., 241 N.W.2d 91 (1976):

> " * * * The enforceability of a lease clause which exculpates a landlord from liability for negligence is a question of balance. The public policy favoring freedom of contract is weighed against the

policy favoring the landlord's observance of the particular duty he is alleged to have breached. Thus, the balance depends on the nature of the particular duty breached. If the landlord's duty is basic and his observance of it is of extreme importance * * *, then the policy favoring his observance of that duty may well be stronger than the policy favoring freedom of contract. * * * [I]f the duty the landlord breaches is less basic and his observance of it is not of such grave importance * * *, then freedom of contract may well be the dominant policy."

The question then becomes whether the alleged duty of the landlord in this case is "basic."

The duty of Apache, if it can be defined as such, was to sufficiently inform Vermes concerning the store which was being considered for rental to the extent that Vermes had enough information from which he would be able to properly assess the store's suitability for his jewelry business. In the commercial context this would seem to be a "basic" duty. A commercial tenant will often have specific needs peculiar to his business which will require the premises to be leased to have certain attributes. Space suitable for a restaurant, for example, might be completely unsuitable for a bank. A part of a building where the air conditioning is ineffective might suit a tenant in need of storage space, but could be useless for a doctor or a business office. In cases where suitability factors might not be obvious upon casual inspection, as with ineffective air conditioning if the premises were inspected in winter, it would be a basic duty of the landlord to inform the prospective tenant of any qualities of the premises which might reasonably be undesirable from the tenant's point of view.

A jewelry store, in addition to the usual requirements for a retail store, requires physical security. The landlord's duty, prior to the signing of the lease, would be to point out any facts about the premises which would tend to make them insecure; for example, a side door accessible from the street or a thin partition separating them from a storage room. In this case it was, in the language of *Rossman v. 740 River Drive, supra,* the "particular duty" of Apache to point out to Vermes any facts about the proposed premises which might reasonably make them unsuitable for his use. As noted by Vermes in his brief, this duty was basic to the relationship between Apache and Vermes. It is fair to say that if Vermes had been informed of his insecure ceiling, he might have insisted that changes be made as conditions to the lease. He did so as to lighting.

Thus, under the *Rossman* decision, the broad exculpatory clause in the lease here should not operate to bar Vermes' negligence claim against Apache. It is not necessary to reach plaintiff's other arguments on precontractual negligence, contractual ambiguity, misrepresentation, and strict construction. * * *

Reversed in part, affirmed in part, and remanded with instructions.

Notes and Questions

1. Should prospective landlords or tenants be allowed to contract away rights or duties? Should the type of intended use of the property being rented—agricultural, commercial, residential—make a difference? As we progress through these materials, we will see that courts and legislatures have tended to create different rules for adjusting rights and responsibilities of landlords and tenants based on the type of intended use.

2. Suppose the rent for the space leased in the principal case was less than half of that for other, more secure buildings that were available at the time the jewelry store owner signed the lease containing the exculpatory clause. Should that have a bearing on cases of this type? Might the lower rent suggest that the parties were allocating the risk of physical security to the tenant?

3. What risk was being allocated by the exculpatory clause in *Vermes*? Did the court allocate the risk differently, or did the court enforce a different duty (disclosure of latent defects)? Did the language of the exculpatory clause cover potential liability to tenants, or was it designed to insulate the landlord from potential claims of third parties?

4. Are there exculpatory clauses in the sample residential leases discussed *supra*? If so, would you expect the *Vermes* court to enforce them?

5. Statutes in some states prohibit lease clauses that are designed to protect landlords from the legal consequences of their conduct or the conduct of third parties. See, e.g., the Maryland Real Property Code Ann., § 8–105 (1988), which declares void as against public policy lease provisions that "indemnify the landlord, hold the landlord harmless, or preclude or exonerate the landlord from any liability * * * for any injury, loss, damage, or liability arising from any * * * negligence * * * of the landlord on or about the leased premises or any * * * appurtenances used in connection with them, and not within the exclusive control of the tenant." Prince Philip Partnership v. Cutlip, 321 Md. 296, 582 A.2d 992 (1990) (landlord's failure to install handicapped-accessible public toilet facilities in medical office building in violation of applicable building code not protected by exculpatory clause in lease to physician whose patient fell and broke her legs while attempting to use a non-handicapped accessible bathroom in the physician's office because the landlord's negligence involved "appurtenances [that were] not within the exclusive control" of the tenant).

6. Another frequent source of disputes is the allocation of repair responsibilities, particularly when it is not articulated clearly in the lease. Who, for example, should be responsible for repairing a pre-existing hole in the roof of a leased building under a lease that required the tenant to keep the building "in as good condition as when received, ordinary wear and tear excepted"? See Jacobi v. Timmers Chevrolet, Inc., 164 Ga.App. 198, 296 S.E.2d 777 (1982) (distinguishing capital "repairs" from ordinary "maintenance" and requiring the landlord to repair the roof as a capital improvement of greater benefit to the landlord than to the tenant).

If the parties do not allocate repair responsibilities in their lease, how should that allocation be made? What reasons can you articulate in favor of an allocation to the landlord? to the tenant? Are there reasons to restrict the ability of the parties to make the allocation decision themselves? Might the parties make the allocation decision without expressly saying so, for example, by adjusting the rent or other terms? Should the rules regarding allocation of repair responsibility be different for commercial and residential tenancies? What about multi-family residential as opposed to single-family residential? What about mixed-use buildings in which both commercial and residential spaces are leased? Should the answer turn on who has possession and control of the premises in question? See *Wohlford v. Quesenberry*, 259 Va. 259, 523 S.E.2d 821 (2000) (lessee in control of entire single family residence has responsibility for roof and furnace repairs under common law and the Uniform Statewide Building Code in the absence of a lease provision to the contrary).

7.   How much should a landlord be required to disclose to a prospective commercial tenant, particularly if the prospective tenant does not make known specific needs? What about lack of storage space for a retail business such as a shoe store? A narrow driveway adjacent to loading docks? Space leased to a competitor in the next block? The traditional common law answer has been *caveat emptor*—let the actor beware. Later we will see that this principle became the focal point for the movement to reform the law affecting residential landlord-tenant relationships.

Is the real issue for lawyers what clients should disclose rather than what the law requires to be disclosed? Suppose one's client asks if a prospective tenant must be told about a situation such as the one in *Vermes*. Would the lawyer be providing better service to the client by responding in a spirit of friendship (collaboration in the good) with suggestions regarding what is morally admirable even though it may not be legally required, or should the lawyer simply stick to the rules of law? See ABA Model Rules of Professional Conduct, Comment to Rule 2.1 (Purely technical legal advice can sometimes be inadequate. It is proper for a lawyer to refer to relevant moral and ethical considerations in giving advice).

T. SHAFFER, AMERICAN LEGAL ETHICS

453–455 (1985).

Here is a landlord-tenant situation from Professors Louis M. Brown and Edward Dauer (Planning by Lawyers, 1978):

Lawyers * * * are enlisted not only in the defense of virtue; they also participate in a process which most often does not occur before or within an impartial tribunal. The lawyer is often engaged as a planner, and as a counsellor for clients not then involved in any dispute whatsoever. There are still decisions that are made, and these decisions may still have better or worse outcomes, but they involve neither adversaries nor the safeguard of a tribunal: In the preventive law area of practice the lawyering process is final and decisive. There is virtually no appeal from the lawyer's preventive law decision that his client sign the irrevocable trust, or the deed conveying property, or a contract, or engage in numerous other events having legal consequences.

Consider then the difficulties which are raised when the role predicate of the profession's responsibilities seems exclusively adversarial. More to the point, consider the following hypothetical problem: Five years ago the state legislature enacted a statute specifically authorizing residential tenants to offset against their liability for rent payments any sums which they expended in improving the premises so that they would conform to the existing housing code's minimum standards of habitability. The intended effect of the act was to prevent evictions for nonpayment of rent when the tenant made necessary repairs, and as a practical matter to encourage such repairs to be made. Almost immediately after the statute became effective the great majority of residential lease forms began including a clause (a lawyer's product, no doubt) whereby the tenant waived his right to offset under section so-and-so of the statutes. Having thus had its purposes thwarted, the legislature recurred to the offensive: three years ago a further statute was enacted, this one making such waivers void. No criminal or other penalties were listed with the second statute. Such a waiver would be a null act—the courts would not aid in its enforcement, and it would not serve to defeat the statutory defense to eviction. The legislative history is clear, and it is well-known that such waivers were considered by the legislature to be against public policy.

A landlord now becomes a client and requests that a lawyer draft a standard lease form for use in his leasing all of the dozen or so tenements which he owns. The client asks that a waiver of the offset right be included. He is advised that such a waiver is unenforceable, but persists: The waiver will have an *in terrorem* effect on those tenants who are not aware of the later statute (all of them, we can suppose *arguendo*) and who are unlikely ever to have their claims adjudicated by a knowing tribunal or with the aid of a knowing counsellor (ditto). The clause will, in addition, deter tenants from unilaterally making repairs at the landlord's expense.

In a somewhat related situation, the Association of the Bar of the City of New York said:

In the opinion of our Committee it is not within the proper standards of ethics for a lawyer to insert such a waiver in a contract if the lawyer knows that such a waiver is against public policy and void as a matter of law.

A lawyer must himself observe and advise his client to observe the statute law * * *. If a waiver in a contract has been held by a court of last resort to be void as against public policy as a matter of law, he should so advise his client. If the client should nevertheless insist on its incorporation in the contract, the lawyer should refuse to do so, for if he should comply with his client's request he would thereby become a party to possible deception of the other party to the contract.

It is the lawyer's duty, the Association said, "to uphold the honor of the profession. He should strive at all times to uphold the honor and to maintain the dignity of the profession and to improve not only the law but the administration of justice."

Professor Monroe Freedman, in his widely discussed book, *Lawyers' Ethics in an Adversary System* (1975), indicated that he and many lawyers might have disagreed with the Association. The cases might be said to turn on a lawyer's obligation to carry out the law—or at least to obey it—and therefore to be within the limitations adopted in Canon Seven. It does not go as far as the cases * * * where the client's means or goal are clearly legal but the lawyer nonetheless believes them to be immoral. That suggests a distinction that may not be defensible, of course, particularly if the relationship between law and morals is one of dependence (of law on morals) rather than of peaceful coexistence.

PROBLEMS

(a) First year law students Ann Bucki, Susie Lewis, and Colleen O'Hara signed a one-year lease for a small house about a mile or so from campus. Willing to accept a Spartan life style during law school and anxious to save money where possible, they negotiated a lease to rent the property "as is" for a 20 per cent reduction in rent. The lease contained the following provisions:

4. In consideration of the reduced rental provided for, the tenant covenants not to sue the landlord and the landlord will not be liable to the tenant for any damage, loss or injury to property or person by reason of any existing or future defect in the premises, including acts, omissions, negligence or nuisance of other persons or tenants or of the landlord or his agent, and including that arising from falling plaster, leaking roofs, or faulty or inadequately lighted or repaired sidewalks, stairs, halls, alleys, yards or cellars.

5. It is understood that the landlord has no public liability insurance. If the tenant desires to eliminate clause four, written notice thereof should be given the landlord, in which event the rent will be increased $10 a month. Following termination of clause four by the tenant, the landlord's liability shall be that provided by the general laws of the State. The landlord *shall not* become an insurer by virtue of such termination.

A New Jersey court in deciding a case involving a clause similar to Clause Four, but without the provision for a reduction in rent, stated that a clause which attempts to immunize the landlord from all liability is contrary to public policy, particularly in situations where the relative bargaining positions of the landlord and tenant are substantially unequal. Kuzmiak v. Brookchester, Inc., 33 N.J.Super. 575, 111 A.2d 425 (1955). Does the addition of Clause Five cure any public policy questions arising from Clause Four? See Cardona v. Eden Realty Company, 118 N.J.Super. 381, 288 A.2d 34 (1972) (clauses in question invalidated as "legalistic effort[s] to circumvent the positive public policy of the State"); Jones v. Hanna, 814 S.W.2d 287, 289 (Ky.Ct.App.1991), distinguishing exculpatory clauses for causing personal injury or for wilful and wanton conduct (invalid as against public policy) from clauses excusing simple negligence affecting property or business activities (public policy not affected). See generally Burnham, Teaching Legal Ethics in Contracts, 41 J.Leg.Ed. 105 (1991).

Can you redraft the lease to reflect the parties' agreement so that it will pass muster under the New Jersey rule?

(b) The *Vermes* case and the *Shaffer* excerpt raise the point about drawing a distinction between (i) moral behavior and legal advice consistent with it, and (ii) what the law will allow. One is as much the business of the law office as is the other. Note also that there is a distinction between the profession's regulatory rules and moral behavior. Would, for example, an attorney who drafts clauses such as those contained in Problem (a), violate her professional responsibility under Rule 1.2(d) of the American Bar Association's Model Rules of Professional Conduct:

> A lawyer shall not counsel a client to engage, or assist a client, in conduct that the lawyer knows is criminal or fraudulent, but a lawyer may discuss the legal consequences of any proposed course of conduct with a client and may counsel or assist a client to make a good faith effort to determine the validity, scope, meaning, or application of the law.

Would the drafting of such clauses be a moral act? Cf. Burnham, Teaching Legal Ethics in Contracts, 41 J.Leg.Ed. 105, 118, n. 42 (1991), noting that the following clause was deleted prior to adoption of Rule 1.2(d): A lawyer shall not counsel or assist a client in conduct "or in the preparation of a written instrument containing terms" the lawyer knows or reasonably should know are legally prohibited.

IV.   SELECTION OF TENANTS

Although the power to exclude incidental to property ownership discussed in Chapter One gives landlords the general right to choose whomever they please as tenants, the following constitutional and statutory prohibitions against various forms of discrimination impose important limitations on landlords' freedom of choice.

A.   PROHIBITED DISCRIMINATION

UNITED STATES CONSTITUTION
Amendment XIII

Section 1. Neither slavery nor involuntary servitude, except as a punishment for crime whereof the party shall have been duly convicted, shall exist within the United States, or any place subject to their jurisdiction.

Section 2. Congress shall have power to enforce this article by appropriate legislation.

Amendment XIV

Section 1. All persons born or naturalized in the United States, and subject to the jurisdiction thereof, are citizens of the United States and of the State wherein they reside. No State shall make or enforce any law which shall abridge the privileges or immunities of citizens of the United States; nor shall any State deprive any person of life, liberty, or property, without due process of law; nor deny to any person within its jurisdiction the equal protection of the laws. * * *

CIVIL RIGHTS ACTS—EXCERPTS
42 U.S.C. § 1982

All citizens of the United States shall have the same right, in every State and Territory, as is enjoyed by white citizens thereof to inherit, purchase, lease, sell, hold, and convey real and personal property.

Fair Housing Act of 1968, as amended

42 U.S.C. § 3602 Definitions

(b) "Dwelling" means any building, structure, or portion thereof which is occupied as, or designed or intended for occupancy as, a residence by one or more families, and any vacant land which is offered for sale or lease for the construction or location thereon of any such building, structure, or portion thereof.

* * *

(h) "Handicap" means, with respect to a person—

(1) a physical or mental impairment which substantially limits one or more of such person's major life activities,

(2) a record of having such an impairment, or

(3) being regarded as having such an impairment, but such term does not include current, illegal use of or addiction to a controlled substance (as defined in section 102 of the Controlled Substances Act (21 U.S.C. 802)).

* * *

(k) "Familial status" means one or more individuals (who have not attained the age of 18 years) being domiciled with—

(1) a parent or another person having legal custody of such individual or individuals; or

(2) the designee of such parent or other person having such custody, with the written permission of such parent or other person.

The protections afforded against discrimination on the basis of familial status shall apply to any person who is pregnant or is in the process of securing legal custody of any individual who has not attained the age of 18 years.

42 U.S.C. § 3604 Discrimination in sale or rental of housing and other prohibited practices

As made applicable by section 803 of this title and except as exempted by sections 803(b) and 807 of this title, it shall be unlawful—

(a) To refuse to sell or rent after the making of a bona fide offer, or to refuse to negotiate for the sale or rental of, or otherwise make unavailable or deny, a dwelling to any person because of race, color, religion, sex, familial status, or national origin.

(b) To discriminate against any person in the terms, conditions, or privileges of sale or rental of a dwelling, or in the provision of services or facilities in connection therewith, because of race, color, religion, sex, familial status, or national origin.

(c) To make, print, or publish, or cause to be made, printed, or published any notice, statement, or advertisement, with respect to the sale or rental of a dwelling that indicates any preference, limitation, or discrimination based on race, color, religion, sex, handicap, familial status, or national origin, or an intention to make any such preference, limitation, or discrimination.

(d) To represent to any person because of race, color, religion, sex, handicap, familial status, or national origin that any dwelling is not available for inspection, sale, or rental when such dwelling is in fact so available.

(e) For profit, to induce or attempt to induce any person to sell or rent any dwelling by representations regarding the entry or prospective entry into the neighborhood of a person or persons of a particular race, color, religion, sex, handicap, familial status, or national origin.

(f)(1) To discriminate in the sale or rental, or to otherwise make unavailable or deny, a dwelling to any buyer or renter because of a handicap of—

(A) that buyer or renter,

(B) a person residing in or intending to reside in that dwelling after it is so sold, rented, or made available; or

(C) any person associated with that buyer or renter.

(2) To discriminate against any person in the terms, conditions, or privileges of sale or rental of a dwelling, or in the provision of services or facilities in connection with such dwelling, because of a handicap of—

(A) that person; or

(B) a person residing in or intending to reside in that dwelling after it is so sold, rented, or made available; or

(C) any person associated with that person.

(3) For purposes of this subsection, discrimination includes—

(A) a refusal to permit, at the expense of the handicapped person, reasonable modifications of existing premises occupied or to be occupied by such person if such modifications may be necessary to afford such person full enjoyment of the premises, except that, in the case of a rental, the landlord may where it is reasonable to do so condition permission for a modification on the renter agreeing to restore the interior of the premises to the condition that existed before the modification, reasonable wear and tear excepted.

(B) a refusal to make reasonable accommodations in rules, policies, practices, or services, when such accommodations may be necessary to afford such person equal opportunity to use and enjoy a dwelling; or

(C) in connection with the design and construction of covered multifamily dwellings for first occupancy after the date that is 30 months after the date of enactment of the Fair Housing Amendments Act of 1988, a failure to design and construct those dwelling in such a manner that—

(i) the public use and common use portions of such dwellings are readily accessible to and usable by handicapped persons;

(ii) all the doors designed to allow passage into and within all premises within such dwellings are sufficiently wide to allow passage by handicapped persons in wheelchairs; and

(iii) all premises within such dwellings contain the following features of adaptive design:

(I) an accessible route into and through the dwelling;

(II) light switches, electrical outlets, thermostats, and other environmental controls in accessible locations;

(III) reinforcements in bathroom walls to allow later installation of grab bars; and

(IV) usable kitchens and bathrooms such that an individual in a wheelchair can maneuver about the space.

* * *

(8) Nothing in this title shall be construed to invalidate or limit any law of a State or political subdivision of a State, or other jurisdiction in which this title shall be effective, that requires dwellings to be designed and constructed in a manner that affords handicapped persons greater access than is required by this title.

(9) Nothing in this subsection requires that a dwelling be made available to an individual whose tenancy would constitute a direct threat to the health or safety of other individuals or whose tenancy would result in substantial physical damage to the property of others.

42 U.S.C. § 3607   Exemption

* * *

b) Numbers of occupants; housing for older persons; persons convicted of making or distributing controlled substances

(1) Nothing in this subchapter limits the applicability of any reasonable local, State, or Federal restrictions regarding the maximum number of occupants permitted to occupy a dwelling. Nor does any provision in this subchapter regarding familial status apply with respect to housing for older persons.

* * *

[Definition of "housing for older persons" omitted. Eds.]

(4) Nothing in this subchapter prohibits conduct against a person because such person has been convicted by any court of competent jurisdiction of the illegal manufacture or distribution of a controlled substance as defined in section 802 of Title 21.

42 U.S.C. § 3616a.   Fair housing initiatives program

b) Private enforcement initiatives

(2) Activities

The Secretary shall use funds made available under this subsection to conduct, through contracts with private nonprofit fair housing enforcement organizations, a range of investigative and enforcement activities designed to—

(A) carry out testing and other investigative activities [of violations of civil rights], including building the capacity for housing investigative activities in unserved or underserved areas...

ASBURY v. BROUGHAM

United States Court of Appeals, Tenth Circuit, 1989.
866 F.2d 1276.

PARKER, DISTRICT JUDGE.

Plaintiff Rosalyn Asbury brought suit under 42 U.S.C. § 1982 and the Fair Housing Act, 42 U.S.C. § 3601 *et seq.* (FHA), claiming that the defendants refused to rent or to allow her to inspect or negotiate for the rental of an apartment or townhouse at Brougham Estates in Kansas City. Defendants Leo Brougham, individually and doing business as Brougham Estates and Brougham Management Company, and Wanda Chauvin, his employee, appeal a jury verdict awarding Asbury compensatory damages of $7,500 against them upon a finding that the defendants discriminated against her on the basis of race and/or sex. Leo Brougham appeals from the jury verdict awarding punitive damages in the amount of $50,000 solely against him. Defendants contend that the jury verdict awarding compensatory damages is unsupported by the evidence because it failed to establish an intent to discriminate. Defendant Leo Brougham appeals the award of punitive damages on the additional ground that any discriminatory motivation that the jury may have found on the part of Wanda Chauvin could not be attributed to Brougham, on whose behalf she managed leasing of apartments and townhouses at Brougham Estates. The defendants argue, therefore, that the district court erred by denying their motion for a new trial.

I. SUFFICIENCY OF EVIDENCE SUPPORTING A FINDING OF RACIAL
DISCRIMINATION IN VIOLATION OF § 1982 AND FHA.

42 U.S.C. § 1982 and the FHA both prohibit discrimination on the basis of race. In order to prevail on a claim made under these statutes, plaintiff must prove a discriminatory intent. A violation occurs when race is a factor in a decision to deny a minority applicant the opportunity to rent or negotiate for a rental, but race need not be the only factor in the decision. In addition, § 3604(d) of the FHA specifically prohibits dissemination of false information about the availability of housing because of a person's race. Accordingly, failure to provide a minority applicant with the same information about availability of a rental until or the terms and conditions for rental as is provided to white "testers," results in false information being provided and is cognizable as an injury under the FHA. [ ]

A. *Asbury's Prima Facie Case under § 1982 and FHA.*

The three-part burden of proof analysis established in *McDonnell Douglas Corp. v. Green*, 411 U.S. 792, 93 S.Ct. 1817, 36 L.Ed.2d 668 (1973), a Title VII employment discrimination case, has been widely applied to FHA and § 1982 claims. [ ] Under the *McDonnell Douglas* analysis, plaintiff first must come forward with proof of a prima facie case of discrimination. Second, if plaintiff proves a prima facie case, the burden shifts to defendants to produce evidence that the refusal to rent or negotiate for a rental was motivated by legitimate, non-racially considerations. [ ] Third, once defendants by evidence articulate non-discriminatory reasons, the burden shifts back to plaintiff to show that the proffered reasons were pretextual. [ ]

The proof necessary to establish a prima facie case under the FHA also established a prima facie case of racial discrimination under § 1982. In order to establish her prima facie case, plaintiff had to prove that:

(1) she is a member of a racial minority;

(2) she applied for and was qualified to rent an apartment or townhouse in Brougham Estates;

(3) she was denied the opportunity to rent or to inspect or negotiate for the rental of a townhouse or apartment; and

(4) the housing opportunity remained available. [ ]

A review of the evidence in this case shows that plaintiff established her prima facie case. Defendants stipulated that Asbury is black. Plaintiff testified that on February 23, 1984, she went to Brougham Estates with her daughter to obtain rental housing. R. Vol. II at 29. At the rental office at Brougham Estates, Asbury encountered Wanda Chauvin, the manager, and explained to Chauvin that she was being transferred to Kansas City and needed to rent housing. R. Vol. II at 29–30. Asbury told Chauvin that she needed to secure housing by the middle of March or the beginning of April. R. Vol. II at 30. In response, Chauvin said there was no vacancies, R. vol. Ii at 30, but told Asbury she could call back at a later time to check on availability. R. Vol. II at 33. Chauvin provided no information concerning availability of rental units that would assist Asbury in her efforts to rent an apartment or townhouse at Brougham Estates. R. Vol. II at 32. Asbury asked for the opportunity to fill out an application, again stating that there were no vacancies and that she kept no waiting list. R. Vol. II at 33. Asbury also requested floor plans or the opportunity to view a model unit, and Chauvin refused. R. Vol. II at 31. Instead, Chauvin suggested Asbury inquire at the Westminister Apartments, R. Vol. II at 33, an apartment complex housing mostly black families. R. Vol. II at 3–4. Although Chauvin did not ask Asbury her qualifications, plaintiff was employed with the Federal Aviation Authority at a salary of $37,599. R. Vol. II at 25. Based on her salary, defendants concede that Asbury would likely be qualified to rent an apartment or townhouse at Brougham Estates. Brief of Appellants at 8.

Defendants argue that Asbury was not rejected because Chauvin courteously invited her to call back. However, there is ample evidence in the record to support the jury's finding that defendants' failure or refusal to provide Asbury the opportunity to rent or inspect or negotiate for the rental of a townhouse or apartment constituted a rejection because of her race cognizable under § 1982 and the FHA.

Although there was a conflict in the evidence as to the availability of housing at the time Asbury attempted to inspect and negotiate for rental, there was abundant evidence from which the jury could find that housing was available. Defendants testified that families with a child are housed exclusively in the townhouses at Brougham Estates, and that there were no townhouses available on the date Asbury inquired. Asbury introduced evidence suggesting that both apartments and townhouses were available and, in addition, that exceptions previously had been created to allow children to reside in the apartments.

On February 24, 1984, the day after Asbury inquired about renting, Asbury's sister-in-law, Linda Robinson, who is white, called to inquire about the availability of two-bedroom apartments. R. Vol. II at 76. The women who answered the telephone identified herself as "Wanda" and invited Robinson to Brougham Estates to view the apartments. R. Vol. II at 76–77. The following day, February 25, 1984, Robinson went to the rental office at Brougham Estates and met with Wanda Chauvin. R. Vol. II at 77–78. Chauvin provided Robinson with floor plans of available one- and two-bedroom apartments at Brougham Estates. R. Vol. II at 78–79. Robinson specifically asked Chauvin about rental to families with children, and Chauvin did not tell Robinson that children were restricted to the townhouse units. R. Vol. II at 80–81. Robinson accompanied Chauvin to inspect a model unit and several available two-bedroom apartments. R. Vol II at 83–85. Upon inquiry by Robinson, Chauvin indicated that the apartments were available immediately and offered to hold an apartment for her until the next week. R. Vol. II at 84.

Asbury also provided evidence indicating that townhouses were available for rent. On February 1, 1984, Daniel McMenay, a white male, notified Brougham Estates that he intended to vacate his townhouse. On April 4, 1984, Brougham Estates rented the townhouse vacated by McMenay to John Shuminski, a white male. R. Vol. III at 9–10. On March 10, 1984, Randall Hockett, a white male, also rented a townhouse at Brougham Estates. In addition, Asbury provided computer data sheets generated by Brougham Estates which indicated that a third townhouse was unoccupied at the time of her inquiry on February 23, 1984 and remained vacant as of April 10, 1984. There was also evidence that a building which included townhouse units had been closed for the winter but would be available for rent beginning in the spring. On February 22, 1984, one day prior to Asbury's inquiry into vacancies, James Vance, a white male, paid a deposit for a townhouse which he occupied when the building opened on April 10, 1984. R. Vol. II at 131, 134. Since Asbury testified that she told Chauvin she did not need to occupy a rental unit until the beginning of April, the jury could have concluded that at least one of the townhouses which was subsequently rented to the white males was available at the time Asbury inquired. Although defendants took the position at trial that the townhouses were closed or out of order for repair and therefore not available to rent, the jury was free to accept the evidence of availability presented by the plaintiff.

Since Asbury met her burden of proving a prima facie case of racial discrimination, the burden shifted to defendants to prove a legitimate, non-discriminatory reason for denial of housing. [   ]

B.   Failure of Proof of Legitimate, Non-discriminatory Reason for Rejection.

Defendants claimed their legitimate, nondiscriminatory reasons for rejecting Asbury arose out of the policies at Brougham Estates that families with one child could rent townhouses but not apartments, and that families with more than one child were not permitted to move into Brougham Estates. [   ] Defendants further argued that they made no exceptions to these rules. Defendants contended that in accordance with these rental policies, no appropriate housing was available for Asbury when she inquired. However, plaintiff introduced evidence indicating that exceptions to these rules had been made on several occasions; families with children had rented apartments, and families with more than one child had been permitted to move into Brougham Estates. [   ] Asbury was not provided information about the terms and conditions that gave rise to an exception to the policy concerning children being restricted to the townhouses. [   ] The jury could therefore find that defendants' reasons for denying Asbury the opportunity to negotiate for rental were not legitimate and nondiscriminatory.

Defendants also argue that evidence of a high percentage of minority occupancy in Brougham Estates conclusively rebuts the claim of intentional racial discrimination. Although such statistical data is relevant to rebutting a claim of discrimination, statistical data is not dispositive of a claim of intentional discrimination. [ ] Moreover, there was other evidence from which the jury could have determined that race was a motivating factor in defendants' decision to refuse to negotiate with Asbury for a rental unit.

II. SUFFICIENCY OF EVIDENCE SUPPORTING PUNITIVE DAMAGES AWARD.

* * *

III. PLAINTIFF'S REQUEST FOR ATTORNEY'S FEES UNDER 42 U.S.C. § 1988 AND FOR DAMAGES AND DOUBLE COSTS FOR FRIVOLOUS APPEAL.

* * *

While we have determined that there was ample evidence to support the jury's findings of intentional racial discrimination, we cannot say that defendants' appeal of the compensatory damages award was utterly meritless. With respect to the award of punitive damages, we believe there was a significant question as to the sufficiency of the evidence on the issues of Brougham's intentional or reckless establishment of discriminatory policies and Brougham's ratification of Chauvin's actions. We conclude that defendants' appeal was not frivolous, and we therefore decline to award damages or double costs.

AFFIRMED AND REMANDED.

JANCIK v. DEPARTMENT OF HOUSING AND URBAN DEVELOPMENT

United States Court of Appeals, Seventh Circuit, 1995.
44 F.3d 553.

ROVNER, CIRCUIT JUDGE.

Stanley Jancik petitions for review of a decision of the Department of Housing and Urban Development ("HUD"), which found that he discriminated in the rental of an apartment on the basis of both race and family status in violation of section 804(c) of the Fair Housing Act ("FHA"), 42 U.S.C. § 3604(c). He also petitions for review of an order awarding attorney fees to the Leadership Council for Metropolitan Open Communities. We affirm.

I.

Stanley Jancik owns Building No. 44 in King Arthur's Court, a large housing complex in the Chicago suburb of Northlake. King Arthur's Court houses people of all ages, including children, and although all of the apartments in Jancik's building have only one bedroom, they are large enough to house more than one occupant under local codes. The claims in this case arise out of Jancik's conduct in the rental of an apartment in that building. On August 29, 1990, Jancik placed this ad in a local suburban newspaper:

> NORTHLAKE deluxe 1 BR apt, a/c, newer quiet bldg, pool, prkg, mature person preferred, credit checked. $395. . . .

Suspecting that the request for a "mature person" might reflect a violation of the Act, the Leadership Council's Investigations Manager Glenn Brewer decided to "test" the property. In that process, "testers" bearing fictitious identities posed as potential renters in order to check for discriminatory practices. In this instance, Brewer chose to use volunteer testers Cindy Gunderson, who is white, and Marsha Allen, who is African American, for the task.

Gunderson spoke with Jancik by telephone on the evening of September 7, 1990. She subsequently related that after asking Gunderson her age and learning that she was 36, Jancik told her "that was good—he doesn't want any teenagers in there." (Int. Ex. 5 at 6.) Jancik also asked Gunderson her name and, upon hearing it, inquired "what kind of name" it was. (*Id.* at 7.) Learning that the name was Norwegian, Jancik asked whether "that's white Norwegian or black Norwegian" and repeated the question a second time after Gunderson failed to answer. (*Id.*) Gunderson asked Jancik whether he was inquiring as to her race, and after he responded affirmatively, told him that she was white. Gunderson then asked to view the apartment and the two arranged for her to do so the following morning.

Marsha Allen spoke with Jancik two hours later the same evening. Jancik asked Allen her occupation, income, age, marital status, race and whether she had any children or pets. Allen did not reveal her race, but in response to that question asked Jancik why he needed this information. He responded, in her words, "that he had to screen the applicants because the tenants in the building were middle-aged and he did not want anyone moving in who was loud, made a lot of noise and had children or pets." When Allen told Jancik that she did not have any children or pets he said "wonderful," and the two arranged for Allen to see the apartment the next morning. Both testers arrived the next morning at approximately 10:00, and Jancik's rental manager separately informed each that the apartment had been rented earlier that morning.

Based on the reports filed by Gunderson and Allen, the Leadership Council filed an administrative complaint with HUD on May 22, 1991. The Council charged that Jancik had violated section 804(c) of the FHA, 42 U.S.C. § 3604(c), which makes it unlawful:

> To make, print, or publish, or cause to be made, printed, or published any notice, statement, or advertisement, with respect to the sale or rental of a dwelling that indicates any preference, limitation, or discrimination based on race, color, religion, sex, handicap, familial

status, or national origin, or an intention to make any such preference, limitation, or discrimination.

The Leadership Council claimed that Jancik's print advertisement violated the section by indicating a preference based on family status and that his interviews with the testers violated the section by indicating a preference based on both race and family status. After HUD's General Council issued a "Determination of Reasonable Cause and Charge if Discrimination," the matter was set for hearing before Administrative Law Judge ("ALJ") William C. Cregar, as provided by 42 U.S.C. § 3612(b). With the Council and Marsha Allen as interveners, the ALJ conducted a two-day hearing in early June of 1993 and issued a 21–page Initial Decision and Order on October 1, 1993, which found that Jancik had violated section 3604(c). The ALJ awarded damages to the Leadership Council ($21,386.14) and to Marsha Allen ($2,000), assessed a civil penalty of $10,000, and enjoined Jancik from engaging in further acts of discrimination, all as authorized by 42 U.S.C. § 3612(g)(3). The ALJ's decision become final on October 31, 1993. *See* 42 U.S.C. § 3612(h). The Leadership Council subsequently filed a petition requesting $23,842.50 in attorney's fees. Although Jancik did not raise any factual objections to the fee petition, which was supported by affidavits, he did request a hearing on the fees issue. In a February 10, 1994 order, the ALJ denied that request and granted the fees petition for the full amount requested. Jancik now seeks review of both of the ALJ's orders, as provided by 42 U.S.C. § 3612(i).

II.

* * *

Section 3604(c) prohibits the making or publishing of any statement or advertisement that "indicates" any preference or limitation based on, among other factors, race or family status. Whether a given statement or advertisement "indicates" such a preference is therefore central to our analysis. Although we have not previously dealt with the "indicates" aspect of section 3604(c), the circuit courts that have done so have employed a relatively straightforward approach, which we also find appropriate. First, every circuit that has considered a claim under section 604(c) has held that an objective "ordinary reader" standard should be applied in determining what is "indicated" by an ad. Thus, "the statute [is] violated if an ad for housing suggest to an ordinary reader that a particular [protected group] is preferred or dispreferred for the housing in question." *Ragin v. New York Times Co.*, 923 F.2d 995, 999 (2d Cir.), *cert. denied*, 502 U.S. 821, 112 S.Ct. 81, 116 L.Ed.2d 54 (1991). [ ] In applying the "ordinary reader" test, courts have not required that ads jump out at the reader with their offending message, but have found instead that the statute is violated by "any ad that would discourage an ordinary reader of a particular [protected group] from answering it." *Ragin*, 923 F.2d at 999–1000.

Significantly, no showing of a subjective intent to discriminate is therefore necessary to establish a violation of the section, [   ] At the same time, however, evidence of such intent is not irrelevant. Evidence that the author or speaker intended his or her words to indicate a prohibited preference obviously bears on the question of whether the words in fact do so. [   ] Thus, if such proof exists, it may provide an alternative means of establishing a violation of the section. [   ]

In view of these guidelines, the ALJ's finding that Jancik's advertisement and statements expressed a preference based on family status in violation of section 804(c) was certainly supported by substantial evidence. First, Jancik told Allen that he did not want any families with children and told Gunderson that he did not want any teenagers in the building. In our view, both of these statements quite clearly would suggest to an "ordinary" listener that Jancik had a preference or limitation based on family status. The advertisement indicating his preference for a "mature person" was similarly problematic. Not only do we view that term as suggesting an unlawful preference to an ordinary reader, the term is noted in the implementing regulation as being among "those most often used in residential real state advertising to convey either overt or tacit discriminatory preferences or limitations." 24 C.F.R. § 109.20(b)(7). Of course, as Jancik points out, use of the listed terms does not violate the Act per se, but it does "indicate a possible violation of the act and establish a need for further proceedings on the complaint, if it is apparent from the context of the usage that discrimination within the meaning of the act is likely to result. *Id.* Here, the context of the usage, which included explicit verification of Jancik's preference to each of two prospective tenants who responded to the ad, makes clear that the usage was meant to convey an unlawful preference.

And, although we have no doubt that the Act has been violated based solely on this objective analysis, the record was also complete with evidence of Jancik's subjective intent to discriminate against families with children. For example, Jancik admitted at the hearing that he had told prospective tenants with children that there was no school in the area, where there was in fact a high school located on adjacent property and an elementary school within one mile. [   ] Jancik also told the HUD investigator that he had previously turned away a single parent with a ten-year-old child. [   ]

Although the question of whether Jancik violated section 3604(c) by asking Gunderson and Allen about their race is somewhat more difficult, the ALJ's determination in that regard is also supported by substantial evidence. Unlike his comments regarding family status, Jancik did not expressly indicate a preference based on race, but merely asked the testers about their race. In the only case that has commented on the issue, the Second Circuit has indicated by way of dicta in *Soules v. HUD*, 967 F.2d 817 (2d Cir.1992) that questions about race standing alone are sufficient to violate the section because "[t]here is simply no legitimate reason for considering an applicant's race." 967 F.2d at 824. We need not decide that question here, however, because the context of the questions make clear they did indicate an intent to discriminate on the basis of race. First, each question came in the midst of conversations in which Jancik was expressing other impermissible preferences. Hearing an inquiry about race immediately after being asked about children and told that applicants with children were undesirable, would, in our view, suggest to an ordinary listener that the racial question was part of the same screening process. Indeed, when Allen asked Jancik the purpose of his question about her race, he admitted that he was, in her words, "screening the applicants." [   ] Jancik's unlawful purpose was similarly revealed in his conversation with Gunderson by the pointedness of his inquiry. After asking the origins of the Gunderson name and learning that it was Norwegian, he twice inquired whether Gunderson was "white Norwegian or black Norwegian" and subsequently admitted, in answer to her question, that he was inquiring as to her race. It is unlikely that if the inquiry had been merely conversational, as Jancik has contended, he would have pursued it with such determination. In addition, the fact that Jancik had never rented to an African–American tenant before the Leadership Counsel filed its complaint to this case further bolsters the ALJ's conclusion that Jancik's question reflected an intent to exclude tenants on the basis of race.

III. ATTORNEY'S FEES

Jancik does not contest the amount of attorney's fees awarded, but argues only that the ALJ abused his discretion in denying Jancik's request for a hearing on the issue. Aside from arguing in general that the fees were excessive, however, Jancik raised no factual objections to the fees petition. The ALJ addressed each of Jancik's legal challenges to the fees petition in a thorough order disposing of the matter. Because no facts were in dispute, the ALJ's determination that an evidentiary hearing was "unnecessary" [   ] was not an abuse of discretion.

IV.

For the foregoing reasons, we find that each of the ALJ's orders is both in accordance with law and supported by substantial evidence. Jancik's petitions for review are therefore DENIED.

Notes and Questions

1. *Asbury* illustrates the so-called prima facie burden of proof analysis commonly used in discrimination cases. In the first phase, plaintiff must produce evidence that is adequate by itself and sufficient, if not explained or contradicted, to establish illegal discrimination. If plaintiff does so, the burden shifts to defendant to show that the refusal to rent was based on legitimate, non-discriminatory business reasons. If defendant succeeds in doing so, plaintiff then must establish that defendants' reasons were merely pretextual in order to prevail on the merits of the case.

2. *Jancik* illustrates the use of "testers," people of different races who pose as prospective tenants or homebuyers in order to test whether landlords

or realtors are engaging in illegal discriminatory practices. Testers are employed by civil rights advocacy groups and the U.S. Department of Justice to enforce anti-discrimination legislation. Local testing programs have been supported by grants from the Department of Housing and Urban Development under statutory authority, 42 U.S.C. § 3616(b)(2). Is there a moral issue in the use of testers? Their use has been defended because of the recognized difficulty in obtaining evidence of illegal discrimination without them. While testing has been criticized as undermining respect for the integrity of the law by use of deceptive practices, realtors and apartment owners have endorsed the practice as a useful "reminder ... that you can't do something ... (and that) makes us better." Mei–Ling Hopgood, 'Renters' Test for Bias In Housing, St. Louis Post–Dispatch, May 9, 1996, at 1, 4 W.

3. *Jancik* also construes the prohibition against discriminatory advertisements and statements in the Fair Housing Act, 42 U.S.C.A. § 3604(c). Note the court's use of the "ordinary reader" perspective in determining whether a particular communication violates the statute. The subjective intent of the speaker or writer is not controlling. See also State v. Keding, 553 N.W.2d 305 (Iowa 1996) (newsletter distributed to mobile home park tenants that owner was "contemplating" turning the mobile home development into an "adult park" violated fair housing act despite defendants' contention that they did not actually intend to implement the change).

4. May a landlord bar a disabled tenant who has pled guilty to possession of drug paraphernalia? Yes, according to Taylor v. Cisneros, 102 F.3d 1334 (3d Cir. 1996). What about a tenant whose guests had illegal drugs in her apartment without her knowledge? Yes, according to Housing Authority of New Orleans v. Green, 661 So.2d 1355 (La.1995) (Anti–Drug Abuse Act of 1988 was applicable because "tenant controlled who had access to the premises"). May a landlord bar guests from tenant's apartments through the use of criminal trespass statutes? Upheld in Williams v. Nagel, 162 Ill.2d 542, 205 Ill.Dec. 525, 643 N.E.2d 816 (1994). But see Charlotte Housing Authority v. Patterson, 120 N.C.App. 552, 464 S.E.2d 68 (1995) (unforeseen criminal acts by tenant's son committed outside tenant's presence and without her knowledge may not serve as a basis for eviction of the tenant).

5. Would the Fair Housing Act be violated by a refusal to rent to someone because of her occupation, e.g., a lawyer? See Kramarsky v. Stahl Management, 92 Misc.2d 1030, 401 N.Y.S.2d 943 (1977) (refusal to rent to black woman lawyer not violative of New York fair housing statute when decision was based on occupation). "[T]here is nothing illegal in a landlord discriminating against lawyers as a group, or trying to keep out of his building intelligent persons, aware of their rights, who may give him trouble in the future." Id. at 944.

6. Does the Fair Housing Act prohibit a landlord from refusing to rent to unmarried, cohabiting couples even though such activity offends the landlord's religious beliefs? How should the interest of landlords and tenants be balanced when their life styles differ? Courts have differed based on whether they consider that such refusal to rent is based on conduct (landlord's refusal is not illegal discrimination) or status (refusal to rent is unlawful). See Smith v. Fair Employment and Housing Com'n, 12 Cal.4th 1143, 51 Cal.Rptr.2d 700, 913 P.2d 909 (1996) (status) (Federal Religious

Freedom Restoration Act (RFRA) does not exempt landlord from complying with California Fair Employment and Housing Act (FEHA). The asserted burden was the result of a "religion-neutral" law rather than a law directed against religious exercise); Swanner v. Anchorage Equal Rights Com'n, 874 P.2d 274 (Alaska 1994) *cert. den.*, 513 U.S. 979, 115 S.Ct. 460, 130 L.Ed.2d 368 (1994) (status) (statutes prohibiting discrimination in housing on basis of marital status are "neutral laws of general applicability" that do not violate Free Exercise Clauses of U.S. or Alaska constitutions); reaffirmed in Thomas v. Anchorage Equal Rights Comm'n, 102 P.3d 937 (Alaska 2004); Attorney General v. Desilets, 418 Mass. 316, 636 N.E.2d 233 (1994) (conduct). For an extensive analysis of the case law interpreting the Free Exercise Clause of the First Amendment and its application to landlord-tenant conflicts, see Maureen Markey, The Price of Landlord's "Free" Exercise of Religion: Tenants' Right to Discrimination—Free Housing and Privacy, 22 Ford. Urb. L.J. 699 (1995) (arguing that courts should not grant individual landlords free exercise exemptions from fair housing legislation, and that legislatures should do so only if particular exemptions are warranted and are narrowly drawn).

For a case resolving the conflict in values in favor of the landlord's religious beliefs, see State by Cooper v. French, 460 N.W.2d 2 (Minn.1990), holding that the prohibition against discrimination on the basis of marital status in the Minnesota Human Rights Act was not intended by the legislature to include unmarried, cohabiting couples, and that the religious liberty clause of the Minnesota Constitution protected the "rights of conscience" of a landlord who refused to rent to unmarried, cohabiting couples. The court held that unless the state can show a "compelling and overriding state interest," the landlord must be granted an "exemption" from the state human rights act. See also North Dakota Fair Housing Council v. Peterson, 625 N.W.2d 551 (N.D. 2001) (conduct); Dane County, Wis. v. Norman, 174 Wis.2d 683, 497 N.W.2d 714 (1993) (landlord's policy of refusing to rent to unrelated individuals seeking to live together is based on "conduct" rather than "marital status" and does not unlawfully discriminate against unmarried cohabitants).

One of the reasons the Minnesota Supreme Court gave for overturning a conviction under the Minnesota Human Rights Act was that there was a "less restrictive" alternative to "forc[ing] a person to break one statute [prohibiting fornication] to obey another [prohibiting discrimination based on marital status]." Is the "exemption" the court granted an appropriate way to resolve such disputes? If so, how should it be worded? Should it make a difference whether the landlord is "some faceless corporation" or an elderly couple who acquired the apartment "as wholly personal investments for their retirement years"? J. Kilpatrick, Living–in–Sin Suit Pits Rights Against Rights, St. Louis Post–Dispatch, August 29, 1989, at p. 3B, suggesting that such a line be drawn. Suppose the landlord were in his mid–30s and rented units as a source of investment income? Layle French, the landlord in the Minnesota case, was 34 at the time of the supreme court decision. Associated Press, Landlord Ruling Reversed, The Cincinnati Enquirer, September 2, 1990, at p. A–12. Should the number of units involved make a difference? In the *French* case, a single two-bedroom house was involved. Is the following compromise, worked out by Congress in the debate over the Fair Housing Act of 1968, an acceptable one?

42 U.S.C. § 3603 * * *

(b) Nothing in section 804 of this title (other than subsection (c)) shall apply to—

(1) any single-family house sold or rented by an owner: **Provided,** That such private individual owner does not own more than three such single-family houses at any one time: **Provided further,** That in the case of the sale of any such single-family house by a private individual owner not residing in such house at the time of such house or who was not the most recent resident of such house prior to such sale, the exemption granted by this subsection shall apply only with respect to one such sale within any twenty-four month period: **Provided further,** That such bona fide private individual owner does not own any interest in, nor is there owned or reserved on his behalf, under any express or voluntary agreement, title to or any right to all or a portion of the proceeds from the sale or rental of, more than three such single family houses at any one time: **Provided further,** That after December 31, 1969, the sale or rental of any such single-family house shall be excepted from the application of this subchapter only if such house is sold or rented (A) without the use in any manner of the sales or rental facilities or the sales or rental services of any real estate broker, agent, or salesman, or of such facilities or services of any person in the business of selling or renting dwellings, or of any employee or agent of any such broker, agent, salesman, or person and (B) without the publication, posting or mailing, after notice, of any advertisement or written notice in violation of section 804(c) of this title; but nothing in this proviso shall prohibit the use of attorneys, escrow agents, abstractors, title companies, and other such professional assistance as necessary to perfect or transfer the title, or

(2) rooms or units in dwellings containing living quarters occupied or intended to be occupied by no more than four families living independently of each other, if the owner actually remains and occupies one of such living quarters as his residence.

7. The Fair Housing Amendments Act of 1988 expanded the coverage of the Act to include persons with disabilities and families with children. For a discussion of the changes, see Kushner, The Fair Housing Amendments Act of 1988: The Second Generation of Fair Housing, 42 Vanderbilt L.Rev. 1049 (1989). Examine the statutory excerpts. May a landlord require an elderly person to be able to "live independently" as a condition of admission? See Cason v. Rochester Housing Authority, 748 F.Supp. 1002 (W.D.N.Y. 1990) (ability to live independently requirement held violative of Fair Housing Act and Rehabilitation Act of 1973). What about a mentally ill person who suffers from auditory hallucinations? Cf. City Wide Associates v. Penfield, 409 Mass. 140, 564 N.E.2d 1003 (1991) (eviction violated Federal Rehabilitation Act where landlord received public subsidies including reimbursement for tenant-caused damage and adverse impact on other tenants was not shown). Suppose a landlord denies an application of a couple who told the landlord that they planned to adopt a foster child. See Gorski v.

Troy, 929 F.2d 1183 (7th Cir.1991) (couple evicted after telling landlord of their plans to adopt foster child were "aggrieved persons" within meaning of Fair Housing Act). Could a landlord deny an application to a homosexual couple? See Braschi v. Stahl Associates Co., 74 N.Y.2d 201, 544 N.Y.S.2d 784, 543 N.E.2d 49 (1989), discussed in Comment, Braschi v. Stahl: Family Redefined, 8 J. Human Rts. 289 (1990) (homosexual couple held legal equivalent of family under state rent control statute).

8.   Can a landlord of a 156–unit apartment complex restrict one bedroom apartments to one person even though local occupancy codes permit two persons? See U.S. v. Badgett, 976 F.2d 1176 (8th Cir.1992) (familial status discrimination found). What about an elderly couple who refuses to rent a small single family house to more than four persons? See Pfaff v. HUD, 88 F.3d 739 (9th Cir.1996) (landlords met their rebuttal burden by showing that a facially neutral, numerical occupancy restriction was based on number of bedrooms and size of the house. "Compelling business necessity" standard was not appropriate in this case because HUD had misled landlords by previously published interpretations of the statute that a less rigorous standard would be reasonable).

9.   Is a landlord required by the "reasonable accommodation" provision (42 U.S.C. § 3604(f)(3)(B)) to evict a tenant whose "meticulous" housecleaning habits aggravated the chemical sensitivity disability of her upstairs neighbor? See Temple v. Gunsalus, 97 F.3d 1452 (6th Cir.1996) ("requirement of reasonable accommodation does not entail an obligation to do everything humanly possible to accommodate a disabled person"). What about a refusal to allow deaf tenants to have a dog? See Bronk v. Ineichen, 54 F.3d 425 (7th Cir.1995) (landlord may not refuse if dog was a hearing dog; may refuse if dog was not a hearing dog); In re Kenna Homes Cooperative Corp., 210 W.Va. 380, 557 S.E.2d 787 (2001) (landlord can require tenant to establish that service animal was properly trained and necessary because of tenant's disability). *See also* Jankowski Lee & Assocs. v. Cisneros, 91 F.3d 891 (7th Cir.1996) (increase in number of handicapped parking spaces from 4 to 8 and addition of one van space was not a reasonable accommodation to a tenant with multiple sclerosis when 27 tenants were registered to park in handicapped spaces).

10.   Would a requirement that prospective tenants have gross monthly incomes of at least three times the rent to be charged be a violation of the Act? Suppose a prospective tenant alleges race or sex discrimination because of findings that minorities and women tend to have lower average incomes than Caucasian men. The Supreme Court of California construed the state civil rights statute to require a showing of intentional discrimination rather than discriminatory impact and upheld the minimum income policy as a reasonable economic test in Harris v. Capital Growth Investors XIV, 52 Cal.3d 1142, 278 Cal.Rptr. 614, 805 P.2d 873 (1991). The court reasoned as follows:

> The minimum income policy is no different in its purpose or effect from stated price or payment terms. Like those terms, it seeks to obtain for a business establishment the benefit of its bargain with the consumer: full payment of the price. In pursuit of the objective of securing payment, a landlord has a legitimate and direct economic interest in the

income level of prospective tenants, as opposed to their sex, race, religion, or other personal beliefs or characteristics. For nearly all tenants, current income is the source of the monthly rental payment. When a tenant ceases paying rent during the term of the tenancy, the landlord must resort to legal process to obtain possession of the premises and to collect any back rent that may be due. [   ]

Even with the use of summary unlawful detainer proceedings, an eviction may take several months, during which the tenant remains in possession, enjoying the benefits of the leasehold without paying rent. [   ] Thus, the landlord bears the economic burdens (what an economist might call the "transaction costs of death") resulting from: (1) loss of income from default to eviction; (2) administrative time and the legal and other expenses incurred in the eviction process; and (3) the delays and expense of collection of back rent from the tenant, as well as the risk of noncollection.

In order to minimize the transaction costs of default, the economically rational landlord might adopt one or more of several approaches. First, a landlord might simply charge higher rents to all tenants to absorb the additional expense. Such a policy, of course, contains its own element of arbitrariness because it penalizes the majority of tenants who pay their rent on a regular basis. Moreover, the charging of higher rents as a means of subsidizing defaults necessarily excludes even more low income persons from tenancy. Second, a landlord might require larger amounts from all tenants as advance rent or security deposits. This policy, too, imposes additional burdens on the paying tenants. In apparent recognition of this fact, it is also subject to statutory limitations on the amount of advance payment a landlord may demand. [   ] Third, a landlord might adopt one or more policies or practices designed to screen out prospective tenants who are likely to default.

The minimum income policy adopted by defendants is, of course, an example of the third approach. It assumes that, at some ratio of rent to income, the burden of paying rent, along with other living expenses, will impose a hardship on a tenant, resulting in default. Although there may be myriad of individual factors operating in cases of particular prospective tenants that might affect the predictive value of the ratio, it does not thereby become "arbitrary" in the same way that race and sex discrimination are arbitrary. On the contrary, it is based on the rational economic interest of the landlord to minimize defaults and maintain the solvency of his business establishment, while extending the opportunity for rental housing to all persons regardless of race, sex, religion, etc. * * * Id., 805 P.2d 885–886, 893. See also Mencer v. Princeton Square Apartments, 228 F.3d 631 (CA 8, 2000) (application of three times rent income qualification upheld).

11.   Does a blanket "no AFDC recipients" policy violate the familial status provision of the Fair Housing Act? In Gilligan v. Jamco Development Corp., 108 F.3d 246 (9th Cir.1997), the U.S. Court of Appeals for the Ninth Circuit held that a prospective tenant did not have to allege sufficient income to pay the rent in order to prosecute a fair housing complaint based on such a policy.

12. Courts have recognized a cause of action for creating a hostile housing environment under the broad language of 42 U.S.C.A. § 3604(b). A claim is actionable "when the offensive behavior unreasonably interferes with use and enjoyment of the premises." Honce v. Vigil, 1 F.3d 1085 (10th Cir.1993). Suppose a male landlord tells a female tenant, while caressing her arm and back, that if she could not pay the rent, she "could take care of it in other ways." When the tenant slammed the door in his face he cursed her. Over the next several months, the parties continued to disagree about the rent until the landlord sued to evict tenant. Shortly thereafter, tenant filed a claim alleging housing discrimination on the basis of sex. What result? See DiCenso v. Cisneros, 96 F.3d 1004, 1008–1009 (7th Cir.1996). In reversing a decision of the Secretary of Housing and Urban Developments's designee and holding that the particular incident was not sufficiently egregious to create a hostile housing environment claim, the court stated:

> In this context, the problem with Brown's complaint is that although DiCenso may have harassed her, he did so only once. Moreover, DiCenso's conduct, while clearly unwelcome, was much less offensive than other incidents which have not violated Title VII. DiCenso's comment vaguely invited Brown to exchange sex for rent, and while DiCenso caressed Brown's arm and back, he did not touch an intimate body part, and did not threaten Brown with any physical harm. There is no question that Brown found DiCenso's remarks to be subjectively unpleasant, but this alone did not create an objectively hostile environment.

> We stress in closing that our decision today should not be read as giving landlords one free chance to harass their tenants. We do not condone DiCenso's conduct, nor do we hold that a single incident of harassment never will support an actionable claim. [ ] Considering the totality of the circumstances in this case, we agree with the [Administrative Law Judge] that DiCenso's conduct was not sufficiently egregious to create an objectively hostile housing environment.

See also Neudecker v. Boisclair Corp., 351 F.3d 361 (8th Cir. 2003) ("disability harassment," such as circulating tenant's private medical information to other tenants, is actionable under the Fair Housing Act); United States v. Koch, 352 F.Supp.2d 970 (D. Neb. 2004) (sexual harassment likewise).

13. Imagine yourself in law practice, saying the following things to two clients, a married couple, who (i) have a vacant apartment over their garage, which they want to offer for rent; (ii) are opposed on moral grounds to cohabitation without marriage; and (iii) are worried about an ordinance forbidding discrimination against unmarried couples. There are many ways, as *Asbury* and *Jancik* illustrate, to deny this apartment to an unmarried couple without giving the real reasons for doing so: credit checks, requiring references, restrictions on use (invented for the occasion) that seem to fit the potential tenants' "lifestyle." As *Asbury* and *Jancik* show, these ways may not succeed; but few potential tenants are willing to pursue administrative and judicial remedies that will end up saying so. You (assume) would never advise such an arsenal to support racial discrimination; but you are willing to respect their consciences in the matter. Should a lawyer be involved in such evasions of the law? See Model Rules of Professional Conduct, Rule

1.2(d),reproduced earlier in this Chapter, and assume that the advice outlined here would be a violation of that rule. Does conscience trump the law?
Does conscience trump professional rules? Why or why not? If you decide
that conscience trumps rule and law, how will you go about giving this
advice in such a way as to avoid professional discipline for doing so? Does the
last sentence in Rule 1.2(d) help?

"A lawyer should not counsel a client to engage, or assist a client, in
conduct that the lawyer knows is criminal or fraudulent, but a lawyer may
discuss the legal consequences of any proposed course of conduct with a
client and may counsel or assist a client to make a good faith effort to
determine the validity, scope, meaning or application of the law."

One way to approach such an ethical question is to define the issue
verbally, and analyze the facts, as if the problem were a legal one that
turned on language in an act of the legislature. The rule (1.2[d]) says
"conduct that the lawyer knows is criminal or fraudulent." Analysis might
lead to the conclusions that excluding an unmarried couple who plan to live
together over one's garage is surely neither a crime nor a fraud, particularly
not if one lets the word "fraud" have full sway and applies to it intuitive
considerations such as honesty and integrity. (I.e., honest acts are not
frauds.) That being the case—this "objective" reasoning might say—it is
surely all right to use devices (credit checks, references) that are in themselves legitimate to achieve the purpose, even if the object of using the
devices is not as important as the client and lawyer might make it appear to
be. And then, if there is doubt as to that ethical conclusion, one can take
advantage of the provision in this rule (1.2[d]) that would permit a lawyer to
advise clients to test the validity of their reasoning on whether exclusion,
using these devices, is within the meaning of Rule 1.2 (whether or not it is
within the meaning of a no-discrimination ordinance). And if it is all right to
do all of that, it is probably all right, even under the Rules, to suggest such
screening devices to one's clients. Notice that what we are doing here is not
deciding whether the landlord's behavior at issue is morally wrong; we have
already decided it is not morally wrong to exclude unmarried people who
plan to live in sin over the garage; what we are deciding is whether the
lawyer who is mixed up in this evasion is or should be subject to the
disapproval of her professional peers. The issue is reminiscent of discussions
on legal advice to take advantage of tax "loopholes." See Randolph Paul,
"The Responsibilities of the Tax Advisor," 63 Harvard Law Review 385
(1950); and the Report of the Committee on Standards of Tax Practice,
(A.B.A.) Section of Taxation Newsletter, Winter 1984.

Rule 1.2 (e) originally attempted to provide guidance to the lawyer who
has a client who "expects assistance not permitted by the rules of professional conduct or other law." The guidance was to "consult with the client
regarding the relevant limitations on the lawyer's conduct." That direction
was reworded slightly and moved to a comment (no. 13) by the A.B.A.
Committee that revised the Rules in 2002. It was also added as Rule
1.4(a)(5). It sounds somewhat like a requirement for a lawyer-to-client
sermon. You might feel, if you were the lawyer in the case we put here, that
you should follow the rule in this respect (why not?); if so, what would you
say?

B.　INTEGRATION MAINTENANCE

In addition to the prohibition against discrimination, the Fair Housing Act requires governmental agencies to "affirmatively further" fair housing efforts. 42 U.S.C. § 3608(d). This is accomplished through a variety of integration maintenance programs, which can by their very nature result in discriminatory treatment. In one celebrated case, United States v. Starrett City Associates, 840 F.2d 1096 (C.A. 2, 1988), the court struck down an admissions policy that established a quota of 64% of the apartments in a large privately-owned cooperative apartment development in New York City for whites, 22% for blacks and 8% for Hispanics as prohibited discrimination even though it was designed to maintain an integrated community. The case that follows examines a similar policy by New York City's housing authority that was designed to implement a consent decree to settle a fair housing lawsuit.

DAVIS v. NEW YORK CITY HOUSING AUTHORITY

Court of Appeals for the Second Circuit, 2002.
278 F.3d 64.

KEARSE, CIRCUIT JUDGE.

This case returns to us following remands in 1999 and 2000 to the United States District Court for the Southern District of New York, Robert W. Sweet, Judge, for further findings, clarification, and supplementation of the record in connection with its issuance of injunctions prohibiting defendant New York City Housing Authority ("NYCHA" or the "Authority") from implementing proposed changes in its method of complying with a 1992 consent decree (the "Consent Decree or "Decree") settling actions alleging that, in accepting tenants for public housing in New York City, the Authority had discriminated against Latinos and African Americans on the basis of race. The district court found that NYCHA' s proposed introduction of a working-family preference into the tenant acceptance procedures would cause a significant perpetuation of past segregation at 20 NYCHA low-income housing projects, and in 1999 it permanently enjoined NYCHA from implementing that preference at those projects. NYCHA appeals, contending principally that the district court erred (a) in its view of what constitutes segregation, and (b) in finding that segregation would be significantly perpetuated. For the reasons that follow, we affirm with respect to 14 of the housing projects, and we reverse with respect to the remaining six....

[Separate lawsuits were filed by the United States and Pauline Davis *et al.* alleging that the NYCHA violated the Civil Rights statutes, 42 U.S.C § 1981, 1982 and 1983, and the Fair Housing Act, 42 U.S.C § 3601 *et seq.*, by engaging in the practice of "racial steering." Both actions were settled by a Consent Decree in 1992. The Consent Decree established a new three-stage tenant selection and assignment plan ("TSAP") involving 1) eligibility determination, 2) a waiting list, and 3) assignment to a unit. The waiting list contained three tiers based on income, with Tier I the lowest and Tier III the highest. When vacancies occur, NYCHA attempts to allocate 25% of such units to Tier III applicants and divide evenly between Tier I and II the remaining 75%.

In 1995, NYCHA proposed to add a working family preference ("WFP") to the eligibility standards, eliminating housing need as a local priority in favor of families who can pay the most. NYCHA's goals were to increase the number of working families and income integration in public housing to promote financial and social stability. Plaintiffs opposed the WFP because of concerns that it would effectively perpetuate racial segregation by favoring white families. In a series of court proceedings over several years, the parties and the district court concluded that projects "more than 30% of whose apartments were rented to white families" were segregated, a standard that the court of appeals accepted as "reasonable."—Eds.]

D.   The Legal Significance of the WFP's Effects

The matter of whether the differences in the pace of desegregation under the original TSAP and the TSAP as it would be modified by the WFP are legally significant is a question of law that we review *de novo*. The caselaw give us little guidance as to what constitutes legal significance. The district court focused primarily on the issue of desegregation and the differences between the existing and the proposed procedures in achieving desegregation. In so doing, the court adopted the reasonable premise that past segregation may be perpetuated by actions that slow the pace of desegregation, even though they do not reverse it. . . . Were the court not to consider the effects of proposed conduct on the pace of desegregation, desegregation could be delayed to such an extent that it effectively would never be achieved. And were there no worthy countervailing considerations, the court's correct findings that proposed modifications would substantially delay desegregation would likely end our inquiry.

In the present case, however, NYCHA has proposed the WFP in pursuit of a valid countervailing interest that is, to some extent, in tension with the goal of expeditious desegregation and that is worthy of consideration. . . . NYCHA's goal in proposing a preference for working families is to increase the number of such families, increase income integration in public housing, and thereby promote financial and social stability in such housing. There can be no doubt that this is a legitimate objective. In providing federal funding for low-income housing, Congress has prohibited recipient public housing agencies from "concentrate[ing] very low-income families (or other families with relatively low incomes) in public housing dwelling units in certain public housing projects or certain buildings within projects," 42 U.S.C. § 1437n(a)(3)(A) (Supp. V 1999), and has required such agencies to adopt plans for deconcentration. . . .

As amended in 1998, § 1437n provides that "public housing agency may establish and utilize income-mix criteria for the selection of residents for dwelling units in public housing projects, subject to the requirements of this section," 42 U.S.C. § 1437n(a)(1) (Supp. V 1999).

Consistent with these statutory provisions, HUD regulations explicitly permit a preference for "working families." See 24 C.F.R. § 960.205(a) (2001); 24 C.F.R. § 960.206(b)(2) (2001). In issuing § 960.205(a), HUD commented that "[t]he Department is convinced that housing agencies must have the flexibility to give preference to working families to assure diversity in the residency of projects and to include families who can serve as role models for other families." 59 Fed.Reg. 36,618 (July 18, 1994).

Notwithstanding that conviction, HUD did not endorse NYCHA's proposed WFP. Nor, however, despite having responsibility under § 602 of Title VI of the Civil Rights Act of 1964 to review plans for federally funded public housing to ensure compliance with federal civil rights law, see 42 U.S.C. § 2000d–1 (1994), did HUD criticize the WFP. Rather, when NYCHA sought HUD's approval for the WFP and Project Choice, HUD's response with respect to the WFP...was to remind NYCHA that it must give notice of the proposed WFP and that it must " 'be mindful of the injunctive relief provided for by the *Davis* consent decree and its responsibilities under civil rights statutes....' "

We too are mindful of NYCHA's responsibilities under the Decree and the civil rights laws, and we conclude that the assessment of whether the effects of the WFP are legally significant involves a balancing of the interest in eradicating the past effects of segregation against the interest in achieving financial stability in public housing. The latter is reflected in the public housing statutes discussed above....

At the same time, we think it plain that Congress did not mean to cause public housing agencies to implement plans for financial deconcentration in a way that would violate the civil rights laws. And we take into account the fact that, in the present case, the concentration of most of the white families in a small percentage of the projects was the consequence of NYCHA policies and practices that—as acknowledged by NYCHA in urging judicial approval of the Consent Decree—included racial steering, withholding of information that could have led minority applicants to rent apartments in predominantly or disproportionately white projects, misrepresentations that deterred such integrated rentals, and favorable treatment for white applicants seeking housing in predominantly or disproportionately white projects. As a result, when the Decree was entered, NYCHA had placed more than 71% of its white families in 35 of its 320–odd projects. More than 51% of the white families (7,929 of 15,530) lived in the 20 projects that are at issue on this appeal and that concentration level declined little after the implementation of the TSAP. As of January 1, 1999, there were a total of 12,185 white families residing in NYCHA projects and 5771 of them lived in the 20 projects covered by the injunction. Thus, when the permanent injunction was entered, 20 of NYCHA's 322 housing projects (6.2%) still housed 47.36% of the white families.

Balancing all of the factors, we conclude that in the circumstances of this litigation, the district court determined correctly, with respect to most—although not all—of the 20 projects in question, that the desegregation delays that would be caused by implementation of the WFP are legally significant. In reaching this conclusion, we consider the delays not just in terms of percentages but also as real-time intervals. With that focus, which is somewhat broader than that of the district court, we see significant distinctions between certain categories of projects: There are two projects that were in effect desegregated prior to the entry of the permanent injunction, four projects at which the WFP is predicted to delay the achievement of desegregation by very small intervals of real time, several others at which desegregation will be delayed for a large number of years, still others that would otherwise eventually be desegregated but that will never reach the 30% level under the WFP, and two projects that will h e 30% level with or without the WFP....

In sum, we conclude that at those six projects where the WFP will not delay the reduction of the white tenant population to 30% either at all or by more than 12 months, the effects of the WFP are not legally significant. At the remaining 14 projects, the delays that would be caused by the WFP are legally significant, and implementation of the WFP at those projects was properly enjoined....

CONCLUSION

We have considered all of NYCHA's contentions on this appeal and, except as indicated above, have found them to be without merit. The order of the district court is reversed to the extent that it enjoined NYCHA from implementing the WFP at the Bay View, Holmes Towers, Isaacs, Pelham Parkway, Sheepshead Bay, and Straus projects; in all other respects, the injunction is affirmed.

JOHN M. WALKER, JR., CHIEF JUDGE, dissenting: [omitted. Eds.]

Notes and Questions

1. *Starrett City* and *Davis* considered the problem of "integration maintenance," the process of maintaining integration once it has been achieved. What would you tell a landlord client can be done to prevent loss of an integrated environment through "tipping" toward a predominant racial group? What about a special marketing plan, leaflets, advertisements in targeted newspapers, etc., to attract one racial group without deterring others? See South–Suburban Housing Center v. Greater South Suburban Board of Realtors, 935 F.2d 868 (7th Cir.1991) (affirmative marketing plan to foster integration without denying equal housing opportunities to all persons upheld).

2. The working family preference at the center of the *Davis* litigation poses a real dilemma for landlords, as the court noted. On the one hand, such a preference offers the landlord a means of selecting a more economically-stable tenant population. On the other hand, it raises the possibility, as the *Davis* court also noted, that it will produce a discriminatory result.

Would such a preference be a permissible part of a tenant selection policy for a *new* development? In *Starrett City* the court distinguished the permissible use of "race-conscious tenanting practices" in the "single event" of initially renting new units from the impermissible use of such techniques to maintain an integrated status. Is that distinction persuasive? Should admission standards be "race blind" at all times?

3. The selection and maintenance of sites for governmentally-assisted housing developments also has been a source of conflict in a number of communities. Federal public housing units, constructed under a program that began in the 1930s and expanded in the 20 years following World War II, along with federally-subsidized private apartment developments constructed in the 1960s and 1970s, often have been located in racially-segregated neighborhoods. Protracted litigation has ensued in an attempt to dismantle segregated public housing and to provide opportunities for persons in subsidized housing to live in an integrated neighborhood. Notable success has been achieved in establishing that site selection procedures which cater to segregated housing patterns violate constitutional protections against racial discrimination if intentional and violate the Fair Housing Act if such practices have the effect of racial discrimination. See, e.g., Hills v. Gautreaux, 425 U.S. 284, 96 S.Ct. 1538, 47 L.Ed.2d 792 (1976) (intentional discrimination in the selection of sites for public housing in Chicago); Charleston Housing Authority v. U.S. Dept. of Agriculture, 419 F.3d 729, 740–741 (8th Cir. 2005) (public housing tenants established prima facie case that Housing Authority's decision to demolish public housing complex had a discriminatory effect in violation of the Fair Housing Act); Huntington Branch, N.A.A.C.P. v. Town of Huntington, 844 F.2d 926, (2d Cir.1988), review declined in part, judgment affirmed 488 U.S. 15, 109 S.Ct. 276, 102 L.Ed.2d 180 (1988) (refusal to rezone to permit construction of a subsidized multi-family development in a white neighborhood violated Fair Housing Act); United States v. Yonkers, 837 F.2d 1181 (2d Cir.1987) (city and board of education held liable for intentionally maintaining segregated housing and public schools through "pattern and practice of confining subsidized housing" to southwest portion of city and "selective adherence to a neighborhood-school policy in light of the City's segregative housing practices"); Young v. Pierce, 628 F.Supp. 1037 (E.D.Tex.1985); 685 F.Supp. 984 (E.D.Tex.1988) (maintenance of racially segregated public and subsidized housing in 36 East Texas counties enjoined).

4. However, fashioning an appropriate remedy has proved to be extraordinarily difficult, primarily because of tension between the "flexible but not unlimited power" of federal courts to remedy constitutional violations, United States v. Yonkers, 837 F.2d at 1235, and the separation of powers principle which allocates to the legislative branch the power and responsibility for spending public funds and exercising public regulatory authority. For discussion of the remedy question, see Spallone v. United States, 493 U.S. 265, 110 S.Ct. 625, 107 L.Ed.2d 644, (1990) (enforcement of order to build subsidized housing outside southwest area of Yonkers); United States v. Secretary of Housing and Urban Development, 239 F.3d 211, 220–221 (2nd Cir. 2001) (reviewing use of consent decrees and approving court-ordered race-conscious modifications to Yonkers consent decree as a "temperate and responsible 'means' of remedying the City's past intentional racial discrimi-

nation''); Low–Income Black Children in White Suburban Schools (1986) and Economic and Social Impacts of Housing Integration (1990), Center for Urban Affairs and Policy Research, Northwestern Univ., Evanston, Ill. (evaluating the success of a consent decree following *Gautreaux* that has enabled over 4,000 households to obtain certificates entitling them to federal subsidies for private rental housing in non-racially impacted neighborhoods of Chicago and surrounding suburbs); Roisman, Keeping the Promise: Ending Racial Discrimination and Segregation in Federally Financed Housing, 48 How. L. J. 913 (2005) (advocating aggressive moves, including use of testers and litigation, to address problems of racial discrimination and segregation in federally assisted housing); Schuck, Judging Remedies: Judicial Approaches to Housing Segregation, 37 Harv. C.R.–C.L. L. Rev. 289 (2002) (examining results of the *Mount Laurel* (reproduced in Chap 7 *supra*), *Gautreaux* and *Yonkers* litigation and arguing that quiet negotiation with individual landlords by tenants who have government financial assistance and the support of mobility professionals is more effective than litigation in increasing racial diversity); Comment, *Colorblind Segregation: Equal Protection as a Bar to Neighborhood Integration*, 92 Cal. L. Rev. 841 (2004) (arguing that "colorblind jurisprudence," as represented by the 5th Circuit's rejection of race-conscious court orders to overcome intentional racial discrimination in public housing, Walker v. City of Mesquite, Tex, 169 F.3d 973 (5th Cir. 1999), may have the effect of "preserving existing patters of neighborhood advantage polarized by race," *Id.*, at 846).

The *Gautreaux* story is told in A. Polikoff, Waiting for Gautreaux: A Story of Segregation, Housing & the Black Ghetto (Northwestern Univ. Press 2006). Alexander Polikoff, the author, was the lead attorney for the late Dorothy Gantreaux and the class of public housing residents she represented.

V. THE LANDLORD–TENANT RELATIONSHIP—A REGULATED CONTRACTUAL RELATIONSHIP

As noted earlier, the modern law governing the landlord-tenant relationship is a blend of common law contract law, property law, and statutory regulation. This section explores the interaction of common law property principles, contract law applied to the lease agreement, and statutory regulation designed to adjust the status of the parties.

A. RIGHT/DUTY TO POSSESS

ADRIAN v. RABINOWITZ

Supreme Court of New Jersey, 1936.
116 N.J.L. 586, 186 A. 29.

HEHER, JUSTICE.

On April 30, 1934, defendant, by an indenture, leased to plaintiff certain store premises in the main business district of the city of

Paterson for the term of six months, commencing on June 15th next ensuing, at a stipulated monthly rent payable in advance; and the gravamen of this action is the breach of an obligation thereby imposed upon the lessor, as is said, to deliver to the lessee possession of the demised premises at the beginning of the term so prescribed. The state of demand is in two counts: The first seems to be grounded upon an asserted implied duty "to give and deliver possession" of the demised premises on the first day of the term; and the second, upon what plaintiff conceives to be an express covenant to put the lessee in possession on that day.

The lessee stipulated to devote the premises to the conduct of the shoe business; and he was given an option to renew the lease for an additional term of six months. Rent for the first month of the term was paid upon delivery of the lease, and the payment was acknowledged therein.

At the time of the execution of the contract, the premises were tenanted by another, who failed to respond to the landlord's notice to vacate on June 15. The landlord deemed himself obliged to institute dispossess proceedings, which terminated in a judgment of removal. This judgment was executed on July 7, 1934, and plaintiff took possession two days later.

The district court judge, sitting without a jury, found for the plaintiff on the basic issue, and measured the damages at $500, "the loss sustained by plaintiff in the resale of the seasonable merchandise." He also ruled that plaintiff was not liable for rent for the portion of the term he was deprived of possession, and, making allowance for this, he awarded $25 to defendant on her set-off for rent due for the month beginning July 15, 1934.

It is apparent that the tenant in possession when the lease was executed wrongfully held over after the termination of the tenancy; and the primary question, raised by motions to nonsuit and direct a verdict in defendant's favor, is whether, expressly or by implication, the contract imposed upon the lessor the duty of putting the lessee in actual and exclusive possession of the demised premises at the beginning of the term.

It seems to be the rule in this state that a covenant for quiet enjoyment, as one of the covenants of title, is not to be implied from the mere relation of landlord and tenant, even when that relation springs from a deed. [ ] But here the lessor expressly covenanted that the lessee, "on paying the said monthly rent, and performing the covenants aforesaid, shall and may peaceably and quietly have, hold and enjoy the said demised premises for the term aforesaid." And it has been held elsewhere that a covenant for quiet enjoyment, similarly phrased, imposed upon the lessor the obligation to deliver possession of the premises on the first day of the term. [ ] Yet a covenant for quiet enjoyment is generally interpreted to secure the lessee against the acts or hindrances of the lessor, and persons deriving their right or title through him, or from paramount title, and does not protect the lessee from interference by strangers with his possession. [   ] It remains to consider whether the lessor, in the absence of an express undertaking to that effect, is under a duty to put the lessee in actual as well as legal possession of the demised premises at the commencement of the term. We are of the view that he is. There seems to be no dissent from the doctrine that the lessor impliedly covenants that the lessee shall have the legal right of possession at the beginning of the term. But there is a contrariety of view as to whether this implied obligation extends as well to actual possession, especially where, as here, the prior tenant wrongfully holds over. [   ]

In some of our American jurisdictions, the rule obtains that, while the lessee is entitled to have the legal right of possession, there is no implied covenant to protect the lessee against wrongful acts of strangers. [   ] The English rule is that, where the term is to commence in futuro, there is an implied undertaking by the lessor that the premises shall be open to the lessee's entry, legally and actually, when the time for possession under the lease arrives. This rule has the support of respectable American authority. [   ] And in an early case in this state, where the premises, while tenanted, were let for a term to begin on a fixed day in the future, and the lessor, in an action of covenant brought by the lessee for failure to deliver possession on the first day of the term, or any time thereafter, pleaded inability to deliver possession because of the wrongful holding over by the tenant, this court construed the stipulation for possession at the commencement of the term "as an express covenant to let the premises, and give possession" on the first day of the term, and held that the lessor, having failed in the performance of the duty thus undertaken, was liable to the action. [   ]

The English rule, so-called, is on principle much the better one. It has the virtue, ordinarily, of effectuating the common intention of the parties—to give actual and exclusive possession of the premises to the lessee on the day fixed for the commencement of the term. This is what the lessee generally bargains for; and it is the thing the lessor undertakes to give. Such being the case, there is no warrant for placing upon the lessee, without express stipulation to that effect, the burden of ousting, at his own expense, the tenant wrongfully holding over, or the trespasser in possession of the premises without color of right at the commencement of the term; and thus to impose upon him who is not in possession of the evidence the burden of establishing the respective rights and duties of the lessor and the possessor of the lands inter se, as well as the consequences of the delay incident to the adjudication of the controversy, and the obligation to pay rent during that period. As was said by Baron Vaughan in Coe v. Clay, supra: "He who lets agrees to give possession, and not merely to give a chance of a law suit." This doctrine is grounded in reason and logic. The underlying theory is that the parties contemplated, as an essential term of their undertaking, without which the lease would not have been made, that the lessor should, at the beginning of the term, have the premises open to the entry and exclusive possession of the lessee. This is certainly the normal course of dealing, and, in the absence of stipulation to the contrary, is to be regarded as the parties' understanding of the lessor's covenant to deliver possession of the demised premises at the time prescribed for the commencement of the term.

There is an obvious distinction, which seems to have been overlooked in some of the cases rejecting the English doctrine [   ] between a wrongful possession at the time fixed for the commencement of the term and the acts of trespassers who intrude after the lessee has been given the possession provided by the contract. [   ]

It is worthy of note that here the lessor, apparently conscious of a contractual obligation in the premises, initiated and prosecuted to a conclusion the proceedings requisite for dispossession of the hold-over tenant. She interpreted the contract as imposing the duty.

Therefore, the motions for a nonsuit and a direction of a verdict in defendant's favor on the ground that there was no evidence of a breach of defendant's undertaking to deliver possession of the demised premises at the stipulated time were rightly denied. * * *

Notes and Questions

1. The Restatement has adopted the English rule of actual possession over the American rule of legal possession, in the absence of a valid lease provision to the contrary, Restatement (Second) of Property, § 6.2, Reporter's Note 2 (1976).

2. Does it surprise you that the American rule has been the majority rule in the United States? The leading case for the American rule is Hannan v. Dusch, 154 Va. 356, 153 S.E. 824 (1930). Clearly, delivery of the right to possession will give the new tenant a host of legal and equitable remedies that can be asserted against a person wrongfully in possession. Who might be said to have a greater incentive to use the available remedies, the landlord (English rule) or the successor tenant (American rule)?

3. Examine the sample leases, supra. Which rule do those leases adopt?

4. Does the tenant have a duty to take possession of leased premises? Does it make a difference whether the premises are to be used for commercial or for residential purposes? The following case explores these questions.

SLATER v. PEARLE VISION CENTER, INC.

Superior Court of Pennsylvania, 1988.
376 Pa.Super. 580, 546 A.2d 676.

BECK, JUDGE:

This is a commercial lease dispute between Maurice Slater and Peter Kanton, t/a Bloomsburg Shopping Center, Associates (the "Shopping Center") and Pearle Vision Center, Inc. ("Pearle"). Appellant Shopping Center is the lessor and appellee Pearle is the tenant under a lease of premises located in Shopping Center's strip shopping mall. Although

Pearle has paid the rent under the lease, it has never occupied the leased premises. Apparently because of Shopping Center's concern that the presence of a vacant store would damage the business of the shopping mall as a whole, in August 1986 Shopping Center filed a complaint in equity seeking an injunction requiring Pearle to occupy and use the premises.

Pearle filed preliminary objections in the nature of a demurrer. Pearle basically alleged that Shopping Center had failed to state a claim for breach of either an express or implied obligation to occupy and use the premises and indeed could not since the lease contains none. Pearle also alleged that Shopping Center had an adequate remedy at law and had no standing to claim relief on behalf of other tenants in the mall.

The trial court sustained Pearle's preliminary objection on the ground that the lease does not expressly obligate Pearle to occupy and use the premises and that as a matter of law, no such obligation could be implied. * * *

We reverse and remand because we find that the complaint, which incorporates the lease in full, is sufficient, albeit minimally, to state a claim for relief based on an implied obligation of Pearle to occupy the premises. * * *

Shopping Center argues that the lease contains both an express and an implied requirement that Pearle occupy the premises. The express requirement is alleged to be found in Section 10 of the lease, which states:

> A. Tenant covenants and agrees that it shall use the Premises solely as a "Pearle Vision Center" or such other name as is used by the other Tenant's businesses within the State of Pennsylvania for the retail sale and repair of eyeglasses, lenses and other optical merchandise and optical services, and eye examinations and lens grinding and preparation and for no other purpose * * *.

The quoted language on its face would appear to impose an obligation on Pearle to occupy the premises and to use it as a vision center. However, Pennsylvania case law requires us to interpret such language in commercial leases to mean only that no use other than the use specified in the lease is permitted. The language does not address the question of the lessee's duty to occupy the premises.

In the seminal case of *Dickey v. Philadelphia Minit–Man Corp.*, 377 Pa. 549, 105 A.2d 580 (1954), the lease provided that the leased premises were to be occupied by the lessee in the business of washing and cleaning automobiles and for no other purpose. [ ] The lease also provided for rent based on a percentage of gross sales, with a fixed minimum annual rental. The defendant tenant occupied and used the premises for a number of years in accordance with the lease, but then limited its business to waxing cars and largely eliminated the car washing aspect of its business.

The lessor sought to eject the defendant, contending that it was in breach of the lease. The Supreme Court affirmed the trial court's grant of a demurrer to the landlord's complaint. * * *

The lessor argued that in a lease where the rental is based upon gross sales, there is an implied obligation of the tenant to continue the business on the premises to the fullest extent possible. The Court rejected this argument, finding that the tenant's decision to change its business was made in good faith and in the exercise of legitimate business judgment and was not forbidden by any implied term of the lease.

* * *

Thus, the holding of *Dickey* would appear to be that a use covenant like that presented here cannot be read as an express requirement that the tenant use the premises for the precise permitted business purpose. Moreover, *Dickey* holds that there is no implied obligation that the tenant under a percentage lease refrain from conducting its business in good faith and in accordance with sound business judgment simply because doing so may decrease the rent payable.

More pertinent to the instant case is the fact that *Dickey* specifically does not address a situation where the tenant conducts no business on the leased premises. It also does not address a lease for premises which are part of a strip of stores where the economic health of each store may be dependent on the others.

Certain of these considerations were addressed, however, in *McKnight–Seibert Shopping Center, Inc. v. National Tea Co.*, 263 Pa.Super. 292, 397 A.2d 1214 (1979). In *McKnight*, the lessor of a shopping center brought an action for ejectment of the tenant, a food market operator, and its assignee and for damages for wrongful retention of the premises. The lease contained a use provision similar to that involved herein and a fixed rental provision. When the tenant experienced financial difficulties, it attempted to assign the lease, which was permitted by the lease, and notified the lessor that it would close the store temporarily to allow for transfer to the assignee. The temporary closing lasted longer than contemplated due to labor difficulties of the tenant, who paid the fixed monthly rental throughout. Eventually, possession of the premises was surrendered to the lessor, but the claim for damages for wrongful retention survived.

The *McKnight* court recognized the general rule expressed in *Dickey* regarding the limited meaning of a use clause. However, it also recognized that "[a] clause that a shopping center tenant 'shall use the demised premises * * * for the purpose of * * * displaying and selling [merchandise]' probably does not contemplate a permanently idle store front." *Id.* at 298, 397 A.2d at 1217. On the other hand, the court noted that the absence of provisions like a percentage rental clause, a continuous operations clause or a clause mandating that the store be open during certain hours would indicate that there was no obligation of continuous use.

Since the only issue before the *McKnight* court was whether the temporary cessation of the tenant's business to accommodate a legitimate assignment, lengthened due to circumstances beyond the tenant's control, was wrongful and in breach of the lease, the court did not specifically hold as to whether permanent vacancy of a store might constitute a breach of the lease. The court simply held that under the facts presented, a temporary vacancy did not constitute a breach of the lease. *Id.* at 298, 397 A.2d at 1218.

The trial court in the instant matter found *Dickey* and *McKnight* controlling and read them as mandating the dismissal of plaintiff's complaint. As the foregoing discussion of these cases indicates, we do not consider them completely dispositive in this case. Although we recognize that *Dickey* precludes our finding that the use provision requires that the tenant actually used the premises for the precise permitted use, and thus precludes our accepting Shopping Center's argument that this provision alone is an express imposition of a use requirement on Pearle, that does not conclude our inquiry. Shopping Center also argues that in consideration of all of the circumstances of this case, including consideration of all of the provisions of the lease, we should find that it has stated a claim for relief based on an implied obligation to occupy and use the premises. Neither *Dickey* nor *McKnight* precludes such a claim since neither of those cases address the specific situation presented here, i.e. a completely vacant store front in an interdependent shopping mall where the lease itself contains provisions other than the use clause from which an obligation to use and occupy might be implied.

Since there is no other directly controlling Pennsylvania precedent, we must necessarily rely on more general principles of lease construction in our analysis of this issue. As our Supreme Court has recently reiterated, "a lease is in the nature of a contract and is controlled by principles of contract law." *Cimina v. Bronich,* 517 Pa. 378, 383, 537 A.2d 1355, 1357 (1988). One such principle of contract law applicable to this case is sometimes called the doctrine of necessary implication, which has been described as follows:

> In the absence of an express provision, the law will imply an agreement by the parties to a contract to do and perform those things that according to reason and justice they should do in order to carry out the purpose for which the contract was made and to refrain from doing anything that would destroy or injure the other party's right to receive the fruits of the contract.

Frickert v. Deiter Bros. Fuel Co., Inc., 464 Pa. 596, 347 A.2d 701 (1975) (Pomeroy, J., concurring) (quoting *D.B. Van Campen Corp. v. Building and Const. Trades Council of Phila.,* 202 Pa.Super. 118, 122, 195 A.2d 134, 136 (1963)). Thus, where it is clear that an obligation is within the contemplation of the parties at the time of contracting or is necessary to carry out their intentions, the court will imply it. [   ] This is true even where the contract itself is not ambiguous. [ ] Since the doctrine of necessary implication serves not to instruct the court as to which of two possible interpretations of a contract should be adopted, but rather to allow the court to enforce the clear intentions of the parties and avoid injustice, the court does not need to find an ambiguity before it will employ the doctrine.

Applying this doctrine to the case at bar, we find ample evidence in this lease that these parties may well have contemplated and intended that Pearle was obligated to occupy and use the premises. For example, sub-paragraph 9(E) of the lease provides that the tenant agrees to "open the Premises for business to the public not later than ninety (90) days after Landlord's approval of Tenant's plans and specifications." Although we recognize that Shopping Center's complaint does not specifically allege when or if it ever approved Pearle's "plans and specifications", thus triggering this provision, the complaint does allege that Pearle "failed to open the premises and utilize it in accordance with" this provision. Although admittedly unclear, the lack of specificity in the complaint on this point should not herald its demise. This is precisely the genre of pleading deficiency that may often be cured by amendment and that should not, therefore, constitute grounds for dismissal.

Moreover, we find that there are other provisions in the lease that suggest that actual occupancy and use of the premises by Pearle was in the contemplation of the parties when they executed the lease. Section 10(B) states that the tenant agrees "that it will conduct its business in the entire Premises." Section 30 includes "abandonment" as an Event of Default and contains the following noteworthy exception:

> Notwithstanding anything to the contrary herein, Tenant may allow the demised premises to be vacant for a period not exceeding sixty (60) days, provided Landlord is given not less than ninety (90) days written notice that such vacancy will occur: said vacancy being necessary due to repairs or remodeling of the demised premises or transfer of possession to a franchisee or assignee pursuant to the terms of this lease.

This exception appears in type that differs from the body of the lease, which otherwise appears to be largely based on a standard form, thus creating at least the suggestion that this provision was a separately negotiated term. The necessary implication of this provision, which severely circumscribes Pearle's ability to leave the premises vacant, is that except under the circumstances specifically outlined, Pearle *cannot* allow the premises to be vacant.

Finally, the lease contains references to the obligations of Pearle vis-a-vis the viability of the shopping mall as a whole. The "affirmative obligations" of Pearle set forth in Section 20(A) refer to Pearle's obligation to keep the premises in a manner consistent with the general character of the shopping mall and to refrain from any action or practice that "may damage, mar or deface the Premises or any other part of the Shopping Center."

In the face of such provisions, we cannot agree with the trial court's conclusion, based only on the complaint and the *Dickey* and *McKnight* decisions, that no implied-in-fact obligation to occupy and use the premises can be found as a matter of law. We note that a similar conclusion has been reached in cases involving similar facts decided in other jurisdictions. * * *

These cases further buttress our conclusion that in construing the lease to ascertain what obligations respecting use and occupancy it imposes on Pearle, and thus in ascertaining the intentions of the parties to the lease, we must construe the lease as a whole in light of the circumstances surrounding its execution. Having done so, we are convinced that Shopping Center has pleaded a minimally sufficient claim for relief, perhaps capable of further support through an amended pleading, based on an implied obligation to occupy and use. In the instant case, the lease is not completely silent on the tenant's duty to occupy. If it were, we would conclude that the tenant had no duty to occupy because the landlord failed to include such a condition in the lease. Here, several provisions on the lease can arguably lead to the conclusion that the parties intended that Pearle would occupy the premises. * * *

Notes and Questions

1.   Whether the tenant has a duty to occupy leased premises normally arises only in commercial settings where a portion of the rent, called percentage rent, is derived from the income generated by the tenant's business. In those situations, the landlord has a direct stake in the tenant's occupation of the leased premises.

Consider, however, whether the landlord might also have a direct interest in a tenant's occupation of residential space. Even if the tenant pays rent on time, might the landlord also desire and expect physical occupation to forestall vandalism and trespass by squatters?

2.   Note the use by the court of the contract law doctrine of necessary implication to hold the tenant obligated to occupy the premises in *Slater*. What provisions of the lease, other than the "use" clause, led the court to the "necessary implication" that the parties contemplated regular occupancy? Are any of these provisions the type that might lead to a similar conclusion with respect to a residential lease? Are any of them present in the sample leases supra?

3.   The common meaning of a "use" clause is as a restrictive covenant prohibiting uses other than those specified in the lease, and not as a promise of continuous operation .. See, e.g. Kilgore Enterprises v. Brookshire Grocery Co., 81 Fed. App. 827 (5th Cir. 2003) (grocery store in shopping center); Universal Health Services, Inc. v. Renaissance Women's Group, P.A., 121 S.W.3d 742 (Tex. 2003) (lease of medical office space in building housing a hospital did not include covenant that hospital would remain open).

4.   Suppose the lease provides that the lessee "may use" the leased premises for a named activity, and provides that rent is the higher of a fixed

sum or a stated percentage of gross sales. Is there an express or implied covenant of continuous operation of the named activity? See Nalle v. Taco Bell Corp., 914 S.W.2d 685 (Tex.App.1996) (language of "possibility, permission, liberty, or power," along with a fixed rent provision, indicates that parties did not contemplate a requirement of continuous operation).

5. Randy Cohen, author of "The Ethicist" column in the New York Times Magazine (also in other newspapers) entertained this inquiry from a tenant in San Diego: "During an election . . . a large political sign supporting an anti-gay proposition we strongly opposed . . . appeared on the front lawn of our rented single-family house. Not knowing who posted it, we took it down and destroyed it. Another appeared. We took that one down too and destroyed it. Then we saw our landlord, who asked us what had happened to the signs he was posting. Did he have a right to put them up?"

Mr. Cohen answered as an arbiter of morals: "Your landlord should not post a sign in your yard if doing so would create the false impression that it proclaimed your views. Even appending his name to his placard would be insufficient. Its mere presence on your lawn would suggest to your neighbors that it spoke for you. He must find a means of expression that makes it clear whose opinions are being expressed."

Then Mr. Cohen obtained and relayed the opinion of Adam Liptak, "The Times's national legal reporter": "I think the landlord has no more right to put a sign up on a lawn I am renting than he does to put a poster up in my living room." (The New York Times Magazine, April 14, 2002, p. 29.) Do you think you, as a lawyer, might be able to argue, as a legal proposition, the distinction Mr. Cohen implies and Mr. Liptak seems to leave out of account? Notice, please, that the Cohen side of the distinction tends to imply a view of landlord-tenant relationships that the Liptak side seems not even to consider.

B. TRANSFER OF LEASEHOLD INTERESTS

As discussed in Chapter Two, transferability is an important "stick" in the Anglo–American property bundle. But the transition from one tenant to another can cause problems. Whom, for example, should the landlord look to for rent if a successor tenant (T_2) fails to pay it, the original tenant (T_1) or the successor (T_2)? The next case discusses the problem.

DAVIS v. VIDAL

Supreme Court of Texas, 1912.
105 Tex. 444, 151 S.W. 290.

DIBRELL, J. This is a suit by Antoinette W. Davis brought in the district court of El Paso county against Lewis Vidal, to recover the sum of $1,200 alleged to be due her by Vidal for the use of certain premises situated in the city of El Paso, of which Vidal was in possession as the assignee of the Dallas Brewery. The sole question of law involved in the case is whether a certain instrument of writing executed by the Dallas Brewery to the defendant, Vidal, on October 1, 1907, was an assignment of its lease from the plaintiff, Antoinette W. Davis, of date April 26, 1907, or a subletting of the premises in question. If the instrument referred to was an assignment of the lease, then plaintiff was authorized to recover of the defendant the rent due on her contract of lease with the Dallas Brewery, by virtue of the privity of estate and contract that subsists between them; but if, on the other hand, the instrument was a subletting of the premises to Vidal by the original lessee, the plaintiff could not recover against defendant as a subtenant, since in such case there is neither privity of estate nor of contract between the original lessor and the undertenant. [   ]

The instrument in question was construed by the trial court and the Court of Civil Appeals to be a subletting of the premises by the Dallas Brewery to the defendant, Vidal, and in accordance with that holding judgment was rendered for the defendant. Upon appeal of the case to the Court of Civil Appeals the judgment of the lower court was affirmed.

That the question involved and decided may be fully understood we embody the instrument executed by the Dallas Brewery to Vidal: "Know all men by these presents, that, whereas, on the 26th day of April, 1907, Mrs. Antoinette W. Davis, acting by her agents, A.P. Coles & Brother, did lease to the Dallas Brewery the following parcel of land with the tenements thereon in the city of El Paso, county of El Paso, state of Texas, to wit, being the one-story and adobe composition roof building situated on lot 1 and south 24 feet of lot 2, block 135, Campbell's addition to the city of El Paso, Texas, known as Nos. 415–419 Utah street, same being leased from the 1st day of May, 1907, for three years, to be ended and completed on the 30th of April, 1910 and in consideration of same lease the said Dallas Brewery yielding and paying therefor during said term the sum of $100.00 per month, payable in advance on the first day of each and every month; and, whereas, said lease provides that said premises or any part thereof may be sublet by said Dallas Brewery without the consent of said Mrs. Davis; and, whereas, it is desired to transfer, assign and sublet all of said above premises so leased by the said Mrs. Davis to said Dallas Brewery to Lou Vidal: Now, therefore, in consideration of the premises and the sum of $300.00 to it in hand paid, the receipt whereof is hereby acknowledged, said the Dallas Brewery does hereby sublet, assign and transfer the said above premises and does assign and transfer the above said lease, to the said Lou Vidal, and in consideration therefor the said Vidal does well and truly agree and promise to pay the rents in said lease agreed to be paid, to wit, the sum of one hundred ($100.00) dollars per month, each and every month hereafter ensuing, beginning on the first day of November, 1907, in advance on the first day of each month so hereinafter ensuing. And the said Vidal does agree and bind himself and obligates himself to in all respects indemnify, save and hold harmless said Dallas Brewery by reason of any of the terms or conditions in said lease contained, including the payment of rent therein provided to be paid, and should the said Dallas Brewery elect to pay any rent therein provided, or be called upon to pay any rent therein provided, upon same being done the said Vidal agrees to pay the same with interest at the rate of ten per cent. per annum; or if the said Vidal neglects or fails to pay said rent promptly, as in said lease provided to be paid, then and in such event the Dallas Brewery can and may at its option declare this transfer null and void, and thereupon oust the said Vidal, and assume possession thereof, and this without notice of any character or kind to the said Vidal; and the failure to pay any rent as in said lease provided to be paid, at the election of the said Dallas Brewery, can and may authorize it without notice to re-enter and repossess said premises."

In construing the effect of the foregoing instrument it is not conclusive as to its form, since it may be in form an assignment and yet be in effect a sublease. The question is one of law to be determined from the estate granted by the instrument. As a general proposition, if the instrument executed by the lessee conveys the entire term and thereby parts with all of the reversionary estate in the property, the instrument will be construed to be an assignment; but, if there remains a reversionary interest in the estate conveyed, the instrument is a sublease. The relation of landlord and tenant is created alone by the existence of a reversionary interest in the landlord. Out of this fact arises the distinction made between assignments and subtenancies. To state the test slightly different from that already stated, if the instrument is of such character by its terms and conditions that a reversionary interest by construction remains in the grantor of the property, he becomes the landlord and the grantee the tenant. The tenant who parts with the entire term embraced in his lease becomes an assignor of the lease, and the instrument is an assignment; but where the tenant by the terms, conditions, or limitations in the instrument does not part with the entire term granted him by his landlord, so that there remains in him a reversionary interest, the transaction is a subletting and not an assignment. [ ] It will be observed that, in stating the general rule as to what constitutes an assignment of a lease as distinguished from a sublease, the requirement is that the instrument must convey the whole *term*, leaving no interest or reversionary interest in the grantor.

By the word "term," as used in the statement of this principle of law, is meant something more than the mere *time* for which the lease is given, and the instrument must convey not only the entire time for which the lease runs, but the entire estate or interest conveyed by the lease. Mr. Blackstone in his Commentaries (book 2, p. 144), in commenting on the significance of the word "term," when used in leases, says: "Thus the word, *term*, does not merely signify the time specified in the lease, but the estate also and interest that passes by the lease; and therefore the *term* may expire, during the continuance of the *time*, as by surrender, forfeiture and the like." The meaning of the word "term," as defined by Blackstone above, was adopted by the Supreme Court of Massachusetts in the case of Dunlap v. Bullard, 131 Mass. 161, and by a number of text-writers on the subject of assignments and subleases.

Mr. Blackstone, in his Commentaries (book 2, p. 327), defines an assignment to be, and draws the distinction between an assignment and a lease of property, as follows: "An *assignment* is properly a transfer, or making over to another, of the right one has in *any* estate; but it is usually applied to an estate for life or years. And it differs from lease only in this: That by a lease one grants an interest less than his own, reserving to himself a reversion; in an assignment he parts with the whole property, and the assignee stands to all intents and purposes in the place of the assignor." If we may accept this definition from so eminent authority upon the common law, which definition and distinction so concisely stated and drawn seems to have met the approval of this court in other cases, and apply it to the facts of the case at bar, the conclusion must be reached that the instrument executed by the Dallas Brewery to Vidal was a sublease and not an assignment. The instrument speaks for itself. By its terms the whole estate granted to the Dallas Brewery by its lease from Mrs. Davis is not conveyed, for the reason there is reserved to the Dallas Brewery a contingent reversionary interest in the estate, to be resumed summarily upon the failure of Vidal to pay rent. More than this, and of equal significance, by the terms of the instrument the Dallas Brewery reserved the right to pay the rent to the original lessor, and thereby the right was reserved to forestall Mrs. Davis, upon the failure of Vidal to pay the rent, from exercising the right to re-enter and possess the premises. That right was reserved to the Dallas Brewery and gave it the power to control the estate in the premises upon failure by Vidal to pay it the rent.

If the instrument was an assignment of the lease, the Dallas Brewery must of necessity have parted with all its estate and interest in said premises, and could therefore exercise no right in or control over the premises. If the instrument was an assignment of the lease, the legal effect was to substitute Vidal in lieu of the Dallas Brewery. But this was not the case. By the terms of the instrument the Dallas Brewery retained the control of the possession of the leased premises, thereby denying the legal effect of an assignment, which would have given Mrs. Davis the right of re-entry and possession of the property upon Vidal's failure to pay the rent.

We are aware that there is great conflict of authority upon this subject, and that it would be futile to attempt to reconcile such conflict. Many of the authors of the textbooks on the subject of the assignment of leases and subletting under leases, and the decisions of a great many of the states in this Union, hold that the fact that the right of re-entry is reserved in the assignment to the assignor upon failure of the assignee to pay rent does not change the instrument of assignment from such to a sublease. The holding of such authors and decisions is based upon the theory that the right of re-entry is not an estate or interest in land, nor the reservation of a reversion. They hold that the reservation of the right of re-entry upon failure to pay rent is neither an estate nor interest in land, but a mere chose in action, and when exercised the grantor comes into possession of the premises through the breach of the condition and not by reverter.

Those authorities which hold the contrary doctrine base their ruling upon the idea that the reservation in the instrument of the right of re-entry is a contingent reversionary interest in the premises resulting from the conveyance of an estate upon a condition subsequent where there has been an infraction of such condition. * * *

We are not able to discern why there may not be a contingent reversionary estate or interest in land, as well as any other contingent estate or interest. It certainly cannot be contended upon sound principle that, because the right of re-entry and resumption of possession of land is contingent, it is thereby any the less an estate or interest in land. The very definition of a contingent estate as distinguished from a *vested* estate is that "*the right to its* enjoyment is to accrue on an event which is dubious and uncertain." 1 Washburn on Real Property, 38.

We think it deducible from respectable authority that where the tenant reserves in the instrument giving possession to his transferee the right of re-entry to the premises demised, upon failure to pay rent, he necessarily retains a part of or an interest in the demised estate which may come back to him upon the happening of a contingency.

The instrument under consideration does not convey the entire estate received by the Dallas Brewery by its lease from Mrs. Davis, but retains by the right of possible re-entry a contingent reversionary interest in the premises. That the interest retained is a contingent reversionary interest does not, it seems to us, change the rule by which an assignment may be distinguished from a sublease. If by any limitation or condition in the conveyance the entire term, which embraces the estate conveyed in the contract of lease as well as the length of time for which the tenancy is created, may by construction be said not to have passed from the original tenant, but that a contingent reversionary estate is retained in the premises the subject of the reversion, the instrument must be said to constitute a subletting and not an assignment.

The following test may be applied to determine whether the instrument in question is an assignment of the original lease, or a subletting of the premises: If it is an assignment, its legal effect must be a transfer of the right of possession of the property conveyed to Vidal and the creation of a privity of estate and contract between Mrs. Davis, the original lessor, and Vidal, to whom the possession was granted by the Dallas Brewery. This would be essential to constitute the instrument an assignment, and if it was an assignment Vidal obligated himself to pay the rent to Mrs. Davis, and the Dallas Brewery had no further connection with or interest in the transaction. But such a result can by no fair or reasonable construction of the language and provisions of the instrument be deduced therefrom. On the contrary, the Dallas Brewery reserved the privilege of paying the rent to its lessor, and upon nonpayment of rent by Vidal it reserved the right to declare the instrument forfeited and to repossess the premises without notice to or the consent of Vidal. There can be but one theory upon which the Dallas Brewery considered itself interested in seeing that the rent was promptly paid by Vidal, and that is that it desired to control the property in question, and therefore intended, and by the language and reservation in the instrument made, it a sublease.

We do not think the proposition tenable that by the express terms of the agreement between the Dallas Brewery and Vidal, or by implication, Vidal obligated himself to pay the rent to Mrs. Davis. The provision of the contract relied upon to establish the fact that Vidal obligated himself to pay the rent to the lessor in the original lease is the following, "and in consideration therefor the said Vidal does well and truly agree and promise to pay the rents in said lease agreed to be paid, to wit, the sum of one hundred dollars per month." Under the uniform rule of construction the latter part of the above sentence explains and qualifies the preceding part. The obligation of Vidal was to pay the rents in said lease agreed to be paid, that is, the sum of $100 per month, payable on the 1st day of each month in advance. There is nothing in the agreement from which it may be inferred that Vidal obligated himself to pay the rents directly to Mrs. Davis.

Having reached the conclusion that the instrument executed by the Dallas Brewery to Vidal conveying the premises in question was a sublease and not an assignment, * * * we conclude there exists no privity of estate or contract between the plaintiff, Mrs. Davis, and the defendant, Lewis Vidal, and that Mrs. Davis has no cause of action authorizing her to recover judgment against Vidal. * * *

The court is of opinion the judgments of the Court of Civil Appeals and of the trial court should be affirmed, and it is, accordingly, so ordered.

Notes and Questions

1.   At common law, for a covenant respecting land, such as a promise to pay rent, to "run with the land" and thus be binding on successors in interest to that land, three requirements must generally be met: 1) the parties to the covenant must intend it to run; 2) the covenant must "touch and concern" the land; and 3) there must be privity of estate. Some formality in the making of the covenant may also be required, such as that the covenant be in writing.

In the landlord-tenant context, as *Davis v. Vidal* illustrates, there is privity of estate between landlord and assignee, but not between landlord and subtenant. The intention of the parties is supplied in most leases by a catch-all "successors and assigns" clause. The absence of a clause binding successors and assigns, however, will not necessarily mean that a covenant does not run with the land. Conversely, the presence of such a clause will not necessarily mean that a covenant does run with the land. This topic is discussed in greater detail in Chapter Six, The Law of Neighbors.

2.   Why should it make a difference whether a transfer of a leasehold interest is an assignment or a sublease? While the original tenant can

transfer her property interest, doesn't she remain liable to the landlord under her contract? Are landlords more likely to seek to have a transfer characterized as an assignment and successor tenants to have it deemed a sublease? What about the original tenant? Will she likely have a preference? Might the presence of income-producing property that is appreciating or depreciating in value affect the parties' viewpoints? Cf. Bob Ferstl Chrysler Plymouth, Inc. v. Budget Rent–A–Car Systems, Inc., 206 F.Supp.2d 853 (S.D. Tex. 2002) (sublessee did not acquire option to purchase leased property held by sublessor, citing *Davis*).

3. The intention of the parties, rather than the presence or absence of a reversionary interest, often is said to be the determining factor in deciding whether a transfer is an assignment or a sublease. See e.g., Ernst v. Conditt, 54 Tenn.App. 328, 390 S.W.2d 703 (1964). How does one determine the intention, if not by examining whether a reversionary interest is present?

4. Assume a five-year commercial lease with four consecutive options to renew for additional five-year periods. The lease contains covenants on the part of the tenant to pay rent, to return the property at the end of the lease term, and to repaint the interior of the leased premises annually.

(a) Tenant transfers her interest in the property "for the balance of my term." Who is responsible for the rent? Is the transferee responsible for repainting the interior? Can the transferee exercise an option to renew?

(b) Suppose instead that tenant transfers her interest for two years. Who is responsible for the rent? Is the transferee responsible for repainting the interior? Can the transferee exercise the option to renew? If the tenant defaults on the lease covenants, can the landlord evict the transferee?

(c) If you represented the landlord, the tenant, or the transferee, what interests would you expect your client to have and what clauses would you seek to add to the lease in anticipation of the situations described in (a) and (b) above. Consider the following observations by an experienced real estate lawyer.

> Preparing and defending a one-sided unfair lease form is a wasteful and foolish activity. It doesn't take long for a property owner or a tenant to fill in the blanks of a printed form or word processing document. On the other hand, the negotiators who have to read the document must spend many boring hours just to discover what everybody knows to begin with—the lease is one-sided, every provision is one-sided, and every sentence is one-sided. * * *

> The fact that a form is printed should be a signal that it is not fair. It is unrealistic to expect a real estate board or a corporation that leases many offices, stores or warehouses to go to the trouble of printing a lease form that is fair to landlords and tenants alike. Landlords and tenants who print their forms often do so to intimidate the other party with the notion that, if it's printed, it can't be changed. * * *

> * * * I've heard of more than one tenant who violently threw a lease proposed by his landlord in the garbage after checking out a few clauses. Most likely, a few chain store printed forms have found their way to landlords' garbage cans as well. The main advantage of drafting a fair lease is that you might get it signed.

Halper, Can You Find a Fair Lease? 14 Real Est.L.J. 99, 100–101, 121 (1985).

JULIAN v. CHRISTOPHER

Court of Appeals of Maryland, 1990.
320 Md. 1, 575 A.2d 735.

CHASANOW, JUDGE.

In 1961, this Court decided the case of *Jacobs v. Klawans*, 225 Md. 147, 169 A.2d 677 (1961) and held that when a lease contained a "silent consent" clause prohibiting a tenant from subletting or assigning without the consent of the landlord, landlords had a right to withhold their consent to a subletting or assignment even though the withholding of consent was arbitrary and unreasonable. * * *

In the instant case, the tenants, Douglas Julian and William J. Gilleland, III, purchased a tavern and restaurant business, as well as rented the business premises from landlord, Guy D. Christopher. The lease stated in clause ten that the premises, consisting of both the tavern and an upstairs apartment, could not be assigned or sublet "without the prior written consent of the landlord." Sometime after taking occupancy, the tenants requested the landlord's written permission to sublease the upstairs apartment. The landlord made no inquiry about the proposed sublessee, but wrote to the tenants that he would not agree to a sublease unless the tenants paid additional rent in the amount of $150.00 per month. When the tenants permitted the sublessee to move in, the landlord filed an action in the District Court of Maryland in Baltimore City requesting repossession of the building because the tenants had sublet the premises without his permission.

At the district court trial, the tenants testified that they specifically inquired about clause ten, and were told by the landlord that the clause was merely included to prevent them from subletting or assigning to "someone who would tear the apartment up." The district court judge refused to consider this testimony. He stated in his oral opinion that he would "remain within the four corners of the lease, and construe the document strictly," at least as it pertained to clause ten. Both the District Court and, on appeal, the Circuit Court for Baltimore City found in favor of the landlord. The circuit judge noted: "If you don't have the words that consent will not be unreasonably withheld, then the landlord can withhold his consent for a good reason, a bad reason, or no reason at all in the context of a commercial lease, which is what we're dealing with."

* * *

Traditional property rules favor the free and unrestricted right to alienate interests in property. Therefore, absent some specific restriction in the lease, a lessee has the right to freely alienate the leasehold interest by assignment or sublease without obtaining the permission of the lessor.[2] [   ]

Contractual restrictions on the alienability of leasehold interests are permitted. [   ] Consequently, landlords often insert clauses that restrict the lessee's common law right to freely assign or sublease.

Probably the most often used clause is a "silent consent" clause similar to the provision in the instant case, which provides that the premises may not be assigned or sublet without the written consent of the lessor.

In a "silent consent" clause requiring a landlord's consent to assign or sublease, there is no standard governing the landlord's decision. Courts must insert a standard. The choice is usually between 1) requiring the landlord to act reasonably when withholding consent, or 2) permitting the landlord to act arbitrarily and capriciously in withholding consent.

Public policy requires that when a lease gives the landlord the right to withhold consent to a sublease or assignment, the landlord should act reasonably, and the courts ought not to imply a right to act arbitrarily or capriciously. If a landlord is allowed to arbitrarily refuse consent to an assignment or sublease, for what in effect is no reason at all, that would virtually nullify any right to assign or sublease.

Because most people act reasonably most of the time, tenants might expect that a landlord's consent to a sublease or assignment would be governed by standards of reasonableness. Most tenants probably would not understand that a clause stating "this lease may not be assigned or sublet without the landlord's written consent" means the same as a clause stating "the tenant shall have no right to assign or sublease." Some landlords may have chosen the former wording rather than the latter because it vaguely implies, but does not grant to the tenant, the right to assign or sublet.

There are two public policy reasons why the law enunciated in *Klawans* should now be changed. The first is the public policy against restraints on alienation. The second is the public policy which implies a covenant of good faith and fair dealing in every contract.

Because there is a public policy against restraints on alienation, if a lease is silent on the subject, a tenant may freely sublease or assign. Restraints on alienation are permitted in leases, but are looked upon with disfavor and are strictly construed. [   ]

If a clause in a lease is susceptible of two interpretations, public policy favors the interpretation least restrictive of the right to alienate freely. Interpreting a "silent consent" clause so that it only prohibits subleases or assignments when a landlord's refusal to consent is reasonable, would be the interpretation imposing the least restraint on alien-

---

2. The common law right may have some limitations. For example, a lessee may not sublet or assign the premises to be used in a manner which is injurious to the property or inconsistent with the terms of the original lease.

ation and most in accord with public policy. * * * [T]his Court has recognized that in a lease, as well as in other contracts, "there exists an implied covenant that each of the parties thereto will act in good faith and deal fairly with the others." *Food Fair v. Blumberg,* 234 Md. 521, 534, 200 A.2d 166, 174 (1964). When the lease gives the landlord the right to exercise discretion, the discretion should be exercised in good faith, and in accordance with fair dealing; if the lease does not spell out any standard for withholding consent, then the implied covenant of good faith and fair dealing should imply a reasonableness standard.

We are cognizant of the value of the doctrine of *stare decisis,* and of the need for stability and certainty in the law. However, as we noted in *Harrison v. Mont. Co. Bd. of Educ.,* 295 Md. 442, 459, 456 A.2d 894, 903 (1983), a common law rule may be modified "where we find, in light of changed conditions or increased knowledge, that the rule has become unsound in the circumstances of modern life, a vestige of the past, no longer suitable to our people." The *Klawans* common law interpretation of the "silent consent" clause represents such a "vestige of the past," and should now be changed.

REASONABLENESS OF WITHHELD CONSENT

In the instant case, we need not expound at length on what constitutes a reasonable refusal to consent to an assignment or sublease. We should, however, point out that obvious examples of reasonable objections could include the financial irresponsibility or instability of the transferee, or the unsuitability or incompatibility of the intended use of the property by the transferee. We also need not expound at length on what would constitute an unreasonable refusal to consent to an assignment or sublease. If the reasons for withholding consent have nothing to do with the intended transferee or the transferee's use of the property, the motivation may be suspect. Where, as alleged in this case, the refusal to consent was solely for the purpose of securing a rent increase, such refusal would be unreasonable unless the new subtenant would necessitate additional expenditures by, or increased economic risk to, the landlord.

PROSPECTIVE EFFECT

The tenants ask us to retroactively overrule *Klawans,* and hold that in all leases with "silent consent" clauses, no matter when executed, consent to assign or sublease may not be unreasonably withheld by a landlord. We decline to do so. In the absence of evidence to the contrary, we should assume that parties executing leases when *Klawans* governed the interpretation of "silent consent" clauses were aware of *Klawans* and the implications drawn from the words they used. We should not, and do not, rewrite these contracts. * * *

For leases entered into after the mandate in this case, if the lease contains a "silent consent" clause providing that the tenant must obtain the landlord's consent in order to assign or sublease, such consent may not be unreasonably withheld. If the parties intend to preclude any transfer by assignment or sublease, they may do so by a freely negotiated provision in the lease. If the parties intend to limit the right to assign or sublease by giving the landlord the arbitrary right to refuse to consent, they may do so by a freely negotiated provision of the lease clearly spelling out this intent. For example, the clause might provide, "consent may be withheld in the sole and absolute subjective discretion of the lessor."

[Reversed and remanded—Eds.]

Notes and Questions

1. If a tenant sublets contrary to the transfer provision in her lease, yet continues to pay the monthly rent in a timely fashion, has the landlord been harmed? What remedies are available to the landlord? If the landlord elects to terminate the lease under a provision authorizing that remedy, would the sublessee have any rights? Against whom? See Lampasas v. Spring Center, Inc., 988 S.W.2d 428 (Tex. App. 1999) (sublessee in violation of lease requirement for landlord's written consent is mere trespasser).

2. Four graduate students leased a large house for one year, beginning August 1 and ending July 31 the next year. The lease, signed by all four students, contained no provisions limiting assignment or subletting. By December, two of the tenants had moved out because of a dispute among the tenants over parties in the house. During the semester break, one of the remaining tenants who lived in town assigned the lease to four law students, assuring the law students that the fourth tenant, who was in Florida for the holidays, was anxious to be relieved of the large rent payment. The third tenant moved out but left the fourth tenant's clothing and furniture. When school resumed for the second semester, the fourth tenant returned and was surprised to find the law students occupying the house. Who is entitled to possession of the house? Who is obligated to pay rent? See Dozier v. Wallace, 169 Ga.App. 126, 311 S.E.2d 839 (1983) (tenant in common has no power to lease the common property without the consent of the remaining co-tenants).

3. Consider the tenant's remedies if the landlord unreasonably withholds consent. If the landlord specifically covenants and agrees not to unreasonably withhold or delay consent, failure to act reasonably subjects the landlord to liability for the tenant's damages. However, if the landlord's agreement is merely a qualification or condition to tenant's covenant not to assign or sublet, then tenant's only remedy is declaratory judgment. ("T's right to sublet or assign shall be subject to its having first obtained the prior written consent of L, which may be withheld by L in the good faith exercise of its reasonable business judgement.") Suppose, after extensive negotiation, the landlord finally concedes the point of not unreasonably withholding consent, but asks in return for tenant's agreement not to sue for damages for breach. If tenant agrees, it has won the battle but may have lost the war. A declaratory judgment that the landlord unreasonably withheld consent may provide little solace to the tenant seeking to assign the leased premises because, during the litigation delay, the typical office or retail space assignee is likely to rent elsewhere.

4. *Julian* illustrates the Restatement (Second) of Property view (§ 15.2(2) (1976)) that landlords may not arbitrarily withhold consent to transfer. As noted, the common law position was the opposite, and some courts adhere to that approach. *See, e.g.*, Dobyns v. Department of Parks, Recreation and Tourism, 325 S.C. 97, 480 S.E.2d 81, 84 (1997) (declining to impose a reasonableness requirement on a landlord's refusal to approve transfer of a long term lease in a state park. "The judicial function of a court of law is to enforce contracts as made by the parties and not to re-write or distort, under the guise of judicial construction, the terms of an unambiguous contract").

5. Review the sample residential leases discussed, supra. What do they say about assignments and subleases?

6. Restatement (Second) of Property, § 15.2, Comment i (1976) adopts the "freely negotiated" standard for determining the validity of clauses giving landlords the absolute right to withhold consent. What is meant by a "freely negotiated" transfer provision? As tenant, what would you seek? As landlord? Should it make a difference whether the proposed use is commercial or residential? To what extent should lawyers attempt to persuade their clients to negotiate "fair" leases? Consider the following excerpt.

BERGER, HARD LEASES MAKE BAD LAW
74 Colum.L.Rev. 791, 792, 813–815 (1974).

[Professor Berger's article is based on a study of 103 reported landlord-tenant cases in the New York courts from 1970 through 1972, about evenly divided between commercial and residential tenancies. Virtually all the cases involved standard form printed leased heavily stacked in favor of the landlord. Thus, landlords should have won most of the cases. However, Professor, Berger expected to find, and did find, "judges reluctant to give landlords what they asked for, and in most cases, literally deserved." In what he called the "rhetoric of decision," Professor Berger identified twelve "principled" reasons for refusing the landlord's proposed relief: plain meaning, waiver, estoppel, ambiguity, failure of proof, unavailability of summary proceeding, non-substantial violations, substantial compliance, rule of reason, prevent unjust results, unconscionable conduct, and unconscionable lease terms. He then posed a question concerning the implications of the "winds of change (that) are stirring landlord-tenant law."]

[A] larger issue remains that the present system fails to moot. It is the issue of "contract integrity"—the integrity of the paper that seals the bargain. Here I use "integrity" in a dual sense. I refer both to the honesty or fairness of the contract and to its even-handed completeness.

In the context of the lease, let me illustrate what I mean. A and B make a lease. What they negotiate, however, is far less detailed than the instrument they sign. The negotiated oral transaction seldom goes beyond the monthly rental and the duration of the lease. These terms often are flexible, and the final bargain responds to the urgency with which each party needs to obtain or get rid of the space. Thus, even during an apartment shortage, some owners may readily make a rent concession if their buildings are renting poorly. Conversely, some tenants will pay dearly for apartments they badly want even during a market glut. Thus, as to the *negotiated* bargain, chronic disparity between landlord and tenant would be hard to prove.

If the negotiated bargain were the entire transaction, the written lease would be one paragraph long. But, of course, the landlord-tenant relation is far more complex, and the non-bargained part of the transaction occupies most of the written form. This is where the principle of contract integrity enters. It would require:

1. That the lease fairly describe all the unspoken expectations of the parties. For example, if the tenant expects to receive and the landlord expects to furnish heat, hot and cold running water, trash removal, a minimum level of security, or janitorial service, these rights and duties should be set forth.

2. That the lease fairly describe all basic statutory and common-law rights of the parties. For example, where statute requires landlord to hold the tenant's security deposit in an interest-bearing account, interest payable annually to the tenant, the lease should say so.

3. That the lease describe the tenant's remedies with the same completeness and detail that it describes the landlord's remedies. Thus, tenants would read in their leases of rent-withholding, repair-and-offset, or rescission, where these remedies were available.

4. That the lease distinguish *fairly* between major ("substantial") and minor ("insubstantial") duties, and indicate what penalties follow the breach of each.

5. That the lease not contain any surprises. A tenant who expected to get delivery of the apartment on April 1 should not discover, if the previous tenant unlawfully holds over, that the landlord may recover rent even though the apartment is not ready. If the landlord wants to bargain for such a surprising right, he must *ask* for it during the oral negotiations.

6. That the lease be written for a layman's understanding.

Contract integrity and contract unconscionability occupy the opposing ends of a spectrum. Between them lie many shades of tolerated agreement. Since unconscionability is a doctrine of last resort, virtually any contract that does not shock the conscience is presumptively valid. But I suggest that the legal system should espouse a higher norm, one that contract integrity can help fulfill. Each party who signs an agreement should sense its truth and essential fairness and should believe that the paper fully states his rights and remedies, that it captures both parties' understanding, that it conceals no hookers, and that it is understandable. Uninformed or misinformed parties to a contract are easily terrorized or disarmed into foregoing their rights and remedies, and contract integrity would help prevent that. I also believe, and have tried to show, that hard leases often make bad law, and while no reform can root out the defects of intellect or of fairness among our judges, contract integrity would allow courts to apply their powers of reason and their spirit of impartiality to a dispute far more readily than does today's standard form lease.

C. CONDITION OF THE PREMISES

The intersection of property law, contract law, and statutory regulation is particularly evident in the evolution of the law governing responsibility for the physical condition, including maintenance and repair of improvements, of leased property.

Since landlord-tenant law developed out of property law concepts, it should not surprise you that the early cases dealing with the condition of the premises placed responsibility on the tenant because she received the possessory rights to the property (land) being transferred. Once the tenant accepted possession, responsibility for maintaining and protecting the land passed to the tenant. Absent an express promise on the part of the landlord to take care of the property, the law looked to the tenant to take care of the leased property. In fact the landlord was said to be incapable of responding because the landlord had given up the right to possess the land during the period of the tenancy.

1. *Implied Covenant of Quiet Enjoyment–Constructive Eviction*

DYETT v. PENDLETON

Court of Errors of New York, 1826.
8 Cow. 727.

[John B. Pendleton sued Joshua Dyett for nonpayment of rent under a lease with a term of "two, three, five or eight years, but not for a less term than two years" for several rooms in a house in New York City. Dyett defended by alleging that Pendleton had "introduced divers lewd women or prostitutes" into portions of the house remaining in Pendleton's control, causing "such noise and riotous proceedings" at night that Dyett was forced to leave the premises. The trial court refused to admit evidence concerning Dyett's allegations. From a verdict in favor of Pendleton, Dyett appealed—Eds.]

SPENCER, SENATOR. It seems to be conceded, that the only plea which could be interposed by the defendant below, to let in the defense which he offered, if any would answer that purpose, was, that the plaintiff had entered in and upon the demised premises, and ejected and put out the defendant. Such a plea was filed, and it is contended on the one side that it must be literally proved, and an actual entry and expulsion established; while on the other side it is insisted that a constructive entry and expulsion is sufficient, and that the facts which tended to prove it, should have been left to the jury. * * *

This distinction, which is as perfectly well settled as any to be found in our books, establishes the great principle that a tenant shall not be required to pay rent, even for the part of the premises which he retains, if he has been evicted from the other part by the landlord. As to the part retained, this is deemed such a disturbance, such an injury to its beneficial enjoyment, such a diminution of the consideration upon which the contract is founded, that the law refuses its aid to coerce the payment of any rent. Here, then, is a case, where actual entry and physical eviction are not necessary to exonerate the tenant from the payment of rent; and if the principle be correct as applied to a part of the premises, why should not the same principle equally apply to the whole property demised, where there has been an obstruction to its beneficial enjoyment, and a diminution of the consideration of the contract, by the acts of the landlord, although those acts do not amount to a physical eviction? If physical eviction be not necessary in the one case, to discharge the rent of the part retained, why should it be essential in the other, to discharge the rent of the whole? If I have not deceived myself, the distinction referred to settles and recognizes the principles for which the plaintiff in error contends, that there may be a constructive eviction produced by the acts of the landlord. * * *

[Reversed—Eds.]

Notes and Questions

1. The decision in *Dyett* was based on the principle that the landlord impliedly covenants not to disturb the tenant's enjoyment of his possessory interest. While the tenant's promise to pay rent was said to be "independent" of any promises the landlord may have made about the condition of the premises being leased, the importance of the tenant's possessory interest was such that interference by the landlord with its "quiet enjoyment" constituted a "total breach of consideration," depriving the landlord of any remedy for the tenant's failure to pay rent. Thus, the duty to pay rent became "dependent" upon the landlord's observing the implied covenant of quiet enjoyment.

2. The first case to require abandonment of the premises by a tenant alleging constructive eviction was Edgerton v. Page, 20 N.Y. 281 (1859).

3. While early cases applying the principle of constructive eviction were not sympathetic to tenants who complained of vermin, see, e.g., Jacobs v. Morand, 59 Misc. 200, 110 N.Y.S. 208 (1908), it is now well settled that vermin infestation which is outside the control of tenants can constitute constructive eviction. See, e.g. Mayers v. Kugelman, 81 Misc.2d 998, 367 N.Y.S.2d 144 (1975); Ianacci v. Pendis, 64 Misc.2d 178, 315 N.Y.S.2d 399 (1970); Streep v. Simpson, 80 Misc. 666, 141 N.Y.S. 863 (1913).

BLACKETT v. OLANOFF

Supreme Judicial Court of Massachusetts, 1977.
371 Mass. 714, 358 N.E.2d 817.

WILKINS, JUSTICE.

The defendant in each of these consolidated actions for rent successfully raised constructive eviction as a defense against the landlords' claim. The judge found that the tenants were "very substantially deprived" of quiet enjoyment of their leased premises "*for a substantial time*" (emphasis original). He ruled that the tenants' implied warranty of quiet enjoyment was violated by late evening and early morning music and disturbances coming from nearby premises which the landlords leased to others for use as a bar or cocktail lounge (lounge). The judge further found that, although the landlords did not intend to create the conditions, the landlords "had it within their control to correct the conditions which * * * amounted to a constructive eviction of each [tenant]." He also found that the landlords promised each tenant to correct the situation, that the landlords made some attempt to remedy the problem, but they were unsuccessful, and that each tenant vacated his apartment within a reasonable time. Judgment was entered for each tenant; the landlords appealed; and we transferred the appeals here. We affirm the judgments.

The landlords argue that they did not violate the tenants' implied covenant of quiet enjoyment because they are not chargeable with the noise from the lounge. The landlords do not challenge the judge's conclusion that the noise emanating from the lounge was sufficient to constitute a constructive eviction, if that noise could be attributed to the landlords.[3] Nor do the landlords seriously argue that a constructive eviction could not be found as matter of law because the lounge was not on the same premises as the tenants' apartments. [ ] The landlords' principal contention, based on the denial of certain requests for rulings, is that they are not responsible for the conduct of the proprietors, employees, and patrons of the lounge.

Our opinions concerning a constructive eviction by an alleged breach of an implied covenant of quiet enjoyment sometimes have stated that the landlord must perform some act with the intent of depriving the tenant of the enjoyment and occupation of the whole or part of the leased premises. [ ] There are occasions, however, where a landlord has not intended to violate a tenant's rights, but there was nevertheless a breach of the landlord's covenant of quiet enjoyment which flowed as the natural and probable consequence of what the landlord did, what he failed to do, or what he permitted to be done. [ ] Although some of our opinions have spoken of particular action or inaction by a landlord as showing a presumed intention to evict, the landlord's conduct, and not his intentions, is controlling. [ ]

The judge was warranted in ruling that the landlords had it within their control to correct the condition which caused the tenants to vacate their apartments. The landlords introduced a commercial activity into an

---

3. There was evidence that the lounge had amplified music (electric musical instruments and singing, at various times) which started at 9:30 P.M. and continued until 1:30 A.M. or 2 A.M., generally on Tuesdays through Sundays. The music could be heard through the granite walls of the residential tenants' building, and was described variously as unbelievably loud, incessant, raucous, and penetrating. The noise interfered with conversation and prevented sleep. There was also evidence of noise from patrons' yelling and fighting.

area where they leased premises for residential purposes. The lease for the lounge expressly provided that entertainment in the lounge had to be conducted so that it could not be heard outside the building and would not disturb the residents of the leased apartments. The potential threat to the occupants of the nearby apartments was apparent in the circumstances. The landlords complained to the tenants of the lounge after receiving numerous objections from residential tenants. From time to time, the pervading noise would abate in response to the landlord's complaints. We conclude that, as matter of law, the landlords had a right to control the objectionable noise coming from the lounge and that the judge was warranted in finding as a fact that the landlords could control the objectionable conditions.

This situation is different from the usual annoyance of one residential tenant by another, where traditionally the landlord has not been chargeable with the annoyance. [   ]⁴ Here we have a case more like *Case v. Minot,* 158 Mass. 577, 33 N.E. 700 (1893), where the landlord entered into a lease with one tenant which the landlord knew permitted that tenant to engage in activity which would interfere with the rights of another tenant. There, to be sure, the clash of tenants' rights was inevitable, if each pressed those rights. Here, although the clash of tenants' interests was only a known potentiality initially, experience demonstrated that a decibel level for the entertainment at the lounge, acoustically acceptable to its patrons and hence commercially desirable to its proprietors, was intolerable for the residential tenants.

Because the disturbing condition was the natural and probable consequence of the landlords' permitting the lounge to operate where it did and because the landlords could control the actions at the lounge, they should not be entitled to collect rent for residential premises which were not reasonably habitable. Tenants such as these should not be left only with a claim against the proprietors of the noisome lounge. To the extent that our opinions suggest a distinction between nonfeasance by the landlord, which has been said to create no liability [   ] and malfeasance by the landlord, we decline to perpetuate that distinction where the landlord creates a situation and has the right to control the objectionable conditions.

Judgments affirmed.

Notes and Questions

1. What is the difference between malfeasance and nonfeasance noted by the court in the principal case? Should it make a difference whether the

---

4. The general, but not universal, rule in this country is that a landlord is not chargeable because one tenant is causing annoyance to another [   ] even where the annoying conduct would be a breach of the landlord's covenant of quiet enjoyment if the landlord were the miscreant. * * *

A tenant with sufficient bargaining power may be able to obtain an agreement from the landlord to insert and to enforce regulatory restrictions in the leases of other, potentially offending, tenants. [   ]

condition which forms the basis of a tenant's complaint is the result of landlord malfeasance or nonfeasance? Is the key question did the landlord have a duty to respond in a way other than he did, regardless of whether the response complained of was a particular action (malfeasance) or a failure to act at all (nonfeasance)? See Fidelity Mutual Life Ins. Co. v. Robert P. Kaminsky, M.D., 768 S.W.2d 818 (Tex.App.1989) (constructive eviction resulted from failure to prevent demonstrators from blocking access to leased premises from common areas).

2. To what extent should a landlord be held responsible for behavior of tenants that is offensive to other tenants? Should it make a difference whether the behavior complained of is a violation of published rules and regulations, such as the ones incorporated into the lease reproduced earlier in this chapter? Would the following clause make a difference?

> Nothing contained in this lease shall be construed to impose upon landlord any duty or obligation to enforce the rules and regulations, or the terms, conditions or covenants in any other lease, as against any other tenant, and landlord shall not be liable to tenant for violation of the same by any other tenant, its employees, agents or invitees.

Would you suggest to a landlord-client, or possibly accept the suggestion from him that he be willing to surrender some of his power as owner to tenants who would meet and decide what they want from one another with regard to the control of offensive behavior? Is this what is done when home owners and condominium owners form community associations? See Chapter Six.

3. Restatement (Second) of Property, § 6.1 Comment d (1976), states: "The conduct of a third person outside of the leased property that is performed on property in which the landlord has an interest, which conduct could be controlled by him, is attributable to the landlord for the purpose of applying the rule of this section [describing remedies for impermissible interference with use and enjoyment]."

Illustrations 10–12 indicate that the section is intended to apply to the landlord's failure to control noisy tenants. The Reporter's Note points out, however, that the noisy tenant rule is a special exception to the "well settled" rule that the landlord is not responsible for third party interference after the tenant has taken possession. Restatement (Second) of Property, § 6.1 Reporter's Note 3, at 231–32 (1976).

4. One of the main elements, and perhaps the chief weakness, of the constructive eviction defense is the requirement that the tenant vacate the premises within a reasonable time after the condition causing the constructive eviction arises. See, e.g., Shaker and Associates, Inc. v. Medical Technologies Group, Ltd., 315 Ill.App.3d 126, 248 Ill.Dec. 190, 733 N.E.2d 865 (2000) (10 months delay constitutes waiver of constructive eviction defense). The Supreme Court of New Jersey described the dilemma this can pose for a tenant as follows:

> Plaintiff's final claim is that assuming the tenant was exposed to a constructive eviction, she waived it by remaining on the premises for an unreasonable period of time thereafter. The general rule is, of course, that a tenant's right to claim a constructive eviction will be lost if he

does not vacate the premises within a reasonable time after the right comes into existence. [ ] What constitutes a reasonable time depends upon the circumstances of each case. In considering the problem courts must be sympathetic toward the tenant's plight. Vacation of the premises is a drastic course and must be taken at his peril. If he vacates, and it is held at a later time in a suit for rent for the unexpired term that the landlord's course of action did not reach the dimensions of constructive eviction, a substantial liability may be imposed upon him. That risk and the practical inconvenience and difficulties attendant upon finding and moving to suitable quarters counsel caution.

Here, plaintiff's cooperative building manager died about nine months before the removal. During that period the tenant complained, patiently waited, hoped for relief from the landlord, and tried to take care of the water problem that accompanied the recurring rainstorms. But when relief did not come and the "crowning blow" put five inches of water in the leased offices and meeting rooms on December 20, 1961, the tolerance ended and the vacation came ten days later after notice to the landlord. The trial court found as a fact that under the circumstances such vacation was within a reasonable time, and the delay was not sufficient to establish a waiver of the constructive eviction. We find adequate evidence to support the conclusion and are of the view that the Appellate Division should not have reversed it.

Reste Realty Corporation v. Cooper, 53 N.J. 444, 251 A.2d 268, 277 (1969).

5. Statutes in some states have codified the covenant of quiet enjoyment and permit the recovery of damages, including reasonable attorney's fees, for breach. See, e.g., N.D.C.C. §§ 47–16.08, 47–16–13 (Lexis 1999); Mass.Ann.Laws ch. 186, § 14 (Michie/Law Co-op 1981); Pfeifle v. Tanabe, 620 N.W.2d 167, 172 (N.D. 2000) (upholding lease termination "based on the cumulative effect of dilapidations or problems concerning the lessee's quiet enjoyment" despite lessee's remaining in possession for about two years); Manzaro v. McCann, 401 Mass. 880, 519 N.E.2d 1337 (1988) (upholding award of three months rent as damages along with reasonable attorney's fees for landlord's failure to silence smoke alarms that sounded for over 24 hours). But see Al–Ziab v. Mourgis, 424 Mass. 847, 679 N.E.2d 528 (1997) (violation of lead paint statute does not constitute a violation of the statutory covenant of quiet enjoyment absent proof of knowledge of the risk and negligence by the landlord).

6. What if the eviction complained of is from only part of the premises? When actual eviction of part of the leased premises occurs, such as by blocking access to an elevator, a hallway or an entrance way, the tenant receives full abatement of rent but does not have to vacate the rest of the premises. See Bijan Designer v. St. Regis Sheraton, 142 Misc.2d 175, 536 N.Y.S.2d 951 (1989) (discussing concept but finding no actual partial eviction from renovation of hotel in which tenant leased space).

But interference with, rather than deprivation of, ingress and egress is not partial actual eviction. Cut–Outs, Inc. v. Man Yun Real Estate Corp., 286 A.D.2d 258, 729 N.Y.S.2d 107 (2001). Suppose one room in an apartment develops a serious leak in the ceiling. Does it make sense to require the tenants to vacate the apartment in order to use constructive eviction as a defense for non-payment of rent or should they be allowed to merely close off the room? See Manhattan Mansions v. Moe's Pizza, 149 Misc.2d 43, 561 N.Y.S.2d 331 (1990) (necessity to close periodically the kitchen of a coffee shop because of water leaking from shower in apartment above the kitchen constituted partial constructive eviction entitling tenant to partial abatement of rent).

7. Some leases, particularly for commercial personality such as computers, contain an unconditional obligation to pay rent clause, known as a "hell or high water" clause. Suppose such a clause is contained in a sublease of computer equipment. If the prime lease is terminated because of failure of the lessee (sublessor) to pay rent due the lessor, can the sublessee assert a defense of constructive eviction and avoid paying the base rent but keep the equipment so long as it pays the sublease rent? See Colorado Interstate Corp. v. CIT Group/Equipment Financing, 993 F.2d 743, 747–48 (10th Cir., 1993) (constructive eviction defense not available to circumvent "hell or high water" clause).

8. The following question was posed by the Michigan Bar Examiners in 1997:

On May 1, 1997, Peter and Bridget Sheringham, newlyweds, signed a lease for the rent of a ground-floor apartment in Peaceful Vista, a three-story, six-apartment complex near the campus of Upper Michigan University. They signed a printed lease form provided by the Peaceful Vista management; it covers a period of one year, at an annual rent of six thousand dollars, from May 1, 1997, with rent payable in monthly installments of five hundred dollars on the first day of each month. The lease says nothing about the behavior of the tenants or other people in other parts of the building. The Sheringhams paid the first month's rent and moved in the day they signed the lease.

All was well in Peaceful Vista until students of U.M.U. began to move into other parts of the building, apparently for the summer session, which began in June. With each day the amount of noise from stereo sets, televisions tuned to ball games, and vigorous youthful reactions to music and sport, came through the walls and down from the ceiling of the Sheringhams' apartment.

Last Saturday night the inconvenience reached a new high (or low) when no fewer than fifty students crowded into the premises above the Sheringhams' apartment for a party that lasted until dawn. Neither Peter nor Bridget got a wink of sleep. They complained on Monday, to the manager of Peaceful Vista, who said, "They're young. What can you expect? By the way, the tenant in that apartment is a fraternity. They use it for parties." As soon as they could arrange an appointment, the Sheringhams went to see a lawyer.

You are the lawyer. The Sheringhams are ready to move and have located a quiet place ten miles from the campus. They have paid Peaceful Vista three months' rent (fifteen hundred dollars); they are worried about having to pay the remaining forty-five hundred. Is there a way for them to give up the apartment without liability for all of that future rent?

2. *Implied Warranty of Habitability*

JAVINS v. FIRST NATIONAL
REALTY CORPORATION

United States Court of Appeals, District of Columbia Circuit, 1970.
428 F.2d 1071, cert. den., 400 U.S. 925, 91 S.Ct. 186, 27 L.Ed.2d 185.

J. Skelly Wright, Circuit Judge:

These cases present the question whether housing code violations which arise during the term of a lease have any effect upon the tenant's obligation to pay rent. The Landlord and Tenant Branch of the District of Columbia Court of General Sessions ruled proof of such violations inadmissible when proffered as a defense to an eviction action for nonpayment of rent. The District of Columbia Court of Appeals upheld this ruling. [   ]

Because of the importance of the question presented, we granted appellants' petitions for leave to appeal. We now reverse and hold that a warranty of habitability, measured by the standards set out in the Housing Regulations for the District of Columbia, is implied by operation of law into leases of urban dwelling units covered by those Regulations and that breach of this warranty gives rise to the usual remedies for breach of contract.

I

The facts revealed by the record are simple. By separate written leases, each of the appellants rented an apartment in a three-building apartment complex in Northwest Washington known as Clifton Terrace. The landlord, First National Realty Corporation, filed separate actions in the Landlord and Tenant Branch of the Court of General Sessions on April 8, 1966, seeking possession on the ground that each of the appellants had defaulted in the payment of rent due for the month of April. The tenants, appellants here, admitted that they had not paid the landlord any rent for April. However, they alleged numerous violations of the Housing Regulations as "an equitable defense or [a] claim by way of recoupment or set-off in an amount equal to the rent claim," as provided in the rules of the Court of General Sessions. They offered to prove

> "[t]hat there are approximately 1500 violations of the Housing Regulations of the District of Columbia in the building at Clifton Terrace, where Defendant resides some affecting the premises of this Defendant directly, others indirectly, and all tending to establish a course of conduct of violation of the Housing Regulations to the damage of Defendants * * *."

Settled Statement of Proceedings and Evidence, p. 2 (1966). Appellants conceded at trial, however, that this offer of proof reached only violations which had arisen since the term of the lease had commenced. The Court of General Sessions refused appellants' offer of proof and entered judgment for the landlord. The District of Columbia Court of Appeals affirmed, rejecting the argument made by appellants that the landlord was under a contractual duty to maintain the premises in compliance with the Housing Regulations. [   ]

II

Since, in traditional analysis, a lease was the conveyance of an interest in land, courts have usually utilized the special rules governing real property transactions to resolve controversies involving leases. However, as the Supreme Court has noted in another context, "the body of private property law * * *, more than almost any other branch of law, has been shaped by distinctions whose validity is largely historical." Courts have a duty to reappraise old doctrines in the light of the facts and values of contemporary life—particularly old common law doctrines which the courts themselves created and developed. As we have said before, "[T]he continued vitality of the common law * * * depends upon its ability to reflect contemporary community values and ethics."

The assumption of landlord-tenant law, derived from feudal property law, that a lease primarily conveyed to the tenant an interest in land may have been reasonable in a rural, agrarian society; it may continue to be reasonable in some leases involving farming or commercial land. In these cases, the value of the lease to the tenant is the land itself. But in the case of the modern apartment dweller, the value of the lease is that it gives him a place to live. The city dweller who seeks to lease an apartment on the third floor of a tenement has little interest in the land 30 or 40 feet below, or even in the bare right to possession within the four walls of his apartment. When American city dwellers, both rich and poor, seek "shelter" today, they seek a well known package of goods and services—a package which includes not merely walls and ceilings, but also adequate heat, light and ventilation, serviceable plumbing facilities, secure windows and doors, proper sanitation, and proper maintenance. * * *

Some courts have realized that certain of the old rules of property law governing leases are inappropriate for today's transactions. In order to reach results more in accord with the legitimate expectations of the parties and the standards of the community, courts have been gradually introducing more modern precepts of contract law in interpreting leases. Proceeding piecemeal has, however, led to confusion where "decisions are frequently conflicting, not because of a healthy disagreement on social policy, but because of the lingering impact of rules whose policies are long since dead."

In our judgment the trend toward treating leases as contracts is wise and well considered. Our holding in this case reflects a belief that leases of urban dwelling units should be interpreted and construed like any other contract.[5]

---

5. This approach does not deny the possible importance of the fact that land is involved in a transaction. The interpretation and construction of contracts between

III

Modern contract law has recognized that the buyer of goods and services in an industrialized society must rely upon the skill and honesty of the supplier to assure that goods and services purchased are of adequate quality. In interpreting most contracts, courts have sought to protect the legitimate expectations of the buyer and have steadily widened the seller's responsibility for the quality of goods and services through implied warranties of fitness and merchantability. Thus without any special agreement a merchant will be held to warrant that his goods are fit for the ordinary purposes for which such goods are used and that they are at least of reasonably average quality. Moreover, if the supplier has been notified that goods are required for a specific purpose, he will be held to warrant that any goods sold are fit for that purpose. These implied warranties have become widely accepted and well established features of the common law, supported by the overwhelming body of case law. Today most states as well as the District of Columbia have codified and enacted these warranties into statute, as to the sale of goods, in the Uniform Commercial Code.

Implied warranties of quality have not been limited to cases involving sales. The consumer renting a chattel, paying for services, or buying a combination of goods and services must rely upon the skill and honesty of the supplier to at least the same extent as a purchaser of goods. Courts have not hesitated to find implied warranties of fitness and merchantability in such situations. In most areas product liability law has moved far beyond "mere" implied warranties running between two parties in privity with each other.

The rigid doctrines of real property law have tended to inhibit the application of implied warranties to transactions involving real estate. Now, however, courts have begun to hold sellers and developers of real property responsible for the quality of their product. For example, builders of new homes have recently been held liable to purchasers for improper construction on the ground that the builders had breached an implied warranty of fitness. In other cases courts have held builders of new homes liable for breach of an implied warranty that all local building regulations had been complied with. And following the developments in other areas, very recent decisions and commentary suggest the possible extension of liability to parties other than the immediate seller for improper construction of residential real estate.

private parties has always required courts to be sensitive and responsive to myriad different factors. We believe contract doctrines allow courts to be properly sensitive to all relevant factors in interpreting lease obligations.

We also intend no alteration of statutory or case law definitions of the term "real property" for purposes of statutes or decisions on recordation, descent, conveyancing, creditors' rights, etc. We contemplate only that contract law is to determine the rights and obligations of the parties to the lease agreement, as between themselves. The civil law has always viewed the lease as a contract, and in our judgment that perspective has proved superior to that of the common law. *See* 2 M. Planiol, Treatise on the Civil Law § 1663 *et seq.* (1959); 11 La.Stat. Ann., Civil Code, Art. 2669 (1952).

Despite this trend in the sale of real estate, many courts have been unwilling to imply warranties of quality, specifically a warranty of habitability, into leases of apartments. Recent decisions have offered no convincing explanation for their refusal; rather they have relied without discussion upon the old common law rule that the lessor is not obligated to repair unless he covenants to do so in the written lease contract. However, the Supreme Courts of at least two states, in recent and well reasoned opinions, have held landlords to implied warranties of quality in housing leases. [   ] In our judgment, the old no-repair rule cannot coexist with the obligations imposed on the landlord by a typical modern housing code, and must be abandoned[6] in favor of an implied warranty of habitability.[7] In the District of Columbia, the standards of this warranty are set out in the Housing Regulations.

IV

A. In our judgment the common law itself must recognize the landlord's obligation to keep his premises in a habitable condition. This conclusion is compelled by three separate considerations. First, we believe that the old rule was based on certain factual assumptions which are no longer true; on its own terms, it can no longer be justified. Second, we believe that the consumer protection cases discussed above require that the old rule be abandoned in order to bring residential landlord-tenant law into harmony with the principles on which those cases rest. Third, we think that the nature of today's urban housing market also dictates abandonment of the old rule.

The common law rule absolving the lessor of all obligation to repair originated in the early Middle Ages.[8] Such a rule was perhaps well suited to an agrarian economy; the land was more important[9] than whatever small living structure was included in the leasehold, and the tenant farmer was fully capable of making repairs himself.[10] These historical

6. As far as tort liability is concerned, we have previously held that the old common law rule has been changed by passage of the housing code and that the landlord has a duty to maintain reasonably safe premises. * * *

7. Although the present cases involve written leases, we think there is no particular significance in this fact. The landlord's warranty is implied in oral and written leases for all types of tenancies.

8. The rule was "settled" by 1485. 3 W. Holdsworth, A History of English Law 122–123 (6th ed. 1934). The common law rule discussed in text originated in the even older rule prohibiting the tenant from committing waste. The writ of waste expanded as the tenant's right to possession grew stronger. Eventually, in order to protect the landowner's reversionary interest, the tenant became obligated to make repairs and liable to eviction and damages if he failed to do so. *Ibid.*

9. The land was so central to the original common law conception of a leasehold that rent was viewed as "issuing" from the land: "[T]he governing idea is that the land is bound to pay the rent * * *. We may almost go to the length of saying that the land pays it through [the tenant's] hand." 2 F. Pollock & F. Maitland, The History of English Law 131 (2d ed. 1923).

10. Many later judicial opinions have added another justification of the old common law rule. They have invoked the time-worn cry of *caveat emptor* and argued that a lessee has the opportunity to inspect the premises. On the basis of his inspection, the tenant must then take the premises "as is," according to this reasoning. As an historical matter, the opportunity to inspect was not thought important when the rule was first devised.

* * *

facts were the basis on which the common law constructed its rule; they also provided the necessary prerequisites for its application.[11]

Court decisions in the late 1800's began to recognize that the factual assumptions of the common law were no longer accurate in some cases. For example, the common law, since it assumed that the land was the most important part of the leasehold, required a tenant to pay rent even if any building on the land was destroyed. Faced with such a rule and the ludicrous results it produced, in 1863 the New York Court of Appeals declined to hold that an upper story tenant was obliged to continue paying rent after his apartment building burned down. The court simply pointed out that the urban tenant had no interest in the land, only in the attached building.

Another line of cases created an exception to the no-repair rule for short term leases of furnished dwellings. The Massachusetts Supreme Judicial Court, a court not known for its willingness to depart from the common law, supported this exception, pointing out:

> " * * * [A] different rule should apply to one who hires a furnished room, or a furnished house, for a few days, or a few weeks or months. Its fitness for immediate use of a particular kind, as indicated by its appointments, is a far more important element entering into the contract than when there is a mere lease of real estate. One who lets for a short term a house provided with all furnishings and appointments for immediate residence may be supposed to contract in reference to a well-understood purpose of the hirer to use it as a habitation. * * * It would be unreasonable to hold, under such circumstances, that the landlord does not impliedly agree that what he is letting is a house suitable for occupation in its condition at the time. * * * "[12]

These as well as other similar cases demonstrate that some courts began some time ago to question the common law's assumptions that the land was the most important feature of a leasehold and that the tenant could feasibly make any necessary repairs himself. Where those assumptions no longer reflect contemporary housing patterns, the courts have created exceptions to the general rule that landlords have no duty to keep their premises in repair.

It is overdue for courts to admit that these assumptions are no longer true with regard to all urban housing. Today's urban tenants, the vast majority of whom live in multiple dwelling houses, are interested,

---

11. Even the old common law courts responded with a different rule for a landlord-tenant relationship which did not conform to the model of the usual agrarian lease. Much more substantial obligations were placed upon the keepers of inns (the only multiple dwelling houses known to the common law). Their guests were interested solely in shelter and could not be expected to make their own repairs. "The modern apartment dweller more closely resembles the guest in an inn than he resembles an agrarian tenant, but the law has not generally recognized the similarity." J. Levi, P. Hablutzel, L. Rosenberg & J. White, Model Residential Landlord–Tenant Code 6–7 (Tent.Draft 1969).

12. Ingalls v. Hobbs, 156 Mass. 348, 31 N.E. 286 (1892).

not in the land, but solely in "a house suitable for occupation." Furthermore, today's city dweller usually has a single, specialized skill unrelated to maintenance work; he is unable to make repairs like the "jack-of-all-trades" farmer who was the common law's model of the lessee. Further, unlike his agrarian predecessor who often remained on one piece of land for his entire life, urban tenants today are more mobile than ever before. A tenant's tenure in a specific apartment will often not be sufficient to justify efforts at repairs. In addition, the increasing complexity of today's dwellings renders them much more difficult to repair than the structures of earlier times. In a multiple dwelling repair may require access to equipment and areas in the control of the landlord. Low and middle income tenants, even if they were interested in making repairs, would be unable to obtain any financing for major repairs since they have no long-term interest in the property.

Our approach to the common law of landlord and tenant ought to be aided by principles derived from the consumer protection cases referred to above. In a lease contract, a tenant seeks to purchase from his landlord shelter for a specified period of time. The landlord sells housing as a commercial businessman and has much greater opportunity, incentive and capacity to inspect and maintain the condition of his building. Moreover, the tenant must rely upon the skill and *bona fides* of his landlord at least as much as a car buyer must rely upon the car manufacturer. In dealing with major problems, such as heating, plumbing, electrical or structural defects, the tenant's position corresponds precisely with "the ordinary consumer who cannot be expected to have the knowledge or capacity or even the opportunity to make adequate inspection of mechanical instrumentalities, like automobiles, and to decide for himself whether they are reasonably fit for the designed purpose." Henningsen v. Bloomfield Motors, Inc., 32 N.J. 358, 375, 161 A.2d 69, 78 (1960).

Since a lease contract specifies a particular period of time during which the tenant has a right to use his apartment for shelter, he may legitimately expect that the apartment will be fit for habitation for the time period for which it is rented. We point out that in the present cases there is no allegation that appellants' apartments were in poor condition or in violation of the housing code at the commencement of the leases. Since the lessees continue to pay the same rent, they were entitled to expect that the landlord would continue to keep the premises in their beginning condition during the lease term. It is precisely such expectations that the law now recognizes as deserving of formal, legal protection.

Even beyond the rationale of traditional products liability law, the relationship of landlord and tenant suggests further compelling reasons for the law's protection of the tenants' legitimate expectations of quality. The inequality in bargaining power between landlord and tenant has been well documented. Tenants have very little leverage to enforce demands for better housing. Various impediments to competition in the rental housing market, such as racial and class discrimination and standardized form leases, mean that landlords place tenants in a take it or leave it situation. The increasingly severe shortage of adequate housing further increases the landlord's bargaining power and escalates the need for maintaining and improving the existing stock. Finally, the findings by various studies of the social impact of bad housing has led to the realization that poor housing is detrimental to the whole society, not merely to the unlucky ones who must suffer the daily indignity of living in a slum.

Thus we are led by our inspection of the relevant legal principles and precedents to the conclusion that the old common law rule imposing an obligation upon the lessee to repair during the lease term was really never intended to apply to residential urban leaseholds. Contract principles established in other areas of the law provide a more rational framework for the apportionment of landlord-tenant responsibilities; they strongly suggest that a warranty of habitability be implied into all contracts for urban dwellings.

B. We believe, in any event, that the District's housing code requires that a warranty of habitability be implied in the leases of all housing that it covers. The housing code—formally designated the Housing Regulations of the District of Columbia—was established and authorized by the Commissioners of the District of Columbia on August 11, 1955. Since that time, the code has been updated by numerous orders of the Commissioners. The 75 pages of the Regulations provide a comprehensive regulatory scheme setting forth in some detail: (a) the standards which housing in the District of Columbia must meet; (b) which party, the lessor or the lessee, must meet each standard; and (c) a system of inspections, notifications and criminal penalties. The Regulations themselves are silent on the question of private remedies.

Two previous decisions of this court, however, have held that the Housing Regulations create legal rights and duties enforceable in tort by private parties.

* * *

This principle of implied warranty is well established. Courts often imply relevant law into contracts to provide a remedy for any damage caused by one party's illegal conduct. In a case closely analogous to the present ones, the Illinois Supreme Court held that a builder who constructed a house in violation of the Chicago building code had breached his contract with the buyer:

"* * * [T]he law existing at the time and place of the making of the contract is deemed a part of the contract, as though expressly referred to or incorporated in it. * * *

"The rationale for this rule is that the parties to the contract would have expressed that which the law implies 'had they not supposed that it was unnecessary to speak of it because the law provided for it.' * * * Consequently, the courts, in construing the existing law as part of the express contract, are not reading into the contract provisions different from those expressed and intended by the parties, as defendants contend, but are merely construing the contract in accordance with the intent of the parties."[13]

We follow the Illinois court in holding that the housing code must be read into housing contracts—a holding also required by the purposes and the structure of the code itself. The duties imposed by the Housing Regulations may not be waived or shifted by agreement if the Regulations specifically place the duty upon the lessor.[14] Criminal penalties are provided if these duties are ignored. This regulatory structure was established by the Commissioners because, in their judgment, the grave conditions in the housing market required serious action. Yet official enforcement of the housing code has been far from uniformly effective. Innumerable studies have documented the desperate condition of rental housing in the District of Columbia and in the nation. In view of these circumstances, we think the conclusion reached by the Supreme Court of Wisconsin as to the effect of a housing code on the old common law rule cannot be avoided:

" * * * [T]he legislature has made a policy judgment—that it is socially (and politically) desirable to impose these duties on a property owner—which has rendered the old common law rule obsolete. To follow the old rule of no implied warranty of habitability in leases would, in our opinion, be inconsistent with the current legislative policy concerning housing standards. * * * "[15]

We therefore hold that the Housing Regulations imply a warranty of habitability, measured by the standards which they set out, into leases of all housing that they cover.

---

13. Schiro v. W.E. Gould & Co., 18 Ill.2d 538, 544, 165 N.E.2d 286, 290 (1960). As a general proposition, it is undoubtedly true that parties to a contract intend that applicable law will be complied with by both sides. We recognize, however, that reading statutory provisions into private contracts may have little factual support in the intentions of the particular parties now before us. But, for reasons of public policy, warranties are often implied into contracts by operation of law in order to meet generally prevailing standards of honesty and fair dealing. When the public policy has been enacted into law like the housing code, that policy will usually have deep roots in the expectations and intentions of most people. *See* Costigan, Implied-in-Fact Contracts and Mutual Assent, 33 Harv.L.Rev. 376, 383–385 (1920).

14. Any private agreement to shift the duties would be illegal and unenforceable.

The precedents dealing with industrial safety statutes are directly in point:

" * * * [T]he only question remaining is whether the courts will enforce or recognize as against a servant an agreement express or implied on his part to waive the performance of a statutory duty of the master imposed for the protection of the servant, and in the interest of the public, and enforceable by criminal prosecution. We do not think they will. To do so would be to nullify the object of the statute. * * * "

Narramore v. Cleveland, C., C. & St. L. Ry. Co., 6 Cir., 96 F. 298, 302 (1899). *See* W. Prosser, Torts § 67 at 468–469 (3d ed. 1964) and cases cited therein.

15. Pines v. Perssion, 14 Wis.2d 590, 596, 111 N.W.2d 409, 412–413 (1961). *Accord,* Buckner v. Azulai, 251 Cal.App.2d Supp. 1013, 59 Cal.Rptr. 806 (1967).

V

In the present cases, the landlord sued for possession for nonpayment of rent. Under contract principles,[16] however, the tenant's obligation to pay rent is dependent upon the landlord's performance of his obligations, including his warranty to maintain the premises in habitable condition. In order to determine whether any rent is owed to the landlord, the tenants must be given an opportunity to prove the housing code violations alleged as breach of the landlord's warranty.[17]

At trial, the finder of fact must make two findings: (1) whether the alleged violations[18] existed during the period for which past due rent is claimed, and (2) what portion, if any or all, of the tenant's obligation to pay rent was suspended by the landlord's breach. If no part of the tenant's rental obligation is found to have been suspended, then a judgment for possession may issue forthwith. On the other hand, if the jury determines that the entire rental obligation has been extinguished by the landlord's total breach, then the action for possession on the ground of nonpayment must fail.[19]

The jury may find that part of the tenant's rental obligation has been suspended but that part of the unpaid back rent is indeed owed to the landlord. In these circumstances, no judgment for possession should issue if the tenant agrees to pay the partial rent found to be due. If the tenant refuses to pay the partial amount, a judgment for possession may then be entered.

The judgment of the District of Columbia Court of Appeals is reversed and the cases are remanded for further proceedings consistent with this opinion.[20]

16. In extending all contract remedies for breach to the parties to a lease, we include an action for specific performance of the landlord's implied warranty of habitability.

17. To be relevant, of course, the violations must affect the tenant's apartment or common areas which the tenant uses. Moreover, the contract principle that no one may benefit from his own wrong will allow the landlord to defend by proving the damage was caused by the tenant's wrongful action. However, violations resulting from inadequate repairs or materials which disintegrate under normal use would not be assignable to the tenant. Also we agree with the District of Columbia Court of Appeals that the tenant's private rights do not depend on official inspection or official finding of violation by the city government. Diamond Housing Corp. v. Robinson, 257 A.2d 492, 494 (1969).

18. The jury should be instructed that one or two minor violations standing alone which do not affect habitability are *de minimis* and would not entitle the tenant to a reduction in rent.

19. As soon as the landlord made the necessary repairs rent would again become due. Our holding, of course, affects only eviction for nonpayment of rent. The landlord is free to seek eviction at the termination of the lease or on any other legal ground.

20. Appellants in the present cases offered to pay rent into the registry of the court during the present action. We think this is an excellent protective procedure. If the tenant defends against an action for possession on the basis of breach of the landlord's warranty of habitability, the trial court may require the tenant to make future rent payments into the registry of the court as they become due; such a procedure would be appropriate only while the tenant remains in possession. The escrowed money will, however, represent rent for the period between the time the landlord files suit and the time the case comes to trial. In the normal course of litigation, the only factual question at trial would be the condition of the apartment during the time the landlord alleged rent was due and not paid.

As a general rule, the escrowed money should be apportioned between the landlord and the tenant after trial on the basis of the finding of rent actually due for the period at issue in the suit. To insure fair apportion-

Notes and Questions

1. Judge J. Skelly Wright's eloquent opinion in *Javins* generally is credited with supplying the impetus for one of the most striking reforms in the common law of property. In less than 20 years after his opinion, virtually all of the states adopted the implied warranty of habitability, either by judicial opinion or by statute, and in the process reversed the common law view of residential landlord-tenant relationships that had been in vogue for centuries. See Merrill v. Jansma, 86 P.3d 270, 275–81 (Wyo. 2004) (reviewing judicial and legislative developments). For a thorough history and analysis of the reform, see Rabin, The Revolution in Residential Landlord–Tenant Law: Causes and Consequences, 69 Cornell L.Rev. 517 (1984) and Glendon, The Transformation of American Landlord–Tenant Law, 23 B.C.L.Rev. 503 (1982). See also Cunningham, The New Implied and Statutory Warranties of Habitability in Residential Leases: From Contract to Status, 16 Urb.L.Ann. 3 (1979).

2. How should "habitability" be defined? Suppose an apartment building in an older section of town has hot and cold running water in the kitchens, but only cold water in the bathrooms. Does the fact that a tenant cannot take a hot shower and must fill a tub with hot water from the kitchen in order to take a bath constitute a breach of the warranty of habitability? See City of St. Louis v. Brune, 515 S.W.2d 471 (Mo.1974) (hot shower a "convenience" rather than a "necessity" for health or safety). See also Solow v. Wellner, 86 N.Y.2d 582, 635 N.Y.S.2d 132, 658 N.E.2d 1005 (1995) (implied warranty of habitability covers only essential amenities necessary to protect life, health or safety, and does not expand as quality or cost of unit increases). Suppose a housing code requires window screens to keep out insects. If such screens are installed, but fail to prevent a young child from falling through an open window and suffering serious injury, is the apartment uninhabitable in violation of the warranty? See Mudusar by Baloch v. V.G. Murray & Co., 100 N.C.App. 395, 396 S.E.2d 325 (1990) (screens that keep out insects but do not keep in children not violative of statutory implied warranty of habitability).

3. What obligation does a tenant have to notify her landlord of conditions affecting habitability? Should failure to notify the landlord affect her ability to pursue a cause of action for breach of the warranty? See Detling v. Edelbrock, 671 S.W.2d 265, 270 (Mo.1984) (tenant must give landlord notice of defects not known to landlord and a reasonable opportunity to cure). Jablonski v. Casey, 2003 WL 23005021 (Mass. App. 2003) (tenant cannot stop paying rent prior to notifying landlord of defects and giving an opportunity to cure).

4. Suppose neither the landlord nor the tenant knew of the defect, for example, faulty wiring concealed in the space between the first and second floor of a house. Is the landlord responsible for injuries or property damage

ment, however, we think either party should be permitted to amend its complaint or answer at any time before trial, to allege a change in the condition of the apartment. In this event, the finder of fact should make a separate finding as to the condition of the apartment at the time at which the amendment was filed. This new finding will have no effect upon the original action; it will only affect the distribution of the escrowed rent paid after the filing of the amendment.

resulting from an electrical fire? See Estate of Vazquez v. Hepner, 564 N.W.2d 426 (Iowa 1997) (landlord is "not required to take extreme measures and expend significant amounts of time and money trying to discover hazards that may not even exist").

5. Judge Wright in *Javins* stressed that all contract remedies, including actions for specific performance, are available for breach of the implied warranty of habitability (IWH). Examples of available remedies include:

(a) *rent withholding*—Green v. Superior Court, 10 Cal.3d 616, 111 Cal.Rptr. 704, 517 P.2d 1168 (1974) (defense of breach of IWH may be raised in action for possession because of non-payment of rent);

(b) *rent abatement*—Berzito v. Gambino, 63 N.J. 460, 308 A.2d 17 (1973) (retroactive rent abatement, as well as other affirmative contract remedies, recognized for breach of IWH);

(c) *self-help repairs and deduction of rent*—Marini v. Ireland, 56 N.J. 130, 265 A.2d 526 (1970) (tenant may deduct costs of necessary repairs when landlord fails to maintain premises in livable condition after timely notice);

(d) *damages*—Mease v. Fox, 200 N.W.2d 791 (Iowa 1972) (damages for breach of implied warranty of habitability are the difference between fair rental value as warranted and fair rental value as is; if tenant vacates, damages are based on loss of bargain difference between fair rental value as warranted and promised rent for balance of term).

6. Courts have had difficulty with the measure of damages for breach of the warranty of habitability. Most have applied the contract measure of damages for breach of warranty. If the buyer keeps the product, his general damages are the difference between the value of the product as promised (warranted) and the value of the product he received. He is obligated to pay the purchase price less his damages. If the buyer returns the product to the seller, his damages are the difference between the value of what he was promised and the amount he promised to pay, i.e., the value of his bargain. In that case, of course, he does not pay the purchase price.

The "value" of what was promised or received is the fair market value (in the lease context, the fair rental), i.e., the price a willing buyer would pay to a willing seller in an arms-length transaction in a free market. The problem with determining the fair rental value of property, especially for lower income or slum housing, is that there are not many willing sellers of slum housing which meet the warranty of habitability standards or willing buyers of unsafe and unsanitary housing. The absence of a free market in housing, resulting from housing shortages and the tenants' consequent lack of bargaining power, was one of the primary reasons for the development of the implied warranty of habitability.

The absence of data on fair rental value has led many courts to assume that the agreed rental represents the fair rental value as warranted, since that is what the tenant bargained for (or would have bargained for if he had enough bargaining power). See, e.g., Hilder v. St. Peter, 144 Vt. 150, 478 A.2d 202, 209 (1984); Berzito v. Gambino, 63 N.J. 460, 469, 308 A.2d 17, 22 (1973). Even if this assumption were valid at the time the lease was made, it is not necessarily so at the time of the breach, since rental values can rise or fall. Other courts have assumed that the agreed rent is equivalent to the fair rental value of the dwelling in its defective condition, i.e. unfit for human habitation. In addition to ignoring possible market fluctuations, does this approach also overlook the tenant's lack of free choice in the market by assuming that he got what he bargained for? See generally R. Schoshinski, American Law of Landlord and Tenant § 3:25 (1980 & 2005 Supp.) (discussing four different views regarding measure of damages that courts have adopted).

7.   Suppose the apartment did not meet habitability standards at the time the tenant rented it. Would that affect her legal position? In Brown v. Southall Realty Co., 237 A.2d 834 (D.C.App.1968), the court held that a lease of property containing violations of the housing code is void. A subsequent case, William J. Davis, Inc. v. Slade, 271 A.2d 412 (D.C.App.1970), also involved a lease that was void because substantial violations of the housing code existed at the time the lease was executed. The court held that the tenant, while in possession of the premises under the void lease, was a tenant at sufferance. Consequently the landlord was entitled to receive the reasonable rental value of the premises in the defective condition for the period of the tenant's occupation.

8.   If T's utility bills are excessive because of the uninhabitable condition of the premises, can T recover the difference between what the bills actually were and what they should have been if the premises had been in a habitable condition? See Fair v. Negley, 257 Pa.Super. 50, 390 A.2d 240 (1978). (Yes. Court also held that boilerplate "as is" clause did not constitute an effective waiver of the implied warranty of habitability.)

9.   Should the implied warranty be limited to multi-family apartment buildings, or should it extend to detached single family homes, commercial facilities, or mixed use buildings? Many courts have rejected an implied warranty of habitability or suitability in commercial leases without analyzing whether the distinctions between residential and commercial leases justify limiting the warranty to residential leases. A standard argument is that commercial lessees normally do not occupy inferior bargaining positions. See, e.g., Service Oil Co. v. White, 218 Kan. 87, 542 P.2d 652 (1975). Is that a persuasive reason for the distinction? What about commercial tenants on the first floor of an apartment building? Do they have a stronger bargaining position than the residential tenants?

The American Law Institute, in adopting the implied warranty of habitability as a warranty that premises will be "suitable for residential use," stated that it was taking "no position at this time" on whether the warranty should be implied in commercial leases. Restatement (Second) of Property §§ 5.1, Caveat; 5.5, Caveat to subsection (1) (1976).

However, in Davidow v. Inwood North Professional Group, 747 S.W.2d 373 (Tex.1988), the Court stated:

When a commercial tenant ... leases office space, many of the same considerations (as are present in residential leases) are involved. A significant number of commentators have recognized the similarities between residential and commercial tenants and concluded that residential warranties should be expanded to cover commercial property. [   ]

It cannot be assumed that a commercial tenant is more knowledgeable about the quality of the structure than a residential tenant. A businessman cannot be expected to possess the expertise necessary to adequately inspect and repair the premises, and many commercial tenants lack the financial resources to hire inspectors and repairmen to assure the suitability of the premises. [ ] Additionally, because commercial tenants often enter into short-term leases, the tenants have limited economic incentive to make any extensive repairs to their premises. [ ] Consequently, commercial tenants generally rely on their landlords' greater abilities to inspect and repair the premises. [ ]

In light of the many similarities between residential and commercial tenants and the modern trend towards increased consumer protection, a number of courts have indicated a willingness to apply residential property warranties to commercial tenancy situations. [ ]

There is no valid reason to imply a warranty of habitability in residential leases and not in commercial leases. Although minor distinctions can be drawn between residential and commercial tenants, those differences do not justify limiting the warranty to residential leaseholds....

Davidow suggests some differences in the application of the implied warranty of suitability for leased commercial space. For example, the warranty can be waived if "the parties to a lease expressly agree that the tenant will repair certain defects." 747 S.W.2d at 377. In considering the enforceability of "as is" clauses, Texas courts apply a five factor test evaluating: (1) the parties, (2) the terms, (3) the negotiation process, (4) the transaction and (5) whether any known facts were misrepresented or concealed. Gym–N–I Playgrounds, Inc. v. Snider, 158 S.W.3d 78, 85 (Tex. App. 2005) (concluding that implied warranty of suitability was waived by "as is" clause). In a mixed-use building, with both residential and commercial tenants, should different standards be applied concerning waivability?

10. Does the implied warranty of habitability pose ethical dilemmas for low income tenants, landlords who rent to them, and lawyers who advise them? Suppose a tenant does not have enough money to pay the agreed rent, regardless of whether the apartment meets habitability standards. Would use of the implied warranty and related tenant-protective rules to delay eviction for months be an abuse of the landlord? Suppose the tenant can afford a lower rent, but the landlord cannot afford to charge the lower rent unless repairs necessary to meet habitability standards are not made. What should be done?

A NOTE ON LANDLORD TORT LIABILITY

(a) Traditional Rules

Historically, landlords have been immune from tort liability because a lease was viewed as a conveyance of land. The landlord gave up control of the premises once possession was transferred to the tenant. With the transfer of possession went the power to exclude the landlord and the responsibility for conditions of the premises. Without control, the landlord had no duty of care for the premises. See, e.g., Adams v. Miller, 908

S.W.2d 112, 115–116 (Ky.1995) (landlord not liable for injuries caused by fire in tenant's rented house that was not equipped with smoke detectors).

Over the years, courts have recognized several exceptions to immunity and have held that landlords could be liable in tort for

"(1) defects in premises leased for admission of the public; (2) a breach of a covenant to repair; (3) negligent repairs; (4) defects in 'common areas' under the landlord's control; and more recently (5) defects constituting a violation of a provision of the applicable building or housing code." Merrill v. Jansma, 86 P.3d 270, 275 (Wy 2004), quoting Old Town Development Company v. Langford, 349 N.E.2d 744, 754–55 (Ind. App. 1976). See also Brooks v. Lewin Realty, 378 Md. 70, 835 A.2d 616 (2003) (violation of housing code prohibiting lead-based paint is presumptive evidence of negligence); McIntyre v. Philadelphia Housing Authority, 816 A.2d 1204, 1211 (Pa. Cmwlth. 2003) (violation of a statute or regulation is negligence per se, quoting Comment to Restatement (Second) of Property § 17.6 (1977)).

(b) Impact of the Implied Warranty of Habitability

The advent of the implied warranty of habitability triggered a reconsideration of the general immunity rule, leading some courts to abrogate it. The Supreme Court of New Hampshire, in Sargent v. Ross, 113 N.H. 388, 308 A.2d 528, 533–534 (1973), stated that " * * * now is the time for the landlord's tort immunity to be relegated to the history books where it more properly belongs." The court found that "landlords, as other persons, must exercise reasonable care not to subject others to an unreasonable risk of harm." The Supreme Court of Wisconsin, in Pagelsdorf v. Safeco Ins. Co. of America, 91 Wis.2d 734, 284 N.W.2d 55, 60 (1979), extended this duty of due care to people on the premises with the tenant's permission, concluding that "[i]t would be anomalous indeed to require a landlord to keep his premises in good repair as an implied condition of the lease, yet immunize him from liability for his failure to do so." In Kline v. 1500 Massachusetts Avenue Apartment, 439 F.2d 477, 483–485 (D.C.Cir.1970), the District of Columbia Circuit Court held that the landlord was bound to protect the tenant against foreseeable risks of crime and that this duty derived from the "logic of the situation itself," the implied warranty of habitability in the lease, which had been recognized three months earlier by the court in *Javins,* and common law precedents regarding innkeepers and guests also used in *Javins* to support the implied warranty rationale.

The Supreme Court of California in Becker v. IRM Corp., 38 Cal.3d 454, 213 Cal.Rptr. 213, 220, 698 P.2d 116, 123 (1985), held a landlord strictly liable in tort for a defect in the premises. In that case, a tenant suffered severe cuts when he slipped and fell against an untempered glass door. The court held that "a landlord engaged in the business of leasing dwellings is strictly liable in tort for injuries resulting from a * * * defect in the premises when the defect existed at the time the premises were let to the tenant." In reaching this conclusion, the court drew heavily on the implied warranty of habitability concept recognized in California 11 years earlier in Green v. Superior Court, 10 Cal.3d 616, 111 Cal.Rptr. 704, 517 P.2d 1168 (1974).

Should a tenant be able to recover for mental distress caused by the landlord's breach of the warranty of habitability?

Restatement (Second) of Torts § 46 provides in part:

(1) One who by extreme and outrageous conduct intentionally causes severe emotional distress to another is subject to liability for such emotional distress, and if bodily harm to the other results from it, for such bodily harm.

Several courts have held that § 46 extends to a landlord who intentionally inflicts emotional distress on a tenant by breaching the implied warranty of habitability. Simon v. Solomon, 385 Mass. 91, 431 N.E.2d 556 (1982); Fair v. Negley, 257 Pa.Super. 50, 390 A.2d 240 (1978); Aweeka v. Bonds, 20 Cal.App.3d 278, 97 Cal.Rptr. 650 (1971). In Detling v. Edelbrock, 671 S.W.2d 265 (Mo.1984), the Missouri Supreme Court held that a tenant cannot recover for emotional harm unless physical injury also was suffered or the emotional distress was "medically diagnosable and medically significant."

Not all courts have accepted the argument that the implied warranty of habitability should be used to abrogate landlords' traditional common law immunity from tort liability. The Supreme Court of Vermont refused to apply the implied warranty of habitability to a case in which a tenant was injured by falling down a steep stairway on the leased premises. The court reasoned as follows:

We believe, however, that in the adjudication of a lawsuit for relief from personal injury, the concepts of tort and negligence law provide the more straightforward way to describe the respective duties and liabilities of the parties. Where a tenant leases substandard premises, she ought recover from the landlord her excess rental payments, her consequential damages for "annoyance and discomfort" and, in certain instances, punitive damages. The landlord broke a promise— at least one implied by the law—and the tenant has the right to recover her losses. But where the tenant seeks a damage award for her personal injuries, other questions arise: What caused the injuries? Were they the result of the landlord's breach? Did they flow from the tenant's own carelessness? The law of negligence is best suited to answer these questions and has developed rules for their accommodation. For example, under Vermont's comparative negligence statute, a plaintiff can recover only if her own negligence contributed to no more than half the cause of the accident, and even then only in proportion to the amount of negligence attributed to the defendant. 12 V.S.A. § 1036. If she was primarily to blame for her fall and injuries, she cannot recover. In essence, plaintiff is asking us to do away with these principles, for, in her view, all damages stemming from defendant's breach of the warranty would be recoverable. Fault would not enter the calculation. We believe it is unwise to abandon negligence principles in this context absent legislative direction.

Favreau v. Miller, 156 Vt. 222, 591 A.2d 68, 73 (Vt.1991).

The Pennsylvania Commonwealth Court, applying decisions of the Supreme Court of Pennsylvania, Staley v. Bouril, 553 Pa. 112, 718 A.2d 283 (1998) (implied warranty of habitability applied to a lease for an improved lot in a mobile home park) and Pugh v. Holmes, 486 Pa. 272, 405 A.2d 897 (1979) (recognizing implied warranty of habitability, concluded that "traditional contract remedies are the only remedies available" and refused to allow damages for injuries caused by exposure to lead-based paint in a residence. McIntyre v. Philadelphia Housing Auth., 816 A.2d 1204, 1209 (Pa. Cmwlth. 2003). See also Bolin Development Corp. v. Indart, 803 S.W.2d 817, 819–820 (Tex. App. 1991) (personal injury and/or property damages recoverable only if the elements of negligence could be established in a negligence action rather than in an action for breach of the implied warranty).

(c) Criminal Activity

Courts generally have concluded that landlords have no common law duty to protect tenants from the criminal acts of strangers. See, e.g., Miller v. Whitworth, 193 W.Va. 262, 455 S.E.2d 821 (1995) (but duty exists if landlord's actions or inactions affirmatively increased risk to tenants); Bartley v. Sweetser, 319 Ark. 117, 890 S.W.2d 250 (1994); Schelp v. Cohen–Esrey Real Estate Services, Inc., 889 S.W.2d 848 (Mo. Ct.App.1994), app. to tr. den.; Cramer v. Balcor Property Management, Inc., 312 S.C. 440, 441 S.E.2d 317 (1994). Nor do landlords have any duty to protect third parties from injuries caused by a tenant. Spencer v. Nesto, 46 Conn.Supp. 566, 764 A.2d 224 (2000).

Exceptions to this no liability rule have been recognized when a "special relationship" exists or "special circumstances" are present. For example, in Aaron v. Havens, 758 S.W.2d 446 (Mo.1988), the Missouri Supreme Court held that a landlord could be liable for the injuries sustained by a tenant as a result of a sexual assault by an intruder who gained entry to her apartment via a window adjoining a fire escape. The court stated that the owner of the building had a recognized duty of due care to make the premises safe against foreseeable risk, and that, in this situation, the landlord had ample reason to know of the danger of the fire escape leading to the tenant's window. Thus, the landlord could be liable for damage resulting from this dangerous condition. The court made no mention of the implied warranty of habitability which had been accepted by the court four years earlier in Detling v. Edelbrock, 671 S.W.2d 265 (Mo.1984). See also Hemmings v. Pelham Wood Limited Liability Limited Partnership, 375 Md. 522, 826 A.2d 443 (2003) (landlord responsible for intruder who broke into apartment by breaking open a patio door); T.W. v. Regal Trace, Ltd., 908 So.2d 499 (Fla. App. 2005) (special relationship triggered duty to warn of foreseeable criminal conduct).

For discussion of the tort liability issue, see J. Page, The Law of Premises Liability 193–253 (2d Ed 1988); R. Schoshinski, American Law of Landlord and Tenant § 3.9 (1980 & 2005 Supp); Browder, The Taming of a Duty—The Tort Liability of Landlords, 81 Mich.L.Rev. 99 (1982); Annot., Dangerous Condition of Rented Premises, 64 A.L.R.3d 339 (1975); Restatement (Second) of Property §§ 17.1–17.7, 18.1–18.4, 19.1–19.3 (1977).

3. *Waste*

RUMICHE CORPORATION v. EISENREICH

Court of Appeals of New York, 1976.
40 N.Y.2d 174, 386 N.Y.S.2d 208, 352 N.E.2d 125.

FUCHSBERG, JUDGE.

The issue is whether certain repairs and alterations made by a tenant to his rent-controlled apartment constitute grounds for eviction under the provisions of subdivision a of section 52 of the New York City Rent, Eviction and Rehabilitation Regulations.

The Civil Court of the City of New York granted the landlord's petition for eviction; the Appellate Term and the Appellate Division, successively, each affirmed. The tenant appeals to this court by leave of the Appellate Division. For the reasons which follow, we believe there should be a reversal.

Subdivision a of section 52 of the Rent, Eviction and Rehabilitation Regulations, in pertinent part, reads:

[A]n action or proceeding to recover possession of any housing accommodation shall be maintainable * * * upon one or more of the following grounds:

"a. The tenant is violating *a substantial obligation of his tenancy* other than the obligation to surrender possession of such housing accommodation and has failed to cure such violation after written notice by the landlord that the violation cease within 10 days; *or within the 3 month period immediately prior to the commencement of the proceeding, the tenant has wilfully violated such an obligation inflicting serious and substantial injury upon the landlord*". (Emphasis added.)

Turning to the facts, the record on this appeal discloses that the tenant has lived in his one-room studio apartment for approximately 10 years. In May of 1973, the building was purchased from its former owner by the landlord, who immediately requested the existing rent-controlled tenants to vacate the building so that he could renovate the premises, offering at least some of them a sum of money as inducement to do so. The tenant before us received such an offer but declined to move. He also called the landlord's attention to the fact that his ceiling was falling in and asked that it be repaired. The landlord did not do so.

The tenant thereupon replaced it with one constructed of three-eighths inch sheetrock and, in the course of doing so, had a licensed electrician install a working ceiling light fixture controlled from a wall switch in place of the pre-existing malfunctioning, old-fashioned, pull-chain one. He also attached a single wooden closet to a wall and erected a small decorative wooden frame around the room's only window. That is the sum total of the "repairs and alterations" involved here.

In essence, in its petition brought pursuant to subdivision a of section 52, the landlord alleged that the repairs to the ceiling did not conform to section 60 of New York City's Fire Code, which specifies five-eighths inch rather than three-eighths inch sheetrock be used, and that the lighting fixture, the closet and the window frame were so permanent or lasting in nature and so materially altered the premises that they violated the "substantial obligation" of the tenancy contemplated by the section. * * *

The question then is whether the repairs and alterations before us constituted waste.

Basically, at common law waste had three different definitions, each related to particular types of conduct on the part of tenants. Involuntary waste was defined as failure to prevent damage to the premises, in other words negligence. Equitable waste was defined as failure to do what a prudent owner would do and was available as a cause of action only in limited circumstances, neither of these concepts is relevant to the facts at hand. But the third, voluntary waste, is. It occurs when a tenant injures the premises by an affirmative act. [　]

Voluntary waste as a concept stems from early English common law concern that the interests in land held by reversioners or remaindermen be protected from depredations by life tenants of scarce natural resources. [　]

For instance, the cutting of trees or exhaustion of coal supplies were regarded as waste because their effects extended well beyond the term of the tenant's temporary interest in the land or premises. It is the impingement upon the ultimate estate of the landlord which is the keynote to the definition of waste. * * *

Its application in a modern landlord-tenant setting is well described in *Pross v. Excelsior Cleaning & Dyeing Co.*, 110 Misc. 195, 201, 179 N.Y.S. 176, 179: "[S]uch a change as to affect a vital and substantial portion of the premises, as would change its characteristic appearance, the fundamental purpose of the erection, or the uses contemplated, or a change of such a nature, as would affect the very realty itself—extraordinary in scope and effect, or unusual in expenditure".

Other courts have also emphasized the definition of waste as permanent or lasting damage. [　]

Thus, not every change or alteration made by a tenant constitutes waste. For instance, prior to modern leasing developments, except as provided in tenement house legislation [   ] it was, and is, the tenant's and not the landlord's obligation to make repairs. [   ]

Short of waste, a tenant may also make nonstructural alterations consistent with the use of the premises contemplated by his possession of them. [   ]

The ready removability of installations is a significant factor. * * *

In this perspective, it becomes apparent that in the case before us there was insufficient proof of any repair or alteration which could be characterized as one causing permanent or lasting injury to the premises. The apartment in issue remains a one-room studio. Its four walls are intact and remain in place. The closet and windowframe built by the tenant are merely nailed to and not built into the walls; there was no showing that either cannot be taken down and removed at minimal, if any, expense or damage. They are clearly consistent with the tenant's use of the apartment as a residence. The ceiling light fixture is a straight replacement of the old and unworkable one by a new and functioning equivalent; the addition of a modern wall switch could hardly have been more *de minimis*. The replacement for the defective ceiling itself, though, according to the parties' stipulation, not as thick as that required by the fire code, was of the required composition and, interestingly, no violation because of it had ever been issued by the city. More pointedly, the landlord made no showing whatsoever, whether by stipulation or otherwise, that the thickness of the falling ceiling which it replaced was any greater than the one of which it complained in this proceeding.

Significant too, especially on the question of the regulation's requirement that there be a showing of willfulness, is the fact that the tenant, though compelled to remedy the ceiling problem on his own and unaware that his choice of materials could be cause for complaint, upon learning that it was, offered to correct it. His offer, never withdrawn, was refused, the landlord insisting on nothing less than eviction.

We conclude, therefore, that, as a matter of law, the landlord did not establish that the tenant inflicted serious and substantial injury upon the landlord by willfully violating a substantial obligation of his tenancy. Accordingly, the order of the Appellate Division should be reversed and the petition dismissed.

COOKE, JUDGE (dissenting) [omitted.]

Notes and Questions

1. As noted in *Rumiche,* the concept of waste stems from the fact that landlord and tenant share contemporaneous property interests, as do the holders of life estates and remainders discussed in Chapter Two and the holders of concurrent interests discussed in Chapter Three. While the tenant

enjoys the benefits of present possession, she must respect the fact that the landlord expects to experience similar possessory enjoyment in the future—when the tenancy ends. In a sense, the tenant is a steward of the landlord's property. The modern doctrine of waste attempts to balance that stewardship responsibility with the recognition that physical changes to the leased property may be necessary to enable the tenant to use the property as intended. See, King's Court Racquetball v. T.E. Dawkins, 62 S.W.3d 229 (Tex. App. 2001) (gutting of building used for racquetball held waste and not exercise of contract right to "alter, reconstruct, rebuild and modify the premises without restriction"); e.g., Wingard v. Lee, 287 S.C. 57, 336 S.E.2d 498 (App.1985) (clear cutting of unimproved land covered with trees by tenant who had 25–year lease for development of mobile home park held reasonable use and not waste); Restatement (Second) of Property § 12.2(1) (1976) (tenant may change physical condition to extent necessary to permit reasonable use).

2. Many states regulate waste by statute, with remedies ranging from multiple damages (double or treble) to forfeiture of the lease. See Restatement (Second) of Property, Statutory Note to Section 12.2 (1976) for a review of the statutes.

3. Waste is a fact-specific doctrine. Courts use a multi-factor test to decide controversies involving allegations of waste, with the key factors being "the nature, purpose and duration of the tenancy; the character of the property; whether the acts complained of are related to the use and enjoyment of the property; whether the use is reasonable in the circumstances; and whether the acts complained of are reasonably necessary to effectuate such use." Wingard v. Lee, 287 S.C. 57, 336 S.E.2d 498, 500 (App.1985). For a well-known analysis of the waste multi-factor test in the life tenant-remainder setting, see Melms v. Pabst Brewing Co., 104 Wis. 7, 79 N.W. 738 (1899) (permitting family home to be demolished by life tenant because of "radical and permanent change in surrounding conditions" (industrial development)).

4. The Uniform Residential Landlord and Tenant Act allocates certain specific responsibilities to tenants, as noted in the following excerpts.

UNIFORM RESIDENTIAL LANDLORD AND TENANT ACT

§ 3.101. [Tenant to Maintain Dwelling Unit]

A tenant shall

(1) comply with all obligations primarily imposed upon tenants by applicable provisions of building and housing codes materially affecting health and safety;

(2) keep that part of the premises that he occupies and uses as clean and safe as the condition of the premises permit;

(3) dispose from his dwelling unit all ashes, garbage, rubbish, and other waste in a clean and safe manner;

(4) keep all plumbing fixtures in the dwelling unit or used by the tenant as clear as their condition permits;

(5) use in a reasonable manner all electrical, plumbing, sanitary, heating, ventilating, air-conditioning, and other facilities and appliances including elevators in the premises;

(6) not deliberately or negligently destroy, deface, damage, impair, or remove any part of the premises or knowingly permit any person to do so; and

(7) conduct himself and require other persons on the premises with his consent to conduct themselves in a manner that will not disturb his neighbors' peaceful enjoyment of the premises.

§ 3.102. [Rules and Regulations]

(a) A landlord, from time to time, may adopt a rule or regulation, however described, concerning the tenant's use and occupancy of the premises. It is enforceable against the tenant only if

(1) its purpose is to promote the convenience, safety, or welfare of the tenants in the premises, preserve the landlord's property from abusive use, or make a fair distribution of services and facilities held out for the tenants generally;

(2) it is reasonably related to the purpose of which it is adopted;

(3) it applies to all tenants in the premises in a fair manner;

(4) it is sufficiently explicit in its prohibition, direction, or limitation of the tenant's conduct to fairly inform him of what he must or must not do to comply;

(5) it is not for the purpose of evading the obligations of the landlord; and

(6) the tenant has notice of it at the time he enters into the rental agreement, or when it is adopted.

(b) If a rule or regulation is adopted after the tenant enters into the rental agreement that works a substantial modification of his bargain it is not valid unless the tenant consents to it in writing.

§ 3.103. [Access]

(a) A tenant shall not unreasonably withhold consent to the landlord to enter into the dwelling unit in order to inspect the premises, make necessary or agreed repairs, decorations, alterations, or improvements, supply necessary or agreed services, or exhibit the dwelling unit to prospective or actual purchasers, mortgagees, tenants, workmen, or contractors.

(b) A landlord may enter the dwelling unit without consent of the tenant in case of emergency.

(c) A landlord shall not abuse the right of access or use it to harass the tenant. Except in case of emergency or unless it is impracticable to do so, the landlord shall give the tenant at least [2] days' notice of his intent to enter and may enter only at reasonable times.

(d) A landlord has no other right of access except

    (1) pursuant to court order;

    (2) as permitted by Sections 4.202 and 4.203(b); or

    (3) unless the tenant has abandoned or surrendered the premises.

§ 3.104. [Tenant to Use and Occupy]

Unless otherwise agreed, a tenant shall occupy his dwelling unit only as a dwelling unit. The rental agreement may require that the tenant notify the landlord of any anticipated extended absence from the premises [in excess of [7] days] no later than the first day of the extended absence.

4. *Security Deposits*

Concerns over waste are one of the main reasons that landlords usually require tenants to pay security deposits.

W. STOEBUCK & D. WHITMAN, THE LAW OF PROPERTY, THIRD EDITION

367–370 (2000).

§ 6.59 Security and Damage Deposits

Presumably on the theory of "a bird in the hand," landlords frequently require their tenants to deposit a sum of money with them at the beginning of the term, to serve as security for the tenant's paying rent and performing other lease covenants. A specialized form of security deposit is the so-called "damage deposit," which the landlord holds to cover the cost of repairing physical damage or perhaps extraordinary cleaning costs caused by the tenant's acts. It is common for leases to require both deposits to secure rent and performance and to pay for damage. * * *

The first and most straightforward mechanism is for the tenant to deposit money or securities upon the understanding that the landlord may draw upon the fund to make up for the tenant's defaults or to pay for physical damage but that all sums not thus withdrawn will be returned to the tenant at the end of the term. Courts agree that the fund remains the tenant's property; for instance, with this kind of deposit, the landlord does not receive income for federal income tax purposes when the deposit is made but only if and when a breach occurs. There is disagreement, however, over the relationship between landlord and tenant with respect to the fund. Most courts consider the landlord to be the tenant's debtor. A few states, New Jersey notably, regard the parties as pledgor and pledgee. Under the creditor-debtor view or the pledgor-pledgee view, the landlord generally is not required to keep the deposit separate from his own funds or to pay interest on it unless, as in a number of jurisdictions, a statute imposes one or both duties. * * *

A second form of security clause is one that, on its face anyway, allows that landlord to retain the entire deposit if the tenant breaches in any way. This is in essence a liquidated damages mechanism. Questions about commingling, interest payment, federal income tax, and accounting should be resolved the same as for the deposit described in the preceding paragraph. A new issue is whether the provision for liquidated damages may be declared void on the ground that it calls for a penalty. Decided cases go both ways on this question. The correct approach, which seems to reconcile most of the decisions, is to begin with the principle that parties may agree for liquidated damages as long as the amount is "reasonable." * * *

The third form of security device, the prepayment of rent for the last period or periods of the term, is not truly a "deposit." When paid at the commencement of the term, the money is the landlord's absolute property. He is required to include it in that year's income for federal income tax purposes. Though it is probably not often done, because advance rent and a security deposit serve overlapping functions, there seems no reason the parties might not use both devices, which do not completely overlap. Apparently the main legal reason a landlord would want rent in advance for the latter part of the term is to avoid the common-law rule that if the landlord entered during the term because the lease authorized it for the tenant's breach, the landlord could not recover rent for the balance of the term. * * *

Statutes in most states affect, to a greater or lesser extent, what has been said thus far about security and damage deposits. Likewise, the Uniform Residential Landlord and Tenant Act and the Model Residential Landlord–Tenant Code regulate such deposits. * * *

Notes and Questions

1. Statutes typically require landlords to return security deposits within a specified period of time, usually 30 or 45 days, or provide tenants itemized lists in writing of claimed damages within that same time frame. Litigation under these statutes tends to focus on whether strict compliance or some lesser degree of compliance is required. See, e.g., Turley v. Hyten, 772 N.E.2d 993, 997 (Ind. 2002) (notice that tells tenant why landlord is keeping the security deposit sufficient. If the landlord believes that tenant damage amounts to more than the security deposit, can the landlord sue the tenant for such damages without first sending an itemized list of the alleged damages to the tenant? See Garcia v. Thong, 119 N.M. 704, 895 P.2d 226 (1995) (failure to provide itemized lists of damages causes landlord to forfeit right to file suit for damages).

2. Statutes that regulate security deposits require landlords to account in detail for the use of security deposits, within thirty to forty-five days of the time the tenant (a) leaves the premises and (b) gives the landlord an address to which to mail the accounting. A landlord who fails to act within the required time is vulnerable to a lawsuit for the security deposit and to paying the tenant's attorneys fees. Case law under the statute holds that

landlords are then also barred from recovering back rent or reimbursement for repairing damages. Here is how that can work, a moral tale one might call, On Keeping Your Head Down in the Legal Aid Office (Tom Shaffer):[21]

In comes a single mom who has a minimum-wage job and three small children. She has been told that her leasehold is ended for failure to pay rent on time and for extensive damage to the apartment she has been renting. I have to tell her that she is vulnerable to judicial eviction, which will take only about a week; Indiana eviction law has tight notice requirements. I also tell her that her complaints that the windows are broken and the upstairs toilet leaks through the floor are not defenses to eviction, nor to liability for at least some of the rent; that she can call the local code enforcement office if she wants, but that any actions it takes cannot keep her in the apartment; and that her best course of action is to locate another place to live and let me bargain a little time from the landlord for her to move her children and her furniture.

That's the bad news. The good news (believe it or not) is maybe that the damages issue is not as bad as it looks, even though the landlord can probably demonstrate liability for damages of a couple of thousand dollars, and liability for unpaid rent of another thousand–say three thousand dollars altogether. If the landlord gets a judgment for these amounts, our client is vulnerable to the loss of her five-hundred dollar security deposit, and to garnishment on her wages, for, say, three thousand dollars plus attorney fees, interest, and costs.

The good news on the bad news is the possibility that she can avoid these liabilities by giving the landlord her new address when she moves, and then keeping her head down for forty-five days. The landlord may fail, for forty-five days, to account on the security deposit, or he may give her an inadequate accounting. But even if he is able to keep the security deposit, it would cover only a fourth or a fifth of his claim, and so he is seeking a judgment for the whole three thousand, and can then, he might think, just deduct the security deposit, which he already has, from the amount of the judgment (plus attorneys fees, interest, and costs). Meanwhile, the clock is ticking toward forty-five days and my well-advised client, who moved after I got an extra week of time for her, and who gave the landlord a new address when she moved, is keeping her head down. She did not tell the landlord why she gave him her new address.

If the landlord does not provide an accounting, or if he provides an inadequate accounting, we can, in the damages hearing, defeat his three thousand dollar claim (and his claim for attorneys fees, interest, and costs), recover the security deposit, and get an order for our fees to help the legal-aid clinic with its expenses. The result we would shoot for is, for example, a six thousand dollar judgment for the tenant, against the landlord, and a judgment of zero for the landlord against the tenant. If, as is unlikely, the landlord has not filed for damages, my client can file her own action, waiting to file until after the forty-five days passes. If the landlord has filed for

---

21. From Thomas L. Shaffer, "Using the Pervasive Method of Teaching Legal Ethics in a Property Course," 46 St. Louis University Law Journal 655, 661–664 (2002). Shaffer, retired from the Notre Dame Law Faculty, is a supervising attorney in the Notre Dame Legal Aid Clinic, in South Bend, Indiana.

damages, but has not accounted for his use of the security deposit, and the hearing date is within forty-five days, I could file for and probably get a continuance, without disclosing why I want more time.

This strategy works, in my experience, more often than one might think. The key to it is to keep our heads down and not let the landlord know what we have in mind. We say nothing about damages or the security deposit when we bargain for the time for her to move out of the apartment; we say nothing about the merits when we seek a continuance on the damages hearing, if we have to do that; and our client says nothing at all when landlord and tenant run into one another at the supermarket.

Moral issue: Would this be fair? Should a lawyer who has been hardened toward landlords by years of helping low-income tenants and the victims of a hundred kinds of creditor oppression even ask that question? What should the lawyer say if his client asks the moral question? How about the fact that mom-and-pop landlords are often as low on the wealth scale as tenants are, and are not represented by lawyers who do not charge fees? If these questions, or some of them, are asked, and the client, a thoughtful and honorable person says, "Go ahead," does the lawyer still have a moral problem? I confess that I have not asked the is-this-fair question and, if my client asked the question, heard my ambivalent answer, and then said, "Go ahead," I have gone ahead.

Lurking in the moral discussion is an important agenda for property-law lawyers, and that, put with an academic cast, is the agenda of social justice—how much (as a left-leaning teacher might think of it) of property law, and especially landlord-tenant law, serves the ruling class and how little of it has to do with decent housing for low-income people? That question can be put in legal-ethics terms, and may be different when taken up that way: Is a lawyer for poor people entitled to a special ethic? That is, if I were representing landlords, would I do anything this sneaky? Would I advise my landlord-client to do anything this sneaky? Does either answer, if "no," preclude a different answer when my client is a tenant? A colleague pondered these questions on sneakiness and said: "It's not any more 'sneaky' than dozens of pro-landlord laws that tenants become aware of only after they suffer because of them."

D. PUBLIC REGULATION OF THE RESPONSIBILITIES FOR LEASED PREMISES

1. *Statutory Responsibilities*

Statutes in a number of states have codified landlord and tenant responsibilities for conditions of the premises, generally following the implied warranty of habitability. The best known statute, the Uniform Residential Landlord and Tenant Act (URLTA), contains the following provisions.

UNIFORM RESIDENTIAL LANDLORD AND TENANT ACT

§ 2.104 [Landlord to Maintain Premises]

(a) A landlord shall

(1) comply with the requirements of applicable building and housing codes materially affecting health and safety;

(2) make all repairs and do whatever is necessary to put and keep the premises in a fit and habitable condition;

(3) keep all common areas of the premises in a clean and safe condition;

(4) maintain in good and safe working order and condition all electrical, plumbing, sanitary, heating, ventilating, air-conditioning, and other facilities and appliances, including elevators, supplied or required to be supplied by him;

(5) provide and maintain appropriate receptacles and conveniences for the removal of ashes, garbage, rubbish, and other waste incidental to the occupancy of the dwelling unit and arrange for their removal; and

(6) supply running water and reasonable amounts of hot water at all times and reasonable heat [between [October 1] and [May 1]] except where the building that includes the dwelling unit is not required by law to be equipped for that purpose, or the dwelling unit is so constructed that heat or hot water is generated by an installation within the exclusive control of the tenant and supplied by a direct public utility connection.

(b) If the duty imposed by paragraph (1) of subsection (a) is greater than any duty imposed by any other paragraph of that subsection, the landlord's duty shall be determined by reference to paragraph (1) of subsection (a).

(c) The landlord and tenant of a single family residence may agree in writing that the tenant perform the landlord's duties specified in paragraphs (5) and (6) of subsection (a) and also specified repairs, maintenance tasks, alterations, and remodeling, but only if the transaction is entered into in good faith.

(d) The landlord and tenant of any dwelling unit other than a single family residence may agree that the tenant is to perform specified repairs, maintenance tasks, alterations, or remodeling only if

(1) the agreement of the parties is entered into in good faith and is set forth in a separate writing signed by the parties and supported by adequate consideration;

(2) the work is not necessary to cure noncompliance with subsection (a)(1) of this section; and

(3) the agreement does not diminish or affect the obligation of the landlord to other tenants in the premises.

(e) The landlord may not treat performance of the separate agreement described in subsection (d) as a condition to any obligation or performance of any rental agreement.

———

The Wisconsin statute is another example of codification of the implied warranty of habitability.

WISCONSIN STATUTES ANNOTATED

§ 704.07 Repairs; untenantability

(1) Application of section. This section applies to any nonresidential tenancy if there is no contrary provision in writing signed by both parties and to all residential tenancies. An agreement to waive the requirements of this section in a residential tenancy is void. Nothing in this section is intended to affect rights and duties arising under other provisions of the statutes.

(2) Duty of landlord. (a) Except for repairs made necessary by the negligence or improper use of the premises by, the tenant, the landlord has a duty do all of the following:

    1.   Keep in reasonable state of repair portions of the premises over which the landlord maintains control;

    2.   Keep in a reasonable state of repair all equipment under the landlord's control necessary to supply services that the landlord has expressly or impliedly agreed to furnish to the tenant, such as heat, water, elevator or air-conditioning;

    3.   Make all necessary structural repairs;

    4.   Except for residential premises subject to a local housing code, and except as provided in sub. (3)(b), repair or replace any plumbing, electrical wiring, machinery, or equipment furnished with the premises and no longer in reasonable working condition ..

    5.   For a residential tenancy, comply with any local housing code applicable to the premises.

(b) If the premises are part of a building, other parts of which are occupied by one or more other tenants, negligence or improper use by one tenant does not relieve the landlord from the landlord's duty as to the other tenants to make repairs as provided in par. (a).

(c) If the premises are damaged by fire, water or other casualty, not the result of the negligence or intentional act of the landlord, this subsection is inapplicable and either sub. (3) or (4) governs.

(3) Duty of tenant. (a) If the premises are damaged by the negligence or improper use of the premises by the tenant, the tenant must repair the damage and restore the appearance of the premises by redecorating. However, the landlord may elect to undertake the repairs or redecoration, and in such case the tenant must reimburse the landlord for the reasonable cost thereof; the cost to the landlord is presumed reasonable unless proved otherwise by the tenant.

(b) Except for residential premises subject to a local housing code, the tenant is also under a duty to keep plumbing, electrical wiring, machinery and equipment furnished with the premises in reasonable working order if repair can be made at cost which is minor in relation to the rent.

(c) A tenant in a residential tenancy shall comply with a local housing code applicable to the premises.

(4) Untenantability. If the premises become untenantable because of damage by fire, water or other casualty or because of any condition hazardous to health, or if there is a substantial violation of sub. (2) materially affecting the health or safety of the tenant, the tenant may remove from the premises unless the landlord proceeds promptly to repair or rebuild or eliminate the health hazard or the substantial violation of sub. (2) materially affecting the health or safety of the tenant; or the tenant may remove if the inconvenience to the tenant by reason of the nature and period of repair, rebuilding or elimination would impose undue hardship on him. If the tenant remains in possession, rent abates to the extent the tenant is deprived of the full normal use of the premises. This section does not authorize rent to be withheld in full, if the tenant remains in possession. If the tenant justifiably moves out under this subsection, the tenant is not liable for rent after the premises become untenantable and the landlord must repay any rent paid in advance apportioned to the period after the premises become untenantable. This subsection is inapplicable if the damage or condition is caused by negligence or improper use by the tenant.

CHICAGO BOARD OF REALTORS
v. CITY OF CHICAGO

United States Court of Appeals, Seventh Circuit, 1987.
819 F.2d 732.

CUDAHY, CIRCUIT JUDGE.

On September 8, 1986, the Chicago City Council enacted the Chicago Residential Landlord and Tenant Ordinance (the "Ordinance"), Municipal Code of Chicago, ch. 193.1 (repealing § 193.11), recasting the relative rights and obligations of most residential landlords and tenants in Chicago. On October 14, 1986, the day before the Ordinance was to become effective, this lawsuit began. Plaintiffs-appellants are Chicago property owners or managers and organizations representing their interests. Defendants-appellees are the City of Chicago and its Mayor. Also before the court are three individual tenants and nine organizations representing Chicago tenants. Plaintiffs challenged the constitutionality of the Ordinance and sought a temporary restraining order and a preliminary injunction to prevent its enforcement. A TRO was issued on October 14. On November 3, 1986, the district court denied the preliminary injunction and dissolved the TRO, pending plaintiffs' immediate interlocutory appeal. We granted an expedited appeal schedule but denied plaintiffs' emergency motion for a stay and an injunction pending appeal. We now affirm the district court's denial of plaintiffs' motion for a preliminary injunction.

I. The Ordinance

The Ordinance, by its own terms, was passed by the Chicago City Council:

> in order to protect and promote the public health, safety and welfare of its citizens, to establish the rights and obligations of the landlord and the tenant in the rental of dwelling units, and to encourage the landlord and the tenant to maintain and improve the quality of housing.

Ordinance, § 193.1–1. By its terms the Ordinance applies to all rental agreements for dwelling units located in Chicago, with exceptions for owner-occupied buildings of six or fewer units; dwelling units in hotels, motels, boarding houses and the like; accommodations in hospitals, not-for-profit shelters and school dormitories; and units in cooperatives occupied by holders of proprietary leases. [ ] The Ordinance governs leases either entered into or to be performed after October 15, 1986.

Landlords are required to maintain dwelling units in compliance with all applicable municipal code provisions and with certain other specified standards. [ ]

Landlords have the authority, after notice to the tenant, to terminate a lease if the tenant fails to pay rent or otherwise comply with lease requirements. If the landlord accepts the full rent due under a lease knowing that payments are in default, the landlord thereby waives the right to terminate the lease for that default.

[ ] Except in case of emergency, the landlord must provide notice two days before entering a unit for maintenance, repairs or inspections. [ ]

After notice to the landlord, tenants are granted authority to withhold rent in an amount reflecting the reasonable value of any material noncompliance with the lease by the landlord. Alternatively, tenants can, again after notice, opt to repair certain minor defects or deficiencies and deduct their reasonable cost from the rent.

[ ] Tenants are required to keep their units clean and safe, to use appliances and utilities in a reasonable manner and to avoid disturbing neighbors' "peaceful enjoyment of the premises."

The Ordinance prohibits a charge greater than ten dollars per month for late payment of rent. [ ] In addition, all security deposits received after January 1, 1987 must be maintained in a federally insured account in a financial institution located in Illinois. * * *

A. The Contract Clause

The Constitution prohibits a state from passing "any * * * law impairing the Obligation of Contract," U.S. Const. art. I, § 10, cl. 1. The plaintiffs contend that the Ordinance violates this provision by destroying pre-existing contractual rights and bargained-for expectations contained in leases entered into before October 15, 1986. Despite the mandatory language of the contract clause, however, the Supreme Court has repeatedly affirmed that the clause does not abrogate a state's inherent power to protect the interests of its citizens. * * *

The extent of this prior regulation [of the landlord-tenant relationship] suggests that the Ordinance in fact might not substantially impair any contract obligations. [   ]

At the least, prior regulation dictates a lowered level of scrutiny.

With a relaxed level of scrutiny, then, we ask whether legitimate and significant purposes support the Ordinance and the contractual impairments that it works. The plaintiffs suggest that the actual purpose behind the Ordinance is simply to "provide[   ] one group with an economic advantage over another group," [   ] rather than to protect the public health or welfare. Of course, regulatory legislation may frequently tip the economic scales but at the same time serve entirely legitimate purposes. The expressed purpose of the Ordinance is to promote public health and welfare by improving the quality of housing in the city. The city apparently concluded that this purpose could be furthered by enacting the Ordinance and redefining some rights and obligations for landlords and tenants. On the record before us, we cannot say that the Ordinance is without a legitimate and significant public purpose. * * *

In any event, and certainly without passing judgment on its advisability, we believe that the Ordinance may represent a rational allocation of rights and responsibilities between landlords and tenants. This is an allocation that the city rationally could have believed would lead to improved public health and welfare.

Accordingly, we agree with the district court that the plaintiffs did not show a reasonable probability of prevailing on their contract clause claim. We have found no case, and none has been cited to us, in which a similar landlord-tenant law has been found unconstitutional under the contract clause. The plaintiffs have failed to present persuasive reasons why the present Ordinance should not similarly pass muster.

B. Procedural Due Process

The plaintiffs assert that the Ordinance deprives them of protected property rights without procedural due process as guaranteed by the fourteenth amendment. The essence of this argument seems to be that the Ordinance is unconstitutional because it delegates to tenants—inherently biased decisionmakers—a broad discretion to withhold rent while retaining possession of a landlord's property. [   ]

The first step in this inquiry, of course, is to determine what, if any, state action exists. We are not convinced that actions taken by tenants, pursuant to the Ordinance, comprise state action. A law that defines rights, obligations or remedies among private parties does not thereby transform every private enforcement of that law into state action. [ ] The Supreme Court considered the issue of what action by a private citizen constitutes state action in *Flagg Brothers, Inc. v. Brooks,* 436 U.S. 149, 98 S.Ct. 1729, 56 L.Ed.2d 185 (1978), where the Court held that a warehouseman's forced sale of a debtor's goods, pursuant to New York law, was not state action, because by merely delegating a power to resolve disputes, New York had not delegated any "exclusive public function." *Id.* at 161, 98 S.Ct. at 1739. To the extent that the Ordinance shifts from the landlord to the tenant the power initially to determine whether the premises are in accordance with the lease terms (and with municipal standards embodied in the terms), the Ordinance has readjusted property rights. But this is not a delegation of an exclusive public function; it does not import state action into every action a tenant or landlord might take. We believe that neither a landlord's unlawful lockout of a tenant nor a tenant's unlawful withholding of rent from a landlord would of itself involve state action.

[ ] This analysis does not end the matter, however, because the plaintiffs charge that the Ordinance itself, enacted by the City, works a deprivation of protected property rights.

The enactment of the Ordinance itself undoubtedly represents state action. The Ordinance, however, does not deprive the plaintiffs of rights in property without due process. The plaintiffs' strongest argument is that the Ordinance provides inadequate post-deprivation remedies by which a landlord can challenge rent withholdings and regain possession. But the Ordinance does not significantly alter the preexisting post-deprivation remedy, the Illinois Forcible Entry and Detainer Act, Ill.Rev. Stat. ch. 110, ¶ 9–101 *et seq.* Plaintiffs have not shown that the Forcible Entry and Detainer Act is an unconstitutionally slow or onerous procedure. [ ] If the Ordinance had established a new post-deprivation procedure by which, for instance, a landlord could not recover possession for five years after a rent default, the plaintiffs would have a much stronger case.

The Ordinance prohibits a late payment penalty exceeding $10 per month. This undoubtedly will cost some landlords some money. But a law that imposes heavier economic burdens on some group of citizens is not thereby rendered unconstitutional. The procedure the landlords were due in this respect was accorded them—in the legislature. [ ]

In addition, the Ordinance requires that landlords attach a copy of the Ordinance to each lease. It is inconceivable that this violates procedural due process.

We conclude that the Ordinance simply readjusts the balance in the long-standing landlord-tenant relationship. Nothing suggests that the Ordinance itself works a deprivation of property without procedural due process. Rather, the Ordinance appears merely to shift some bargaining power to the tenant. This in itself does not violate procedural due process. [ ] * * *

[The Court's discussion of void-for-vagueness, substantive due process, equal protection and preemption is omitted.—Eds.]

The judgment of the district court is Affirmed.

POSNER, CIRCUIT JUDGE, with whom EASTERBROOK, CIRCUIT JUDGE, joins.

We agree with Judge Cudahy's opinion as far as it goes, and we therefore join it. But in our view it does not go far enough. It makes the rejection of the appeal seem easier than it is, by refusing to acknowledge the strong case that can be made for the unreasonableness of the ordinance. It does not explain how the district judge's denial of a preliminary injunction against such an interference with contract rights and economic freedom can be affirmed without violating the contract clause and the due process clause of the Constitution. So we are led to write separately, and since this separate opinion commands the support of two members of this panel, it is also a majority opinion.

The new ordinance rewrites present and future leases of apartments in Chicago to give tenants more legal rights than they would have without the ordinance. It requires the payment of interest on security deposits; requires that those deposits be held in Illinois banks; allows (with some limitations) a tenant to withhold rent in an amount reflecting the cost to him of the landlord's violating a term in the lease; allows a tenant to make minor repairs and subtract the reasonable cost of the repair from his rent; forbids a landlord to charge a tenant more than $10 a month for late payment of rent (regardless of how much is owing); and creates a presumption (albeit rebuttable) that a landlord who seeks to evict a tenant after the tenant has exercised rights conferred by the ordinance is retaliating against the tenant for the exercise of those rights.

The stated purpose of the ordinance is to promote public health, safety, and welfare and the quality of housing in Chicago. It is unlikely that this is the real purpose, and it is not the likely effect. Forbidding landlords to charge interest at market rates on late payment of rent could hardly be thought calculated to improve the health, safety, and welfare of Chicagoans or to improve the quality of the housing stock. But it may have the opposite effect. The initial consequence of the rule will be to reduce the resources that landlords devote to improving the quality of housing, by making the provision of rental housing more costly. Landlords will try to offset the higher cost (in time value of money, less predictable cash flow, and, probably, higher rate of default) by raising rents. To the extent they succeed, tenants will be worse off, or at least no better off. Landlords will also screen applicants more carefully, because the cost of renting to a deadbeat will now be higher; so marginal tenants will find it harder to persuade landlords to rent to them. Those who do find apartments but then are slow to pay will be subsidized by responsible tenants (some of them marginal too), who will be paying higher rents, assuming the landlord cannot determine in advance who is likely to pay rent on time. Insofar as these efforts to offset the ordinance fail, the cost of rental housing will be higher to landlords and therefore less will be supplied—more of the existing stock than would otherwise be the case will be converted to condominia and cooperatives and less rental housing will be built.

The provisions of the ordinance requiring that interest on security deposits be paid and that those deposits be kept in Illinois banks are as remote as the provision on late payment from any concern with the health or safety of Chicagoans, the quality of housing in Chicago, or the welfare of Chicago as a whole. Their only apparent rationale is to transfer wealth from landlords and out-of-state banks to tenants and local banks—making this an unedifying example of class legislation and economic protectionism rolled into one. However, to the extent the ordinance seeks to transfer wealth from landlords to tenants it could readily be undone by a rent increase; the ordinance puts no cap on rents. Cf. Coase, *The Problem of Social Cost,* 3 J.Law & Econ. 1 (1960).

The provisions that authorize rent withholding, whether directly or by subtracting repair costs, may seem more closely related to the stated objectives of the ordinance; but the relation is tenuous. The right to withhold rent is not limited to cases of hazardous or unhealthy conditions. And any benefits in safer or healthier housing from exercise of the right are likely to be offset by the higher costs to landlords, resulting in higher rents and less rental housing.

The ordinance is not in the interest of poor people. As is frequently the case with legislation ostensibly designed to promote the welfare of the poor, the principal beneficiaries will be middle-class people. They will be people who buy rather than rent housing (the conversion of rental to owner housing will reduce the price of the latter by increasing its supply); people willing to pay a higher rental for better-quality housing; and (a largely overlapping group) more affluent tenants, who will become more attractive to landlords because such tenants are less likely to be late with the rent or to abuse the right of withholding rent—a right that is more attractive, the poorer the tenant. The losers from the ordinance will be some landlords, some out-of-state banks, the poorest class of tenants, and future tenants. The landlords are few in number (once owner-occupied rental housing is excluded—and the ordinance excludes it). Out-of-staters can't vote in Chicago elections. Poor people in our society don't vote as often as the affluent. See Filer, An Economic Theory of Voter Turnout 81 (Ph.D. thesis, Dept. of Econ., Univ. of Chi., Dec. 1977); Statistical Abstract of the U.S., 1982–83, at pp. 492–93 (tabs. 805, 806). And future tenants are a diffuse and largely unknown class. In contrast, the beneficiaries of the ordinance are the most influential group in the city's population. So the politics of the ordinance are plain enough, cf. DeCanio, *Rent Control Voting Patterns, Popular Views, and Group Interests,* in Resolving the Housing Crisis 301, 311–12 (Johnson ed. 1982), and they have nothing to do with either improving the allocation of resources to housing or bringing about a more equal distribution of income and wealth.

A growing body of empirical literature deals with the effects of governmental regulation of the market for rental housing. The regulations that have been studied, such as rent control in New York City and Los Angeles, are not identical to the new Chicago ordinance, though some—regulations which require that rental housing be "habitable"— are close. The significance of this literature is not in proving that the Chicago ordinance is unsound, but in showing that the market for rental housing behaves as economic theory predicts: if price is artificially depressed, or the costs of landlords artificially increased, supply falls and many tenants, usually the poorer and the newer tenants, are hurt. See, e.g., Olsen, *An Econometric Analysis of Rent Control*, 80 J.Pol.Econ. 1081 (1972); Rydell et al., The Impact of Rent Control on the Los Angeles Housing Market, ch. 6 (Rand Corp. N–1747–LA, Aug. 1981); Hirsch, *Habitability Laws and the Welfare of Indigent Tenants*, 61 Rev.Econ. & Stat. 263 (1981). The single proposition in economics from which there is the least dissent among American economists is that "a ceiling on rents reduces the quantity and quality of housing available." Frey et al., *Consensus and Dissension Among Economists: An Empirical Inquiry*, 74 Am.Econ.Rev. 986, 991 (1984) (tab. 2).

Article I, § 10, cl. 1 of the Constitution—the "contract clause"— forbids a state to pass "any * * * Law impairing the Obligation of Contracts." If the contract clause were taken seriously, the Chicago ordinance, to the extent it modifies existing leases as well as prescribing terms for future ones, would certainly violate the clause. And even though the clause isn't taken very seriously nowadays by those whose views matter the most (Justices of the Supreme Court), the plaintiffs may conceivably be able to prove a violation when the case is tried on the merits. No one argues that the ordinance is not a "law" for purposes of the contract clause or that a lease is not a contract, and no one could doubt that the ordinance impairs the contractual obligations of the tenants: abrogating an obligation impairs the obligation. One might suppose, by analogy to the just-compensation clause, that the hardest cases under the contract clause would be those where the state, without actually abrogating a contract in whole or part, did something that made a person's contractual rights much less valuable. [ ]

This is not such a case. The ordinance transfers contractual entitlements from the party on one side of the contract to the party on the other side.

The Supreme Court, however, has rewritten the contract clause, by inserting the word "unreasonably" before "impairing" and by adopting a radically undemanding definition of "reasonableness." * * *

At all events it is clear that the plaintiffs in this case have an extremely uphill battle against the ordinance on contract clause grounds, [ ] a battle they cannot possibly win on the basis of the evidence they presented in seeking a preliminary injunction. An even stronger conclusion is possible with regard to their challenge on the ground of "substantive due process." The due process clauses of the Fifth and Fourteenth

Amendments forbid government to deprive a person of life, liberty, or property without due *process* of law; and if due process is accorded, it is very hard to see how the person can complain about the *substance* of the government's action. So the text is inhospitable to the concept of "substantive due process"; nor does the history of the Constitution support it.

* * *

The plaintiffs have brought their case in the wrong era. Chicago's new ordinance indeed strikes at the heart of freedom of contract, but the Supreme Court's current conception of substantive due process does not embrace freedom of contract; a provision once questionably interpreted to guarantee economic freedom is now questionably interpreted to guarantee sexual and reproductive freedom instead. The Court is not about to cut the welfare state down to size by invalidating unreasonable economic regulation such as the ordinance under attack in this case. [ ] Thus it is clear that the Chicago ordinance does not deny "substantive due process," though not because it is a reasonable ordinance, which it is not.

Clearly, if reasonableness means the same thing in applying the contract clause as in applying the due process clause, the plaintiffs' claim of impairment of contract is also doomed, no matter what evidence they put in at the trial on the merits. Maybe, though, * * * it is a somewhat more demanding requirement in the former than in the latter setting. * * *

Notes and Questions

1. Although concurring in the decision, Judge Posner criticized the Chicago ordinance based on the economic theory that artificial depression of prices (e.g., through public regulation of rents) or increases in costs (e.g., through public imposition of higher standards of quality) will cause the supply of affordable housing to fall. Most ordinances regulating rents also restrict the ability of landlords to refuse to renew tenancies so long as tenants are paying the controlled rent and abiding by reasonable rules and regulations. Landlords often argue that these provisions amount to an illegal taking of their power to exclude, discussed in Chapter One, without payment of just compensation, discussed in Chapter Seven. The results have been mixed. See Yee v. City of Escondido, 503 U.S. 519, 112 S.Ct. 1522, 118 L.Ed.2d 153 (1992); Pennell v. City of San Jose, 485 U.S. 1, 108 S.Ct. 849, 99 L.Ed.2d 1 (1988) (taking issue held premature); Pinewood Estates of Michigan v. Barnegat Township Leveling Board, 898 F.2d 347 (3d Cir.1990) (illegal taking of power to exclude by owners of mobile home park); Troy Ltd. v. Renna, 727 F.2d 287 (3d Cir.1984) (no taking resulted from law prohibiting conversion of apartments occupied by elderly and disabled into condominiums).

Should the landlord's power to exclude outweigh a tenant's "right to shelter (tenure)" in a situation where the landlord wishes to convert occupied apartments to condominiums for wealthier persons? Would your answer be different if the building in question was a dilapidated, unoccupied, single room occupancy hotel that the city believes can provide housing for homeless persons? See Seawall Associates v. City of New York, 74 N.Y.2d 92, 544 N.Y.S.2d 542, 542 N.E.2d 1059 (1989), cert. den., 493 U.S. 976, 110 S.Ct. 500, 107 L.Ed.2d 503 (1989) (requirement that owners of SROs restore units and offer them at controlled rents held a taking requiring compensation). Do the selections in Chapter One from different perspectives on the concept of property help in answering these questions?

2.   A number of studies, some cited by Judge Posner, have found that low income tenants often are not represented by lawyers and thus do not raise available defenses to eviction actions. In addition, these studies have found that often little or no positive improvement in housing quality results when warranty of habitability issues are raised by low income tenants, primarily because of the inability of such tenants to pay the fair rental value of housing that has been brought up to warranty quality. If these findings are true, should tenant-protective changes continue to be supported without a corresponding willingness to publicly subsidize land owners who are willing to rent to low income families?

3.   What if a tenant was aware of habitability standards but was willing to accept an apartment "as is" because of a lower rent? Is the warranty available under URLTA? The Wisconsin statute? Should it be? Suppose a landlord cannot meet habitability standards and still make a profit on investment in residential rental housing because required repairs are too costly or persons who would consider renting the apartments would not or could not pay the rent the landlord would have to charge to recover the costs of repairs. What is a landlord is this situation likely to do? Should the parties be able to bargain for a lower standard of quality?

4.   Are the statutory standards broader or narrower than the standard adopted by Judge Wright in *Javins*? Who is better able to define an inherently vague term such as habitability, the judiciary or the legislature? Are the legislative definitions based on notions of a *contract* between a residential landlord and a residential tenant, as Judge Wright envisioned his definition, or is it based on what the legislature believes the *status* of residential landlord and residential tenant should mean? Cf. Cunningham, The New Implied and Statutory Warranties of Habitability in Residential Leases: From Contract to Status, 16 Urb.L.Ann. 3 (1979).

5.   Statutes codifying the implied warranty of habitability can have important implications for third parties providing services to occupants of leased premises. Note that Sec. 2.104(a)(6) of URLTA requires the landlord to supply running water. Suppose the landlord does not pay a water bill to the city supplying water service to the leased property. Is the city required to give tenant reasonable notice before shutting off the water? See Turpen v. Corvallis, 26 F.3d 978 (9th Cir. 1994), cert. den., 513 U.S. 963, 115 S.Ct. 426, 130 L.Ed.2d 339 (1994) (failure to give notice of pending water shut off to tenants deprived them of property interest in statutory cause of action for injunctive relief against landlord without due process). But cf. Golden v. City of Columbus, 404 F.3d 950 (6th Cir. 2005) (tenant had no constitutionally protected property right to water service which was shut off because prior

tenant had left an unpaid bill); James v. City of St. Petersburg, 33 F.3d 1304 (11th Cir.1994) (no constitutionally protected property right to continued water service).

2. *Retaliatory Eviction*

EDWARDS v. HABIB

United States Court of Appeals, District of Columbia Circuit, 1968.
397 F.2d 687, cert. den., 393 U.S. 1016, 89 S.Ct. 618, 21 L.Ed.2d 560 (1969).

J. SKELLY WRIGHT, CIRCUIT JUDGE:

In March 1965 the appellant, Mrs. Yvonne Edwards, rented housing property from the appellee, Nathan Habib, on a month-to-month basis. Shortly thereafter she complained to the Department of Licenses and Inspections of sanitary code violations which her landlord had failed to remedy. In the course of the ensuing inspection, more than 40 such violations were discovered which the Department ordered the landlord to correct. Habib then gave Mrs. Edwards a 30–day statutory notice to vacate and obtained a default judgment for possession of the premises. Mrs. Edwards promptly moved to reopen this judgment, alleging excusable neglect for the default and also alleging as a defense that the notice to quit was given in retaliation for her complaints to the housing authorities. Judge Greene, sitting on motions in the Court of General Sessions, set aside the default judgment and, in a very thoughtful opinion, concluded that a retaliatory motive, if proved, would constitute a defense to the action for possession. At the trial itself, however, a different judge apparently deemed evidence of retaliatory motive irrelevant and directed a verdict for the landlord.

Mrs. Edwards then appealed to this court for a stay pending her appeal to the District of Columbia Court of Appeals, and on December 3, 1965, we granted the stay, provided only that Mrs. Edwards continue to pay her rent. [ ] She then appealed to the DCCA, which affirmed the judgment of the trial court. [ ] In reaching its decision the DCCA relied on a series of its earlier decisions holding that a private landlord was not required, under the District of Columbia Code, to give a reason for evicting a month-to-month tenant and was free to do so for any reason or for no reason at all. The court acknowledged that the landlord's right to terminate a tenancy is not absolute, but felt that any limitation on his prerogative had to be based on specific statutes or very special circumstances. Here, the court concluded, the tenant's right to report violations of law and to petition for redress of grievances was not protected by specific legislation and that any change in the relative rights of tenants and landlords should be undertaken by the legislature, not the courts. We granted appellant leave to appeal that decision to this court. We hold that the promulgation of the housing code by the District of Columbia Commissioners at the direction of Congress impliedly effected just such a change in the relative rights of landlords and tenants and that proof of a retaliatory motive does constitute a defense to an action of eviction.

Accordingly, we reverse the decision of the DCCA with directions that it remand to the Court of General Sessions for a new trial where Mrs. Edwards will be permitted to try to prove to a jury that her landlord who seeks to evict her harbors a retaliatory intent.

* * *

[Discussion of constitutional issues that were not decided is omitted.— Eds.]

III

* * *

45 D.C.Code § 910, in pertinent part, provides:

"Whenever * * * any tenancy shall be terminated by notice as aforesaid [ ], and the tenant shall fail or refuse to surrender possession of the leased premises, * * * the landlord may bring an action to recover possession before the District of Columbia Court of General Sessions, as provided in sections 11–701 to 11–749."

And 16 D.C.Code § 1501, in pertinent part, provides:

"When a person detains possession of real property * * * after his right to possession has ceased, the District of Columbia Court of General Sessions * * * may issue a summons to the party complained of to appear and show cause why judgment should not be given against him for restitution of possession."

These provisions are simply procedural. They neither say nor imply anything about whether evidence of retaliation or other improper motive should be unavailable as a defense to a possessory action brought under them. It is true that in making his affirmative case for possession the landlord need only show that his tenant has been given the 30–day statutory notice, and he need not assign any reason for evicting a tenant who does not occupy the premises under a lease. But while the landlord may evict for any legal reason or for no reason at all, he is not, we hold, free to evict in retaliation for his tenant's report of housing code violations to the authorities. As a matter of statutory construction and for reasons of public policy, such an eviction cannot be permitted.

The housing and sanitary codes, especially in light of Congress' explicit direction for their enactment, indicate a strong and pervasive congressional concern to secure for the city's slum dwellers decent, or at least safe and sanitary, places to live. Effective implementation and enforcement of the codes obviously depend in part on private initiative in the reporting of violations. Though there is no official procedure for the filing of such complaints, the bureaucratic structure of the Department of Licenses and Inspections establishes such a procedure, and for fiscal year 1966 nearly a third of the cases handled by the Department arose from private complaints. To permit retaliatory evictions, then, would clearly frustrate the effectiveness of the housing code as a means of upgrading the quality of housing in Washington.

As judges, "we cannot shut our eyes to matters of public notoriety and general cognizance. When we take our seats on the bench we are not struck with blindness, and forbidden to know as judges what we see as men." Ho Ah Kow v. Nunan, C.C.D.Cal., 12 Fed.Cas. 252, 255 (No. 6546) (1879). In trying to effect the will of Congress and as a court of equity we have the responsibility to consider the social context in which our decisions will have operational effect. In light of the appalling condition and shortage of housing in Washington, the expense of moving, the inequality of bargaining power between tenant and landlord, and the social and economic importance of assuring at least minimum standards in housing conditions, we do not hesitate to declare that retaliatory eviction cannot be tolerated. There can be no doubt that the slum dweller, even though his home be marred by housing code violations, will pause long before he complains of them if he fears eviction as a consequence. Hence an eviction under the circumstances of this case would not only punish appellant for making a complaint which she had a constitutional right to make, a result which we would not impute to the will of Congress simply on the basis of an essentially procedural enactment, but also would stand as a warning to others that they dare not be so bold, a result which, from the authorization of the housing code, we think Congress affirmatively sought to avoid.

The notion that the effectiveness of remedial legislation will be inhibited if those reporting violations of it can legally be intimidated is so fundamental that a presumption against the legality of such intimidation can be inferred as inherent in the legislation even if it is not expressed in the statute itself. Such an inference was recently drawn by the Supreme Court from the federal labor statutes to strike down under the supremacy clause a Florida statute denying unemployment insurance to workers discharged in retaliation for filing complaints of federally defined unfair labor practices. While we are not confronted with a possible conflict between federal policy and state law, we do have the task of reconciling and harmonizing two federal statutes so as to best effectuate the purposes of each. The proper balance can only be struck by interpreting 45 D.C.Code §§ 902 and 910 as inapplicable where the court's aid is invoked to effect an eviction in retaliation for reporting housing code violations.

This is not, of course, to say that even if the tenant can prove a retaliatory purpose she is entitled to remain in possession in perpetuity. If this illegal purpose is dissipated, the landlord can, in the absence of legislation or a binding contract, evict his tenants or raise their rents for economic or other legitimate reasons, or even for no reason at all. The question of permissible or impermissible purpose is one of fact for the court or jury, and while such a determination is not easy, it is not significantly different from problems with which the courts must deal in a host of other contexts, such as when they must decide whether the employer who discharges a worker has committed an unfair labor practice because he has done so on account of the employee's union activities. As Judge Greene said, "There is no reason why similar factual judgments cannot be made by courts and juries in the context of economic retaliation [against tenants by landlords] for providing information to the government."

Reversed and remanded.

McGOWAN, CIRCUIT JUDGE (concurring except as to Parts I and II).

[omitted]

DANAHER, CIRCUIT JUDGE (dissenting).

[omitted]

Notes and Questions

1.   Restatement (Second) of Property § 14.8, Caveat (1976) takes no position on whether the retaliatory eviction defense should be extended to residential leases not involving code violations, residential leases from landlords who are not in the rental business, or to commercial leases. Are there any policy reasons for limiting the retaliatory eviction defense in this manner? See Espenschied v. Mallick, 633 A.2d 388 (D.C. 1993) (retaliatory eviction defense is not available to commercial lessees) Custom Parking, Inc. v. Superior Court, 138 Cal.App.3d 90, 187 Cal.Rptr. 674 (1982) (extending retaliatory eviction defense to commercial tenancies). Port of Longview v. International Raw Materials, 96 Wash.App. 431, 979 P.2d 917 (1999) (retaliatory eviction defense permitted in unlawful detainer action by government landlord who sought to evict commercial tenant following publication of letter critical of landlord. The Restatement's description identifies five elements of the defense: 1) a protective housing statute, such as a housing code, is the basis for the defense, 2) the defense is asserted against a landlord who is in the business of renting residential units, 3) the tenants are not in breach of the lease at the time of service of an eviction notice, 4) the tenants have established that the landlord's primary motive for eviction was retaliation, and 5) the tenants' complaints were made in good faith and after reasonable notice was given to the landlord. See Building Monitoring Systems, Inc. v. Paxton, 905 P.2d 1215 (Utah 1995) (applying the Restatement description).

2.   For purposes of retaliatory eviction, is there any reason to distinguish between termination and refusal to renew? See Houle v. Quenneville, 173 Vt. 80, 787 A.2d 1258, 1263 (2001) (statutory retaliatory eviction prohibition applies to refusals to renew); Restatement (Second) Property § 14.8 (1976) (both covered) and URLTA § 5.101 (covers any action for possession). Is there a difference, in terms of the elements of retaliatory eviction, or in moral terms, between giving the tenant a short-term lease, with implicit or explicit provisions allowing the landlord to refuse to renew, and a lease which is renewed automatically every time a rent payment is due? (Note that under some statutes a lease without provisions for renewal is probably a lease for the term of the current rent. Note, too, that sometimes it's the tenant who benefits from a month-to-month tenancy.) Should a landlord be able to refuse to renew a lease in order to take property off the market, even if the decision to do so is in response to tenant-iniated code enforcement proceeding? See Robinson v. Diamond Housing Corp., 463

F.2d 853 (D.C. Cir. 1972) (defense of retaliatory eviction is available against landlord who attempted to evict complaining tenant after taking property off the market instead of bringing it to code compliance).

3. A number of states have prohibited retaliatory eviction and related acts by statute. For a review of the statutes and commentary, see Restatement (Second) of Property §§ 14.8 & 14.9 (1977). Other acts prohibited include retaliatory rent increases and retaliatory reductions in services. See e.g., Cal. Civ. Code § 1942.5(c.) (retaliatory rent increases and retaliatory actions against lawful tenant organization efforts), (b) & (g) (authorizing recovery of actual and punitive damages, as well as attorney's fees); Rich v. Schwab, 63 Cal.App.4th 803, 75 Cal.Rptr.2d 170 (1998) (applying statute to space tenants in mobile home park). Statutes may differ on the extent of coverage and who has burden of proof. See e.g., 9 V.S.A. § 4465(a)(2), construed in Houle v. Quenneville, 173 Vt. 80, 787 A.2d 1258, 1265–66 (2001) (tenants have burden of proof by an objective standard, distinguishing cases from other jurisdictions because of statutory language differences.

In addition to retaliatory eviction statutes, some states have enacted statutes that protect landlords' right to go out of the residential rental business by withdrawing property from the market. See e.g. Cal. Gov. Code § 7060 et seq., which was enacted originally in response to a court decision prohibiting a landlord from withdrawing property from a rent-controlled market if such withdrawal would displace low-or moderate-income persons. Nash v. City of Santa Monica, 37 Cal.3d 97, 207 Cal.Rptr. 285, 688 P.2d 894 (1984). Can a tenant assert a retaliatory eviction defense against a landlord seeking to take property off the market in accordance with such a statute? See Drouet v. Superior Court, 31 Cal.4th 583, 3 Cal.Rptr.3d 205, 73 P.3d 1185, 1195 (2003) (landlord may overcome statutory defense of retaliatory eviction "by demonstrating a bona fide intent to withdraw the property from the market").

4. For an imaginative proposal advocating the creation of nonrenewal insurance to compensate tenants who suffer eviction without cause as an alternative to rent control and a remedy for retaliatory eviction, see G. Samuel Zucker, Insurance for Eviction Without Cause: A Middle Path for Tenant Tenure Rights and a New Remedy for Retaliatory Eviction, 28 Urb. Law 113 (1996) (12th Annual R. Marlin Smith Student Writing Competition Award Winner). The author argues that modern rent control legislation, which combines moderate restrictions on rent increases with prohibitions against eviction without cause, imposes "enormous transaction costs on tenant and landlord alike." A rental market without rent control, however, "swerves in the opposite extreme . . . victimiz(ing) poor tenants in particular by leaving them with no useful defense against retaliatory eviction and leaving them uncompensated for the loss of their home when evicted without cause." As an alternative, the author proposes an insurance system that would provide tenants evicted without cause a low flat rate payment roughly equal to one month's low-income rent typical for the area per year of tenancy.

5. The student article discussed in note 4 calls attention to the question whether modern landlord-tenant law has resulted in better housing conditions for persons who rent rather than own their homes, particularly

for those who do so out of necessity rather than choice. Effective implementation of the implied warranty of habitability, the retaliatory eviction defense, and the enforcement obligations of local housing codes requires a degree of energy and sophistication, not to mention access to lawyers, that low and moderate income landlords and tenants may not possess. In commenting on this reality and giving qualified support to landlord-tenant mediation programs, a legal services attorney told a 1994 meeting of the American Bar Association's Commission on Homelessness and Poverty chaired by one of the authors that he keeps the following sign on his desk:

POSSESSION OF A LAWYER IS NINE–TENTHS OF THE LAW

That same lawyer cautioned against mediation programs that tend to split the difference between the parties, saying this was not always the fair result. Self help remedies such as rent withholding can be useful, he said, if two major weaknesses can be overcome: the inability of low income people to hold their withheld rent in escrow for future payment because of competing needs for food and other household necessities, and the temptation to settle for less than might be obtained because of the fear of homelessness if possession is lost.

A NOTE ON MAINTAINING AFFORDABLE HOUSING THROUGH GOVERNMENT SUBSIDY, RENT CONTROL, AND LONG TERM LEASES

While homeownership has been and remains the dream of most Americans, it is little more than a faint glimmer for millions of persons in the bottom economic quartile. For the most part, persons making less than $20,000 per year (which will include two-income families if both incomes do not exceed full-time minimum wage rates) must depend on rental housing for their shelter. See, e.g., National Low Income Housing Coalition, OUT OF REACH (2003) (family of four needs almost three times the minimum wage to afford average two bedroom apartment in metropolitan areas); John E. Schwarz, Illusions of Opportunity: The American Dream In Question (W.W. Norton, 1997) (four-member household needs at least $27,000 a year for a minimally acceptable livelihood".

Increasing pressures on rents resulting from a variety of factors, including inflation and higher standards of housing quality, have reduced the number of affordable units of decent quality in the private rental market. See, e.g., Joint Center for Housing Studies of Harvard University, The State of the Nations Housing 23 (2005) (shortfall of affordable and available rental units for households with incomes of $16,000 or less exceeded 5 million units).

The dramatic rise in homelessness among individuals and families since the mid–1980s, passage of major welfare reform legislation in 1996 putting strict time limits on receipt of public assistance (Personal Responsibility and Work Opportunity Reconciliation Act of 1996, Pub L. No. 104–193, 110 Stat. 2105), and drastic reductions in the amount of federal assistance for housing over the past 20 years have raised serious questions about the ability of low income individuals and families to obtain such housing.

Governments and non profit organizations have responded to this situation in a number of ways.

Public housing. Since 1937, the United States has offered financial assistance to local communities for the development and management of rental units that are owned by local public bodies called housing authorities. 42 U.S.C. § 1437 et seq. (1999). The public housing program is a complex exercise in federalism, with the federal government offering financial assistance, state governments regulating the governing public authorities through state enabling legislation, and local governments establishing public authorities that own the housing units. Financial assistance comes in several forms: 1) sale of government backed, tax-free bonds to finance construction, 2) long-term "annual contributions contracts" for the payment of interest and principal on the bonds, 3) annual operating subsidies, and 4) periodic grants for maintenance and repairs. Controversial from its inception, the public housing program remains the most significant form of government housing assistance for low income persons. A new program designed to encourage transfer of ownership of public housing units to tenant organizations and individuals was authorized by the Cranston–Gonzales National Affordable Housing Act of 1990. For a discussion of major changes taking place in the policies affecting public housing, See David P. Varady, Wolfgang F.E. Preiser, and Francis P. Russell, New Directions in Urban Public Housing (1998); Susan Popkin, Mary Cunningham & Martha Burt, Public Housing Transformation and the Hard-to-House, 16 Housing Policy Debate 1 (2005).

Because public housing landlords are public agencies governed by statutes establishing criteria for tenant selection and admission, federal and state courts "have uniformly concluded that an applicant has a property interest in his or her eligibility for public housing, and, that consequently, some measure of due process was required in the consideration of the application." Madera v. Secretary of Executive Office, 418 Mass. 452, 636 N.E.2d 1326, 1331 (1994), citing cases.

Assisted Housing. Since the 1960s, the federal government has offered a variety of incentives to private owners of rental housing, including subsidies to lenders to reduce the cost of financing the development of housing, 12 U.S.C. § 1715z–1 (2000), rental subsidies tied to particular units that were constructed or renovated in accordance with government standards, and vouchers issued to eligible low income persons that can be redeemed for rental subsidies by owners of existing units who agree to rent to the persons holding the vouchers. 42 U.S.C. § 1437f (2000). Concerns over the cumulative budgetary effect of multi-year interest and rental subsidies led to sharp reductions in appropriations for new expenditures after 1978. For a review of the Section 8 housing voucher program, see William Grigsby & Steven Bourassa, Section 8: The Time for Fundamental Program Change? 15 HOUSING POLICY DEBATE 805 (2004).

Courts have split on the question whether applicants for assisted housing have due process rights similar to applicants for public housing. See Hill v. Group Three Hous. Dev. Corp., 799 F.2d 385 (8th Cir.1986) and Eidson v. Pierce, 745 F.2d 453 (7th Cir.1984) (because admission is left to business judgment of private landlord, applicants for assisted housing do not have constitutionally protected property interest in such housing); Ressler v. Pierce, 692 F.2d 1212 (9th Cir.1982) *contra.*

Low Income Housing Tax Credit. In 1986, a new program of tax credits to individuals and corporations who invest in the development of multi-family housing for persons of low and moderate-income was approved by Congress, 26 U.S.C. § 42 (2004). By the mid–1990s, it had become the Federal Government's major housing development program and continued to be so during the first decade of the Twenty First Century. In many housing tax credit developments, tenants also receive assistance through Section 8 vouchers.

While leases in public assisted and tax-credit housing typically offer one year terms, legislative and judicial restrictions on refusals to renew except for "good cause" effectively convert the leases into long-term tenancies called statutory tenancies in the *Moynihan* excerpt *supra.*

Rent Control. As noted by Judge Posner, governmental restriction on the amount of rent that can be charged by private landlords is an approach often advocated and sometimes implemented in tight housing markets. Rent control usually is coupled with a restriction on refusing to renew leases for other than "good cause," similar to good cause restrictions on public housing and assisted housing landlords.

The most well-known, and controversial, rent control program is in New York City. The following description is drawn from Resolution Trust Corp. v. Diamond, 18 F.3d 111 (2d Cir.1994) (Diamond I) and Resolution Trust Corp. v. Diamond, 45 F.3d 665 (2d Cir.1995), (Diamond II) which held that the federal Financial Institutions Reform, Recovery, and Enforcement Act of 1989 ("FIRREA") preempted contrary state and local rent control laws.

Owners of residential rental property in New York City were first subjected to regulation by the federal government during World War II. State legislation in 1946 and local ordinances in 1962 continued the program under findings of housing emergencies that have been renewed periodically, most recently in 1985. Maximum rents are set every two years by a local administrative board. Landlords may petition for increases but have to show extraordinary considerations such as increases in operating expenses. Tenants cannot be evicted so long as they pay the specified rent. Rents are regulated whether or not a written lease is used.

A second and more flexible program, rent stabilization, was adopted in 1969 because of concerns over the effectiveness of rent control. Rent stabilization requires a written lease and regular renewal offers. See e.g., South Park Assocs., L.L.C. v. Renzulli, 94 F.Supp.2d 460 (S.D.N.Y. 2000) (failure to state factual basis for termination of rent stabilization lease in termination notice bars eviction proceedings; tenant's refusal to sign renewal lease that contains terms and conditions different from the expiring lease does not provide cause for eviction. Maximum rent increases, rather than maximum rents, are promulgated regularly for one and two year leases, with allowable increases pegged at least in part to market conditions.

Rent regulation also is achieved through New York's anti-fraud securities statute, which requires sellers of condominium and cooperative interests in an existing rental building being converted to those forms of ownership to disclose eviction procedures and rent regulations for non-purchasing tenancies.

New York rent control statutes prohibit landlords from evicting tenants so long as the tenants continue to pay the regulated rent, unless certain specified grounds occur (generally failure to comply with reasonable rules and regulations). The termination prohibition provisions of rent control ordinances have survived constitutional challenges as unlawful takings of property without just compensation (discussed in Chapter Seven). See Yee v. City of Escondido, 503 U.S. 519, 112 S.Ct. 1522, 118 L.Ed.2d 153 (1992).

Rent control has been controversial from its inception. Except during times of war, it generally has not spread beyond New York, New Jersey and a few cities in California. Periodic efforts at reform or abolition have been mounted in the New York State legislature. For a comprehensive analysis of rent control, including examinations of rent control programs in Berkeley and Los Angeles, California, New Jersey, New York City, Toronto, Canada, and Washington, D.C., See W. Dennis Keating, Michael B. Teitz, and Andrejs Skaburskis, Rent Control: Regulation and the Rental Housing Market (1998).

Long Term Leases. Public controversies over abandonment of apartment buildings by private owners, conversion of apartments to condominiums, and withdrawal of apartments from the assisted housing market have dramatized the importance of maintaining a predictable supply of affordable rental units. A number of techniques involving long term leases have been used.

(a) *Limited equity cooperatives.* In a limited equity cooperative, a non profit corporation owns the building and maintains it as affordable housing. Members of the cooperative purchase shares of stock in the corporation, which entitle them to a vote on corporate governance and a long-term lease of one of the units in the cooperative. Transfer of memberships is regulated by the cooperative and members agree to limit their profit potential should the units appreciate in value.

(b) *Mutual Housing Associations.* The housing cooperative principle is expanded in the mutual housing association through the addition of representatives of business, community groups and government to the governing board, although a majority of the board is made up of residents. Mutual housing associations emphasize long term affordability by offering a life-time right to occupy, along with a right to pass on the unit to a family or household member.

(c) *Community land trusts.* Community land trusts are non-profit corporations that are organized to acquire and hold land for the benefit of a particular community. Community land trusts may emphasize goals of protecting agricultural land, preserving the environment and safeguarding cultural treasures, as well as providing permanent affordable housing. When affordable housing is the goal, long term leases of the land will be executed, enabling lessees to acquire existing units or build new units on the land. Private restrictions on land use, discussed in Chapter Six, combined with long term leases and repurchase options for improvement, are used to ensure that the land is permanently dedicated to affordable housing. See, generally, Institute for Community Relations, The Community Land Trust Handbook (1982).

PROBLEM

Suppose you are a new associate assigned to represent an important client of your law firm who has inherited rental property in a low-income neighborhood.

Current tenants generally are long-standing residents, some with month-to-month tenancies and others with one-year term leases that have been renewed on a regular basis. Some tenants have lost their jobs because of a recent plant closing. Most of the rental units need repairs, and the client is weighing alternatives of retaining the rental units "as is," making repairs and raising rents, converting the units to condominiums for middle income persons, or demolishing the building in favor of commercial use. You have been asked to advise the client concerning property law aspects of the alternatives under study, including consideration of the harm that might be caused the tenants and steps that might be taken to alleviate that harm. Prepare a memorandum discussing your analysis and conclusions.

Suppose the client does not ask about potential hardships that might result. Should you raise that possibility? If so, how would you do it?

VI. SPECIAL PROCEDURAL RULES

A. PROHIBITION AGAINST SELF HELP

HARKINS v. WIN CORPORATION

District of Columbia Court of Appeals, 2001.
771 A.2d 1025.

PRYOR, SENIOR JUDGE:

Michael Harkins, Jr., appellant, appeals from the trial court's grant of summary judgment in favor of WIN Corp., appellee in Harkins's suit for wrongful eviction. The trial court found that appellant was a roomer or lodger, as opposed to a tenant, and concluded that self-help "was a permissible method of eviction." Appellant contends that the exclusive legislative remedy required for a landlord to regain possession from a tenant also must be used to evict a roomer. Being unpersuaded by this contention, we affirm the judgment of the trial court.

I.

The facts of this case are undisputed. WIN Corp. operated the Allen–Lee Hotel in the District of Columbia. It had obtained both a valid license and a Certificate of Occupancy to operate a rooming house. Appellant was among the occupants of the hotel. Appellant became an occupant of a room in the hotel in September 1994 when he agreed, by signing a hotel registration card, to a weekly occupancy charge of $85 (plus tax and expenses). WIN Corp. provided linens, maid service, as well as furniture for the room during Harkins's stay. By April 1995, appellant was in arrears with respect to his weekly payments, and the manager of the hotel informed him that he would be evicted if he did not pay the arrearage due on his account. Harkins, however, continued to be delinquent in his payments. Appellee did not file a complaint in the Landlord and Tenant Branch of the Superior Court seeking repossession of the room for nonpayment of rent. Rather, on May 3, 1995, appellee changed the locks for Harkins's room, thereby effectively locking him out of the premises.

Harkins subsequently filed a complaint against WIN Corp. alleging, *inter alia,* wrongful eviction. Both parties then moved for summary judgment. In deciding the cross-motions, the trial court found that Harkins was a roomer, not a tenant, since he did not have exclusive possession of the room and was not a tenant under the Rental Housing Act of 1985 ("Housing Act"). The trial judge concluded that the common law remedy of self-help to evict a roomer was still permissible, though no longer available to evict a tenant. Accordingly, the trial court granted summary judgment for WIN Corp. This appeal followed.

II.

In his brief, Harkins states that "the straightforward, but not simple question" for this court is "whether the operator of a rooming house may utilize self-help to evict a roomer." Relying primarily on our holding in *Mendes v. Johnson*, 389 A.2d 781, 786–87 (D.C.1978) (en banc), and his reading of the present version of the District's eviction statute, D.C.Code § 16–1501 (1997), appellant contends that a judicial possessory action is the sole remedy for matters related to repossession of real property, as here.

D.C.Code § 16–1501 presently provides:

> When a person detains possession of real property without right, or after his right to possession has ceased, the Superior Court of the District of Columbia, on complaint under oath verified by the person aggrieved by the detention, or by his agent or attorney having knowledge of the facts, may issue a summons in English and Spanish to the party complained of to appear and show cause why judgment should not be given against him for the restitution of possession.

Before 1953, D.C.Code § 11–735 (1940), the predecessor to the modern statutory summary possessory provision, was unavailable in situations other than the unlawful entry and detainer or unlawful detention of property by a tenant. [   ] Then in 1953, section 11–735 was amended, replacing the forcible entry and detainer provisions with a general remedy for any unlawful detention of property. [   ] Section 11–735 gave rise to section 16–1501, which is substantially the same today as the 1973 version at issue in *Mendes, supra,* 389 A.2d at 783 n. 5. The one difference is that now the required summons must be in English and Spanish. Appellant urges that the statute, in its present form, referring to "a *person* [who] detains possession of real property without right," when read along with our decision in *Mendes*, should include all "persons" and not just tenants.

A.

Commentators have long surveyed the question surrounding the eviction of roomers or lodgers and tenants. *See* 2 Richard R. Powell & Patrick J. Rohan, Powell on Real Property § 16.02[3][ii], at 16–28 to 16–30 (Michael A. Wolf ed.2000). As one leading commentator suggests, however, the distinction between a roomer and a tenant can be elusive. *See id.* at 16–28. At one end of the spectrum is the transient one-night roomer; at the other end is the long-term tenant with a written lease. "The central conceptual distinction [between these two ends] is usually phrased in terms of whether the occupant has or lacks a right of possession or exclusive control. . . ." *Id.* at 16–28 to 16–29; *see also Beall, [v. Everson]*, 34 A.2d, 41, 41 (D.C. 1943)" 'The principal distinction between the two relation[ships] is that the tenant acquires an interest in the real estate and has the exclusive possession of the leased premises, while the lodger acquires no estate and has merely the use without the actual or exclusive possession.' "(quoting *Coggins v. Gregorio*, 97 F.2d 948, 950 (10th Cir.1938))). In many, if not all instances, a licensee, such as a roomer or lodger, may be subjected to self-help eviction, *see*

POWELL, *supra*, at 16–29 (citing examples), whereas a tenant generally may not be so evicted, *see id.;* P.A. Agabin, Annotation, *Right of Landlord Legally Entitled to Possession to Dispossess Tenant Without Legal Process,* 6 A.L.R.3d 177, 186–189 (1966 & Supp.2000). For the first time since our holding with regard to tenants in *Mendes,* we encounter the question of self-help with regard to roomers or lodgers.

Resolution of this question requires us to revisit our holding in *Mendes.* In *Mendes,* we considered whether a landlord could resort to self-help to evict a tenant notwithstanding the summary possessory action provided by D.C.Code § 16–1501. *See* 389 A.2d at 782. In that case, the landlord had evicted the tenant, who was a tenant by the month, by packing up and removing all of the tenant's possessions. *See id.* After reviewing the evolution of self-help into more current times, we held that "in this jurisdiction, the *landlord's* common law right of self-help has been abrogated, and the legislatively created remedies for reacquiring possession are exclusive. A *tenant* has a right not to have his or her possession interfered with except by lawful process...." *Id.* at 787 (emphasis added). Foremost among the reasons for our decision in *Mendes* were: (1) the use of self-help would be avoided or obviated only if the statutory remedy was deemed to be exclusive; (2) sanctioning the use of self-help in an urban area with housing shortages would invite violence; (3) a tenant evicted by self-help is deprived of an opportunity to assert various equitable defenses and rights afforded by statute or case law; and (4) a law abiding society often requires redress only through established political, legislative, and judicial processes. *See id.* at 786–87. Our holding expressly overruled *Snitman v. Goodman,* 118 A.2d 394 (D.C.1955), which held that the "judicial remedy" was an additional, not the exclusive, means for a landlord to repossess his property from a tenant. *See Mendes, supra,* 389 A.2d at 787. We did not, however, address the propriety of self-help in the context of a roomer.

B.

As a threshold consideration, we observe that in order for Harkins to prevail in this instance it would be necessary to expressly overrule *Davis v. Francis Scott Key Apartments,* 140 A.2d 188 (D.C.1958), which held, parallel with our holding in *Snitman, supra,* 118 A.2d at 397, that in the case of a roomer, summary judicial action was an alternative remedy to self-help eviction.

We turn now to each of the four policy reasons motivating our conclusion in *Mendes.* The first reason underlying our holding was that self-help would continue to be used in the landlord-tenant context unless the legislative remedy was deemed exclusive. *See* 389 A.2d at 786. In discussing the intent of the statute to abrogate the common law, we limited any such abrogation to landlord-tenant relationships only. We stated that "the landlord's common law right of self-help has been abrogated," and that "[a] tenant has a right not to have his or her possession interfered with except by lawful process." *Id.* at 787. Therefore when we discussed the necessity to abrogate the common law, our discussion was limited to the context of landlords and their tenants only, not to all situations involving real property. A broader construction of our holding could have unforeseen consequences.

The second rationale for our decision in *Mendes* was that self-help against tenants is likely to cause violence. The potential for violence in the context of a roomer is somewhat diminished. First, the roomer is less likely to consider his or her transient accommodation as their "castle" as a tenant may view their rental unit. Roomers may have brought fewer possessions with them into their accommodation. A roomer may not have as much need to remain in a particular accommodation and may be less affected by any housing shortage that may exist within a particular city. Tenants, on the other hand, often cannot as easily find a new permanent residence to house all of their possessions, thus increasing the likelihood of violence when dispossessed. Since the likelihood of violence is diminished in the context of a roomer, though admittedly not altogether absent, our holding in *Mendes* abrogating the common law, to the extent it was predicated upon the likelihood of violence, is not applicable to the same degree in the context of a roomer.

The remaining two policy considerations underpinning our holding in *Mendes* do not advance Harkins's argument any further than the first two. The equitable defenses available to tenants are applicable to roomers, at most, in a limited degree. A roomer does not have an equivalent need for the equitable defenses that a tenant may have when committed to a long-term lease, since the roomer generally has less of a need to remain in possession of a particular accommodation while engaging in litigation. Moreover, Harkins has not explained how any of those equitable defenses would apply in this particular case. Lastly, the parties have not cited, and our research has not revealed, any precedent which squarely supports appellant's contentions in this latter regard. In light of the foregoing, the general policy grounds invoked in *Mendes* have limited application here.

As we turn to the crux of this case, appellant, though acknowledging that he was a roomer, emphasizes that the relationship was of long standing. He occupied the room at appellee's hotel for approximately eight months. Given his broad reading of the eviction statute, he urges that our holding in *Mendes* should be extended to include him. However, it is also true that the only document executed between the parties was the registration card completed upon appellant's initial arrival. We note that, appellant was obliged, on a weekly basis, to pay for his furnished room and to make the room accessible for linen and cleaning service. In the context of our present eviction statute, our existing judicial decisions on the subject, and relevant treatises, we decline appellant's invitation to extend the *Mendes* holding to this case.... Close scrutiny of this question reveals that there are a range of legitimate concerns to be considered regarding a roomer of long-standing. However, resolution of these concerns both of the landowner and persons seeking rooming accommodations of various durations is probably better suited, and prudently left, to the legislative forum. *See, e.g.*, N.Y. REAL PROP. ACTS Law § 711

(McKinney 2001) (providing status of "tenant" and corresponding protections to non-transient occupants of a rooming house or hotel).

III.

Accordingly, we hold that a transient-accommodation provider may utilize self-help as an alternative means of evicting a nonpaying roomer or lodger.

Affirmed.

Notes and Questions

1. Were the Court's reasons for distinguishing between tenants and roomers persuasive? Homelessness has been a serious problem in major urban areas since the mid–1980s. Because a large number of homelss persons are single men or women, many of whom have chemical dependency and other disabilities, advocates and caregivers have recommended a return to single room occupancy (SRO) and other forms of permanent housing that include provision of needed social services as an alternative to homeless shelters and/or park benchers. See e.g., Rae Bridgman, Housing Chronically Homeless Women: "Inside" a Safe Haven, 13 HOUSING POLICY DEBATE 51 (2002). These would necessarily have to be furnished units and would likely be occupied for extended periods of time. Should occupants of such housing have the procedural safeguards afforded tenants or does their status imply a dependency that doesn't merit recognition of possessory rights?

2. Are there any reasons for treating commercial tenants differently from residential tenants with respect to permissible levels of self-help? Also, should the activities of the tenants be taken into consideration in determining whether self-help is available to recover possession of leased premises? Suppose, for example, tenants are suspected of associating with criminal elements and the landlord feels threatened by their activities. Should the landlord be able to use self-help, say by changing locks while the tenants are out, to remove such "threatening" tenants? See Restatement (Second) of Property § 14.2 (1977) (landlord or incoming tenant may not use self-help if a speedy judicial remedy for recovery of possession is available unless self-help is permitted by controlling law).

3. The modern rule with regard to tenants is illustrated by Berg v. Wiley, 264 N.W.2d 145, 151 (Minn. 1978):

> To make clear our departure from the common-law rule for the benefit of future landlords and tenants, we hold that, subsequent to our decision in this case, the only lawful means to dispossess a tenant who has not abandoned nor voluntarily surrendered but who claims possession adversely to a landlord's claim of breach of a written lease is by resort to judicial process. We find that Minn. St. 566.02 to 566.17 summary proceedings provide the landlord with an adequate remedy for regaining possession in every such case. Where speedier action than provided in §§ 566.02 to 566.17 seems necessary because of threatened destruction of the property or other exigent circumstances, a temporary restraining order under Rule 65, Rules of Civil Procedure, and law

enforcement protection are available to the landlord. Considered together, these statutory and judicial remedies provide a complete answer to the landlord. In our modern society, with the availability of prompt and sufficient legal remedies as described, there is no place and no need for self-help against a tenant in claimed lawful possession of leased premises. *Id., at 151.*

4. *Summary proceeding statutes*

As the *Harkins* court noted restrictions on landlord self-help often are justified as the "quid pro quo" for summary proceeding statutes enacted in all the states. The statutes were designed to provide a quick and simple forum to determine who has the right to possession when disputes arise between landlords and tenants "The usual scheme is that the landlord must give the tenant a notice in a prescribed manner, requiring the tenant either to cure the breach, if it is curable, within a certain period of time or to vacate. Times of notice, generally short, vary from state to state and according to the nature of the breach; from three to 10 days' notice is typical for a rent default. If the tenant vacates, lease and leasehold terminate. If not, the tenant falls into a status usually called "unlawful detainer." At that point the landlord has the summary court action for possession and, in most states, for back rent with perhaps a penalty. In Lindsey v. Normet, 405 U.S. 56, 92 S.Ct. 862, 31 L.Ed.2d 36 (1972), the United States Supreme Court upheld the constitutionality of the summary form of action with accelerated trial date." W. STOEBUCK & D. WHITMAN, THE LAW OF PROPERTY, THIRD EDITION 395 (2000). Landlords often complain that recalcitrant tenants can manipulate the statutory process to delay eviction by weeks and months, particularly by alleging breach of the implied warranty of habitability. For a review of the use of summary proceeding statutes and recommendation that landlord self-help be prohibited, see DeGraffe, The Development of Unlawful Evictions and Tenant Remedies for Injurious Conduct in New York, 41 Syracuse L.Rev. 1179 (1990).

PROBLEM

Margaret Thomas placed an advertisement in the local newspaper seeking a roommate. She had several responses, but decided to lease her extra bedroom to Laura Witt. Laura gave Margaret a security deposit and moved in. The next day, Margaret asked Laura to sign a lease. Laura refused. Therefore Margaret asked Laura to move out. She refused to do that as well.

About 20 days later, Margaret decided she'd had enough. She demanded that Laura leave immediately. Laura refused this request and locked herself in the bedroom. Margaret called the police, who arrested Laura for trespass.

What do you think of Laura's actions? Of Margaret's? Should Margaret have used a different approach? See People v. Evans, 163 Ill.App.3d 561, 114 Ill.Dec. 662, 516 N.E.2d 817 (1987) (summary proceedings statute provided sole means for resolving dispute concerning who had "better right of possession").

One of the complaints landlords have about the summary eviction process is that sometimes it is nearly impossible to get tenants out once they have taken possession. Consider this problem in light of both the traditional view of the lease as a conveyance of property and the view that a lease is simply a contractual arrangement. What about the situation, as with Margaret and Laura, where there is no written lease? Should self help be available?

A 1990 movie, "Pacific Heights", portrayed a situation similar, although more extreme, to that of Margaret and Laura. A tenant moved in before he signed a lease, did not sign the lease and proceeded to systematically destroy the apartment before the landlords were finally able to have him evicted.

B. HOLDOVERS

BOCKELMANN v. MARYNICK

Supreme Court of Texas, 1990.
788 S.W.2d 569.

PHILLIPS, CHIEF JUSTICE.

The issue in this appeal of a landlord-tenant dispute is whether a tenant who has vacated the leased premises before the end of the term is liable for rent and repairs accruing during a cotenant's holdover tenancy. The court of appeals held that the tenant is liable unless the tenant gives notice to the landlord that he or she ceases to hold the leased premises. [ ] We reverse the judgment of the court of appeals and render judgment for the vacating tenant, holding that one tenant is not jointly liable for the holding over of another.

Brenda Bockelmann and her then husband, Hermann Bockelmann, rented one side of a duplex from Samuel and Sharon Marynick for several years. Their last written lease was jointly executed in 1984, for a twelve-month term ending on February 28, 1985. The lease included the following holdover provision:

> Should Tenant remain in possession of the demised premises with the consent of Lessor after the natural expiration of this lease, a new tenancy from year to year shall be created between Lessor and Tenant which shall be subject to all the terms and conditions hereof but shall be terminable by 60 days notice.

Ten days before the lease expired, Brenda separated from her husband and vacated the premises.

After the lease expired, Hermann remained in possession of the duplex and continued to pay rent. During part of 1985, however, Hermann was unable to pay his rent. Hermann and Samuel agreed, in writing, to a "loan" that suspended Hermann's rent payments for seven months and required repayment with interest. Hermann resumed his rent payments in November 1985 and began making loan payments in January 1986.

At the conclusion of the first holdover year, Hermann again retained possession of the duplex. He continued to make both rent and loan payments through June 1986, when he defaulted on both obligations. At the insistence of the Marynicks, Hermann vacated the duplex on September 7, 1986.

The Marynicks brought suit against Hermann and Brenda to recover unpaid rent, the expense of repairs, and the balance due under the loan contract. The trial court rendered summary judgment for the Marynicks against Hermann but ordered that they take nothing against Brenda. The Marynicks appealed from the take-nothing judgment against Brenda. The court of appeals, with one justice dissenting, affirmed in part and reversed in part. The court agreed that Brenda was not liable under the loan contract, thus affirming part of the trial court's judgment. However, the court reversed the remainder of the trial court's judgment, holding that Brenda was liable for unpaid rent and repairs because her "joint obligations under the lease continued through the first and second holdover terms by virtue of Hermann's holding over."
[ ]

Although this issue is one of first impression in this state, it has been addressed by at least four other jurisdictions. The earliest reported decision was by the South Carolina Supreme Court, which held that when a lease is executed by two tenants jointly and only one occupies after expiration of the term, the law will presume that both tenants are holdovers unless the tenant not in actual possession gives notice to the landlord that he or she ceases to hold. *Fronty v. Wood,* 20 S.C.L. (2 Hill) 367 (1834). The court below relied on this decision. The Supreme Court of Arizona and an appellate court in New York, however, have rejected the South Carolina presumption, holding instead that one tenant cannot be involuntarily bound to a new tenancy by the acts of another. *Mosher v. Sabra,* 34 Ariz. 536, 541, 273 P. 534, 535 (1929) (the contract arising from a holdover is between the tenant continuing to occupy the premises and the landlord; the cotenant not in possession is not liable simply because he or she jointly leased the premises); *Foster v. Stewart,* 196 A.D. 814, 816, 188 N.Y.S. 151, 152 (App.Div.1921) (a cotenant cannot, by the act of holding over, exercise an option to renew and thereby create a new contract which would bind a cotenant not in possession). More recently, a California intermediate court followed *Fronty v. Wood* and distinguished the Arizona and New York decisions by concluding that California treats a holdover tenancy as an extension of the original agreement rather than a new tenancy. *Schmitt v. Felix,* 157 Cal.App.2d 642, 645, 321 P.2d 473, 475 (1958) (a cotenant who vacates remains in constructive possession of the premises by virtue of the other cotenant's continuing occupancy and, in the absence of notice to the landlord of any change in the occupancy of the premises, may be bound as a holdover).

The court below held that notice was required in order to terminate Brenda's continuing obligations under the joint lease. We disagree. The lease created a tenancy for a definite term (a tenancy with a specified beginning and ending date). The general rule is that a tenancy for a definite term does not require a tenant to give notice in order to terminate the tenancy, because a tenancy for a definite term simply expires at the end of the contract period. [   ] The tenancy created under this lease thus terminated regardless of notice and regardless of whether either tenant vacated.

A tenant who remains in possession of the premises after termination of the lease occupies "wrongfully" and is said to have a tenancy at sufferance. [   ] Under the common law holdover rule, a landlord may elect to treat a tenant holding over as either a trespasser or as a tenant holding under the terms of the original lease. [   ] The lease incorporated this rule of holdover, providing that, if the landlord consents, a "new tenancy" would be created if the tenant remained in possession beyond expiration of the lease. The lease stated that this new tenancy would be subject to the same terms and conditions as the original tenancy, except that the holdover tenancy would be "from year to year * * * terminable by 60 days notice." Thus, under the express terms of the lease, this holdover tenancy was a new tenancy rather than an extension or renewal of the original lease. Therefore, Hermann's holdover tenancy was not, as the court below held, a continuation of the original tenancy he held jointly with Brenda, but was rather a new tenancy for which he alone was liable.

The court of appeals bound Brenda to this new tenancy by presuming that a holding over by Hermann was also a holding over by Brenda, absent notice to the contrary. However, a presumption that one cotenant's holding over binds another cotenant is contrary to the general principles of cotenancy under Texas law. The relationship of cotenancy exists only so long as the parties own rights in common property. [   ] At the moment the original lease expired, neither Hermann nor Brenda had any legal right to possession of the duplex, and their relationship as cotenants was extinguished. Because they were no longer cotenants, there was no basis from which to presume a joint holding over. Moreover, under Texas law, "each owner in a co-tenancy acts for himself and no one is the agent of another or has any authority to bind him merely because of the relationship." *Lander v. Wedell*, 493 S.W.2d 271, 274 (Tex.Civ.App.—Dallas 1973, writ ref'd n.r.e.). Thus, where a lease contains an option to renew, one tenant may not unilaterally exercise that option and bind nonconsenting cotenants. [   ] Since Texas does not permit Hermann to renew the lease for another term on Brenda's behalf, it similarly should not presume that he was authorized to hold over on her behalf.

Accordingly, the judgment of the court of appeals is reversed, and we render judgment that the Marynicks take nothing.

Notes and Questions

1. What constitutes "holding over"? Suppose a tenant sends a letter to the landlord stating an intention not to renew a lease upon its expiration in

compliance with the notice provisions of the lease. The tenant vacates on the appointed date, but retains the keys and leaves items of personal property in the vacated premises. Is the tenant holding over? See Longmier v. Kaufman, 663 S.W.2d 385 (Mo.App.1983),(retention of keys and failure to remove property constitutes sufficient control to support finding of a holding over). See also Caudill v. Acton, 175 S.W.3d 617 (Ky. App. 2004) (construing URLTA holdover provision and holding that daughter who signed lease along with her father and paid her father's rent, but never occupied the unit, has a sufficient possessory interest to be considered a holdover tenant along with her father).

2.   As noted in the principal case, the common law holdover rule gives the landlord a choice to treat the holdover as a trespasser or as a tenant under the terms of the original lease. Controversies often arise over the terms of the new lease when the parties do not anticipate the holdover possibility. For example, if a tenant holding over after the expiration of a five year term tenders rent equal to one month under the expired lease and the landlord accepts it, has a new five year term been created, or a periodic tenancy from year to year or month to month? See, W. Stoebuck & D. Whitman, The Law of Property, Third Edition 265 (2000) (new tenancy is periodic, by same period if prior tenancy was periodic for less than a year, by year to year if old tenancy was for a term of a year or more).

C. MITIGATION OF DAMAGES

AUSTIN HILL COUNTRY REALTY, INC. v. PALISADES PLAZA, INC.

Supreme Court of Texas, 1997.
948 S.W.2d 293.

Spector, Justice.

The issue in this case is whether a landlord has a duty to make reasonable efforts to mitigate damages when a tenant defaults on a lease. The court of appeals held that no such duty exists at common law. 938 S.W.2d 469. We hold today that a landlord has a duty to make reasonable efforts to mitigate damages. Accordingly, we reverse the judgment of the court of appeals and remand for a new trial.

I.

Palisades Plaza, Inc., owned and operated an office complex consisting of four office buildings in Austin. Barbara Hill, Annette Smith, and David Jones sold real estate in Austin as a Re/Max real estate brokerage franchise operating through Austin Hill Country Realty, Inc. On September 15, 1992, the Palisades and Hill Country executed a five-year commercial office lease for a suite in the Palisades office complex. An addendum executed in connection with the lease set the monthly base rent at $3,128 for the first year, $3,519 for the second and third years, and $3,910 for the fourth and fifth years. The parties also signed an improvements agreement that called for the Palisades to convert the shell office space into working offices for Hill Country. The lease was to begin on the "commencement date," which was defined in the lease and the improvements agreement as either (1) the date that Hill Country occupied the suite, or (2) the date that the Palisades substantially completed the improvements or would have done so but for "tenant delay." All parties anticipated that the lease would begin on November 15, 1992.

By the middle of October 1992, the Palisades had nearly completed the improvements. Construction came to a halt on October 21, 1992, when the Palisades received conflicting instructions about the completion of the suite from Hill on one hand and Smith and Jones on the other. By two letters, the Palisades informed Hill Country, Hill, Smith, and Jones that it had received conflicting directives and would not continue with the construction until Hill, Smith and Jones collectively designated a single representative empowered to make decisions for the trio. Hill, Smith, and Jones did not reply to these letters.

In a letter dated November 19, 1992, the Palisades informed Hill Country, Hill, Smith, and Jones that their failure to designate a representative was an anticipatory breach of contract. The parties tried unsuccessfully to resolve their differences in a meeting. The Palisades then sued Hill Country, Hill, Smith, and Jones (collectively, "Hill Country") for anticipatory breach of the lease.

At trial, Hill Country attempted to prove that the Palisades failed to mitigate the damages resulting from Hill Country's alleged breach. In particular, Hill Country introduced evidence that the Palisades rejected an offer from Smith and Jones to lease the premises without Hill, as well as an offer from Hill and another person to lease the premises without Smith and Jones. Hill Country also tried to prove that, while the Palisades advertised for tenants continuously in a local newspaper, it did not advertise in the commercial-property publication "The Flick Report" as it had in the past. Hill Country requested an instruction asking the jury to reduce the Palisades' damage award by "any amount that you find the [Palisades] could have avoided by the exercise of reasonable care." The trial judge rejected this instruction, stating "Last time I checked the law, it was that a landlord doesn't have any obligation to try to fill the space." The jury returned a verdict for the Palisades for $29,716 in damages and $16,500 in attorney's fees. The court of appeals affirmed that judgment. 938 S.W.2d 469.

II.

In its only point of error, Hill Country asks this Court to recognize a landlord's duty to make reasonable efforts to mitigate damages when a tenant breaches a lease. . . .

Today we face the issue . . . whether a landlord has a duty to make reasonable efforts to mitigate damages upon the tenant's breach. Because there is no statute addressing this issue, we look to the common law. [　]

The traditional common law rule regarding mitigation dictates that landlords have no duty to mitigate damages. See Dawn R. Barker, Note, Commercial Landlords' Duty Upon Tenants' Abandonment—To Mitigate?, 20 J. Corp. L. 627, 629 (1995). This rule stems from the historical concept that the tenant is owner of the property during the lease term; as long as the tenant has a right to possess the land, the tenant is liable for rent. [   ] Under this rule, a landlord is not obligated to undertake any action following a tenant's abandonment of the premises but may recover rents periodically for the remainder of the term. . . .

Texas courts have consistently followed this no-mitigation rule in cases involving a landlord's suit for past due rent. [   ]

Some Texas courts have, however, required a landlord to mitigate damages when the landlord seeks a remedy that is contractual in nature, such as anticipatory breach of contract, rather than a real property cause of action. . . .

Other Texas courts have required a landlord to mitigate damages when the landlord reenters or resumes control of the premises. [   ] Thus, a landlord currently may be subject to a mitigation requirement depending upon the landlord's actions following breach and the type of lawsuit the landlord pursues.

III.

In discerning the policy implications of a rule requiring landlords to mitigate damages, we are informed by the rules of other jurisdictions. Forty-two states and the District of Columbia have recognized that a landlord has a duty to mitigate damages in at least some situations: when there is a breach of a residential lease, a commercial lease, or both.

Only six states have explicitly held that a landlord has no duty to mitigate in any situation. In South Dakota, the law is unclear.

Those jurisdictions recognizing a duty to mitigate have emphasized the change in the nature of landlord-tenant law since its inception in medieval times. At English common law, the tenant has only contractual rights against the landlord and therefore could not assert common-law real property causes of action to protect the leasehold. Over time, the courts recognized a tenant's right to bring real property causes of action, and tenants were considered to possess an estate in land. [   ] The landlord had to give the tenant possession of the land, and the tenant was required to pay rent in return. As covenants in leases have become more complex and the structures on the land have become more important to the parties than the land itself, courts have begun to recognize that a lease possesses elements of both a contract and a conveyance. [   ] Under contract principles, the lease is not a complete conveyance to the tenant for a specific term such that the landlord's duties are fulfilled upon deliverance of the property to the tenant. Rather, a promise to pay in a lease is essentially the same as a promise to pay in any other contract, and a breach of that promise does not necessarily end the landlord's ongoing duties. [   ] Because of the contractual elements of the modern lease agreement, these courts have imposed upon the landlord the contractual duty to mitigate damages upon the tenant's breach.

Public policy offers further justification for the duty to mitigate. First, requiring mitigation in the landlord-tenant context discourages economic waste and encourages productive use of the property. As the Colorado Supreme Court has written:

> Under traditional property law principles a landlord could allow the property to remain unoccupied while still holding the abandoning tenant liable for rent. This encourages both economic and physical waste. In no other context of which we are aware is an injured party permitted to sit idly by and suffer avoidable economic loss and thereafter to visit the full adverse economic consequences upon the party whose breach initiated the chain of events causing the loss.

Schneiker v. Gordon, 732 P.2d 603, 610 (Colo.1987). A mitigation requirement thus returns the property to productive use rather than allowing it to remain idle. Public policy requires that the law "discourage even persons against whom wrongs have been committed from passively suffering economic loss which could be averted by reasonable efforts." Wright v. Baumann, 239 Or. 410, 398 P.2d 119, 121 (1965) (quoting C. McCormick, Handbook on the Law of Damages, § 33 (1935)).

Second, a mitigation rule helps prevent destruction of or damage to the leased property. If the landlord is encouraged to let the property remain unoccupied, "the possibility of physical damage to the property through accident or vandalism is increased." Schneiker, 732 P.2d at 610.

Third, the mitigation rule is consistent with the trend disfavoring contract penalties. [ ] Courts have held that a liquidated damages clause in a contract must represent a reasonable estimate of anticipated damages upon breach. [ ] "Similarly, allowing a landlord to leave property idle when it could be profitably leased and forc[ing] an absent tenant to pay rent for that idled property permits the landlord to recover more damages than it may reasonably require to be compensated for the tenant's breach. This is analogous to imposing a disfavored penalty upon the tenant." Reid v. Mutual of Omaha Ins. Co., 776 P.2d 896 905–06 (Utah 1989).

Finally, the traditional justifications for the common law rule have proven unsound in practice. Proponents of the no-mitigation rule suggest that the landlord-tenant relationship is personal in nature, and that the landlord therefore should not be forced to lease to an unwanted tenant. [ ] Modern lease arrangements, however, are rarely personal in nature and are usually business arrangements between strangers. [ ] Further, the landlord's duty to make reasonable efforts to mitigate does not require that the landlord accept replacement tenants who are financial risks or whose business was precluded by the original lease. [ ]

The overwhelming trend among jurisdictions in the United States has thus been toward requiring a landlord to mitigate damages when a tenant abandons the property in breach of the lease agreement. Those courts adopting a mitigation requirement have emphasized the contractual elements of a lease agreement, the public policy favoring productive use of property, and the practicalities of the modern landlord-tenant arrangement as supporting such a duty.

IV.

We are persuaded by the reasoning of those courts that recognize that landlords must mitigate damages upon a tenant' abandonment and failure to pay rent. This Court has recognized the dual nature of a lease as both a conveyance and a contract. [   ] Under a contract view, a landlord should be treated no differently than any other aggrieved party to a contract. Further, the public policy of the state of Texas calls for productive use of property as opposed to avoidable economic waste.... Finally, we have recognized that contract penalties are disfavored in Texas. [   ] A landlord should not be allowed to collect rent from an abandoning tenant when the landlord can, by reasonable efforts, relent the premises and avoid incurring some damages. We therefore recognize that a landlord has a duty to make reasonable efforts to mitigate damages when the tenant breaches the lease and abandons the property.

V.

To ensure the uniform application of this duty by the courts of this state, and to guide future landlords and tenants in conforming their conduct to the law, we now consider several practical considerations that will undoubtedly arise. We first consider the level of conduct by a landlord that will satisfy the duty to mitigate. The landlord's mitigation duty has been variously stated in other jurisdictions.... We hold that the landlord's duty to mitigate requires the landlord to use objectively reasonable efforts to fill the premises when the tenant vacates in breach of the lease.

We stress that this is not an absolute duty, nor does the landlord's failure to mitigate give rise to a cause of action by the tenant. Rather, the landlord's failure to use reasonable efforts to mitigate damages bars the landlord's recovery against the breaching tenant only to the extent that damages reasonably could have been avoided. Similarly, the amount of damages that the landlord actually avoided by releasing the premises will reduce the landlord's recovery.

Further, we believe that the tenant properly bears the burden of proof to demonstrate that the landlord has mitigated or failed to mitigate damages....

The final issue to resolve regarding the duty to mitigate is to which types of actions by the landlord the duty will apply. Traditionally, Texas courts have regarded the landlord as having four cause of action against a tenant for breach of the lease and abandonment. [   ] First, the landlord can maintain the lease, suing for rent as it becomes due. Second, the landlord can treat the breach as an anticipatory repudiation, repossess, and sue for the present value of future rentals reduced by the reasonable cash market value of the property for the remainder of the lease term. Third, the landlord can treat the breach as anticipatory, repossess, release the property, and sue the tenant for the different between the contractual rent and the amount received from the new tenant. Fourth, the landlord can declare the lease forfeited (if the lease so provides) and relieve the tenant of liability for future rent. [ ]

The landlord must have a duty to mitigate when suing for anticipatory repudiation. Because the cause of action is contractual in nature, the contractual duty to mitigate should apply. The landlord's option to maintain the lease and sue for rent as it becomes due, however, is more troubling. To require the landlord to mitigate in that instance would force the landlord to reenter the premises and thereby risk terminating the lease or accepting the tenant's surrender. [ ] We thus hold that, when exercising the option to maintain the lease in effect and sue for rent as it becomes due following the tenant's breach and abandonment, the landlord has a duty to mitigate only if (1) the landlord actually reenters, or (2) the lease allows the landlord to reenter the premises without accepting surrender, forfeiting the lease, or being construed as evicting the tenant. [ ] A suit for anticipatory repudiation, and actual reentry, or a contractual right of reentry subject to the above conditions will therefore give rise to the landlord's duty to mitigate breaches upon the tenant's breach and abandonment.

VI.

In their first amended answer, Hill Country and Barbara Hill specifically contended that the Palisades failed to mitigate its damages. Because the court of appeals upheld the trial court's refusal to submit their mitigation instruction, we reverse the judgment of the court of appeals and remand for a new trial.

Notes and Questions

1. What is the basis for the traditional common law rule that the landlord has no responsibility to mitigate damages in cases of tenant abandonment? Are there reasons for continued adherence to the no-mitigation rule, or has the rule outlived its usefulness? See Bowdoin Square, L.L.C. v. Winn–Dixie Montgomery, Inc., 873 So.2d 1091, 1098–1101 (Ala. 2003) (construing lease clause containing mitigation provision as permissive rather than mandatory); Restatement (Second) of Property, § 12.1 (3), Comment i (1977) (no-mitigation rule helps discourage tenant abandonment and subsequent threat of vandalism). See generally Flynn, Duty to Mitigate Damages upon a Tenant's Abandonment, 34 Real Prop. Prob. & Tr. J. 721 (2000) (reviewing history of landlord mitigation issue and examining how state courts determine what are acceptable mitigation efforts); Weissenberg, The Landlord's Duty to Mitigate Damages on the Tenant's Abandonment: A Survey of Old Law and New Trends, 53 Temple L.Q. 1 (1980).

2. What constitutes abandonment? Suppose a tenant leaves on a trip for three weeks without telling the landlord. Is the landlord justified in

treating the tenant as having abandoned the premises? Would it make a difference whether the rent was not yet due, or that it was overdue? Would a landlord be justified in including in a lease the requirement that tenants inform the landlord whenever they will be absent for more than seven days, and that failure to do so would enable the landlord to treat the tenant as having abandoned? See URLTA, § 3.104, reproduced earlier (authorizing notice requirement for extended absences).

3. Suppose a landlord re-lets an abandoned apartment for more than the original contract rent. Who is entitled to the difference? Suppose the apartment is re-let for half the remaining time of the original lease but for twice the contract rent. How would the landlord's damages be calculated?

4. Ordinarily, the landlord who refuses to accept surrender and elects to leave the property vacant must wait to collect rent until it falls due. If the abandoning tenant refuses to pay, and the landlord does not want to sue for each installment, he may wait until several installments have accrued or even until the term has expired to begin legal action. Some jurisdictions, however, will allow the landlord to recover damages on a theory of breach by anticipatory repudiation. What would be the measure of the landlord's damages under that theory?

5. To enable the landlord to sue for the rent for the balance of the term immediately upon a tenant's abandonment, leases frequently include rent acceleration clauses, which render the balance of the rent due, at the landlord's option, if any rental installment is past due. Should the rent acceleration clause be enforceable in a no-mitigation jurisdiction? In a mitigation jurisdiction? See Ricker v. Rombough, 120 Cal.App.2d Supp. 912, 261 P.2d 328 (1953) (held unenforceable as either a penalty or an agreement for liquidated damages when actual damages are readily ascertainable); W. Stoebuck & D. Whitman, The Law of Property, Third Edition 360–61 (2000) (majority of courts accept acceleration clauses under freedom of contract principles, but apply strict construction rules).

VII.   A SECOND LOOK AT DISPUTE RESOLUTION

SALSICH AND FITZGERALD, MEDIATION OF LAND-LORD–TENANT DISPUTES: NEW HOPE FOR THE IMPLIED WARRANTY OF HABITABILITY?

19 Creighton L.R. 791–795, 809–815 (1986).

* * *

While the revolution in residential landlord-tenant law has resulted in one of the quickest and most dramatic changes in American history to a major aspect of law, it has not produced the improvement in housing standards for low-and moderate-income families that its leaders expected. Legal literature is replete with analysis and commentary about the implied warranty of habitability as a legal concept and about the expectations that were created by it. In many locations, the results have fallen far short of the expectations. Empirical studies in Boston, Chicago,

Detroit, and San Francisco, as well as observations of activity in Kansas City and St. Louis, have noted a disappointing, harsh, but observable reality: landlord-tenant law reform, as administered by the courts, has not improved the housing conditions of low-and moderate-income tenants. One of the most distressing findings is the evidence that some courts, responsible for administering landlord-tenant law, have taken a hostile view to the doctrine of implied warranty of habitability or have ignored the doctrine and its attendant tenant remedies.

This Article does not attempt to reanalyze this problem but, instead, looks at a parallel development, alternative dispute resolution, as a possible approach to the administration of the new landlord-tenant law. This approach may enable some of the hopes regarding better housing to be realized. Some particular characteristics of the residential landlord-tenant relationship, particularly with respect to the low-and moderate-income tenants in urban environments, suggest that alternatives to litigation as a means of resolving disputes and administering this relationship have greater potential for success than a continued tinkering with the litigation process.

* * *

Because the landlord remains the owner of the property, a complexity is introduced into this relationship. Two people share the property "bundle" represented by the leased premises. The landlord has an obligation not to harm the tenant's possessory interest, while the tenant has both an obligation not to harm the landlord's ownership interest and an obligation to pay rent. The technical articulation of the tenant's responsibility is that the tenant may not commit waste. Most written leases incorporate the tenant's responsibility through language providing that the tenant agrees to return the property in the same condition as received, normal wear and tear excepted. When a dispute develops involving allegations that waste has been committed, the security deposit usually becomes the center of attention.

Another point of importance, particularly with respect to residential rental property occupied by families of low-and moderate-income, is that short-term tenancies often are created by oral agreements. Most states require written leases for tenancies that are one year or longer in duration. Many low-and moderate-income urban tenants occupy housing under oral arrangements that can be terminated by either party at the end of a rental period, which is usually one month in duration. Traditionally, landlord-tenant law focused on the administration of the termination process by concentrating on notice requirements, summary eviction proceedings, and regulation of the use of self-help.

* * *

III.   NONADVERSARIAL DISPUTE RESOLUTION

A parallel development of potential significance to landlords and tenants has been the increased attention given to non-adversarial methods of resolving disputes. A wide range of techniques are being touted, with arbitration and mediation the most popular. The basic distinction between arbitration and mediation is the role assumed by the person to whom the dispute has been brought and the amount of pressure which that person can bring to bear on the parties to the dispute.

Under an arbitration system, the parties usually transfer control over the dispute to a neutral arbitrator who will impose a resolution which will bind the parties if they have agreed in advance to be bound. Arbitration resembles adjudication in this respect, but it is conducted in a far less formal manner. If the parties have agreed in advance to accept the arbitrator's decision, courts will enforce that decision unless the arbitrator clearly exceeded his authority.

Mediation, on the other hand, focuses primarily on the parties themselves coming to an agreement. In these situations, the mediator acts only as a facilitator without the authority to impose a decision on the parties. The mediator seeks to be accepted by the parties as a neutral conciliator rather than a partisan participant or adjudicator.

Proponents of both mediation and arbitration emphasize the speed, lack of expense, informality, de-emphasis of adversary relationships, voluntary nature, privacy, and potential expertise of the dispute resolution officials as factors favoring the use of alternatives to litigation. They, however, caution that mediation typically presumes the possibility of compromise between the parties. If one of the parties is considerably more powerful than the other, that party may not have sufficient incentives to compromise.

In addition to the benefits noted, proponents argue that more extensive use of mediation and arbitration would alleviate some of the problems arising from use of the traditional judicial system. The courts are often a hostile environment for landlord-tenant disputes. This hostility can flow from such things as overburdened caseloads, the built-in conflict between human and property rights, traditional court procedures, lack of familiarity with conditions of housing involved, and even the lack of standards for determining such things as damages from a breach of the implied warranty of habitability. Some courts, recognizing these difficulties, have begun encouraging parties to participate in a mediation process before the court enters its final judgment.

Landlord-tenant disputes—especially conflicts between individual tenants and their landlords over conditions within their particular apartments because of which rent payments or security deposits are held hostage, while emotions rage out of control—may be particularly suited to nonadjudicatory, dispute-resolution processes. In dealing with these issues, property law in general, and landlord-tenant law in particular, has traditionally recognized few legal theories that permit courts to compromise claims. Thus, litigation takes the form of an "either/or, winner/loser" process. Because of the continuing nature of the relationship and the often blurred facts as to who bears responsibility for the damages, litigation may be the least satisfactory approach toward resolving the typical landlord-tenant dispute.

In part, this ineffectiveness is due to the subject matter of the dispute. When parties are in litigation over possessory or ownership rights to real property, usually one side must be declared the winner, with the corresponding right to possess or exclude, and the other, the loser. Ownership and possessory interests and corresponding responsibilities for maintenance and protection of those interests generally must be clear and undiluted in order to enhance the property's productivity and transferability. The long-term nature of most property investments makes predictability an essential element of property law.

The "either/or" choices that prevail in property law litigation can destroy the continuity that is an essential attribute of landlord-tenant relationships. The modern residential landlord-tenant relationship resembles a family in one crucial aspect—mutual interdependence. Because the landlord normally does not live in the building that is being rented, and may, in fact, not even be present in the same jurisdiction, the landlord depends upon the tenants to be "good" tenants and to take care of the landlord's property. At the same time, the tenants depend upon the landlord to be a "good" landlord and to provide the essential services which enable the tenants to live in peace and dignity. The reality of these mutual but often unstated interests was recognized in the pathbreaking, implied-warranty-of-habitability cases. The nature of mediation, with its emphasis on direct communication between the parties to the relationship, assists in defining such interests.

These mutual interests often stem from the purely interpersonal disputes which arise among parties involved in an ongoing relationship. For example, a landlord might believe that a tenant's young children will be likely to damage the common areas of the premises and, therefore, will be less tolerant of any normal childlike activity. The tenant, on the other hand, might believe that the landlord has failed to provide an adequate area where the children may play without them worrying about damage to the premises. In this situation, mediation can be of immeasurable help because it can get the parties talking to one another. With this conversation, the parties may realize that there is no genuine conflict between them. Meshing the concept of "kids will be kids" with the landlord's legitimate concern for the preservation of his property is just one circumstance which is better suited for dispute resolution through communication rather than through a formal judicial process.

Satisfactory protection of the mutual interests of landlords and tenants requires a stable, predictable relationship in which each party can rely on the other to perform in accordance with the mutual understandings. It, however, does not require that landlords or tenants subordinate their self-interests. In fact, responding to the others' concerns actually maximizes the responders' self-interests. The landlord who wants the tenants to be "good" tenants and to take care of the property, as well as to pay the rent on time, is more likely to get these results if he delivers the services that his tenants justifiably expect to receive. Conversely, the tenant who seeks services of a particular quality, such as prompt responses to repair and maintenance requests, is more likely to obtain such responses if he pays the rent on time and takes reasonable care of the premises. In short, both parties desire that the other be "good."

Unfortunately, as is the case with all families, disputes often mar the day-to-day life of the landlord-tenant family. Comparable to other families, resorting to the courts for a resolution of a landlord-tenant dispute generally presages the destruction of the relationship. Whatever possibilities for conciliation and compromise which might exist and which could save the relationship are generally lost once litigation is commenced. This loss is due to the way an adversarial proceeding often transforms a dispute over competing interests into a conflict over hardened positions. Regardless of who wins a landlord-tenant lawsuit, whatever trust and respect that might have been present at one time and which is so essential to the achievement of a "good" landlord-tenant relationship, has probably been destroyed by the bitterness engendered in the litigation. Litigation can be quite costly to both the winner and the loser. If the tenant leaves as a result of the conflict, the landlord faces the additional expense and uncertainty of a vacant apartment until a new tenant can be found, plus the cost of redecorating or repairing the apartment to attract a new tenant. Likewise, the departing tenant faces the cost and uncertainty of seeking a new place to live. If the tenant stays after the litigation has been completed, the obstacles that must be overcome before a "good" relationship can be restored are enormous.

The seeds of urban tragedy can be found in this state of affairs. The great hope that the revolution in residential landlord-tenant law would result in improved housing conditions for low-income families has dissolved like a desert mirage. Wholesale abandonment of apartment buildings or their conversion into condominiums has occurred in many urban neighborhoods. Of course, placing all of the housing ills of the urban poor on the doorstep of the landlord-tenant courthouse is about as fair as blaming all of the ills of society on the failure of the public school system. However, the fact remains that reliance on litigation, even after the substantial shift in the law toward the tenant's point of view, has not resulted in a measurable improvement in the living conditions of the low- or moderate-income urban tenant. Continued reliance on litigation as the basic mechanism for resolution of landlord-tenant disputes is, thus, open to serious question.

The shift in landlord-tenant law has laid the foundation for the use of alternatives to litigation in dispute resolution. Two of the major concerns that have been raised about the use of arbitration and mediation in landlord-tenant disputes are: (1) the perceived imbalance of power between the landlord and the tenant; and (2) the corresponding lack of incentive for the landlord to participate in noncoercive dispute resolution proceedings. Under the common law, the landlord certainly held the upper hand, in that the tenant had an absolute obligation to pay rent and usually had all the responsibility for maintenance and repair, even if he did not have control or the wherewithal to discharge that responsibility. The typical response of the landlord to a tenant's protest of that state of affairs was that no one was forcing the tenant to stay. This has changed. Society, through the courts and the legislatures, has shifted much of the repair and maintenance responsibility back to the landlord. In the eyes of the law, a state of equilibrium has been approached. If anyone may cry in the future that the system is out of balance, it may be the landlords.

While these changes in the law are not yet reflected in the realities of the landlord-tenant courts, they can dispel the power-imbalance concern because the tenant today has a wide range of legal weapons at his disposal. Effective dissemination of information about the power-shifts in the landlord-tenant law may help tenants overcome the intimidation which results from their sense of powerlessness, while also giving landlords a greater incentive to accept and, perhaps, even to seek out nonadversarial means of settling disputes. If a seeking of nonadversarial means were to occur, the use of the techniques of conciliation and compromise, heart of the mediation process, could enable the disputing parties to preserve the essential unity of the landlord-tenant relationship, while resolving their differences in a reasonably efficient and less costly manner. One of the most positive results that could come about is an increase in direct communication regarding the disputed matter. Communication between the affected parties could occur at an earlier stage so as to prevent irreparable damage to the landlord-tenant relationship. * * *

MEDIATION FROM A LAW STUDENT PERSPECTIVE*

Two Case Studies

During the Spring, 1984 Semester, five Saint Louis University law students participated in an experimental settlement program designed to resolve disputes among litigants in the small claims division of the St. Louis City Circuit Court. As court-appointed mediators, the students met with litigants on the date their cases were scheduled to be heard and attempted to settle the disputes without the need for adjudication. The judge explained to the parties that they were under no obligation to settle, but he expressed his desire that they attempt settlement before requesting a trial of their cause.

Students generally followed a three-step procedure. First, they explained their role as a neutral third party whose duty was simply to facilitate an agreement. Second, they met with each party to the dispute in a private conference for ten to fifteen minutes to obtain a basic understanding of the dispute and gauge the interests of the respective

* Reprinted with permission of Timothy Blanchard (J.D., M.H.A., 1986, Saint Louis University) and William K. Meehan (J.D., 1985, Saint Louis University). Names of parties are changed to protect privacy.

parties. Finally, they met with both parties in a joint conference in which they attempted to help the parties reach agreement. Each student was assigned four or five cases during a one-month period. Following are illustrative case evaluations from two students who participated in the program.

JOHN O. MARLEY v. HOUSE CIRCLE APARTMENTS

Marley v. House Circle Apartments was an action for property damage arising out of a landlord-tenant relationship. One morning in December, 1983, John Marley, a tenant in defendant's building, noticed a leak emanating from his dishwasher before leaving for work. Marley reported the leak to the management and left for work. He returned later that evening and found his kitchen flooded by approximately a foot and a half of water. Marley again called the management, which responded the next day to remove the water and clean up the mess. As a result of the flooding, Marley claimed damage to his personal effects, groceries, and household items in the amount of $338.00.

The events in question occurred during a prolonged period of unreasonably cold temperatures in the St. Louis area. While the flooding could have logically been caused by the rupture of frozen water pipes, Marley ruled out this possibility since he had taken the precaution of letting his taps run in an effort to avoid this problem. Thus, he concluded that management had been negligent in responding to his report of a leaky dishwasher. Marley made several requests for compensation with regard to his damaged property, but received only a letter dated two days after the incident. The letter, authored by the unit manager, denied his claims for compensation and implied that he was negligent in failing to let his taps run during the cold snap. In the face of this response, Marley brought this action.

The apartment complex was represented by the community director, the unit manager, and the maintenance supervisor. At the time of the letter, the source of the flooding had yet to be determined. By the time of the hearing, management had ascertained the source of the flooding and they brought a detailed account of the problem with them to the hearing. Acting as spokesman for the group, the maintenance supervisor explained, with the aid of graphics, that the flooding of the apartment had been caused by a rupture in a water main leading to the outside of the building. The main was located in a locked access area behind the wall of the kitchen and was not an area regularly checked by the management's maintenance staff. When the break occurred, management was unaware of its existence and the water flowed into the apartment.

After speaking with both sides, I became convinced that this dispute had arisen due to poor communication between the parties. Marley had been informed of the true cause behind the flooding and still was under the impression that the apartment complex was unjustly attempting to hold him negligent. House Circle contributed to this misconception by failing to clear the matter up and ignoring his claims for compensation. I believed that once the misunderstanding was corrected, the parties would be able to reach some sort of settlement.

To their credit, both sides to this dispute were extremely objective. Although I sensed a bit of tension and annoyance on both sides, the parties were able to separate their emotions from the merits of the dispute. The maintenance supervisor was especially adept in his handling of the negotiations. Judging from his performance, it was obvious to me that he was well experienced in just this type of bargaining. Using his graphics and citing relevant portions of the lease agreement, he explained to Marley the cause behind the flooding, noted the unanticipated cold spell, and reminded Marley that management was not responsible for damage resulting from breaks in water or gas lines pursuant to the lease. The argument was flawless in that it employed an objective criterion and was tied to a rationale supported by evidence. Marley was equally objective in his response to the maintenance supervisor's explanation and argument. He didn't attack its premise, but, rather, accepted the explanation as plausible. Yet, he adhered to principle by arguing that he was not responsible for the flooding and felt victimized.

Once the misunderstanding had been resolved, I recognized each party desired to settle the dispute without going to trial. The maintenance supervisor acknowledged that Marley had been a good tenant and House Circle wanted him to continue residency there. Marley also indicated that he had been satisfied with the House Circle management and wished to continue his residence there. This gave me the opening I was looking for. Both sides had recognized their mutual interests at stake (their desire to preserve the satisfactory landlord-tenant relationship) and now needed an option which would allow both to gain at neither's expense. This meant that the issue of culpability would have to be resolved.

Marley had worded his complaint in terms alleging that House Circle had been negligent. House Circle would not settle if it meant they would be held negligent. Such a judgment would have reflected poorly on their maintenance man, and it was clear he was not at fault. At this point, I suggested that Marley waive his allegation of negligence in return for a cash settlement. Moreover, I reviewed Marley's list of damages and suggested he drop some of the more frivolous items. Both parties were receptive to such a proposed settlement, and after a short discussion over some of the damage items, they agreed on terms. In return for $170.00 as settlement of his claims, Marley agreed to waive his claim of negligence on the part of House Circle Apartments.

In summary, this was simply a case of failed communication between parties engendering a lawsuit. Acting out of ignorance of the true cause behind the disputed event, both sides retreated to positions and resisted any effort to move towards rational discussion. After the addition of a disinterested third party, the parties were able to recognize their interests, improve their communications, and work towards an option meeting both of their needs. The parties preserved their existing relationship and avoided the risk of realizing their perceived BATNAs (Best Alternative to Negotiated Agreement) which would have resulted in dismissal of Marley's claim or a judgment against House Circle for the entire amount asked. Mediation allowed both parties to walk away content, if not pleased.

ROSS v. GRAHAM

This case involved a dispute between a landlord and former tenants. The Grahams rented the upper flat from Ross, who lived in the lower flat. There was no written lease, but the parties agree that rent of $225.00 was due monthly. It is disputed whether the term began on the eleventh or the seventh of the month, however, and with the exception of the first month, the rent had been tendered and accepted in installments as the Grahams were able to pay. In December the Grahams were unable to pay rent, but they paid the December rent, less $19.00, in early January. They then agreed to pay the January rent at $50.00 per week for two weeks then $125.00 two weeks later. The Grahams made the first $50.00 payment then moved out without notice, leaving a balance due of $194.00. Mrs. Ross's prayer for $234.00 included $194.00 in rent due, a penalty of $25.00 for failure to give 30 days notice prior to vacating, and $15.00 for an allegedly missing fluorescent lamp fixture.

During Mrs. Ross's rendition of the facts, neither of the Grahams gave any indication of disagreement with anything she said, so, rather than ask for their side of the story, I simply asked if what she said was correct. They admitted that they owed the $194.00 and that they were willing to pay. They were unable to pay the total due at one time, however, because of cash flow problems. They maintained, however, that no penalty was discussed at any time prior to their moving out, and that they did not take the lamp fixture. Mrs. Graham then began an attempt to legitimate the fact that they moved out by complaining that promised repairs had not been effected by Ross. For a moment I was afraid that the momentum generated by the Graham's quick admission of responsibility would be lost in counterproductive ancillary counter-claims. In order to avoid this without having to separate them, which would likewise destroy the momentum, I interrupted by asking, "Excuse me, but was there a written lease?" The response was that there was not. Since I suspected that Ross's primary objective was to recover the rent due, I wanted to reduce her expectation of recovering the penalty. Toward this end I pointed out that in the absence of a written lease, the court would probably require the landlord to prove that such a clause had been agreed to from the outset. I also recognized that the Grahams already felt guilty about not having been able to pay the rent. Since this coupled with their admission gave Mrs. Ross a stronger power position, I sought to equalize the bargaining positions because when one side is in the dominant position or perceives itself to be, effective negotiation is less likely to occur. More powerful parties tend to exhibit behavior leading to inequitable agreements. Therefore, effective bargaining should be enhanced to the extent that a mediator can bring about a perception of balance of power.

I think I was able to do this by phrasing my comments in such a way as to make Ross feel a bit guilty or at least foolish for not having a written lease. Ross admitted that the provision for a penalty had never been discussed. I then asked, "Your real interest then is that $194.00," to which she responded, "Yes," and that she would settle for that, but that it had to be all in one payment. The Grahams both interjected that they couldn't do that. When I asked why it had to be a single payment she said that was how the rent was to have been paid all along, and that she couldn't wait for it anymore. She was in effect saying to the Grahams, We've been nice to you, but now that you're going we want our money now. The perceived balance of power was shifting once again, so to avoid the risk of losing the "bargaining relationship," I once again sought to equalize the relative power positions. I pointed out that the law may imply a waiver of even explicit terms in light of a course of dealing to the contrary, such as the payment schedule in this case. To this Ross responded that she just wanted to be sure that she got the money once and for all. Thus, her primary concern was certainty of collection. I then explained that even if the judge ruled in her favor, it would be up to her to collect on the judgment, that this would involve another court appearance in a collection or garnishment proceeding (making it sound as complicated and cumbersome as possible), and that given the Grahams' income, even this would not pay her "all at once."

Having adequately reduced her expectations, I restated the situation as I saw it in a light most favorable to both parties. I said that it looked to me as though the Grahams really just wanted a chance to pay what they owed, and that Ross was mainly interested in the certain recovery of her money as quickly as reasonably possible. My goal in making this statement was to make use of an impression I had drawn from observing Ross. It was my impression that she was not there for the purpose of punishing the Grahams but only to insure the recovery of the rent due. I further speculate that Mr. Ross actually decided to sue, but that Mrs. Ross had to appear since he was at work. At one point Mrs. Ross said that Mr. Ross had demanded a single payment of the late January rent but she had convinced him to allow them to make installments—to give them another chance, as it were. Thus, through this statement and my delivery, I was attempting to reinforce Ross's self-perception as a good, generous person and at the same time revive her prior perception of the Grahams as good people having some tough times, who deserved one more chance. One might have expected an entirely different attitude from Mrs. Ross, who might have felt double-crossed by the Grahams, who had, in effect, bitten the hand that fed them (with another chance). Accordingly were it not for the contrary impression I got from non-verbals, I would have expected "face-restoration" behavior since the Grahams' vacation of the flat with rent past due must have made Ross look foolish to her husband. Fortunately, this was not the case.

I waited for both parties to volunteer agreement to this characterization of the situation. Having put the rationale before the solution, I suggested, "Suppose I can work it out to where both of these interests are met—do you think we can settle this case?" When both parties had agreed, I explained that a payment schedule could be set forth in a consent judgment entered by the Judge, and that this would afford Ross the security of a judgment which she could execute if the Grahams failed to make the scheduled payments. We then worked out a payment schedule with three payments of $50.00 every other week and the balance due two weeks after the third payment. I then asked if this was entirely agreeable to everyone. Both sides answered affirmatively and I simply allowed the allegedly missing lamp fixture to be forgotten. The case was settled.

I made an error, however, that could have ruined the whole thing. I forgot to deal with court costs. When the issue arose before the judge the Grahams accepted it as a formality and the costs were added on to the final payment. This could have been a serious practical problem, given the Grahams' cash flow situation, even though they acknowledged their duty to pay the back rent and that they would have lost on that issue at trial. Even if the issue of victory at trial had been at issue, I could have suggested that the court costs be set up to cancel out the $15.00 lamp fixture. In spite of feeling a bit foolish if not negligent, about forgetting the issue of court costs, I left the courtroom tired but strangely satisfied, despite the rain.

Notes and Questions

1.   Compare the approaches of the two students. In the first case, the student emphasized the use of mediation techniques, while in the second one, greater use was made of landlord-tenant law in an attempt to persuade the parties that they may achieve a more satisfactory result by themselves than one that might be imposed through litigation.

2.   The author of the first paper was more successful in mediating the four disputes assigned to him than the author of the second paper. Does this suggest that:

   a.   mediation skills and their effective use by the mediator,

   b.   the cases/parties themselves and their suitability for mediation, or

   c.   some necessary combination of the above,

is the distinguishing feature of those cases which are successfully resolved without litigation?

3.   Did the student mediators maintain neutrality? Were their statements of law accurate? Did the student mediators appear to have achieved success?

4.   As counsel for either Kelly Green or Lance Lord, prepare a proposal for a negotiated settlement. Identify the issues upon which agreement may

be relatively easy to obtain, and the ones which will most likely require hard bargaining. To use a baseball analogy, prepare a list of goals, from "home-run" (best possible achievement) through "triple," "double," "single," and "strikeout," for review with your client.

5.   Consider the use of a grievance procedure to resolve landlord-tenant disputes. For example, Federal law requires local public housing authorities to offer administrative grievance procedures for disputes which "adversely affect the tenant's rights, duties, welfare or status." 24 C.F.R. § 966.50 et seq. (1997). The grievance procedure includes an informal settlement conference, a hearing before an impartial hearing officer, and an administrative appeal. What advantages or disadvantages might such a procedure have over litigation? Over mediation?

Chapter Five

REAL ESTATE TRANSACTIONS

I. THE PARTICIPANT AND THEIR ROLES

A. THE SERVICE GROUPS

With this chapter we finally arrive at the subject that most lay persons assume real property law is really about: conveyancing. We begin with an examination of the participants in the real estate transfer process and their roles in that process. Next we examine the primary legal documents involved in real estate transfers and legal problems that arise with respect to them. Finally we turn to the primary problems with which conveyancing law is concerned: protection against defects in the condition or title of the property and the financing of real estate purchases. Many of the cases that follow involve residential real estate.

Although the lawyer's role in the residential real estate transaction has decreased in recent years, the residential real estate transaction is important for law students to study. First, despite the general trend discussed in the following article, many lawyers, particularly in rural areas, remain involved in residential transactions. Second, the same rules and concepts that govern the residential transactions govern commercial transactions. The lawyer's involvement in commercial transactions is frequent and intense. Thirds, as the cases that follow reveal, the residential real estate transaction is a frequent source of litigation. So while residential transactions may not be important for the real estate lawyer, they may be very important for the litigator.

BRAUNSTEIN, STRUCTURAL CHANGE AND
INTER–PROFESSIONAL COMPETITIVE
ADVANTAGE: AN EXAMPLE DRAWN FROM
RESIDENTIAL REAL ESTATE CONVEYANCING
62 Missouri Law Review 241 (1997).

I. INTRODUCTION

[Lawyers] have become marginalized in the residential real estate transaction. They are involved only in about forty percent of residential transactions, and even when they are involved, their involvement is typically late and shallow. In almost all states the real estate agent drafts and negotiates the contract of sale without the aid of an attorney. Lawyers are not involved in the closing most of the time, and the trend is toward less lawyer involvement rather than more. The article explains how United States lawyers lost the monopoly they once enjoyed over residential real estate conveyancing and how structural change, whether economic, technological or both, influences the demand for professional, including legal services.

* * *

II. BRIEF REVIEW OF THE LITERATURE—PRINCIPALLY THE CASE BOOKS

Academic legal literature draws a distorted picture of the role of the lawyer in the residential real estate transaction. Details aside, the portrayal is inaccurate in three major respects. First, this literature portrays the involvement of the lawyer in residential conveyancing as much more desirable than it really is; second, it portrays the role of the lawyer as much more central to the transaction than it really is; and third, it portrays the residential real estate transaction as much more complex (hence demanding of legal skills) than it really is.

* * *

IV. PATTERNS OF LAWYER USE AND NON-USE THROUGHOUT THE UNITED STATES

A. Introduction

This section describes what lawyers do, and do not do, in the residential real estate transaction from the perspectives both of the organized real estate profession and the lawyers in the United States who are engaged in residential real estate work. * * *

The Perspective of the Organized Real Estate Profession

Concurrent with the diminution of the lawyers' role in residential transactions has been an increase in the role of the real estate agent. Indeed, the real estate agent is the dominant player in the residential real estate transaction in almost all parts of the United States. By this I mean that the real estate agent is the "gate keeper" and either does the work or assigns various aspects of it to other professionals, as deemed necessary. While there is some regional variation, most of the work of residential conveyancing is controlled or performed by real estate agents.

In 1992 a survey was conducted of the executive directors and the general counsel of the Board of Realtors of all fifty states. Each board was asked to respond to four questions concerning local customs and procedures for the purchase and sale of residential real estate in their respective state. The purpose of this survey was to determine the relative prominence of the various professions involved in the typical residential real estate transaction.

The survey results indicate a great deal of uniformity throughout the U.S. in professional roles and duties in residential real estate transactions, notwithstanding the conventional wisdom to the contrary. These results also corroborate the paucity of attorney involvement in residential real estate transactions.

1. The Pre–Contract and Contract Stage

Respondents indicated that in 35 of the 40 states responding, the real estate agent typically negotiates and drafts the contract of purchase and sale without the aid or assistance of an attorney. In these states, the real estate agent prepares the contract and other necessary documentation on standardized forms. Usually, these forms have been approved by the local board of realtors, the local bar association or both. In these states, attorney involvement is often limited to transactions in which no realtor is involved or transactions that are unusually complicated, such as those involving contract for deed or seller financing.

Within the general framework of real estate agent dominance there are still a few contested services that may require attorney involvement. For example, in a few states, the realtor is permitted to fill in forms commonly in use in the community, "but may not modify terms or conditions of the contract that would effect the legal relationship of the parties." A few states have attorney approval clauses. These clauses provide that either party may have the contract reviewed by an attorney within a specified number of days after the execution of the contract. If the attorney does not approve of the contract as written she may suggest changes and if these are not agreed to by the other party the contract is nullified. Even in states where such clauses are used, however, actual attorney review and involvement is rare.

There are only five states where it is still customary for the attorney to draw the contract of sale.[1] In each of these states, although procedures differ slightly, it is customary for the real estate agent to draft a "binder" which outlines the terms of the agreement, but typically for the attorney to draw the contract.

2. The Post–Contract and Closing Stage

Moving a transaction from the contract stage to the closing[2] involves a number of steps.

At least to the uninitiated the quantity and technicality of these steps may be daunting. Although most real estate professionals would

---

1. Even in the handful of states where lawyer use is prevalent in residential real estate transactions, the practice varies within the state and lawyer use is generally limited to those parts of the state involving large population centers. Thus, in Massachusetts, lawyer use is limited to the Boston area, in New York to New York City and the upper Hudson River Valley and in Illinois to Cook County and the area surrounding Chicago.

2. In some states the closing is referred to as the settlement. Whatever the terminology, this is the time when the obligations of the contract are performed by both buyer and seller and the contract thus becomes fully executed. While closing may involve a number of technical steps, the most important of these are the payment of the purchase price by the buyer and the delivery of the deed by the seller.

agree that these steps are routine and largely mechanical, lawyer involvement after the purchase contract is executed is greater than in the pre-contract stage. Still, in most cases attorneys are not involved in readying the transaction for closing and frequently are not present at the closing. In only eight states of the forty states reporting is it customary for either the buyer's or the seller's attorney to ready the transaction for closing. In the rest of the states the preparation of the closing documentation and the closing itself are handled by the real estate agent, the title insurance company, a corporate closing company, an escrow agency, or some combination of them.

The historical trend is in favor of even less lawyer involvement during the closing. A 1983 survey conducted by First America Title Insurance Company listed fifteen states where it was common for residential real estate transactions to be closed by lawyers. The 1992 survey reported in this article obtained responses from thirteen of those fifteen states. Of the thirteen responding states it was still common for lawyers to conduct the closing in only five of them. In the remaining eight states, closings were conducted by lay conveyancers. No state that reported using lay conveyancers to close residential real estate transactions in the 1983 survey reported using lawyers for this work in the 1992 survey. Thus, in the nine years between the 1983 and the 1992 survey, the number of states in which closings were conducted primarily by lawyers declined by sixty percent.

The Perspective of the Practicing Lawyer in the United States

* * *

Interviewees had been members of the bar between three and thirty-six years. On average, they had spent 14.2 years in residential real estate practice. Residential real estate as a percentage of the attorney's total work varied greatly: between five percent and ninety percent, with an average of twenty-eight percent. Residential real estate as the percentage of a firm's work ranged from one percent to ninety percent. Residential real estate work was twice as important to rural lawyers than to urban ones (38.1 percent vs. 17.9 percent) and more important to solo practitioners than to lawyers in firms (35 percent vs. 22.3 percent). Generally, as firm size increased, the time devoted to residential real estate decreased. Lawyers in the very largest firms reported that they did virtually no residential real estate (1 percent) and that what they did was usually undertaken as an accommodation only to those who were already clients of the firm. Residential real estate is not an "elite" practice.

1. Attorney Practices: Overview

The following is a brief outline of what the respondents stated an attorney should do in residential conveyancing:

1. Review contract with buyer.

2. Make any addenda to the contract and try to negotiate with seller on the addenda.

3. Search the title and clear any title defects.

4. Certify the title or issue a lawyer's opinion of title.

5. Advise client as to types of title insurance.

6. Order surveys and review them to make sure there are no encroachments.

7. Solve any problems revealed by the survey.

8. Review deed restrictions and easements.

9. Render tax advice to the client.

10. Collect and disburse funds.

11. Record documents such as the deed and the mortgage.

12. After settlement, make sure liens are satisfied on the record and check that other title matters are completed.

13. Handle any escrows created at settlement.

14. After recorded documents are returned from Recorders, send them to appropriate parties.

As seen below, most attorneys do not perform most of these services most of the time. Indeed, most of the time none of these services are performed by an attorney.

2. Attorney Practices: Point of Involvement

Seventy-five percent of the attorneys interviewed stated that they are usually contacted by the buyer after the buyer has entered into a real estate purchase contract. Although attorneys say it is important for them to be involved in the process from the beginning, only one attorney * * * stated that she would refuse representation unless she was involved in the transaction from the point of the offer.

In the usual case, where the buyer executes a contract before retaining an attorney, respondents stated that they review the contract and make necessary changes or addenda. Respondents "rarely" or "infrequently" made changes to the contract, however. This was true even in states requiring that contracts drafted by a real estate agent have an "attorney review period" clause in the agreement. This clause gives the attorney for either the buyer or seller the opportunity to disapprove the contract within a specified number of days after execution.

3. Attorney Practices: Structural Factors

* * *

Age of Property

When asked if the age of a property is likely to have any influence on the work they do, about three-fourths of the attorneys stated "yes." Surprisingly, many attorneys stated that it was their duty to ensure that the property was physically suitable for their client. Traditional legal doctrine would place responsibility for this not with the attorney but with the seller, builder or realtor. Among the concerns expressed by attorneys were leaking roofs, termites, and compliance with environmental laws enacted after the construction of the home. Respondents believed that recent construction presented fewer inspection issues because, in the attorneys' opinion, problems of defective quality are less frequent.

On the other hand, title problems may be more likely with newer property. Several attorneys noted that there may be easements or uses that are unknown, or other problems that have not had a chance to be exposed. With older property the attorneys felt it was more likely that these matters would have become apparent and been previously addressed.

Requirements of Mortgage Lenders

About half of the respondents stated that mortgage lenders have no influence on the services they perform. If this statement is taken at face value it is surprising because the lending industry is generally perceived as dictating the structure of the residential real estate transaction. When probed, however, what these attorneys reveal is that lending industry demands are contained in non-negotiable, standardized forms, including such things as the form of mortgage, note, disclosure documents and the form and necessity of the title insurance policy.

The lending industry's comprehensive control of the residential real estate transaction leaves the attorney little room to operate within the sphere of its influence. It is against this background that one must understand statements such as that of one respondent * * *, who described the mortgage lending industry as very standardized and said, consequently, "its only influence is its timetable and whether the mortgage will be approved." Or that of another attorney * * * who depicted mortgage lenders as creating various contingencies, all of which must be met in order to get a loan; however, "these contingencies have no effect on the services" that the attorney himself performs.

All of the attorneys agreed that the lenders' documents were not negotiable. Because the lender wants to preserve the option to sell the mortgage on the secondary mortgage market, standardization is very important and alteration of the documents, except to fill in blanks concerning interest rate, term, etc., is not permitted. The lender presents documents on a "take it or leave it" basis. Thus, while the attorney can explain the documents, he cannot change them.

4. Attorney Practices: Securing Good Title

Attorneys do not search titles because "this is what the title company does." Title insurance is vital in these transactions "because there is not a lender around that will give mortgage money unless there is a title policy." The title company delivers to the attorneys the title insurance commitment, which commits the company to issue its policy subject to some exceptions if specified conditions are met. These exceptions are the title defects, such as restrictions, liens, easements, etc., that the company finds in its search. Most attorneys said that they review the title documents once they receive them to see if there are any problems they do not "feel uncomfortable with." If the attorney finds such a problem, he will try to resolve it. The attorneys revealed, however, that in many cases they do not see the title commitment until the day of the closing. One wonders, therefore, how meaningful a review could occur and whether there is time to remedy objectionable matters.

5. *Attorney Practices: Lengths of Transaction*

When the attorneys were asked how long a typical transaction takes from offer to closing, the responses ranged from as short as 4 weeks to as long as one year. The average time reported was 60 days, with about half of the attorneys stating between 45 to 60 days and the other half 60 to 90 days. Only 3 attorneys suggested that the length of these transactions could be as little as 30 days. One attorney remarked that the length of time from offer to closing depended on the type of financing. For instance, the time frame may be longer or shorter depending on whether the buyer obtains a VA, FHA or a conventional loan. In addition, contingencies in the contract had an effect on the length of the whole transaction.

B.   CONVEYANCING AND THE PRACTICE OF LAW

As the Braunstein excerpt notes, the importance of lawyers in residential real estate transactions has diminished in recent years as other professionals or institutions have taken on an increasingly dominant role. Under these circumstances, three questions must be addressed: Is there a continuing role for lawyers in real estate transactions? If so, is it necessary that all participants in the transaction be represented by their own lawyer? Is it appropriate for non-lawyers to undertake tasks traditionally performed by lawyers as part of the conveyancing process?

As to the first question, lawyers clearly have a role in conveyancing, if only to review documents for lenders and for title insurers. Certainly, major commercial transactions cannot go forward without extensive involvement of lawyers. Lawyer involvement in residential transactions, however, varies at this point from locality to locality. In some jurisdictions, representation of the buyer or seller or both is common; in others it is rare. In favor of lawyer involvement, it can be argued that the purchase of a dwelling is the biggest investment most lower and middle-class persons make in their lifetime, and is, as should be clear by the end of this chapter, potentially fraught with legal perils. On the other hand, individual residential real estate transactions rarely result in serious legal problems, and real estate transactions are costly enough without adding lawyer's fees. Buyers often assume that their interests are adequately protected by their lender, title insurer, and loan guarantor (such as the Federal Housing Administration, FHA), who also have a stake in the transaction. Ask again when you finish these materials whether lawyers are necessary.

IN RE OPINION NO. 26 OF THE COMMITTEE ON THE UNAUTHORIZED PRACTICE OF LAW

Supreme Court of New Jersey, 1995.
139 N.J. 323, 654 A.2d 1344.

PER CURIAM.

I

PROCEEDINGS BELOW

Opinion No. 26 of the Committee on the Unauthorized Practice of Law, 130 N.J.L.J. 882 (March 16, 1992), was issued in response to an inquiry, one of many, from the New Jersey State Bar Association. The inquiry sought a determination of whether the South Jersey practice constituted the unauthorized practice of law. That practice, described in detail later, concerns the sale of a home generally financed by a purchase money mortgage. The essence of the South Jersey practice is that from the beginning of the transaction to the end, neither seller nor buyer is represented by counsel. Every aspect of the transaction is handled by others, every document drafted by others, including the contract of sale, affidavit of title, bond and mortgage. The Committee on the Unauthorized Practice of Law (the Committee), relying largely on our decisions in New Jersey State Bar Association v. New Jersey Association of Realtor Boards, 93 N.J. 470, 461 A.2d 1112 (1983); Cape May County Bar Association v. Ludlam, 45 N.J. 121, 211 A.2d 780 (1965); New Jersey State Bar Association v. Northern New Jersey Mortgage Associates, 32 N.J. 430, 161 A.2d 257 (1960), and its own prior determination in Opinion No. 11 of the Committee on the Unauthorized Practice of Law, 95 N.J.L.J. 1345 (December 28, 1972), ruled that the ordering of a title search by the broker, the preparation of conveyancing and other documents by title officers, their clearing of title questions, and indeed the activities of both broker and title officers at the closing itself, where neither buyer nor seller was represented by counsel, that all of these activities constituted the unauthorized practice of law. The decision was interpreted widely as prohibiting the South Jersey practice, in effect prohibiting a seller and buyer from proceeding with the sale of a home without counsel.

II

THE SOUTH JERSEY PRACTICE

Although the variations are numerous, the South Jersey practice complained of typically involves residential real estate closings in which neither buyer nor seller is represented by counsel, and contrasts most sharply with the North Jersey practice if one assumes both parties are represented there. Obviously, that is not always the case: the record shows that about sixty percent of the buyers and about sixty-five percent of the sellers in South Jersey are not represented by counsel. In North Jersey, only one half of one percent of buyers, and fourteen percent of sellers, proceed without counsel.

In North Jersey, when both seller and buyer are represented by counsel, they sign nothing, agree to nothing, expend nothing, without the advice of competent counsel. If, initially without counsel, they sign a contract of sale prepared by the broker, they ordinarily then retain counsel who can revoke that contract in accordance with the three-day attorney review clause. They are protected, and they pay for that protection. The seller in North Jersey spends on average $750 in attorney fees, and the buyer in North Jersey spends on average $1,000. The buyer in South Jersey who chooses to proceed without representation spends nothing. . . .

The typical South Jersey transaction starts with the seller engaging a broker who is ordinarily a member of the multiple listing system. The first broker to find an apparently willing buyer gets in touch with the seller and ultimately negotiates a sale price agreeable to both. The potential buyer requires financing arrangements which are often made by the broker. Before the execution of any sales contract the broker puts the buyer in touch with a mortgage company to determine if the buyer qualifies for the needed loan.

At this preliminary stage, no legal obligations of any kind are likely to have been created, except for those that arise from the brokerage relationship itself.

Assuming the preliminary understanding between the seller and buyer remains in effect, the broker will present the seller with the standard form of contract used in that area (usually a New Jersey Association of Realtors Standard Form of Real Estate Contract). That form includes . . . notice that the attorney for either party can cancel the contract within three business days. If the seller signs the contract, and does not within three days retain counsel, the seller will have become legally bound to perform numerous obligations without the benefit of any legal advice whatsoever, some of which may turn out to be onerous, some costly, some requiring unanticipated expense, and some beyond the power of the seller to perform, with the potential of substantial liability for such nonperformance. Many sellers will not understand just what those obligations are, and just what the risks are. Not only has the seller not retained a lawyer, the only person qualified to explain those risks. Worse yet, the only one the seller has had any contact with in the matter is the broker, whose commission depends entirely on consummation of the transaction, and whose interest is primarily—in some cases it is fair to say exclusively—to get the contract signed and the deal closed.

After the seller signs the contract, the broker delivers it to the buyer for execution. The buyer may not know if the description of the property is precisely that assumed to be the subject of the purchase. The buyer may have no idea if the title described in the contract is that with which he would be satisfied, no sound understanding of what the numerous obligations on the part of the seller mean, and no fair comprehension of whether all of the possible and practical concerns of a buyer have been addressed by the contract. No lawyer is present to advise or inform the buyer; indeed, there is no one who has the buyer's interest at heart, only the broker, whose interests are generally in conflict with the buyer's. . . . Therefore, without independent advice, the buyer signs the contract. If no attorney is retained within three days, the buyer is bound by all of its terms.

For both seller and buyer, it is that contract that substantially determines all of their rights and duties. Neither one of them can be regarded as adequately informed of the import of what they signed or indeed of its importance. At that point the broker, who represents only the seller and clearly has an interest in conflict with that of the buyer (the broker's interest is in consummation of the sale, the buyer's in making certain that the sale does not close unless the buyer is fully protected) performs a series of acts on behalf of the buyer, and is the only person available as a practical matter to explain their significance to the buyer. The broker orders a binder for title insurance, or a title commitment to make sure that the buyer is going to get good title. The buyer has no idea, and hopefully never will have, whether the broker ordered the right kind of title search, a fairly esoteric question that only an experienced attorney can determine.

The broker also orders numerous inspection and other reports, all primarily of interest to the buyer, to make certain that not only is the title good, but that there are no other problems affecting the premises, the house and their use. Those reports can have substantial legal consequences for both seller and buyer. For example, at what threshold dollar amount of required repairs should the seller (or the buyer) be able to cancel the contract? At what dollar amount should the buyer ignore the repairs? At what dollar amount should the buyer be able to compel the seller to make the repairs, and within what time frame? At this stage of the transaction the help of a lawyer could be invaluable, and the advice of a broker problematic.

The seller in the meantime is happy to hear from no one, for it suggests there are no problems. Eventually, the seller is told that a deed will be arriving drafted by an attorney selected by the broker, the instrument that our decisions clearly require may be drafted only by the seller's attorney. Cape May County Bar Ass'n v. Ludlam, 45 N.J. 121, 211 A.2d 780 (1965). Of course, the purpose of that ruling was to assure competent counsel in the drafting of such a uniquely legal document, but "competent" always meant counsel who understood the entire transaction. In South Jersey, the attorney selected by the broker, while theoretically representing the seller, may be primarily interested in the broker, the source of the attorney's "client" and the likely source of future "clients," and consequently primarily interested in completing the sale. That attorney is likely to prepare a deed satisfactory to the title company—in fact that attorney often does not even contact the seller. He or she may have no idea of anything in the contract of sale other than the description of the land and the fact that a certain kind of deed is required. No advice on the substance of the transaction comes from such an attorney even though the seller may get the impression that, since an attorney drafted the deed, the seller's interests are somehow being protected. In fact, the only protection those interests ever received, other than those that happened to appear in the form contract, is in the numbers inserted in that contract, the total purchase price, the down payment, and the closing date, for those are probably the only terms of that contract fully understood by the seller.

The buyer's position is even worse when the closing occurs. The seller will at least know that he or she got paid. Legal training is not required for that fact, even though there is no practical assurance that the seller will not thereafter be sued. The buyer, on the other hand, wants something that is largely incomprehensible to almost all buyers, good and marketable title, one that will not result in problems in the future. What the buyer gets before closing is a "title binder," a piece of paper that may suggest something about the quality of the seller's title, but that is very much in need of explanation for any substantial understanding of its meaning. The title company is required to mail to the unrepresented buyer notice of any exceptions or conditions associated with the title insurance policy. N.J.S.A. 17:46B–9. This notice, which must be sent five days prior to the closing, must also notify the buyer of the right to review the title commitment with an attorney. Ibid. If the buyer chooses not to retain an attorney, there is no one to give the buyer that understanding other than the broker and the title agent. The broker's knowledge will often be inadequate, and the conflicting interest apparent. The title company similarly has a conflicting interest, for it too is interested in completion of the transaction, the sine qua non of its title premium. But the title company is also interested in good title, for it is guaranteeing that to the mortgage company, as well as to the buyer. "Good title," however, may be one on which the title company and the mortgagee are willing to take a risk, but one on which a buyer might or should not be willing to, if the buyer knew what the risk was. Again, there is no one to tell the buyer what those risks are, and in some cases the explicit exceptions found in a title policy, those matters that the title company will not guarantee, are of the greatest importance. The significance of those matters is conceded by all to be something that only attorneys can give advice on, and it is contended by all that they never give such advice. Yet such exceptions exist, and title still closes, and the buyer is totally unrepresented by counsel. One must assume that somewhere, somehow, the buyer is satisfied that there is nothing to worry about, leading to the inescapable conclusion that either the broker or the title officer provides some modicum of assurance or explanation.

The day for closing arrives and everyone meets, usually at the offices of the title company. Seller and buyer are there, each without an attorney; the broker is there, and the title officer is there, representing both the title company and the mortgagee. The funds are there. And the critical legal documents are also on hand: the mortgage and the note, usually prepared by the mortgagee; the deed, along with the affidavit of title, prepared by the attorney selected by the broker or by the title company; the settlement statement, usually prepared by the title company, indicating how much is owed, what deductions should be made for taxes and other costs and what credits are due; and the final marked-up title binder, which evidences the obligation of the title company to issue a title policy to the buyer, and which at that point is probably practically meaningless to the buyer. All are executed and delivered, along with other documents, and the funds are delivered or held in escrow until the title company arranges to pay off prior mortgages and liens.

It would take a volume to describe each and every risk to which the seller and buyer have exposed themselves without adequate knowledge. But it takes a very short sentence to describe what apparently occurs: the deal closes, satisfactory to buyer and seller in practically all cases, satisfactory both at the closing and thereafter.

III

The Unauthorized Practice of Law

This transaction in its entirety, the sale of real estate, especially real estate with a home on it, is one that cannot be handled competently except by those trained in the law. The most important parts of it, without which it could not be accomplished, are quintessentially the practice of law. The contract of sale, the obligations of the contract, the ordering of a title search, the analysis of the search, the significance of the title search, the quality of title, the risks that surround both the contract and the title, the extent of those risks, the probability of damage, the obligation to close or not to close, the closing itself, the settlement, the documents there exchanged, each and every one of these, to be properly understood must be explained by an attorney. And the documents themselves to be properly drafted, must be drafted by an attorney. Mixed in with these activities are many others that clearly do not require an attorney's knowledge, such as the ordering of inspection and other reports, and the price negotiation. But after that, even though arguably much can be accomplished by others, practically all else, to be done with full understanding, requires the advice of counsel.

. . . Having answered the question whether the practice of law is involved, we must decide whether the public interest is served by such prohibition. Not every such intrusion by laypersons into legal matters disserves the public: this Court does not wear public interest blinders when passing on unauthorized practice of law questions. We have often found, despite the clear involvement of the practice of law, that nonlawyers may participate in these activities, basing our decisions on the public interest in those cases in allowing parties to proceed without counsel. . . . The resolution of the question is determined by practical, not theoretical, considerations; the public interest is weighed by analyzing the competing policies and interests that may be involved in the case;

the conduct, if permitted, is often conditioned by requirements designed to assure that the public interest is indeed not disserved.

... In re Baker, 8 N.J. 321, 334, 85 A.2d 505 (1951), this Court, holding respondents in contempt for their unauthorized practice of law, ... observed that "[t]he reason for prohibiting the unauthorized practice of the law by laymen is not to aid the legal profession but to safeguard the public from the disastrous results that are bound to flow from the activities of untrained and incompetent individuals," those not only lacking the many years of preparation, but also the high standards of professional conduct imposed on members of the bar and enforced by the Court.

* * *

In this case, the record clearly shows that the South Jersey practice has been conducted without any demonstrable harm to sellers or buyers, that it apparently saves money, and that those who participate in it do so of their own free will presumably with some knowledge of the risk; as Judge Miller found, the record fails to demonstrate that brokers are discouraging the parties from retaining counsel, or that the conflict of interest that pervades the practice has caused material damage to the sellers and buyers who participate in it. Given that record, and subject to the conditions mentioned hereafter, we find that the public interest will not be compromised by allowing the practice to continue. ...

Of decisive weight in our determination is the value we place on the right of parties to a transaction to decide whether or not they will retain counsel. We should not force them to do so absent persuasive reasons. ...

The public needs protection in these matters. The Legislature has recognized such need and afforded statutory protection for both buyers and sellers at various stages of the real estate transaction. ...In addition, Congress has recognized the need for uniformity in consumer real estate transactions. 12 U.S.C.A. §§ 2601–2617 (Real Estate Settlement Procedures Act); 15 U.S.C.A. §§ 1601–1693 (Truth in Lending Act); see Gerald S. Meisel, RESPA: Federal Control of Residential Real Estate, 98 N.J.L.J. 713 (August 21, 1975).

We do not here adopt a "consumerism" that invariably requires that services be made available at the lowest price no matter how great the risk. The record suggests that despite their conflict of interest, brokers' ethical standards have resulted in some diminishment of those risks. Unlike prior cases, there is no finding here, for instance, that brokers are discouraging retention of counsel, no suggestion that title companies are paying rebates to referring brokers. Today's public, furthermore, not only has the benefit of the attorney-review clause, but is presumably better educated about the need for counsel, the function of attorneys, and the legal aspects of the sale of the home. The public continues, in South Jersey, to choose not to be represented. We assume that the public has simply concluded that the perceived advantages are worth those risks.

We do not adopt a rule, however, that so long as informed consent from the parties is obtained, any conduct that might otherwise constitute the unauthorized practice of law is permitted. Most of the practices restricted to attorneys can be performed, and may be performed, only by them regardless of the informed consent of the parties and regardless of the lower cost of using non-attorneys. All we decide is that in this case, concerning this practice, the record demonstrates that the public interest will not be compromised by allowing what would otherwise be the unauthorized practice of law if the parties are adequately informed of the conflicting interests of brokers and title officers and of the risks involved in proceeding without counsel.

We emphasize the nature of the public interest standard applied in this case.... We do not conclude that the public is better off without lawyers in the South Jersey practice. As stated several times above, we firmly believe the parties should retain counsel. We decide only that given the history and experience of the South Jersey practice, the public interest will not be disserved by allowing the parties, after advance written notice of their right to retain counsel and the risk of not doing so, to choose to proceed without a lawyer; we decide only that the public interest does not require that the protection of counsel be forced upon the parties against their will. ...

There is a point at which an institution attempting to provide protection to a public that seems clearly, over a long period, not to want it, and perhaps not to need it—there is a point when that institution must wonder whether it is providing protection or imposing its will. It must wonder whether it is helping or hurting the public.[5] We have reached that point in this case. Although we have strong doubts, the evidence against our doubt requires that we allow this practice to continue with some form of added protection, recognizing, however, that like the attorney-review clause, the added protection may not be effective.

IV

CONCLUSION AND CONDITIONS

We premise our holding on the condition that both buyer and seller be made aware of the conflicting interests of brokers and title companies in these matters and of the general risks involved in not being represented by counsel. ...If that notice is not given, the broker will be engaged in the unauthorized practice of law. Furthermore, anyone who participates in the transaction, other than buyer and seller, knowing that the

5. We note that in Arizona, after its Supreme Court prohibited brokers from preparing real estate sales contracts, the people approved a constitutional amendment that provided that licensed real estate brokers "shall have the right to draft or fill out and complete" real estate documents, including deeds, mortgages, and contracts of sale. Ariz. Const. art. XXVI, § 1.

notice has not been given when and as required, will also be engaged in the unauthorized practice of law. As for any attorney who, under the same circumstances, continues to participate in the transaction, that attorney will also be subject to discipline for unethical conduct. . . .

Assuming such notice is given in accordance with the terms and conditions mentioned above, we hold that attendance and participation at the closing or settlement where neither party has been represented by counsel, or where one has not been so represented, does not constitute the unauthorized practice of law; that brokers may order abstracts, title binders, and title policies; that an attorney retained by the broker to draft a deed and/or affidavit of title for the seller may do so but only if the attorney personally consults with the seller; regardless of the prior restriction, any attorney retained by the broker for that purpose, or any attorney acting for the title company, may draft any of the documents involved in the transaction upon written request of the party, be it buyer, seller, lender, mortgagee, bank, or others;[7] that the title company may participate in clearing up those minor objections which Judge Miller refers to as categories one and two: standard exceptions such as marital status and money liens customarily paid at closing, but not those classified as categories three and four: easements, covenants or other serious legal objections to title.

. . .

The decision of the Committee, Opinion No. 26, is affirmed in part, and reversed in part, and judgment entered declaring the rights of the participants in New Jersey residential real estate transactions in accordance with this opinion.

Notes and Questions

1. You may recall that in Chapter Two we considered the circumstances in which lawyers may represent multiple parties in a single matter. See page 135, note 4(f). Here, we further examine the implications of dual-representation in regard to the sale of real property. The New Jersey Supreme Court, in In re Dolan, 76 N.J. 1, 384 A.2d 1076 (1978), considered a real estate transaction in which the same attorney represented both the buyer and the seller. A developer who was building a townhouse project for the Borough of Carteret hired Dolan to represent it during the sale of the individual townhouses to buyers. Dolan also represented buyers at these closings. Thus, a potential conflict of interest arose, and the court held that disciplinary action against Dolan was appropriate. Consent was not obtained from the buyers until the closing, which "amounted to little more than a perfunctory effort" to comply with the requirement that consent be obtained from the client before an attorney may take up dual representation. Dolan had been representing these purchasers for weeks before closing, giving ample time to explain the possible conflicts which might arise. Waiting until

---

7. Of course, the title company may continue to prepare non-conveyance documents such as the settlement statement.

the "eleventh hour" of closing implied that "execution of the form was due more to the exigencies of the situation than to an unfettered will." Nonetheless, the court refused to adopt a per se ban on representation of both buyer and seller during real estate transactions, because under this rule "many prospective purchasers in marginal financial circumstances would be left without representation."

2. New Jersey Supreme Court Justice Pashman, in a concurring opinion in Dolan, argued for a per se rule totally forbidding dual representation. He noted the obvious difference between the value to Dolan's law firm of the business generated by the primary client (the developer-seller) and the derivative clients (the townhouse buyers). "Dual representation in these circumstances forces the derivative client to play with a stacked deck. I cannot countenance the Court's continued tolerance of such farcical and often duplicitous behavior by some members of the legal profession," he wrote. Justice Pashman had previously criticized the court's majority for refusing to adopt a per se rule. In In re Lanza, 65 N.J. 347, 322 A.2d 445 (1974), Justice Pashman wrote, "It is virtually impossible for one attorney in any manner and under any circumstances to faithfully and with undivided allegiance represent both a buyer and seller ... The potential conflict in home buying or selling may never come to fruition. However, when it does surface, both sides explode in anger and accusations. The attorney will then withdraw, leaving the situation no better than when it occurred and, for that matter, probably a bit worse. This is not fair to either party..." Do you agree or disagree?

In Baldassare v. Butler, 132 N.J. 278, 625 A.2d 458 (1993), the New Jersey Supreme Court ultimately adopted the rule proposed by Justice Pashman strictly prohibiting dual representation in the context of commercial real estate transactions, citing the complex contract contingencies and large sums of money involved as reasons why the potential for conflict is too great to permit even consensual dual representation.

3. Rule 2.2 of the 1983 proposed Rules of Professional Conduct of the American Bar Association offered a new category of law-office practice called "lawyer as intermediary." The initial comment to the new rule said, "A lawyer acts as intermediary ... when the lawyer represents two or more parties with potentially conflicting interests" (emphasis supplied). Other rules—e.g., R.P.C. 1.7—dealt with actual conflicts of interests; and the A.B.A. revision of the Rules in 2002 dealt with situations in which the lawyer acts as mediator between or among people who are not clients (Rule 2.4, "Lawyer Serving as Third–Party Neutral"). An intermediary is neither an advocate nor a mediator. Being an intermediary is, rather, a hybrid assignment that, as things turned out, disturbed many lawyers, some of whom had rule-making clout in the A.B.A. The background of Rule 2.2—well hidden in the A.B.A. proposal, by the way—was Louis D. Brandeis's law office in Boston and Professor Geoffrey Hazard's book Ethics in the Practice of Law (1979). (See pp. 135–136.)

Rule 2.2, said, "A lawyer acts as intermediary in seeking to establish or adjust a relationship between clients on an amicable and mutually advantageous basis; for example, in helping to organize a business in which two or more clients are entrepreneurs, working out the financial reorganization of an enterprise in which two or more clients have an interest, arranging a property distribution in settlement of an estate or mediating a dispute between clients." The examples might have included facts such as those in the Dolan case—buyer and seller of real property come to the buyer's lawyer to work out the legal details. Or a married couple come to a lawyer to have wills done for each of them; or a landlord and her tenant come to her lawyer, who becomes, at least for a while, their lawyer, to get the lease drafted and signed.

Rule 2.2 requires that clients be told, by their lawyer, of "the implications of the common representation, including the advantages and risks involved, and the effect on the attorney-client privileges," and it requires that each client "consent to the common representation." Rule 2.2(a). The Rule seems to contemplate a writing, and many lawyers, as a standard practice, have provided a written statement of what the lawyer proposes to do, endorsed by the clients, to show that the clients understand the lawyer's undertaking. Regardless of the form of the communication, the Rule required of the lawyer:

— consultation with clients on implications, including advantages, risks, and effect on privilege;

— the lawyer's reasonable belief that she can (a) tend to the legal job "on terms compatible with the clients' best interests"; (b) that each client will be able to "make adequately informed decisions"; (c) "that there is little risk of material prejudice to the interests of any of the clients if the contemplated resolution is unsuccessful;" (d) that the lawyer be able to remain impartial; and (d) that the present business will not have "improper effect on other [of the lawyer's] responsibilities . . . to any of the clients."

— The lawyer is then required to consult with each client on each of the "decisions . . . and considerations" that come to be involved in this intermediative work.

The lawyer is required to withdraw from the assignment as intermediary if any client asks her to do so, or if any of the conditions outlined here "is no longer satisfied." Once the lawyer withdraws she is not permitted to represent any of the clients "in the matter that was the subject of the intermediation."

(It is significant to the normal commerce of law practice that these rules allow, without being specific enough about it, for the situation [as in Dolan] in which the lawyer has represented one of the parties to the intermediation, or hopes to continue working for that client when the intermediation is completed, or both, whether or not the intermediation is completed successfully. Does it seem to you that the rule is sufficiently cautious in preserving a requirement of lawyer impartiality without impairing the lawyer's pre-existing or enduring relationships with one or some of the clients but not all of them?)

With few exceptions, the state supreme courts that adopted the 1983 A.B.A. rules adopted Rule 2.2. Then, in 2001–2002, the A.B.A. committee considering changes in the Rules decided to "delete" Rule 2.2. Since then (and this is early days) some states have "deleted" it and some have not.

One of the relatively cryptic reasons the A.B.A. committee gave <u>for</u> the deletion was that Rule 1.7, which deals with actual (rather than potential) conflicts of interest, deals sufficiently with what the 1983 Rules called "intermediation." The committee seemed to have some doubt about that conclusion, though, because it made significant changes in Rule 1.7, beginning with a change in the title from "Conflict of Interest: General Rule" to "Conflict of Interest: Current Clients," along with changes in text apparently meant to include both potential and active conflicts of interest. The committee recommended "deleting" provisions in Rule 1.7 that paralleled Rule 2.2 and substituting a more concise set of requirements for situations in which there is "a concurrent conflict of interest"—that is, a situation in which the representation of one client will have a direct adverse impact on another client or will materially limit representation of someone else.

Does it seem to you that all of this solution is too much trouble in a busy law practice? Maybe it is better for a lawyer in the <u>Dolan</u> situation to tell his client's customer to go down the hall and get a different lawyer. Here is a sort of mushy argument against doing that: There is a somewhat recondite tension in this part of the literature of lawyer regulation, a tension between a persistent moral interest in building and preserving communities (which is what collections of people owning and occupying business or residential real property often are or hope to be) and a narrow interest in saving legal expense. The commentary to the R.P.C. 2.2 (1983) acknowledged that one reason people with potential conflicts of interest might want to do their business with a single lawyer is to save legal fees. But the same commentary also recognized that separate representation can lead to unnecessary hostility between people who started out determined not to be hostile toward one another, who came to their lawyer—a single lawyer "for the situation"—for help in carrying out that objective.

Here is a poetic reflection that may show how more is involved than saving legal fees: Anne Tyler's story <u>Accidental Tourist</u> presents a wonderfully ditzy woman named Muriel who makes her living by walking other people's dogs. (She was played in the movie version by Geena Davis.) Muriel takes the relentlessly dull protagonist, the accidental tourist (travel writer) Macon (William Hurt), and Macon's dog, for a walk. They wander into a second-hand store; Muriel points to something that should have been in a trash can: Look, she says, "There's a magnifying glass all cracked and broken, and when you look at broken things through the lens you'd swear they'd turned whole again." The commentary to Rule 2.2 is, in places, like that: Its aspirational language, tied to the probably unfortunate word "intermediation," seems to have been put there by rule-makers who want lawyers to <u>be</u> broken magnifying glasses, to be people who, when you see what they see, cause you to see broken things turned whole again. It is relatively easy to detect that aspiration when "intermediation" means doing wills for married couples (two people, one lawyer, <u>one family?</u>), or when a lawyer is helping proud and habitually independent entrepreneurs arrive at a common and mutually enriching way to do business as a partnership or close corporation. It may be a bit harder to detect the hope for community in property transactions, but it is usually nonetheless in there somewhere.

MORGAN, THE EVOLVING CONCEPT OF
PROFESSIONAL RESPONSIBILITY

90 Harv.L.Rev. 702 (1977).

A lawyer certainly cannot sit at both counsel tables in contested litigation. However by no means all legal problems involve going to court, and when they do not, having more than one lawyer to accomplish the parties' objectives may be an unnecessary and wasteful luxury. Individuals entering upon a contractual relationship, for example, might find it significantly less expensive and less disruptive to hire a single lawyer to draft a contract incorporating the business consensus of both sides than to have two lawyers, each trying to exact the marginal pound of flesh for his client. * * *

The response to this argument from many lawyers is that a situation which appears nonlitigious at the moment may develop into a contested situation in the future. This is not an unreasonable concern and may appear to go in part to the interest of the client. But having two lawyers from the outset in every case is expensive insurance against the unknown. Moreover, in many situations where things go badly, both sides can simply bring in separate counsel. The only person hurt by such a procedure would be the first lawyer who will now represent neither party. That the lawyer might not like this result is understandable. That his unhappiness should rise to the level of an ethical precept is less clear.

Do you agree or disagree? Is involvement of lawyers representing all parties necessarily an unnecessary extravagance? See Residential Real Estate Transactions: The Lawyer's Proper Role—Services—Compensation, 14 Real Prop., Prob., & Trust J. 581, 590–595 (1979) (each party to the transaction needs separate representation).

If a lawyer chooses to represent both the buyer and the seller (or any other two or more parties in a real estate transaction), how should the lawyer disclose the potential conflict? Is an oral disclosure sufficient? If a written disclosure is necessary, how should it be worded? Should it disclose some or all potential areas of conflict between the parties? What must the lawyer do if a conflict actually emerges? Is ABA Model Rule 1.7 helpful in resolving these issues?

4. A lawyer representing the purchaser in a real estate transaction drafts both a deed granting the property to the purchaser and a deed of trust—securing the interest of the vendor for later payment of the purchase price. The lawyer fails to advise the vendor of the necessity of recording the deed of trust to protect her security interest in the property. The vendor fails to record the deed of trust. Subsequently the property is sold to a purchaser who takes free of the unrecorded deed of trust under the recording act, and the original purchaser declares bankruptcy. Can the initial seller sue the lawyer for malpractice? See Stinson v. Brand, 738 S.W.2d 186 (Tenn.1987) (recognizing a cause of action on similar facts).

5. Can a lawyer adequately represent both a buyer and a title insurer? Are the title insurer's interests necessarily more compatible with those of

the buyer than are the interests of the seller or broker? See, ABA Formal Opinion 331. (No necessary conflict of interest between representing buyer and acting as agent for title insurance company if full disclosure and no breach of other rules).

6. Ask many real estate brokers whether lawyers should be involved in real estate transactions and the broker will tell you that lawyers kill deals. This is clearly a good reason for brokers not to want lawyers involved. Is it a good reason for buyers not to want lawyers involved? Or is that view of lawyers too cynical? Consider the following:

The common reality is that decisions arrived at by lawyers and their clients talking together are mutual decisions. Sometimes the conscience involved is like a new, third conscience. Here is an example from the late Professor Louis M. Brown, the grandfather of preventive-law jurisprudence in the United States and the founder of the national client-counseling competition. This dialogue, which Professor Brown recorded, takes place in a law office after the client has received a demand that he pay a real-estate broker who did not have a written listing agreement with the client (quoted in T. Shaffer, American Legal Ethics 623–624 [1985]):

L: Have you had any prior dealings with this broker?

C: No, only in the purchase of this property.

L: And you had no written agreement with him concerning this deal [acquiring a tenant], only his request to you for this money, after the fact.

C: Yes. That's right. He didn't say anything about getting a six per cent commission until after the tenant was in. As far as I was concerned, I shouldn't have to pay him anything. I don't know if I really have to. However, I assume I do. I don't know. Do I have an obligation to pay?

L: Under our law, any arrangement or agreement which is made between you and a broker which is not written down is not enforceable.

C: And I could have told him good-bye and leave me alone.

L: There was nothing he could do about it. I think also you have some extra-legal considerations that you shouldn't lose sight of, in terms of your business reputation, in terms of if you are ever going to have dealings with other brokers.

C: What are you telling me then? That I should pay him or that I shouldn't?

L: Well, I'm not telling you that you should pay him or not pay him, but I think, in making your decision you have to consider not just your legal obligation but other considerations which are up to you, to decide how significant they are to you. You see, the point is that we don't know how difficult it would have been for you to get somebody to become a tenant in that building, and, after all, he did so out of his way to get somebody in that building, and that person is now paying you for leasing. So you're getting a benefit conferred on you right now. Now, it's true that you may not technically be liable to him, and we're not saying that that shouldn't be an important consideration to you, obviously.

C: Well, all right. I said before I suppose I have to pay him.

(An exacting reader might notice—or claim—that this lawyer did not make a moral argument here. But then where did the phrase "benefit conferred" come from? If you remember, wherein is that source a moral source?)

7. If neither the buyer nor seller is represented by counsel, someone other than a lawyer must draft the documents necessary to consummate the conveyance. These are likely to be drafted by the real estate broker, the title company, or the lender. In drafting these documents, and in advising the buyer and seller as to what should be included in these documents, are these entities practicing law? If so, is their conduct illegal or unethical?

In State Bar of Arizona v. Arizona Land Title and Trust Co., 90 Ariz. 76, 366 P.2d 1 (1961), the integrated State Bar of Arizona and individual attorneys filed complaints for a declaratory judgment against several real estate brokers and title companies claiming that in connection with the conduct of their businesses and transactions the real estate brokers and title companies regularly prepared, drafted, and formulated documents affecting title to real property, and that their giving legal advice regarding the transactions and instruments constituted the unauthorized practice of law. The bar sought an injunction restraining and enjoining the real estate brokers and title companies from any further legal involvement in real estate transactions, except preparation of the customary preliminary purchase agreement executed on printed forms.

The Arizona Supreme Court held that, while it was impossible to give an exhaustive definition of "the practice of law," it was "sufficient to state that those acts, whether performed in court or in the law office, which lawyers customarily have carried on from day to day through the centuries must constitute 'the practice of law'." It was "obvious to anyone familiar with the work of attorneys that most of the activities engaged in by [the real estate brokers and title companies], traditionally have been and presently are conducted in the regular course of their practice by members of the bar." The court rejected the argument that the defendants were not practicing law since they did not charge separately for preparing legal documents, noting that "[r]eliance by the client on advice or services rendered, rather than the fact that compensation is received, is more pertinent in determining whether certain conduct is the purported or actual practice of law."

The court was particularly concerned that the title company employees who prepared the documents for customers of the title companies owed their first allegiance to "the company's rights and obligations rather than [to] the parties to the transaction." This the court contrasted with the position of lawyers representing the buyer or seller, who under professional ethics owed sole allegiance to the interest of their clients. The court further observed that "[t]itle company witnesses consistently testified that when dealing with customers, they carefully avoided conversation which would involve a discussion of the customers' objectives, or legal rights and obligations with respect to the property being conveyed. Nevertheless, the title company employee, in 'filling in a form,' obviously exercises his own discretion as to what form should be used, and what language is to be inserted in the blank spaces.

* * * The title company employee, treading on doubtful ground, is hesitant to ask relevant questions and even more reluctant to make positive recommendations regarding the legal aspects of a prospective transaction, although he is nevertheless willing to draft legal instruments in order that a title policy may be issued. * * * "

The court rejected the argument that the complained—of acts were not the practice of law because of long-standing custom and because experience had proved that protection of the public interest did not require that the acts in question be performed by lawyers. The court argued: "This is tantamount to saying, 'We have been driving through red lights for so many years without a serious mishap that it is now lawful to do so.' " It went on to say that, "neither the public blissful acquiescence nor the bar's confessed lethargy can clothe the activities with validity. There is no prescriptive right to practice law." The court concluded by enjoining the title companies and realtors from assisting or advising in the preparation of documents affecting the title to real or personal property, including filling in the blanks in legal forms.

Subsequent to the Arizona decision, a popular initiative, sponsored by the real estate industry, amended the Arizona Constitution as follows:

ARTICLE XXVI

§ 1.　Powers of real estate broker or salesman

Section 1. Any person holding a valid license as a real estate broker or a real estate salesman regularly issued by the Arizona State Real Estate Department when acting in such capacity as broker or salesman for the parties, or agent for one of the parties to a sale, exchange, or trade, or the renting and leasing of property, shall have the right to draft or fill out and complete, without charge, any and all instruments incident thereto including, but not limited to, preliminary purchase agreements and earnest money receipts, deeds, mortgages, leases, assignments, releases, contracts for sale of realty, and bills of sale.

What arguments can be made in favor of or in opposition to such an amendment? See Marks, The Lawyers and the Realtors: Arizona's Experience, 49 A.B.A.J. 139 (February 1963). In the course of the debate concerning the initiative, Marks relates, a Tucson attorney offered a $100 prize to any real estate salesman (not a lawyer) who could pass a real property examination at the College of Law of the University of Arizona (supra at 141).

In subsequent cases, Arizona courts have held that real estate brokers completing legal documents can be held to full understanding of the implications and ramifications of legal doctrines, Olson v. Neale, 116 Ariz. 522, 570 P.2d 209 (App.1977), and to an obligation to inform their clients as to the legal consequences of documents they draft, Morley v. J. Pagel Realty and Ins., 27 Ariz.App. 62, 550 P.2d 1104 (1976).

Although some courts have reserved certain legal instruments solely for preparation by lawyers, the current trend and the current practice are to permit lay conveyancers to fill in the blanks of standard form deeds, mortgages, and other instruments of conveyance, as well as escrow documents, title insurance papers, abstracts, earnest money agreements, purchase and sale agreements, affidavits, short form leases, bills of sale, options, and more. Indeed, in most parts of the United States there is no service required in the typical residential real estate transactions that is prohibited to lay conveyancers. See New Jersey State Bar Ass'n v. New Jersey Realtor Boards, 93 N.J. 470, 461 A.2d 1112 (1983), modified, 94 N.J. 449, 467 A.2d 577 (1983); Duncan & Hill Realty, Inc. v. Department of State, 62 A.D.2d 690, 405 N.Y.S.2d 339 (1978), appeal denied, 45 N.Y.2d 821, 409 N.Y.S.2d 210, 381 N.E.2d 608 (1978); Cultum v. Heritage House Realtors, Inc., 103 Wash.2d 623, 694 P.2d 630 (en banc 1985). Are participants in real estate transactions adequately protected by form contracts?

8. A study of 132 recent home buyers in Columbus, Ohio, found that only 41 per cent of home buyers hired their own lawyer to represent them in some aspect of the purchase. Twenty-one per cent of the buyers who did not use lawyers stated that they relied on the realtor to assist them with title matters, while 40 per cent of the purchasers stated that they relied mainly on the title insurance company. Seventy-eight per cent of the purchasers believed that if their lender was satisfied with the condition and title of the house, their investment was in all likelihood safe. Others stated that they relied on the seller's or builder's attorney to take care of the legalities. The study found that the purchasers were remarkably uninformed as to basic matters like the type of deed they received or their coverage under the title insurance policy (only seven per cent realized that there were exceptions in the title insurance policy). It also found, however, that purchasers represented by lawyers were: (i) no better informed than those who were not; (ii) slightly less satisfied with the purchase transaction (78 per cent compared to 84 per cent satisfied); (iii) just as likely to find after signing the contract that it contained matters not explained to them; and (iv) no less likely to avoid disputes. See Braunstein & Genn, Odd Man Out: Preliminary Findings Concerning the Diminishing Role of Lawyers in the Home–Buying Process, 52 Ohio St.L.J. 469, 479–480 (1991).

II.   THE BASIC DOCUMENTS IN THE REAL ESTATE TRANSACTION

Real estate lawyering is fundamentally a process of negotiating and problem solving. The function of the real estate lawyer is to achieve the client's lawful and ethical investment objectives. Frequently, this requires the creative real estate lawyer to think of ways to structure the transaction so it results in a win-win and not a win-lose situation. Once the deal is struck, the real estate lawyer's work turns to drafting to document the transaction. We begin this part with the consideration of the documents that govern routine real estate transactions, and the relationships they establish and memorialize.

Many if not most of the documents involved in routine real estate transactions are forms that have evolved over time and are uniform in their terms. Attempts to tailor such forms are often met with considerable resistance. Nevertheless, it is important that the attorney seek to ascertain that her client has had the opportunity both to read and understand the documents presented for her signature. An attorney is expected not only to forward documents to the client with instructions to review them, but also to direct the client's attention to clauses with the greatest impact. Sufficient time should be set aside to discuss the documents. Clients should be asked whether they have read the documents, how much time they spent, whether they understand the provisions, and whether they have any questions. Beware that certain types of clients, including highly educated, successful people with controlling personalities, often disguise or fail to volunteer their lack of understanding, or think they understand provisions when in fact they do not. Clients should be provided with concrete examples of how particular clauses operate, without jargon or buzz words.

A.　THE BROKERAGE AGREEMENT

TYPE				REMARKS		
CONST		DRAPES				
APPROX. AGE		CARPETS				
APPROX. LOT SZ.		STRM. WNDO.				
C & C TAX		SCREENS				
POSS.		FIREPLACE		MAP LOC	DIRECTIONS	
FQNT		AIR COND/C ☐	W ☐			
BSMT		C. WSHR. ☐	DISP ☐			
HEAT		RANGE/GAS ☐	ELEC ☐	SUBDIV	SUB ASSMT	
WT. HTR.		CLOSETS	STRM. DR	LR	BR	
GARAGE		FEN YD ☐	PATIO ☐	DR	BP	
SCH. DIST		SEWER ☐	SEPTIC ☐	KIT	BR	
ELEM		GAS ☐	W'R ☐　220V ☐	FR	BR	
JR./SR.		SGN ☐	KEY ☐	BATHS	BR	
LENDER		TYPE	RATE	OWNER	PH	
L.B.		TERM	MO. PAY	AGENT	PH	
Sell FHA ☐	G/C　Conv. ☐　ASM ☐　%/L		S	BROKER	PH	
#	Area　Add		Zip	RMS	BR	B　$

This information is not intended for advertising purposes but is prepared for office use only. Purchasers are cautioned not to rely upon the information contained hereon but to verify all information to their own satisfaction before entering into contract to purchase.

This is a legally binding contract;　　　　　　　　　　　　　　　　ST. LOUIS ASSOCIATION OF REALTORS 1992
if not understood, seek legal advice.　　　　　　　　　　　©Approved by Counsel for the St. Louis Association of Realtors® and by the
Form #2047　　6/92　　　　　　　　　　　　　　　　　　St. Louis Association of Realtors® to be used exclusively by Realtors

LISTING CONTRACT
(EXCLUSIVE RIGHT TO SELL)

In consideration of the agreement of the undersigned REALTOR to endeavor to procure a Buyer, we, the undersigned Owners of property known as and numbered _____ for ourselves, our heirs and assigns and representing by our signatures hereto that jointly and severally we have a legal right to make an absolute sale of the property, hereby appoint said REALTOR as our sole and exclusive agent with the exclusive right to sell the property described above for $_____ or for any other price to which we shall consent and under the following special terms (if any) _____

We agree to pay said REALTOR a commission of _____ of the total selling, lease or exchange price under any of the following circumstances: (1) If, by 11:59 p.m. of _____, 19__ (hereinafter the "termination date"), a ready, willing and able Buyer is procured by the undersigned REALTOR, or by us, or by any other person; or (2) by termination date said property is contracted by us to be sold to, leased to or exchanged with any person or organization; or (3) within an additional term of _____ days after termination date (hereinafter "protection period"), said property is contracted by us to be sold to, leased to or exchanged with anyone with whom the Owner, REALTOR or REALTOR'S agent (including an agent working under a Buyers Agency Agreement), has introduced to the property prior to termination date, provided we have received by said termination date written notice of the names of said prospective Buyers and further provided that no commission is owed as to registered prospective Buyers if the undersigned Owners enter into a valid listing agreement with another licensed real estate Broker during such protection period and the sale, lease or exchange is made during the protection period.

The total selling, lease or exchange price shall be determined as follows: (1) in the case of a sale, it shall be the total sale price for the property, without reduction for closing adjustments, points or other charges; (2) in the case of a lease, it shall be the total lease payments due to the Owner by the tenant during the term of the lease, without adjustment for utilities, taxes and other charges which may be imposed on the tenant; and (3) in the case of an exchange, it shall be the total value of the consideration received by the undersigned Owners, including, but not limited to, real property and cash. In the event the undersigned Owners effect the terms of ownership in the said real estate by means of delivering stock in a corporation, the commissions shall be due and shall be a lien on said stock.

In the event that said property shall be sold, leased or exchanged in cooperation with another Broker (including a Broker working under a Buyer's Agency Agreement), the undersigned REALTOR shall receive not less than _____ of the total selling, leasing or exchange price.

In the event subject property shall be sold, leased or exchanged by or through another Broker in cooperation with the undersigned REALTOR within said protection period, the total commission shall not exceed the rates set forth above.

The undersigned Owners hereby authorize the undersigned REALTOR to offer to, and pay to, any agent working under a Buyer's Agency Agreement a portion of the REALTOR'S commission hereunder. The Owners acknowledge that if such an agent working under a Buyer's Agency Agreement is licensed with the undersigned REALTOR, there is a dual agency - that is, the undersigned REALTOR is working on behalf of the Buyer and the Owners.

The commission shall be a lien on the property and on earnest money until paid.

WE REPRESENT THAT WE KNOW OF NO MATERIAL STRUCTURAL DEFECTS, LATENT OR APPARENT IN THE IMPROVEMENTS, INCLUDING, BUT NOT LIMITED TO, THE ROOF, FOUNDATION AND BASEMENT (except as noted). WE FURTHER REPRESENT THAT, AS OF THE DATE HEREOF, WE KNOW OF NO SPECIAL CONDOMINIUM ASSESSMENTS OR SPECIAL SUBDIVISION UPKEEP ASSESSMENTS WHICH MAY BE ASSESSED AGAINST THIS PROPERTY DURING THE TERM HEREOF, INCLUDING EXTENSIONS (except as noted). WE THE OWNERS FURTHER REPRESENT THAT TO OUR BEST KNOWLEDGE ALL THE MECHANICAL ELEMENTS OF THE PROPERTY AND THE APPLIANCES BEING SOLD HEREWITH, INCLUDING, BUT NOT LIMITED TO, THE HEATING, COOLING, PLUMBING AND ELECTRICAL EQUIPMENT OF THE PROPERTY ARE IN PROPER WORKING CONDITION (except as noted) OR WILL BE RESTORED TO PROPER WORKING CONDITION AS OF THE DATE OF CLOSING OF THE PROPERTY. THIS REPRESENTATION SHALL NOT BE CONSTRUED TO BE A WARRANTY OF CONDITION, BUT SHALL CONSTITUTE THE OWNER'S OPINION. EXCEPTIONS/NOTATIONS _____

Flood plain:
☐　Property is located in flood plain which requires insurance.
☐　Property is not located in flood plain which requires insurance.
☐　Owner does not know whether property is located in flood plain which requires insurance, and authorizes REALTOR to obtain flood letter at Owner's expense.
If property is located in flood plain which requires insurance, REALTOR is authorized to disclose to prospective Buyer.

In endeavoring to obtain a Buyer for the subject property, the REALTOR will have the right to use all reasonable and recognized professional practices including, but not limited to, the association and cooperation with other licensed Brokers, and the right to submit subject property to any Multiple Listing organization; to provide sales data information, including the final sale price obtained for said property to the Regional Multiple Listing Service and its members, and authority is hereby granted to authorize the REALTOR to use the undersigned Owners' names for advertising and trade papers in connection with this sale. The undersigned Owners authorize the REALTOR to place/erect a suitable sign on the property.

"REALTOR, his client and agents of prospective Buyers authorized by REALTOR shall have access to the property at all reasonable times to show the property. If the undersigned Owners authorize the use of the Multacc or other system allowing access during the absence of Owners, such authorization shall include agents of prospective Buyers authorized by REALTOR."

By our signatures hereto, we the Owners acknowledge that we have read and approved the above information regarding the above addressed property, and that we authorize the undersigned REALTOR to rely upon said information in advertising and promoting the property.

We hereby authorize you, as our agent, and any subagents appointed by you, to disclose the above information to prospective Buyers.

This property is offered without respect to race, color, religion, sex, national origin, handicap or family status.

REALTOR _____ Date _____　　　　　　Owner _____ Date _____

By _____
　(Authorized Agent)　　　　　　　　　　　　Owner _____ Date _____

Address _____　　　　　　　　　　　　Address _____

_____

Tel.: _____　　　　　　　　　　　　　Tel.: _____

　　　　　　　　　　　　　　　　　　　　　Witness _____

MARGARET H. WAYNE TRUST v. LIPSKY

Supreme Court of Idaho, 1993.
123 Idaho 253, 846 P.2d 904.

REINHARDT, JUSTICE PRO TEM.:

This contract dispute arises from a Real Estate Purchase and Sale Agreement entered into between the plaintiff/respondent Margaret H. Wayne Trust ("Wayne" hereafter), as seller, and the defendant/appellant Allan G. Lipsky ("Lipsky" hereafter) as purchaser. The sale was not closed, and Wayne brought an action for damages which was tried without a jury. Lipsky appeals from the Court's judgment in favor of Wayne.

FACTS

The Margaret H. Wayne Trust owned a condominium in Ketchum, Idaho, which was listed for sale by its Trustee, Margaret Wayne, who is a licensed real estate salesperson. The property was shown to Mr. Lipsky by Alan Reynolds, an associate real estate broker for Sun Valley Realty.

Lipsky (who is also a licensed real estate salesman) made three offers to purchase the Wayne property, using a standard printed real estate purchase and sale agreement (earnest money agreement) form provided by Mr. Reynolds. Mrs. Wayne rejected the first offer as too low; the second offer was for a higher amount, but failed because it was contingent on financing which did not occur. The third agreement, dated September 23, 1987, was also on a standard form prepared by Mr. Reynolds and mailed to Lipsky for his signature. It provided for Lipsky to pay $1,000 in earnest money and contained a liquidated damages clause. This offer was made subject to the acceptance of seller on or before September 28; however, Lipsky felt that time was inadequate and changed the acceptance date to October 2, 1987, placing his initials by the change before returning the form to Reynolds.

In anticipation of receiving an acceptable offer from Lipsky, Mrs. Wayne had moved out of the condominium prior to leaving on a vacation. She returned on October 12, 1987 and signed the agreement, also initialing the change in acceptance date. Upon receiving the signed agreement, Reynolds telephoned Lipsky and told him that the offer had been accepted. Whether Reynolds informed Lipsky at that time that the acceptance was ten days late is unclear. Reynolds testified that his normal procedure would be to mail a copy of the agreement to the purchaser once it was accepted. Closing was set for November 2, 1987, and Lipsky proceeded to insure the property, obtain a bank loan, and negotiate through Reynolds for the purchase of some of Wayne's furniture.

On October 19, the stock market began a precipitous decline which caused Lipsky to reconsider his decision to invest in a vacation home. Sometime in late October, he called Reynolds and informed him that he did not intend to close the purchase and would forfeit the earnest money he had paid, but would be interested in renting the condominium for six months at $1,000 per month. He also stated that he did not have a copy of the executed agreement and asked Reynolds to mail a copy to him. On the proposed closing date, Lipsky again spoke with Reynolds to confirm the fact that he did not intend to buy the property and would release the earnest money. During that conversation, Lipsky for the first time mentioned the fact that Mrs. Wayne had not accepted within the time period required by the agreement.

Wayne declined to rent the unit to Lipsky, and also refused to accept the earnest money as liquidated damages, choosing instead to file a suit for specific performance. She subsequently sold the property and proceeded with a claim for actual damages she alleged were caused by Lipsky's breach. After a one-day court trial, a decision issued which incorporated findings of fact and conclusions of law proposed by Wayne, and a judgment was entered in favor of Mrs. Wayne.

* * *

IV

The Trial Court Erred in Awarding Damages Which Represented a Commission for the Broker's Services

In spite of the fact that Wayne did not seek recovery for a commission to Reynolds and presented no evidence that Reynolds sought payment, the trial court granted $4,460 to Mrs. Wayne for "real estate commission owed" to Reynolds. We believe that the trial court erred in this regard.

Idaho has, in the past, adopted the traditional rule that a broker earns his commission when he procures a buyer who is ready, willing and able to purchase on terms acceptable to the seller. Rogers v. Hendrix, 92 Idaho 141, 438 P.2d 653 (1968). A growing number of courts have, however, added a requirement that there must be a closing of title for the broker to receive a commission, adopting the rationale of Ellsworth Dobbs, Inc. v. Johnson, 50 N.J. 528, 236 A.2d 843 (1967):

> When a broker is engaged by an owner of property to find a purchaser for it, the broker earns his commission when (a) he produces a purchaser ready, willing and able to buy on the terms fixed by the owner, (b) the purchaser enters into a binding contract with the owner to do so, and (c) the purchaser completes the transaction by closing the title in accordance with the provisions of the contract.

236 A.2d at 855.

This position was addressed by our Court of Appeals in Strout Realty, Inc. v. Milhous, 107 Idaho 330, 689 P.2d 222 (Ct.App.1984), where a seller under an installment land contract claimed that he was not liable for the commission because the buyer defaulted before he had fully performed and was therefore not "ready, willing, and able." In analyzing the point in time when the ability of the buyer is to be determined, the Court of Appeals employed the Ellsworth Dobbs rule in finding that the commission had been earned at the time the transaction was closed. We also adopt the three-part test set out in Ellsworth Dobbs as the general rule to determine when a real estate broker earns his commission. Because the transaction between Lipsky and Wayne was never closed, Reynolds did not earn his commission.

The adoption of this rule does not, however, alter the obligation to pay the commission if the sale is not completed due to the fault of the seller. This is also recognized in *Ellsworth Dobbs* where the court, after setting out the three-part test, went on to say:

> If the contract is not consummated because of lack of financial ability of the buyer to perform or because of any other default of his * * * there is no right to commission against the seller. On the other hand, if the failure of completion of the contract results from a wrongful act or interference of the seller, the broker's claim is valid and must be paid. In short, in the absence of default by the seller, the broker's right to commission against the seller comes into existence only when his buyer performs in accordance with the contract of sale.

236 A.2d at 855.

Paragraph 15 of the agreement executed by Lipsky and Wayne provides:

> In the event of default in the performance of the terms and conditions of this agreement by either party, the defaulting party agrees to pay the broker the commission which the broker is entitled to receive from the Seller for his/her services in connection with the sale of the premises.

It is clear that Wayne, as the non-breaching party, is not liable for any commission to Reynolds under this provision of the agreement. In determining whether Lipsky is liable for payment of a commission to Reynolds, we note that Lipsky joined Reynolds in this action with a third-party complaint, alleging that Reynolds had represented that Lipsky would only be required to forfeit his earnest money if he chose not to close the sale. Reynolds cross-claimed for the commission he claimed was due from Lipsky as the defaulting party. Prior to trial, Lipsky and Reynolds reached a settlement and dismissed these claims. We hold that Reynolds' claim for a commission on this transaction has been extinguished, and that under the circumstances, it was error for the trial court to award a sum for Reynolds' commission to Wayne.

Notes and Questions

1. List all of the duties sellers generally expect their brokers to perform in connection with the sale of real property. Now examine carefully the form listing agreement reproduced above on page 472. Which of these duties does the broker agree to perform, if any?

2. The contract in *Lipsky* provided that the defaulting party would pay the brokerage commission. Lipsky, who was the defaulting buyer, settled the contract claim against him by the broker Reynolds. Suppose that the contract was silent on this issue, and Lipsky defaults. How should the court decide whether Reynolds is entitled to his commission? If Reynolds cannot recover his commission from the seller Wayne, may he recover from Lipsky?

3. May the rule regarding when the broker earns his commission be changed by contract? Compare Tristram's Landing, Inc. v. Wait, 367 Mass. 622, 626, 327 N.E.2d 727, 729 (1975) ("The purchase and sale agreement provided that the commission was to be paid 'on the said sale,' and we construe this language as requiring that the said sale be consummated before the commission is earned.") with Ellsworth Dobbs, Inc. v. Johnson, 50 N.J. 528, 555, 236 A.2d 843, 857 (1967) ("Whenever there is substantial inequality of bargaining power, position or advantage between the broker and the other party involved, any form of agreement [which purports to grant the broker his commission after a contract of sale is signed regardless of whether the deal closes requires] a court to condemn it as unconscionable.").

4. The court in *Lipsky* relied heavily on Ellsworth Dobbs, Inc. v. Johnson, 50 N.J. 528, 236 A.2d 843 (1967). Only a minority of courts follow the rule of *Ellsworth Dobbs*. The majority rule remains to be that when a broker obtains a buyer who is ready, willing and able to purchase the property, the commission is earned regardless of whether the sale is actually consummated. Which rule is better supported by policy?

5. How might a seller seek to modify the brokerage agreement form in light of the rule of Ellsworth Dobbs? Consider the following provision:

"The commission shall be due and payable at closing if and only if closing occurs, and only out of the net proceeds of sale due seller at closing."

Is this provision fair to the broker?

6. Suppose the improvements on the property are destroyed by fire or other casualty in the period between contract formation and closing. Should the broker be entitled to the commission on the grounds that the seller was in a position to control the risk, or insure against it? See Hecht v. Meller, 23 N.Y.2d 301, 296 N.Y.S.2d 561, 244 N.E.2d 77 (1968).

7. Though the Statute of Frauds in most states requires that most transactions affecting real property must be in writing (see below), the statutes of a majority of states exclude brokerage agreements, permitting oral agreements to be enforced. Even where the Statute of Frauds does not explicitly extend to brokerage agreements, some agreements may still need to be in writing under other provisions of the Statute, for example, agreements that cannot be performed within one year. Where a state statute of frauds requires brokerage commissions to be in writing, it is important that essential terms, such as the fact of employment, the authority of the agent, and the description of the property, be clearly spelled out.

8. There are several ways a seller may "list" his property with a real estate broker. Under an "open listing", the seller authorizes a broker to attempt to sell the property, while also retaining for himself the right to sell the property independently, or to procure the services of other brokers in

marketing the property. Where several brokers hold an open listing on a property, the broker who actually was the procuring cause of a sale can claim the commission. An "exclusive agency" limits the seller to one broker during the duration of the agreement, but permits the seller to attempt to sell the property also on his own to buyers other than those procured by the broker. Finally, an "exclusive right to sell" authorizes only the broker to sell the property. If any buyer purchases the property during the duration of the agreement, a commission is owed.

A "multiple listing" arrangement permits brokers holding exclusive listings in a particular area to pool their listings through a common clearing house. Any broker belonging to the multiple listing arrangement may attempt to sell multiple listed properties. If a broker is successful, the commission will be split between the listing and the selling broker. The courts are split on the question of whether multiple listing arrangements that restrict access of realtors are restraints on trade, but the trend seems to be to permit multiple listing where restrictions on access are reasonable. See 7 R. Powell & P. Rohan, Real Property, ¶ 938.16[2].

9. Under the terms of a "net listing" the brokerage agreement contains the seller's taking price and the broker is entitled to retain as a commission any amount paid by purchaser in excess of this sum. Some jurisdictions prohibit net listings. Do you see why net listings present an inherent conflict of interest in the principal-agent relationship?

10. The broker's primary fiduciary obligation is to the seller of real estate rather than to the buyer. When the property turns out to be defective, however, the buyer often attempts to hold the broker responsible. We examine the broker's obligations under these circumstances in Section IV below.

11. Can a seller avoid paying a commission by waiting to sign a contract of sale until after the term of the listing has expired? How does the listing contract reproduced above on page 472 address this problem? For an example of how difficult it can be to avoid paying the broker a commission under such circumstances, see Gundaker v. Templer, 560 S.W.2d 306 (Mo. App. 1977) (broker entitled to receive commission despite failure to notify seller of name of prospective buyer).

B. THE CONTRACT

The residential real estate purchase contract is easily the most important document in what is often the most important transaction in a client's life. What turns out to be the contract of sale normally begins as an offer from the purchaser (responding to the vendor's listing of the property) which in turn results in a counter-offer or acceptance from the vendor. Negotiations can go on for some time, and in the case of commercial real estate, normally do. The contract, once signed, governs the relationship between the vendor and purchaser during the time, often lasting several weeks or months, between the contract and the closing—the date on which the deed is delivered. In some instances, as will be explored further below, some contractual obligations extend beyond the closing as well.

During the period between the signing of the contract and the closing, important tasks must be completed. In the course of completing those tasks, numerous problems can arise. It is during this period that the title record of the property is usually examined to discover any defects. (Why would the seller wait until a contract is signed to examine the title, rather than having a title examination completed before placing the property on the market?) Providing evidence of good title is usually the obligation of the seller, though in some eastern states the buyer undertakes the responsibility of examining the title. Once defects are uncovered (as they often are), the vendor must undertake to resolve them. The buyer must usually secure financing for part of the purchase price during this time. This will often require satisfying the lender as to the value of the property through an appraisal. Often the buyer or lender will also require a survey of the premises and the purchase of title insurance. The buyer may want to have buildings on the property examined for defects: leaky roofs, termite infestation, structural problems, defective appliances.

During the time that these tasks are underway, other problems may arise. The buildings on the property may be destroyed by fire, eminent domain proceedings against the property may be initiated, mechanics liens or tax liens may be filed encumbering the property.

Ideally, the contract will be sufficiently clear and detailed to resolve any disputes that may arise prior to the closing. As residential real estate contracts are often drafted, however, by brokers more eager to make a sale than to identify potential problems, this is not always the case. There are widespread variations from state to state in the form of contract used in real estate transactions. Examine the following contract, and compare it to one commonly used in your jurisdiction. Consider how they address common real estate transaction problems. Specifically, note how the contract allocates the risks and potential problems inherent in the acquisition and disposition of real property. Consider how you might modify the contract to limit your client's liability with respect to these risks.

PURCHASE AGREEMENT

The undersigned, ROBERT T. SMITH, whose address is 123 Presidents Ave., Columbus, Ohio 43222 (hereinafter referred to as "Buyer"), offers to purchase from ROBERT AND MAXINE HALER, whose address is 1738 Kaiser Dr., Columbus, Ohio 43068 (hereinafter referred to as "Seller"), that real property commonly known as 125 Lincoln Ave., Columbus, Ohio and being at least 90 feet by 150 feet in size, together with all improvements thereon and all appurtenant rights, privileges and easements thereto (hereinafter referred to as the "Property"), at the price and upon the terms and conditions set forth below:

1. PURCHASE PRICE.

The purchase price for the Property (the "Purchase Price") is FIVE HUNDRED AND SEVENTY THOUSAND DOLLARS ($570,000.00). The

Purchase Price shall be paid by Buyer in cash, or by a check at the Closing (as hereinafter defined). Buyer shall be entitled to a credit against the purchase price for the amount of the earnest money deposit paid herewith.

2. APPURTENANCES AND PERSONAL PROPERTY.

This Agreement covers all appurtenances, fixtures and personal property now located at or used in the operation or maintenance of the Property including without limitation:

> All lighting, electrical, heating and air conditioning, plumbing and bathroom fixtures and equipment, all machinery, equipment and trade fixtures, all window and door shades, Venetian blinds, awnings, curtain and drapery rods, window and door screens, storm windows and storm doors, landscaping, shrubbery, television aerials, affixed wall mirrors, attached linoleum, carpeting, stair carpeting, humidifiers, de-humidifiers, refrigerators, stoves, ovens and other kitchen appliances if any, which are now on the premises and used in connection therewith.

3. CLOSING; POSSESSION.

(a) If this Agreement is accepted by Seller within the time provided herein, the delivery of the Deed conveying the Property to the Buyer and, if necessary, the Bill of Sale conveying the fixtures and personal property covered by this Agreement (the "Closing") shall be at a mutually agreed upon time and place in Columbus, Ohio not more than ninety (90) days after the date of acceptance of this Offer to Purchase.

(b) Seller shall deliver occupancy and possession of the Property to Buyer at the Closing; provided, however, that during the period between the acceptance of this Offer to Purchase and the Closing, Buyer may enter onto the Property for the purpose of making any and all inspections of the Property that he shall deem necessary. Also prior to closing, Buyer shall have the right, at his expense, to make such applications, in Seller's name, to commissions and agencies of Columbus and Franklin County as Buyer shall deem necessary or convenient.

(c) The property is sold subject to the existing month to month lease to David Love. Seller shall deliver a true copy of said lease within 10 days of the date of this agreement. At the Closing, Seller will deliver to Buyer a letter from said tenant confirming the terms of said lease, that no rent has been pre-paid, that the amount of the rent is $550 per month and the amount of the security deposit.

4. DEED; TITLE INSURANCE.

Conveyance shall be by recordable general warranty deed with release of dower, if any, and shall convey to Buyer marketable title, free, clear and unencumbered except for the lease to David Love and other matters approved by Buyer's attorney in writing as set forth in paragraph 9(a) hereof. Seller shall furnish and pay for an owner's title insurance commitment and policy (ALTA form B (1970 Rev. 10–17–70 & Rev. 10–17–84)) in the amount of the purchase price. Seller shall pay any and all conveyance fees required to be paid prior to or at the recording of the deed to Buyer. Unless Buyer otherwise notifies Seller in writing prior to the Closing, Buyer shall take title to the Property in the name of Robert T. Smith. At Closing, Buyer shall also deliver to Seller a completed affidavit in the form customary in Franklin County, with content consistent with this Agreement and otherwise satisfactory to Buyer.

5. REAL ESTATE TAXES, ASSESSMENTS, RENTS AND CURRENT OPERATING EXPENSES.

Real estate taxes, installments of assessments, current operating costs and rents, if any, shall be pro-rated as of the date of Closing based on the relevant bills most recently received therefor. Seller shall deliver to Buyer all security or other deposits held, or required to be held by Seller with respect to the Property.

6. CONDITION OF PREMISES.

Seller represents and warrants to Buyer that the Property is in good and habitable condition and that the improvements constructed thereon have been fully and satisfactorily completed in a workmanlike manner.

7. DAMAGE OR DESTRUCTION.

In the event that prior to the Closing the Property is damaged or destroyed by fire or other casualty in an amount (i) less than $1,000.00, Seller shall repair the Property prior to the Closing, or (ii) exceeding $1,000.00, Buyer shall have the option of: (1) accepting the Property in its damaged condition, in which event Seller shall assign to Buyer at the Closing the proceeds of insurance as a result of said damage or destruction; or (2) terminating the contract formed by the acceptance of this Offer to Purchase, in which event the Earnest Money shall be returned to Buyer and all obligations of Buyer and Seller hereunder shall terminate.

8. BROKER'S COMMISSIONS.

No Broker Commissions are payable in connection with this purchase and sale.

9. CONDITIONS.

The obligations of Buyer hereunder are conditioned, at Buyer's option, upon:

(a) Buyer's attorney's approval of the condition of title to the Property (including, without limitation, approval of easements, restrictions, and other conditions of record on the Property), any leases of the Property, the assessments against and the zoning of the Property, which shall not be withheld unreasonably. If Buyer's attorney does not approve of the condition of such title, Buyer, or Buyer's attorney shall so notify Seller in writing on or before ten (10) days prior to the Closing.

(b) Seller's warranties being true and correct as of the date of Closing.

(c) Buyer, at his expense, obtaining a certified survey, which shall be satisfactory to Buyer, showing the boundary lines of the Property and all improvements located thereon. If Buyer is not satisfied with respect to any such item, Buyer shall so notify Seller in writing no more than ten (10) days after delivery of the survey to Buyer.

(d) Inspections, at Buyer's expense, showing to Buyer's satisfaction that the heating and air conditioning units in the building on the Property are in good working order, that the improvements on the Property are not infested or previously damaged by termites or other wood-destroying pests, and that there are no structural or other defects materially and adversely affecting said improvements, or any part thereof, including the roof. Such inspections, if made, must be completed, and any disapproval of such conditions must be made in writing on or before twenty-five (25) days after the acceptance of this Offer to Purchase, or the right to make such inspections shall be waived.

(e) Buyer obtaining a 30 year conventional mortgage secured by the Property, the principal amount of which shall be not less than 80% of the purchase price, with interest thereon not to exceed 10% and 1 point.

10.   RETURN OF EARNEST MONEY; DEFAULT.

If for any reason the Seller cannot perform pursuant to the terms and conditions of this Agreement, or if any one or more of the contingencies set forth in Paragraph 10 above is not satisfied and is not waived in writing by Buyer, the Earnest Money shall be immediately returned to Buyer, without limitation of any other rights Buyer may have hereunder or at law or in equity. If Buyer defaults in the performance of his obligations hereunder, Seller shall be entitled to retain the Earnest Money as liquidated damages, and such shall be his sole remedy.

11.   ENTIRE AGREEMENT.

This Agreement shall constitute the entire agreement between Buyer and Seller as to the terms it contains and no oral or verbal or implied agreement or understanding shall cancel or vary the terms of this Agreement. The terms of this Agreement shall survive the Closing. Buyer may assign his rights and obligations under this Agreement.

This offer shall remain open for acceptance until 10:00 p.m. on March 6, 1990. Signed at Columbus, Ohio on March 5, 1990.

Buyer:

—————————————————————

Robert T. Smith

The undersigned as Seller, accepts the above offer. The undersigned warrant to Buyer they are the sole owners of the Property and acknowledge receipt of the earnest money in the amount of FIVE HUNDRED DOLLARS $500.

Date:

Seller:

_____

Robert Haler

_____

Maxine Haler

Notes and Questions

1. The typical seller's principal legal objectives are first to receive the agreed purchase price in exchange for delivering the deed of conveyance on a date certain, or to be free to promptly offer the property for sale to other prospective purchasers without interference; and second, to limit seller's continuing liability with respect to the property after closing occurs. How does the contract accomplish these objectives?

2. Examining both the contract above and a contract commonly used in your jurisdiction, determine the rights of the parties to a residential real estate transaction if after the contract is signed but prior to the closing:

(a) The residence is destroyed by fire. (We return shortly to the issue of allocation of risk of loss if the contract is silent on this issue.)

(b) Extensive termite damage and active termite infestation are discovered.

(c) The roof of the residence leaks during a heavy rain storm, causing serious damage to the plaster and carpets in several rooms.

(d) The main drain leading from the house to the city sewer line is found to be seriously damaged by a tree in the front yard.

(e) An inspection reveals that the level of radon gas in the house is ten times acceptable levels.

(f) The financial markets suffer a shock and the purchaser finds that she can only secure financing by paying interest rates three per cent higher than the rates on which she had planned.

(g) A title examination discovers an unreleased 1903 mortgage and a possible outstanding dower interest in the wife of a previous owner who sold the property in 1948.

(h) A survey reveals easements for telephone, electric, gas, water, sewer, and cable TV lines. It also establishes that the residence is only nine feet, nine inches from the west lot line, in violation of ten–foot set back requirements established by the municipal zoning ordinance and by private covenants.

(i) The purchaser is transferred to a different part of the country by his employer.

3.   The Statute of Frauds of 1677 provided:

And be it further enacted by the authority aforesaid that * * * no action shall be brought * * * (4) or upon any contract for sale of lands, tenements or hereditaments, or any interest in or concerning them; * * * (6) unless the agreement upon which such action shall be brought, or some memorandum or note thereof, shall be in writing and signed by the party to be charged therewith, or some other person thereunto by him lawfully authorized. Stat. 29 Car. II, ch. 3 § 17 (1677).

Every American jurisdiction similarly provides that contracts for the sale of land must be in writing, though the statutes vary somewhat as to whether unwritten agreements are void or just unenforceable, and as to how long the term of a lease may be before it must be in writing. Though there is considerable variation among jurisdictions as to what contract terms must be in writing for a contract to be enforceable, most require identification of the parties, a description of the premises to be conveyed, language indicating intention to sell or purchase, and a signature of the party against whom the contract is to be enforced. Many jurisdictions also require the price term to be in writing, though some courts will imply a reasonable price if no price term is included.

Despite the absolute language of the statute, many jurisdictions will enforce oral land-sale contracts under the exception of part performance. The extent of performance necessary to take a contract out of the Statute of Frauds varies considerably. In most jurisdictions, partial payment alone is not sufficient, but a combination of partial payment with taking of possession or making improvements might suffice. A few jurisdictions require all three elements to establish part performance; a few refuse to recognize any exception for partial performance. Some courts treat part performance as the evidentiary equivalent of a writing, others liken part performance to estoppel, grounding the exception in justifiable reliance. The exception causes considerable uncertainty and contributes to a great deal of litigation. See, on the Statute of Frauds and its exceptions, W. Stoebuck and D. Whitman, The Law of Property, §§ 10.1, 10.2 (3rd ed. 2000); 3 American Law of Property, §§ 11.2–11.12 (J. Casner, ed., 1952); Braunstein, Remedy, Reason and the Statute of Frauds: A Critical Economic Analysis, 1989 Utah L.Rev. 383.

4.   One of the most common conditions in contemporary residential real estate contracts is the "subject to financing" clause. This condition makes the purchaser's obligation to purchase the property subject to the purchaser being able to secure a financing commitment from a lending institution to finance that part of the purchase which the purchaser cannot afford to pay from his own funds. Subject to financing clauses can be drafted with great specificity—"subject to the purchaser obtaining a commitment for a thirty-year conventional fixed mortgage at a rate not exceeding 12% per annum and two points"—or with great generality—"subject to the purchaser obtaining satisfactory financing."

Obviously, subject to financing clauses, particularly vague and indefinite clauses, provide a great opportunity for the purchaser who has second thoughts about a purchase commitment to back out of a real estate transaction. Indeed a sufficiently vague subject to financing clause may raise questions as to whether a contract obligates the buyer at all, and if not, whether it is unenforceable for not creating mutual obligations. See Imas Gruner & Associates, Limited v. Stringer, 48 Md.App. 364, 427 A.2d 1038 (1981); Nodolf v. Nelson, 103 Wis.2d 656, 309 N.W.2d 397 (App.1981).

Courts commonly interpret subject to financing clauses as creating an obligation on the buyer to exercise good faith in pursuing financing. See Brack v. Brownlee, 246 Ga. 818, 273 S.E.2d 390 (1980); Smith v. Vernon, 6 Ill.App.3d 434, 286 N.E.2d 99 (1972). If the buyer is unable to secure financing, despite good faith efforts, his performance is excused. If, however, the buyer fails to make good faith efforts, he can be held in breach of contract. Other conditions, such as that of the purchaser selling another home to raise the down payment, have similarly been held to impose an obligation of good faith effort.

Should a buyer who fails to qualify for conventional financing from an institutional lender be required to accept financing from the seller? Compare Kovarik v. Vesely, 3 Wis.2d 573, 89 N.W.2d 279 (1958), with Gardner v. Padro, 164 Ill.App.3d 449, 115 Ill.Dec. 445, 517 N.E.2d 1131 (1987). Why would the buyer even care about the source of financing?

5. People make significant plans in reliance on the occurrence of real estate closings at the appointed time. The buyer's financing commitment has an expiration date. Either buyer or seller may have scheduled simultaneous closings on other property. A contract may or may not specify the time by which conditions specified in the contract must be met and the closing occur. If it fails to do so, compliance must occur within a reasonable time. If a date for compliance with conditions or for closing is specified in the contract, it may not be determinative. Delay, if it does not become unreasonable, may subject the party in breach to damages, but not excuse performance by the other party. The party whose performance was delayed may still sue the other party at equity for specific performance.

If, however, the contract uses the magic formula, "time is of the essence," performance must be tendered on the date specified in the contract. In Gorrie v. Winters, 214 N.J.Super. 103, 518 A.2d 515 (1986), sellers were present and prepared to close at the stated time of 11 a.m., and declared the contract terminated when buyer had not appeared by 11:45 a.m. In response to buyer's suit for specific performance, the court held that buyer's failure to close at the stated time effectively terminated the contract because time was made of the essence. Even if the contract fails to contain this formula, however, time may be made essential by either party giving the other reasonable notice that strict compliance must be forthcoming by a set date. As is often the case where form triumphs over fairness, courts often attempt to mitigate the strict application of these doctrines, usually by finding waiver by the party demanding performance. W. Stoebuck and D. Whitman, The Law of Property, § 10.9 (3rd ed. 2000).

6. Suppose your client (the buyer, say) would like to keep his options open on buying an existing commercial building, but that the other side insists on a tight deal. Can you think of a condition that would let your client escape from what otherwise appears to be a tight deal, if your client changes his mind? What you seem to need here is something like the conditions on financing or time but free of the judicial garnish of reasonableness. (Suppose, for example, the condition that the local

zoning authority approve the reasonable remodeling of the building your client contemplates, when the political realities are that your client controls decisions of the zoning authority and the seller does not realize what the political realities are. [You can probably think of better examples.]) Is there, in your perception, a moral objection to drafting such a clause for your client? See the brief description of "the equitable sanction" taught by the late Kurt F. Pantzer of the Indianapolis Bar, T. Shaffer, C. Mooney, and A. Boettcher, The Planning and Drafting of Wills and Trusts 157 (4th ed. 2001). A non-lawyer friend read this note and commented: "This is why people hate lawyers."

7. Most residential real estate transactions are first formalized by real estate brokers, not lawyers, and on contract forms prepared by local boards of Realtors, not by bar associations. There are usually material differences, most of them tracing to the fact that most real estate brokers represent sellers, not buyers. Suppose, to illustrate the point, a young married couple come to the law offices with a real estate broker form of contract, filled in by the seller's broker, for the purchase of a home they very much want to buy, for a price they think is a bargain. They ask for legal advice on whether they should sign the contract (which, signed by them, will be presented to the seller as in effect an offer to purchase from them). The lawyer reads the contract, consults her knowledge and experience in such transactions, and compares it with the form of contract prepared by her local bar association (e.g., the contract on pp. 478–482). This lawyer has three problems with the Board of Realtors contract her clients show her:

(i) The contract puts all risk of loss from latent defects (those not known to seller or discovered by the clients or their inspectors) on the buyers.

(ii) The contract refers to descriptions of the house contained in material circulated to brokers by the local multiple listing service. The clients tell the lawyer that the broker quoted such material when he described the property to these clients. (For example, the nearby elementary school is the best in the city; the roof on the house is new; and no water softener is necessary in this part of the city.) But the contract provides that this material "is for the sole purpose of providing general guidance to Realtors * * * and is not represented to be accurate. Therefore the Seller and Purchaser represent that they have not relied on any of the said publications or materials and are contracting based solely on their personal inspection of the real estate. * * * "

(iii) The contract requires that the buyers pay for all inspections.

Using the brokers' form, therefore, puts significant (but probably not fatal) risks on these clients that using a modification of it (drafted by the lawyer) or the bar association form would not put on them. However, this lawyer's experience is that brokers tend to insist on using their own form, and lawyers who want to vary the form or provide another form often end up ruining a good deal for their clients. What course of action is best for this lawyer to take? If this lawyer is one of those who answers such professional questions by saying to herself, "I explain all the options and let the clients decide," and the clients ask, "What would *you* do?" what should the lawyer's response be?

KUHN v. SPATIAL DESIGN, INC.

Superior Court of New Jersey
Appellate Division, 1991.

245 N.J.Super. 378, 585 A.2d 967.

R.S. Cohen, J.

Plaintiffs John and Marlene Kuhn contracted to buy a home from defendant Spatial Design, Inc. The sale was contingent on the Kuhns' obtaining a mortgage to finance the purchase. They applied to Prudential Home Mortgage Company through a mortgage broker, defendant Sterling National Mortgage Company, Inc., with the help of Sterling employees, defendants Ellberger and Wolf. Prudential issued a mortgage commitment but later withdrew it. The Kuhns then sought to void their purchase contract with Spatial Design for failure of the mortgage contingency. When they did not get their deposit back, they started suit. Spatial Design counterclaimed for damages for breach of contract. Judge Patrick J. McGann, Jr., heard the matter and found that the Kuhns had breached. He therefore denied their claim and awarded Spatial Design damages on the counterclaim. We affirm . . .

Judge McGann concluded on compelling evidence that the Kuhns and Sterling's people purposely submitted a mortgage application that presented a materially false picture of the Kuhns' income and assets, because they knew that revealing their true financial situation would not produce the loan they sought. The judge further found that the Kuhns and Sterling were encouraged to submit such an application by Prudential's dependably credulous way of dealing with income and asset information submitted to it.

The Kuhns knew that their application showed that Kuhn was an Air Force colonel, but did not reveal that he had already been approved for retirement; that Mrs. Kuhn had a substantial income from "Plants–R–You," a florist business which existed only in the minds of the Kuhns and Sterling's people; that the fictitious business had assets of $50,000, which did not exist at all; that the $50,000 deposit on the purchase came from savings, when in fact it was borrowed on a second mortgage on the Kuhns' present home, and that the Kuhns had jewelry, antiques, stamps and the like worth $123,000, which Kuhn actually thought would fetch some $47,000.

Kuhn knew that his true current income and assets would not support the mortgage application. He and his wife also knew that Wolf had left some figures blank in the application they signed. Wolf had said they were not going to be "boy scouts" in the matter. Predictably, Sterling's president, Ellberger, who knew what numbers it took to make the application viable, supplied some impressive ones. They showed bank balances of some $240,000 instead of the real $10,000, and total family income of some $218,000 instead of the real $65,000 or even the fictitious $95,000 that earlier appeared. Not surprisingly, Prudential issued a commitment for a $300,000 mortgage for the $515,000 purchase.

All of this was possible because the Kuhns were making a "no documentation" loan application. That meant that Prudential would probably not check to see if the represented facts showing the career Air Force officer's improbably comfortable financial situation were true.

Colonel Kuhn expected the whole business to be ultimately supported by a high-salaried but not-yet-identified private sector job he hoped to find before he retired. The $30,000 in income he thought was going to be attributed to "Plants–R–You" (Ellberger eventually settled on $9400 per month) was really his Air Force pension. The $65,000 he thought he showed as service income (Ellberger made it $8800 per month) would be covered by the private sector job he had not yet sought.

When Kuhn put the present home up for sale and looked for a private sector job, he found both the real estate market and the job market unwelcoming. He heard that Spatial Design might have sold the house across the street from their new one for much less than they were paying. He therefore decided to climb down from the shaky limb he was on. He telephoned Prudential and wrote to Sterling, stating that he had decided to retire from the Air Force, and would thus lose some $40,000 in annual income. He inquired innocently if that would affect the mortgage commitment.

Almost simultaneously, Kuhn wrote to the Air Force to withdraw his approved retirement, thus falsifying the sole expressed basis of his communications with Prudential and Sterling. Prudential withdrew its commitment on the basis of the new information. It had retained the right to withdraw "if any material facts appear that have not previously been revealed by [the applicant]." Kuhn then unsuccessfully tried to cancel the purchase contract on the thesis that the mortgage contingency was not satisfied.

The Kuhns sued Spatial Design, which counterclaimed for the deposit and damages. They then sued Sterling, Wolf and Ellberger for indemnification against the counterclaim. Spatial Design crossclaimed against Sterling, Wolf and Ellberger for fraud, tortious interference, conspiracy and negligence.

After a bench trial, Judge McGann found in favor of Spatial Design and against the Kuhns, and assessed damages at almost $100,000, less the retained deposit of $50,000. He denied the Kuhns' indemnification claim and Spatial Design's damage claim against the mortgage brokers.

Spatial Design has not crossappealed from the denial of its damage claim against the mortgage brokers. We therefore do not comment on it. In all respects material to this appeal, however, Judge McGann's findings and conclusions on the conduct of the parties are supported by compelling evidence. We have considered his conclusions that as wrongdoers the Kuhns are not entitled to indemnification, and that whatever limited knowledge the Kuhns' real estate broker Flo Pulda had about the mortgage application was not attributable to Spatial Design. Those conclusions were factually supported and legally sound.

Now, as to damages. The contract price was $515,000, subject to a real estate commission of 5% or $25,750. The house was eventually sold, free of commission, for $434,000. In the interim, there were carrying charges for taxes and interest. There was no reason suggested by the evidence to doubt the reasonableness either of the time it took to resell the house or the sale price obtained.

Damages arose from two different sources. The first was the decreasing value of the house due to general market conditions. The second was the cost of holding the house until it could be resold. The holding costs are not the subject of this appeal. The Kuhns have two arguments, however, about the loss-of-value damages.

The first argument is that the true measure of a seller's damages for breach of contract by a buyer of real estate is the difference between the contract price and the market value at the time of the breach, less credit for any deposit retained by the seller. They point out that if values were steadily declining, as the judge found, they had declined very little in the few months between contract and breach, and certainly much less than at the time of resale, many months later. Thus, the Kuhns argue, it was error to measure Spatial Design's damages by the difference between the two contract prices.

Neither of the cases cited by the Kuhns involved the assessment of damages resulting from a breach in a falling market. In such circumstances, two basic rules must be consulted. One is that contract damages are designed to put the injured party in as good a position as if performance had been rendered as promised. The other, from *Hadley v. Baxendale,* is that damages should be such as may fairly be considered either arising naturally, *i.e.,* according to the usual course of things, from the breach, or such as may reasonably be supposed to have been in the contemplation of both parties, at the time they contracted, as the probable result of the breach. *Donovan v. Bachstadt,* 91 N.J. 434, 444–445, 453 A.2d 160 (1982).

In the usual course of things, a $515,000 house cannot be resold the instant a contract buyer breaches, and a reasonable time for resale must therefore be allowed. In addition, it is not uncommon for property values to experience a general fall-off after a period of intense run-up. In a falling market, buyers take longer to find, and they buy at reduced prices.

A rule that restricts damages for breach of a contract to buy real estate to the difference between contract price and value at the time of breach (plus expenses) works fairly only in a static market. A damage rule works fairly in a declining market only if it takes account of slowing sales and falling values. In such cases, where the seller puts the property back on the market and resells, the measure is not contract price less value at the time of breach, but rather the resale price, if it is reasonable as to time, method, manner, place and terms. These are matters for the factfinder, who may or may not conclude from the evidence that what actually occurred after breach by way of resale was reasonable and thus provides an accurate measure of damages. Judge McGann found that it did here, on sufficient credible evidence.

We adopt for these purposes, the essence of the sellers' damage rules provided for sellers of goods in the Uniform Commercial Code, *N.J.S.A.* 12A:2–706 and 708, and adapted for sellers of real estate in §§ 504–507 of the Uniform Land Transactions Act (ULTA), which New Jersey has not adopted. We adopt these rules because they take account of the effect of changing market conditions in sound ways which New Jersey's reported decisions have not yet taken into account.

Where a buyer of real estate wrongfully rejects, repudiates or materially breaches as to a substantial part of the contract, the seller may resell in a manner that is reasonable as to method, manner, time, place and terms. The defaulting buyer must have reasonable notice of the time after which resale will take place. If the resale is a public sale, the defaulting buyer must have notice of the time and place, and may buy. The seller may then recover the amount by which the unpaid contract price and any incidental and consequential damages exceed the resale price, less expenses avoided because of the buyer's breach. *See* ULTA § 2–504, 13 U.L.A. 552 (1977); N.J.S.A. 12A:2–706.

A seller's incidental damages include any reasonable out-of-pocket expenses incurred because of the buyer's breach. A seller's consequential damages include any loss the buyer knew or at the time of contracting had reason to know would result from the buyer's breach and which reasonably could not be avoided by the seller. *See* ULTA § 507, 13 U.L.A. 555 (1977).

The case may be different where the seller does not put the property back on the market. In such a case, the measure of the seller's damages is the amount by which the unpaid contract price and any incidental and consequential damages exceed the fair market value of the property at the time of breach, less expenses avoided because of the buyer's breach. *See* ULTA § 2–505(a), 13 U.L.A. 553 (1977) (using the value at the time set for conveyance instead of at the time of breach); *see also* N.J.S.A. 12A:2–708(1). Without a resale, value at the time of breach is used, even in a declining market, because the choice of any other time would be so speculative. We need not explore application of the exceptions made by ULTA 2–505(b) and N.J.S.A. 12A:2–708(2) for situations in which the difference between contract price and fair market value is inadequate to put the seller in as good a position as performance would have.* * *

Notes and Questions

1. The standard measure of damages for breach of contract for the purchase and sale of land is the difference between the contract price and the market value of the property at the time of breach. Why does the court in Kuhn apply a different measure of damages? From what source is this

measure of damages derived? Is it not the height of judicial activism for the court to adopt a measure of damages that had been explicitly considered and rejected by the state legislature?

2. How would the result in <u>Kuhn</u> been different if the parties had used the contract reproduced above on pages 478–482?

C. THE DEED

The laws of most states contain statutory forms of deeds. Examine the following statutory deeds and warranties from Ohio.

5302.01 CREATION OF STATUTORY FORMS; ALTERATION

The forms set forth in sections 5302.05, [et seq.] of the Revised Code may be used and shall be sufficient for their respective purposes. They shall be known as "Statutory Forms" and may be referred to as such. They may be altered as circumstances require, and the authorization of such forms shall not prevent the use of other forms. Wherever the phrases defined in sections 5302.06, 5302.08, 5302.10, and 5302.13 of the Revised Code are to be incorporated in instruments by reference, the method of incorporation as indicated in the statutory forms shall be sufficient, but shall not preclude other methods.

5302.05 DEED IN FEE SIMPLE, GENERAL WARRANTY DEED

A deed in substance following the form set forth in this section, when duly executed in accordance with Chapter 5301. of the Revised Code, has the force and effect of a deed in fee simple to the grantee, the grantee's heirs, assigns, and successors, to the grantee's and the grantee's heirs', assigns', and successors' own use, with covenants on the part of the grantor with the grantee, the grantee's heirs, assigns, and successors, that, at the time of the delivery of that deed the grantor was lawfully seized in fee simple of the granted premises, that the granted premises were free from all encumbrances, that the grantor had good right to sell and convey the same to the grantee and the grantee's heirs, assigns, and successors, and that the grantor does warrant and will defend the same to the grantee and the grantee's heirs, assigns, and successors, forever, against the lawful claims and demands of all persons.

GENERAL WARRANTY DEED

_____ (marital status), of _____ County, _____ for valuable consideration paid, grant(s), with general warranty covenants, to _____, whose tax-mailing address is _____, the following real property: (description of land or interest therein and encumbrances, reservations, and exceptions, if any) Prior Instrument Reference: Volume _____, Page _____, wife (husband) of the grantor, releases all rights of dower therein.

Executed this _____ day of _____.

(Execution in accordance with Chapter 5301. of the Revised Code)

5302.06 GENERAL WARRANTY COVENANTS

In a conveyance of real estate, or any interest therein, the words "general warranty covenants" have the full force, meaning, and effect of the following words: "The grantor covenants with the grantee, his heirs, assigns, and successors, that he is lawfully seized in fee simple of the granted premises; that they are free from all encumbrances; that he has good right to sell and convey the same, and that he does warrant and will defend the same to the grantee and his heirs, assigns, and successors, forever, against the lawful claims and demands of all persons."

5302.07 LIMITED WARRANTY DEED

_____ (marital status), of _____ County, _____ for valuable consideration paid, grant(s), with limited warranty covenants, to _____, whose tax-mailing address is _____, the following real property: (description of land or interest therein and encumbrances, reservations, and exceptions, if any) Prior Instrument Reference: Volume _____, Page _____, wife (husband) of said grantor, releases to said grantee all rights of dower therein.

Executed this _____ day of _____.

(Execution in accordance with Chapter 5301. of the Revised Code)

5302.08 LIMITED WARRANTY COVENANTS DEFINED

In a conveyance of real estate, or any interest therein, the words "limited warranty covenants" have the full force, meaning, and effect of the following words: "The grantor covenants with the grantee, his heirs, assigns, and successors, that the granted premises are free from all encumbrances made by the grantor, and that he does warrant and will defend the same to the grantee and his heirs, assigns, and successors, forever, against the lawful claims and demands of all persons claiming by, through, or under the grantor, but against none other."

5302.11 QUIT–CLAIM DEED

_____ (marital status), of _____ County, _____ for valuable consideration paid, grant(s) to _____, whose tax-mailing address is _____, the following real property: (description of land or interest therein and encumbrances, reservations, and exceptions, if any) Prior Instrument Reference: Volume _____, Page _____, wife (husband) of the grantor, releases all rights of dower therein.

Executed this _____ day of _____.

(Execution in accordance with Chapter 5301. of the Revised Code)

Notes and Questions

1. If the parties choose to use a deed different from the statutory form, will the deed be valid? What are the advantages of using the statutory form?

Seller sold a house to Buyer. Unknown to either, the title to the house was defective because the person from whom Seller had purchased had granted a right of way across the property to a neighbor. Is Seller liable to Buyer for breach of the warranties of title *to Seller* conveyed by warranty deed, special warranty deed, or quitclaim deed? Why would a seller want to use a quitclaim deed? Why would a buyer be willing to accept it?

2. Conveyancing by deed replaced the earlier process of feoffment by livery of seisin. Livery of seisin, as you recall, was accomplished by the parties going to the parcel of land to be conveyed and there, in the sight of witnesses, handing over a clod or twig to symbolize the transfer of ownership. The ingenuity of conveyancers and the rise of the use made possible a variety of alternatives to transfer by livery of seisin, which was too public and inconvenient for many grantors. These alternatives included the bargain and sale deed, the lease and release, and the covenant to stand seized. They were supplemented as devices for transferring property by the fine and common recovery, which were used to defeat the fee tail, and the grant for non-freehold interests. The Statute of Uses of 1536 and the Statute of Frauds of 1677 effectively ended transfer of property by livery of seisin, and gave birth to the modern deed. Many deeds remain archeological artifacts, however, containing all the atavistic formulae effective at one time or another for transferring one interest or another in real property: i.e. "The grantor * * * does give, grant, bargain, sell, release, and convey unto the grantee * * *."

3. Under the Statute of Frauds, a deed must be in writing. The essential elements which must be written include the names of the grantor and grantee, a description of the property, and a statement of intention to convey. The deed must also be signed by the grantor. Historically, a seal was also required for some forms of conveyancing, and a deed may still require a seal in a few states. Many states require that a deed be acknowledged before it can be recorded. A few require attestation by witnesses as an alternative to, or in addition to, acknowledgment.

Occasionally deeds are executed by a grantor with the grantee's name left blank. Traditionally, such deeds were considered void and of no effect. If the grantee's name is inserted subsequently, however, some courts uphold the validity of the transfer for equitable reasons. See Mehus v. Thompson, 266 N.W.2d 920 (N.D.1978); Kindred v. Crosby, 251 Iowa 198, 100 N.W.2d 20 (1959).

As a deed is not a contract, neither consideration nor recitation of consideration is necessary to its validity. Recitation of consideration may be significant, however, for purposes of determining whether a grantee is a bona fide purchaser for value, protected by a recording act. Some states also require that deeds specify the amount of consideration for which the property was transferred as a "condition for recordation" to facilitate determination of the transfer tax and for property tax assessment.

To effectively transfer property, a deed must adequately describe the property transferred. In the United States, several methods of property description are in use. In the Atlantic seaboard states, Kentucky, Tennessee and West Virginia, property is commonly described through the use of metes and bounds descriptions. Such descriptions commonly begin at a geographic point of beginning, then specify, or call, the direction and distance of each boundary line around the lot back to the beginning. Where possible, reference is made to natural or artificial monuments.

The old Northwest territories and most of the land added to the United States since the colonial period has been surveyed according to the Government Survey System designed by Thomas Jefferson and adopted by the Continental Congress in 1785. Pursuant to this system the nation has been divided into six-mile-square blocks known as Townships, which each in turn are subdivided into mile square Sections, all numbered according to the same formula. Sections can be further divided into halves, quarters, or smaller units for describing properties located within them. Each township in the country can be located with reference to Range lines, running north and south parallel to Principal Meridian lines, or to township lines running east and west parallel to Base lines. There are 36 sets of such Principal Meridian and Base lines within the Government Survey System. So for example, a property could be described under the government system as the S 1/2 of the SW 1/4 of Section 25 of Township 3 North, Range 3 West, First Principal Meridian.

Finally, residential property in the United States is commonly described by reference to a subdivision plat. A plat is a recorded survey map of a subdivided property. A deed may describe a property by lot and block number in a particular subdivision, and then refer to the recorded plat of that subdivision, and, perhaps to the location of the subdivision under the Government Survey System. For example, a property could be described as "Lot 7, West River Terrace, part of Sections 3 and 10, Township 8 South, Range 17 West, Bertrand Township, Berrein County, Michigan, according to the Plat thereof, recorded July 23, 1957, in Book 15 of Plats, page 40."

Because surveying was not an exact science at the time much of the United States was surveyed, and because of transcription errors as descriptions in deeds have been transcribed or copied over time, inconsistencies and conflicts in the deeds of neighboring lots, or within the description of a single lot, occur not infrequently, as is illustrated by the following case.

THERIAULT v. MURRAY

Supreme Judicial Court of Maine, 1991.
588 A.2d 720.

GLASSMAN, JUSTICE.

Robert P. and Anita B. Theriault appeal from a judgment of the Superior Court (Penobscot County, Alexander, J.), contending that the court erred in relying solely on the distance calls in the Theriaults' deed to fix the southern boundary of their land in the Town of Charleston. The Theriaults' disputed southern boundary is the northern boundary of the land owned by the defendants, Joseph C. and Linda M. Murray. We agree with the Theriaults' contention and vacate the judgment.

By a deed dated June 15, 1972, the Theriaults acquired land from Merle S. Bradford, described in pertinent part as follows:

Commencing on the County Road at the southwest corner of land now or formerly owned by Elizabeth Chute, being the generally northwesterly corner of a certain lot or parcel of land conveyed by Clarence H. Dyer to John B. Bradford, ... thence in a generally southerly direction by and along said County Road Twenty (20) rods to a stake driven into the ground; thence at right angles to said County Road in a generally easterly direction Fifty (50) rods to a stake driven into the ground; thence at right angles in a generally northerly direction Twenty-eight (28) rods more or less to land now or formerly of Edwin Bickmore, ... thence in a generally westerly direction by and along said northerly line of said premises ... Thirty (30) rods more or less to the generally northeasterly corner of said premises now or formerly of said Elizabeth Chute; thence in a generally southerly direction by and along said easterly line of said premises of said Elizabeth Chute Eight (8) rods more or less to the generally southeasterly corner of said premises of said Elizabeth Chute; thence in a generally westerly direction by and along the southerly line of said premises of said Elizabeth Chute Twenty (20) rods more or less to the point of beginning.

A sketch of the property described in the Theriaults' deed is attached to this opinion as Appendix A. Elizabeth Chute, referred to in the Theriaults' deed, previously had a smaller lot. At the time of Bradford's conveyance to the Theriaults, however, Chute had increased her holdings to include the lot bounded at its southwest corner by point "B" on the sketch. Bradford later conveyed the property south of the Theriault property to Gary Jackson, who deeded it to the Murrays in 1987. The deeds to Jackson and the Murrays defined the northern boundary of the Murray land as being the southern boundary of the Theriault land.

The instant dispute arose from two features of the 1972 deed from Bradford to the Theriaults. The deed defines the starting point both by a primary description, which corresponds to the southwest corner of the new Chute lot (point B), and by an auxiliary description which corresponds to the southwest corner of the old Chute lot (point A). The deed also describes the Theriaults' southern boundary by measurements of 20 rods along and 50 rods at right angles to a county road and by the locations of two stakes at either end of the boundary. From 1972 to 1987 the Theriaults treated the boundary as the line defined by a stake located 20 rods south of the southwest corner of the new Chute lot (point D) and another stake perpendicular to it (point E). In 1987, when the stakes no longer existed, the Murrays asserted that the boundary belonged further north. Relying on the auxiliary description of the starting point in the Theriaults' deed, the Murrays contended that the boundary was located 20 rods south of the southwest corner of the old Chute lot (point C). The Theriaults sought a declaratory judgment to determine the true location of the boundary.

The Superior Court heard unrebutted testimony that the location of the original stakes still can be discerned from vegetation patterns and an old roadbed. A surveyor testified that the starting point at the new Chute lot is 20 rods from this original stake line. But if the new Chute lot is used, then the other measurements of the Theriaults' land along the abutting Bickmore and new Chute boundaries do not closely match the Theriaults' deed distance calls. If the original stake line is ignored and the old Chute lot starting point is used, then the measurements along the Bickmore and old Chute boundaries match the deed distance calls precisely. The court concluded from this precise match that the deed intended to convey to the Theriaults the land described solely by the old Chute starting point and that the distance calls in the deed prevailed over the monuments referred to in the deed. The court accordingly entered judgment for the Murrays.

We consistently have held that what boundaries a deed refers to is a question of law, while the location of those boundaries on the face of the earth is a question of fact. [   ] If facts extrinsic to the deed reveal a latent ambiguity, then we determine the intent from contemporaneous circumstances and from standard rules of construction. [   ] A basic rule is that boundaries are controlled, in descending priority, by monuments, courses, distances, and quantity, unless this priority produces absurd results. Id. at 158. The physical disappearance of a monument does not end its use in defining a boundary if its former location can be ascertained. [   ]

The Theriaults' deed describes their property both by monuments and by courses and distances. The court properly found that the boundaries of land owned by the abutters Bickmore and Chute are monuments that define the Theriaults' northern boundaries. [   ] But the deed also defines the southern boundary by monuments: the two stakes. The court has a duty to determine, if possible, the original locations of these stakes on the face of the earth. If they can be located, these monuments as a matter of law must prevail over the deed's course and distance calls. The deed's reference to the new Chute lot as the starting point, which is consistent with the original stake boundary, cannot be impaired by an auxiliary reference to the old Chute lot as a starting point, [B6] No absurd result manifestly inconsistent with the intent of the deed is produced by the use of the monuments called out in the deed to define the disputed boundary. On remand the court may accept additional evidence relative to the plaintiffs' burden of proving the original location of the monuments. [   ]

The entry is:

Judgment vacated. Remanded to the Superior Court for proceedings consistent with the opinion herein.

All concurring.

Not To Scale

Notes and Questions

1. The principle on which the court in *Theriault* relies for construction is supplemented by others, such as: "the construction prevails which is most favorable to the grantee"; "if the deed contains two descriptions, one ambiguous and the other unambiguous, the latter prevails in order to sustain the deed" or "when a tract of land is bound by a monument which has width, such as a highway or stream, the boundary line extends to the center * * *." See J. Cribbet & C. Johnson, Principles of the Law of Property, 210–212 (3rd ed. 1989) listing and commenting on these and other principles.

2. In Kauka Farms, Inc. v. Scott, 256 Ga. 642, 352 S.E.2d 373 (1987), the seller reserved a life estate in part of the land conveyed to the buyer. The description of the life estate reserved was the seller's "home and 20 acres of land immediately surrounding his home." The court found that this descrip-

tion was "clear on its face as to size, shape, and location," and that the term "surrounding" described a circle centered on the home, having the proper radius to result in an area of 20 acres.

3. According to the old chestnut, a deed is effective when "signed, sealed, and delivered." Though the seal has fallen into desuetude, execution and delivery are still key to the passage of property by deed, with delivery being the final act necessary before the deed becomes effective. Delivery is often straightforward; after signing the deed, the grantor hands it to the grantee. Increasingly, however, deeds are handled through commercial escrows supervised by financial institutions or title companies, where the deed may be delivered to the grantee sometime after the grantor executes it. In commercial escrows, an escrow agent is appointed with instructions from both the grantor (vendor) and grantee (purchaser). The escrow agent receives the deed from the vendor and the purchase money from the purchaser and lender. The agent determines the various charges and credits due each party, and ultimately records the deed and security interests and makes disbursements. Because escrow closings do not require the presence of the purchaser and vendor, the ceremony that attended traditional delivery of the deed is absent from them.

Delayed delivery of a deed is also used by grantors from time to time as an estate planning device. Whenever delivery is delayed problems can arise, as is evidenced in the following case.

PIPES v. SEVIER

Missouri Court of Appeals, 1985.
694 S.W.2d 918.

SHANGLER, JUDGE.

This action, an intra-family squabble over the title to certain parcels of land under successive—and incompatible—conveyances from the mother to several family members, commenced as a petition for declaratory judgment, and was adjudicated on a petition [the fourth amendment] to remove a cloud from the title. The dispute ranged the two children of Leone Pipes—Keith and Beverly—against the other, while the mother aligned first with the cause of Keith, and then after his death, with the cause of Beverly.

The action was tried to the court, and the court adjudged that the fee simple title to the subject parcel [the Home Place] was vested in Violet Pipes and children Jerry, Gary, Walter and Kathy—all as heirs at law of grantee Keith Pipes, then deceased, subject only to the life estate reserved in the grantor, Leone Pipes.

The appellants, Beverly Sevier and son Roddy and mother Leone Pipes, contend that the evidence does not support the judgment, and other errors.

The evidence was that Ralph and Leone Pipes, parents of Keith and Beverly, owned three tracts of land in Sullivan County: the Cott Farm, the Sheppy Farm and the Home Place. The parents purchased the Home Place in 1948. That acquisition [a tract of some 297 acres] was induced by the agreement of son Keith to remain with the father in the farm operation. The son Keith faithfully worked with the father from that time until year 1967, when the elder Pipes died, and thereafter continued to operate or work all three farms on a crop-share basis with mother Leone Pipes, until Keith died in 1982.

In about the year 1960, Ralph Pipes had a will prepared by attorney Leman Atherton whereby the Home Place was devised to son Keith and the Cott Farm and the Sheppy Farm to daughter Beverly, in the event wife Leone predeceased the children. The widow of son Keith, Violet Pipes, testified that it was understood within the family that the ultimate division of the farms intended by the parents was as provided in the Ralph Pipes will. Accordingly, in order to give effect to that shared intention, in November of 1972, Leone Pipes directed attorney Atherton to prepare two sets of deeds—a conveyance of the Home Place to son Keith and conveyances of the Cott Farm and the Sheppy Farm to daughter Beverly. She instructed attorney Atherton to keep them, and to deliver them only upon her death. The attorney advised her that upon delivery of the deeds to him for that purpose, "nobody could get them, not even herself." Leone Pipes understood and responded that was exactly what she wanted, "what she and [deceased husband] Ralph wanted." The attorney thereupon prepared the deeds as directed, Leone Pipes executed them, the attorney acknowledged them and affixed the notary seal, and then placed them in envelopes. There was a legend on the outside of each wrapper, respectively:

"This envelope is to be delivered to my daughter Beverly J. Sevier on my death.

/s/Leone Pipes"

and

"This envelope is to be delivered to my son Keith Pipes on my death.

/s/Leone Pipes"

These containers, sealed, were kept by attorney Atherton until they were produced as exhibits in the litigation we review.

The daughter, Beverly, accompanied the mother to the office of attorney Atherton on that occasion, but was excluded from their company at the direction of the attorney. She left at the request of Atherton. That was the version of the events given by the attorney. The narrative of daughter Beverly was different. She testified that she was present during the discussions between her mother and the attorney. The mother wanted the deeds "so that she could sell it at any time." Attorney Atherton advised, Beverly testified, that the deeds could be recalled at any time, whenever the mother decided that "[she] wanted to do anything different." That was the sense, also, of the testimony of the conveyancer, mother Leone Pipes—then, from her own choice, a party defendant to the suit. The mother freely acknowledged that she directed the deeds and signed them, but only on the assurance that "I could get them when I wanted them." The mother testified also that, although it was her signature that appeared upon the face of each envelope, there was no "printing on it" when she signed each one. That testimony, however, was contradicted by her written statement made to [then] attorney Kenneth Lewis [now circuit judge] who was counsel for Keith Pipes, and given at a time before mother Pipes aligned formally with any party to the suit. That statement recited that she directed attorney Atherton to make the three deeds, two to daughter Beverly and the Home Place to son Keith, that she signed the instruments, delivered the deeds to Atherton with the direction that they were to be recorded upon her death, and that she understood the counsel of attorney Atherton "that the delivery of the deeds to him was final and that I could not thereafter cancel the deeds or change my mind. I knew that the delivery of the deeds to Mr. Atherton was unconditional."

In March of 1981, almost ten years after mother Leone executed the deeds, Beverly accompanied her mother to the office of attorney Atherton to retrieve the deeds, but he refused to deliver them up. The mother then made two visits to another attorney, Merrill Montgomery—first in the company of son Keith and wife Violet, and then in the company of daughter Beverly. [The relations between the brother and sister were strained.] On that first visit, Leone informed attorney Montgomery concerning the deeds executed by her and given over to attorney Atherton, and of his refusal to give them back. Montgomery advised that those deeds were of no effect because unrecorded. The mother, Leone, on that first visit informed Montgomery that she wanted son Keith to have a lifetime share in the Home Place but that neither Violet nor her children were "to have any of it." The deeds to the other lands were to be "fixed" to Beverly and herself. Keith and Violet became displeased, and they left. Leone returned with Beverly the next day, and the deeds were fixed as the mother had directed. To begin with, Montgomery presented to the mother a deed which conveyed the Home Place to son Keith and mother Leone as joint tenants, but she refused it. The attorney then prepared two other deeds at the direction of Leone Pipes. One conveyed a life estate in the Home Place to Keith, and reserved a life estate to Leone, herself. The other conveyed one of the two other properties to daughter Beverly and to Leone, herself, as joint tenants. They were recorded. In April of 1981, Leone fell ill and was interned in the hospital. While there, she executed another deed which purported once again to convey the Home Place—this time to daughter Beverly in fee "subject to any interest that Keith Pipes has, if any." That deed was also duly recorded. Then, in August of 1981, Beverly conveyed the Home Place—now titled of record in her sole name—to Beverly J. Sevier and Roddy Sevier [her son] as joint tenants. That deed was also promptly recorded.

On September 1, 1981, Keith brought a petition against Beverly Sevier and Roddy Sevier for a declaratory judgment that all the conveyances of the lands, other than the deeds executed by Leone Pipes and delivered to attorney Atherton for recordation upon her death, are null and void. The mother, Leone Pipes, joined the suit as a party plaintiff, by amendment. The plaintiffs were represented by attorney Atherton. When it became evident that his witness would be necessary, attorney Atherton withdrew from the case, and [then] attorney Kenneth Lewis entered appearance and filed a second amended petition for declaratory judgment. In November of 1982, attorney Lewis assumed duty as circuit judge, and attorney Gordon Cox, a partner, assumed the representation. The plaintiff Keith Pipes died on November 9, 1982, and his widow, Violet Pipes and their four children, Jerry, Gary, Kathy and Walter, were substituted as plaintiffs in lieu. The mother, Leone Pipes, in turn, moved to be deleted as a party plaintiff and to be added as a party defendant, and for leave to file a counterclaim. The petition was amended into a petition to remove a cloud from the title and for the cancellation of deeds. The defendants [Beverly and Roddy] counterclaimed to quiet title and for trespass. The counterclaim of [now] defendant Leone Pipes to remove a cloud from the title was not thereafter repleaded.

The judgment adjudicated that the title to the Home Place was vested in fee simple absolute in Violet Pipes, widow of the deceased Keith Pipes, and in their children, Jerry, Gary, Walter and Kathy, subject to the life estate reserved by the grantor, Leone Pipes. The judgment rested on findings of fact that the deeds drafted by attorney Atherton were drawn upon the instructions of mother Leone Pipes, executed by her, then deposited in the envelopes with the written instructions for delivery to Keith and Beverly upon her death subscribed by the signature of the grantor mother, and then only after full explanation by attorney Atherton that the delivery of the enveloped deeds to him for that purpose—made without a reserved right of recall—was a final and irrevocable act. The court found as a fact, also, that the deed was accepted by the grantee, Keith Pipes, during his lifetime, and that he thereafter died intestate and was survived by the wife and four children. The judgment also adjudicated the counterclaims against the defendants. The demand for a jury trial was properly refused.

* * *

THE ATTORNEY-CLIENT PRIVILEGE

The defendants contend that at the times described in the testimony of attorney Atherton and [then] attorney Lewis, the attorney-client relationship subsisted between Leone Pipes and each of the named attorneys, hence the communications between them on subject matter encompassed by the professional relationship were privileged and could not be disclosed without the consent of the client. Atherton, as our discussion discloses, prepared the three deeds in November of 1972 to the three tracts then owned by Leone Pipes: the Home Place to son Keith, and the Cott Farm and the Sheppy Farm to daughter Beverly. Atherton testified in detail as to the circumstances of the preparation, execution and delivery of the instruments to his care with directions from the grantor mother Leone. * * * Atherton testified, most tellingly, that he informed Leone Pipes if he carried out her instructions as to the transactions "there was no way she or anyone else could get them [the deeds]." The defendants contend that these communications were incidents of the attorney-client relationship, and therefore were privileged and incompetent as evidence, over objection. The defendants did lodge objection at the trial, but that objection was ineffectual and properly refused for the simple reason that Leone Pipes had executed a formal waiver of her privilege—a waiver obtained from the witness by [then] attorney Lewis, counsel for Keith and Violet Pipes. That waiver [received as Exhibit 19] was executed by Leone Pipes on July 19, 1982, and recites:

> "I, Leone Pipes, hereby waive the attorney-client privilege regarding confidential communications with L.E. Atherton and hereby authorize him to testify in any legal action pertaining to any land which I now own or formerly owned.

/s/Leone Pipes"—

The attorney-client privilege dates from the common law. Section 491.060, RSMo 1978 enacts that developed principle:

> "The following persons shall be incompetent to testify:
>
> * * *
>
> (3) An attorney, concerning any communication made to him by his client in that relation, or his advice thereon, without the consent of such client."

* * * There is no doubt that the communications between Leone Pipes and attorney Atherton were at the time the attorney-client relation subsisted between them, and that his advice on them was given in that capacity and on that account. That is to say, that the communications were privileged. Nor is there doubt that the privilege that they remain confidential, owned by the client, was waived by the client. Thus, the testimony of attorney Atherton was properly received.

The defendants assert that the testimony of [then] attorney Lewis was incompetent, and for the same reason. The original suit for declaratory judgment and for cancellation of the post-Atherton deeds was filed on September 11, 1981 by attorney Atherton on behalf of Keith Pipes as plaintiff and against Beverly Sevier and son Roddy as defendants. It became evident that the testimony of attorney Atherton was necessary to prove the cause of action, so he withdrew as counsel and referred the suit to [then] attorney Lewis. On June 15, 1982, Keith Pipes and wife Violet engaged the Lewis firm: Cleaveland, Macoubrie, Lewis and Cox as counsel to prosecute the petition. The contract of employment specified payment at a designated rate per hour, and required an advance of $2000. The Pipes husband and wife executed the contract at the home, and the mother Leone was then present. The retainer for $2000 was paid by a check signed by Leone Pipes. On that occasion, Lewis interrogated all three—Leone, Keith and Violet—in the presence of each other concerning the transactions involved, particularly the three Atherton deeds. On that June 15, 1982 occasion, attorney Lewis took from Leone Pipes a written statement subscribed by her signature concerning the Atherton deeds transactions—received at the trial as Exhibit 20. * * *

Attorney Lewis returned to the Pipes residence on July 19, 1982, to prepare Leone Pipes for her deposition on the next day. * * * Attorney Lewis testified at the trial that during the course of the deposition testimony, witness Leone Pipes was asked several times, and answered without variance, that Atherton advised her that "a delivery to him was final, absolute, unconditional and irrevocable and that she could not get the deed back." * * *

The defendants contend that the statements contained in Exhibit 20, as well as the testimony narrated by attorney Lewis at the trial concerning the communications from Leone Pipes were disclosures of confidential communications between attorney and client, and hence incompetent as evidence upon objection of the client.

The contention that the attorney-client relation subsisted between Lewis and Leone from June 15, 1982, rests altogether on the circumstance that the $2000 retainer was paid by a check signed by Leone and drawn upon her account. * * * The contract of employment in evidence, executed on June 15, 1982, was between attorney Lewis and Keith and Violet Pipes exclusively. The mother, Leone, was not a party. Attorney Lewis considered the retainer check, albeit drawn by Leone, as payment from the clients, Keith and Violet. The trial court expressly accepted that evidence as true. To be sure, Leone Pipes later [in October of 1982] joined son Keith as a party plaintiff on the petition against Beverly and son Roddy to cancel the latter deeds, but the attorney-client relationship did not arise until some time after July 20, 1982 [when the deposition of Leone was taken] and before October of 1982 [when Leone was formally joined as a plaintiff]. The trial court expressly found that the attorney-client relationship between attorney Lewis and Leone Pipes did not come into being until after July 20, 1982, so that the evidence given by Lewis at the trial concerning the Leone Pipes communications to him as to the Atherton transactions was competent.

To exclude the testimony of an attorney on the ground of privilege, the relation of attorney and client must have actually subsisted between the principals at the time the communication was made or the advice given. [   ] The communication, moreover, must have been made to the attorney on account of the relation of attorney and client. * * * Nor does the circumstance that the declarant herself later becomes a client cloak communications between them before the onset of that relation with confidentiality and privilege from disclosure. [   ] The determination by the trial court that Leone was not a client of attorney Lewis until after the deposition event is valid, and we sustain it.

The Delivery of the Atherton Deeds

The defendants contend that the evidence does not sustain a valid delivery of the Home Place deed to Atherton. They argue the evidence given by Leone Pipes [by then, no longer a plaintiff, but a defendant aligned with daughter Beverly] that she gave the deed [and the two others] over to attorney Atherton for "safekeeping," and not as an irrevocable conveyance. The defendants argue that her attempt to retrieve them ten years later and the execution of the successor deeds when Atherton refused to yield them up prove that the placement into his escrow was without intention to pass title—that is, make delivery. They argue, moreover, that the legend on the envelope: "This envelope is to be delivered to my son, Keith Pipes, on my death" not only does not evince an intention for delivery, but expressly contradicts any such purpose.

The intention of the principals, particularly that of the grantor, *Delivery of deed* determines whether a delivery of a deed has been accomplished. The essential inquiry, therefore, is whether the grantor intended a complete transfer: that is, whether the grantor parted with the instrument with the intention to relinquish all dominion and control over it so as to make the deed a presently effective and operative conveyance of title to the land. [   ] It is not essential to delivery that the deed be manually given *No manual* over to the grantee or to another person for the grantee; there may be *delivery necessary* delivery notwithstanding that the deed remains in the custody of the grantor. [   ] A delivery to a third party, to be held by that party for delivery to the grantee upon the death of the grantor operates as a valid delivery when there is no reservation in the deed nor any right of control over the instrument retained by the grantor. In such case, the deed in the hands of the custodian has the same effect "as if it had been manually delivered by the grantor to the grantee." [   ] A deed unconditional in terms and placed beyond control of the grantor upon its delivery to the third party escrow holder, moreover, although not a conferral of an immediate right to present possession, constitutes "such an investiture of title as to give the grantee a present fixed right of future enjoyment although the use of the premises [is] retained by the grantor during [her] life * * * The time of acceptance will not affect the validity of the transfer * * * Acceptance after the death of the grantor dates back to the time of the delivery of the deed to the * * * [escrow holder] and renders it a transfer as of that date." [   ] On this principle, upon final delivery by the depositary of the deed given in escrow, "the instrument will be treated as relating back to, and taking effect at the time of the original deposit *in escrow* * * * [*and this*] *appl[ies] even though one of the parties to the deed dies before the second delivery.* [   ] On this principle, the death of the grantee Keith Pipes which intervened before the second delivery from depositary Atherton is of no legal consequence—the validity of the delivery by Leone to Atherton in the first instance, assumed."

The defendants argue that Leone did not intend a delivery, but only to vouchsafe the keeping of the executed deeds. The evidence on the essential issue of delivery was in conflict—and in the case of Leone, herself, in utter contradiction. The court found her trial testimony not credible, and gave it no belief. * * * The court found as fact that Leone executed the deed to the Home Place in favor of son Keith and delivered the instrument in escrow with attorney Atherton with instruction to deliver to Keith upon her death only after full advice from him that such an act of delivery, when made without a reserved right of recall, was irrevocable and final. The court also found the testimony of attorney Atherton disinterested and credible, believed his testimony of the deed transactions with Leone Pipes, and rendered judgment accordingly. We concur in the thoughtful and meticulously-wrought judgment of the trial court: that the deed executed by Leone Pipes and delivered to attorney Atherton as escrow holder placed fee simple title to the Home Place in Keith Pipes, subject only to a reserved life estate in the grantor, Leone Pipes; that on the death of Keith Pipes, that interest passed to his wife and children as his sole heirs at law, and that the counterclaims of the defendants be disallowed with prejudice.

The judgment is affirmed.

Notes and Questions

1. What advantages and disadvantages of having an attorney serve as an escrow agent are illustrated by the *Pipes* case? Although the court held the testimony of Atherton and Lewis to be unprivileged, was it ethical for them to testify against a client? Would it have been ethical for them to have failed to testify? Do A.B.A. Rules 1.6 and 3.7 help? See also A.B.A. Model Code of Professional Responsibility, Disciplinary Rules 4–101, 5–102.

The traditional rule against a lawyer being both witness and advocate in the same litigation is now in Rule 3.7, which was not changed in 2002. That codified rule contains an exception that dispenses with the usual principle that lawyers from the same law firm are treated as if they were a single lawyer. In this one instance (the advocate-witness rule): "A lawyer may act as advocate in a trial in which another lawyer in the lawyer's firm is likely to be called as a witness unless precluded from doing so by Rule 1.7 [conflicts of interest] or Rule 1.9 [duties to former clients]." See also Harold A. Brown and Louis M. Brown, "Disqualification of the Testifying Advocate–A Firm Rule?" 57 North Carolina Law Review 597 (1979).

2. The *Pipes* case recites the traditional law with respect to "death escrows": that unconditional delivery to the escrow agent with instructions to deliver to the grantee on the death of the grantor effectively creates a remainder in the grantee, subject to a life estate in the grantor. Grantors occasionally attempt to achieve the same result through other forms of conditional delivery. The key issue in litigation resulting from these transfers is (or should be) the grantor's intent, as delivery is primarily a question of intent.

First, a grantor may deliver to a grantee a deed which conveys an interest to commence on the death of the grantor. The grantor's intent in such transactions is to transfer a future interest, and this intent is uniformly enforced. A grantor may also deliver to a grantee a deed absolute on its face, but accompanied by an oral condition that the deed will only take effect upon the occurrence of a certain contingency. If the contingency is the grantor's death, many cases hold the deed void as an improper testamentary transfer. If the contingency is other than death, some courts hold the deed valid and the condition void, others the deed void (because the grantor lacked intent presently to deliver the deed), and still others hold both the condition and the deed valid. A few cases have also upheld deeds expressly on their face conditional on the death of the grantor, and also reserving in the grantor the power to dispose of the property in fee and revoke the future interest, though such deeds seem clearly testamentary in nature. Whenever a deed is delivered conditionally and not recorded, of course, the opportunity exists for the grantor to subsequently transfer the property unconditionally to a bona fide purchaser for value, whose rights may be superior to those of the conditional grantee under the jurisdiction's recording acts. For a fuller discussion of conditional delivery, see H. Hovenkamp and S. Kurtz, The Law of Property, § 16.4 (5th ed. 2001); W. Stoebuck and D. Whitman, The Law of Property, § 11.3 (3rd ed. 2000); 6A R. Powell & P. Rohan, Powell on Real Property, ¶ 898[2][a].

3. Under a commercial escrow, the vendor/grantor delivers a signed deed to the escrow agent (an escrow company, financial institution, title insurer, abstract company or lawyer) to be released to the purchaser/grantee upon the grantee's compliance with the terms of the sales contract, including, most importantly, payment for the property. If the grantor delivers the deed to the escrow agent pursuant to an enforceable contract of sale, retaining no right to recover the deed if the purchaser complies with the terms of the sales contract, the ultimate delivery from the escrow agent to purchaser is considered to relate back and to be effective as of the date the grantor delivered the deed to the escrow agent. Thus, if the grantor dies or becomes incapacitated in the interim period, an effective transfer can still be accomplished. If the escrow agent improperly releases the deed to the grantee prior to the fulfillment of the conditions of the contract, the deed is void and unenforceable against the grantor by the grantee, and, in most jurisdictions, also by subsequent purchasers from the grantee.

IN THE MATTER OF DAVID T. AUSTERN, RESPONDENT

District of Columbia Court of Appeals, 1987.
524 A.2d 680.

Pryor, Chief Judge:

Respondent is charged with violating DR1–102(A)(4) and DR7–102(A)(7) of the Code of Professional Responsibility by engaging in conduct involving dishonesty and misrepresentation and by counseling or assisting a client in conduct that the lawyer knows to be illegal or fraudulent. Specifically, he is alleged to have assisted in closing a real estate transaction despite being told by his client that the client's escrow account would have insufficient funds to accomplish its stated purpose. The Board on Professional Responsibility finds that respondent's conduct violated both DR1–102(A)(4) and DR7–102(A)(7) and recommends a sanction of public censure,[2] Upon review of the record, we are satisfied

---

2. DR1–102(A)(4) provides: Misconduct.

(A) A lawyer shall not:

* * *

that the Board's findings of fact are supported by substantial evidence, and accept its conclusion that respondent knowingly assisted his client in conduct involving dishonesty and misrepresentation. Moreover, we conclude that respondent was under a duty to withdraw from representation of his client in this situation. We also adopt the Board's recommended sanction of public censure.

I

The relevant facts in this case are largely uncontested. The Hearing Committee found that respondent represented Milton Viorst and a corporation largely controlled by Viorst known as Harmony House Corporation. Viorst and Harmony House converted several buildings to condominiums. Respondent's clients were anxious to go to closing on the various condominium units as quickly as possible with a number of prospective purchasers. Several of these prospective purchasers had been tenants in the buildings before the conversion and were actually in possession of their units. However, the work necessary to bring the units into compliance with the District of Columbia Housing Code had not yet been completed to the satisfaction of the prospective purchasers.

On January 27, 1981, the parties met to attempt to close on as many of the units as then had committed purchasers. Respondent was not able to be present at the beginning of this closing because of other commitments. He arrived later in the evening as the closing was continuing; before his arrival, Viorst was represented by one of respondent's partners. During this time, Viorst and the purchasers drafted an escrow agreement in order to facilitate closing on that date.

Despite the fact that the purchasers were suspicious of Viorst and entertained doubts concerning his willingness to complete the repairs necessary to the units, they were willing to go to closing on the condition that Viorst deposit $10,000 into the escrow account. The funds in the account were to be available to complete the work on the units if Viorst or Harmony House did not perform. If Viorst did perform, the escrow funds were to be released back to the sellers upon agreement by all parties that the relevant work had indeed been satisfactorily performed.

For their protection, the purchasers insisted that the escrow account be under the control of two co-escrow agents-respondent, who represented the sellers, and Arnold Spevak, who represented the purchasers and who was also acting as the settlement attorney.

(4) Engage in conduct involving dishonesty, fraud, deceit, or

misrepresentation.

DR7–1 02(A)(7) provides:

Representing a Client Within the Bounds of the Law.

(A) In his representation of a client, a lawyer shall not:

* * *

(7) Counsel or assist his client in conduct that the lawyer knows to be illegal or fraudulent.

Upon respondent's late arrival at the closing, the substance of the escrow agreement had already been agreed upon by the parties. According to respondent, the escrow agreement had been fully drafted, typed, and signed by all the other parties before he arrived. Respondent testified that he was put under considerable pressure to agree to act as the co-escrow agent and that he ultimately yielded and signed the agreement that same evening.

Notwithstanding respondent's testimony,[3] the Hearing Committee found that the escrow agreement, although dated January 27, 1981, had not been finally typed and signed by respondent until the following day.

After respondent's arrival at the closing, Viorst wrote a check in the amount of $10,000, which was intended to fund the escrow account. The check was exhibited to the purchasers and to their attorney, Spevak. It was decided that respondent, as one of the two escrow agents, would take possession of the check and deposit it. Either before or after respondent gained possession of the check, respondent and Viorst stepped out into the hall, out of earshot of the other parties to the transaction. Viorst then informed respondent that there were no funds in the account upon which the check had been written. Respondent considered the ramifications of this revelation, but took the necessary steps to complete the closing on January 28.

Respondent held the worthless check but did not inform his co-escrow agent about the situation. Subsequently, on March 23, 1981, Viorst received a $10,000 non refundable deposit from a purchaser in connection with the sale of one of the condominium units. He then gave this deposit check to respondent. Respondent promptly opened an interest-bearing savings account at a local bank into which this check was deposited on March 27, 1981. Respondent did not notify his co-escrow agent that the funds were finally on hand, nor did he ever arrange to have his co-escrow agent obtain signature authority over the account.

It was not until the beginning of April, after the time the funds were actually placed in the escrow account, that one of the purchasers made the first claim against the account. That claim was paid from the account, and there is no question that the $10,000 was properly administered by respondent once it was placed into the account.

II

The Board concluded that the Hearing Committee's findings were supported by substantial evidence, and adopted them. We, in turn, must adopt the Board's conclusions if they are supported by substantial evidence in the record. * * * We conclude that the Board's conclusions are supported by substantial evidence, and adopt them.

3. Respondent maintained that he signed the escrow agreement the evening of January 27, and agreed to act as the co-escrow agent before he was informed by Viorst that his check for the escrow account was worthless. The Hearing Committee found that he signed the agreement at the following day's continuation of the closing, on January 28, after he was informed that Viorst's check was worthless.

The Board, like the Hearing Committee, concluded that respondent assisted his client in committing a fraud-the placement in escrow of a worthless check to induce the purchasers to go to settlement. The Board found that the client and respondent failed to disclose a material fact: namely, that there were insufficient funds to cover the check to be deposited in the escrow account. The Board concluded that this material omission induced the purchasers to go forward to settlement at a time when the repairs of their units had not yet been completed. The Board further determined that by signing the escrow agreement and by continuing to conceal the fact that the check funding the escrow account was worthless during the closing, respondent lulled the purchasers into a false sense of security that their repairs were funded, and thereby used his status as an attorney to lend legitimacy to a transaction which had none. The Board then concluded, as did the Hearing Committee, that by agreeing to act as an escrow agent in this sham transaction, respondent actively and affirmatively assisted his client in completing a fraud, and by doing so violated DR1–102(A)(4) and DR7–102(A)(7).

We agree with these conclusions. While a client is entitled to representation by his attorney for any objective within the bounds permitted by law, [   ], he is not entitled to affirmative assistance by his attorney in conduct that the lawyer knows to be illegal or fraudulent. DR7–102(a)(7). Generally, a lawyer should abide by a client's decisions concerning the objectives of the representation, and the lawyer can determine the means to accomplish these objectives, so long as the lawyer does not knowingly assist the client to engage in illegal conduct. [   ] When the attorney is presented with a situation where the client's wishes call for conduct that is illegal or fraudulent, the attorney is under an affirmative duty to withdraw from representation. [   ]* * *

In the instant case, therefore, respondent was under an affirmative duty to withdraw from his representation of Mr. Viorst once he knew that the escrow account Viorst purported to establish to induce settlement was funded with a worthless check. We do not deem crucial the question of whether respondent signed the escrow agreement before rather than after being informed that the check was worthless. In either event, his conduct in furthering the transaction and acquiescing in its fraudulent purpose is violative of DR 1–102(A)(4) and DR 7–102(A)(7).

III

Turning to the issue of an appropriate sanction, the Board rejected the recommendation of the Hearing Committee that respondent receive a reprimand by the Board * * * and concluded that respondent should receive a sanction of public censure by this court. The Board concluded that this case involved dishonesty and misrepresentation on the part of an attorney, and, in a broad sense, the appropriate sanction should be influenced by our decision in In re Reback, 513 A.2d 226 (D.C. 1986) (en banc) (imposing six-month suspensions against attorneys who neglected a matter and falsified a client's signature, representing it as genuine to both a notary and the court). The Board noted, however, that a similar suspension here would be too severe a penalty because the focus in Reback was on subversion of the judicial process, a more serious violation than is involved here.

The Board determined that a public censure by this court would be the most appropriate sanction in this case because the culpability of the conduct at issue here fell short of that in other cases where attorney dishonesty resulted in a brief suspension. * * *

The Board also considered many mitigating factors in this case. It observed that respondent has no prior disciplinary record, and has indeed made notable contributions in the area of legal ethics. The Board also took into account the fact that respondent's conduct was not motivated by the desire for personal gain, and caused no pecuniary injury to the purchasers of the client's units who relied on the escrow account.[9] The Board further observed that respondent's decision making may have been affected by the extreme animosity which existed between him and his client, Mr. Viorst. The Board noted that respondent may have been too anxious to overcompensate for this ill will and "may have bent over backwards in the client's favor" by taking part in the fraudulent transaction, concluding that respondent's participation may have been motivated in part by a desire to bring the troubled attorney-client relationship to a speedy close.

* * *

To be sure, no monetary harm befell anyone as a result of respondent's failure to disclose that the check funding the escrow account was worthless. * * * But it is important to remember that for a number of weeks the purpose of the escrow account was in fact defeated. The protection the account was supposed to offer did not exist. Respondent, as co-escrow agent, owed a fiduciary duty to the client's purchasers to protect their investment; instead, he aided his client in inducing the buyers to proceed to settlement although there was no escrow protection. Therefore, considering the gravity of respondent's misconduct, the mitigating factors considered by the Board, and viewing respondent's violations "in light of all relevant factors," Reback, supra, 513 A.2d at 231, we conclude that the Board's recommended sanction of public censure is appropriate.

Accordingly, it is ORDERED that respondent be, and hereby is, publicly censured.

So ordered.

Notes and Questions

1. Why do you suppose Mr. Austern was reluctant to serve as escrow agent in this situation? Perhaps he was aware that title insurance companies

---

9. The Board noted that since this case is not a civil action for damages, the fact that the purchasers actually suffered no injury is immaterial to the consideration of the ethical obligation of an attorney not to assist in fraud or other conduct involving dishonesty or misrepresentation.

suffer more losses in connection with the performance of escrow services then for insured losses under policies of title insurance.

2. As illustrated by the Pipes and Austern cases, the lawyer's service in the additional capacity of escrow agent is fraught with ethical implications. That David Austern was regarded as an expert in legal ethics was noted in the following discussion of the case, which appeared in the Washington Post on May 25, 1987:

> Austern, who writes an ethics column for the Association of Trial Lawyers of America, argued that his duty of confidentiality to his client outweighed his duty to withdraw from the case to avoid furthering the fraud.

> But the appeals court, in an opinion by Chief Judge William C. Pryor, said Austern's conduct was wrong even though no harm resulted.

> "When an attorney is presented with a situation where the client's wishes call for conduct that is illegal or fraudulent, the attorney is under an affirmative duty to withdraw from representation," the three-judge panel said.

> Austern, whose ethics course at Georgetown University Law Center was "delisted" after 19 years when the ethics charges became public, said he disagreed with the court's reasoning but noted a silver lining: "I guess one needs a perverse sense of humor to think this is funny," he said, "but never in my 20 years of lecturing and teaching on legal ethics have I received so many invitations to speak."

3. In determining the appropriate sanction, the court noted that Mr. Austern's violation was not as serious as lying directly to the court, which had happened in *Reback*. Do you agree? Can you make the argument that Mr. Austern's conduct was no less if not more deserving of punishment because of the context in which it occurred? Consider the following excerpt:

> "An an advocate in open court, the lawyer faces the opposition of a presumably equally able and well-prepared advocate whose counter-partisanship will offset his own ... But when the lawyer is in his office devising a course of business conduct, a standard form contract, or a complex scheme of land acquisition and development, no opposing lawyer is there to represent the equities of the many persons who may be affected by the lawyer's plans, no judge is present to monitor the fairness of the arrangements, and there are no fires of controversy to keep the counselor honest and purge his client's specifications of over-reaching self-interest. Is there a lawyer anywhere who has not felt the twinges of ethical uneasiness in so hidden and *ex parte* a professional context?"

T. Shaffer, American Legal Ethics: Text, Readings and Discussion Topics 440–41 (1985).

4. Why did the court consider the animosity that existed between Mr. Austern and his client, Mr. Viorst, to be a mitigating factor in determining the appropriate sanction? In your opinion, did Mr. Austern deserve the leniency afforded by the court by reason of this situation?

III. TITLE ASSURANCE

A person purchasing an interest in real property normally demands and expects to receive the most secure and unrestricted title to that interest that our legal system allows. Productive use of property requires that one who invests in purchasing or improving property be able to do so with assurance that he or she will be able to claim and enjoy the fruits of the investment and not lose it to one with a superior claim to the property. A purchaser of a fee estate in residential property should realistically expect some limitation on her rights to that property—reasonable public zoning regulations, servitudes limiting the property to uses appropriate to the neighborhood, and beneficial easements for sewer, water, gas, electric, telephone and cable TV lines. The purchaser should insist, however, that the vendor in fact has title to the property that would be recognized by a court of law and that all encumbrances affecting the property—unpaid taxes, liens, mortgages, easements, use restrictions—are fully disclosed and either removed or accepted before the purchase is completed. What is needed, therefore, is a system that encourages the vendor to identify and cure title defects prior to the completion of the sale. Finally, the purchaser wants insurance, either provided by the vendor or a third party, against undisclosed risks that may appear after the closing either as adverse claims or suits asserted against the purchaser as owner or as hindrances to a future resale.

Several approaches have evolved in the United States for protecting the title of purchasers of real property. First, most real estate contracts require the vendor to produce title of a certain quality (usually stipulated as marketable, merchantable, record, or insurable) before the purchaser is obligated to accept the property and to come forth with the purchase price. Second, the vendor through common law covenants of title warrants the title she conveys to the purchaser. Third, the recording acts protect the title of purchasers who search carefully before purchase and promptly record thereafter. Fourth, a few jurisdictions have adopted systems of title registration that offer further protection of titles. Finally, title insurance insures against title defects.

A. THE CONTRACTUAL OBLIGATION OF THE VENDOR TO PROVIDE MARKETABLE TITLE

The contract reproduced above requires the vendor to provide the purchaser with marketable title. As the following case illustrates, marketable title is not perfect title. It can, indeed, be very imperfect.

VOORHEESVILLE ROD & GUN CLUB, INC. v. E.W. TOMPKINS CO., INC.

Court of Appeals of New York, 1993.
82 N.Y.2d 564, 606 N.Y.S.2d 132, 626 N.E.2d 917.

HANCOCK, JUDGE.

The first issue in this case is whether the subdivision regulations of the Village of Voorheesville apply to a conveyance of a portion of a parcel of land where it is intended by the parties to the transaction that the lands shall remain undeveloped. If the regulations apply, then the primary issue is whether defendant seller's failure to seek subdivision approval before the transfer renders the title unmarketable. We conclude that the Village's subdivision regulations apply to this sale of property. But we further hold that defendant's refusal to seek the subdivision approval here does not cause the title to be unmarketable. Because no provision in the contract requires defendant to obtain subdivision approval and the only basis for plaintiff's specific performance claim is its failed assertion of unmarketable title, we reverse, deny plaintiff's summary judgment motion for specific performance, and dismiss the complaint.

I

On January 15, 1986, plaintiff Voorheesville Rod & Gun Club, Inc., signed a standard preprinted contract with defendant E.W. Tompkins Company, Inc., to purchase a portion of defendant's property located in the Village of Voorheesville, Albany County, for $38,000. The contract specified that the property would be conveyed by warranty deed subject to all covenants, conditions, restrictions and easements of record, and also to zoning and environmental protection laws, "provided that this does not render the title to the premises unmarketable." The property to be conveyed consisted of 24.534 acres of undeveloped land used for recreational purposes. The parties agree that plaintiff buyer did not intend to change the existing condition or use of the property after the purchase.

On August 23, 1986, prior to the revised closing date, plaintiff's attorney sent defendant's attorney a copy of the Village of Voorheesville's subdivision regulations and requested that defendant comply with them. Defendant did not seek subdivision approval. Defendant sent plaintiff a time-of-the-essence notice, demanded a closing on August 29, 1986, and notified plaintiff that if it did not close, that would be considered an anticipatory breach of contract. When plaintiff failed to close, defendant canceled the contract and returned plaintiff's $5,000 deposit. On September 4th, plaintiff informed defendant that the cancellation was unacceptable because defendant's failure to obtain subdivision approval had rendered the title unmarketable and, for that reason, plaintiff's financing bank was unwilling to close. Plaintiff then sought the requisite approval from the Village of Voorheesville Planning Commission. The Commission denied the application, stating that the subdivision regulations required that the application be submitted "by the [property] owner or an agent of the owner."

Plaintiff commenced this action on September 12, 1986, for specific performance or damages for breach of contract and then moved for partial summary judgment seeking specific performance. Supreme Court ordered that the contract be specifically performed by defendant and directed that defendant apply to the Village for subdivision approval and close on the subject property within a reasonable time after approval. The court held that defendant's failure to obtain subdivision approval made the title unmarketable and relieved plaintiff from closing until the approval was obtained [   ]

The Appellate Division affirmed, stating that the sale of a portion of defendant's real property subjected the sale to the subdivision regulations of the Village of Voorheesville, even though development of the land was not then contemplated. The Court concluded that defendant's refusal to obtain subdivision approval rendered the title unmarketable, particularly because it appeared that plaintiff "would be 'plagued by zoning problems' "[   ]

Thereafter, plaintiff moved in Supreme Court for an order compelling defendant to file the subdivision application and convey the property. Noting that the subdivision application had been made and approved, Supreme Court directed defendant to transfer the property. Then the parties stipulated to discontinue all causes of action interposed in the pleadings except plaintiff's claim for specific performance of the contract. This Court granted defendant leave to appeal from the stipulation, deemed a judgment, bringing up for review the prior nonfinal Appellate Division order pursuant to CPLR 5602(a)(1)(ii).

II

The preliminary issue is whether the Village's subdivision regulations apply at all under the circumstances presented. [The court's discussion of this issue is omitted.]

III

Given that the subdivision regulations apply, we turn to the main issue: whether lack of subdivision approval constitutes a cloud on the title which renders the title unmarketable. It is undisputed that the contract is silent as to the specific issue of subdivision approval. Thus nothing in the contract imposes upon defendant the affirmative obligation of obtaining subdivision approval.[3] Rather, paragraph 4 of the

---

3. To the extent that plaintiff now claims—distinct from its argument that lack of subdivision approval renders the title unmarketable—that defendant has an implied good-faith contractual duty to obtain subdivision approval as a precondition of performing the contract, this issue was not raised by plaintiff in its summary judgment motion papers and thus is not preserved for our review.

We also note that this is not a case where the seller is seeking specific performance of a contract to compel a buyer to purchase contract, entitled "Existing Conditions", provides that the property would be conveyed by warranty deed "subject to all covenants, conditions, restrictions and easements of record. *Subject also to zoning and environmental protection laws*; any existing tenancies; * * * and any state of facts which an inspection and/or accurate survey may show, *provided that this does not render the title to the premises unmarketable"* (emphasis added).

As stated, plaintiff was to purchase the property subject to zoning laws, which are closely related to subdivision regulations. [ ] This requirement conforms to the well-settled rule that "where a person agrees to purchase real estate, which, at the time, is restricted by laws or ordinances, he will be deemed to have entered into the contract subject to the same [and] [h]e cannot thereafter be heard to object to taking the title because of such restrictions." [ ]

The only limitation that the contract places upon plaintiff's duty to purchase the property subject to zoning laws is when the application of such laws would render title to the property unmarketable. It was not necessary for the contract to specify that a marketable title was required because, in the absence of a stipulation to the contrary, it is presumed that a marketable title is to be conveyed. [ ] Accordingly, the issue reduces to whether the lack of subdivision approval constitutes a defect in the title which makes it unmarketable.

The test of the marketability of a title is "whether there is an objection thereto such as would interfere with a sale or with the market value of the property." [ ] A marketable title is "a title free from reasonable doubt, but not from every doubt." [ ] We have said that a "purchaser ought not to be compelled to take property, the possession or title of which he may be obliged to defend by litigation. He should have a title that will enable him to hold his land free from probable claim by another, and one which, if he wishes to sell, would be reasonably free from any doubt which would interfere with its market value" [ ]. As can be seen from these definitions, marketability of title is concerned with impairments on title to a property, i.e., the right to unencumbered ownership and possession, not with legal public regulation of the use of the property. [ ] Accordingly, a zoning ordinance, existing at the time of the contract, which regulates only the use of the property, generally is not an encumbrance making the title unmarketable. [ ]

Where, however, a contract expressly provides that the seller warrants and represents that, upon purchase, the property will not be in violation of any zoning ordinance, the purchaser "is entitled to demand that the vendor rectify the same or return any moneys paid on account." [ ] Contrary to plaintiff's claim, the present case does not fall within this exception to the general rule. Defendant did not warrant or represent that it would obtain subdivision approval; rather, plaintiff agreed to purchase the property subject to the zoning laws. In effect, plaintiff is

property lacking subdivision approval or where a municipality is trying to block such a conveyance, and we do not address such situations here.

attempting to add a term to the contract after the deal has been made. Thus, although defendant's failure to obtain subdivision approval was a violation of the regulations which were in effect when the parties contracted, such violation did not make the title unmarketable. [   ]

We recognize, as noted by the courts below, the increasing sophistication of municipalities regarding subdivision regulation and their ability to prevent the purchaser from developing property as allowed by the zoning laws until the requisite subdivision approval is obtained. [   ] The solution for avoiding such problems, however, is not for the courts to expand the conditions which render title unmarketable, thereby altering the concept of marketability of title, but for the parties to real estate contracts to include specific provisions dealing with the duty to obtain subdivision approval.

Accordingly, the judgment appealed from and the order of the Appellate Division brought up for review should be reversed, with costs, plaintiff's motion for partial summary judgment should be denied, and defendant's cross motion for summary judgment dismissing the complaint should be granted.

KAYE, C.J., and SIMONS, TITONE, BELLACOSA and SMITH, JJ., concur.

LEVINE, J., taking no part.

Judgment appealed from and order of the Appellate Division brought up for review reversed, etc.

Notes and Questions

1. Few titles to property are record perfect. A thorough search of the title records of a particular property will often turn up old unreleased mortgages, potential dower interests, questionable legal descriptions, flawed acknowledgments, outstanding mineral interests, and a host of other problems. If a contract requires that the vendor produce marketable or merchantable title, the parties must determine whether such flaws render the title unmarketable. The question is usually one of judgment—in the first instance the judgment of an attorney, abstractor, or insurer—then the judgment of the parties, and ultimately, possibly, the judgment of a court. As the principal case notes, the question is one of reasonableness: Is the title free from reasonable doubt? Or, conversely, does it subject the purchaser to sufficiently great risks of future litigation or unmarketability on resale that it would not be equitable to force him to go through with the purchase?

If the parties do not stipulate the quality of title that the purchaser expects, the law will imply an obligation to provide marketable title. The parties may alter this standard, however, for example, by agreeing instead to accept insurable title or insisting on record title. The purchaser may also agree to accept certain disclosed defects in the vendor's title.

Defects that render a title unmarketable can either be defects in the vendor's ownership of the property (e.g. claims of adverse possessors or of holders of paramount title), or encumbrances that do not affect the vendor's fee title but limit the use of the land. A host of encumbrances—liens, mortgages, easements, covenants, equitable servitudes, leases, dower interests, boundary disputes and encroachments, etc.—can raise the latter sort of problem. Visible servitudes that benefit the land, such as utility easements or public roads along the edge of the property, usually are held not to affect marketability. Similarly, public zoning laws are not usually considered encumbrances, though violation of zoning ordinances may be. However, any encumbrances on title that detract from the value of the property to any significant extent, render the property unmarketable.

2.   Whether the vendor is obligated to provide evidence of marketable title or the purchaser is responsible for discovering title defects depends on the contract between the parties and the custom of the jurisdiction. Normally, however, the purchaser is responsible for giving the vendor notice of any objections he may have to the vendor's title. Failure to object may result in waiver of defects that the vendor could have cured had they been called to her attention.

3.   At what point must the vendor be able to produce marketable title? One position the law could have taken would be that a vendor should not contract to sell more than she owns at the time the contract is signed. What problems would this approach cause? Another logical approach would be to require the vendor to be able to produce marketable title on "law day," the day set by the contract for closing. In fact, unless the contract specifies that "time is of the essence," courts usually allow the vendor a reasonable time to cure defects identified by the purchaser, even if the vendor is in fact not fully able to provide marketable title by the date set for closing.

4.   The remedy sought by the vendee in the *Voorheesville Rod & Gun* case was specific performance. Specific performance is granted much more commonly with respect to property transactions than elsewhere in contract law because of the belief that land is unique and damages for the breach of land-sale contracts are difficult to determine. Should this rule apply when the vendor is suing for specific performance, rather than the purchaser, since the vendor is seeking money (the purchase price) which is certainly not a unique commodity? Should it apply when the sale of a condominium in a large development of similar condominiums is at issue? In Centex Homes Corporation v. Boag, 128 N.J.Super. 385, 320 A.2d 194 (Ch.Div.1974), the court refused to grant specific performance to a seller where breach concerned one of 360 nearly identical condominium units. Though *Centex* has never been explicitly overruled, the same court that decided *Centex* has since held that a buyer can enforce a contract for the sale of a designated condominium unit by specific performance "irrespective of any special proof of its uniqueness." Pruitt v. Graziano, 215 N.J.Super. 330, 521 A.2d 1313, 1314 (1987). Most commentators share the opinion that "it would be unwise to read too much into the *Centex* case." J. Cribbett and C. Johnson, Principles of the Law of Property 181 (3rd ed. 1989).

5.   Alternatively the injured party may sue for damages. The vendor often holds the earnest money deposit as liquidated damages specified by the contract, a permitted remedy where the damages are reasonable. The vendor may also sue for compensatory damages where the purchaser is in breach.

If the vendor is in breach, the purchaser may sue for restitution of any earnest money deposit and for compensatory damages. Where the vendor is unable to perform, however, because of a defect in the title, but is not in bad faith or willful breach, the common law limited the purchaser to recovery of the earnest money deposit, interest, and expenses. This rule, the "English" rule, was justified by the problems faced by a title examiner in determining clear title in eighteenth and nineteenth century England at the time the rule was formed. Many states have abandoned this rule, permitting purchasers loss-on-the-bargain damages where the seller is unable to provide good title. See Donovan v. Bachstadt, 91 N.J. 434, 453 A.2d 160 (1982) (abandoning English rule in favor of allowing compensatory damages to buyer where vendor unable to provide good title).

6. The suit for specific performance is a potent weapon in the hands of a disappointed purchaser. Whether or not the purchaser ultimately prevails in a suit for specific performance, once such a suit is filed, it renders the property unmarketable in the hands of the vendor. If court dockets portend lengthy litigation and the vendor must pay carrying charges until the litigation is resolved, the vendor has little choice but to settle with the purchaser for whatever terms can be obtained. See, e.g. Safeco Title Ins. Co. v. Moskopoulos, 116 Cal.App.3d 658, 172 Cal.Rptr. 248, 18 A.L.R. 4th 1301 (1981). Is it unethical for a purchaser to sue for specific performance where his rights under a real estate contract are doubtful if the main purpose of the suit is to extract a favorable settlement from the vendor? Does A.B.A. Model Rule 3.1 help resolve this dilemma?

B. DEED COVENANTS

If a grantor of real property fails to provide a grantee with marketable title as promised under the contract of sale at the time the deed is delivered, the merger doctrine may very well preclude the grantee from further recourse under the contract. Under the merger doctrine, acceptance of a deed that conveys a lesser title than that promised by a contract excuses the grantor from any obligation to provide any greater title. Questions as to the title would almost never be held collateral to the deed, thus it would rarely be the case that an agreement to provide marketable title would expressly survive the deed.

Subsequent to the closing, therefore, recourse by the grantee against the grantor must normally be based on covenants as to title found expressly in the deed or incorporated into the deed by statute. Subsequent grantees may also sue a grantor on the basis of deed covenants if it turns out that the title the grantor warranted was defective. The following case illustrates the limitations of reliance on deed covenants for title security.

ST. PAUL TITLE INSURANCE CORPORATION v. OWEN

Supreme Court of Alabama, 1984.
452 So.2d 482.

MADDOX, JUSTICE.

The question here is what liability do grantors have to remote grantees or their assigns under a warranty deed and a statutory warranty deed where certain covenants of title contained in the deeds are found to run with the land?

On February 18, 1976, Albert M. Owen, an unmarried man, executed a warranty deed purporting to convey certain real property in Baldwin County to his brother and sister-in-law, James R. Owen, Jr., and Cheryl C. Owen. The deed, which was recorded on March 8, 1976, in Baldwin County, contained the following covenants of title:

> "The party of the first part [Albert Owen] for himself, his heirs, executors and administrators, hereby covenants and warrants to and with the said parties of the second part [James and Cheryl Owen], their heirs and assigns, that he is seized of an indefeasible estate in and to the said property; that he has a good right to convey the same as herein contained; that he will guarantee the peaceable possession thereof; that the said property is free from all liens and encumbrances, and that he will, and his heirs, executors and administrators will forever warrant and defend the same unto the said parties of the second part, their heirs and assigns, against the lawful claims of all persons."

The warranty deed form was obtained from the law office of James R. Owen, Sr., the father of Albert and James Owen.

Subsequently, James and Cheryl Owen conveyed the Baldwin County property, purportedly conveyed to them, by statutory warranty deed[4] to Dennis C. Carlisle Jr., the brother of Cheryl Owen. The property was conveyed June 6, 1976, and the deed recorded in Baldwin County on July 14, 1976.

On June 10, 1976, Dennis Carlisle mortgaged the property to United Companies Mortgage and Investment of Mobile 2, Inc., for $17,159.52. This mortgage was recorded on July 14, 1976, in both Mobile and Baldwin counties.

Dennis Carlisle mortgaged the property to GECC Financial Services (GECC) for $17,671.29, on November 8, 1977, apparently substituting mortgages and paying off the original mortgage. The mortgage to GECC was recorded in Baldwin County and a policy of title insurance naming GECC as the insured was issued shortly thereafter by Eastern Shore Title Insurance Corp., of Daphne, the agent for St. Paul Title Insurance Corp. (St. Paul Title). The title insurance was issued at the request of Dennis Carlisle.

When Dennis Carlisle subsequently defaulted on his mortgage payments, GECC attempted to foreclose on the property. The Circuit Court of Baldwin County found, however, that because Dennis Carlisle held no right, title, or interest in or to any of the property on the day the mortgage was executed, GECC was not entitled to foreclose on the property. GECC then brought suit against St. Paul Title, to collect its

---

4. The deed provided that " * * * the Grantee, does hereby Grant, Bargain, Sell   and convey unto said Grantee * * *."

debt, and in addition the costs of litigation involved, all as provided for under the terms of the title insurance policy.

St. Paul Title, as subrogee of GECC, then filed a complaint against Albert Owen, James R. Owen, Jr., and Cheryl Owen, wherein St. Paul alleged that they had breached the covenants of title contained in the deeds executed and delivered by them. The trial court, after a non-jury trial, entered a judgment on behalf of the defendants. St. Paul appeals.

I.   THE LIABILITY OF ALBERT OWEN UNDER THE EXPRESS COVENANTS OF TITLE CONTAINED IN HIS WARRANTY DEED

The deed executed by Albert Owen, an unmarried man, purporting to convey property to James and Cheryl Owen, contained the following express covenants of title: a covenant of seizin; a covenant of right to convey; a covenant for quiet enjoyment; a covenant against encumbrances; and a covenant of warranty. [ ] Of these covenants, however, only the covenants of quiet enjoyment and warranty are said to operate in futuro for the benefit of the ultimate grantee. [ ] Until broken, these two covenants run with the land to the heirs of the grantee, or if the land is conveyed or assigned, to the assignee, so that when they are broken, the heir or assignee injured by the breach can maintain an action against the covenantor. [ ] Thus, it is generally recognized and held that when a covenant of title runs with the land, all grantors, back to and including the original grantor-covenantor, become liable upon a breach of the covenant to the assignee or grantee in possession or entitled to the possession at the time, and the latter may sue the original or remote grantor, regardless of whether he has taken from the immediate grantor with a warranty. [ ]

Because the covenants of quiet enjoyment and of warranty are virtually identical in operation, whatever constitutes a breach of one covenant is a breach of the other. [ ] Neither covenant is breached until there is an eviction under paramount title. [ ] The eviction may be either actual or constructive. [ ]

It has been said that an outstanding title that could be asserted in a judicial proceeding against the party in possession is equivalent to an eviction. [ ] Likewise, a final judgment or decree adverse to the covenantee's title or right to possession constitutes a sufficient constructive eviction to entitle the covenantee to sue for breach of the covenant of warranty. [ ]

Here, the breach occurred when the trial court ruled in the foreclosure proceedings that Dennis Carlisle possessed no interest in the property which had been mortgaged, thereby frustrating GECC's attempt to foreclose on the property purportedly conveyed to Carlisle in fee simple.

We hold that the covenant of quiet enjoyment and warranty provided by the terms of the warranty deed executed by Albert Owen ran with the land purportedly conveyed by that instrument. We further hold that because someone other than the original grantor-covenantor in fact possessed paramount title, appellant is entitled to assert a claim for the breach of the covenants of title, as its subrogor was the ultimate grantee or assignee who was in possession at the time the covenants were broken.

II.   THE LIABILITY OF JAMES AND CHERYL OWEN UNDER THE COVENANTS OF TITLE CONTAINED IN TTHEIR STATUTORY WARRANTY DEED.

The deed executed by James and Cheryl Owen contained no express covenants of title, but it did use the words, "grant, bargain, sell and convey." In all conveyances of estates in fee where the words "grant, bargain, and sell" appear, the deed is construed by statute as containing the following covenants of title: a covenant of seizin; a covenant against encumbrances; and a covenant of quiet enjoyment. Code 1975, § 35–4–271.

Appellant asserts that James and Cheryl Owen are liable for a breach of the implied covenant of quiet enjoyment contained in the statutory warranty deed, and that such a covenant runs with the land so as to benefit a remote grantee or assign. Unlike the express covenants of title found in a general warranty deed, however, the implied covenants of title contained in a statutory warranty deed are more limited in effect.

In the early case of Heflin v. Phillips, 96 Ala. 561, 11 So. 729 (1892), the Court noted: "In construing this statute [predecessor of § 35–4–271] this Court declared that the words 'grant, bargain, sell' do not import an absolute general covenant of seizin against incumbrances and for quiet enjoyment, but that they amount to a covenant only against acts done or suffered by the grantor and his heirs." [   ] More than twenty years after Heflin, the Court remarked: "All authorities hold that the covenants implied by statute are limited to the acts of the grantor and those claiming under him, and do not extend to defects of title anterior to the conveyance to him." Mackintosh v. Stewart, 181 Ala. 328, 333, 61 So. 956, 958 (1913).

* * *

James and Cheryl Owen conveyed their complete, albeit non-existent interest, in the subject property to Dennis Carlisle by statutory warranty deed. By so doing, they merely warranted that they had not conveyed title to anyone else; that they had not allowed the property to become encumbered while they held purported title; and that they had not caused or suffered anyone to do anything that would interfere with the property's quiet enjoyment by the grantee, the grantee's heirs or assigns. Because the record indicates that James and Cheryl did nothing to affect the purported title they conveyed, they did not breach any of the covenants of title contained in the statutory warranty deed delivered to Dennis Carlisle and are therefore not liable to the appellant, as subrogee of GECC.

III.   DAMAGES FOR BREACH OF COVENANTS OF TITLE

Appellant asserts that it is entitled to recover, as damages, the amount of mortgage proceeds paid to Dennis Carlisle by its subrogor, plus litigation costs and interest. Appellant further contends its recovery should neither be barred nor be limited to merely nominal damages, even though appellees received no consideration for their conveyances.

In situations where there has been a complete failure of title and a grantee has sought recovery from his immediate grantor, the maximum recovery allowed has been the purchase price paid. [   ] With respect to an action against a remote grantor, however, there appears to be a difference of opinion as to whether damages are to be determined by the consideration paid by the grantee bringing the suit to his immediate grantor or by the consideration paid to the original grantor or covenantor, not exceeding in either case, however, the consideration paid for the conveyance by the defendant in the action. [   ] Here, however, the facts indicate that no consideration was ever paid to or received by any of the appellees, Albert Moore Owen, James R. Owen, Jr., or Cheryl C. Owen. Consequently, since there was no evidence that the remote grantors received any consideration for their conveyances purportedly conveying title to the subject property, appellant, as subrogee of GECC, is entitled to an award of nominal damages only, for the breach of the covenant of quiet enjoyment contained in Albert Owen's deed, and not the amount of the mortgage made by GECC. [   ]

* * *

The judgment of the trial court is hereby reversed and the cause remanded to that court for a determination of the amount of nominal damages appellant is entitled to recover as consistent with the holding of this opinion.

Notes and Questions

1.   The "general warranty" deed from Albert Owen to James and Cheryl Owen contained five of the six common deed covenants. The covenant of seisin guaranties that the grantor is seised of an estate in the land to be conveyed. In most jurisdictions this means that the grantor owns the land, but in a few it means that the grantor is in possession of the land. The covenant of right to convey promises that the grantor has the right to convey the property. Normally, a grantor with a right to convey a property is seised of it, and visa versa. Under what circumstances might one be true, but not the other?

The covenant against encumbrances promises that the land is free from a variety of potential rights and interests encumbering the land that could exist in third parties. First, it promises freedom from interests that affect the use and enjoyment of the land physically, i.e. servitudes. Second, it promises freedom from liens and charges. Third, it guarantees the absence of other interests that might limit the rights of the grantee, while not affecting seisin, such as leases, dower interests, etc. It is not breached by the existence of zoning ordinances that affect use of the property.

The covenants of warranty and of quiet enjoyment are identical. Under these covenants the grantor promises to defend the grantee's title and use of the property against any future adverse claims put forward by others. A sixth covenant, further assurances, is more common in England than in the United States, but appears in some warranty deeds. This promise to execute any documents or take further steps necessary to protect the grantee's title is specifically enforceable.

2. The first three covenants, seisin, right to convey, and against encumbrances, are present covenants. This means that they are breached only to the extent that the grantor's title is defective or encumbered at the time the deed is delivered. Several consequences follow from this. First, the statute of limitations for enforcing these covenants begins to run at the date of delivery of the deed. Even though outstanding claims and interests exist in third parties, if these claims are not asserted during the statutory period, the grantee may only claim nominal damages, and is barred from claiming damages under the present covenants thereafter. Further, these covenants, being present covenants, do not run with the land for the benefit of future grantees. They only benefit the immediate grantee of the land and covenant. A few jurisdictions permit a cause of action for breach of these covenants to be assigned with the resale of the property to remote grantees, Rockafellor v. Gray, 194 Iowa 1280, 191 N.W. 107 (1922), but in most jurisdictions the cause of action for breach of the present covenants may only be brought by the original grantee to whom the covenant was made.

3. The covenants of warranty, quiet enjoyment, and further assurances are future covenants. They are breached whenever a third party successfully asserts paramount title against the beneficiary of the covenant, and they run with the land. They thus benefit both immediate and future grantees. They are breached only in the event of actual or constructive eviction of the grantee. It is not sufficient that a claim is asserted, or even that it affects marketability of the title. Purchase of an outstanding interest to avoid eviction, however, may constitute a sufficient breach to ground an action.

4. In most jurisdictions, the rule of damages established in the principal case is followed: Damages for failure of title are limited to the consideration received by the original covenantor. If title is lost to only a portion of the total area covered by the deed, recovery is limited to a proportionate share of the consideration. Where the defect that appears is an encumbrance, the damages recoverable are measured by the cost of removing the encumbrance, or, alternatively in some jurisdictions, the diminution in value of the property. Interest expenses for the time the grantee is deprived of the property and attorney's fees for defending against adverse claims may also be recoverable damages.

5. Statutes in many jurisdictions imply the presence of certain covenants from the use of specific language or deed forms. For example, in Illinois the use of the word "warrants" in a deed implies the covenants of seisin, right to convey, freedom from encumbrances, warranty and quiet enjoyment. IL St. Ch. 765 § 5/9 .. The use of the term in Iowa only implies

a covenant of general warranty, Iowa Code Ann. § 558.19. See 6A Powell on Real Property, ¶ 897[2].

6. The deed of Albert Owen in the principal case is a "general warranty" deed. It covenants against any problems that subsequently may arise affecting the property, regardless of the covenantor's responsibility for causing those problems. The deed from James and Cheryl Owen to Dennis Carlisle is a "special warranty" deed. The grantor of a special warranty deed only warrants against problems which he may himself have caused or created while owning the property, not those attributable to predecessors in title. Finally, a grantor may "quitclaim" the property to the grantee, making no covenants at all as to the state of the title.

7. Why did the plaintiff title insurance company in the principal case not sue on the present covenants against Albert Owen? Against James and Cheryl Owen? Assuming that a remote grantor has transferred property for consideration, why might a suit on the future covenants still yield an unsatisfactory result? Had James and Cheryl quitclaimed the property to Carlisle, what would be their liability? What would be the liability of Albert Owen, their grantor? See 6A R. Powell & P. Rohan, Powell on Real Property, ¶ 900[4]; W. Stoebuck and D. Whitman, The Law of Property § 11.13 (3rd ed. 2000).

C. RECORDING ACTS

The most important device for protecting land titles in the United States, on which other forms of title assurance are ultimately based, is the recording system. The maintenance of pervasive records of land titles is an American innovation. Antecedents for it can be found in the English enrollment of bargain and sale deeds and in the local customs of some English counties, which required registration of land titles. See Cribbet, Conveyancing Reform, 35 N.Y.U.L.Rev. 1291, 1293–1296 (1960). Security of English land titles, however, was initially dependent on public enfeoffment ceremonies, and then, once written evidence of land transfers became more common, on the passing on at each transfer of relevant muniments of title. As early as 1640, however, the Massachusetts Bay colony adopted a recording act. Other colonies followed suit, and as the country spread westward, the practice of requiring recording of land-title transactions spread with it. See Marshall, A Historical Sketch of the American Recording Acts, 4 Cleve.–Mar.L.Rev 56 (1955). The laws of every state in the United States now provide for recording or registration of land-title transactions.

Nowhere is recording necessary to the validity of a transaction between the transferor and transferee: Regardless of whether a purchaser (or donee) of property records his title, it is good against the vendor (or donor). Recording does serve a number of other purposes, however. First, it provides a public record of land-title transactions. If a person wants to know who owns the trash-covered vacant lot down the street, or how much her neighbor's house just sold for, or whether a potential debtor really owns the property listed on a loan application, the public land records may provide an answer. In most states, properly authenticated copies of recorded documents are also admissible evidence in judicial proceedings in which questions relating to the land titles arise.

The most important purpose of the recording acts, however, is to assure the security of the title of land owners. They do this in two ways. First, a potential purchaser (or his title insurer), by examining a vendor's title to property, can discover any outstanding clouds on the title of the vendor. These can then be cleared up before the purchase is completed, or, if they cannot be, the purchaser can abandon the purchase as too risky. Second, once a purchase is completed, the recording acts protect the title of the purchaser (who, depending on the type of recording act, either takes without notice, records first, or both) from prior unrecorded interests in the property.

Recording systems are established by statute. Three different types of recording statutes are found in the United States.[5] The simplest, and most primitive are the race statutes. Under a pure race statute, the first to record of two holders of conflicting interests prevails. If O sells Blackacre first to A and second to B, and B records first, B's interest takes precedence over A's in a race jurisdiction. Pure race statutes operate very efficiently—the only question before a court in a title dispute is who recorded first, a matter usually quite simply determined. They are, however, inequitable in the situation where B was aware of A's prior unrecorded interest.

Faced with the potential for fraud and inequity raised by pure race recording acts, courts began to interpret them so as to refuse protection to subsequent purchasers with notice, even if the subsequent purchaser recorded first. Legislatures eventually amended the recording acts to incorporate notice requirements as well, resulting in notice acts. Notice statutes permit a purchaser to prevail in a dispute with a previous purchaser, even though the subsequent purchaser failed to record, thus defeating, to some extent, the goal of the recording acts to encourage universal recording of land transactions.

Under the final form of statute, the race-notice statute, a subsequent purchaser, to prevail in a dispute with a prior purchaser, must not only take without notice of the prior interests, but also must record before the holder of the prior interest records.

5. Some commentators recognize a fourth category of recording acts, grace-period acts, which allow a prior grantee of land to take precedence over a subsequent transfer if the earlier transaction is recorded within a "grace period" provided by statute. See 6A R. Powell & R. Rohan, Powell on Real Property, ¶ 905[1][c][iv]. Grace periods were common in early recording statutes, as the large areas covered by a single recorder's office and primitive means of transportation impeded immediate recordation of land transactions. It is obviously contrary to the policies underlying the recording acts, however, to hold a subsequent purchaser subject to an undiscoverable prior interest recorded after the subsequent purchase but within the grace period, thus grace-period statutes have been generally repealed. The only modern example of grace-period statutes are mechanic's lien statutes, which permit laborers or building suppliers to record a mechanics lien against a property if bills are not paid within a statutory period (usually 60–120 days). A purchaser of real property is well advised, therefore, to ascertain if any work has recently been done on the property, and, if so, to make certain that all bills are paid prior to closing.

American states are today about evenly divided between notice and race-notice recording statutes, with a few pure race statutes remaining (see IV American Law of Property, § 17.5 for a complete list).

How would you classify each of the following statutes?

All deeds, mortgages and other instruments of writing which are authorized to be recorded, shall take effect and be in force from and after the time of filing the same for record, and not before, as to all creditors and subsequent purchasers, without notice; and all such deeds and title papers shall be adjudged void as to all such creditors and subsequent purchasers, without notice, until the same shall be filed for record. IL St. Ch. 765 § 5/30.

A conveyance of real property, within the state, on being duly acknowledged by the person executing the same, or proved as required by this chapter, * * *, may be recorded in the office of the clerk of the county where such real property is situated * * * Every such conveyance not so recorded is void as against any person who subsequently purchases or acquires by exchange or contracts to purchase or acquire by exchange, the same real property or any portion thereof, * * *, in good faith and for a valuable consideration, from the same vendor or assignor, his distributees or devisees, and whose conveyance, contract, or assignment is first duly recorded. . . . * * * N.Y.Real Prop.L. § 291.

An instrument affecting real estate is of no validity against subsequent purchasers for a valuable consideration, without notice, * * * unless the instrument is filed and recorded in the county in which the real estate is located, as provided in this chapter. Iowa Code Ann. § 558.41.

No (i) conveyance of land, or (ii) contract to convey, or (iii) option to convey, or (iv) lease of land for more than three years shall be valid to pass any property interest as against lien creditors or purchasers for a valuable consideration from the donor, bargainor or lessor but from the time of registration thereof in the county where the land lies. * * * Gen.Stat.N.C. § 47–18.

Though the law of recording is fundamentally statutory, as with the law of adverse possession, the simple language of the statutes has been subjected to considerable judicial interpretation. See Mattis, Recording Acts: Anachronistic Reliance, 25 Real Prop., Prob. & Trust J. 17, 22–40 (1990).

The classic recording act dispute involves three parties: O, the original owner of the land; A, to whom O first transferred title to the land (or an interest in the land, such as a lien or an easement); and B, to whom O subsequently transferred a conflicting interest in the same land.[6] To determine who prevails in a dispute between A and B in a particular jurisdiction it is necessary to know:

---

6. Note that, consistent with what was said earlier about the recording acts not affecting the validity of transfers between grantors and grantees, either A or B will

(1) Does the jurisdiction have a race, notice, or race-notice statute?

(2) Is A's interest an interest that must be recorded under the recording act to be protected against subsequent purchasers?

(3) Is B a purchaser protected by the recording acts?

(4) Did A record before B's purchase?

(5) Did B record before A (relevant only in race and race-notice jurisdictions)?

(6) Did B purchase without notice (constructive, actual, or inquiry) of A's interest (relevant only in notice or race-notice jurisdictions)?

(7) Were the formalities of the recording act properly observed (instruments properly acknowledged, transcribed, indexed)?

(8) If A's interest was recorded prior to B's purchase, was A's interest recorded in B's chain of title?

All of these questions must be considered against the background of the common law which preceded the recording acts. Under the common law, the general rule was first in time, first in right. Between two conflicting interests if both were legal or both were equitable, the earlier created interest would prevail. Thus A would always win in the dispute we have posed above. This rule makes a great deal of sense: If O has transferred an interest in property to A, O no longer owns that interest and cannot transfer it subsequently to B, thus the transfer to B is a nullity, and in a dispute between A and B, A must prevail. The only exception to this rule at the common law was that if A's interest was equitable (for example a constructive or resulting trust) and B was a purchaser who took for value without notice of A's interest, B would prevail. Equity thus protected bona fide purchasers for value from secret equities. See J. Pomeroy, Equity Jurisprudence, §§ 677–734 (5th ed. 1941)

We begin with the questions two and three above, which As must record to be protected by the recording act? Which Bs are protected by the act from unrecorded interests?

MUGAAS v. SMITH ET UX.

Supreme Court of Washington, 1949.
33 Wash.2d 429, 206 P.2d 332.

HILL, JUSTICE.

This is an action by Dora B. Mugaas, a widow, to quiet title to a strip of land 135 feet in length and with a maximum width of 3 1/2 feet

prevail over O in a dispute regardless of considerations of recordation or notice. Note also that, depending on the facts of the transaction, the losing party in the A versus B dispute may be able to recover from O under a fraud or constructive trust theory.

which she claims by adverse possession, and to compel Delmar C. Smith and his wife to remove therefrom any and all buildings and encroachments. From a judgment quieting title to the strip in Mrs. Mugaas and directing the removal of any and all buildings and encroachments, the Smiths appeal.

The appellants contend that the respondent has failed to establish adverse possession of the tract in question. The character of the respondent's possession over the statutory period is one of fact, and the trial court's finding in that regard is to be given great weight and will not be overturned unless this court is convinced that the evidence preponderates against that finding. We are of the opinion that the evidence was sufficient to sustain the trial court's findings, and the conclusions based thereon, that the respondent had acquired title to the strip in question by adverse possession. The evidence would have warranted a finding that her adverse possession dated back to 1910.

The only serious questions raised by this appeal are attributable to the fact that the fence which between 1910 and 1928 clearly marked the boundary line for which respondent contends, disappeared by a process of disintegration in the years which followed, and, when appellants purchased the property in 1941 by a legal description and with a record title which included the disputed strip, there was no fence and nothing to mark the dividing line between the property of appellants and respondent, or to indicate to the appellants that the respondent was claiming title to the strip in question.

We have on several occasions approved a statement which appears in Towles v. Hamilton, 94 Neb. 588, 143 N.W. 935, 936, that:

> " * * * It is elementary that, where the title has become fully vested by disseisin so long continued as to bar an action, it cannot be divested by parol abandonment or relinquishment or by verbal declarations of the disseizor, nor by any other act short of what would be required in a case where his title was by deed." [ ]

The fact that the respondent had ceased to use the strip in question in such a way that her claim of adverse possession was apparent did not divest her of the title she had acquired.

Appellants' principal contention is that we have held, in a long line of cases, that a bona fide purchaser of real property may rely upon the record title. The cases cited by appellants construe our recording statute, Rem.Rev.Stat. §§ 10596–1, 10596–2, and involve contests between those relying upon the record title and those relying upon a prior unrecorded conveyance as conveyances are defined by Rem.Rev.Stat. § 10596–1. The holdings in the cases cited give effect to that provision of § 10596–2 which states that any unrecorded conveyance " * * * is void as against any subsequent purchaser or mortgagee in good faith and for a valuable consideration from the same vendor, his heirs or devisees, of the same real property or any portion thereof whose conveyance is first duly recorded. * * * "

Appellants cite no cases, and we have found none, supporting their contention that, under a recording statute such as Rem.Rev.Stat. §§ 10596–1, 10596–2, a conveyance of the record title to a bona fide purchaser will extinguish a title acquired by adverse possession. The trial judge, in his admirable memorandum decision, quoted the following from the opinion in Ridgeway v. Holliday, 59 Mo. 444, 454:

> " * * * But it is contended by the defendant that he is a purchaser for value from Voteau who appeared from the record to be the owner, and was in possession, without any notice of the prior adverse possession which passed the title to Ridgeway, or of any claim on his part to the premises; and that as against him, the defendant, Ridgeway, cannot assert his title; that to permit him to do so, would be giving to an adverse possession greater force and efficacy than is given to an unrecorded conveyance. These objections, it must be admitted, are very forcible. The registry act, however, cannot, in the nature of things, apply to a transfer of the legal title by adverse possession, and such title does not stand on the footing of one acquired and held by an unrecorded deed, and of such title, the purchaser may not expect to find any evidence in the records."

He quoted, also, the following from Schall v. Williams Valley R. Co., 35 Pa. 191, 204:

* * *

> "The first observation we have to make on his ruling is, that titles matured under the statute of limitations, are not within the recording acts. However expedient it might be to require some public record of such titles to be kept, and however inconvenient it may be to purchasers to ascertain what titles of that sort are outstanding, still we have not as yet any legislation on the subject, and it is not competent for judicial decision to force upon them consequences drawn from the recording acts. Those acts relate exclusively to written titles."

These cases seem to us to be directly in point, and to afford a complete answer to appellants' contention. * * *

* * *

The judgment is affirmed.

Notes and Questions

1. If A's interest is not subject to recordation and thus does not need to be recorded under the recording act, a dispute between A and a subsequent purchaser B will be settled under the common law rules, i.e. normally A will win (subject to the exception that prior equitable interests are subordinate to the interests of subsequent bona fide purchasers). A's interest may be exempt from recording for several reasons. First, as in the principal case, A's

interest may not be based on a document, and thus may not be recordable. Adverse possession claims, easements created by necessity, implication or prescription, (See Chapter 6), dower or courtesy rights, and beneficial interests in constructive or resulting trusts fall in this category. Second, there are interests that are noted on public records elsewhere, such as tax and assessment liens kept in the county treasurer or tax office, wills filed in the probate court, and bankruptcy records in the bankruptcy court, of which a purchaser will be treated as having constructive notice, whether or not the interests are recorded. See Leary and Blake, Twentieth Century Real Estate Business and Eighteenth Century Recording, 22 Am.U.L.Rev. 275, 283–84 (1973). Thus, these records must be checked as part of a thorough title search. Third, some instruments are specifically not recordable, and thus need not be recorded. In earlier times, many kinds of instruments were not subject to recordation, but today the most common example of this category is the short-term lease, see N.Y.Real Prop.Law § 290 (McKinney) (leases not over 3 years), Mass.Gen.L.Ann. ch. 183 § 4 (leases not over 7 years). Finally, federal land patents need not be recorded under state recording acts. Which As must record under each of the recording acts set out above?

2. The obvious effect of the fact that the recording acts do not protect Bs against the unrecorded interests of As who are not required by law to record their interests is that a simple search of the recording acts is not sufficient to protect prospective Bs from subsequent unpleasant surprises. This in turn means that a title search is not complete until the examiner has studied not only the records of the recorder's office, but also examined probate, bankruptcy and divorce court records and made a trip out to the property to discover the interests of those in possession. But what could the Smiths do to protect themselves against the claims of Dora Mugaas? If you cannot think of anything they could have done differently, what does that say about the protection afforded by the recording acts?

3. If B is protected by the recording act, B will prevail in a dispute with A who claims under a prior recordable but unrecorded interest. Most recording acts only protect Bs who are purchasers, defined as any person who acquires an interest in property for valuable consideration. The interest need not be a fee interest—mortgagees, purchasers of easements or mineral estates, and lessees are protected. Donees, heirs, devisees, persons who file a lis pendens, and, in many jurisdictions, general creditors, are not, however, protected by the recording acts. Neither are persons who pay a nominal consideration. Some acts explicitly identify those protected by the recording act ("purchasers for value"), others explicitly identify those not protected by the act ("the grantor, his heirs and devisees"). Which Bs are protected by each of the statutes set out above?

About half of the states protect general creditors. (See the North Carolina and Illinois statutes above). Even in these jurisdictions, however, only creditors who have filed a lien against the property by judgment or attachment are protected. Further, in most jurisdictions that protect creditors, only creditors who take without notice are protected. Purchasers at judgment sales are protected if they purchase without notice of prior unrecorded interests. If the recording act protects creditors, however, even a purchaser with notice is protected if the creditor who obtained a judgment against the property obtained her lien without notice. See, 4 American Law of Property, §§ 17.9, 17.10, 17.29, 17.30 (J. Casner, ed. 1952); Johnson, Purpose and Scope of Recording Statutes, 47 Iowa L.Rev. 231, 235–237 (1962).

4. Recording acts only protect Bs who are purchasers for "value." Problems arise if value is not extended at the same time the property interest is obtained: if, for example, the subsequent purchaser extends value first and acquires a property interest later; or acquires a property interest first and extends value later. Bs who acquire mortgages or transfers of title for an antecedent debt are not protected by the recording acts from prior unrecorded interests. Neither are Bs who receive an interest in property in exchange for a promise to pay, at least unless the promise to pay is in the form of a negotiable instrument which is negotiated to a holder in due course. Where the transfer and payment are part of the same transaction, the fact that one precedes the other will not be fatal unless in the interim between the transfer and the payment, the subsequent purchaser receives notice of the interest of an A in a notice or race-notice jurisdiction. Some courts have held that where B receives notice of the claim of an A after the B has given value but before the transfer has occurred, B will not be protected from A's interest by the recording act. On the other hand, a B who has obtained title but only paid part of the purchase price when she receives notice of the existence of an A, will only prevail to the extent of consideration already paid. See IV American Law of Property at § 17.10; Johnson, 47 Iowa L.Rev. at 234; Mattis, Recording Acts: Anachronistic Reliance, 25 Real Prop., Prob. & Trust J. 17, 55–94 (1990).

5. To be protected by the recording acts, a B must also, in a notice or race-notice jurisdiction, purchase without notice. Much more will be said about this below.

6. What kinds of documents should be recorded? Deeds and documents evidencing encumbrances on title, for example mortgages securing the owner's debt, obviously ought to be recorded. What about documents relating to the property, but not affecting the validity of title? At least one commentator has suggested that sellers should be required to give buyers an environmental disclosure statement, and buyers should be required to record this document. See Russell James III, Requiring Environmental Information Disclosure on the Deed: Shining the Light on Residential Transactions, 2 Mo. Envtl. L. & Pol'y Rev. 81 (1994). This statement would reflect whether any of the four major environmental problems found in residential property—lead, radon, underground storage tanks, and asbestos—exist on the property. Is this a good idea, or would it clutter up an already overburdened recording system?

D. THE CHAIN OF TITLE

The recording acts seem literally to say that if A is first to place his interest of record in a race or race-notice jurisdiction, or if A places his interest of record before B purchases in a notice jurisdiction, then A will prevail over B in a dispute between them. In practice, however, A's obligation of prior recording has been largely replaced with an obligation to record within B's "chain of title." This change has been dictated by the nature of the American recording system.

In virtually any American recorder's office, far more instruments are of record than could ever be examined by a title searcher examining the title of a particular parcel of property. Title examiners must, therefore, depend on an index to identify documents relevant to a particular piece of property.[7] Traditionally, and still in most jurisdictions, recorded documents are indexed under the names of the parties to the recorded transaction. Separate indices are kept by the names of grantors and grantees. When a document is brought in for recording, it is microfilmed or photocopied, and assigned an index number (traditionally a volume and page number) which will facilitate its retrieval. The recorder then notes the document in two indices, one listing grantors and the other listing grantees.

Traditionally, these indices were arranged alphabetically by the first two or three letters of the last name. For example, a page might be headed Sho and include Shorrs, Shorts, Shooks, Shoops and Shopovskis, in chronological order of the filing of instruments rather than in strictly alphabetical order. From time to time indices are consolidated, so that a search might require reviewing a current index, annual indices for the last several years, and decennial indices for earlier times.

To illustrate, assume that you represent a client who wants to purchase Greenacre, which Johnson claims to own. You would search the grantee indices (probably searching the Jo pages) until you found the date where Johnson received the property from Salsich. Noting the date and index number of that transaction, you would then search the grantee books further back looking for the name Salsich until you found a point where Salsich received the property from Shaffer. Noting again the date and index number of the transaction, you would search back until you found the deed by which Shaffer had received the property. You would continue your search backwards in time until you reached a deed from the sovereign, or until you reached the point where title searching standards in your jurisdiction or your marketable title act permit you to stop. You would at that point have a list of successive owners of the property, and of the index numbers of the instruments by which they transferred title to the property.

At that point you would move over to the grantor books. Starting from the earliest deed you discovered, you would search forward for the names of a grantor from the date of the deed to that grantor to the date at which a deed from that grantor to the next was recorded. (Can you explain why your search would cover this time frame?) You would note the dates and index numbers of all instruments recorded in the name of each grantor during the time he or she had title to the property. If Shaffer, for example, had executed a mortgage to First Bank and Trust during the time he had title to the property, this would be noted. So would the fact that Shaffer had granted an easement to Jost, a neighbor.

7. For a good description of title indices, see Leary and Blake, Twentieth Century Real Estate Business and Eighteenth Cen-tury Recording, 22 Am.U.L.Rev. 275, 283–286 (1973).

The grantor indices would then be searched forward under these names as well, to determine if the mortgage or easement was ever released. When you finally had searched Johnson's name forward through the grantor index to the day of the search, your search of the indices would be completed. You would then retrieve the copies of the documents identified and examine them to determine which, if any, had any continuing effect on the title to Greenacre.

The series of successive interests in land identified by this search would constitute the chain of title for Greenacre. It is possible, however, that documents purporting to affect the title of Greenacre might be recorded out of this chain of title. Suppose, for example, that at some point in time Smith, who had no interest in Greenacre, deeded Greenacre to Jones and that Jones recorded the deed. This deed would in fact be prior of record to any deed your client could obtain or record, and thus literally, under the language of the recording act, would take precedence over that to your client. But should the claim of Jones prevail over that of your client? In fact, the courts have often placed a practical construction on the recording acts, holding a purchaser subject, not to all previously recorded deeds, but only to deeds recorded in that purchaser's "chain of title." The following cases explore the "chain of title" notion.

These cases also begin to explore the concept of "notice." Under notice or race-notice statutes, a B is only protected if he or she purchases without "notice" of prior unrecorded interests. Different types of notice are recognized by the cases. First, purchasers are considered to have "constructive" notice of all claims memorialized in recorded documents. Second, purchasers are held responsible for any claims to the property of which they have full "actual" notice. Finally, purchasers may be put on "inquiry" notice by various circumstances, most commonly by possession inconsistent with record title, or by information appearing in recorded documents suggesting unrecorded claims. A purchaser with inquiry notice has an obligation to make reasonable inquiries to discover the existence of prior adverse claims.

PALAMARG REALTY COMPANY v. REHAC

Supreme Court of New Jersey, 1979.
80 N.J. 446, 404 A.2d 21.

MOUNTAIN, J.

Plaintiffs brought suit to quiet title to two tracts of land in Burlington County. Title to one tract is claimed by defendants Joseph Rehac and Alexander Piatkowski; title to the other tract is claimed by defendants David W. Worth and Ezra B. Sharp. All defendants answered and filed counterclaims demanding relief similar to that sought by plaintiffs. Both plaintiffs and defendants moved for summary judgment. The trial court, in an unreported opinion, denied plaintiffs' motion and granted those of defendants. The Appellate Division reversed and entered judgment in favor of plaintiffs. * * *

Defendants Rehac and Piatkowski claim title to their tract by deed from Kupire Corporation dated November 21, 1973 and recorded November 26 of that year. The claim of title to the other tract, asserted by Worth and Sharp, rests upon a deed from the same grantor, Kupire Corporation, dated September 13, 1971 and recorded the following day. Although the two sets of defendants received deeds to their respective tracts from a common grantor on different dates, their back titles, to the extent here relevant, are otherwise identical.

Plaintiffs' chain of title as well as the common chain of all defendants derives from a common grantor, the Asbury Company. By quitclaim deed, on February 12, 1913, Asbury Company conveyed to a corporation named Appleby Estates a tract of land which included all the property here in question. The description in the deed is not by metes and bounds, but merely by reference to the earlier deeds that had conveyed the various parcels to the grantor. The instrument was recorded February 18, 1913. On February 15 of the same year, Asbury Company conveyed the particular land here in question (apparently all the land now claimed by both sets of defendants)[8] to one Robert E. Taylor by warranty deed,[9] the tract being described by metes and bounds. Taylor did not record this deed until April 25, 1913. Plaintiffs claim through the Asbury Company–Appleby Estates (Appleby Estates) chain; defendants, through the Asbury Company–Taylor (Taylor) chain.

The next instrument in plaintiffs' chain of title is a warranty deed from Appleby Estates back to Asbury Company dated and recorded in 1924. The description by earlier deed references only describes the lands that had been conveyed by Asbury Company to Appleby Estates in 1913, together with an additional tract. The description, however, includes the following proviso:

> Excepting therefrom the following named conveyances made by the said party of the first part; 429 acres to Robert E. Taylor,

(There follow like references to a number of other excepted tracts.) "The said party of the first part" was, of course, Appleby Estates, the grantor named as such in the deed, and Appleby Estates had made no conveyance to Robert E. Taylor. The conveyance of 429 acres to him had been made by its predecessor in title, Asbury Company. The exception quoted above made no reference to the date of the deed to Taylor, nor to the book and page where it had been recorded.

The next significant transaction in the plaintiffs' chain of title occurred about 40 years later. On August 15, 1966, Asbury Company, Appleby Estates and Appleby & Wood Company[10] conveyed to Anthony J. Del Tufo Agency, Inc., by quitclaim deed,

---

8. Some deed descriptions are so imprecise that we cannot make this statement with absolute certainty.

9. Inadvertently, the Appellate Division described this deed as being one of bargain and sale. 159 N.J.Super. at 290, 387 A.2d 1233. This point has importance, as will be seen below.

10. An earlier owner of some of the property.

* * * all of the real property owned by the grantors herein, wherever situate within the boundaries of the County of Burlington in the State of New Jersey.

This instrument was accompanied by a second quitclaim deed, dated August 12, 1966, running in favor of Anthony J. Del Tufo Agency, Inc., and executed by 34 persons purporting to be "all of the surviving heirs at law of J. Randolph Appleby and Maria DuBois Appleby, his wife, and their respective spouses," as well as by the five executors of the last will and testament of J. Randolph Appleby, deceased. The description of the property in this deed reads as follows:

Being all of the real property owned by the grantors herein, wherever situate within the boundaries of the County of Burlington in the State of New Jersey, to which any of them may have derived title through the estates of J. Randolph Appleby or Maria DuBois Appleby, his wife, or from Appleby and Wood Company, Appleby Estates, or the Asbury Company, all being corporations of the State of New Jersey.

Plaintiffs are successors in title, by virtue of a number of mesne conveyances, to the Del Tufo Agency.

Two observations should be made with respect to Appleby Estates' chain of title. First, all instruments in the chain are quitclaim deeds with the exception of the deed of reconveyance in 1924 from Appleby Estates to Asbury Company. It is urged by defendants that plaintiffs' position is fatally weakened by this fact. The law is well settled, however, that a quitclaim deed passes the same estate to a grantee as does a deed of bargain and sale. The point is, therefore, without significance.

Secondly, J. Randolph Appleby was president and majority stockholder of both Asbury Company and Appleby Estates. In his capacity as president of the former he executed the first conveyance from Asbury Company to Appleby Estates and as president of the latter he executed the deed of reconveyance. This fact may be significant.

The Taylor chain, upon which all defendants rely, can be simply described. It will be recalled that Taylor ostensibly took title from Asbury Company by deed dated February 15, 1913 and recorded April 25, 1913. Taylor and his wife thereafter conveyed to Ruth McCrae on July 7, 1932, by deed of bargain and sale with covenant against grantors' acts. The deed was recorded May 23, 1933. There follow a series of warranty deeds culminating in the conveyances to defendants described above. The descriptions in all deeds in this chain of title are by metes and bounds.

The Appellate Division decided that plaintiffs should prevail. While we agree with much of the reasoning of the Appellate Division, we have concluded, for reasons set forth below, that the judgment of that court should be vacated and the case remanded to the trial court for further proceedings consistent with what is set forth herein.

Generally speaking, and absent any unusual equity, a court should decide a question of title such as this in the way that will best support and maintain the integrity of the recording system. The underlying purpose of the Recording Act is clear.

An historical study of the (Recording) Act, as well as an analysis of the cases interpreting it, leads to the conclusion that it was designed to compel the recording of instruments affecting title, for the ultimate purpose of permitting purchasers to rely upon the record title and to purchase and hold title to lands within this state with confidence. The means by which the compulsion to record is accomplished is by favoring a recording purchaser, both by empowering him to divest a former non-recording title owner and by preventing a subsequent purchaser from divesting him of title. This ability to deprive a prior and bona fide purchaser for value of his property shows a genuine favoritism toward a recording purchaser. It is a clear mandate that the recording purchaser be given every consideration permitted by the law, including all favorable presumptions of law and fact. It is likewise a clear expression that a purchaser be able to rely upon the record title. (Jones, The New Jersey Recording Act—A Study of its Policy, 12 Rutgers L.Rev. 328, 329–30 (1957))

This policy is clearly established in the New Jersey Recording Act, pertinent parts of which provide as follows:

Except as otherwise provided herein, whenever any deed * * * shall have been or shall be duly recorded * * * such record shall, from that time, be notice to all subsequent * * * purchasers * * * of the execution of the deed * * * so recorded and of the contents thereof. (N.J.S.A. 46:21–1)

Every deed * * * shall, until duly recorded * * *, be void and of no effect against * * * all subsequent bona fide purchasers * * * for valuable consideration, not having notice thereof, whose deed shall have been first duly recorded * * *. (N.J.S.A. 46:22–1)

This legislation makes New Jersey a "notice/race" type jurisdiction. 4 American Law of Property § 17.5, at 541–45 & n. 63 (Casner ed. 1952). This means that if a common grantor sells the same land to two persons, the first to record even though he may have been the second to purchase will prevail, but only so long as he had no actual notice of the earlier sale. Id. at 544.

We examine first the deed from Asbury Company to Appleby Estates dated February 12, 1913 and recorded six days later. It was executed by J. Randolph Appleby as president of Asbury Company. It is not denied that Appleby was also at that time president of the grantee corporation, Appleby Estates. He, alone or with his wife, owned a substantial majority of the shares of both corporations. In fact it may also be reasonably inferred from the rather meager record though not certainly determined that the other shareholders of both corporations were all members of the Appleby family. It was also in his capacity as president of Asbury Company that he executed the deed dated February 15, 1913 from that corporation to Robert E. Taylor. Were it not for these facts, we would agree with the Appellate Division's conclusion that, because the Asbury Company–Appleby Estates deed was the first recorded, "Appleby Estates title was, in 1913, superior to that of Taylor * * *." 159 N.J.Super. at 292, 387 A.2d at 1236.

Although Taylor, had he been made aware of the conflicting conveyance to Appleby Estates, might have brought a suit for damages against Asbury Company on the warranty in his deed, it is much more likely that he would have sought equitable relief against Asbury Company, Appleby Estates and J. Randolph Appleby by way of cancellation or removal of cloud on title. Had there been such a title contest in 1913, Taylor would most surely have won. We need cite no authority to support the obvious conclusion that J. Randolph Appleby's personal knowledge of the deed to Taylor would have been attributed to Appleby Estates. As far as the rights of third persons were concerned, one corporation was simply the *alter ego* of the other, and both stood in that position with respect to J. Randolph Appleby. This would have prevented Appleby Estates from successfully asserting its prior recording as a defense to Taylor's claim. It is, therefore, imprecise to say that Appleby Estates' title was superior to Taylor's in 1913. There was, however, no title contest at that time.

The prospects for a successful title suit by Taylor would not have been diminished by the deed of reconveyance to Asbury Company in 1924.[11] Notice of the Taylor deed still would have been attributed to both Appleby Estates and Asbury Company. In 1924 the latter, upon reacquiring title, did not become a purchaser for value without notice. Up to this point an action by Taylor, of the kind suggested above, presumably would have succeeded.

The superiority of the Taylor chain fades, however, with the 1966 conveyances to the plaintiffs' predecessor in interest, the Del Tufo Agency. It will be recalled that Asbury Company conveyed to Appleby Estates by deed dated February 12, 1913 and recorded February 18, 1913. The Taylor deed was dated February 15, 1913 and recorded April 25 of the same year. Therefore, when the Del Tufo Agency took title by virtue of the two deeds of which mention is made above, it did not have record notice of the Taylor deed. A leading treatise states that:

> If after the recording of a deed from an owner there is later recorded another deed from the same grantor to a different grantee, whether earlier or later in date, a purchaser from the first grantee is without notice of any rights of the second grantee unless it is by reason of some fact other than the record; the purchaser's obligation to examine the grantor's indices as to that grantor ceased at the date of recording of the first deed. This principle has general application in the case of two successive deeds from the same grantor, both

11. The question raised by the exception contained in the deed of reconveyance as well as the issue of estoppel by deed presented thereby, are both discussed below.

deeds recorded in the order of their execution; a party thereafter purchasing from the first grantee is not charged with notice by reason of the record then existing of the second deed. (4 American Law of Property § 17.21, at 596–97 (Casner ed. 1952))

Although the New Jersey Recording Act appears to say that a subsequent purchaser will *always* be deemed to have notice of, and be bound by, a prior recorded deed touching the same property, this is not in fact the case. The statutes have been consistently interpreted to mean that the subsequent purchaser will be bound only by those instruments which can be discovered by a "reasonable" search of the particular chain of title. That is, a prospective purchaser need only search the records to discover conveyances or other significant acts of an owner from the date the deed into that person was recorded until the date he relinquishes record title. A leading case in New Jersey is Glorieux v. Lighthipe, 88 N.J.L. 199, 96 A. 94 (E. & A.1915). There Justice Swayze, speaking for a unanimous court said,

> A purchaser may well be held bound to examine or neglect at his peril, the record of the conveyances under which he claims, but it would impose an intolerable burden to compel him to examine all conveyances made by every one in his chain of title. (88 N.J.L. at 203, 96 A. at 96)

* * *

Although it is thus clear that Del Tufo Agency had no record notice, it still may have had *actual* notice. Because the case was decided on motion for summary judgment, this particular point was not adequately explored. Defendants will be given an opportunity to examine that question on remand.[12]

On remand, except in the respect noted below, the court need not concern itself with the 1924 deed of reconveyance from Appleby Estates to Asbury Company containing, as it does, the exception with respect to 429 acres described as having been previously conveyed by Appleby Estates to Robert E. Taylor.[13] As we have seen, there had been no such conveyance by Appleby Estates, although there had been such a convey-

---

12. It is appropriate in this connection to bear in mind that defendants would not be entitled to succeed merely by showing that Del Tufo Agency had actual notice. It must also be shown that subsequent purchasers had such actual notice.

Unless the contrary appears from the record, the question of whether prior owners in a chain of title were innocent purchasers is not material to an examiner, provided only his client is such at the time he completes his purchase. This is because, in all jurisdictions, a purchaser without notice from an owner who has notice is protected. This is not peculiar to the recording acts, but is merely the application of a long-established equity doctrine as to the effect

of notice. It is further the case that a purchaser will be protected, even though he has notice of an unrecorded title or claim, provided his vendor was an innocent purchaser. (Patton on Titles, § 15 at 68–69 (1938))

3 Pomeroy, Equity Jurisprudence §§ 754, 754a, at 55–61 (5th ed. 1941).

13. We do not wish to be understood as foreclosing the possibility that expert testimony presented on remand may suggest that the exception in this deed should be deemed sufficient notice to spur further inquiry. In this latter event, the point should be considered anew in the light of such evidence and relevant law.

ance by its predecessor in title, Asbury Company. Defendant argues that this recital of an exception should be deemed to constitute notice of the Taylor deed to subsequent purchasers in plaintiffs' chain of title. Although we reserve final judgment, we tentatively feel that contention lacks merit. The recital gives notice only of a non-existent conveyance. Had the exception either referred to the proper grantor—Asbury Company—or to the book and page where the record of the instrument could be found, then indeed there would have been notice. Here, both were lacking. Nevertheless, final decision on this point should await the taking of expert proofs on remand.

Defendants' final and most vigorously pressed argument is that they are entitled to prevail upon a proper application of the doctrine of estoppel by deed. This issue was not addressed by the Appellate Division, perhaps because, as mentioned above, that court mistakenly thought the deed from Asbury Company to Taylor to have been one of bargain and sale rather than of warranty. Defendants contend that even if Taylor did not acquire title to the premises in question in 1913—the deed to Appleby Estates having been first recorded—nevertheless he did acquire title in 1924 when the property was reconveyed to Asbury Company.

Under the well-settled doctrine of estoppel by deed, a grantor who executes a general warranty deed purporting to convey land to which he has no title will not be heard to claim title against his grantee, if he (the grantor) subsequently acquires title. It will be seen that an application of this doctrine would, presumptively at least, either place title in Taylor upon the execution and delivery of the deed of reconveyance from Appleby Estates to Asbury Company in 1924 or give Taylor a right to equitable relief by way of specific performance. Plaintiffs answer by saying that estoppel by deed operates only to vest title in the original grantee and his successors in interest if the grantor, subsequent to his acquisition of good title, does not thereafter convey the property to a purchaser for value without notice. Such a conveyance apparently took place, plaintiffs point out, upon the transfer of title to the Del Tufo Agency in 1966.

Whether under circumstances such as this, title should be held to inure to the original grantee and his successors or pass to the subsequent grantee has been the subject of much controversy. See 3 American Law of Property § 15.22, at 849–50 (Casner ed. 1952). The case law in our state clearly favors the subsequent purchaser for value without notice. [   ]

Furthermore, this conclusion is in conformity with the requirements of our Recording Act and supports the integrity of the recording system. See especially, Philbrick, Limits of Record Search and Therefore of Notice, 93 U.Pa.L.Rev. 125, 181–86 (1944). It is likely that a correctly undertaken title search by the Del Tufo Agency in 1966 or by any of its successors in title would not have discovered the original deed from Asbury Company to Taylor. * * *

There is a further point that must be considered, but which has been neither briefed nor argued. As we set forth at the beginning of this opinion, defendants Rehac and Piatkowski ostensibly acquired title to the premises which they claim to own in November 1973. We may take judicial notice of the fact that it is the custom of title searchers and conveyancers in New Jersey to search a title only for sixty years and until a warranty deed is found in the chain of title. A sixty-year search undertaken in November, 1973 would extend back to November, 1913. A further search for a warranty deed would presumably end upon discovery of the Asbury Company to Taylor deed recorded in April of that year. Thus the deed from Asbury Company to Appleby Estates would not be discovered. Would such a title search meet the customary requirements as established by conveyancing practice in New Jersey? If so, how much force should be given to this fact? Should we adopt the custom of conveyancers and make the sixty-year search convention a rule of law? How could this be made to harmonize with the Recording Act and other relevant statutes? To what extent and over what period of time has reliance been placed on the sixty-year search? How did this custom develop and upon what law does it rest? What is the attitude of title companies to the problem that this case presents? We would prefer not to decide questions with such potentially far-reaching effects in a factual vacuum.

We are mindful that the art of title searching, upon which so much of our conveyancing practice rests, has been created in very large part without the aid of legislation and has received little attention in judicial decisions.

> No statute has ever mentioned search, much less indicated the time or records over which it must extend * * *. (Philbrick, supra, 93 U.Pa.L.Rev. at 137)

On remand to the trial court, expert testimony should be offered and received as to the customs and usages of the conveyancing bar and title companies with respect to what has been discussed above. * * *

* * *

Notes and Questions

1. The principal case illustrates two of the most commonly discussed chain of title problems. The archetype of the first problem is as follows: First O transfers to A. A does not record. Then O transfers to B. B takes with notice of A's claim, but records. Subsequently A records. Then B transfers to C, who takes without notice of A's claim. Analytically, at the point O transferred to B, B would, in a notice or race-notice jurisdiction, take subordinate to A's interest, since B had notice of it. Since B's claim is subordinate to A's, C can only prevail in a dispute between C and A if C can prevail in her own right. Assuming C takes without actual or inquiry notice of A's claim, C will prevail unless A's interest is considered to be of prior record to C's claim. In fact, A's claim is recorded before C's, but to discover A's claim, C would have to make a title search more extensive than that

described above. C could not stop searching for O's name in the indices once the first recorded O to B transfer was found, but would need to keep searching forward until the prior in time, but later in record, O to A transfer was found. Presumably, C would then need to further inquire as to whether B had knowledge of the O to A transfer to determine if C could claim shelter under the O to B transfer.

The *Palamarg* case raised the problem of when a title examiner can cease searching the indices as to a particular grantor, and with some twisting, its facts can be made to fit the aforementioned archetype. The Asbury Company is obviously O, Taylor is A, and the February 15, 1913 transfer from Asbury Company to Taylor is the O to A transfer. The transfer from Asbury Company to Appleby Estates on February 12, 1913 is the O to B transfer. (In fact this transfer was prior in time to the Asbury to Taylor transfer, but because of the identity of Asbury and Appleby, the court is willing to subordinate the transfer between them to the transfer between Asbury and Taylor, effectively treating Appleby Estates as a B rather than an A.) Asbury Company, of course, is on notice of its earlier transfer to Taylor, and therefore cannot claim the benefit of the fact that Appleby recorded before Taylor. Del Tufo may, however, be the C, who takes without notice, and who will not find the A (Taylor) record because it appears after the Asbury to Appleby deed is recorded.

Is the solution *Palamarg* reaches to this conundrum, limiting C to a "reasonable" search and permitting C to win over A unless C in fact had notice of A's claim, consistent with the language of the recording acts? Is it consistent with their policy? Should the answer to this question vary depending on whether the jurisdiction is a race or race-notice jurisdiction? See 4 American Law of Property, § 17.22 (J. Casner ed. 1952); Philbrick, Limits of Record Search and Therefore of Notice, 93 U.Pa.L.Rev. 125, 391–440 (1944); Cross, The Record "Chain of Title" Hypocrisy, 57 Colum.L.Rev. 787, 793–794 (1957); Mattis, Recording Acts: Anachronistic Reliance, 25 Real Prop., Prob. & Trust J. 17, 40–55 (1990). The jurisdictions are split on this issue, though a majority of the cases that have addressed the issue favor a literal reading of the recording acts, and give the victory to A.

2. Many areas of the country employ a tract index rather than a grantor-grantee index for locating recorded documents.[14] Normally under a tract index system, each parcel of property in the locality is given a parcel-identifier number. This can usually be discovered by locating the parcel on a map which gives the identifier numbers. Each parcel will then be assigned a page (or several pages) in the property indices. As documents are recorded, the recorder indexes them with respect to each tract which they affect. In a jurisdiction with a tract index, a title examiner need only study the pages of the indices affecting that particular piece of property to discover any interests affecting a particular parcel of property.

Would a tract index solve the problem identified in the preceding note? How?

---

14. A recent survey of recorder's offices found that of the 1330 respondent jurisdictions, 1059 used grantor-grantee indices, and 271 used a tract index, U.S. Dept. of Agriculture, Economic Research Serv. Natl. Resource Economics Div., Information Contained in Real Property Transfer Records, Rep. No. A–GE–S–840711 (August 1984).

3. The second problem encountered in the *Palamarg* case can be described as follows: A transfers an interest in property which A does not own to B by warranty deed. B records. Then O, the previous owner, transfers the property interest to A and A records. (Note at this point that by virtue of the doctrine of estoppel by deed, A's interest in the property becomes B's.) Finally, A transfers the property interest to C, who takes without notice of the earlier transfer to B and records. Subsequently C and B both claim the property interest. Note that, literally, B has recorded before C, and therefore ought to take priority under the recording acts. Again, however, this result would dramatically expand the scope of search required of C. He cannot begin his search with respect to each grantor in the chain, but must go back beyond that point for an undetermined previous period of time.

Under the facts of the *Palamarg* case, B is Taylor, who was transferred an interest in the property by warranty deed by Asbury (the A) at a time when Asbury had no interest in the property. Asbury subsequently receives the property from Appleby Estates (O) but then transfers it to Del Tufo (C).

The result reached by the *Palamarg* case to this problem, that C triumphs over B, is consistent with the weight of authority, though there are some cases to the contrary, See 4 American Law of Property, § 17.20; Philbrick, 93 U.Pa.L.Rev. at 303–306; Cross, 57 Colum.L.Rev. at 794–796; Mattis, 25 Real Prop., Prob. & Trust J. at 40–55.

Would a tract index solve this problem? How?

4. *Palamarg* dismisses offhandedly the notion that grantees under a quitclaim deed should be entitled to less protection under the recording acts than grantees under a warranty deed. A few jurisdictions hold, however, that a quitclaim grantee cannot claim recording act protection. The most common argument for this result is that the grantor's lack of confidence in his own title should put the grantee on notice of potential adverse claims. Other cases argue that a quitclaim transfers only the interest of the grantor, which, where there has been a prior conveyance, is no interest at all. Modern cases, following two Supreme Court decisions, Moelle v. Sherwood, 148 U.S. 21, 13 S.Ct. 426, 37 L.Ed. 350 (1893) and United States v. California and Oregon Land Co., 148 U.S. 31, 13 S.Ct. 458, 37 L.Ed. 354 (1893), generally take the *Palamarg* approach.

5. Do the concluding paragraphs of the opinion suggest that the court is proposing judicial adoption of a marketable title act? (See Section F infra.) It is perhaps sensible for the court not to get tied up in the literal language of the recording act, instead limiting searches to a reasonable time period. Is the court suggesting, however, that the defendants would win in 1973, the plaintiffs in 1974, despite the multiple intervening transfers of the land?

BALL v. VOGTNER

Supreme Court of Alabama, 1978.
362 So.2d 894.

Torbert, Chief Justice.

Appellant, Kitty Ball, filed suit against appellees, William and Rebecca Vogtner, to establish a judgment lien on certain real property in

Mobile County. The Vogtners filed an answer and a third party claim against cross-appellant Mississippi Valley Title Insurance Company (hereinafter referred to as Mississippi Valley). The Vogtners denied the validity of the judgment lien and raised the defense that they were good faith purchasers for value without notice of appellant's judgment, and the judgment recorded in the probate court was outside their chain of title. The third party claim averred that the Vogtners had purchased a title insurance policy from Mississippi Valley and, if they were liable to appellant, then Mississippi Valley was liable to them. Mississippi Valley filed an answer denying liability based upon a policy exclusion, and the Vogtners filed an amended third party complaint alleging timely notice of the claim and asserting an additional claim for failure to defend.

The appellant then, with leave of court, amended the complaint to join as parties defendant in the original action Cooper Realty Company, Martin Ramon and Barbara Jolene Carrera, and Mississippi Valley alleging against such defendants, and the Vogtners, a count for fraud and conspiracy. The trial court dismissed with prejudice the count for fraud as to all parties, but allowed appellant to amend the original action against the Vogtners as a suit to impress a lien against the property.

The case was tried on the issues of the superiority of the judgment lien and the title company's duty to defend. The court entered its final decree holding that the Vogtners had neither actual nor constructive knowledge of the judgment against Mary Morgan; therefore, the judgment did not constitute a lien against the property. Furthermore, the trial court determined that Mississippi Valley had a duty to defend and awarded the Vogtners $1800 for attorney fees. After denial of her motion for new trial, appellant filed this appeal. Cross-appellant Mississippi Valley appeals that portion of the trial court's order awarding the Vogtners attorney fees which was based on the trial court's finding that Mississippi Valley had the duty to defend the action of appellant.

Appellant filed suit for damages for assault and battery on May 20, 1971 in the Circuit Court of Mobile County against Mary Morgan. Appellant recovered a judgment against Mary Morgan and recorded the judgment on May 17, 1972. During the interim between the filing of suit and judgment, Mary Morgan married B.B. Collins and subsequently acquired the property in question. Although appellant and her attorney knew of the marriage at the time of entry of judgment, the judgment was entered against Mary Morgan, not Mary Collins.

On December 15, 1971, the property in question consisting of a house and lot was conveyed to Mary C. Collins as grantee by Leon Gavin and Margaret Susan Young Helton, grantors. Mary Collins conveyed the property to Martin and Barbara Carrera on October 10, 1973 by a deed reciting a valuable consideration including the assumption of an existing mortgage. However, Mary Collins remained in possession of the house and lot and made the installment payments on the mortgage in lieu of rent to the Carreras. Both deeds were recorded.

Subsequently, the Vogtners became interested in the property and contacted Cooper Realty Company which had the listing. A representative of the company took them to the house where Mrs. Collins showed them around. Mrs. Collins had placed the house with Cooper Realty. Believing Mrs. Collins to be the owner, the Vogtners submitted a written offer through the realtor naming Mrs. Collins as owner. This offer was rejected. However, a subsequent offer was accepted but was signed by the Carreras as owners. Upon the Vogtners' inquiry concerning the signature of the Carreras, the agent of the realty company replied that there were some marital problems and they didn't want the house mixed up in the divorce.

Later, Mrs. Collins contacted the Vogtners in an effort to rescind the transaction, so the Vogtners retained counsel, Mr. Walter Lee, to represent them in the purchase of the home. Mr. Lee came to the conclusion that the Carreras were "straw people," and Mrs. Collins was the real owner of the property. Accordingly, he required a letter of attornment from Mrs. Collins and that the Vogtners' check at closing be endorsed by the Carreras over to Mrs. Collins.

Attorney Lee, before commencement of his representation of the Vogtners, learned through social contacts with appellant that she might have a judgment against Mary Collins whom he knew at that time only as "Mary." At the closing, he told the representative of Mississippi Valley, Mrs. Flinn, that there might be a judgment against Mary Collins, but he never communicated such to the Vogtners. Mrs. Flinn quickly checked the company's in-house records and found no judgment against Mrs. Collins, and the transaction was closed.

* * *

Appellant * * * contends that the property should be subject to the judgment lien since the Vogtners had actual or constructive notice of the lien.

For a judgment to create a lien on the property of the defendant, a certificate must be filed in the office of the judge of probate of the county in which the property is situated which shows: (1) the style of the court which entered the judgment, (2) the amount and date thereof, (3) the amount of costs, (4) the names of the parties thereto, (5) the name of the plaintiff's attorney, and (6) the address of each defendant or respondent, as shown in the court proceedings. Ala.Code §§ 6–9–210 to 211 (1975). To create a lien, the statutory requirements as to the contents of the certificate must be strictly observed. [   ]

Appellant properly filed a certificate; however, she listed the judgment debtor as Mary Morgan instead of Mary Collins. The certificate, as filed, does establish a valid lien between appellant and Mary Collins, but not as to the Vogtners since the name shown in the certificate is insufficient to impart constructive notice to third parties.

As between the judgment creditor and judgment debtor a judgment may afford a valid lien despite inaccuracies or omissions in the docket or index in respect of the names or descriptions of the parties. In order to make the lien of a judgment effective as against third persons, however, it is ordinarily necessary that the docket and index should disclose the names of both parties, plaintiff as well as defendant, and designate them with such a degree of accuracy as to charge persons searching such records with notice of the judgments or to put them on inquiry. [   ]

Mary Collins both acquired and conveyed title to the property in her name as such. Nowhere in the Vogtners' chain of title does the name Mary Morgan appear. The Vogtners possessed no facts sufficient to put them on inquiry or to enable them to discover the existence of the judgment lien against Mary Morgan. An instrument executed by a married woman in her name prior to marriage without mention of her married name imparts no notice. [   ] 8 G. Thompson, Commentaries on the Modern Law of Real Property § 4300, at 275 (1963). In the absence of actual knowledge, the purchaser is charged with notice of that which appears on the face of all the instruments by which he takes title, but is not bound to inquire into collateral circumstances. [   ] A reasonable search of the records in the instant case would have revealed nothing of the judgment lien since the parties would be searching under the name Mary Collins, not Mary Morgan.

The Vogtners had no actual notice of the judgment lien. Their attorney did not inform them of the possibility of a judgment against Mrs. Collins. To impart constructive notice to the Vogtners, the certificate would have to be in their chain of title. [   ] Since it was not, the only way for the Vogtners to have any knowledge of the judgment is if the knowledge of their attorney, Mr. Lee, is imputed to them.

Our cases hold that for knowledge of the attorney to be imputed to the client, the knowledge must have come to the attorney while engaged in a service for his client after the attorney-client relationship began. [   ] "Information to an agent is not notice to the principal when given to the agent upon a casual conversation at a time when he is not engaged in business for his principal and no act or transaction of the agency is then pending." [   ] Mr. Lee acquired his knowledge of the possibility of a judgment during a "casual conversation" with social acquaintances approximately two years before his representation of the Vogtners; therefore, any knowledge he may have possessed is not imputed to the Vogtners. Since the Vogtners had neither actual nor constructive notice of the judgment lien, they acquired the property free of the lien.

Cross-appellant Mississippi Valley contends that it had no duty to defend the action against the Vogtners since a policy exclusion exempts the judgment lien from coverage. Therefore, awarding the Vogtners attorney fees was improper.

The policy provided that "(t)he company, at its own cost and without undue delay, shall provide for the defense of the insured in all litigations * * * founded upon defect, lien or encumbrance insured against by this policy." The policy expressly excluded from coverage:

"(D)efects, liens, encumbrances, adverse claims against the title as insured or other matters * * * known to the Insured either at the date of this policy or at the date such Insured acquired an estate or interest insured by this policy and not shown by the public records, unless disclosure thereof in writing by the Insured shall have been made to the company prior to the date of the policy * * *." Public records are defined in the policy as "those records which impart constructive notice of matters relating to said land."

The certificate in this case did not impart constructive notice of the lien because it contained the judgment debtor's maiden name only, and accordingly, was outside the Vogtners' chain of title. The name Mary Morgan was insufficient to alert anyone interested in the property as to the existence of the lien. Therefore, the lien was not "shown by public records" and would be excluded from coverage if the Vogtners had knowledge of it and failed to notify the company in writing. However, since the Vogtners had no knowledge, either actual or constructive, of the judgment lien, the lien was not within those defects excluded by the policy and Mississippi Valley was obligated to defend.

For the above mentioned reasons, the order of the trial court is due to be affirmed.

AFFIRMED.

Notes and Questions

1. As the court views the facts in the principal case, it presents the classical wild deed problem: A (Mary Morgan) transfers Orangeacre to B (Kitty Ball), then O (Mary Collins), the record owner, transfers it to C (the Vogtners). (Here we have, of course, a variation on the classical problem in that O and A are, in fact, the same person. Normally A would be a complete stranger to the chain of title in which O was found.) A standard title search by C, as described above, will never find A's deed to B. How extensive a search would C have to carry out to find it? Courts uniformly rule for the subsequent purchaser without notice in this situation.

2. Who could most easily protect himself or herself in the principal case, Ms. Ball or the Vogtners? What would each have had to do to assure protection of his or her interest?

3. Would a tract index solve this problem? How?

4. Variances in names can arise not just from changes in marital status, but also from spelling variants and misspellings, or from variant usage of given names and initials. A reasonable title search should not require an examiner to check different letters of the alphabet for the same surname (Jost and Yost, Coons and Kuhns), but might require checking for variant spellings beginning with the same letter (Frazier and Fraser, Johnson and Johnstone). See 4 American Law of Property § 17.18 (J. Casner ed. 1952).

5. Why are the Vogtners not treated as having "actual knowledge" of Ms. Ball's claim, since their attorney was aware of it? Is the decisive fact

here that the information was obtained by their attorney through a "casual conversation" or that it was obtained before the attorney-client relationship began? The first question goes to what constitutes "actual notice" under the recording acts. Should it be sufficient to charge B with actual notice of A's claim that B is aware of the assertion of a claim, or must B have knowledge of the validity of the adverse claim? Surely the former information could be obtained through a casual conversation, the latter might require more. If a casual conversation cannot give actual knowledge of a claim, can it give inquiry notice? If so, was the extent of the inquiry in the principal case sufficient? See 6A R. Powell & P. Rohan, Powell on Real Property, ¶ 905[1][d]; Philbrick, Limits of Record Search and Therefore of Notice, 93 U.Pa.L.Rev. 125, at 259–273 (1944).

Turning to the second issue, under what circumstances should the knowledge of an attorney be attributed to a client? Clearly, if the information is gained during the attorney-client relationship as a result of work done for the client, it is attributable to the client. What if, however, the attorney became aware of the claim during a previous title search of the same property, for example for a previous owner? What if he learned of it representing Ms. Morgan Collins in previous litigation? What if he learned of it representing Ms. Ball? If, by the way, the attorney had represented Ms. Ball in the earlier litigation, would he have an ethical obligation to decline to represent the Vogtners in their efforts to purchase the property? See A.B.A. Model Rules 1.6, 1.9.

6. The Vogtners failed to discover the Ball claim because it was indexed under Ms. Collins' maiden name. Assume, however, that the lien was properly filed against Ms. Collins, but the recorder erroneously failed to index it, or indexed it under the wrong name or with respect to the wrong property (i.e., the legal description of the property in the index was in error). Should the courts treat such an improperly indexed document as a wild deed, and consider a subsequent purchaser to be without notice of it? Or should the court hold that once the instrument is recorded with the recorder, all subsequent purchasers have constructive notice of it? Who can most easily avoid this problem? What must Bs do to find such improperly indexed documents? What must As do to avoid mis-indexing?

In most states the first purchaser must make sure that in fact her instrument is placed of record. The effect of subsequent indexing errors, however, is less certain. The majority of states have held that a subsequent purchaser can be held to have constructive notice of a recorded claim even though it was not properly indexed. Brown v. United States, 496 F.Supp. 903 (D.N.J.1980); Luthi v. Evans, 223 Kan. 622, 576 P.2d 1064 (1978); Cross, The Record "Chain of Title" Hypocrisy, 57 Colum.L.Rev. 787, 790–793 (1957). A significant minority, however, (probably representing the modern trend) hold that proper indexing is necessary to proper recording, Compiano v. Jones, 269 N.W.2d 459 (Iowa 1978); Badger v. Benfield, 78 N.C.App. 427, 337 S.E.2d 596 (1985). A party injured by recorder error may be able to sue the recorder, if permitted to do so by state law. Recovery will usually be limited to the amount of the recorder's bond, however, which is usually very low by modern standards. See Basye, A Uniform Land Parcel Identifier—Its Potential for All our Land Records, 22 Am.U.L.Rev. 251, n. 29 at 262 (1973).

7. A fourth situation in which the common law definition of "chain of title" may triumph over the literal words of the recording act commonly occurs in subdivision development. In the archetypical example of this problem, O conveys parcel 1 to A, conveying with it a servitude of some sort (easement, real covenant, equitable servitude) in his retained property. Subsequently he conveys parcel 2 to B, in which he previously granted a servitude when he transferred parcel 1 to A. If B searches only for transactions affecting parcel 2, she will not find the previously conveyed servitude unless the deed to parcel 1 was indexed as affecting parcel 2. There are, in effect, two chains of title branching from a common root.

Which party can more easily avoid the loss in this situation, the owner of parcel 1 or of parcel 2? Note that the deed to A here was from O, a grantor in B's chain of title, so the problem faced by B may not be as unmanageable as in other cases. Nevertheless, in large subdivisions with hundreds of lots the search can still be very burdensome. Would a tract index resolve this problem? Why or why not?

The courts seem fairly split on this issue. See 6A R. Powell & P. Rohan, Powell on Real Property, ¶ 906[2][b][iii]; Bishop v. Rueff, chapter six below.

8. The problem raised by the subdivision hypothetical is often resolved through a finding that B had inquiry notice of A's claim. If B purchases a property that clearly has a driveway leading across it to a neighboring property, the purchaser can realistically be required to inquire as to whether the neighbor owns an easement. The concept of inquiry notice is somewhat more problematic when applied to restrictions on the use of property imposed by real covenants and equitable servitudes. Should a purchaser in a subdivision be held responsible for inquiring as to the possible existence of restrictions limiting the property to residential use simply because all properties in the subdivision are occupied with dwelling units? See Sanborn v. McLean, 233 Mich. 227, 206 N.W. 496, 60 A.L.R. 1212 (1925) (yes). Should the fact that all buildings in a subdivision are set back the same uniform distance from the street alert a purchaser to inquire regarding setback requirements?

9. The subdivision problem can easily be avoided. The subdivider can, for example, prior to subdividing the property, deed the entire subdivision to a straw and then back to himself with restrictions and easements attached. The servitudes are then easily discoverable in the chain of title of each purchaser in the subdivision. Alternatively, the subdivider can record a declaration of restrictions and reference it in every deed in the subdivision. Finally, in many jurisdictions he can record a plat for the subdivision, reciting restrictions and easements, which puts any purchaser of lots in the subdivision on notice of them. The paucity of cases in recent years raising the subdivision problem indicates that subdividers are in fact pursuing these strategies.

E. NOTICE

HATCHER v. HALL

Court of Appeals of Missouri, 1956.
292 S.W.2d 619.

STONE, JUDGE.

In this action for a declaratory judgment [ ], plaintiff seeks a determination of rights and status under a written agreement between C.E. and Helen Whartenby, as "lessors," and Melvin Hall (one of the defendants herein), as "lessee," dated July 1, 1941, and recorded in the office of the Recorder of Deeds of McDonald County, Missouri, on September 20, 1941. (Except as otherwise specifically stated, statutory references herein are to RSMo 1949, V.A.M.S.) By this agreement, the "lessors," for a recited consideration of "One Dollar and other valuable consideration," purported to "lease, grant, bargain and sell unto the lessee the exclusive right to furnish all gasoline and oil products to be sold at a certain filling station" on a described tract (hereinafter called "the tract") at Lanagan, McDonald County, Missouri (then owned by the Whartenbys and presently owned by plaintiff), "for a period of ten years from the date of this instrument," with the further provision that "at any time said station is no longer used * * * to dispense motor fuel and lubricants, then this agreement shall suspend during such discontinuance and if re-opened then this agreement shall be reinstated and the time that such station was not being operated shall not run against this lease." By its terms, the agreement was "binding upon any and all persons or corporations which take possession of said premises" and granted to the "lessee * * * prior rights to renew this agreement for a like period of time." Since the case was tried below and has been presented here on that theory, we assume for the purposes of this opinion (without, however, so deciding) that the agreement was an instrument "whereby * * * real estate may be affected" [Section 442.380], and that the obligation, which it purported to impose, might run with the land; and, adopting the terminology of the parties, we hereinafter refer to the agreement as "the lease."

Defendant Hall, a distributor of Phillips "66" products, supplied the filling station on the tract until the Whartenbys closed the station in September, 1946; but, the evidence is clear and undisputed that, when Gilbert F. Willard (joined as a defendant herein) purchased the tract on July 28, 1950, there were no pumps or "filling station equipment" on the tract, the abstract of title to the tract did not show the lease, and defendant Willard had no knowledge of it. As will become apparent from our subsequent discussion, we think it unnecessary to resolve the issue of credibility raised by the sharply-conflicting testimony as to whether Willard thereafter learned of the lease during the period of his ownership. "Right after" he purchased the tract, Willard leased a portion of it to one Norman Gast; and, under "a reseller's contract" with Gast, defendant Hall installed storage tanks, two pumps and some signs on the tract and supplied Phillips "66" products to Gast, who operated a filling station thereon from August 11, 1950, until he "went broke" about June 30, 1951.

When plaintiff purchased the tract from defendant Willard on May 15, 1952, a cafe and package liquor store were being operated on the tract, but the filling station was not in operation. The only description of the unused station equipment then on the tract came from plaintiff who said that there were "two abandoned pumps at the place," which "were broken down, doors off of them" and "weren't in condition to work," that there were "a couple of light globes, they were off," and that there was "a Phillips sign * * * at the other end of the property." At the time of his purchase, plaintiff was informed by Willard that Hall owned the filling station equipment on the tract. However, Willard also told plaintiff that he (Willard) had asked Hall "to come get those pumps"; and, in response to plaintiff's specific inquiry as to whether "Hall had any kind of lease whatsoever," Willard had replied, "No, he has not." The abstract of title still did not show the lease, and the conveyance by Willard to plaintiff made no reference thereto. Plaintiff first learned of the lease about two months after the date of his purchase of the tract, when defendant Hall notified plaintiff of his (Hall's) intention to enforce the lease. Upon the foregoing state of facts, the trial court found that plaintiff "had no actual knowledge or constructive notice of the lease" and that "the lease is not binding" upon the tract. Defendant Hall appeals.

The first issue is as to whether plaintiff, a subsequent purchaser of the tract, is charged with constructive notice of the lease by reason of its recordation on September 20, 1941. Plaintiff's position is that, for the reason (inter alia) that the acknowledgment was incomplete and insufficient, the lease was not entitled to record and that, therefore, recordation thereof did not impart constructive notice. The "acknowledgment" on the lease consists of the simple statement "Subscribed and sworn to before me this the 15th day of August, 1941," followed by the signature (without seal attached) of one "B.F. St. Clair," whose official status or position (if any) is not suggested and who remains utterly unidentified either in the lease or in the record before us.

We quickly recognize that the language of Section 442.210 (including the forms of acknowledgment which "may be used in * * * written instruments affecting real estate") is permissive and not mandatory, and we heartily endorse the salutary principle, which has found application in a variety of circumstances, that substantial compliance with statutory provisions pertaining to acknowledgments will suffice. But, although the law requires nothing more than such substantial compliance, it is satisfied with nothing less. And, since the power to take acknowledgments is derived from the statutory provisions pertaining thereto and acknowledgments may be taken only by a person designated by statute, [ ], we do not impose "hypercritical requirements of technical nicety" [ ] in concluding, as we do, that "no rational liberality of construction can cure" [ ] the patent defects in the "acknowledgment" to the lease in the instant case, which does not even indicate whether the individual purporting to take such "acknowledgment" in 1941 was a person then authorized so to do. Section 3408, RSMo 1939. Lacking an acknowledgment substantially complying with statutory requirements, the lease was not entitled to record [see Sections 442.380 and 59.330(1)], and recordation thereof did not impart constructive notice under Section 442.390 to plaintiff, a subsequent purchaser for value.

* * *

Finally, defendant Hall asserts that plaintiff's knowledge, when he purchased the tract, that Hall owned the filling station equipment thereon should have provoked further investigation which would have disclosed existence of the lease, and that, therefore, plaintiff is chargeable with actual notice thereof. It is true that, as our courts have reiterated many times, notice is regarded in law as actual where the person sought to be charged therewith either knows of the existence of the particular fact in question or is conscious of having the means of knowing it, even though such means may not be employed by him; and that, since notice does not mean positive information brought directly home to the person sought to be affected thereby, whatever fairly is sufficient to put an ordinarily prudent person on inquiry constitutes notice to him of such facts as would be disclosed by reasonable pursuit and proper inquiry. For, justice is not so indulgent as to encourage one to shut his eyes to circumstances which would excite the zetetic impulse in an ordinarily prudent individual [   ] or to throw away the key to the door of exploration through which the facts reasonably might be ascertained [   ]; and, from early times, our courts "have always recognized that the still small voice of suggestion, emanating as it will from contiguous facts and surrounding circumstances, pregnant with inference and provocative of inquiry, is as potent to impart notice as a presidential proclamation, or an army with banners." [   ]

However, one is put on inquiry and charged with notice of the facts which would be disclosed thereby, only when "the inquiry becomes a duty, and the failure to make it a negligent omission" [   ] or, as otherwise stated, "(w)here there is a duty of finding out and knowing, negligent ignorance has the same effect in law as actual knowledge." Whether the circumstances are sufficient to give rise to a duty of further inquiry is ordinarily a question of fact [at least where the evidence is conflicting or is such that more than one inference of fact might be drawn therefrom (Merrill on Notice, Vol. 1, Section 64, p. 61)], frequently fraught with appreciable difficulty and always determinable in the light of the circumstances of the particular case under consideration; and whether, when one is put on inquiry, the exercise of common prudence and ordinary diligence [   ] in further investigation would have led to discovery of the information, knowledge of which is sought to be charged, likewise usually becomes a question of fact.

Being mindful that one of these questions of fact necessarily was found in favor of plaintiff [   ] and that, in this court-tried case, "(t)he judgment shall not be set aside unless clearly erroneous, and due regard shall be given to the opportunity of the trial court to judge of the credibility of the witnesses" [ ], we would not be inclined, upon the record before us, to disagree with the finding of the capable trial judge that plaintiff did not have actual notice of the lease. However, we need not and do not rest disposition of the case on this basis alone, for, on the undisputed testimony, defendant Willard, who was plaintiff's immediate predecessor in title, acquired the tract on July 28, 1950, as a bona fide purchaser for value without notice, either actual or constructive, of the lease. "(I)t is a commonplace of the law of real property that an innocent purchaser for value takes the title discharged of secret outstanding equities * * * not of record, and that, having a good title himself, he can transfer one to a grantee who even had notice" [subject only to the exception that the title may not be conveyed] free from such equities, to a former owner charged with notice [ ], the classic statement of the reason for the rule, in the words of Chancellor Kent, being "to prevent a stagnation of property, and because the first purchaser, being entitled to hold and enjoy, must be equally entitled to sell." Thus, the title to the tract being clear of "silent, unknown equities" when defendant Willard purchased in 1950 remained clear thereafter [ ] and so descended to plaintiff, a purchaser for value, irrespective of whether he had actual notice of the lease at the time of his acquisition.

The judgment of the trial court should be and is affirmed.

Notes and Questions

1. The "shelter rule," relied on by the court in *Hatcher v. Hall,* is a powerful tool for resolving recording act disputes. If O conveys to A, who fails to record, and then to B, who takes without notice (and in a race or race-notice jurisdiction records before A), it does not matter that C, a subsequent purchaser from B, has actual, constructive, or inquiry notice of A's claim. C is sheltered by B's good title.

2. Most states require that prior to recordation, an instrument affecting title to property must be witnessed or acknowledged. Some jurisdictions further require seals or transfer stamps. Where documents do not comply with these recording technicalities, they have no standing of record and do not give constructive notice to subsequent purchasers. See 4 American Law of Property, §§ 17.27, 17.31 (J. Casner ed. 1952).

3. If Hatcher (or his attorney) had discovered the improperly acknowledged lease while searching the title to the property, would he have actual notice of it, and not be able to claim bona fide purchaser status? Alternatively, would his actual discovery of the defectively acknowledged lease put him on inquiry notice of Hall's claim, i.e. would he have a duty to inquire as to the validity of Hall's claim? How would Hatcher's status be affected if Willard had actually discovered the improperly acknowledged lease? Does the language of the recording acts set out above help with this problem? See 6A R. Powell & P. Rohan, Powell on Real Property, ¶ 906[1]; Philbrick, Limits

of Record Search and Therefore of Notice, 93 U.Pa.L.Rev. 125 at 281–296 (1944).

4. Recorded documents actually reviewed by a title examiner may also, in some instances, give notice of unrecorded claims. If a recorded document, for example, refers specifically to an unrecorded mortgage, or to a mortgage recorded outside of the purchaser's chain of title, most jurisdictions would hold the purchaser to a duty of inquiry to determine the status of the mortgage. Specific reference in a recorded interest to a deed on a specific date between two specific parties should probably excite the curiosity of a title examiner to determine whether such a document ever existed, and, if so, whether it supports an existing claim to the property. Many deeds, however, contain general exceptions such as "subject to existing encumbrances." Do such phrases give notice of anything? More specific statements such as "subject to existing mortgages" or "excepting so much of the described premises as have been heretofore conveyed" are more problematic. Though cases have imposed a duty of inquiry where such phrases appear in recorded documents, such decisions obviously have potential for undermining the protection the recording acts are supposed to afford subsequent purchasers. Thus some reform statutes take approaches similar to that of the Uniform Simplification of Land Transfers Act § 3–207(a):

> Unless a reference in a document is a reference to another document by its record location, a person by reason of the reference is not charged with knowledge of the document or an adverse claim founded thereon, and the document is not in the record chain of title by reason of the reference to it.

5. A purchaser of real property cannot rest secure even with a completely clear title examination unless the property itself has also been inspected. Signs of possession of the property inconsistent with the record should stimulate the "zetetic impulse" of potential purchasers as to adverse claims. Thus a purchaser is held, in most jurisdictions, to have inquiry notice of any claims that could have been discovered by an inspection of the premises.

Possession by a tenant in many jurisdictions gives notice, not only of the tenant's interest under her lease, but also of any other claims the tenant may have, such as the option in the principal case. Moreover, possession not only gives notice of the claim of the possessor, but also of those through whom the possessor claims. Thus, possession by a tenant gives notice of the landlord's title, possession by a vendee under an installment sales contract gives notice of the vendor's title. Possession consistent with the record, however, does not give notice of unrecorded claims of the party in possession. Thus, possession of property by a wife as a tenant in common with her husband under a recorded deed does not put a purchaser on notice of the fact that she also claims under an unrecorded quitclaim deed from the husband of his interest. Ildvedsen v. First State Bank, 24 N.D. 227, 139 N.W. 105 (1912). Possession is not limited to human occupancy. A form of possession adequate to ground a claim for adverse possession is likely also to be sufficient to put a purchaser on inquiry notice of a claim to the property.

6. Assume O conveys to A and B as tenants in common by deed which is properly recorded. Thereafter, A conveys his undivided one-half interest as

tenant in common to B, his logical purchaser. Although B fails to record, he immediately goes into possession of the entire property. Next, A unscrupulously conveys his interest for the second time to C, a purchaser for value who both searches the land records and inspects the property, finding B in possession. Who prevails as between C and B? Is B's possession of the property inconsistent with the status of record title so as to charge C with inquiry notice of the prior transfer of A's interest to B?

7. In Obernay v. Chamberlin, 506 S.W.2d 446 (Mo. 1974), a married couple sold property to the wife's parents who went into possession but failed to record the deed. Subsequently, the couple executed a mortgage to a lender as security for a loan. When the loan went into default, the lender commenced proceedings to foreclose the mortgage. The parents filed suit to enjoin the foreclosure, claiming the lender was charged with inquiry notice of their prior interest in the property by reason of their possession. The evidence showed that the mortgagee had no actual knowledge of the parents' title. The son-in-law had told the lender that his in-laws lived on the property paying a nominal rent. The mortgagee had driven by the property but made no effort to interview the occupants. The Missouri Supreme Court held *en banc* that possession of the property under these circumstances is insufficient to charge the mortgagee with notice so as to upset its priority. Some commentators believe the case stands for the proposition that the inquiry form of notice is not recognized in Missouri. Do you believe this is a correct interpretation of the court's decision?

REVIEW PROBLEMS

For each of the three problems which follow, state how your answer would differ depending upon whether the jurisdiction had enacted a race, notice or race-notice recording statute.

1. O conveyed Blackacre to A by warranty deed. A did not record her deed or occupy Blackacre. O subsequently died, leaving all his property to H, who then conveyed Blackacre to B by quit claim deed for good and valuable consideration. B knew nothing of the earlier conveyance to A, and did not record. Who owns Blackacre?

2. On Monday, O conveyed Blackacre to A. A never recorded his deed. On Tuesday, A conveyed Blackacre to B who recorded his deed immediately. On Wednesday, O conveyed Blackacre to C who recorded his deed immediately. Assuming that A, B and C were bona fide purchasers for value, how is a court likely to decide C's quiet title action against B?

3. Owner conveyed Blackacre to A on August 1 and A recorded on November 1. Owner also conveyed Blackacre to B on October 1. B recorded immediately. In that same year, B conveyed Blackacre to C on December 1. C recorded immediately. Neither B nor C had actual notice of Owner's conveyance to A. However, A had posted "No Trespass" notices (signed by A) on Blackacre promptly upon acquiring title from Owner. Assuming that all deeds were delivered for valuable consideration, how is a court likely to decide A's quiet title action against C?

F. TITLE RECORD REFORM

It should be clear by now that public title recording systems, as they have evolved in America, are far from perfect. An A may not be protected by the system, even if she promptly records her interest in a property, if: (i) a recording technicality is not properly complied with; (ii) the interest is not properly indexed (in some jurisdictions); or (iii) the record of the interest, for whatever reason, falls outside of the chain of title of a subsequent B. Bs are even more at risk of prior interests recorded outside of their chain of title or not subject to the recording acts.

Several approaches have been proposed, and to varying extents adopted, for improving the protections afforded property owners by public recording systems. First, a variety of statutes address specific defects such as defective acknowledgments, or problematic interests such as ancient mortgages or rights of entry and possibilities of reverter. More radical reform is offered by the marketable title acts, which attempt to set a statutory limit to the scope of a search necessary to identify interests affecting a piece of property, and eliminate interests recorded outside such a limited search. Finally, the most radical reform is title registration, which attempts to make the title records the sole and authoritative source of authentic title.

1. Specific Statutory Reform

Among the most basic of title reforms are curative acts. A curative act is "a form of retroactive legislation which reaches back into the past to operate upon past events, acts or transactions in order to correct errors and irregularities and to render valid and effective many attempted acts which would otherwise be ineffective for the purpose intended." Bayse, Clearing Land Titles § 201 (2d ed. 1970). Curative acts are generally aimed at specific types of commonly occurring mistakes and errors, and normally operate by validating acts taken before a certain date. Often they address trivial problems that are unlikely to result in litigation, but nevertheless clog commerce in real estate as overly scrupulous or anxious lawyers "fly-speck" a title.

One of the most common problems addressed by curative acts is that of formalities of recorded instruments, such as defective acknowledgments or missing seals. The Ohio statute is typical:

Ohio Rev. Code § 5301.07

When any instrument conveying real estate, or any interest therein, is of record for more than twenty-one years * * * and the record shows that there is a defect in such instrument, such instrument and the record thereof shall be cured of such defect and be effective in all respects as if such instrument had been legally made, executed, and acknowledged, if such defect is due to any one or more of the following:

(A) Such instrument was not properly witnessed.

(B) Such instrument contained no certificate of acknowledgment.

(C) The certificate of acknowledgment was defective in any respect.

Curative acts also address defects regarding the capacity of the parties to an instrument or the interests of persons not explicitly parties to the instrument. Examples of such defects include improper exercise of powers of attorney, conveyances by corporate officers which are not properly authorized or not signed in representative capacity, conveyances by trustees, executors, or foreclosing mortgagees not fully complying with proper formalities, and conveyances without proper release of dower or homestead rights by the grantor's spouse. See Bayse, supra §§ 261–355. These defects are often not apparent from the face of the record, and are thus troublesome to a purchaser who desires a perfectly secure title. With respect to these problems, curative acts usually provide that if the defect is not raised to challenge the rights of a subsequent purchaser within a specified period of time, it cannot be raised thereafter.

Other statutes aim at specific troublesome interests. One common target of such statutes is ancient mortgages. Prior to this century, property was often purchased with borrowed money secured by short-term lump-sum mortgages. In time these mortgages were usually paid off, but often no formal discharge was recorded. Moreover, when mortgages were not paid off in a timely manner, payment was often extended through extension agreements or partial payment. Agreed-upon extensions were often not reflected on the record. Although suit on a mortgage is eventually barred by the statute of limitations, partial payment during the statutory period may extend the limitations period. As a result, within the title chains of many properties in the United States are found ancient mortgages of uncertain legal status. Ancient mortgage statutes address this problem, See Bayse, supra, ch. 5. The Oklahoma statute is a good example of such legislation:

Okl.St.Ann. tit. 46 § 301

A. Before November 1, 2001, no suit, action or proceeding to foreclose or otherwise enforce the remedies in any mortgage, contract for deed or deed of trust shall be had or maintained after the expiration of ten (10) years from the date the last maturing obligation secured by such mortgage, contract for deed or deed of trust becomes due as set out therein, and such mortgage, contract for deed or deed of trust shall cease to be a lien, unless the holder of such mortgage, contract for deed or deed of trust either:

* * *

2. After October 1, 1981, and within the above described ten-year period, files or causes to be filed of record a written notice of extension * * *

* * *

C. No suit, action or proceeding to foreclose or otherwise enforce the remedies in any mortgage, contract for deed or deed of trust filed of record in the office of the county clerk, in which the due date of the last maturing obligation secured by such mortgage, contract for deed or deed of trust cannot be ascertained from the written terms thereof, shall be had or maintained after the expiration of thirty (30) years from the date of recording of the mortgage, contract for deed or deed of trust, and said mortgage, contract for deed or deed of trust shall cease to be a lien, unless the holder of such mortgage, contract for deed or deed of trust either:

* * *

2. After October 1, 1981, and within the above described thirty-year period, files or causes to be filed of record a written Notice of Maturity Date * * *

* * *

E. Any mortgage, contract for deed or deed of trust barred under this section shall not be a defect in determining marketable record title.

Similar statutes address the problem of ancient possibilities of reverter and rights of entry. As you remember, these interests are not subject to the rule against perpetuities and thus can persist almost indefinitely. Statutes limiting such interests take several different approaches. Some of the earlier statutes barred covenants, conditions and restrictions of "merely nominal, and of no actual and substantial benefit," Minn.Stat.Ann. § 500.20, effectively applying the equitable "changed conditions doctrine" to such interests. Other statutes bar such interests absolutely after a period of time, or bar such interests if not rerecorded within a statutory period. Unlike ancient repaid or abandoned mortgages, reversionary interests often serve an ongoing purpose in restricting land to a specific charitable or public purpose. Some state courts have therefore held statutes cutting them off to be unconstitutional as denying due process or impairing contract rights, Board of Educ. v. Miles, 15 N.Y.2d 364, 259 N.Y.S.2d 129, 207 N.E.2d 181 (1965); Biltmore Village v. Royal, 71 So.2d 727 (Fla.1954). Other courts have held that the goal of protecting land from stale interests that unreasonably restrict the use of that land to be sufficiently important to justify such legislation, Trustees of Schools v. Batdorf, 6 Ill.2d 486, 130 N.E.2d 111 (1955); Presbytery of Southeast Iowa v. Harris, 226 N.W.2d 232 (Iowa 1975).

2. *Marketable Title Acts*

By the mid-twentieth century, advocates of conveyancing reform realized that piece-meal solutions were not adequate. The increasing frequency and variety of recorded interests affecting land made traditional title searches more cumbersome and less certain. What was needed was a new approach; one that would radically cut off dormant and outdated interests and limit the period of necessary search. See Aigler, Clearance of Land Titles—A Statutory Step, 44 Mich.L.Rev. 45

(1945); Basye, Trends and Progress—The Marketable Title Acts, 47 Iowa L.Rev. 261 (1962); Cribbet, Conveyancing Reform, 35 N.Y.U.L.Rev. 1291 (1960). In response to this need, a number of states enacted marketable title legislation. These formed the basis for the Model Marketable Title Act, drafted by Professor Lewis Simes and Charles Taylor in conjunction with the Michigan Research Project. L. Simes and C. Taylor, The Improvement of Conveyancing by Legislation (1960). The Ohio statute, like that of most states that have adopted a marketable title act, tracks this Model to a considerable extent.

OHIO REV. CODE §§ 5301.47 ET SEQ.

§ 5301.47   Definitions

As used in sections 5301.47 to 5301.56, inclusive, of the Revised Code:

(A) "Marketable record title" means a title of record, as indicated in section 5301.48 of the Revised Code, which operates to extinguish such interests and claims, existing prior to the effective date of the root of title, as are stated in section 5301.50 of the Revised Code.

(B) "Records" includes probate and other official public records, as well as records in the office of the recorder of the county in which all or part of the land is situate.

(C) "Recording," when applied to the official public records of the probate or other court, includes filing.

(D) "Person dealing with land" includes a purchaser of any estate or interest therein, a mortgagee, levying or attaching creditor, a land contract vendee, or any other person seeking to acquire an estate or interest therein, or impose a lien thereon.

(E) "Root of title" means that conveyance or other title transaction in the chain of title of a person, purporting to create the interest claimed by such person, upon which he relies as a basis for the marketability of his title, and which was the most recent to be recorded as of a date forty years prior to the time when marketability is being determined. The effective date of the "root of title" is the date on which it is recorded.

(F) "Title transaction" means any transaction affecting title to any interest in land, including title by will or descent, title by tax deed, or by trustee's, assignee's, guardian's, executor's, administrator's, or sheriff's deed, or decree of any court, as well as warranty deed, quit claim deed, or mortgage.

* * *

§ 5301.48   Unbroken chain of title; determination

Any person having the legal capacity to own land in this state, who has an unbroken chain of title of record to any interest in land for forty years or more, has a marketable record title to such interest as defined in section 5301.47 of the Revised Code, subject to the matters stated in section 5301.49 of the Revised Code.

A person has such an unbroken chain of title when the official public records disclose a conveyance or other title transaction, of record not less than forty years at the time the marketability is to be determined, which said conveyance or other title transaction purports to create such interest, either in:

(A) The person claiming such interest; or

(B) Some other person from whom, by one or more conveyances or other title transactions of record, such purported interest has become vested in the person claiming such interest; with nothing appearing of record, in either case, purporting to divest such claimant of such purported interest.

* * *

§ 5301.49   Limitations on record marketable title

Such record marketable title shall be subject to:

(A) All interests and defects which are inherent in the muniments of which such chain of record title is formed; provided that a general reference in such muniments, or any of them, to easements, use restrictions, or other interests created prior to the root of title shall not be sufficient to preserve them, unless specific identification be made therein of a recorded title transaction which creates such easement, use restriction, or other interest; * * *;

(B) All interests preserved by the filing of proper notice or by possession by the same owner continuously for a period of forty years or more, in accordance with section 5301.51 of the Revised Code;

(C) the rights of any person arising from a period of adverse possession or user, which was in whole or in part subsequent to the effective date of the root of title;

(D) Any interest arising out of a title transaction which has been recorded subsequent to the effective date of the root of title from which the unbroken chain of title or record is started; provided that such recording shall not revive or give validity to any interest which has been extinguished prior to the time of the recording by the operation of section 5301.50 of the Revised Code;

(E) The exceptions stated in section 5301.53 of the Revised Code.

§ 5301.50   Prior interests

Subject to the matters stated in section 5301.49 of the Revised Code, such record marketable title shall be held by its owner and shall be taken by any person dealing with the land free and clear of all interests, claims, or charges whatsoever, the existence of which depends upon any act, transaction, event, or omission that occurred prior to the effective date of the root of title. All such interests, claims, or charges, however denominated, whether legal or equitable, present or future, whether such interests, claims, or charges are asserted by a person sui juris or under a disability, whether such person is within or without the state, whether such person is natural or corporate, or is private or governmental, are hereby declared to be null and void.

§ 5301.51   Preservation of interests

(A) Any person claiming an interest in land may preserve and keep effective the interest by filing for record during the forty-year period immediately following the effective date of the root of title of the person whose record title would otherwise be marketable, a notice in compliance with section 5301.52 of the Revised Code. No disability or lack of knowledge of any kind on the part of anyone suspends the running of the forty-year period. * * *

(B) If the same record owner of any possessory interest in land has been in possession of the land continuously for a period of forty years or more, during which period no title transaction with respect to such interest appears of record in his chain of title, and no notice has been filed by him on his behalf as provided in division (A) of this section, and such possession continues to the time when marketability is being determined, the period of possession is equivalent to the filing of the notice immediately preceding the termination of the forty-year period described in division (A) of this section.

§ 5301.52   Contents and filing of notice; false statements

* * *

(B) The notice shall be filed for record in the office of the recorder of the county or counties where the land described in it is situated. The recorder of each county shall accept all such notices presented to him which describe land situated in the county in which he serves, shall enter and record them in the deed records of that county, and shall index each notice in the grantee deed index under the names of the claimants appearing in that notice and in the grantor deed index under the names of the record owners appearing in that notice. Such notices also shall be indexed under the description of the real estate involved in a book set apart for that purpose to be known as the "Notice Index." Each recorder may charge the same fees for the recording of such notices as are charged for recording deeds.

* * *

---

§ 5301.53   provides that the Marketable Title Act shall not extinguish any lessor or reversioner following a lease, any railroad or public utility easement, and "easement or interest in the nature of an easement, the existence of which is clearly observable by physical evidence of its use"; easements, visible or invisible, for any "pipe, valve, road, wire, cable, conduit, duct, sewer, track, pole, tower, or other physical facility;" interests in coal; mortgages recorded by railroads, public utilities or government corporations; or interests of the United States, Ohio, or any of its political subdivisions.

Notes and Questions

1. The basic concept of marketable title acts is elegantly simple: The title examiner need only search the title indices back for 40 (or 30 or 50) years and then prior to that point to the "root of title," the most recently recorded instrument prior to that time purporting to transfer the interest in which the examiner is interested. The examiner thereafter need only concern herself with interests created subsequent to the root of title; all prior interests are nullified.

For example, assume O transferred Blackacre to X in 1948 and that X recorded this transfer. O then transferred the same interest again to Y in 1949, Y also recording. Under the common law, and under any form of recording act, X prevails over Y. Under the marketable title acts, however, as of 1990, Y would have marketable title as the most recently recorded interest prior to 1950 (1990—40 years), and X's interest would be nullified.

2. Like Hydra, however, title defects are not so easily slain. The interests of some property claimants are simply too powerful or sympathetic to be cut off summarily simply because they are more than 40 years old. First, note that § 5301.53 exempts a host of prior interests. One can certainly understand why the legislature would be hesitant to cut off these interests, but if a title examiner stops after a 40–year search, will she find them?

Second, any claimant of an interest more than 40 years old can preserve it by filing a notice of the interest within the 40 year period immediately following the root of title. This is certainly sensible. If an interest is of value, there ought to be a means to preserving it for more than 40 years. But, how will the title examiner discover such a claim in a jurisdiction that depends on grantor-grantee indices? (Do you see how this problem is solved by a tract index?) Section 5301.52 provides for indexing the claim under the name of the claimant in the grantee index and under the name of the record owner in the grantor index. If we return to our earlier example, however, if X records a properly drafted notice of his claim to the property in 1987, the interest will be indexed under X's name in the grantor indices, and will not be discoverable by an examiner searching only Y's chain back to the root of title in 1990. See Barnett, Marketable Title Acts: Panacea or Pandemonium? 53 Cornell L.Rev. 45, 81–83 (1967).

Third, what is meant by a defect "inherent in the muniments of which such chain of record title is formed"? If the root of title deed to Y is forged, or executed by one without capacity, does X remain the owner, even though a search terminating at the root of title will not discover X's interest? See Barnett, supra, 67–69.

It is not hard to imagine clients and associations of clients approaching legislatures with proposals to shorten the time for title searches and to cut off interests that do not appear of record. It is not hard to imagine lawyers appearing before legislative committees in support of such legislation—sometimes in the public interest, sometimes in the interest of lawyers, and sometimes for clients (e.g., title insurance companies or land developers). And it is not hard to imagine that lawyers appearing for clients, as lobbyists for legislation, are paid for their efforts and their time. It is not too hard to imagine such a lawyer arguing for legislation he does not much believe in. (Would that raise a moral problem that the adversary ethic in court does not raise?)

When an appearance before a legislative committee, by a lawyer, is not clearly in one of these capacities rather than the others, do sound morals (or for that matter rules of ethics) require a lawyer to identify the capacity in which she appears and to reveal whether she is being paid for the appearance? John P. Frank, "The Legal Ethics of Louis D. Brandeis," 17 Stanford Law Review 707 (1965), discusses an array of cases that became sources of criticism by the Senate committee that considered President Wilson's nomination of Mr. Brandeis to be a Supreme Court justice. Most of these cases came up in Mr. Brandeis's busy law practice in Boston. One or two involved lobbying for legislation; in one case when he was in the employ of the Shoe Manufacturers' Alliance in Massachusetts: The accusation there, in the Senate, was that he "made believe that he was appearing . . . in the public interest and without pay when he was acting directly for and in the interest of private individuals." This charge was false, as Judge Frank demonstrates from the record; Mr. Brandeis had said he was appearing in his own behalf and for his client, and he identified his client. Nonetheless, Judge Frank let himself imagine that the charge was not false and opined that it would not have violated either ethical rules or sound morals for Mr. Brandeis to fail to mention that he had a client, nor to mention that he was being paid to appear. Do you agree on these points—(a) representative capacity or (b) fee or (c) both? Maybe R.P.C. 3.9 helps: "A lawyer representing a client before a legislative body or administrative agency in a nonadjudicative proceeding shall disclose that the appearance is in a representative capacity and shall conform to the provisions of Rule 3.3(a) through (c) [candor and truthfulness], 3.4 (a) through (c) [fairness, truthfulness, rules of tribunal] and 3.5 [decorum]."

Note that there is a professional tradition that forbids a lawyer to "vouch" for her client. E.g.: "A lawyer shall not . . . in a trial . . . state a personal opinion as to the justness of a cause, the credibility of a witness, the culpability of a civil litigant or the guilt or innocence of an accused." R.P.C. Rule 3.4(e). See Thomas L. Shaffer, "The Legal Profession's Rule Against Vouching for Clients: Advocacy and 'The Manner That Is the Man Himself,'" 7 Notre Dame Journal of Law, Ethics and Public Policy 145 (1993). Should that rule apply when a lawyer appears for a client in a legislative hearing?

3.   Finally, what is the meaning of Ohio Rev.Code § 5301.49(D)?

HEIFNER v. BRADFORD

Supreme Court of Ohio, 1983.
4 Ohio St.3d 49, 446 N.E.2d 440.

In 1916, Elvira Sprague and her husband, owners in fee simple of a tract of real estate located in Monroe Township, Muskingum County, conveyed their interest by deed to Fred H. Waters. By this instrument, the grantors reserved the oil and gas rights in the land. This transaction was recorded in Muskingum County that same year.

Elvira Sprague died testate in Tuscarawas County in 1931. Her will was probated in Tuscarawas County and devised the reserved oil and gas rights in the land equally to her two daughters, Lottie E. Rogers and Sarah A. Bradford.

In 1936, Fred H. Waters and his wife, without mention of the reservation of the oil and gas rights, conveyed the property by warranty deed to Charles B. Waters, Emma M. Waters, Sarah K. Waters, and William H. Waters. This conveyance was recorded in 1936.

An authenticated copy of Elvira Sprague's will was filed in Muskingum County in 1957. In accordance with the terms of the will, an affidavit of transfer was filed and recorded in Muskingum County evidencing the transfer of the oil and gas rights by inheritance from Elvira Sprague to her daughters. However, both Lottie E. Rogers and Sarah A. Bradford had died intestate prior to this transfer. Thus, Lottie E. Rogers' one-half share in the oil and gas rights was divided equally among her four children and Sarah A. Bradford's share was equally divided among her three children. These conveyances were evidenced by affidavits of transfer which were duly recorded in Muskingum County in 1957.

In 1980, Charles B. Waters et al. conveyed their interest in the property to William H. Waters and his wife Shirley S. Waters.

Appellants, Charlotte Heifner, Jean Stewart and Doris Schaevitz, own three undivided fractional shares of the oil and gas rights in the property. Appellants instituted this action in the court of common pleas seeking to quiet title and partition the undivided fractional shares in the oil and gas rights. Defendants represent the remaining fractional oil and gas rights owners, as well as the record surface owner, William H. and Shirley S. Waters.

Relevant to this appeal, the record surface owners claim also to be owners of the oil and gas rights in the land contrary to the claim of appellants. Appellees, William H. and Shirley S. Waters, base their claim upon an operation of R.C. 5301.47 through 5301.56, Ohio's Marketable Title Act.

Upon appellants' motion for summary judgment, the trial court ruled that appellants were owners of the oil and gas rights and ordered a partition of the undivided fractional interests. The court of appeals reversed, holding that the Marketable Title Act operated to extinguish appellants' interest and vest complete ownership of the property in William S. and Shirley H. Waters.[15]

The cause is now before this court upon the allowance of a motion to certify the record.

* * *

Frank D. Celebrezze, Chief Justice.

This case involves a controversy between independent competing claims of ownership to the oil and gas rights in a particular tract of land. For purposes of this decision, appellants are the purported owners of the oil and gas rights while appellees are the undisputed owners of the surface land. The question involved is one of first impression in this state and deals exclusively with the operation of R.C. 5301.47 through 5301.56, otherwise known as the Ohio Marketable Title Act. The issue presented by this appeal is whether appellees, who have an unbroken chain of title of record of forty years or more, have a marketable record title even though appellants' competing interest arose from an independent chain of title recorded during the forty-year period subsequent to appellees' root of title.

At the outset, the Marketable Title Act sets forth several definitions germane to the instant cause. R.C. 5301.47(A) defines "marketable record title" as a "title of record, as indicated in section 5301.48 of the Revised Code, which operates to extinguish such interests and claims, existing prior to the effective date of the root of title * * *." A "root of title" is defined in subsection (E) as "that conveyance or other title transaction in the chain of title of a person, upon which he relies as a basis for the marketability of his title, and which was the most recent to be recorded as of a date forty years prior to the time when marketability is being determined. * * * "Subsection (F) defines "title transaction" as "any transaction affecting title to any interest in land, including title by will or descent * * *."

R.C. 5301.48 provides that one "who has an unbroken chain of title of record to any interest in land for forty years or more, has a marketable record title to such interest * * * subject to the matters stated in section 5301.49 of the Revised Code."

In relevant part, R.C. 5301.49 states:

"Such record marketable title shall be subject to:

" * * *

---

15. The trial court distributed the oil and gas interests as follows:

Charlotte Heifner an undivided 1/8

Jean Stewart an undivided 1/8

Doris Schaevitz an undivided 1/6

Lane S. Bradford an undivided 1/6

Jeanne Weaver Reed an undivided 1/12

Edith Morris Rogers an undivided 1/4

Charles Weaver an undivided 1/12

Further, the determination by the trial court with respect to the fractionalization of the oil and gas ownership is not before us.

"(D) Any interest arising out of a title transaction which has been recorded subsequent to the effective date of the root of title from which the unbroken chain of title of record is started; provided that such recording shall not revive or give validity to any interest which has been extinguished prior to the time of the recording * * *."

Appellants' root of title is the 1916 deed from Elvira Sprague and her husband to Fred H. Waters which reserved to the grantors the oil and gas rights in the land. Appellees' root of title is the 1936 conveyance from Fred H. Waters and his wife to Charles B. Waters, Emma M. Waters, Sarah K. Waters, and William H. Waters which failed to mention the reservation of oil and gas rights. Consequently, unless subject to R.C. 5301.49, appellees hold a marketable record title to the oil and gas rights, as well as title to the surface land, by virtue of having an "unbroken chain" of record title for over forty years which extinguishes prior claims and interests, including that of appellants. R.C. 5301.47(A) and 5301.48.

The Act defines a "title transaction" to include the passage of "title by will or descent." Thus, the 1957 conveyance of the oil and gas rights which passed under the terms of Elvira Sprague's will must be considered a "title transaction" under R.C. 5301.49(D).

Appellees argue that we should construe R.C. 5301.49(D) to require that a title transaction under that section arise from the same chain of title as that under which there is claimed to be a marketable record title. For the reasons to follow, we feel the proper construction should be otherwise.

Ohio's Marketable Title Act is taken primarily from the Model Marketable Title Act.[16] In fact, R.C. 5301.49(D) is virtually identical to Section 2(d) of the Model Act.1[17] This being the case, we are convinced that the General Assembly and the drafters of the Model Act intended that a title transaction under R.C. 5301.49(D) and Section 2(d), respectively, may be part of an entirely independent chain of title.

In Simes & Taylor, Model Title Standards (1960) 32, the drafters of the Model Act proposed comprehensive model title standards to accompany the Model Act. Standard 4.10 states:

"The recording of an instrument of conveyance subsequent to the effective date of the root of title has the same effect in preserving any interest conveyed as the filing of the notice provided for in § 4 of the Act. (See § 2[d] of the Model Act.)"

Perhaps more significant is the comment to the above standard which provides that, "[t]his standard is operative both where there are claims under a single chain of title and where there are two or more independent chains of title." Id. (Emphasis added.)

---

16. The Model Marketable Title Act was first proposed in Simes & Taylor, The Improvement of Conveyancing by Legislation (1960).

17. Bayse, Clearing Land Titles (1970) 378, Section 174.

Moreover, the Ohio Standards of Title Examination drafted and adopted by the Ohio State Bar Association have embraced an identical approach. See 55 Ohio Bar No. 19 (May 10, 1982), at page 763.

Hence, we are satisfied that R.C. 5301.49(D) ought to be construed in the manner that Simes and Taylor, as drafters of Section 2(d) of the Model Act, intended.[18] Accordingly, a "marketable title," as defined in R.C. 5301.47(A) and 5301.48, is subject to an interest arising out of a "title transaction" under R.C. 5301.49(D) which may be part of an independent chain of title. Further, the effect of R.C. 5301.49(D) is identical to that obtained by the filing of a preservation notice. R.C. 5301.51 provides for the preservation of interests by the filing of a notice of claim during the forty-year period. As a result, the recording of a "title transaction" under R.C. 5301.47(F) and 5301.49(D) is equivalent to the filing of a notice of claim during the forty-year period as specified in R.C. 5301.51 and 5301.52.12[19]

Thus, the 1957 conveyance under the terms of Elvira Sprague's will was a "title transaction" within the meaning of R.C. 5301.49(D), and

---

18. Appellees contend, however, that under the present grantor-grantee indexing system, in order to locate title transactions in an independent chain of title, the title examiner will have to search the title to its origin and then forward to discover such transactions. It is appellees' position that the purpose of the Act is to limit title searches to forty years.

The approach taken by the court of appeals and advanced by the appellees is not without support. See Barnett, Marketable Title Acts—Panacea or Pandemonium? 53 Cornell L.Rev. 45, 54–56 (1967). However, we are left unpersuaded by Professor Barnett's analysis. Initially, Barnett concedes his approach is contrary to that of the drafters of the Model Act [Barnett, supra, at page 89, fn. 122] and, further, Barnett views the purpose of marketable title acts solely to shorten title examinations. Barnett, at page 91.

We are not inclined to view the purpose of the Marketable Title Act so narrowly. The Supreme Court of Florida in Miami v. St. Joe Paper Co. (Fla.1978), 364 So.2d 439, 442, aptly stated that the purpose of marketable title acts is three-fold:

"The Marketable Record Title Act is a comprehensive plan for reform in conveyancing procedures. * * *

"The Marketable Record Title Act is also a statute of limitations in that it requires state demands to be asserted within a reasonable time after a cause of action has accrued. * * *

"The Marketable Record Title Act is also a recording act in that it provides for a simple and easy method by which the owner of an existing old interest may preserve it. If he fails to take the step of filing the notice as provided, he has only himself to blame if his interest is extinguished. The legislature did not intend to arbitrarily wipe out old claims and interests without affording a means of preserving them and giving a reasonable period of time within which to take the necessary steps to accomplish that purpose." [ ]

19. This precise conclusion was reached by the Supreme Court of Oklahoma in Allen v. Farmers Union Co–Operative Royalty Co. (Okl.1975), 538 P.2d 204, 209, in interpreting similar provisions of Oklahoma's Marketable Record Title Act.

We do recognize, as a practical matter, the difficulty faced by title examiners in locating these title transactions in a common title examination. We note that the General Assembly has mandated a "Notice Index" by which notices under R.C. 5301.51 are indexed under the description of the real estate. R.C. 5301.52. It would seem consistent to similarly require such an indexing procedure of at least the title transactions falling under R.C. 5301.49(D). See Webster, The Quest for Clear Land Titles—Making Land Title Searches Shorter and Surer in North Carolina via Marketable Title Legislation, 44 N.C.L.Rev. 89, 108–109 and 122 (1965). However, that is in the nature of a legislative determination beyond the scope of our consideration.

appellants' interest was not extinguished by operation of the Marketable Title Act. Accordingly, the judgment of the court of appeals is reversed.

Judgment reversed.

Notes and Questions

1.   How extensive a search must a title examiner conduct to discover subsequently recorded interests under § 5301.49(D)? Is the search any less extensive than that necessary before the marketable title act was adopted? See Charles B. Allott, The New Marketable Title Act—Will It Chase the Clouds Away in Rhode Island?, R.I. B.J., November 1995, at 7, 8 ("When each of these exceptions are reviewed closely it becomes clear that the Act will change the nature and extent of the title search, but it will not nullify the need for a traditional 50–year search," even though the Act tries to limit search to 40 years). If the Marketable Title Act does not, in fact, significantly limit the extent of the search necessary to assure perfect record title, is it therefore of no value? Is it more difficult to find or to clear up problematic interests?

2.   Marketable Title Acts also have the potential for terminating property interests that can present sympathetic arguments for preservation. Returning to our original hypothetical, for example, X's interest in the property certainly seems worthy of some protection. What can X do to protect his claim?

First, X can possess the property continuously for 40 years or more, during which no title transactions appear in his chain of title and no notice is filed by another claimant. Apparently, however, if X transfers his interest to another during the 40–year period, the interest may be extinguished by Y's subsequently recorded interest, even if X and his grantee are continuously in possession. Alternatively, the marketable title acts of some states preserve interests carried on the real property tax roles for three years prior to the time marketability is to be determined. This serves to protect fee interests, but will not protect interests such as mortgages or servitudes ordinarily not subject to real estate taxes.

X can, of course, record a notice of his interest, but if he has no knowledge of Y's claim, what would cause him to do this? Assume, moreover, that the interest to be preserved is not a fee, but rather an equitable servitude imposing restrictions in favor of each lot owner in a 250–lot planned subdivision against each other lot owner. Must each lot owner record a notice in the chain of each other lot owner in the subdivision to preserve the planned, restricted, nature of the community?

X   can also establish title through adverse possession under § 5301.49(C). When is such adverse possession established however? Does this exception help if interests are not possessory?

Finally, X's interest may be preserved under § 5301.49(A) if it is noted in the muniments of title of contrary chains. Note, however, that even though every deed in the chain of title states that it is subject to a specific interest (for example a possibility of reverter) held by a specific person but antedating the root of title, that interest will nevertheless be nullified if the documents do not also specify where that interest is recorded.

3. The constitutionality of the destruction of prior interests wrought by marketable title acts has been vigorously debated in the courts. The issue seems now, however, to have been settled in favor of such legislation by the United States Supreme Court in Texaco, Inc. v. Short, 454 U.S. 516, 102 S.Ct. 781, 70 L.Ed.2d 738 (1982).

PROBLEM: SUBURBAN SECRETS

One of the town's nicest residential areas, Orchard Hills, has been built on the site of an elegant old nineteenth-century farm house and orchard. Orchard Hills consists of 30 homes, several of which have changed hands in recent years. The transfers have taken place in amicable, green-eyeshade fashion. One of the older lawyers in town, however, knows that the deed from the family that owned the orchard to the developer 29 years ago contained a defective acknowledgment. This defect is beyond curing, as the deed to the developer was from a dozen heirs, some of whom are dead and some unavailable. The other lawyers in town, however, have not discovered the defect because title searching is done with abstracts and the abstracter did not note the defective acknowledgment.

Two years ago, Peter McPherson, a lawyer neither old nor young, discovered the fact of the defective acknowledgment from the older lawyer, who had a bit too much to drink, at a bar-association golf outing. Peter dug up the deed in the recorder's office and found out that what the older lawyer said was so. Peter was at that time representing the seller of a lot in Orchard Hills; it was not to his client's advantage to call attention to the defect, and he did nothing.

Now Peter has as a prospective client the purchaser of another lot in Orchard Hills. Should Peter disclose the defective acknowledgment to his client? Is there here an obligation to keep confidences? See A.B.A. Rule 1.6. Can Peter represent the buyer at all? Is there a conflict of interest? What is the moral thing to do? Would your answer change if the jurisdiction had a marketable title act that would make the acknowledgment moot in two more years (30 years from the first transfer from the developer of the subject lot)?

G.   TITLE REGISTRATION

The deficiencies of the recording acts both for securing the rights of owners of existing property interests, and for disclosing a definitive record of such interests for the benefit of potential purchasers, are manifest and manifold. Clearly a better system must be possible. In fact, such a system exists and is in use in central Europe, England, much of the former British empire (including Australia, New Zealand, and most of Canada) and in several American states. Title registration is often referred to as the "Torrens system," after Sir Richard Torrens, who introduced the system to South Australia in the mid–19th century.

Under a Torrens system property title is based on registration. A person claiming title to land and desiring to register that title must initiate judicial proceedings to determine ownership. The title history of the land is then searched and an abstract prepared. This abstract is in turn examined by an official examiner who reports to the court. Parties who are identified as possibly having an interest in the property are notified and a hearing is held to establish title. A final decree is then issued declaring title in the owner subject to any proven outstanding interests.

Title as established by the registration decree is considered absolute, subject to limited exceptions, such as claims based on federal law. Any challenges to the title must be brought by appeal of the original action. The decree is registered with the register of titles. Any subsequent transfers of the property or new interests created in the property must be registered and appear on the official certificate to be valid. Transfers may only be effected by surrender of the owner's duplicate certificate and issuance of a new duplicate certificate in the name of the new owner. Interests may not be gained by adverse possession or prescription. For a complete description of Torrens Systems, see B. Schick and I. Plotkin, Torrens in the United States (1978).

The theoretical advantages of title registration are obvious. The rights of a holder of a registered property interest are nearly indefeasible. In theory, at least, they are only subject to fraud or an error by the register, for which the owner may be able to recover against the compensation fund. A potential purchaser, on the other hand, need only review a certificate at most a few pages long to determine definitively all interests affecting a parcel of property. Virtually all of the uncertainties of the recording system could be eliminated.

Because of these obvious advantages, it would seem that title registration would have been widely adopted as an alternative to recording. In fact, title registration was quite popular in the United States in the early twentieth century, and at one point 21 states legally recognized the Torrens system. Since then nine states have repealed title registration however, and it has been extensively used only in parts of Hawaii, Illinois, Massachusetts, Minnesota, New York and Ohio. Though articles advocating giving title registration another chance appear from time to time,[20] its prospects in the United States at this point in time appear very dim.

Why has title registration failed to take hold in the United States? First, since Constitutional constraints required that registration be accomplished initially through a judicial rather than an administrative process, initial registration of title has proved quite costly and time consuming. Because title registration has always been voluntary rather

20. See McCormack, Torrens and Recording: Land Title Assurance in the Computer Age, 18 Wm. Mitchell L. Rev. 61 (1992); Bostick, Land Title Registration: An English Solution to an American Problem, 63 Ind.L.J. 35 (1987); Janczyk, Land Title Systems, Scale of Operations and Operating and Conversion Costs, 8 J.Leg. Studies 569 (1979).

than compulsory, landowners in jurisdictions with registration often opt to transfer unregistered land through the conventional system rather than through registration to avoid this initial expense. Second, registration statutes, like the marketable title acts, frequently except a variety of interests, weakening the conclusiveness of registered title. Subsequent judicial decisions upholding unregistered interests presenting appealing equities have further undermined the conclusiveness of registration. See Couey v. Talalah Estates Corp., 183 Ga. 442, 188 S.E. 822 (1936); Sheaff v. Spindler, 339 Ill. 540, 171 N.E. 632 (1930); Kirk v. Mullen, 100 Or. 563, 197 P. 300 (1921). Finally, it is widely believed that vigorous opposition from the conveyancing establishment, particularly from the title insurance companies, has contributed significantly to limiting and reversing the growth of title registration.

H. TITLE INSURANCE

In many parts of the United States, before a financial institution will agree to finance a real property purchase, it will insist that the seller or buyer procure a mortgagee policy of title insurance. If the financial institution intends to sell the mortgage on the secondary mortgage market, this will almost certainly be the case. Moreover, many purchasers of residential real property rely on their title insurance policy as the primary protection of their title. Indeed, in some jurisdictions general warranty deeds have been replaced by special warranty or quitclaim deeds and purchasers of residences rarely seek the assistance of attorneys because of the pervasiveness of reliance on title insurance as the primary means to securing title.

Title insurance is a peculiar form of insurance. Most forms of insurance cover the insured during a specified period of time against designated risks that may occur during that time period. In contrast, title insurance covers the insured only against risks already in existence at the time the policy is issued but for an unlimited time after issuance. Most forms of insurance insure against risks that are at least partially under the control of the insured. Title insurance insures against risks that are generally beyond the control of the insured, but often discoverable by, and thus, to some extent, subject to the control of the insurer.

Title insurance policies insure either the mortgagee or the owner. The mortgagee policy insures the title of the mortgagee against encumbrances and defects. It also insures the marketability and assignability of the mortgagee's title and access to and from the land subject to the mortgage. Mortgagee policies are generally assignable with the mortgage.

A copy of the current American Land Title Association owner's policy is reproduced below:

POLICY OF TITLE INSURANCE ISSUED BY

STEWART TITLE
GUARANTY COMPANY

SUBJECT TO THE EXCLUSIONS FROM COVERAGE, THE EXCEPTIONS FROM COVERAGE CONTAINED IN SCHEDULE B AND THE CONDITIONS AND STIPULATIONS, STEWART TITLE GUARANTY COMPANY, a Texas corporation, herein called the Company, insures, as of Date of Policy shown in Schedule A, against loss or damage, not exceeding the Amount of Insurance stated in Schedule A, sustained or incurred by the insured by reason of:

1. Title to the estate or interest described in Schedule A being vested other than as stated therein;

2. Any defect in or lien or encumbrance on the title;

3. Unmarketability of the title;

4. Lack of a right of access to and from the land.

The Company will also pay the costs, attorneys' fees and expenses incurred in defense of the title, as insured, but only to the extent provided in the Conditions and Stipulations.

IN WITNESS WHEREOF, Stewart Title Guaranty Company has caused this policy to be signed and sealed by its duly authorized officers as of the date of Policy shown in Schedule A.

STEWART TITLE
GUARANTY COMPANY

_____
Chairman of the Board

Countersigned:

_____
Authorized Signatory

U.S. Title Guaranty, Inc.
Company 8135 Forsyth
Lower Level
City Clayton, MO 63105

_____
President

EXCLUSIONS FROM COVERAGE

The following matters are expressly excluded from the coverage of this policy and the Company will not pay loss or damage, costs, attorneys' fees or expenses which arise by reason of:

1. (a) Any law, ordinance or governmental regulation (including but not limited to building and zoning laws, ordinances, or regulations) restricting, regulating, prohibiting or relating to (i) the occupancy, use, or enjoyment of the land; (ii) the character, dimensions or location of any improvement now or hereafter erected on the land; (iii) a separation in ownership or a change in the dimensions or area of the land or any parcel of which the land is or was a part; or (iv) environmental protection, or the effect of any violation of these laws, ordinances or governmental regulations, except to the extent that a notice of the enforcement thereof or a notice of a defect, lien or encumbrance resulting from a violation or alleged violation affecting the land has been recorded in the public records at Date of Policy.
   (b) Any governmental police power not excluded by (a) above, except to the extent that a notice of the exercise thereof or a notice of a defect, lien or encumbrance resulting from a violation or alleged violation affecting the land has been recorded in the public records at Date of Policy.
2. Rights of eminent domain unless notice of the exercise thereof has been recorded in the public records at Date of Policy, but not excluding from coverage any taking which has occurred prior to Date of Policy which would be binding on the rights of a purchaser for value without knowledge.
3. Defects, liens, encumbrances, adverse claims or other matters:
   (a) created, suffered, assumed or agreed to by the insured claimant;
   (b) not known to the Company, not recorded in the public records at Date of Policy, but known to the insured claimant and not disclosed in writing to the Company by the insured claimant prior to the date the insured claimant became an insured under this policy;
   (c) resulting in no loss or damage to the insured claimant;
   (d) attaching or created subsequent to Date of Policy; or
   (e) resulting in loss or damage which would not have been sustained if the insured claimant had paid value for the estate or interest insured by this policy.
4. Any claim, which arises out of the transaction vesting in the Insured the estate or interest insured by this policy, by reason of the operation of federal bankruptcy, state insolvency, or similar creditors' rights laws, that is based on:
   (a) the transaction creating the estate or interest insured by this policy being deemed a fraudulent conveyance or fraudulent transfer; or
   (b) the transaction creating the estate or interest insured by this policy being deemed a preferential transfer except where the preferential transfer results from the failure:
      (i) to timely record the instrument of transfer; or
      (ii) of such recordation to impart notice to a purchaser for value or a judgment or lien creditor.

Page 1 of
Policy
Serial No.   O-9993- 2427230

ALTA OWNER'S POLICY - 10-17-92

CONDITIONS AND STIPULATIONS

1.   DEFINITION OF TERMS.

The following terms when used in this policy mean:

(a) "insured": the insured named in Schedule A, and, subject to any rights or defenses the Company would have had against the named insured, those who succeed to the interest of the named insured by operation of law as distinguished from purchase including, but not limited to, heirs, distributees, devisees, survivors, personal representatives, next of kin, or corporate or fiduciary successors.

(b) "insured claimant": an insured claiming loss or damage.

(c) "knowledge" or "known": actual knowledge, not constructive knowledge or notice which may be imputed to an insured by reason of the public records as defined in this policy or any other records which impart constructive notice of matters affecting the land.

(d) "land": the land described or referred to in Schedule A, and improvements affixed thereto which by law constitute real property. The term "land" does not include any property beyond the lines of the area described or referred to in Schedule A, nor any right, title, interest, estate or easement in abutting streets, roads, avenues, alleys, lanes, ways or waterways, but nothing herein shall modify or limit the extent to which a right of access to and from the land is insured by this policy.

(e) "mortgage": mortgage, deed of trust, trust deed, or other security instrument

(f) "public records": records established under state statutes at Date of Policy for the purpose of imparting constructive notice of matters relating to real property to purchasers for value and without knowledge. With respect to Section 1(a)(iv) of the Exclusions From Coverage, "public records" shall also include environmental protection liens filed in the records of the clerk of the United States district court for the district in which the land is located.

(g) "unmarketability of the title": an alleged or apparent matter affecting the title to the land, not excluded or excepted from coverage, which would entitle a purchaser of the estate or interest described in Schedule A to be released from the obligation to purchase by virtue of a contractual condition requiring the delivery of marketable title.

2.   CONTINUATION OF INSURANCE AFTER CONVEYANCE OF TITLE.

The coverage of this policy shall continue in force as of Date of Policy in favor of an insured only so long as the insured retains an estate or interest in the land, or holds an indebtedness secured by a purchase money mortgage given by a purchaser from the insured, or only so long as the insured shall have liability by reason of covenants of warranty made by the insured in any transfer or conveyance of the estate or interest. This policy shall not continue in force in favor of any purchaser from the insured of either (i) an estate or interest in the land, or (ii) an indebtedness secured by a purchase money mortgage given to the insured.

3.   NOTICE OF CLAIM TO BE GIVEN BY INSURED CLAIMANT.

The insured shall notify the Company promptly in writing (i) in case of any litigation as set forth in Section 4(a) below, (ii) in case knowledge shall come to an insured hereunder of any claim of title or interest which is adverse to the title to the estate or interest, as insured, and which might cause loss or damage for which the Company may be liable by virtue of this policy, or (iii) if title to the estate or interest, as insured, is rejected as unmarketable. If prompt notice shall not be given to the Company, then as to the insured all liability of the Company shall terminate with regard to the matter or matters for which prompt notice is required; provided, however, that failure to notify the Company shall in no case prejudice the rights of any insured under this policy unless the Company shall be prejudiced by the failure and then only to the extent of the prejudice.

4.   DEFENSE AND PROSECUTION OF ACTIONS; DUTY OF INSURED CLAIMANT TO COOPERATE.

(a) Upon written request by the insured and subject to the options contained in Section 6 of these Conditions and Stipulations, the Company, at its own cost and without unreasonable delay, shall provide for the defense of an insured in litigation in which any third party asserts a claim adverse to the title or interest as insured, but only as to those stated causes of action alleging a defect, lien or encumbrance or other matter insured against by this policy. The Company shall have the right to select counsel of its choice (subject to the right of the insured to object for reasonable cause) to represent the insured as to those stated causes of action and shall not be liable for and will not pay the fees of any other counsel. The Company will not pay any fees, costs or expenses incurred by the insured in the defense of those causes of action which allege matters not insured against by this policy.

(b) The Company shall have the right, at its own cost, to institute and prosecute any action or proceeding or to do any other act which in its opinion may be necessary or desirable to establish the title to the estate or interest, as insured, or to prevent or reduce loss or damage to the insured. The Company may take any appropriate action under the terms of this policy, whether or not it shall be liable hereunder, and shall not thereby concede liability or waive any provision of this policy. If the Company shall exercise its rights under this paragraph, it shall do so diligently.

(c) Whenever the Company shall have brought an action or interposed a defense as required or permitted by the provisions of this policy, the Company may pursue any litigation to final determination by a court of competent jurisdiction and expressly reserves the right, in its sole discretion, to appeal from any adverse judgment or order.

(d) In all cases where this policy permits or requires the Company to prosecute or provide for the defense of any action or proceeding, the insured shall secure to the Company the right to so prosecute or provide defense in the action or proceeding, and all appeals therein, and permit the Company to use, at its option, the name of the insured for this purpose. Whenever requested by the Company, the insured, at the Company's expense, shall give the Company all reasonable aid (i) in any action or proceeding, securing evidence, obtaining witnesses, prosecuting or defending the action or proceeding, or effecting settlement, and (ii) in any other lawful act which in the opinion of the Company may be necessary or desirable to establish the title to the estate or interest as insured. If the Company is prejudiced by the failure of the insured to furnish the required cooperation, the Company's obligations to the insured under the policy shall terminate, including any liability or obligation to defend, prosecute, or continue any litigation, with regard to the matter or matters requiring such cooperation.

5.   PROOF OF LOSS OR DAMAGE.

In addition to and after the notices required under Section 3 of these Conditions and Stipulations have been provided the Company, a proof of loss or damage signed and sworn to by the insured claimant shall be furnished to the Company within 90 days after the insured claimant shall ascertain the facts giving rise to the loss or damage. The proof of loss or damage shall describe the defect in, or lien or encumbrance on the title, or other matter insured against by this policy which constitutes the basis of loss or damage and shall state, to the extent possible, the basis of calculating the amount of the loss or damage. If the Company is prejudiced by the failure of the insured claimant to provide the required proof of loss or damage, the Company's obligations to the insured under the policy shall terminate, including any liability or obligation to defend, prosecute, or continue any litigation, with regard to the matter or matters requiring such proof of loss or damage.

In addition, the insured claimant may reasonably be required to submit to examination under oath by any authorized representative of the Company and shall produce for examination, inspection and copying, at such reasonable times and places as may be designated by any authorized representative of the Company, all records, books, ledgers, checks, correspondence and memoranda, whether bearing a date before or after Date of Policy, which reasonably pertain to the loss or damage. Further, if requested by any authorized representative of the Company, the insured claimant shall grant its permission, in writing, for any authorized representative of the Company to examine, inspect and copy all records, books, ledgers, checks, correspondence and memoranda in the custody or control of a third party, which reasonably pertain to the loss or damage. All information designated as confidential by the insured claimant provided to the Company pursuant to this Section shall not be disclosed to others unless, in the reasonable judgment of the Company, it is necessary in the administration of the claim. Failure of the insured claimant to submit for examination under oath, produce other reasonably requested information or grant permission to secure reasonably necessary information from third parties as required in this paragraph shall terminate any liability of the Company under this policy as to that claim.

6.   OPTIONS TO PAY OR OTHERWISE SETTLE CLAIMS; TERMINATION OF LIABILITY.

In case of a claim under this policy, the Company shall have the following additional options:

(a) **To Pay or Tender Payment of the Amount of Insurance.**

To pay or tender payment of the amount of insurance under this policy together with any costs, attorneys' fees and expenses incurred by the insured claimant, which were authorized by the Company, up to the time of payment or tender of payment and which the Company is obligated to pay.

Upon the exercise by the Company of this option, all liability and obligations to the insured under this policy, other than to make the payment required, shall terminate, including any liability or obligation to defend, prosecute, or continue any litigation, and the policy shall be surrendered to the Company for cancellation.

(b) **To Pay or Otherwise Settle With Parties Other than the Insured or With the Insured Claimant.**

(i) to pay or otherwise settle with other parties for or in the name of an insured claimant any claim insured against under this policy, together with any costs, attorneys' fees and expenses incurred by the insured claimant which were authorized by the Company up to the time of payment and which the Company is obligated to pay; or

(ii) to pay or otherwise settle with the insured claimant the loss or damage provided for under this policy, together with any costs, attorneys' fees and expenses incurred by the insured claimant which were authorized by the Company up to the time of payment and which the Company is obligated to pay.

Upon the exercise by the Company of either of the options provided for in paragraphs (b)(i) or (ii), the Company's obligations to the insured under this policy for the claimed loss or damage, other than the payments required to be made, shall terminate, including any liability or obligation to defend, prosecute or continue any litigation.

(continued and concluded on last page of this policy)

CONDITIONS AND STIPULATIONS Continued

(continued and concluded from reverse side of Policy Face)

7. DETERMINATION, EXTENT OF LIABILITY AND COINSURANCE.

This policy is a contract of indemnity against actual monetary loss or damage sustained or incurred by the insured claimant who has suffered loss or damage by reason of matters insured against by this policy and only to the extent herein described.

(a) The liability of the Company under this policy shall not exceed the least of:

(i) the Amount of Insurance stated in Schedule A; or,

(ii) the difference between the value of the insured estate or interest as insured and the value of the insured estate or interest subject to the defect, lien or encumbrance insured against by this policy.

(b) In the event the Amount of Insurance stated in Schedule A at the Date of Policy is less than 80 percent of the value of the insured estate or interest or the full consideration paid for the land, whichever is less, or if subsequent to the Date of Policy and improvement is erected on the land which increases the value of the insured estate or interest by at least 20 percent over the Amount of Insurance stated in Schedule A, then this Policy is subject to the following:

(i) where no subsequent improvement has been made, as to any partial loss, the Company shall only pay the loss pro rata in the proportion that the amount of insurance at Date of Policy bears to the total value of the insured estate or interest at Date of Policy; or

(ii) where a subsequent improvement has been made, as to any partial loss, the Company shall only pay the loss pro rata in the proportion that 120 percent of the Amount of Insurance stated in Schedule A bears to the sum of the Amount of Insurance stated in Schedule A and the amount expended for the improvement.

The provisions of this paragraph shall not apply to costs, attorneys' fees and expenses for which the Company is liable under this policy, and shall only apply to that portion of any loss which exceeds, in the aggregate, 10 percent of the Amount of Insurance stated in Schedule A.

(c) The Company will pay only those costs, attorney's fees and expenses incurred in accordance with Section 4 of these Conditions and Stipulations.

8. APPORTIONMENT.

If the land described in Schedule A consists of two or more parcels which are not used as a single site, and a loss is established affecting one or more of the parcels but not all, the loss shall be computed and settled on a pro rata basis as if the amount of insurance under this policy was divided pro rata as to the value on Date of Policy of each separate parcel to the whole, exclusive of any improvements made subsequent to Date of Policy, unless a liability or value has otherwise been agreed upon as to each parcel by the Company and the insured at the time of the issuance of this policy and shown by an express statement or by an endorsement attached to this policy.

9. LIMITATION OF LIABILITY.

(a) If the Company establishes the title, or removes the alleged defect, lien or encumbrance, or cures the lack of a right of access to or from the land, or cures the claim of unmarketability of title, all as insured, in a reasonably diligent manner by any method, including litigation and the completion of any appeals therefrom, it shall have fully performed its obligations with respect to that matter and shall not be liable for any loss or damage caused thereby.

(b) In the event of any litigation, including litigation by the Company or with the Company's consent, the Company shall have no liability for loss or damage until there has been a final determination by a court of competent jurisdiction, and disposition of all appeals therefrom, adverse to the title as insured.

(c) The Company shall not be liable for loss or damage to any insured for liability voluntarily assumed by the insured in settling any claim or suit without the prior written consent of the Company.

10. REDUCTION OF INSURANCE; REDUCTION OR TERMINATION OF LIABILITY.

All payments under this policy, except payments made for costs, attorneys' fees and expenses, shall reduce the amount of the insurance pro tanto.

11. LIABILITY NONCUMULATIVE.

It is expressly understood that the amount of insurance under this policy shall be reduced by any amount the Company may pay under any policy insuring a mortgage to which exception is taken in Schedule B or to which the insured has agreed, assumed, or taken subject, or which is hereafter executed by an insured and which is a charge or lien on the estate or interest described or referred to in Schedule A, and the amount so paid shall be deemed a payment under this policy to the insured owner.

12. PAYMENT OF LOSS.

(a) No payment shall be made without producing this policy for endorsement of the payment unless the policy has been lost or destroyed, in which case proof of loss or destruction shall be furnished to the satisfaction of the Company.

(b) When liability and the extent of loss or damage has been definitely fixed in accordance with these Conditions and Stipulations, the loss or damage shall be payable within 30 days thereafter.

13 SUBROGATION UPON PAYMENT OR SETTLEMENT.

(a) **The Company's Right of Subrogation.**

Whenever the Company shall have settled and paid a claim under this policy, all right of subrogation shall vest in the Company unaffected by any act of the insured claimant.

The Company shall be subrogated to and be entitled to all rights and remedies which the insured claimant would have had against any person or property in respect to the claim had this policy not been issued. If requested by the Company, the insured claimant shall transfer to the Company all rights and remedies against any person or property necessary in order to perfect this right of subrogation. The insured claimant shall permit the Company to sue, compromise or settle in the name of the insured claimant and to use the name of the insured claimant in any transaction or litigation involving these rights or remedies.

If a payment on account of a claim does not fully cover the loss of the insured claimant, the Company shall be subrogated to these rights and remedies in the proportion which the Company's payment bears to the whole amount of the loss.

If loss should result from any act of the insured claimant, as stated above, that act shall not void this policy, but the Company, in that event, shall be required to pay only that part of any losses insured against by this policy which shall exceed the amount, if any, lost to the Company by reason of the impairment by the insured claimant of the Company's right of subrogation.

(b) **The Company's Rights Against Non-insured Obligors.**

The Company's right of subrogation against non-insured obligors shall exist and shall include, without limitation, the rights of the insured to indemnities, guaranties, other policies of insurance or bonds, notwithstanding any terms or conditions contained in those instruments which provide for subrogation rights by reason of this policy.

14. ARBITRATION

Unless prohibited by applicable law, either the Company or the insured may demand arbitration pursuant to the Title Insurance Arbitration Rules of the American Arbitration Association. Arbitrable matters may include, but are not limited to, any controversy or claim between the Company and the insured arising out of or relating to this policy, any service of the Company in connection with its issuance or the breach of a policy provision or other obligation. All arbitrable matters, when the Amount of Insurance is $1,000,000 or less shall be arbitrated at the option of either the Company or the insured. All arbitrable matters when the Amount of Insurance is in excess of $1,000,000 shall be arbitrated only when agreed to by both the Company and the insured. Arbitration pursuant to this policy and under the Rules in effect on the date the demand for arbitration is made or, at the option of the insured, the Rules in effect at Date of Policy shall be binding upon the parties. The award may include attorneys' fees only if the laws of the state in which the land is located permit a court to award attorneys' fees to a prevailing party. Judgment upon the award rendered by the Arbitrator(s) may be entered in any court having jurisdiction thereof.

The law of the situs of the land shall apply to an arbitration under the Title Insurance Arbitration Rules.

A copy of the Rules may be obtained from the Company upon request.

15. LIABILITY LIMITED TO THIS POLICY; POLICY ENTIRE CONTRACT.

(a) This policy together with all endorsements, if any, attached hereto by the Company is the entire policy and contract between the insured and the Company. In interpreting any provision of this policy, this policy shall be construed as a whole.

(b) Any claim of loss or damage, whether or not based on negligence, and which arises out of the status of the title to the estate or interest covered hereby or by any action asserting such claim, shall be restricted to this policy.

(c) No amendment of or endorsement to this policy can be made except by a writing endorsed hereon or attached hereto signed by either the President, a Vice President, the Secretary, an Assistant Secretary, or validating officer or authorized signatory of the Company.

16. SEVERABILITY.

In the event any provision of the policy is held invalid or unenforceable under applicable law, the policy shall be deemed not to include that provision and all other provisions shall remain in full force and effect.

17. NOTICES, WHERE SENT.

All notices required to be given the Company and any statement in writing required to be furnished the Company shall include the number of this policy and shall be addressed to the Company at P. O. Box 2029, Houston, Texas 77252-2029.

STEWART TITLE

GUARANTY COMPANY

OFFICE USE ONLY:
  Agent I.D. #:   SIMUL. #:-
  Prior Liability: DATED: Prior Policy #:
Endorsements:
Total Charges: Risk Rate:

STEWART TITLE GUARANTY COMPANY
ALTA OWNERS POLICY
SCHEDULE A

Abstract No.:   Policy No.:
                                                  M -

Date of Policy: February 18, 2004 at 11:40 am

Amount of Insurance: $ 97,000.00

1. Name of Insured:

2. The estate or interest in the land which is covered by this policy is:

   FEE SIMPLE

3. Title to the estate or interest in the land is vested in:

4. The land referred to in this policy is described as follows:

Parcel 1: The Southern 35 feet of the Northern 40 feet of Lot 23 in Block 2
of Laclede J. Howard's Subdivision and in Block 5495 of the City of St. Louis,
fronting 35 feet 2-1/4 inches on the West line of Graham Street by a depth
Westwardly between parallel lines 35 feet apart of 125 feet 2-5/8 inches along
the North line of said property and of 128 feet 8-1/4 inches along the South
line of said property to an alley, having a radius thereon of 35 feet,
according to survey executed by Claude Myers, City Surveyorduring January
1950.

Parcel 2: 24-239 C.B. 4 feet 6 inches/55 feet 6-7/8 inches X 125 feet 1-3/8
inches 141 feet, 2-1/2 inches, part of Lot 23 in Block 2 of Laclede J.
Howard's Subdivision, City Block 5495, all part of 1529 Graham, City of St.
Louis, Missouri.

BY:_____
        Authorized Officer/Signatory

SCHEDULE B

Abstract No.:   Policy No.:

This policy does not insure against loss or damage (and the Company will not pay costs, attorneys' fees or expenses) which arise by reason of:

General Exceptions:
1. Rights or claims of parties in possession not shown by the public records.
2. Encroachments, overlaps, boundary line disputes, and any other matters which would be disclosed by an accurate survey an inspection of the premises.
3. Easements, or claims of easements, not shown by the public records.
4. Any lien, or right to a lien, for services, labor, or material heretofore or hereafter furnished, imposed by law and not shown by the public records.
5. Taxes or special assessments which are not shown as existing liens by the public records.

    ITEMS 1-5 OF THE ABOVE EXCEPTIONS ARE HEREBY DELETED.

Special Exceptions:

6. All assessments and taxes for the year 2004 and all subsequent years for the City of St. Louis, none now due and payable.

7. Any discrepancy between the actual boundaries of the land and the apparent boundaries as indicated by fences, plantings or other improvements.

Notes and Questions

1. The policy reproduced is the Form B policy. The form A policy differs only in that it does not insure marketability of the property. What difference does this make to the insured?

2. In addition to the general exceptions listed in the policy, the title policy will also generally except from coverage any non-trivial defects discovered during the title company's search. Indeed, it is possible to view the title insurer's job to be discovering all real risks to the title of a property and excluding these risks. Of course, the buyer or mortgagee dissatisfied with the exceptions specifically identified by the title insurer can refuse to issue a mortgage or to proceed with the property purchase.

3. Considering the exceptions and exclusions found in the policy, would a purchaser of property be insured against:

(a) claims of an adverse possessor to part of the insured property?

(b) a prescriptive easement across the property?

(c) an encroachment across the boundary by a fence erected by a neighboring landowner?

(d) a sewer line running across the property and used by a neighbor?

(e) a mechanic's lien filed against the property after the closing for work performed before the closing, which under state law takes precedence over the title of the purchaser?

(f) a violation of the zoning ordinance?

(g) a preexisting unrecorded mortgage of which the purchaser has heard unconfirmed rumors?

(h) a dower interest stemming from a sale of the property twenty years previously, which is discovered after the conveyance of the property to the purchaser, but never asserted against the property by its owner?

What exactly does a title insurance policy insure against?

4. Note that Schedule B of the policy reproduced provides that the five enumerated General Exceptions are deleted. On what basis did the title insurance company agree to delete these exceptions, thus adding value to the insurance coverage?

5. Value may also be added to title insurance coverage through endorsements. For example, counsel for buyers typically request an inflation endorsement so that, in the event of an insured loss, buyer will receive the appreciation in the value of their property.

6. When a defect is discovered that is covered by a title insurance policy, the extent of liability of a title insurer will usually be determined by interpreting the policy. One common measure where a claim is presented for a partial failure of title is the difference between the market value of the insured property with and the market value without the defect; another considers the cost of removing the defect. Where failure of title is complete, the measure of damages is usually the fair market value of the property to which title failed. Policies also vary as to the date on which damages are to be determined, some specifying the date of the policy; others specifying the date the defect was discovered. Damages can never exceed the total value of the policy (usually the purchase price of the property for owners' policies, the value of the loan for mortgagee policies) and the extent of the insured's

loss. For a mortgagee, for example, the damages cannot exceed the amount unpaid on the loan at the time title fails. Most policies also provide for coverage of litigation costs for defending the title of the insured in addition to any damages recoverable by the insured. See D. Burke, The Law of Title Insurance (1986).

Though contract damages against title insurers are often quite limited, tort damages may be more substantial where tort liability is established. Tort litigation may also impose on title insurance companies responsibilities not clearly imposed by the insurance contract.

MOORE v. TITLE INSURANCE CO. OF MINNESOTA

Court of Appeals of Arizona, 1985.
148 Ariz. 408, 714 P.2d 1303.

HOWARD, JUDGE.

Plaintiffs filed this action against the defendant title company alleging that the defendant was negligent in failing to discover certain liens against property plaintiffs were purchasing and further alleging that this misconduct resulted in a breach of contract. * * * [Plaintiffs appealed a judgment for the title company]

* * *

The facts considered in the light most favorable to defendant are as follows. On July 10, 1979, Michael C. Moore, acting on behalf of the partnership of Moore and Bale, attended a meeting at the offices of Title Insurance Company of Minnesota (Minnesota) in Tucson. The meeting concerned the purchase by the partnership of certain apartments located in Sierra Vista, Arizona, owned by Mr. Nieman. Present at the meeting were Nieman, his real estate broker, Moore, Bale and Roy Rogers, an escrow officer of Minnesota. The purpose of the meeting was to work out the details of a deposit receipt and agreement in connection with the partnership's proposed purchase of the apartments.

The partnership was concerned about purchasing the property because Sierra Solar Systems, Inc., a corporation owned by Nieman, was in bankruptcy and there were serious delinquencies on the first deed of trust on the apartments held by Security Savings and Loan. Unless immediate cash was provided to Security Savings it was going to foreclose. Moore informed everyone at the meeting that the partnership did not want to enter into the transaction at all if there was any danger that Nieman personally would file bankruptcy or if there was any problem concerning the property that would bring it into the bankruptcy court.

A deposit receipt and agreement was typed at the Minnesota office. It provided for a purchase price of approximately $100,000. It disclosed the existence of three liens on the property: first lien to Security Savings in the approximate sum of $30,000, a second lien to S & D Cattle Company in the approximate sum of $30,000 to $40,000 and a third lien to First National Bank in the approximate sum of $30,000. The agreement also contained the following terms and conditions:

"(1) If the subject property is subject to any liens other than the three liens described on page one, buyer shall have the option to terminate this agreement and all deposits shall be returned to buyer and buyer shall not be liable to seller for any amount nor may seller enforce this agreement."

* * *

Prior to signing the deposit receipt and agreement, Rogers told Moore that Minnesota had made a title search and there were no problems. Indeed, the record discloses that a preliminary title report was made searching the title up to July 10, 1979. It discloses no liens other than the realty mortgage owed to Security Savings, and the deeds of trust securing loans owed to S & D Cattle Company and First National Bank of Arizona.

The partners signed the agreement and took possession of the apartments. Although there were 14 apartments in existence at the time, only one of them was in shape to be rented and it was the duty of Bale to see to it that the remaining units were brought into a rentable condition. During their discussions with Nieman prior to signing the deposit receipt and agreement, Nieman represented to the partnership that the amount of money due and owing on the mortgage to S & D Cattle Company was closer to $30,000 with a discount and that the lienholder was cooperative. In fact, after taking possession, the partners discovered that the amount of the lien was claimed to be closer to $40,000 and that the S & D Cattle Company was not cooperative. It was also discovered that some of the fixtures and equipment in the apartments did not work and that there was cement in part of the sewer system. Bale commenced to repair the apartments and succeeded in getting six of them rented. Eventually the amount of rents came close to giving the partners a positive cash flow.

* * *

On December 13, 1979, the partners closed the deal in anticipation of persuading S & D Cattle Company to accept a lesser amount. At the time of the closing they did not have any financing.

Prior to the closing, Minnesota had prepared an amended preliminary title report which was given to the escrow officer. The only liens shown on this amended report were the liens that were previously known. Neither partner saw either of the preliminary title reports prior to closing the sale. The closing statement, which both partners saw, showed only the existence of the three liens previously mentioned and the closing statement showed that the partners were taking the property subject to these liens. Moore asked Rogers at the time about the three liens, and Rogers told him that he would let him know the balance due on each. Upon closing, the partnership released the $6,000 note which was given as security for the $45,000 earnest money and voided it. They also released Nieman's home in Sierra Vista, which was being held as security.

After the closing, Bale continued to work on improving the property. In April 1980, Bale moved to Kansas City. In November 1980, he made up a sales packet for the property showing a sale price of $155,000. He tried to sell the property to a prospect who, after checking into the deal, told Bale that the deal was not as represented since there were other outstanding liens on the property. About one month earlier, Moore was discussing financing with Lou Wallace of the First National Bank. Wallace told him that the bank would be happy to lend him money to pay off the first three liens, but asked Moore who was going to pay off the additional liens that his research showed existed on the property. This was the first time that Moore had any notice that there were additional liens.

Minnesota had failed to list the following liens of record on the property against Sierra Solar Systems, Inc.: Arizona Department of Economic Security, $329.36, recorded November 6, 1978; Arizona Department of Economic Security, $604.93, recorded November 29, 1978; United States Internal Revenue Service, $9,141.45, recorded January 15, 1979; Arizona Department of Economic Security, $214.82, recorded February 22, 1979, and United States Internal Revenue Service, $2,925.29, recorded March 13, 1979. Although a deed transferring the property from Sierra Solar Systems, Inc. to Nieman, individually, was executed and recorded on December 29, 1978, this deed was subsequently re-recorded by the title company on December 13, 1979 because of a defective acknowledgment.

Both personally and through his attorney, Moore communicated with Minnesota asking it to compensate the partnership for its failure to include all liens of record. The title company responded that it was responsible to protect and defend them with respect to the first two undisclosed liens on the subject property totalling about $1,000, but that it was not responsible for the other liens since they were filed after the debtor, Sierra Solar Systems, Inc., had transferred the property to Nieman in his individual capacity. This response did not satisfy the partnership. In the meantime, trustee's sales were noticed as to the deeds of trust held by S & D Cattle Company and First National Bank. Furthermore, the suit against S & D Cattle Company had not been resolved. Although the partnership had enough cash to pay off the liens that had not been disclosed by the title company, if they did so, they would not have the funds necessary to operate the apartments. First National Bank would not lend them the money unless they paid off the liens. The net result was that the partnership lost the property through the trustee's sales since it could not find permanent financing. This suit ensued.

At trial, both an expert witness on behalf of the plaintiffs and defendant's own employee, an escrow officer, testified that the title company had fallen below the standard of care of title companies under the circumstances by failing to discover and disclose all liens of record prior to closing.

It is plaintiffs' contention that the defendant was negligent in searching the title and that this negligence prevented them from exercising their option to terminate the contract. Plaintiffs contend that the title company should have the same liability as an abstractor of title. The title company contends that it is not an abstractor of title, that it is only an insurer and that it can only be liable for breach of contract. It argues that any duty on the part of an insurer to search the records has to be expressed and/or implied from the title policy issued to the plaintiff and that where, as here, the title company has no such duty under the title policy, any search that it may have actually undertaken was undertaken solely for its own protection against losses covered by its policy. See Anderson v. Title Insurance Company, 103 Idaho 875, 655 P.2d 82 (1982), and Horn v. Lawyers Title Insurance Corporation, 89 N.M. 709, 557 P.2d 206. See also Maggio v. Abstract Title & Mortgage Corporation, 277 App.Div. 940, 98 N.Y.S.2d 1011 (1950).

We start with the proposition that an abstractor of title is negligent as a matter of law when it fails to include in its abstract liens which are of record. Phoenix Title and Trust Company v. Continental Oil Company, 43 Ariz. 219, 29 P.2d 1065 (1934), overruled on other grounds, Donnelly Const. Co. v. Oberg/Hunt/Gilleland, 139 Ariz. 184, 677 P.2d 1292 (1984). Other jurisdictions have held that a title insurance company has the liability of an abstractor of title when it inspects records and prepares title reports. Garton v. Title Insurance and Trust Company, 106 Cal.App.3d 365, 165 Cal.Rptr. 449 (1980); Jarchow v. Transamerica Title Insurance Company, 48 Cal.App.3d 917, 122 Cal.Rptr. 470 (1975); Hawkins v. Oakland Title Insurance and Guaranty Company, 165 Cal. App.2d 116, 331 P.2d 742 (1958); Shada v. Title & Trust Company of Florida, 457 So.2d 553 (Fla.App.1984); Heyd v. Chicago Title Insurance Company, 218 Neb. 296, 354 N.W.2d 154 (1984);[21] and see the dicta in Laurence v. Kruckmeyer, 124 Ariz. 488, 605 P.2d 466 (App.1979).

The rationale for imposing liability is best expressed in Heyd v. Chicago Title Insurance Company, supra:

"We now hold that a title insurance company which renders a title report and also issues a policy of title insurance has assumed two distinct duties. In rendering the title report the title insurance company serves as an abstractor of title and must list all matters of public record adversely affecting title to the real estate which is the subject of the title report. When a title insurance company fails to perform its duty to abstract title accurately, the title insurance company may be liable in tort for all damages proximately caused by such breach of duty. A title company's responsibility for its tortious conduct is distinct from the insurance company's responsibility existing on account of its policy of insurance. Different duties and responsibilities imposed on the title insurance company, therefore,

---

21. See also Shotwell v. Transamerica Title Insurance Company, 91 Wash.2d 161, 588 P.2d 208 (1978). The Washington court has discussed the issue but has not yet decided it.

can be the basis for separate causes of action—one cause of action in tort and another in contract." 354 N.W.2d at 158–159.

Support for the foregoing can also be found in § 552(1) of the Restatement (Second) of Torts, which states:

"One who, in the course of his business, profession or employment, or in any other transaction in which he has a pecuniary interest, supplies false information for the guidance of others in their business transactions, is subject to liability for pecuniary loss caused to them by their justifiable reliance upon the information, if he fails to exercise reasonable care or competence in obtaining or communicating the information."

The preliminary title report was given to the escrow by the title insurance company. On the preliminary report, there is a section of "requirements." The requirements contained a list of documents that had to be drafted and executed by the escrow in order for the title insurance company to insure title. The title insurance company knew and intended that the escrow officer would use its preliminary title report both to comply with the requirements and to prepare a closing escrow statement for the parties. Clearly, the above section of the Restatement applies.

To hold otherwise would be to completely ignore reality. In addition, we note what one authority has said about this issue:

"Applicants for a title insurance policy are interested in obtaining the insurance coverage, but they are sometimes more interested in what the company examination of title discloses. This is perhaps partly at the base of the prevailing philosophy of title insurance companies—stressing the service of risk delineation rather than risk coverage." Johnstone, Title Insurance, 66 Yale L.J. 492, 494 (1957).

The insurance company holds itself out as a searcher of titles and provides the information for the applicants to act upon, and the applicants expect and rely on this information in closing their deals. We agree fully with the decision of the Nebraska court in Heyd v. Chicago Title Insurance Company, supra.

Having concluded that the title company can be held liable in tort for its negligence, we turn our attention to the issue upon which the trial court based its decision: reliance or, in other words, proximate cause. It is helpful to reiterate the plaintiffs' theory of liability. They claimed that the failure of the title company to disclose the liens of record prevented them from exercising their option to cancel the contract and that, had they known of the existence of the liens, they would have canceled.

Thus the case really hinged on their assertion that they would have canceled the contract. On the other hand, the trial court had the testimony of the plaintiffs saying they would have canceled, pointing out that they had included special provisions in the agreement regarding the existence of any other undisclosed liens. On the other hand, there was evidence that Nieman had lied to them about the S & D Cattle Company loan, that the sewage system was damaged, that there were defective fixtures and appliances and that the partners were unable to obtain satisfactory financing prior to closing. In spite of these deficiencies, the plaintiffs chose to close the sale. They did not have to do so because of another special provision which allowed them to cancel the contract if they did not have the necessary financing.

We believe that the evidence in this case was capable of two conclusions. The trial court could have believed that, in view of their decision to close the sale in the face of the adverse circumstances which were known to them, the partners would not have exercised the option of cancellation because of additional liens, but would have gone forward and closed the sale anyway in the hope of securing additional financing. Alternatively, it could have decided to believe the plaintiffs and found that the additional liens would have been the straw that broke the camel's back. It chose the former conclusion and not the latter.

An appellate court will not disturb the findings of fact of the trial court unless they are clearly erroneous. * * * Deciding what the plaintiffs would have done in this case, had they had knowledge of the liens, was peculiarly for the trial court to decide and there is substantial evidence to support its conclusion.

Affirmed.

Notes and Questions

1. Title insurance policies often attempt to limit the insurer's liability to the indemnity specified in the policy and to disclaim the insurer's responsibility to search the title. Nevertheless, the representations of title companies as to the services they provide frequently identify title searching as one of these services. Binders or title commitments provided prior to a closing also may create the bases of subsequent tort suits for negligent search. A recent review of the cases revealed that 18 states now impose a duty on title insurers to do a competent title search, while seven reject such a duty. See Palomar, Title Insurance Companies' Liability for Failure to Search Title and Disclose Record Title, 20 Creighton L.Rev. 455 (1987). Note, however, that the insurer is only liable in these suits for a negligent search. It is not liable for a competent search that fails to reveal a title defect.

2. Who may claim the benefit of the title company's title search? May a mortgagor claim reliance on the search carried out before issuance of the mortgagee policy? See Fox v. Title Guaranty and Abstract Co. of Mobile Inc., 337 So.2d 1300 (Ala.1976) (yes). May a purchaser who relies on a title company's abstract prepared for the vendor? See Williams v. Polgar, 391 Mich. 6, 215 N.W.2d 149 (1974) (yes). When should the statute of limitations begin to run, on the date the search is completed, or on the date a defect is subsequently discovered?

3. The contractual nature of title insurance was emphasized in Citibank, N.A. v. Commonwealth Land Title Ins. Co., 228 A.D.2d 635, 645

N.Y.S.2d 826 (1996), where the title insurance policy was held to insure against an encumbrance that was not recorded until after the policy was issued. The policy, dated October 25, 1988, did not exclude a mortgage which was entered into by the homeowners on October 11, 1988, but not recorded until November 2, 1988. Citibank, relying on the title insurance policy, loaned money to the homeowners, secured by a mortgage which was recorded on October 25, 1988 (the date of the title insurance policy). Citibank's mortgage was held inferior to the October 11 mortgage, and the foreclosure proceeds could not satisfy the homeowner's debt to Citibank.

The court stated, "[T]he liability of the title insurer to its insured is essentially based on contract law and not negligence law. * * * Thus, it is no defense to a title insurer to assert that the matter which caused a loss to its insured could not have been ascertained by a reasonably competent search, examination and legal consideration of the land records. As previously stated the title insurer will be liable for hidden defects and all matters affecting title within the policy coverage and not excluded or specifically excepted from said coverage." Because the policy did not exclude the prior mortgage, it covered any loss sustained by Citibank as a result of that mortgage having priority over Citibank's mortgage.

4. In Lick Mill Creek Apartments v. Chicago Title Ins. Co., 231 Cal.App.3d 1654, 283 Cal.Rptr. 231 (1991), the buyer of an apartment complex sued its title insurer to recover the cost of cleaning up hazardous waste on the property left by the previous owner. At the time of the purchase, three separate state agencies had records disclosing the presence of hazardous waste on the property. The policy insured "against loss or damage * * * sustained or incurred by reason of: (1) Title to the estate or interest described in Schedule A being vested otherwise than as stated therein; (2) Any defect in or lien or encumbrance on such title: (3) Lack of a right of access to and from the land; or (4) Unmarketability of such title."

The buyer relied on clauses 2 and 4 of the policy. First, the court held that the hazardous waste did not render the title unmarketable, so clause 4 did not cover plaintiff's loss. "Because marketability of title and the market value of the land itself are separate and distinct, plaintiffs cannot claim coverage for the property's physical condition * * *." Second, the court held that the hazardous waste was not a "lien or encumbrance" under clause 2 for similar reasons: the clause protected against rights being asserted by third parties, not the physical condition of the land. Thus the court affirmed the dismissal of buyer's suit. The question of liability based on environmental condition is dealt with again in the context of real estate finance, infra.

5. Is it ethical for a lawyer to act both as agent for the title insurance company and as attorney for the buyer in a residential real estate transaction? See In re Opinion 682 of the Advisory Committee on Professional Ethics, 147 N.J. 360, 371–72, 687 A.2d 1000, 1005–06 (1997), which outlines three possible approaches to this issue. In that case, the New Jersey Supreme Court held that this dual representation is unethical. However, the court noted that the ABA permits the dual representation if both the buyer and the title insurance company give their informed consent. See ABA Comm. on Professional Ethics and Professional Responsibility, Formal Opinion 331 (1972). Other jurisdictions follow a "middle-of-the-road approach,"

where dual representation is proper if the attorney acts as an agent of the title insurance company, but does not own an interest in the company. See N.Y. State Bar Ass'n Committee on Professional Ethics, Opinion 595 (1988) and Opinion 621 (1991). See also Paul Bintinger, Conflict of Interest: Attorney as Title Insurance Agent, 4 Geo. J. Legal Ethics 687, 687 (1991) (describing the "inherent conflicts that arise when an attorney [representing either buyer or seller] functions as an agent for a title insurance corporation"). The relevant rule seems to be the one that forbids conflicts between the interests of a client and the lawyer's personal interests. The rule for that is R.P.C. Rule 1.8, which is extensive and which was extensively revised in the proposed 2002 A.B.A. amendments. Comment "1" in those revisions:

> A lawyer's legal skill and training, together with the relationship of trust and confidence between lawyer and client, create the possibility of overreaching when the lawyer participates in a business, property or financial transaction with a client, for example . . . a . . . sales transaction. . . . The rule applies to lawyers engaged in the sale or goods or services related to the practice of law, for example, the sale of title insurance . . . to existing clients of the lawyer's legal practice. . . .

See further quoted provisions of Rule 1.8 in Note "3," pages 685–686 infra.

6. Whenever a title insurance company hires a lawyer to represent an insured against an adverse claim, the potential exists for confusion as to whom the lawyer represents, the insured or the insurer. When the insured subsequently turns on the insurer, claiming inadequate defense or bad faith failure to settle within the policy limits, this conflict can raise major problems. In Lake Havasu Community Hospital, Inc. v. Arizona Title Insurance and Trust Co., 141 Ariz. 363, 687 P.2d 371 (App.1984), overruled in part on other grounds, 155 Ariz. 519, 747 P.2d 1218, for example, the insurer hired an attorney, Miller, to represent the insured in litigation involving the insured property. During the course of the litigation, the attorney disclosed to the insurer his belief that the insured was trying to settle the litigation and then to make a claim against the company. The court stated: "There is no question that Miller's letter to Arizona Title includes confidential and privileged information obtained by Miller as attorney for Community Hospital." 687 P.2d at 384. The court then held, under earlier Arizona precedent, that " * * * when an attorney, who is an insurance company's agent, uses the confidential relationship between an attorney and a client to gather information so as to deny an insured coverage under the policy, such conduct constitutes a waiver of any policy defense, and is so contrary to public policy that the insurance company is estopped as a matter of law from disclaiming liability under an exclusionary clause in the policy." Id. Finally, the court held that the company was estopped from claiming that it would not have settled for the policy limits absent the disclosure of privileged information by Miller. It awarded the insured the full value of the policy limits, plus $50,000 in punitive damages against the insurer for the attorney's unfaithfulness (holding the insurance company vicariously liable for the attorney's acts), even though the court otherwise concluded that the insurer would have been liable only for a much smaller amount.

7.   Consider the following excerpt describing how title insurance companies have displaced lawyers in residential real estate conveyances:

A.   The Growth of Title Insurance

The growth of title insurance in the United States is accounted for by three factors. First, it was early established by judicial decision that conveyancers and other real estate professionals were liable only for their negligence, and thus certain losses that fell on the purchasers of real estate could not be shifted to the real estate professionals who had assisted them. In response to these decisions, the first title insurance company in the United States, the Real Estate Title Insurance Company, was formed in 1876. Title insurance provides coverage against hidden risks that lawyer's opinions do not. Thus, title insurance protects the purchaser against such defects as a forged, stolen or undelivered deed, while the lawyer's opinion will not. Moreover, title insurance companies provide this coverage at lower cost than lawyers, at least in some markets. This relative efficiency reflects the inferiority of the publicly maintained land records compared to the privately maintained "title plants" owned by the title companies.

The second reason for the growth of title insurance was the rapid development of the western United States at the end of World War II. During this period, the demand for development capital outpaced the locally available supply. The traditional sources of development capital were banks and savings and loans. These institutions typically invested the great bulk of their mortgage loan portfolio in mortgages secured by real estate in the locality in which the institution operated. Consequently, western developers could not look to eastern savings and loans for funds. "Life insurance companies, however, are national lenders, and the larger companies hold mortgages on lands located in all parts of the United States." Because the insurance companies were in need of title protection, it is not surprising that they readily accepted the idea of title insurance as the source of that protection. Moreover, life insurance companies are regulated by state laws that require that their real estate loans be secured by a first lien; title insurance provided an easy means of establishing regulatory compliance.

The third reason for the growth in popularity of title insurance is accounted for by the growth in size and importance of the secondary mortgage market. Briefly, the secondary mortgage market is a securities-like market organized by the federal government, in which residential mortgages originated by local mortgage lenders are bundled into large packages, usually in excess of $1 million, insured by the federal government, and then sold on a national market to private investors located all over the country and, increasingly, the world. The principal players in this market are three government-chartered secondary market corporations: The Federal National Mortgage Association (Fannie Mae), The Federal Home Loan Mortgage Corporation (Freddie Mac), and The Government National Mortgage Association (Ginnie Mae). The purpose of the secondary market is two-fold: to smooth out cyclical periods of tight money, and to enable capital-rich regions of the county to provide mortgage funds to areas of the country where demand exceeds local supply. It has been estimated that 65 to 70 percent of all new mortgage loans each year are sold on the secondary market.

The ability to participate in the secondary market is a great advantage to a lending institution. Participation enables the lender to increase liquidity, obtain a hedge against future inflation, and engage in the profitable mortgage servicing business. In order to participate in these markets, however, federal government regulations require title insurance.

Michael Braunstein, Structural Change and Inter–Professional Competitive Advantage: An Example Drawn from Residential Real Estate Conveyancing, 62 Mo. L. Rev. 241 (1997).

I. LENDER LIABILITY

Many purchasers of residential real property who purchase without legal representation apparently think that if the lender is willing to accept the title, the title must be acceptable for the purchaser as well. How valid is this reasoning? What does the lender stand to lose if the title to a property proves defective or encumbered? What does the purchaser stand to lose? How do the interests of each change over time? Can you think of encumbrances that might affect the use of the property by the purchaser but not the security of the lender's loan? Moreover, what recourse does the purchaser have against the lender or its attorney if title proves defective? Consider the following case.

PAGE v. FRAZIER

Supreme Judicial Court of Massachusetts, 1983.
388 Mass. 55, 445 N.E.2d 148 (1983).

LYNCH, JUSTICE.

The plaintiffs appeal from an adverse decision on the merits of their claims of negligent misrepresentation against defendants Attorney Charles E. Frazier, Jr., and the Cape Cod Five Cents Savings Bank (bank), which retained Frazier to perform a real property title examination on property being purchased by the plaintiffs. A judge of the Superior Court, who heard the case without a jury, dismissed the complaint after making comprehensive findings of fact and rulings of law, summarized below. We granted the plaintiffs' motion for direct appellate review. We affirm the judgments.

The plaintiffs, husband and wife, purchased a house in Wellfleet in 1964. Beginning in 1967, the plaintiff Robert G. Page (Page) sought to ascertain the ownership of an abutting, unimproved parcel of slightly over 1.1 acres; * * * In November, 1972, Page entered into an agreement to purchase the parcel for $14,500, from heirs of Lorenzo Dow Baker (sellers). * * * Page applied to the bank for an $8,700 mortgage loan on November 21, 1972. The bank's mortgage application form included the following language: "(1) The responsibility of the attorney for the mortgagee is to protect the interest of the mortgagee, notwithstanding the fact that (a) the mortgagor shall be obligated to pay the legal fees of said attorney, and (b) the mortgagor is billed for such legal services by the mortgagee. (2) The mortgagor may, at his own expense, engage an attorney of his own selection to represent his own interests in the transaction."[22]

Page's application was approved on November 22, 1972. Thereafter the bank retained Frazier, an experienced conveyancing attorney, and a vice-president and trustee of the bank as well, to certify the title to the property and to draft the necessary legal instruments. The judge found that it was the bank's practice at that time to require an attorney so retained to certify a good, clear, marketable title. The bank also requested from the sellers' attorney, and received on or about December 8, 1972, a general list of title references to deeds, probate decrees, and wills to assist Frazier in his examination of the title. In February, 1973, the sellers' attorney forwarded to the bank a proposed deed without title references. When executed ultimately in April, 1973, the quitclaim deed from the sellers to the plaintiffs was in the same form as the proposed deed. The title references in the December 8 communication from the sellers' attorney were photocopied and appended to the quitclaim deed and were recorded with it, on April 17, 1973, by Frazier, or at his direction. In his title examination Frazier had also relied on five separate survey plans of abutting owners and an unrecorded survey plan prepared in 1926 which, upon his research, yielded a reference to a deed to Lorenzo Dow Baker in 1900. Frazier searched that chain of title from 1926 onward. The 1900 deed, however, had no connection with the subject locus, and the property which it described had been conveyed out in 1909. A survey plan prepared for the sellers in January, 1973, and available to Frazier during his examination, referred to a 1932 deed which the parties stipulated during trial did not describe the subject locus.

The judge found that Page was not "particularly conversant with the intricate elements or ramifications of title examinations. However, Robert Page [was] a high-level executive possessing concomitant intelligence, ability and knowledge of business transactions. [He had] both purchased and sold real property for his personal use on a number of occasions prior to the transaction in issue." Page had engaged Frazier in 1967 to review his will and had from time to time inquired of Frazier as to possible real estate sites in Wellfleet. In purchasing property prior to 1972, Page had retained another attorney.

22. The plaintiffs have noted the use of this language, which appeared on the application for a mortgage loan on unimproved land, and which the judge termed as "statutory." General Laws c. 184, § 17B, inserted by St.1969, c. 423, required the language to be printed in large type only on applications for loans "on real estate consisting of a dwelling house with accommodations for four or less separate households and occupied or to be occupied in whole or in part by the obligor on the mortgage debt." By St.1972, c. 547, § 2, approved June 29, 1972, and in effect at the time of Page's application, a portion of the language required to appear on application forms was deleted. As the judge noted, St.1972, c. 547, § 1, also amended G.L. c. 93, by inserting § 70, which provided for limited liability of a bank's attorney to a borrower paying the attorney's fee, subject to the same dwelling and occupancy conditions contained in c. 184, § 17B. The judge ruled that G.L. c. 93, § 70, had no application to the case at bar.

With respect to the instant transaction, in addition to the mortgage application form, the following documents involving Page or Frazier were in evidence: (1) a letter from Frazier to Page, dated March 3, 1973, requesting the plaintiffs' signatures on an enclosed proposed mortgage deed, mortgage note, and disclosure form showing a bank attorney's charge of $125 for recording and for title certification, payable by the plaintiffs;[23] (2) a letter from Page to Frazier, dated March 6, 1973, indicating that all forms forwarded on March 3 had been signed and were being returned; (3) a letter from Page to Frazier, dictated on March 28, 1973, enclosing a check for the balance of the purchase price, and adding: " * * * I would appreciate it very much if you would have the deed properly recorded for me. I will not be represented by an attorney in this transaction"; (4) a letter from Frazier to a vice-president of the bank, dated April 19, 1973, certifying that he had examined the record title to the parcel and had recorded the mortgage note on April 17, 1973, also stating that "[t]itle at the time of said recording was free and clear of any and all encumbrances of record," and requesting that a check for the mortgage loan proceeds be forwarded "payable to me as Attorney for the Pages." The bank assumed this letter indicated a good, clear, marketable title. A copy of the letter was sent to Page by the bank. In July, 1974, Page entered into an agreement of first refusal on the parcel with Stanford and Dorothy Ross. In December, 1975, the Pages and the Rosses executed a purchase and sale agreement. When the prospective buyers' attorney was unable to find good record and marketable title, Page contacted Frazier, who attempted without success to obtain a release of the Rosses' right of first refusal on the parcel. An attorney subsequently retained by the bank and a title researcher engaged by Page's attorney could not find title in the plaintiffs from the reference on their quitclaim deed. The title researcher determined that the deed reference upon which Frazier had relied did not convey the subject locus as a matter of record. The plaintiffs then commenced this action against Frazier and the bank.

The judge found that no record title had been established in the plaintiffs and that no good, clear, marketable title in them was ascertainable, based on Frazier's examination. She further found that, although the plaintiffs had shown by a fair preponderance of the evidence that Frazier was negligent in the performance of his title examination, they had failed to show the existence of an attorney-client relationship between them and Frazier.[24] As she found that Frazier was an independent contractor retained by the bank to represent its interests, the judge declined to impute his negligent performance to the bank, which she

23. Page was neither billed for this charge nor did he pay it. This fact, however, would not preclude a finding that an attorney-client relationship existed. * * *

24. The judge specifically found: "Despite the one statement to the [b]ank at the conclusion of the transaction wherein Frazier referred to himself as the 'Attorney for the Pages,' I find that the only express contract between the plaintiff and Frazier was relative to the recording of the deed. As Frazier was representing the bank, I find no privity of contract between Page and Frazier nor any attorney-client relationship."

* * *

found had neither expressly nor impliedly warranted title to Page. On appeal, the plaintiffs argue that an attorney-client relationship did exist between Frazier and them; that even if such a relationship did not exist, their action for negligent misrepresentation against Frazier should not be barred; that Frazier's negligence must be imputed to the bank; and that the bank negligently misrepresented to them the sufficiency of title to the parcel.

We consider first the plaintiffs' contention that there is a statutory basis for their claim against Frazier. We recognize that the Legislature has modified the common law, to a certain extent, through the provisions of G.L. c. 93, § 70. As enacted by St.1972, c. 547, § 1, and in effect at the time of the present transaction, § 70 provided in material part:

"Whenever, in connection with the granting of any loan or credit to be secured by a mortgage on real estate improved with a dwelling designed to be occupied by not more than four families and occupied or to be occupied in whole or in part by the mortgagor, the mortgagor is required or agrees to pay or to be responsible for any fee or expense charged or incurred by any attorney acting for or on behalf of the mortgagee, the mortgagor or his attorney shall be given a copy of any certification of title to the mortgaged property rendered by the mortgagee's attorney, and such certification shall be deemed to have been rendered for the benefit of the mortgagor to the same extent as it is for the mortgagee." * * * The plaintiffs urge us to extend the principle of G.L. c. 93, § 70, to the case before us. We can find, however, no suggestion or implication in the clear language of the statute that it is intended to be applicable to purchasers of unimproved land. * * *

We turn next to the plaintiffs' argument that an attorney-client relationship existed between them and Frazier. * * * Whether an attorney-client relationship existed between Frazier and the plaintiffs was a disputed issue to be resolved by the trier of fact. * * * The judge's finding that no attorney-client relationship was created between Frazier and the plaintiffs is amply supported by the evidence. [ ] Such a relationship may be, but need not be, express; the relationship can be implied from the conduct of the parties. [ ] Here, the judge weighed all the evidence, including Page's education and experience, his communications with Frazier, the mortgage application's language relative to the attorney's fee and representation, and Frazier's conduct in making no direct certification at all to Page and in certifying to the bank after the transaction had closed. She concluded, from conflicting evidence, that the plaintiffs had not carried their burden of proving an express or implied attorney-client relationship. * * *

The plaintiffs argue that the absence of an attorney-client relationship should not preclude them from recovering from Frazier for negligent misrepresentation of good, clear, marketable title to the property they wished to purchase. While they cite to us no case wherein a mortgagee's attorney has been held liable to a mortgagor for negligent performance of a real property title examination, the plaintiffs point to a general common law trend permitting recovery by injured nonclients for the negligent conduct of attorneys. Cf. Lucas v. Hamm, 56 Cal.2d 583, 15 Cal.Rptr. 821, 364 P.2d 685 (1961), cert. denied, 368 U.S. 987, 82 S.Ct. 603, 7 L.Ed.2d 525 (1962) (lack of privity was not a bar to an action by beneficiaries of a will alleging negligent drafting by the testator's attorney). We do not find the plaintiffs' authorities persuasive here, as we deal with the attorney's liability to another where the attorney is also under an independent and potentially conflicting duty to a client. [ ] See also Attorney Negligence in Real Estate Title Examination and Will Drafting: Elimination of the Privity Requirement as a Bar to Recovery by Foreseeable Third Parties, 17 New Eng.L.Rev. 955 (1982). As the judge noted in the instant case, "It is not only in the matter of items such as prepayment rights, disclosure law, late charge provisions and special mortgage provisions where a conflict of interest could arise if the attorney represented both bank and borrower, but many experienced conveyancers would acknowledge that there is a conflict of interest even with respect to title as there are some title defects which will not make the property unsatisfactory as a security but which would concern a buyer." Compare Lucas v. Hamm, supra, with Amey, Inc. v. Henderson, Franklin, Starnes & Holt, P.A., 367 So.2d 633 (Fla.Dist.Ct.App.1979) (allowance of defendants' motion for summary judgment on claims of attorney-client relationship and third-party beneficiary theory upheld where bank's attorneys were alleged by mortgagor to have negligently failed to discover a tax lien on the subject property).

* * *

* * * The present plaintiffs signed a mortgage application, conspicuous upon which was the bank's cautionary advice that its attorney would represent its interests, and that the plaintiffs might retain their own attorney to represent their interests. Because of what she termed this "strong exculpatory language," the judge concluded that the plaintiffs were not "entitled * * * to rely upon the defendant's performance." * * * In the case at bar, Frazier's contract with the bank was exclusively and expressly for the benefit and protection of the bank. Quite conceivably, the bank's interest could have differed materially from the plaintiffs' and the plaintiffs have not shown that they knew what type of certification the bank would require of Frazier at the time they claim reliance upon his performance. Nor do we think they have shown that Frazier could foresee their reliance from a letter dictated by Page five days before he expected the transaction to close, in which he informed Frazier that he was not represented by an attorney.

* * * The judge noted that Page's belief "that Frazier's role as the [b]ank's attorney in searching the title was representative of his interest as well * * * is not unusual * * * when a bank requires the borrower to pay the attorney's fee." Inherent in such a belief is the surmise that the client's interest is identical to the nonclient's. "However, this is a calculated risk, and if it proves to be unfounded, the buyer has no claim that the lawyer violates a duty owed to him." Amey, Inc. v. Henderson,

Franklin, Starnes & Holt, P.A., 367 So.2d 633, 635 (Fla.Dist.Ct.App. 1979). Where, as here, a nonclient takes the chance that the client's interests are in harmony with his own, and does so in the face of an express warning that the interests may differ, his claim of foreseeable reliance cannot be rescued simply because, in retrospect, the interests are shown not to have differed. * * *

The plaintiffs also seek recovery from the bank for its alleged negligent misrepresentation that Frazier's title examination had revealed no irregularities. * * * Page testified that he telephoned a vice-president of the bank to inquire whether his loan application had been approved, and that during the conversation he said that he "would be using the bank's attorney, * * * would not be using an attorney [because] it was a simple transaction * * * [and he] saw no sense in employing two attorneys to do the same job, or words to that effect." Beyond this testimony, the record does not show that the plaintiffs made any inquiry with respect to the condition of the title, nor does it show that either defendant made any representation whatsoever to the plaintiffs with respect to the status of the title examination or the sufficiency of the title prior to the closing. In the absence of some evidence of affirmative conduct on the part of the bank, there could be no reasonable understanding or reliance by the plaintiffs at the time the plaintiffs would have had to rely on such conduct, i.e., before they closed the sale. [ ] It follows that there could be no knowledge of reliance by the bank. [ ] The evidence supports the judge's finding of "no express or implied warranty on the part of the [b]ank to Page relative to the title of the locus." Since there was no evidence of any representations on behalf of the bank to Page, this finding also precludes recovery on the basis of negligent misrepresentation.

On our view that this case presents no demonstrated duty by Frazier or the bank to the plaintiffs with respect to performance of the title examination, the plaintiffs' arguments advancing liability on the theory that Frazier was an employee or agent of the bank are unavailing.

Judgment affirmed.

Notes and Questions

1. In addition to the theories argued in the principal case, a purchaser might also argue breach of contract, if contractual terms obligate the lender to establish clear title for the benefit of the purchaser, or breach of fiduciary duty. In the absence of a statute like the Massachusetts provision distinguished in the principal case, however, the courts are reluctant to find lenders liable to purchaser. See Note, Mortgage Lender Liability to the Purchasers of New or Existing Homes, 1988 U.Ill.L.Rev. 191.

2. Would it be unethical for an attorney to represent both a lender and a purchaser in conducting a title search?

3. What protection is in fact enjoyed by a purchaser of residential real property who does not retain an attorney for the transaction, but rather

relies on the issuance of a title policy without significant specific exceptions
and the fact that a lender will finance most of the purchase price? Would the
purchaser be significantly better protected if she retained an attorney to
handle the purchase? Would the purchaser be more or less likely to end up
in disputes or litigation if he or she retained an attorney to handle the
transaction? Does the added cost of an attorney exceed the added benefit?
How would you go about answering these questions?

IV. THE CONDITION OF THE PREMISES

Under modern conditions the purchaser of real property is often at
least as interested in the physical condition of the building that sits on
the property as in the condition of the title to the property underlying
the building. Legal disputes concerning the condition of the improvements on the premises commonly arise under two circumstances. First, if
the condition of the improvements changes dramatically (because of fire,
flood, or other disaster) while the property is under contract (i.e.
between the time the contract is signed and the time that title changes
hands), the parties argue over who bears the risk of loss. Second, if
improvements prove to be defective, the purchaser turns to those who
participated in the sale of the property for compensation for the damages
attributable to the defects.

A. RISK OF LOSS WHILE THE PROPERTY IS UNDER CON-TRACT

SKELLY OIL COMPANY v. ASHMORE

Supreme Court of Missouri, 1963.
365 S.W.2d 582.

HYDE, JUDGE.

* * *

This is a suit by the purchaser, Skelly Oil Company, a corporation,
against the vendors, Tom A. Ashmore and Madelyn Ashmore, husband
and wife, in two counts. Count One is for the specific performance of a
contract to sell the north half of a certain described southwest corner lot
(fronting 97 1/2 feet on Main and 195 feet on 42nd Streets) in that part
of Joplin lying in Newton County. Count Two seeks an abatement in the
purchase price of $10,000, being the proceeds received by the vendors
under an insurance policy on a building on the property, which building
was destroyed by fire in the interim between the execution of the
contract of sale and the time for closing of said sale by the exchange of
the $20,000 consideration for the deed to the property. * * * The trial
court found the issues in favor of the purchaser, decreed specific performance, and applied the $10,000 insurance proceeds on the $20,000
purchase price. The vendors have appealed.

The vendors acquired this property about 1953, and operated a
grocery store in the concrete block building, with fixtures and furniture,
and a one story frame "smoke house" thereon. * * *

Joe Busby, of the Kansas City office of the Skelly Oil Company real estate department, and Mr. Ashmore conducted the negotiations resulting in the contract of sale. * * * Busby secured the execution of a Skelly printed form of option by the vendors, dated July 31, 1957, for Skelly "to purchase" for the sum of $20,000, "payable in cash upon delivery of deed" said property, "together with the buildings, driveways, and all construction and equipment thereon, at any time before" August 31, 1957. * * * The option provided in typewriting (referring to the Jones lease): "Purchaser agrees to honor present lease on above property until expiration." * * *

* * *

[After attempts to terminate the lease proved unsuccessful] Busby informed Ashmore Skelly had decided to purchase under its option with Jones in possession under his lease. * * *

* * *

* * * By letter to the Ashmores under date of March 4, 1958, Skelly explicitly stated: "This letter is to inform you that Skelly Oil Company does hereby exercise its option to purchase the above described property for the sum of $20,000.00, subject to all the terms and conditions of the above referred to option, * * * "

The latter part of March Busby telephoned to Ashmore in Lawton and they agreed to meet in Joplin on April 16, 1958, to close the transaction.

The concrete block building, furniture and fixtures were destroyed by fire on April 7, 1958, without fault of either party.

Skelly's Kansas City headquarters advised Busby, who was in St. Joseph, on April 7 of the fire. The next day Busby telephoned Ashmore from Kansas City. In this conversation Ashmore said he had insurance on the building and fixtures, naming the company in Kansas City carrying it. * * * Busby called the insurance company and was informed there was $10,000 insurance on the building and $4,000 on the fixtures. He reported this to the purchaser's legal department. Then, after research, the legal department concluded that Skelly was entitled to have the insurance on the building applied on the purchase price. The closing papers were prepared accordingly.

The closing of the transaction was considered by the parties on April 15, 16 and 17. Busby [and Skelly's lawyer] * * * informed Ashmore * * * that Skelly thought it was entitled to the insurance proceeds on the building and would like an assignment of the insurance proceeds. When Ashmore disagreed, they informed him Skelly would close the deal and pay him the contract price but would not waive its rights to the insurance proceeds in so doing. Ashmore would not agree to this. * * *

By letter dated April 26, 1958, the Ashmores notified Skelly that the "option agreement" was rescinded "because it was given without consideration and is therefore not binding on us and for the further reason that you have refused to complete the purchase unless we reduce the agreed price, which constitutes a breach of the terms of the agreement.''

A month or so later the Phoenix Insurance Company, under the standard mortgage clause, paid the Bank of Neosho the balance due on the vendors' notes, $7,242.46, and $2,757.54, the balance of the $10,000 insurance on the building, to the vendors, and also paid the vendors the $4,000 insurance carried on the furniture and fixtures.

This purchaser's claims are founded on the contract of sale in its letter of March 4, 1958, and the option therein referred to, which letter was "acknowledged and agreed to" by the vendors. * * *

* * *

The contract of sale here involved contained no provision as to who assumed the risk of loss occasioned by a destruction of the building, or for protecting the building by insurance or for allocating any insurance proceeds received therefor. When the parties met to close the sale on April 16, the purchaser's counsel informed vendors and their attorney he was relying on Standard Oil Co. v. Dye, 223 Mo.App. 926, 20 S.W.2d 946, for purchaser's claim to the $10,000 insurance proceeds on the building. Purchaser made no claim to the $4,000 paid vendors for the loss of the furniture and fixtures. It is stated in 3 American Law of Property, § 11.30, p. 90, that in the circumstances here presented at least five different views have been advanced for allocating the burden of fortuitous loss between vendor and purchaser of real estate. We summarize those mentioned: (1) The view first enunciated in Paine v. Meller (Ch. 1801, 6 Ves.Jr. 349, 31 Eng. Reprint 1088, 1089) is said to be the most widely accepted; holding that from the time of the contract of sale of real estate the burden of fortuitous loss was on the purchaser even though the vendor retained possession. (2) The loss is on the vendor until legal title is conveyed, although the purchaser is in possession, stated to be a strong minority. (3) The burden of loss should be on the vendor until the time agreed upon for conveying the legal title, and thereafter on the purchaser unless the vendor be in such default as to preclude specific performance, not recognized in the decisions. (4) The burden of the loss should be on the party in possession, whether vendor or purchaser, so considered by some courts. (5) The burden of loss should be on the vendor unless there is something in the contract or in the relation of the parties from which the court can infer a different intention, stating "this rather vague test" has not received any avowed judicial acceptance, although it is not inconsistent with jurisdictions holding the loss is on the vendor until conveyance or jurisdictions adopting the possession test. As to the weight of the authority, see also 27 A.L.R.2d 448; Tiffany, Real Property, 3rd ed., § 309.

We do not agree that we should adopt the arbitrary rule of Paine v. Meller, supra, and Standard Oil Co. v. Dye, supra, that there is equitable conversion from the time of making a contract for sale and purchase of land and that the risk of loss from destruction of buildings or other

substantial part of the property is from that moment on the purchaser.
* * *

We take the view stated in an article on Equitable Conversion by Contract, 13 Columbia Law Review 369, 386, Dean Harlan F. Stone, later Chief Justice Stone, in which he points out that the only reason why a contract for the sale of land by the owner to another operates to effect conversion is that a court of equity will compel him specifically to perform his contract. He further states: "A preliminary to the determination of the question whether there is equitable ownership of land must therefore necessarily be the determination of the question whether there is a contract which can be and ought to be specifically performed *at the very time when the court is called upon to perform it.* This process of reasoning is, however, reversed in those jurisdictions where the 'burden of loss' is cast upon the vendee. The question is whether there shall be a specific performance of the contract, thus casting the burden on the vendee, by compelling him to pay the full purchase price for the subject matter of the contract, a substantial part of which has been destroyed. The question is answered somewhat in this wise: equitable ownership of the vendee in the subject matter of the contract can exist only where the contract is one which equity will specifically perform. The vendee of land is equitably entitled to land, therefore the vendee may be compelled to perform, although the vendor is unable to give in return the performance stipulated for by his contract. The *non sequitur* involved in the proposition that performance may be had because of the equitable ownership of the land by the vendee, which in turn depends upon the right of performance, is evident. The doctrine of equitable conversion, so far as it is exemplified by the authorities hitherto considered, cannot lead to the result of casting the burden of loss on the vendee, since the *conversion depends upon the question whether the contract should in equity be performed.* In all other cases where the vendee is treated as the equitable owner of the land, it is only because the contract is one which equity first determines should be specifically performed.

"Whether a plaintiff, in breach of his contract by a default which goes to the essence, as in the case of the destruction of a substantial part of the subject matter of the contract, should be entitled to specific performance, is a question which is answered in the negative in every case except that of destruction of the subject matter of the contract. To give a plaintiff specific performance of the contract when he is unable to perform the contract on his own part, violates the fundamental rule of equity that * * * *equity will not compel a defendant to perform when it is unable to so frame its decree as to compel the plaintiff to give in return substantially what he has undertaken to give* or to do for the defendant.

"The rule of casting the 'burden of loss' on the vendee by specific performance if justifiable at all can only be explained and justified upon one of two theories: first, that since equity has for most purposes treated the vendee as the equitable owner, it should do so for all purposes, although *this ignores the fact that in all other cases the vendee is so treated only because the contract is either being performed or in equity ought to be performed; or,* second, which is substantially the same proposition in a different form, the specific performance which casts the burden on the vendee is an incident to and a consequence of an equitable conversion, whereas in all other equity relations growing out of the contract, the equitable conversion, if it exists, is an incident to and consequence of, a specific performance. Certainly nothing could be more illogical than this process of reasoning." (Emphasis ours.)

For these reasons, we do not agree with the rule that arbitrarily places the risk of loss on the vendee from the time the contract is made. Instead we believe the Massachusetts rule is the proper rule. It is thus stated in Libman v. Levenson, 236 Mass. 221, 128 N.E. 13, 22 A.L.R. 560: When "the conveyance is to be made of the whole estate, including both land and buildings, for an entire price, and the value of the buildings constitutes a large part of the total value of the estate, and the terms of the agreement show that they constituted an important part of the subject matter of the contract * * * the contract is to be construed as subject to the implied condition that it no longer shall be binding if, before the time for the conveyance to be made, the buildings are destroyed by fire. The loss by the fire falls upon the vendor, the owner; and if he has not protected himself by insurance, he can have no reimbursement of this loss; but the contract is no longer binding upon either party. If the purchaser has advanced any part of the price, he can recover it back. [ ] If the change in the value of the estate is not so great, or if it appears that the building did not constitute so material a part of the estate to be conveyed as to result in an annulling of the contract, specific performance may be decreed, with compensation for any breach of agreement, or relief may be given in damages." [ ] * * * The reason for the Massachusetts rule is that specific performance is based on what is equitable; and it is not equitable to make a vendee pay the vendor for something the vendor cannot give him.

However, the issue in this case is not whether the vendee can be compelled to take the property without the building but whether the vendee is entitled to enforce the contract of sale, with the insurance proceeds substituted for the destroyed building. We see no inequity to defendants in such enforcement since they will receive the full amount ($20,000.00) for which they contracted to sell the property. Their contract not only described the land but also specifically stated they sold it "together with the buildings, driveways and all construction thereon." While the words "Service Station Site" appeared in the caption of the option contract and that no doubt was the ultimate use plaintiff intended to make of the land, the final agreement made by the parties was that plaintiff would take it subject to a lease of the building which would have brought plaintiff about $6,150.00 in rent during the term of the lease. Moreover, defendants' own evidence showed the building was valued in the insurance adjustment at $16,716.00 from which $4,179.00 was deducted for depreciation, making the loss $12,537.00. Therefore, defendants are not in a very good position to say the building was of no value to plaintiff. Furthermore, plaintiff having contracted for the land with the building on it, the decision concerning use or removal of the building, or even for resale of the entire property, was for the plaintiff to make. Statements were in evidence about the use of the building and its value to plaintiff made by its employee who negotiated the purchase but he was not one of plaintiff's chief executive officers nor possessed of authority to bind its board of directors. The short of the matter is that defendants will get all they bargained for; but without the building or its value plaintiff will not.

We therefore affirm the judgment and decree of the trial court.

STORCKMAN, JUDGE (dissenting).

I agree that the parties on March 7, 1958, entered into a valid contract for the transfer of the real estate, but in the circumstances I cannot assent to the holding that the plaintiff is entitled to specific performance on any terms other than those of the purchase contract without reduction in the contract price. * * *

The evidence is convincing that Skelly Oil Company was buying the lot as a site for a service station and that in so using it they not only wanted the Jones's lease terminated but intended to tear down and remove the building in question. * * * This conduct is consistent with its prior activities, but is inconsistent with plaintiff's present contention that the building and its rental under the lease represented a substantial part of the consideration for the purchase of the real estate.

* * *

The plaintiff introduced no evidence of the market value of the property before or after the fire in support of the allegations in Count 2. The amount paid by the insurance company is of little or no benefit as evidence of the actual value of the building * * *. Defendants' evidence tended to prove that the real estate was worth more as a site for a service station after the fire than before and that the value of the real estate after the fire was in excess of $20,000.

The claim of neither party is particularly compelling insofar as specific performance in this case is concerned. The destruction of the building by fire, its insurance, and the disposition of the insurance proceeds were matters not contemplated by the parties and not provided for in the purchase contract documents. Skelly's representative did not know that Mr. Ashmore carried insurance on the building until after the fire, and he then told Mr. Ashmore that despite the fire the deal would be closed on the agreed date. Skelly's present claims are an afterthought inconsistent with its conduct throughout the negotiations and prior to the closing date.

In short, as to both Skelly and the Ashmores, the destruction of the insured building was a fortuitous circumstance supplying the opportunity to rid the property of a vexatious lease, to dispose of the building, and at the same time resulting in a windfall of $10,000. And the problem, in fact the only seriously contested issue between the parties, is which of them is to have the advantage of this piece of good fortune. Skelly contracted to pay $20,000 for the property. If it is awarded the $10,000 windfall, it will receive a $20,000 lot for $10,000. If the Ashmores retain the $10,000, they will in fact have realized $30,000 for a piece of property they have agreed to sell for $20,000.

In claiming the proceeds of the Ashmores' fire insurance policy, Skelly did not contend that the value of the real estate as a service station site had decreased. * * * [Skelly relied on cases following Paine v. Meller, (1801) 6 Ves.Jr. 349, 31 Eng.Reprint 1088. The holding of that case] is "that a contract to sell real property vests the equitable ownership of the property in the purchaser, with the corollary that any loss by destruction of the property through casualty during the pendency of the contract must be borne by the purchaser." Annotation 27 A.L.R.2d 444, 446. The two-fold rationale of this doctrine is a maxim that "equity regards as done that which should have been done," from which it is said the "vendor becomes a mere trustee, holding the legal title for the benefit of the purchaser or as security for the price." 27 A.L.R.2d 444, 448, 449. All of the experts and scholars seem to agree that this doctrine and its rationale is misplaced if not unsound. To illustrate see only 4 Williston, Contracts, §§ 928–943B, pp. 2605–2639. As to the maxim, Williston said, "Only the hoary age and frequent repetition of the maxim prevents a general recognition of its absurdity." 4 Williston, Contracts, § 929, p. 2607. As to the corollary, Williston points out that while the purchaser may have an interest in the property, it is equally clear that the vendor likewise has an interest, and as for the vendor's being a trustee for the purchaser observes, "However often the words may be repeated, it cannot be true that the vendor is trustee for the purchaser." 4 Williston, Contracts, § 936, p. 2622. See also Pound "The Progress of The Law—Equity", 33 Harv.L.R. 813, 830.

Nevertheless, adapting this doctrine and following a majority opinion in another English case, Rayner v. Preston, (1881) L.R. 18 Ch.Div. 1 (CA), the rule as stated in the Dye case has evolved: "Where the purchaser as equitable owner will bear the loss occasioned by a destruction of the property pending completion of the sale, and the contract is silent as to insurance, the rule quite generally followed is that the proceeds of the vendor's insurance policies, even though the purchaser did not contribute to their maintenance, constitute a trust fund for the benefit of the purchaser to be credited on the purchase price of the destroyed property, the theory being that the vendor is a trustee of the property for the purchaser." Annotation 64 A.L.R.2d 1402, 1406. Many jurisdictions have modified or do not follow this doctrine, some take the view that the vendor's insurance policy is personal to him, and Parliament has enacted a statute which entirely changes the English rule. 4 Mo.L.R. 290, 296. The rule is not as general as the annotator indicated, and as with the rule upon which it is founded, all the experts agree that it is unsound, their only point of disagreement is as to what the rule should be. See 4 Williston, Contracts, §§ 928–943; Vance, Insurance, § 131, p. 777, and 34 Yale L.J. 87; Vanneman, "Risk of Loss, Between Vendor and Purchaser", 8 Minn.L.R. 127; Pound, "The Progress of The

Law", 33 Harv.L.R. 813, and the excellent student note to Standard Oil Co. v. Dye in 4 Mo.L.R. 290. * * *

* * *

Automatic application of the doctrine that "equity regards that as done which ought to be done", in the circumstances of this case, begs the question of what ought to be done. Because the insurance proceeds may be a windfall to those legally entitled does not necessarily mean that justice will be accomplished by transferring them elsewhere. * * *

A valid legal excuse is a sufficient reason for refusal of specific performance. * * * Destruction of a particular thing upon which the contract depends is generally regarded as a legal excuse for nonperformance. * * *

* * *

If plaintiff's contention is that there has been a substantial failure or impairment of the consideration of the contract by reason of the destruction of the building, then I do not think that the Ashmores should be entitled to specific performance, and because of the theory of mutuality it would seem that Skelly would not be entitled to specific performance unless it was willing to perform its legal obligations under the purchase contract as drawn. We would not be justified in making a new contract for the parties to cover the building insurance, and a court of equity will not decree specific performance of a contract that is incomplete, indefinite or uncertain. * * *

* * *

But Skelly did not after the fire or in this action elect to abandon the contract although the Ashmores gave it the opportunity to do so rather than to sell at the reduced price. It is quite evident that Skelly has received one windfall as the result of the fire in that the lease is terminated and the site can be cleared at less cost. It has not shown itself to be entitled to another, the one now legally vested in the Ashmores. Ideally the purchase contract should be set aside so that the parties could negotiate a new one based on the property in its present condition. But the plaintiff by its election to take title has foreclosed this possibility.

[The majority] * * * professes to repudiate the equitable conversion theory and to adopt unequivocally the Massachusetts rule, * * *.

Obviously the majority opinion did not find that the value of the building constituted "a large part of the total value of the estate" or "an important part of the subject matter of the contract", else it would have declared the sales contract no longer binding under the Massachusetts rule. What it had to find was that the value of the building was not so great or such a material part of the estate to be conveyed as to interfere with the decree of specific performance.

But at this point the majority opinion abandons any pretense of following the Massachusetts rule and switches back to the equitable conversion theory and awards the insurance proceeds as such to the vendee without a determination of compensation for breach or relief to be given in damages. The value of the building for insurance purposes or as a structure to house a retail store is not necessarily the proper measure of the compensation or damages to which the plaintiff is entitled. It might be considerably less than such a figure if Skelly intended to remove the building as soon as it had the legal right to do so. Obviously the Massachusetts rule is not tied in with insurance at all and that is as it should be. Logically the majority opinion should have remanded the case for a determination of the amount of actual damages suffered by Skelly or the compensation to which it is entitled if it still wants specific performance. This is undoubtedly what the Massachusetts rule contemplates. I would find no fault with such a procedure.

Such evidence would also have a bearing on whether specific performance should be decreed at all, which was the first matter to be determined. Actually without such evidence the court does not have any basis for its finding as to the value of the building to the vendee and whether it was "an important part of the subject matter of the contract". Such a determination is a necessary prerequisite to granting or denying specific performance under the Massachusetts rule before the assessment of damages is reached. As the opinion stands, the adoption of the Massachusetts rule is more imaginary than real. The equitable conversion theory is applied, not the Massachusetts rule.

* * *

Notes and Questions

1.   As a practical matter, there is necessarily a hiatus between the time when the parties enter into a contract for sale of real property and the time when closing, or transfer of possession, occurs. During this so-called "executory period," buyer searches title, obtains a survey and financing, and performs structural and other inspections in order to satisfy the conditions set forth in the contract. Because of this hiatus, the operative facts upon which the transaction was structured may change, the most dramatic being a destruction of the improvements by fire, hurricane or other casualty. How does the contract reproduced above at pages 478–482 handle the problem of risk of loss? Why does it not adopt the common-law equitable conversion approach?

Frequently the parties avoid the doctrine of equitable conversion by allocating the risk of loss by contract. Allocation of the risk of loss takes on large proportions following natural disasters. A flurry of cases arose in Florida following hurricane Andrew in 1992. Compare Munshower v. Martin, 641 So.2d 909 (Fla.Dist.Ct.App.1994) (holding that the contract, which stated "The risk of loss or damage to said premises by fire or other cause until closing, is assumed by the seller," placed the risk of loss on the seller), with Alvarez v. Garcia, 662 So.2d 1312 (Fla.Dist.Ct.App.1995) (placing the risk of loss on the buyer in the absence of such a provision).

2. The doctrine of equitable conversion represents the triumph of doctrinal elegance over common sense and the expectations of the parties to a transaction. The *Skelly* case explores fully the roots of the doctrine and its most important application: the situation where the property is destroyed during the contract period. The doctrine has been applied also, however, where a vendor or purchaser dies with real property passing to one person or groups of persons and the personal property passing to another by will or intestate succession. Under a rigorous application of the doctrine of equitable conversion, equitable title to the property would pass as realty to those who inherit the real property from the purchaser; the obligation to pay for, or exonerate, the land would be imposed on the personal representative, to be satisfied from the personal property. Conversely, legal title would pass to those who inherited real property from the vendor, but would be held subject to the equitable obligation to convey the property. The proceeds from the property equitably would belong to the personal representative of the vendor, to be turned over to the legatees or next-of-kin.

In most states, heirs and next-of-kin are the same persons, so the rule is only important if property passes under a will that distinguishes between those who inherit real and those who inherit personal property. Where a will is involved, courts should be more concerned with the intent of the testator than with doctrinal elegance, but the rule of equitable conversion is still applied in some cases, particularly where the testator's intent is unclear. To explore the vagaries of this application of the doctrine further, consult III The American Law of Property, §§ 11.26 and 11.27.

When creditors of the vendor attempt to attach a judgment lien against property under contract, some courts also apply the doctrine of equitable conversion, finding that the property is no longer equitably that of the vendor. The lien, which attaches to all real property of the judgment debtor, thus does not attach. Other cases reject the doctrine and allow the lien to attach. The rights of the purchaser, however, are not affected unless he has notice of the lien, and even then, he is merely obligated to pay the creditor rather than the vendor payments due under the contract.

Should the doctrine of equitable conversion apply if property under contract is seized under the eminent domain authority? Should it apply if changed zoning or environmental regulations deprive the land of much of its value between the contract and closing?

3. The Uniform Vendor and Purchaser Risk Act (UVPRA) is one of several model acts drafted to address the risk of loss problem. It was drafted by Professor Samuel Williston and has been adopted by twelve jurisdictions.

Any contract hereafter made in this State for the purchase and sale of realty shall be interpreted as including an agreement that the parties shall have the following rights and duties, unless the contract expressly provides otherwise:

(a) If, when neither the legal title nor the possession of the subject matter of the contract has been transferred, all or a material part thereof is destroyed without fault of the purchaser or is taken by eminent domain, the vendor cannot enforce the contract, and the purchaser is entitled to recover any portion of the price that he has paid;

(b) If, when either the legal title or the possession of the subject matter of the contract has been transferred, all of any part thereof is destroyed without fault of the vendor or is taken by eminent domain, the purchaser is not thereby relieved from a duty to pay the price, nor is he entitled to recover any portion thereof that he has paid.

See also § 2–406 of the Uniform Land Transactions Act.

Does the UVPRA solve the problem presented in the *Skelly* case? Was the loss material in *Skelly*? If not, what relief, if any, does the UVPRA afford *Skelly*?

B.   REMEDIES FOR DEFECTS IN THE PREMISES AFTER THE PROPERTY IS TRANSFERRED

Not uncommonly the purchaser of real property is disappointed with the building he has bought. The land beneath it settles, the walls, ceilings, and basement floors crack, the roof leaks, termite infestation is discovered, the plumbing or wiring is defective, the well is poisoned. The purchaser then looks to those with whom he dealt in the conveyancing process for relief. If he bought the property from a builder or developer, he may make, along with other claims, a straightforward breach of warranty claim for defective merchandise. If the property was a used building, purchased from a previous owner, analogies to the commercial law setting are less obvious. The buyer also may look to those he trusted and depended on to protect his interests in the purchase process: the real estate broker, the lender, an appraiser, perhaps even a loan guarantor such as the VA or FHA. Traditionally, the doctrine of caveat emptor left the buyer unprotected, wherever he may have turned. But this is changing, as the following materials illustrate.

ROSE, CRYSTALS AND MUD IN PROPERTY LAW
40 Stan. L. Rev. 577 (1988).

THE DEMISE OF CAVEAT EMPTOR

For several hundred years, and right up to the last few decades, caveat emptor was the staple fare of the law of real estate purchases, at least for buildings already constructed. The purchaser was deemed perfectly capable of inspecting the property and deciding for himself whether he wanted it, and if anyone were foolish enough to buy a pig in a poke, he deserved what he got. Short of outright fraud that would mislead the buyer, the seller had no duties to disclose anything at all.

One chink in this otherwise smooth wall was the doctrine of "latent defects," which, like the exception for fraud, suggested that perhaps the buyer really can't figure things out entirely. For some time now, in at least some states, a seller has had to tell a buyer about material problems with the property known to the seller but undiscoverable by the purchaser upon reasonable inspection. The doctrine began to raise a few problems of muddiness: What defects are "material"? What does the seller "know"? To what extent should the buyer "reasonably" have to inspect for herself?

Within the last few decades, the movement to mud in this area has become even more pronounced as some courts and legal commentators maintain that builder/vendors implicitly warrant a new house "habitable." But what does habitability mean? Is the house's habitability coterminous with the local housing code, or does "habitability" connote some less definite standard? What if the defects were obvious, and just what does "obvious" mean, anyway? We don't know until we litigate the issues.

Even if a builder/vendor's warranties do muddy up property rights, there are some plausible reasons for them. After all, the builder/vendors are professionals, and they should know more about their own construction; they even might have avoided the problems in the first place by building more carefully. It is somewhat more difficult to extend those arguments to sellers who are themselves merely homeowners instead of builder/vendors, yet we find that even these nonprofessional sellers have increasing obligations to anticipate the buyers' desires, and to inform buyers about disagreeable factors that might make the buyers think twice. A California court, for example, has ruled that the sellers had to inform the buyer that a mass murder had taken place a decade previously in a particular house. The courts now seem to presume a buyer who can't figure out much at all, and to protect that buyer they have adopted a mud standard: like good neighbors, sellers must tell buyers about any "material" defects—whatever those may be. . . .

But there is a countermove as well: Even if the legal rules have moved toward mud, private bargainers often try to install their own little crystalline systems through contractual waivers of warranties or disclosure duties (for example, the "as is" or "no warranty" sale). These private efforts in effect move things into the pattern of a circle, from crystal to mud and back to crystal. And the circle turns once again when the courts ban such waivers, as they sometimes do, and firmly reestablish a rule of mud—only to be followed by even more artful waivers. . . .

TUSCH ENTERPRISES v. COFFIN

Supreme Court of Idaho, 1987.
113 Idaho 37, 740 P.2d 1022.

DONALDSON, JUSTICE.

Tusch Enterprises appeals from an order of the district court granting summary judgment in favor of Robert and Elizabeth Vander Boegh, husband and wife, and Rex T. Coffin. Tusch Enterprises brought this action after discovering that residential duplexes it had recently purchased suffered from major structural infirmities. The complaint advanced the following theories of recovery: (1) negligence, (2) misrepresentation, (3) express warranty, and (4) implied warranty of habitability. We reverse the entry of summary judgment as to the misrepresentation and implied warranty of habitability counts.

I

FACTS

We present the facts in the light most favorable to Tusch Enterprises. Robert Vander Boegh, a man with considerable experience in the road construction business, and his wife owned land in Pocatello, Idaho, and decided to build three duplexes. The rolling foothill upon which the duplexes were to be built was levelled for construction by Bengal Construction. The Vander Boeghs then contracted with Rex Coffin, a building contractor, to erect the duplexes. Pursuant to their agreement, Coffin was to prepare plans for the duplexes, secure all the necessary building permits, and build the structures. The site preparation and the outside work, such as gutters, lawns, curbs, and grading, were left to Robert Vander Boegh to do, or to contract out.

Coffin began working on the site in the fall of 1975. In his deposition, he describes some difficulties he encountered in securing a permit:

* * *

Throughout his deposition, Coffin testifies that Robert Vander Boegh told him the site had been cut from the mountain, and that no fill dirt had been used. The presence of fill dirt is significant because it tends to compact more and is thus more likely to cause foundations to settle and crack. During construction, Coffin became concerned enough about the "softness" of the soil where the south duplex was to be built that he asked a building inspector to investigate. Coffin testifies that the softness was brought to Vander Boegh's attention:

* * *

In early 1976, after the duplexes were completed, the Vander Boeghs began renting out the duplex apartments. Later, they listed the properties for sale with a realtor. * * *

On June 7, 1978, Tusch Enterprises offered to purchase the duplexes for $125,000. The offer was rejected. During this time period, Marianne Tusch met with Robert Vander Boegh and his realtor. In her deposition, Marianne Tusch testifies that Vander Boegh informed her he worked for a construction company, had access to site preparation equipment, and had participated in the site preparation. She also testifies that Vander Boegh stated the buildings were of "good quality construction." By affidavit, she asserts that she relied upon these representations. On June 15, 1978, a second offer of about $140,000 was communicated to the Vander Boeghs. Vander Boegh told Marianne Tusch that he would either accept the second offer or take the property off the market. He chose the latter.

Sometime later, the duplexes were re-listed. Tusch Enterprises became aware of this, and on March 27, 1979, submitted an offer of $140,000. The Vander Boeghs accepted this third offer, though it was substantially the same as the one they had rejected only nine months earlier.

Prior to purchasing the units, Tusch Enterprises had inspected them and noticed no major defects. However, about one month after purchasing the duplexes, Tusch Enterprises discovered from a tenant that the south unit was having problems. The walls had begun cracking around the windows and many of the doors would not close properly. Further investigation revealed that the foundation was cracking. Geotechnical and construction experts have submitted affidavits and testified by deposition of their opinion that the foundation had been partially constructed on fill dirt, which had compacted causing the foundation to settle and crack. They are of the opinion that the foundation was improperly constructed given the fill dirt conditions.

Marianne Tusch testifies in her deposition that she was not told of the fill dirt conditions, or of the possible problems with the foundation. She further testifies that one of the cracks in the south unit appeared to have been filled in, or patched, with cement. After discovering the problems with the foundation, Tusch Enterprises learned from the Vander Boeghs that Coffin had actually constructed the duplexes and attempted, without success, to discuss the problems with Coffin. Tusch Enterprises expended a great deal of money remedying the problems. The structural defects have caused damage to the duplexes themselves and to the parking lot, and have caused losses in rental income, but Tusch Enterprises has suffered no personal injuries and has suffered no damage to property other than that which was the subject of the duplex sales transaction.

Suit was filed against the Vander Boeghs and Coffin to seek compensation for these structural defects. Tusch Enterprises alleged negligence, misrepresentation, express warranty, and implied warranty and prayed for damages for loss of rental value and costs of repair. The case was before a number of district judges at different stages, and eventually summary judgment was entered against Tusch Enterprises as to all four theories of recovery.

* * *

II

Negligence

Tusch Enterprises alleges negligence on the part of the Vander Boeghs and Coffin in the design and construction of the duplexes. However, the only damages it alleges are lost rental income and property damage to the duplexes and the parking lot. These losses are economic.
* * *

In Clark v. International Harvester Co., 99 Idaho 326, 581 P.2d 784 (1978), we had to decide whether the purchaser of a defective product who has suffered only economic losses may recover those losses in a negligence action against the manufacturer. We ruled that purely economic losses are not recoverable in negligence. Other courts have criticized limiting the negligence theory in this manner. See, e.g., Council of

Co–Owners v. Whiting–Turner, 308 Md. 18, 517 A.2d 336, 344–45 (1986), and the cases cited therein. These courts argue that the distinction between economic and other loss is arbitrary. However, as we explained in Clark with the words of Justice Traynor, in our view:

> "[t]he distinction that the law has drawn between tort recovery for physical injuries and warranty recovery for economic loss is not arbitrary and does not rest on the 'luck' of one plaintiff in having an accident causing physical injury. The distinction rests, rather, on an understanding of the nature of the responsibility a manufacturer must undertake in distributing his products. He can appropriately be held liable for physical injuries caused by defects by requiring his goods to match a standard of safety defined in terms of conditions that create unreasonable risks of harm. He cannot be held for the level of performance of his products in the consumer's business unless he agrees [expressly or impliedly] that the product was designed to meet the consumer's demands." Clark, supra, 99 Idaho at 334, 581 P.2d at 792, quoting Seely v. White Motor Co., 63 Cal.2d 9, 45 Cal.Rptr. 17, 23, 403 P.2d 145, 151 (1965). (Addition ours.)

* * *

We adhere to the view expressed in Clark, and, accordingly, affirm the decision of the court below dismissing Tusch Enterprises' negligence claims.

III

MISREPRESENTATION

In its complaint, Tusch Enterprises alleges misrepresentation on the part of Robert Vander Boegh. Tusch Enterprises directs the court's attention to Faw v. Greenwood, 101 Idaho 387, 613 P.2d 1338 (1980), and argues that the elements of misrepresentation outlined therein have been satisfied. The elements are as follows:

> "(1) a representation; (2) its falsity; (3) its materiality; (4) the speaker's knowledge of its falsity or ignorance of its truth; (5) his intent that it should be acted on by the person and in the manner reasonably contemplated; (6) the hearer's ignorance of its falsity; (7) his reliance on the truth; (8) his right to rely thereon; and (9) his consequent and proximate injury." Id., at 389, 613 P.2d at 1340, quoting Mitchell v. Siqueiros, 99 Idaho 396, 401, 582 P.2d 1074, 1079 (1978).

We do not believe Tusch Enterprises' misrepresentation claim should be analyzed only with reference to the elements recited in Faw, supra. It must also be considered whether the facts here fall within the category of cases finding a misrepresentation on the basis of nondisclosure.

We addressed the instances where nondisclosure may amount to misrepresentation in Bethlahmy v. Bechtel, 91 Idaho 55, 415 P.2d 698 (1966). In Bethlahmy, the defendant, Bechtel, was the builder and vendor of a residential home. Bechtel told the plaintiffs that the houses he built were the finest, and that the house at issue was of first quality construction. However, Bechtel did not disclose to the plaintiffs that a tiled water line ran underneath the garage and to within seven or nine feet of the north wall of the residence. * * *

Relying upon § 551 of a tentative draft of the Restatement (Second) of Torts,[25] the court found that the plaintiffs had presented facts entitling them to relief:

> "Defendant did not testify that he called attention to, or advised plaintiffs of, the ditch running under the lot and garage; nor that the ditch was constructed of drainage tile without sealed joints; nor that the basement was not of waterproof construction. These facts were known to defendant and unknown to plaintiffs. They were not discoverable by inspection. Defendant had superior knowledge. Plaintiffs were ignorant of the facts. The parties did not deal at arms length. Defendant dealt from a position of superior knowledge. A confidential relationship arose between the parties. Stearns v. Williams, 72 Idaho 276, 288, 240 P.2d 833 (1952). Plaintiffs relied, and were entitled to rely, upon defendant's representation that the house would be a quality home. The facts essential to a finding of constructive fraud * * * are not in dispute." Id., at 62, 415 P.2d at 705.

The rationale for recognizing such a cause of action was explained in Bethlahmy with the following quotation from Kaze v. Compton, 283 S.W.2d 204, 207 (Ky.1955):

> "It cannot be controverted that actionable fraud or misrepresentation by a vendor may be by concealment or failure to disclose a hidden condition or a material fact, where under the circumstances there was an obligation to disclose it during the transaction. If deception is accomplished, the form of the deceit is immaterial. And the legal question is not affected by the absence of an intent to deceive, for the element of intent, whether good or bad, is only important as it may affect the moral character of the representation." Bethlahmy, supra, 91 Idaho at 60, 415 P.2d at 703.

25. The tentative draft provision relied upon in Bethlahmy was adopted after only minor cosmetic changes. Restatement (Second) of Torts § 551 (1977) provides in pertinent part: "§ 551. Liability for Nondisclosure (1) One who fails to disclose to another a fact that he knows may justifiably induce the other to act or refrain from acting in a business transaction is subject to the same liability to the other as though he had represented the nonexistence of the matter that he has failed to disclose, if, but only if, he is under a duty to the other to exercise reasonable care to disclose the matter in question. (2) One party to a business transaction is under a duty to exercise reasonable care to disclose to the other before the transaction is consummated, (a) matters known to him that the other is entitled to know because of a fiduciary or other similar relation of trust and confidence between them; and (b) matters known to him that he knows to be necessary to prevent his partial or ambiguous statement of the facts from being misleading; and * * * (e) facts basic to the transaction, if he knows that the other is about to enter into it under a mistake as to them, and that the other, because of the relationship between them, the customs of the trade or other objective circumstances, would reasonably expect a disclosure of those facts."

Kaze v. Compton explained that actual intent to deceive need not be shown where the seller knew of facts which would have apprised a person of ordinary prudence of the truth: if a reasonable person would have been so apprised, and the seller was under a duty to inform the buyer of the concealed facts, then intent to deceive is not necessary to make a prima facie showing. Kaze, supra, at 208.

After his conversation with Coffin, Vander Boegh knew, or should have known, that the south duplex was, at least partially, built upon fill dirt. A person of ordinary prudence with a background similar to Vander Boegh's (e.g., with extensive road construction experience and knowledge of compaction), who knew of the fill dirt would have been apprised of the truth (e.g., that problems with the foundation were likely). Yet, by Tusch Enterprises' account, Vander Boegh did not disclose the fill dirt problems, and, instead, assured Marianne Tusch that the duplexes were quality dwellings. * * *

We hold that it was error to dispose of Tusch Enterprises' misrepresentation claim against the Vander Boeghs at the summary judgment stage. Genuine issues of material fact exist whether the nondisclosure of the soil problems, coupled with the assurance that the duplexes were quality constructed, amounted to a misrepresentation. See Restatement (Second) of Torts § 551(2)(a), (b) and (e). * * *

IV

Express Warranty

Tusch Enterprises alleges that the Vander Boeghs and Coffin breached an express warranty to the effect that the duplexes were well-constructed. Regarding Coffin, Tusch Enterprises readily admits that it did not know of Coffin until after it had purchased the duplexes and problems had become evident. There being nothing in the record to show that Coffin made any warranties to the Vander Boeghs or had any discussions with Tusch Enterprises, we affirm the dismissal of the express warranty claim against Coffin. With regard to the Vander Boeghs, the facts alleged in support of an express warranty are essentially those discussed in the preceding section under misrepresentation. Tusch Enterprises argues that these representations of quality construction became part of the bargain. However, we find that the parol evidence rule precludes Tusch Enterprises from making such an assertion and, accordingly, affirm the decision below dismissing the express warranty claim against the Vander Boeghs.

Before further addressing the applicability of the parol evidence rule, it is necessary to supplement the facts previously recited. When the third offer was accepted by the Vander Boeghs, they and Tusch Enterprises signed an earnest money agreement. This written document was prepared by Marianne Tusch, and included the following language with which she had become familiar through her employment with a real estate agency:

"The undersigned Buyer hereby acknowledges further that he has not received or relied upon any statements or representation by the undersigned broker or his representatives or by the Seller which are not herein expressed. The Buyer has entered into this agreement relying solely upon information and knowledge obtained from his own investigation or personal inspection of the premises. This agreement constitutes the whole agreement between the parties and no warranties, agreements or representations have been made or shall be binding upon either party unless herein set forth."

A short time after executing the earnest money agreement, the parties entered into a written real estate contract, which was prepared by the Vander Boeghs. This contract provided that it incorporated the terms and conditions of the earnest money agreement, except as modified by the real estate contract. The portions of the real estate contract pertinent to the present inquiry are as follows:

"12. EXCLUSIVE TERMS: This contract is the entire agreement between the parties and all other agreements heretofore entered into, either written or oral, are hereby either abrogated or contained in this agreement. All prior oral agreements and conditions are expressly waived unless stated in this agreement and the parties expressly understand they have no mutual understanding or agreement other than as herein set forth.

"13. WARRANTIES: The Purchasers have fully inspected the above described premises and know just exactly what they are purchasing. Sellers warrant that they have a good and sufficient title, and that the premises have no code violations or governmental restrictions as of May 15, 1979, and that further as of May 15, 1979, Sellers warrant that they know of no defects in the sewers, plumbing, electrical items, and mechanical items in and about the property. Other than as set forth in this paragraph, Sellers make no further warranties with regard to the condition of the sewer lines, utility poles, fences, curbs, sidewalks, streets, patios or any other mechanical item of any description whatsoever within the described premises."

The features of the parol evidence rule are aptly stated in Chapman v. Haney Seed Co., Inc., 102 Idaho 26, 624 P.2d 408 (1981):

"It is the general rule that when a contract has been reduced to writing, which the parties intend to be a complete statement of their agreement, any other written or oral agreements or understandings (referred to in many cases as extrinsic evidence) made prior to or contemporaneously with the written 'contract' and which relate to the same subject matter are not admissible to vary, contradict or enlarge the terms of the written contract." Id., at 28, 624 P.2d at 410.

* * *

From these facts, it is apparent that the parties intended the real estate contract, and the earnest money agreement by incorporation, to be a complete and exclusive statement of the terms of their agreement. The evidence proffered by Tusch Enterprises to the effect that the Vander Boeghs, prior to execution of these agreements, warranted that the duplexes were well-constructed is evidence that would vary, contradict or enlarge the terms of the written contract. Thus, under the parol evidence rule, this evidence was properly excluded, and the express warranty count against the Vander Boeghs was properly dismissed.[26]

V

IMPLIED WARRANTY

The final theory of recovery which we need address is implied warranty of habitability. Tusch Enterprises alleges a breach on the part of both Coffin and the Vander Boeghs. First, the Court will examine whether the integrated writings of the parties preclude the implied warranty of habitability. Next, we will address the issue whether the implied warranty of habitability extends to dwellings purchased for income-producing purposes which have never been occupied by the buyers. Then, we will determine if genuine issues of material fact exist as to whether the Vander Boeghs may have been builders or builder-developers and, thus, warrantors of habitability; and, if so, whether issues of material fact exist as to a breach of that warranty. Finally, we have to determine if genuine issues of material fact exist as to whether Coffin may have been a builder and, thus, a warrantor of habitability; and, if so, whether the implied warranty of habitability would extend to subsequent purchasers.

A. Disclaimers

As noted in the preceding section, the integrated agreement of the parties purports to set forth all the warranties which attached to the duplexes. However, the warranty of habitability is not specifically mentioned or disclaimed in either the earnest money agreement or the real estate contract.

The majority of states permit a disclaimer of an implied warranty of habitability, but the disclaimer must be clear and unambiguous and such disclaimers are strictly construed against the builder-vendor. Belt v. Spencer, 41 Colo.App. 227, 585 P.2d 922, 925 (1978); Bridges v. Ferrell, 685 P.2d 409, 411 (Okla.Ct.App.1984); Crowder v. Vandendeale, 564 S.W.2d 879 (Mo.1978) (en banc). We agree with these courts * * *.

* * *

The disclaimers in the instant case fall woefully short of fulfilling these requirements. Because the implied warranty of habitability is a

26. It may appear odd that we did not address the parties' merger clauses in our discussion above of misrepresentation, especially since Tusch Enterprises advances the same facts in support of both express warranty and misrepresentation, and since the merger clauses, when read together provide that the buyer has relied upon no representations other than those expressed in the two written agreements. The parol evidence rule, however, does not apply to averments of fraud, misrepresentation, mutual mistake or other matters which render a contract void or voidable. See 3 Corbin on Contracts § 580 (1960); and Restatement (Second) of Contracts § 214 (1981). * * *

creature of public policy, public policy dictates that it be waived only with difficulty. The party asserting that it has been waived bears the burden of proving that it has been knowingly waived. Clearly, when no mention is made of the implied warranty of habitability in a contract, and the contract contains only general language stating there are no warranties other than those contained within its four corners, any purported waiver of the implied warranty of habitability is ineffective.

Because we find that the implied warranty of habitability has not been disclaimed, we proceed to the next topic.

B. Buyers

Next, we consider whether the implied warranty of habitability extends only to buyers who reside in dwellings after they are purchased. The uncontroverted facts show that Tusch Enterprises purchased the duplexes at issue for income-producing purposes and, rather than residing in them, has leased them to others. * * *

* * *

We refuse to restrict the implied warranty of habitability to buyers who personally reside in dwellings after they are purchased. It is of no matter who ultimately inhabits the home after purchase, be it the buyer, a relative or lessee. The implied warranty is that the structure will be fit for habitation, and resolution of the question whether the buyer has received that which he bargained for does not depend upon the status of the buyer or ultimate user; it depends upon the quality of the dwelling delivered and the expectations of the parties. In transactions in goods, our Uniform Commercial Code implies warranties of merchantability and fitness for a particular purpose when certain circumstances are present. See I.C. §§ 28–2–314 and 28–2–315 (1980). Yet, the UCC does not distinguish, as Hopkins does with sales of homes, between buyers who seek income through the use of purchased goods and buyers who merely acquire them for personal use. The focus must be upon the product, be it a typewriter or a home, and not upon the buyer. * * *

* * *

Therefore, we hold that the implied warranty of habitability extends to residential dwellings purchased for income-producing purposes which have never been occupied by the buyers.

C. Vander Boeghs

The court below granted summary judgment in favor of the Vander Boeghs on Tusch Enterprises' implied warranty of habitability count.

In Bethlahmy, supra, we recognized that when builder-vendors sell newly constructed buildings there is an implied warranty that the buildings will be habitable. Our rejection of the doctrine of caveat emptor as applied to the sale of new houses is consistent with the vast weight of authority. [ ] The trend away from the doctrine of caveat emptor in transactions of this nature is rooted in considerations of public policy:

"The mores of the day have changed and the ordinary home buyer is not in a position to discover hidden defects in a structure. A home buyer should be able to place reliance on the builder or developer who sells him a new home, the purchase of which in so many instances, is the largest single purchase a family makes in a lifetime. Courts will judicially protect the victims of shoddy workmanship. Consumer protection demands that those who buy homes are entitled to rely on the skill of the builder and that the house is constructed so as to be reasonably fit for its intended use. The average purchaser is without adequate knowledge or opportunity to make a meaningful inspection of the component parts of a residential structure." Moxley v. Laramie Builders, Inc., 600 P.2d 733, 735 (Wyo.1979) (footnote omitted).

Economic policy considerations come into play as well:

"[B]y virtue of superior knowledge, skill, and experience in the construction of houses, a builder-vendor is generally better positioned than the purchaser to know whether a house is suitable for habitation. He also is better positioned to evaluate and guard against the financial risk posed by a [latent defect], and to absorb and spread across the market of home purchasers the loss therefrom. In terms of risk distribution analysis, he is the preferred or 'least cost' risk bearer. Finally, he is in a superior position to develop or utilize technology to prevent such defects: and as one commentator has noted, 'the major pockets of strict liability in the law' derived from 'cases where the potential victims * * * are not in a good position to make adjustments that might in the long run reduce or eliminate the risk.' R. Posner, Economic Analysis of Law 140–41 (2d ed. 1977)." Gaito v. Auman, 70 N.C.App. 21, 318 S.E.2d 555, 559 (1984), aff'd, 313 N.C. 243, 327 S.E.2d 870 (1985).

Further, the implied warranty of habitability is not limited to builder-developers:

"We can see no difference between a builder or contractor who undertakes construction of a home and a builder-developer. To the buyer of a home the same considerations are present, no matter whether a builder constructs a residence on the land of the owner or whether the builder constructs a habitation on land he is developing and selling the residential structures as part of a package including the land. It is the structure and all its intricate components and related facilities that are the subject matter of the implied warranty. Those who hold themselves out as builders must be just as accountable for the workmanship that goes into a home * * * as are builder-developers." Moxley, supra, at 735.

However, the implied warranty of habitability only applies to those who are in the business of building dwellings. Hibbler v. Fisher, 109

Idaho 1007, 712 P.2d 708 (Ct.App.1985); Klos v. Gockel, 87 Wash.2d 567, 554 P.2d 1349, 1352 (1976) (en banc); Moxley, supra.

By adopting the implied warranty of habitability, we did not intend to make builders or developers the insurers against any and all defects in a home:

> "The implied warranty of fitness [for habitability] does not impose upon the builder an obligation to deliver a perfect house. No house is built without defects, and defects susceptible of remedy ordinarily would not warrant rescission. But major defects which render the house unfit for habitation, and which are not readily remediable, entitle the buyer to [relief]. The builder-vendor's legitimate interests are protected by the rule which casts the burden upon the purchaser to establish the facts which give rise to the implied warranty of fitness [for habitability], and its breach." Bethlahmy, supra, 91 Idaho at 68, 415 P.2d at 711.

* * *

Construing the facts in favor of Tusch Enterprises, we note that Robert Vander Boegh had many years of experience in the road construction business. Regarding the duplexes, he contracted with Coffin to have the structures built. He contracted with others to level the land and make other site preparations. He periodically visited the site during the construction phase and consulted with Coffin about the possibility of fill dirt existing under the south duplex. Coffin stated that he relied upon Vander Boegh's expertise in these matters. From these facts it cannot be concluded that there is no genuine issue as to whether Vander Boegh was a developer-builder or merely an ordinary person with little expertise who contracted with others to have a house built for him. * * *

Having found that genuine issues of material fact exist, we hold that it was error for the court below to dismiss Tusch Enterprises' implied warranty of habitability claim against Vander Boeghs.

D. Coffin

Construing the facts again in favor of Tusch Enterprises, we conclude that they are sufficient to raise an issue as to whether Coffin was a builder in the sense that an implied warranty of habitability would flow from him. The Court, however, must consider a remaining issue: whether a subsequent purchaser of residential dwellings may assert a claim for breach of the implied warranty of habitability against the builder of the dwellings when there is no privity of contract between them.

The growing trend among other jurisdictions is to extend the implied warranty of habitability to subsequent purchasers. The following courts have so extended the doctrine: Barnes v. Mac Brown & Co., Inc., 264 Ind. 227, 342 N.E.2d 619 (1976) (cracks in basement walls); Moxley, supra, (Wyo.1979) (defective electrical wiring); Terlinde v. Neely, 275 S.C. 395, 271 S.E.2d 768 (1980) (foundation settled causing walls to crack, floors to sink, doors to not close properly, etc.); Hermes v. Staiano,

181 N.J. Super. 424, 437 A.2d 925 (N.J. Super. Ct. Law Div.1981) (defects in foundations wall and underground sewage disposal system); Blagg v. Fred Hunt Co., Inc., 272 Ark. 185, 612 S.W.2d 321 (1981) (strong odor and fumes from formaldehyde); Elden v. Simmons, 631 P.2d 739 (Okla.1981) (defective bricks); Redarowicz, supra, (1982) (defects in chimney and wall); Keyes v. Guy Bailey Homes, Inc., 439 So.2d 670 (Miss.1983) (foundation cracked); Gupta v. Ritter Homes, Inc., 646 S.W.2d 168 (Tex.1983) (foundation settled excessively causing walls to crack, roof to leak, and patio to pull away from house); and Richards v. Powercraft Homes, Inc., 139 Ariz. 242, 678 P.2d 427 (1984) (en banc) (faulty pipes, separation of floors from walls, cracking of walls, doors that would not close, etc.).

In choosing to follow this trend, the Arizona Supreme Court explained that limiting the implied warranty to first buyers would not only be arbitrary, but might encourage sham first sales calculated to insulate builders from liability. They explained further:

> "The same policy considerations that lead to [our adoption of the implied warranty of habitability for sales of new homes]—that house-building is frequently undertaken on a large scale, that builders hold themselves out as skilled in the profession, that modern construction is complex and regulated by many governmental codes, and that homebuyers are generally not skilled or knowledgeable in construction, plumbing, or electrical requirements and practices— are equally applicable to subsequent homebuyers. Also, we note that the character of our society is such that people and families are increasingly mobile. Home builders should anticipate that the houses they construct will eventually, and perhaps frequently, change ownership. The effect of latent defects will be just as catastrophic on a subsequent owner as on an original buyer and the builder will be just as unable to justify improper or substandard work. Because the builder-vendor is in a better position than a subsequent owner to prevent occurrence of major problems, the cost of poor workmanship should be his to bear." Richards, supra, 678 at 430.

We adopt the reasoning of these courts, but with the following proviso:

> "This extension of liability is limited to latent defects, not discoverable by a subsequent purchaser's reasonable inspection, manifesting themselves after the purchase. The standard to be applied in determining whether or not there has been a breach of warranty is one of reasonableness in light of surrounding circumstances. The age of the home, its maintenance, the use to which it has been put, are but a few factors entering into this factual determination at trial." Barnes, supra, 342 N.E.2d at 621.

This extension to subsequent purchasers is also limited to latent defects which manifest themselves within a reasonable time. Redarowicz, supra, 65 Ill.Dec. at 411, 441 N.E.2d at 331; Moxley, supra. Further:

"The burden is on the subsequent owner to show that the defect had its origin and cause in the builder-vendor. * * * Defenses are, of course, available. The builder-vendor can demonstrate [that the suit was not brought within the appropriate statute of limitations,] that the defects are not attributable to him, that they are the result of age or ordinary wear and tear, or that previous owners have made substantial changes." Richards, supra, 678 P.2d at 430.

* * *

We hold only that subsequent purchasers of residential dwellings, who suffer purely economic losses from latent defects manifesting themselves within a reasonable time, may maintain an action against the builder (or builder-developer, as the case may be,) of the dwelling based upon the implied warranty of habitability despite the fact that no privity of contract exists between the two. Any other holding would lead to an absurd result. For example, suppose an unscrupulous builder constructed a home of inferior quality and sold it to another. Suppose further, that for whatever reason, the buyer after three months sold the home to a second purchaser. And one month later the foundation of the house split apart rendering the home valueless. Should the common law deny the subsequent purchaser a remedy against the builder merely because there is no privity of contract and because the damages happen to be purely economic, when it was the conduct of the builder which created the latent defect in the first place?

We conclude that it was error for the court below to enter summary judgment in favor of Coffin on Tusch Enterprises' implied warranty of habitability count.

The decision of the court below is affirmed as to the negligence and express warranty counts. The decision granting summary judgment against Tusch Enterprises on the misrepresentation and implied warranty counts is reversed, and remanded for further proceedings not inconsistent with this opinion.

Notes and Questions

1. As the principal case illustrates, claims involving damages from latent defects in new or relatively new buildings may involve a variety of combinations of plaintiffs and defendants. Such claims may be brought against either the builder, who constructed the building, or the developer, who is responsible for putting it on the market. The developer and builder may be the same or different entities. Claims may also be presented by initial or subsequent purchasers. Such claims may be asserted on a variety of theories based either in tort (negligence, strict liability, or misrepresentation), or contract (express or implied warranty).

The easiest case is probably an original purchaser's claim based on express warranty against an entity which is both the builder and developer. Many courts have also recognized implied warranty claims brought by initial purchasers against builders or developers. Several states have imposed warranties on new residential construction by statute. See Md.Real Prop. Code Ann. § 10–203; N.J.Stat.Ann § 46:3B; Va.Code Ann. § 55–70.1. Courts are generally receptive to tort claims where purchasers are injured because of defects in the premises, but where the only injuries are economic (i.e., loss of the expectancy interest), a number of courts have rejected tort claims for defects as noncompensable. Few courts have accepted strict liability claims.

Where claims are brought by subsequent purchasers against a builder or developer, or by an initial purchaser against a builder who was not the developer, the court must consider whether the lack of privity between the plaintiff and defendant defeats the claim. Lack of privity is probably a bar to recovery on an express warranty claim. The courts are split on the question of whether an implied warranty of habitability extends to subsequent purchasers of dwelling units, with a majority requiring privity. But see Von-Holdt v. Barba & Barba Constr., Inc., 175 Ill.2d 426, 432, 222 Ill.Dec. 302, 305, 677 N.E.2d 836, 839 (1997) (holding "that a subsequent purchaser has a cause of action for damages resulting from a breach of the implied warranty of habitability for latent defects caused in the construction of a significant structural addition to an existing residence."). Jurisdictions permitting recovery to subsequent purchasers in tort are less likely to find lack of privity to be fatal, though the economic loss rule often effectively bars recovery by subsequent purchasers for the cost of the defects themselves. See Briggs v. Riversound Ltd. Partnership, 942 S.W.2d 529 (Tenn.App.1996) (holding that a subsequent purchaser may maintain a suit for negligence against the home's builder despite a lack of privity).

The same requirements have barred suits against builders where the initial purchaser bought the property from a developer rather than from the builder itself; though if, as is sometimes the case, the developer is merely a shell corporation created by the builder, it can be argued that the court should consider the realities of the situation rather than its form. Jurisdictions permitting subsequent purchasers to recover do so for only a reasonable period of time, recognizing that as a home ages, defects are expected and are less often directly attributable to initial construction.

The principal case also addresses the efficacy of disclaimers of tort and contract liability. Disclaimers of tort liability for personal injury are generally held to be against public policy. Courts are more receptive to disclaimers against warranty liability, but are reluctant to accept vague or ambiguous attempts to disclaim liability. If a court permits a subsequent purchaser to recover, should disclaimers found in the contract between the initial purchaser and builder or developer be a bar?

Recovery is generally limited, in any event, to damages attributable to latent defects. Where defects are immediately evident, recovery is limited to rights that exist under contract.

Why might the right to recover against a builder or developer often prove an empty right? If you were representing a home purchaser, what protection would you prefer for your client? Is this a problem better handled through insurance rather than through tort or contract liability?

See, discussing these issues further, Annotation, Liability of Builder of Residence for Latent Defects Therein as Running to Subsequent Purchasers From Original Vendee, 10 A.L.R.4th 385 (1981); Annotation, Liability of

Builder–Vendor or Other Vendor of New Dwelling for Loss, Injury or Damage Occasioned by Defective Condition Thereof, 25 A.L.R.3d 383 (1969); Barrett, Recovery of Economic Loss in Tort for Construction Defects: A Critical Analysis, 40 S.C.L.Rev. 891 (1989); Cherry, Builder Liability for Used Home Defects, 18 Real Est.L.J. 115 (1989); Grand, Implied and Statutory Warranties in the Sale of Real Estate: The Demise of Caveat Emptor, 15 Real Est.L.J. 44 (1986); Note, Latent Defects: Subsequent Home Purchasers Beware, 40 S.C.L.Rev. 1017 (1989).

THOMSON v. McGINNIS

Supreme Court of Appeals of West Virginia, 1995.
195 W.Va. 465, 465 S.E.2d 922.

WORKMAN, JUSTICE:

This is an appeal by Rebecca A. Thomson (hereinafter "the Appellant"), from a final order of the Circuit Court of Kanawha County granting summary judgment to the Appellees, Erma McGinnis, Robert R. Vitello, and The Property Centre, Inc., in an action instituted by the Appellant alleging negligence and fraud in connection with her purchase of a home. The Appellant contends that genuine issues of material fact existed which should have precluded the lower court from granting summary judgment. We agree with the contentions of the Appellant, reverse the decision of the lower court, and remand this matter for consideration on the merits.

I.

On April 20, 1992, the Appellant contracted to purchase a home located in Charleston, West Virginia. The Appellant was represented by Ms. Pam Grey of Home Finders Associates, Inc., and the seller was represented by Appellee Erma McGinnis, a real estate agent employed by Appellee The Property Centre, Inc. At the request of the Appellant, the Appellees agreed to have the furnace inspected and to certify the working condition of the heating system. The approval of the mortgage loan was also conditioned upon this inspection.

David Stephens, owner of Appellee D & R Builders, was retained by Ms. McGinnis and The Property Centre, Inc., to inspect the residence for termites and to install smoke detectors. During his performance of these duties on June 4, 1992, he was contacted by Ms. McGinnis and asked to inspect the heating system. Mr. Stephens testified that he had previously been employed by Ms. McGinnis and The Property Centre, Inc., to inspect heating systems and that his performance of the inspection upon the home in question consisted of listening to the furnace running while he was in the home. He was later provided with a Heating Certification form by Ms. McGinnis upon which he certified that the furnace was in proper working condition. Having received certification of the condition of the furnace, the Appellant purchased the home.

On October 7, 1992, upon discovering that the furnace was not functioning, the Appellant telephoned Kerstein's Heating and Air–Conditioning. A representative of that business went to the Appellant's home and informed the Appellant that it would be dangerous to light the pilot light because the furnace had no safety shut-off switch. The Property Centre, Inc., was thereafter informed of the furnace problems, and Mr. Stephens and an associate went to the Appellant's residence to service the furnace. When the Appellant asked whether the associate was certified in heating and air-conditioning, it is the Appellant's testimony that Mr. Stephens informed her that neither Mr. Stephens nor his associate was certified in heating and air-conditioning. According to the testimony of both Mr. Stephens and the Appellant, Mr. Stephens also advised the Appellant that he never should have signed the certification and that he did so only at the direction of Ms. McGinnis. The Appellant thereafter obtained three estimates for a new furnace and accepted the bid of $1450. All three companies inspecting the furnace emphasized that the heating pipes connected to the furnace were wrapped in asbestos. The Appellant was informed by these companies that the asbestos could not be removed from the pipes due to the danger of asbestos fibers. The only recommendation they offered the Appellant was to wrap the pipes with tape to encase the asbestos insulation.

The Appellant filed a civil action alleging fraudulent misrepresentation and negligence on October 13, 1993. On September 22, 1994, the lower court granted the Appellees' motion for summary judgment. It is from that order that the Appellant appeals.

II.

In syllabus point one of Teter v. Old Colony Co., 190 W.Va. 711, 441 S.E.2d 728 (1994), we explained as follows:

> A vendor's real estate broker may be liable to a purchaser if the broker makes material misrepresentations with regard to the fitness or habitability of residential property or fails to disclose defects or conditions in the property that substantially affect its value or habitability, of which the broker is aware or reasonably should be aware, but the purchaser is unaware and would not discover by a reasonably diligent inspection. It also must be shown that the misrepresentation or concealment was a substantial factor in inducing the purchaser to buy the property.

Id. at 713, 441 S.E.2d at 730.

In *Teter*, the prospective purchasers had expressed concern about a crack in a retaining wall, and the real estate agent agreed to secure the services of an engineer to examine the wall. 190 W.Va. at 715, 441 S.E.2d at 732. Based upon a written report indicating that the wall was in good condition, the Teters purchased the property. Id. Upon the collapse of the retaining wall, the Teters sought to establish liability of the real estate company on the theories that it had failed to make a reasonably diligent inspection and that the engineering firm negligently inspecting the wall was an agent of the real estate company. Id. We held that a broker has no "independent duty to inspect and uncover latent defects on residential premises." 190 W.Va. at 719, 441 S.E.2d at 736.

We also concluded in *Teter* that the real estate company, by hiring an engineering firm to conduct an investigation, did not create an agency relationship whereby the real estate company could become liable for negligent acts of the engineering firm. Id. We based this latter determination upon the absence of any "evidence demonstrating that the broker retained any control over the manner in which the engineering firm performed its inspection of the premises." Id. at 720, 441 S.E.2d at 737. As we noted in syllabus point three of *Teter*, "[o]ne of the essential elements of an agency relationship is the existence of some degree of control by the principal over the conduct and activities of the agent." Id. at 713, 441 S.E.2d at 730. In syllabus point two of *Teter*, we also explained as follows:

> "An agent in the restricted and proper sense is a representative of his principal in business or contractual relations with third persons; while a servant or employee is one engaged, not in creating contractual obligations, but in rendering service, chiefly with reference to things but sometimes with reference to persons when no contractual obligation is to result." Syllabus Point 3, State ex rel. Key v. Bond, 94 W.Va. 255, 118 S.E. 276 (1923).

190 W.Va. at 713, 441 S.E.2d at 730.

In syllabus point four of Painter v. Peavy, 192 W.Va. 189, 451 S.E.2d 755 (1994), we explained the following:

> Summary judgment is appropriate where the record taken as a whole could not lead a rational trier of fact to find for the nonmoving party, such as where the nonmoving party has failed to make a sufficient showing on an essential element of the case that it has the burden to prove.

Id. at 190, 451 S.E.2d at 756.

We emphasized the necessity for the nonmoving party to "take initiative and by affirmative evidence demonstrate that a genuine issue of fact exists." 192 W.Va. at 192, 451 S.E.2d at 758 n. 5. Doubt regarding the existence of a genuine issue of material fact, however, is to be resolved against the moving party. [   ]. Moreover, as we emphasized in syllabus point four of Henderson v. Coombs, 192 W.Va. 581, 453 S.E.2d 415 (1994), " '[t]he question to be decided on a motion for summary judgment is whether there is a genuine issue of fact and not how that issue should be determined.' Syl. pt. 5, Aetna Casualty & Surety Co. Federal Ins. Co. of N.Y., 148 W.Va. 160, 133 S.E.2d 770 (1963)." Id. at 582, 453 S.E.2d at 416.

In the present case, unlike the scenario in *Teter*, there was some evidence tending to demonstrate that the broker retained an element of control over the actions of the individual inspecting the furnace. Despite the Appellees' contention that Mr. Stephens acted only as an independent contractor, the Appellant testified in her deposition that she was informed by Mr. Stephens that he signed the certification upon the direction of Ms. McGinnis. Mr. Stephens also testified that Ms. McGinnis contacted him while he was at the home performing the termite inspection and requested him to inspect the furnace, and that she actually provided him with the written heating certification to sign. We have previously noted that where factual conflict exists regarding the degree of control exercised and the nature of the relationship thereby created, jury resolution is warranted. [ ]. In *Spencer*, we stated that "[a]s a general rule, where the evidence relating to an independent contractor or employee is conflicting, or if not conflicting, where more than one inference can be derived therefrom, the question is one of fact for jury determination...." [ ]. In syllabus point five of Pasquale v. Ohio Power Co., 187 W.Va. 292, 418 S.E.2d 738 (1992), we elaborated:

> "One who would defend against tort liability by contending that the injuries were inflicted by an independent contractor has the burden of establishing that he neither controlled nor had the right to control the work, and if there is a conflict in the evidence and there is sufficient evidence to support a finding of the jury, the determination of whether an independent contractor relationship existed is a question for jury determination." Syllabus Point 1, Sanders v. Georgia–Pacific Corp., 159 W.Va. 621, 225 S.E.2d 218 (1976).

187 W.Va. at 295, 418 S.E.2d at 741.

Based upon the foregoing, we find that there exists a genuine issue of material fact regarding the existence of an agency relationship between the Appellees and Mr. Stephens, precluding the summary judgment granted by the lower court.[27]

III.

As an alternative to her position that the Appellees are liable for the negligent acts of Mr. Stephens based upon an employer/employee relationship, the Appellant also alleges in her complaint that the Appellees owed her "a duty to use reasonable care to discover and communicate truthful information about the subject property, and in particular ... the qualifications of the Defendant, David R. Stephens, to inspect furnaces and heating systems." The Appellant further asserts that the Appellees "breached this duty of reasonable care to obtain and communicate truthful and accurate information concerning the subject property, and in particular ... the qualifications of the Defendant, David R. Stephens, to inspect furnaces and heating systems."

The Appellant is essentially asserting a claim of negligent hiring against the Appellees. While West Virginia has not previously addressed

27. If, upon remand, an agency relationship between Mr. Stephens and the Appellees is determined to exist, the rule of respondeat superior would apply to bind the Appellees for the negligent acts of their employee. As we noted in Barath v. Performance Trucking Co., 188 W.Va. 367, 424 S.E.2d 602 (1992), "[t]he fundamental rule in West Virginia is that if it can be shown that an individual is an agent and if he is acting within the scope of his employment when he commits a tort, then the principle is liable for the tort as well as the agent." Id. at 370, 424 S.E.2d at 605.

the specific issue of negligent hiring of an employee or an independent contractor, we have explained our approach to liability of an employer for the actions of an independent contractor as follows:

> The general rule is that where one person has contracted with a competent person to do work, not in itself unlawful or intrinsically dangerous in character, and who exercise no supervision or control over the work contracted for, such person is not liable for the negligence of such independent contractor or his servants in the performance of the work.

Syl. Pt. 1, Chenoweth v. Settle Eng'rs, Inc., 151 W.Va. 830, 156 S.E.2d 297 (1967), overruled in part on other grounds by Sanders, 159 W.Va. at 628, 225 S.E.2d at 222. (emphasis added). Other jurisdictions have entertained a cause of action for negligent hiring of an independent contractor, reasoning that negligently securing the services of the independent contractor falls within one of several typically recognized exceptions to the rule that an employer is not liable for the actions of his independent contractor.[28]

* * *

Accordingly, we hold that while a real estate broker bears no responsibility to conduct an independent investigation of a latent defect, when such broker volunteers to secure an inspection of the premises, or some part thereof, by retaining on behalf of the buyer a third party to conduct the inspection, then that real estate broker may be held liable to the buyer for civil damages if the broker in retaining said third party is negligent in the selection and retention of the third party and if such negligence proximately causes harm to the buyer. By so ruling, we do not impose upon a real estate broker the affirmative duty to conduct a comprehensive inquiry into the credentials of an individual hired as an independent contractor. Where the independent contractor selected is a licensed, reputable individual or firm, for instance, the broker is not obligated to engage in a personal inquiry into the credentials or training of the contractor. However, where the exercise of reasonable diligence would disclose facts demonstrating that the contractor was clearly incompetent for the particular task contemplated, a reasonably prudent broker should not retain the contractor.

The Appellant in the instant case has alleged a cause of action for negligent hiring by asserting that the Appellees knew or should have known that Mr. Stephens was not qualified to inspect furnaces or heating systems. The questions of whether the Appellees created an agency relationship in retaining Mr. Stephens, and whether the Appellees knew or should have known that Mr. Stephens was not qualified to

---

28. The traditional rule regarding liability of employers for negligent acts of an independent contractor is that the employer is not liable for such acts committed in the performance of the work the contractor was hired to perform. [   ]. Exceptions previously recognized by this Court include work which is in itself unlawful, work which is intrinsically dangerous, and work which is likely to cause injury to another person if proper care is not taken. [   ].

inspect heating systems create genuine issues of material facts precluding summary judgment and justifying the remand of this matter for examination of those issues.

IV.

* * *

Based upon the foregoing, we find that the Appellant presented sufficient evidence to preclude summary judgment, we reverse the decision of the lower court, and we remand for consideration of the merits of this action.

Reversed and remanded.

MILLER, RETIRED JUSTICE, sitting by temporary assignment.

ALBRIGHT, J., did not participate.

Notes and Questions

1. The real estate broker, you will remember, is normally the agent of the seller. Therefore, imposing obligations on the broker to protect the purchaser confronts the broker with an inevitable and often difficult conflict of interest. In residential purchases, however, buyers often believe that the broker is on their side, and rely on the broker for assurances that the house they are buying is in good condition. Brokers often do little to disabuse buyers of either belief. Buyers can, of course, engage their own broker to represent their interests, but most do not.

Courts, and occasionally legislatures, have recognized the reality of buyer reliance on brokers, and have steadily expanded the responsibilities of brokers to buyers. Intentional misrepresentation of facts concerning the condition of the property relied on by the buyer will probably lead to broker liability, although mere "puffing" or statements of opinion may be excused. Most jurisdictions will also impose liability for intentional concealment of material facts that are known to the broker but which the broker knows are not known to the buyer.

Many, though not all, courts further hold the broker liable for negligent misrepresentation. If the broker merely passes on incorrect information supplied by the seller where the broker, by exercising reasonable care, could have discovered the falsity of the seller's statement, the broker may be liable. This theory does not require the broker to independently assess the conditions of the premises for the buyer; it merely requires the broker to avoid making statements about such conditions that the broker would have verified were the broker acting reasonably.

Some jurisdictions go further, holding the broker liable for innocent misrepresentation—i.e., for innocently passing on false information to the buyer, whether or not it was reasonable to expect the broker to verify the information. This effectively imposes a strict liability standard on the broker, though the broker may still avoid liability by disclaiming knowledge as to certain problems rather than making assertions regarding the premises.

Finally, a few courts have gone even further, imposing a duty on the broker to make a reasonable inspection of the premises and to disclose to the buyer any defects discovered in such an inspection. The California case of Easton v. Strassburger, 152 Cal.App.3d 90, 199 Cal.Rptr. 383 (1984), which established the doctrine, held that a broker who failed to note soil defects that were suggested by various "red flags" and could have been discovered with reasonable diligence, was liable for not disclosing such defects. This position has also been endorsed by the California legislature, Cal.Civ.Code §§ 2079–2079.5.

Finally, various courts interpreting their states' consumer protection acts or real estate licensure acts have also imposed duties of disclosure on real estate brokers.

As between the broker and the buyer, who is better able to discover defects in the premises? What difficulties does imposing a duty to disclose create for the broker? What alternatives does the buyer have to relying on the broker? Would a disclaimer, or disclosure of the broker's obligations to the seller, protect the buyer adequately? Might brokers object to such a requirement? Would greater involvement of attorneys representing buyers in real estate transactions alleviate this problem in any respect?

See, among the many sources addressing this topic, Annotation, Real–Estate Broker's Liability to Purchaser for Misrepresentation or Nondisclosure of Physical Defects in Property Sold, 46 ALR 4th 546 (1986); Hagglund & Weimer, Caveat Broker: The Brokers Liability for Negligent and Innocent Misrepresentation, 20 Real Est.L.J. 149 (1991); Murray, The Real Estate Broker and the Buyer: Negligence and the Duty to Investigate, 32 Vill.L.Rev. 989 (1987); Comment, Broker Liability After Easton v. Strassburger: Let the Buyer be Aware, 25 Santa Clara L.Rev. 651 (1985); Note, Imposing Tort Liability on Real Estate Brokers Selling Defective Housing, 99 Harv.L.Rev. 1861 (1986).

2.   Can the seller's broker be held liable for not disclosing conditions which are not a part of the property being conveyed, but materially affect the value of that property? The court in Strawn v. Canuso, 140 N.J. 43, 65, 657 A.2d 420, 431 (1995) thought so. In that case, neither the seller nor the broker told the plaintiff-buyers that the property was located near an abandoned hazardous waste dump. "[A] builder-developer of residential real estate or a broker representing it is not only liable to a purchaser for affirmative and intentional misrepresentation, but is also liable for nondisclosure of off-site physical conditions known to it and unknown and not readily observable by the buyer if the existence of those conditions is of sufficient materiality to affect the habitability, use, or enjoyment of the property and, therefore, render the property substantially less desirable or valuable to the objectively reasonable buyer." The court held that it was an issue for the jury whether the presence of the hazardous waste dump site met this standard, thus rendering summary judgment for the defendants improper.

STAMBOVSKY v. ACKLEY

Supreme Court, Appellate Division, First Department, New York, 1991.
169 A.D.2d 254, 572 N.Y.S.2d 672, 60 USLW 2070.

OPINION OF THE COURT

RUBIN, J.

Plaintiff, to his horror, discovered that the house he had recently contracted to purchase was widely reputed to be possessed by poltergeists, reportedly seen by defendant seller and members of her family on numerous occasions over the last nine years. Plaintiff promptly commenced this action seeking rescission of the contract of sale. Supreme Court reluctantly dismissed the complaint, holding that plaintiff has no remedy at law in this jurisdiction.

The unusual facts of this case, as disclosed by the record, clearly warrant a grant of equitable relief to the buyer who, as a resident of New York City, cannot be expected to have any familiarity with the folklore of the Village of Nyack. Not being a "local", plaintiff could not readily learn that the home he had contracted to purchase is haunted. Whether the source of the spectral apparitions seen by defendant seller are parapsychic or psychogenic, having reported their presence in both a national publication (Readers' Digest) and the local press (in 1977 and 1982, respectively), defendant is estopped to deny their existence and, as a matter of law, the house is haunted. More to the point, however, no divination is required to conclude that it is defendant's promotional efforts in publicizing her close encounters with these spirits which fostered the home's reputation in the community. In 1989, the house was included in five-home walking tour of Nyack and described in a November 27th newspaper article as "a riverfront Victorian (with ghost)." The impact of the reputation thus created goes to the very essence of the bargain between the parties, greatly impairing both the value of the property and its potential for resale.* * *

While I agree with Supreme Court that the real estate broker, as agent for the seller, is under no duty to disclose to a potential buyer the phantasmal reputation of the premises and that, in his pursuit of a legal remedy for fraudulent misrepresentation against the seller, plaintiff hasn't a ghost of a chance, I am nevertheless moved by the spirit of equity to allow the buyer to seek rescission of the contract of sale and recovery of his down payment. New York law fails to recognize any remedy for damages incurred as a result of the seller's mere silence, applying instead the strict rule of caveat emptor. Therefore, the theoretical basis for granting relief, even under the extraordinary facts of this case, is elusive if not ephemeral.

* * *

From the perspective of a person in the position of plaintiff herein, a very practical problem arises with respect to the discovery of a paranormal phenomenon: "Who you gonna' call?" as a title song to the movie "Ghostbusters" asks. Applying the strict rule of caveat emptor to a contract involving a house possessed by poltergeists conjures up visions of a psychic or medium routinely accompanying the structural engineer and Terminix man on an inspection of every home subject to a contract of sale. It portends that the prudent attorney will establish an escrow account lest the subject of the transaction come back to haunt him and his client—or pray that his malpractice insurance coverage extends to supernatural disasters. In the interest of avoiding such untenable consequences, the notion that a haunting is a condition which can and should be ascertained upon reasonable inspection of the premises is a hobgoblin which should be exorcised from the body of legal precedent and laid quietly to rest.

* * * New York adheres to the doctrine of caveat emptor and imposes no duty upon the vendor to disclose any information concerning the premises [   ] unless there is a confidential or fiduciary relationship between the parties * * * or some conduct on the part of the seller which constitutes "active concealment." [   ] Normally, some affirmative misrepresentation [   ] or partial disclosure [   ] is required to impose upon the seller a duty to communicate undisclosed conditions affecting the premises. [   ]

Caveat emptor is not so all-encompassing a doctrine of common law as to render every act of nondisclosure immune from redress, whether legal or equitable. * * * Common law is not moribund. *Ex facto jus oritur* (law arises out of facts). Where fairness and common sense dictate that an exception should be created, the evolution of the law should not be stifled by rigid application of a legal maxim.

The doctrine of caveat emptor requires that a buyer act prudently to assess the fitness and value of his purchase and operates to bar the purchaser who fails to exercise due care from seeking the equitable remedy of rescission. It should be apparent, however, that the most meticulous inspection and the search would not reveal the presence of poltergeists at the premises or unearth the property's ghoulish reputation in the community. Therefore, there is no sound policy reason to deny plaintiff relief for failing to discover a state of affairs which the most prudent purchaser would not be expected to even contemplate. [   ]

The case law in this jurisdiction dealing with the duty of a vendor of real property to disclose information to the buyer is distinguishable from the matter under review. The most salient distinction is that existing cases invariably deal with the physical condition of the premises, [   ] defects in title, [   ] liens against the property, [   ] expenses or income [   ] and other factors affecting its operation. No case has been brought to this court's attention in which the property value was impaired as the result of the reputation created by information disseminated to the public by the seller (or, for that matter, as a result of possession by poltergeists).

Where a condition which has been created by the seller materially impairs the value of the contract and is peculiarly within the knowledge of the seller or unlikely to be discovered by a prudent purchaser exercising due care with respect to the subject transaction, nondisclosure constitutes a basis for rescission as a matter of equity. Any other outcome places upon the buyer not merely the obligation to exercise care in his purchase but rather to be omniscient with respect to any fact which may affect the bargain. No practical purpose is served by imposing such a burden upon a purchaser. To the contrary, it encourages predatory business practice and offends the principle that equity will suffer no wrong to be without a remedy.

* * *

In the case at bar, defendant seller deliberately fostered the public belief that her home was possessed. Having undertaken to inform the public-at-large, to whom she has no legal relationship, about the supernatural occurrences on her property, she may be said to owe no less a duty to her contract vendee. * * * Where, as here, the seller not only takes unfair advantage of the buyer's ignorance but has created and perpetuated a condition about which he is unlikely to even inquire, enforcement of the contract (in whole or in part) is offensive to the court's sense of equity. Application of the remedy of rescission, within the bounds of the narrow exception to the doctrine of caveat emptor set forth herein, is entirely appropriate to relieve the unwitting purchaser from the consequences of a most unnatural bargain.

Accordingly, the judgment of the Supreme Court, * * * which dismissed the complaint * * * should be modified, * * * and the first cause of action seeking rescission of the contract reinstated, without costs.

Smith, J. (Dissenting).

I would affirm the dismissal of the complaint by the motion court.

Plaintiff seeks to rescind his contract to purchase defendant Ackley's residential property and recover his down payment. Plaintiff alleges that Ackley and her real estate broker, defendant Ellis Realty, made material misrepresentations of the property in that they failed to disclose that Ackley believed that the house was haunted by poltergeists. Moreover, Ackley shared this belief with her community and the general public through articles published in Reader's Digest (1977) and the local newspaper (1982). In November 1989, approximately two months after the parties entered into the contract of sale but subsequent to the scheduled October 2, 1989 closing, the house was included in a five-house walking tour and again described in the local newspaper as being haunted.

Prior to closing, plaintiff learned of this reputation and unsuccessfully sought to rescind the $650,000 contract of sale and obtain return of his $32,500 down payment without resort to litigation. The plaintiff then commenced this action for that relief and alleged that he would not have entered into the contract had he been so advised and that as a result of the alleged poltergeist activity, the market value and resaleability of the property was greatly diminished. Defendant Ackley has counterclaimed for specific performance.

"It is settled law in New York State that the seller of real property is under no duty to speak when the parties deal at arm's length. The mere silence of the seller, without some act or conduct which deceived the purchaser, does not amount to a concealment that is actionable as a fraud. [ ] The buyer has the duty to satisfy himself as to the quality of his bargain pursuant to the doctrine of caveat emptor, which in New York State still applies to real estate transactions." [ ]

The parties herein were represented by counsel and dealt at arm's length. This is evidenced by the contract of sale which, inter alia, contained various riders and a specific provision that all prior understandings and agreements between the parties were merged into the contract, that the contract completely expressed their full agreement and that neither had relied upon any statement by anyone else not set forth in the contract. There is no allegation that defendants, by some specific act, other than the failure to speak, deceived the plaintiff. Nevertheless, a cause of action may be sufficiently stated where there is a confidential or fiduciary relationship creating a duty to disclose and there was a failure to disclose a material fact, calculated to induce a false belief. [ ] However, plaintiff herein has not alleged and there is no basis for concluding that a confidential or fiduciary relationship existed between these parties to an arm's length transaction such as to give rise to a duty to disclose. In addition, there is no allegation that defendants thwarted plaintiffs efforts to fulfill his responsibilities fixed by the doctrine of caveat emptor. [ ]

Finally, if the doctrine of caveat emptor is to be discarded, it should be for a reason more substantive than a poltergeist. The existence of a poltergeist is no more binding upon the defendants than it is upon this court.

Based upon the foregoing, the motion court properly dismissed the complaint.

Notes and Questions

1. Because most used dwellings will possess some sort of problem at the time of sale, nearly every such transfer of real estate invites litigation instituted by a disappointed buyer. Purchasers of existing housing who find the premises to be defective are likely to want to sue their seller, the previous owner. The traditional rule has been caveat emptor—look it over well before you decide to buy it because seller has no duty to disclose known defects. Exceptions to caveat emptor were long recognized if a seller intentionally misrepresents or conceals defects in the premises and the buyer justifiably relies on these misrepresentations. In such cases the seller may be liable for fraud. A court that finds a seller liable for fraud may rescind the

transaction and award damages to the purchaser. A seller will also be liable, of course, if it offers and breaches an express warranty as to the condition of the premises.

2.   Caveat emptor was a time-honored principle of both Anglo–Saxon and Roman legal traditions, and was firmly entrenched in the common law of this country until the latter part of the last century. The nationwide erosion of the common law doctrine of caveat emptor in residential real estate is one of the most extraordinary legal reforms of the past generation. Most states today recognize a common law duty on the part of the seller of residential real property to disclose defects that are material and known to the seller. In such states, buyers may seek rescission and monetary damages as remedies for breach of sellers' disclosure obligation. New York is idiosyncratic in limiting relief to rescission. Similarly, New York is unique in carving out only the narrowest of exceptions to caveat emptor, for nonphysical defects created by the seller. Can you explain the likely rationale for New York's approach?

3.   About half the states have adopted statutes requiring sellers to disclose certain information about property that they sell. See e.g., Cal. Civ. Code §§ 1102–1102.18 (West Supp. 2005); Ill. Ann. Stat. ch. 765, §§ 77/1–77/99 (Smith–Hurd Supp. 2005); Ohio Rev. Code Ann. § 5302.30 (Anderson Supp. 2005); Tex. Prop. Code Ann. § 5.008 (West Supp. 2005). For an example of a typical seller disclosure form, see the following from the Texas statute cited above. Real estate brokers have often lobbied for such laws. Can you explain why? Such statutes often protect sellers from liability for failure to disclose psychologically stigmatizing conditions such as when a suicide, homicide or death by AIDS occurred on the property. See Lefcoe, Property Condition Disclosure Forms: How the Real Estate Industry Eased the Transition from Caveat Emptor to "Seller Tell All," 39 Real Prop., Prob. & Tr. J. 193 (2004); and Weinberger, "Let the Buyer Be Well Informed–Doubting the Demise of Caveat Emptor," 55 Md. L. Rev. 387 (1996).

CONCERNING THE PROPERTY AT_____

SELLER'S DISCLOSURE NOTICE

(Street Address and City)

THIS NOTICE IS A DISCLOSURE OF SELLER'S KNOWLEDGE OF THE CONDITION OF THE PROPERTY AS OF THE DATE SIGNED BY SELLER AND IS NOT A SUBSTITUTE FOR ANY INSPECTIONS OR WARRANTIES THE PURCHASER MAY WISH TO OBTAIN. IT IS NOT A WARRANTY OF ANY KIND BY SELLER OR SELLER'S AGENTS.

Seller _____ is _____ is not occupying the Property.

If unoccupied, how long since Seller has occupied the Property?_____

1.   The Property has the items checked below:

Write Yes (Y), No (N), or Unknown (U).

___ Range	___ Oven	___ Microwave
___ Dishwasher	___ Trash Compactor	___ Disposal
___ Washer/ Dryer Hookups	___ Window Screens	___ Rain Gutters

— Security System   — Fire Detection Equipment   — Intercom System
— TV Antenna   — Cable TV Wiring   — Satellite Dish
— Ceiling Fan(s)   — Attic Fan(s)   — Exhaust Fan(s)
— Central A/C   — Central Heating   — Wall/Window Air Conditioning
— Plumbing System   — Septic System   — Public Sewer System
— Patio/Decking   — Outdoor Grill   — Fences
— Pool   — Sauna   — Spa — Hot Tub
— Pool Equipment   — Pool Heater   — Automatic Lawn Sprinkler System
— Fireplace(s) & Chimney (Woodburning)   — Fireplace(s) & Chimney (Mock)
— Gas Lines (Nat./LP)   — Gas Fixtures

Garage: — Attached   — Not Attached   — Carport
Garage Door Opener(s):   — Electronic   — Control(s)
Water Heater: — Gas   — Electric
Water
Water Supply: — City   — Well — MUD   — Co-op
Roof Type: _____ Age: — (approx)

Are you (Seller) aware of any of the above items that are not in working condition, that have known defects, or that are in need of repair? _____ Yes _____ No _____ Unknown.

If yes, then describe. (Attach additional sheets if necessary):_____
_____
_____

2. Are you (Seller) aware of any known defects/malfunctions in any of the following?

Write Yes (Y) if you are aware, write No (N) if you are not aware.

— Interior Walls   — Ceilings   — Floors
— Exterior Walls   — Doors   — Windows
— Roof   — Foundation/ Slab(s)   — Basement
— Walls/Fences   — Driveways   — Sidewalks
— Plumbing/ Sewers/Septics   — Electrical Systems   — Lighting Fixtures

_____ Other Structural Components (Describe): _____
_____
_____

If the answer to any of the above is yes, explain. (Attach additional sheets if necessary):_____
_____
_____

3. Are you (Seller) aware of any of the following conditions?

Write Yes (Y) if you are aware, write No (N) if you are not aware.

—— Active Termites
(includes wood-destroying
insects)

—— Previous Structural
or Roof Repair

—— Termite or Wood Rot
Damage Needing Repair

—— Hazardous or Toxic
Waste

—— Previous Termite Damage

—— Asbestos Components

—— Previous Termite
Treatment

—— Urea formaldehyde
Insulation

—— Previous Flooding

—— Radon Gas

—— Improper Drainage

—— Lead Based Paint

—— Water Penetration

—— Aluminum Wiring

—— Located in 100–Year
Floodplain

—— Previous Fires

—— Present Flood Insurance
Coverage

—— Unplatted Easements

—— Landfill, Settling, Soil
Movement, Fault Lines

—— Subsurface
Structure or Pits

If the answer to any of the above is yes, explain. (Attach additional sheets if necessary): _____

_____

4.   Are you (Seller) aware of any item, equipment, or system in or on the property that is in need of repair? _____ Yes (if you are aware) _____ No (if you are not aware). If yes, explain (attach additional sheets as necessary)._____

5.   Are you (Seller) aware of any of the following?

Write Yes (Y) if you are aware, write No (N) if you are not aware.

_____ Room additions, structural modifications, or other alterations or repairs made without necessary permits or not in compliance with building codes in effect at that time.

_____ Homeowners' Association or maintenance fees or assessments.

_____ Any "common area" (facilities such as pools, tennis courts, walkways, or other areas) co-owned in undivided interest with others.

_____ Any notices of violations of deed restrictions or governmental ordinances affecting the condition or use of the Property.

_____ Any lawsuits directly or indirectly affecting the Property.

_____ Any condition on the Property which materially affects the physical health or safety of an individual.

If the answer to any of the above is yes, explain. (Attach additional sheets if necessary): _____

_____

_____

_____   _____
Date   Signature of Seller

The undersigned purchaser hereby acknowledges receipt of the foregoing

_____   _____
Date   Signature of Purchaser

4. The doctrine of caveat emptor enjoys continued vitality in the purchase and sale of commercial property. See, e.g., Savage v. KGE Associates Ltd. Partnership, 260 Ga.App. 770, 580 S.E.2d 591 (2003); Green Acres, Inc. v. First Union Nat'l Bank, 637 So.2d 363 (Fla. Dist. Ct. App. 1994) (finding no duty to disclose to home builder that 63 acre parcel in South Florida was the first home and burial ground of the Seminole Tribe).

5. Courts generally hold that a buyer is under no duty to disclose information to seller of facts within buyer's knowledge that render the property more valuable than seller is aware. See, e.g., Nussbaum v. Weeks, 214 Cal.App.3d 1589, 263 Cal.Rptr. 360 (1989); Zaschek v. Traverse Corp., 123 Mich.App. 126, 333 N.W.2d 191 (1983).

PARKER v. COLUMBIA BANK

Court of Special Appeals of Maryland, 1992.
91 Md.App. 346, 604 A.2d 521.

MOTZ, JUDGE.

In these difficult economic times with falling real estate prices, lender liability suits have become one of the few "growth industries." This appeal is a part of that "industry," involving, as it does, a number of issues concerning a bank's duties and responsibilities to its borrowers. This case arises out of two actions, now consolidated, relating to a residential construction loan secured by appellants, Robert and Margaret Parker ("the Parkers"), from appellee, The Columbia Bank ("Columbia"). The Parkers appeal the order of the Circuit Court for Montgomery County granting Columbia's motion to dismiss the Parkers' suit for fraud, fraudulent concealment, negligent misrepresentation, negligence, breach of fiduciary duty, and breach of contract; and the order of that court ratifying the foreclosure sale by Columbia of real estate used by the Parkers to secure this construction loan.

(i)

During 1988, the Parkers, physicians employed at the National Institutes of Health, began to look for a larger home in Montgomery County. After "many drives throughout Montgomery County" they met George Evangelos Paleologos ("Paleologos"), a builder who had contracted with friends of the Parkers to construct a custom home in Brookeville, Maryland. Paleologos introduced the Parkers to a project in which his construction company, Evangelos Enterprises, Ltd. ("Evangelos"), planned to build a group of seven custom homes in a subdivision known as "Brookeville Farms." Dr. Parker spoke with Paleologos and other subdivision buyers, "observed the displays" in Paleologos' sale office and "the work under way" on Paleologos' own house. From these conversations and observations, Dr. Parker "gained the impression that he [Paleologos] was competent." After several meetings with Paleologos, the

Parkers believed that Paleologos "could build the house" the Parkers "wanted at a price [they] could afford."

On September 21, 1988, the Parkers entered into a contract with Evangelos for the construction of a 5,000–square-foot house at a cost of $385,000. The Parkers "selected a floor plan and numerous features that customized the house to meet the specific needs of [their] family. The construction documents called for more than 5,000 square feet of finished living space, 7 bedrooms, 5 full and 2 half baths, 10–foot ceilings on the first floor, a soaring cathedral ceiling 27 feet high in the family room, 3 fireplaces, huge arched windows, and other features that made this the home [the Parkers] felt [they] could keep forever." In order to verify that Paleologos could build this house for $385,000, Dr. Parker asked him if he could and the builder "said yes."

On October 15, 1988, the Parkers entered into a contract with the "Brookeville Development Partnership" for the purchase, at the price of $160,000, of the lot on which the house was to be built. While the land contract stated that the seller of the property, the Brookeville Development Partnership, "is not involved in the construction or development of the home," Paleologos signed the land contract on behalf of the seller. The land contract, but not the construction contract, included a provision that its execution would be contingent on the Parkers' obtaining a loan to finance the purchase.

Over the following weeks, the Parkers sought a lender to finance the purchase of the land, the construction of the house, and the mortgage. They spoke with representatives of three banks regarding financing. In late October and early November, they contacted Mr. Clements, a loan officer at Sandy Spring Bank, who had provided funding for two other couples, friends of the Parkers, in the Brookeville Farms development. Dr. Parker told Mr. Clements that he was "looking for financing that would provide 80% of the appraised value, which was expected to be between $700,000 and $750,000." As Dr. Parker recognized, "this would result in financing essentially 95–100% of the construction and land costs." Mr. Clements, according to Dr. Parker, "did not believe his Bank's loan board would allow such a financing package." Accordingly, the Parkers submitted no loan application to Sandy Spring. Dr. Parker next spoke to Mr. Bollinger at First Annapolis Savings & Loan. Paleologos, who told Dr. Parker that "he was also dealing" with First Annapolis, referred Dr. Parker to that institution. Again, Dr. Parker "asked for a package that would essentially finance 95% of the construction and land costs, based on 80% of the appraised value as completed." Again, the loan officer indicated that the "Bank could not do that." Again, no loan application was submitted.

Dr. Parker then spoke with Michael T. Galeone, a senior vice president of Columbia Bank. On January 7, 1990, the Parkers made an application to Columbia for a construction loan. Dr. Parker again explained that he "was looking for financing on 80% of the appraised price rather than 80% of the purchase price." Moreover, Dr. Parker alleges he told Galeone that "if the house could not be built for this, we could not proceed with the project." Mr. Galeone asked Dr. Parker "what he knew about" Paleologos and "how" Dr. Parker "came to know" Paleologos. Dr. Parker, in response, related his conversations with Paleologos and observations of Paleologos' own house and sales displays, which are outlined above. Dr. Parker provided Galeone with Paleologos' address and telephone number so Columbia could do its own check on the qualifications of the builder.

The Parkers allege that, over the next two months, they spoke with Galeone on numerous occasions and he "intentionally cultivated a relationship of trust and confidence with" them and they "came to regard him and Columbia as an adviser and consultant with respect to the project." They further allege that, to induce them to enter into a construction loan with Columbia, Galeone represented that: (1) he was "experienced in the placement and administration of loans similar to the construction loan needed for the house" while in fact he had never administered a loan involving draw payments to a builder; (2) Columbia had "thoroughly investigated" Paleologos and determined he was qualified to undertake this project, while in fact this investigation was "perfunctory" and overlooked information which would show he was not qualified; (3) Galeone and Columbia would protect the Parkers' interest, as well as Columbia's, throughout construction of the house, while in fact Galeone had no intention of protecting the Parkers' interest unless it coincided with Columbia's; (4) construction draws would only be issued after Columbia had obtained inspections to insure that work had been done in accordance with the draw schedule, while in fact Columbia intended to advance funds, if requested by Paleologos, ahead of the draw schedule and regardless of inspections; and (5) in response to the Parkers' specific inquiries, "Galeone told them that in the event of a default by the builder, Columbia would find or recommend another builder and would see that the house was completed within budget," while in fact Columbia intended to provide no such protection to the Parkers.

On March 3, 1989, Columbia issued a commitment letter to the Parkers for financing the project. The bank undertook to provide financing for 96% to 97% of the costs of the project, *i.e.*, the Parkers would provide $21,290 and Columbia would loan them $529,000. The Parkers accepted Columbia's offer of financing the next day, March 4, 1989. On March 17, 1989, the Parkers and Columbia entered into a written construction loan agreement in the amount of $529,000 to cover the Parkers' purchase of the land and the construction loan. They allege that they had "little or no experience in matters relating to real estate," that Galeone knew this, and that "but for" Galeone's representations set forth above, they "would not have entered into the loan agreement with Columbia." At closing, Columbia disbursed $234,290 of the loan proceeds to the Parkers, $85,000 of which was paid by the Parkers to Evangelos and the remainder of which was used by the Parkers to pay the balance of the purchase price for the land.

In administering the loan, Columbia did not adhere to the draw schedule set forth in the Parkers' construction contract with Evangelos. The Parkers allege in their amended complaint that another draw schedule was substituted by Columbia and Evangelos without the Parkers being advised of its terms, but Dr. Parker explains in his affidavit that he and Galeone did discuss amending the draw schedule. In any event, the construction loan entered into by Columbia and the Parkers provides that disbursements of the construction loan "will be made by two party checks payable to both the Borrowers and their general contractor, unless Lender exercises its rights hereunder to make disbursements directly to any party." Columbia, in fact, released all loan draws to the Parkers in the form of a two-party check payable to the Parkers and Paleologos as follows: $85,000 at closing on March 17, 1989; $55,000 on May 31, 1989; $50,000 on June 29, 1989; and $110,000 on September 18, 1989. In addition to personally signing each draw check, the Parkers talked with Paleologos "at least 2–3 times a week from mid-March, 1989 through mid-November, 1989." They also frequently talked with other families who were having houses built by Evangelos in Brookeville Farms.

At the same time that Columbia was developing its relationship with the Parkers, it was, according to the amended complaint, "developing a relationship" with Paleologos and Evangelos in order to bring Columbia significant lending business from the builder. None of the details of how this "relationship" was developed are set forth in the complaint except that it is alleged that "one or more" managing agents of Columbia obtained construction services from Paleologos and Evangelos during 1989 "at little or no charge." It is not alleged, however, that either Paleologos or Evangelos had any banking relationship with Columbia until March 10, 1989, after Columbia had offered, and the Parkers had accepted, financing. On that date, Evangelos opened an account with Columbia by depositing $500. Over the course of the summer, nearly 100 checks drawn upon that account were returned for insufficient funds. On August 15, 1989, Columbia approved a line of credit to Evangelos in the amount of $250,000, which was immediately drawn upon and exhausted within a day. During the next four months, another seventy checks drawn on the Evangelos account were returned for insufficient funds; however, all required interest payments were made on the $250,000 line of credit until January 1990. Columbia did not contemporaneously disclose any of its transactions with, or information about, Paleologos to the Parkers; the Parkers allege that these nondisclosures are fraudulent.

After the last draw, in September 1989, Evangelos performed little, if any, additional work on the Parkers' house. The Parkers assert that as of that date, although 80% of the construction loan funds had been paid, the project was only 40% complete. In September, Paleologos advised Columbia and the Parkers that he needed additional financing in order to proceed with the project and that he intended to use his residence and adjacent land as collateral. Dr. Parker asked Galeone to have the bank's attorneys examine the builder's condition; he asserts that he repeated this request weekly for six weeks and Galeone repeatedly refused it, stating that "the value is in the ground," and there was nothing to worry about. In November 1989, when the Parkers received a supplier's notice of intent to file a mechanic's lien, they asked Paleologos and Galeone about the builder's financial status. Galeone told Dr. Parker that he "knew nothing of" the liens and "would look into it." Paleologos told Dr. Parker that he was experiencing a cash-flow problem but was seeking refinancing to continue the project and that the "lien would be taken care of." Dr. Parker spoke the next day to Galeone who purportedly reassured him; Dr. Parker then relayed to Galeone the builder's assurances.

In February, 1990, the Parkers learned that in order to complete the project according to its original specifications and to build the necessary road mandated by county regulations, a sum of approximately $350,000 would be necessary, in addition to the existing construction balance of $300,000 and the land loan of $144,000. Even if this amount was reduced by $160,000 in proceeds from their former home, the remaining balance of $634,000 was "far beyond Plaintiffs' means" and "substantially higher than the $385,000 mortgage balance originally contemplated." The Parkers ceased making payments on their loan to Columbia. The Parkers assert that if Columbia had not "engaged in the misrepresentations, concealments and silence" alleged in the complaint, they would never have entered into the loan agreement and/or "would have timely undertaken steps to investigate further and would have sought competent professional assistance to salvage the project within budget" and thereby avoided thousands of dollars in damages.

In November, 1990, the Parkers filed a complaint against Columbia for fraud, fraudulent concealment, negligence, negligent misrepresentation, breach of fiduciary duty, and civil conspiracy. They subsequently amended their complaint to include as defendants Galeone and John M. Bond, a director of the bank, and to add counts for fraud in the inducement and breach of contract. On May 24, 1991, the action was dismissed. Also in November, 1990, Galeone as trustee and Louis J. Ebert as substitute trustee acted to foreclose on a deed of trust, which encumbered the Parkers' building lot and the partially completed house. The Parkers sought an interlocutory injunction and a stay of the foreclosure sale, which were denied. After the foreclosure sale, the Parkers filed exceptions to the trustees' report of sale, which were overruled after a hearing on the merits. The Parkers appealed the order to dismiss, except for the dismissal of the civil conspiracy count, and the order ratifying the foreclosure sale.

(ii)

Many of the counts in the Parkers' complaint involve their central claim that special circumstances exist here which trigger a duty on the part of appellees to the Parkers; two counts, however, are not premised on any claim of duty. These are: fraud (including fraudulent misrepresentation and fraudulent inducement) and breach of contract. We consider these counts first.

In order to recover on a claim for fraud, a plaintiff must show: (1) that the defendant made a false representation; (2) that its falsity was either known to the defendant, or the misrepresentation was made with such reckless indifference to the truth as to be equivalent to actual knowledge; (3) that it was made for the purpose of defrauding the person claiming to be injured thereby; (4) that such person not only relied upon the misrepresentation, but had a right to rely upon it in the full belief of its truth, and would not have done the thing from which the injury had resulted had not such misrepresentation been made; and (5) that such person actually suffered damage directly resulting from such fraudulent misrepresentation.

* * *

In the amended complaint, * * * the Parkers have alleged a cause of action in fraud against the appellees (except for Bond), as to the following alleged misrepresentations by Galeone: (1) Galeone and Columbia would protect the Parkers' interest, as well as Columbia's, throughout the construction of the house, while in fact Galeone had no intention of protecting the Parkers' interest unless it coincided with Columbia's; (2) construction draws would only be issued after Columbia had obtained inspections to insure that work had been done in accordance with the draw schedule, while in fact Columbia intended to advance funds ahead of the draw schedule and regardless of draw inspections if requested by Paleologos; and (3) in the event of default by Paleologos and Evangelos, Columbia "would find or recommend another builder and would see that the house was completed within budget" while, in fact, Columbia intended to provide no such protection to the Parkers.

(iii)

The Parkers' breach of contract claim alleges a violation of the express terms of the contract and of an implied duty of good faith. First, the Parkers assert that Columbia breached the express terms of Article 9, Section 9.1 of the loan agreement by disbursing draws when the loan was out of balance. Section 9.1 provides:

Lender's Duty to Disburse—Lender agrees, upon Borrower's compliance with all conditions precedent to the Opening of the Loan, and provided the Loan is in balance, to open the Loan hereunder and to continue to disburse the same so long as the Loan remains in balance and Borrowers have complied with all conditions precedent from time to time and is not in default hereunder.

This section does not prohibit Columbia from disbursing draws if the loan is out of balance; it merely provides that Columbia is not obligated to disburse draws when the loan is out of balance. By its terms, Section 9.1 is for Columbia's protection, not the Parkers'. Columbia was not contractually obligated to make sure that the Parkers' loan remained in balance. Rather, it was the Parkers who were obligated to maintain the loan in balance. Indeed, to the extent that the loan became out of balance, the Parkers were expressly obligated, under Section 8.1 of the loan agreement, to invest additional funds in the project to rectify the problem.

The Parkers also allege that Columbia breached an implied duty of good faith and fair dealing "by advancing the builder funds for work not done, failing to disclose to the Parkers the true financial condition of the project and by actively misleading" the Parkers as to its condition. Under Maryland law, a duty of good faith and fair dealing is an implied term in certain contracts, [ ] but this duty simply prohibits one party to a contract from acting in such a manner as to prevent the other party from performing his obligations under the contract. [ ] Thus, the duty of good faith merely obligates a lender to exercise good faith in performing its contractual obligations; it does not obligate a lender to take affirmative actions that the lender is clearly not required to take under its loan documents. * * *

Here, the Parkers have not alleged that Columbia prevented them from performing any of their contractual obligations under the loan agreement. The Parkers have merely alleged that Columbia failed to take certain actions that Columbia was clearly not required to take under the loan agreement. In essence, the Parkers contend that Columbia should have protected their interests by monitoring Evangelos's work to make sure that the loan was in balance and that Evangelos was performing the work covered by each draw. Columbia, however, as discussed above, had no obligation under the loan agreement to make sure that the loan was in balance. Similarly, Columbia had no obligation under the loan agreement to inspect Evangelos's work to make sure that the work covered by each draw had been performed. Rather, Section 12.10 of the loan agreement expressly provided that any actions taken by Columbia to inspect or monitor the builder's work was exclusively for Columbia's benefit. Accordingly, Columbia had no contractual obligation to do any of the things that the Parkers alleged it should have done, and so the court below did not err in dismissing the Parkers' breach of contract claim.

(iv)

In order to state a cause of action as to all of their remaining claims—fraudulent concealment, negligent misrepresentation, negligence, and breach of fiduciary duty—the Parkers must demonstrate a duty owed to them by Columbia. * * *

In pressing these claims, the Parkers heavily rely upon Jacques v. First Nat'l Bank, supra. There, the Court of Appeals held that a bank, which contracted for a specified fee to process a residential loan application, was required to "use reasonable care" in doing so. [ ] Thus, as Judge McAuliffe carefully explained for the Court in *Jacques*, the basis for the duty of care was an express, albeit oral, contract. As we have held, supra, here Columbia did not breach its contract with the Parkers. Accordingly, unlike *Jacques,* no contractual promise provides a predicate for a tort duty of reasonable care here.

Moreover, recently in Yousef v. Trustbank Sav., F.S.B., 81 Md.App. 527, 568 A.2d 1134 (1990), we reiterated a long-standing principle of Maryland law that the relationship of a bank to its customer in a loan transaction is ordinarily a contractual relationship between a debtor and a creditor, and is not fiduciary in nature. * * * In *Yousef,* disgruntled commercial borrowers appealed an order dismissing their claims in contract, negligence and civil conspiracy against a lender; we affirmed the order. The borrowers, who were shopping center tenants seeking to purchase the shopping center, asserted that a clause within the loan agreement with the defendant bank, which provided that the borrowers would provide the lender with documentation that 85% of the shopping center had been leased, imposed a duty on the lender to review the shopping center leases for validity and enforceability. When it turned out that less than 50% of the space had been leased, the borrowers alleged that the lender was negligent in its failure to inspect the leases. Such an interpretation of the lender's obligations, we said, was, "to put it mildly, misplaced." Thus, we refused to permit the borrower in *Yousef* "to attach to the appellee the assumption of any greater duty than that specified in [the contract between the parties]".

If the Parkers' situation were clearly analogous to that of the borrowers in *Yousef*—that is, if the Parkers were business people with more experience dealing with banks and if they were relying on a contractual provision designed for the exclusive benefit of the lender as the sole source of the affirmative duty they allege—then we would, without further elaboration, affirm the circuit court's order to dismiss. There are, however, sufficient facts alleged here, which distinguish the Parkers from the borrowers in *Yousef,* to prompt us to evaluate the merits of the Parkers' assertion that "special circumstances" exist here such that Columbia owed them a fiduciary duty over and above any contractual obligations.

Courts have been exceedingly reluctant to find special circumstances sufficient to transform an ordinary contractual relationship between a bank and its customer into a fiduciary relationship or to impose any duties on the bank not found in the loan agreement. [ ] Some cases do state that such special circumstances "may" exist where "the bank knows or has reason to know that the customer is placing his trust and confidence in the bank and relying on the bank to counsel and inform him." [ ] Yet even in those cases, courts generally have refused to hold the bank liable to its customer, reasoning that a borrower cannot "abandon all caution and responsibility for his own protection and unilaterally impose a fiduciary relationship on another without a conscious assumption of such duties by the one sought to be held to be liable as a fiduciary." [ ] Moreover, precisely this conclusion has been reached on facts far more sympathetic than those at hand.

In Tokarz v. Frontier Federal Sav. & Loan Ass'n, 33 Wash.App. 456, 656 P.2d 1089 (1982), a case relied on by both parties, the Court of Appeals of Washington, after reviewing the case law, and recognizing the general rule, enunciated in *Yousef*, that the relationship between a bank and its customer does not ordinarily impose a fiduciary duty on the bank, identified four "special circumstances" which might nonetheless "dictate" such a duty. The analysis of the *Tokarz* court is compelling here, not only because it attempts to synthesize the abundant caselaw in the field and set forth an identifiable test, but also, and just as significantly, because the facts involved there have, as the Parkers acknowledge, "many similarities" to those at hand.

In *Tokarz*, as here, the plaintiffs were borrowers who contracted for a residential construction loan with their bank. In *Tokarz*, as here, the bank learned, shortly after agreeing to make the construction loan to the borrowers, that the borrowers' builder was having "evident" financial problems but did not disclose those problems to the borrowers. Finally, in *Tokarz*, as here, the borrowers ultimately sued the bank alleging it breached its fiduciary duty and fraudulently failed to disclose the builder's financial condition to them. The trial court granted summary judgment to the bank in *Tokarz*. The Washington appellate court affirmed, holding that it found "none of the special circumstances which may impose a fiduciary duty." Specifically, the *Tokarz* court found "no allegation or evidence" that the lender "(1) took on any extra services on behalf of [the borrowers] other than furnishing the money for construction of a home; (2) received any greater economic benefit from the transaction other than the normal mortgage; (3) exercised extensive control over the construction; or (4) was asked by [the borrowers] if there were any lien actions pending." [ ] The Parkers do not assert that *Tokarz* is wrongly decided or inapplicable here. Rather, they embrace it and claim that such "special circumstances" are alleged here. That claim is belied by the authorities relied on in *Tokarz*, the facts there, and the similarity of the *Tokarz* facts to those alleged here.

First, *Tokarz* makes clear that the "extra services" triggering a lender's duty are, contrary to the Parkers' argument, something more than the normal investigations, evaluations, and inspections that a prudent lender makes as a part of any construction loan since those normal services were presumably provided by the defendant bank in *Tokarz* without it incurring any liability to its borrower. Rather, the *Tokarz* court pointed to Hutson v. Wenatchee Fed. Savings & Loan Ass'n, 22 Wash.App. 91, 588 P.2d 1192 (1978) and Burien Motors, Inc. v. Balch, 9 Wash.App. 573, 513 P.2d 582 (1973) as cases in which the defendant had performed "extra services" for the plaintiffs. In *Hutson*, the defendant savings & loan institution undertook to provide its customers with credit life insurance and so was held to have a duty to disclose fully the nature of the insurance the customers were purchasing, [ ] in *Burien*, a real estate broker who undertook to draft lease assignment papers was held to have a duty to disclose the adverse zoning law status of the real estate or the broker's ignorance of this status. [ ]

See also Walters v. First Nat'l Bank of Newark, 69 Ohio St.2d 677, 433 N.E.2d 608 (1982) (bank which undertook to procure credit life insurance for borrower held to have a duty of care in procuring insurance); Stewart v. Phoenix Nat'l Bank, 49 Ariz. 34, 44, 64 P.2d 101, 106 (1937) (bank which acted as financial advisor to borrower for 23 years held to have duty to him).

Thus, all four cases cited above involve truly extra, out of the ordinary services and so are very different from *Tokarz* and the case at hand where all of the services performed by the lender were services normally provided by a bank for its customer. Such normal services, even if performed over a far more extended period of time than that involved here, do not constitute "extra services" creating a duty of care in the lender. * * *

Secondly, as in *Tokarz*, no economic benefit was received by the bank here from the loan other than the normal mortgage. Again, *Tokarz* itself makes clear that the fact that a bank is lending, or wants to lend, money to the plaintiffs' builder does not mean that it has received from the plaintiff's loan an economic benefit, other than the mortgage itself. Rather, it is only when the bank will receive a direct economic benefit it would not otherwise have had, through the fraud of one of its depositors and/or at the expense of one of its clients, that it has been held to have a duty to disclose the fraud to its customer. [　]

Thirdly, again contrary to the Parkers' assertions, they do not allege that the bank exercised the "extensive control over the construction" identified by the *Tokarz* court as possibly creating a special duty to the borrower. See Bradler v. Craig, 79 Cal.Rptr. 401, 407, 274 Cal.App.2d. 466 (1969) ("Approval of plans and specifications, and periodic inspection of houses during construction is normal procedure for any construction money lender" and triggers no special duty to the borrower). Thus, although the Parkers assert that Columbia received numerous calls from contractors and suppliers inquiring about payment, and designated one of its employees to "field" those calls and make representations to callers, they do not allege that, while they were making payments on their mortgage, Columbia ever disbursed funds to anyone except them or took charge of supervision of construction.

Nor is there any allegation of the last special circumstance identified by the *Tokarz* court, that the borrowers inquired of the bank as to whether there were "any lien actions pending" and were given false information. In *Tokarz*, the bank knew that there were lien actions pending against the builders. The court held, however, that in the absence of the borrower's specific inquiry, the bank had no duty to disclose the liens. Here, there is no allegation that the Parkers asked Columbia about liens and received an untruthful answer. Indeed, the very paragraphs of the complaint upon which the Parkers rely for their argument to the contrary indicate that the Parkers knew about the liens before Columbia.

In sum, in cases like the one at hand where there are none of these special circumstances and no contractual basis for a special duty of care is alleged, a lender owes no duty of care to its borrower. Accordingly, the Parkers have not alleged sufficient facts to establish that Columbia owes them a duty and so the circuit court was correct in dismissing their fraudulent concealment, negligent misrepresentation, negligence and breach of fiduciary duty claims.

Judgment affirmed in part and reversed in part.

Costs to be paid 80% by appellants and 20% by appellees.

Notes and Questions

1. For a case holding the construction lender liable for defects in the property, see Terrace Condominium Ass'n v. Midlantic Nat'l Bank, 268 N.J.Super. 488, 633 A.2d 1060 (1993). In *Terrace Condominium*, the builder-vendor gave a deed to Midlantic in lieu of a foreclosure on the construction mortgage. Midlantic completed the construction, and attempted to make several repairs. When the condominium association sued for the cost of repairs it made after Midlantic ceased remedial activity, Midlantic claimed it could not be liable because it was only a lender. The court disagreed: "[S]ince Midlantic took over construction, it must be held to have assumed all of the obligations and responsibilities of the initial builder and developer and to have become a full-fledged 'builder-vendor,' responsible for all defects, including those beyond the scope of what it perceives to be its own limited construction activities."

2. Many home purchasers no doubt believe that if there were something seriously wrong with the property, the lender, who has had the home independently inspected and appraised, would not be willing to finance 80 per cent, 90 per cent, or more of the home's value. When defects subsequently appear, however, the buyer who turns to the lender or its appraiser to claim damages for reliance is usually disappointed. Courts are particularly reluctant to recognize obligations where the lender and purchaser have no direct contractual relationship. In Connor v. Great Western Savings & Loan Ass'n, 69 Cal.2d 850, 73 Cal.Rptr. 369, 447 P.2d 609, (1968) the California Supreme Court did hold a lender liable to subsequent purchasers for construction defects where the lender was extensively and intimately involved in the construction process. However, *Connor* was later abrogated by statute. See Cal. Civ. Code § 3434 (West 1996). Subsequent cases have rejected *Connor* or limited it to its facts. A few courts have been willing to hold lenders liable to their own borrowers who have relied on appraisals done by the lender in purchasing a property. See Larsen v. United Federal Savings and Loan Association, 300 N.W.2d 281 (Iowa 1981). By and large, however, a purchaser's reliance on the lender will not render the lender liable for damages. See, on this topic, Note, Mortgage Lender Liability to the Purchasers of New or Existing Homes, 1988 U.Ill.L.Rev. 191 (1988).

3. Recent heightened sensitivity to environmental hazards has added a dimension to condition of the premises litigation. In particular, the discovery of high levels of radon in a house, or of pesticides in a water supply, or the

presence of hazardous wastes previously disposed of on a property, create serious problems for a purchaser of property, which might well cause the purchaser to look elsewhere for relief. Moreover, federal superfund legislation holds purchasers (as well as prior owners) liable for the cost of cleaning up toxic wastes, unless a purchaser can prove that, despite diligent efforts to determine its presence, he was unaware of toxic contamination. 42 U.S.C.A. § 9601(35)(A). A purchaser tagged with such liability may well look towards the prior owner who created the condition, a builder who built on contaminated property, or a real estate broker who failed to mention it, for indemnification. See Powell, Builder–Vendor Liability for Environmental Contamination in the Sale of New Residential Property, 58 Tenn.L.Rev. 231 (1991); Comment, A Toxic Nightmare on Elm Street: Negligence and the Real Estate Broker's Duty in Selling Previously Contaminated Residential Property, 15 B.C.Envtl.Aff.L.Rev. 547 (1988). See also pages 616–622 below, discussing further the implications of the superfund legislation for real estate transactions.

Suppose you are the lawyer for the seller of business property, a seller (client) who assures her lawyer, in answer to your routine question, of her "diligent efforts" to determine the presence of toxic wastes on the property. As her lawyer, you go ahead with the sale. Then, one day, your client tells you the reason she gave the toxic waste matter diligent effort is because she knew, as the buyer did not, that electric transformers (a source of PCBs, a toxic chemical) had been stored on the property. And suppose the regulators and the purchaser later discover the history of the PCBs and the purchaser sues your client to recover the costs of cleaning up the residues. You suspect that your client the seller knew about the transformer storage before the sale, and just kept her head down. What could you have done about your suspicion at the time, and what can you do about it now that the issue is in court? Consider the law-office dilemma given to the New York Times Magazine ethics columnist, Randy Cohen (July 29, 1999): "I am the attorney for a former employee of a tobacco company who has evidence that it purchased tobacco contaminated with radioactive residue for use in cigarettes. His wife has prevailed upon him not to allow the information to be made public, because it might affect his future job prospects, although he bears no responsibility. The Virginia State Bar advises me that I may not violate attorney-client privilege here. What should I do?" See Rules of Professional Conduct, Rule 1.6(a) and (b)(2003 A.B.A. revision):

> (a) A lawyer shall not reveal information relating to the representation of a client unless the client gives informed consent, the disclosure is impliedly authorized in order to carry out the representation, or the disclosure is permitted by paragraph (b).

> (b) A lawyer may reveal information relating to the representation of a client ...

> > (4) to comply with other law or a court order.

Do you agree with what the Virginia State Bar told Mr. Cohen's correspondent?

* * *

Where the context is less clearly tied to financial gain and loss, Mr. Cohen is relatively severe. For example, on whether a high school student should disclose a disciplinary record, expunged by the high school, on an application for college admission, he ruled: "[K]nowing that the high school no longer has any record ... might make the temptation to conceal nearly overwhelming: There's little chance [you] would be caught in a lie. But [you] should not yield to that temptation.... With luck, colleges will admire [your] integrity ... and display ... savvy and humanity." (South Bend Tribune, January 27, 2005, p. D–1.)

V. FINANCING THE ACQUISITION AND DEVELOPMENT OF LAND

With rare exceptions, land acquisition and development is accomplished with borrowed money. As discussed earlier in this chapter, a wide variety of financial institutions regularly lend money to finance real estate transactions. Real estate lenders generally have two basic interests: 1) recovery of borrowed money (the "principal"); and 2) realization of a profit on the transaction (the return on investment). In order to cover the costs of lending money and to make a profit on the transactions, lenders commonly charge "interest" on the "principal" amount of the loan. In this context, "interest" is an annual charge, expressed as a percentage of the amount of the loan, for the use of someone else's money.

Interest rates traditionally have been regulated by state laws prohibiting the charging of exorbitant rates, known as usury. However, in 1980 and 1982, Congress preempted state usury laws for most residential real estate loans. 12 U.S.C.A. § 3701 et seq.; 12 U.S.C.A. § 3801 et seq. See generally G. Nelson & D. Whitman, Real Estate Finance Law, 4th Ed, § 11.6 (2001). Actual rates charged for particular real estate loans represent a combination of limits established by the marketplace as well as by government regulators. In recent years, interest rate volatility has made adjustable rate mortgages (the interest rate is adjusted to "market rate" periodically) more attractive than fixed rate mortgages (the interest rate is "fixed" over the term of the mortgage, usually 15–30 years). Do you see why both borrowers and lenders prefer the adjustable rate mortgage?

Although real estate loans come in all sorts of packages, each one contains combinations of four basic variables, termed the "credit quartet" by Professors Curtis Berger and Quintin Johnstone, Land Transfer and Finance 177 (4th ed.1993): 1) amount borrowed ("principal"); 2) length of time for repayment ("term"); 3) interest rate; and 4) method of repayment (amortization). The amount borrowed also is described in a loan-to-value ratio (amount of the loan expressed as a percentage of the value of the property offered as security for the loan, or of the value of the total real estate investment, e.g., an $80,000 loan secured by a house valued at $100,000, or being used to complete a $100,000 real estate investment, has a loan-to-value ratio of 80 percent and is known as an 80 percent loan).

The four variables can be manipulated to accomplish a variety of objectives. For example, a person with reasonable expectations for economic advancement, but little accumulated savings may be able to afford the monthly payments for a 20–year, $80,000 loan at ten per cent ($772.04 per month), but may not be able to purchase a $100,000 house because of the $20,000 down payment required to complete the transaction. However, if the loan-to-value ratio were increased to 95 per cent, the down-payment problem would be resolved, but the monthly payments on a $95,000 loan at ten per cent ($916.80 per month) might be prohibitive. The monthly payment problem can be resolved either by lengthening the term of the loan, e.g., from 20 to 30 years (reducing the monthly payment to $702.07), or by reducing the interest rate, e.g., from ten per cent to eight per cent (lowering the monthly payment to $669.19 (20 years) or $587.03 (30 years)). When a 95 percent loan-to-value ratio is combined with a 30 year term and an eight per cent interest rate, the resulting smaller down-payment ($5000) and lower monthly payments for principal and interest ($697.10), may make a $100,000 house affordable to a median-income family.

The Federal Housing Administration (FHA), established by Congress in the 1930s, pioneered the use of high loan-to-value, long term, lower interest, fixed-rate loans with self-amortizing features to reduce the cost of housing for moderate and middle-income families by offering mortgage insurance to lenders who would make such loans. FHA-insured loans also reduced a risk of default at the end of the loan term by providing for amortization of principal over the term of the loan through application of a gradually-increasing portion of each monthly payment to reduce the outstanding principal balance, rather than requiring a lump-sum ("balloon") payment at the end of the loan term.

The following table illustrates the effect of variations in loan-to-value ratio, down payment, length of term, and interest rate on the monthly principal and interest costs of a $100,000 house.

Interest Rate		Amount Borrowed	
8%	$80,000	$90,000	$95,000
Loan Term		Monthly Payment	
20 yrs.	$669.19/mo.	$752.84/mo.	$794.67/mo.
25 yrs.	617.48	694.67	733.26
30 yrs.	587.03	660.41	697.10
10%			
20 yrs.	$772.04/mo.	$868.54/mo.	$916.80/mo.
25 yrs.	726.97	817.85	863.28

30 yrs.	702.07	789.82	833.77
12%			
20 yrs.	$880.08/mo.	$990.09/mo.	$1045.95/mo.
25 yrs.	842.40	947.70	1000.35
30 yrs.	823.20	926.10	977.55

———

Effect of below-market interest rate subsidy

4%	**$80,000**	**$90,000**	**$95,000**
20 yrs.	$484.80/mo.	$545.40/mo.	$575.70/mo.
25 yrs.	442.40	475.20	501.60
30 yrs.	381.60	429.30	453.15

———

The concept of leverage plays an important role in real estate finance. Leverage in real estate finance is a reflection of the success a purchaser has in using other people's money to finance a real estate transaction. A highly-leveraged transaction is one with a high loan-to-value ratio and correspondingly low down payment (investment) by the purchaser. Leverage offers the potential for dramatically increasing the rate of return on a purchaser's investment. If, for example, property purchased for $100,000 in cash is sold in one year for $110,000, the seller obtains a 10 per cent return on her investment. If, however, that same property was purchased with a 90 per cent loan ($10,000 down payment), a sale for $110,000 nets the seller $20,000 or double her initial investment.

From a lender's standpoint, highly-leveraged loans are risky because highly-leveraged borrowers have less to lose from default, and thus may be less inclined to take steps to avoid default. In addition, a decline in real estate values may cause a lender to lose money on a loan default if the foreclosure sale price of highly-leveraged property is not sufficient to cover the unpaid balance of the loan.

The long-term nature of most real estate loans, coupled with the large amounts usually borrowed, make real estate loans inherently risky for both lender and borrower. Because of the high risks, it is common for real estate loans to be "secured" by property of the borrower. A "security interest" or "lien" on the property is conveyed by the borrower to the lender. The interest conveyed, called a mortgage, or in some states a deed of trust, is a non-possessory right to sell the property and use the proceeds of the sale to retire the loan should the borrower fail to make timely payments. It is called a security interest because the lender is supposed to feel more secure about the prospects of ultimate recovery of its investment should a default occur, and the borrower is supposed to be more motivated to honor her promise to repay because of the prospect of losing the property if the loan is not repaid.

Lenders commonly cluster their perceptions of the risks of real estate loans into two groups: 1) credit risks; and 2) interest rate risks.

Credit risks are of two types, the risk that the borrower will not have enough money to make the promised monthly payments, and the risk that, if a default occurs, the value of the property will not be high enough to generate sale proceeds sufficient to recoup the lender's investment. These risks are evaluated through a process called loan underwriting, using income and credit histories of the borrower, and appraisals of the value of the property which will secure the loan. Loan underwriting can be time consuming, and is one of the reasons why a substantial delay (30–90 days) usually occurs between the time a real estate sale contract is signed and a deed is transferred.

Interest rate risks arise out of increased unpredictability concerning the cost of money. Lenders typically obtain money for real estate loans by "buying" the use of other peoples' money through various types of deposit accounts, insurance premiums, pension accumulations, etc. They "pay" for such use by crediting interest to the accounts of the depositors. The interest rate risk that concerns lenders is the possibility that they may find themselves paying more to acquire money for lending purposes than they are receiving in repayment of previous loans. For example, lenders who routinely made 25 year-to–30–year loans at fixed interest rates in the six per cent range in the 1950s and early 1960s were not happy people when they had to offer 10–12 per cent rates in order to attract depositors in the 1970s and 1980s. Fears about interest rate risk returned in 1992 in the wake of a "tidal wave" of homeowners seeking to refinance home loans to take advantage of sharply lower interest rates. Labaton, Lower Interest Rates Revive Fears of Banks and S. & L.'s, New York Times, January 13, 1992, at p. A1, col. 3. The growth in popularity of various forms of adjustable rate mortgage loans (ARMs) is a result of lenders' concerns about interest rate risks.

A. ELEMENTS OF THE LOAN

The basic real estate loan consists of two parts: 1) a written promise to pay back the money borrowed upon the agreed terms (the note), and 2) a conveyance of a property interest to the lender to secure the borrower's performance of her promise (the mortgage or deed of trust).

1. The Note

The note is the contract between the borrower and the lender. It describes the particular cluster of variables described above that have been agreed upon by the parties, and expresses the borrower's promise to repay, along with agreements concerning the right to pay the loan off early ("prepayment"), late charges, rights of the lender upon default, notice requirements for exercising those rights, and an acknowledgment that the note is secured by a mortgage, deed of trust, or other property interest.

NOTE

_____, _____ _____ _____

[Date]   [City]   [State]

[Property Address]

1. BORROWER'S PROMISE TO PAY

In return for a loan that I have received, I promise to pay U.S. $_____ (this amount is called "Principal"), plus interest, to the order of the Lender. The Lender is _____

_____. I will make all payments under this Note in the form of cash, check or money order.

I understand that the Lender may transfer this Note. The Lender or anyone who takes this Note by transfer and who is entitled to receive payments under this Note is called the "Note Holder."

2. INTEREST

Interest will be charged on unpaid principal until the full amount of Principal has been paid. I will pay interest at a yearly rate of _____%.

The interest rate required by this Section 2 is the rate I will pay both before and after any default described in Section 6(B) of this Note.

3. PAYMENTS

(A) Time and Place of Payments

I will pay principal and interest by making a payment every month.

I will make my monthly payment on the _____ day of each month beginning on _____, _____. I will make these payments every month until I have paid all of the principal and interest and any other charges described below that I may owe under this Note. Each monthly payment will be applied as of its scheduled due date and will be applied to interest before Principal. If, on _____, 20_____, I still owe amounts under this Note, I will pay those amounts in full on that date, which is called the "Maturity Date."

I will make my monthly payments at _____ _____ or at a different place if required by the Note Holder.

(B) Amount of Monthly Payments

My monthly payment will be in the amount of U.S. $_____.

4. BORROWER'S RIGHT TO PREPAY

I have the right to make payments of Principal at any time before they are due. A payment of Principal only is known as a "Prepayment." When I make a Prepayment, I will tell the Note Holder in writing that I am doing so. I may not designate a payment as a Prepayment if I have not made all the monthly payments due under the Note.

I may make a full Prepayment or partial Prepayments without paying a Prepayment charge. The Note Holder will use my Prepayments to reduce the amount of Principal that I owe under this Note. However, the Note Holder may apply my Prepayment to the accrued and unpaid interest on the Prepayment amount, before applying my Prepayment to reduce the Principal amount of the Note. If I make a partial Prepayment, there will be no changes in the due date or in the amount of my monthly payment unless the Note Holder agrees in writing to those changes.

5. LOAN CHARGES

If a law, which applies to this loan and which sets maximum loan charges, is finally interpreted so that the interest or other loan charges collected or to be collected in connection with this loan exceed the permitted limits, then: (a) any such loan charge shall be reduced by the amount necessary to reduce the charge to the permitted limit; and (b) any sums already collected from me which exceeded permitted limits will be refunded to me. The Note Holder may choose to make this refund by reducing the Principal I owe under this Note or by making a direct payment to me. If a refund reduces Principal, the reduction will be treated as a partial Prepayment.

6. BORROWER'S FAILURE TO PAY AS REQUIRED

(A) Late Charge for Overdue Payments

If the Note Holder has not received the full amount of any monthly payment by the end of _____ calendar days after the date it is due, I will pay a late charge to the Note Holder. The amount of the charge will be _____% of my overdue payment of principal and interest. I will pay this late charge promptly but only once on each late payment.

(B) Default

If I do not pay the full amount of each monthly payment on the date it is due, I will be in default.

(C) Notice of Default

If I am in default, the Note Holder may send me a written notice telling me that if I do not pay the overdue amount by a certain date, the Note Holder may require me to pay immediately the full amount of Principal which has not been paid and all the interest that I owe on that amount. That date must be at least 30 days after the date on which the notice is mailed to me or delivered by other means.

(D) No Waiver By Note Holder

Even if, at a time when I am in default, the Note Holder does not require me to pay immediately in full as described above, the Note Holder will still have the right to do so if I am in default at a later time.

(E) Payment of Note Holder's Costs and Expenses

If the Note Holder has required me to pay immediately in full as described above, the Note Holder will have the right to be paid back by me for all of its costs and expenses in enforcing this Note to the extent not prohibited by applicable law. Those expenses include, for example, reasonable attorneys' fees.

7. GIVING OF NOTICES

Unless applicable law requires a different method, any notice that must be given to me under this Note will be given by delivering it or by mailing it by first class mail to me at the Property Address above or at a different address if I give the Note Holder a notice of my different address.

Any notice that must be given to the Note Holder under this Note will be given by delivering it or by mailing it by first class mail to the Note Holder at the address stated in Section 3(A) above or at a different address if I am given a notice of that different address.

8. OBLIGATIONS OF PERSONS UNDER THIS NOTE

If more than one person signs this Note, each person is fully and personally obligated to keep all of the promises made in this Note, including the promise to pay the full amount owed. Any person who is a guarantor, surety or endorser of this Note is also obligated to do these things. Any person who takes over these obligations, including the obligations of a guarantor, surety or endorser of this Note, is also obligated to keep all of the promises made in this Note. The Note Holder may enforce its rights under this Note against each person individually or against all of us together. This means that any one of us may be required to pay all of the amounts owed under this Note.

9. WAIVERS

I and any other person who has obligations under this Note waive the rights of Presentment and Notice of Dishonor. "Presentment" means the right to require the Note Holder to demand payment of amounts due. "Notice of Dishonor" means the right to require the Note Holder to give notice to other persons that amounts due have not been paid.

10. UNIFORM SECURED NOTE

This Note is a uniform instrument with limited variations in some jurisdictions. In addition to the protections given to the Note Holder under this Note, a Mortgage, Deed of Trust, or Security Deed (the "Security Instrument"), dated the same date as this Note, protects the Note Holder from possible losses which might result if I do not keep the promises which I make in this Note. That Security Instrument describes how and under what conditions I may be required to make immediate payment in full of all amounts I owe under this Note. Some of those conditions are described as follows:

If all or any part of the Property or any Interest in the Property is sold or transferred (or if Borrower is not a natural person and a beneficial interest in Borrower is sold or transferred) without Lender's prior written consent, Lender may require immediate payment in full of all sums secured by this Security Instrument. However, this option shall not be exercised by Lender if such exercise is prohibited by Applicable Law.

If Lender exercises this option, Lender shall give Borrower notice of acceleration. The notice shall provide a period of not less than 30 days from the date the notice is given in accordance with Section 15 within which Borrower must pay all sums secured by this Security Instrument. If Borrower fails to pay these sums prior to the expiration of this period, Lender may invoke any remedies permitted by this Security Instrument without further notice or demand on Borrower.

WITNESS THE HAND(S) AND SEAL(S) OF THE UNDERSIGNED.

_____(Seal)   _____(Seal)
　　　　　　　　-Borrower   　　　　　　　　-Borrower

_____(Seal)   _____(Seal)
　　　　　　　　-Borrower   　　　　　　　　-Borrower

_____(Seal)   _____(Seal)
　　　　　　　　-Borrower   　　　　　　　　-Borrower

_____(Seal)   _____(Seal)
　　　　　　　　-Borrower   　　　　　　　　-Borrower

[Sign Original Only]

Notes and Questions

1. Examine the note carefully. Does the borrower have a grace period for making payments? What constitutes default? What procedure is to be followed when default occurs? Is the note transferable? By the lender? By the borrower? If the borrower wins the lottery, does she have the right to eliminate her debt by prepaying the note? If the borrower makes a double payment (two months), can she skip the next month's payment if she should become ill or be laid off from work? What happens to the balance of the double payment that remains after the regular monthly payment is credited? Does the note contain any restrictions on transfer of the property by the borrower?

2. The following excerpt describes a variety of mortgage loans designed to offer more flexibility to borrowers and lenders. In recent years, lenders have introduced new loans to attract first-time homebuyers with low monthly payments. Interest-only loans allow buyers to pay only interest for a fixed period of time. Negative amortization loans allow buyers to repay even less than the interest owed for a specific period, but add any accrued but unpaid interest to the total loan amount. Such loans have become increasingly popular notwithstanding criticism that they present an unacceptably high risk of default and foreclosure in the event of a dramatic rise in interest rates or decline in housing values. It was estimated that these loans accounted for 35% of new home loans nationwide in 2005, and as much as

70% in some markets such as San Francisco. As you study the excerpt, consider what changes you would make to the sample note in order to create a particular kind of mortgage note.

NELSON & WHITMAN, REAL ESTATE

881–884 (4th ed. 2001).

§ 11.4 Alternative Mortgage Instruments

The great majority of mortgage loans made in America since the great depression are of the level-payment self-amortizing type * * *. Interest is fixed for the life of the loan and payments are the same each month or other period, and fully amortize the debt with no "balloon" payment upon maturity. While this format eliminates the need for periodic refinancing which existed in pre-depression mortgage loans, in which only interest was paid monthly, it also has certain disadvantages. The disadvantages fall into two basic categories, as do various proposals for reform.

The first troublesome aspect of the standard loan format is its failure to take into account changes in the ability of the mortgagors to make payments over their life spans. For example, young families purchasing a first house are likely to experience significant increases in income as they grow older. Yet the standard loan provides for level payments in terms of nominal dollars; in an inflationary economy, the real value of the monthly payments will decline over time, even though the mortgagors' ability to pay will probably be increasing. Hence their maximum initial loan amount will be fixed by an income which rapidly becomes irrelevant with the passage of time; after a few years they will easily be able to afford payments on a larger home, but can make such a change only through the rather costly method of selling the existing house and buying another.

At the other end of the mortgagors' life span an opposite mismatch occurs. They usually retire and experience a sharp drop in income, but their monthly mortgage payment obligation remains constant despite the fact that principal amortization and inflating house values have combined to produce a very low loan-to-value ratio. The mortgagors might prefer to reduce their payments, or even to stop them entirely, but the standard loan format makes no provision for doing so.

The second major problem with the standard loan relates not to the preferences and incomes of mortgagors, but to the ability of lenders, particularly thrift institutions, to retain deposits and hence to continue lending during periods of sharply increasing interest rates. The United States economy has experienced a series of large fluctuations in interest rates during the post-war period, especially since 1966. These credit cycles are produced by the interaction of a complex set of factors, including consumer behavior, federal and state borrowing demands, domestic and international trade and economic conditions, and the periodic efforts of the Federal Reserve Board to tighten the supply of money in the economy in order to slow inflation. Interest rate peaks can be clearly discerned in 1966, 1969–70, 1974, 1978, 1981, 1984, 1989–90, and 1995. In each case rates have subsequently fallen, but in some cases did not return to pre-peak levels.

The effect of these credit cycles on thrift institutions has been highly damaging. When short-term rates on alternative investments, such as Treasury bills and commercial paper, rise above the rates being paid on savings deposits by thrift institutions, many sophisticated depositors withdraw their funds from savings accounts and place them in these alternative investments. The institutions may literally run out of money to lend, and the housing market suffers. This phenomenon is known as disintermediation, since it involves the removal of funds from the thrift institutions, which are financial intermediaries. To forestall disintermediation, thrift institutions may attempt to raise the interest rates on their own deposits, thereby inducing investors to keep their funds on deposit. * * *

* * *

* * * [L]enders that invest primarily in standard mortgages still have difficulty raising their deposit interest rates to competitive levels during periods of generally rising rates. The reason is that their mortgage portfolios consist of mortgages made in prior years as well as those made in the current year. Even if the institution raises the interest rates on mortgage loans currently being made to very high levels, that action has relatively little impact on the overall yield of the portfolio, since it consists largely of fixed-interest loans made in earlier periods when rates were lower. This "portfolio lag" phenomenon virtually precludes the institutions from raising deposit interest rates quickly, no matter how much they would like to do so. Thus thrift institutions may be caught in a fundamental structural dilemma; by their nature they violate the well-known axiom of finance: "Never borrow short and lend long." In an economy characterized by volatile interest rates, their problem is an acute one.

Two approaches to this problem can be taken, and the thrift institutions and their regulators moved toward both. The first is to change the maturity structure of the institutions' liabilities—that is, their deposits—in order to make them less volatile. A number of regulatory changes have been made to allow thrifts to offer a broader range of longer-term instruments to savers. . . .

The other approach is to shorten the effective maturity of the institutions' assets, their mortgage loans. Although most home mortgages today have nominal maturities of twenty-five to thirty years, they are typically prepaid in ten to twelve years or less. These early payments have historically been in part the result of inflating housing prices, which tend to make property sales with assumptions and subject-to transfers impractical within a few years after a mortgage loan has been placed on a home. The widespread use of due-on-sale clauses is also an important factor in causing early payoffs. But most portfolio lenders wish to reduce the effective term of the average home mortgage loan a great deal more than the reduction which results from ordinary prepayments associated with home transfers. Hence, since the beginning of the 1980's they have engaged in a major shift away from the standard fixed-rate loan and toward instruments with adjustable rates, with the adjustment indexed to short-term or medium-term market rates such as those on United States government securities. Such mortgages are viewed as the economic equivalent of short-term loans, even though their monthly payment schedules might continue to be based on thirty year amortization of principal.

There are, then, two reasons for the development in recent years of alternative mortgage instruments: the desire to conform payment schedules to borrowers' abilities to pay, and the desire to make mortgage loans which are not locked into fixed interest yields for long time periods, but on which yields will tend to match those available in the current market from time to time. Certain types of new mortgage formats are associated with each of these two objectives.

* * *

———

3. As discussed earlier the secondary mortgage market plays a vital role in real estate finance. The rise of the secondary mortgage market gives added weight to the importance of the mortgage note, because secondary market investors must look to the note, as well as the mortgage, for their rights should disputes arise concerning payment or procedures to follow in case of default. Investors in the secondary market typically seek protection of the "holder in due course" concept of negotiable instruments in order to insulate themselves from defenses that may be raised by the original borrower against the original lender in case of default. For a case illustrating the importance of careful drafting of the mortgage note, see Taylor v. Roeder, 234 Va. 99, 360 S.E.2d 191 (1987) (adjustable mortgage note failed to qualify as negotiable instrument under Uniform Commercial Code).

2. *The Mortgage (and Mortgage Substitutes)*

The property part of a real estate loan transaction is the conveyance of a non-possessory property interest by the borrower to the lender. This takes place simultaneously with the execution of the note, and provides the "security" for repayment of the debt represented by the note. The document evidencing the conveyance is called a mortgage, although in some jurisdictions a similar document called a deed of trust is used. Except where indicated, we can use the terms interchangeably. Indeed, it is not uncommon for mortgages to be used in parts of a state, and deeds of trust to be used in other areas of the same state, as a matter of local practice. In reviewing the sample deed of trust below, pay particular attention to the language of conveyance. What legal relationships are created? What obligations are undertaken by the grantor (usually called the mortgagor)? By the grantee (the mortgagee)? By the trustee?

Return To: U.S. Bank N.A.
              1550 American Blvd East   Lender address located on page 2
              Bloomington MN 55425   Trustee address located on page 2
                                       Full Legal Description located on page 3

———[Space Above This Line For Recording Data]———

DEED OF TRUST

DEFINITIONS

Words used in multiple sections of this document are defined below and other words are defined in Sections 3, 11, 13, 18, 20 and 21. Certain rules regarding the usage of words used in this document are also provided in Section 16.

(A) "Security Instrument" means this document, which is dated ———, ———, together with all Riders to this document.

(B) "Borrower" is ———————————————————————.
Borrower is the trustor under this Security Instrument.

(C) "Lender" is ———————————————————————.
Lender is a ——— organized and existing under the laws of ———.
Lender's address is ———. Lender is the beneficiary under this Security Instrument.

(D) "Trustee" is ———.

(E) "Note" means the promissory note signed by Borrower and dated ———, ———. The Note states that Borrower owes Lender ——— Dollars (U.S. $———) plus interest. Borrower has promised to pay this debt in regular Periodic Payments and to pay the debt in full not later than ———.

(F) "Property" means the property that is described below under the heading "Transfer of Rights in the Property."

(G) "Loan" means the debt evidenced by the Note, plus interest, any prepayment charges and late charges due under the Note, and all sums due under this Security Instrument, plus interest.

(H) "Riders" means all Riders to this Security Instrument that are executed by Borrower. The following Riders are to be executed by Borrower [check box as applicable]:

☐ Adjustable Rate Rider   ☐ Condominium Rider   ☐ Second Home Rider
☐ Balloon Rider   ☐ Planned Unit Development Rider   ☐ Other(s) [specify] ———
☐ 1–4 Family Rider   ☐ Biweekly Payment Rider

(I) "Applicable Law" means all controlling applicable federal, state and local statutes, regulations, ordinances and administrative rules and orders (that have the effect of law) as well as all applicable final, non-appealable judicial opinions.

(J) "Community Association Dues, Fees, and Assessments" means all dues, fees, assessments and other charges that are imposed on Borrower or the Property by a condominium association, homeowners association or similar organization.

(K) "Electronic Funds Transfer" means any transfer of funds, other than a transaction originated by check, draft, or similar paper instrument, which is initiated through an electronic terminal, telephonic instrument, computer, or magnetic tape so as to order, instruct, or authorize a financial institution to debit or credit an account. Such term includes, but is not limited to, point-of-sale transfers, automated teller machine transactions, transfers initiated by telephone, wire transfers, and automated clearinghouse transfers.

(L) "Escrow Items" means those items that are described in Section 3.

(M) "Miscellaneous Proceeds" means any compensation, settlement, award of damages, or proceeds paid by any third party (other than insurance proceeds paid under the coverages described in Section 5) for: (i) damage to, or destruction of, the Property; (ii) condemnation or other taking of all or any part of the Property; (iii) conveyance in lieu of condemnation; or (iv) misrepresentations of, or omissions as to, the value and/or condition of the Property.

(N) "Mortgage Insurance" means insurance protecting Lender against the nonpayment of, or default on, the Loan.

(O) "Periodic Payment" means the regularly scheduled amount due for (i) principal and interest under the Note, plus (ii) any amounts under Section 3 of this Security Instrument.

(P) "RESPA" means the Real Estate Settlement Procedures Act (12 U.S.C. § 2601 et seq.) and its implementing regulation, Regulation X (24 C.F.R. Part 3500), as they might be amended from time to time, or any additional or successor legislation or regulation that governs the same subject matter. As used in this Security Instrument, "RESPA" refers to all requirements and restrictions that are imposed in regard to a "federally related mortgage loan" even if the Loan does not qualify as a "federally related mortgage loan" under RESPA.

(Q) "Successor in Interest of Borrower" means any party that has taken title to the Property, whether or not that party has assumed Borrower's obligations under the Note and/or this Security Instrument.

TRANSFER OF RIGHTS IN THE PROPERTY

This Security Instrument secures to Lender: (i) the repayment of the Loan, and all renewals, extensions and modifications of the Note; and (ii) the performance of Borrower's covenants and agreements under this Security Instrument and the Note. For this purpose, Borrower irrevocably grants, bargains, sells, conveys and confirms to Trustee, in trust, with power of sale, the following described property located in the _____ of

[Type of Recording Jurisdiction]

_____:

[Name of Recording Jurisdiction]

which currently has the address of _____

[Street]

_____, Missouri _____ ("Property Address"):

[City][Zip Code]

TOGETHER WITH all the improvements now or hereafter erected on the property, and all easements, appurtenances, and fixtures now or hereafter a part of the property. All replacements and additions shall also be covered by this Security Instrument. All of the foregoing is referred to in this Security Instrument as the "Property."

BORROWER COVENANTS that Borrower is lawfully seised of the estate hereby conveyed and has the right to grant and convey the Property and that the Property is unencumbered, except for encumbrances of record. Borrower warrants and will defend generally the title to the Property against all claims and demands, subject to any encumbrances of record.

THIS SECURITY INSTRUMENT combines uniform covenants for national use and non-uniform covenants with limited variations by jurisdiction to constitute a uniform security instrument covering real property.

UNIFORM COVENANTS. Borrower and Lender covenant and agree as follows:

1. Payment of Principal, Interest, Escrow Items, Prepayment Charges, and Late Charges. Borrower shall pay when due the principal of, and interest on, the debt evidenced by the Note and any prepayment charges and late charges due under the Note. Borrower shall also pay funds for Escrow Items pursuant to Section 3. Payments due under the Note and this Security Instrument shall be made in U.S. currency. However, if any check or other instrument received by Lender as payment under the Note or this Security Instrument is returned to Lender unpaid, Lender may require that any or all subsequent payments due under the Note and this Security Instrument be made in one or more of the following forms, as selected by Lender: (a) cash; (b) money order; (c) certified check, bank check, treasurer's check or cashier's check, provided any such check is drawn upon an institution whose deposits are insured by a federal agency, instrumentality, or entity; or (d) Electronic Funds Transfer.

Payments are deemed received by Lender when received at the location designated in the Note or at such other location as may be designated by Lender in accordance with the notice provisions in Section 15. Lender may return any payment or partial payment if the payment or partial payments are insufficient to bring the Loan current. Lender may accept any payment or partial payment insufficient to bring the Loan current, without waiver of any rights hereunder or prejudice to its rights to refuse such payment or partial payments in the future, but Lender is not obligated to apply such payments at the time such payments are accepted. If each Periodic Payment is applied as of its scheduled due date, then Lender need not pay interest on unapplied funds. Lender may hold such unapplied funds until Borrower makes payment to bring the Loan current. If Borrower does not do so within a reasonable period of time, Lender shall either apply such funds or return them to Borrower. If not applied earlier, such funds will be applied to the outstanding principal balance under the Note immediately prior to foreclosure. No offset or claim which Borrower might have now or in the future against Lender shall relieve Borrower from making payments due under the Note and this Security Instrument or performing the covenants and agreements secured by this Security Instrument.

2.   Application of Payments or Proceeds. Except as otherwise described in this Section 2, all payments accepted and applied by Lender shall be applied in the following order of priority: (a) interest due under the Note; (b) principal due under the Note; (c) amounts due under Section 3. Such payments shall be applied to each Periodic Payment in the order in which it became due. Any remaining amounts shall be applied first to late charges, second to any other amounts due under this Security Instrument, and then to reduce the principal balance of the Note.

If Lender receives a payment from Borrower for a delinquent Periodic Payment which includes a sufficient amount to pay any late charge due, the payment may be applied to the delinquent payment and the late charge. If more than one Periodic Payment is outstanding, Lender may apply any payment received from Borrower to the repayment of the Periodic Payments if, and to the extent that, each payment can be paid in full. To the extent that any excess exists after the payment is applied to the full payment of one or more Periodic Payments, such excess may be applied to any late charges due. Voluntary prepayments shall be applied first to any prepayment charges and then as described in the Note.

Any application of payments, insurance proceeds, or Miscellaneous Proceeds to principal due under the Note shall not extend or postpone the due date, or change the amount, of the Periodic Payments.

3.   Funds for Escrow Items. Borrower shall pay to Lender on the day Periodic Payments are due under the Note, until the Note is paid in full, a sum (the "Funds") to provide for payment of amounts due for: (a) taxes and assessments and other items which can attain priority over this Security Instrument as a lien or encumbrance on the Property; (b) leasehold payments or ground rents on the Property, if any; (c) premiums for any and all insurance required by Lender under Section 5; and (d) Mortgage Insurance premiums, if any, or any sums payable by Borrower to Lender in lieu of the payment of Mortgage Insurance premiums in accordance with the provisions of Section 10. These items are called "Escrow Items." At origination or at any time during the term of the Loan, Lender may require that Community Association Dues, Fees, and Assessments, if any, be escrowed by Borrower, and such dues, fees and assessments shall be an Escrow Item. Borrower shall promptly furnish to Lender all notices of amounts to be paid under this Section. Borrower shall pay Lender the Funds for Escrow Items unless Lender waives Borrower's obligation to pay the Funds for any or all Escrow Items. Lender may waive Borrower's obligation to pay to Lender Funds for any or all Escrow Items at any time. Any such waiver may only be in writing. In the event of such waiver, Borrower shall pay directly, when and where payable, the amounts due for any Escrow Items for which payment of Funds has been waived by Lender and, if Lender requires, shall furnish to Lender receipts evidencing such payment within such time period as Lender may require. Borrower's obligation to make such payments and to provide receipts shall for all purposes be deemed to be a covenant and agreement contained in this Security Instrument, as the phrase "covenant and agreement" is used in Section 9. If Borrower is obligated to pay Escrow Items directly, pursuant to a waiver, and Borrower fails to pay the amount due for an Escrow Item, Lender may exercise its rights under Section 9 and pay such amount and Borrower shall then be obligated under Section 9 to repay to Lender any such amount. Lender may revoke the waiver as to any or all Escrow Items at any time by a notice given in accordance with Section 15 and, upon such revocation, Borrower shall pay to Lender all Funds, and in such amounts, that are then required under this Section 3.

Lender may, at any time, collect and hold Funds in an amount (a) sufficient to permit Lender to apply the Funds at the time specified under RESPA, and (b) not to exceed the maximum amount a lender can require under RESPA. Lender shall estimate the amount of Funds due on the basis of current data and reasonable estimates of expenditures of future Escrow Items or otherwise in accordance with Applicable Law.

The Funds shall be held in an institution whose deposits are insured by a federal agency, instrumentality, or entity (including Lender, if Lender is an institution whose deposits are so insured) or in any Federal Home Loan Bank. Lender shall apply the Funds to pay the Escrow Items no later than the time specified under RESPA. Lender shall not charge Borrower for holding and applying the Funds, annually analyzing the escrow account, or verifying the Escrow Items, unless Lender pays Borrower interest on the Funds and Applicable Law permits Lender to make such a charge. Unless an agreement is made in writing or Applicable Law requires interest to be paid on the Funds, Lender shall not be required to pay Borrower any interest or earnings on the Funds. Borrower and Lender can agree in writing, however, that interest shall be paid on the Funds. Lender shall give to Borrower, without charge, an annual accounting of the Funds as required by RESPA.

If there is a surplus of Funds held in escrow, as defined under RESPA, Lender shall account to Borrower for the excess funds in accordance with RESPA. If there is a shortage of Funds held in escrow, as defined under RESPA, Lender shall notify Borrower as required by RESPA, and Borrower shall pay to Lender the amount necessary to make up the shortage in accordance with RESPA, but in no more than 12 monthly payments. If there is a deficiency of Funds held in escrow, as defined under RESPA, Lender shall notify Borrower as required by RESPA, and Borrower shall pay to Lender the amount necessary to make up the deficiency in accordance with RESPA, but in no more than 12 monthly payments.

Upon payment in full of all sums secured by this Security Instrument, Lender shall promptly refund to Borrower any Funds held by Lender.

4. Charges; Liens. Borrower shall pay all taxes, assessments, charges, fines, and impositions attributable to the Property which can attain priority over this Security Instrument, leasehold payments or ground rents on the Property, if any, and Community Association Dues, Fees, and Assessments, if any. To the extent that these items are Escrow Items, Borrower shall pay them in the manner provided in Section 3.

Borrower shall promptly discharge any lien which has priority over this Security Instrument unless Borrower: (a) agrees in writing to the payment of the obligation secured by the lien in a manner acceptable to Lender, but only so long as Borrower is performing such agreement; (b) contests the lien in good faith by, or defends against enforcement of the lien in, legal proceedings which in Lender's opinion operate to prevent the enforcement of the lien while those proceedings are pending, but only until such proceedings are concluded; or (c) secures from the holder of the lien an agreement satisfactory to Lender subordinating the lien to this Security Instrument. If Lender determines that any part of the Property is subject to a lien which can attain priority over this Security Instrument, Lender may give Borrower a notice identifying the lien. Within 10 days of the date on which that notice is given, Borrower shall satisfy the lien or take one or more of the actions set forth above in this Section 4.

Lender may require Borrower to pay a one-time charge for a real estate tax verification and/or reporting service used by Lender in connection with this Loan.

5. Property Insurance. Borrower shall keep the improvements now existing or hereafter erected on the Property insured against loss by fire, hazards included within the term "extended coverage," and any other hazards including, but not limited to, earthquakes and floods, for which Lender requires insurance. This insurance shall be maintained in the amounts (including deductible levels) and for the periods that Lender requires. What Lender requires pursuant to the preceding sentences can change during the term of the Loan. The insurance carrier providing the insurance shall be chosen by Borrower subject to Lender's right to disapprove Borrower's choice, which right shall not be exercised unreasonably. Lender may require Borrower to pay, in connection with this Loan, either: (a) a one-time charge for flood zone determination, certification and tracking services; or (b) a one-time charge for flood zone determination and certification services and subsequent charges each time remappings or similar changes occur which reasonably might affect such determination or certification. Borrower shall also be responsible for the payment of any fees imposed by the Federal Emergency Management Agency in connection with the review of any flood zone determination resulting from an objection by Borrower.

If Borrower fails to maintain any of the coverages described above, Lender may obtain insurance coverage, at Lender's option and Borrower's expense. Lender is under no obligation to purchase any particular type or amount of coverage. Therefore, such coverage shall cover Lender, but might or might not protect Borrower, Borrower's equity in the Property, or the contents of the Property, against any risk, hazard or liability and might provide greater or lesser coverage than was previously in effect. Borrower acknowledges that the cost of the insurance coverage so obtained might significantly exceed the cost of insurance that Borrower could have obtained. Any amounts disbursed by Lender under this Section 5 shall become additional debt of Borrower secured by this Security Instrument. These amounts shall bear interest at the Note rate from the date of disbursement and shall be payable, with such interest, upon notice from Lender to Borrower requesting payment.

All insurance policies required by Lender and renewals of such policies shall be subject to Lender's right to disapprove such policies, shall include a standard mortgage clause, and shall name Lender as mortgagee and/or as an additional loss payee. Lender shall have the right to hold the policies and renewal certificates. If Lender requires, Borrower shall promptly give to Lender all receipts of paid premiums and renewal notices. If Borrower obtains any form of insurance coverage, not otherwise required by Lender, for damage to, or destruction of, the Property, such policy shall include a standard mortgage clause and shall name Lender as mortgagee and/or as an additional loss payee.

In the event of loss, Borrower shall give prompt notice to the insurance carrier and Lender. Lender may make proof of loss if not made promptly by Borrower. Unless Lender and Borrower otherwise agree in writing, any insurance proceeds, whether or not the underlying insurance was required by Lender, shall be applied to restoration or repair of the Property, if the restoration or repair is economically feasible and Lender's security is not lessened. During such repair and restoration period, Lender shall have the right to hold such insurance proceeds until Lender has had an opportunity to inspect such Property to ensure the work has been completed to Lender's satisfaction, provided that such inspection shall be undertaken promptly. Lender may disburse proceeds for the repairs and restoration in a single payment or in a series of progress payments as the work is completed. Unless an agreement is made in writing or Applicable Law requires interest to be paid on such insurance proceeds, Lender shall not be required to pay Borrower any interest or earnings on such proceeds. Fees for public adjusters, or other third parties, retained by Borrower shall not be paid out of the insurance proceeds and shall be the sole obligation of Borrower. If the restoration or repair is not economically feasible or Lender's security would be lessened, the insurance proceeds shall be applied to the sums secured by this Security Instrument, whether or not then due, with the excess, if any, paid to Borrower. Such insurance proceeds shall be applied in the order provided for in Section 2.

If Borrower abandons the Property, Lender may file, negotiate and settle any available insurance claim and related matters. If Borrower does not respond within 30 days to a notice from Lender that the insurance carrier has offered to settle a claim, then Lender may negotiate and settle the claim. The 30–day period will begin when the notice is given. In either event, or if Lender acquires the Property under Section 22 or otherwise, Borrower hereby assigns to Lender (a) Borrower's rights to any insurance proceeds in an amount not to exceed the amounts unpaid under the Note or this Security Instrument, and (b) any other of Borrower's rights (other than the right to any refund of unearned premiums paid by Borrower) under all insurance policies covering the Property, insofar as such rights are applicable to the coverage of the Property. Lender may use the insurance proceeds either to repair or restore the Property or to pay amounts unpaid under the Note or this Security Instrument, whether or not then due.

6. Occupancy. Borrower shall occupy, establish, and use the Property as Borrower's principal residence within 60 days after the execution of this Security Instrument and shall continue to occupy the Property as Borrower's principal residence for at least one year after the date of occupancy, unless Lender otherwise agrees in writing, which consent shall not be unreasonably withheld, or unless extenuating circumstances exist which are beyond Borrower's control.

7. Preservation, Maintenance and Protection of the Property; Inspections. Borrower shall not destroy, damage or impair the Property, allow the Property to deteriorate or commit waste on the Property. Whether or not Borrower is residing in the Property, Borrower shall maintain the Property in order to prevent the Property from deteriorating or decreasing in value due to its condition. Unless it is determined pursuant to Section 5 that repair or restoration is not economically feasible, Borrower shall promptly repair the Property if damaged to avoid further deterioration or damage. If insurance or condemnation proceeds are paid in connection with damage to, or the taking of, the Property, Borrower shall be responsible for repairing or restoring the Property only if Lender has released proceeds for such purposes. Lender may disburse proceeds for the repairs and restoration in a single payment or in a series of progress payments as the work is completed. If the insurance or condemnation proceeds are not sufficient to repair or restore the Property, Borrower is not relieved of Borrower's obligation for the completion of such repair or restoration.

Lender or its agent may make reasonable entries upon and inspections of the Property. If it has reasonable cause, Lender may inspect the interior of the improvements on the Property. Lender shall give Borrower notice at the time of or prior to such an interior inspection specifying such reasonable cause.

8. Borrower's Loan Application. Borrower shall be in default if, during the Loan application process, Borrower or any persons or entities acting at the direction of Borrower or with Borrower's knowledge or consent gave materially false, misleading, or inaccurate information or statements to Lender (or failed to provide Lender with material information) in connection with the Loan. Material representations include, but are not limited to, representations concerning Borrower's occupancy of the Property as Borrower's principal residence.

9. Protection of Lender's Interest in the Property and Rights Under this Security Instrument. If (a) Borrower fails to perform the covenants and agreements contained in this Security Instrument, (b) there is a legal proceeding that might significantly affect Lender's interest in the Property and/or rights under this Security Instrument (such as a proceeding in bankruptcy, probate, for condemnation or forfeiture, for enforcement of a lien which may attain priority over this Security Instrument or to enforce laws or regulations), or (c) Borrower has abandoned the Property, then Lender may do and pay for whatever is reasonable or appropriate to protect Lender's interest in the Property and rights under this Security Instrument, including protecting and/or assessing the value of the Property, and securing and/or repairing the Property. Lender's actions can include, but are not limited to: (a) paying any sums secured by a lien which has priority over this Security Instrument; (b) appearing in court; and (c) paying reasonable attorneys' fees to protect its interest in the Property and/or rights under this Security Instrument, including its secured position in a bankruptcy proceeding. Securing the Property includes, but is not limited to, entering the Property to make repairs, change locks, replace or board up doors and windows, drain water from pipes, eliminate building or other code violations or dangerous conditions, and have utilities turned on or off. Although Lender may take action under this Section 9, Lender does not have to do so and is not under any duty or obligation to do so. It is agreed that Lender incurs no liability for not taking any or all actions authorized under this Section 9.

Any amounts disbursed by Lender under this Section 9 shall become additional debt of Borrower secured by this Security Instrument. These amounts shall bear interest at the Note rate from the date of disbursement and shall be payable, with such interest, upon notice from Lender to Borrower requesting payment.

If this Security Instrument is on a leasehold, Borrower shall comply with all the provisions of the lease. If Borrower acquires fee title to the Property, the leasehold and the fee title shall not merge unless Lender agrees to the merger in writing.

10. Mortgage Insurance. If Lender required Mortgage Insurance as a condition of making the Loan, Borrower shall pay the premiums required to maintain the Mortgage Insurance in effect. If, for any reason, the Mortgage Insurance coverage required by Lender ceases to be available from the mortgage insurer that previously provided such insurance and Borrower was required to make separately designated payments toward the premiums for Mortgage Insurance, Borrower shall pay the premiums required to obtain coverage substantially equivalent to the Mortgage Insurance previously in effect, at a cost substantially equivalent to the cost to Borrower of the Mortgage Insurance previously in effect, from an alternate mortgage insurer selected by Lender. If substantially equivalent Mortgage Insurance coverage is not available, Borrower shall continue to pay to Lender the amount of the separately designated payments that were due when the insurance coverage ceased to be in effect. Lender will accept, use and retain these payments as a non-refundable loss reserve in lieu of Mortgage Insurance. Such loss reserve shall be non-refundable, notwithstanding the fact that the Loan is ultimately paid in full, and Lender shall not be required to pay Borrower any interest or earnings on such loss reserve. Lender can no longer require loss reserve payments if Mortgage Insurance coverage (in the amount and for the period that Lender requires) provided by an insurer selected by Lender again becomes available, is obtained, and Lender requires separately designated payments toward the premiums for Mortgage Insurance. If Lender required Mortgage Insurance as a condition of making the Loan and Borrower was required to make separately designated payments toward the premiums for Mortgage Insurance, Borrower shall pay the premiums required to maintain Mortgage Insurance in effect, or to provide a non-refundable loss reserve, until Lender's requirement for Mortgage Insurance ends in accordance with any written agreement between Borrower and Lender providing for such termination or until termination is required by Applicable Law. Nothing in this Section 10 affects Borrower's obligation to pay interest at the rate provided in the Note.

Mortgage Insurance reimburses Lender (or any entity that purchases the Note) for certain losses it may incur if Borrower does not repay the Loan as agreed. Borrower is not a party to the Mortgage Insurance.

Mortgage insurers evaluate their total risk on all such insurance in force from time to time, and may enter into agreements with other parties that share or modify their risk, or reduce losses. These agreements are on terms and conditions that are satisfactory to the mortgage insurer and the other party (or parties) to these agreements. These agreements may require the mortgage insurer to make payments using any source of funds that the mortgage insurer may have available (which may include funds obtained from Mortgage Insurance premiums).

As a result of these agreements, Lender, any purchaser of the Note, another insurer, any reinsurer, any other entity, or any affiliate of any of the foregoing, may receive (directly or indirectly) amounts that derive from (or might be characterized as) a portion of Borrower's payments for Mortgage Insurance, in exchange for sharing or modifying the mortgage insurer's risk, or reducing losses. If such agreement provides that an affiliate of Lender takes a share of the insurer's risk in exchange for a share of the premiums paid to the insurer, the arrangement is often termed "captive reinsurance." Further:

(a) Any such agreements will not affect the amounts that Borrower has agreed to pay for Mortgage Insurance, or any other terms of the Loan. Such agreements will not increase the amount Borrower will owe for Mortgage Insurance, and they will not entitle Borrower to any refund.

(b) Any such agreements will not affect the rights Borrower has—if any—with respect to the Mortgage Insurance under the Homeowners Protection Act of 1998 or any other law. These rights may include the right to receive certain disclosures, to request and obtain cancellation of the Mortgage Insurance, to have the Mortgage Insurance terminated automatically, and/or to receive a refund of any Mortgage Insurance premiums that were unearned at the time of such cancellation or termination.

11. Assignment of Miscellaneous Proceeds; Forfeiture. All Miscellaneous Proceeds are hereby assigned to and shall be paid to Lender.

If the Property is damaged, such Miscellaneous Proceeds shall be applied to restoration or repair of the Property, if the restoration or repair is economically feasible and Lender's security is not lessened. During such repair and restoration period, Lender shall have the right to hold such Miscellaneous Proceeds until Lender has had an opportunity to inspect such Property to ensure the work has been completed to Lender's satisfaction, provided that such inspection shall be undertaken promptly. Lender may pay for the repairs and restoration in a single disbursement or in a series of progress payments as the work is completed. Unless an agreement is made in writing or Applicable Law requires interest to be paid on such Miscellaneous Proceeds, Lender shall not be required to pay Borrower any interest or earnings on such Miscellaneous Proceeds. If the restoration or repair is not economically feasible or Lender's security would be lessened, the Miscellaneous Proceeds shall be applied to the sums secured by this Security Instrument, whether or not then due, with the excess, if any, paid to Borrower. Such Miscellaneous Proceeds shall be applied in the order provided for in Section 2.

In the event of a total taking, destruction, or loss in value of the Property, the Miscellaneous Proceeds shall be applied to the sums secured by this Security Instrument, whether or not then due, with the excess, if any, paid to Borrower. In the event of a partial taking, destruction, or loss in value of the Property in which the fair market value of the Property immediately before the partial taking, destruction, or loss in value is equal to or greater than the amount of the sums secured by this Security Instrument immediately before the partial taking, destruction, or loss in value, unless Borrower and Lender otherwise agree in writing, the sums secured by this Security Instrument shall be reduced by the amount of the Miscellaneous Proceeds multiplied by the following fraction: (a) the total amount of the sums secured immediately before the partial taking, destruction, or loss in value divided by (b) the fair market value of the Property immediately before the partial taking, destruction, or loss in value. Any balance shall be paid to Borrower. In the event of a partial taking, destruction, or loss in value of the Property in which the fair market value of the Property immediately before the partial taking, destruction, or loss in value is less than the amount of the sums secured immediately before the partial taking, destruction, or loss in value, unless Borrower and Lender otherwise agree in writing, the Miscellaneous Proceeds shall be applied to the sums secured by this Security Instrument whether or not the sums are then due.

If the Property is abandoned by Borrower, or if, after notice by Lender to Borrower that the Opposing Party (as defined in the next sentence) offers to make an award to settle a claim for damages, Borrower fails to respond to Lender within 30 days after the date the notice is given, Lender is authorized to collect and apply the Miscellaneous Proceeds either to restoration or repair of the Property or to the sums secured by this Security Instrument, whether or not then due. "Opposing Party" means the third party that owes Borrower Miscellaneous Proceeds or the party against whom Borrower has a right of action in regard to Miscellaneous Proceeds.

Borrower shall be in default if any action or proceeding, whether civil or criminal, is begun that, in Lender's judgment, could result in forfeiture of the Property or other material impairment of Lender's interest in the Property or rights under this Security Instrument. Borrower can cure such a default and, if acceleration has occurred, reinstate as provided in Section 19, by causing the action or proceeding to be dismissed with a ruling that, in Lender's judgment, precludes forfeiture of the Property or other material impairment of Lender's interest in the Property or rights under this Security Instrument. The proceeds of any award or claim for damages that are attributable to the impairment of Lender's interest in the Property are hereby assigned and shall be paid to Lender.

All Miscellaneous Proceeds that are not applied to restoration or repair of the Property shall be applied in the order provided for in Section 2.

12. Borrower Not Released; Forbearance By Lender Not a Waiver. Extension of the time for payment or modification of amortization of the sums secured by this Security Instrument granted by Lender to Borrower or any Successor in Interest of Borrower shall not operate to release the liability of Borrower or any Successors in Interest of Borrower. Lender shall not be required to commence proceedings against any Successor in Interest of Borrower or to refuse to extend time for payment or otherwise modify amortization of the sums secured by this Security Instrument by reason of any demand made by the original Borrower or any Successors in Interest of Borrower. Any forbearance by Lender in exercising any right or remedy including, without limitation, Lender's acceptance of payments from third persons, entities or Successors in Interest of Borrower or in amounts less than the amount then due, shall not be a waiver of or preclude the exercise of any right or remedy.

13. Joint and Several Liability; Co-signers; Successors and Assigns Bound. Borrower covenants and agrees that Borrower's obligations and liability shall be joint and several. However, any Borrower who co-signs this Security Instrument but does not execute the Note (a "co-signer"): (a) is co-signing this Security Instrument only to mortgage, grant and convey the co-signer's interest in the Property under the terms of this Security Instrument; (b) is not personally obligated to pay the sums secured by this Security Instrument; and (c) agrees that Lender and any other Borrower can agree to extend, modify, forbear or make any accommodations with regard to the terms of this Security Instrument or the Note without the co-signer's consent.

Subject to the provisions of Section 18, any Successor in Interest of Borrower who assumes Borrower's obligations under this Security Instrument in writing, and is approved by Lender, shall obtain all of Borrower's rights and benefits under this Security Instrument. Borrower shall not be released from Borrower's obligations and liability under this Security Instrument unless Lender agrees to such release in writing. The covenants and agreements of this Security Instrument shall bind (except as provided in Section 20) and benefit the successors and assigns of Lender.

14. Loan Charges. Lender may charge Borrower fees for services performed in connection with Borrower's default, for the purpose of protecting Lender's interest in the Property and rights under this Security Instrument, including, but not limited to, attorneys' fees, property inspection and valuation fees. In regard to any other fees, the absence of express authority in this Security Instrument to charge a specific fee to Borrower shall not be construed as a prohibition on the charging of such fee. Lender may not charge fees that are expressly prohibited by this Security Instrument or by Applicable Law.

If the Loan is subject to a law which sets maximum loan charges, and that law is finally interpreted so that the interest or other loan charges collected or to be collected in connection with the Loan exceed the permitted limits, then: (a) any such loan charge shall be reduced by the amount necessary to reduce the charge to the permitted limit; and (b) any sums already collected from Borrower which exceeded permitted limits will be refunded to Borrower. Lender may choose to make this refund by reducing the principal owed under the Note or by making a direct payment to Borrower. If a refund reduces principal, the reduction will be treated as a partial prepayment without any prepayment charge (whether or not a prepayment charge is provided for under the Note). Borrower's acceptance of any such refund made by direct payment to Borrower will constitute a waiver of any right of action Borrower might have arising out of such overcharge.

15. Notices. All notices given by Borrower or Lender in connection with this Security Instrument must be in writing. Any notice to Borrower in connection with this Security Instrument shall be deemed to have been given to Borrower when mailed by first class mail or when actually delivered to Borrower's notice address if sent by other means. Notice to any one Borrower shall constitute notice to all Borrowers unless Applicable Law expressly requires otherwise. The notice address shall be the Property Address unless Borrower has designated a substitute notice address by notice to Lender. Borrower shall promptly notify Lender of Borrower's change of address. If Lender specifies a procedure for reporting Borrower's change of address, then Borrower shall only report a change of address through that specified procedure. There may be only one designated notice address under this Security Instrument at any one time. Any notice to Lender shall be given by delivering it or by mailing it by first class mail to Lender's address stated herein unless Lender has designated another address by notice to Borrower. Any notice in connection with this Security Instrument shall not be deemed to have been given to Lender until actually received by Lender. If any notice required by this Security Instrument is also required under Applicable Law, the Applicable Law requirement will satisfy the corresponding requirement under this Security Instrument.

16. Governing Law; Severability; Rules of Construction. This Security Instrument shall be governed by federal law and the law of the jurisdiction in which the Property is located. All rights and obligations contained in this Security Instrument are subject to any requirements and limitations of Applicable Law. Applicable Law might explicitly or implicitly allow the parties to agree by contract or it might be silent, but such silence shall not be construed as a prohibition against agreement by contract. In the event that any provision or clause of this Security Instrument or the Note conflicts with Applicable Law, such conflict shall not affect other provisions of this Security Instrument or the Note which can be given effect without the conflicting provision.

As used in this Security Instrument: (a) words of the masculine gender shall mean and include corresponding neuter words or words of the feminine gender; (b) words in the singular shall mean and include the plural and vice versa; and (c) the word "may" gives sole discretion without any obligation to take any action.

17. Borrower's Copy. Borrower shall be given one copy of the Note and of this Security Instrument.

18. Transfer of the Property or a Beneficial Interest in Borrower. As used in this Section 18, "Interest in the Property" means any legal or beneficial interest in the Property, including, but not limited to, those beneficial interests transferred in a bond for deed, contract for deed, installment sales contract or escrow agreement, the intent of which is the transfer of title by Borrower at a future date to a purchaser.

If all or any part of the Property or any Interest in the Property is sold or transferred (or if Borrower is not a natural person and a beneficial interest in Borrower is sold or transferred) without Lender's prior written consent, Lender may require immediate payment in full of all sums secured by this Security Instrument. However, this option shall not be exercised by Lender if such exercise is prohibited by Applicable Law.

If Lender exercises this option, Lender shall give Borrower notice of acceleration. The notice shall provide a period of not less than 30 days from the date the notice is given in accordance with Section 15 within which Borrower must pay all sums secured by this Security Instrument. If Borrower fails to pay these sums prior to the expiration of this period, Lender may invoke any remedies permitted by this Security Instrument without further notice or demand on Borrower.

19. Borrower's Right to Reinstate After Acceleration. If Borrower meets certain conditions, Borrower shall have the right to have enforcement of this Security Instrument discontinued at any time prior to the earliest of: (a) five days before sale of the Property pursuant to any power of sale contained in this Security Instrument; (b) such other period as Applicable Law might specify for the termination of Borrower's right to reinstate; or (c) entry of a judgment enforcing this Security Instrument. Those conditions are that Borrower: (a) pays Lender all sums which then would be due under this Security Instrument and the Note as if no acceleration had occurred; (b) cures any default of any other covenants or agreements; (c) pays all expenses incurred in enforcing this Security Instrument, including, but not limited to, reasonable attorneys' fees, property inspection and valuation fees, and other fees incurred for the purpose of protecting Lender's interest in the Property and rights under this Security Instrument; and (d) takes such action as Lender may reasonably require to assure that Lender's interest in the Property and rights under this Security Instrument, and Borrower's obligation to pay the sums secured by this Security Instrument, shall continue unchanged. Lender may require that Borrower pay such reinstatement sums and expenses in one or more of the following forms, as selected by Lender: (a) cash; (b) money order; (c) certified check, bank check, treasurer's check or cashier's check, provided any such check is drawn upon an institution whose deposits are insured by a federal agency, instrumentality or entity; or (d) Electronic Funds Transfer. Upon reinstatement by Borrower, this Security Instrument and obligations secured hereby shall remain fully effective as if no acceleration had occurred. However, this right to reinstate shall not apply in the case of acceleration under Section 18.

20. Sale of Note; Change of Loan Servicer; Notice of Grievance. The Note or a partial interest in the Note (together with this

Security Instrument) can be sold one or more times without prior notice to Borrower. A sale might result in a change in the entity (known as the "Loan Servicer") that collects Periodic Payments due under the Note and this Security Instrument and performs other mortgage loan servicing obligations under the Note, this Security Instrument, and Applicable Law. There also might be one or more changes of the Loan Servicer unrelated to a sale of the Note. If there is a change of the Loan Servicer, Borrower will be given written notice of the change which will state the name and address of the new Loan Servicer, the address to which payments should be made and any other information RESPA requires in connection with a notice of transfer of servicing. If the Note is sold and thereafter the Loan is serviced by a Loan Servicer other than the purchaser of the Note, the mortgage loan servicing obligations to Borrower will remain with the Loan Servicer or be transferred to a successor Loan Servicer and are not assumed by the Note purchaser unless otherwise provided by the Note purchaser.

Neither Borrower nor Lender may commence, join, or be joined to any judicial action (as either an individual litigant or the member of a class) that arises from the other party's actions pursuant to this Security Instrument or that alleges that the other party has breached any provision of, or any duty owed by reason of, this Security Instrument, until such Borrower or Lender has notified the other party (with such notice given in compliance with the requirements of Section 15) of such alleged breach and afforded the other party hereto a reasonable period after the giving of such notice to take corrective action. If Applicable Law provides a time period which must elapse before certain action can be taken, that time period will be deemed to be reasonable for purposes of this paragraph. The notice of acceleration and opportunity to cure given to Borrower pursuant to Section 22 and the notice of acceleration given to Borrower pursuant to Section 18 shall be deemed to satisfy the notice and opportunity to take corrective action provisions of this Section 20.

21. Hazardous Substances. As used in this Section 21: (a) "Hazardous Substances" are those substances defined as toxic or hazardous substances, pollutants, or wastes by Environmental Law and the following substances: gasoline, kerosene, other flammable or toxic petroleum products, toxic pesticides and herbicides, volatile solvents, materials containing asbestos or formaldehyde, and radioactive materials; (b) "Environmental Law" means federal laws and laws of the jurisdiction where the Property is located that relate to health, safety or environmental protection; (c) "Environmental Cleanup" includes any response action, remedial action, or removal action, as defined in Environmental Law; and (d) an "Environmental Condition" means a condition that can cause, contribute to, or otherwise trigger an Environmental Cleanup.

Borrower shall not cause or permit the presence, use, disposal, storage, or release of any Hazardous Substances, or threaten to release any Hazardous Substances, on or in the Property. Borrower shall not do, nor allow anyone else to do, anything affecting the Property (a) that is in violation of any Environmental Law, (b) which creates an Environmental Condition, or (c) which, due to the presence, use, or release of a Hazardous Substance, creates a condition that adversely affects the value of the Property. The preceding two sentences shall not apply to the presence, use, or storage on the Property of small quantities of Hazardous Substances that are generally recognized to be appropriate to normal residential uses and to maintenance of the Property (including, but not limited to, hazardous substances in consumer products).

Borrower shall promptly give Lender written notice of (a) any investigation, claim, demand, lawsuit or other action by any governmental or regulatory agency or private party involving the Property and any Hazardous Substance or Environmental Law of which Borrower has actual knowledge, (b) any Environmental Condition, including but not limited to, any spilling, leaking, discharge, release or threat of release of any Hazardous Substance, and (c) any condition caused by the presence, use or release of a Hazardous Substance which adversely affects the value of the Property. If Borrower learns, or is notified by any governmental or regulatory authority, or any private party, that any removal or other remediation of any Hazardous Substance affecting the Property is necessary, Borrower shall promptly take all necessary remedial actions in accordance with Environmental Law. Nothing herein shall create any obligation on Lender for an Environmental Cleanup.

NON–UNIFORM COVENANTS. Borrower and Lender further covenant and agree as follows:

22. Acceleration; Remedies. Lender shall give notice to Borrower prior to acceleration following Borrower's breach of any covenant or agreement in this Security Instrument (but not prior to acceleration under Section 18 unless Applicable Law provides otherwise). The notice shall specify: (a) the default; (b) the action required to cure the default; (c) a date, not less than 30 days from the date the notice is given to Borrower, by which the default must be cured, and (d) that failure to cure the default on or before the date specified in the notice may result in acceleration of the sums secured by this Security Instrument and sale of the Property. The notice shall further inform Borrower of the right to reinstate after acceleration and the right to bring a court action to assert the non-existence of a default or any other defense of Borrower to acceleration and sale. If the default is not cured on or before the date specified in the notice, Lender at its option may require immediate payment in full of all sums secured by this Security Instrument without further demand and may invoke the power of sale and any other remedies permitted by Applicable Law. Lender shall be entitled to collect all expenses incurred in pursuing the remedies provided in this Section 22, including, but not limited to, reasonable attorneys' fees and costs of title evidence.

If Lender invokes the power of sale, Lender or Trustee shall mail copies of a notice of sale in the manner prescribed by Applicable Law to Borrower and to the other persons prescribed by Applicable Law. Trustee shall give notice of sale by public advertisement for the time and in the manner prescribed by Applicable Law. Trustee, without demand on Borrower, shall sell the Property at public auction to the highest bidder for cash at the time and place and under the terms designated in the notice of sale in one or more parcels and in any order Trustee determines. Trustee may postpone sale of all or any parcel of the Property to any later time on the same date by public announcement at the time and place of any previously scheduled sale. Lender or its designee may purchase the Property at any sale.

Trustee shall deliver to the purchaser Trustee's deed conveying the Property without any covenant or warranty expressed or implied. The recitals in the Trustee's deed shall be prima facie evidence of the truth of the statements made therein. Trustee shall apply the proceeds of the sale in the following order: (a) to all expenses of the sale, including, but not limited to, reasonable Trustee's and attorneys' fees; (b) to all sums secured by this Security Instrument; and (c) any excess to the person or persons legally entitled to it.

23. Release. Upon payment of all sums secured by this Security Instrument, Lender shall release this Security Instrument. Borrower shall pay any recordation costs. Lender may charge Borrower a fee for releasing this Security Instrument, but only if the fee is paid to a third party for services rendered and the charging of the fee is permitted under Applicable Law.

24. Substitute Trustee. Lender, at its option, may from time to time remove Trustee and appoint a successor trustee to any Trustee appointed hereunder by an instrument recorded in the county in which this Security Instrument is recorded. Without conveyance of the Property, the successor trustee shall succeed to all the title, power and duties conferred upon Trustee herein and by Applicable Law.

25. Lease of the Property. Trustee hereby leases the Property to Borrower until this Security Instrument is either satisfied and released or until there is a default under the provisions of this Security Instrument. The Property is leased upon the following terms and conditions: Borrower, and every person claiming an interest in or possessing the Property or any part thereof, shall pay rent during the term of the lease in the amount of one cent per month, payable on demand, and without notice or demand shall and will surrender peaceable possession of the Property to Trustee upon default or to the purchaser of the Property at the foreclosure sale.

26. Homestead Exemption. Borrower hereby waives all homestead exemptions in the Property to which Borrowers would otherwise be entitled under Applicable Law.

27. Notice. Oral agreements or commitments to loan money, extend credit or to forebear from enforcing repayment of debt including promises to extend or renew such debt are not enforceable. To protect you (Borrower(s)) and us (Creditor) from misunderstanding or disappointment, any agreements we reach covering such matters are contained in this writing, which is the complete and exclusive statement of the agreement between us, except as we may later agree in writing to modify it.

BY SIGNING BELOW, Borrower accepts and agrees to the terms and covenants contained in this Security Instrument and in any Rider executed by Borrower and recorded with it.

_____   _____ (Seal)
                                                              -Borrower

_____   _____ (Seal)
                                                              -Borrower

_____**[Space Below This Line For Acknowledgment]**_____

STATE OF MISSOURI,   County ss:

On this   day of   , before me personally appeared

To me known to be the person(s) described in and who executed the foregoing instrument, and acknowledged that he/she/they executed the same as his/her/their free act and deed.

IN TESTIMONY WHEREOF, I have hereunto set my hand and affixed my official seal in the and State aforesaid, the day and year first above written.

My Term Expires:

_____
                          Notary Public

PREPARED BY:

U.S. BANK N.A.

9321 OLIVE BOULEVARD

ST. LOUIS, MO 63132

Notes and Questions

1. Examine the deed of trust carefully. It is intended to accomplish two objectives. The first is to give the lender an interest in the borrower's real property to secure the repayment of the indebtedness evidenced by the borrower's promissory note. The second objective is to preserve the status quo. Specifically, it is important to the lender that the secured property not deteriorate in value before the loan is repaid, or foreclosure occurs in the event of default. Can you identify which provisions of the deed of trust accomplish each of these two objectives?

2. How would you describe the state of the title to property secured by the sample deed of trust? Who holds legal title? Equitable title? Are there encumbrances? If so, in favor of whom?

3. Suppose more than one person owns an interest in the property, such as a lessor and lessee, or concurrent owners? Can both persons pledge

their property interest as security for a loan that one is obtaining without also becoming liable on the loan? See paragraph 13.

4. What happens to the proceeds of insurance in the event of fire or other insured casualty? To the proceeds of condemnation? Why are these treated differently?

5. Can a borrower safely transfer her interest in secured property without obtaining permission from the lender, for example, by selling the property to someone who will assume the loan? See paragraph 18. How do these paragraphs compare with regulations of assignment and subleasing by tenants?

Paragraph 18 is an example of a due-on-sale clause that enables the lender to declare the entire balance of the mortgage loan immediately due and payable if the secured premises are sold without its consent. The real significance of the clause lies in its ability to maintain the lending institution's long-term investment portfolio at the current market interest rates. This is accomplished by accelerating the maturity of older, below-market rate loans upon disposition of the property by the borrower. The lender thus uses the due-on-sale clause as a yield-maintenance device. Do you understand why an adjustable rate mortgage would not need to contain a due-on-sale clause?

During a period of sharply rising interest rates in the 1970's, borrowers challenged the enforceability of the due-on-sale clause as an impermissible indirect restraint on alienation. The issue ultimately reached the Supreme Court in Fidelity Fed. Sav. & Loan Assoc. v. de la Cuesta, 458 U.S. 141, 102 S.Ct. 3014, 73 L.Ed.2d 664 (1982). The outcome not surprisingly was in favor of the lenders' position. Faced with an indirect restraint on alienation, courts assess reasonableness by measuring the quantum of restraint against the lender's justification for imposing the restraint. The owner of encumbered property remains free to convey the property. The owner, however, is not free to "sell" the existing financing to a third party. Doing so would provide automatic financing for the buyer in a tight money market in disregard of lender's wishes. Thus, due-on-sale clauses only affect the price that sellers receive on the sale of mortgaged property by placing them in the same position as sellers of unencumbered property.

Many people took advantage of the historic low interest rates in recent years to refinance loans and finance the purchase of new homes. If interest rates rise sharply again, there will be renewed interest in the due-on-sale clause.

Might a seller and buyer agree that it is in their mutual interest to seek to conceal the transfer from the lender by not recording the deed, and by having the seller continue to make monthly payments with funds provided by the buyer? What are the potential consequences to the buyer of failing to record the deed? Does your answer depend upon the type of recording statute in the jurisdiction?

As a matter of professional responsibility, can a lawyer assist the parties in the closing of a real estate transfer without recording the deed in order to conceal the fact of the transfer from seller's lender? Do the activities of the parties to the transaction necessarily involve more than mere non-disclosure? Might these activities, specifically designed to prevent the lender from acquiring material information, constitute active concealment and actionable fraud?

According to an opinion by the Oregon State Bar,

"A lawyer may represent the seller of property in a real estate transaction when the real estate in question is encumbered and the seller and buyer both agree to effectuate the sale without notifying the mortgage company which holds the encumbrance. The transaction, although legally precarious, is not fraudulent or illegal. It does constitute a breach of contract creating a potential detriment to the mortgagee. The lawyer, however, does not assist the client in an illegal or fraudulent transaction by his representation." Formal Opinion 464, ABA/BNA Lawyers Manual on Professional Conduct 801: 7107–08 (1984).

The foregoing opinion has been sharply criticized. See Roszkowski, Drafting Around Mortgage Due-on-Sale Clauses: The Danger of Playing Hide and Seek, 21 Real Property Probate and Trust Journal 23, 54–55 (1986). The transaction that gave rise to the opinion occurred at the height of the controversy over the enforceability of the due-on-sale clause. Since the resolution of this issue, it is more likely that an attorney's involvement in concealment of a real estate transfer could be considered "fraudulent" under the terms of Rule 1.2 of the Model Rules of Professional Conduct which provides that a lawyer shall not counsel a client to engage, or assist the client, in "conduct that the lawyer knows is criminal or fraudulent." See G. Nelson and D. Whitman, Real Estate Finance Law 356–361 (4th ed. 2001).

(a) The Mortgage Concept

PREBLE & CARTWRIGHT, CONVERTIBLE AND SHARED APPRECIATION LOANS: UNCLOGGING THE EQUITY OF REDEMPTION

20 Real Prop., Prob. & T.J. 821, 823–824 (1985).

I. Introduction

For nearly six centuries, lenders have used mortgages on real property to secure loans made to individual and commercial borrowers. The mortgage of the fourteenth century, however, is but a distant cousin of the various security devices used by commercial lenders today. For most of the period since the fourteenth century, the evolutionary process has been a gradual one. The past ten years, however, have witnessed dramatic changes in real estate secured lending. Inflation, high real and nominal interest rates, the deregulation of financial institutions, the growth of pension funds, the changing role of life insurance companies, the impact of new tax laws and the development of computer programs for sophisticated financial forecasting have all combined to radically change the capital markets and the structure of real estate financing.

* * *

II. THE ENGLISH AUTHORITIES

A. *Evolution of the Mortgage*

The original mortgage form was the nominal equivalent of a fee simple subject to a condition subsequent. The borrower conveyed seisin and a deed to the lender, subject to a condition subsequent which would revest seisin in the borrower upon repayment of the debt. Payment had to be made on what came to be known as "law day." The right of repayment, which effectively defeated the lender's title, appeared as the "defeasance" clause in the deed.

In accordance with the common law courts' strict view of property law, a default by the borrower on law day destroyed the contingency and vested full title in fee simple absolute in the lender. The old English common law courts never mixed concepts of property law and contract law. Thus, no matter how much of the debt had been repaid, if the borrower failed to extinguish the obligation in full on law day, he lost the entire property.

* * * Under the Chancellor's parallel court system, "equity" responded to the harsh results perpetrated by common law decisions. As a result, in the seventeenth century, the chancery courts began a sustained attack upon the forfeiture imposed by the common law courts. Two significant legal rights were born: (i) the borrower was permitted to petition the King to set aside the deed; and (ii) if the debt was repaid, albeit not in strict compliance with the terms of the mortgage, the chancery courts would order reconveyance of the deed. It was the right of appeal to equity which spawned the equity of redemption.

Although the original purpose of the Chancellor's intervention was to protect the borrower against forfeiture and fraud, the remedy created by the equity courts, the borrower's equity of redemption, clouded every lender's title with the possibility that a defaulting borrower might eventually seek equitable relief. How long would the borrower have to redeem? When would the lender's title be immune from attack? A response and counterattack by the lender was inevitable. Thus, the lender was given the right to petition the chancery court to foreclose the equity of redemption. The court usually responded by setting a date at which the borrower's equity would be cut off if the default continued. Nevertheless, judicial relief was an uncertain, time-consuming and expensive process. In order to avoid the cumbersome appeals to equity and the uncertainty of property rights in the interim, lenders began a long process of changing the form and purpose of the mortgage deed. Not all of the steps in this evolutionary process met the standards of equity as viewed by the Chancellor.

Indeed, the initial step—a waiver of the equity of redemption executed by the borrower—was ultimately rejected by courts of equity. To protect the substantive equitable redemption right of the borrower, the equity courts countered the waiver and other unconscionable attempts to circumvent equitable jurisdiction with the doctrine against "clogging" the equity of redemption. In essence, the clogging doctrine restricted the lender to only one method of cutting off the borrower's equity of redemption—foreclosure. * * *

As the following case indicates, the concept of a mortgage has changed considerably since the days when it had the characteristics of a fee simple defeasible.

HARMS v. SPRAGUE

Supreme Court of Illinois, 1984.
105 Ill.2d 215, 85 Ill.Dec. 331, 473 N.E.2d 930.

THOMAS J. MORAN, JUSTICE.

Plaintiff, William H. Harms, filed a complaint to quiet title and for declaratory judgment in the circuit court of Greene County. Plaintiff had taken title to certain real estate with his brother John R. Harms, as a joint tenant, with full right of survivorship. The plaintiff named, as a defendant, Charles D. Sprague, the executor of the estate of John Harms and the devisee of all the real and personal property of John Harms. Also named as defendants were Carl T. and Mary E. Simmons, alleged mortgagees of the property in question. Defendant Sprague filed a counterclaim against plaintiff, challenging plaintiff's claim of ownership of the entire tract of property and asking the court to recognize his (Sprague's) interest as a tenant in common, subject to a mortgage lien. At issue was the effect the granting of a mortgage by John Harms had on the joint tenancy. Also at issue was whether the mortgage survived the death of John Harms as a lien against the property.

The trial court held that the mortgage given by John Harms to defendants Carl and Mary Simmons severed the joint tenancy. Further, the court found that the mortgage survived the death of John Harms as a lien against the undivided one-half interest in the property which passed to Sprague by and through the will of the deceased. The appellate court reversed, finding that the mortgage given by one joint tenant of his interest in the property does not sever the joint tenancy. Accordingly, the appellate court held that plaintiff, as the surviving joint tenant, owned the property in its entirety, unencumbered by the mortgage lien. * * *

Two issues are raised on appeal: (1) Is a joint tenancy severed when less than all of the joint tenants mortgage their interest in the property? and (2) Does such a mortgage survive the death of the mortgagor as a lien on the property?

A review of the stipulation of facts reveals the following. Plaintiff, William Harms, and his brother John Harms, took title to real estate located in Roodhouse, on June 26, 1973, as joint tenants. The warranty deed memorializing this transaction was recorded on June 29, 1973, in the office of the Greene County recorder of deeds.

Carl and Mary Simmons owned a lot and home in Roodhouse. Charles Sprague entered into an agreement with the Simmons whereby Sprague was to purchase their property for $25,000. Sprague tendered $18,000 in cash and signed a promissory note for the balance of $7,000. Because Sprague had no security for the $7,000, he asked his friend, John Harms, to co-sign the note and give a mortgage on his interest in the joint tenancy property. Harms agreed, and on June 12, 1981, John Harms and Charles Sprague, jointly and severally, executed a promissory note for $7,000 payable to Carl and Mary Simmons. The note states that the principal sum of $7,000 was to be paid from the proceeds of the sale of John Harms' interest in the joint tenancy property, but in any event no later than six months from the date the note was signed. The note reflects that five monthly interest payments had been made, with the last payment recorded November 6, 1981. In addition, John Harms executed a mortgage, in favor of the Simmonses, on his undivided one-half interest in the joint tenancy property, to secure payment of the note. William Harms was unaware of the mortgage given by his brother.

John Harms moved from his joint tenancy property to the Simmons property which had been purchased by Charles Sprague. On December 10, 1981, John Harms died. By the terms of John Harms' will, Charles Sprague was the devisee of his entire estate. The mortgage given by John Harms to the Simmonses was recorded on December 29, 1981.

Prior to the appellate court decision in the instant case no court of this State had directly addressed the principal question we are confronted with herein—the effect of a mortgage, executed by less than all of the joint tenants, on the joint tenancy. * * *

Clearly, this court adheres to the rule that a lien on a joint tenant's interest in property will not effectuate a severance of the joint tenancy, absent the conveyance by a deed following the expiration of a redemption period. [ ] It follows, therefore, that if Illinois perceives a mortgage as merely a lien on the mortgagor's interest in property rather than a conveyance of title from mortgagor to mortgagee, the execution of a mortgage by a joint tenant, on his interest in the property, would not destroy the unity of title and sever the joint tenancy.

Early cases in Illinois, however, followed the title theory of mortgages. In 1900, this court recognized the common law precept that a mortgage was a conveyance of a legal estate vesting title to the property in the mortgagee. [ ] Consistent with this title theory of mortgages, therefore, there are many cases which state, in *dicta*, that a joint tenancy is severed by one of the joint tenants mortgaging his interest to a stranger. [ ] Yet even the early case of *Lightcap v. Bradley,* cited above, recognized that the title held by the mortgagee was for the limited purpose of protecting his interests. The court went on to say that "the mortgagor is the owner for every other purpose and against every other person. The title of the mortgagee is anomalous, and exists only between him and the mortgagor * * *.'' *Lightcap v. Bradley* (1900), 186 Ill. 510, 522–23, 58 N.E. 221.

Because our cases had early recognized the unique and narrow character of the title that passed to a mortgagee under the common law title theory, it was not a drastic departure when this court expressly characterized the execution of a mortgage as a mere lien in *Kling v. Ghilarducci* (1954), 3 Ill.2d 454, 121 N.E.2d 752. In *Kling,* the court was confronted with the question of when a separation of title, necessary to create an easement by implication, had occurred. The court found that title to the property was not separated with the execution of a trust deed but rather only upon execution and delivery of a master's deed. The court stated:

> "In some jurisdictions the execution of a mortgage is a severance, in others, the execution of a mortgage is not a severance. In Illinois the giving of a mortgage is not a separation of title, for the holder of the mortgage takes only a lien thereunder. After foreclosure of a mortgage and until delivery of the master's deed under the foreclosure sale, purchaser acquires no title to the land either legal or equitable. Title to land sold under mortgage foreclosure remains in the mortgagor or his grantee until the expiration of the redemption period and conveyance by the master's deed." 3 Ill.2d 454, 460, 121 N.E.2d 752. * * *

[The Court also held that a joint tenancy is not severed by the execution of a mortgage by one joint tenant and that such a mortgage executed by one joint tenant does not survive the death of that joint tenant because the property right to which the mortgage lien originally attaches is extinguished automatically by the death of the mortgaging tenant—Eds.]

Judgment affirmed.

Notes and Questions

1.   As a result of *Harms,* what should a lender do to protect itself if the borrower is a joint tenant of the property securing the loan? Does paragraph 13 of the sample deed of trust resolve the problem? Under *Harms,* is the surviving joint tenant a "successor" or "assign"? Should the lender insist that both joint tenants sign the security instrument?

2.   As the court in *Harms* noted, the early view was that mortgagees held defeasible title to the mortgaged property, giving rise to the "title" theory of mortgages. Today, the majority of states follow the "lien" theory espoused in *Harms.* A third group of states follows an "intermediate" theory under which the mortgagee has a title, but no possessory right until after default and may only exercise the rights of a lienholder through foreclosure and sale of the property. See generally, G. Nelson and D. Whitman, Real Estate Finance Law 10–11 (4th ed. 2001).

3.   What theory of mortgages is adopted by the Restatement Third, Property (Mortgages)? Section 4.1 provides:

(a) A mortgage creates only a security interest in real estate and confers no right to possession of that real estate or the mortgages.

(b) The Purchase Money Mortgage

Mortgages are used to secure a variety of loans, but one of the most common is the loan to enable someone to purchase land. A mortgage given to secure a loan to buy the property that is pledged as security for repayment of the loan is called a purchase money mortgage. It may be given either to a seller who is willing to accept a note and mortgage in lieu of cash ("seller financing") or it may be given to a third party who advances the money for the purchase. In either event, the purchase money mortgage is given a special priority.

The theoretical basis for the special priority extended to purchase money mortgages was the common law belief that seisin did not leave the hands of the seller who accepted a purchase money note and mortgage in lieu of cash, but passed through the hands of the purchaser and came back immediately to the seller, albeit in altered form as a defeasible fee rather than an absolute fee. Since title had never left the seller, there was no time for a lien arising out of other actions of the purchaser to attach to the land *ahead* of the seller's lien. See generally G. Nelson & D. Whitman, Real Estate Finance Law 781–788 (4th ed. 2001).

Is the special priority policy justified today, especially in lien or intermediate theory states? A creditor that has reduced a claim to judgment and obtained a lien against a purchaser's property prior to a purchase money mortgage land transaction clearly has priority in time against the seller's purchase money mortgage lien. Is the commonly accepted policy that creditor's rights follow debtor's rights sufficient basis for favoring the seller over the innocent and prior judgment creditor? Suppose the purchaser-mortgagor agreed with the prior creditor that the creditor's lien would attach to after-acquired property. Would that change the equation in favor of the prior creditor? Of the two innocent parties, the prior judgment creditor and the purchase money mortgage seller, who is better able to guard against the risk of loss from default? Should that be the basis for a decision regarding priority of lien claims? See G. Nelson & D. Whitman, Real Estate Finance Law 783 (4th ed. 2001); Restatement Third, Property (Mortgages) § 7.2 and illustrations following.

(c) Mortgage Alternatives

DUVALL v. LAWS, SWAIN & MURDOCH, P.A.

Court of Appeals of Arkansas, 1990.
32 Ark.App. 99, 797 S.W.2d 474.

JENNINGS, JUDGE.

In 1982, appellant Fred Duvall was charged with theft in connection with the buying and selling of oil and gas leases. He asked Ike Allen

Laws, Jr., the appellee, a Russellville lawyer, to represent him. The two had known each other since grade school.

Laws quoted Duvall a fee of $5,000.00. Duvall paid $2,498.00 but then he was unable to raise the balance. He and Laws entered into an agreement, which later became the subject matter of this lawsuit. Duvall and his wife executed a deed which purported to convey outright the mineral rights to 160 acres of land in Pope County. The deed was dated September 27, 1982 and recited a consideration of $5,000.00. Revenue stamps were purchased reflecting that amount. Also on September 27 Laws sent Duvall the following letter:

> This will acknowledge that you have on this date transferred to our firm certain minerals by mineral deed, representing our attorney's fee of Five Thousand Dollars ($5,000.00) to defend Fred E. Duvall in the State of Arkansas v. Fred E. Duvall.

> This letter will serve as evidence of our agreement that you may repurchase these minerals at any time within one (1) year from the date of this letter upon payment in full of my said fee.

It is undisputed that the letter was received by Duvall. On October 5, 1982, the law firm sent Duvall an invoice showing a balance of $2,502.00. This was the last bill sent to Duvall.

During the summer of 1983, Duvall located a prospective purchaser for the mineral rights who was apparently willing to pay more than $30,000.00 for them. The transaction did not go through due to title problems. At trial, the testimony was conflicting as to whether Laws cooperated in the attempt to sell the mineral rights to the third party.

In 1987 Laws leased the mineral rights for $12,740.00. On June 28, 1988, Duvall sued Laws, alleging that their 1982 transaction ought to be construed as an equitable mortgage. The chancellor held that the transaction was a deed with an option to purchase and not an equitable mortgage. He nevertheless awarded Duvall judgment for $2,498.00. Duvall appeals the first holding; Laws cross appeals the second. We affirm on direct appeal and reverse on cross appeal.

On direct appeal, Duvall argues that the chancellor applied the wrong burden of proof and that his refusal to hold that the transaction was an equitable mortgage was clearly erroneous. The case is governed by two distinct sets of rules. In equity, a grantor may show that a deed, absolute on its face, was intended only to be security for the payment of a debt and thus was in actuality a mortgage. [ ] The burden of proving that the transaction was truly a mortgage rests upon the grantor because there is a presumption that the instrument is what it purports to be. [ ] The burden may be met only by clear and convincing evidence. [ ] When a vendor, at the time of a sale, is indebted to a purchaser, and continues to be indebted after the sale, with the right to call for a reconveyance upon payment of the debt, a deed absolute on its face will be considered in a court of equity as a mortgage. [ ] On the other hand the parties may enter into a contract for the purchase and sale of land, with a reservation to the vendor of a right to repurchase the property at a fixed price and at a specific time. If such a transaction is security for a debt, then it is a mortgage—otherwise it is a sale. [ ] The line of demarcation between the two has been said to be "shadowy." [ ] The question whether a deed to realty, absolute on its face, when construed together with a separate agreement or option to repurchase by the grantor amounts to a mortgage or is a conditional sale, depends on the intention of the parties in the light of all attendant circumstances. * * *

While it is true that during his testimony, Laws said that Duvall never made any attempt to "pay the balance of the fee," there was also evidence from which the chancellor could have found that Duvall's failure to pay "the balance" for more than six years indicates his awareness that the transaction was an absolute conveyance. * * * [O]ne test which may be helpful in determining whether a transaction is a mortgage or a conditional sale is to decide whether the grantee has the right to compel the grantor to pay the consideration named in the stipulation for reconveyance. In the case at bar it seems clear that Laws would not have been successful in a suit to compel the payment of "the balance" of his fee. In any event we cannot say that the chancellor's determination that the transaction was not intended as a mortgage is clearly erroneous.

In contending that the chancellor applied the "wrong burden of proof," Duvall relies upon the principle that an attorney who enters into a business transaction with a client has the burden of proving the fairness and equity of that transaction and the adequacy of the consideration therefor. [ ] We agree that the principle is applicable to the case at bar. Once the chancellor found that the grantor had not met his burden of proving by clear and convincing evidence that the transaction was intended as a mortgage, the burden was then upon Laws to establish that he dealt fairly and justly with Fred Duvall. [ ] In contending that the trial court applied the wrong burden, appellant relies on two remarks made by the chancellor.

> One of the problems in deciding this case that bothers me is the fact that the defendant is an attorney; [I] want to be very careful that he's not treated improperly one way or the other just because he's a lawyer.

> * * *

> If I ruled otherwise it would be simply because Mr. Laws is an attorney whom I have never met or seen before as far as I know ever in my life or had any correspondence with him. And I don't think that's right either.

When the two statements are viewed in the context of the court's other remarks, we are not persuaded that they indicate the chancellor was unaware of the burden imposed on Laws * * *. It is not an incorrect statement of the law to say that a decision should not be made *solely* on the basis that one of the parties is a lawyer. * * * In the case at bar there was evidence from which the trial court could find that mineral rights conveyed from Duvall to Laws were essentially without market value at the time of the conveyance. It was therefore not improper for the chancellor to find, as he clearly did, that the transaction was fair to appellant, viewed from the time of its making.

Finally, if the chancellor was correct in holding that the transaction was an absolute conveyance, we can find no justification for upholding his award of damages to the appellant and that award must be reversed.

Affirmed on direct appeal and reversed on cross appeal.

WRIGHT, ACTING CHIEF JUDGE, dissenting.

In September 1982, appellant and his wife, residents of Pope County, found themselves in a vulnerable position. Appellant was under criminal indictment in Conway County and needed an attorney to defend him. At trial he was acquitted. Appellant's wife had been seriously ill and the couple owed various debts, including a civil judgment in Conway County, hospital bills approximating $90,000.00 and other debts. Appellant was unemployed as he had been caring for his sick wife. Their assets were exhausted except for some mineral interests. Appellant's wife died after the commencement of this suit.

Appellant made an agreement with attorney Ike Laws, Jr. to defend him in the criminal case for a fee of $5,000.00. Appellant could raise only half of the fee at the time of employment. Appellant told Laws he had some mineral interests he wanted to sell and would pay the balance of the fee upon sale of the mineral interests. However, very shortly after half of the fee was paid, Laws called appellant on the phone and suggested appellant deed the mineral interests to him to assure payment of the balance of the agreed fee, and suggested further that appellant's judgment creditors could attach and execute upon the mineral interests and deprive appellant of all benefits in the mineral interests.

In keeping with Laws' recommendation, appellant and his wife on September 27, 1982, executed a deed prepared by Laws conveying to the appellee law firm the mineral rights in 160 acres of land in Pope County. On that date or shortly thereafter Laws sent appellant the letter set out in the majority opinion.

When the letter was written, Laws had already received $2,498.00 on the fee and was owed a balance of $2,502.00. However, the letter refers to the deed as "representing our attorney's fee of Five Thousand Dollars ($5,000.00)."

On October 5, 1982, some eight days after delivery of the deed to Laws, his office sent a statement to appellant reflecting a total fee of $5,000.00 in the criminal case, credits of $2,498.00 and a balance of $2,502.00 unpaid.

Laws gave testimony at the trial "so far as I'm concerned" the deed for the mineral interests was in settlement of the balance of the fee but that he gave appellant the right to have the minerals reconveyed upon payment of the balance within one year from date. However, during Laws' testimony with reference to a conversation he had with a Mr. Womack who was attempting in July 1983 to purchase for $30,000 the subject mineral interests, together with some 50 acres of additional mineral interests in which appellant and wife had an interest, he stated he told Mr. Womack his office had a deal with appellant and they wanted their name on the draft. In reference to his deposition, Laws admitted to the following at trial:

Q. "You stood to get your fee out of this?" And your answer was?

A. I stood to get what he still owed me on my fee.

The statement by appellee Laws was in direct conflict with his testimony at trial that the deed for the mineral interests was in settlement of the balance of the fee. The sale to Womack was never closed.

Appellant sought to employ attorney Ernie Witt to recover the mineral interests at least as early as July 1985. The evidence shows that attorney Cliff Hoofman had sent Laws a letter about appellant's claim for recovery of his mineral interests from Laws and Laws wrote Hoofman a letter in February 1988 in which he stated:

Dear Cliff: I thought you might be interested in a computer check I ran on judgments against Fred DuVall. With these judgments against him, it is my opinion that he would not be able to keep the minerals he claims, even if he could get them. I thought this may be of some interest to you in determining the manner that you took employment.

The letter was written after Laws had in December 1987 entered into two oil and gas leases for the mineral interests for an up front consideration of $12,700.00. Laws also wrote attorney Hoofman in February 1988 and in referring to appellant, stated: "he had not made any attempt to pay a single penny on our fee since his trial." The statement is in conflict with appellees' contention the mineral deed settled the fee.

Appellant gave the following unrebutted testimony:

A. I went to Ike's office and asked him if I borrowed the money, could I pay him in full and he issued a challenge to me if I could find an attorney to represent me.

Q. Was this following the * * * was this still within the one year period?

A. Yes, that was within the one year period.

Q. What did he say?

A. He said, "You just do whatever you think you're big enough to do."

Appellant testified that he had leased the mineral interests in years past for figures from $40.00 to $50.00 per acre and this was not rebutted.

Appellant testified he went to Laws' office promptly after he got the letter concerning his right to have the minerals reconveyed to him and complained that the letter did not show he would only be required to pay $2,500.00, the unpaid part of the fee, to have the minerals reconveyed, and also complained that the letter did not show the agreement was that the $2,500.00 would be paid when he sold the mineral interests. He said Laws' response was:

> He said it was necessary for him to word the letter like that. That that represented the full fee in case the judgment people came out * * * came after me and said that I overpaid him 110 acres of minerals for just $2,500.00.

The chancellor found that the deed from appellant and wife to the appellees for the mineral interests was not a security for the debt, but was an absolute conveyance.

In an effort to show the $2,502.00 balance of the fee was fair consideration for the mineral interests appellees' witness Dale Braden, a fellow attorney and member of the Russellville Bar, who worked with Arkansas Oil and Gas Co., testified he offered "nothing" for the subject mineral interests in 1982. Of course, this had no significance for establishing the value of the mineral interests. There was no evidence any offer from him was solicited in 1982, and whether he offered "nothing" has no evidentiary value as to the market value. This witness admitted he paid Laws $129.00 per acre for a five-year lease on 80 acres of the mineral interests in 1987.

There are two reasons for reversing. First, when an attorney contracts with his client and litigation arises over the transaction, the attorney has the burden of proving that no advantage has been taken of the client. Appellant alleged that appellees' actions constituted a gross ethical breach of the duties a lawyer owes his client in an ongoing lawyer-client relationship. The reason for the rule is that the relation of attorney and client is one of trust and confidence requiring high degree of fidelity and good faith. The burden is upon the attorney to prove the fairness and equity of the transaction and the adequacy of the consideration. [ ] It is apparent from the findings and rulings of the chancellor from the bench that he did not follow this rule. * * * When the evidence as a whole is carefully weighed, it is apparent appellees failed to meet the burden of proving the transaction with appellant was fair and equitable. Appellees completely failed to present evidence of the market value of the mineral interests as of September 1982, the date of the deed. There is substantial evidence the value of the mineral interests greatly exceeded the amount of the balance of the fee. The court failed to make a finding as to the fairness of the transaction * * *. There is a total absence of evidence of negotiation between the parties as to the relative value of the minerals with relation to the balance of fee owed, and the testimony of Laws at trial was at variance with his own documentary evidence. His testimony sought to impeach his own documents and prior admissions. * * *

Secondly, it is clear from the evidence appellee Laws continued to consider appellant still owed the unpaid balance on the agreed fee after the receipt of the mineral deed as evidenced by the bill sent to appellant, Laws' letter to attorney Hoofman, and some of Laws' testimony that appellant had not paid the balance of the fee owed. When the evidence is considered in its entirety it is clear the chancellor's finding the mineral deed to Laws was in effect a sale with no equitable security interest attached was clearly against the preponderance of the evidence. * * * The evidence is abundantly clear, not only from the testimony of appellant, but from evidence flowing from Laws that appellant continued to owe the balance of the fee after delivery of the mineral deed. The letter from Laws to appellant, coupled with the rest of the evidence, nails down the fact that the deed was security for the balance of the fee. It was after litigation was in the offing that Laws' posture about the nature of the transaction changed and in his testimony he sought to change the meaning of the bill for the balance of the fee sent after receipt of the deed and to impeach his prior statements about appellant still owing the balance of the fee. It is undisputed that appellant had the right to reconveyance on payment of the fee balance. The fact the letter purported to limit that right to one year is of no consequence here as the transaction constituted an equitable mortgage that required foreclosure. * * *

* * *

This case should be reversed and judgment entered in favor of appellant against appellees for $12,700.00 less $2,502.00 and interest thereon from September 27, 1983. The mineral deed to appellee should be canceled, but appellant's mineral interests should be decreed subject to the rights of the two innocent purchasers of mineral leases who leased from appellees.

MAYFIELD, J., joins in dissent.

Notes and Questions

1. Since the essence of a mortgage is the conveyance of an interest in land to secure performance of a promise to repay borrowed money, it should come as no surprise that a variety of other property techniques can be used to accomplish the same result. These techniques are designed by lender's counsel to obtain all of the principal benefits of being a secured creditor, but without exposing lender to the problems associated with holding an interest in the property of another. What might be some of the problems associated with being a real property secured creditor?

(a) We have already mentioned the deed of trust, in which the property is conveyed to a third party as trustee for the benefit of the lender but also the borrower.

(b) Another device is the installment land contract, or "contract for deed," in which the seller allows the purchaser to obtain possession while making periodic payments, and agrees to transfer title to the purchaser when the final installment of the purchase price is paid. In effect, the seller is financing the buyer's purchase of the land. Since title is not transferred at the time that possession is transferred, the relationship of purchaser and seller during the period before transfer of title resembles that of landlord and tenant. Thus, when a default occurs, the creditor-seller seeks to regain possession of the land by obtaining a judicial decree that the debtor-purchaser has forfeited her right to possession by defaulting on her obligations under the contract. Under the terms of the contract, the seller is also entitled to retain all of the installments paid by the buyer prior to default. Why might a court be unwilling to enforce the contract strictly in accordance with its terms?

(c) Still another technique is the long term ground lease, with or without an option to purchase at the end of the term. The ground lessee obtains long term control, which in many cases is the practical equivalent of a fee interest, and finances the acquisition of control through the periodic payments mechanism of the long term lease.

(d) The equitable mortgage, or deed absolute, illustrated by the principle case, is yet another device to accomplish the purpose of a mortgage. Courts will look through the form of a purported sale and construe the conveyance of a deed as the conveyance of a mortgage when they are persuaded that the parties really intended the transaction to serve as security for a deed.

For discussion of mortgage alternatives, see G. Nelson & D. Whitman, Real Estate Finance Law 34–128 (4th ed. 2001).

2. As noted by the *Duvall* court, whether a deed coupled with an agreement that the seller may repurchase the property should be construed as a sale with an option to repurchase or as a mortgage to secure repayment of a debt is a question of intent. What did the plaintiff in *Duvall* fail to prove? The presence of a debt? The desire to obtain repayment of that debt? The intent to use the mineral rights as security for the debt? Was the fact that the plaintiff apparently made no payments for six years persuasive? What about the fact that no bills were sent? What is the significance of construing the transaction in *Duvall* as a mortgage? Who would be entitled to the $12,000 proceeds from the mineral lease?

3. The dissent in *Duvall* was highly critical of the lawyer defendant's conduct in first entering into a property transaction with a client in a "vulnerable" position, and then being imprecise in the description of the transaction. Should attorneys be barred from business transactions of this sort with clients? If so, what should an attorney do in cases such as *Duvall* where a client cannot pay the full fee—waive the unpaid amount, accept an unsecured promise to pay, or refuse the case? Would a straight mortgage be acceptable? Cf. ABA Model Rules of Professional Conduct, Rule 1.8:

(a) A lawyer shall not enter into a business transaction with a client or knowingly acquire an ownership, possessory, security or other pecuniary interest adverse to a client unless:

(1) the transaction and terms on which the lawyer acquires the interest are fair and reasonable to the client and are fully disclosed and

transmitted in writing in a manner that can be reasonably understood by the client;

(2) the client is advised in writing of the desirability of seeking and is given a reasonable opportunity to seek the advice of independent legal counsel on the transaction; and

(3) the client gives informed consent, in a writing signed by the client, to the essential terms of the transaction and the lawyer's role in the transaction, including whether the lawyer is representing the client in the transaction.

(b) a lawyer shall not use information relating to representation of a client to the disadvantage of the client unless the client gives informed consent, except as permitted or required by these Rules.

* * *

(i) A lawyer shall not acquire a proprietary interest in the cause of action or subject matter of litigation the lawyer is conducting for a client, except that the lawyer may:

(1) acquire a lien authorized by law to secure the lawyer's fee or expenses; and

(2) contract with a client for a reasonable contingent fee in a civil case.

This incorporates 2002 revisions in the American Bar Association version of Rule 1.8. The 2002 revisions included extensive changes in the commentary to Rules 1.8(a), 1.8(b), and 1.8(i) as well as extensive changes in the rules governing gifts from clients to lawyers; settlements; representing relatives; and sexual relationships with clients, along with commentary to those changed rules. Finally, the revisions added an express attribution rule (Rule 1.8[k]): "While lawyers are associated in a firm, a prohibition in the foregoing paragraphs ... that applies to any one of them shall apply to all of them."

The 2002 revisions included, throughout the Rules, as in the quoted parts of Rule 1.8, specific provisions on obtaining informed consent from clients. New Rule 1.0(b) and (e):

"Informed consent" denotes the agreement by a person to a proposed course of conduct after the lawyer has communicated adequate information and explanation about the material risks of and reasonably available alternatives to the proposed course of conduct.

* * *

"Confirmed in writing," when used in reference to the informed consent of a person, denotes informed consent that is given in writing by the person or a writing that a lawyer promptly transmits to the person confirming an oral informed consent.

(d) Possessory Rights of Mortgagees

As the Preble & Cartwright excerpt notes, the common law lender had an absolute right to take possession of the property if the borrower failed to repay the loan in full on "law day." What happens to the right to possession under *Harms*? See Martinez v. Continental Enterprises, 730 P.2d 308 (Colo.1986) (mortgagee may not recover possession in the absence of foreclosure and sale).

A lender who does take possession of secured property faces a new set of risks, as illustrated by the following case.

UNITED STATES v. MARYLAND BANK AND TRUST COMPANY

United States District Court, D. Maryland, 1986.
632 F.Supp. 573.

NORTHROP, SENIOR DISTRICT JUDGE.

This case presents the novel question of whether a bank, which formerly held a mortgage on a parcel of land, later purchased the land at a foreclosure sale and continues to own it, must reimburse the United States for the cost of cleaning up hazardous wastes on the land, when those wastes were dumped prior to the bank's purchase of the property.

The United States instituted this action pursuant to section 107 of the Comprehensive Environmental Response, Compensation, and Liability Act of 1980 ("CERCLA"), 42 U.S.C. § 9607 (1983), to recover the expenses incurred by the United States Environmental Protection Agency ("EPA") for removal of hazardous wastes from the toxic dump site known as the McLeod property or the California Maryland Drum site, located near the town of California in St. Mary's County, Maryland. Named as defendant in this suit is the Maryland Bank & Trust Company ("MB & T"), the owner of the property since May, 1982, and before that, the mortgagee of the tract beginning in December, 1980.

Pending before the Court are defendant Maryland Bank & Trust Co.'s motion for summary judgment and plaintiff United States' motion for partial summary judgment on the issue of liability.

FACTS

From July 7, 1944 to December 16, 1980, Herschel McLeod, Sr. and Nellie McLeod owned the piece of property now the subject of this litigation, a 117 acre farm located near the town of California, Maryland in St. Mary's County. The parties have dubbed this property the California Maryland Drum site or "CMD site".

During the period of the McLeod's ownership, the McLeods engaged in a business relationship with Maryland Bank & Trust Co., the contours of which are disputed by the parties. It is undisputed, however, that during the 1970's, MB & T loaned money to Herschel McLeod, Sr. for two of his businesses—Greater St. Mary's Disposal, Inc. and Waldorf Sanitation of St. Mary's, Inc. The bank knew that McLeod operated a trash and garbage business on the site, but the record does not state at what point the bank became aware of this.

During 1972 or 1973, McLeod permitted the dumping of hazardous wastes on the CMD site. The wastes included organics such as toluene, ethylbenzene and total xylenes and heavy metals such as lead, chromium, mercury, and zinc.

In 1980, Mark Wayne McLeod applied for a $335,000 loan from MB & T to purchase the CMD site from his parents. On or about September 2nd of that year, MB & T sent Farmers Home Administration a request for loan guarantees relating to the McLeod loan * * *. FmHA issued Loan Note Guarantees for 90% of the loan on January 2, 1981.

Mark Wayne McLeod purchased the CMD site on December 16, 1980 through the MB & T loan, but soon failed to make payments on the loan. Consequently, MB & T instituted a foreclosure action against the CMD site in 1981 and purchased the property at the foreclosure sale on May 15, 1982 with a bid of $381,500. MB & T then took title to the property. From that date to the present, MB & T has been the record owner of the CMD site. FmHA continues to be a 90% guarantor of that loan.

On June 20, 1983, Mark Wayne McLeod informed Walter E. Raum, Director of Environmental Hygiene for St. Mary's County Department of Health, of the existence of the dumped wastes on the CMD site. After inspecting the site the following day, the State of Maryland contacted the EPA. Tests were conducted to identify the substances. On the basis of the test results, the EPA requested and received funding to conduct a removal action under CERCLA. The agency notified MB & T president John T. Daugherty that MB & T would be given until October 24, 1983 to initiate corrective action at the site or EPA would use its funds to clean-up the wastes. The bank declined the EPA's offer, so the agency proceeded to clean the site itself, removing two hundred thirty-seven drums of chemical material and 1180 tons of contaminated soil at a cost of approximately $551,713.50. After completing the clean-up, the EPA sent a letter to MB & T President Daugherty summarizing the costs incurred in the response action and demanding payment. To date, MB & T has not tendered payment. This action ensued.

CERCLA

Congress enacted CERCLA in 1980 in response to the environmental and public health hazards posed by improper disposal of hazardous wastes. [ ] CERCLA empowers the federal government to clean-up and otherwise respond to hazardous dump sites. The EPA has been delegated primary responsibility for this task. [ ]

"Response" actions undertaken by the EPA are financed primarily from the Hazardous Substance Response Trust Fund, commonly known as the "Super Fund" * * *. The Act also authorizes the government to recover costs from certain "responsible parties". [ ] This section extends liability to four categories of persons: 1) current owners and operators of the hazardous substance facility; 2) past owners or operators of the hazardous substance facility at the time of disposal; 3) persons who arranged for treatment or disposal of hazardous substances at the facility; and 4) persons who transported hazardous substances for treatment or disposal at the facility selected by them.

To establish liability under section 107(a) of the Act, the government must establish the following:

1) The site is a "facility";

2) A "release" or "threatened release" of any "hazardous substance" from the site has occurred;

3) The release or threatened release has caused the United States to incur "response costs"; and

4) The defendant is one of the persons designated as a party liable for costs.

Section 107 imposes strict liability. * * *

DISCUSSION

Defendant Maryland Bank & Trust does not dispute the fact that the first three elements of the prima facie case under section 107(a) have been met by the United States. [ ] The question central to both the defendant's and the plaintiff's motions for summary judgment concerns the final element, specifically, whether Maryland Bank & Trust is an "owner and operator" within the meaning of sections 107(a)(1) and 101(20)(A).

Additionally, Maryland Bank & Trust has raised in its answer an affirmative defense based upon section 107(b)(3), the so-called "third party defense". The United States argues in its motion for partial summary judgment that the bank cannot meet its burden of proof on that defense, an assertion disputed by the defendant in its opposition memorandum.

* * *

A. The Court initially turns to the question of whether MB & T falls within section 107(a)(1). That section holds liable "the owner and operator" of the facility. It is undisputed that MB & T has been the owner of the facility since May, 1982. The parties dispute whether the bank has been the operator of the facility since that time. The dispute over the term "operator" is not determinative, however, for the Court holds that current ownership of a facility alone brings a party within the ambit of subsection (1). Notwithstanding the language "the owner and operator", a party need not be both an owner and operator to incur liability under this subsection.

The structure of section 107(a), like so much of this hastily patched together compromise Act, is not a model of statutory clarity. It is unclear from its face whether subsection (1) holds liable both owners and operators or only parties who are both owners and operators. This ambiguity stems in large part from the placement of the definite article "the" before the term "owner" and its omission prior to the term "operator". Proper usage dictates that the phrase "the owner and operator" include only those persons who are both owners and opera-tors. But by no means does Congress always follow the rules of grammar when enacting the laws of this nation. In fact, to slavishly follow the laws of grammar while interpreting acts of Congress would violate sound canons of statutory interpretation. [ ] Misuse of the definite article is hardly surprising in a hastily conceived compromise statute such as CERCLA, since members of Congress might well have had no time to dot all the i's or cross all the t's. [ ]

An examination of the legislative history, sparse as it is, and the lone relevant case convinces the Court to interpret the language of subsection (1) broadly to include both owners and operators. The House Report accompanying H.R. 85, one of the four bills to coalesce into CERCLA, explains the definition of "operator" as follows: "In the case of a facility, an 'operator' is defined to be a person who is carrying out operational functions for the owner of the facility pursuant to an appropriate agreement." [ ] By its very definition, an operator cannot be the same person as an owner. Therefore, a class defined as consisting of persons who are both owners and operators would contain no mem-bers. Such a definition would render section 107(a)(1) a totally useless provision.

The Court of Appeals for the Second Circuit recently held a current owner of a facility responsible for response costs under section 107(a)(1) even though that party had not owned the site at the time of the dumping and had apparently not "operated" the facility. [ ] The court stated that "section 9607(a)(1) [107(a)(1)] unequivocally imposes strict liability on the current owner of a facility from which there is a release or a threat of release, without regard to causation." [ ] This Court agrees.

B. The definition of "owner or operator" contained in section 101(20)(A), 42 U.S.C. § 9601(20)(A), excludes from liability "a person, who, without participating in the management of a vessel or facility, holds indicia of ownership primarily to protect his security interest in the * * * facility." MB & T disclaims liability on the basis of this exemption.

Relying upon a statutory exemption to a Congressionally imposed rule of general liability, MB & T has the burden of proving that it is entitled to that exemption. [ ]

It is undisputed that MB & T held a mortgage on the site beginning on December 16, 1980, instituted foreclosure proceedings in 1981, and purchased the property at the foreclosure sale on May 15, 1982. MB & T contends that it is entitled to the benefit of this exclusion because it acquired ownership of the CMD site through foreclosure on its security interest in the property and purchase of the land at the foreclosure sale. The government asserts that the bank is not entitled to the exemption as a matter of law. The Court finds the government's position more persuasive and holds that MB & T is not exempted from liability by the exculpatory clause of section 101(20)(A).

The exemption of subsection (20)(A) covers only those persons who, at the time of the clean-up, hold indicia of ownership to protect a then-held security interest in the land. The verb tense of the exclusionary language is critical. The security interest must exist at the time of the clean-up. The mortgage held by MB & T (the security interest) terminated at the foreclosure sale of May 15, 1982, at which time it ripened into full title. [   ]

MB & T purchased the property at the foreclosure sale not to protect its security interest, but to protect its investment. Only during the life of the mortgage did MB & T hold indicia of ownership primarily to protect its security interest in the land. Under the law of Maryland (and twelve other states), the mortgagee-financial institution actually holds title to the property while the mortgage is in force. [   ] Congress intended by this exception to exclude these common law title mortgagees from the definition of "owner" since title was in their hands only by operation of the common law. The exclusion does not apply to former mortgagees currently holding title after purchasing the property at a foreclosure sale, at least when, as here, the former mortgagee has held title for nearly four years, and a full year before the EPA clean-up.

A review of the legislative history and policies underlying the Act support this narrow construction. * * * This [review] indicates that Congress intended to protect banks that hold mortgages in jurisdictions governed by the common law of mortgages, and not all mortgagees who later acquire title.

The interpretation of section 101(20)(A) urged upon the Court by MB & T runs counter to the policies underlying CERCLA. Under the scenario put forward by the bank, the federal government alone would shoulder the cost of cleaning up the site, while the former mortgagee-turned-owner, would benefit from the clean-up by the increased value of the now unpolluted land. At the foreclosure sale, the mortgagee could acquire the property cheaply. All other prospective purchasers would be faced with potential CERCLA liability, and would shy away from the sale. Yet once the property has been cleared at the taxpayers' expense and becomes marketable, the mortgagee-turned-owner would be in a position to sell the site at a profit.

In essence, the defendant's position would convert CERCLA into an insurance scheme for financial institutions, protecting them against possible losses due to the security of loans with polluted properties. Mortgagees, however, already have the means to protect themselves, by making prudent loans. Financial institutions are in a position to investigate and discover potential problems in their secured properties. For many lending institutions, such research is routine. CERCLA will not absolve them from responsibility for their mistakes of judgment.

* * *

NOTE: THE IMPACT OF ENVIRONMENTAL REGULATION ON REAL ESTATE FINANCE

1. As noted in <u>Maryland Bank</u>, liability under CERCLA is joint and several. It is also strict and retroactive, in the sense that defendants are liable for conduct that may have occurred many years before the enactment of environmental protection legislation. Liability is unlimited in amount, and includes the cost to remediate contamination of adjacent properties. Liability is endless in the sense that there is no statute of limitation protection against liability for conduct that occurred many years ago. Potentially responsible parties include the owner at the time of the release of a hazardous substance as well as the current owner, subject to an affirmative defense available to innocent landowners. The "innocent purchaser" defense requires proof that, at the time of acquisition, the purchaser did not know and had no reason to know the condition of the property. A purchaser is required to demonstrate that he or she made appropriate inquiry into the previous ownership of the property. See Patterson, A Buyer's Catalogue of Prepurchase Precautions to Minimize CERCLA Liability in Commercial Real Estate Transactions, 15 U. Puget Sound L. Rev. 469 (1992). Many environmental law practitioners believe that the onerous due diligence requirements of the innocent landowner defense make it difficult to establish, and something of a Catch–22.

2. Enactment of comprehensive environmental laws and decisions such as *Maryland Bank* spawned a whole new industry—environmental audits—involving engineers, lawyers and other professionals. Real estate departments of large law firms found themselves scrambling to hire lawyers with environmental law backgrounds, or sending members back to school to add environmental law to their repertoires.

A surprisingly large number of important issues were left ambiguous or simply unaddressed in the statute. CERCLA was passed during the final hectic days of the 96th Congress, a lame-duck Congress, just prior to the first inauguration of Ronald Reagan, under a suspension of the rules that precluded amendments. No House–Senate conference was held on the measure, so no conference report exists. For example it is unclear from the statute whether intervening landowners (those in the chain of title between the owner at the time of the release and the current owner) are liable for the cost of remediation. Courts in recent years have grappled with the question of whether a property owner may be held liable as a responsible party on a "passive" disposal theory. See, e.g., Carson Harbor Village, Ltd. v. Unocal Corp., 227 F.3d 1196 (9th Cir. 2000), rev'd en banc, 270 F.3d 863 (9th Cir. 2001).

The cost to clean up the almost 400,000 hazardous waste sites identified through 1990 has been estimated to exceed $100 billion. To bridge the gap between the cost and available government resources,

EPA has urged expansive theories of CERCLA liability. Does *Maryland Bank* represent acceptance of such theories, or is it consistent with a careful but not strained reading of the statute?

3. Note the Court's use of the distinction between "title" and "lien" theories of mortgages to support its decision to give a narrow construction to the secured creditor exemption from liability under the statute. Is the court's rationale persuasive or is it an example of form over substance?

4. What is a lender to do after *Maryland Bank*? Would the lender be better off not foreclosing and then asserting the "security interest" exception of CERCLA, which exempts from liability any "person, who, without participating in the management of a * * * facility, holds indicia of ownership primarily to protect his security interest in the * * * facility" (42 U.S.C. § 9601(20)(A))? If so, what happens to its possessory rights under the foreclosure process? How can it protect its security interest from additional devaluation? Note that the costs of cleanup that Maryland Bank was assessed (more than $550,000) exceeded its investment in the property ($381,500).

5. In *Maryland Bank,* the lender became involved with CERCLA because it purchased the contaminated property at a foreclosure sale. Suppose that environmental cleanup costs are incurred before a secured lender takes title through the foreclosure sale process. If the landowner goes bankrupt, can the government recover from the secured lender? In United States v. Fleet Factors Corp., 901 F.2d 1550, 1556–1558 (11th Cir.1990), the court construed the "secured creditor" exemption as follows:

> The construction of the secured creditor exemption is an issue of first impression in the federal appellate courts. The government urges us to adopt a narrow and strictly literal interpretation of the exemption that excludes from its protection any secured creditor that participates in any manner in the management of a facility. We decline the government's suggestion because it would largely eviscerate the exemption Congress intended to afford to secured creditors. Secured lenders frequently have some involvement in the financial affairs of their debtors in order to insure that their interests are being adequately protected. To adopt the government's interpretation of the secured creditor exemption could expose all such lenders to CERCLA liability for engaging in their normal course of business.

> Fleet in turn, suggests that we adopt the distinction delineated by some district courts between permissible participation in the financial management of the facility and impermissible participation in the day-to-day or operational management of a facility * * *

> The court below * * * interpreted the statutory language to permit secured creditors to provide financial assistance and general, and even isolated instances of specific, management advice to its debtors without risking CERCLA liability if the secured creditor does not

participate in the day-to-day management of the business or facility either before or after the business ceases operation.

Fleet Factors Corp., 724 F.Supp. at 960 (S.D.Ga.1988); * * *

[W]e find its construction of the statutory exemption too permissive towards secured creditors who are involved with toxic waste facilities. In order to achieve the "overwhelmingly remedial" goal of the CERCLA statutory scheme, ambiguous statutory terms should be construed to favor liability for the costs incurred by the government in responding to the hazards at such facilities.

The district court's broad interpretation of the exemption would essentially require a secured creditor to be involved in the operations of a facility in order to incur liability. This construction ignores the plain language of the exemption and essentially renders it meaningless. * * *

Under the standard we adopt today, a secured creditor may incur section 9607(a)(2) liability, without being an operator, by participating in the financial management of a facility to a degree indicating a capacity to influence the corporation's treatment of hazardous wastes. It is not necessary for the secured creditor actually to involve itself in the day-to-day operations of the facility in order to be liable—although such conduct will certainly lead to the loss of the protection of the statutory exemption. Nor is it necessary for the secured creditor to participate in management decisions relating to hazardous waste. Rather, a secured creditor will be liable if its involvement with the management of the facility is sufficiently broad to support the inference that it could affect hazardous waste disposal decision if it so chose. * * *

The Court of Appeals for the Ninth Circuit suggested, without deciding, that it believed the *Fleet Factors* rule was too broad, stating that "whatever the precise parameters of 'participation,' it is clear that there must be some actual management of the facility before a secured creditor will fall outside the exception." In re Bergsoe Metal Corporation (Hill v. The East Asiatic Company Ltd.), 910 F.2d 668 (9th Cir.1990). For an exhaustive analysis of the lender liability issue, see Howard and Gerard, Lender Liability Under CERCLA: Sorting Out the Mixed Signals, 64 S.Cal.L.Rev. 1187 (1991); Anno. Secured Lender Liability: Application of Security Interest Exemption Under CERCLA, 131 A.L.R. Fed. 293 (1996).

6. The debate over the proper scope of the security interest exemption under CERCLA is ongoing. In 1996 Congress enacted the Asset Conservation, Lender Liability and Deposit Insurance Act as part of the Omnibus Consolidated Appropriations Act, 1997, P.L. 104–208, Div. A, Title II, Subtitle E. § 2501, et. seq. The Act provides as follows:

(b) DEFINITION OF OWNER OR OPERATOR.—Section 101(20) of the Comprehensive Environmental Response, Compensation, and Liability Act of 1980 (42 U.S.C. 9601(20)) is amended by adding at the end the following:

"(E) EXCLUSION OF LENDERS NOT PARTICIPANTS IN MANAGEMENT.—

"(i) INDICIA OF OWNERSHIP TO PROTECT SECURITY.—The term 'owner or operator' does not include a person that is a lender that, without participating in the management of a vessel or facility, holds indicia of ownership primarily to protect the security interest of the person in the vessel or facility.

"(ii) FORECLOSURE.—The term 'owner or operator' does not include a person that is a lender that did not participate in management of a vessel or facility prior to foreclosure, notwithstanding that the person—

"(I) forecloses on the vessel or facility; and

"(II) after foreclosure, sells, re-leases (in the case of a lease finance transaction), or liquidates the vessel or facility, maintains business activities, winds up operations, undertakes a response action under section 107(d)(1) or under the direction of an on-scene coordinator appointed under the National Contingency Plan, with respect to the vessel or facility, or takes any other measure to preserve, protect, or prepare the vessel or facility prior to sale or disposition, if the person seeks to sell, re-lease (in the case of a lease finance transaction), or otherwise divest the person of the vessel or facility at the earliest practicable, commercially reasonable time, on commercially reasonable terms, taking into account market conditions and legal and regulatory requirements.

"(F) PARTICIPATION IN MANAGEMENT.—For purposes of subparagraph (E)—

"(i) the term 'participate in management'—

"(I) means actually participating in the management or operational affairs of a vessel or facility; and

"(II) does not include merely having the capacity to influence, or the unexercised right to control, vessel or facility operations;

"(ii) a person that is a lender and that holds indicia of ownership primarily to protect a security interest in a vessel or facility shall be considered to participate in management only if, while the borrower is still in possession of the vessel or facility encumbered by the security interest, the person—

"(I) exercises decisionmaking control over the environmental compliance related to the vessel or facility, such that the person has undertaken responsibility for the hazardous substance handling or disposal practices related to the vessel or facility; or

"(II) exercises control at a level comparable to that of a manager of the vessel or facility, such that the person has assumed or manifested responsibility—

"(aa) for the overall management of the vessel or facility encompassing day-to-day decisionmaking with respect to environmental compliance; or

"(bb) over all or substantially all of the operational functions (as distinguished from financial or administrative functions) of the vessel or facility other than the function of environmental compliance;

"(iii) the term 'participate in management' does not include performing an act or failing to act prior to the time at which a security interest is created in a vessel or facility; and

"(iv) the term 'participate in management' does not include—

"(I) holding a security interest or abandoning or releasing a security interest;

"(II) including in the terms of an extension of credit, or in a contract or security agreement relating to the extension, a covenant, warranty, or other term or condition that relates to environmental compliance;

"(III) monitoring or enforcing the terms and conditions of the extension of credit or security interest;

"(IV) monitoring or undertaking 1 or more inspections of the vessel or facility;

"(V) requiring a response action or other lawful means of addressing the release or threatened release of a hazardous substance in connection with the vessel or facility prior to, during, or on the expiration of the term of the extension of credit;

"(VI) providing financial or other advice or counseling in an effort to mitigate, prevent, or cure default or diminution in the value of the vessel or facility;

"(VII) restructuring, renegotiating, or otherwise agreeing to alter the terms and conditions of the extension of credit or security interest, exercising forbearance;

"(VIII) exercising other remedies that may be available under applicable law for the breach of a term or condition of the extension of credit or security agreement; or

"(IX) conducting a response action under section 107(d) or under the direction of an on-scene coordinator appointed under the National Contingency Plan, if the actions do not rise to the level of participating in management (within the meaning of clauses (i) and (ii)).

"(G) OTHER TERMS.—As used in this Act:

"(i) EXTENSION OF CREDIT.—The term 'extension of credit' includes a lease finance transaction—

"(I) in which the lessor does not initially select the leased vessel or facility and does not during the lease term control the daily operations or maintenance of the vessel or facility; or

"(II) that conforms with regulations issued by the appropriate Federal banking agency or the appropriate State bank supervisor (as those terms are defined in section 3 of the Federal Deposit Insurance Act (12 U.S.C. 1813)) or with regulations issued by the National Credit Union Administration Board, as appropriate.

"(ii) FINANCIAL OR ADMINISTRATIVE FUNCTION.—The term 'financial or administrative function' includes a function such as that of a credit manager, accounts payable officer, accounts receivable officer, personnel manager, comptroller, or chief financial officer, or a similar function.

"(iii) FORECLOSURE; FORECLOSE.—The terms 'foreclosure' and 'foreclose' mean, respectively, acquiring, and to acquire, a vessel or facility through—

"(I)(aa) purchase at sale under a judgment or decree, power of sale, or nonjudicial foreclosure sale;

"(bb) a deed in lieu of foreclosure, or similar conveyance from a trustee; or

"(cc) repossession, if the vessel or facility was security for an extension of credit previously contracted;

"(II) conveyance pursuant to an extension of credit previously contracted, including the termination of a lease agreement; or

"(III) any other formal or informal manner by which the person acquires, for subsequent disposition, title to or possession of a vessel or facility in order to protect the security interest of the person.

"(iv) LENDER.—The term 'lender' means—

"(I) an insured depository institution (as defined in section 3 of the Federal Deposit Insurance Act (12 U.S.C. 1813));

"(II) an insured credit union (as defined in section 101 of the Federal Credit Union Act (12 U.S.C. 1752));

"(III) a bank or association chartered under the Farm Credit Act of 1971 (12 U.S.C. 2001 et seq.);

"(IV) a leasing or trust company that is an affiliate of an insured depository institution;

"(V) any person (including a successor or assignee of any such person) that makes a bona fide extension of credit to or takes or acquires a security interest from a nonaffiliated person;

"(VI) the Federal National Mortgage Association, the Federal Home Loan Mortgage Corporation, the Federal Agricultural Mortgage Corporation, or any other entity that in a bona fide manner buys or sells loans or interests in loans;

"(VII) a person that insures or guarantees against a default in the repayment of an extension of credit, or acts as a surety with respect to an extension of credit, to a nonaffiliated person; and

"(VIII) a person that provides title insurance and that acquires a vessel or facility as a result of assignment or conveyance in the course of underwriting claims and claims settlement.

"(v) OPERATIONAL FUNCTION.—The term 'operational function' includes a function such as that of a facility or plant manager, operations manager, chief operating officer, or chief executive officer.

"(vi) SECURITY INTEREST.—The term 'security interest' includes a right under a mortgage, deed of trust, assignment, judgment lien, pledge, security agreement, factoring agreement, or lease and any other right accruing to a person to secure the repayment of money, the performance of a duty, or any other obligation by a nonaffiliated person.".

In light of the foregoing, is *Fleet Factors* still good law? See Monarch Tile, Inc. v. City of Florence, 212 F.3d 1219, 1223 (11th Cir. 2000). How would *Maryland Bank* have been decided? Did the lender in *Maryland Bank* seek to "divest * * * the facility at the earliest practicable commercially reasonable time"?

7.   Note that under CERCLA, the United States can impose a lien on property to recover cleanup costs. This environmental lien, as a government lien, takes priority over all non-governmental liens. Review the material on title insurance earlier in this chapter. How should title insurance companies respond to environmental liens? Many state environmental laws provide for similar cleanup liens. See, e.g., N.J.Stat., § 58:10–23.11 f.f.

B.   THE FORECLOSURE PROCESS—BALANCING DEBTOR AND CREDITOR INTERESTS

The vast majority of real estate loans are paid off on time and in accordance with the loan covenants. When the loan is retired, the mortgagee's lien is released, usually by the return of the note and mortgage to the borrower with a release notation added. In addition, the mortgagee should file with the recorder a deed of release, or request the recorder to enter a marginal note of release on the recorded mortgage or deed of trust.

However, when a mortgagor incurs a default by failure to pay as required, the mortgagee may take steps to protect its security interest. The following excerpt discusses the two most popular procedures, judicial foreclosure and power-of-sale foreclosure. Other procedures available to mortgagees are the common-law strict foreclosure, in which title is transferred directly to the mortgagee following a judicial decree of foreclosure, and acceptance by the mortgagee of a deed from the defaulting mortgagor in satisfaction of the debt, called a deed in lieu of foreclosure, or simply a deed in lieu.

NELSON & WHITMAN, REAL ESTATE FINANCE LAW
558–560, 581–587 (4th ed. 2001).

D. JUDICIAL FORECLOSURE

§ 7.11 Judicial Foreclosure—General Characteristics

Judicial foreclosure by sale in a court action in equity is a major, if not predominant method of foreclosure in the United States. It is the exclusive or generally used method of foreclosure in at least forty percent of the states. Moreover, it is available in every jurisdiction, either by virtue of express statutory enactment or as an incident to the inherent jurisdiction of courts of equity. Even in jurisdictions where power of sale foreclosure is dominant, judicial foreclosure is required in certain special situations. For example, it will be necessary where the mortgage fails to create a power of sale. This situation will arise where the mortgage form omits any reference to a power of sale. It can also occur where one is seeking to foreclose an absolute deed as a mortgage because, by its very nature, the absolute deed will not contain a power of sale. Judicial foreclosure will also be required where there is a serious lien priority dispute. In such a situation a judicial determination of lien priority will enable potential foreclosure sale purchasers to know the state of the title they will be bidding on and thus judicial foreclosure will be encouraged. On the other hand, if power of sale foreclosure were used, the uncertainty as to lien priority would discourage bidding and create title problems for the ultimate sale purchaser....

In spite of being a widely used method of foreclosure in America today, it has serious disadvantages. It is complicated, costly, and time-consuming. A typical action in equity to foreclose and sell involves a long series of steps: a preliminary title search to determine all parties in interest; filing of the foreclosure bill of complaint and lis pendens notice; service of process; a hearing, usually by a master in chancery who then reports to the court; the decree or judgment; notice of sale; actual sale and issuance of certificate of sale; report of the sale; proceedings for determination of the right to any surplus; possible redemptions from foreclosure sale; and the entry of a decree for a deficiency.

* * *

E. POWER OF SALE FORECLOSURE

§ 7.19 General Considerations

The other main foreclosure method, permitted in about sixty percent of the jurisdictions, is power of sale foreclosure. After varying types and degrees of notice, the property is sold at a public sale, either by a public official, such as a sheriff, by some other third party, or by the mortgagee.

In some states utilizing the power of sale method, the deed of trust is the most commonly used mortgage instrument. The mortgagor-trustor conveys the real estate to a trustee who holds the property in trust for the mortgagee-beneficiary until full payment of the mortgage debt. In the event of foreclosure, the power of sale is exercised by the trustee, who holds a public sale of the mortgaged property; the sale is usually not judicially supervised.

As previously indicated, the notice requirements under power of sale foreclosure vary, but are usually less rigorous than those associated with judicial foreclosure. Notice, as used here, may be simply notice of foreclosure or notice of default or a combination of the two. While some states require that notice by mail or personal service be provided for any person having a record interest in the real estate junior to the mortgage being foreclosed, many do not. A few states require only notice of publication. This publication sometimes takes the form of newspaper advertisement and sometimes consists only of public posting. Other states, in addition to published notice, require notice either by mail or personal service to the mortgagor and the owner of the mortgaged real estate, but not to junior lienors and others holding an interest subordinate to the mortgage being foreclosed. A few states attempt to protect those interested parties who are neither mortgagors nor owners by requiring that the notice of foreclosure be mailed to any person who has previously recorded a request for such notice. In any event, whatever the notice requirements of the foregoing statutes, federal legislation makes power of sale foreclosure ineffective against a junior federal tax lien unless written notice is provided to the United States at least 25 days prior to the sale by registered or certified mail or by personal service. Finally, almost no power of sale foreclosure statutes provide for an opportunity for a hearing prior to the foreclosure sale.

* * *

The underlying theory of power of sale foreclosure is simple. It is that by complying with the above type statutory requirements, the mortgagee accomplishes the same purposes achieved by judicial foreclosure without the substantial additional burdens that the latter type of foreclosure entails. Those purposes are to terminate all interests junior to the mortgage being foreclosed and to provide the sale purchaser with a title identical to that of the mortgagor as of the time the mortgage being foreclosed was executed. Moreover, where it is in common use, power of sale foreclosure has provided an effective foreclosure remedy with a cost in time and money substantially lower than that of its judicial foreclosure counterpart.

Notwithstanding the fact that power of sale foreclosure generally works and that it is more efficient and less costly than judicial foreclosure, the titles it produces have been somewhat less stable than those resulting from judicial foreclosure. As we noted earlier, there are at least three reasons for this. First, the court supervision involved in judicial foreclosure will prevent many defects from arising. Second, because judicial foreclosure is an adversary proceeding, the presence of other parties who will bring possible defects to the court's attention constitutes added protection against a faulty end product. Finally, the concept of judicial finality provides substantial insulation against subsequent collateral attack even on technically defective judicial foreclosure proceedings. None of these protections are inherent in power of sale foreclosure. . . .

§ 7.20 Defective Power of Sale Foreclosure—The "Void–Voidable" Distinction

* * * Generally, defects in the exercise of a power of sale can be categorized in at least three ways. Some defects are so substantial as to render the sale void. In this situation no title, legal or equitable, passes to the sale purchaser or subsequent grantees, except perhaps by adverse possession. Such a result typically occurs where, notwithstanding mortgagee compliance with the prescribed foreclosure procedure, there was no right to exercise the power of sale. A forged mortgage, for example, would fall into this category. The most common example, however, of a defect that would render a sale void is where the power of sale is exercised when there has been no default in the mortgage obligation. So too will a sale be characterized as void where the person foreclosing did not own the note or where a trustee under a deed of trust forecloses without being authorized by the noteholder to do so. Moreover, the failure to follow certain fundamental procedural requirements may render a sale void. For example, the omission of part of the mortgaged real estate from the notice of sale has been held to render the sale of omitted land void. . . .

Most defects * * * render the foreclosure *voidable* and not void. This means that bare legal title passes to the sale purchaser, subject to the rights of redemption of those injured by the defective foreclosure. Typically such a defect is "an irregularity in the execution of a foreclosure sale" and must be "substantial or result in a probable unfairness." A common example of a voidable sale in many jurisdictions is the purchase by a trustee under a deed of trust at his own sale. Further examples include the publication of the notice of sale for slightly fewer than the statutorily prescribed number of times or the sale at the east door instead of the west front door of the county courthouse. However, where the defect only renders the sale voidable, the rights of redemption can be cut off if the land falls into the hands of a bona fide purchaser for value. Where this occurs, an action for damages against the foreclosing mortgagee or trustee may be the only remaining remedy.

Finally, some defects are treated as so inconsequential as to render the sale neither void nor voidable. Such defects commonly involve minor discrepancies in the notice of sale. For example, where the first of four published notices of sale omitted the place of sale, the court held that since there was "substantial compliance" with the requirements specified by the deed of trust and since the parties were not affected in a "material way", the sale was valid. Similarly, a sale was deemed valid where the notice of sale was sent by regular rather than by the statutorily required certified or registered mail and the mortgagor had actual notice of the sale for more than the statutory period prior to the sale.

* * *

FIRST STATE BANK OF FORSYTH
v. CHUNKAPURA

Supreme Court of Montana, 1987.
226 Mont. 54, 734 P.2d 1203.

SHEEHY, JUSTICE.

We hold in this case that a lender, electing to foreclose on its security under a trust deed by judicial procedure, is not entitled to remedies inconsistent with the Small Tract Financing Act of Montana, [ ] Specifically, the lender (mortgagee) may not recover a deficiency judgment against the borrower (mortgagor), and the borrower has no right of redemption as is accorded borrowers in judicial foreclosures of conventional mortgages.

First State Bank of Forsyth and William F. Meisburger appealed from an order of the District Court, Sixteenth Judicial District, Rosebud County, the Honorable C.B. Sande, District Judge, presiding, that § 71–1–317, MCA, prohibits the Bank from recovering a deficiency judgment on judicial foreclosure. No final judgment has been entered in the cause pending this appeal, and the cause has been properly certified to us for appeal * * *.

On October 20, 1980, the Chunkapuras executed a promissory note to the First State Bank of Forsyth in the amount of $17,000 with interest on the unpaid principal thereon accruing at the rate of 14% per annum to be paid by the Chunkapuras in monthly payments. The note was secured by a deed of trust executed the same day from the Chunkapuras to First Montana Title Insurance Company as trustee, naming the Bank as beneficiary, covering Lots 17 and 18 in Block 54 of the original town, now city, of Forsyth, Montana.

Under the terms of the note the Chunkapuras would have paid to the Bank $226.40 per month until October 20, 1995 to pay off the note, and under the terms of the deed of trust, were to provide such additional sums monthly as would be sufficient to pay taxes, assessments, insurance premiums, and other charges.

William S. Meisburger succeeded First Montana Title Insurance Company as trustee under the deed of trust. He appears in this action as a plaintiff trustee, and as attorney for the Bank and himself as plaintiffs. * * *

The Chunkapuras made payments under the note and deed of trust to the Bank until April 20, 1985, at which time they went into default, the principal of the indebtedness having been reduced to $14,957.02. On September 11, 1985, the plaintiffs filed an action in the District Court to foreclose judicially the security interest of the Bank. Their complaint was amended on October 4, 1985. Under the amended complaint plaintiffs prayed for judgment against the defendants for the unpaid principal, accrued interest and other costs, for a sale of the real estate premises by the sheriff of Rosebud County, and for a deficiency judgment against the defendants after applying all the proceeds of the sale of the premises.

By stipulation, the parties agreed that the District Court could enter judgment, issue an order for a sheriff's sale, and proceed with the sheriff's sale, reserving until a later time the question of whether a deficiency judgment could be recovered. At the sheriff's sale, the Bank, being the only bidder, bid on the property in the sum of $10,000.00 which after deducting sheriff's fees and attorneys fees, left a net sum of $8,965.50. Thereupon the plaintiffs sought a deficiency judgment in the amount of $8,556.93.

* * *

I.

The issues in this case involve interpretation of the Small Tract Financing Act of Montana, enacted in 1963. The history of the legislative adoption of that Act, not unknown to some members of this Court, needs telling at this point for perspective.

Prior to 1963, Montana was a "one action" state with respect to foreclosures of mortgages. Our statute provided that there was but one action for the recovery of debt, or the enforcement of any rights incurred by mortgage upon real estate, which action had to be in accordance with the foreclosure provisions of our statutes. [   ] Whereas in other states with differing statutes the lender had the option of suing on the promissory note, or suing to foreclose the mortgage securing the note, our "one action" statute was construed by us to mean that a creditor could not waive the mortgage and sue on the debt but was limited to foreclosure of the mortgage indebtedness. [   ] A mortgage instrument could and still may contain a power of sale provision to which the mortgagee could resort for foreclosure without judicial proceedings. [   ] No provision however is made in our statutes for a deficiency judgment where foreclosure under power of sale occurs. In a judicial foreclosure, after the court entered judgment that the mortgager had defaulted on his obligations and that the mortgagee was entitled to the benefit of his security, the court could and still can order sale of the secured premises by the sheriff of the county involved. If the proceeds from the sheriff's sale are insufficient and a balance still remains due, a deficiency judgment can then be docketed against the defendant or defendants personally liable for the debt which becomes a lien upon the real estate of the judgment debtors. [   ]

Two legal consequences attended, and still attend a judicial foreclosure of mortgaged real property. The judgment debtor has the right to redeem the property from the purchaser at the sheriff's sale any time within one year after the sale. [   ] The purchaser was not and is not now entitled to the possession of the real property as against the judgment debtor during the period of redemption while the debtor personally occupied the land as a home for himself and his family. [   ]

The banking and lending industry came to the legislature in 1963, contending that the "one action" rule and the attendant right of redemption and right of possession rules hampered the financing of improvements on small tracts in Montana because banks and investors were unwilling to invest in mortgages when on default their funds would be tied up during the period of redemption. A *quid pro quo* was proposed to the legislature: the lenders would give up their deficiency judgment rights on default, if the borrowers would give up their rights of possession and redemption. The result was the adoption by the legislature of the Small Tract Financing Act of Montana, originally limited to tracts of three acres, but now may involve tracts as large as fifteen acres.

Under the Small Tract Financing Act, instead of mortgages, trust indentures (sometimes called "deeds of trust" or "trust deeds") are authorized. Such instruments have the effect of transferring the title of the borrower to a private trustee to be held by the trustee to secure the performance of the obligation by the borrower. A power of sale is by the law granted to the trustee to be exercised after a breach of the obligation for which the trust transfer is security. [   ] The trust indenture is considered to be a mortgage on real property, [   ] and provisions are made in the law for the method whereby a trustee may foreclose a trust indenture by advertisement and sale. [   ] It is certain that when a trustee conducts a foreclosure sale, a deficiency judgment is not allowed [   ], and the purchaser at the trustee sale is entitled to possession of the property on the tenth day following the sale. [   ]

It may be safely said, although it does not appear in this record, that in the time since the enactment of the Small Tract Financing Act, the use of trust deeds for security purposes has become nearly exclusive in this state.

II.

The issues in this cause arise out of certain provisions of the Small Tract Financing Act which are subject to judicial interpretation. Section 71–1–304(3), MCA, provides that a trust indenture may be foreclosed by an advertisement and sale through the trustee, or at the option of the beneficiary (lender) by judicial procedure as provided by law for the foreclosure of mortgages on real property. The foreclosure of a trust indenture by advertisement and sale or by judicial procedure is limited to the times provided by law for the foreclosure of a mortgage on real property. Section 71–1–311, MCA. The provision prohibiting deficiency judgment states:

Deficiency judgment not allowed. When a trust indenture executed in conformity with this part is foreclosed by advertisement and sale, no other or further action, suit, or proceedings shall be taken or judgment entered for any deficiency against the grantor or his surety, guarantor, or successor in interest, if any, on the note, bond, or other obligation secured by the trust indenture or against any other person obligated on such note, bond, or other obligation.

Section 71–1–317, MCA.

With respect to possession, the Act provides:

Possession. The purchaser at the trustee's sale shall be entitled to possession of the property on the 10th day following the sale, and any persons remaining in possession after that date under any interest, except one prior to the trust indenture, shall be deemed to be tenants at will.

Section 71–1–319, MCA.

The First State Bank of Forsyth contends that under the Act, it has the option of either foreclosing on the security by means of a trustee sale, or by resorting to judicial foreclosure. It further contends that when it elects to proceed by judicial foreclosure, it then becomes entitled to the legal consequences that follow the judicial foreclosure of a conventional mortgage, that is, the right to a deficiency judgment. It admits that if it is entitled to a deficiency judgment, the borrower also then becomes entitled to the right of redemption granted in the foreclosure of conventional mortgages.

The Chunkapuras on the other hand, contend that because the lender chose to finance this obligation under the Small Tract Financing Act, it thereupon elected the benefits conferred upon lending institutions by the Act, the immediate transfer of title in exchange for no deficiency judgment, and that these results apply whether the lender elects to proceed by trustee sale on default, or by judicial foreclosure. The Chunkapuras rely especially on § 71–1–305, MCA, which provides:

Trust indenture considered to be a mortgage on real property. A trust indenture is deemed to be a mortgage on real property and is subject to all laws relating to mortgages on real property except to the extent that such laws are inconsistent with the provisions of this part, in which event the provisions of this part shall control. For the purpose of applying the mortgage laws, the grantor in a trust indenture is deemed the mortgagor and the beneficiary is deemed the mortgagee.

They point also to the provisions of § 71–1–317, MCA, which we have quoted above, contending that whether a trustee sale occurs or a judicial foreclosure is utilized, the trust indenture is foreclosed "by advertisement and sale" in either case, and under § 71–1–317, a deficiency judgment is not allowed. To grant a deficiency judgment, the Chunkapuras contend, would be in effect giving life to a provision of the judicial foreclosure statutes which is inconsistent with the provisions of the Small Tract Financing Act under § 71–1–305.

III.

This Court is confronted in this case with a statutory situation wherein it is clear that in cases of trustee sales under trust deeds, there is no right of redemption given to the borrower, and the borrower must surrender possession within ten days; and the lender under a trustee sale has no right to a deficiency judgment. The provisions of the Small Tract Financing Act, permitting an election to the lender to resort to judicial foreclosure, [   ], and setting out time limitations [   ], do not clearly provide that under judicial foreclosures, the legal consequences of redemption and deficiency judgment follow. It becomes a matter of judicial interpretation whether the sense and intent of the legislature, in adopting the Small Tract Financing Act, and permitting judicial foreclosure, was also to permit deficiency judgments to the lenders and the rights of redemption to the borrowers.

* * *

We are directed to the case law of other states.

* * *

It may be stated therefore, as a broad general policy in the western states, with Alaska the sole exception, the lender has the option of proceeding by trustee sale under trust instruments, or by judicial foreclosure under the mortgage statutes; but if the latter procedure is elected, the deficiency judgment provisions of those statutes limit the deficiency judgment to the difference between the amount of the indebtedness sought and the fair market value of the property at the time of the sale, or the amount realized at the sale, whichever figure results in the lesser deficiency. Montana statutes on judicial foreclosure do not have a "fair market value" provision. A consideration of those provisions brings us to the crux of the problem in this case.

IV.

Generally, since 1963, with the exception of the last few years, real estate values in Montana have been subjected to the same inflationary pressures that existed elsewhere in the nation. At or about the time that the Chunkapuras borrowed on their property in this case, inflation had reached its highest stage. But Montana, since 1981, has been enduring a depressed economy of sorts, which has resulted in a marked depreciation in the values of real property. In the past five to six years foreclosures because of defaulted debts on farms, businesses, and homes have increased notably in this state. In this case, the Bank was the only bidder for the Chunkapuras property. Its bid of $10,000 may represent the fair market value of the property at the time of the sheriff's sale, or it may be an opportunistic bid which takes advantage of the circumstances so that later the Bank may sell the property for a sum in excess of $10,000. In the meantime the deficiency judgment of $8,556.93, plus accrued interest and costs, if allowed would become a lien on any other real estate the Chunkapuras now own or may own during the period that the judgment lien is in effect. The right of possession of their home which the Chunkapuras would have for one year might have some value, but the right of redemption is valueless, because if the Chunkapuras redeemed, the deficiency judgment lien would immediately adhere to the redeemed property. This result is not the *quid pro quo* which the legislature intended when it acceded to the lending industries' urging and adopted the Small Tract Financing Act in 1963.

We therefore determine and hold that District Judge Sande was correct when he determined that under § 71–1–317, MCA, a deficiency judgment may not be allowed when trust indentures are executed in conformity with the Act, and are foreclosed by advertisement and sale, whether through the trustee or by judicial proceedings; and that to allow a deficiency judgment would be inconsistent with the provisions of the Small Tract Financing Act of Montana and accordingly forbidden * * *.

The decision in the District Court therefore that no deficiency judgment may be obtained against the Chunkapuras is affirmed. It should go without saying that in like manner, the Chunkapuras are not entitled either to a right of possession after ten days from the sale, or to a right of redemption for a period of one year.

* * *

WEBER, JUSTICE, dissents. * * * [The dissent argued that the majority disregarded the interests of lenders and failed to follow the plain meaning of the statutes. If modification were necessary, that should be done by the legislature, the dissent concluded—Eds.]

ORDER ON REHEARING

[The Court limited its order to trust deeds related to occupied, single family residential property, holding that the restrictions on deficiency judgments did not apply to commercial lending or investment settings—Eds.]

Notes and Questions

1. If the foreclosure proceeds are insufficient to satisfy the balance of the secured indebtedness at the time of foreclosure, plus the expenses of sale, a deficiency is said to exist. For example, assume that the unpaid balance of the debt secured by the mortgage is $75,000, and that the expenses of conducting the foreclosure sale are $3,000. Under the circumstances of a distress sale, property is likely to be sold for a price at the low end of the range of fair market value. If the foreclosure sale price is only $72,000, then the secured creditor is entitled to seek a $6,000 deficiency judgment.

In an effort to prevent real estate recessions from spiraling into depressions, Montana and some of her sister states have enacted statutes to protect borrowers from being sued to collect deficiency judgments. California, which has the most comprehensive anti-deficiency legislation of any state, extends its protection to commercial borrowers.

If you were asked to advise a state legislator contemplating introducing antideficiency legislation, what are the comparative advantages and disadvantages that should be taken into consideration?

2. Note the trade-offs in the Montana legislation: Lenders gave up the right to obtain deficiency judgments in return for borrowers giving up the right to retain possession after foreclosure while they attempted to raise money to pay off the debt and redeem the property. Does this strike you as a fair approach? Does this legislation increase or decrease the lenders' credit risk? The borrowers'?

3. A recurring theme of mortgage law development is the attempt to balance the risks of debtors and creditors. Creditors tend to have the upper hand because mortgage finance is a contractual activity in which persons with money generally can dictate the terms under which persons seeking money can obtain it. A major concern of lenders is the protection of their credit risk. To reduce this risk, lenders generally prefer to be able to transfer possession quickly to foreclosure sale purchasers, and to be able to recoup any deficiencies after foreclosure sale from the defaulting borrowers. Periodically courts of equity and legislatures have intervened, particularly in times of severe economic distress, such as the great depression, to cushion the impact of such risk-reduction techniques on defaulting borrowers in the hopes of alleviating some of the social problems resulting from residential default. As noted in *Chunkapura,* three basic techniques that originated in the depression are in use in a number of states: (a) "fair value" legislation that limits any deficiency that may be realized after foreclosure sale to the difference between an established "fair value" and the outstanding debt; (b) "anti-deficiency" legislation that prohibits deficiency judgments when power-of-sale foreclosure is used, or in cases where the foreclosed mortgage is a purchase money mortgage rather than a construction mortgage; and (c) "one action" rules that require mortgagees to choose either a contractual action on the promissory note or a foreclosure action under the mortgage, or limit mortgagees to the foreclosure sale proceeds. For a succinct analysis of such legislative intervention, see G. Nelson & D. Whitman, Real Estate Finance Law 658–688 (4th ed. 2001).

4. During the inflationary-recessionary period of the late 1970s and early 1980s, high rates of default on farm and home mortgages led a number of states to enact additional consumer protection measures including temporary mortgage-payment forbearance periods of up to six months, court ordered restructuring of mortgage debt, and mortgage assistance payments to homeowners by state agencies. See e.g., Conn. Gen. Stat. §§ 49–31d through 49–31j. Similar programs enacted in Minnesota and Pennsylvania have since been repealed. For a review of these programs, see Sclar, From the Legislatures: Mortgage Foreclosure Relief, 12 Real Est.L.J. 366 (1984).

5. One of Randy Cohen's "Everyday Ethics" correspondents wrote the expert for moral comfort as he, the correspondent, considered whether to buy a home from "an acquaintance" who "purchased [the] house from a bank that had foreclosed on it, acquiring it for half its value with no down." Mr. Cohen's words of comfort turned, but with some uncertainty, on legal devices such as those described in these notes: "I believe you may honorably purchase a foreclosed property. It is not just that you didn't cause any family to lose its home [which, one supposes, would not be an <u>honorable</u> thing to do]—you did not—but that foreclosure can be an acceptable part of a financial system," which Mr. Cohen goes on to demonstrate, by explaining the need for collateral in lending as consistent with <u>honorable</u> systems.

"What is necessary is that the borrower be given every opportunity to repay. Contingencies must be established to cope with illness or job loss or other unexpected catastrophes that could befall a borrower.

"That is, the mortgage system must be fair, flexible and humane. If it is, foreclosures should be few and buying a home that has been through one is legitimate. You might query the bank about its policies and about the history of the particular house you want to buy." (A property casebook editor wonders if these criteria for inquiry would be morally useful for a lawyer deciding whether to represent the plaintiff in the foreclosure.)

"That said, I myself would be reluctant to buy one. A home is suffused with feeling; it's where you live. I wouldn't want it tainted with the residue of the previous owner's ill fortune.

"But it is emotion, not ethics, that would keep me from buying a foreclosed house." (The South Bend Tribune, January 22, 2004, page C–1.) This column first appeared in the New York Times Magazine.

6.   The foreclosure relief statutes discussed above become effective after the foreclosure process has begun. An alternative approach, using mediation, is designed to intervene before debt problems reach the desperate stage of foreclosure. Farmer-lender mediation programs have been established in a number of midwestern states, some voluntary and some mandatory.

As we discussed in the landlord-tenant chapter, mediation is typically a voluntary procedure that depends in large measure for its success on the willing participation of the protagonists. Whether the mediation program is a required step in a loan default process, or merely a recommended step in the process, the parties must believe in mediation or at least be willing to approach mediation with an open mind if it is to have a chance to contribute to the resolution of a dispute. In Graham v. Baker, 447 N.W.2d 397 (Iowa 1989), the Supreme Court of Iowa held that an attorney for a lender who attended a mediation session but refused to cooperate with the mediator satisfied the Iowa statute requiring "participation" in mediation before foreclosing on farm loans. Did the court give the correct interpretation to the Iowa legislation, or should it have implied a standard of "good faith" before a mediation release could be obtained? Does such legislation make any sense the way the Iowa court construed it?

Would an attorney retained by a lender to pursue remedies upon default by a borrower be acting in an ethical/professional manner in refusing to cooperate with a mediation process? Would it make a difference whether the process was mandatory or voluntary? Would such an attorney merely be loyal to his client, or would he go beyond the bounds of loyalty and fail to live up to his obligation to serve the public as an officer of the court, particularly if the legislature had determined that efforts to resolve mortgage loan defaults short of forfeiture were required as a matter of public policy?

Proponents of mediation between farmers and creditors have identified "four outcomes that can be considered successful:

* clarification of the impasses including the recognition that the issues cannot be resolved;

* management of the communication system so that the parties can interact effectively;

* resolution of the goals and issues and management of the communications; and

* reconciliation of the relationship so that both parties' interests, issues and goals are met."

Thompson, Crisis in Rural America: The Genesis of Farmer–Lender Mediation, Nat. Inst. for Dispute Res. Forum, p. 4 (Fall 1990).

7. The constitutionality of power of sale foreclosure has been challenged on due process grounds. Borrowers have argued that due process requires notice reasonably calculated to inform them of the pendency of the sale of their property, and that the advertising requirements of the typical state power of sale foreclosure statutes fall short of meeting this standard. Most courts have rejected constitutional challenge to power of sale foreclosure on the theory that there is inadequate state action. See generally, G. Nelson and D. Whitman, Real Estate Finance Law, 615–643 (4th ed. 2001).

8. What are the advantages to the borrower and the lender of a deed in lieu over foreclosure? Can you think of any disadvantages?

Chapter Six

THE LAW OF NEIGHBORS: SERVITUDES AND NUISANCES

This chapter is about the law of neighbors. Real property does not exist in a vacuum. Except perhaps for isolated islands, any particular parcel owned by one or more persons is bounded by other parcels owned by other persons. Correspondingly, the use of real property affects and is affected by the use of neighboring properties. The owner of a remote mountain ranch, for example, may need an access easement across a neighbor's land to get to a public road, or may damage neighboring properties through poor logging practices. Neighbors in a suburban residential development are far more interdependent. Their houses are hooked into pipes and wires that crisscross the neighborhood. They may be annoyed by each other's children, dogs, parties, fences, or satellite dishes. Developers attempt to define the character of neighborhoods through restrictions that limit permissible uses, or the placement of buildings, or the architectural style of the neighborhood. Neighbors litigate concerning these restrictions when nonconforming persons or uses attempt to settle in the neighborhood. Restrictions may also create property owners' associations—miniature private governments that may collect taxes (assessments), maintain common improvements, decide what sort of architecture will be permitted within the development, and amend their fundamental laws as the development progresses. Finally, residents in a cooperative or condominium are even more interdependent, and thus even more dependent on complex and detailed deed restrictions for accommodating each other as they live their common life.

Neighboring uses are accommodated through a variety of legal doctrines. The law of adverse possession, which you have already studied, is commonly used to decide boundary disputes between neighboring owners. The public law of zoning and planning, which comes later in this course, plays an increasingly important role in reconciling neighboring uses. Most of the law relevant to legal accommodations and disputes among neighbors, however, is found in this chapter.

The chapter begins with consideration of servitudes, then examines the law of nuisance, and concludes with a brief discussion of a variety of doctrines that play a lesser role in the law of neighbors: lateral and subjacent support and the law of surface waters.

I. SERVITUDES

Servitudes serve three primary functions. First, they permit persons affirmatively to use land that they do not own or possess. For example, A can own servitudes that allow her to get to her own land by driving down her neighbor, B's, lane; or to run telephone or electric wire, or gas, water, or sewer pipes across B's land to permit the development of her own land. Second, servitudes allow land owners to restrict their neighbors' use of their own land. A can own servitudes that forbid her neighbor, B, from using his property for uses other than residential development, from building within 30 feet of the street, from constructing a building not approved by an architectural review committee, or from posting political signs in his front yard. Finally, servitudes allow landowners to impose affirmative obligations on their neighbors. B, for example, may be obligated to pay $50 a year to a property owners' association, or to maintain a fence, or to provide his neighbor, A, with water from a stream.

Servitudes are most commonly based on agreements between or among landowners. They are often based on language in deeds or independent grants: A, for example, deeds the back half of her 320–acre farm to B and in doing so grants to B a servitude of way across A's retained 160 acres to get to B's purchased land. Increasingly servitudes are created by subdivision plats or declarations of restrictions. A developer establishes a 120–lot exclusive residential development, and before selling any lots, records a declaration binding the entire subdivision with certain restrictions.

Insofar as servitudes are based on agreements, they resemble contracts. They differ from contracts, however, in an important respect: they run with the land. A contract only binds parties who agree to be bound by it. When the appropriate requirements are met, however, a servitude binds and benefits not only the initial owners of the burdened and benefited properties, but also their successors. Moreover, unlike contracts, which bind their signatories until the obligations imposed by the contract are fulfilled or released, servitudes normally bind landowners only for so long as they own burdened land.

Though most servitudes are appurtenant to particular parcels of burdened and benefited properties, servitudes may also be created in gross. They may, that is, be created for the benefit of a particular individual or entity independent of property ownership. The telephone company may, for example, own an easement across a property to run its wires, or an environmental organization may own a conservation easement limiting the development of farmland.

Some kinds of servitudes may be created not only by express agreement, but also by implication. If A had not granted a servitude of way to B in the hypothetical above, for example, and if the conveyance cut B's land off from any access to any public road, the law would in all likelihood imply a servitude of way across A's land in B's favor. If the deed failed to mention a servitude of way, but B used A's lane without her permission to get to his land for 10 years, the law might recognize a servitude based on prescription. If the developer in the example above had not recorded a declaration of restrictions, but rather had advertised a restricted development and sold off successive lots each with identical restrictions in their deeds, the law might very well at some point imply the restrictions against a lot sold off subsequently without the restrictions. Because of a general public policy favoring preservation of land free from encumbrances, however, courts imply restrictions reluctantly and only under limited circumstances when they believe public policy requires it.

The law of servitudes could be relatively straightforward, but, unfortunately, it is not. Here, as elsewhere in property law, doctrine is a creature of history. Where the law of estates and future interests represents the continuous organic development of nearly a millennium of English and American law, servitude law in its modern form is largely a creation of the nineteenth and twentieth century. It thus represents the simultaneous uncoordinated attempts of the English law and chancery courts and of a number of American jurisdictions to arrive at a law suited to a period of rapid development.

The results are singularly confusing. Five primary tools—easements, licenses, profits, real covenants, and equitable servitudes—were created to serve the three functions set out above. To complicate matters further, several of these servitudes can serve more than one function. Real covenants and equitable servitudes can in many jurisdictions be used both to restrict land and to impose affirmative obligations on land owners. Easements permit one to use affirmatively another's property, but negative easements restrict the use of property, and, under very limited circumstances, easements can impose affirmative obligations.

The law of servitudes is also burdened by confusing doctrine which often either serves no contemporary purpose, or which strives by indirection to achieve goals more properly addressed directly. The requirement of horizontal privity for the creation of real covenants, for example, was probably created to deal with the lack of a recording system in Britain, but serves no purpose in modern America. The "touch and concern" requirement limits the subject matter of servitudes that impose negative restrictions or affirmative obligations on land, but often results in obfuscation and tautological reasoning instead of clear discussion of policy questions.

Much of this confusing doctrine was unfortunately enshrined in the 1944 Restatement of Property, which on the whole assumed a hostile attitude towards restrictions on real property, and adopted a variety of archaic doctrines of questionable authority to limit their use. A new Restatement, which adopts the more modern attitude recognizing the value of servitudes for many purposes was adopted in 2000. It will greatly simplify servitude law if its reasoning is adopted by the courts. This goal may be achieved in your lifetime, but for the present, you must, regrettably, come to terms with the doctrine that still appears in court decisions. For these reasons, the text continues to cite the 1944 Restatement as well as the 2000 Restatement where relevant.

Because existing traditional servitudes cannot be fit neatly into functional categories, this text adopts a functional as well as doctrinal approach. Affirmative rights to use the property of another—easements, licenses, and profits—are treated together first. Negative and affirmative obligations—real covenants, equitable servitudes, and negative easements—are considered next. Within each of these categories we consider creation; validity, succession, and scope; and modification and termination.

A. AFFIRMATIVE RIGHTS TO USE PROPERTY: EASEMENTS, LICENSES, AND PROFITS

1. *Definitions*

Three legal devices are used to permit affirmative use of property owned by another: easements, profits, and licenses. A license is a privilege to use property possessed by another. See Restatement, Property (1944) § 512. Examples of a license include tickets to a theatre or sporting event, or the privilege of being seated in a restaurant or of being allowed in a shopping mall. A license is revocable at the will of the licensor except where it has become irrevocable under one of several doctrines discussed below. An irrevocable license looks a great deal like an easement. The Restatement (Third) Property (2000) § 1.2(4) takes the quite sensible position that irrevocable licenses are easements.

A profit (or profit à prendre) is the right to sever and take the "profits"—i.e. produce or substance—of the land of another. Examples of traditional English profits include turbary (the right to dig turf), estovers (the right to remove timber as needed for good husbandry), and pannage (the right to feed swine on acorns and mast). Of more contemporary importance, the right to remove oil and gas can be considered a profit, see Gerhard v. Stephens, 68 Cal.2d 864, 69 Cal.Rptr. 612, 442 P.2d 692 (1968).

The 1944 Restatement (§ 450, Special Note) took the sensible position that under contemporary American law there was no distinction between easements and profits, and that, therefore, the use of both terms was unnecessary. Other authorities have followed this approach (see 3 R. Powell & P. Rohan, Powell on Real Property), ¶ 404(1) (1991). Unfortunately, the 2000 Restatement defines a profit as an easement but, somewhat inconsistently, perpetuates the semantic, but not the substantive, distinction between easements and profits. *Id.* § 1.2(2).

The most common device for creating affirmative rights in the property of another is the easement. The 1944 Restatement, § 450, defines an easement as:

"An interest in land in the possession of another which

(a) entitles the owner of such interest to a limited use or enjoyment of the land in which the interest exists;

(b) entitles him to protection as against third persons from interference in such use or enjoyment;

(c) is not subject to the will of the possessor of the land;

(d) is not a normal incident of the possession of any land possessed by the owner of the interest; and

(e) is capable of creation by conveyance."

The 2000 Restatement § 1.2(1) defines "easement" as follows:

An easement creates a nonpossessory right to enter and use land in the possession of another and obligates the possessor not to interfere with the uses authorized by the easement.

Problem: Do the following situations involve easements, licenses, profits, or something else? How do you know?

(a) A permits B to place a billboard on the side of A's building.

(b) A University sells B student a parking permit which permits B to park in any available student parking place on campus.

(c) B purchases from A the right to dig gravel from a gravel pit on A's property.

(d) B parks her car in A's parking garage. B turns the car and its keys over to A upon entering the garage. A parks the car and keeps the keys until B returns.

(e) B permits A to hunt on B's property every year during hunting season.

(f) A uses B's lane to get from his farm across B's property to the county road.

(g) The eaves of A's house overhang B's property by one foot.

2. *Creation*

(a) By Express Conveyance

Most easements are created through express conveyances. Easements can be created in deeds conveying the fee to which they are appurtenant; through separate written grants; by reference to plats, maps, or declarations; and even by wills. Easements can also be created by contract to the extent that a contract to make an easement will be specifically enforced at equity. At common law, easements were incorporeal hereditaments, not subject to creation by livery of seisin. Instead, they had to be created through deeds, which had to be sealed instruments. The requirement of a seal has been abolished in most jurisdictions by statute or court decision, but appears to remain in force in a handful of jurisdictions.

Although there was some early confusion as to whether the Statute of Frauds applied to easements, since on its face it only applied to estates that could be created by livery of seisin or parole, it now clearly applies to easements. The Statute thus requires (subject to exceptions considered below) that grants of easements be in writing and signed. Though the writing must identify the burdened estate, it is not necessary to specify the location of the servitude upon the burdened estates, and grants are often indefinite in this particular. It is also not necessary that the grant identify the benefited estate if its identity is clear from the context. Finally, easements are often created by deeds that independently convey a fee, and which are signed only by the grantor. Even though the deed is a deed poll, not signed by the grantee (as is commonly the case), the grantor may retain an easement across the granted property, with the grantee's acceptance serving in place of a signature. Traditionally, the word "grant" was appropriate for creating an easement. While under contemporary practice other words can be used if their purpose is clear, lawyers never forget, and easements are still commonly granted. Easements are subject to the recording act and must normally be recorded to bind future parties.

Formalities retain their greatest vitality with respect to grants to third parties.

WILLARD v. FIRST CHURCH OF CHRIST, SCIENTIST, PACIFICA

Supreme Court of California, 1972.
7 Cal.3d 473, 102 Cal.Rptr. 739, 498 P.2d 987.

PETERS, ASSOCIATE JUSTICE.

In this case we are called upon to decide whether a grantor may, in deeding real property to one person, effectively reserve an interest in the property to another. We hold that in this case such a reservation vests the interest in the third party.

Plaintiffs Donald E. and Jennie C. Willard filed an action to quiet title to a lot in Pacifica against the First Church of Christ, Scientist (the church). After a trial judgment was entered quieting the Willards' title. The church has appealed.

Genevieve McGuigan owned two abutting lots in Pacifica known as lots 19 and 20. There was a building on lot 19, and lot 20 was vacant. McGuigan was a member of the church, which was located across the street from her lots, and she permitted it to use lot 20 for parking during services. She sold lot 19 to one Petersen, who used the building as an office. He wanted to resell the lot, so he listed it with Willard, who is a realtor. Willard expressed an interest in purchasing both lots 19 and 20, and he and Petersen signed a deposit receipt for the sale of the two lots.

Soon thereafter they entered into an escrow, into which Petersen delivered a deed for both lots in fee simple.

At the time he agreed to sell lot 20 to Willard, Petersen did not own it, so he approached McGuigan with an offer to purchase it. She was willing to sell the lot provided the church could continue to use it for parking. She therefore referred the matter to the church's attorney, who drew up a provision for the deed that stated the conveyance was "subject to an easement for automobile parking during church hours for the benefit of the church on the property at the southwest corner of the intersection of Hilton Way and Francisco Boulevard * * * such easement to run with the land only so long as the property for whose benefit the easement is given is used for church purposes." Once this clause was inserted in the deed, McGuigan sold the property to Petersen, and he recorded the deed.

Willard paid the agreed purchase price into the escrow and received Petersen's deed 10 days later. He then recorded this deed, which did not mention an easement for parking by the church. While Petersen did mention to Willard that the church would want to use lot 20 for parking, it does not appear that he told him of the easement clause contained in the deed he received from McGuigan.

Willard became aware of the easement clause several months after purchasing the property. He then commenced this action to quiet title against the church. At the trial, which was without a jury, McGuigan testified that she had bought lot 20 to provide parking for the church, and would not have sold it unless she was assured the church could thereafter continue to use it for parking. The court found that McGuigan and Petersen intended to convey an easement to the church, but that the clause they employed was ineffective for that purpose because it was invalidated by the common law rule that one cannot "reserve" an interest in property to a stranger to the title.

The rule derives from the common law notions of reservations from a grant and was based on feudal considerations. A reservation allows a grantor's whole interest in the property to pass to the grantee, but revests a newly created interest in the grantor.[1] [ ] While a reservation could theoretically vest an interest in a third party, the early common law courts vigorously rejected this possibility, apparently because they mistrusted and wished to limit conveyance by deed as a substitute for livery by seisin. (See Harris Reservations in Favor of Strangers of the Title (1953) 6 Okla.L.Rev. 127, 132–133.) Insofar as this mistrust was the foundation of the rule, it is clearly an inapposite feudal shackle today. Consequently, several commentators have attacked the rule as groundless and have called for its abolition. [ ]

1. The effect of a reservation should be distinguished from an exception, which prevents some part of the grantor's interest from passing to the grantee. The exception cannot vest an interest in the third party, and the excepted interest remains in the grantor. (6 Powell, The Law of Real Property (Rohan ed. 1971) § 892.)

California early adhered to this common law rule. [ ] In considering our continued adherence to it, we must realize that our courts no longer feel constricted by feudal forms of conveyancing. Rather, our primary objective in construing a conveyance is to try to give effect to the intent of the grantor. [ ] In general, therefore, grants are to be interpreted in the same way as other contracts and not according to rigid feudal standards. [ ] The common law rule conflicts with the modern approach to construing deeds because it can frustrate the grantor's intent. Moreover, it produces an inequitable result because the original grantee has presumably paid a reduced price for title to the encumbered property. In this case, for example, McGuigan testified that she had discounted the price she charged Petersen by about one-third because of the easement. Finally, in some situations the rule conflicts with section 1085 of the Civil Code.[2]

In view of the obvious defects of the rule, this court has found methods to avoid it where applying it would frustrate the clear intention of the grantor. In Butler v. Gosling, 130 Cal. 422, 62 P. 596 (1900), the court prevented the reserved title to a portion of the property from vesting in the grantee by treating the reservation as an exception to the grant. In Boyer v. Murphy, *supra,* 202 Cal. 23, 259 P. 38, the court, noting that its primary objective was to give effect to the grantor's intention (Id., at pp. 28–29, 259 P. 38), held that the rule was inapplicable where the third party was the grantor's spouse. [ ] Similarly, the lower courts in California[3] and the courts of other states[4] [ ] have found ways of circumventing the rule.

2. Section 1085 provides that "(a) present interest, and the benefit of a condition or covenant respecting property, may be taken by any natural person under a grant, although not named a party thereto." We have been unable to find a California case that cites the section. Similar provisions in the codes of other states have also lain unused on the books. (See Mont.Rev. Codes Ann. (1962) § 67–1524; N.D.Cent.Code (1962) § 47–09–17; R.I.Gen.Laws Ann. (1956) § 34–11–10.) The language of the section clearly does not apply in this case because the church is a corporation and not a natural person.

3. In Sutter Butte Canal Co. v. Richvale Land Co., 40 Cal.App. 451, 181 P. 98 (1919), a developer provided, in its subdivision proposal, that certain easements for streets were reserved to its assigns and successors. Faced with a challenge to the easement based on the rule against reservation to a stranger, the court noted that it was "not justified in resorting to technical refinement as to the meaning of 'reversions' to defeat the manifest intent of the parties * * *." (Id., at pp. 456–457, 181 P. at p. 100.) It held that the complaining landowner was estopped to object to the easement because of his express consent to it. Simi-

larly, in Smith v. Kraintz, 201 Cal.App.2d 696, 20 Cal.Rptr. 471 (1962), the court upheld a reservation to the general public because the intent to dedicate can be shown by even an ineffective instrument.

4. (See generally Harris, Reservations in Favor of Strangers to the Title, *supra,* 6 Okla.L.Rev. 127, 139–150.) Some courts, like the court in Butler, supra, mitigate the harshness of the rule by treating the reservation as an exception that retained the interest in the grantor. [ ]. While this approach did prevent the reserved interest from passing to the grantee, it did not achieve the grantor's intention of vesting that interest in the third party. Other courts gave effect to the grantor's intention by estopping those who claimed under a chain of title including the deed containing the reservation from challenging it on the basis of the common law rule. [ ] This approach has the effect of emasculating the common law rule without expressly abandoning it. One court found that a reservation created a trust in favor of the stranger [ ], but this approach seems unduly elaborate to achieve the grantor's intent. Finally, several courts, like the court in Boyer, supra, will disregard the rule entirely when

The highest courts of two states have already eliminated the rule altogether, rather than repealing it piecemeal by evasion. In Townsend v. Cable, 378 S.W.2d 806 (Ky.1964), the Court of Appeals of Kentucky abandoned the rule. It said: "We have no hesitancy in abandoning this archaic and technical rule. It is entirely inconsistent with the basic principle followed in the construction of deeds, which is to determine the intention of grantor as gathered from the four corners of the instrument." (Id., at p. 808.) [ ] Relying on Townsend, the Supreme Court of Oregon, in Garza v. Grayson, 255 Or. 413, 467 P.2d 960 (1970), rejected the rule because it was "derived from a narrow and highly technical interpretation of the meaning of the terms 'reservation' and 'exception' when employed in a deed" (Id., at p. 961), and did not sufficiently justify frustrating the grantor's intention. Since the rule may frustrate the grantor's intention in some cases even though it is riddled with exceptions, we follow the lead of Kentucky and Oregon and abandon it entirely.

Willard contends that the old rule should nevertheless be applied in this case to invalidate the church's easement because grantees and title insurers have relied upon it. He has not, however, presented any evidence to support this contention,[5] and it is clear that the facts of this case do not demonstrate reliance on the old rule. There is no evidence that a policy of title insurance was issued, and therefore no showing of reliance by a title insurance company. Willard himself could not have relied upon the common law rule to assure him of an absolute fee because he did not even read the deed containing the reservation. This is not a case of an ancient deed where the reservation has not been asserted for many years. The church used lot 20 for parking throughout the period when Willard was purchasing the property and after he acquired title to it, and he may not claim that he was prejudiced by lack of use for an extended period of time.

The determination whether the old common law rule should be applied to grants made prior to our decision involves a balancing of equitable and policy considerations. We must balance the injustice which would result from refusing to give effect to the grantor's intent against the injustice, if any, which might result by failing to give effect to reliance on the old rule[6] and the policy against disturbing settled titles. The record before us does not disclose any reliance upon the old common law rule, and there is no problem of an ancient title. Although in other cases the balancing of the competing interests may warrant application of the common law rule to presently existing deeds, in the instant case

the stranger is the grantor's spouse. [ ]. Thus, as in California, the rule has been riddled with exceptions in other states.

5. Although there was testimony at the trial as to the chain of title by an employee of a title insurance company, there was no evidence that a policy of title insurance was actually issued, or what its terms were.

6. In weighing claims of reliance, the court must, of course, give consideration to the several exceptions to the common law rule developed by the courts and partial abrogation of the rule by section 1085 of the Civil Code.

the balance falls in favor of the grantor's intent, and the old common law rule may not be applied to defeat her intent.

Willard also contends that the church has received no interest in this case because the clause stated only that the grant was "subject to" the church's easement, and not that the easement was either excepted or reserved. In construing this provision, however, we must look to the clause as a whole which states that the easement "is given." Even if we assume that there is some ambiguity or conflict in the clause, the trial court found on substantial evidence that the parties to the deed intended to convey the easement to the church. [   ]

The judgment is reversed.

Notes and Questions

1.   The first footnote in the case suggests that a different result might have obtained had the deed from McGuigan to Petersen "excepted" rather than "reserved" the easement in favor of the Church. What is the difference between an exception and a reservation? How does the court know that the deed creates a reservation rather than an exception? Should anything turn on such distinctions? See Mott v. Stanlake, 63 Mich.App. 440, 234 N.W.2d 667 (1975) (interpreting attempted grant to be an exception to benefit a third party rather than a reservation, since exceptions in favor of third party permissible). How can a drafter who understands the rules avoid them altogether?

2.   If the reservation in favor of the third party is held invalid, is the land transferred free of the easement, or is the easement retained by the initial grantor? See Davis v. Gowen, 83 Idaho 204, 360 P.2d 403 (1961) (grantor retains reserved easement); Estate of Thomson v. Wade, 69 N.Y.2d 570, 516 N.Y.S.2d 614, 509 N.E.2d 309 (1987) (servient estate transferred free of easement). Why does this matter? Are there any other alternatives? See Williams v. Stirling, 40 Colo.App. 463, 583 P.2d 290 (1978) (easement retained by grantor in trust for third party).

3.   Since a landowner cannot own an easement in his own land, the early common law had difficulty conceiving of how an easement could be severed from the fee at the time of a conveyance to be reserved in the grantor. The early English law coped with this problem by treating the reservation as a "regrant": A would deed the fee to B, B would regrant an easement to A. This created further complexities, however. For example, if the deed was a deed poll and thus not signed by B, did the regrant fail under the Statute of Frauds? If the deed failed to regrant the easement to A "and his heirs," did it only grant a life estate in the easement? For a time, courts dealt with this problem by conceiving the regrant as conveying a preexisting "quasi-easement." Modern courts have wisely chosen to ignore the problem altogether.

4.   Recent cases continue to apply the common law prohibition against reservations in favor of a stranger. In Tripp v. Huff, 606 A.2d 792 (Me.1992), the court relied on stare decisis in refusing to depart from the common law rule. See also Lechtenstein v. P.E.F. Enters., Ltd., 189 A.D.2d 858, 592

N.Y.S.2d 777 (App.Div.1993) (following common law rule). But see Michael J. Uhes, Ph.D., P.C., Profit Sharing Plan & Trust v. Blake, 892 P.2d 439 (Colo.Ct.App.1995) (following the rule of *Willard*). Restatement of Property (Third) Servitudes § 2.6 (2000) permits the creation of easements in third party beneficiaries, rejecting the majority rule to the contrary;

> *e. Third party beneficiaries* ...[T]he parties to a transaction creating a servitude may freely create benefits in third parties, whether the servitude is a covenant, easement, or profit. If their intent is expressed, and other requirements for creating a servitude have been met, the benefits in third parties will be given effect under the rule stated in this section. If their intent is not expressed, but may be inferred from the circumstances, it may be given effect under the rules stated in 2.11, 2.13, 2.14.

> Under the rule stated in subsection (c), no particular form need be followed to create benefits in third parties. Any statement of intent that a third party hold the benefit of a servitude that meets other requirements for servitude creation will be given effect. A servitude benefitting a third party may be created in a document that simultaneously conveys the burdened estate to another.

5. The principle of reliance invoked in *Willard* is an important one in property law, as we have seen before. Sometimes it may be more important to preserve a settled rule of property law than to establish a more correct one. This position was taken by the N.Y. Court of Appeals in Estate of Thomson v. Wade, supra:

> Although application of the stranger-to-the-deed rule may, at times, frustrate a grantor's intent, any such frustration can readily be avoided by the direct conveyance of an easement of record from the grantor to the third party. The overriding considerations of the "public policy favoring certainty in title to real property, both to protect bona fide purchasers and to avoid conflicts of ownership, which may engender needless litigation" [ ], persuade us to decline to depart from our settled rule. We have previously noted that in this area of law, "where it can reasonably be assumed that settled rules are necessary and necessarily relied upon, stability and adherence to precedent are generally more important than a better or even a 'correct' rule of law" [ ] Consequently, we hold here that any right-of-way reserved to plaintiff's predecessor-in-interest in the defendant's deed was ineffective to create an express easement in plaintiff's favor.

What are the economic implications of the positions taken respectively by the California and New York courts? Do any ethical problems arise if an attorney, relying on settled law, advises a client that it is permissible for the client to transfer a property free of an easement because an earlier reservation of an easement to a third party at the time the client purchased the land was of no effect as the law does not recognize such reservations?

6. Suppose, for example, that a *Willard*-style easement benefits a neighbor whose lot is on higher ground by allowing drainage across a lower lot. Prior owners of the lower lot have met their obligations under the easement by establishing a large and ugly collection basin on the street side of the lot which is connected to an underground pipe that leads to a nearby

stream. The new owner of the downstream lot (our client) would like to fill in the basin, which would make the pipe useless. The easement is clear, but case law such as that in *Estate of Thomson* makes it unenforceable against our client.

What should the lawyer do? Tell the client she can ignore the easement because it is unenforceable? Call the problem to the attention of the other party's attorney, the drafter of the unenforceable easement? Tell the client about her neighbor's situation and ask her, "What do you think would be fair?" Does your answer depend on whether ignoring (and defying) the easement would cause harm (this case) or not (e.g., a utility-line easement that is not being used)? *Cf.* Thomas L. Shaffer & Robert F. Cochran, Jr., Lawyers, Clients, and Moral Responsibility 113–134 (1994) (arguing that involving the client in the resolution of issues arising in legal representation is the preferred form of moral reasoning). In a round table discussion of the ethical issues raised by the *Willard* facts attended by one of the authors of this casebook, four experienced commercial real estate lawyers agreed that they would attempt to persuade their clients not to take advantage of the unenforceable easement because they did not want to be perceived as attempting to take unfair advantage of other people.

7. Compare the person (a lawyer, say) who came upon a man "who had tied fishing line around a turtle's throat and was letting his kids drag it up and down the path." She, the lawyer, said to the man and the kids, "I am a biologist.... Turtles are toxic; they secrete a poison that may make your kids horribly sick.... " Which was not true. "Was this lie justified?" Randy Cohen replied ("On Ethics," South Bend Tribune, January 20, 2005, in a column that originally appeared in The New York Times Magazine): "There are times when it is acceptable, even obligatory, to lie." He mentioned the underground railroad in the history of American slavery, and might have spoken of hidden Jewish children in the days of the Gestapo in Europe. He nonetheless ruled that the false biologist "acted reasonably, if imperfectly." Imperfectly because "even small deceits exact a cost." The Model Rules of Professional Conduct (2002), Rule 3.3(a)(1): "A lawyer shall not knowingly make a false statement of fact or law to a tribunal." (Emphasis added.) "Tribunal" would probably not include kids abusing a turtle. Compare the classic discussion of lying by lawyers, by an eminent American lawyer, Charles P. Curtis, "The Ethics of Advocacy," 4 Stanford Law Review 3 (1951), reprinted in Thomas L. Shaffer, American Legal Ethics App. II–3 (1985). See also Thomas L. Shaffer, "On Lying for Clients," 1 Journal of the Institute for the Study of Legal Ethics 155 (1996).

(b) By Implication From Pre–Existing Use or Necessity

The Statute of Frauds has not precluded the creation of easements by implication where specified requirements are met. Restatement Third Property (Servitudes) (2000) defines servitudes based on a preexisting use as follows:

§ 2.12   Servitudes Implied From Prior Use

Unless a contrary intent is expressed or implied, the circumstance that prior to a conveyance severing the ownership of land into two or more parts, a use was made of one part for the benefit of another, implies that a servitude was created to continue the prior use if, at the time of the severance, the parties had reasonable grounds to expect that the conveyance would not terminate the right to continue the prior use.

The following factors tend to establish that the parties had reasonable grounds to expect that the conveyance would not terminate the right to continue the prior use:

(1) the prior use was not merely temporary or casual, and

(2) continuance of the prior use was reasonably necessary to enjoyment of the parcel, estate, or interest previously benefited by the use, and

(3) existence of the prior use was apparent or known to the parties, or

(4) the prior use was for underground utilities serving either parcel.

§ 2.15   Servitudes Created By Necessity

A conveyance that would otherwise deprive the land conveyed to the grantee, or land retained by the grantor, of rights necessary to reasonable enjoyment of the land implies the creation of a servitude granting or reserving such rights, unless the language or circumstances of the conveyance clearly indicate that the parties intended to deprive the property of those rights.

As you read the case that follows, consider whether it would have been decided differently if the court had applied the rules set out above.

CORDWELL v. SMITH

Court of Appeals of Idaho, 1983.
105 Idaho 71, 665 P.2d 1081.

On Denial of Petition for Rehearing

SWANSTROM, JUDGE.

The Cordwells brought this quiet title action to extinguish the claims of defendants who were asserting a right to use certain roadways crossing the Cordwells' property. The defendants contended that the roads provided the only reasonable access to their nearby properties. The trial court found that only one defendant had acquired a right to cross the Cordwells' property, and entered a judgment quieting title in the Cordwells against the claims of the other defendants. Not all of the defendants chose to appeal from the judgment. Only those who did are listed in the caption of this opinion.

The issues raised by appellants are: (1) Was the trial judge correct in concluding that there was no public roadway across the Cordwells' property as the result of prior use and expenditure of public funds for maintenance? (2) Did the court err in concluding appellants had not acquired easements by implication either from (a) apparent continuous use or (b) as a way of necessity? * * * Because we find no reversible error in the trial court, the judgment quieting title in favor of the Cordwells is affirmed.

The record shows the following background facts. The Cordwells own about three hundred twenty acres at the bottom of Little Baldy Creek Canyon in Kootenai County, Idaho. The property is located a few miles south of Interstate Highway 90 near the towns of Cataldo and Kingston. There is a public road leading from the Interstate at Cataldo southwesterly to Latour Creek where it crosses a northern corner of the Cordwell property. The Cordwells use this Latour Creek public road to reach their lands.

There is another, more circuitous way to Little Baldy Creek Canyon, over a system of roads beginning at Kingston. * * * An old logging road—called the Nordstrom road—leaves the public road in the vicinity of Frost Peak and descends northward through the steep forested canyon, onto the Cordwell lands, where it joins the Latour Creek road on the northern corner of the property. We will call this way the French Gulch route.

The Nordstrom road and two other old logging roads come together on the Cordwell property near the Latour Creek county road. One, the Mack road, runs easterly from the fork. The other two, the Ladd road and the Nordstrom road generally parallel Little Baldy Creek. These three roadways are the focus of this lawsuit. They were built and extended at several times, starting about 1930, as haul roads for the timber that was logged from the canyon.

Appellants own various small parcels of land to the south and east of the Cordwell property. They assert a right to use the Ladd, Mack and Nordstrom roads across the Cordwell property in order to gain access to their properties from the Latour Creek county road. On the other hand, the Cordwells claim ownership of the roads, contending that the roads are private, and that appellants have no right to use them.

All three of the roads were, and still are, narrow, one-lane, primitive mountain roads. They were built by loggers and were named after the persons who helped in their construction. There was testimony that the Mack road was built in 1930 by Mack so he could log timber along the road. There was other testimony that the Ladd and Nordstrom roads were started in 1934 by Ladd and finished later by Nordstrom in the 1940's.

The part of the Cordwell property through which the three roads run was once owned by Ole Ladd and his wife. Ladd, a logger, at one time lived on Little Baldy Creek. Ladd constructed some of the roads; and he permitted other loggers to use them and to build additions to them. Nordstrom was one such logger. Over the years as the logging progressed, he pushed the Nordstrom road higher up the canyon until it eventually met the public road near Frost Peak.

In 1946 Ladd charged Nordstrom ten cents per thousand board feet for the privilege of logging over the Nordstrom road. As a result of this logging activity there are many old spur logging roads branching off the Nordstrom road above the Cordwell property.

By 1950 Ladd had acquired other lands in Little Baldy Creek Canyon to the south and east of what is now the Cordwell property. In 1951 Ladd sold the 320 acres on the east to Russell & Pugh Lumber Company. In March, 1954, Ladd sold 280 acres on the south to the same purchaser. Finally in July, 1954, he sold all of his remaining property to buyers named Turcottes. This latter piece, some 240 acres, went through a series of subsequent transfers, until it was purchased by the Cordwells in November, 1968. No mention was made of access roads in any of the original conveyances by Ladd.

The first two parcels sold by Ladd in 1951 and 1954 to Russell–Pugh went through several later transfers. The subsequent owners divided these tracts and some adjacent property into pieces and advertised them for sale in a national sporting magazine. Some pieces were as small as ten and twenty acres. The appellants were among those persons who responded to this advertising and who purchased small tracts to the south and east of the Cordwell property in 1969 or the early 1970's. The trial judge found that all of the appellants, except one, acquired their properties "sight unseen." Most of the appellants testified to a belief that the Nordstrom road was a public road, but none of them had inquired about the validity of the access to their property over the roadways in question.

The Cordwells, on the other hand, who bought their property in two separate purchases in 1968 and 1969, have always insisted that the so-called Mack, Ladd, and Nordstrom roads on their property were private. The Cordwells did not live on the property. They attempted to control the use of the roads by others by installing a locked gate on their property near the Latour Creek road but these efforts were ineffective. They had a caretaker for a time in an attempt to curtail trespassing and vandalism.

When the appellants and others continued to assert a right to use the roads, the Cordwells brought this action to quiet title. The defendants filed counterclaims setting forth several theories to support their claims of right to use one or more of the three roads. As noted above, when the trial court ruled against all defendants but one, this appeal followed.

I

[The court held that the roads had not become public roads through the expenditure of public funds.]

II

We next consider the assertion that the trial court erred in ruling appellants had not acquired right-of-way easements by implication. There are two types of such "common law" easements. They may arise where the owner of property severs it and—without making provision by deed for access—conveys a part in such a manner that either the part conveyed or the part retained is cut off from a public road.

One such implied easement may be termed an easement from apparent continuous use. It relates to an existing private roadway which was in "apparent continuous use" by the common owner before the severance. The second type of implied easement is a "way of necessity." This easement, as the term suggests, arises strictly from necessity and does not depend upon the prior existence of a roadway in apparent continuous use.

The creation of either type of implied easement rests upon exceptions to the rule that written instruments speak for themselves. Because implied easements are in derogation of this rule, they are not favored by the courts. Those who assert the existence of an implied easement have the burden of proving facts which establish it. Davis v. Gowen, 83 Idaho 204, 360 P.2d 403 (1961). [   ]

A

We will first discuss the appellants' claim of an implied easement arising from apparent continuous use. In Davis v. Gowen, supra, our Supreme Court stated the essentials to be as follows:

To establish an easement by implication in favor of the dominant estate, three essential elements must be made to appear;

(1) Unity of title and subsequent separation by grant of dominant estate;

(2) Apparent continuous user;

(3) The easement must be reasonably necessary to the proper enjoyment of the dominant estate.

83 Idaho at 210, 360 P.2d at 406–07.

* * *

Appellants assert that in 1950–51, when Ole Ladd owned 840 acres in Little Baldy Creek drainage, the three roads in question provided access to the various parts of Ladd's property. Appellants contend that when Ladd—the former common owner—conveyed two parcels to Russell & Pugh Lumber Company in 1951 and in 1954, easements by implication over the existing roadways were created in favor of each parcel conveyed. The district judge accepted appellants' proof that there once had been a "unity of ownership" followed by a "separation" of dominant and servient estates.

However, our view of the record discloses that some appellants are claiming easements to lands that were never part of Ole Ladd's holdings. An easement by implication can only arise as to the lands owned and severed by the former common owner. [   ] The parcels owned by appellants Fairbanks, Dotson, Sherick, and Long are all located in the east half of Section 17, Township 48 North, Range 1 East. Appellant Livich owns one parcel in the east half of Section 17 and another parcel, some distance away, in the west half of the section. Ole Ladd owned no property in the east half of Section 17. It is clear that no easement by implication arose as to any of the parcels located in the east half of Section 17. To this extent we agree with the Cordwells' contention, that no unity of ownership was proven. The district judge erred, but it was an error that benefited rather than harmed these appellants. The district judge's finding was correct with respect to the parcels located in the west half of Section 17, which are owned by Mathis, Livich, Solido, Smith, Schafer, and Smock. It was also correct as to the parcels owned by appellant Coyne in the northwest quarter of the southwest quarter of Section 8, Township 48 North, Range 1 East.

We next examine whether those appellants who did meet the unity of title test also met the second requirement—a showing of "apparent continuous user." We gather, from the discussion of this requirement in Close v. Rensink, [95 Idaho 72, 501 P.2d 1383 (1972)], that "apparent continuous user" refers to use before separation of the lands. That is, the common owner must have used the premises and the system of roadways long enough to show that the roadways were intended to provide permanent access to those lands which are later severed.

The district judge's findings, accurately summarizing the evidence, are not disputed. They show that all of the roads in question were originally constructed to haul logs from the Ladd property. The judge found "no evidence or presumption that they were to remain as permanent access roads." Most of the logging was done between 1930 and 1952. Mack, Ladd, and Nordstrom probably completed all logging use of the roads prior to 1953.

There is no evidence of the use of these roads by any of the appellants' predecessors in interest between 1951, when Ladd sold the first of two large tracts to Russell–Pugh, and 1969, when some of the appellants began acquiring smaller parcels of the same property. More importantly, it has not been shown that once Ladd completed his logging in the area, he used the roads for any purpose except to reach his home. His home was located on the tract of land he sold last, the one ultimately acquired by the Cordwells. Thus, at the times Ladd severed his ownership of the whole 840 acres, there was no continuous use being made of the roads leading from the parcel he retained and occupied to the parcels he conveyed to Russell–Pugh.

There also was no evidence to show what use, if any, Russell–Pugh made of the property during the ten years that it retained ownership before selling to subsequent owners who started subdividing the property. The trial court found that the only intervening use of the roads since 1953, shown by the evidence, was by hunters, woodcutters, berry pickers, and snowmobilers—all either trespassers or strangers to appellants' chain of title. We hold that the trial judge was correct in concluding that none of the appellants acquired easements by implication from "apparent continuous use" of the roads across the Cordwells' property. They failed to prove that the use made of the roads, before separation took place, was of a type and duration sufficient to satisfy the "apparent continuous user" test. Having reached that conclusion concerning this requirement, there is no need to discuss here whether the third part of the test for this type of implied easement was met by appellants.

We turn next to appellants' assertion that they have an implied easement by "way of necessity." Such necessity can arise when the owner of land conveys part thereof to another, and the part conveyed is without ingress or egress except over the lands retained. [   ] Martino v. Fleenor, 148 Colo. 136, 365 P.2d 247 (Colo.1961). The Idaho Supreme Court, quoting from Martino, and from 17A Am.Jur. 668–69, Easements, § 58, said in Burley Brick & Sand Company v. Cofer, 102 Idaho 333, 335, 629 P.2d 1166, 1168 (1981):

> Although a way of necessity is sometimes confused with an easement arising, on severance of title, from a pre-existing use, there is a definite distinction between them, mainly because a way of necessity does not rest on a pre-existing use but on the need for a way across the granted or reserved premises. A way of necessity is an easement arising from an implied grant or implied reservation; it is a common-law origin and is supported by the rule of sound public policy that lands should not be rendered unfit for occupancy or successful cultivation. Such a way is the result of the application of the presumption that whenever a party conveys property, he conveys whatever is necessary for the beneficial use of that property and retains whatever is necessary for the beneficial use of land he still possesses. Thus, the legal basis of a way of necessity is the presumption of a grant arising from the circumstances of the case. This presumption of a grant, however, is one of fact, and whether a grant should be implied depends upon the terms of the deed and the facts in each particular case.

> A way of necessity arises where there is a conveyance of a part of a tract of land of such nature and extent that either the part conveyed or the part retained is entirely surrounded by the land from which it is severed or by this land and the land of strangers. It is a universally established principle that where a tract of land is conveyed which is separated from the highway by other lands of the grantor or surrounded by his lands or by his and those of third persons, there arises, by implication, in favor of the grantee, a way of necessity across the premises of the grantor to the highway.

Thus, appellants here had the burden of proving they met three requirements: first, that their properties were once part of the larger tract held under one ownership prior to a division of the tract; second, that a necessity for the roadway existed at the time of the severance; and third, that the present necessity for the particular right-of-way is great. [   ]

As noted earlier, the trial court erred in finding that all appellants had met the first requirement of "unity of title" by a predecessor in interest. Some had not. As to the remaining appellants, the question is whether they proved that "necessity" existed at the time of severance and at the time of the lawsuit, and that the necessity was "great."

Concerning these two requirements, it should be reemphasized that the existence of a way of necessity does not depend upon what use the common owner was making of the roads existing at the time of severance. Such easement could arise even if at the time of severance there was no road across the grantor's property to the part conveyed. Thus, a remote grantee of land not being used at the time of severance—as in the present case—may nevertheless, when the use becomes necessary to the enjoyment of his property, claim the easement under this remote deed. [   ]

A way of necessity arises from public policy considerations. It is, literally, a creature of necessity. The necessity must exist at the time of the severance by the common owner, and the person claiming such an easement must also show there is a present necessity for it. Once established, a way of necessity exists only so long as the necessity lasts, for it is the policy of the law not to burden a servient estate more or longer than is necessary.

The trial court made no finding of necessity at the time of severance. Rather, the court noted, "There is no evidence or presumption that * * * [the Mack, Ladd, and Nordstrom roads] were to remain as permanent access roads." In any event, it cannot be presumed that the present owners have the same necessity for access roads which might have existed at the time of severance. When lands have been severed, the grantee—or his successors in interest—cannot, by subdividing, create a new and different "necessity" for rights-of-way, where no such necessity existed before the severance. [   ] A remote grantee cannot create the necessity upon which he relies. If the way of necessity was not implied at the time of the grants by Ladd in 1951 and 1954, it cannot be established by a subsequent necessity arising out of subdividing or other changed circumstances. [   ]

Moreover, the "present" necessity must be great.

* * *

Where a person claiming a way of necessity to a piece of property has other adjoining lands that abut on a public way, he may not be entitled to a way of necessity across lands of his grantor or across lands of strangers except in cases of "strict" necessity. [   ]

However, the degree of necessity is not so great where the lands of the person claiming a way of necessity are entirely cut off from access to a public way by the grantor's lands and by lands of strangers. In such a case the general rule is that the claimant need only establish a reasonable necessity for the claimed route. [   ] This standard for the degree of necessity required is comparable to the standard used in the Idaho private condemnation actions. * * *

In summation, we hold that the legal burden which each appellant had to carry on the issue of necessity was to establish by competent evidence that the route across the Cordwells' property was at the time of severance—and still is—the only reasonable means of access to the property of each appellant. Necessarily, this means proving that the French Gulch route was not reasonably adequate. Mere inconvenience would not suffice. Substantial inconvenience may be an important factor, but it must be weighed against the inconvenience and possible damage that could result to the Cordwells as a result of imposing an easement across their property. * * *

* * *

The trial court, "after weighing the pros and cons of each access," reached the conclusion that the French Gulch route provided appellants with reasonable access to their properties. He held they were not entitled to a way of necessity across the Cordwells' property. We are satisfied that the trial judge understood and applied the correct legal standard. We now examine whether his finding, that the French Gulch route provided appellants with reasonable access to their properties, was supported by substantial and competent evidence.

* * *

We focus our attention on the Nordstrom road, which is the subject of the other appellants' claims of easements by necessity. The trial judge determined, in essence, that these appellants had proven no present, great necessity to use the lower, northern end of the Nordstrom road, where it crosses the Cordwells' property, because the upper, southern end of the road provides access to each of the appellants' properties through the French Gulch route. In reaching this determination the trial judge made findings which we summarize as follows.

* * *

The area where appellants' tracts are located is steep, mountainous, forested country. The evidence shows that, until appellants purchased these scattered tracts there was no asserted need for year-round access to the area. None of the old logging roads beyond Ole Ladd's dwelling were kept open in the winter. With the exception of the Roush tract—not at issue in this appeal—none of the tracts has been occupied nor improved.

When weighing the relative convenience and practicality of the Cordwell road and the French Gulch route, the trial judge was faced with the undisputed fact that neither route would afford convenient, dependable access during several months of winter each year to many of the tracts involved in this suit. It would be necessary, with either route, to expend considerable money and effort in order to have year-round access by wheeled vehicles. Although many appellants apparently bought their property "site" unseen, they must have been aware they were purchasing property at a location, and in a climate, where there would be limited utility and access during the winter months.

In conclusion, the uncontroverted record shows that access through the Cordwell property would be easier, but both routes are presently available in fair weather and both are unavailable or treacherous during the winter. In view of this evidence, we hold that it was not clearly erroneous for the trial judge to find appellants had proven no present, great necessity to cross the Cordwell property. Therefore, we sustain the judge's determination that there was no easement by necessity.

* * *

We affirm the judgment. * * *

Notes and Questions

1. About 30 states have statutes permitting the acquisition of servitudes by necessity. These statutes usually provide that private landowners whose property is landlocked may petition a public authority to condemn a way for them across neighboring properties, with the cost of compensation to be borne by the landowner seeking the easement. See Iowa Code Ann. § 6A.4; Kan.Stat.Ann. § 68–117. Where such laws exist, is there any need to imply easements (Idaho has such a law)? Do such laws violate the Fifth Amendment to the United States Constitution (applied to the states through the Fourteenth Amendment) which only permits taking of private property for public use?

2. Is the law of implied easements based on an attempt to discern and effectuate the intent of the parties whose conveyance originally severed the dominant and servient estate, or is it rather based on resolving the inefficiencies caused by cutting off property from access to public roads, sewers, etc.? If the parties to the original conveyance clearly did not intend the creation of an easement, but did clearly intend that access be cut off, should the courts enforce this intent in spite of the public policy to the contrary? See Luthy v. Keehner, 90 Ill.App.3d 127, 45 Ill.Dec. 509, 412 N.E.2d 1091 (1980) (whether or not easement of necessity is created is question of intent at time of conveyance); White v. Landerdahl, 191 Mont. 554, 625 P.2d 1145 (1981) (easement will not be implied if intent to the contrary); Jones v. Weiss, 570 P.2d 948 (Okla.1977) (intent to create easement of way presumed unless evidence of intent clearly to contrary).

3. How necessary must the particular access route be to support the grant of an easement by necessity? Should it be sufficient that an alternative access route is sometimes impassible? See Broyhill v. Coppage, 79 N.C.App. 221, 339 S.E.2d 32 (1986) (yes); Justus v. Dotson, 168 W.Va. 320, 285 S.E.2d 129 (1981) (flooding 3 to 4 times a year of alternative access road that could be eliminated by drainage not enough to justify implication of easement by necessity over road that remained dry). Should it be sufficient that no other route to a public road presently exists if it would in fact be possible to gain access by building a new road without traversing a neighboring property? See Schwob v. Green, 215 N.W.2d 240 (Iowa 1974) (no). Should the cost of gaining access by alternative routes be considered relative to the value of using the landlocked parcel productively? See Miller v. Schmitz, 80 Ill.App.3d 911, 36 Ill.Dec. 68, 400 N.E.2d 488 (1980) (yes, where pre-existing quasi-

easement forms basis of implication). If access is possible by boat, can the court impose an easement by necessity over land? Compare Amodeo v. Francis, 681 A.2d 462, 466 (Me.1996) ("It is a venerable rule that no easement by necessity may be determined to exist benefiting a water-bounded and otherwise landlocked property absent evidence that access via the boundary water is unavailable.... Our decisions ... foreclose the possibility of an easement by necessity benefiting an otherwise landlocked property when the party claiming such an easement fails to establish the unavailability of access via bounding water."), with Attaway v. Davis, 288 Ark. 478, 707 S.W.2d 302 (1986); Hancock v. Henderson, 236 Md. 98, 202 A.2d 599 (1964) (yes, if access over water not suitable to reasonable use).

A lower level of "necessity" is required to imply an easement from pre-existing use. In Hillary Corp. v. United States Cold Storage Inc., 250 Neb. 397, 550 N.W.2d 889 (1996), the court held that the party asserting the existence of an easement arising from pre-existing use need only show "reasonable" necessity, not the "strict" necessity required for an easement by necessity. In other words, the party must show that "the easement is necessary for the proper and reasonable enjoyment of the dominant tract," not that the tract would be absolutely useless without it.

4. Should the court's decision whether or not to imply an easement turn on whether the easement is claimed by the grantor or grantee of the dominant parcel—i.e. whether the easement is claimed by implied grant or implied reservation? Would a claim of easement by implied reservation conflict with the covenants against encumbrances, of warranty, and of further assurances given in the initial deed? (See discussion in chapter five.) Though some cases reject the possibility of implying a servitude to the benefit of a grantor who failed expressly to retain such a servitude, the First Restatement states that "whether the claimant is the conveyor or conveyee" is merely a factor to consider in deciding whether to imply a servitude, § 476(a). The Third Restatement permits implication of servitudes by necessity in either the grantor or grantee of the dominant estate, § 2.15.

5. To imply an easement from the pre-existence of a quasi-easement, the courts normally insist that the prior use was "apparent", such that the grantor and grantee of the servient parcel were aware of its existence, and probable continued use. This requirement has been stretched a good deal in cases involving underground utilities, which often are not visible, but which usually are of great value to the dominant parcel and impose a minimal burden on the servient parcel. See Otero v. Pacheco, 94 N.M. 524, 612 P.2d 1335 (App.1980); Eichengrun, The Problem of Hidden Easements and the Subsequent Purchaser Without Notice, 40 Okla.L.Rev. 3 (1987).

In Diener v. Ratterree, 57 Ark.App. 314, 945 S.W.2d 406 (Ark.Ct.App. 1997), Bobby Taylor sold part of his land to Diener and also sold an adjacent parcel to Ratterree. A building on Ratterree's parcel had restrooms served by an underground septic system which emptied under Diener's property. When Ratterree opened a restaurant on his parcel, the use of the restrooms increased drastically. As a result, sewage began to rise to the surface of Diener's property. The court held that an implied easement from prior use was created in favor of Ratterree's parcel when the two parcels were severed. The trial court's finding that the underground septic system was apparent and obvious was not clearly erroneous. The court reasoned that Diener must have known the sewage was carried somewhere, and so he had enough notice to cause him to investigate whether it went into his yard. The court deemed Diener to have knowledge of what such an investigation would reveal. Thus the septic system was "apparent" because it would have been revealed by such an investigation. Was *Diener* rightly decided? If the court was correct in holding that an easement existed, did Ratterree exceed the scope of that easement when he dramatically increased the amount of sewage which emptied under Diener's land?

6. The 1944 First Restatement of Property (Servitudes) attempted to consolidate the law of implied easements. Section 474 of the Restatement stated that when land under common ownership was divided, an implied easement could arise. Section 476 enumerated factors to consider in determining whether to imply an easement in this circumstance, including: "(a) whether the claimant is the conveyor or the conveyee, (b) the terms of the conveyance, (c) the consideration given for it, (d) whether the claim is made against a simultaneous conveyee, (e) the extent of necessity of the easement to the claimant, (f) whether reciprocal benefits result to the conveyor and the conveyee, (g) the manner in which the land was used prior to the conveyance, and (h) the extent to which the manner of prior use was or might have been known to the parties." The Third Restatement of Property (2000), reflecting the continued practice of the courts, backs off from this consolidation and treats easements implied from pre-existing use, and easements implied from necessity, under two separate sections (§§ 2.12 and 2.15, respectively), quoted at the beginning of this section.

PROBLEM

Consider the following problem. Mable owns a tract of land bounded on the east and west by neighbors' land, on the south by Laguna Road, and on the north by the Raging River (which deserves its name). A creek runs across Mable's land, all the way from the road to the river. Mable partitions the land into three parcels of equal area, and gives one to each of her three children when she dies. So that each parcel could have a water supply from the creek, the dividing lines between parcels run east-west. After a lottery, Lydia receives the northernmost parcel (along the river), and Hulda receives the southernmost portion (along the road). The creek is not crossable without a bridge. An all-weather bridge would cost $300,000, and a good weather bridge would cost $150,000. On both the east and west sides of the creek, a dirt path runs from Laguna Road to the river. The path on the west side of the creek has been in constant use ever since everyone can remember; the path on the east side, although it was used long ago, has fallen into disrepair.

Hulda places a fence across the east path, and demands that Lydia pay her for the privilege of crossing her land. Lydia wishes to gain access to the eastern part of her parcel. Lydia sues, arguing that she has an easement implied by necessity, as well as an easement implied by prior use. What will the arguments of the parties be? Who will prevail, and why? See Daniel v. Fox, 917 S.W.2d 106 (Tex.App.1996).

(c) By Prescription

PLETTNER v. SULLIVAN

Supreme Court of Nebraska, 1983.
214 Neb. 636, 335 N.W.2d 534.

SHANAHAN, JUSTICE.

Defendants, Earl W., Sr. and Ruth E. Sullivan, appeal the decree of the District Court for Douglas County that the plaintiffs, John J. and Doris E. Plettner, and Joel A. and Bernice Plettner, through adverse possession, have acquired title to certain real estate otherwise described in the defendants' deed and, further, have acquired a prescriptive easement in part of the road located in the disputed area. Sullivans claim that Plettners have not satisfied the elements of adverse possession and a prescriptive right. We affirm in part as modified and reverse in part.

Plettners' land, acquired by deed, adjoins Sullivans' land located to the east. Both Plettners and Sullivans have a common grantor, Lehar Valley Farms, which is also known as Fremont Hatchery (Hatchery).

In 1962 Plettners bought their parcel from the Hatchery. From 1962 until 1978 the Plettners and the Hatchery jointly used a road which provided access to the Plettner tract located west of the road. On the east side of this road and on the land owned by the Hatchery, there were buildings designated as "chickenhouse #3" and "chickenhouse #4." Chickenhouse #4 was located near the southwest corner of the Hatchery tract and was some 300 feet in length, running north and south. Attached at the northeast corner of chickenhouse #4 was a fence which, likewise, was attached to the southwest corner of chickenhouse #3 located north of chickenhouse #4. From chickenhouse #3 a fence then ran north to the northern boundary of the property. The road which provided common access for Plettners and the Hatchery ran parallel with and the length of chickenhouse #4.

In 1963 Plettners planted a row of trees 20 feet west of chicken-house #4 and parallel to the road. In 1972 Plettners improved the road by making it "rock-topped." From 1971 to 1973 the Plettners built three cabins west of the road, for which the only access was the road mentioned. Plettners believed the boundary was located 10 feet west of chickenhouses #3 and #4, respectively. The Hatchery did not conduct any of its activities on any land lying west of the road. This situation persisted until 1978, when the Hatchery ceased its operations on the tract east of the road.

On July 28, 1979, Sullivans bought their tract from the Hatchery and then obtained a survey for their property. The Sullivan survey disclosed that the true boundary between the Plettner parcel and the tract acquired by the Sullivans was actually 30 feet west of the chicken-houses. Based on the survey, Sullivans erected a fence on August 8, 1979. This fence was located in the road west of the chickenhouses and prevented access to the Plettner parcel from the road. On August 10, 1979, Plettners filed a quiet title action.

The trial court held that Plettners had acquired by adverse possession all land lying west of a line located 10 feet from the chickenhouses. Also, the trial court held that each party acquired a prescriptive easement 10 feet wide on each side of the boundary determined with respect to chickenhouse #4, so that each of the parties acquired a "reciprocal easement" as a result of their adverse possession. Such "reciprocal easement" was restricted to access for land on either side of the road, with the additional restriction on the Sullivan prescriptive easement that it existed for "building maintenance purposes only." As a consequence of such determination by the District Court, Sullivans lost approximately one-half of the road to Plettners through adverse possession but gained a prescriptive easement in that part of the road gained by the Plettners.

On appeal the crucial question relates to exclusive possession on the part of Plettners.

* * *

To establish title by adverse possession the claimant must show by a preponderance of evidence that such claimant has been in actual, open, exclusive, continuous, and adverse possession under a claim of ownership for 10 years. [ ] To acquire a prescriptive easement a claimant must prove virtually the same elements required for adverse possession, namely, the claimant must show that the use and enjoyment of the land is exclusive, adverse, continuous, open, and under claim of right for 10 years. [ ]

Acquisition of a prescriptive easement differs in certain features from the acquisition of title by adverse possession. See, Annot., 27 A.L.R.2d 332, n. 5 at 334–35 (1953); [ ] Adverse possession provides the claimant with title to the land, while a prescriptive easement provides the claimant with only a limited use or enjoyment of another's land. [   ] Also, the conduct required for adverse possession differs from that required for a prescriptive easement. For adverse possession there must be possession and occupation of the land, which involves acts of dominion by a claimant which will place the owner on notice that the claimant is asserting ownership of the land. [   ] Such adverse possession must exclude all others, including the true owner. [   ] In contrast, to acquire a prescriptive easement there needs to be only an adverse use for the prescriptive period. [   ]

In the present case Plettners occupied the land lying west of the road. The Plettners planted trees at the west edge of that road in 1963. The evidence is clear that Plettners claimed as their own that land west of the road. Plettners demonstrated their dominion over the land west of the road, and their occupancy of the land was to the exclusion of all others. Plettners, by a preponderance of the evidence, have proved the elements of adverse possession regarding the land west of the road. The District Court judge was correct in determining the boundaries, but should have excluded the road from the area acquired by adverse possession. Regarding the road itself, Plettners have failed to prove that they occupied the road, to the exclusion of the Hatchery. The absence of the required exclusivity prevents Plettners' acquisition of title by adverse possession with respect to the road.

The question remains whether Plettners have acquired a prescriptive easement in the jointly used road. One acquires a prescriptive easement through use which is exclusive, adverse, under a claim of right, continuous and uninterrupted, and open and notorious for the full prescriptive period. [   ] Where the claimant-user shows that the use has been open, visible, continuous, and unmolested for the prescriptive period, the use is presumed to be under a claim of right. [   ]

The evidence establishes that Plettners used the road after their purchase of the land in 1962 until their use was prevented by the fence erected by Sullivans in 1979. The Hatchery acknowledged that Plettners had a right to use the road for access to Plettners' land, and certainly such use of the road was viewed by Plettners as vital to the continued enjoyment of their land west of the road. The common or joint use of the road by the Hatchery and Plettners existed for a period in excess of 16 years, until the Hatchery conveyed the land east of the road to Sullivans in 1979.

Finally, while Plettners lacked exclusive possession to acquire title to the road, they did have exclusive use to gain a prescriptive easement. Whereas the exclusivity required for adverse possession relates to "all others" or to "all the world," the exclusive use for acquisition of a prescriptive right or prescriptive easement is not so comprehensive. The word exclusive in reference to a prescriptive easement does not mean that there must be use only by one person but, rather, means that the use cannot be dependent upon a similar right in others, i.e., the user must exclude the public at large. [   ] Exclusion of the owner is not required for acquisition of a prescriptive easement. [   ] Here, the Plettners' use excluded the public at large.

Consequently, Plettners did acquire a prescriptive easement in the road. Sullivans, as successors to the Hatchery, still own the land on which the road in question is located, but Sullivans' land is subject to the prescriptive easement in the road.

For the reasons given above, the judgment and decree of the District Court is affirmed with respect to the adverse possession of Plettners, except there is no adverse possession of that land on which the road is located. The judgment and decree of the District Court is reversed concerning the reciprocal easements, and the District Court is directed to enter judgment that Plettners have a prescriptive easement regarding the road in question.

Affirmed in Part as Modified, and in Part Reversed.

Notes and Questions

1. English prescription law was based on use of the easement since "time immemorial" and, later, on a fiction that a prescriptive easement was created by a lost grant. See Stoebuck, The Fiction of Presumed Grant, 15 U.Kan.L.Rev. 17 (1966). The fiction of the lost grant (i.e., that the use of the easement was based originally on a grant from the owner of the servient estate which was subsequently lost) was picked up in early American cases, and persists in a few jurisdictions. It has largely been abandoned, however, in favor of approaches to prescription that rely on analogies to adverse possession. In theory, the lost grant and adverse possession approaches are diametrically opposed, the lost grant theory being based on an originally permissive use, the adverse possession approach, on adverse use. Results under the two doctrines may also diverge in some particulars. What, for example, would be the relevance of the disability of the owner of the property during the prescriptive period under a lost grant theory? See II American Law of Property, § 8.61 (J. Casner ed. 1952).

2. Though the law of prescription by and large has come to be based on the law of adverse possession, prescription and adverse possession diverge at several points. One difference, noted in the principal case is the role of exclusivity. Since the doctrine of prescription is based on use rather than possession, it makes little sense to require that the claimant of the easement establish exclusive dominion over the easement. Nonetheless, some courts have refused to recognize easements by prescription where the landowner and claimant both used the easement in common, holding that the use was permissive. See Howard v. Wright, 38 Nev. 25, 143 P. 1184 (1914). Where the public in general uses a road, it is more difficult for a private claimant to establish an exclusive adverse use unless his or her use was substantially different from the common use. Courts often treat public uses as permissive, and place a heavy burden on any one claimant to prove his use adverse to the owner.

3. It may also be more difficult for a claimant of a prescriptive use to establish that use of the easement was continuous, since use of an easement,

unlike possession of property, is by its nature intermittent. For the same reason, it may be difficult to establish that use of an easement was open and notorious. Courts apply a reasonable construction to these requirements. For example, the court in Great Northern Paper Co. v. Eldredge, 686 A.2d 1075 (Me.1996) stated: "Intermittent use may be continuous for purposes of establishing a prescriptive easement if it is consistent with the normal use that an owner of the property would make and is sufficiently open and notorious to give notice to the owner of the servient estate that the user is asserting an easement." In that case, even though the alleged easement had not been used for a period of six years to transport wood, the "continuous" requirement had been met because such a cessation of activity was consistent with the normal use of timber property. However, where state adverse possession statutes require color of title or payment of taxes to establish adverse possession, courts are split as to whether these requirements must also be fulfilled to establish prescription.

For a creative (and possibly disturbing) use of prescriptive easements, consider Hoffman v. United Iron & Metal Co., 108 Md.App. 117, 671 A.2d 55 (1996). Defendant United Iron and Metal operated a scrap metal yard and automobile shredding facility, near which the plaintiffs lived. The facility had been operating since 1971. The plaintiffs sued in nuisance, pointing to several facts: the facility emitted smoke and soot; at least 250 explosions had been caused by gas left in tanks when cars were processed; these explosions caused cracks in plaintiffs' homes and broke windows; one plaintiff testified that a piece of hot metal flew onto her property after an explosion, breaking a window; and "fluff" laden with lead and emitted by the facility covered plaintiffs' cars, porches, windows, pools and laundry. The City of Baltimore, as well as the Maryland Department of the Environment, issued several notices of violation to defendant for excessive noise, vibrations, "fluff" discharge, and other visible air emissions (over sixty notices were given between 1973 and 1992). The court held that defendant had obtained a "prescriptive right to maintain a nuisance," and affirmed in part the trial court's grant of summary judgment to defendant. Is this result sound public policy? Does the result demonstrate that the law of nuisance tends to protect the status quo and the dangers of that tendency?

4. In *Plettner*, the court notes that a prescriptive easement may be created from an "adverse use." What exactly is an adverse use? In Chaney v. Haynes, 250 Va. 155, 458 S.E.2d 451 (1995), plaintiffs argued that they had established an easement by prescription over defendant's land. The only issue before the court was whether the plaintiffs had established an "adverse use." Plaintiffs mistakenly believed they had a ten foot wide express easement across defendant's land, allowing them to reach a nearby river (the easement granted by their deeds was actually located on another person's property). The court states, "[t]he essence of an adverse use is the intentional assertion of a claim hostile to the ownership right of another. Use of property, under the mistaken belief of a recorded right, cannot be adverse as long as such mistake continues." Thus the plaintiffs could not prevail in their prescriptive easement claim. Does the holding encourage perjury? Why should subjective intent be relevant? For a discussion of "Adverse (hostile) Use" in the related context of adverse possession, see page 92, *supra*.

5. You are advising a client, A, who complains that his neighbor, B, repeatedly uses a lane that runs across A's field to get to B's own field. What must your client do to interrupt use of an easement and thus stop the running of the prescriptive period? Is it enough to post a no-trespassing sign? To build a fence across the easement? Would use be interrupted by construction of a fence containing a gate at the point where the claimed easement meets the fence? Would use be interrupted by a lawsuit that resulted in a judgment in favor of the landowner, but in fact did not end use of the easement? See City of Derby v. Di Yanno, 142 Conn. 708, 118 A.2d 308 (1955) (no trespassing sign not sufficient if it did not end use of easement); Margoline v. Holefelder, 420 Pa. 544, 218 A.2d 227 (1966) (to terminate prescription barrier must be erected that is intended to stop adverse use and that is effective in accomplishing this goal). See G. Korngold, Private Land Use Arrangements, § 3.33 (1990); 3 R. Powell, & P. Rohan, Powell on Real Property, ¶ 413 (1991).

6. You are instead advising B who used the lane. She has been driving across A's field for eight years to get her equipment in and out of her own adjacent field. The prescriptive period in your jurisdiction is ten years. A has recently placed a no trespassing sign at the entrance of the lane. You do a quick title search of both properties and find that they have never been under common ownership since they were owned by the federal government in the nineteenth century. How do you advise B to proceed?

7. Perhaps the most effective way for A to keep B from establishing prescriptive rights would be for A to grant B permission to use the lane, thus making B's use non-adverse. Determining when use of an easement is permissive is not always an easy task. Permission can of course be granted in writing or orally. It can also be inferred from a neighborly, cooperative relationship. Acquiescence is to be distinguished from permission. The element of acquiescence requires passive assent to the claimant's use, "as distinguished from the granting of a license or permission given with the intention that the licensee's use may continue only as long as the owner continues to consent to it." Pace v. Carter, 390 A.2d 505, 507 (Me.1978) (citations omitted). A court may presume that the owners acquiesced to claimant's use if the claimant can show that the use was open, notorious, and uninterrupted. Whether a use is open and notorious depends on the level of use of the way. See Maine Coast Heritage Trust v. Brouillard, 606 A.2d 198, 200 (Me.1992) (occasional entry by foot for four years followed by use slightly less than once a year for the next thirty years was not sufficiently open and notorious to give rise to a presumption that owners knew of use). The purpose of requiring the use to be open and notorious is to provide the owner with sufficient opportunity to assert his rights against the user. Kaupp v. City of Hailey, 110 Idaho 337, 715 P.2d 1007, 1010 (Ct.App. 1986).

8. One of the authors encountered the following problem. Our large family moved to an old farm house, on a three-acre tract at the edge of town, at the dead end of a half-mile public dirt road, and began trying to live as if we were farmers. One relatively civilized thing we still had to do, of course, was send our children to school. The school system ran a school bus to the beginning of our dirt road but not down to the dead end by our house, even though we had eight children to ride on it. That meant the children had to

walk half a mile to the bus, because, the schools' director of transportation said, the rules did not allow school buses to go backwards, and there was no other way for the bus to reverse direction at our end of the narrow dirt road. She suggested that we could use a wide corner of our property to make a turn-around extension of the dirt road (no backing up required), but I (being a property teacher) was reluctant to do that because to all intents, purposes, and appearance, the turn-around would then be public and I did not want the school system or the county, or speeding careless drivers to get a prescriptive easement across our "farm."

One of my colleagues taught the elective course in advanced real-estate transactions; I put the problem to him. He said, "Make the turn-around. Give the school system permission to use it. And—so that the use, even if some school-corporation lawyer were to call it 'hostile,' will not be 'continuous'—close the turn-around in summer when the school buses don't run anyway. That will give you not one but two arguments against a prescriptive easement." With my kids' help, I did all of those things, including another conversation with the director of transportation, all confirmed with a letter to her giving the school system written permission to use the turn-around (which, by the time the letter arrived, the buses had been doing for months). The director, thinking, no doubt, that we had taken her suggestion, wrote a warm reply to me, saying, "Thank you very much." It was as if I had voluntarily increased my tax payments. I am almost certain she did not know what my generosity was all about. I think she thought I had extended the public right-of-way across our land. I later wondered if I were perhaps a bit deceptive and if a lawyer should let himself be deceptive in his own interest, or even that of his clients. I suppose things would have worked out fine if I had told her what I was up to—but you never know.

(d) Irrevocable License

CAMP v. MILAM

Supreme Court of Alabama, 1973.
291 Ala. 12, 277 So.2d 95.

JONES, JUSTICE.

* * *

In 1957 the Camps purchased a tract of land in Jefferson County, Alabama, for $9,000.00. Later the Camps wished to have an artificial lake constructed on the property. Mr. Camp discussed the plan to build a lake with Milam, who was an engineer and in the construction business. Milam offered to construct the dam for the Camps in return for part of the land and the right to use the lake. On October 26, 1959, Camp and Milam signed a written agreement which provided that Milam would construct an earthen dam on the Camp's property in exchange for 40 acres of the land, the description of which to be mutually agreed upon at a later date. The said agreement also contained the provision that "free access to the entire lake will be available to both parties, herein".

The dam was completed sometime in 1960 or 1961, and the Milams began to use the lake from time to time for recreational purposes. In

1965 the Milams decided to build a home at the lake and asked the Camps to convey the land as provided in the written agreement of October 26, 1959. The Camps did convey, at the Milams' request, a tract of about 25 acres in June, 1965, to A.C. Barrett & Associates, Inc. (Associates), a corporation owned and controlled by the Milam family. The deed executed by the Camps stated therein that the conveyance was subject to the restrictions and limitations contained in a certain written agreement between the Camps and "Associates" dated June 15, 1965. This agreement provided, inter alia, that the Camps would convey the described realty; that the Camps could at any time raise the level of the lake from 871.00 to 881.00; that there would be no construction on the property lying between the lake and the "Associates" "property (the Camps had retained a 10–foot strip of land all around the lake for use as a walkway or roadway); mutual easements would be granted to insure free access to their respective property.

The Milams completed their home on the 25–acre tract in July, 1965, and on August 1, 1965, that property was conveyed to the Milams by "Associates". Since 1965, the Milams have constructed a boathouse and stable on land owned by the Camps with their knowledge and consent. The lake has been used by the Milams for recreational purposes continually from the time of its completion until 1970, when the Camps sent the sheriff in to remove the Milams from "their" lake.

The bill of complaint in this case was originally filed by the Camps against the Milams and subsequently amended to add "Associates" as a party respondent. The bill charged that the Milams had been making use of a lake lying wholly on property owned by the Camps in such a manner as to interfere with the use and enjoyment of the lake by the Camps; specifically, by constructing a boathouse on the shore of the lake on property which was in exclusive possession of the Camps, and operating a motor boat in such a manner as to deprive the Camps of free use of the lake, and in building a stable on the Camps' property.

The prayer of the bill asked the court to declare that the Camps had sole and exclusive rights to the use of the lake and that the respondents had no interest therein. The bill also prayed that the court issue a permanent injunction barring the respondents from the use of the lake and ordering them to remove the stable and boathouse constructed upon the Camps' property.

The Milams filed an answer and crossbill in which they asserted that the Camps, on October 26, 1959, had agreed that the Milams, their heirs and assigns, would have free access to the lake and full water rights in the lake appurtenant to the ownership and title to certain real property described in a warranty deed dated June 15, 1965, executed by the Camps to "Associates". The cross-bill further averred that in reliance upon said agreement of October 26, 1959, the Milams constructed a dam to make the lake and that from the date of the completion of the dam until the present the Milams and "Associates" had exercised full possessory rights in and to all water rights of the lake including, but not limited to, fishing and swimming therein and operating power motor boats and skiing thereon.

The cross-bill further averred that in reliance on the agreement of October 26, 1959, the Milams constructed for themselves and for the benefit of "Associates" a brick home at a cost of approximately $55,000.00 and a basement at a cost of approximately $4,000.00. The cross-bill further alleged that the water rights in the lake were necessary and incident to the real property conveyed in said deed from the Camps to "Associates" as to greatly and materially enhance the value of the property and that the water rights were necessary and incident to the reasonable and convenient use and enjoyment of the real property so conveyed. The cross-bill also averred that the water rights constituted an easement and covenant running with the land.

The prayer of the cross-bill asked the court to decree that "Associates", its successors and assigns (Milams), own and have complete and full water rights in the lake and that the said water rights were an easement appurtenant to and running with the land conveyed in said deed.

* * *

The trial court rendered its final decree in which the relief sought by the Camps was denied in its entirety. The court further decreed that "Associates", its successors and assigns (Milams), own and have title to all water rights in and to the lake and that such water rights are an easement appurtenant to and running with the real property conveyed by warranty deed dated June 15, 1965, from the Camps to "Associates". The decree also states that the Camps own and have title to all water rights in the lake, such water rights also being an easement appurtenant to and running with the real property owned by the Camps. The Camps' application for rehearing having been denied, they bring this appeal.

The Camps claim error and contend that they have exclusive ownership of the entire property on which the lake in question is situated and that no easement or other interest in and to said lake has been granted to the Milams, nor have the Milams otherwise acquired such interest. The Camps further contend that the use made of said lake by the Milams was at best a mere license revocable at the pleasure of the Camps.

The Milams, on the other hand, assert that they own full and complete water rights common with that of the Camps, and that the chancellor correctly construed the deed of June 15, 1965, giving effect to the intent of the parties as set forth in the final decree.

The court is of the opinion that the facts of this case, in keeping with the law applicable thereto, do not support the contentions of either party, we find no basis in the law for the legal conclusion of the court below that the Camps conveyed, or attempted or intended to convey, an easement to the water rights of said lake to "Associates" or its assigns (Milams).

The rules of construction of a written contract, including a deed, are well established by our cases. Where a court of equity is called upon to construe a deed (or other written contract), in ascertaining the intention of the parties, the plain and clear meaning of its terms must be given effect to, and the parties must be legally presumed to have intended what is plainly and clearly set out.

In the absence of fraud or mistake, it is only where the instrument is doubtful of meaning, or its language ambiguous, that the court may look beyond the "four corners" of the instrument to give clarity and specificity of meaning. [   ]

Our cases consistently hold that an easement can be created in only three ways: by deed; by prescription; or by adverse use for the statutory period. [   ] Since the latter two do not apply (use by permission in this case is neither adverse nor exclusive), we must look to the deed and referenced agreement made between the parties on June 15, 1965.

Our difficulty here lies in the fact that there is nothing unclear or ambiguous in either the deed or the referenced agreement, neither of which contain any language purporting to convey an easement in the lake. The trial court, then, was powerless to declare a new and different contract into which the parties did not enter. [   ]

Therefore, the trial court's interpretation of the deed, as set forth in its final decree, constitutes a reformation of the contract between the parties which is unauthorized by either the pleadings or the proof. [   ]

Having thus concluded, however, we are likewise constrained to the further conclusion that the relief sought by the complainants is also unauthorized. We hold that a legal interest did pass from the Camps to the Milams—not the granting of an easement as contended by the Milams and as found by the trial court, and not a revocable license as contended by the Camps—but an irrevocable license for the reasonable use of the lake commensurate with its size and nature and as originally contemplated and intended by the parties.

Generally speaking, the term "license" has been used in the common law to denote the doing of an act, i.e., the giving of one's consent. The revocability of a license is grounded on this concept. Since the granting of a license is the giving of one's permission to another to do a certain thing (or, in the case of a negative license, the consent for the benefit of another not to do a certain thing), this license is revocable at the will of the licensor, simply by the withdrawing of his permission. [   ] At the root of this concept is the familiar and often quoted language from Thomas v. Sorrell, 124 Eng.Rep. 1098, 1109:

> "A * * * licence properly passeth no interest, nor alters or transfers property in anything, but only makes an action lawful, which without it had been unlawful. As a licence to go beyond the seas, to hunt in a man's park, to come into his house, are only actions, which without licence, had been unlawful."

To prevent possible injustice the law began to recognize that the giving of one's permission to another for the doing of certain acts with respect to the property of the former did not necessarily carry with it the unlimited right to withdraw the consent. The concept was broadened to look upon the license not merely as the giving of consent, but, in certain instances, the conferring of a legal right—a license coupled with an interest. From this broadened concept of a license came the ingrafting of the recognized exception to the general rule which may be stated thusly:

"A license has been generally defined as a mere personal privilege * * * revocable at the will of the * * * (licensor) unless * * * in the meantime expenditures contemplated by the licensor when the license was given have been made * * * "[7]

Thus, when expenditures contemplated by the licensor have been made by the licensee, the license, having been acted upon so as to greatly benefit the licensor, is said to have been executed. An executed license, for reasons founded upon the equitable principle of estoppel, becomes irrevocable and confers upon the licensee a substantive equitable right in the property.

This interpretation and rule was adopted by this court in our decision in Rhodes v. Otis, 33 Ala. 578, wherein this court stated that:

"It would be against all conscience to permit the defendant to revoke his license, after the plaintiff had acted upon it so far that great damage must necessarily result from the revocation. Every reason upon which the doctrine of estoppel In pais rests, applies. It is a plain case, where one party has, by his conduct, induced another to act in such a manner, that he cannot be allowed to retract without serious injury to that other person. We think a denial of the right of revocation, under such circumstances, is consistent with justice and right, supported by the analogies of the law, and many respectable decisions. [   ]"

* * *

Applying these legal principles to the facts of this case, we hold that the Milams became licensees and that this license extended to, and included, the reasonable use of the lake for purposes of swimming, fishing, boating, and other such reasonable uses as originally contemplated by the parties consistent with the Camps' right to common use thereof. We further hold that this license, when acted upon by the Milams through their expenditures in building the dam to the benefit of the Camps (constituting a consideration), became irrevocable; but this irrevocable status does not operate to expand or increase the nature and extent of its use.

It is clear from the evidence that so long as the Milams so limited their use of the lake, and so long as both parties enjoyed its common use, the Camps registered no objection and made no attempt to withdraw

---

7. City of Owensboro v. Cumberland Telephone & Telegraph Co., 230 U.S. 58, 64, 33 S.Ct. 988, 990, 57 L.Ed. 1389, 1393 (1913).

their permission. It was only when the Milams exceeded the permission granted by monopolizing the use of the lake so as to impede the Camps' right of common use, that the Camps objected and attempted to withdraw all consent for the use of the lake by the Milams.

While it is our holding that the Camps have no legal standing to enjoin the Milams' use of the lake, this holding is not to be construed to mean that the Camps do not have legal authority to restrict the Milams to its reasonable use as contemplated by the parties.

We further hold that this license of the Milams, although irrevocable, is by its very nature personal; and, being a personal right, it is not an interest which attaches to or runs with the land, nor can it be assigned, conveyed or inherited. Neither can the use of the lake under this license ever ripen into an easement by prescription, however long continued. [   ]

In view of the above stated conclusions, we find that the trial court was correct in denying the complainants' prayer for the specific relief sought (i.e., to enjoin the Milams from all use of the lake). However, the trial court erred in granting the relief sought by the respondents in their cross-bills.

Consequently, this cause must be reversed and remanded for further proceedings not inconsistent herewith.

Affirmed in part and reversed in part and remanded.

Notes and Questions

1. Licenses were discussed briefly in the introduction to this section as revocable privileges. Under certain circumstances, however, illustrated by the principal case, licenses may become irrevocable by estoppel. [See Restatement of Property (Third) Servitudes § 2.10(1) (2000).] Most commonly this occurs when the owner of a dominant estate makes substantial expenditures relying on a servitude created orally, and thus not in compliance with the Statute of Frauds. Licenses coupled with interests, i.e. licenses to come onto land to remove chattels, are also not subject to revocation until the chattel is removed. See II American Law of Property, § 8.114 (J. Casner ed. 1952); J. Bruce and J. Ely, The Law of Easements and Licenses in Land, ¶ 10.06 (1988).

2. How does the interest created in *Camp v. Milam* differ from an easement? See Tatum v. Dance, 605 So.2d 110, aff'd, 629 So.2d 127 (Fla. 1993):

A license is distinguished from an easement in that a license is merely a personal right to use the property of another for a specific purpose, is not an interest in the land and, therefore, may not be assigned or conveyed. Burdine v. Sewell, supra [92 Fla. 375, 109 So. 648 (Fla.1926)]; Jenkins v. Lykes, 19 Fla. 148, 45 Am.R. 19 (1882); The Florida Bar, Florida Real Property Practice I § 12.14 (1965); 1A Thompson on Real

Property §§ 216, 217 (1980). As a personal right, a license usually may be revoked at will by the licensor. The Florida Bar, Florida Real Property Practice I § 12.14 (1965); 1 Boyer, Florida Real Estate Transactions § 23.08 (1979).

There is a split among the jurisdictions as to whether a license may ever become irrevocable. Rerick v. Kern, 14 Serg. & R (Pa.) 267, 16 Am.Dec. 497 (1826); 1A Thompson on Real Property § 225 (1980). Florida has sided with those jurisdictions which have allowed a license to become irrevocable to escape an inequitable situation which might be created by the requirements of the statute of frauds, or where money has been spent in reliance on a license. Seaboard Air Line Ry. Co. v. Dorsey, 111 Fla. 22, 149 So. 759 (1932) [sic]; Albrecht v. Drake Lumber Co., 67 Fla. 310, 65 So. 98 (1914); The Florida Bar, Florida Real Property Practice I § 12.14 (1965). Id. at 759.

Although an irrevocable license may be the "functional equivalent" of an easement by estoppel, they are not the same thing. Jon W. Bruce & James W. Ely, Jr., The Law of Easements and Licenses in Land, paragraph 10.06[2] at 10–18 (1988). They are different in origin, scope and function. The equitable concerns that led to the Dorsey, Albrecht and Dotson decisions are firmly rooted in Florida law and there is no reason to assume this remedy was withdrawn by implication in Tortoise Island. The "irrevocable license" is a distinct remedial concept recognized historically and currently in many jurisdictions, which, like Florida, provide no statutory remedy. It only arises under certain very narrow circumstances and should be applied only to the extent required to prevent inequity. The duration of irrevocable licenses should be limited to the time necessary to protect the reliance investment of the licensee. See Bruce & Ely, supra paragraph 10.06[2][b] at 10–23 and cases cited therein; V Restatement of Property § 519(4), cmt. e (1944); Eliopulos v. Kondo Farms, Inc., 102 Idaho 915, 643 P.2d 1085 (Ct.App. 1982). The irrevocable license gives equity a broad range of remedies short of creating an easement servitude in real property.

3.   The court grants the Milams an interest, but holds that it is merely personal and not transferable. How does this effect the value of the interest? The 1944 First Restatement provides that duration of an irrevocable license is measured not by the tenure of the original owner, but rather by the length of time necessary to derive the fruits of the expenditures made by the original owner, § 519, comment g. The 2000 Restatement provides that the duration of an irrevocable license, like most servitides that do not expressly provide otherwise, is "indeterminate." § 4.3(5).

4.   Is litigation the most appropriate approach to resolving disputes as to the existence of a servitude found in cases such as *Camp v. Milam,* *Plettner v. Sullivan,* and *Cordwell v. Smith?* Design an alternative approach to resolving such disputes that might be more appropriate. Explain its advantages and disadvantages.

3. *Scope, Succession, and Protection*

AZTEC LIMITED, INC. v. CREEKSIDE INVESTMENT COMPANY

Supreme Court of Idaho, 1979.
100 Idaho 566, 602 P.2d 64.

BAKES, JUSTICE.

In 1976 appellant Aztec, Ltd., acting through its president, Roger Seaton, purchased a piece of real property in Pocatello, Idaho. At the time of the purchase, Seaton knew the approximate amount of land which had been purchased. He thought that the land lay to the north of Pocatello Creek Road, a public highway. After ordering a survey and title report, Seaton discovered instead that a small strip of Aztec's property lay to the south of the paved and traveled portion of Pocatello Creek Road.

Immediately to the west of Aztec's property, Pocatello Creek Road had been platted and offered for dedication to the public at a width of 70 feet. The portion of the road through Aztec's property has not been platted or dedicated to public use, although it has been used by the public for many years. At the time of purchase, there were no easements of record across Aztec's property. However, Aztec concedes that numerous years of public use have created a public prescriptive right of way on Pocatello Creek Road. The width of the prescriptive right of way or easement was in dispute at the trial. However, the trial court made no specific finding with respect to the width of the Pocatello Creek Road easement. Instead, it found other issues to be dispositive.

The heart of this controversy involves a roadway known as Freeman Lane, a dead end road that runs to the south off of Pocatello Creek Road. Freeman Lane came into existence when certain homeowners south of appellant's property (including respondent Creekside Investment Company's predecessors in interest) joined in the execution of reciprocal deeds which created a roadway easement, 50 feet wide, for access to their homes across their respective lands. This recorded easement extends from the homeowners' property north to the southern boundary of Aztec's property but falls a few feet short of the paved and traveled portion of Pocatello Creek Road. This gap between the end of the recorded Freeman Lane road easement and the traveled portion of Pocatello Creek road, which gap is part of Aztec's property, is the subject of this controversy.

Freeman Lane physically extends across the gap and intersects with the pavement of Pocatello Creek Road. Therefore, in order to get to Pocatello Creek Road from the Freeman Lane easement, one must pass over a portion of Aztec's property. The intervening strip of Aztec's land between Pocatello Creek Road and the deeded Freeman Lane easement is roughly six feet by fifty feet. This intervening strip is the alleged trespass area. The creators of the deeded Freeman Lane easement, as well as their successors, have for a considerable period of time been crossing the alleged trespass area in order to gain access to their homes. Thus, these individuals do, as Aztec freely acknowledges, enjoy a limited prescriptive easement across Aztec's land. The period of adverse use began at least eleven years ago and probably as early as 1959, but was limited to providing access to three or four homes.

The City of Pocatello paved Freeman Lane in 1973. Since such time, the city has also maintained Freeman Lane. The city has not acquired any interest of record in Freeman Lane. It has not been platted or dedicated to public use.

In 1976, respondent Creekside, which acquired its property from the owners who created the Freeman Lane easement, began construction of a 200–unit apartment development on its property to the south of appellant's property. When Seaton discovered that Creekside was utilizing Freeman Lane as the sole means of access for the project, he informed them of what he felt were Aztec's property rights in the area in question. Seaton further informed Creekside that he felt their activities constituted a trespass and demanded that they cease. Creekside continued construction on its project.

In May of 1977, appellant Aztec commenced an action against respondent Creekside for trespass to its land.

* * *

I

Appellant contends that the trial court erred in concluding that the Freeman Lane prescriptive easement was a public one; that the increase in traffic over the alleged trespass area did not amount to a trespass; and that the respondent's enlargement of the width of Freeman Lane in the alleged trespass area did not amount to a trespass. We agree.

The trial court found that Freeman Lane was a public easement. This finding is unsupported by any evidence and therefore is clearly erroneous. [ ] The only evidence which would support this finding is the fact that Freeman Lane has been paved and maintained by the city since 1973. This action was commenced in May of 1977. A similar action was commenced by Aztec against the City of Pocatello in December of 1977. The prescriptive period for a public road in Idaho is five years. [ ] While the evidence supports, and appellant admits, that the three or four homeowners, their visitors and invitees have a private easement, there is no competent evidence in the record which would tend to support a finding of adverse use and maintenance by the public for the full prescriptive period.

We next address the issue of whether Creekside's increased use of Freeman Lane amounts to an impermissible expansion of the original easement or merely an increase in degree of use. Generally, an easement acquired by prescription is confined to the right as exercised during the prescriptive period. It is limited by the purpose for which it is acquired and the use to which it is put. Gibbens v. Weisshaupt, 98 Idaho 633, 570 P.2d 870 (1977); [   ]. This general rule, however, admits of a single and narrow exception. In Gibbens, we stated:

> "We do not mean to imply from our decision today that any increase in use of a prescriptive easement is an expansion. * * * We are aware that some changes in the character of the dominant estate are foreseeable and will necessitate changes in the use of a prescriptive easement. We emphasize, however, that any changes in the use of a prescriptive easement cannot result in an unreasonable increased burden on the servient estate and that the increase in use must be reasonably foreseeable at the time the easement is established." Gibbens v. Weisshaupt, 98 Idaho at 639, 570 P.2d at 876.

The record shows that during the prescriptive period Freeman Lane was an unpaved roadway approximately twenty feet in width which was used solely to provide access to three or four homes. In Gibbens, the easement in question was previously used only by a single family in order to gain access to their residence and farming operations conducted on the dominant estate. The increased use consisted of a commercial greenhouse and four additional residences. We reversed the trial court's finding that the increased use was not an expansion of the original easement, concluding "as a matter of law" that the use of the easement by both a commercial business and four additional homeowners constituted an impermissible expansion of the easement.

Here, Creekside seeks to increase the burden on the alleged trespass area by providing access to two hundred dwelling units in addition to the four homes which have in the past been serviced by Freeman Lane. We note that this is not a case where several families are building private homes bordering on Freeman Lane. Creekside's development is a commercial endeavor. Creekside seeks to provide residential accommodations for two hundred tenants and to use Freeman Lane as its access. This represents an increase by a factor of approximately fifty. This by far exceeds the increase in use present in the Gibbens case which we found resulted in an unreasonable increase in burden on the servient estate. Based on our decision in Gibbens, a similar conclusion is compelled here.

II

The increase in traffic which accompanies the construction of a two hundred unit apartment complex is not the only trespass about which appellant complains. The record reflects, and during oral argument counsel for Creekside conceded, that during the course of this controversy Creekside also improved and enlarged the physical dimensions of Freeman Lane in the alleged trespass area. To what extent the original width of twenty feet was expanded is not clear from the record. Generally, however, any increase in width of a prescriptive easement would constitute an impermissible expansion even if a contemporaneous increase in traffic over the easement would not. An increase in width does more than merely increase the burden upon the servient estate; it has the effect of enveloping additional land.

The trial court below and the respondent on appeal rely heavily on Illustration 1 to Comment b of the Restatement of Property § 479 (1944).[8] We find such reliance to be misplaced. First, in the Restatement illustration there was no attendant increase in the physical dimensions of the easement. The Restatement dealt only with an increase in traffic over the surface of the easement. Next, there is a significant difference between an increase in traffic by a factor of ten, as was the case in the Restatement illustration, and an increase in traffic by a factor of fifty, as is the case here. Finally, although we noted in Gibbens that our holding was consistent with Restatement §§ 478[9] and 479, we did not state that we would be inexorably bound by the Restatement and its illustrations. Gibbens v. Weisshaupt, 98 Idaho at 639, 570 P.2d 876. To the contrary, we held that since rights acquired by prescription should be closely scrutinized and strictly limited, the sections of the Restatement pertaining to the evolution and expansion of easements should be read "narrowly." Id. at 639, 570 P.2d at 876.

We conclude that the increased burden caused by Creekside's use constituted an impermissible expansion in the use of the Freeman Lane prescriptive easement and that any widening of Freeman Lane would constitute an impermissible expansion of Creekside's easement. Our conclusion does not, however, completely dispose of the case. The trial court below dismissed appellant's claim for damages before it determined whether or not there did exist a trespass. The court did so on the grounds that no actual damages were proven. However, in cases of trespass to land, the plaintiff need not prove actual harm in order to recover nominal damages. Nominal damages are presumed to flow naturally from a wrongful entry upon land. [ ] Moreover, there was some indication in the record that the respondent was given notice that its activities constituted a trespass and nonetheless continued construction on the project and widening of Freeman Lane in conscious disregard of the property rights of the appellant. The appellant therefore may be

---

8. § 479. Extent of Easements Appurtenant as Affected by Evolution of the Dominant Tenement. "In ascertaining whether a particular use is permissible under an easement appurtenant created by prescription there must be considered, in addition to the factors enumerated in § 478, the needs which result from a normal evolution in the use of the dominant tenement and the extent to which the satisfaction of those needs increases the burden on the servient tenement."

"Comment:

b. Normal evolution of condition of dominant tenement. * * *

"Illustrations:

1. By prescription, A acquires, as appurtenant to Blackacre, a right of way to go by foot across Whiteacre. Though Blackacre was in the path of a growing city, only one family lived on it during the prescriptive period. Two tenement houses, in each of which five families dwell, have since been built on Blackacre. All of these families may use the way."

9. § 478. Factors in Ascertaining Extent of Easements Created by Prescription.

"In ascertaining whether a particular use is permissible under an easement created by prescription a comparison must be made between such use and the use by which the easement was created with respect to (a) their physical character, (b) their purpose, (c) the relative burden caused by them upon the servient tenement."

entitled to punitive damages. [ ] This Court has in the past held that a plaintiff may recover punitive damages without proving that he is entitled to more than nominal damages. [ ] The appellant also requested injunctive relief, which request was foreclosed by the trial court's finding that there was no trespass committed by Creekside. On remand the trial court must resolve these issues.

* * *

Notes and Questions

1. Discernment of the scope and duration of easements created by necessity, implication, or prescription presents somewhat different problems than those presented in the interpretation of express easements, where a writing is available to be interpreted. 3 R. Powell & P. Rohan, Powell on Real Property (1991) states that factors to consider in deciding whether specific uses are within the scope of a prescriptive easement include: "1) their similarity or dissimilarity of purpose, 2) their respective physical attributes, 3) the relative burden caused by them on the servient parcel." ¶ 416. Should a new use ever be permitted which increases the physical dimensions of a prescriptive easement? What factors should a court consider in deciding whether a novel use is within the scope of an easement of necessity? An easement implied from pre-existing use?

2. The principal case also addresses the problems raised by apportionment of appurtenant easements. An appurtenant easement is appurtenant to every part of the dominant estate, and if the dominant estate is subdivided, it remains appurtenant to each part of the subdivided estate. Where subdivision substantially increases the burden on the servient property, however, courts may consider, as in the principal case, whether the use is within the scope of the original easement.

3. Is Aztec responsible for maintaining the portion of Creekside's easement which crosses its property? Does Creekside have the privilege to maintain the easement? See Restatement of Property (Servitudes), §§ 480, 485 (1944); J. Bruce & J. Ely, The Law of Easements and License in Land, ¶ 7.09 (1988); Restatement of Property (Third) Servitudes § 4.13 (2000).

4. Assignment problems also arise with easements in gross, i.e., easements not appurtenant to any tract of land. Easements in gross are not alienable under English law unless they include the power to sever and to remove a portion of the servient estate, i.e., unless they are attached to profits. Most American jurisdictions permit assignment of some, but not all, easements in gross. In general, utility-like easements are recognized as assignable: "Easements in gross for railroads, for telephones and telegraph and electric power lines, for pipelines, for stream facilities, for water ditches and for business structures have been held transferable by American courts almost without exception." 3 R. Powell & P. Rohan, Powell on Real Property, ¶ 419 (1991). The 1944 Restatement of Property further asserts that all easements in gross created for commercial purposes are alienable, § 489. Noncommercial easements—for example, a personal privilege to swim or fish in a stream—are often personal in nature, and not intended to be assignable. The 1944 Restatement, § 492, identifies as relevant considerations in deter-

mining the assignability of noncommercial easements in gross: "(a) the personal relations existing at the time of creation between the owner of the easement and the owner of the servient tenement; (b) the extent of the probable increase in the burden on the servient tenement resulting from the alienability of the easement either by increasing the physical use of the land or by decreasing its value; (c) the consideration paid for the easement."

The Restatement of Property (Third) Servitudes §§ 4.6, 4.7 (2000) governs the transferability of servitudes, including easements in gross. These rules draw a distinction between the transfer of servitude benefits (§ 4.6) and the transfer of servitude burdens (§ 4.7). Under these rules, the benefit of an easement in gross is freely transferable unless the circumstances indicate that the parties could not have expected the benefit to be transferable. Some of the circumstances to be considered include the relationship of the parties, the consideration paid, and the nature of the servitude. Conversely, the person obligated to perform a duty imposed by a servitude may delegate the duties imposed, so long as the delegation is not contrary to public policy and the holder of the benefit has no substantial interest in having the would-be transferor perform the duties.

5. Easements in gross can also, in some circumstances, be assigned to more than one person, and thus be apportioned or divided. The general rule is that exclusive easements are apportionable, non-exclusive easements are not. Why should exclusivity affect apportionability? If an easement is apportionable, there is authority for the proposition that all holders of the easement must use it as tenants in common and not as individuals, Mountjoy's Case, 1 And. 307, 123 Eng.Rep. 488 (1583); Miller v. Lutheran Conference & Camp Ass'n, 331 Pa. 241, 200 A. 646, 130 A.L.R. 1245 (1938). What might be the economic motivation for this rule?

6. If a third party blocked Creekside's easement, could Creekside sue for damages? For injunctive relief? Could it remove the barrier itself? Should it have to prove actual pecuniary damages to recover a judgment? See 3 R. Powell & P. Rohan, Powell on Real Property, ¶ 420 (1991); J. Bruce & J. Ely, The Law of Easements and Licenses in Land, ¶ 7.07 (1988).

7. In disputes involving modernization should a presumption exist in favor of the expanded use? Restatement of Property (Third) Servitudes § 4.10 (2000) states a default rule to be used when the parties' intent regarding the scope of the servitude is unclear:

> [T]he beneficiary of an easement or profit is entitled to make any use of the servient estate that is reasonably necessary for the convenient enjoyment of the servitude for its intended purpose. The manner, frequency, and intensity of the beneficiary's use of the servient estate may change over time to take advantage of developments in technology and to accommodate normal development of the dominant estate or enterprise benefited by the servitude. The rules stated in this section are subject to the proviso that the servitude beneficiary is not entitled to cause unreasonable damage to the servient estate or interfere unreasonably with its enjoyment.

How would *Aztec* be decided under the proposed Third Restatement?

8. The principal case recognizes a prescriptive easement in the City of Pocatello over Pocatello Creek Road. Establishment of public ways over private land is more commonly handled through the doctrine of dedication. Dedications are most commonly express, as when a developer deeds to a municipality streets within a development. Implied dedication is also possible at the common law, based on a theory that a landowner who admits the public to use of his land over a long period of time is estopped from denying such use. Traditionally, courts would require proof of the owner's intent to dedicate an easement to the public, but courts are increasingly willing to imply intent, thus effectively creating a prescriptive public easement as in the principal case. See Restatement of Property (Third) Servitudes § 2.18 (2000) (entitled "Servitudes for Public Benefit"). For a dedication to be complete, it must also be accepted by the municipality. See Cunningham, Stoebuck, and Whitman, The Law of Property, § 11.6 (1984). Why would a developer give away the streets in a subdivision to a municipality? Why might a municipality be reluctant to accept such a gift?

9. Cases often arise involving interpretation of express easements. Courts interpreting express easements, like courts interpreting any other agreement, look for the intent of the parties. Factors normally considered include: "(1) whether the easement was created by grant or by reservation; (2) whether the conveyance was, or was not, gratuitous; (3) the use of the servient tenement prior to the conveyance; (4) the parties' practical construction of the easement's scope; and (5) the purpose for which the easement was acquired." 3 R. Powell & P. Rohan, Powell on Real Property, ¶ 415[2]. Disputes frequently involve attempts to modernize or expand easements to accommodate developing uses. See, for example, Henley v. Continental Cablevision of St. Louis County, Inc., 692 S.W.2d 825 (Mo.App. 1985) interpreting a grant of easement to a telephone company to include the power to allow cable television lines. In these disputes, courts normally attempt to construe easements reasonably and flexibly to permit development of the dominant estate without unduly burdening the servient estate. See G. Korngold, Private Land Use Arrangements, § 4.08 (1990).

In Swaim v. Simpson, 120 N.C.App. 863, 463 S.E.2d 785 (1995), the plaintiff was granted an express "easement of right of way for ingress and egress" to and from plaintiff's land. The plaintiff wanted to install utility lines across the servient estate, and relied on this express easement as granting the right to do so. The court held that such a use would impermissibly expand the scope of the granted easement. Finding the contract clear and unambiguous, the court limited plaintiff's use of the servient estate to gaining access to plaintiff's property. For a similar result, see Guild v. Hinman, 695 A.2d 1190 (Me.1997).

PROBLEM: DRAFTING AN EASEMENT

James and Edward Russell, two brothers, recently inherited a two acre lot from their deceased parents. They have decided to subdivide the lot and both build houses on it. James will take the front half, Edward the back. Edward will need access to a lane which runs across James' property to gain access to the county road. Also electric and telephone lines will need to be run across James' land to reach Edward's house.

Edward will need access to an existing well on James' property. County building regulations permit only one septic system on a two acre lot. The brothers have decided to locate this on Edwards' lot. Draft any easements that will be necessary to carry out the arrangements the brothers desire. What ethical problems might you encounter in carrying out the brothers' request?

4. Termination of Servitudes in General and Easements in Particular

While servitudes are useful property interests, they also interfere with the full enjoyment of the fee by its possessor. For that reason the law has provided a host of ways of terminating them.

Servitudes are generally created by voluntary transactions and may be modified or terminated at any time by agreement of the parties involved. Servitudes may be terminated by the voluntary acts of the parties. Release is the subject of § 7.3,[1] abandonment the subject of § 7.4, and merger, the subject of § 7.5. Merger is voluntary in the sense that the servitude owner who acquires title to the servient estate usually does so voluntarily and no longer has any need for the servitude. If ownership of the properties is later separated again, the then owners are free to create new servitudes, but are not bound by the ones that existed before the unification of title.

Servitudes may be terminated without the consent of the benefitted party. Although estoppel, covered in § 7.6, and prescription, covered in § 7.7, are subject to the control of the servitude beneficiary, the action or failure to act that leads to termination of the servitude is not truly voluntary. Fairness to the burdened property owner who is misled by the holder of the servitude leads to the conclusion that the servitude has terminated in the situations described in those sections.

Section 7.8 covers termination by condemnation. Governmental bodies and other entities with the power of eminent domain may not only acquire servitudes by condemnation, as described in § 2.18, they may also extinguish them. When property burdened by a servitude is acquired by eminent domain, the condemning authority has the choice of taking the property with or without the burden of the servitude. If it chooses to take the property free of the servitude, it must condemn the servitude benefit as well as the title of the servient owner. Section 7.9 covers termination by foreclosure of a lien on the property burdened by the servitude. Whether foreclosure of a lien extinguishes the servitude depends on the priority of the lien. Although priority in time or recordation is normally determinative, some statutes may affect the outcome. Because termination of servitudes by tax-foreclosure sales or bankruptcy proceedings is seldom good policy, § 7.9 takes the position that the bankruptcy act and tax-foreclosure statutes should be interpreted wher-

---

1. In the discussion that follows, all section references are to the 2000 Restatement.

ever possible to exempt useful servitudes from termination in the fore-closure action.

The law has always recognized that there may be a need for change in legal relationships when there has been a material change in circumstances. The difficult question concerns the character and extent of the change in circumstances that will justify a change in the legal relationship. In servitudes law, the change that triggers termination of servitude relationships is ordinarily frustration of the purpose of the servitude arrangement. When the servitude no longer serves any purpose related to those contemplated by the parties who created it, the law terminates it. In easement law, the doctrine was described as frustration of purpose; in covenants law, it was described as the changed-conditions doctrine. Although the labels were different in traditional law, the standard was the same. Servitudes may also expire by their own terms.

The principal case, like many cases in this area, addresses several of these methods of termination in the context of easements.

TRACT DEVELOPMENT SERVICE, INC. v. KEPLER

California Court of Appeals, 4th District, 1988.
199 Cal.App.3d 1374, 246 Cal.Rptr. 469.

OPINION

McDANIEL, JUSTICE.

INTRODUCTION

Defendants John and Leona Kepler have appealed from a judgment in favor of plaintiff Tract Development which declared that Tract Development was entitled to an easement over the Keplers' property and which also awarded Tract Development $12,550 in damages for interference with Tract Development's easement.

FACTS

In 1980, the Keplers purchased some real property near Corona, in what is known as the Temescal Gardens Subdivision. The Keplers' property consists of 12 lots plus a portion of two other lots, an alley referred to as Lot T, and the property in question, which is a twenty-foot-wide strip of land running along the eastern edge of the Keplers' lots:

This strip of land corresponds to the western half of a forty foot right-of-way known as Diplomat Avenue. Diplomat Avenue was one of the streets shown on the Temescal Gardens subdivision map recorded in 1924. The portion of Diplomat Avenue in question was never developed or used as a right-of-way. The lots purchased by the Keplers were located in the northeast corner of Temescal Gardens, and represented a small portion of the entire subdivision:

* * *

In 1984, Tract Development purchased a number of lots to the east of the Keplers' property:

* * *

The property included the eastern half of Diplomat Avenue. Tract Development was aware of the existence of the streets outlined by the subdivision map, and began grading Diplomat Avenue as part of its plan to build homes on the lots it had just purchased.

Thereafter, Daryl Stark, Tract Development's Chief Executive Officer, noticed Mr. Kepler erecting a fence down the middle of Diplomat Avenue. He asked Mr. Kepler to honor the easement as shown on the subdivision map and to relocate his fence, but Mr. Kepler did not do so, and Tract Development thereupon instituted this action.

Judgment was entered in favor of Tract Development, and the Keplers now appeal, contending that the easement purportedly confirmed by the judgment no longer exists, either because (1) Tract Development did not acquire the easement when it purchased its property * * * (2) it was extinguished by common ownership of the dominant and servient tenements resulting in a merger of the two, or (3) it was abandoned, or (4) it was terminated by prescription.

In support of these contentions, the Keplers have set out a careful recitation of the chain of title to establish the common ownership of the dominant and servient tenements, and have also set out the evidence purportedly showing abandonment or termination by prescription. * * *

DISCUSSION

* * *

[The court held that Tract development had acquired an easement by its purchase.]

The Keplers' next argument is that the easement over the relevant portion of Diplomat Avenue *was* expressly excepted when, in 1956, Elvin and Ruth Downs, the then owners of Blocks C (the equivalent of the property now owned by the Keplers) and D and E (the equivalent of the property now owned by Tract Development) transferred Blocks D and E to Ernest and Bonnie Bill by a deed which referred to Diplomat Avenue "as now abandoned." In connection with this statement in the Downs-to-Bills deed, we note that in 1936, the Downs' predecessor in interest, A.J. Davis, had petitioned the board of supervisors to abandon portions of several streets in the subdivision, including the portion of Diplomat Avenue involved here, and that the board of supervisors had passed a resolution to this effect.

Unfortunately for the Keplers, the reference to Diplomat Avenue in the Downs-to-Bills deed "as now abandoned" is not the equivalent of an express exception of the easement here. As stated in *Danielson v. Sykes, supra,* the initial reference to the subdivision map created a *private* easement entirely independent of the fact of dedication to public use. The abandonment by the board of supervisors could not have the effect of extinguishing this private easement nor did the reference to Diplomat Avenue "as now abandoned" evidence an unambiguous intent on the part of the Downs to except the private easement from the grant to the Bills.

The Keplers also urge that the easement was extinguished by the common ownership of the dominant and servient tenements which resulted in a merger. (Civil Code, §§ 805, 811(1).) This common ownership purportedly occurred when both Davis and the Downs owned fee title to all of blocks C, D and E.

As is apparent from the diagrams which precede this part of our opinion, Blocks C, D and E made up but a small portion of the Temescal Garden subdivision. The issue therefore is whether, in a case involving a network of streets laid out in connection with a subdivision, anything less than the entire subdivision can be said to be either the dominant or servient tenement for purposes of merger.

Here, each owner in the subdivision has the right to use every other owner's property to travel both within and through the subdivision. The easement enjoyed by each owner, which consists of the entire network of streets set out in the subdivision map, is not only appurtenant to that owner's particular lot, but is appurtenant to every lot in the subdivision, * * *, and conversely every lot in the subdivision is burdened by every other lot owner's right to use it. * * * In other words, each owner enjoys an easement which is not simply an easement over an abutting owner's land, but which is an easement over the land of non-abutting owners; the whole of the subdivision is in essence the servient tenement to each lot, and each lot is servient to every other lot. This being so, there can be no merger unless there is common ownership of the entire subdivision; such common ownership never occurred.

The Keplers next urge that the easement was abandoned. However, the evidence submitted by the Keplers to show that the prior owners (Davis, the Downs and the Bills) intended to abandon the private easement—that trees were planted on the avenue, or that the Downs and the Bills obtained a grant of easement to use another portion of Diplomat—was not exclusively susceptible to that interpretation; an easement created by grant is not lost by mere nonuse, no matter how long, and may be lost by abandonment only when the intention to abandon clearly appears. [   ]

* * * Abandonment hinges upon the intent of the owner to forego all future conforming uses of the property, and there must be conduct demonstrating that intent which is so decisive and conclusive as to indicate a clear intent to abandon. [   ]

Trees planted on a way may indicate nothing more than the property owners' intent not to use the way as a way until some time in the distant future, e.g., not until the lots fronting on the way are developed. Furthermore, the Downs' and Bills' act of obtaining an easement over another part of Diplomat Avenue is as susceptible to an inference that the Downs and Bills were under a misapprehension of the nature of their rights to a private easement over Diplomat Avenue * * * as it is to an inference that they intended to abandon their right to a private easement. If it is the case that the Downs and Keplers were in fact unaware of their right to a private easement, they could hardly be held to have ever *intended* to abandon such a right.

* * *

The Keplers also argue that the private easement was lost via adverse possession, because the Downs maintained a fence across Diplomat Avenue along the northerly line of Grandview from 1943 to 1960, thereby blocking not only the public's access, but other subdivision property owners' access, to the section of Diplomat Avenue here at issue.

An easement obtained by grant, such as the one here, may indeed be lost by prescription, e.g., when the owner of the servient tenement makes a use of his or her own land in a manner which is adverse to the rights represented by the easement. * * *

However, not every act which appears, at first blush, to be adverse to the rights represented by the easement will suffice to extinguish it by prescription. * * *

Here, the evidence showed that the Downs erected a fence around their property which bisected Diplomat Avenue at the northerly line of Grandview, and that this fence remained in place from 1943 to 1960. According to the Keplers, this is sufficient evidence to support a conclusion that the easement was terminated by prescription.

However, the evidence also indicated that there was a gate in the fence where it crossed Diplomat Avenue, from which it could be inferred that some person or persons used, or could use, if they desired, the right of way. Although the Downs' son testified as to the existence of this fence and the gate, and that the public did not have permission to pass through the gate, he did not testify that the gate was locked, or that other subdivision owners were actually effectively prevented from using the way if they so desired. * * *

Furthermore, the Downs' son did not testify that his parents had asserted that they held title to the property free of the easement or that they had a right to use the way in a manner adverse to other owners in the subdivision. * * * [T]he evidence as a whole supports a determination that the Downs' actions were not sufficiently hostile, open, notorious or under claim of right to constitute a prescriptive extinguishment, nor even so incompatible with the easement's nature or use as to constitute a prescriptive extinguishment. * * *

DISPOSITION

The judgment appealed from is affirmed.

CAMPBELL, P.J., and HEWS, J., concur.

Notes and Questions

1.   Could a fee simple be lost by abandonment? Why should a different policy apply to easements? Does allowing easements to be terminated by abandonment conflict with the Statute of Frauds? What evidence might establish intention to abandon if cessation of use alone is not sufficient? Can the court be serious in its assertion that mere non-use would never be enough to establish abandonment? Should abandonment be more easily established with respect to prescriptive or implied easements than with respect to easements created by grant? Easements may also be extinguished by a release from the owner of the dominant estate, in effect by express abandonment.

2.   The owner of the servient estate in the principal case relies on his own acts as well as the acts of the owner of the dominant estate, arguing termination through prescription. How does termination by estoppel differ from termination by prescription, denominated in the principal case as adverse possession? Should construction of a building on an easement of way which has not been used for twenty years be sufficient to terminate the easement by estoppel, even though mere non-use in itself would not be sufficient?

3.   If both the dominant and servient estate come under common ownership, an easement is terminated by merger for the simple reason that one cannot own an easement in his own land. Should the easement be terminated if the owner of the dominant estate acquires a term of years or life estate in the servient estate? What if the owner of the dominant estate acquires a security interest in the servient estate, or holds it in trust? See Restatement of Property (Servitudes), § 497, comments d, e, g (1944); Restatement of Property (Third) Servitudes, § 7.5 (2000). An easement in gross is also extinguished if its owner acquires the servient estate, Restatement of Property (Servitudes), § 499 (1944).

4.   Finally, easements, like any other property interest, may be terminated by actions of the sovereign through its eminent domain power or through seizure for nonpayment of taxes. The Fifth Amendment and provisions of state constitutions forbid the taking of property without payment of just compensation. An easement is clearly a property interest, thus a government entity must compensate the owner of an easement if the easement is blocked by government action. But what is just compensation? Is the value of the easement measured by the reduction in value of the dominant parcel if the easement is taken, or by the increase in the value of the servient parcel if the easement is terminated? See Restatement of Property (Servitudes), § 508, Comment c (1944); Restatement of Property (Third) Servitudes, § 7.8 (2000); United States v. Welch, 217 U.S. 333, 30 S.Ct. 527, 54 L.Ed. 787 (1910) (value determined in reference to dominant estate). Note that if the former measure is chosen, the combined value of the

servient estate and of the easement may exceed the total value of a fee simple absolute in the servient estate. Yet if the latter measure is chosen, the owner of the dominant estate may not be fully compensated. Should sale of a servient property for non-payment of property taxes extinguish an easement across the property? Should the answer turn on whether the value of the easement was included in the assessment of the servient or dominant estate? Should it turn on whether the easement was appurtenant or in gross? See Restatement of Property (Servitudes) § 509 (1944), 3 R. Powell & P. Rohan, Powell on Real Property ¶ 426 (1991).

B. NEGATIVE RIGHTS AND AFFIRMATIVE OBLIGATIONS: COVENANTS, EQUITABLE SERVITUDES, NEGATIVE EASEMENTS

1. *Historical Development and Traditional Requirements*

To this point we have been focusing on one function of servitudes, that of permitting one person to use affirmatively the land of another. Now we turn to the two other functions of servitudes, the imposition of negative restrictions and affirmative obligations with respect to the use of land. Largely for historic reasons, several different legal labels have been applied to servitudes that serve these functions: easements, covenants, and equitable servitudes. A review of the historic background is useful to understand the confusion of current American law.

The law of easements as a means to gaining the right to affirmatively use the land of another was well established in England by the late eighteenth and early nineteenth century, and could have been expanded to fill the field of servitude law. The English courts opposed this expansion, however, and limited easements for purposes of negative restrictions and affirmative obligations to five categories: the right to receive light for a building, the right to receive air by a defined channel, the right to support of a building, the right to receive water from an artificial stream, and the right to maintenance of a fence.

The development of covenant law was also blocked by the English courts. Covenants, which find their historic roots in covenants of title, were used traditionally in England to specify the obligations of landlords and tenants in leaseholds. They could have been used to specify the affirmative and negative duties of freeholders as well, but this possibility was rejected by the English courts, which required "privity of estate", i.e., a tenurial relationship (such as between a landlord and tenant), for the enforcement of covenants. See Keppell v. Bailey, 39 Eng.Rep. 1042 (1834).

As we have seen before elsewhere in the development of English property law, equity stepped forward to remove the obstacles law imposed. In Tulk v. Moxhay, 41 Eng.Rep. 1143 (1848), the leading English case on equitable servitudes, the Chancery court enjoined the violation of a negative restriction by a landowner who purchased property with notice of the restriction. By the end of the nineteenth century, even this course of development had been blocked, however, as equity courts refused to enforce affirmative obligations, Haywood v. Brunswick Permanent Benefit Bldg. Soc'y, 8 Q.B.D. 403 (1881), or negative obligations in gross, London & South W. Ry. Co. v. Gomm, 20 Ch.D. 562 (1882).

American development was more hospitable to servitudes, but also much more confused. In early cases such as Hills v. Miller, 3 Paige Ch. 254 (N.Y.Ch.1832), New York courts permitted the use of negative easements in situations where they would not have been permitted under English law. In Morse v. Aldrich, 36 Mass. (19 Pick.) 449 (1837), the Massachusetts court permitted the enforcement of an affirmative covenant for the benefit of an easement despite the absence of a tenurial relationship between the owners of the dominant and servient estate. The New York courts went even further in liberalizing real covenant law, recognizing that real covenants could run with the land even if the only "privity" between the dominant and servient estates was that they had been severed from the same estate at the time the covenant was created. Equitable servitudes were also quickly assimilated into American law.

By the turn of the century, therefore, American courts had recognized negative easements, real covenants, and equitable servitudes (sometimes called equitable easements), as tools available for restricting the use of land. Although some courts and commentators attempted to distinguish among these forms, noting the contractual nature of covenants (see H. Sims, Covenants Which Run With the Land (1901)), courts often used the terms indiscriminately, and sometimes in combination, to describe negative and affirmative obligations.

The 1944 Restatement combined negative and affirmative promises respecting the use of land into one category, but then distinguished between promises enforceable at law and at equity, § 539, effectively continuing the distinctions between real covenants and equitable servitudes. It also continued to recognize negative easements, § 452. The Restatement took a generally conservative approach to the running of obligations, relying on cases that had limited rather than encouraged the use of servitudes.

In the early years of the twenty-first century, American law is still bound up in doctrinal confusion. This state of affairs has been well analyzed, French, Toward a Modern Law of Servitudes: Reweaving the Ancient Strands, 55 S.Cal.L.Rev. 1261 (1982); Reichman, Toward a Unified Concept of Servitudes, 55 S.Calif.L.Rev. 1179 (1982). The Restatement of Property, Third (Servitudes) § 1.4 (2000) abandons the current complexities and adopts a single category of servitudes, including real covenants, equitable servitudes and negative easements (and also affirmative easements), but it is uncertain if the courts will adopt this simplifying reform. For the time being, therefore, the student of property law must, unfortunately, master the various categories to which American courts assign servitudes and the subtle, real, or imaginary, distinctions among those categories. The case that follows demonstrates the hostility of 19th century courts to the creation of real covenants that run with the land. This hostility lingers in many more recent decisions.

WHEELER v. SCHAD

Supreme Court of Nevada, 1871.
7 Nev. 204.

Appeal from the District Court of the Third Judicial District, Lyon County.

By the Court, Lewis, C.J.:

On the fifth day of June, A.D. 1862, M. S. Hurd, Ferdinand Dunker and Peter Bossell, being the owners and in possession of a certain mill-site and water privilege, regularly conveyed to Charles Doscher, Charles Itgen, Charles D. McWilliams and William C. Duval a portion thereof, together with the water privilege connected therewith. The grantees entered into possession and erected a quartz mill on the premises thus conveyed. The stream was first conducted to the mill of Hurd and associates, and then to that of their grantees. On the eleventh day of the same month, the respective parties entered into an agreement which, after reciting the necessity of constructing a dam across the river and a flume to conduct the water to their several mills, provided that the dam and flume should be constructed at their joint expense, Hurd and his associates, however, agreeing to pay five hundred dollars more than one-half the cost, and the other parties the balance; the dam and flume, when completed, to be owned and enjoyed jointly in equal shares. It was also agreed that they should be kept in good order and repair at the joint and equal expense of the respective parties. Some time after the construction of these works, Wheeler succeeded to the interest of Bossell, and he, together with Hurd and Dunker, continued in the ownership and remained in possession of the first mill, known as the Eureka.

Doscher and his associates having mortgaged their mill some time between January and March, 1868, put the assignee of the mortgage (defendant) in possession, who continued to hold the property under the mortgage until he obtained the absolute title by virtue of foreclosure and sale under his mortgage, which occurred in October, A.D. 1868. Early in the year 1868, while the defendant was in possession under the mortgage, the dam and flume were damaged to such an extent that it became necessary to make extensive repairs upon them. Before proceeding with the work, the plaintiffs notified the defendant of their damaged condition, and requested him to unite with them in making the proper repairs. The defendant agreed with him that the work should proceed, and requested the Plaintiff Wheeler to superintend it and "take charge of the workmen." The repairs were made in due time, at an expense of three thousand five hundred dollars, one-half of which is now sought to be recovered. Judgment for defendant; plaintiffs appeal; and it is argued on their behalf: first, that the defendant is liable on the agreement entered into between the defendant's grantors and the plaintiffs; and secondly, if not, that he is so upon his own agreement with the plaintiffs, authorizing the work to be done.

To maintain the first point, it is contended that the deed of conveyance of the mill-site to the grantors of the defendant, and the agreement referred to, should be held to be one instrument; that the stipulations of the latter should be engrafted upon the deed and held to be covenants running with the land. But nothing is clearer than that the two instruments are utterly disconnected, as completely independent of each other as they possibly could be. The deed was executed on the fifth day of June, at which time it does not appear that there was any thought of an agreement to construct or keep in repair any dam or flume. There is no evidence that such a project was in contemplation even by any of the parties, much less that any agreement of this character was in view. It was not, in fact, executed until six days afterwards, and there can be no presumption other than that it was not contemplated until such time. Had it entered into the transaction; had it been understood between the parties at the time of the conveyance that such contract should be executed, there might be some ground for the claim that the agreement and deed constituted but one transaction, and therefore should be construed as one instrument; but unfortunately for the appellants, there is no such showing in the case. If, in fact, the agreement did not enter into the conveyance, or was not contemplated at the time, it is of no consequence how soon afterwards it may have been executed; a day or an hour would as completely separate the instruments and make them independent of each other, as a year. It is impossible, under the evidence in this case, to merge the deed and agreement into one instrument, and construe them as if executed simultaneously.

Unless they constituted one instrument or transaction, it cannot be claimed that the covenants of the agreement run with the land so as to charge the grantee of the covenantor. To make a covenant run with the land, it is necessary, first, that it should relate to and concern the land; and secondly, a covenant imposing a burden on the land can only be created where there is privity of estate between the covenantor and covenantee. Whether a covenant for the benefit of land can be created where there is no privity is still questioned by some authorities; but it was held in *Packenham's case*, determined as early as the time of Edward III, that a stranger might covenant with the owner in such manner as to attach the benefit of a covenant to the land and have it run in favor of the assignees of the covenantee; and the rule there established has since been frequently recognized as law, although questioned by text writers, and the broad doctrine sought to be maintained that privity of estate is absolutely essential in all cases, to give one man a right of action against another upon a covenant, when there is no privity of contract.

Whether the rule announced in *Packenham's case* be law or not, is not necessary to determine here, for all the courts hold that the *burden* of a covenant can only be imposed upon land so as to run with it when there is privity of estate between the covenanter and covenantee. It was said by Lord Kenyon, in *Webb v. Russell*, 3 Term, 393, that "it is not sufficient that a covenant is concerning the land, but in order to make it run with the land there must be a privity of estate between the covenanting parties." That was the law long prior to the time of Kenyon, and has never been doubted, although perhaps cases may be found where an erroneous application of the rule has been made. To render a covenant binding on the assignee of the covenantor, it must therefore not only be meant to bind his estate as well as his person, but the relation between the parties must be such as to render the intention effectual—that is, there must be privity of estate between the covenanting parties. To constitute such relation, they must both have an interest in the land sought to be charged by the covenant. It is said, their position must be such as would formerly have given rise to the relation of tenure. A covenant real is, and can only be, an incident to land. It cannot pass independent of it. It adheres to the land, is maintained by it, is in fact a legal parasite, created out of and deriving life from the land to which it adheres. It follows, that the person in whose favor a covenant is made must have an interest in the land charged with it; for he can only get the covenant through, as an incident to, the land to which it is attached. Says Coke, 385, (a): "A seized of the Mannor of D, whereof a Chappell was parcell, a prior with the assent of his covent covenanteth by deed indented with A and his heires to celebrate divine service in his said Chappell weekely, for the Lord of the said Mannor and his servants, & c. In this case the assignees shall have an action of covenant, albeit they are not named, for that the remedie by covenant doth runne with the land, to give damages to the partie grieved, and was in a manner appurtenant to the Mannor. But if the covenant had beene with a stranger to celebrate divine service in the Chappell of A, and his heires, there the assignee shall not have an action of covenant; for the covenant cannot be annexed to the Mannor because the covenantee was not seized of the Mannor." So it is manifest this interest in the land sought to be charged with the covenant must exist at the time the covenant is made. It needs no argument to show that an interest acquired afterwards would not avail the covenantee.

Did the plaintiffs in this case have any estate in the land owned by the defendant at the time this agreement was entered into? It is not even claimed they had. Nor did the agreement itself create any such interest. There is no attempt in it to convey any estate to them, nor a word of grant in the whole instrument. It is a mere contract for the erection of a dam, which does not appear to be on the premises either of the plaintiffs or defendant, and a flume to conduct water to their respective mills, and to maintain them in good order. Suppose the grantors of the defendant had entered into an agreement binding themselves to build the dam and flume for the benefit of the plaintiffs, for a stipulated sum of money; will it be claimed that such an agreement could be held a covenant running with land owned by such grantors, and which was entirely distinct from that upon which the work was to be performed? We apprehend not. Where the distinction, as to its capacity to run with the land, between such a covenant and that entered into here, where instead of compensation in money the defendant's grantors were to receive a benefit from the improvement itself?

As the grantors had no estate in the land owned by the defendant when the agreement was entered into, but were mere strangers to it, the case comes directly within the rule announced by Lord Coke, and very uniformly followed both by the English and American courts since his time. *Webb v. Russell*, 3 Term, and *Stokes v. Russell*, Id.; *Hurd v. Curtis* 19 Pick. 459; *Plymouth v. Carver*, 16 Pick. 183. See also an elaborate review of the question in 1 Smith's Leading Cases, note to *Spencer's Case*; 2 Washburn on Real Property, 16 Pick. 183.

The case of *Plymouth v. Carver* was of this character. A town granted certain land on condition that the grantees should become bound by bond to maintain a portion of the highway passing by such land, but did not reserve a right of entry in case the highway should be suffered to be out of repair; and the grantee gave a bond accordingly, by which he bound himself, his heirs, executors, administrators and assigns. It was held that the obligation in the bond was not a covenant running with the land; the court saying: "The plaintiffs claim to recover upon the writing declared upon as a covenant which runs with the land. But with what land is this covenant running? No right or estate in any land is conveyed by the covenantor to the inhabitants of the town. Nor did the town in their deed reserve any right of entry, or any interest whatever, in the land which they granted to Barnaby and Shurleff. But on the contrary, the town conveyed the land on a condition that the grantees would give a bond that they would maintain the highway. The grantees gave a bond to that effect, and thereupon the estate vested in them absolutely. We think it very clear that the bond was a formal obligation of the obligors, not subjecting the land which the town had conveyed to them in any other way than any of the estate of the obligors might be liable to the performance of their personal covenants or obligations." There are cases in equity holding that covenants entered into touching or concerning land, but which are not such as will run with it, may be enforced against the assignee of the covenantor *who takes the land with notice of the covenant*. Such are the cases of *Whitman v. Gibson*, 9 Simon, and *Mann v. Stephens*, 15 Simon, 379. But in this case there is no showing that the mortgagee had notice of the covenants sought to be charged upon the land at the time the mortgage was executed, or that the defendant had such notice at the time he bought in the property at the foreclosure sale; therefore, if the cases referred to correctly declare the law, they do not control this case in the absence of the essential element of notice.

There being no privity of estate, or of contract between the parties, it only remains to determine whether the defendant is holden on his own promise made to the plaintiffs. First, the action is not based on any such promise or contract. The complaint is framed with reference exclusively to the written agreement, and upon that alone relief is sought. Nothing is charged in the complaint tending to charge the defendant with any personal obligation, except that the repairs were made with his knowledge. As the complaint does not allege any personal promise or contract on the part of the defendant, it would hardly be conformable to the rules of law to award relief upon the assumption of its existence. No personal promise or agreement by the defendant could properly be proven under the complaint; for proof is only admissible to establish the case made by the allegations of the pleading.

But again, if any such promise was made, it is undoubtedly barred by the statute of limitations, not being evidenced by writing. It cannot be said that the defendant adopted the written agreement as his own, and thereby bound himself to it, for it is not shown that he knew of its existence. But even if he knew of it, the only evidence of his obligation upon it was in parol, and therefore it cannot with any degree of reason be said that if he had directly adopted the contract by a parol promise, his obligation would not be barred by the limitation prescribed for parol contracts.

The judgment below must be affirmed.

Notes and Questions

1. According to the traditional law as set out in the 1944 Restatement, promises respecting the use of land only become property interests (i.e. obligations enforceable not only against the original promisor for the benefit of the original promisee, but also against successors in interest of the original promisor or by successors in interest of the original promisee) if several requirements are met. First, the parties to the original promise must intend it to "run with the land"—to bind and benefit successors. Second, the promise must "touch and concern" the land. Third, if the promise is to be enforced at law (in a suit for damages) as a real covenant, the following privity requirements must be met: (i) For the burden of the covenant to bind successors, there must be "horizontal privity" between the original promisor and promisee, i.e., the original promisor and promisee must have a relationship between themselves that meets certain requirements. (ii) There must be "vertical privity" between the original parties to the promise and their successors against or for whom enforcement is sought, i.e., the successor must succeed to a specified interest of the original promisor. Was horizontal or vertical privity at issue in *Wheeler*? For the promise to be enforced at equity (i.e., by injunction or specific performance), privity between the initial promisor and promisee, or between the original promisor and its successor, is not necessary. All that is necessary is that the successor to the promisor purchase with notice of the promise (and, perhaps, vertical privity between the promisee and a successor to the promisee).

The meaning and continuing validity of these requirements, as well as emerging additional limitations on negative and affirmative servitudes, will now be explored.

2. Creation

(a) Express Provision

Servitudes imposing negative and affirmative obligations, like easements, are most commonly created by express grants. Such restrictions are within the coverage of the Statute of Frauds and, unless they fall within an exception to the statute, must be in writing.

A developer creating a restricted subdivision may record a declaration of restrictions establishing building lines, restricting construction to residential buildings, establishing the minimum square footage for buildings, and restricting, depending on the nature of the subdivision, such things as clotheslines, pets, satellite dishes, or signs. The declaration may also impose affirmative obligations, such as an obligation to pay an annual assessment for the support of a property owners' association or for the maintenance of common facilities. The declaration is then recorded and incorporated by reference into deeds from the developer to purchasers in the subdivision. Alternatively, the subdivider can deed the entire subdivision to a straw, incorporating the restrictions into this deed. This deed is then recorded, after which the straw deeds the subdivision back to the developer, with all property within it bound by the restrictions. Finally, a subdivider can attempt to incorporate the restrictions into each deed individually. This strategy is the most risky, because the subdivider may inadvertently (or intentionally) leave the restrictions out of some deeds. In this situation the courts must decide whether to imply restrictions, essentially rejecting the applicability of the Statute of Frauds.

(b) By Implication

WARREN v. DETLEFSEN

Supreme Court of Arkansas, 1984.
281 Ark. 196, 663 S.W.2d 710.

HICKMAN, JUSTICE.

Mike Detlefsen and others filed suit to enjoin the construction of two duplexes in the Warren Subdivision 3 in El Dorado, Arkansas. This subdivision is one of three adjoining residential neighborhoods which were part of a development by the Warrens through their partnership, the Warren Construction Company. The chancellor held that the Warrens should be enjoined from building the duplexes based on the restrictive covenants contained in the deeds of the appellees and the representations made by the Warrens concerning the development of the three subdivisions. In finding that these were enforceable restrictive covenants for single family use, the chancellor relied on the language in the deeds that the property was to be used for residential purposes, and that "carport" was used singularly in the deeds. Those factors coupled with the oral representations of the Warrens led the chancellor to conclude the restrictive covenants were enforceable. We find no error under these facts.

The chancellor received into evidence deeds to the lots which the Warrens had sold in each of the three units. In Unit One, there are nine lots, with five of the deeds containing covenants restricting use to "residential purposes only" and requiring a minimum of fourteen hundred square feet. One deed recites similar language except it requires a minimum of twelve hundred square feet. One deed states that the lot can be "used only for residential purposes" and requires a minimum cost of $30,000. Two deeds contain no covenants.

Unit Two consists of 21 lots with three of the deeds restricting use to "residential purposes only," "the dwelling," and require a minimum of fourteen hundred square feet. Four deeds are restricted to "residential purposes only," "the residence dwelling," and a minimum of fourteen hundred square feet. Four deeds contain this same language except the area is reduced to a minimum of twelve hundred square feet. Eight deeds in Unit Two contain no covenants.

In Unit Three, 20 lots had been sold at the time of trial. Of those, 11 deeds contain the restriction "for residential purposes only," "the residence dwelling," and require a minimum of twelve hundred square feet. One deed is restricted to "residential purposes only," "the residence," and requires a minimum of fourteen hundred square feet.

In promoting the development, the Warrens did not make a distinction between the three units, selling the area as a single neighborhood. There are no visible boundaries or divisions between the units. The Warrens, through Warren Construction Company, are the grantors, the developers, and the builders of the subdivisions. The Warrens displayed a master plat of the entire development on the wall of their office for prospective purchasers to view. This master plat was not recorded.

The Warrens argue that the chancellor erred in allowing witnesses to testify concerning oral representations allegedly made by them at the time the appellees were considering purchasing lots and homes within the units. This concerned the type of homes being built and the general scheme or plan of development which the Warrens intended to pursue. Testimony reflected that the Warrens had discussed these intentions with the prospective buyers, assuring them that only single family homes would be constructed, that no apartments would be constructed and that no mobile homes would be placed in any of the three units. Further, the appellees testified that they relied on these statements, at least in part, in deciding to purchase from the Warrens. At least one witness said he was told no duplexes would be built. Generally, duplexes were not mentioned.

While parol evidence is generally inadmissible to vary or contradict the language of a restrictive covenant, [ ] such evidence is admissible to establish a general building plan or scheme of development and improvement. Such plan or scheme can be proven by express covenant, by implication from a field map, or by parol representation made in sales brochures, maps, advertising, or oral statements upon which the purchaser relied in making his decision to purchase. [ ] This general scheme is shown by the deeds and by the oral statements of the Warrens. Seven of the nine deeds in Unit One are restricted to residential use. Thirteen of 21 deeds in Unit Two are restricted to residential use. In Unit Three, 12 of the 20 deeds contain similar restrictions. Mrs. Warren testified that she and Mr. Warren intended to insert the restrictions in all deeds in the three units. She also testified that they were aware that the prospective purchasers were relying on their oral representations in deciding whether or not to buy. The subdivisions, themselves, consisted of single-family dwellings only at the time the appellees purchased their lots and homes. Both Warrens testified that the economy dictated they change their plans and build the duplexes rather than single family residences.

The Warrens argue that the chancellor erred in finding that the restrictions contained in the deeds of the appellees were the proper basis for enjoining the construction of the duplexes. They contend that the wording of the restrictions does not limit their development to single family dwellings, but rather, that multi-family use was permissible, citing Shermer v. Haynes, 248 Ark. 255, 451 S.W.2d 445 (1970). There, we held that covenants which restrict use to "residence" or "dwelling" purpose alone, generally do not have the effect of forbidding the erection or maintenance of multiple family dwellings. However, the chancellor in this case had testimony and facts of a total building and selling scheme which indicate single residence purposes only. Further, the testimony reflects that the oral representations, combined with the express covenants, were the basis of the purchasers' decisions to buy lots in the neighborhood. The homes in the units display a uniformity of development, further indication of the general plan and scheme.

These restrictions are enforceable against the lots retained by the Warrens in the three units as a reciprocal negative easement. When the grantor places an express restriction in deeds to his grantees within the particular development, the restriction attaches to the lots retained to prevent their use in a manner detrimental to the enjoyment and value of neighboring lots sold with the restriction. 20 Am.Jr.2d Covenants § 173. The Warrens had the restrictions placed in their grantees' deeds, and the chancellor's findings support a conclusion that the Warrens intended to bind all the lots sold within the three units.

Finally, the Warrens challenge the standing of homeowners in Units One and Two to seek enforcement of the restrictions against the lots retained by the Warrens in Unit Three. They argue that these first two subdivisions are legally separate subdivisions and, as such, the owners within them can not have the restrictions enforced in the third, separate subdivision. However, in the negotiations leading to the purchase, the Warrens represented that the development would consist of some 350 homes, all being single family dwellings. The buyers were shown a master plat which depicted the three subdivisions as a single development, with only a line distinguishing the boundaries of each unit. Otherwise, there are no visible boundaries or divisions between the units. The buyers relied upon these factors in making their decision to purchase. Also, at least two of the appellees were homeowners in Unit Three.

While the chancellor based his decision on narrow reasoning, we must affirm unless the decision is clearly erroneous. [   ] The distinctive facts in this case support the chancellor's conclusion and since we cannot say he was clearly erroneous, we affirm his decision.

Affirmed.

Notes and Questions

1. The implied reciprocal servitudes doctrine is of use for addressing three problems. First, there is the situation found in the principal case. A developer purports to create a restricted subdivision, selling off lots with restrictions in the deeds. Subsequently the market changes and the developer decides to sell off or to develop lots in the subdivision in violation of the restrictions. Courts will then imply restrictions binding the retained lots, essentially estopping the developer from developing the land for purposes other than those represented to earlier purchasers.

A second situation arises where a developer sells off some lots with deed restrictions, then subsequently, and perhaps inadvertently, sells others without. A purchaser of an unrestricted lot (or her successors) attempts to develop the lot for a purpose prohibited by the restrictions on the other lots. If a court finds that the earlier restrictions were imposed as part of a common scheme of which subsequent purchasers had notice, they will again imply a restriction, attaching with the earlier sale of restricted lots.

Finally, the implied reciprocal servitude doctrine addresses the conceptual problem raised when early purchasers in a subdivision attempt to enforce express servitudes against subsequent purchasers. There is no conceptual problem, of course, with subsequent purchasers in a subdivision enforcing written restrictions in the deeds of prior purchasers. Such restrictions are made for the benefit of the developer's retained land, and run to the benefit of subsequent purchasers of that land. Prior purchasers, however, are strangers to the transactions between the developer and subsequent purchasers and cannot claim to succeed to the benefit of that promise. Note there is no problem with the Statute of Frauds in these cases—the restrictions are in writing—rather the problem is how to connect them up with prior purchasers. Several theories have evolved for permitting enforcement. The prior purchasers could be treated as third-party beneficiaries to the subsequent agreement, the approach taken by the 1944 Restatement, § 541, comments c and f, and a few cases, Snow v. Van Dam, 291 Mass. 477, 197 N.E. 224 (1935). As courts do not commonly allow enforcement of negative servitudes by third-party beneficiaries, however, this theory is problematic, see 2 American Law of Property § 9.30 (J. Casner ed. 1952). More commonly, courts hold that at the time of the prior purchases, reciprocal servitudes were implied against the retained land of the developer of the common scheme for the benefit of the prior purchasers, and that these restrictions continue to bind the land in the hands of subsequent purchasers, see Sanborn v. McLean, 233 Mich. 227, 206 N.W. 496 (1925), Lehmann v.

Wallace, 510 S.W.2d 675 (Tex.Civ.App.1974). This is the position taken by the Restatement of Property (Third) Servitudes § 2.14 (2000):

Unless the facts or circumstances indicate a contrary intent, conveyance of land pursuant to a general plan of development implies the creation of servitudes as follows:

(1) Implied Benefits: Each lot included within the general plan is the implied beneficiary of all express and implied servitudes imposed to carry out the general plan.

(2) Implied Burdens:

(a) Language of condition that creates a restriction or other obligation, in order to implement the general plan, creates an implied servitude imposing the same restriction or other obligation.

(b) A conveyance by a developer that imposes a servitude on the land conveyed to implement a general plan creates an implied reciprocal servitude burdening all the developer's remaining land included in the general plan, if injustice can be avoided only by implying the reciprocal servitude.

2. Some jurisdictions continue to reject the implied reciprocal servitudes doctrine for any purpose because of its conflict with the Statute of Frauds, see Riley v. Bear Creek Planning Committee, 17 Cal.3d 500, 131 Cal.Rptr. 381, 551 P.2d 1213 (1976) (also relying on the parol evidence rule); Houghton v. Rizzo, 361 Mass. 635, 281 N.E.2d 577 (1972). What facts must a court find in such a jurisdiction before it would permit a prior (or a subsequent) purchaser in a subdivision to enforce a restriction against another lot owner in the subdivision? See Trahms v. Starrett, 34 Cal.App.3d 766, 110 Cal.Rptr. 239 (1973):

* * * To create an equitable servitude, both the grantor and a grantee must intend that a parcel of land conveyed from the grantor to the grantee be restricted pursuant to a general plan. [ ] That intent must appear in the instruments exchanged between them. [ ] The agreement between the two parties must show 'that the parcel conveyed (is) subject to restrictions in accordance with the plan for the benefit of all the other parcels and also that all other parcels (are) subject to such restrictions for its benefit.' [ ] The dominant and servient tenements must be shown. [ ] If these conditions have been met the grantee of the first deed from the developer of a tract will be entitled to enforce the covenants as to all the remaining area placed under equitable servitude; operation of the recording statutes will prevent the developer from exempting other grantees by omitting reference to restrictions in drawing later deeds. [ ]

* * * But a grantee possessed of a dominant interest could not enforce the restrictions as to lots that were deeded without restriction by Marinero prior to the execution of the grantee's deed. This conclusion follows from the fact that a grantor cannot place restrictions on land he does not own, or contract for third parties without their consent. * * *

Therefore the grantees whose deeds incorporated the restrictions, and were issued prior to the issuance of appellants' deeds, could enforce the restrictions on appellants. But neither appellants' deeds nor respondents' deed expressly or by reference adopted the restrictions. The facts that respondents may have known of the recorded tract restrictions by virtue of references in the report of the Real Estate Commissioner and in documents received from the title insurance company did not act as an agreement on their part to abide by the tract restrictions. [   ] The deed was the 'final and exclusive memorial of the intention and rights of the parties.' [   ]

Since neither appellants nor respondents agreed in their deeds to abide by the restrictions, appellants cannot enforce the restrictions on respondents. The fact that a few lot owners, who were granted deeds incorporating the restrictions prior to the grant to respondents, can enforce the restriction on respondents' lot does not determine the question whether appellants can enforce the restrictions. The servitudes created by those prior deeds run from respondents' lot to each of the lots conveyed by prior deeds which adopted the restrictions, not between appellants' lots and respondents' lot.

3.   The principal case also raises the problem of what land will be included in the general plan for purposes of implying servitudes where a subdivision is not yet fully developed when a lot is sold off, or when the subdivision is developed in phases. Particular problems arise where an effort is made by a prior purchaser to enforce restrictions against land that was subsequently acquired by the subdivider but developed as part of the same scheme. The problem is usually handled as a question of fact, looking to the intentions and representations of the developer. How is this issue resolved under Restatement of the Law of Property (Third) Servitudes (see note 1, *supra*).

4.   Implied servitudes are generally negative restrictions enforced at equity and are denominated as negative easements or equitable servitudes. Traditional doctrine forbids implication of real covenants—servitudes enforceable at law. Cases implying affirmative obligations are rare, see R & R Realty Co. v. Weinstein, 4 Ariz.App. 517, 422 P.2d 148 (1966) (implied reciprocal servitude to contribute to maintenance of park). Why should courts be more willing to imply negative than affirmative restrictions?

(c) By Prescription

PROBLEM: ANCIENT LIGHTS

Fifteen years ago, Samuel Kent bought a lot on a gentle hill on the north shore of Sandy's cove. Immediately after the purchase, he built a house with a sweeping view of the ocean. Eight years ago he built a swimming pool below the house, heated by a solar collector placed next to the swimming pool, ten feet from the southern boundary of Samuel's property. Last year Bill Littleton acquired the lot immediately south of Samuel's lot. Bill is building a two story A-frame home on his lot, which will substantially obstruct the view of the Ocean from Samuel's deck and cut off sunlight from the solar collector (as well as from the pool) much of the day during most of the year. There are no express restrictive servitudes affecting either lot, and Bill's proposed home complies with local zoning and development restrictions. The prescriptive period for establishing servitudes is five years. Samuel learns of the English "ancient lights" doctrine which permits acquisition of a negative easement for access to light by use for the prescriptive period. He brings a suit seeking an injunction against the construction of Bill's house, claiming that the courts of his jurisdiction should recognize the ancient lights doctrine. What result should obtain, and why? Would an argument of implication from necessity or pre-existing use fare any better? See Prah v. Maretti, 108 Wis.2d 223, 321 N.W.2d 182 (1982); Fontainebleau Hotel Corp. v. Forty–Five Twenty–Five, Inc., 114 So.2d 357 (Fla.App.1959); Maioriello v. Arlotta, 364 Pa. 557, 73 A.2d 374 (1950).

3. Validity, Interpretation, and Scope

When courts refuse to enforce restrictive and affirmative servitudes they usually offer one of two categories of reasons in explanation. First, they may refuse to enforce servitudes that violate explicit public policies, that, e.g., discriminate against protected groups, unduly restrain alienation, or restrain trade. Second, they may refuse to enforce restrictions created in violation of traditional servitude doctrine, e.g., where there was no "horizontal privity" between the initial covenantor and covenantee, or where the restriction does not "touch and concern" the land. The former doctrines normally render the servitude wholly unenforceable. The latter doctrines render the restrictions unenforceable against, and, sometimes, by, subsequent owners of burdened or benefited land, but do not affect their enforceability as contracts. This section begins with a consideration of restrictions imposed on servitudes by traditional law. It then moves on to consider public policy constraints on the enforcement of servitudes.

(a) Traditional Servitude Law

A traditional requirement for the enforcement of promises respecting the use of land against or by successors of the original promisor or promisee is that the original parties intend that the promise bind or benefit successors. Since servitudes originate in consensual relationships, it makes sense that the intent of the initial creators of the servitude should be considered in determining whether it runs with the land.

While this requirement has clear continuing validity, its operation has changed somewhat over time. At one time there was authority for the proposition that, at least for some servitudes, it was necessary to state that the servitude was binding on "assigns" to designate that the benefit or burden of the servitude was intended to run with the land. Modern courts try to discern the intent of the parties, unbound by particular verbal formulae. See American Law of Property, § 9.10 (J. Casner, ed. 1952).

Under the traditional law of servitudes, however, the mere intention of the parties that the promise "run with the land" was not enough to insure that it would. In addition, the law required that the promise "touch and concern" the land. Also, for a real covenant to be enforceable (i.e., for a negative or affirmative servitude to be enforceable at law), the initial covenantor and covenantee had to be in a special relationship known as "horizontal privity". What purposes do these doctrines serve? Do they, and should they, have continuing vitality? Consider these questions as you study the following materials.

(i) Horizontal Privity

MOSELEY v. BISHOP

Court of Appeals of Indiana, Fourth District, 1984.
470 N.E.2d 773.

Young, Judge.

Edith Moseley brought suit against Merrill and Joanna Gates and sixteen others (hereinafter defendants) seeking damages for the defendants' failure to maintain a tile drain that served Moseley's farm and ran across the Gateses' land. This suit was based upon a contract made in 1896 by Henry Moseley, who then owned what is now the plaintiff's farm, and William Bohn, the defendants' predecessor in interest. The trial court ruled that this contract, which required Bohn to "permanently maintain" the drain at issue, did not run with the land and thus was not binding upon the defendants, Bohn's successors. The trial court also ruled that Moseley had not proved the defendants' failure to repair the drain caused the losses of which she complained. Moseley appeals, claiming the trial court's judgment was contrary to law.

We reverse.

In 1896, Henry Moseley and William Bohn owned adjoining farms in Miami County, Indiana. Moseley's land was drained by an open ditch across Bohn's land. In August, 1896, they entered into a contract (hereinafter termed the Moseley–Bohn agreement), which read in part as follows:

> That Whereas; There exists an open public ditch known as the 'Moseley Ditch' in the West half of the East half of Section 23 in Township 26 North, of Range 4 East, which real estate is owned by said Bohn, and Whereas; said Moseley is the owner of real estate lying immediately South of and adjoining said real estate and which has the ditch above referred to for the out-let for its drainage, and Whereas said Moseley and divers other persons have heretofore been assessed for the construction and repair of said Moseley Ditch, and said Bohn is desirous of straightening and placing drain tile the entire length of said ditch; Now Therefore, in consideration that said Moseley will consent to such straightening and tiling of said ditch, and in the further consideration of the sum of Forty Dollars to be paid by said Moseley when the tiling through that portion of said ditch which has been assigned to him for repairs shall have been completed, said William C. Bohn hereby agrees that he will place through the entire length of said ditch and permanently maintain

drain tile of sufficient capacity to furnish adequate out-let for drainage from a twelve inch tile at the North line of said Moseley's land, being the south line of said Section 23. Backwater at said point to be conclusive evidence of lack of said capacity. In consideration of the foregoing premises, said Moseley hereby consents to the straightening and tiling of said ditch and agrees to pay to said Bohn the sum of $40.00 on the terms above stated.

This contract was duly recorded in the Miami County Recorder's Office.

In the course of time, Henry Moseley's farm came into the hands of Edith Moseley, the plaintiff. Bohn's farm has had several subsequent owners, most recently the Gateses—who farm the land—and the other defendants, most of whom own small residential tracts. Beginning in 1976, Moseley's son Harold noticed that her farm seemed to lack good drainage. This condition worsened each year to the point that, in 1981, there was standing water on Moseley's farm. In 1981 and again in 1982 Harold walked along the course of the drain at issue, which ran exclusively across the Gateses' land. On both occasions he observed eroded holes in the ground, some filled with water, indicating that the drain tile was broken or blocked. Harold requested Mr. Gates to fulfill his obligation under the Moseley–Bohn agreement and repair the drain tile. Gates refused to do so without Moseley's help, and he petitioned the Miami County Drainage Board to repair the drain and assess the cost equally against all the affected landowners. Moseley then brought this suit against the defendants, based on the Moseley–Bohn agreement, seeking damages for losses caused by flooding on her farm and asking that the defendants be made to pay any repair charges assessed against Moseley by the drainage board. After a bench trial the court entered judgment against Moseley, and this appeal ensued.

Moseley contends the trial court's ruling that the defendants had no contractual duty to repair the ditch was contrary to law. The central issue here is whether the Moseley–Bohn agreement runs with the land, so as to bind the defendants to "permanently maintain" the drain tile on their land. Generally, a covenant imposing an affirmative burden will run with the land if (1) the covenantors intend it to run, (2) the covenant touches and concerns the land, and (3) there is privity of estate between subsequent grantees of the original covenantor and covenantee. [ ] J. Cribbet, Principles of the Law of Property 353 (2d ed. 1975). Because Moseley had the burden of establishing these elements, we may reverse the trial court's ruling against her only if the evidence is undisputed and shows that she is entitled to judgment as a matter of law. [ ]

The first element, the parties' intent that their covenant should run with the land, must be determined from the specific language used and from the situation of the parties when the covenant was made. [ ] Cribbet, supra, at 354. Although a statement in the covenant that it is binding on the covenantor's heirs and assigns is strong evidence of intent that the covenant should run with the land, the omission of such language here, as the defendants concede, does not conclusively prove the covenant was not intended to run. [ ]

In the contract at issue, Bohn agreed to "permanently maintain" a tile drain across his property. This language indicates an intention to bind not only Bohn but later grantees of the burdened property as well. Also relevant are the facts surrounding the covenant. Even before the agreement, Moseley's land was drained by an open ditch across Bohn's property. Thus, the installation of buried drain tile benefitted only Bohn, whose property gained additional usable surface area. Moseley, on the other hand, incurred an increased risk that his property might not be adequately drained, since it is more difficult to remove obstructions from a buried drain than from an open ditch. Under these circumstances, the importance of Bohn's promise to "permanently maintain" the drain is clear. Given the importance of this drain to Moseley's land, it is improbable that the parties intended their agreement to be purely personal and not binding on subsequent grantees of the land. Faced with similar agreements relating to ditches and drains, courts in other jurisdictions have generally found an intent that the covenant run with the land. See 20 Am.Jur.2d Covenants, Conditions, and Restrictions § 42 (1965). We find as a matter of law that the facts surrounding the written agreement and the language used in it show an intent to create a covenant running with the land.

Having proved this intent, Moseley was also required to show the covenant touched and concerned the land with which it was to run. This requirement ensures that one purchasing land will be bound by his grantor's contract only where the contract has some logical connection to his use and enjoyment of the land. Thus, a successor to the covenantor's interest in property may be bound by the covenant if it is logically connected to that property interest. Conversely, a successor to the covenantee's property interest may enforce the covenant if it is logically connected to his property. See C. Clark, Real Covenants and Other Interests Which "Run With Land" 97 (1947). The covenant to maintain the tile drain at issue here is logically connected both to the Gateses' property—in which the drain is buried—and to the plaintiff's land, which is served by the drain. Because the drain runs exclusively across the Gateses' land, however, the agreement to maintain it has no logical connection to the land held by the other defendants, who own residential tracts in the old Bohn farm. Thus, the "touch and concern" requirement is met as to Moseley, the plaintiff, and the Gateses, but not as to the other defendants.

Finally, to establish a covenant running with the land, Moseley was required to prove she was in privity of estate with the defendants. Where, as here, neither of the original covenantors is a party to the suit, both "vertical privity" and "horizontal privity" must be proved. "Vertical privity" is established where the party seeking to enforce the covenant and the party against whom it is to be enforced are successors in title to the property of the covenantee and covenantor respectively. See Cribbet, supra, at 354. Vertical privity clearly exists in this case.

The concept of "horizontal privity," however, is more difficult. "Horizontal privity" is generally established by evidence that the original parties to the covenant had some mutual or successive interest either in the land burdened by the covenant or the land benefitted by it. The requirement of horizontal privity may be met by proof that the covenantee has a leasehold and the covenantor has the reversion in the affected land. [ ] Similarly, the parties are in privity where one has an easement in land owned by the other, so long as the covenant concerns the easement. [ ] Finally, privity of estate may be found between the original covenantors even where they did not hold simultaneous interests in the land if the covenant concerns land transferred by one party to the other. [ ] Additionally, to establish privity, the plaintiff generally must prove the covenant was made in the context of a transfer of an interest in the affected land, whether by lease or by deed conveying the property or an easement therein. Wheeler v. Schad, 7 Nev. 204 (1871); Cribbet, supra, at 354.[8]

We believe Moseley established the required privity of estate in this case. Where one landowner agrees to construct a drain across his

---

8. For several reasons, we make the foregoing statements of the law regarding horizontal privity with some trepidation. First, most of the legal scholars who have discussed real covenants argue that no privity of estate between the original covenantors should be required for their covenant to run with the land. Clark, supra, 111–37; O.W. Holmes, The Common Law 403, 404; Newman & Losey, Covenants Running with the Land, and Equitable Servitudes; Two Concepts, or One? 21 Hastings L.J. 1319 (1970); Stoebuck, Running Covenants: An Analytical Primer, 52 Wash.L.Rev. 861 (1977). These writers point out that the requirement of horizontal privity, while frequently stated in dictum, is seldom used to bar the running of an otherwise valid real covenant. Clark, supra, at 116. They also argue that this requirement is purely arbitrary, not vindicating any interest of the landowners involved or of society at large. Id. at 116–17. Second, the courts have made significant exceptions to the privity requirement. Thus, it has been held that a covenant need not be made as part of a transfer of an interest in land if "the promise is made in the adjustment of the mutual relationships arising out of the existence of an easement held by one of the parties to the promise in the land of the other." Restatement of Property § 534(b) (1944); see Morse v. Aldrich, 36 Mass. 449 (1837). Further, it is unnecessary to prove privity of estate where the benefit of the covenant, rather than the burden, is to run with the land. City of Reno v. Matley, 79 Nev. 49,

378 P.2d 256 (1963); Restatement of Property § 548 (1944); 21 C.J.S. Covenants § 58 (1940 & Supp.1984). Finally, the horizontal privity requirement has been undermined by the courts' frequent resort to the doctrine of equitable servitudes. Under this doctrine, a landowner who has actual or constructive notice of a covenant concerning the land made by his predecessor in interest may be bound by the covenant even though the original covenantors were not in privity of estate. Tulk v. Moxhay, 2 Phillips 774, 41 Eng.Rep. 1143 (1848); Cribbet, supra, at 356; see Howard D. Johnson Co. v. Parkside Development Corp., 169 Ind.App. 379, 348 N.E.2d 656 (1976). Because virtually all promises giving rise to a real covenant also create an equitable servitude, this equitable doctrine has become a popular means of circumventing the technical requirements that govern real covenants— most notably the requirement of horizontal privity. See, e.g., Neponsit Property Owners' Ass'n v. Emigrant Industrial Savings Bank, 278 N.Y. 248, 15 N.E.2d 793 (1938); Merrionette Manor Homes Improvement Ass'n v. Heda, 11 Ill.App.2d 186, 136 N.E.2d 556 (1956); see generally Stoebuck, supra, 52 Wash.L.Rev. at 919–21. For all these reasons, although we find the technical requirement of horizontal privity has been satisfied in this case, we doubt whether this requirement has much continuing vitality in Indiana.

property for the benefit of a neighbor's land, the agreement will generally create an easement appurtenant to the adjacent land. [   ] Thus, we find that Bohn's agreement to construct a tile drain across his land for Moseley's benefit created an easement appurtenant to Moseley's land. Since Bohn's agreement to maintain the drain was contained in the same document, the covenant was clearly made in the context of a transfer to Moseley of an easement in Bohn's land. This satisfies the requirement of privity of estate between the original covenantors. [   ] We accordingly hold that the Moseley–Bohn agreement runs with the land now held by Moseley and the Gateses. Because the agreement does not affect the other defendants' property, however, the trial court correctly found it did not run with their land.

* * *

Notes and Questions

1. The "horizontal" relationship in servitude law is the relationship between the initial promisor and promisee. Whether these two parties are in "privity" depends on the nature of that relationship, and the horizontal privity requirement applied in the jurisdiction. As the principal case points out, the requirement has been interpreted variously in different jurisdictions, with England requiring a landlord-tenant relationship, Massachusetts and other jurisdictions requiring that the servitude be attached to a "mutual" relationship, usually an easement, and other jurisdictions merely requiring that the servitude be created through a conveyance. Would the following landowners be in horizontal privity, and, if so, under what definition?

a. Two neighbors who each promise to contribute half to the maintenance of a common sewer line that both use.

b. A purchaser of a lot in a subdivision who accepts a deed which includes a promise to use the land only for residential purposes.

c. Two neighbors who each agree to use their land only for residential purposes.

d. A person who buys a lot from his neighbor and promises not to build within 20 feet of the property line of the neighbor who sells him the lot.

2. The horizontal privity requirement is largely based on older cases; modern cases honor it principally in dicta. The Restatement of the Law of Property (Third) Servitudes (2000) states:

§ 2.4 No Horizontal Privity Required

No privity relationship between parties is necessary to create a servitude.

Its rationale for this position is:

b. *Rationale.* In American law, the horizontal privity requirement serves no function beyond insuring that most covenants intended to run with the land will be created in conveyances. Formal creation of covenants is desirable because it tends to assure that they will be recorded. However, the horizontal privity requirement is no longer needed for this purpose. In modern law, the Statute of Frauds and recording acts perform that function.

Application of the horizontal privity requirement prevents enforcement at law of covenants entered into between neighbors and between other parties who do not transfer or share some other interest in the land. The rule can easily be circumvented by conveyance to a strawperson who imposes the covenant in the reconveyance. Since the rule serves no necessary purpose and simply acts as a trap for the poorly represented, it has been abandoned. As a matter of common law, horizontal privity between the covenanting parties is no longer required to create a servitude obligation.

(ii) The Touch and Concern Requirement

The touch and concern requirement may prove more durable. The position is commonly taken that the benefit of a servitude must touch and concern some estate in the dominant parcel to run with the land. Similarly, the burden must touch and concern some estate in the burdened parcel to run with that land. See Cunningham, Stoebuck and Whitman, The Law of Property, § 8.15 (1984); G. Korngold, Private Land Use Arrangements, § 9.10 (1990). The content of the requirement, however, is subject to debate. Must the benefit or burden physically affect the land in some way, or would, for example, an obligation to pay money to a property owners association touch and concern the land? See Neponsit Property Owners' Ass'n v. Emigrant Industrial Savings Bank, 278 N.Y. 248, 15 N.E.2d 793 (1938) (the obligation to pay money touches and concerns the land where the money is used to maintain common easements). The most famous explication of the rule was created by Dean Harry Bigelow and elaborated by Judge Charles E. Clark:

> If the promisor's legal relations in respect to the land in question are lessened—his legal interest as owner rendered less valuable by the promise—the burden of the covenant touches or concerns that land; if the promisee's legal relations in respect to that land are increased—his legal interest as owner rendered more valuable by the promise—the benefit of the covenant touches or concerns that land.

C. Clark, Covenants and Interests Running with the Land, 97 (2d ed. 1947).

Try to apply this test in the *Kotseas* case which follows.

Professor French, the author of the 2000 Restatement, proposes abolition of the requirement in favor of more policy oriented analysis:

FRENCH, SERVITUDES REFORM AND THE NEW RE-
STATEMENT OF PROPERTY: CREATION DOC-
TRINES AND STRUCTURAL SIMPLIFICATION

73 Cornell L.Rev. 928, 939–940 (1988).

* * *

The touch and concern doctrine has traditionally been stated in the form of an ex ante limit on the creation of servitudes. If the benefit or burden of the covenant does not touch or concern the land, then it does not run with the land. As it applies to benefits, I continue to regard the requirement as such as an ex ante control, and I have treated it as a prohibition on benefits in gross. As it applies to burdens, however, I think the touch and concern requirement is more in the nature of an ex post control, operating after the fact to give the court a discretionary power to terminate a servitude. The concept is so difficult to pin down that it can rarely be used as a basis for predicting the enforceability of a particular covenant. Each covenant must be litigated to determine whether it touches and concerns or not.

To the extent that the burden side of the touch and concern requirement does operate as a limit on covenant creation, I propose that it be eliminated along with the other old ex ante controls. Its only significant operation is in the realm of affirmative covenants, where it serves to prevent the creation of particular types of covenants. Why it prevents them, however, remains a mystery. Some have suggested that it only prevents creation of covenant obligations that people would expect not to be bound by if they bought the land. But why would they expect not to be bound? If there is notice of the covenant, and the intent that it run is clear, the only basis for such an expectation is precedent.

When a court invalidates a covenant obligation on the ground that it does not touch and concern the land, it makes a substantive judgment that the obligation should not be permitted to run with land. Such judgments have been passed with respect to mortgage covenants, a variety of lease covenants, and a few other covenants. The real reasons for the invalidation are seldom, if ever, given. Sometimes it appears that the covenant restrains trade or competition; sometimes it appears that the covenant takes unfair advantage of a consumer; sometimes it simply appears that the conditions have changed and the agreement no longer produces the benefits that the original covenantor expected.

In my view, servitudes law should separate initial-validity questions from modification and termination questions, and should tackle both directly. The vice of the touch and concern doctrine is that it permits commingling of the two types of questions and treats both behind such a screen of hocus-pocus that we have to guess at the reasons for a decision. It is often difficult to know whether the arrangement was invalidated because it violated some important public policy, or whether it was terminated because it was unfair in the beginning or had become obsolete or unduly burdensome later on.

We will make a major advance in improving the quality of servitudes law if we abandon the rhetoric of touch and concern. Servitudes law should address separately and directly the questions whether an arrangement would violate a constitutional, statutory, or public policy norm if permitted to operate as a servitude, and whether the arrangement, while valid as a servitude, should be terminated because it has become obsolete, unduly burdensome, or something else.

Professor Uriel Reichman, on the other hand, argues that the doctrine serves a useful purpose:

REICHMAN, TOWARD A UNIFIED CONCEPT OF SERVITUDES

55 S.Cal.L.Rev. 1177, 1232–1233 (1982).

In situations where a promise has no bearing on land use regulation, the courts treat the arrangement as a contract between the original parties and exempt the promisor's transferees from liability. In such cases, it is irrelevant whether or not the transacting parties clearly expressed their written intention that the promise would "run with the land," or that the promisor's transferee had actual or constructive notice of the obligation. As a matter of positive law, where land use efficiency gains could not conceivably be accomplished, servitudes are not recognized. By applying the "touch and concern" test, the courts are actually exercising their power to fix the boundaries of servitudes.

This somewhat unusual interventionist theory is justified because the permanent attachment to land of merely personal obligations is likely to frustrate the objectives of a private land holding system.

In the first place, obligations not related to actual property use are highly individualized. They tend, therefore to become inefficient in the short run following a transfer. Consensual termination of such rights might not occur because of prohibitive transaction costs. The best way to insure efficient termination of such arrangements is to shift the burden of negotiation; instead of making the transferee negotiate for a release, the aspiring beneficiary will have to reach agreement with each new owner. Personal contracts remain the subject of personal bargains.

There is another reason for the "touch and concern" rule. Private property is sanctioned by society not only to promote efficiency, but also to safeguard individual freedom. Servitudes are a kind of private legislation affecting a line of future owners. Limiting such "legislative powers" to an objective purpose of land planning eliminates the possibility of creating modern variations of feudal serfdom. There might be nothing objectionable in personal agreements concerning personal labor, adherence to ideologically prescribed modes of behavior, or promises to buy from a certain supplier. When such obligations however, become permanently enforced against an ever-changing group of owners, the matter acquires different dimensions. One point needs emphasis: The courts are not involved in measuring efficiency gains; this is clearly the prerogative of the parties. The courts only deny the permanency of agreements clearly unrelated to land use.

Consider how the touch and concern requirement was dealt with in a recent case, addressing one of the most persistent problems for which the touch and concern requirement has been invoked, the problem of covenants not to compete. Does the court's shift in analysis deal with the problem more rationally? Does it make the problem easier to deal with?

WHITINSVILLE PLAZA, INC. v. KOTSEAS

Supreme Judicial Court of Massachusetts, 1979.
378 Mass. 85, 390 N.E.2d 243.

QUIRICO, JUSTICE.

These are civil actions commenced by Whitinsville Plaza, Inc. (Plaza), against Charles H. Kotseas and Paul Kotseas (Kotseas) and against Whitinsville CVS, Inc. (CVS). In its further amended complaint against Kotseas, Plaza alleged imminent violations of certain anticompetitive deed restrictions and requested declaratory, injunctive, and monetary relief under theories of breach of contract and unfair acts or practices within the meaning of M.G.L.A. c. 93A, § 2. Plaza's amended complaint against CVS likewise alleged imminent violations of the deed restrictions, and it requested declaratory, injunctive, and monetary relief on theories of breach of contract, unfair trade practices, and interference with contractual relations. A judge of the Superior Court granted the defendants' motions to dismiss for failure to state a claim. [   ]

* * * We hold that dismissal for failure to state a claim was erroneous as to some counts of each complaint.

* * * [The allegations] are as follows. In 1968, Kotseas conveyed certain land identified as "Parcel A" to four individuals as trustees of the "122 Trust" (Trust), a wholly owned subsidiary of Plaza. The deed set forth numerous, detailed, reciprocal restrictions and covenants designed to assure the harmonious development of a shopping center on Parcel A and on abutting land retained by Kotseas. In particular, Kotseas promised (a) not to use the retained land in competition with the discount store contemplated by the grantee and (b) to use the retained land only for enumerated business purposes. Among the permitted business uses of the land retained by Kotseas was a "drug store," defined in an appendix to the deed as a store selling prescribed types of merchandise. In addition, the deed recited that "(t)he foregoing restrictions shall be considered as covenants running with the land to which they are applicable and shall bind and inure to the benefit of the heirs and assigns of the respective parties to whom any part of the lands made subject to the above restrictions covenants and conditions shall at any time become or belong during the period hereinbefore set forth."

In 1975, the Trust conveyed Parcel A to Plaza and, thereafter, ceased operations. The deed to Plaza expressly made Plaza subject to, and gave it the benefit of, the restrictions and covenants in the 1968 deed from Kotseas to the Trust. At some later time, Kotseas leased a portion of its abutting land to CVS for use as a "discount department store and pharmacy." Plaza's complaints state that the lease to CVS, dated May 10, 1977, was expressly subject to the 1968 deed restrictions and that operation of the contemplated CVS store would violate those restrictions. Although the defendants controvert these allegations, we must, as we have said, accept them as true in ruling on the motion to dismiss.

As against Kotseas, Plaza sought (a) an injunction prohibiting the use of the retained land in violation of the restrictions and (b) damages suffered because of the alleged violations. In the alternative, Plaza prayed for a declaration that its own land was no longer subject to the anticompetitive restrictions. Plaza also requested the court to find that Kotseas had knowingly and wilfully violated M.G.L.A. c. 93A, § 2, and to award double or treble damages and counsel fees. As against CVS, Plaza requested similar relief and also requested damages on the theory that CVS had tortiously interfered with Plaza's contract by inducing Kotseas to violate its restrictions. The defendants filed motions to dismiss, stating as grounds that Plaza lacked standing to sue on the covenants and that the covenants were, in any event, unreasonable and in restraint of trade. * * *

I.   Theories of Recovery

A.   Real covenant analysis. Plaza has primarily sought to maintain its actions on the theory that the covenants contained in the 1968 deed run with the land. In our view, Plaza has alleged sufficient facts to be entitled to a hearing on its claims for legal and equitable relief on this theory. See generally 5 R. Powell, Real Property pars. 672–675, at 149–185 (Rohan rev. ed. 1979) (summarizing requirements for covenants to run with land). The covenants in question are evidenced by a writing signed by Kotseas, the covenantor. [   ] M.G.L.A. c. 259, § 1, Fourth (Statute of Frauds for interests in land). The language of the 1968 deed aptly expresses the intention of the original parties that the covenants run with the land. [   ] The deed also grants mutual easements sufficient to satisfy the requirement that Plaza and CVS be in privity of estate. See, e.g., Morse v. Aldrich, 19 Pick. 449, 454 (1837) (action at law). Plaza's complaint alleges that CVS had actual knowledge of the restrictions and shows, in any event, that the restrictions were recorded with the deed. [   ]

One additional prerequisite for either legal or equitable relief is, however, arguably lacking in this case on the present state of our case law. It is essential that both the benefit and the burden of a real covenant "touch and concern" the affected parcels of land before it will be considered to run. [   ] This court has long held that a covenant not to compete contained in a deed, such as is involved in this case, does not "touch and concern" the land to be benefited and that, in consequence, such a covenant does not run with the land. Shade v. M. O'Keeffe, Inc., 260 Mass. 180, 183, 156 N.E. 867 (1927); Norcross v. James, 140 Mass. 188, 192, 2 N.E. 946 (1885). In Shell Oil Co. v. Henry Ouellette & Sons, 352 Mass. 725, 227 N.E.2d 509 (1967), we intimated that we might overrule Norcross and Shade in an appropriate case. Id. at 730–731 & n. 8, 227 N.E.2d 509. We believe this is such a case.

It is essential to our task that we identify precisely the holding and rationale of the cases we propose to overrule. Norcross was an action seeking specific performance of a covenant not to quarry stone from a parcel of land. The covenant in question was contained in a deed by which one Kibbe conveyed a stone quarry to one Flynt, and it concerned adjoining land retained by Kibbe. The defendant James, a successor to Kibbe's interest, began operating a quarry on the restricted land. The plaintiff Norcross, a successor to Flynt's interest, sought an injunction to halt that operation. 140 Mass. at 188, 2 N.E. 946. In an opinion by Justice Holmes, this court denied relief. Id. at 192, 2 N.E. 946.

Justice Holmes analyzed the case before him in two steps. He first noted a distinction drawn in early English decisions between promises resembling warranties of title and those resembling grants of easements. Warranty-like covenants ran "with the estate" to grantees from the covenantee, but were enforceable only against the covenantor. Easement-like covenants, on the other hand, ran "with the land" in favor of and against subsequent owners. Id. at 188–190, 2 N.E. 946. See also O.W. Holmes, The Common Law 371–409 (1881) (developing historical analysis summarized later in Norcross opinion).

Having traced the development of the law of real covenants, Justice Holmes proceeded to determine whether the covenant could be encompassed within the easement-like class.[11] He stated that a real covenant must "touch or concern" the land by conferring "direct physical advantage in the occupation of the dominant estate." 140 Mass. at 192, 2 N.E. at 949. The covenant against operating a quarry did not do so because "(i)t does not make the use or occupation of (the dominant estate) more convenient. It does not in any way affect the use or occupation; it simply tends indirectly to increase its value, by excluding a competitor from the market for its products." Id. In addition, the covenant transgressed a

---

11. Because Kibbe, the original covenantor, was not a party to the Norcross case, it was obvious that classifying the covenant with warranties of title would not assist the plaintiff.

supposed rule against attaching "new and unusual incidents" to land, for it attempted to create "an easement of monopoly, an easement not be competed with" not theretofore recognized. Id.

Two observations about Norcross are appropriate before we consider later developments. First of all, the benefit of the covenant surely touched and concerned the dominant estate within the ordinary sense and meaning of the phrase "touch and concern." Justice Holmes's analysis has been described as "overlook(ing) the purpose of all building restrictions, which is to enhance the market value of the promisee's land, whether for residential or for business purposes." 2 American Law of Property § 9.28, at 414 (Casner ed. 1952). It has been suggested that Justice Holmes's "real objection to (the covenant was) the policy against monopolies, and not any policy with reference to real covenants as such." C. Clark, Real Covenants and Other Interests Which "Run with Land" 84 n. 26 (1929). Cf. 140 Mass. at 193, 2 N.E. 946 (unnecessary to decide whether covenant would be invalid restraint of trade if enforcement attempted against Kibbe). If free-competition policies were indeed the basis for the Norcross decision, it would now seem preferable for us to deal with them explicitly rather than to condemn all anticompetitive covenants regardless of reasonableness.

Second, Norcross seems to turn on an assumption that there could be no other class of covenants, differing both from easements and from warranties, but which might nevertheless run with the land. Justice Holmes reasoned that neither the benefit nor the burden of the covenant could run because the benefit was personal to the original covenantee and was therefore inconsistent with the existence of any easement-like right appurtenant to the dominant land. Underlying such reasoning is the peculiar Massachusetts requirement of privity of estate, created by the existence of an easement between the parties to an action on a real covenant. Clark, *supra* at 88. Cf. Morse v. Aldrich, supra at 452–454 (statement of Massachusetts privity rule); 140 Mass. at 191, 2 N.E. 946 (citing Massachusetts privity cases). Yet, privity of estate in this sense had never been thought essential to an action in equity for specific performance of a covenant. [   ]

* * *

Massachusetts has been practically alone in its position that covenants not to compete do not run with the land to which they relate. It has long been the opinion of text writers that our rule is anachronistic and in need of change. See 2 American Law of Property § 9.28, at 414 (J. Casner ed. 1952); 5 Powell, *supra* par. 678, at 197. The American Law Institute has suggested that an otherwise enforceable covenant not to compete should be held enforceable in the same manner as an equitable servitude. Restatement of Property § 539, Comment k (1944). Reasonable anticompetitive covenants are enforceable in the great majority of States where the issue has arisen. See Comment, Covenants Not to Compete: Do They Pass?, 4 Cal.W.L.Rev. 131, 133–134 (1968). Modern judicial analysis of cases like the one at bar appears to concentrate on the effects of particular covenants on competition and to avoid the esoteric convolutions of the law of real covenants. See, e.g., Hall v. American Oil Co., 504 S.W.2d 313, 316 n. 3 (Mo.App.1973); Quadro Stations, Inc. v. Gilley, 7 N.C.App. 227, 231–235, 172 S.E.2d 237 (1970).

In addition to the doctrinal questions about the Norcross rule and the preference of most authorities for a more flexible approach, we may note the unfairness that would result from applying that rule to the facts of this case. In what appears to have been an arm's-length transaction, Kotseas agreed in 1968 not to use retained land in competition with the Trust. We may assume (a) that Kotseas received compensation for thus giving up part of his ownership rights by limiting the uses he could make of the retained land, and (b) that freedom from destructive, next-door competition was part of the inducement for the Trust's purchase and of the price paid by the Trust. Plaza, a closely associated business entity, succeeded to the Trust's interest in 1975. One of these entities established a business, presumably at great cost to itself and in reliance on the contractually obtained limitation of competition in its own narrow market area. Notwithstanding the promise not to do so, Kotseas proceeded to lease land to CVS for the purpose of carrying on the business that it knew would, at least in part, compete with Plaza and divert customers from Plaza's premises. Acting with full knowledge of the 1968 arrangement, CVS participated in this inequitable conduct by Kotseas. If we assume for the moment that the 1968 covenants are reasonable in their application to the present facts, we cannot condone the conduct of Kotseas and CVS. Yet, if Norcross remains the law, we are powerless to prevent Kotseas and CVS from indirectly destroying or diminishing the value of Plaza's investment in its business.

We think the time has come to acknowledge the infirmities and inequities of Norcross. Prior decisions by this court establish what we believe is the proper direction. With respect to covenants in commercial leases, we have long held that reasonable anticompetitive covenants are enforceable by and against successors to the original parties. [ ] We have applied a similar rule with respect to covenants between fee owners when we could identify intelligible land-use planning goals. * * * In short, our decisions support what we hereby state to be the law: reasonable covenants against competition *may* be considered to run with the land when they serve a purpose of facilitating orderly and harmonious development for commercial use. To the extent they are inconsistent with this statement, Norcross, Shade, and Ouellette are hereby expressly overruled.

We recognized in our decision in Ouellette that "(t)he fact of bar reliance in the past, however, must be given weight where a rule affecting real estate is involved." 352 Mass. at 730, 227 N.E.2d at 512. The fact of such reliance is a persuasive reason for excluding all covenants executed before June 13, 1967, the date of the Ouellette decision, from the operation and effect of the new rule which we have declared in the preceding paragraph of the present opinion. [ ] We believe that parties who, after the date of the Ouellette decision, executed restrictive covenants of the kind involved in this case could reasonably have relied on the expectation that on the next appropriate occasion thereafter this court would overrule the Shade and Norcross decisions, as we have done by our present decision. We believe further that parties who executed such covenants after Ouellette could not reasonably expect that the covenants would continue to be unenforceable under the rule of the Shade and Norcross decisions. We therefore hold that our overruling of the rule of the Shade and Norcross decisions shall apply to all such covenants executed after the Ouellette decision. [ ]

What we have said should not be construed as an invitation to legal draftsmen to insert unlimited, "boilerplate"-type covenants against competition in real estate documents. As we have said, an enforceable covenant will be one which is consistent with a reasonable overall purpose to develop real estate for commercial use. In addition, the ordinary requirements for creation and enforcement of real covenants must be met. We have summarized many of these requirements earlier in this opinion. Others are found in G.L. c. 184, §§ 27, 30, which regulate enforcement of land-use restrictions generally. Within these limits, however, commercial developers may control the course of development by reasonable restrictive covenants free from resort to devious subterfuges in their attempts to avoid the doubts created by the Norcross rule and our efforts to apply or reconcile it in later cases.

* * *

[The court proceeded to hold that claims of unreasonable restraint of trade raised factual questions that would have to be resolved on remand.]

III. Conclusion

To the extent that they dismiss Plaza's claims under c. 93A, the judgments are affirmed without prejudice to Plaza's right to amend its complaints within a reasonable time hereafter. To the extent they dismiss Plaza's claims for violation of real covenants or for interference with contractual relations, the judgments are erroneous and must be vacated. The cases are remanded to the Superior Court for further proceedings consistent with this opinion.

So ordered.

Notes and Questions

1. Was Kotseas' conduct inequitable and Plaza's reliance justified, given the previous state of Massachusetts law?

2. One implication of the position of the 1944 Restatement of Property (Servitudes) that the burden of a servitude was only enforceable as a real covenant if the benefit touched and concerned land was that covenants could not be created in gross. Restatement of the Law of Property (Servitudes) § 537(a) (1944). The Restatement did, however, permit equitable servitudes

in gross, § 539, Comment k. Servitudes in gross serve a variety of useful purposes. Conservation groups, for example, can acquire development easements, permitting an owner to continue using his land for agricultural uses, but prohibiting development. Restrictions promoting historical preservation could also be owned by groups dedicated to that goal. Finally, property owners' associations often hold rights to enforce servitudes, including the right to enforce affirmative obligations like the payment of dues, even though they themselves own no property. Covenants against competition, like that found in the principal case, may be held in gross, as may covenants created for the benefit of governmental entities. The Restatement of Property (Third) Servitudes (2000) takes the position that:

> (b) The benefit of a servitude may be held personally, in gross, or as an appurtenance to an estate or other interest in land. § 2.6

While decisions are divided on whether this statement accurately represents the law (see Roberts, Promises Respecting Land Use—Can Benefits be Held in Gross, 51 Mo.L.Rev. 933 (1986)) there is much to commend it.

3. The English courts prohibited running of servitudes that imposed affirmative obligations. A similar result has been reached by some American courts, which have held that affirmative covenants, such as covenants to pay money, do not touch and concern the land. See Eagle Enterprises, Inc. v. Gross, 39 N.Y.2d 505, 384 N.Y.S.2d 717, 349 N.E.2d 816 (1976) (obligation to purchase water from developer does not touch and concern the land). Most American courts, however, permit the running of affirmative servitudes.

(b) Interpretation or Invalidation to Promote Public Policy

Kotseas reaches beyond traditional servitude law to a more public policy-based approach to servitude law. Could an approach to questions of validity and interpretation be devised that was based solely on public policy, without consideration of traditional notions such as horizontal privity or touch and concern?

Some problems of servitude law are well-suited to such an approach. One of the most common uses of restrictive covenants in the early part of the twentieth century was to create racially restricted subdivisions. In some parts of the country virtually all deeds in new subdivisions had covenants or conditions prohibiting the sale of the property to African–Americans or limiting purchase to caucasians. Asians and Jews were also frequently singled out by such restrictions. In Shelley v. Kraemer, 334 U.S. 1, 68 S.Ct. 836, 92 L.Ed. 1161 (1948), the United States Supreme Court held that, while such covenants were not void, enforcement of them by the courts through the grant of injunctive relief would violate the Fourteenth Amendment. Subsequently, the Court in Barrows v. Jackson, 346 U.S. 249, 73 S.Ct. 1031, 97 L.Ed. 1586 (1953), held that such covenants could not be enforced through the grant of money damages. They would also currently violate Title VIII of the Civil Rights Act of 1968, 42 U.S.C.A. §§ 3601–3631. Such covenants continue to exist pervasively, however, in the chains of title of American real estate. Can anything be done to remove such restrictions? Is there any reason for attempting to do so if they cannot be enforced under *Shelley v. Kraemer*?

Since servitudes are based on private agreements, their existence does not require state action. Enforcement of servitudes requires judicial action, however, and it is here that the Court in *Shelley* found state action. How broad is this principle? Should a servitude that prohibits religious uses be found to violate the Free Exercise Clause? Compare West Hill Baptist Church v. Abbate, 24 Ohio Misc. 66, 261 N.E.2d 196 (Com.Pl.1969) (yes), with Ireland v. Bible Baptist Church, 480 S.W.2d 467 (Tex.Civ.App.1972), cert. den., 411 U.S. 906, 93 S.Ct. 1529, 36 L.Ed.2d 195 (1973); Ginsberg v. Yeshiva of Far Rockaway, 45 A.D.2d 334, 358 N.Y.S.2d 477 (1974), aff'd, 36 N.Y.2d 706, 366 N.Y.S.2d 418, 325 N.E.2d 876 (1975) (no). Does a court's holding that a servitude is invalid constitute the taking of a property interest without compensation, also prohibited by the Constitution?

Servitudes can also under some circumstances be challenged as restraints on alienation.

The Restatement of Property (Third) Servitudes (2000) states at § 3.4:

> A servitude that imposes a direct restraint on alienation of the burdened estate is invalid if the restraint is unreasonable. Reasonableness is determined by weighing the utility of the restraint against the injurious consequences of enforcing the restraint.

Section 3.5 states:

> (1) An otherwise valid servitude is valid even if it indirectly restrains alienation by limiting the use that can be made of property, by reducing the amount realizable by the owner on sale or other transfer of the property, or by otherwise reducing the value of the property.
>
> (2) A servitude that lacks a rational justification is invalid.

For an example of this approach, see Taormina Theosophical Community, Inc. v. Silver, 190 Cal.Rptr. 38, 140 Cal.App.3d 964 (1983). In that case a covenant prohibited sales of land within a restricted community except to Theosophists over 50 years of age. The court held the covenant was an invalid restraint on alienation, as there were only 6000 Theosophists in the United States, and even fewer over 50. Should a servitude that requires construction of a residence of at least 3000 square feet in area, or of at least $500,000 in value, also be held to be a restraint on alienation? Do such restrictions substantially limit the number of prospective purchasers of a particular property? Should cooperatives or condominiums be given greater latitude in restricting sales of units than developments involving separately owned single-family dwellings?

Another approach to dealing with discriminatory restrictions is to limit their restrictive nature through a narrow interpretation rather than to eliminate them through invalidation. Such an approach leaves the restrictions intact, but may substantially diverge from the intent of the initial drafter of the servitude.

BLEVINS v. BARRY–LAWRENCE COUNTY ASSOCIATION FOR RETARDED CITIZENS

Supreme Court of Missouri, 1986.
707 S.W.2d 407.

WELLIVER, JUDGE.

This is an appeal from a circuit court judgment enjoining appellant, Barry–Lawrence County Association for Retarded Citizens, from using its property as a group home for retarded individuals. Respondents, Jess and Nedra Blevins, brought this equitable action alleging that said use violates a restrictive covenant on the lot. * * * We reverse.

Appellant owns Lot 23 and the residence thereon in the Wildwood Estates Subdivision of Cassville, Missouri, and it plans on establishing a group home for eight unrelated mentally retarded persons. Respondents own Lot 24, which is across the street from appellant's property. The subdivision is protected by restrictive covenants, which provide in relevant part:

> 1. The aforesaid real property shall be used for residential purposes only. No buildings shall be erected, altered, placed or permitted to remain on said real property other than single or double family dwellings not to exceed two and one-half stories in height and private garages for not more than two cars. No detached structures shall be permitted.

Respondents argue that appellant's intended use of its property will contravene this covenant. Appellant responds by alleging (1) that its intended use does not violate the covenant; (2) that awarding an equitable injunction would violate public policy, as illustrated by the recently enacted § 89.020, RSMo Supp.1985 which forbids either zoning ordinances or restrictive covenants from excluding group homes for mentally retarded individuals; and (3) that § 89.020 must be given retroactive effect and, therefore, the provision of the restrictive covenant is void.

* * *

It is a well-established rule that restrictive covenants are not favorites of the law, and when interpreting such covenants, courts should give effect to the intent of the parties as expressed in the plain language of the covenant; but, when there is any ambiguity or substantial doubt as to the meaning, restrictive covenants will be read narrowly in favor of the free use of property. [ ] It might be noted that respondent attempted to establish the intent of the parties to the covenant by offering the testimony of one of the original developers. Such evidence, however, is neither binding as a matter of law nor usually admissible. [ ]

The initial question is whether the group home for eight unrelated persons and two house parents violates the restriction against any use other than for "residential purposes only." In Shepherd v. State, 427 S.W.2d 382 (Mo.1968), this Court interpreted the phrase "residential purposes" in a restrictive covenant. This Court quoted with approval the following definition of "residential purposes":

> Giving the words their plain and ordinary meaning, we would say that * * * it is, one in which people reside or dwell, or which they make their homes, as distinguished from one which is used for commercial or business purposes.

Shepherd v. State, supra, at 388. [ ] Apartment buildings, therefore, were permitted under the covenant.

It is beyond doubt that the operation of the group home in question has all the characteristics of a residential as opposed to a commercial use. The home is owned and run by a non-profit organization, and the underlying theory behind establishing such a home is that it serves as a surrogate family arrangement. There is no commercial enterprise, and the home is neither a boarding house nor an institutional facility. The trial court found the following facts relative to the operation of the home:

> [Appellant] operates a number of "group homes" in which mentally retarded adults live in a residential setting with "house parents", often a husband and wife, who provide supervision and care for the retarded adults.

* * *

> The group home as contemplated to be operated in Wildwood Estates by defendant is designed to allow the residents to develop their social, emotional and intellectual skills by living in a stable family-type environment. The house parents and residents function in an integrated family-style unit instead of as independent individuals who share only a place to sleep and eat. Residents are involved in performing simpl[e] household duties and participate in discussing, and if possible, resolving problems existing in the home and in making decisions as to the nature of group activities. Although ultimate decisions are left to house parents and/or the defendants board. The entire group often attends church, goes shopping and travels about the community in a body.

> * * * [F]ormal training for the retarded residents does not take place in the group home, but rather is conducted at an activity center or sheltered workshop during the workweek. Within the group home, the house parents encourage the development of social skills and simple homemaking skills by the individuals living there. The primary purpose of a residential group home is to provide a living situation as normal as possible for developmentally disabled residents of the community and is ordinarily not a temporary living arrangement but, depending upon the individual, a resident may remain in the group home months, years or for their entire lifetime.

The trial court also found that prospective occupants of group homes are carefully screened and are admitted, at first, only on a trial basis. We believe that these findings of fact clearly indicate that appellant's intended use of Lot 23 as a group home is a residential purpose under the restrictive covenant.

Faced with a similar factual situation, a substantial number of courts have held that the operation of a group home is a residential purpose within the meaning of a covenant with such a restriction. [ ] See generally Annot., Restrictive Covenant Limiting Land Use to "Private Residence" or "Private Residential Purposes": Interpretations and Application, 43 A.L.R.4th 71 (1986); Annot., Use of Property for Multiple Dwellings as Violating Restrictive Covenant Permitting Property to be used for Residential Purposes Only, 99 A.L.R.3d 985 (1980).

* * *

The remaining question is whether appellant's intended use of the property violates the second sentence of the restrictive covenant, which prohibits erecting, altering, placing or permitting any building "other than single or double family dwellings not to exceed two and one-half stories in height and private garages for not more than two cars." Respondents argue that this restriction is a restriction on the use of the property; and, if a restriction on use, appellant's group home is neither a single nor a double family dwelling.

By its plain terms, however, this restriction applies only to structures and not to the use of the property.

* * *

A number of other jurisdictions have reached a similar conclusion.[12] [ ]

The record indicates that appellant does not intend to alter the structure of the residence on its lot. We hold, therefore, that appellant's intended use of its property does not violate the terms of the restrictive covenant. The trial court judgment granting the injunction is reversed.

Notes and Questions

Interpretation of negative or affirmative servitudes is necessary where a property owner wants to use the property for uses not clearly permitted by the restrictions. A host of cases, for example, address the question of whether restrictions limiting property to "residential purposes" or to a "dwelling house" excludes use for apartments, duplexes, or boarding homes, or for home occupations. Limitations governing types of commercial uses permitted or locations of buildings on lots also have resulted in litigation.

---

12. We need not reach the issue of whether the group home would satisfy a single or double family use restriction. However, it might be noted that a number of jurisdictions, whether interpreting a restrictive covenant or a zoning ordinance, hold that certain group homes may be a "family" unless an explicit definition contained in the covenant or ordinance dictates otherwise. [ ] Recently the United States Supreme Court held that the application of a particular ordinance to prohibit a group home for mentally disabled persons was unconstitutional. City of Cleburne, Tex. v. Cleburne Living Center, 473 U.S. 432, 105 S.Ct. 3249, 87 L.Ed.2d 313 (1985). [ ]

Courts commonly construe restrictions strictly so as to promote the use of land, as in the principal case. See 5 R. Powell, & P. Rohan, Powell on Real Property, ¶ 674 (1991).

Interpretation may also be necessary where a land-owner proposes to use property for uses not contemplated at the time the restriction was drafted. In Breeling v. Churchill, 228 Neb. 596, 423 N.W.2d 469 (1988), a landowner was enjoined from erecting a satellite dish on her lot in violation of a 1972 restriction prohibiting any "outside radio, television, Ham broadcasting, or other electronic antenna or aerial." The court sensibly read the restriction to preclude satellite dishes, even though the technology was not in use at the time the restriction was granted.

4. *Succession to Servitudes*

If a servitude is determined to be valid and enforceable, and to run with the land generally to bind or benefit persons who subsequently hold interests in the burdened or benefited properties, the question still remains which particular individual subsequent purchasers will be bound or benefited.

(a) *The Running of Burdens*

(i) *The Vertical Privity Requirement*

The running of the burden of servitudes is limited both by the law of servitudes and by the recording acts. The most important of the limits imposed by the law of servitudes is the requirement of vertical privity, mentioned in the *Moseley* case above. While horizontal privity refers to the relationship between the initial promisor and promisee, vertical privity refers to the relationships between the initial promisor and promisee and their successors. The labels relate to a diagram used by generations of property teachers:

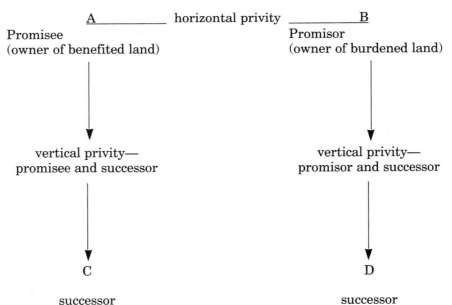

A ———————— horizontal privity ———————— B
Promisee   Promisor
(owner of benefited land)   (owner of burdened land)

vertical privity—   vertical privity—
promisee and successor   promisor and successor

C   D

successor   successor

The 1944 Restatement of the Law of Property (Servitudes), § 535 describes the sorts of relationships that can meet the vertical privity requirements for succession to the benefit or burden of promises respecting the use of land enforceable at law.

§ 535. PRIVITY AS BETWEEN PROMISOR AND SUCCESSOR

The successors in title to land respecting the use of which the owner has made a promise are not bound as promisors upon the promise unless by their succession they hold

(a) the estate or interest held by the promisor at the time the promise was made, or

(b) an estate or interest corresponding in duration to the estate or interest held by the promisor at that time.

Note that the same relationship that can serve to establish horizontal privity can also serve to establish vertical privity. A purchaser purchasing a lot in a subdivision is in a successive relationship with the developer (i.e. the purchaser succeeds to the interest of the developer in the purchased lot). This successive relationship meets the requirements of either horizontal privity or vertical privity. Whether it is considered under one category or the other depends on the relationship of the purchaser to the promise which is being enforced. If the purchaser/developer relationship is the initial relationship pursuant to which the promise was made that is now being enforced, the relevant category is horizontal privity. If the purchaser succeeds to a previously burdened or benefited parcel (i.e., the developer has earlier made a promise binding or received a promise to benefit the retained land now being purchased), the relevant category is vertical privity.

What sorts of relationships meet the requirements of Restatement § 535? A sells Blackacre, bound by a servitude which requires the payment of an annual fee to a neighbor for maintenance of a common fence, to B. Is B bound by the servitude under Restatement § 535? A leases the property to B for one year. Must B make the payment? B takes the property from A by adverse possession. Must B continue to pay the fee? If you reach a different result for the different questions, is the result defensible in principle? Should the requirements be different if the servitude were negative in nature, e.g., a servitude prohibiting commercial uses in a residential neighborhood? Should tenants be treated differently from adverse possessors? Compare Reichman, Toward a Unified Concept of Servitudes, 55 S.Cal.L.Rev. 1179, 1249–1252 (1982) (vertical privity requirement makes no sense with respect to negative servitudes, affirmative obligations should be governed by rule that looked to nature of relationships and burdens) with French, Toward a

Modern Law of Servitudes: Reweaving the Ancient Strands, 55 S.Cal.L.Rev. 1261, 1294–96 (1982) (vertical privity requirement as applied to limit the running of affirmative burdens is efficient and fair).

The 1944 Restatement required a looser privity—succession to title or possession of a property—for enforcement of the benefit of a servitude at equity. Does it make sense to have different standards for enforcement at law and at equity? Might your answer turn on whether affirmative obligations, as well as negative, were enforceable at equity?

The Restatement of Property (Third) Servitudes (2000) adopts a nuanced approach to the vertical privity requirement. The general rule of the 2000 Restatement is that vertical privity is not required for the benefit or burden of a servitude to run to a subsequent possessor. See section 5.2. Certain subsequent possessors who hold lesser interests than the original covenanting party are treated separately. Section 5.3 covers lessees and life tenants and provides as follows:

(1) The benefits of the following affirmative covenants run to the lessee:

> (a) a covenant to repair, maintain, or render services to the property; and

> (b) a covenant benefit that can be enjoyed by the lessee without diminishing its value to the lessor and without materially increasing the burden of performance on the person obligated to perform the covenant.

(2) The burden of an affirmative covenant that can more reasonably be performed by a person in possession than by the holder of a reversion in the burdened property runs to the lessee.

(3) The benefits and burdens of other affirmative covenants do not run to the lessee.

Section 5.4 deals with the running of benefits and burdens to life tenants and provides as follows:

> Except as otherwise provided by its terms, the benefits and burdens of an affirmative covenant created prior to creation of a life estate in the property to which the benefits or burdens are appurtenant run to the life tenant, subject to the proviso that the life tenant's liability for performance of affirmative covenants is limited to the value of the life estate. Performance rendered to the life tenant satisfies the current obligation imposed by a covenant that benefits the property.

Section 5.5 deals with the running of benefits and burdens to adverse possessors and provides as follows:

> Except as otherwise provided by its terms, the benefit of the following described affirmative covenants runs to an adverse possessor who has not gained title to the benefitted property:

(1) the benefit of covenants to repair, maintain, or render services to the property;

and

(2) covenant benefits that can be enjoyed by the person in possession without diminishing their value to the owner of the property and without materially increasing the burden of perform-ance on the person obligated to perform the covenant.

(ii) Notice

Equitable servitudes are only enforceable against persons who take with notice. By virtue of the recording acts, the same is true with all servitudes. Questions of notice are often, therefore, very important when enforcement of servitudes is sought. The notice requirement seldom causes problems where a servitude is expressly placed in a recorded deed of a particular property against which the servitude is later enforced. A standard title search would find the servitude, and imposition of con-structive notice is certainly defensible where such a title search is not done. Where servitudes are created by implication, however, or where the servitude is imposed by a deed from a common grantor to the owner of a benefited property but does not appear in the subsequent deed to the purchaser of the burdened parcel, locating the servitude through a title search becomes much more difficult. The question then arises whether the owner of the burdened parcel had sufficient notice of the servitude to be bound by it.

BISHOP v. RUEFF

Court of Appeals of Kentucky, 1981.
619 S.W.2d 718.

REYNOLDS, JUDGE.

Mrs. Nancy Bishop, appellant (plaintiff below), was awarded $1,801 damages in an action instituted against adjoining property owners, William and Patricia Rueff. This is an appeal and cross-appeal from the judgment.

The Rueffs had constructed a backyard patio and enclosed it with a 7–foot high "wooden slab" fence. One section of the fence was erected upon the parties' common boundary which was in near proximity to the side of the Bishop home. As a result of this improvement, appellant alleged damages resulting in changes from the water-flow across her property, as well as from the interference with her use and enjoyment of the property, and, additionally, she had sought injunctive relief to bring the fence into compliance with cited restrictive covenant.

Mr. George Imorde initially owned a sizeable tract of property, and from a portion of the tract he established four lots, one of which he sold to Mrs. Bishop in June of 1957, and her deed contained the following restriction:

> As a further consideration for this conveyance, it is hereby agreed that the property herein conveyed shall be subject to the following restrictions:
>
> No. 4 No solid board fence shall be erected on the property. Fencing, if any, shall be of rail, picket or shrub. Fences, other than shrub, shall not exceed four feet in height.
>
> It is further agreed that the restrictions hereinabove set out shall apply to and affect all the remaining property of the parties of the first part as was conveyed to George H. Imorde by deed of record in Deed Book 2672, Page 566, in the aforesaid Clerk's office.

Subsequent to this transaction, and before June 17, 1959, three additional lots were sold by Mr. Imorde, and with only one of those deeds (Lot 251 sold on July 3, 1957) containing notice of these restrictions. On March 29, 1962, Mr. Imorde disposed of a larger tract constituting the remainder of this property to developers David H. Wilson and Bobby J. Welsh. A subdivision containing eleven lots, being known as Trough Springs, was then developed with separate restrictions, none of which mentioned, nor did the deeds refer to, or notice, the restrictions contained in Mrs. Bishop's deed. On June 1, 1973, appellees became owners of a Trough Springs Subdivision lot which abutted the Bishop property.

Appellees were unaware of the restrictions until their backyard construction was substantially complete. This area had been graded, as well as elevated, which allowed water to flow/stand upon appellant's property.

In its instructions to the jury, the court ruled that the restrictions serving as the basis for appellant's claim for injunctive relief were inapplicable. The court reasoned that in the absence of notice in the direct chain of title, appellees were not charged with duty of notice. * * * [The jury awarded damages for diverted surface water and nuisance (not for violation of the servitude).]

Appellant argues that the deed restrictions ran with the land and were therefore binding on any subsequent purchasers of remaining portions of the original tract, and that the court's instructions were contrary to law and erroneous. On cross-appeal it is asserted that the court erred in not directing a verdict in their favor at the close of all evidence regarding the claims for water damage and nuisance.

Generally, the grantee is charged with notice of an encumbrance upon property created by an instrument which is of record, notwithstanding the fact that it may exist only collaterally in the chain of title. Harp v. Parker, 278 Ky. 78, 128 S.W.2d 211 (1939). The trial court determined that the restrictive covenant from the Bishop deed had no application to the lot subsequently acquired by appellees. The criteria for determining whether a covenant runs with the land or is merely personal between the grantor and the grantee include the intent of the parties, whether the covenant must affect or concern the land with which it runs, and whether privity of estate exists between the party claiming the benefit and the party who rests under the burden. 21 C.J.S. Covenants § 54. While the Bishops' deed was not in appellees' chain of title, we are aware of no rule that a restrictive covenant of this nature must meet such requirement. We believe that appellees were on constructive notice as to the restriction limiting fences, and there is some evidence of actual notice. The "chain of title" argument seems to have been disposed of by Harp v. Parker, supra.

We believe the governing principle involved is stated in McLean v. Thurman, Ky., 273 S.W.2d 825, 829 (1954). Where the owners of two or more lots situated near one another convey one of the lots with express restrictions applying thereto in favor of the land retained by the grantor, the servitude becomes mutual, and during the period of restraint the owner of the lots retained may do nothing that is forbidden to the owner of the lot sold. The restriction is enforceable against the grantor, or subsequent purchaser, with notice, actual or constructive. [ ]

The deed of conveyance between Imorde and appellant contains words indicating that the parties intended for the restrictive covenants to run with Imorde's remaining lands and thus be binding on subsequent purchasers. After the Bishop sale, Imorde sold three additional residential lots. One of the deeds contained the restriction. We hold that the trial court erred by denying injunctive relief.

* * *

The judgment of the trial court is reversed in part, and appellant is entitled to the enforcement of the restrictive covenant which provides:

> No solid board fence shall be erected on the property. Fencing, if any, shall be of rail, picket or shrub. Fences, other than shrub, shall not exceed four feet in height.

The judgment of the trial court, in all other respects, is affirmed.

HOWERTON, JUDGE, concurring.

I would like to affirm Judge Eckert in all respects, but I must concur in the result reached by this Court. Perhaps our Supreme Court will see fit to bring the law regarding reciprocal negative easements and/or covenants running with the land into the late Twentieth Century. This case disturbs me, because we are giving effect to land restrictions which are not within a chain of title, nor are they contained in an instrument which should necessarily be checked to insure a clear title.

Three Kentucky cases which have dealt with the problem and which have helped establish the law are Anderson v. Henslee, 226 Ky. 465, 11 S.W.2d 154 (1928); Harp v. Parker, 278 Ky. 78, 128 S.W.2d 211 (1939); and McLean v. Thurman, Ky., 273 S.W.2d 825 (1954). Each of the cases, if limited to its facts, could be distinguished from the case at bar, but the language of the opinions expresses the law in such a way that such restrictions are enforceable, if reasonable. Constructive notice was considered to be given, because the restrictions were recorded in a deed from a common grantor, although the deed was outside the chain of title of the party to be bound by the restrictions.

* * *

Generally, the law is that reciprocal negative easements, which are enforceable against a grantor, are also enforceable against a subsequent purchaser of the common grantor's restricted remaining property, if the purchaser has notice, actual or constructive. I find no fault with that general principle, but the problem comes in what constitutes constructive notice of such off-shoot restrictions.

In attempting to "settle" the chain of title argument in Harp, the court adopted a passage from 2 Tiffany on Real Property, (2d Ed.) p. 2188. The passage concludes:

> And if, in conveying lot A the grantor enters into a restrictive agreement as to the improvement of lot B, retained by him, a subsequent purchaser of lot B would ordinarily be charged with notice of the agreement, by reason of its record as a part of the conveyance of lot A. Harp v. Parker, 278 Ky. 78, at 82, 128 S.W.2d 211.

Lot A is a conveyance from a common grantor with lot B, but the deed to lot A is outside the chain of title for lot B. The restrictive agreement is not in any conveyance to the common grantor.

It appears to me that the question of what is reasonable should not only apply to the nature of the restriction, but also to the manner of recording and what should constitute constructive notice. None of the three cited cases reach unreasonable results on the basis of their facts. However, to blindly apply Tiffany's principle in today's world is absurd. We are no longer dealing with a few conveyances or the examples of "blackacre" and "whiteacre."

Today, we may find a subdivision of 1,000 acres divided into 2,000 lots. If the owner of the subdivision agreed with the buyer of the twenty-fifth lot to have a reciprocal negative easement against fences on the remainder of his land, is every lot sold thereafter to be bound solely from the restriction written in the twenty-fifth deed? If so, it means that the buyer of lot number 2,000 would have to examine all 1,999 preceding deeds.

Buyers and lenders already have legitimate complaints regarding costs of title examinations, but we have heard nothing compared to what we will hear, if such useless and unreasonable burdens are mandated. It would be far more reasonable to require the buyer of lot A or 25 to require the grantor to record a separate instrument putting the restrictions squarely on the common grantor and in all chains of title from him. If the buyer of lot A or 25 desires to have the restrictions run with the land, he could require that the necessary instrument be prepared and recorded.

There will be times when a proper title examination will reveal restrictions which are nevertheless outside the chain of title. Examples of these situations would be similar to Anderson, Harp, and McLean, supra. Actual knowledge may come from any source, but constructive notice should not be applied to any situation where reciprocal negative restrictions are recorded only outside the chain of title.

Notes and Questions

1. In a jurisdiction that implies servitudes from the existence of a common scheme, what would a title examiner have to do before pronouncing whether or not a lot in a subdivision was bound by express servitudes? When searching the title of a subdivision lot in a jurisdiction which permits implication of restrictions, is it possible to do an adequate title search if the search is restricted solely to documents found in a recorder's office or title plant? See Sanborn v. McLean, 233 Mich. 227, 206 N.W. 496, 60 A.L.R. 1212 (1925) (inquiry notice from "strictly uniform" character of development of lots).

Bishop v. Rueff was overruled in part by Oliver v. Schultz, 885 S.W.2d 699, 701 (Ky.1994):

[I]t has become obvious to this Court that the law in this area needs to be clarified. In response to Judge Howerton's concurring opinion in Bishop, we hold that Bishop is only applicable under two circumstances: first, where the remainder of the grantor's property is restricted in a deed of conveyance in such a manner that the restriction runs with the land; and second, that a subdivision plat, a deed of restrictions, or some other instrument of record is filed that would place an ordinary and reasonably prudent attorney performing a title search on notice of the restrictions in question. To the extent that Bishop allows a restriction placed in a collateral chain of title to bind a subsequent grantee in the absence of a recorded subdivision plat or deed of restrictions, it is overruled. In the future, restrictive covenants will be enforced under Kentucky law only when the restriction is placed in a recorded instrument, actual notice of a purported restriction notwithstanding.

2. 4 The American Law of Property, § 17.24 (J. Casner ed. (1952)) states that the courts are equally divided between the positions of the majority and concurring opinion in the principal case.

(b) The Running of Benefits

The 1944 Restatement takes the position that the only privity necessary for the benefit of a servitude (either enforceable at law as a real covenant or at equity as an equitable servitude) is that the successor "succeeds to some interest of the beneficiary." § 547. This language was intended to exclude adverse possessors, but why should they be excluded if a servitude is in fact a property rather than a contract interest? Professor French, the author of the 1989 Draft Restatement, argues that there is no case authority to support the position of the 1944 Restatement, and no reason other than dislike of adverse possessors for barring them from enforcement of servitudes. French, Toward a Modern Law of Servitudes: Reweaving the Ancient Strands, 55 S.Cal.L.Rev. 1261, 1294–96 (1982). The 2000 Restatement adopts this position in large part and provides as follows:

> Except as otherwise provided by its terms, the benefit of the following described affirmative covenants runs to an adverse possessor who has not gained title to the benefitted property:
>
> 1. (1) the benefit of covenants to repair, maintain, or render services to the property; and
>
> (2) covenant benefits that can be enjoyed by the person in possession without diminishing their value to the owner of the property and without materially increasing the burden of performance on the person obligated to perform the covenant.

C. TERMINATION

EL DI, INC. v. TOWN OF BETHANY BEACH

Supreme Court of Delaware, 1984.
477 A.2d 1066.

HERRMANN, CHIEF JUSTICE for the majority:

This is an appeal from a permanent injunction granted by the Court of Chancery upon the petition of the plaintiffs, The Town of Bethany Beach, et al., prohibiting the defendant, El Di, Inc. ("El Di") from selling alcoholic beverages at Holiday House, a restaurant in Bethany Beach owned and operated by El Di.

I.

The pertinent facts are as follows:

El Di purchased the Holiday House in 1969. In December 1981, El Di filed an application with the State Alcoholic Beverage Control Commission (the "Commission") for a license to sell alcoholic beverages at the Holiday House. On April 15, 1982, finding "public need and convenience," the Commission granted the Holiday House an on-premises license. The sale of alcoholic beverages at Holiday House began within 10 days of the Commission's approval. Plaintiffs subsequently filed suit to permanently enjoin the sale of alcoholic beverages under the license.

On appeal it is undisputed that the chain of title for the Holiday House lot included restrictive covenants prohibiting both the sale of alcoholic beverages on the property and nonresidential construction.[13]

---

13. The restrictive covenant stated: "This covenant is made expressly subject to and upon the following conditions: viz; That no intoxicating liquors shall ever be sold on the said lot, that no other than dwelling or cottage shall be erected thereon and but one to each lot, which must be of full size according to the said plan, excepting, however, suitable and necessary out or back building, which may be erected on the rear

The same restriction was placed on property in Bethany Beach as early as 1900 and 1901 when the area was first under development.

As originally conceived, Bethany Beach was to be a quiet beach community. The site was selected at the end of the nineteenth-century by the Christian Missionary Society of Washington, D.C. In 1900, the Bethany Beach Improvement Company ("BBIC") was formed. The BBIC purchased lands, laid out a development and began selling lots. To insure the quiet character of the community, the BBIC placed restrictive covenants on many plots, prohibiting the sale of alcohol and restricting construction to residential cottages. Of the original 180 acre development, however, approximately ⅓ was unrestricted.

The Town of Bethany Beach was officially incorporated in 1909. The municipal limits consisted of 750 acres including the original BBIC land (hereafter the original or "old-Town"), but expanded far beyond the 180 acre BBIC development. The expanded acreage of the newly incorporated Town, combined with the unrestricted plots in the original Town, left only 15 percent of the new Town subject to the restrictive covenants.

Despite the restriction prohibiting commercial building ("no other than a dwelling or cottage shall be erected * * * "), commercial development began in the 1920's on property subject to the covenants. This development included numerous inns, restaurants, drug stores, a bank, motels, a town hall, shops selling various items including food, clothing, gifts and novelties and other commercial businesses. Of the 34 commercial buildings presently within the Town limits, 29 are located in the old-Town originally developed by BBIC. Today, Bethany Beach has a permanent population of some 330 residents. In the summer months the population increases to approximately 10,000 people within the corporate limits and to some 48,000 people within a 4 mile radius. In 1952, the Town enacted a zoning ordinance which established a central commercial district designated C–1 located in the old-Town section. Holiday House is located in this district.

Since El Di purchased Holiday House in 1969, patrons have been permitted to carry their own alcoholic beverages with them into the restaurant to consume with their meals. This "brown-bagging" practice occurred at Holiday House prior to El Di's ownership and at other restaurants in the Town. El Di applied for a license to sell liquor at Holiday House in response to the increased number of customers who were engaging in "brown-bagging" and in the belief that the license would permit restaurant management to control excessive use of alcohol and use by minors. Prior to the time El Di sought a license, alcoholic

of said lot, and no building or buildings shall be erected thereon within ten feet of the front building line of said lot and, if said lot be a corner lot within ten feet of the building line of the side street on which it abuts, and that all buildings erected or to be erected on said lot shall be kept neatly painted; a breach of which said conditions, or any of them, shall cause said lot to revert to and become again the property of the grantor, his heirs and assigns; and upon such breach of said conditions or restrictions, the same may be restrained or enjoined in equity by the grantor, his heirs or assigns, or by any co-lot owner in said plan or other party injured by such breach."

beverages had been and continue to be readily available for sale at nearby licensed establishments including: one restaurant ½ mile outside the Town limits, 3 restaurants within a 4 mile radius of the Town, and a package store some 200–300 yards from the Holiday House.

The Trial Court granted a stay pending the outcome of this appeal.

II.

In granting plaintiffs' motion for a permanent injunction, the Court of Chancery rejected defendant's argument that changed conditions in Bethany Beach rendered the restrictive covenants unreasonable and therefore unenforceable. Citing Restatement of Property, § 564 [ ]. The Chancery Court found that although the evidence showed a considerable growth since 1900 in both population and the number of buildings in Bethany Beach, "the basic nature of Bethany Beach as a quiet, family oriented resort has not changed." The Court also found that there had been development of commercial activity since 1900, but that this "activity is limited to a small area of Bethany Beach and consists mainly of activities for the convenience and patronage of the residents of Bethany Beach."

The Trial Court also rejected defendant's contention that plaintiffs' acquiescence and abandonment rendered the covenants unenforceable. In this connection, the Court concluded that the practice of "brown-bagging" was not a sale of alcoholic beverages and that, therefore, any failure to enforce the restriction as against the practice did not constitute abandonment or waiver of the restriction.

III.

We find that the Trial Court erred in holding that the change of conditions was insufficient to negate the restrictive covenant.

A court will not enforce a restrictive covenant where a fundamental change has occurred in the intended character of the neighborhood that renders the benefits underlying imposition of the restrictions incapable of enjoyment. [ ] Review of all the facts and circumstances convinces us that the change, since 1901, in the character of that area of the old-Town section now zoned C–1 is so substantial as to justify modification of the deed restriction. We need not determine a change in character of the entire restricted area in order to assess the continued applicability of the covenant to a portion thereof. [ ]

It is uncontradicted that one of the purposes underlying the covenant prohibiting the sale of intoxicating liquors was to maintain a quiet, residential atmosphere in the restricted area. Each of the additional covenants reinforces this objective, including the covenant restricting construction to residential dwellings. The covenants read as a whole evince an intention on the part of the grantor to maintain the residential, seaside character of the community.

But time has not left Bethany Beach the same community its grantors envisioned in 1901. The Town has changed from a church-affiliated residential community to a summer resort visited annually by thousands of tourists. Nowhere is the resultant change in character more evident than in the C–1 section of the old-Town. Plaintiffs argue that this is a relative change only and that there is sufficient evidence to support the Trial Court's findings that the residential character of the community has been maintained and that the covenants continue to benefit the other lot owners. We cannot agree.

In 1909, the 180 acre restricted old-Town section became part of a 750 acre incorporated municipality. Even prior to the Town's incorporation, the BBIC deeded out lots free of the restrictive covenants. After incorporation and partly due to the unrestricted lots deeded out by the BBIC, 85 percent of the land area within the Town was not subject to the restrictions. Significantly, nonresidential uses quickly appeared in the restricted area and today the old-Town section contains almost all of the commercial businesses within the entire Town. [   ] Moreover, these commercial uses have gone unchallenged for 82 years. [   ]

The change in conditions is also reflected in the Town's decision in 1952 to zone restricted property, including the lot on which the Holiday House is located, specifically for commercial use. Although a change in zoning is not dispositive as against a private covenant, it is additional evidence of changed community conditions. [   ]

Time has relaxed not only the strictly residential character of the area, but the pattern of alcohol use and consumption as well. The practice of "brown-bagging" has continued unchallenged for at least twenty years at commercial establishments located on restricted property in the Town. On appeal, plaintiffs rely on the Trial Court finding that the "brown-bagging," practice is irrelevant as evidence of waiver inasmuch as the practice does not involve the sale of intoxicating liquors prohibited by the covenant. We find the "brown-bagging" practice evidence of a significant change in conditions in the community since its inception at the turn of the century. Such consumption of alcohol in public places is now generally tolerated by owners of similarly restricted lots. The license issued to the Holiday House establishment permits the El Di management to better control the availability and consumption of intoxicating liquors on its premises. In view of both the ready availability of alcoholic beverages in the area surrounding the Holiday House and the long-tolerated and increasing use of "brown-bagging," enforcement of the restrictive covenant at this time would only serve to subvert the public interest in the control of the availability and consumption of alcoholic liquors.

Plaintiffs contend that the covenant prohibiting the sale of intoxicating liquors is separate from the other covenants. In the plaintiffs' view, the alcohol sale restriction serves a purpose distinct from the prohibition of nonresidential uses. Plaintiffs argue, therefore, that despite evidence of commercial uses, the alcohol sale restriction provides a substantial benefit to the other lot owners. We find the cases on which plaintiff relies distinguishable:

In Jameson v. Brown, 109 F.2d 830 (D.C.Cir.1939), all of the lots were similarly restricted and there was no evidence of waiver or abandonment of the covenant prohibiting the sale of spiritous liquors. The court found evidence of one isolated violation—in contrast to the long-tolerated practice of "brown-bagging" in Bethany Beach. * * * In Benner v. Tacony Athletic Ass'n, Pa.Supr., 328 Pa. 577, 196 A. 390 (1938), it was found that commercial encroachments were few and that residential properties still closely surrounded the commercial lots. In Bethany Beach commercial uses have not simply crept in, but have been given official sanction through the 1952 Zoning Ordinance.

It is further argued that the commercial uses are restricted to a small area within the old–Town section. But significantly, the section in which Holiday House is located is entirely commercial. The business uses, the availability of alcohol in close proximity to this section, and the repeated use of "brown-bagging" in the C–1 district render the originally intended benefits of the covenants unattainable in what has become an area detached in character from the strictly residential surroundings to the west.

In view of the change in conditions in the C–1 district of Bethany Beach, we find it unreasonable and inequitable now to enforce the restrictive covenant. To permit unlimited "brown-bagging" but to prohibit licensed sales of alcoholic liquor, under the circumstances of this case, is inconsistent with any reasonable application of the restriction and contrary to public policy.

We emphasize that our judgment is confined to the area of the old–Town section zoned C–1. The restrictions in the neighboring residential area are unaffected by the conclusion we reach herein.

Reversed.

CHRISTIE, JUSTICE, with whom MOORE, JUSTICE, joins, dissenting:

I respectfully disagree with the majority.

I think the evidence supports the conclusion of the Chancellor, as finder of fact, that the basic nature of the community of Bethany Beach has not changed in such a way as to invalidate those restrictions which have continued to protect this community through the years as it has grown. Although some of the restrictions have been ignored and a portion of the community is now used for limited commercial purposes, the evidence shows that Bethany Beach remains a quiet, family-oriented resort where no liquor is sold. I think the conditions of the community are still consistent with the enforcement of a restrictive covenant forbidding the sale of intoxicating beverages.

In my opinion, the toleration of the practice of "brown bagging" does not constitute the abandonment of a longstanding restriction against the sale of alcoholic beverages. The restriction against sales has, in fact, remained intact for more than eighty years and any violations thereof have been short-lived. The fact that alcoholic beverages may be purchased right outside the town is not inconsistent with my view that the quiet-town atmosphere in this small area has not broken down, and that it can and should be preserved. Those who choose to buy land subject to the restrictions should be required to continue to abide by the restrictions.

I think the only real beneficiaries of the failure of the courts to enforce the restrictions would be those who plan to benefit commercially.

I also question the propriety of the issuance of a liquor license for the sale of liquor on property which is subject to a specific restrictive covenant against such sales.

I think that restrictive covenants play a vital part in the preservation of neighborhood schemes all over the State, and that a much more complete breakdown of the neighborhood scheme should be required before a court declares that a restriction has become unenforceable.

I would affirm the Chancellor.

Notes and Questions

1. The typical changed conditions case occurs because a residential neighborhood is gradually surrounded by commercial development, making the bordering lots of little value for residential use, but of great value for commercial development. The courts must then decide whether to lift the restriction, freeing the border lots up for their most valued use, or to retain it, thus protecting the interior lots from encroaching commercial development. In applying the changed conditions doctrine, courts are effectively nullifying a property right (or a contract right, depending on how one views servitudes) of the owner of the dominant estate, in order to enhance the value of the servient estate. Whether or not courts should do this has proved quite controversial. The doctrine thus serves as a useful point of departure for considering a wider debate as to the proper role of the courts in enforcing servitudes, and, indeed, of the respective roles generally of private consent and public policy in property law.

Professor Richard Epstein takes a strong stance against judicial interference with contractual arrangements governing the use of land. He further argues that the protection of strangers to such contracts, including future purchasers of restricted property, is normally guaranteed adequately by recordation of restrictions. He then goes on to address the question of whether changed conditions justify modification or termination of private restrictions:

EPSTEIN, NOTICE AND FREEDOM OF CONTRACT IN THE LAW OF SERVITUDES

55 S.Cal.L.Rev. 1353 (1982).

This argument in favor of expanding the scope of the changed conditions doctrine contains three familiar elements. First, it is said that the original parties cannot anticipate changed circumstances and, therefore, cannot guard against them. Second, it is asserted that servitudes that persist over time give their holders the power to "blackmail" others long after their servitudes have become obsolete. Third, it is argued that such servitudes generate excessive transaction costs. Eliminating obsolete servitudes or allowing their modification is said to be beneficial on all three counts. A changed condition doctrine indeed is superior to a doctrine that strikes down many servitudes *ab initio* because its proponents are fearful of the future. But, even a limited doctrine of the sort advocated here is inferior to a complete denial of public intervention based on changed conditions.

The argument that parties who wish to create a servitude are incapable of providing for future contingencies presumes that such parties rarely, if ever, consider changed conditions in the course of their negotiations. The argument continues with the additional presumption that, even if the parties had considered the possibility of changed conditions, they would have agreed to apply the doctrine and allow for the modification or termination of the servitude in question. * * * [M]ost servitudes are not casual affairs. If they are recorded, there is a strong likelihood that the property in question is of sufficient value that both sides have been represented by lawyers. As a matter of construction, therefore, there is much to be gained by demanding that the parties to a transaction deal with the contingency of future uncertainty, just as they must deal with all other contingencies * * *

The parties involved in a transaction can be expected to shape their joint future in a way that promotes their mutual benefit. They may choose to create discretionary powers in anticipation of changed conditions. For example, in the case of planned unit communities, discretionary interests granted to the developer or the homeowners' association commonly function as a device for continuous corporate governance. The fact that discretion is often a good thing, however, is no justification for imposing it from without by terminating servitudes that are deemed obsolete. With discretion comes uncertainty, and this parties may rightly (and expressly) fear. * * * The point is that, given the pervasive ignorance over the trade-off between the virtues of flexibility and certainty, and between the vices of indefiniteness and rigidity, there is simply no persuasive reason to embrace one extreme to the exclusion of the other.

Professor Reichman suggests that courts should be permitted to modify as well as terminate servitudes that are considered obsolete because of changed conditions. Long temporal horizons make *any* present determination of utility imperfect by definition. The relevant question, therefore, is whether judicial determinations are superior to private ones. The original parties can provide for changed conditions if they so desire at the time when servitudes are created. And when disputes arise there is no apparent reason to consider judicial coercion superior to consensual renegotiation.

The second argument, that permanent easements encourage the holders of servitudes to extort large sums from those who wish to buy them out, is misplaced in principle. Here it is worth taking note of what ownership means in the context of the fee simple absolute in possession, i.e., the right to hold out. Suppose that *A* owns land which he does not wish to develop and that *B* wants this land as part of a larger parcel assembled for the most modern and productive use. *B* cannot simply take the land and escape all payment by showing the social superiority of his plans and intentions. Nor can *B* take the land from *A* even if he is prepared to pay him some reserve price, reflective of its value in current use. Ownership is meant to be a bulwark against the collective preferences of others; it allows one, rich or poor, to stand alone against the world no matter how insistent or intense its collective preferences.

In contrast Professor Sterk argues that servitudes create inefficiencies that under some circumstances justify public intervention:

STERK, FREEDOM FROM FREEDOM OF CONTRACT: THE ENDURING VALUE OF SERVITUDE RESTRICTIONS

70 Iowa L.Rev. 615 (1985).

This Article argues that to leave landowners unrestricted in their right to impose by contract obligations that run to successors-in-interest of land would be to ignore, or to subordinate as unworthy of decisive consideration, at least two problems. First, a number of servitudes create externalities. They affect not only the owners of burdened and benefited land, but third parties whose interests are not represented in the negotiation process. Second, many servitudes, particularly those that bind or benefit multiple parties, are difficult to remove because of high transaction costs. Even when parties to the original agreement consider the costs of removing the restrictions and take steps to reduce those costs, their actions do not eliminate the need for subsequent consideration. Current landowners have limited foresight; permitting their restrictions to govern land use for long periods or periods of unlimited duration might frustrate even their own preferences for the future. More important, even if current landowners possessed perfect foresight, to permit their preferences to govern for long periods or forever would be to resolve against future generations difficult questions of intergenerational fairness.

Of course, many servitudes impose no substantial external diseconomies. Nevertheless, high transaction costs—such as the cost associated with negotiating removal—may prevent removal of a servitude. Particularly if the servitude was imposed as part of a neighborhood scheme, with many parties holding the right to enforce the servitude, private negotiations for removal may be fraught with holdout and free rider problems. * * *

Sterk further argues that our legal system does not always protect the rights of hold-outs. The promisee of a contract, for example, cannot invariably insist on specific performance. He argues that leaving landowners to private negotiations when servitudes become inefficient may lead to strategic bargaining by hold-outs that ultimately prevents reaching agreements terminating the inefficient servitudes. He then states:

The chance that an exchange will not be completed is particularly high when multiple parties are involved. * * * When an exchange cannot be accomplished without the agreement of multiple parties, * * * both the difficulty of bringing all parties together and the uncertainty each party will face in assessing and reacting to the strategies of other parties make the exchange less likely. * * *

* * *

When landowners express their land use preferences in a privately negotiated servitude, the terms of the servitude establish the efficiency of the arrangement only as of the time of the agreement. But preferences and circumstances can change, and if modification of the original servitude cannot be achieved by private negotiation, the continued existence of the servitude would not establish its continued efficiency. It is true that the parties, in negotiating a servitude in the first instance, have the opportunity to consider the possibility that their preferences will change. An agreement that leaves the parties without flexibility to account for altered preferences is a strong indication that the parties expect their preferences to be stable over time. But no one is blessed with perfect foresight. There will be cases in which preferences have changed but the parties have left themselves no mechanism to accommodate the changes. In those cases the argument for governmental interventions is as strong as the argument for governmental intervention in any instance in which high transaction costs prevent private parties from reaching agreements that would promote their mutual interests.

Sterk concludes by arguing that the changed conditions doctrine is necessary to promote intergenerational equity:

Protecting future generations from dead-hand control has been a pervasive theme in property law. The rule against perpetuities, prohibitions against novel estates, and more modern regulations of the environment and of historic landmarks are all designed at least in part to prevent one generation from controlling the destiny of its successors. In the specific area of servitudes, the changed conditions doctrine, statutory limits on the duration of servitudes, and perhaps even the touch and concern requirement reflect in part a persistent if not easily quantifiable concern for intergenerational fairness. * * *

The [changed conditions] doctrine operates to protect present and future landowners from dead-hand control of land perpetuated through the use of servitudes that, because of high transaction costs, cannot be removed practically by private negotiations. The doctrine provides this protection by permitting judicial intervention to remove obsolete servitudes when private negotiations likely would be fruitless. This understanding of the changed conditions doctrine is supported by study of the doctrine's application. First, the doctrine is rarely, if ever, invoked to remove a servitude imposed on a single land-owner for the benefit of another. Instead, the doctrine relieves land-owners of burdens imposed on an entire neighborhood, where the transaction costs of removing restrictions are likely to be higher. * * * The doctrine itself is often framed to require a burdened landowner to establish changed conditions in the neighborhood—a difficult task if the only affected parcel is the benefited land and the benefited landowner refuses to consent to removal of the restriction.

In addition, in many jurisdictions changed conditions excuse the restricted landowner from specific enforcement of a servitude; the doctrine does not deprive benefited landowners of money damages for breach. * * * And because the litigation costs accompanying judicial removal are themselves substantial, affected landowners retain an incentive to remove obsolete restrictions by private agreement if at all possible. Only when the transaction costs accompanying private negotiations are higher than the litigation costs accompanying judicial removal will there be cause for invocation of the changed conditions doctrine.

For further elaboration of the consent-versus-intervention debate, see Alexander, Dilemmas of Group Autonomy: Residential Associations and Community, 75 Cornell L.Rev. 1 (1989); Ellickson, Cities and Homeowners Associations, 130 U.Pa.L.Rev. 1519 (1982); Korngold, Resolving the Flaws of Residential Servitudes and Owners Associations: For Reformation not Termination, 1990 Wis.L.Rev. 513; Natelson, Consent, Coercion, and "Reasonableness" in Private Law: The Special Case of the Property Owners Association, 51 Ohio St.L.J. 41 (1990); Winokur, The Mixed Blessing of Promissory Servitudes: Toward Optimizing Economic Utility, Individual Liberty and Personal Identity, 1989 Wis.L.Rev. 1; Winokur, Reforming Servitude Regimes: Toward Associational Federalism and Community, 1990 Wis.L.Rev. 537; Note, the Rule of Law in Residential Associations, 99 Harv.L.Rev. 472 (1985).

2.   Do Epstein and Sterk adequately address the situation raised by the *El Di* case? What transactions would have had to take place for El Di to have freed itself from the servitude? Could the interests of the dominant estate (whatever that may be) be protected by damages? Is the problem in *El Di* an initial lack of foresight as to future efficient uses?

3.   Note that the servitude in the principal case includes a defeasible fee. Are defeasible fees subject to the changed conditions doctrine, or can the initial grantor claim a reversion if the property is used in violation of the condition? See Jost, The Defeasible Fee and the Birth of the Modern Residential Subdivision, 49 Mo.L.Rev. 695, 731–732 (1984). Should the changed conditions doctrine apply to affirmative use servitudes (easements) if the law of servitudes is unified?

4.   Absent changed conditions, should the owner of a servient estate be able to argue that the burden caused by the servitude far exceeds its value to the owner of the dominant estate? More specifically, if enforcement is sought through an injunction, should the equitable doctrine of balancing of the hardships apply, or should the injunction be granted regardless of the burdens this imposes on the defendant? Compare Beeler Development Co. v. Dickens, 254 Iowa 1029, 120 N.W.2d 414 (1963) (balancing of hardships inappropriate where injunction sought to enforce restriction to maintain the status quo of development) with Gilpin v. Jacob Ellis Realties, Inc., 47 N.J.Super. 26, 135 A.2d 204 (App.Div.1957) (damage award instead of injunction where injury to defendant if injunction issued grossly disproportionate to injury to plaintiff if injunction denied).

5.   In addition to the changed conditions doctrine, several other means exist for terminating negative or affirmative obligation servitudes. The duration of a servitude is occasionally specified in the deed or declaration

that creates it. In these instances, the servitude expires naturally at the end of the period specified in the document. Statutes in some states achieve the same result, see, e.g., Ga.Code Ann. § 44–5–60, limiting the running of a covenant to 20 years in a municipality that has adopted zoning. Why might the presence or absence of zoning be relevant to the duration of servitudes?

6.   Negative and affirmative obligation servitudes may also be terminated by the same devices that would terminate affirmative-use servitudes (easements). They will be terminated by merger of the dominant and servient estate. See Aull v. Kraft, 286 S.W.2d 460 (Tex.Civ.App.1956). They may also be terminated by release by the owner of the dominant estate, see Chimney Hill Owners' Ass'n v. Antignani, 136 Vt. 446, 392 A.2d 423 (1978), or by an agreement to rescind or modify the servitude by all affected parties. Where a servitude binds all of the lots in a subdivision, however, merger and release issues can become complicated. Thus, if a developer reacquires lots it has earlier sold under a general plan of development, these lots are not thereby freed from servitudes which still benefit other lots the developer has sold. Similarly, the developer cannot unilaterally release a particular lot from restrictions that also benefit other lot owners in the subdivision.

7.   When an attempt is made to enforce a servitude at equity, equitable defenses may also apply. These include abandonment, waiver, estoppel, acquiescence, laches, and unclean hands. Estoppel is argued when the restriction has been violated following assurances that it would not be enforced; laches when enforcement attempts are tardy and the delay has prejudiced the defendant. Acquiescence is raised when violations of the servitude have been tolerated elsewhere in the neighborhood, unclean hands when the plaintiff himself has violated the servitude previously. Abandonment and waiver are vaguer and more general terms, which may include any of the other concepts. All of these defenses raise factual questions, and where servitudes vary from lot to lot, or where the servitudes that have been violated by the plaintiff or by others in the neighborhood are different from those violated by the defendant, these questions can become quite complex.

8.   Finally, servitudes may be terminated by eminent domain, where the servient estate is used for a public use contrary to the restriction. This situation raises the questions of whether the servitude is a property interest, the loss of which must be compensated under the United States or state constitutions, and how it should be valued. Although it is clear that easements are property interests which must be paid for if taken, there is still controversy as to whether affirmative obligations or restrictive covenants are compensable interests. Compare Southern California Edison Co. v. Bourgerie, 9 Cal.3d 169, 107 Cal.Rptr. 76, 507 P.2d 964 (1973) (restriction is compensable property interest) and Restatement of Property (Servitudes) § 566 (1944), with Burma Hills Development Co. v. Marr, 285 Ala. 141, 229 So.2d 776 (1969) (restriction not property interest that must be compensated). Courts arguing the latter position hold that they are contract rather than property rights, that they were not intended to bind the government or to be enforced against government policy, or that compensation would be too expensive or procedurally cumbersome. The cost of compensating all property owners benefited by a terminated servitude is a real concern where the restriction runs to the benefit of a large subdivision.

Is it fair to permit a property benefited by a servitude to collect damages caused by a power station or prison built next door in violation of a restrictive covenant, but to refuse damages to an adjacent property not benefited by a restriction? Could the whole problem perhaps be better handled through nuisance rather than servitude law? See Note, Nuisance Damages as an Alternative to Compensation of Land Use Restrictions in Eminent Domain, 47 S.Cal.L.Rev. 998 (1974).

If a zoning ordinance inconsistent with a servitude is adopted (e.g., an ordinance permitting only commercial use in a neighborhood restricted to residential use), should the zoning ordinance or the servitude control future development? If the zoning ordinance controls, should the owners of the servitude be compensated for its termination?

II. NEIGHBORHOOD GOVERNANCE

A. GENERALLY

Servitudes make neighborhood governance possible. To the extent that the law also permits neighborhoods to choose those primarily responsible for enforcing servitudes, to amend the servitudes by which they govern themselves, to exercise discretion in the interpretation and enforcement of servitudes, to tax themselves through assessments, and to own and manage common facilities, neighborhoods begin to resemble municipalities, clothed in the powers traditionally exercised by governments. These functions are commonly exercised through property owners associations.

Property owners associations can exist in residential subdivisions, condominiums or cooperatives. Even without the existence of formal associations, some of the functions exercised by property owners associations can be carried on within neighborhoods. Neighbors can, for example, vote from time to time to modify the servitudes by which they govern themselves.

Servitudes found in deeds and in covenant declarations effectively serve as the constitutions of property owners associations. Problems addressed in the previous sections regarding the creation, interpretation, modification, and termination of servitudes take on new dimensions when the servitudes create and are enforced by residential private governments. These problems are explored in the materials that follow.

B. DEVELOPER–PROPERTY OWNER RELATIONS

BROWN v. McDAVID

Colorado Court of Appeals, 1983.
676 P.2d 714.

SMITH, JUDGE.

This case arises from the attempt, by the owners of a ranch in Grand County, to develop and subdivide their property.

Although several tracts were sold pursuant to a subdivision development plan, the original owners and their successors ultimately determined to abandon the entire plan. Plaintiffs Mackintosh and Sylvia Brown whose predecessors in title had purchased one of the tracts during the development stage, brought this action seeking to compel the developers and the owners of the ranch to provide them with certain easements, and to enforce certain covenants which were to be part of the development plan and upon which the tract purchasers alleged they relied at the time of the purchase of their respective tracts.

Ultimately, the owners of the other four tracts were made parties to this action, and at trial were aligned as plaintiffs. The case was tried to the court without a jury, and at the conclusion thereof, the trial court entered findings of fact and conclusions of law, and issued its decree determining, in essence, that the covenants, easements, and undertakings to provide easements, which had come into being during the developmental stage, ran with the land, were perpetual, and were not terminable. Having so decreed, the court entered certain orders designed to assure that the affirmative duties, which it found had arisen under the covenants, would be complied with. Upon appeal, we reverse and remand with directions.

Lewis, George, and J. Donald Yager were the joint owners of land in Grand County, commonly known as Devil's Thumb Ranch. In September of 1973, the Yagers entered into a contract with Charles Badsley, C.B. Jensen, and Jack Randall, who, as joint venturers, acting under the name "B.J.R. Associates" (BJR), agreed to develop and sell Devil's Thumb Ranch.

Under this contract, BJR was permitted to take possession of the ranch, have it surveyed, and to divide it into 26 separate parcels for resale as a ranch subdivision. Ultimately, a plan for development evolved which contemplated that certain protective and restrictive covenants were to be drafted and recorded as sales inducements in connection with the offering of Devil's Thumb Ranch. Pursuant to this plan, five lots were sold to various parties in November 1974. The purchasers were Bennett (Brown's predecessor in title), Mountain Valley Investment Corporation, the Greenwoods, Colskilo Inc., and the Hilbs.

Since the entire ranch was still under contract between the Yagers and B.J.R., it was necessary that the Yagers convey the five parcels to B.J.R., who in turn delivered deeds to the five respective purchasers. The promotional material used by B.J.R. included copies of the proposed restrictive covenants covering "Devil's Thumb Ranch Estates," and which we will refer to as the "Covenant Document."

The purchase contracts between B.J.R. and the above five parties had copies of the Covenant Document attached. At the time of closing of the five sales transactions, the Covenant Document had not been recorded nor was it attached, nor made a part of the deeds transferring title to the respective purchasers. By stipulation, however, the parties agreed that all of the purchasers (including McDavid) had relied on the Covenant Document at the time they purchased their respective lots.

The Hilbs, however, requested that their lot be exempted from the benefits and burdens of the Covenant Document in exchange for an express 60 foot easement, which was, in fact, granted to them across the southern end of the ranch.

B.J.R. recorded the Covenant Document in September 1975, with the county clerk and recorder. Subsequent to that recording, Bennett, Mountain Valley, the Greenwoods and Colskilo each executed a letter ratifying, adopting and confirming the recorded Covenant Document.

Eight months later, in May 1976, the Browns purchased their tract from Bennett. Later in 1976, the Browns and Mountain Valley made a request of B.J.R. and the Yagers for an express, legally described, written grant of easement. These demands were not met, and the Browns subsequently commenced this action and recorded a lis pendens in Grand County.

Following the commencement of this action and the filing of a lis pendens by the Browns, the Yagers, together with B.J.R. sold the balance of the tracts to McDavid. As a result of this transaction, McDavid became the title owner of 21 of the 26 tracts or lots which comprised "Devil's Thumb Ranch Estates."

On May 9, 1977, McDavid recorded with the county clerk and recorder a document entitled "Declaration and Consent to Elimination of Protective Covenants," which document we will refer to as the "Termination Document," and which was recorded for the purpose of terminating the Covenant Document. After McDavid had acquired title and recorded the termination document, he was made a party to this action. He thereafter conveyed his interest in "Devil's Thumb Ranch Estates" to a corporation, Devil's Thumb Ranch and Cross–Country Center, Inc.

I. THE COVENANT DOCUMENT

The dispute here revolves around the language of the covenant document, and whether it could be, and was, properly terminated. This document, after describing generally its purposes, as being in furtherance of a plan for development, improvement, and sale of tracts within Devil's Thumb Ranch Estates, declares, inter alia:

> "These Covenants shall run with said property, and shall be binding upon and inure to the benefit of the Developer, each subsequent owner of said real property, or any part thereof, and each successor in interest of each such subsequent owner."

The document then discusses certain easements to be reserved to all of the owners for horseback riding, hiking, cross-country skiing, fishing, and other similar uses, and further purports to require each owner to grant a 60 foot wide easement for access and utility purposes to the owners of all other parcels. These easements were undescribed and unlocated at the time of the execution and recording of the Covenant Document.

The last two paragraphs of the document then read as follows:

"ALL OF THE FOREGOING covenants, conditions, reservations and restrictions shall continue and remain in full force and effect at all times as against the owner of any parcel in Devil's Thumb Ranch Estates, regardless of how he acquired title, until the commencement of the calendar year 2000 A.D., on which date these covenants, conditions, reservations and restrictions shall terminate and end, and thereinafter be of no further legal or equitable effect on such premises, or any owner thereof.

NOTWITHSTANDING THE FOREGOING, the Covenants agreements, conditions, reservations, restrictions and charges created and established herein for the benefit of the foregoing owners, and each parcel therein, may be waived, terminated or modified as to the whole of Devil's Thumb Ranch Estates only, with the written consent of the owners of sixty-six per cent (66%) of the parcels in Devil's Thumb Ranch Estates. No such waiver, termination or modification shall be effective until the proper instrument in writing shall be executed and recorded in the office of the Clerk and Recorder in the County of Grand and State of Colorado."

The trial court, in construing this document, concluded, inter alia, as follows:

"[T]he recorded Covenants purport to provide for a grant of perpetual easements binding on the grantors, their successors and assigns, and then to provide that the easements are not perpetual and that they do not run with the land but have a fixed expiration date and are terminable at any time. These conflicting terms are irreconcilable and must therefore be construed against the drafters, particularly where, as here, the covenants affect substantial property interests of all the parties. The Court therefore concludes that those provisions of the covenants reserving or providing for a grant of easements should be preserved and specifically enforced in accord with the parties' clear intent."

Inasmuch as the trial court's determination proceeds solely from its interpretation of the written document, we are not bound thereby. [   ] We do not agree with the trial court's interpretation.

Despite the preliminary language in the covenant document providing that the covenants "run with the land," we conclude that there is no material ambiguity within the document. Reading it as a whole, it is apparent that the developers and owners of tracts who subsequently agreed to the document, intended that the covenants, easements, and other agreements, should terminate by the document's own terms, on the commencement of the calendar year 2000 A.D., unless they should be sooner terminated by the execution and recording of an appropriate document so reciting, consented to by the owners of 66% of the parcels in Devil's Thumb Ranch Estates. We construe the reference to covenants running with the land to express the intention that these covenants and agreements should be binding upon all owners of the land, their successors, and assigns, until the same be terminated, either by the terms of the agreement or by the filing and recording of a proper termination agreement.

Thus, reading the termination document as a whole, we conclude that it is not ambiguous, nor do we find in its terms any irreconcilable conflicts. We conclude that the trial court's interpretation is erroneous.

II. TERMINATION

Implicit in the trial court's lengthy ruling, however, is its conclusion that it would be inequitable to allow McDavid to terminate the covenants and thereby abandon the development plan upon which the other purchasers had relied in buying their lots. The parties argue here, in support of the trial court's ruling, that particularly the easements for utilities and access are essential to their use of the land. They assert that they should be, as the trial court determined, perpetual and not subject to termination. We disagree.

We do not disagree with the assertion that such easements may be a necessity, but rather with the argument that such necessity precludes exercise of the termination clause. No Colorado cases have been cited to us, nor have we found any dealing with the effect of similar termination clauses. However, the general law is well established that a covenant running with the land in a subdivision may be modified or terminated, when the covenant permits termination, upon the consent of a specified percentage of lot owners.

Such a case, closely analogous to the instant one, is Matthews v. Kernewood, Inc., 184 Md. 297, 40 A.2d 522 (1945). In Matthews, a development corporation subdivided parcels of land into thirty-four separate lots and imposed stringent protective covenants. Seventeen years later, only half of the lots had been sold. The developer then exercised his right which had been reserved in the covenants, to annul or change or modify the restrictions, and resubdivided the unsold lots into smaller parcels with reduced restrictions. Seven owners of the original lots filed suit, charging that they had purchased their lots in reliance on the development plan and original restrictions. The Maryland court observed that the rights of the parties who purchased the original lots must be determined by the agreement they voluntarily made, and that they could not be judicially relieved of a bad bargain into which they themselves had entered. Where covenants terminate on the consent of a specified percentage of lot owners, consent of the proper percentage will terminate the covenants. [   ]

Since developers and potential lot purchasers are free to contract for the price, terms, and conditions of any sale, when such parties elect to provide for covenants which, by their nature, may be terminated upon certain conditions, then a court must presume that such a contingency is reflected in the consideration paid, and will not rewrite the covenants years later for one of the parties. [ ] Where, as here, the covenant document containing the termination clauses in question, was admittedly relied upon and accepted by all parties, all parties knew the covenants could be terminated and this knowledge became part of the basis of their bargain. [ ]

We have examined the "Termination Document" and conclude that it is sufficient to comply with the provisions of the "Covenant Document" relative to termination. Thus, we hold that all of the covenants, easements, and servitudes created by the Covenant Document were terminated on the date that the Termination Document was recorded. Accordingly, we conclude that each tract owner has no rights or benefits in the land at Devil's Thumb Ranch Estates except those expressly granted by their deeds and as otherwise found in the law. It necessarily follows that the same rule applies as to burdens upon each of the parcels.

III. ISSUES REMAINING

Our determination that the Covenant Document and all of the rights and obligations which it created has been properly terminated does not, however, resolve all of the issues existing between the parties.

There remain to be determined factual questions relative to location and extent of the access for ingress and egress and for utilities to certain of the parcels which appear to be landlocked. Easements may arise in any number of ways. They may arise by express grant or reservation, covenant, prescription, or implication. Colorado expressly recognizes implied easements which may arise by reason of grant and reservation, [ ] or even by preexisting use. [ ]

Here, Mountain Valley Investment Corporation appears to have an express easement created by grant apart from the terminated covenants. In its deed there appears the following language:

"Purchasers are hereby granted an easement for access to this tract of land across the presently existing ranch road, a diagram of said road is attached hereto * * *."

Defendants Thomas and Susan Hilb likewise appear to have an express easement created by grant. As these grants are wholly separate from the easements granted in the covenant document, they are therefore unaffected by the termination document filed by McDavid. Plaintiffs, Mackintosh and Sylvia Brown, however, do not have a specific grant of easement. They may well, however, have an implied easement under one of the theories previously mentioned.

Because the evidence contained in the record before us discloses facts which may well entitle the Browns to an implied easement we remand this case to the trial court for location and determination of the extent of such easements as may have arisen outside of the covenants, specifically as to Mountain Valley and the Browns, as well as to consider if such easements should be decreed as to the other parcels.

The intent of the parties, as disclosed by the evidence, at the time the respective parcels were severed from the original tract, may provide guidance for the trial court in determining the location as well as the reasonable extent and dimensions of such easements. [   ]

We conclude that appellants' other contentions are without merit.

* * *

Notes and Questions

1. Modern residential developments are often quite large and represent a considerable capital investment for which a developer is responsible. In the early stages of the development, the developer faces a quandary. It may want to aim the development at a certain market—residential rather than commercial, upscale rather than moderate-income residential—and may want to include servitudes in the deeds or declaration of restrictions that will be attractive to this market. At the same time, the developer may not want to lock itself in. If it turns out that the developer's market research was faulty, it may want to change the nature of the subdivision to include some lower-priced housing or even rental units or commercial uses. In some jurisdictions, the developer may preserve this flexibility simply by not binding its retained land when it sells off restricted properties, but in many it cannot. Can you explain why?

In most jurisdictions, developers have attempted to retain flexibility by reserving to themselves the right to amend restrictions. This is often done through establishing the right to amend restrictions in the property owners association, and then retaining control of the property owners association until the development is substantially complete. This can be done, as in the principal case, by giving the developer one vote for each lot it retains, allowing it to retain control until it has sold off a considerable number of its lots. Model forms developed by the Urban Land Institute go further, allowing the developer three votes for every unit, effectively giving the developer control until 75% of the units in the development are sold. The developer may also want to retain control over architectural review committees and over the expenditure of funds collected through assessments.

Developer retention of control, however, poses problems for residents in a development. The developer can, as in the principal case, abandon the restrictions the lot owners thought they would be protected by, creating a much different sort of community. It could even use assessments from the community for its own purposes, such as marketing the development. Should these problems be addressed by the courts? By legislation? How? See Reichman, Residential Private Governments: An Introductory Survey, 43 U.Chi.L.Rev. 253, at 285–291 (1976).

2. As the development progresses and lots are sold, the developer will usually lose interest in the development. If the developer has maintained tight control over the property owners association until this point, however, there may not be any residents with the knowledge and ability to take over managing the association. Should a developer have an obligation to assist property owners in establishing a viable association once it loses interest? See Reichman, 43 U.Chi.L.Rev. at 290–291.

3. Does it help, in such local arrangements, to move from the neighborly expectations of members of a voluntary association to rules that can be–and are–enforced with law? One part of that answer is that it sometimes helps, particularly among neighbors who live together cordially, to have the police or code-enforcement office take the blame for enforcing such things as use restrictions. One reason it helps, perhaps, is that the public enforcer has not only coercion behind her but also a certain amount of discretion. (One thinks of the legendary Irish cop who did not arrest the disruptive teen-ager but seized him by the neck and took him home to his mother.) On the other hand, the fact that the enforcer is a public official, not a neighbor, carries a formal risk. For example, one of Randy Cohen's correspondents was annoyed at what a police officer no doubt thought of as a kindness: "I was pulled over on a rural state parkway, clocked doing 71 mph in a 55–mph zone. I was wearing a seat belt. The officer ticketed me for driving without a seat belt, which is often less likely than a speeding violation to carry points or affect insurance.... [S]hould I ... just pay the fine?" Mr. Cohen recommended paying the fine and likened the situation to a plea bargain in a weightier criminal case. But he disapproved of what the officer did, because it amounted to charging the correspondent with an offense he did not commit. Excessive formality? Perhaps the police officer was Irish. (The South Bend Tribune, May 27, 2004, originally published in the New York Times Magazine.)

4. Other concerns that must be faced as a developer withdraws from management of a development and a property owners association takes over include transfer of common property, accounting for and transfer of funds collected to maintain common property, and transfer of books and records.

5. How should votes be allocated in an association once the developer has completed the development? Should they be distributed on a "one person, one vote" principle, or on a unit-by-unit basis, or with each owner having a number of votes proportionate to the value of his or her investment? What justifies the application of different principles than those followed with respect to public corporations, where one person, one vote is the rule? See Ellickson, Cities and Homeowners Associations, 130 U.Pa. L.Rev. 1519 (1982).

6. See generally on litigation by property owners associations against developers, R. Natelson, Law of Property Owners Associations, chapter 9 (1989).

C. INTERPRETATION AND ENFORCEMENT OF SERVITUDES BY PROPERTY OWNERS ASSOCIATIONS

SMITH v. BUTLER MOUNTAIN ESTATES PROPERTY OWNERS ASSOCIATION, INC.

Court of Appeals of North Carolina, 1988.
90 N.C.App. 40, 367 S.E.2d 401.

JOHNSON, JUDGE.

Plaintiffs are the owners of a lot in Butler Mountain Estates. Butler Mountain Estates is a residential development containing 48 lots, and at the time of this action, consisted of twelve lots upon which houses have been constructed and three lots upon which houses are under construction. The lots in Butler Mountain Estates are subject to restrictive covenants set forth in a restrictive agreement. The restrictive covenants provide that the lots are to be used for single family residential houses and specify that any dwelling erected thereon is to have a habitable floor space on the main level of at least 1100 square feet. Furthermore, the restrictive covenants provide that:

> * * * all building plans * * * shall require the approval of the developer and/or Property Owners Association * * *. No structure of any kind, the plan, elevations, and specifications which have not received the written approval of the developer and/or Property Owners Association and which does not comply fully with such approved plans and specifications, shall be erected, constructed, placed or maintained upon any lot * * *

In the beginning, prior to the formation of an architectural review board, proposed plans were submitted to each existing homeowner and approved or disapproved, by the individual homeowners based on square footage and on the design.

On 29 February 1984, Elbert S. Brown and Dorothy S. Brown, the developers of Butler Mountain Estates, signed a Grant of Architectural Review, by the terms of which they granted to Butler Mountain Estates Property Owners Association Corporation, all rights of review and approval reserved by the developer under the above quoted restrictive covenant regarding building plans. In January of 1985, an architectural review board was formed to review all proposed building plans for each dwelling unit to be constructed. The architectural review board consists of the Board of Directors and the existing homeowners in Butler Mountain Estates.

In October, 1985, plaintiffs submitted a set of plans for a proposed dwelling unit to the architectural review committee for approval. Plaintiffs' plans, which were not for a geodesic dome house, were rejected solely because they failed to meet the restrictive covenant's square footage requirement.

In December 1985, plaintiffs submitted a second set of plans for a proposed dwelling unit, a geodesic dome house, to the architectural review committee for approval. The architectural review committee rejected these plans because of the roofline and the geodesic design of the house. It was also determined that the plans did not meet the minimum square footage requirement, but the architectural review committee did not express that failure as a prime consideration for rejecting plaintiffs' plans. On 23 January 1986, the president of the Property Owners Association mailed plaintiffs a letter indicating that the "proposed structure reflects a marked departure from home-building styles prevailing throughout the area" and that plaintiffs "might consider a design closer to the home-building styles that exist on Butler Mountain Estates."

The primary manner in which this plan was such a radical departure from the existing homes was in its roofline. Plaintiffs' home would have an irregular domed roofline, which is built out of a series of triangles and pentagons, whereas the existing houses have conventional horizontal rooflines.

The architectural review committee did not have written standards as to design acceptability of plans but did establish among themselves a format to review plans submitted by owners. The committee believed that the homes should "conform and blend together." (See Illustrations.)

**Illustration of existing houses in
Butler Mountain Estates**

**Illustration of
Plaintiffs' geodesic house plans**

On 11 April 1986, plaintiffs filed their complaint seeking a declaratory judgment and alternatively for injunctive relief, against defendant. Defendant filed its answer on 13 June 1986. On 18 September 1986, plaintiffs filed a motion for summary judgment which was denied by order of the court on 5 November 1986. On 17 December 1986, a trial without jury was conducted before Judge Robert M. Burroughs, Sr. On 18 December 1986, after making findings of fact and conclusions of law, an order was filed granting defendant's motion for involuntary dismissal pursuant to Rule 41(b) of the North Carolina Rules of Civil Procedure. Plaintiffs appeal.

Plaintiffs bring forth sixteen assignments of error grouped into three arguments for this Court's review. For the following reasons, we find no error and affirm the order of the trial court.

First, plaintiffs contend that the trial court erred in finding as fact and concluding as a matter of law that plaintiffs' second set of plans did not meet the restrictive covenant square footage requirement and that the plans were rejected on this basis. We disagree.

* * *

In the case *sub judice,* there was sufficient competent evidence to support the court's findings of fact and conclusions of law. The restriction in question states in part that:

> No structure or building shall be erected, altered, placed, or permitted to remain on any property or tract of land conveyed in Butler Mountain Estates other than one detached single family dwelling, permanent in nature, *the habitable floor space of which, exclusive of basements, porches, garages, is less than 1,100 square feet on the main level of said residence.* (Emphasis added).

Evidence was also admitted in response to questions tendered by plaintiffs, that the habitable living space on the main level of the house proposed by plaintiffs was 30 to 50 feet short of the required square footage. Thus, there was competent evidence to support the court's findings of fact and conclusions of law that plaintiffs failed to meet the 1100 minimum square footage requirement and that the architectural review committee "rejected [the plans] invariably" on that basis.

Next, plaintiffs contend the trial court erred in finding as fact that (a) defendants had developed an architectural style as construction took place; (b) that the existing housing was of a common, similar or like design; and (c) that the plaintiffs' second set of plans was a marked departure from existing homes in the development and did not meet the roofline designs of homes in the area. Again, we disagree.

We have thoroughly examined the record and find that there is sufficient evidence in the record to support the trial court's findings of fact. The photographs of the 12 houses that exist in the development establishes that they are of common, similar or like design, though they are not all exactly alike. The plans submitted by the plaintiffs revealed that the roofline of plaintiffs' house was not of the same or similar design of the other houses. The remaining houses had flat roofs, or pitched roofs with flat planes, and plaintiffs' geodesic home roofline was dome shaped. Furthermore, each house as it was built, maintained the same or similar design as each house previously built, thereby establishing the architectural style of the community. Therefore, plaintiffs' assignments of error on these findings of fact are overruled.

Finally, plaintiffs contend that the trial court erred in entering its judgment against them for the reason that the evidence showed that the restrictive covenants are void and unenforceable as applied because (1) they contain no standards by which proposed plans are to be judged; (2) they are not connected to any general plan or scheme of development; (3) they are ambiguous and (4) they were applied in an arbitrary and unreasonable manner and in bad faith. Again, we disagree.

"In North Carolina restrictive covenants are strictly construed against limitations upon the beneficial use of property, but such construction must be reasonable and not applied in such a way as to defeat the plain and obvious purposes of a restriction." Boiling Spring Lakes v. Coastal Services Corp., 27 N.C.App. 191, 195, 218 S.E.2d 476, 478 (1975). In Boiling Springs, a restrictive covenant required building plans to be submitted to and approved by the grantor prior to construction. This Court laid out the following rules governing approval of building plans by a grantor.

> The exercise of the authority to approve the house plans cannot be arbitrary. There must be some standards. Where these standards are not within the restrictive covenant itself, they must be in other covenants stated or designated, or they must be otherwise clearly established in connection with some general plan or scheme of development. (Citations omitted) * * * [A] restrictive covenant requiring approval of house plans is enforceable only if the exercise of the power in a particular case is reasonable and in good faith. (Citations omitted)

Id. at 195–96, 218 S.E.2d at 478–79.

In support of this rule, this Court relied upon decisions in other jurisdictions. See Syrian Antiochian Orthodox Archdiocese v. Palisades Associates, 110 N.J.Super. 34, 264 A.2d 257 (1970); Rhue v. Cheyenne Homes, Inc., 168 Colo. 6, 449 P.2d 361 (1969).

In Syrian, the court held that a covenant which prohibited the creation of structures or improvements unless plans and specifications in a grading plan of a plot to be built upon were approved by the grantor, and that the grantor could refuse to approve any such plans, which were not suitable in his opinion, was valid and enforceable, though no objective standards were set forth within the covenant to guide the grantor. The court stated,

> [t]he purpose of such a provision is to afford mutual protection to the property owners living in the development against injury, whether taking the form of diminished property values or otherwise, that would result from the construction of a residence or other improvement that was unsightly, in singularly bad taste, *discordantly at variance with neighboring homes in architectural appearance,* or otherwise offensive to the proposed or developed standards of the neighborhood.

Syrian, 110 N.J.Super. at 40, 264 A.2d at 261. (Emphasis added).

Similarly, in Rhue, that court was called upon to consider a covenant which required plans for construction of houses to be submitted to an architectural committee for approval. In Rhue, an owner of property in whose chain of title the covenant appeared, wished to move to the site a 30–year old Spanish style home with a stucco exterior and a red tile roof. The development in which the house was to be located was 80% improved with modern ranch style and split level homes. The grantor refused approval upon the ground that the proposed improvement, if allowed would diminish the value of other properties in the neighborhood and would be an unsightly variation from the architectural pattern that had been established. In sustaining the disapproval the court observed:

> [i]t is no secret that housing today is developed by subdividers who, through the use of restrictive covenants, guarantee to the purchaser that his house will be protected against adjacent construction which will impair its value, and that a general plan of construction will be followed. Modern legal authority recognizes this reality and recognizes also that the approval of plans by an architectural control committee is one method by which guarantees of value and general plan of construction can be accomplished and maintained.

Rhue, 168 Colo. at 8, 449 P.2d at 362.

In the case *sub judice,* the restrictive covenant at issue requires building plans to be submitted to and approved by the Property Owners Association which in turn formed an architectural review committee to serve the same function. The record establishes that this architectural review committee rejected plaintiffs' second set of plans because (1) the design of the house reflected a marked departure from the home building styles in the area and (2) the plans did not meet the general roofline design of the houses in the area. In addition, plaintiffs' plans did not meet the square footage requirement but the architectural review committee did not rely solely on this failure as the primary basis for rejection of the plans.

As shown earlier in the opinion, the plans of the main level of a proposed home had to contain 1100 square feet of habitable floor space. Thus, the architectural review committee could have justifiably rejected plaintiffs' second set of plans on this basis alone. Nevertheless, assuming arguendo, that plaintiffs had met the minimum square footage requirement, the record reveals that the 12 houses constructed were conventional type homes of the same or similar design, and had similar flat roof designs. Plaintiffs' second set of plans for their geodesic home was not of the same or similar design, and their dome shaped roofline, which is built out of a series of triangles and pentagons, was a radical departure from the other houses' rooflines.

Despite the architectural review committee's failure to put in writing the specific architectural style of the houses to be erected, all legitimate considerations which an architectural review committee may assess when determining the aesthetic value in approving house plans which fit into a general plan or development scheme of the neighborhood was attempted in the case sub judice. Without such consideration, there would have been no reasonable or good faith determination for approval or nonapproval of house plans.

The majority view, which this Court has adopted, with respect to covenants requiring submission of plans and prior consent to construction, is that such clauses, even if vesting the approving authority with broad discretionary power, are valid and enforceable so long as the authority to consent is exercised reasonably and in good faith. Therefore, applying the test of reasonableness and good faith to the case sub judice, we find that the rejection of plaintiffs' house plans was not arbitrary or capricious because the record clearly shows that plaintiffs' proposed house plans did not fit into the present and existing general plan or development scheme of the homes in the area.

Accordingly, for all the aforementioned reasons, the judgment is affirmed.

COMMERCIAL WHARF EAST CONDOMINIUM ASSOCIATION v. WATERFRONT PARKING CORP.

Supreme Court of Massachusetts, 1990.
407 Mass. 123, 552 N.E.2d 66.

NOLAN, JUSTICE. * * *

The subject of this litigation is the land in Boston known as Commercial Wharf. In 1967, Commercial Wharf was purchased by the developer, which rehabilitated the granite block warehouse in the center of the wharf and, in 1978, decided to convert the building into condominium units. * * *

Immediately prior to recording the condominium master deed, which covers the granite building and a portion of the wharf known as the "parking and driveway area," the developer recorded a document entitled "Commercial Wharf East Condominium—Declaration of Covenants and Easements" (Declaration). The Declaration purports to retain certain rights for the benefit of the retained land over the parking area which was deeded to the condominium. The retained rights include the right "to control and collect fees for the parking of vehicles in such area." The Declaration also provides that the owner of the retained land must maintain and manage the parking area and rent parking spaces to condominium unit owners at reasonable and competitive rates. The condominium master deed, recorded shortly after the Declaration, recites that it is subject to the easement pronouncement in the Declaration. The master deed also provides that each unit owner has the right to rent one parking space, as stated in the Declaration.

From 1978 to 1984 the developer sold the condominium units in the granite building and managed the entire parking lot, including the parking and driveway area deeded to the Association. Then, in 1984, the developer began to sell its remaining interests on Commercial Wharf. First, in June, 1984, it conveyed lots 2 and 3 to the defendants Wharf Nominee Trust and Marina Nominee Trust (Nominee Trusts). The deeds to the Nominee Trusts include the right to irrevocable licenses to park ten cars in the parking and driveway area. In April, 1985, the developer conveyed lots 4, 5, and 6 and the right "to control and collect fees" in the parking and driveway area to the defendant Waterfront Park Limited Partnership (Waterfront). This deed grants the right to irrevocable licenses for sixteen parking spaces to Waterfront and retains the right to irrevocable licenses for fifty-two spaces in the developer, which then sold lot 1 and the right to twenty-six of its fifty-two irrevocable parking licenses to East Commercial Wharf Limited Partnership (East Commercial Wharf). Next, in February, 1986, the developer conveyed lot 8 to One Hundred Atlantic Avenue Limited Partnership (Atlantic). The deed to Atlantic includes the right to eleven parking licenses. The right to licenses for the remaining spaces of the fifty-two reserved by the developer is included in an option to purchase lot 7, granted to defendant Arthur B. Blackett.

Reference to the accompanying simplified map is helpful in visualizing the various interests on Commercial Wharf.

The granite building and the area surrounding it entitled "parking and driveway" area are condominium property. Lots 2 and 3 are owned by the Nominee Trusts. Lots 4, 5, and 6, together with the right "to control" parking in the parking and driveway area, are owned by Waterfront. Lot 1 and the surrounding marinas are owned by East Commercial Wharf. Lot 7 is under option to Arthur B. Blackett and lot 8 is owned by Atlantic. Further facts appear in our discussion of the various issues raised in the cross appeals. * * *

General Laws c. 183A, § 10(b)(1) (1988 ed.), provides that the condominium association "shall have" the right and power "[t]o lease, manage, and otherwise deal with such community and commercial facilities as may be provided for in the master deed as being common areas and facilities." Since the parking and driveway area is part of the common area, the Association contends that the developer's retention of control over that area cannot be reconciled with § 10(b)(1). * * *

We think it is clear that, by enacting G.L. c. 183A and providing that land can be placed into the condominium form of ownership, the Legislature did not intend to preclude the existence of nonownership interests in the condominium land. The law of real property has long recognized the coexistence of possessory interests in land with limited nonownership interests in the same land. Nothing in c. 183A expressly precludes such nonownership interests. We will not presume that the Legislature intended such a radical change in the common law without a clear expression of such intent. * * *

Similarly, the Association's argument under G.L. c. 183A, § 5(c) (1988 ed.), fails also. Section 5(c) provides that the common area shall remain undivided and that any provision to the contrary is void. The Association contends that the developer's retention of rights in the parking and driveway area is a division of the common area and is therefore void. * * * Section 5(c) provides: "The common areas and facilities shall remain undivided and no unit owner or any other person shall bring any action for partition or division of any part thereof. * * * Any covenant or provision to the contrary shall be null and void." The clear meaning of this provision is that the ownership of the common areas shall not be divided; in other words, the common areas must remain in common ownership with each unit owner entitled to an undivided interest in the common areas. Nothing in § 5(c) purports to prevent the existence of nonownership interests in the common areas. The fee interest remains undivided and in common ownership. That the master deed makes the fee interest subject to a prior interest is not violative of § 5(c).

A valid interest in a common area, to which the master deed is expressly subject, is not part of the common area. Section 1 of G.L. c. 183A makes it clear that certain land granted to a condominium, including the parking area, shall be considered part of the common area, but adds "except as otherwise provided or stipulated in the master deed." In this case the master deed makes it clear that the fee simple title to the parking and driveway area is in the Association. However, the master deed also makes that grant subject to the interests reserved in the Declaration. It follows that the interests retained by the developer in the Declaration are not "common areas." Since the interest retained by the developer never became part of the condominium common area, its retention does not constitute a division of the common area. * * *

"Deeds should be 'construed as to give effect to the intent of the parties, unless inconsistent with some law or repugnant to the terms of the grant.'"*Harrison v. Marcus* * * * (1985). * * * The intent of the parties is gleaned from "the words used, interpreted in the light of the material circumstances and pertinent facts known to them at the time [the deed] was executed." * * * The Declaration provides that the retained land shall benefit from and the condominium land shall be subject to "the non-exclusive right and easement to use the Condominium Land for vehicular and pedestrian access to the Retained Land for all purposes over the * * * 'Parking and Driveway' [area] ... including the right * * * to control and collect fees for the parking of vehicles in such area. * * * "While a strict grammatical reading of the latter phraseology might mean that the owner of the retained land only has the right to control the fees he collects, we think that the intent was to retain the right to control the parking of vehicles on the land. It is clear that the developer intended, when it executed and recorded the Declaration and the master deed, to convey the fee interest in the parking and driveway area to the Association. The Land Court judge found that the developer also intended to create a "common scheme" of sorts, whereby the parking rights of the wharf would be managed for the benefit of all the parcels on the wharf. To effectuate its plan, the developer intended to retain control over the parking activities in the parking and driveway area. Hence, it retained the right "to control and collect fees for the parking of vehicles."

The remainder of the Declaration is indicative of the developer's intent to retain the right to control all parking activities in the parking and driveway area. Paragraph 2 of the Declaration provides, in part, that "[t]he owners of the Retained Land at its [*sic*] own cost and expense shall maintain and manage the said Parking and Driveway area in the same condition as said land is in on the date hereof * * *." The remainder of paragraph 2 lists specific obligations, traditionally associated with management, which were imposed on the owner of the retained land. This implies that the power to control and manage the parking area was meant to be retained. Paragraph 3 obliges the owners of the retained land to rent parking spaces to condominium unit owners at reasonable rates, again indicating that the Declaration envisaged a retention of management rights by the owners of the retained land. In context we think that there is little doubt that the power "to control and collect fees" includes the power to manage the parking activities in the parking and driveway area.

To the extent that there remains any doubt, we think that the actions of the parties clarify the arrangement. "[W]here the language of an instrument is doubtful, evidence of the practical construction by the parties is admissible to explain and remove the doubt." *Oldfield v. Smith* * * * (1939). From 1978 until 1985, when it sold the management rights to Waterfront, the developer controlled all parking activities, set parking rates, and maintained the parking facilities. Neither the Association nor any of the unit owners objected to this control. This practical construction of the terms in the Declaration is in accord with our interpretation of that provision. * * *

The Land Court judge held that the Declaration impliedly retained the right for the developer, as owner of the retained land, to park vehicles other than those of condominium unit owners on condominium land. We agree. As discussed above, the purpose of the Declaration was to retain control over parking for the benefit of all the parcels on the wharf. Absolutely essential to that purpose is the right to park noncondominium vehicles in the parking and driveway area. Moreover, the unit owners and the Association acquiesced in such a construction of the Declaration from 1978 until 1985.

The Land Court judge determined that the Declaration and the master deed envisaged a "common scheme" of "unified control of parking on the Wharf for the benefit of all owners without differentiation of the parking areas on Condominium or Retained Land." What was earlier said about the nature of the expressly reserved right to control parking supports this conclusion, as does the impliedly reserved right to park vehicles other than those of condominium unit owners on condominium land. This is not a "common scheme" in the sense that similar restrictions were imposed upon all the lots in a subdivision. * * *

When it began to sell the remaining parcels on the wharf the developer included in the deeds the rights to obtain licenses to park in the parking lots on the wharf, including in the parking and driveway area. These rights are referred to as "deeded parking rights." In our view, this was a division of the easement rights retained by the developer. Such a division of rights is valid. * * * Indeed, since the retained rights were for the benefit of the land owners on the wharf, those rights were appurtenant to the land. There was nothing wrong with the manner in which the developer divided those rights, according to the needs of each parcel.

Thus, the "deeded parking rights" are valid. * * *

The Land Court judge expressed the view that the retained rights are subject to some durational limit, but reserved the question of what that time limit is. The Land Court judge explicitly noted that she would rule on this question after any appeals from the judgment. * * *

In *Barclay v. DeVeau* * * * (1981), we suggested that a finding of overreaching or fraud might have invalidated the management agreement that we upheld in that case. The Association argues that the arrangement in this case, even if permissible, is invalid because it is the product of overreaching or a breach of fiduciary duty. We disagree.

The Association claims that both procedural and substantive aspects of the parking arrangement are unconscionable. * * * The judge found that the unit owners had notice of the terms of the Declaration. * * * The judge also found that the design of the project was not concealed from the unit owners, that many of the unit owners had "considerable negotiating clout," and that there was no "bad faith" in the submission of the property to c. 183A. The principal point relied upon by the Association is that, despite the notice of the terms of the Declaration, there was some uncertainty as to the extent of the right "to control" parking on the wharf. In the circumstances, we think this falls short of a showing that there was overreaching.

Substantively, we think the parking arrangement is fair and reasonable. The developer submitted the parking and driveway area to condominium ownership in order to comply with zoning requirements. It retained the right to control parking, however, because it had concerns regarding the allocation of the limited parking rights among the various parcels on the wharf. The Declaration and master deed exhibit an attempt by the developer to allocate various burdens and benefits among the parcels on the wharf. Thus, in addition to retaining the right to control parking and to collect fees, the Declaration provides that the owner of the retained land (the developer and its successors) must maintain the parking area. Maintenance includes, "without limitation, making necessary repairs and replacements thereto, clearing snow therefrom, providing for reasonable security at reasonable hours and obtaining and maintaining public liability insurance on said land with limits of not less than a single limit of $1,000,000 * * * said insurance to name the owners of the Condominium Land as additional insureds." The Declaration also provides that the owners of the retained land must assume the cost of maintaining the main horizontal sewer line serving the properties. Unit owners are guaranteed the right to rent parking spaces at "reasonable and competitive" rates. Accordingly, there was both a legitimate reason for the arrangement and a reasonable allocation of the burdens and benefits associated with it. * * *

We need not address the Association's contention that a developer of a condominium owes a fiduciary duty to the future residents. Even if we so held, we would find no breach of that duty in the circumstances presented here. For the reasons discussed above we think the developer acted in a fair and evenhanded manner.

Notes and Questions

1. One study notes that reported state court appellate decisions involving property owners associations and servitudes increased seven-fold from 1977 to 1982, and doubled again between 1982 and 1987. Winokur, The Mixed Blessing of Promissory Servitudes: Toward Optimizing Economic Utility, Individual Liberty, and Personal Identity, 1989 Wis.L.Rev. 1, 63–64.

One classification of disputes within property owners associations breaks them down into six categories. First, are property disputes involving rights to the homeowner's unit or to common elements. Second, are financial disputes, involving assessments or money owed the association by third parties (such as the developer). Disputes involving services and maintenance of the common elements are third. Governance issues involving elections and board governance come next. Fifth are lifestyle disputes, involving noisy children, dogs, stereos, etc. Finally, are disputes involving personal injury or injury to reputation. Walker and Masotti, The Dynamics of Dispute Processing in Condominium Associations, CAI News, January 1983. Disputes involve both substantive issues—is the servitude itself valid—and procedural issues—did the association follow its own procedures and are these procedures reasonable?

Should courts follow a public or private-law model in addressing these questions? Is the property owners association a close enough cognate to the municipality to bring it under the requirements of the United States Constitution or state constitutions? The limits of the *Shelley v. Kraemer* doctrine with respect to servitudes generally have been explored earlier. Should *Shelley v. Kraemer* be applied more expansively where servitudes are enforced by a property owners association? In states where property owners associations exist by virtue of state enabling acts and are regulated by the state, does a sufficiently close nexus exist between the actions of the association and the state to find state action? Should state action be found under the public-function doctrine of Marsh v. Alabama, 326 U.S. 501, 66 S.Ct. 276, 90 L.Ed. 265 (1946)? See Rosenberry, The Application of the Federal and State Constitutions to Condominiums, Cooperatives and Planned Developments, 19 Real Prop., Prob. & Trust J. 1 (1985).

2. Alternatively, should property owners associations be viewed as private entities not subject to public-law controls? As such, should they be permitted to take actions the state is constitutionally barred from taking, such as barring religious uses or discriminating against certain societal groups? What limits may courts place on the procedures followed by associations?

3. The principal case considers the reasonableness and good faith of the substantive decision reached by the association. An alternative approach available in some cases is to focus on the procedures the association followed in making its decision or on the authority of the decisionmaker. In Ironwood Owners Association IX v. Solomon, 178 Cal.App.3d 766, 224 Cal.Rptr. 18 (1986), a property owners association sought a mandatory injunction requiring the removal of eight date palm trees planted by the Solomons. On appeal from the trial court grant of the injunction, the appellate court reversed, noting:

> When a homeowners' association seeks to enforce the provisions of its CCRs to compel an act by one of its member owners, it is incumbent upon it to show that it has followed its own standards and procedures prior to pursuing such a remedy, that those procedures were fair and reasonable and that its substantive decision was made in good faith, and is reasonable, not arbitrary or capricious. [   ]

The Court went on to hold that the record did not show either that the Architectural Control Committee had made findings on the compliance of the trees with the covenants, or that the board had made a decision with respect to the trees. Discussions at members' meetings or polls of the members were not, the court held, an adequate substitute for appropriate decisions by the governing body or proper committee. See, R. Natelson, Law of Property Owners Associations, chapters 4 & 5 (1989).

4. Litigation arises not only when associations sue their members for breach of servitudes, but also when members sue the association for failing

to fulfill its responsibilities. This may happen, for example, when the association misuses assessments, acts beyond its authority, fails to maintain common property, or takes action which results in the injury of a member. A variety of arguments are raised in these actions, including corporate, fiduciary, and tort theories of liability. See R. Natelson, Law of Property Owners Associations, chapter 10 (1989); Rosenberry, Actions of Community Association Boards: When are They Valid and When do they Create Liability, 13 Real Est.L.J. (1985). Should the directors of property owners' associations be held to the same standard of care or to a higher or lower standard than the directors of commercial corporations? See Natelson, Keeping Faith: Fiduciary Obligations in Property Owners Associations, 11 Vt.L.Rev. 421 (1986).

5. An inquiry to Randy Cohen, the ethics columnist, bore the headline, "Home Sale Doesn't Require Sainthood" (South Bend Tribune, July 24, 2003, a column that originated in The New York Times Magazine.): "An oil company has offered us three times the current value of our rural property. If we accept, our neighbors will be looking at a gas station-convenience store instead of open green space." Mr. Cohen:

"As you suspect, that oil company is dangling the big money to tempt you to discard your scruples. The saintly response is to say, 'Get thee behind me, Exxon Mobil ...,' refuse to gain by harming your neighbors, and sell your land as a residence.

"Fortunately, ethics does not demand that you be a saint, only that you be reasonably decent. You're free to sell your property, but you also must balance your desire for maximum profit and your neighbors' desire to preserve their bucolic paradise. That's what it means to live in a community.

"So go with the oil company ... but try to negotiate conditions in the sale to mitigate the gas station's ill effects.... Your neighbors also might have ideas about this.

"In fact, saintly self-sacrifice would most likely yield a pyrrhic victory. The proliferation of malls and minimarts suggests that even if you rebuff the oily offer, eventually someone will accept it. What's needed is not just individual rectitude but also civic action.

"Communities should regulate land use ... through zoning laws and other measures. Were your community prudent, it would have done so already.

"There is something naggingly Nimby about your neighbors. Presumably they all have cars. How else do they get to their Arcadia? Why shouldn't they have the gas stations that go with them?"

(NIMBY—all caps—is an acronym for "not in my backyard.")

Would it be fair ("saintly"? "decent"?) to ask Mr. Cohen if his answer would be the same if the offer to buy came from a gambling casino. A brothel? Buyers from a minority religious or racial background that one might reasonably expect to be unwelcome among some of the neighbors?

By the way, does Mr. Cohen's last paragraph raise a significantly different ethical argument? H.R. Niebuhr said there were two questions in ethics: 1) To whom am I responsible? (2) And in what community? Does Mr. Cohen focus in a useful way on either or both of these?

6. Litigation is often a wholly unsatisfactory means of resolving disputes in property owners' associations. However irritated they may be with each other, neighbors must usually continue to coexist, and thus means of dispute resolution that emphasize cooperation and reconciliation rather than division and conflict are to be favored. How might documents establishing property owners' associations be drafted so as to facilitate more helpful approaches to dispute resolution? What effect might the following Montgomery County, Maryland ordinance have?

MONTGOMERY COUNTY CODE, CHAPTER 24B

Article 2. Dispute Resolution.

10B–2. Definitions.

In this Chapter, the following words have the following meanings:

(a) Commission means the Commission on Common Ownership Communities.

(b) Common ownership community includes:

(1) a development subject to a declaration enforced by a homeowners' association, as those terms are used in state law;

(2) a condominium, as that term is used in state law; and

(3) a cooperative housing project, as that term is used in state law.

(c) Office means the Office of Common Ownership Communities.

* * *

10B–8. Defined terms.

In this Article and Article 3, the following terms

* * *

(3) Dispute means any disagreement between 2 or more parties that involves:

(A) the authority of a governing body, under any law or association document, to:

(i) require any person to take any action, or not to take any action, involving a unit;

(ii) require any person to pay a fee, fine, or assessment;

(iii) spend association funds; or

(iv) alter or add to a common area or element; or

(B) the failure of a governing body, when required by law or an association document, to:

(i) properly conduct an election;

(ii) give adequate notice of a meeting or other action;

(iii) properly conduct a meeting;

(iv) properly adopt a budget or rule;

(v) maintain or audit books and records; or

(vi) allow inspection of books and records.

(4) Dispute does not include any disagreement that only involves:

(A) title to any unit or any common area or element;

(B) the percentage interest or vote allocable to a unit;

(C) the interpretation or enforcement of any warranty;

(D) the collection of an assessment validly levied against a party; or

(E) the judgment or discretion of a governing body in taking or deciding not to take any legally authorized action.

* * *

(7) Party includes:

(A) an owner;

(B) a governing body; and

(C) an occupant of a dwelling unit in a common ownership community.

10B–9. Filing of disputes; exhaustion of association remedies.

(a) The Commission may hear any dispute between or among parties.

(b) A party must not file a dispute with the Commission until the party makes a good faith attempt to exhaust all procedures or remedies provided in the association documents.

(c) However, a party may file a dispute with the Commission 60 days after any procedure or remedy provided in the association documents has been initiated before the association.

(d) After a community association finds that a dispute exists, the association must notify the other parties of their rights to file the dispute with the Commission. The association must not take any action to enforce or implement its decision for 14 days after it notifies the other parties of their rights.

(e) When a dispute is filed with the Commission, a community association must not take any action to enforce or implement the association's decision, except filing a civil action under subsection (f), until the process under this Article is completed.

(f) Any party may file a civil action arising out of an association document or a law regulating the association's powers and procedures at any time. However, the court may stay all proceedings for at least 90 days after the court is notified that a dispute has been properly filed under this Article so that a hearing under Section 10B–13 may be completed.

* * *

10B–11. Mediation.

(a) The Office may investigate facts and assemble documents relevant to a dispute filed with the Commission, and may summarize the issues in the dispute. The Office may notify a party if, in its opinion, a dispute was not properly filed with the Commission, and may inform each party of the possible sanctions under Section 10B–13(d).

(b) Any party may request mediation.

(c) If a party requests mediation, the Commission must notify all parties of the filing and of the mediation session.

(d) The Commission must provide a qualified mediator to meet with the parties within 30 days after a party requests mediation to attempt to settle the dispute.

(e) If any party refuses to attend a mediation session, or if mediation does not successfully resolve the dispute within 10 days after the first mediation session is held, the Commission must promptly schedule a hearing under Section 10B–13 unless a hearing has already been held under Section 10B–13.

10B–12. Hearing Panel.

(a) If a hearing is scheduled, the chair of the Commission must convene a 3–member panel to hear the dispute.

(b) The chair must choose 2 members of the panel from the voting members of the Commission. They must represent 2 different membership groups. At least one member must be a resident of a common ownership community. The 2 Commission members must designate the third member from a list of volunteer arbitrators trained or experienced in common ownership community issues maintained by the Commission. The third member must chair the panel.

(c) Each panelist must not have any interest in the dispute to be heard.

10B–13. Administrative hearing.

(a) A hearing panel appointed under Section 10B–12 must hold a hearing on each dispute that is not resolved by mediation under Section 10B–11 unless the Commission finds that:

(1) the dispute is essentially identical to another dispute between the same parties on which a hearing has already been held under this Section; or

(2) the dispute is clearly not within the jurisdiction of the Commission.

* * *

(d) The hearing panel may award costs, including a reasonable attorney's fee, to any party if another party;

(1) filed or maintained a frivolous dispute, or filed or maintained a dispute in other than good faith;

(2) unreasonably refused to accept mediation of a dispute, or unreasonably withdrew from ongoing mediation; or

(3) substantially delayed or hindered the dispute resolution process without good cause.

The hearing panel may also award costs or attorney's fees if an association document so requires and the award is reasonable under the circumstances.

* * *

(g) The court hearing an appeal must sustain the decision of the hearing panel unless the decision is:

(1) inconsistent with applicable law;

(2) not supported by substantial evidence on the record; or

(3) arbitrary and capricious, considering all facts before the hearing panel.

* * *

10B–14. Settlement of disputes; assistance to parties.

(a) Settlement of a dispute by mediation agreed to by the parties is binding, has the force and effect of a contract, and may be enforced accordingly.

* * *

7. A study of 599 condominium owners in Chicago, including 43 individuals who had been personally involved in condominium disputes, determined that nearly half of the disputants first attempted to resolve their disputes through negotiations, and one quarter through mediation. Only 2.3% began with litigation. Lifestyle and property disputes are most likely to be settled informally; disputes over finances, services, governance and personal well-being are less amenable to informal resolution. See Walker and Masotti, supra.

8. If the members of a property owners association are evenly divided on an issue—for example, whether to raise assessments, enforce a servitude, or undertake expensive remodeling of community facilities—who is the client of the association's lawyer? See A.B.A. Model Rule 1.13.

D. EXTENSION, MODIFICATION, AND TERMINATION OF RE-STRICTIONS BY PROPERTY OWNERS ASSOCIATIONS

RIDGE PARK HOME OWNERS v. PENA

Supreme Court of New Mexico, 1975.
88 N.M. 563, 544 P.2d 278.

SOSA, JUSTICE.

This is a case involving building and use restrictions in a subdivision and concerns the effect of amending restrictive covenants of that subdivision. Plaintiffs-appellants filed an action in the district court of Bernalillo County to enjoin the construction of a drug store and physician's office on two lots in the Ridge Park Addition subdivision in Albuquerque. The lots in question were subject to residential restrictions of record that forbade such construction.

After granting a preliminary injunction, in a subsequent hearing the district court ruled that the restrictions had been amended by a vote of the majority of the owners in the Ridge Park Addition, and that such amendment allowed the construction of the drug store and physician's office on the two lots, and found that the objection was moot. From the dismissal of the complaint and their request for a permanent injunction, the plaintiffs appeal.

Since the amendment relieved only a small portion of the residential lots from the residential restrictions, changing them to multiple dwelling or commercial, it altered the existing restrictions to less than all of the property in the subdivision. The plaintiffs urge for reversal that the district court erred as a matter of law in upholding such amendment. We agree. This issue being dispositive of the appeal, we do not need to reach the other points raised by the appellants.

Building and use restrictions for the Ridge Park Addition were filed with the county clerk of Bernalillo County on January 18, 1951. The Ridge Park Addition to the city of Albuquerque provided for both a commercial and a residential area. The restrictions provided that all lots in all blocks would be used for residential, single dwelling purposes, except for blocks 4 and 9 which could be commercial or residential. Subsequent to the filing of the building and use restrictions, the city of Albuquerque zoned the two lots in question, lots 9 and 10 of block 8 (among others) as commercial, although these two lots were covered with the residential restrictive covenants. The general rule is that zoning ordinances if less stringent do not diminish the legal effect of more restrictive private building restrictions, and the rezoning of property for purposes other than residential does not supersede the original plat restrictions so as to prevent the enforcement of such restrictions. Kosel v. Stone, 146 Mont. 218, 404 P.2d 894 (1965); 20 Am.Jur.2d Covenants, Conditions, and Restrictions § 277 at 837–41 (1965).

Since the zoning did not abrogate the restrictive covenants, defendants assert that the consent of a majority of the owners of all of the lots in the Ridge Park Addition to the changing of lots 9 and 10 in block 8 from residential to commercial abrogated those covenants with respect to the two lots. The method for amending the restrictive covenants was contained in Provision VI of the restrictions which provided as follows:

1. All protective covenants herein shall apply to and be binding upon all parties to this agreement, and their successors in interest, from the date of recording of this agreement with the County Clerk of Bernalillo County, State of New Mexico, for a period of twenty years and shall run with the land. At the expiration of twenty years said covenants shall be extended automatically for successive ten year periods unless a majority of the then owners of the lots vote to alter or eliminate said covenants.

The twenty year period had expired at the time the vote was taken. Passing by approximately an 85% majority, the amendment allowed all lots zoned C—1 by the city to be taken out of the residential restrictions and put under the business restrictions section of the subdivision agreement. The dissenting minority consisted mostly of the individuals living near and around the lots subject to the amendment.

The issue is whether the majority (or whatever percentage is required by an agreement) can amend or delete restrictive covenants on fewer than all lots subject thereto. Absent a specific provision in the agreement stating otherwise, we hold that the requisite vote cannot change the applicability of restrictive covenants to a few of the lots; the change must apply to all lots. Montoya v. Barreras, 81 N.M. 749, 473 P.2d 363 (1970). Defendants seek to distinguish Montoya supra by pointing out that the subdivision in that case was solely residential whereas Ridge Park is residential and commercial. This argument has little merit. "Restrictions as to the use of land are mutual, reciprocal, equitable easements in the nature of servitudes in favor of owners of other lots within the restricted area, and constitute property rights which run with the land." Montoya, 81 N.M. at 751, 473 P.2d at 365. In the instant case the residential restrictions burdened all residential lots; the commercial restrictions burden all commercial lots. The mutuality of restrictive covenants would be destroyed if we were to allow the majority of owners, who might not be adversely affected because of their insulated location in the subdivision, to authorize offensive consequences for the minority by removing or imposing restrictions only on certain lots within the minority's area. Thus, we find that the fact that the Ridge Park Addition was not merely residential, but was residential and commercial, makes no difference. No changes may be made with respect to any one lot without affecting all the others subject to the restrictions.

* * *

Notes and Questions

1. If the servitudes that establish and delineate the powers of a property owners' association are conceived of as its constitution, particular

problems arise when an attempt is made to amend that constitution, especially when the modification will disadvantage some members of the community more than others. Is majority rule acceptable in these circumstances? Are supramajority voting requirements more acceptable, or should absolute unanimity be required? What problems does a unanimity requirement create? If a municipality could take the action at issue in the principal case, essentially a rezoning, why do we not permit it of a property owners association? Would such changes be more palatable if property owners associations were required to compensate losers in wealth-transfer modifications, along the lines of public eminent domain requirements? See Ellickson, Cities and Homeowners Associations, 130 U.Pa.L.Rev. 1519, 1532–1539 (1982).

2. An impressive literature has arisen in the past decade debating whether property owners associations are on the one hand voluntary, consensual communities, that ought to be left largely free to chart their own course, or, on the other, tyrannical and oppressive arrangements that must be subjected to public control. See, e.g., Alexander, Dilemmas of Group Autonomy: Residential Associations and Community, 75 Cornell L.Rev. 1 (1989); Ellickson, Cities and Homeowners Associations, 130 U.Pa.L.Rev. 1519 (1982); Korngold, Resolving the Flaws of Residential Servitudes and Owners Associations: For Reformation not Termination, 1990 Wis.L.Rev. 513; Natelson, Consent, Coercion, and "Reasonableness" in Private Law: The Special Case of the Property Owners Association, 51 Ohio St.L.J. 41 (1990); Winokur, The Mixed Blessing of Promissory Servitudes: Toward Optimizing Economic Utility, Individual Liberty and Personal Identity, 1989 Wis.L.Rev. 1; Winokur, Reforming Servitude Regimes: Toward Associational Federalism and Community, 1990 Wis.L.Rev. 537; Note, The Rule of Law in Residential Associations, 99 Harv.L.Rev. 472 (1985). Do purchasers of property in a restricted subdivision in fact at the time of purchase consider and embrace the servitudes that bind that subdivision? Do most residents in restricted subdivisions experience the servitudes that govern their subdivision as limiting their individual creative expression or as facilitating the creation of a communal identity? Are restrictions the mindless creations of form-book writers or bureaucratic drones, or are they the market's response to the desires of consumers? What legal consequences should follow from how you answer these questions?

And, for that matter, what _moral_ considerations? Suppose somebody in the subdivision began to worry about the safety of children on the streets and sidewalks, particularly those near two busy streets that pass through the subdivision, and lobbied for and got a very local twenty-mile-per-hour speed limit. Given even fairly routine enforcement of such a local law, drivers come soon—to quote one of Randy Cohen's correspondents—to resent and collectively plot against "police cars [which] lie in wait for speeders." And so, "Many drivers flash their headlights to alert others to slow down and avoid a ticket." That, from one point of view (commuters'), is creative communal response. And even from the other point of view, the situation slows the cars down: The flashing-headlight response "results in the same type of driving the police are trying to enforce."

But Mr. Cohen is not happy about it. For one thing, flashing headlights are ineffective means to increase safety: "[A] moment after being flashed, a driver so inclined can blithely resume warp speed, secure that he's back in a copless zone." For another, the commuters' communal strategy is morally corrupt: "[T]he intent of headlight flashing is not to encourage safe legal driving but to help speeders avoid getting caught. . . . [I]t hardly seems like an effective long-term anticrime stratagem." (The New York Times Magazine, August 5, 2001.) This situation is, though, perhaps, pedagogically useful: It seems to present the same sort of communal action—in both directions, speed limit and collective evasion of speed limit—that the proponents of "voluntary" servitudes (use covenants) like to see. And perhaps, like so many restrictions, the situation Mr. Cohen presents illustrates twice over the tension between individual creative identity and communal identity. Here, and with regard to a householder who is annoyed by the neighbor who parks his motor home and ocean-going speed boat in the driveway, an objective ethicist might come out admiring zoning ordinances and salaried local officials who enforce them. Compare the discussion, below, of the zoning alternative, ch. 7, sec. 2, [pp. 969–1036].

Another way to approach both communal adjustments (both the speeding ordinance and the headlights) is with the concept introduced by the creative social psychologist Erving Goffman, in his Asylums: Essays on the Social Situation of Mental Patients and Other Inmates (1961). The concept is "secondary adjustment," that is, "any habitual arrangement by which a member of an organization employs unauthorized means, or obtains unauthorized ends, or both, thus getting around the organization's assumptions as to what he should do and get . . . ways in which the individual stands apart from the role and the self that were taken for granted for him by the institution." The driver who ignores the law and drives too fast where children play is not adjusting or getting around assumptions. The driver coming the other way who flashes headlights to warn of police officers looking for drivers who drive too fast where children play is. Goffman shows how such secondary adjustments become communal when the speeder, the violator, becomes an adjuster (slows down). He shows also how such communal secondary adjustments (driver and flasher in splendid democratic concord) often become acceptable in the community (with many examples of how prisoners behave) and then—in splendid irony—how the secondary adjustment to the rule becomes enforcement of the rule: Drivers who see the flashing headlights of their fellow citizens and slow down are perhaps an example. All of which is enough to cause an anxious freeholder to go along with anything that works, Randy Cohen to the contrary notwithstanding.

3.   The issues raised in these materials are increasingly being addressed by state statutes and uniform laws. See, Codifying the Law of Homeowner Associations: The Uniform Planned Community Act, 15 Real Prop., Prob., and Trust J., 854 (1980); Geis, Beyond the Condominium: The Uniform Common–Interest Ownership Act, 17 Real Prop., Prob. & Trust J. 757 (1982).

SPRING LAKE ESTATES

Adapted from Johnson and Salsich, "Springlake Estates"
in Riskin and Westbrook, Dispute Resolution and
Lawyers, Teachers' Manual (West 1988).

Spring Lake Estates is a planned residential development in an "exurban" part of the metropolitan area. Located approximately 25 miles from the central business district, it features a 200–acre lake and 300 acres of gently rolling meadows interspersed with strands of oak and pine. The developer, Spring Lake Properties, Inc., plans a first phase of 60 one-acre lots and a second phase of 40 additional lots. The first phase of 60 has been platted. The dam has been completed and the lake is filling. Roads have been laid out according to the plat, but have not yet been constructed. At present they are nothing more than dirt trails.

A brochure describing the development contains the following information. Spring Lake Estates will be "an outstanding residential community featuring amenities certain to appeal to executive homeowners." All lot owners will be expected to complete construction of a residence suitable for year-round occupancy or vacationing within two years of purchase. Lot owners and their guests will have full use of the lake, beaches, boat docks, club house, jogging trails, swimming pool, hot tub and tennis courts. Lot owners may have pets, but only if they do not constitute a nuisance. All roads will be paved within the next 12 months. The club house and sporting facilities will be completed within 24 months. All common facilities will be maintained by the developer until a property owners association is established.

Water supply must be purchased from a private utility company that will be organized by the developer. Water lines will be extended to the individual lots. A completion bond has been purchased by the developer. A well has been sunk by the developer that appears adequate for all anticipated water uses. A $10 per month flat rate has been established for each lot serviced by hookup.

Electricity and telephone services are available from local utilities regulated by the State Public Service Commission. Facilities will be extended to the individual lots upon request by a lot purchaser who constructs a residence. Costs of the facilities and service will be the responsibility of the lot owner. There is no gas service to the subdivision.

The sewage system is owned by the developer, which is responsible for the installation and operation of the system. Lines will be extended to individual lots. A connection (hookup) cost of $75 will be borne by the lot owner. No alternative method of sewage disposal will be permitted in the boundaries of the subdivision.

A home owners' association, Spring Lake Estates Home Owners' Association, will be organized when the development is complete. Title to the common areas, such as the lake, dam, roads, pools, clubhouse, and tennis courts will be conveyed to the home owners' association. Each lot owner will pay a maintenance fee of $250 per month. This fee may be modified annually if common area expenses so warrant. In addition, special assessments may be levied to respond to unanticipated repair and maintenance problems. Fees and assessments will be paid to the developer until such time as the home owners association is organized.

Fire and police protection, garbage and trash collection, schools, medical and dental facilities are available from local entities and are not the responsibility of the developer. A small shopping center will be developed at the periphery of the development, which will include a convenience store, drug store, laundromat, movie theater, gasoline station, and restaurant.

PROBLEMS

1. As attorney for the developer, describe the provisions that must be drafted to accomplish the developer's goals as outlined in the narrative. Identify the property interests those provisions create. Pay particular attention to establishing a process to manage change as the development evolves through different stages.

2. Draft one clause creating an affirmative right to use the property of others, one negative obligation servitude, and one affirmative

obligation servitude that will accomplish the developer's goals identified above.

3.   Design a system for resolving disputes arising out of the relationships created by the common interest community and draft the appropriate clauses necessary to establish that system.

Dispute Resolution Exercise

Assume that it is now ten years later. Assume further that the following clauses were included, among others, in the declaration of restrictions:

"(1) No animals, livestock or poultry of any kind shall be raised, bred, or kept on any lot, except that dogs, cats and other household pets may be kept, provided that they are not kept, bred, or maintained for any commercial purpose.

"(2) The grantor reserves to itself the right to alter or amend these restrictions at any time, and such alterations and amendments shall apply to all lots in the subdivision whether owned by the grantor or its successors or assigns, provided that such amendment shall not diminish the protection provided by these restrictions.

"(3) The board of directors of the home owners' association may issue temporary permits to free owners of lots in the subdivision from any obligations express or implied by this declaration, provided the board of directors acts in accordance with adopted guidelines and procedures and shows good cause.

"(4) No noxious or offensive activity shall be carried on upon any lot, nor shall anything be done thereon which may be or may become an annoyance or nuisance to the neighborhood.

"(5) Lots within Spring Lake Estates shall only be used for single-family residential use."

As Spring Lake has developed over the past ten years, several problems have arisen.

(a) Lots 13, 14, and 15 have never been sold. Rather than drive to the common beach, the families owning lots 51 and 52 have simply cut across these lots to get to the lake. They have been doing this for as long as they have lived there. No one ever said anything to them about this, although a couple of "no trespassing" signs have been posted on the trees. Now Spring Lake Properties, Inc. (SLP) has strung a chain between the trees to block access to lots 13, 14 and 15. The owners of lots 51 and 52 seek your advice.

(b) SLP has had some financial difficulties. It recently sold ten acres in the area described as Phase II on the plat to Golden Age Properties (GAP), which plans to construct a 100–unit retirement condominium development. SLP has also transferred "perpetual rights" to use the common area of the development, including the lake, beach, pools and tennis courts, to GAP. Homeowners from several of the lots in the original Spring Lakes development have sought your advice.

(c) The homeowners in the original development have recently discovered that the sewer lines for lots 44 through 33 pass under the land sold to GAP, and that SLP did not reserve an easement in the deed to GAP. GAP has recently discovered the sewer line and wishes to remove it as it interferes with construction in GAP. GAP has come to you for advice.

(d) The original purchaser of lot 5 sold her house and lot to a family that has placed a two bedroom, factory-built, modular house for their grandparents on the lot behind the existing house without seeking approval for the extra unit.

(e) Mrs. Smith's 100 pound golden retriever, Ginger, whom Mrs. Smith claims is "a very gentle animal," barked ferociously and terrorized the six year old daughter of the Browns who live across the street, when she ran into Mrs. Smith's yard to retrieve a ball. Mrs. Smith has accused the eleven year old son of her next door neighbor, Ed Harris, of provoking the dog by constant teasing and harassment. The Browns are threatening legal action against Mrs. Smith unless she removes the dog from the development.

(f) Spring Lake Estates originally was situated about a quarter mile from Highway 103, a two-lane state highway. The area between lots 53 and 60 and the highway was left heavily wooded as a barrier between the highway and Spring Lake Estates. Two years ago, the state made 103 a four-lane divided highway. In doing so, it condemned the wooded land. This area has been replaced with chain-link fence and non-descript highway foliage. The fronts of the homes on lot 53–60 face directly to the highway, separated only by the street and the chain-link fence. The homes were originally built at a cost of approximately $250,000 each.

The owner of lot 53 has a contract to sell his house to Le Petit Enfant Day Care Center. The center would serve about 40 children each day. The center is willing to purchase the house for $180,000. The center expects to do well because Spring Lake Estates is entirely residential, and there is an "office park" on the other side of the highway. The house has been for sale for nine months. The best offer received prior to that from the center was $150,000. The contract of sale is conditional on the absence of restrictions that would prohibit the day care center. What advice do you give the owner of lot 53?

III. NUISANCE

A. PRIVATE NUISANCE

Many disputes that arise between neighbors can be conceptualized alternatively as servitude or as nuisance problems. Servitude law invokes the authority of restrictions or affirmative obligations to which the parties have, at least constructively, consented. Nuisance law, on the other hand, invokes the authority of the more general obligations imposed by the law of tort.

The most general duty imposed by the law of nuisance is articulated by the latin phrase "Sic utere tuo ut alienum non laedas"—use your property so as not to injure others. The difficulty of applying this maxim in the context of relations between neighbors becomes readily apparent if one considers the contexts in which nuisance disputes are likely to arise. One neighbor's beloved pets create noise or odors that offend another. One neighbor's prized tree rains leaves and twigs into another's gutter. The diligent practice of one neighbor's son, an aspiring rock musician, arouses the fury of the entire block on a somnolent Sunday afternoon. Residential uses also come in conflict with agricultural, commercial or industrial uses, which uses in turn conflict among themselves. Feedlots breed odors and vermin, which afflict neighboring residences. Industries belch smoke, which their neighbors must breathe. Bright lights from shopping centers dim the screens of neighboring drive-in theatres. If an offending neighbor's conduct is sufficiently offensive or a receiving neighbor is sufficiently sensitive, offense becomes injury, and a nuisance dispute ends up in court. Courts must then struggle with whose rights must prevail, the rights of one landowner to use her land as she chooses, or the right of another landowner to be free from interference in the use of his land.

A private nuisance (more on public nuisances later) is defined by the Restatement (Second) of Torts (1979) as "a nontrespass invasion of another's interest in the private use and enjoyment of land." § 821D. Nuisance is, therefore, an invasion of property which is not a trespass. Conceptually, trespass is a direct invasion of plaintiff's land, nuisance an indirect interference with use and enjoyment. If your neighbor walks across your land or dumps dirt onto it, he is guilty of trespass. If his noisy air conditioner keeps you awake at night, or flies from his manure pile keep you from enjoying barbecues on your deck, he may be guilty of a nuisance. The conceptual distinction between trespass and nuisance is important because a trespasser is liable irrespective of whether the trespass causes harm, Restatement (Second) of Torts, § 158 (1979), while one who commits nuisance is liable only if significant harm results, Restatement (Second) of Torts, Second, § 821F.

Why does this distinction exist between trespass and nuisance? Does it make economic sense? See Merrill, Trespass, Nuisance, and the Costs of Determining Property Rights, 14 J. Legal Stud. 13 (1985). Practically, the distinction is often difficult to make. See, e.g., Martin v. Reynolds Metals Co., 221 Or. 86, 342 P.2d 790 (1959), cert. den., 362 U.S. 918, 80 S.Ct. 672, 4 L.Ed.2d 739 (1960) (invasion by gas held to be direct physical invasion).

BLANKS v. RAWSON

Court of Appeals of South Carolina, 1988.
296 S.C. 110, 370 S.E.2d 890.

CURETON, JUDGE:

This is a dispute between next door neighbors. Benjamin and Mary Ann Blanks claim their neighbor, Gary W. Rawson, has violated certain neighborhood restrictions by the construction of a dog pen, basketball goal, and ten-foot privacy fence. The trial judge ordered Mr. Rawson to remove or relocate the dog pen and basketball goal. He also ordered Rawson to remove or reduce the height of the fence. Rawson appeals. We affirm in part and reverse in part.

The Blanks and Rawson reside in the Indian Fork subdivision on Lake Murray in Lexington County. Both parties bought vacant lots and constructed homes. The subdivision was developed by Indian Fork Development Company. The company filed a "Declaration of Restrictions" which covered the lots in question. Rawson purchased his lot first. He constructed a home substantially identical to his prior home. In purchasing the property Mr. Rawson had discussions with a representative of Indian Fork Development Company. This representative was aware Rawson desired to build a house identical to his current home. The developer approved Rawson's house plans. The developer specifically gave permission to Rawson to vary the minimum set back requirements in the Declaration of Restrictions to accommodate his home on the lot and to locate the dog pen and basketball goal. The basketball goal is near the edge of the driveway close to the property line. The dog pen is on the property line behind the driveway.

Mr. and Mrs. Blanks purchased the lot to the right of Mr. Rawson. The developer advised the Blanks of Mr. Rawson's name because they desired to know who their neighbor would be. The Blanks rode by Rawson's old home to view it. At that time, the dog pen was behind the driveway on the property line. The dog pen in controversy is in the same location behind the driveway. The difference is Rawson has re-oriented the new house so the driveway is on the right side of the house as opposed to the left. This is the side next to the Blanks.

As the homes were being constructed, Mr. Blanks expressed objections personally and through counsel to Rawson about the dog pen and basketball goal because he felt they violated the minimum setback limits. Rawson had already obtained the approval of the developer to vary the setback limits when these objections were raised. Paragraph Seven of the Declaration of Restrictions provides "no building shall be closer to any side boundary than fifteen (15) feet * * * provided further that the Declarant [Indian Fork Development Co. Inc.] reserves the right to vary all such setback lines at will."

Shortly after the complaint was served, Rawson constructed a ten foot privacy fence. The fence shields the basketball goal and dog pen from the Blanks. As with the dog pen and goal, Rawson obtained the permission of Indian River Development Company to build the fence. This permission was received in December of 1985 although construction of the fence did not occur until May 1986.

The Blanks complain the dog pen and basketball goal violate the minimum setback limits and are a nuisance. They claim the dog barks and the dog pen is not properly maintained thereby creating a foul odor. They complain Rawson's son plays loud music and his basketball comes into their yard. As to the fence, they complain it is too high and blocks the view of the lake they previously enjoyed across Rawson's property. The trial court found the nearness of the basketball goal to the property line created a nuisance whenever the basketball was thrown toward the goal. The court found that if the ball hits the goal it creates a noise and if it misses the goal, it can go into the Blanks' yard. The court found the nearness of the dog pen to the property line created a nuisance because it was not properly maintained and the sight and smell of dog feces was revolting. As to the fence, the court called it a "hate fence" not in keeping with the intentions of a high level residential neighborhood and not in keeping with what is right as opposed to what is wrong. The court held it was wrong for the fence to obstruct the Blanks' view of the lake across the Rawsons' backyard.

The complaint alleges violation of restrictions and seeks an injunction. As previously noted, Paragraph Seven of the Declaration of Restrictions deals with setback requirements. Paragraph Eight provides "no noxious or offensive activity * * * shall be had or done upon any lot in the subdivision and nothing shall be had or done thereon which constitutes or becomes an annoyance or nuisance to the neighborhood or constitutes an unsanitary condition." Paragraph Twelve indicates the restrictions shall run with the land. Paragraph Thirteen gives an owner a right to sue any other owner of real property in the subdivision in order to restrain a violation of the restrictions.

* * *

Mr. Rawson did not violate Paragraph Seven of the subdivision restrictions concerning the setback limits. The evidence is undisputed he received express permission from Indian Fork Development Company to locate the dog pen, basketball goal, and fence. The restrictions in Paragraph Seven concerning setbacks specifically provide the company has the right to vary all setback lines at will.

The trial court rested its conclusions on a concept of nuisance. Paragraph Eight prohibits the creation of an annoyance or nuisance to the neighborhood. Neither a basketball goal nor a dog pen is a nuisance per se. They may be a nuisance per accidens if they become a nuisance by reason of circumstances, location, or surroundings. A nuisance has been defined as "anything which works hurt, inconvenience, or damages; anything which essentially interferes with the enjoyment of life or property [ ]." Strong v. Winn–Dixie Stores, Inc., 240 S.C. 244, 253, 125 S.E.2d 628, 632 (1962).

The South Carolina Supreme Court has recognized that the resolution of the issue of a private nuisance involves the conflicting interests of landowners. "The right of one to make such lawful use of his property as he may desire must be applied with due regard to the correlative right of the other to be protected in the reasonable enjoyment of his property." Winget v. Winn–Dixie Stores Inc., 242 S.C. 152, 159, 130 S.E.2d 363, 367 (1963). Each case must be decided upon its own facts, and the observation of the Supreme Court regarding neighbors is particularly relevant:

> "[E]very annoyance or disturbance of a landowner from the use made of property by a neighbor does not constitute a nuisance. The question is not whether the plaintiffs have been annoyed or disturbed * * * but whether there has been an injury to their legal rights. People who live in organized communities must of necessity suffer some inconvenience and annoyance from their neighbors and must submit to annoyances consequent upon the reasonable use of property by others."

Winget, 242 S.C. at 159, 130 S.E.2d at 367.

From our review of the record, we do not find evidence to support the conclusion the basketball goal is a nuisance. Mr. Blanks testified to only one instance when Mr. Rawson's son was playing basketball and he asked the boy to turn down the radio. He also complained the ball could bounce over into his yard and damage his air conditioner unit or shrubs. There is no evidence this damage has occurred. The pictures in the record do not show any shrubs in the yard although Blanks stated they planned to plant some. At most, the Blanks complain about an anticipatory nuisance in this respect.

The debate over the dog pen concerns how often and how well it is cleaned. The trial court heard the testimony and reviewed photographs. The dog is a large breed. The Rawsons testified they cleaned the pen daily. Mr. Blanks stated it was not cleaned on a regular basis. Blanks testified the odor was still present with the fence in place. The trial court found the dog pen was maintained in a filthy condition and an odor was created by its condition. In this equity action, the Court of Appeals has the authority to make findings of fact in accordance with its own view of the preponderance of the evidence, however, it is not required to disregard the findings of the trial judge who saw and heard the witnesses and was in a better position to judge their credibility. [ ] Given the conflicting evidence on this issue, we affirm the trial judge.

The final issue is the fence. The Blanks object to its height primarily because it restricts their view of the lake. Before the fence was constructed, they could sit on their back porch and look at the lake across the Rawson property. Rawson received permission from the developer to construct the fence.

The Declaration of Restrictions does not contain language creating a covenant of view for any lot owner. South Carolina does not recognize a prescriptive easement of view. [ ]

Perhaps recognizing the inherent problem in arguing there could be no fence, Mr. Blanks testified he would be satisfied if the fence were reduced to eight feet near the basketball goal and six feet down to the water. The trial court apparently felt the fence was ill motivated, but did not find it was a nuisance. The court stated the fence was not in keeping with the intentions of a high-level residential development.

Motive in constructing the fence is not relevant to this case. The question is whether the fence violates a restriction. Based upon our view of the evidence, it does not. It is unfortunate relations among neighbors have degenerated to this point, but it appears the fence may be the best resolution of this controversy. While the Blanks no longer have a panoramic view of the lake, both parties have their privacy.

The decision of the trial court is affirmed in part and reversed in part.

Notes and Questions

1. What sorts of "annoyances and disturbances" rise to the level of a nuisance? The principal case rejects the plaintiff's position that interference with a view can constitute a nuisance. Should nuisance law ever be available to protect aesthetic sensibilities? Compare Cahill v. Heckel, 87 N.J.Super. 201, 208 A.2d 651 (1965); Robie v. Lillis, 112 N.H. 492, 299 A.2d 155 (1972) (unsightly commercial uses in residential neighborhood not nuisance), with Woodbury, Aesthetic Nuisances: The Time has come to Recognize It, 27 Nat.Res.J. 877 (1987). Should courts find "spite fences" to be nuisances? See 5 R. Powell, Powell on Real Property, § 696 (1991). Conduct that physically harms another's property (e.g., injury to crops or trees caused by polluting the soil or water) is grounds for nuisance litigation, as is conduct that diminishes the value of property. Should conduct that causes mental annoyance or physical discomfort also be grounds for a nuisance action independently of its affect on the value of the injured party's land? See Prosser & Keeton on Torts, § 88 (5th ed. 1984). Could a use that causes psychological discomfort, such as a funeral home or cemetery, constitute a nuisance? See Frederick v. Brown Funeral Homes, Inc., 222 La. 57, 62 So.2d 100 (1952) (the majority rule permits enjoining a funeral home in a strictly residential neighborhood). Should a landowner be liable in nuisance if the natural condition of his land (e.g., as overgrown with weeds) injures an adjoining land owner? See Restatement (Second) of Torts, §§ 839, 840 (1977). As nuisance is a property tort, should it make any difference whether the person harmed is the owner of the property or merely another who lives there, such as a family member or employee? See Prosser & Keeton on Torts, § 87 (5th ed. 1984).

2. Nuisance law is permeated with Latin. The principal case raises the distinction between nuisance per se and nuisance per accidens. A nuisance per se (or absolute nuisance) is a use that is unreasonable in itself, wherever located and however conducted. What uses fit that description? As a practical matter, a court will rarely hold a use to be a nuisance per se unless it is specifically outlawed by statute or ordinance. See Vianello v. State of Texas,

627 S.W.2d 530 (Tex.App.1982) (dog kennel illegal under local ordinance). Most nuisances fall into the per accidens category. They are offensive because of where or how they are conducted.

3.   A related distinction applies when a suit is brought to enjoin a prospective nuisance. The plaintiff in such a suit must establish that it is highly probable that a nuisance will result, however the use is operated. It is not sufficient to merely show that a nuisance may result if the use is operated improperly. Usually this means showing that the use in itself is inappropriate for the locality for which it is proposed.

CARPENTER v. DOUBLE R CATTLE COMPANY, INC.

Court of Appeals of Idaho, 1983.
105 Idaho 320, 669 P.2d 643.

BURNETT, JUDGE.

* * *

This lawsuit was filed by a group of homeowners who alleged that expansion of a nearby cattle feedlot had created a nuisance. The homeowners claimed that operation of the expanded feedlot had caused noxious odors, air and water pollution, noise and pests in the area. The homeowners sought damages and injunctive relief. * * * The jury returned a verdict simply finding that no nuisance existed. The court entered judgment for the feedlot proprietors, denying the homeowners any damages or injunctive relief. This appeal followed. For reasons appearing below, we vacate the judgment and remand the case for a new trial.

The homeowners contend that the jury received improper instructions on criteria for determining the existence of a nuisance. The jury was told to weigh the alleged injury to the homeowners against the "social value" of the feedlot, and to consider "the interests of the community as a whole," in determining whether a nuisance existed. In Part I of this opinion we consider the adequacy of the record upon which to review the jury instructions. In Part II we establish an historical framework for reviewing the instructions, by examining the development of American nuisance law. In Part III we turn to pertinent sections from the nuisance chapter of the Restatement (Second) of Torts (1977). We explain how these sections limit the utilization of such concepts as "social value" and "the interests of the community as a whole" in determining whether a nuisance exists. We discuss the implications of these sections; and we adopt them. Finally, in Part IV, we return to the jury instructions in this case, holding them to be erroneous and offering guidance to the trial court upon remand.

I

* * *

Although the record on appeal is limited, the detailed minute records of the court and the exhibits indicate the general nature of evidence adduced. There was evidence tending to show a cattle operation involving several thousand head at the feedlot; swarms of insects on various properties near the feedlot; flocks of birds near the feedlot; manure piles at the feedlot; and drainage of waste water from the feedlot. The evidence identified the nature of the homeowners' properties and fixed their location relative to the feedlot. There was expert testimony regarding the economic values of the properties. * * * A comprehensive plan and a zoning ordinance of Washington County were presented. At the close of the homeowners' evidence, and at the conclusion of trial, the proprietors moved for dismissal of the homeowners' complaint. Both motions were denied.

* * *

II

The concept of nuisance originated in the law of property. At common law, a distinction was maintained between two encroachments upon property rights—interference with possession of land, and interference with the use and enjoyment of land. The first type of encroachment was subject to an "assize of novel disseisen," a remedy for trespass. The latter form of encroachment was subject to an "assize of nuisance," a remedy for a variety of invasions which diminished the owner's enjoyment of his property without dispossessing him of it. Thus, nuisance and trespass have common roots in property law, and occasionally it is difficult to distinguish between them. But where an invasion of property is merely incidental to the use of adjoining property, and does not physically interfere with possession of the property invaded, it generally has been classified as a nuisance rather than as a trespass. See cases collected in 58 Am.Jur.2d Nuisances, § 2, 556–57 (1971).

The early concepts of nuisance and trespass shared the common law's reverence for property rights. Invasions of property were deemed wrongful per se, and the parties responsible for such invasions were subject to a form of strict liability. * * *

The property-oriented, English concept of a nuisance had its analogue in early American law. In one illustrative case of the nineteenth century, an American court held that title to land gave the owner the right to impregnate the air with odors, dust and smoke, pollute his own water and make noises, provided that he did not substantially interfere with the comfort of others or injure the use or enjoyment of their property. Pennoyer v. Allen, 56 Wis. 502, 14 N.W. 609 (1883).

This broad description of nuisance was incorporated into Idaho law. Idaho Code § 52–101, which has antecedents dating to 1881, defines a nuisance as "[a]nything which is injurious to health or morals, or is indecent, or offensive to the senses, or an obstruction to the free use of property, so as to interfere with the comfortable enjoyment of life or property * * *."

However, as the English concept of nuisance was assimilated into American law, it underwent a transformation. It ceased to be solely a creature of property law. As exemplified by the Idaho statutes, nuisance law came to protect life and health, as well as property. * * *

American tort law in the nineteenth and early twentieth centuries was founded upon the rock of "fault." As the notion of fault burrowed into the concept of nuisance, the strict liability which had attended nuisance in property law began to deteriorate. American courts stressed that liability for nuisance would arise only from "unreasonable" uses of property. * * *

* * * Our courts also underscored the distinction between conditions which are inherently nuisances (nuisances per se) and those conditions which may or may not constitute nuisances, depending upon the surrounding circumstances (nuisances per accidens). Of cases in the latter category, it became customary for the courts to say that whether an invasion of another's enjoyment of property was unreasonable would depend upon all circumstances in the case. These circumstances typically would include the location of the claimed nuisance, the character of the neighborhood, the nature of the offending activity, the frequency of the intrusion, and the effect upon the enjoyment of life, health and property.
[ ]

Moreover, the American transformation resulted in diminished application of the principle—derived from property law—that where property rights were substantially impaired by a nuisance, the complaining party was entitled to an injunction. This principle, which had complemented the property-based concept of strict liability, entitled a property owner to block an offensive activity on neighboring property, regardless of disparate economic consequences. American courts apparently found this approach ill-suited to the demands of a developing nation.

There evolved two lines of American response to the problem of injunctions. One response was to narrow the scope of cases in which injunctions would be granted, while continuing to recognize an entitlement to damages for injury to property rights. Thus, in Clifton Iron Co. v. Dye, 87 Ala. 468, 6 So. 192 (1889), the Alabama Supreme Court held that a mining company would not be enjoined from washing its ores simply because the operation polluted a stream below. The court held that the aggrieved parties' recourse was in damages. * * *

Ultimately, the approach exemplified by these cases developed into the "comparative injury" doctrine. Under this doctrine, the comparative benefits and hardships of discontinuing one activity for the protection of another would be weighed in determining whether injunctive relief or damages represented the more appropriate remedy for a nuisance. The Idaho Supreme Court adopted the comparative injury doctrine in Koseris v. J.R. Simplot Co., 82 Idaho 263, 352 P.2d 235 (1960). As explained later in this opinion, our Supreme Court in Koseris acknowledged the right to recover damages for the invasion of one's property, even where the comparative injury doctrine might bar injunctive relief.

The second line of American response to the injunction problem was to narrow the scope of cases in which nuisances were found to exist. This was achieved by incorporating the social value—the "utility"—of the offending activity into the litany of circumstances to be weighed in determining whether a particular use of property was "unreasonable." Thus, the utility of an offending activity militated not merely against the issuance of an injunction, but also against a determination that the offending activity was a nuisance at all. This second line of response found expression in the general ("black letter") principles set forth by the Restatement of Torts (1932) (herein cited as the First Restatement). Section 826 of the First Restatement declared that an invasion of another's enjoyment of property would be deemed unreasonable, and therefore a nuisance, unless the utility of the actor's conduct outweighed the gravity of the harm.

The Idaho Supreme Court never explicitly adopted the First Restatement. However, in McNichols v. J.R. Simplot Co., [74 Idaho 321, 262 P.2d 1012 (1953)], the Court may have intimated a similar approach. * * *

Thus, when confronted with a choice between the two American lines of response to the problem of injunctions in nuisance cases, Idaho appeared to choose both. Koseris adopted the "comparative injury" doctrine, restricting the cases qualifying for injunctions without narrowing the scope of nuisance cases in which an aggrieved party was entitled to be compensated in damages. However, McNichols and IDJI 491 allowed the offending activity's value to the community to be considered in determining whether any nuisance existed at all.

* * *

Dissatisfaction with the First Restatement also was expressed by the courts. In Boomer v. Atlantic Cement Co., 26 N.Y.2d 219, 309 N.Y.S.2d 312, 257 N.E.2d 870 (1970), the New York Court of Appeals held that parties adversely affected by dust from a cement plant would be entitled to recover damages for the harm, although the value of the cement plant to the community was so great that its operation would not be enjoined.

* * *

Thus, it was clear by 1970 that the First Restatement's black letter test for existence of a nuisance had ceased to be—if, indeed, it ever was—an adequate expression of case law. The days were drawing to a close when an economic activity could escape all liability under nuisance law for harm caused to its neighbors, simply because a large measure of social utility was ascribed to it.

III

The seeds of reform had been sown. They took root in fertile soil when the American Law Institute (ALI), which had begun to write a new restatement of the law of torts, turned its attention to the subject of nuisances in 1970.

* * *

B.   The Second Restatement

Ultimately, the provisions of Tentative Draft No. 18 were approved and incorporated into the private nuisance sections of chapter 40, Restatement (Second) of Torts (1977) (herein cited as the Second Restatement). The Second Restatement, like its predecessor, divides such nuisances into two groups: (a) "intentional and unreasonable" invasions of another's interest in the use and enjoyment of property, and (b) invasions which are "unintentional" but otherwise actionable under general tort principles. Second Restatement at § 822.

The first category is broader than the term "intentional" at first glance might suggest. Section 825 of the Second Restatement explains that an invasion is "intentional" if the actor knows that the invasion is resulting, or is substantially certain to result, from his activity. Thus, the purpose of an activity, such as a feedlot, may not be to invade its neighbors' interests in the use and enjoyment of their property; but the invasion is "intentional" within the meaning of the Second Restatement if the proprietors of the activity know that such an invasion is resulting—or is substantially certain to result—from the intended operation of their business. We focus upon "intentional" invasion, in this sense, because it is the type of nuisance alleged to exist in the present case.

The Second Restatement treats such an "intentional" invasion as a nuisance if it is "unreasonable." Section 826 of the Second Restatement now provides two sets of criteria for determining whether this type of nuisance exists:

An intentional invasion of another's interest in the use and enjoyment of land is unreasonable if

(a) the gravity of the harm outweighs the utility of the actor's conduct, or

(b) the harm caused by the conduct is serious and the financial burden of compensating for this and similar harm to others would not make the continuation of the conduct not feasible.

The present version of § 826, unlike its counterpart in the First Restatement, recognizes that liability for damages caused by a nuisance may exist regardless of whether the utility of the offending activity exceeds the gravity of the harm it has created. This fundamental proposition now permeates the entire Second Restatement. * * *

* * *

C.   Evaluation of The Second Restatement

The Second Restatement clearly has rejected the notion that if an activity's utility exceeds the harm it creates, the activity is not a nuisance and therefore is free from all liability in damages or for injunctive relief. * * * It discards those earlier authorities which had responded to the problem of disparate economic consequences of injunctions by narrowing the concept of nuisance. Thus, the Second Restatement today is inconsistent with the Idaho Supreme Court's decision in McNichols, supra, insofar as that decision is said to support IDJI 491. * * *

* * *

Both the Second Restatement and Koseris recognize that utility of the activity alleged to be a nuisance is a proper factor to consider in the context of injunctive relief; but that damages may be awarded regardless of utility. Evidence of utility does not constitute a defense against recovery of damages where the harm is serious and compensation is feasible. Were the law otherwise, a large enterprise, important to the local economy, would have a lesser duty to compensate its neighbors for invasion of their rights than would a smaller business deemed less essential to the community. In our view, this is not, and should not be, the law in Idaho.

Koseris and the Second Restatement also share a recognition of the fundamental difference between making an activity compensate those whom it harms, and forcing the activity to discontinue or to modify its operations. The damage question goes to a person's basic right in tort law to recover for harm inflicted by another. The injunction question is broader; it brings into play the interest of other persons who may benefit from the activity. * * *

We believe that Koseris and the Second Restatement furnish better guidance than IDJI 491 for the future path of nuisance law in Idaho. The law of nuisance profoundly affects the quality of life enjoyed by all Idahoans. It should be broad in coverage, as our statutes provide, and fair in its application. It should not contain blind spots for large or important enterprises.

However, our view is not based simply upon general notions of fairness; it is also grounded in economics. The Second Restatement deals effectively with the problem of "externalities" identified in the ALI proceedings. Where an enterprise externalizes some burdens upon its neighbors, without compensation, our market system does not reflect the true cost of products or services provided by that enterprise. Externalities distort the price signals essential to the proper functioning of the market.

This problem affects two fundamental objectives of the economic system. The first objective, commonly called "efficiency" in economic theory, is to promote the greatest aggregate surplus of benefits over the costs of economic activity. The second objective, usually termed "equity" or "distributive justice," is to allocate these benefits and costs in accordance with prevailing societal values. The market system best serves the goal of efficiency when prices reflect true costs; and the goal of distributive justice is best achieved when benefits are explicitly identified to the correlative costs.

Although the problem of externalities affects both goals of efficiency and distributive justice, these objectives are conceptually different and may imply different solutions to a given problem. In theory, if there were no societal goal other than efficiency, and if there were no impediments to exchanges of property or property rights, individuals pursuing their economic self-interests might reach the most efficient allocation of costs and benefits by means of exchange, without direction by the courts. See Coase, The Problem of Social Cost, 3 J.L. & Econ. 1 (1960). However, the real world is not free from impediments to exchanges, and our economic system operates within the constraints of a society which is also concerned with distributive justice. Thus, the courts often are the battlegrounds upon which campaigns for efficiency and distributive justice are waged.

* * *

In order to address the problem of externalities, the remedies of damages and injunctive relief must be carefully chosen to accommodate the often competing goals of efficiency and distributive justice. See generally Polinsky, Resolving Nuisance Disputes: The Simple Economics of Injunctive and Damage Remedies, 32 Stan.L.Rev. 1075 (1980); Ellickson, Alternatives to Zoning: Covenants, Nuisance Rules, and Fines as Land Use Controls, 40 U.Chi.L.Rev. 681 (1973). Koseris and the Second Restatement recognize the complementary functions of injunctions and damages. Section 826(a) of the Second Restatement allows both injunctions and damages to be employed where the harm created by an economic activity exceeds its utility. Section 826(b) allows the more limited remedy of damages alone to be employed where it would not be appropriate to enjoin the activity but the activity is imposing harm upon its neighbors so substantial that they cannot reasonably be expected to bear it without compensation.

We follow Koseris and adopt § 826 of the Second Restatement. To the extent that IDJI 491 is inconsistent with our decision today, we urge that it be modified. In any event, IDJI 491 is merely recommendatory in nature; it is not mandatory. I.R.C.P. 51(a)(2).

D. Implications of the Second Restatement

Each of the parties in the present case has viewed the Second Restatement with some apprehension. We now turn to those concerns.

The homeowners, echoing an argument made during the ALI proceedings, have contended that the test of nuisance set forth in § 826 grants large enterprises a form of private eminent domain. They evidently fear that if the utility of a large enterprise exceeds the gravity of the harm it creates—insulating it from an injunction and subjecting it to liability only in damages—the enterprise might interfere at will with the enjoyment and use of neighboring property, upon penalty only of paying compensation from time to time. Such a result might be consistent with the economic goal of efficiency, but it may conflict with the goal of distributive justice insofar as it violates a basic societal value which opposes forced exchanges of property rights. See Calabresi, Some Thoughts on Risk Distribution and the Law of Torts, 70 Yale L.J. 499, 536 (1961).

Even those legal scholars who advocate the most limited role for injunctions as a remedy against nuisances acknowledge that damages may be inadequate, and injunctions may be necessary, where the harm in question relates to personal health and safety, or to one's fundamental freedom of action within the boundaries of his own property. Ellickson, supra, 40 U.Chi.L.Rev. at 740–41. Ordinarily, plaintiffs in such cases would prevail on the test which balances utility against gravity of the harm. Moreover, in the exceptional cases, the offending activity might be modified or eliminated through legislative or administrative controls such as environmental protection laws or zoning. Therefore, we expect that few cases would remain in need of a judicial remedy. However, we do not today close the door on the possibility that an injunction might lie, to protect personal health and safety or fundamental freedoms, in cases missed by the balancing test and by non-judicial controls. To this extent, our adoption of the Second Restatement's test of nuisance stops short of being absolute.

The Second Restatement also has encountered a host of objections from the feedlot proprietors and from the amicus curiae. These objections reflect genuine, legitimate concerns of Idaho business, particularly the agricultural community. The concerns have been eloquently presented by able counsel. We recognize that business is an anchor of our state. We believe that Idaho business will find that it can operate responsibly and profitably within the contours of nuisance liability defined by the Second Restatement. Every business person is someone else's neighbor. Business people are as much benefited by protecting our quality of life as are other Idaho residents. We further note that business enterprises which do not depend for their viability upon an asserted right to impose serious harm upon their neighbors will not be threatened by the nuisance tests articulated in the Second Restatement.

Beyond these general observations, we address several particular objections to the Second Restatement. First, our attention has been invited to the Idaho "Right to Farm Act," I.C. §§ 22–4501 et seq. This Act recites the Legislature's concern that agricultural activities conducted on farmland in urbanizing areas often are subjected to nuisance lawsuits. The Act imposes restrictions upon such lawsuits. However, we find that these restrictions are inapposite to the present case. The Act does not apply to lawsuits commenced before March 31, 1981. See I.C. § 22–4504. The homeowners' complaint in the instant case was filed on March 28, 1978.

More fundamentally, even assuming, without deciding, that a feedlot constitutes an "agricultural operation" within the meaning of the Act, the Act precludes a finding of nuisance only with respect to an activity which would not have been a nuisance but for a change in surrounding non-agricultural uses more than one year after the activity began. See

I.C. § 22–4503. In contrast, the pleadings in the present case disclose that the feedlot is alleged to be a nuisance, not because of changes in surrounding non-agricultural uses, but because of an expansion of the feedlot itself.

The proprietors and amicus curiae recognize that the Act does not strictly apply in this case, but they suggest that it is a legislative statement of policy which should inhibit our adoption of the Second Restatement. However, the Act in essence represents a statutory adaptation of the common law doctrine of "coming to the nuisance." This doctrine does not conflict with the Second Restatement.

At early common law, the doctrine of "coming to the nuisance" was thus expressed:

> If my neighbor makes a tan-yard so as to annoy and render less salubrious the air of my house or gardens, the law will furnish me with a remedy; but if he is first in possession of the air, and I fix my habitation near him, the nuisance is of my own seeking, and may continue.

2 W. Blackstone, Commentaries on the Laws of England, 402 (17th ed. 1830). This rigid doctrine later was changed to provide that coming to the nuisance was not an absolute bar to the finding of a nuisance, but was merely one factor to be considered. [   ] This change stemmed from recognition that an absolute bar to a finding of nuisance would, in effect, give the offending activity a perpetual servitude upon the land of its neighbors without the payment of any compensation.

In keeping with this case law development, the Second Restatement recites, at § 840D, that coming to the nuisance is not a total bar to relief, but is a factor to be considered * * *. We conclude that the Act affords no basis to view the Second Restatement as contrary to legislative policy.

The feedlot proprietors and amicus curiae also contend that the Second Restatement should be rejected because it assertedly contains a rule of absolute liability, making an enterprise liable in damages to anyone adversely affected by its operations. However, this argument overlooks the requirement in § 826(b) that the harm be "serious." A plaintiff who fails to demonstrate harm exceeding the utility of a defendant's conduct will fail to establish a nuisance under § 826(a). The plaintiff also will fail under § 826(b) unless the trier of fact is persuaded that the harm shown is "serious." * * *

In determining seriousness, the factors for evaluating gravity of harm, as set forth in § 827, may be utilized. They include the extent and character of the harm, the suitability of the particular use or enjoyment invaded to the character of the locality, the burden on the injured person to avoid such harm, and the value which the law attaches to the type of use or enjoyment invaded. The last factor—the value attached to the type of use or enjoyment invaded—obviously relates to its intrinsic value when applied under § 826(b); its relative value, in comparison with the utility of the offending activity, should be considered only when applying § 826(a).

* * *

The feedlot proprietors and amicus curiae also assert that the Second Restatement will prove uneven in its application, because damages may be awarded only in those cases where the payment of such compensation is "feasible." They contend that the element of feasibility subjects a profitable enterprise to greater potential liability than that which would attend a similar activity conducted by a marginal business. However, we believe this contention misperceives the thrust of the feasibility requirement.

As used in § 826(b), the term "feasible" does not refer to the financial condition of the business conducting the activity, but refers to the activity itself. Section 826(b) merely recognizes that if the burden of paying compensation in damages would make it unfeasible to continue the activity, the effect of a damage award would be to discontinue operation of the activity. In those circumstances, the result would be the same as an injunction. In order to qualify for injunctive relief under § 826(a), a plaintiff would be required to show that the gravity of the harm exceeded the utility of the defendant's conduct. Thus, as noted in comment f to § 826, "[i]f imposition of this financial burden would make continuation of the activity not feasible, the weighing process for determining unreasonableness is similar to that in a suit for injunction." * * *

The element of feasibility illustrates the interrelationship between § 826(a) and § 826(b). If a plaintiff suffers serious harm from an intentional invasion of the use and enjoyment of his property, he is entitled to injunctive relief or damages—or a mix of these remedies—if the trier of fact determines that the gravity of the harm exceeds the utility of the defendant's conduct. If the harm does not outweigh the utility, but remains serious, the plaintiff's remedy is limited to damages—subject, however, to the further limitation that if the nature of the activity (not the particular enterprise conducting it) is such that payment of compensation in damages would cause the activity to be discontinued, then the damage award will be viewed as having the same impact as an injunction. In those circumstances, full compensation will not be awarded unless the gravity of the harm has been found to exceed the utility of the defendant's conduct.

IV

We now resume our focus upon the instant case. * * *

* * * [T]he district judge gave the jury a set of instructions which did not conform precisely to, but were consistent with, the First Restatement and IDJI 491 * * *. We conclude that the jury was improperly instructed, in light of our adoption today of the Second Restatement's criteria for determining existence of a nuisance.

The feedlot proprietors argue that even if the instructions failed adequately to state the entire standard contained in the Second Restatement, nevertheless, the instructions sufficiently stated the test of balancing harm against utility under § 826(a). Accordingly, the proprietors urge us not to disturb that part of the district court's judgment which denied injunctive relief. They contend that any remand in this case should be limited to a determination of damage liability—that is, whether the harm claimed by the plaintiff was "serious" and the payment of compensation was "feasible" under § 826(b). This argument is attractive because it comports with a surface reading of the tests set forth in the two subsections of § 826. However, we believe the argument overlooks the deeper interrelationships between these subsections, and between the remedies of damages and injunctive relief.

* * *

[W]e believe that a rigid separation of § 826(a) from § 826(b) would be inconsistent with the nexus between the remedies of damages and injunctive relief in nuisance cases. A nuisance may be alleviated by no fewer than four possible remedies: (1) an injunction; (2) damages; (3) a conditional injunction, which may be dissolved or modified upon payment of damages; or (4) in unusual circumstances, the "purchased injunction" which is imposed upon condition that a plaintiff may make some offsetting payment to the defendant. Calabresi & Malamed, Property Rules, Liability Rules, and Inalienability: One View of the Cathedral, 85 Harv.L.Rev. 1089 (1972). Moreover, where a nuisance can be abated, and the harm is not permanent but would stop when the nuisance is abated, a plaintiff would not necessarily be entitled to permanent damages. Rather, he could receive temporary or conditionally continuing damages, until the abatement occurs. [   ]

* * *

We conclude that the entire judgment of the district court, entered upon the verdict of a jury which had been improperly instructed, must be vacated. The case must be remanded for a new trial to determine whether a nuisance exists under the full criteria set forth in § 826 of the Second Restatement.

* * *

The judgment of the district court is vacated. The case is remanded for further proceedings consistent with this opinion.

Notes and Questions

1. The Court of Appeals decision in *Carpenter* was reversed by the Idaho Supreme Court at 108 Idaho 602, 701 P.2d 222 (1985). The Idaho Supreme Court rejected the Second Restatement approach, holding to the earlier McNichols precedent. In dissent Judge Bistline observed, "We have before us today a most remarkable event: two appellate courts, each obvious-

ly unaware of its true appellate function. The Court of Appeals, in reviewing the instant case, acted as a court of law, while the Idaho Supreme Court functioned as a court of error correction. In my mind, the roles have been reversed—I always understood that the Court of Appeals was a court of error correction, and it was our function to act as a court of law."

2. The nineteenth-century transformation of nuisance law in the American courts from absolute protection of property rights to a balancing of relative interests is described in Bone, Normative Theory and Legal Doctrine in American Nuisance Law: 1850–1920, 59 S.Cal.L.Rev. 1101 (1986). This article is a masterful piece of legal scholarship, describing the evolution of nuisance law in the context of developing legal theory at the time, and illustrating how the law developed along different lines in different jurisdictions at the same time.

3. Nuisance disputes, as the principal case notes, are normally resolved by striking a balance between the utility of the defendant's conduct and the gravity of the harm experienced by the plaintiff. Relevant factors are outlined in the Restatement (Second) of Torts (1977): "(a) the extent of the harm involved; (b) the character of the harm involved; (c) the social value that the law attaches to the type of use or enjoyment invaded; (d) the suitability of the particular use or enjoyment invaded to the character of the locality; and (e) the burden on the person harmed of avoiding the harm." Restatement (Second) of Torts, § 827 (1977). Relevant factors for assessing the utility of the defendant's conduct include: "(a) The social value which the law attaches to the primary purpose of the defendant's conduct; (b) the suitability of defendant's activity to the character of the locality; and (c) the practicability of preventing or avoiding the invasion." Restatement (Second) of Torts § 828(a) (1977).

If the court finds the nuisance to be a nuisance per se, the balancing process may be short-circuited in the plaintiff's favor. The balance will also tilt more readily against the defendant where the defendant's conduct is motivated solely by malice, as it is clearly without utility. See Dunbar v. O'Brien, 117 Neb. 245, 220 N.W. 278 (1928).

A variety of defenses may also cut short the balancing process. First, the hypersensitive plaintiff, abnormally susceptible to conduct that would not bother most persons, is unlikely to recover. See Beckman v. Marshall, 85 So.2d 552 (Fla.1956) (day care center complained of by elderly neighbors not nuisance). Where the plaintiff has permitted the defendant's conduct, or led the defendant to believe that the plaintiff would not object to it, and the defendant has detrimentally relied on this, estoppel or acquiescence may be argued against a nuisance claim. Laches may also be asserted where the plaintiff fails to pursue a claim diligently, and the delay prejudices the defendant. Finally, the statute of limitations may bar a nuisance claim where the plaintiff has suffered substantial injury for the statutory period without taking action.

A more controversial defense is the "coming to the nuisance" defense. Should a person be permitted to construct a residence in the midst of an industrial area and then demand that all surrounding industries shut down? English courts have rejected the "coming to the nuisance" defense. Bliss v. Hall, 4 Bing (NC) 183, 132 Eng.Rep. 758 (1838). American courts have divided on the question, but the prevailing view is that "coming to the nuisance" is not, in itself, a total bar to a nuisance action. Curry v. Farmers Livestock Market, 343 S.W.2d 134 (Ky.1961) (only equitable consideration); Kellogg v. Village of Viola, 67 Wis.2d 345, 227 N.W.2d 55 (1975) (consideration in weighing equities). Should it be? Should notions of "first in time, first in right", which play such an important role elsewhere in property law, hold sway here? Further, if the plaintiff in a "coming to the nuisance" action acquired the property adjoining the existing offensive use for a price that reflected its limited value for development, is it fair to give the plaintiff a windfall by enjoining neighboring uses that caused the diminution in property value? On the other hand, allowing an offensive use in effect to block all conflicting uses for surrounding property for all time raises the specter of an unparalleled extension of private eminent domain. See, Wittman, First Come, First Served: An Economic Analysis of "Coming to the Nuisance," 9 J. Legal Stud. 557 (1980).

Legislative authorization of offensive conduct may also be raised as a defense to a nuisance action. This defense is particularly likely to be raised when the government is the source of the nuisance. Osborn v. City of Akron, 171 Ohio St. 361, 171 N.E.2d 492 (1960) (municipal garbage dump). "Right to farm laws" such as that discussed in *Carpenter,* are an example of this exception as applied to private uses. See, Comment: The Ethics and Economics of Right-to-Farm Statutes, 9 Harv.J.L. & Pub.Pol'y 525 (1986). Offensive uses must be specifically authorized, however. It is not sufficient that they be permitted under a general zoning ordinance.

The Second Restatement mandates consideration of the social value of both the plaintiff's and defendant's uses of their property. Historically, as *Carpenter* notes, courts have been more sensitive to this consideration in evaluating the defendant's conduct than in assessing the plaintiff's loss, particularly where the plaintiff is seeking injunctive relief. Thus, in Boomer v. Atlantic Cement Co., 26 N.Y.2d 219, 309 N.Y.S.2d 312, 257 N.E.2d 870 (1970), in denying injunctive relief, the court noted in passing that 300 jobs were at stake. On the other hand, more recent cases have also recognized the public interest in the plaintiff's uses as well. For example, in Prah v. Maretti, 108 Wis.2d 223, 321 N.W.2d 182 (1982), the court recognized the public interest in expanding alternative energy sources as one reason for recognizing the applicability of nuisance law for protecting the plaintiff's solar collector.

4. As *Carpenter* recognizes, a key problem in nuisance law is determining the appropriate role of the balancing process. One approach is to balance harm and utility up front to determine whether there is a nuisance at all, the approach ultimately taken by the Idaho Supreme Court. A second approach is to hold any substantial harm to be a nuisance, and then to apply a balancing test to determine whether the nuisance should be enjoined. Under this approach, even if the balance favors the defendant, damages may be appropriate. The Restatement (Second) of Torts (1977) seems to advocate the latter position, recognizing in § 821F that a nuisance should be found whenever there is significant harm, and then in § 826(b) recognizing that it might be appropriate to find a nuisance and award damages in circumstances where conduct is serious, even if the gravity of harm did not outweigh the utility of the defendant's conduct.

5. Nuisance is generally regarded as an intentional tort (Prosser on Torts, § 87), though the Restatement (Second) of Torts takes the position that negligent or reckless conduct, or injuries caused by abnormally dangerous conditions or activities can also result in nuisance liability. What does it mean to say that nuisance results from intentional conduct, as the Restatement does? Must the actor intend the harm, or merely intend the action that causes harm? Is it sufficient that the actor knows (or should know) that his conduct is likely to result in harm? See Restatement (Second) Torts, § 825 (1977); Morgan v. High Penn Oil Co., 238 N.C. 185, 77 S.E.2d 682 (1953) (intention includes actions that the actor knows is substantially certain to result in injury); Keeton, Trespass, Nuisance and Strict Liability, 59 Columb.L.Rev. 457 (1959). If liability for intentional nuisance is only imposed after the court has balanced the utility of the defendant's conduct with the gravity of the harm, how does the test of liability differ from negligence, in which liability is found only when the harm of an action outweighs the cost of avoiding the harm?

6. Much of the scholarship regarding nuisance law over the last three decades has elaborated on themes developed in two seminal articles, Coase, The Problem of Social Cost, 3 J.L. & Econ. 1 (1960), and Calabresi and Melamed, Property Rules, Liability Rules, and Inalienability: One View of the Cathedral, 85 Harv.L.Rev. 1089 (1972). Nobel prize winner Coase noted that it is useful to view nuisance disputes as arising because neighboring lands are used for inconsistent purposes rather than because of wrongdoing. "The question [of nuisance] is commonly thought of as one in which A inflicts harm on B and what has to be decided is: how should we restrain A? But this is wrong. We are dealing with a problem of a reciprocal nature. To avoid the harm to B would inflict harm on A. The real question that has to be decided is: should A be allowed to harm B or should B be allowed to harm A? The problem is to avoid the more serious harm." Id. at 2.

If both polluting and receiving uses were under common ownership, Coase noted, conflicts would not arise, because the owner would choose whatever mix of polluting and receiving uses was optimal, thus achieving an efficient use of the land as a whole. In the absence of transactions costs independent neighboring landowners could reach the same result. Bargaining with each other, the polluting landowner could pay the receiving landowner enough to purchase his acquiesence in the polluting use, if the polluting use were more productive. Alternatively, the receiving landowner could pay the polluter enough to end the pollution if the receiving use was more valuable. The efficient result would be reached regardless of whether legal rules initially favored polluters or receivers, though the final allocation of wealth would differ depending on the legal rule.

The insight of the Calabresi and Melamed article is that there are four possible resolutions to nuisance disputes. Three of these are contemplated as possible results in Carpenter. First, the defendant might be found liable, and an injunction can issue restraining its conduct. Second, the defendant might be found liable, and damages may be ordered to compensate the plaintiff. Third, the defendant might be found innocent, and an injunction may be refused. The fourth possibility, necessary for the sake of symmetry, is to find the defendant innocent, but allow the plaintiff to terminate (or limit) the defendant's offensive conduct by paying damages as determined by the court to the defendant. As an illustration of this fourth alternative, in Spur Industries, Inc. v. Del E. Webb Development Co., 108 Ariz. 178, 494 P.2d 700 (1972), a developer who had built a large housing development next to a feed lot was permitted an injunction against the feed lot, but was required to compensate the feed lot for the cost of moving or shutting down.

The synergy of these two articles has produced a torrent of commentary of ever increasing elaboration, elegance, and abstraction from reality. Coase's theorem argues that, absent transaction costs, regardless of which of the four remedies is chosen to resolve a nuisance dispute, the parties can bargain to an efficient result. Absent transaction costs, therefore, entitlements could be awarded solely on the basis of considerations of fairness or equity, with no need to worry about efficiency. Such fairness rules might be based on considerations such as normal neighborly behavior, or, first in time, first in right.

Transaction costs are always a factor in nuisance disputes, however, and in some cases play a larger role than they do in others. Where many parties are involved, for example, the costs of bargaining for the reallocation of an entitlement awarded by the court to the less productive use might be very high. Conversely, where only two parties are involved, strategic bargaining by the parties might prevent an efficient bargained resolution of the dispute.[14] Efficiency considerations, therefore, should be a factor in awarding entitlements, at least in some cases. Early solutions proposed, therefore, awarding the right to pollute or to be free from pollution initially to the most productive use, thus obviating the need for costly bargaining to reach an efficient result.

Further examination of the problem, however, suggested that both the efficient and fair result could be achieved by proper use of the four remedial options identified by Calabresi and Melamed. Assume, for example, that the fair thing to do is to protect the receiver, who was there first, but that it would be inefficient to close down the polluter, whose use is more productive. Assume also that transaction costs of bargaining to a solution are high. The efficient and fair result could be reached, it was argued, by awarding the entitlement to the receiver, but protecting it with damages rather than an injunction. Thus, the fair result would be reached (the receiver is protected) but the efficient result would also obtain (the polluter continues to operate). Alternatively, if distributional concerns favored the polluter, but the receiving use was more efficient, solution four, the compensated injunction, might be appropriate.

For a time, damage and compensated injunction remedies enjoyed favor among the commentators. See Ellickson, Alternatives to Zoning: Covenants,

---

14. Strategic bargaining results when parties fail to bargain to an efficient result because each bluffs or misreads the other. For example, if continuation of the defendant's feedlot at a given level of production produces $120,000 in profits to the defendant, but will damage the plaintiff's property to the extent of $80,000, and an injunction shutting down the feedlot is awarded to the plaintiff, the defendant could pay pay the plaintiff any amount between $80,000 and $120,000 and both parties come out ahead. If, however, the plaintiff judges the defendant's use to be worth more, and refuses to accept a sum less than $121,000, or the defendant misjudges the plaintiff's injury, and refuses to offer more than $79,000, a bargain may not be struck, the feedlot will close, and both parties and society will be worse off than they would have been had the parties bargained successfully.

Nuisance Rules, and Fines as Land Use Controls, 40 U.Chi.L.Rev. 681 (1973); Rabin, Nuisance Law: Rethinking Fundamental Assumptions, 63 Va.L.Rev. 1299 (1977). These commentators criticized reliance on injunctions to remedy nuisance injuries. If an injunction failed to achieve an efficient solution, it was argued, strategic bargaining on the part of the parties was likely to stand in the way of negotiations leading to an efficient solution. It was also argued that the party holding an injunction might use it to "extort" money from the enjoined party, if the enjoined party happened to be the one who could use the resource most efficiently. Finally, in a situation involving many parties, it was argued, it would be difficult to bargain to a more efficient solution once an injunction was issued or denied. In each of these situations, it was asserted, damage or compensated injunction solutions, were more likely to achieve the efficient result. This position was largely adopted by the appellate court in *Carpenter* with respect to the situation it faced.

The most recent scholarship in the area, however, returns to the injunction as the remedy of choice, or at least argues a more limited role for the damage or compensated injunction remedy. See Polinsky, Resolving Nuisance Disputes: The Simple Economics of Injunctive and Damage Remedies, 32 Stan.L.Rev. 1075 (1980); Compensated Injunctions and the Evolution of Nuisance Law, 71 Iowa L.Rev. 775 (1986) (arguing for more limited use of compensated injunctions); Travalio, Pay Up or Shut Down: Some Cautionary Remarks on the Use of Conditional Entitlements in Private Nuisance Cases, 38 U.Fla.L.Rev. 209 (1986). Assessing damages is a costly and uncertain business. Damage remedies also award all of the "profit" to be made in a transaction to the party against whom damages are awarded, a result that is not obviously fair.[15] Damage awards may further fail to consider the interests of the public or of persons not party to the litigation, which interests should be considered in equitable balancing. Damage awards may not take adequate account of the uncertainty present in modern pollution problems. Damages often, in effect, become a form of private eminent domain: the defendant can violate the plaintiff's property interest as long as it pays a court-determined sum. This raises serious constitutional problems. Finally, injunctions need not be all or nothing remedies. An injunction can be fine-tuned to permit a certain level of pollution, but not more, thus achieving an efficient result as effectively as might a damage remedy. See, reviewing the extensive literature on this subject, Lewin, Boomer and the American Law of Nuisance: Past, Present and Future, 54 Albany L.Rev. 189 (1990).

After three decades of debate, it is not clear that this literature yet gives courts much practical guidance for resolving nuisance disputes. Use of the damage remedy is probably more common now than formerly. With the exception of the Spur case, however, compensated injunctions have not been

---

15. In the example given in the previous note, for example, the prevailing plaintiff would be, under a damage solution, awarded $80,000, and thus be compensated for his damages. The defendant would therefore clear $40,000 ($120,000 − 80,000) from the use of a resource, the air, in which both he and the plaintiff had rights. Why should not the plaintiff share in this wealth? Had the defendant desired to purchase land which the plaintiff owned to pursue a profitable activity, he would have to pay a price which shared the potential profit with the plaintiff. Why should not the same be true if he seeks to use the plaintiff's air?

embraced by the courts. Few courts, moreover, have expressly relied on economic reasoning in resolving nuisance disputes.

B. PUBLIC NUISANCE

ARMORY PARK NEIGHBORHOOD ASSOCIATION v. EPISCOPAL COMMUNITY SERVICES IN ARIZONA

Supreme Court of Arizona, 1985.
148 Ariz. 1, 712 P.2d 914.

FELDMAN, JUSTICE.

On December 11, 1982, defendant Episcopal Community Services in Arizona (ECS) opened the St. Martin's Center (Center) in Tucson. The Center's only purpose is to provide one free meal a day to indigent persons. Plaintiff Armory Park Neighborhood Association (APNA) is a non-profit corporation organized for the purpose of "improving, maintaining and insuring the quality of the neighborhood known as Armory Park Historical Residential District." The Center is located on Arizona Avenue, the western boundary of the Armory Park district. On January 10, 1984, APNA filed a complaint in Pima County Superior Court, seeking to enjoin ECS from operating its free food distribution program. The complaint alleged that the Center's activities constituted a public nuisance and that the Armory Park residents had sustained injuries from transient persons attracted to their neighborhood by the Center.

The superior court held a hearing on APNA's application for preliminary injunction on March 6 and 7, 1984. At the commencement of the hearing, the parties stipulated that

> * * * there is no issue concerning any State, County, or Municipal zoning ordinance, or health provision, before the Court. And, the Court may find that defendants are in compliance with the same.

The residents then testified about the changes the Center had brought to their neighborhood. Before the Center opened, the area had been primarily residential with a few small businesses. When the Center began operating in December 1982, many transients crossed the area daily on their way to and from the Center. Although the Center was only open from 5:00 to 6:00 p.m., patrons lined up well before this hour and often lingered in the neighborhood long after finishing their meal. The Center rented an adjacent fenced lot for a waiting area and organized neighborhood cleaning projects, but the trial judge apparently felt these efforts were inadequate to control the activity stemming from the Center. Transients frequently trespassed onto residents' yards, sometimes urinating, defecating, drinking and littering on the residents' property. A few broke into storage areas and unoccupied homes, and some asked residents for handouts. The number of arrests in the area increased dramatically. Many residents were frightened or annoyed by the transients and altered their lifestyles to avoid them.

Following the hearing, ECS filed a motion to dismiss the complaint based on three grounds: 1) that compliance with all applicable zoning and health laws constituted a complete defense to a claim of public nuisance; 2) that there had been no allegation or evidence of a violation of a criminal statute or ordinance, which it argues is a prerequisite to a finding of public nuisance; and 3) that APNA lacked standing to bring an action to abate a public nuisance because it had neither pled nor proved any special injury differing in kind and degree from that suffered by the public generally.

Based on the hearing testimony, the trial court granted the preliminary injunction and denied ECS' motion to dismiss. In its order, the court noted that ECS could be enjoined because its activities constituted both a public and a private nuisance. After its motion for reconsideration was denied, ECS filed a special action in the court of appeals, and shortly thereafter filed a notice of appeal from the order granting the injunction. The court of appeals consolidated the proceedings and stayed enforcement of the trial court's order pending a final decision.

A divided court of appeals reversed the trial court's order. In the view of the majority, a criminal violation was a prerequisite to a finding of public nuisance; because plaintiff had alleged no criminal violation, the injunction was improperly granted. The majority also concluded that the trial court abused its discretion by finding both a public and a private nuisance when the plaintiff had not alleged a private nuisance. Finally, the court held that compliance with zoning provisions was a complete defense. The court vacated the order for preliminary injunction and remanded the matter to the trial court with directions to grant ECS' motion to dismiss. * * * We granted review in this case because of the importance of the following questions:

1) When does a voluntary association have standing to bring an action for public nuisance on behalf of its members?

2) May a lawful business be enjoined for acts committed off its premises by clients who are not under its control or direction?

3) Is it necessary to plead and prove a zoning or criminal violation by the defendant, or may a lawful activity be enjoined because the manner in which it is conducted is unreasonable and therefore constitutes a public nuisance?

The Concept of "Nuisance"

Now considered a tort, a public nuisance action originated in criminal law. Early scholars defined public nuisance as "an act or omission 'which obstructs or causes inconvenience or damage to the public in the exercise of rights common to all her Majesty's subjects.'" Prosser, W. and W.P. Keeton, Handbook on the Law of Torts, § 90, at 643 (5th ed. 1984), quoting Stephen, General View of the Criminal Law in England 105 (1890). The sole remedy was criminal prosecution. Prosser, supra, § 86, at 618.

Historically, the remedy for a private nuisance was an action "upon the case," as it was an injury consequential to the act done and found its roots in civil law. Pearce, E. and D. Meston, Handbook on the Law Relating to Nuisances 2 (1926). A private nuisance is strictly limited to an interference with a person's interest in the enjoyment of real property. The Restatement defines a private nuisance as "a nontrespassory invasion of another's interest in the private use and enjoyment of land." Restatement (Second) of Torts § 821D. A public nuisance, to the contrary, is not limited to an interference with the use and enjoyment of the plaintiff's land. It encompasses any unreasonable interference with a right common to the general public. Restatement, supra, § 821B. Accord, Prosser, supra, § 86, at 618.

We have previously distinguished public and private nuisances. In City of Phoenix v. Johnson, 51 Ariz. 115, 75 P.2d 30 (1938), we noted that a nuisance is public when it affects rights of "citizens as a part of the public, while a private nuisance is one which affects a single individual or a definite number of persons in the enjoyment of some private right which is not common to the public." Id. at 123, 75 P.2d at 34. A public nuisance must also affect a considerable number of people. Id. * * * The legislature has adopted a similar requirement for its criminal code, defining a public nuisance as an interference "with the comfortable enjoyment of life or property by an entire community or neighborhood, or by a considerable number of persons * * *." A.R.S. § 13–2917.

The defendant contends that the trial court erred in finding both public and private nuisances when the plaintiff had not asserted a private nuisance claim. The defendant has read the trial court's minute entry too strictly. While we acknowledge that public and private nuisances implicate different interests, we recognize also that the same facts may support claims of both public and private nuisance. As Dean Prosser explained:

> When a public nuisance substantially interferes with the use or enjoyment of the plaintiff's rights in land, it never has been disputed that there is a particular kind of damage, for which the private action will lie. Not only is every plot of land traditionally unique in the eyes of the law, but in the ordinary case the class of landowners in the vicinity of the alleged nuisance will necessarily be a limited one, with an interest obviously different from that of the general public. The interference itself is of course a private nuisance; but is none the less particular damage from a public one, and the action can be maintained upon either basis, or upon both. (Citations omitted.)

Prosser, Private Action for Public Nuisance, 52 Va.L.Rev. 997, 1018 (1966).

Thus, a nuisance may be simultaneously public and private when a considerable number of people suffer an interference with their use and enjoyment of land. [ ] The torts are not mutually exclusive. Some of plaintiff's members in this case have suffered an injury to the use and enjoyment of their land. Any reference to both a public and a private nuisance by the trial court was, we believe, merely a recognition of this well-accepted rule and not error. However, both because plaintiff did not seek relief under the theory of private nuisance and because that theory might raise standing issues not addressed by the parties, we believe plaintiff's claim must stand or fall on the public nuisance theory alone.

STANDING TO BRING THE ACTION

1. Do the residents have standing?

Defendant argues that the Association has no standing to sue and that, therefore, the action should be dismissed. The trial court disagreed and defendant claims it erred in so doing. Two standing questions are before us. The first pertains to the right of a private person, as distinguished from a public official, to bring a suit to enjoin the maintenance of a public nuisance. The original rule at common law was that a citizen had no standing to sue for abatement or suppression of a public nuisance since

> such inconvenient or troublesome offenses [sic], as annoy the whole community in general, and not merely some particular persons; and therefore are indictable only, and not actionable; as it would be unreasonable to multiply suits, by giving every man a separate right of action, by what damnifies him in common only with the rest of his fellow subjects.

IV Blackstone Commentaries 167 (1966). It was later held that a private individual might have a tort action to recover personal damages arising from the invasion of the public right. Y.B. 27 Hen. VIII, Mich, pl. 10, cited in Restatement, supra, § 821C comment a. However, the individual bringing the action was required to show that his damage was different in kind or quality from that suffered by the public in common. Prosser, supra, § 90, at 646; Harper & James, the Law of Torts § 1.23, at 64–5 (1956).

The rationale behind this limitation was two-fold. First, it was meant to relieve defendants and the courts of the multiple actions that might follow if every member of the public were allowed to sue for a common wrong. Second, it was believed that a harm which affected all members of the public equally should be handled by public officials. Restatement, supra, § 821C comment a. See also Engle v. Clark, 53 Ariz. 472, 90 P.2d 994 (1939). Considerable disagreement remains over the type of injury which the plaintiff must suffer in order to have standing to bring an action to enjoin a public nuisance. However, we have intimated in the past that an injury to plaintiff's interest in land is sufficient to distinguish plaintiff's injuries from those experienced by the general public and to give the plaintiff-landowner standing to bring the action.
* * *

We hold, therefore, that because the acts allegedly committed by the patrons of the neighborhood center affected the residents' use and enjoyment of their real property, a damage special in nature and different in kind from that experienced by the residents of the city in general, the residents of the neighborhood could bring an action to recover damages for or enjoin the maintenance of a public nuisance.

2.   May the Association bring the action on behalf of its members?

* * *

[The court found that under Arizona law the Association had standing to bring an action to redress injuries done to its members]

Defendant's Derivative Responsibility

Defendant claims that its business should not be held responsible for acts committed by its patrons off the premises of the Center. It argues that since it has no control over the patrons when they are not on the Center's premises, it cannot be enjoined because of their acts. We do not believe this position is supported either by precedent or theory.

* * *

Under general tort law, liability for nuisance may be imposed upon one who sets in motion the forces which eventually cause the tortious act; liability will arise for a public nuisance when "one person's acts set in motion a force or chain of events resulting in the invasion." Restatement, supra, § 824 comment b. We hold, therefore, that defendant's activity may be enjoined upon the showing of a causal connection between that activity and harm to another.

The testimony at the hearing establishes that it was the Center's act of offering free meals which "set in motion" the forces resulting in the injuries to the Armory Park residents. * * * We find the testimony sufficient to support the trial judge's finding of a causal link between the acts of ECS and the injuries suffered by the Armory Park residents. * * *

Reasonableness of the Interferences

Since the rules of a civilized society require us to tolerate our neighbors, the law requires our neighbors to keep their activities within the limits of what is tolerable by a reasonable person. However, what is reasonably tolerable must be tolerated; not all interferences with public rights are public nuisances. As Dean Prosser explains, "[t]he law does not concern itself with trifles, or seek to remedy all of the petty annoyances and disturbances of everyday life in a civilized community even from conduct committed with knowledge that annoyance and inconvenience will result." Prosser, supra, § 88, at 626. Thus, to constitute a nuisance, the complained-of interference must be substantial, intentional and unreasonable under the circumstances. Restatement, supra, § 826 comment c and 821F. Our courts have generally used a balancing test in deciding the reasonableness of an interference. [ ] The trial court should look at the utility and reasonableness of the conduct and balance these factors against the extent of harm inflicted and the nature of the affected neighborhood. We noted in the early case of MacDonald v. Perry:

> What might amount to a serious nuisance in one locality by reason of the density of the population, or character of the neighborhood affected, may in another place and under different surroundings be deemed proper and unobjectionable. What amount of annoyance or inconvenience caused by others in the lawful use of their property will constitute a nuisance depends upon varying circumstances and cannot be precisely defined.

32 Ariz. 39, 50, 255 P. 494 (1927). [   ]

The trial judge did not ignore the balancing test and was well aware of the social utility of defendant's operation. His words are illuminating:

> It is distressing to this Court that an activity such as defendants [sic] should be restrained. Providing for the poor and the homeless is certainly a worthwhile, praisworthy [sic] activity. It is particularly distressing to this Court because it [defendant] has no control over those who are attracted to the kitchen while they are either coming or leaving the premises. However, the right to the comfortable enjoyment of one's property is something that another's activities should not affect, the harm being suffered by the Armory Park Neighborhood and the residents therein is irreparable and substantial, for which they have no adequate legal remedy.

Minute Entry, 6/8/84, at 8. We believe that a determination made by weighing and balancing conflicting interests or principles is truly one which lies within the discretion of the trial judge. [   ] We defer to that discretion here. The evidence of the multiple trespasses upon and defacement of the residents' property supports the trial court's conclusion that the interference caused by defendant's operation was unreasonable despite its charitable cause.

The common law has long recognized that the usefulness of a particular activity may outweigh the inconveniences, discomforts and changes it causes some persons to suffer. We, too, acknowledge the social value of the Center. Its charitable purpose, that of feeding the hungry, is entitled to greater deference than pursuits of lesser intrinsic value. It appears from the record that ECS purposes in operating the Center were entirely admirable. However, even admirable ventures may cause unreasonable interferences. [   ] We do not believe that the law allows the costs of a charitable enterprise to be visited in their entirety upon the residents of a single neighborhood. The problems of dealing with the unemployed, the homeless and the mentally ill are also matters of community or governmental responsibility.

Zoning

ECS argues that its compliance with City of Tucson zoning regulations is a conclusive determination of reasonableness. We agree that compliance with zoning provisions has some bearing in nuisance cases.

We would hesitate to find a public nuisance, if, for example, the legislature enacted comprehensive and specific laws concerning the manner in which a particular activity was to be carried out. Accord Restatement, supra, § 821B comment f. We decline, however, to find that ECS' compliance with the applicable zoning provisions precludes a court from enjoining its activities. The equitable power of the judiciary exists independent of statute. Although zoning and criminal provisions are binding with respect to the type of activity, they do not limit the power of a court acting in equity to enjoin an unreasonable, albeit permitted, activity as a public nuisance. [   ]

The determination of the type of business to be permitted in a particular neighborhood, therefore, may be left to administrative agencies or legislative bodies. However, the judgment concerning the manner in which that business is carried out is within the province of the judiciary. Restatement, supra, § 821B comment f. See also J. Joyce, Treatise on the Law Governing Nuisances § 73, at 115 (1906). Zoning provisions may permit one's neighbor to operate a business. This does not give him license to use one's yard, nor permit his customers to do so.

* * *

CRIMINAL VIOLATION

Occasionally we have indicated that conduct which violates a specific criminal statute is an element of public nuisance for civil tort claims. [   ] These cases did not face the issue whether a tort claim for public nuisance exists independent of statute. * * *

In MacDonald v. Perry, supra, we indicated that the inquiry in a nuisance claim is not whether the activity allegedly constituting the nuisance is lawful but whether it is reasonable under the circumstances. The Restatement states that a criminal violation is only one factor among others to be used in determining reasonableness. That section reads:

(1) A public nuisance is an unreasonable interference with a right common to the general public.

(2) Circumstances that may sustain a holding that an interference with a public right is unreasonable include the following:

(a) Whether the conduct involves a significant interference with the public health, the public safety, the public peace, the public comfort or the public convenience, *or*

(b) whether the conduct is proscribed by a statute, ordinance or administrative regulation, *or*

(c) whether the conduct is of a continuing nature or has produced a permanent or long-lasting effect, and, as the actor knows or has reason to know, has a significant effect upon the public right. (Emphasis supplied.)

Restatement, supra, § 821B. Comment d to that section explains:

It has been stated with some frequency that a public nuisance is always a criminal offense. This statement is susceptible of two interpretations. The first is that in order to be treated as a public nuisance, conduct must have been already proscribed by the state as criminal. This is too restrictive * * *. [T]here is clear recognition that a defendant need not be subject to criminal responsibility.

Restatement, supra, § 821B comment d, at 89.

Our earlier decisions indicate that a business which is lawful may nevertheless be a public nuisance. * * *

We hold, therefore, that conduct which unreasonably and significantly interferes with the public health, safety, peace, comfort or convenience is a public nuisance within the concept of tort law, even if that conduct is not specifically prohibited by the criminal law.

* * *

CONCLUSION

The trial court's order granting the preliminary injunction is affirmed. By affirming the trial court's preliminary orders, we do not require that he close the center permanently. It is of course, within the equitable discretion of the trial court to fashion a less severe remedy, if possible. The opinion of the court of appeals is vacated. The case is remanded for further proceedings.

Notes and Questions

1. Public nuisance grows out of a class of crimes known as purprestures, involving encroachments on the king's right. Though the classic public nuisance was obstruction of a public road, the concept has encompassed publicly offensive conduct as various as keeping of diseased animals, Fevold v. Board of Supervisors of Webster County, 202 Iowa 1019, 210 N.W. 139 (1926); practice of medicine without a license, State ex rel. Collet v. Scopel, 316 S.W.2d 515 (Mo.1958); holding a rock concert, Planning & Zoning Commission v. Zemel Brothers, Inc., 29 Conn.Sup. 45, 270 A.2d 562 (1970); or nude sunbathing, State v. Rocker, 52 Hawai'i 336, 475 P.2d 684 (1970). Creating a public nuisance is often proscribed by state statute or local ordinance. Because the concept is such an amorphous one, however, there is considerable potential for its abuse. Particular problems arise when public nuisance litigation is used to control conduct arguably protected by the First Amendment, such as adult entertainment. Compare Vance v. Universal Amusement Co., 445 U.S. 308, 100 S.Ct. 1156, 63 L.Ed.2d 413 (1980) (enjoining future showings of allegedly obscene films under public nuisance statute was an unconstitutional prior restraint) with Arcara v. Cloud Books, Inc., 478 U.S. 697, 106 S.Ct. 3172, 92 L.Ed.2d 568 (1986) (use of nuisance statute to close adult book store used as place of prostitution does not violate First Amendment). See Gorman, The Demise of Civil Nuisance Actions in Obscenity Control, 14 Loy.U.Chi.L.J. 31 (1982); Note, Enjoining Obscenity

as Public Nuisance and the Prior Restraint Doctrine, 84 Colum.L.Rev. 1616 (1984); Note, Pornography, Padlocks and Prior Restraints: The Constitutional Limits of the Nuisance Power, 58 N.Y.U.L.Rev. 1478 (1983).

2. As *Armory Park* illustrates, conduct that can be classified as a public nuisance may also harm neighbors in the use and enjoyment of their land. The injured neighbor may then either sue for private nuisance or attempt to establish the standing to sue for public nuisance. *Armory Park* presents a typical discussion of how a plaintiff may attempt to meet the special injury requirement for establishing a private right to sue for public nuisance. Unique or special injury may also be shown by establishing harm to health, physical harm to land or chattels, or pecuniary loss. Some state statutes, moreover, permit private suits to enjoin a public nuisance without showing special injury. See Wyo.Stat.Ann. § 6–6–202. Should private individuals be permitted to enjoin any conduct offensive to the public? Should they be permitted to sue for damages? Or should private litigation be limited to conduct that independently causes a private nuisance?

3. The *Armory Park* case illustrates the "not in my backyard" problem, a hardy perennial of property law. Society may need shelters for the homeless, group homes for ex-offenders, nuclear power plants, or hazardous waste dumps, but who wants to live next door to one? In reality, such uses often end up being imposed on neighborhoods or localities that are most politically vulnerable. Is this fair? How might the problem of siting such uses be addressed? Might solutions that depend on mediation or education be more effective than approaches based on litigation or on local politics? Might it be more appropriate to deal with these problems on a state, regional, or national level, because of the strength of opposition that appears when they are addressed locally? Might opposition to some of these uses suggest that they are never appropriate for any locality, and therefore should not be permitted anywhere? Do lawyers have any responsibility to society to seek equitable solutions to such problems, or is it enough that lawyers zealously represent their own clients opposing or supporting such uses?

C. NUISANCE LAW AND THE ENVIRONMENT

Nuisance law has obvious applications for protecting the environment. Persons whose property is damaged by air or water pollution from point sources, for example, can bring nuisance actions to enjoin the continuation of pollution. Alternatively, they can sue for damages against the polluter, thus forcing the internalization of the otherwise externalized costs of pollution. Public nuisance actions brought by municipal governments, for example, may be even more promising as an approach to dealing with widespread pollution. Increasingly, however, pollution has been addressed by federal and state statutory and regulatory law enforced by public administrative agencies.

This development results in obvious problems when the mandates of federal or state statutes and of court judgments enforcing nuisance law come in conflict. If the Environmental Protection Agency, for example, authorizes a certain level of discharge of a pollutant, or imposes a certain timetable for correcting a pollution problem, can a federal or state court impose stricter standards under a nuisance action? This question was addressed by a series of cases involving the attempts of the State of Illinois to stop the City of Milwaukee, Wisconsin, from discharging raw sewerage into Lake Michigan. In 1972, Illinois sued Milwaukee in the United States Supreme Court, seeking to enjoin this discharge. The Supreme Court's opinion, Illinois v. City of Milwaukee, 406 U.S. 91, 92 S.Ct. 1385, 31 L.Ed.2d 712 (1972), remanded the case to the district court for trial, but recognized a federal common law of nuisance giving the district court jurisdiction over the problem. By the time the case was resolved in the district court on remand, however, Congress had adopted the Federal Water Pollution Control Act Amendments of 1972, 33 U.S.C.A. § 1251 et seq., comprehensively amending the federal water pollution laws. The case reached the Supreme Court again in 1981 with the City of Milwaukee on the one hand subject to a state court judgment based on federal permit standards imposing on it one level of effluent discharge and a timetable for correction, and, on the other hand, a federal court nuisance judgment imposing stricter effluent limitations and a shorter time for correction. The Supreme Court held this time, in City of Milwaukee v. Illinois, 451 U.S. 304, 101 S.Ct. 1784, 68 L.Ed.2d 114 (1981), that the federal statute preempted the federal common law of nuisance for cases of interstate water pollution. In Middlesex County Sewerage Authority v. National Sea Clammers Association, 453 U.S. 1, 101 S.Ct. 2615, 69 L.Ed.2d 435 (1981), the Court held, two months later, that the federal water pollution statute had "entirely" preempted federal nuisance law with respect to water pollution, a decision followed by some lower courts as to federal air pollution laws. See New England Legal Foundation v. Costle, 666 F.2d 30 (2d Cir.1981); United States v. Kin–Buc, Inc., 532 F.Supp. 699 (D.N.J.1982); Connecticut v. Long Island Lighting Co., 535 F.Supp. 546 (E.D.N.Y.1982).

What institutional considerations might make legislative or regulatory strategies superior to nuisance litigation for addressing pollution problems? Why might a statewide, regional, or national program for regulating point sources of pollution be superior to a case-by-case approach under private nuisance law? Are there any respects in which nuisance litigation is a superior strategy to regulation for addressing pollution? Should courts in enforcing federal environmental protection law employ the discretion they traditionally exercise in nuisance litigation, or should they demand rigid compliance with the law? See, Farber, Equitable Discretion, Legal Duties, and Environmental Injunctions, 45 U.Pitt.L.Rev. 513 (1984). Why should federal water or air pollution control legislation be held to preempt nuisance litigation, when local zoning ordinances apparently do not? Might there be alternatives to nuisance litigation and regulatory strategies, superior to both?

IV. SURFACE WATER AND SUPPORT

WESTLAND SKATING CENTER, INC.
v. GUS MACHADO BUICK, INC.

Supreme Court of Florida, 1989.
542 So.2d 959.

GRIMES, JUSTICE.

* * *

This case involves a dispute among occupiers of adjacent parcels of land that used to be part of the Everglades and later became pasture-land, but which now comprise commercially developed property in Dade County. Petitioner, Westland Skating Center, Inc., operated a skating rink on property leased from petitioner, Hialeah Skating Center, Ltd. An auto dealership, now operated by respondent, Gus Machado Buick, Inc., occupied abutting property. There has been some alteration of all the land involved, but the parties agree that the natural drainage flow was generally and gradually toward the southwest, that is, from the skating rink property onto and toward the rear of the auto dealership property. When the auto dealership was built in 1970, a miniature-golf course occupied the skating rink property, and apparently neither landowner had unusual problems in dealing with rainwater.

Trouble began in April 1980, however, after the construction of the skating rink. The building's roof was 200 by 120 feet. A 200–by–60 foot section sloped toward the auto dealership; it ended about 10 feet from the property line. Water drained off the roof through five downspouts. During a rainstorm the auto dealership, then Seipp Buick, experienced flooding extensive enough to damage several cars. This sort of flooding had occurred only once before, and then during much heavier rain. Seipp blamed the new skating rink, with its sloping roof and downspouts, for increasing the flow of water onto his property.

Talks between Seipp and Revitz to alleviate the problem were unavailing, and in 1980 Seipp decided to take action. He built a wall, 8 feet high and 2 feet deep between the two tracts along the 900–foot length of his property. This project took several months to complete; the skating center did not object to the presence of the wall during that time.

August of 1981 brought a heavy rain and profoundly different results than the 1980 downpour. This time, water ran off the roof and down toward Seipp's wall, which acted as a dam. The water then backed up under the skating rink's floor, inflicting heavy damage. The floor was replaced, but another heavy rain a month or so later resulted in more flooding, which the skating rink's employees alleviated by sledgehammering holes in Seipp's wall. More repairs to the rink ensued, but eventually it closed.

Westland and Hialeah sued Seipp for damages and sought a mandatory injunction to remove the wall. Seipp counterclaimed for damages and to enjoin Westland from damaging the wall. During the litigation, Machado bought the Seipp land and the dealership and was substituted as a party.[16]

Before trial, Westland and Hialeah obtained a partial summary judgment to the effect that as long as the skating rink was constructed in accordance with the South Florida Building Code, Machado's lower-elevation lot remained the servient tenement for all surface water flowing from the skating center. The case proceeded to trial where the jury, after receiving an instruction that tracked the language of the partial summary judgment, found in favor of Westland and Hialeah in excess of one million dollars in damages.

The Third District Court of Appeal reversed the judgment against Machado in a six-to-three split decision. The court held that the trial judge had applied an incorrect rule of law in granting the summary judgment and that the jury instruction based on the summary judgment also was error.

Originally, disputes involving the interference of surface waters were resolved by one of two doctrines: the common enemy rule or the civil law rule. See generally F. Maloney, S. Plager, R. Ausness, B. Canter, Florida Water Law 589 (1980), [hereinafter Maloney & Plager]; Kunyon & McClure, Interference With Surface Water, 24 Minn.L.Rev. 891 (1940); Annotation, Modern Status of Rules Governing Interference With Drainage of Surface Waters, 93 A.L.R.3d 1216 (1979). The common enemy rule held that landowners had an unlimited privilege to deal with the surface water on their land as they pleased without regard to the harm which may be caused to others. The civil law rule recognized that higher elevation tracts had an easement or servitude over lower tracts for all surface water that naturally flowed downhill. However, anyone who increased or interfered with the natural flow of surface waters so as to cause invasion of another's interests was subject to liability to the other.

Neither of these doctrines, in its pure form, was perfect, especially as the population increased. While the common enemy rule permitted the free improvement of property, it also carried with it the potential of self-help engineering contests in which the winner was the person who most effectively turned the excess water upon his neighbor's land. On the other hand, the civil law rule acted as an impediment to the improvement of land since almost any development by an upper landowner was likely to increase the flow of surface water upon the land below and most efforts by the lower owner to dam the natural flow had the effect of throwing the water back onto the land of the upper owner. As a consequence, some jurisdictions adopted a third rule, known as the

---

16. The counterclaim was dismissed in return for Westland and Hialeah agreeing not to seek punitive damages. The record is silent as to the fate of the injunction, but apparently improvements to both lots eliminated the flooding and mooted the issue.

reasonable use rule. Under this rule, a possessor of land is not unqualifiedly entitled to deal with surface waters as he pleases nor is he absolutely prohibited from increasing or interfering with the natural flow of surface waters to the detriment of others. Each possessor is legally privileged to make reasonable use of his land even though the flow of surface waters is altered thereby and causes some harm to others. He incurs liability only when his harmful interference with the flow of surface waters is unreasonable.

Because of the inequities which would result from a strict application of either the common enemy or the civil law rule, most of the states which had adopted either of these rules began to apply modifications in given cases. Often, these hybrid rules produced the same result as would have occurred through the application of the reasonable use rule. The reasonable use rule has been adopted by Restatement (Second) of Torts § 833 (1979), which recommends that claims of interference with the flow of surface waters should be decided under principles of nuisance. See Pendergrast v. Aiken, 293 N.C. 201, 236 S.E.2d 787 (1977) (if the interference is intentional, the conduct of the offending party is measured in terms of reasonableness; if unintentional, the test is negligence).

The Florida position with respect to the interference with surface waters is not entirely clear. After explaining the common enemy and the civil law rules in Brumley v. Dorner, 78 Fla. 495, 83 So. 912 (1919), this Court noted that both of these rules had been modified considerably by the courts to the extent that each case must stand upon its own facts. The Court then stated:

> The almost universal rule, as gathered from the decisions, is that no person has the right to gather surface waters that would naturally flow in one direction by drainage, ditches, dams, or otherwise, and divert them from their natural course and cast them upon the lands of the lower owner to his injury.

Id. at 501, 83 So. at 914. * * *

* * *

Upon analysis, we have elected to adopt the reasonable use rule in cases involving the interference with surface waters. In so doing, we join approximately twenty-one other states, Case Comment, Waters and Water Courses—Torts—Owners of Property Damaged by Unlawful Ditching or Unreasonable Discharge of Waters May Obtain Relief by Statute or by the Tort Concept of Reasonable Use, 60 N.D.L.Rev. 741, 745 (1984), many of which have taken this position in recent years. E.g., Page Motor Co. v. Baker, 182 Conn. 484, 438 A.2d 739 (1980); Cootey v. Sun Inv., Inc., 690 P.2d 1324 (Haw.App.), cert. granted, 67 Haw. 685, 744 P.2d 781 (1984), rev'd in part, 718 P.2d 1086 (Haw.1986); Hall v. Wood, 443 So.2d 834 (Miss.1983); McGlashan v. Spade Rockledge Terrace Condo. Dev. Corp., 62 Ohio St.2d 55, 402 N.E.2d 1196 (1980); Butler v. Bruno, 115 R.I. 264, 341 A.2d 735 (1975).

The rule we announce appears much like the modified civil law rule; however, we believe it desirable to state our position through the adoption of the separate rule of reasonable use. As noted by Maloney and Plager, supra, at 596:

> Although the courts have treated the doctrine of reasonable use as a separate rule on equal footing with the civil law and common enemy rules, it is in reality merely the general tort principle which would decide such cases in the absence of the application of either of the two "property" rules. The relationship between adjoining landowners, in the absence of specific property rights, has always been governed by the maxim "Sic utere two [sic] ut alienum non laedas" ("Use your property in such a manner as not to injure that of another"). Much confusion and strained reasoning could be avoided if the courts would limit the application of the traditional rules to the narrowest possible situation or discard them altogether.

The principle that an upper landowner enjoys an easement across the lower tract for all naturally occurring surface water continues to apply to land in its natural state. However, when any party improves his land, thereby causing surface waters to damage his neighbor's property, the reasonable use rule shall be applied in order to settle the controversy. The rule applies not only in cases involving the conduct of the upper owner but also to improvements by the lower owner, such as the construction of dams designed to protect against the natural flow of surface waters across the lower land. See Mulder v. Tague, 85 S.D. 544, 186 N.W.2d 884 (1971). Regardless of whether a counterclaim has been filed when both parties have made improvements, the reasonableness of the conduct of each will be in issue and may be compared in order to arrive at a fair determination.

We recognize that the application of the reasonable use rule may make the outcome of certain controversies less predictable. Yet, if the rigidity of the traditional doctrines made cases predictable, it also led to such arbitrary results that the courts began to modify those rules. Predictability should not be achieved at the expense of justice. We believe that the rule of reasonable use employs the proper balance and will best enable surface water controversies to be fairly decided. As stated in McGlashan v. Spade Rockledge Terrace Condominium Development Corp.:

> The basic issue in these controversies is normally whether liability for the damage resulting from an interference with surface water flow should be borne by the person causing it. In this regard, an analysis centering on the reasonableness of a defendant's conduct, in view of all the circumstances, is more likely to produce an equitable result than one based on arbitrary property concepts. It is true that the law should not inhibit reasonable land development, but neither should it allow a landowner to expel surface water without regard to the consequences. As eloquently stated by Justice Brennan in Armstrong v. Francis Corp. (1956), 20 N.J. 320, 330, 120 A.2d 4, 10, "no

reason suggests itself why, in justice, the economic costs incident to the expulsion of surface waters in the transformation of the rural or semi-rural areas of our State into urban or suburban communities should be borne in every case by adjoining landowners rather than by those who engage in such projects for profit. Social progress and the common well-being are in actuality better served by a just and right balancing of the competing interests according to the general principles of fairness and common sense which attend the application of the rule of reason."

62 Ohio St.2d at 59, 402 N.E.2d at 1199–1200.

While it is evident that we do not accept the application of the strict civil law rule by the district court of appeal, we do not disagree with its analysis of the disputed jury instruction. * * *

* * *

This instruction had the practical effect of requiring the jury to determine the reasonableness of Westland's conduct based upon whether or not it complied with the South Florida Building Code. As noted by the court below, while one's compliance with a statute or an ordinance may amount to evidence of reasonableness, such compliance is not tantamount to reasonableness as a matter of law. Thus, evidence of Westland's compliance with the code could be properly considered as evidence of the reasonableness of its conduct, but not to the exclusion of other relevant evidence on that issue. Moreover, this case involved an evaluation and comparison of the reasonableness of the conduct of both parties. Therefore, the entry of the partial summary judgment and the resultant giving of the disputed jury instruction constituted reversible error.

Accordingly, while we have expressed differing views with respect to the law applicable to the interference with surface waters, we approve the decision of the district court of appeal reversing the judgment and directing a new trial.

It is so ordered.

Notes and Questions

1. Does the law of nuisance adequately address problems caused by diversion of surface water, or is the development of separate doctrine necessary?

2. Stormwater runoff from intensely developed urban or suburban land (and from intensely farmed agricultural land) is a major source of water silting and pollution. The Washington, D.C. metropolitan area, for example, constituting 2% of the Potomac River Basin, contributes 25% of the Potomac's sediment load. Runoff from a typical American city during the first hour of a storm may carry many more pollutants than the city's untreated sewerage would carry. Surface water also causes far more significant erosion of soil in developing and developed areas than in areas covered by natural vegetation.

Does the common law of surface waters adequately address these problems? The law discussed in the principal case is supplemented by common-law doctrines regarding the quality of surface waters. In this area, the traditional application of the natural flow doctrine—a landowner cannot alter and diminish the natural quality of water flowing through her land—has increasingly given way to a reasonable-use doctrine, much like general nuisance law. Can such doctrines deal with the problem of surface water pollution?

Increasingly, governments at all levels have addressed the problem of surface water pollution through regulatory solutions. The 1987 Clean Water Act requires states to put in place management programs identifying "best management practices and measures" to control nonpoint pollution sources, and requires permits to regulate municipal and industrial stormwater discharges. 33 U.S.C.A. §§ 1329, 1342(p). A model stormwater runoff control ordinance similarly relies on approved water management plan, see Maloney, Hamann, & Canter, Stormwater Runoff Control: A Model Ordinance for Meeting Local Water Quality Management Needs, 20 Nat. Resources J. 713 (1980). For an example of stormwater management planning for a major development adjoining Austin, Texas, see Marsh & Hill–Rowley, Water Quality, Stormwater Management, and Development Planning on the Urban Fringe, 35 Wash.Univ.J.Urb. & Contemp.L. 3 (1989).

Will regulatory solutions help resolve disputes among neighbors, such as that involved in the principal case?

3. The principal case addresses the rights of persons over whose property water passes to get rid of that water. An even more important issue for landowners, particularly for those who own land in the drier parts of the western United States, is the rights of landowners to withdraw water from streams, rivers, or lakes that pass through or adjoin the landowner's land for domestic, industrial, or agricultural uses.

Different states approach this problem through three different doctrines, two of which are rough cognates of doctrines discussed in the principal case. First, the traditional common-law doctrine of natural flow allows only uses that do not reduce the natural flow of the water course. The owner could only consume water for domestic uses (personal human use and watering domestic animals) and for reasonable commercial uses that did not materially diminish the flow. This doctrine has in many states yielded to a "reasonable-use" doctrine that attempts to weigh economic and social considerations in accommodating uses of flowing water among riparian owners.

Finally, the prior-appropriation doctrine, applied exclusively, or in combination with reasonable-use doctrines, in the western United States, allows the first person to use water for beneficial purposes to establish property rights in the water. It is, like the common-enemy theory of surface water, a doctrine that favors individualism and development over communitarianism and balanced use, but unlike the common-enemy doctrine, establishes property rights in the first claimant that cannot be overcome by later developers. The prior-appropriation doctrine is now generally administered through administrative permit programs that allow the possibility of shifting water rights to later claimants with greater needs for the water, albeit often with compensation. What other doctrines that we have studied earlier does the prior-appropriation doctrine resemble? What incentives does it create? Why might it have been adopted in arid regions?

See generally, on water law, A.D. Tarlock, Law of Water Rights and Resources (1988).

4. Also related to nuisance law is the law of lateral support. At common law, a landowner had a right to have land left in its natural condition supported by the land of her neighbors. If a neighbor's excavation removed support from neighboring land in its natural state causing such land to subside, the excavating neighbor was strictly liable for damages caused thereby. Where supported land was altered or burdened by structures, however, a neighbor who gave notice and then proceeded to excavate without negligence, was not liable for damages to the neighboring land. Support rights of artificial structures can be obtained by contract or by implication. Should they also be obtained by prescription? American courts have generally said no. What supports this position? While American courts have neither permitted prescription nor adopted a general reasonableness standard, they have meliorated the harsh effects of the common law on burdened land by permitting consequential damages for damaged structures where the burdened land would have subsided even if left in its natural state, and by interpreting the concept of negligence rather broadly. The problem is also often addressed by statute or ordinance. Should it be wholly subsumed within the law of nuisance? Are there particular characteristics of the problem of excavation that make separate treatment necessary? See generally on support, 5 R. Powell & P. Rohan, Powell on Real Property ¶ ¶ 698–702 (1991).

Chapter Seven

PUBLIC REGULATION OF LAND USE

I. THE "TAKINGS" QUESTION

The Fifth Amendment to the Constitution of the United States, applicable to the States by operation of the Fourteenth Amendment, provides, in part, that **"no person (shall) be deprived of life, liberty, or property, without due process of law; nor shall private property be taken for public use, without just compensation."** This short declaration has been the subject of thousands and thousands of pages of analysis in court opinions and in scholarly articles. Despite this attention, it can fairly be said that the meaning of this "Takings Clause" in application to particular situations is not entirely clear.

This is not surprising if one realizes that resolution of the takings question requires resolution of the irreducible tensions in private property ownership, especially ownership understood in its more complete sense of both a relationship of a person to a thing (in these cases most often land) *and* a relationship among persons with respect to a thing. The employment of government coercion in all of these cases only intensifies the issue. The cases clearly evidence changing perspectives on the relative balance of government power and private property rights through several generations.

The genesis of all conflicts involving a takings issue is a government action that, at least according to the claimant, interferes with constitutionally protected property rights. A broad range of federal, state or local government actions raises takings claims. In some, the government exercises its power of eminent domain by directly acquiring, through a judicial process, privately held land; for example, the government agency acquires privately owned land for a highway, for a park, for streets, or for a shopping mall or some other economic development. Eminent domain differs from other property transfers in that the owner's consent to the transfer is not required. If the owner rejects the government's offer, a court will settle the matter and may order the transfer and set the price. In other cases raising takings issues, the government simply restricts the ability of the property owner to use his or her property. Common examples of such regulation include historic preservation laws, environmental protection statutes and health and safety regulations.

In applying the constitutional standards of the Fifth Amendment to any of these situations, four separate questions must be answered. First, does the government action further a "public use"? Second, has something been "taken"? Third is that something "private property?" And fourth, has the property owner been justly compensated for his or her loss?

In reviewing the following cases, you will be making a return visit to some of the basic concepts presented early in this course. You will see, for example, some notion of the "column of dirt/column of air" description of property ownership and reliance on the bundle of rights/bundle of sticks description of property ownership. Should these metaphors have constitutional significance?

A. PUBLIC PURPOSE

Introductory Note—The Lead Up To Kelo

Kelo v. City of New London, 125 S.Ct. 2655, 162 L.Ed.2d 439 (2005) is the most recent Supreme Court attempt to define the public use requirement. *Kelo* is the most controversial eminent domain decision by the Supreme Court in recent times. The controversy over *Kelo* emanates from the Court's approval of the taking of a private home for the purpose of transferring it to a private real estate developer. *Kelo* thus pits a homeowner against both the government and big business. A true David and Goliath story, but in this case, unlike the biblical one, David loses. Before examining *Kelo*, a little historical background is in order

In most cases, the public use requirement of the constitution is easily satisfied and does not present a serious issue. When private property is appropriated to construct a highway, an airport or a public utility, such as a gas transmission line, the public use is apparent. To be sure, there is often some private benefit as well. The exit ramp off the highway becomes a valuable site for a gas station, the airport is home to many private businesses including restaurants and hotels, and the utility company that transmits natural gas from the fields of Texas to users in New England is in business to make a profit for its shareholders. But in all these examples, the private benefit is clearly incidental to the public use. One of the hallmarks of these cases that makes the public use so apparent is that at the time of the appropriation it is contemplated that the property will be owned after the appropriation by a public or quasi-public entity. The highway will be owned and operated by the state or federal government, the airport by a municipality and the gas transmission line by a public utility.

A more difficult class of cases arise when at the time of the appropriation it is contemplated that the property taken from private individual A will be transferred to private individual B. Just because the appropriation accomplishes a private to private transfer does not mean that the public use requirement is not satisfied. In *Berman v. Parker*, 348 U.S. 26, 75 S.Ct. 98, 99 L.Ed. 27 (1954) eminent domain was used as part of an urban renewal project. At the time of the appropriation it was contemplated that the property would be transferred from one private entity to another for redevelopment. The Supreme Court held in sweeping language that the public use requirement was satisfied and that the legislature that authorized the appropriation was primarily responsible for determining if the appropriation served the public interest. "[W]hen the legislature has spoken, the public interest has been declared in terms well-neigh conclusive. In such cases the legislature, not the judiciary, is the main guardian of the public needs to be served by social legislation." *Id.*, at 32.

The next major Supreme Court decision in this area was *Hawaii Housing Authority v. Midkiff*, 467 U.S. 229, 104 S.Ct. 2321, 81 L.Ed.2d 186 (1984). In *Midkiff* the Hawaii legislature had authorized the use of eminent domain to take private residential property from its owner and transfer the property to the tenant who occupied it. The justification for the taking was that, for historical reasons, land ownership in Hawaii was highly concentrated: only a few families owned most of the land. These families for a variety of reasons including a desire to avoid a heavy income tax burden had proven unwilling to sell the land. They were willing to lease the property to residential tenants, but not to sell it to them. The Hawaii legislature determined that this situation had resulted in an oligopoly and the attendant failure of the market for fee ownership of single family residences. The legislature chose eminent domain as the remedy for this failure. The legislation was challenged on the ground that it was unconstitutional for failure to satisfy the Constitution's public use requirement. The Supreme Court rejected this challenge and held the legislation constitutional. "Redistribution of fee simples to correct deficiencies in the market determined by the state legislature to be attributable to land oligopoly is a rational exercise of the eminent domain power." *Id.*, *at 243*. More broadly, the Court stated that " . . . where the exercise of the eminent domain power is rationally related to a conceivable public purpose, the Court has never held a compensated taking to be proscribed by the Public Use Clause." *Id.*, at 241.

Two things should be noted about the *Berman—Midkiff* line of cases. First, public use is redefined by them to mean public purpose. There is no claim, for example in *Midkiff* that the private houses that were taken from A and sold to B would be used by the public. In the Court's opinion, however, it was enough if a public purpose would be achieved by the transfer, i.e. elimination of market failure, even if a public use would not be.

Second, in both *Berman* and *Midkiff* the justification for the use of the power of eminent domain was some characteristic of the land while it was owned by A and not the benefit that would accrue to B as a result of the transfer. That is to say that the taking of the land cured the perceived social evil, urban blight in *Berman*, oligopoly in Midkiff, and the transfer to the private entity was merely incidental to accomplishing this purpose. Understood this way, this line of cases is not as far reaching as it may at first seem.

But at the same time that *Berman* and Midkiff were being decided another line of cases was coming up in the state courts. The most prominent of these was *Poletown Neighborhood Council v. Detroit*, 410 Mich. 616, 304 N.W.2d 455 (1981). In *Poletown*, legislation of the City of Detroit was challenged. In the 1980s, Detroit was going through difficult economic times. Many businesses had left the "rust belt" to relocate in the "sun belt," and the Detroit economy was reeling. To make matters worse, General Motors, the area's largest employer, was threatening to relocate some its manufacturing plants out of the Detroit area. In an effort to reverse this trend, Detroit enacted the "Economic Development Corporations Act" to promote industry and commerce and thereby increase jobs and the tax base of the City and the State. The City of Detroit used the Act to condemn a large number of properties in a working class area of the City called *Poletown*. The condemnation contemplated that the assembled properties would be transferred from their former owners to General Motors for the construction of a manufacturing facility. In a *per curium* opinion over a strong dissent by Justice Ryan, the Michigan Supreme Court held that furthering economic development was a public purpose that satisfied the public use requirement of the Michigan Constitution. The only limitation that the court placed on the power of eminent domain in the private to private context was that when eminent domain "is exercised in a way that benefits specific and identifiable private interests, a court inspects with heightened scrutiny the claim that the public interest is the predominant interest being advanced." *Id.*, at 459–460.

Poletown was widely followed. Westlaw's citing reference reveals that the decision was followed or cited positively more than 50 times. *Poletown* was not without its critics, however. For example in *Southwestern Illinois Development Authority v. National City Environmental, L.L.C.*, 199 Ill.2d 225, 263 Ill.Dec. 241, 768 N.E.2d 1 (2002) the Illinois Supreme Court declined to give the broad deference to the legislature that *Poletown* and *Midkiff* had, and held, at least in the factual setting of that case, that a private to private condemnation to promote economic development violated the Illinois constitution. Then, in a decision that surprised many observers, the Michigan Supreme Court reversed itself and overruled *Poletown* in *County of Wayne v. Hathcock*, 471 Mich. 445, 684 N.W.2d 765 (2004). *Hathcock*, in an opinion that relies heavily on the Ryan dissent in *Poletown*, virtually eliminates the ability of governments to use eminent domain for private to private transfers designed to promote economic development. *Hathcock* is discussed in the notes following *Kelo*.

Against this background, observe how the U.S. Supreme Court attempted to resolve the private to private condemnation conundrum.

KELO, ET AL., v. CITY OF NEW LONDON, CONNECTICUT, ET AL.

Supreme Court of the United States, 2005.
125 S.Ct. 2655, 162 L.Ed.2d 439.

JUSTICE STEVENS delivered the opinion of the Court.

In 2000, the city of New London approved a development plan that, in the words of the Supreme Court of Connecticut, was "projected to create in excess of 1,000 jobs, to increase tax and other revenues, and to revitalize an economically distressed city, including its downtown and waterfront areas." 268 Conn. 1, 5, 843 A.2d 500, 507 (2004). In assembling the land needed for this project, the city's development agent has purchased property from willing sellers and proposes to use the power of eminent domain to acquire the remainder of the property from unwilling owners in exchange for just compensation. The question presented is whether the city's proposed disposition of this property qualifies as a "public use" within the meaning of the Takings Clause of the Fifth Amendment to the Constitution.

I

The city of New London (hereinafter City) sits at the junction of the Thames River and the Long Island Sound in southeastern Connecticut. Decades of economic decline led a state agency in 1990 to designate the City a "distressed municipality." In 1996, the Federal Government closed the Naval Undersea Warfare Center, which had been located in the Fort Trumbull area of the City and had employed over 1,500 people. In 1998, the City's unemployment rate was nearly double that of the State, and its population of just under 24,000 residents was at its lowest since 1920.

These conditions prompted state and local officials to target New London, and particularly its Fort Trumbull area, for economic revitalization. To this end, respondent New London Development Corporation (NLDC), a private nonprofit entity established some years earlier to assist the City in planning economic development, was reactivated. In January 1998, the State authorized a $5.35 million bond issue to support the NLDC's planning activities and a $10 million bond issue toward the creation of a Fort Trumbull State Park. In February, the pharmaceutical company Pfizer Inc. announced that it would build a $300 million research facility on a site immediately adjacent to Fort Trumbull; local planners hoped that Pfizer would draw new business to the area, thereby serving as a catalyst to the area's rejuvenation. After receiving initial approval from the city council, the NLDC continued its planning activities and held a series of neighborhood meetings to educate the public about the process. In May, the city council authorized the NLDC to formally submit its plans to the relevant state agencies for review.[2] Upon

2. Various state agencies studied the project's economic, environmental, and so-cial ramifications. As part of this process, a team of consultants evaluated six alternaobtaining state-level approval, the NLDC finalized an integrated development plan focused on 90 acres of the Fort Trumbull area.

The Fort Trumbull area is situated on a peninsula that juts into the Thames River. The area comprises approximately 115 privately owned properties, as well as the 32 acres of land formerly occupied by the naval facility (Trumbull State Park now occupies 18 of those 32 acres). The development plan encompasses seven parcels. Parcel I is designated for a waterfront conference hotel at the center of a "small urban village" that will include restaurants and shopping. This parcel will also have marinas for both recreational and commercial uses. A pedestrian "riverwalk" will originate here and continue down the coast, connecting the waterfront areas of the development. Parcel 2 will be the site of approximately 80 new residences organized into an urban neighborhood and linked by public walkway to the remainder of the development, including the state park. This parcel also includes space reserved for a new U.S. Coast Guard Museum. Parcel 3, which is located immediately north of the Pfizer facility, will contain at least 90,000 square feet of research and development office space. Parcel 4A is a 2.4–acre site that will be used either to support the adjacent state park, by providing parking or retail services for visitors, or to support the nearby marina. Parcel 4B will include a renovated marina, as well as the final stretch of the riverwalk. Parcels 5, 6, and 7 will provide land for office and retail space, parking, and water-dependent commercial uses. 1 App. 109–113.

The NLDC intended the development plan to capitalize on the arrival of the Pfizer facility and the new commerce it was expected to attract. In addition to creating jobs, generating tax revenue, and helping to "build momentum for the revitalization of downtown New London," Id., at 92, the plan was also designed to make the City more attractive and to create leisure and recreational opportunities on the waterfront and in the park.

The city council approved the plan in January 2000, and designated the NLDC as its development agent in charge of implementation. See Conn. Stat 8–188 (2005). The city council also authorized the NLDC to purchase property or to acquire property by exercising eminent domain in the City's name. § 8–193. The NLDC successfully negotiated the purchase of most of the real estate in the 90–acre area, but its negotiations with petitioners failed. As a consequence, in November 2000, the NLDC initiated the condemnation proceedings that gave rise to this case.

II

Petitioner Susette Kelo has lived in the Fort Trumbull area since 1997. She has made extensive improvements to her house, which she prizes for its water view. Petitioner Wilhelmina Dery was born in her

tive development proposals for the area, which varied in extensiveness and emphasis. The Office of Planning and Management, one of the primary state agencies undertaking the review, made findings that the project was consistent with relevant state and municipal development policies. See 1 App. 89–95.

Fort Trumbull house in 1918 and has lived there her entire life. Her husband Charles (also a petitioner) has lived in the house since they married some 60 years ago. In all, the nine petitioners own 15 properties in Fort Trumbull—4 in parcel 3 of the development plan and 11 in parcel 4A. Ten of the parcels are occupied by the owner or a family member; the other five are held as investment properties. There is no allegation that any of these properties is blighted or otherwise in poor condition; rather, they were condemned only because they happen to be located in the development area.

In December 2000, petitioners brought this action in the New London Superior Court. They claimed, among other things, that the taking of their properties would violate the "public use" restriction in the Fifth Amendment. After a 7–day bench trial, the Superior Court granted a permanent restraining order prohibiting the taking of the properties located in parcel 4A (park or marina support). It, however, denied petitioners relief as to the properties located in parcel 3 (office space). 2 App. to Pet. for Cert. 343–350.

After the Superior Court ruled, both sides took appeals to the Supreme Court of Connecticut. That court held, over a dissent, that all of the City's proposed takings were valid. It began by upholding the lower court's determination that the takings were authorized by chapter 132, the State's municipal development statute. See Conn. Gen.Stat. 8–186 et seq. (2005).That statute expresses a legislative determination that the taking of land, even developed land, as part of an economic development project is a "public use" and in the "public interest." 268 Conn., at 18–28, 843 A.2d, at 515–521. Next, relying on cases such as *Hawaii Housing Authority v. Midkiff ... and Berman v. Parker*, ... the court held that such economic development qualified as a valid public use under both the Federal and State Constitutions. 268 Conn., at 40, 843 A.2d, at 527.

Finally, adhering to its precedents, the court went on to determine, first, whether the takings of the particular properties at issue were "reasonably necessary" to achieving the City's intended public use, ... and, second, whether the takings were for "reasonably foreseeable needs." ... The court upheld the trial court's factual findings as to parcel 3, but reversed the trial court as to parcel 4A, agreeing with the City that the intended use of this land was sufficiently definite and had been given "reasonable attention" during the planning process.. . .

The three dissenting justices would have imposed a "heightened" standard of judicial review for takings justified by economic development. Although they agreed that the plan was intended to serve a valid public use, they would have found all the takings unconstitutional because the City had failed to adduce "clear and convincing evidence" that the economic benefits of the plan would in fact come to pass. *Id.* at 144, 146. 843 A.2d, at 587, 588 (Zarella, J., joined by Sullivan, C. J., and Katz, J., concurring in part and dissenting in part).

We granted certiorari to determine whether a city's decision to take property for the purpose of economic development satisfies the "public use" requirement of the Fifth Amendment. . . .

III

Two polar propositions are perfectly clear. On the one hand, it has long been accepted that the sovereign may not take the property of A for the sole purpose of transferring it to another private party B, even though A is paid just compensation. On the other hand, it is equally clear that a State may transfer property from one private party to another if future "use by the public" is the purpose of the taking; the condemnation of land for a railroad with common-carrier duties is a familiar example. Neither of these propositions, however, determines the disposition of this case.

As for the first proposition, the City would no doubt be forbidden from taking petitioners' land for the purpose of conferring a private benefit on a particular private party. . . . Nor would the City be allowed to take property under the mere pretext of a public purpose, when its actual purpose was to bestow a private benefit. The takings before us, however, would be executed pursuant to a "carefully considered" development plan. . . . The trial judge and all the members of the Supreme Court of Connecticut agreed that there was no evidence of an illegitimate purpose in this case. Therefore, as was true of the statute challenged in *Midkiff*, the City's development plan was not adopted "to benefit a particular class of identifiable individuals." . . .

On the other hand, this is not a case in which the City is planning to open the condemned land—at least not in its entirety—to use by the general public. Nor will the private lessees of the land in any sense be required to operate like common carriers, making their services available to all corners. But although such a projected use would be sufficient to satisfy the public use requirement, this "Court long ago rejected any literal requirement that condemned property be put into use for the general public." . . . Indeed, while many state courts in the mid–19th century endorsed "use by the public" as the proper definition of public use, that narrow view steadily eroded over time. Not only was the "use by the public" test difficult to administer (e.g., what proportion of the public need have access to the property? at what price?),[7] but it proved to be impractical given the diverse and always evolving needs of society.[8]

---

7. See, e.g., Dayton Gold & Silver Mining Co. v. Seawell, 11 Nev. 394, 410, 1876 WL 4573, *11 (1876 ("If public occupation and enjoyment of the object for which land is to be condemned furnishes the only and true test for the right of eminent domain, then the legislature would certainly have the constitutional authority to condemn the lands of any private citizen for the purpose of building hotels and theaters. Why not? A hotel is used by the public as much as a railroad. The public have the same right, upon payment of a fixed compensation, to seek rest and refreshment at a public inn as they have to travel upon a railroad").

8. From upholding the Mill Acts (which authorized manufacturers dependent on power-producing dams to flood upstream lands in exchange for just compensation), to approving takings necessary for the economic development of the West through mining and irrigation, many state courts either circumvented the "use by the public"

Accordingly, when this Court began applying the Fifth Amendment to the States at the close of the 19th century, it embraced the broader and more natural interpretation of public use as "public purpose." See, e.g., *Fallbrook Irrigation Dist. v. Bradley*, 164 U.S. 112, 158–164, 17 S.Ct. 56, 41 L.Ed. 369 (1896). Thus, in a case upholding a mining company's use of an aerial bucket line to transport ore over property it did not own, Justice Holmes' opinion for the Court stressed "the inadequacy of use by the general public as a universal test." *Strickley v. Highland Boy Gold Mining Co.*, 200 U.S. 527, 531, 26 S.Ct. 301, 50 L.Ed. 581 (1906). We have repeatedly and consistently rejected that narrow test ever since.

The disposition of this case therefore turns on the question whether the City's development plan serves a "public purpose." Without exception, our cases have defined that concept broadly, reflecting our longstanding policy of deference to legislative judgments in this field.

In *Berman v. Parker* . . . , this Court upheld a redevelopment plan targeting a blighted area of Washington, D. C., in which most of the housing for the area's 5,000 inhabitants was beyond repair. Under the plan, the area would be condemned and part of it utilized for the construction of streets, schools, and other public facilities. The remainder of the land would be leased or sold to private parties for the purpose of redevelopment, including the construction of low-cost housing.

The owner of a department store located in the area challenged the condemnation, pointing out that his store was not itself blighted and arguing that the creation of a "better balanced, more attractive community" was not a valid public use. . . . Writing for a unanimous Court, Justice Douglas refused to evaluate this claim in isolation, deferring instead to the legislative and agency judgment that the area "must be planned as a whole" for the plan to be successful. . . . The Court explained that "community redevelopment programs need not, by force of the Constitution, be on a piecemeal basis—lot by lot, building by building." . . . The public use underlying the taking was unequivocally affirmed:

> "We do not sit to determine whether a particular housing project is or is not desirable. The concept of the public welfare is broad and inclusive. . . . The values it represents are spiritual as well as physi-

test when necessary or abandoned it completely. See Nichols, The Meaning of Public Use in the Law of Eminent Domain, 20 B.U.L.Rev. 15, 619–624 (1940) (tracing this development and collecting cases). For example, in rejecting the "use by the public" test as overly restrictive, the Nevada Supreme Court stressed that "[m]ining" is the greatest of the industrial pursuits in this state. All other interests are subservient to it. Our mountains are almost barren of timber, and our valleys could never be made profitable for agricultural purposes except for the fact of a home market having been created by the mining developments in different sections of the state. The mining and

milling interests give employment to many men, and the benefits derived from this business are distributed as much, and sometimes more, among the laboring classes than with the owners of the mines and mills.

. . . The present prosperity of the state is entirely due to the mining developments already made, and the entire people of the state are directly interested in having the future developments unobstructed by the obstinate action of any individual or individuals." Dayton Gold & Silver Mining Co., 11 Nev., at 409–410, 1876 WL, at *11.

cal, aesthetic as well as monetary. It is within the power of the legislature to determine that the community should be beautiful as well as healthy, spacious as well as clean, well-balanced as well as carefully patrolled. In the present case, the Congress and its authorized agencies have made determinations that take into account a wide variety of values. It is not for us to reappraise them. If those who govern the District of Columbia decide that the Nation's Capital should be beautiful as well as sanitary, there is nothing in the Fifth Amendment that stands in the way." *Id.*, at 33, 75 S.Ct. 98.

In Hawaii Housing Authority v. Midkiff ..., the Court considered a Hawaii statute whereby fee title was taken from lessors and transferred to lessees (for just compensation) in order to reduce the concentration of land ownership. We unanimously upheld the statute and rejected the Ninth Circuit's view that it was "a naked attempt on the part of the state of Hawaii to take the property of A and transfer it to B solely for B's private use and benefit." *Id.*, at 235, 104 S.Ct. 2321 (internal quotation marks omitted). Reaffirming *Berman's* deferential approach to legislative judgments in this field, we concluded that the State's purpose of eliminating the "social and economic evils of a land oligopoly" qualified as a valid public use.... Our opinion also rejected the contention that the mere fact that the State immediately transferred the properties to private individuals upon condemnation somehow diminished the public character of the taking. "[I]t is only the taking's purpose, and not its mechanics," we explained, that matters in determining public use....

In that same Term we decided another public use case that arose in a purely economic context. In *Ruckelshaus v. Monsanto, Co.*, 467 U.S. 986, 104 S.Ct. 2862, 81 L.Ed.2d 815 (1984), the Court dealt with provisions of the Federal Insecticide, Fungicide, and Rodenticide Act under which the Environmental Protection Agency could consider the data (including trade secrets) submitted by a prior pesticide applicant in evaluating a subsequent application, so long as the second applicant paid just compensation for the data. We acknowledged that the "most direct beneficiaries" of these provisions were the subsequent applicants, ... but we nevertheless upheld the statute under *Berman* and *Midkiff*. We found sufficient Congress' belief that sparing applicants the cost of time-consuming research eliminated a significant barrier to entry in the pesticide market and thereby enhanced competition....

Viewed as a whole, our jurisprudence has recognized that the needs of society have varied between different parts of the Nation, just as they have evolved over time in response to changed circumstances. Our earliest cases in particular embodied a strong theme of federalism, emphasizing the "great respect" that we owe to state legislatures and state courts in discerning local public needs.... For more than a century, our public use jurisprudence has wisely eschewed rigid formulas and intrusive scrutiny in favor of affording legislatures broad latitude in determining what public needs justify the use of the takings power.

IV

Those who govern the City were not confronted with the need to remove blight in the Fort Trumbull area, but their determination that the area was sufficiently distressed to justify a program of economic rejuvenation is entitled to our deference. The City has carefully formulated an economic development plan that it believes will provide appreciable benefits to the community, including—but by no means limited to—new jobs and increased tax revenue. As with other exercises in urban planning and development, the City is endeavoring to coordinate a variety of commercial, residential, and recreational uses of land, with the hope that they will form a whole greater than the sum of its parts. To effectuate this plan, the City has invoked a state statute that specifically authorizes the use of eminent domain to promote economic development. Given the comprehensive character of the plan, the thorough deliberation that preceded its adoption, and the limited scope of our review, it is appropriate for us, as it was in Berman, to resolve the challenges of the individual owners, not on a piecemeal basis, but rather in light of the entire plan. Because that plan unquestionably serves a public purpose, the takings challenged here satisfy the public use requirement of the Fifth Amendment.

To avoid this result, petitioners urge us to adopt a new bright-line rule that economic development does not qualify as a public use. Putting aside the unpersuasive suggestion that the City's plan will provide only purely economic benefits, neither precedent nor logic supports petitioners' proposal. Promoting economic development is a traditional and long accepted function of government. There is, moreover, no principled way of distinguishing economic development from the other public purposes that we have recognized. In our cases upholding takings that facilitated agriculture and mining, for example, we emphasized the importance of those industries to the welfare of the States in question, ...; in *Berman*, we endorsed the purpose of transforming a blighted area into a "well-balanced" community through redevelopment[13] ... Had the public use in Berman been defined more narrowly, it would have been difficult to justify the taking of the plaintiffs nonblighted department store; in *Midkiff* we upheld the interest in breaking up a land oligopoly that "created artificial deterrents to the normal functioning of the State's residential land market," 467 U.S., at 242. 104 S.Ct. 2321 and in Monsanto, we accepted Congress' purpose of eliminating a "significant barrier to entry in the pesticide market," 467 U.S., at 1014–1015, 104

13. It is a misreading of Berman to suggest that the only public use upheld in that case was the initial removal of blight. See Reply Brief for Petitioners 8. The public use described in *Berman* extended beyond that to encompass the purpose of developing that area to create conditions that would prevent a reversion to blight in the future. See 348 U.S., at 34–35, 75 S.Ct. 98 ("It was not enough, [the experts] believed, to remove existing buildings that were insanitary or unsightly. It was important to redesign the whole area so as to eliminate the conditions that cause slums.... The entire area needed redesigning so that a balanced, integrated plan could be developed for the region, including not only new homes, but also schools, churches, parks, streets, and shopping centers. In this way it was hoped that the cycle of decay of the area could be controlled and the birth of future slums prevented").

S.Ct. 2862 It would be incongruous to hold that the City's interest in the economic benefits to be derived from the development of the Fort Trumbull area has less of a public character than any of those other interests. Clearly, there is no basis for exempting economic development from our traditionally broad understanding of public purpose.

Petitioners contend that using eminent domain for economic development impermissibly blurs the boundary between public and private takings. Again, our cases foreclose this objection. Quite simply, the government's pursuit of a public purpose will often benefit individual private parties. For example, in *Midkiff* the forced transfer of property conferred a direct and significant benefit on those lessees who were previously unable to purchase their homes. In *Monsanto*, we recognized that the "most direct beneficiaries" of the data-sharing provisions were the subsequent pesticide applicants, but benefitting them in this way was necessary to promoting competition in the pesticide market[14] ... The owner of the department store in Berman objected to "taking from one businessman for the benefit of another businessman," ... referring to the fact that under the redevelopment plan land would be leased or sold to private developers for redevelopment. Our rejection of that contention has particular relevance to the instant case: "The public end may be as well or better served through an agency of private enterprise than through a department of government—or so the Congress might conclude. We cannot say that public ownership is the sole method of promoting the public purposes of community redevelopment projects." *Id.*, at 34, 75 S.Ct. 98.[16]

It is further argued that without a bright-line rule nothing would stop a city from transferring citizen A's property to citizen B for the sole reason that citizen B will put the property to a more productive use and thus pay more taxes. Such a one-to-one transfer of property, executed outside the confines of an integrated development plan, is not presented

14. Any number of cases illustrate that the achievement of a public good often co-incides with the immediate benefitting of private parties. See, e.g., *National Railroad Passenger Corporation v. Boston & Maine Corp.*, 503 U.S. 407, 422, 112 S.Ct. 1394, 118 L.Ed.2d 52 (1992) (public purpose of "facilitating Amtrak's rail service" served by taking rail track from one private company and transferring it to another private company); *Brown v. Legal Foundation of Wash*, 538 U.S. 216, 123 S.Ct. 1406, 155 L.Ed.2d 376 (2003) (provision of legal services to the poor is a valid public purpose). It is worth noting that in *Hawaii Housing Authority v. Midkiff*, ... *Monsanto*, and *Boston & Maine Corp.*, the property in question retained the same use even after the change of ownership.

16. Nor do our cases support Justice O'CONNOR's novel theory that the government may only take property and transfer it to private parties when the initial taking eliminates some "harmful property use." Post, at 2675 (dissenting opinion). There was nothing "harmful" about the non-blighted department store at issue in *Berman*, ...; nothing "harmful" about the lands at issue in the mining and agriculture cases, ...; and certainly nothing "harmful" about the trade secrets owned by the pesticide manufacturers in *Monsanto*. In each case, the public purpose we upheld depended on a private party's *future* use of the concededly nonharmful property that was taken. By focusing on a property's future use, as opposed to its past use, our cases are faithful to the text of the Takings Clause.... Justice O'Connor's intimation that a "public purpose" may not be achieved by the action of private parties, ... confuses the purpose of a taking with its mechanics, a mistake we warned of in *Midkiff*....

in this case. While such an unusual exercise of government power would certainly raise a suspicion that a private purpose was afoot, the hypothetical cases posited by petitioners can be confronted if and when they arise. They do not warrant the crafting of an artificial restriction on the concept of public use.

Alternatively, petitioners maintain that for takings of this kind we should require a "reasonable certainty" that the expected public benefits will actually accrue. Such a rule, however, would represent an even greater departure from our precedent. "When the legislature's purpose is legitimate and its means are not irrational, our cases make clear that empirical debates over the wisdom of takings—no less than debates over the wisdom of other kinds of socioeconomic legislation—are not to be carried out in the federal courts."... Indeed, earlier this Term we explained why similar practical concerns (among others) undermined the use of the "substantially advances" formula in our regulatory takings doctrine. See *Lingle v. Chevron U.S.A. Inc.*, 544 U.S. 528, ___, 125 S.Ct. 2074, 2085, 161 L.Ed.2d 876, 892 (2005) (noting that this formula "would empower—and might often require—courts to substitute their predictive judgments for those of elected legislatures and expert agencies"). The disadvantages of a heightened form of review are especially pronounced in this type of case. Orderly implementation of a comprehensive redevelopment plan obviously requires that the legal rights of all interested parties be established before new construction can be commenced. A constitutional rule that required postponement of the judicial approval of every condemnation until the likelihood of success of the plan had been assured would unquestionably impose a significant impediment to the successful consummation of many such plans.

Just as we decline to second-guess the City's considered judgments about the efficacy of its development plan, we also decline to second-guess the City's determinations as to what lands it needs to acquire in order to effectuate the project. "It is not for the courts to oversee the choice of the boundary line nor to sit in review on the size of a particular project area. Once the question of the public purpose has been decided, the amount and character of land to be taken for the project and the need for a particular tract to complete the integrated plan rests in the discretion of the legislative branch." *Berman*, 348 U.S., at 35–36, 75 S.Ct. 98.

In affirming the City's authority to take petitioners' properties, we do not minimize the hardship that condemnations may entail, notwithstanding the payment of just compensation. We emphasize that nothing in our opinion precludes any State from placing further restrictions on its exercise of the takings power. Indeed, many States already impose "public use" requirements that are stricter than the federal baseline. Some of these requirements have been established as a matter of state constitutional law, while others are expressed in state eminent domain statutes that carefully limit the grounds upon which takings may be exercised. As the submissions of the parties and their *amici* make clear, the necessity and wisdom of using eminent domain to promote economic development are certainly matters of legitimate public debate. This Court's authority, however, extends only to determining whether the City's proposed condemnations are for a "public use" within the meaning of the Fifth Amendment to the Federal Constitution. Because over a century of our case law interpreting that provision dictates an affirmative answer to that question, we may not grant petitioners the relief that they seek.

The judgment of the Supreme Court of Connecticut is affirmed.

It is so ordered.

JUSTICE KENNEDY concurring.

I join the opinion for the Court and add these further observations.

This Court has declared that a taking should be upheld as consistent with the Public Use Clause, U.S. Const., Amdt. 5., as long as it is "rationally related to a conceivable public purpose." *Hawaii Housing Authority v. Midkiff....* This deferential standard of review echoes the rational-basis test used to review economic regulation under the Due Process and Equal Protection Clauses.... The determination that a rational-basis standard of review is appropriate does not, however, alter the fact that transfers intended to confer benefits on particular, favored private entities, and with only incidental or pretextual public benefits, are forbidden by the Public Use Clause.

A court applying rational-basis review under the Public Use Clause should strike down a taking that, by a clear showing, is intended to favor a particular private party, with only incidental or pretextual public benefits, just as a court applying rational-basis review under the Equal Protection Clause must strike down a government classification that is clearly intended to injure a particular class of private parties, with only incidental or pretextual public justifications. See *Cleburne v. Cleburne Living Center, Inc.*, 473 U.S. 432, 446–447, 450, 105 S.Ct. 3249, 87 L.Ed.2d 313 (1985).... *Department of Agriculture v. Moreno*, 413 U.S. 528, 533–536, 93 S.Ct. 2821, 37 L.Ed.2d 782 (1973). As the trial court in this case was correct to observe, "Where the purpose [of a taking] is economic development and that development is to be carried out by private parties or private parties will be benefited, the court must decide if the stated public purpose—economic advantage to a city sorely in need of it—is only incidental to the benefits that will be confined on private parties of a development plan." 2 App. to Pet. for Cert. 263. See also *ante*, at 2661.

A court confronted with a plausible accusation of impermissible favoritism to private parties should treat the objection as a serious one and review the record to see if it has merit, though with the presumption that the government's actions were reasonable and intended to serve a public purpose. Here, the trial court conducted a careful and extensive inquiry into "whether, in fact, the development plan is of primary benefit to ... the developer [*i.e.*, Corcoran Jennison], and private businesses which may eventually locate in the plan area [*e.g.*, Pfizer], and in that regard, only of incidental benefit to the city." 2 App. to Pet. for Cert. 261. The trial court considered testimony from government officials and corporate officers; id, at 266–271; documentary evidence of communications between these parties, *ibid*; respondents' awareness of New London's depressed economic condition and evidence corroborating the validity of this concern, Ed, at 272–273, 278–279; the substantial commitment of public funds by the State to the development project before most of the private beneficiaries were known, *id.*, at 276; evidence that respondents reviewed a variety of development plans and chose a private developer from a group of applicants rather than picking out a particular transferee beforehand, *id.*, at 273, 278; and the fact that the other private beneficiaries of the project are still unknown because the office space proposed to be built has not yet been rented, *id.*, at 278.

* * *

JUSTICE O'CONNOR, with whom THE CHIEF JUSTICE, JUSTICE SCALIA, and JUSTICE THOMAS join, dissenting.

Over two centuries ago, just after the Bill of Rights was ratified, Justice Chase wrote:

> "An ACT of the Legislature (for I cannot call it a law) contrary to the great first principles of the social compact, cannot be considered a rightful exercise of legislative authority.... A few instances will suffice to explain what I mean.... [A] law that takes property from A. and gives it to B: It is against all reason and justice, for a people to entrust a Legislature with SUCH powers; and, therefore, it cannot be presumed that they have done it." *Calder v. Bull*, 3 Dall. 386, 388, 1 L.Ed. 648 (1798 (emphasis deleted).

Today the Court abandons this long-held, basic limitation on government power. Under the banner of economic development, all private property is now vulnerable to being taken and transferred to another private owner, so long as it might be upgraded—*i.e.*, given to an owner who will use it in a way that the legislature deems more beneficial to the public—in the process. To reason, as the Court does, that the incidental public benefits resulting from the subsequent ordinary use of private property render economic development takings "for public use" is to wash out any distinction between private and public use of property— and thereby effectively to delete the words "for public use" from the Takings Clause of the Fifth Amendment. Accordingly I respectfully dissent.

I

Petitioners are nine resident or investment owners of 15 homes in the Fort Trumbull neighborhood of New London, Connecticut. Petitioner Wilhelmina Dery, for example, lives in a house on Walbach Street that has been in her family for over 100 years. She was born in the house in 1918; her husband, petitioner Charles Dery, moved into the house when they married in 1946. Their son lives next door with his family in the house he received as a wedding gift, and joins his parents in this suit. Two petitioners keep rental properties in the neighborhood.

In February 1998, Pfizer Inc., the pharmaceuticals manufacturer, announced that it would build a global research facility near the Fort Trumbull neighborhood. Two months later, New London's city council gave initial approval for the New London Development Corporation (NLDC) to prepare the development plan at issue here. The NLDC is a private, nonprofit corporation whose mission is to assist the city council in economic development planning. It is not elected by popular vote, and its directors and employees are privately appointed. Consistent with its mandate, the NLDC generated an ambitious plan for redeveloping 90 acres of Fort Trumbull in order to "complement the facility that Pfizer was planning to build, create jobs, increase tax and other revenues, encourage public access to and use of the city's waterfront, and eventually 'build momentum' for the revitalization of the rest of the city." App. to Pet. for Cert. 5.

Petitioners own properties in two of the plan's seven parcels— parrcel 3 and Parcel 4A. Under the plan, Parcel 3 is slated for the construction of research and office space as a market develops for such space. It will also retain the existing Italian Dramatic Club (a private cultural organization) though the homes of three plaintiffs in that parcel are to be demolished. Parcel 4A is slated, mysteriously, for " 'park support.' " *Id.*, at 345–346. At oral argument, counsel for respondents conceded the vagueness of this proposed use, and offered that the parcel might eventually be used for parking. Tr. of Oral Arg. 36.

To save their homes, petitioners sued New London and the NLDC, to whom New London has delegated eminent domain power. Petitioners maintain that the Fifth Amendment prohibits the NLDC from condemning their properties for the sake of an economic development plan. Petitioners are not hold-outs; they do not seek increased compensation, and none is opposed to new development in the area. Theirs is an objection in principle: They claim that the NLDC's proposed use for their confiscated property is not a "public" one for purposes of the Fifth Amendment. While the government may take their homes to build a road or a railroad or to eliminate a property use that harms the public, say petitioners, it cannot take their property for the private use of other owners simply because the new owners may make more productive use of the property.

The Fifth Amendment to the Constitution, made applicable to the States by the Fourteenth Amendment, provides that "private property [shall not] be taken for public use, without just compensation." When interpreting the Constitution, we begin with the unremarkable presumption that every word in the document has independent meaning, "that no word was unnecessarily used, or needlessly added." *Wright v. United States*, 302 U.S. 583, 588, 58 S.Ct. 395, 82 L.Ed. 439 (1938). In keeping with that presumption, we have read the Fifth Amendment's language to impose two distinct conditions on the exercise of eminent domain: "the taking must be for a 'public use' and 'just compensation' must be paid to the owner." *Brown v. Legal Foundation of Wash.*, 538 U.S. 216, 231–232, 123 S.Ct. 1406, 155 L.Ed.2d 376 (2003).

These two limitations serve to protect "the security of Property," which Alexander Hamilton described to the Philadelphia Convention as one of the "great obj of Gov 1 Records of the Federal Convention of 1787, p. 302 (M. Farrand ed.1934). Together they ensure stable property ownership by providing safeguards against excessive, unpredictable, or unfair use of the government's eminent domain power—particularly against those owners who, for whatever reasons, may be unable to protect themselves in the political process against the majority's will.

* * *

The Court's holdings in *Berman* and *Midkiff* were true to the principle underlying the Public Use Clause. In both those cases, the extraordinary, precondemnation use of the targeted property inflicted affirmative on society—in *Berman* through blight resulting from extreme poverty and in *Midkiff* through oligopoly resulting from extreme wealth. And in both cases, the relevant legislative body had found that eliminating the existing property use was necessary to remedy the harm. Berman, supra, at 34–35, 75 S.Ct. 98; *Midkiff supra*, at 232, 104 S.Ct. 2321 Thus a public purpose was realized when the harmful use was eliminated. Because each taking directly achieved a public benefit, it did not matter that the property was turned over to private use. Here, in contrast, New London does not claim that Susette Kelo's and Wilhehnina Dery well-maintained homes are the source of any social harm. Indeed, it could not so claim without adopting the absurd argument that any single-family home that might be razed to make way for an apartment building, or any church that might be replaced with a retail store, or any small business that might be more lucrative if it were instead part of a national franchise, is inherently harmful to society and thus within the government's power to condemn.

In moving away from our decisions sanctioning the condemnation of harmful property use, the Court today significantly expands the meaning of public use. It holds that the sovereign may take private property currently put to ordinary private use, and give it over for new, ordinary private use, so long as the new use is predicted to generate some secondary benefit for the public—such as increased tax revenue, more jobs, maybe even aesthetic pleasure. But nearly any lawful use of real private property can be said to generate some incidental benefit to the public. Thus, if predicted (or even guaranteed) positive side-effects are enough to render transfer from one private party to another constitutional, then the words "for public use" do not realistically exclude any takings, and thus do not exert any constraint on the eminent domain power.

There is a sense in which this troubling result follows from errant language in *Berman* and *Midkiff*. In discussing whether takings within a blighted neighborhood were for a public use, *Berman* began by observing: "We deal, in other words, with what traditionally has been known as the police power." 348 U.S., at 32, 75 S.Ct. 98. From there it declared that "[o]nce the object is within the authority of Congress, the right to realize it through the exercise of eminent domain is clear." *Id.,* at 33, 75 S.Ct. 98. Following up, we said in *Midkiff* that "[t]he 'public use' requirement is coterminous with the scope of a sovereign's police powers." 467 U.S., at 240, 104 S.Ct. 2321. This language was unnecessary to the specific holdings of those decisions. *Berman* and *Midkiff* simply did not put such language to the constitutional test, because the takings in those cases were within the police power but also for "public use" for the reasons I have described. The case before us now demonstrates why, when deciding if a taking's purpose is constitutional, the police power and "public use" cannot always be equated.

The Court protests that it does not sanction the bare transfer from A to B for B's benefit. It suggests two limitations on what can be taken after today's decision. First, it maintains a role for courts in ferreting out takings whose sole purpose is to bestow a benefit on the private transferee—without detailing how courts are to conduct that complicated inquiry. *Ante,* at 2661. For his part, Justice KENNEDY suggests that courts may divine illicit purpose by a careful review of the record and the process by which a legislature arrived at the decision to take—without specifying what courts should look for in a case with different facts, how they will know if they have found it, and what to do if they do not. *Ante,* at 2669–2670 (concurring opinion). Whatever the details of Justice KENNEDY's as-yet-undisclosed test, it is difficult to envision anyone but the "stupid staff[er]" failing it. See *Lucas v. South Carolina Coastal Council,* 505 U.S. 1003, 1025–1026, n. 12, 112 S.Ct. 2886, 120 L.Ed.2d 798 (1992). The trouble with economic development takings is that private benefit and incidental public benefit are, by definition, merged and mutually reinforcing. In this case, for example, any boon for Pfizer or the plan's developer is difficult to disaggregate from the promised public gains in taxes and jobs. See App. to Pet. for Cert. 275–277.

Even if there were a practical way to isolate the motives behind a given taking, the gesture toward a purpose test is theoretically flawed. If it is true that incidental public benefits from new private use are enough to ensure the "public purpose" in a taking, why should it matter, as far as the Fifth Amendment is concerned, what inspired the taking in the first place? How much the government does or does not desire to benefit a favored private party has no bearing on whether an economic development taking will or will not generate secondary benefit for the public. And whatever the reason for a given condemnation, the effect is the same from the constitutional perspective—private property is forcibly relinquished to new private ownership.

A second proposed limitation is implicit in the Court's opinion. The logic of today's decision is that eminent domain may only be used to upgrade—not downgrade—property. At best this makes the Public Use Clause redundant with the Due Process Clause, which already prohibits irrational government action. See *Lingle,* 544 U.S. 528, 125 S.Ct. 2074

(2005). The Court rightfully admits, however, that the judiciary cannot get bogged down in predictive judgments about whether the public will actually be better off after a property transfer. In any event, this constraint has no realistic import. For who among us can say she already makes the most productive or attractive possible use of her property? The specter of condemnation hangs over all property. Nothing is to prevent the State from replacing any Motel 6 with a Ritz–Carlton, any home with a shopping mall, or any farm with a factory...

JUSTICE THOMAS dissenting. [Omitted.—Eds.]

Notes and Questions

1. You will notice that while the language of the Fifth Amendment refers to "public use," the Court in *Kelo* instead requires only "public purpose." This is a change that was effected in *Berman v. Parker.* Is this a significant change? Does it anticipate or allow any broader government functions than might be allowed under a requirement that property may be taken only for a public use? Is this a case about whether the courts or elected bodies are in a "better" position to determine the common good?

2. Does the Court in *Kelo* set a substantive standard for "public purpose" or a process standard? Does its requirement that the public purpose be "conceivable" and the method chosen to achieve the purpose be "rational" and part of an integrated development plan limit the authority of the government? Or, is the standard in *Kelo* a process standard; i.e., the government entity must simply "*determine* [that] there are substantial reasons for an exercise of the taking power"? (Emphasis added.)

3. What purposes does the public purpose limitation serve? If the property owner is justly compensated, what more is needed?

4. Under *Kelo,* could a city council exercise its power of eminent domain, within the bounds set by the state, to acquire land for a privately owned shopping mall? What is the public purpose served by such an acquisition? Is a mall the modern equivalent of a public park? Could the council simply grant the power of eminent domain directly to the mall developers, skipping the middleman?

5. Do you agree with the majority that a "bright-line" rule rejecting private to private transfers to promote economic development is not feasible because "there is no principled way of distinguishing economic development from the other public purposes that [the Court has] recognized?" Recall *County of Wayne v. Hathcock,* 471 Mich. 445, 684 N.W.2d 765 (2004) discussed in the introductory note preceding *Kelo.* In *Hathcock* the Michigan Supreme Court, relying heavily on Justice Ryan's dissent in *Poletown,* defined the public use requirement of the Michigan Constitution to limit the power of eminent domain to the following classes of cases:

> [T]he exercise of eminent domain for private corporations has been limited to those enterprises generating public benefits whose very *existence* depends on the use of land that can be assembled only by the coordination central government alone is capable of achieving (emphasis in original).

Justice Ryan listed "highways, railroads, canals, and other instrumentalities of commerce" as examples of this brand of necessity. A corporation constructing a railroad, for example, must lay track so that it forms a more or less straight path from point A to point B. If a property owner between points A and B holds out—say, for example, by refusing to sell his land for any amount less than fifty times its appraised value—the construction of the railroad is halted unless and until the railroad accedes to the property owner's demands. And if owners of adjoining properties receive word of the original property owner's windfall, they too will refuse to sell.

The likelihood that property owners will engage in this tactic makes the acquisition of property for railroads, gas lines, highways, and other such "instrumentalities of commerce" a logistical and practical nightmare. Accordingly, this Court has held that the exercise of eminent domain in such cases—in which collective action is needed to acquire land for vital instrumentalities of commerce—is consistent with the constitutional "public use" requirement. * * *

Second, this Court has found that the transfer of condemned property to a private entity is consistent with the constitution's "public use" requirement when the private entity remains accountable to the public in its use of that property. Indeed, we disapproved of the use of eminent domain in *Portage Twp. Bd. of Health* in part because the entity acquiring the condemned land would not be subject to public oversight. As Justice Ryan observed:

[T]his Court disapproved condemnation that would have facilitated the generation of water power by a private corporation because the power company "will own, lease, use, and control" the water power. In addition, [we] warned, "Land cannot be taken, under the exercise of the power of eminent domain, unless, after it is taken, it will be devoted to the use of the public, *independent of the will of the corporation taking it.*"

In contrast, we concluded in *Lakehead Pipe Line Co. v. Dehn* that the state retained sufficient control of a petroleum pipeline constructed by the plaintiff on condemned property. We noted specifically that the plaintiff had "pledged itself to transport in intrastate commerce," that plaintiffs pipeline was used pursuant to directions from the Michigan Public Service Commission, and that the state would be able to enforce those obligations, should the need arise.

Finally, condemned land may be transferred to a private entity when the selection of the land to be condemned is itself based on public concern. In Justice Ryan's words, the property must be selected on the basis of "facts of independent public significance," meaning that the underlying purposes for resorting to condemnation, rather than the subsequent use of condemned land, must satisfy the Constitution's public use requirement. The primary example of a condemnation in this vein is found in *In re Slum Clearance*, a 1951 decision from this Court. In that case, we considered the constitutionality of Detroit's condemnation of blighted housing and its subsequent resale of those properties to private persons. The city's *controlling purpose* in condemning the properties was to remove unfit housing and thereby advance public health and safety; subsequent resale of the land cleared of blight was "incidental" to this goal. We concluded, therefore, that the condemnation was indeed a "public use," despite the fact that the condemned properties would inevitably be put to private use. *In re Slum Clearance* turned on the fact that the act of condemnation *itself* rather than the use to which the condemned land eventually would be put, was a public use. Thus, as Justice Ryan observed, the condemnation was a "public use" because the land was selected on the basis of "facts of independent public significance"—namely, the need to remedy urban blight for the sake of public health and safety.

Does *Hathcock* draw a bright-line test for the use of eminent domain in private to private transfers? Is the test a principled one? Does it give government sufficient flexibility to address the evolving needs of society?

6. As the Court expressly noted in *Kelo*, nothing in that decision or the U.S. constitution restricts the States from adopting a more restrictive definition of the public use requirement. Many States have commenced to do just that. See for example Ohio Senate Bill 167 (2005) which establishes "until December 31, 2006, a moratorium on the use of eminent domain by any entity of the state government or any political subdivision of the state to take, without the owner's consent, private property that is in an unblighted area when the primary purpose for the taking is economic development that will ultimately result in ownership of the property being vested in another private person . . . "

The U.S. House of Representatives has taken similar action as the following article from the Associated Press (November 11, 2005) discusses:

> Conservative defenders of private property and liberal protectors of the poor joined in an overwhelming House vote to prevent local and state governments from seizing homes and businesses for use in economic development projects.
>
> The House legislation, passed 376–38, was in response to a widely criticized 5–4 ruling by the Supreme Court last June that allowed eminent domain authority to be used to obtain land for tax revenue-generating commercial purposes.
>
> That decision, said the House's third-ranked Republican, Deborah Pryce of Ohio, "dealt a blow to the rights of property owners across the country."
>
> The bill would withhold for two years all federal economic development funds from states and localities that use economic development as a rationale for property seizures. It also would bar the federal government from using eminent domain powers for economic development.
>
> It now goes to the Senate, where Sen. John Corwyn, R–Texas, has introduced similar legislation.
>
> The ruling in *Kelo v. City of New London* allowed the Connecticut city to exercise state eminent domain law to require several homeowners to cede their property for commercial use.

Conservatives were in the forefront in arguing that this was a dangerous interpretation of the "takings clause" in the Fifth Amendment of the Constitution that allows the government to seize property for public use, with just compensation.

"Governments should not be able to bulldoze a person's home or business to benefit other individuals," said Rep. Henry Bonilla, R–Texas.

Liberals warned that it could make it easier to tear down poor neighborhoods. "We don't need you on this one," Rep. Maxine Waters, D–Calif., said to those arguing that eminent domain can lead to beneficial urban renewal projects." We need you to respect the right of those minorities and those poor people to hold on to what is their own."

B. HAS PROPERTY BEEN TAKEN?

In *Kelo,* the government entity involved did not deny that it had "taken" property. It had, after all, acquired title to the land, extinguishing all property rights of the landowners, through eminent domain. Other situations are not so clear on this issue, however; and they produce the most difficult questions in takings litigation. Bright lines are hard to come by, but consider the following case:

1. *Per Se Takings*

LORETTO v. TELEPROMPTER MANHATTAN CATV CORP. ET AL.

Supreme Court of the United States, 1982.
458 U.S. 419, 102 S.Ct. 3164, 73 L.Ed.2d 868.

Justice Marshall delivered the opinion of the Court.

This case presents the question whether a minor but permanent physical occupation of an owner's property authorized by government constitutes a "taking" of property for which just compensation is due under the Fifth and Fourteenth Amendments of the Constitution. New York law provides that a landlord must permit a cable television company to install its cable facilities upon his property. In this case, the cable installation occupied portions of appellant's roof and the side of her building. The New York Court of Appeals ruled that this appropriation does not amount to a taking. 53 N.Y.2d 124, 423 N.E.2d 320 (1981). Because we conclude that such a physical occupation of property is a taking, we reverse.

* * * The New York Court of Appeals described the installation as follows:

"On June 1, 1970 TelePrompter installed a cable slightly less than one-half inch in diameter and of approximately 30 feet in length along the length of the building about 18 inches above the roof top, and directional taps, approximately 4 inches by 4 inches by 4 inches, on the front and rear of the roof. By June 8, 1970 the cable had been extended another 4 to 6 feet and cable had been run from the directional taps to the adjoining building at 305 West 105th Street."

TelePrompter also installed two large silver boxes along the roof cables. The cables are attached by screws or nails penetrating the masonry at approximately two-foot intervals, and other equipment is installed by bolts.

Initially, TelePrompter's roof cables did not service appellant's building. They were part of what could be described as a cable "highway" circumnavigating the city block, with service cables periodically dropped over the front or back of a building in which a tenant desired service. Crucial to such a network is the use of so-called "crossovers"— cable lines extending from one building to another in order to reach a new group of tenants. Two years after appellant purchased the building, TelePrompter connected a "noncrossover" line—*i.e.,* one that provided CATV service to appellant's own tenants—by dropping a line to the first floor down the front of appellant's building.

Prior to 1973, TelePrompter routinely obtained authorization for its installations from property owners along the cable's route, compensating the owners at the standard rate of 5% of the gross revenues that TelePrompter realized from the particular property. To facilitate tenant access to CATV, the State of New York enacted § 828 of the Executive Law, effective January 1, 1973. Section 828 provides that a landlord may not "interfere with the installation of cable television facilities upon his property or premises," and may not demand payment from any tenant for permitting CATV, or demand payment from any CATV company "in excess of any amount which the [State Commission on Cable Television] shall, by regulation, determine to be reasonable." The landlord may, however, require the CATV company or the tenant to bear the cost of installation and to indemnify for any damage caused by the installation. Pursuant to § 828(1)(b), the State Commission has ruled that a one-time $1 payment is the normal fee to which a landlord is entitled. The Commission ruled that this nominal fee, which the Commission concluded was equivalent to what the landlord would receive if the property were condemned pursuant to New York's Transportation Corporations Law, satisfied constitutional requirements "in the absence of a special showing of greater damages attributable to the taking."

* * *

* * * We conclude that a permanent physical occupation authorized by government is a taking without regard to the public interests that it may serve. * * *

The Court [has] noted that no "set formula" exists to determine, in all cases, whether compensation is constitutionally due for a government restriction of property. Ordinarily, the Court must engage in "essentially ad hoc, factual inquiries." [ ] But the inquiry is not standardless. * * *

When faced with a constitutional challenge to a permanent physical occupation of real property, this Court has invariably found a taking. * * *

* * *

The historical rule that a permanent physical occupation of another's property is a taking has more than tradition to commend it. Such an appropriation is perhaps the most serious form of invasion of an owner's property interests. To borrow a metaphor, [   ], the government does not simply take a single "strand" from the "bundle" of property rights: it chops through the bundle, taking a slice of every strand.

Property rights in a physical thing have been described as the rights "to possess, use and dispose of it." [   ] To the extent that the government permanently occupies physical property, it effectively destroys *each* of these rights. First, the owner has no right to possess the occupied space himself, and also has no power to exclude the occupier from possession and use of the space. The power to exclude has traditionally been considered one of the most treasured strands in an owner's bundle of property rights. [   ]

* * *

Second, the permanent physical occupation of property forever denies the owner any power to control the use of the property; he not only cannot exclude others, but can make no nonpossessory use of the property. Although deprivation of the right to use and obtain a profit from property is not, in every case, independently sufficient to establish a taking, [   ], it is clearly relevant. Finally, even though the owner may retain the bare legal right to dispose of the occupied space by transfer or sale, the permanent occupation of that space by a stranger will ordinarily empty the right of any value, since the purchaser will also be unable to make any use of the property.

Moreover, an owner suffers a special kind of injury when a *stranger* directly invades and occupies the owner's property. [P]roperty law has long protected an owner's expectation that he will be relatively undisturbed at least in the possession of his property. To require, as well, that the owner permit another to exercise complete dominion literally adds insult to injury. [   ] Furthermore, such an occupation is qualitatively more severe than a regulation of the *use* of property, even a regulation that imposes affirmative duties on the owner, since the owner may have no control over the timing, extent, or nature of the invasion.

The traditional rule also avoids otherwise difficult line-drawing problems. Few would disagree that if the State required landlords to permit third parties to install swimming pools on the landlords' rooftops for the convenience of the tenants, the requirement would be a taking. If the cable installation here occupied as much space, again, few would disagree that the occupation would be a taking. But constitutional protection for the rights of private property cannot be made to depend on the size of the area permanently occupied.

* * *

Finally, whether a permanent physical occupation has occurred presents relatively few problems of proof. The placement of a fixed structure on land or real property is an obvious fact that will rarely be subject to dispute. Once the fact of occupation is shown, of course, a court should consider the *extent* of the occupation as one relevant factor in determining the compensation due. For that reason, moreover, there is less need to consider the extent of the occupation in determining whether there is a taking in the first instance.

TelePrompter's cable installation on appellant's building constitutes a taking under the traditional test. The installation involved a direct physical attachment of plates, boxes, wires, bolts, and screws to the building, completely occupying space immediately above and upon the roof and along the building's exterior wall.

In light of our analysis, we find no constitutional difference between a crossover and a noncrossover installation. The portions of the installation necessary for both crossovers and noncrossovers permanently appropriate appellant's property. Accordingly, each type of installation is a taking.

* * * [O]ur holding today in no way alters the analysis governing the State's power to require landlords to comply with building codes and provide utility connections, mailboxes, smoke detectors, fire extinguishers, and the like in the common area of a building. So long as these regulations do not require the landlord to suffer the physical occupation of a portion of his building by a third party, they will be analyzed under the multifactor inquiry generally applicable to nonpossessory governmental activity.[17] [   ]

The judgment of the New York Court of Appeals is reversed, and the case is remanded for further proceedings not inconsistent with this opinion.

JUSTICE BLACKMUN, with whom JUSTICE BRENNAN and JUSTICE WHITE join, dissenting.

* * *

In a curiously anachronistic decision, the Court today acknowledges its historical disavowal of set formulae in almost the same breath as it constructs a rigid *per se* takings rule: "a permanent physical occupation authorized by government is a taking without regard to the public interests that it may serve." * * *

* * *

[W]hat does the Court mean by "permanent"? Since all "temporary limitations on the right to exclude" remain "subject to a more complex

---

17. If § 828 required landlords to provide cable installation if a tenant so desires, the statute might present a different question from the question before us, since the landlord would own the installation. Ownership would give the landlord rights to the placement, manner, use, and possibly the disposition of the installation. * * *

balancing process to determine whether they are a taking," the Court presumably describes a government intrusion that lasts forever. But as the Court itself concedes, § 828 does not require appellant to permit the cable installation forever, but only "[s]o long as the property remains residential and a CATV company wishes to retain the installation." This is far from "permanent."

The Court reaffirms that "States have broad power to regulate housing conditions in general and the landlord-tenant relationship in particular without paying compensation for all economic injuries that such regulation entails." Thus, § 828 merely defines one of the many statutory responsibilities that a New Yorker accepts when she enters the rental business. If appellant occupies her own building, or converts it into a commercial property, she becomes perfectly free to exclude Tele-Prompter from her one-eighth cubic foot of roof space. But once appellant chooses to use her property for rental purposes, she must comply with all reasonable government statutes regulating the landlord-tenant relationship. If § 828 authorizes a "permanent" occupation, and thus works a taking "without regard to the public interests that it may serve," then all other New York statutes that require a landlord to make physical attachments to his rental property also must constitute takings, even if they serve indisputably valid public interests in tenant protection and safety.

The Court denies that its theory invalidates these statutes, because they "do not require the landlord to suffer the physical occupation of a portion of his building by a third party." But surely this factor cannot be determinative, since the Court simultaneously recognizes that temporary invasions by third parties are not subject to a *per se* rule. Nor can the qualitative difference arise from the incidental fact that, under § 828, TelePrompter, rather than appellant or her tenants, owns the cable installation. * * *

In any event, under the Court's test, the "third party" problem would remain even if appellant herself owned the cable. So long as TelePrompter continuously passed its electronic signal through the cable, a litigant could argue that the second element of the Court's formula—a "physical touching" by a stranger—was satisfied and that § 828 therefore worked a taking. Literally read, the Court's test opens the door to endless metaphysical struggles over whether or not an individual's property has been "physically" touched. * * *

In sum, history teaches that takings claims are properly evaluated under a multifactor balancing test. By directing that all "permanent physical occupations" automatically are compensable, "without regard to whether the action achieves an important public benefit or has only minimal economic impact on the owner," the Court does not further equity so much as it encourages litigants to manipulate their factual allegations to gain the benefit of its *per se* rule. I do not relish the prospect of distinguishing the inevitable flow of certiorari petitions attempting to shoehorn insubstantial takings claims into today's "set formula."

Notes and Questions

1. The dissent spends considerable effort in arguing that the majority's distinction between permanent physical occupation and temporary physical occupation is not persuasive in the situation in *Loretto*. Aside from the question of whether the cable TV installations in *Loretto* are permanent or temporary, should the distinction generally make such a difference? Why or why not? Why did the majority want to draw such an impenetrable fortress around permanent physical occupations?

2. The majority holds that the Constitution requires that a landowner must be compensated for the value of the property lost due to the CATV installation, even though the financial loss is negligible. (The $1 compensation was found adequate by the New York Court of Appeal at *Loretto,* 58 N.Y.2d 143, 459 N.Y.S.2d 743, 446 N.E.2d 428 (1983).) But, it also states that regulations requiring landlords to install fire extinguishers or other devices, presumably at an expense far exceeding $1, would not be a *per se* taking requiring compensation, but would, instead, require a "multifactor" analysis. Why does the Court value, in terms of constitutional protection, what might be called the symbolic significance of property ownership in *Loretto* over the substantial financial losses of these other government-imposed burdens?

3. Loretto did not contest the public purpose of the cable TV statute. Could she have succeeded? In fact, did she "succeed" in her takings claim? Why might she have pursued this to the United States Supreme Court?

4. So far, we have seen two situations in which a taking is *always* found to have occurred and compensation is *always* required: 1) acquisition by the government of fee title, and 2) permanent physical occupation of property by the government or by a government-authorized third party. Beyond this lies the gray area of "regulation," sometimes a taking and sometimes not. Consider the following case in which the Court seventy years ago identified several of the factors that still define whether a taking has occurred in these gray areas.

2. Ad Hoc Takings

PENNSYLVANIA COAL COMPANY v. MAHON

Supreme Court of the United States, 1922.
260 U.S. 393, 43 S.Ct. 158, 67 L.Ed. 322.

MR. JUSTICE HOLMES delivered the opinion of the Court:

This is a bill in equity, brought by the defendants in error to prevent the Pennsylvania Coal Company from mining under their property in such way as to remove the supports and cause a subsidence of the surface and of their house. The bill sets out a deed executed by the Coal Company in 1878, under which the plaintiffs claim. The deed conveys the surface, but in express terms reserves the right to remove all the coal under the same, and the grantee takes the premises with the risk, and waives all claim for damages that may arise from mining out the coal. But the plaintiffs say that whatever may have been the Coal Company's rights, they were taken away by an Act of Pennsylvania, approved May 27, 1921, commonly known there as the Kohler Act. The court of common pleas found that, if not restrained, the defendant would cause the damage to prevent which the bill was brought, but denied an injunction, holding that the statute, if applied to this case, would be unconstitutional. On appeal, the supreme court of the state agreed that the defendant had contract and property rights protected by the Constitution of the United States, but held that the statute was a legitimate exercise of the police power, and directed a decree for the plaintiffs. A writ of error was granted, bringing the case to this court.

The statute forbids the mining of anthracite coal in such way as to cause the subsidence of, among other things, any structure used as a human habitation, with certain exceptions, including among them land where the surface is owned by the owner of the underlying coal, and is distant more than 150 feet from any improved property belonging to any other person. As applied to this case, the statute is admitted to destroy previously existing rights of property and contract. The question is whether the police power can be stretched so far.

Government hardly could go on if, to some extent, values incident to property could not be diminished without paying for every such change in the general law. As long recognized, some values are enjoyed under an implied limitation, and must yield to the police power. But obviously the implied limitation must have its limits or the contract and due process clauses are gone. One fact for consideration in determining such limits is the extent of the diminution. When it reaches a certain magnitude, in most if not in all cases there must be an exercise of eminent domain and compensation to sustain the act. So the question depends upon the particular facts. The greatest weight is given to the judgment of the legislature, but it always is open to interested parties to contend that the legislature has gone beyond its constitutional power.

This is the case of a single private house. No doubt there is a public interest even in this, as there is in every purchase and sale and in all that happens within the commonwealth. Some existing rights may be modified even in such a case. [   ] But usually, in ordinary private affairs the public interest does not warrant much of this kind of interference. A source of damage to such a house is not a public nuisance even if similar damage is inflicted on others in different places. The damage is not common or public. [   ] The extent of the public interest is shown by the statute to be limited, since the statute ordinarily does not apply to land when the surface is owned by the owner of the coal. Furthermore, it is not justified as a protection of personal safety. That could be provided for by notice. Indeed, the very foundation of this bill is that the defendant gave timely notice of its intent to mine under the house. On the other hand, the extent of the taking is great. It purports to abolish what is recognized in Pennsylvania as an estate in land,—a very valuable estate,—and what is declared by the court below to be a contract hitherto binding the plaintiffs. If we were called upon to deal with the plaintiffs' position alone we should think it clear that the statute does not disclose a public interest sufficient to warrant so extensive a destruction of the defendant's constitutionally protected rights.

* * *

It is our opinion that the act cannot be sustained as an exercise of the police power, so far as it affects the mining of coal under streets or cities in places where the right to mine such coal has been reserved. What makes the right to mine coal valuable is that it can be exercised with profit. To make it commercially impracticable to mine certain coal has very nearly the same effect for constitutional purposes as appropriating or destroying it. This we think that we are warranted in assuming that the statute does.

It is true that in Plymouth Coal Co. v. Pennsylvania, 232 U.S. 531, 58 L.Ed. 713, 34 Sup.Ct.Rep. 359, it was held competent for the legislature to require a pillar of coal to be left along the line of adjoining property, that, with the pillar on the other side of the line, would be a barrier sufficient for the safety of the employees of either mine in case the other should be abandoned and allowed to fill with water. But that was a requirement for the safety of employees invited into the mine, and secured an average reciprocity of advantage that has been recognized as a justification of various laws.

The rights of the public in a street purchased or laid out by eminent domain are those that it has paid for. If in any case its representatives have been so shortsighted as to acquire only surface rights, without the right of support, we see no more authority for supplying the latter without compensation than there was for taking the right of way in the first place, and refusing to pay for it because the public wanted it very much.

* * *

The general rule, at least, is that while property may be regulated to a certain extent, if regulation goes too far it will be recognized as a taking. We are in danger of forgetting that a strong public desire to improve the public condition is not enough to warrant achieving the desire by a shorter cut than the constitutional way of paying for the change. As we already have said, this is a question of degree—and therefore cannot be disposed of by general propositions. * * *

But the question at bottom is upon whom the loss of the changes desired should fall. So far as private persons or communities have seen fit to take the risk of acquiring only surface rights, we cannot see that the fact that their risk has become a danger warrants the giving to them greater rights than they bought.

Decree reversed.

MR. JUSTICE BRANDEIS, dissenting:

The Kohler Act prohibits, under certain conditions, the mining of anthracite coal within the limits of a city in such a manner or to such an extent "as to cause the subsidence of any dwelling or other structure used as a human habitation, or any factory, store, or other industrial or mercantile establishment in which human labor is employed." Coal in place is land; and the right of the owner to use his land is not absolute. He may not so use it as to create a public nuisance; and uses, once harmless, may, owing to changed conditions, seriously threaten the public welfare. Whenever they do, the legislature has power to prohibit such uses without paying compensation; and the power to prohibit extends alike to the manner, the character, and the purpose of the use.

Every restriction upon the use of property, imposed in the exercise of the police power, deprives the owner of some right theretofore enjoyed, and is, in that sense, an abridgment by the state of rights in property without making compensation. But restriction imposed to protect the public health, safety, or morals from dangers threatened is not a taking. The restriction here in question is merely the prohibition of a noxious use. The property so restricted remains in the possession of its owner. The state does not appropriate it or make any use of it. The state merely prevents the owner from making a use which interferes with paramount rights of the public. Whenever the use prohibited ceases to be noxious—as it may because of further change in local or social conditions,—the restriction will have to be removed, and the owner will again be free to enjoy his property as heretofore.

The restriction upon the use of this property cannot, of course, be lawfully imposed, unless its purpose is to protect the public. But the purpose of a restriction does not cease to be public because incidentally some private persons may thereby receive gratuitously valuable special benefits. * * *

It is said that one fact for consideration in determining whether the limits of the police power have been exceeded is the extent of the resulting diminution in value; and that here the restriction destroys existing rights of property and contract. But values are relative. If we are to consider the value of the coal kept in place by the restriction, we should compare it with the value of all other parts of the land. That is, with the value not of the coal alone, but with the value of the whole property. The rights of an owner, as against the public, are not increased by dividing the interests in his property into surface and subsoil. The sum of the rights in the parts cannot be greater than the rights in the whole. The estate of an owner in land is grandiloquently described as extending ab orco usque ad coelum. But I suppose no one would contend that by selling his interest above 100 feet from the surface he could prevent the state from limiting, by the police power, the height of structures in a city. And why should a sale of underground rights bar the state's power? For aught that appears the value of the coal kept in place by the restriction may be negligible as compared with the value of the whole property, or even as compared with that part of it which is represented by the coal remaining in place, and which may be extracted despite the statute. Ordinarily a police regulation, general in operation, will not be held void as to a particular property, although proof is offered that, owing to conditions peculiar to it, the restriction could not reasonably be applied.

* * *

[W]here the police power is exercised, not to confer benefits upon property owners, but to protect the public from detriment and danger, there is, in my opinion, no room for considering reciprocity of advantage. * * *

Notes and Questions

1. Justice Brandeis argues that the Kohler Act merely prohibits a nuisance by regulating anthracite mining methods. Review the material on nuisance that you covered earlier. Clearly, there is no property right to use land in a manner that injures another; so, a regulation prohibiting a nuisance does not take property. Do the facts in *Mahon* better support Holmes' or Brandeis' conclusion as to nuisance?

In Hadacheck v. Sebastian, 239 U.S. 394, 36 S.Ct. 143, 60 L.Ed. 348 (1915), the Court upheld as a legitimate use of the police power a city ordinance that made the operation of a brickyard or brick kiln within city limits illegal. The Court was not persuaded by the property owner's claim that his operation had been a legal and appropriate use of his land. The Court stated that protection of a vested interest by first occupation and use "would preclude development and fix a city forever in its primitive conditions. There must be progress and if in its march private interests are in the way they must yield to the good of the community." The Court commented that the clay on the land could still be used by removing it to another location for processing. How elastic should the concept of nuisance be in a takings case? See, for example, Just v. Marinette County, 56 Wis.2d 7, 201 N.W.2d 761 (1972), in which a state wetlands protection act was held not to constitute a taking: "We have here a restriction on the use of a citizen's property, not to secure a benefit for the public, but to prevent a harm from the change in the natural character of the citizen's property."

See also, Sax, Takings and the Police Power, 74 Yale L.J. 36 (1964) and Sax, Takings, Private Property and Public Rights, 81 Yale L.J. 149 (1971).

2. Justice Holmes in *Mahon* established three of the factors that have been used ever since to determine whether a regulation effects a taking of property. The opinion in *Mahon* is a model of brevity, especially by more modern Supreme Court standards; and Holmes' "tests" are stated in no more than a few words. Perhaps his most cryptic rule is that only regulation that goes "too far" is a taking. The other Holmes' tests are:

(a) The Balancing Test: The public interest in *Mahon*, according to Holmes, was inconsequential while the loss was "great." Recall that all takings of property by the government, even those for which the owner is compensated, require a public purpose. Here, though, the intensity or strength or breadth of the purpose apparently is balanced against the loss to detect whether a taking has occurred and compensation for the loss caused by the regulation is constitutionally required.

(b) Reciprocity of Advantage: Property ownership exists in a society. Although some regulations restricting property rights result in some loss, they also create gains. Things tend to average out over the long run, at least if the loss is not too heavily visited on a few. This analysis is most often used to justify zoning.

(c) Diminution in Value: If the loss reaches a "certain magnitude," a taking occurs. Holmes' single sentence leaves some questions unanswered, and the Court has spent seventy years trying to answer them.

3.   In 1987, the court decided a "triology" of cases in the takings area. In one of those cases, the Court revisited the coal mines. In Keystone Bituminous Coal Ass'n v. DeBenedictis, 480 U.S. 470, 107 S.Ct. 1232, 94 L.Ed.2d 472 (1987), the Court held that Pennsylvania's Bituminous Mine Subsidence and Land Conservation Act, which required that about 50 percent of the coal lying under certain structures be left unmined in order to avoid surface subsidence, did not take private property in violation of the Constitution. The 5–4 majority of the Court worked hard to distinguish *Keystone* from *Pennsylvania Coal.* According to the Court, "Unlike the Kohler Act, the character of the governmental action involved [in *Keystone*] leans heavily against finding a taking; the Commonwealth of Pennsylvania has acted to arrest what it perceives to be a significant threat to the common welfare." The Court in *Keystone* also commented that "there is no record in this case to support the finding, [unlike in *Pennsylvania Coal*], that the Subsidence Act makes it impossible for petitioners to profitably engage in their business, or that there has been undue interference with their investment-backed expectations." Observing that *Pennsylvania Coal* "has for 65 years been the foundation of our regulatory takings jurisprudence," the dissent by Justice Rehnquist argues that the public safety purpose of the Kohler Act was quite clear and, in fact, was quite similar in purpose to the Subsidence Act. The dissent also took issue with the majority's implication that this Act fell within the nuisance exception, discussed in the first note above: "We should hesitate to allow a regulation based on essentially economic concerns to be insulated from the dictates of the Fifth Amendment * * *". Finally the dissent criticizes the majority's conclusion that the Act did not take property because the mines could still be profitable: "There is no question that this coal is an identifiable and separable property interest. * * * [T]he 'bundle' of rights in this coal is sparse. * * * [T]his interest has been destroyed every bit as much as if the government had proceeded to mine the coal for its own use. The regulation, then, does not merely inhibit one strand in the bundle, but instead destroys completely any interest in a segment of property." Which analysis—the majority or the dissent—is more consistent with Holmes' opinion in *Pennsylvania Coal*? Does the result in *Keystone* simply reflect an increased acceptability of economic regulation?

PENN CENTRAL TRANSPORTATION COMPANY
v. CITY OF NEW YORK

Supreme Court of the United States, 1978.
438 U.S. 104, 98 S.Ct. 2646, 57 L.Ed.2d 631, reh. den.,
439 U.S. 883, 99 S.Ct. 226, 58 L.Ed.2d 198 (1978).

MR. JUSTICE BRENNAN delivered the opinion of the Court.

The question presented is whether a city may, as part of a comprehensive program to preserve historic landmarks and historic districts, place restrictions on the development of individual historic landmarks—in addition to those imposed by applicable zoning ordinances—without effecting a "taking" requiring the payment of "just compensation." Specifically, we must decide whether the application of New York City's Landmarks Preservation Law to the parcel of land occupied by Grand Central Terminal has "taken" its owners' property in violation of the Fifth and Fourteenth Amendments.

I

A

Over the past 50 years, all 50 States and over 500 municipalities have enacted laws to encourage or require the preservation of buildings and areas with historic or aesthetic importance. These nationwide legislative efforts have been precipitated by two concerns. The first is recognition that, in recent years, large numbers of historic structures, landmarks, and areas have been destroyed without adequate consideration of either the values represented therein or the possibility of preserving the destroyed properties for use in economically productive ways. The second is a widely shared belief that structures with special historic, cultural, or architectural significance enhance the quality of life for all. Not only do these buildings and their workmanship represent the lessons of the past and embody precious features of our heritage, they serve as examples of quality for today. * * *

New York City, responding to similar concerns and acting pursuant to a New York State enabling Act, adopted its Landmarks Preservation Law in 1965. See N.Y.C.Admin.Code, ch. 8–A, § 205–1.0 et seq. (1976). The city acted from the conviction that "the standing of [New York City] as a world-wide tourist center and world capital of business, culture and government" would be threatened if legislation were not enacted to protect historic landmarks and neighborhoods from precipitate decisions to destroy or fundamentally alter their character. § 205–1.0(a). The city believed that comprehensive measures to safeguard desirable features of the existing urban fabric would benefit its citizens in a variety of ways: e.g., fostering "civic pride in the beauty and noble accomplishments of the past"; protecting and enhancing "the city's attractions to tourists and visitors"; "support[ing] and stimul[ating] business and industry"; "strengthen[ing] the economy of the city"; and promoting "the use of historic districts, landmarks, interior landmarks and scenic landmarks for the education, pleasure and welfare of the people of the city." § 205–1.0(b).

The New York City law is typical of many urban landmark laws in that its primary method of achieving its goals is not by acquisitions of historic properties,[18] but rather by involving public entities in land-use decisions affecting these properties and providing services, standards, controls, and incentives that will encourage preservation by private owners and users. While the law does place special restrictions on landmark properties as a necessary feature to the attainment of its larger objectives, the major theme of the law is to ensure the owners of any such properties both a "reasonable return" on their investments and maximum latitude to use their parcels for purposes not inconsistent with the preservation goals.

The operation of the law can be briefly summarized. The primary responsibility for administering the law is vested in the Landmarks Preservation Commission (Commission), a broad based, 11–member agency[19] assisted by a technical staff. The Commission first performs the function, critical to any landmark preservation effort, of identifying properties and areas that have "a special character or special historical or aesthetic interest or value as part of the development, heritage or cultural characteristics of the city, state or nation." § 207–1.0(n); see § 207–1.0(h). If the Commission determines, after giving all interested parties an opportunity to be heard, that a building or area satisfies the ordinance's criteria, it will designate a building to be a "landmark," § 207–1.0(n), situated on a particular "landmark site," § 207–1.0(*o*), or will designate an area to be a "historic district," § 207–1.0(h). After the Commission makes a designation, New York City's Board of Estimate, after considering the relationship of the designated property "to the master plan, the zoning resolution, projected public improvements and any plans for the renewal of the area involved," § 207–2.0(g)(1), may modify or disapprove the designation, and the owner may seek judicial review of the final designation decision. Thus far, 31 historic districts and over 400 individual landmarks have been finally designated, and the process is a continuing one.

---

18. The consensus is that widespread public ownership of historic properties in urban settings is neither feasible nor wise. Public ownership reduces the tax base, burdens the public budget with costs of acquisitions and maintenance, and results in the preservation of public buildings as museums and similar facilities, rather than as economically productive features of the urban scene. See Wilson & Winkler, The Response of State Legislation to Historic Preservation, 36 Law & Contemp.Prob. 329, 330–331, 339–340 (1971).

19. The ordinance creating the Commission requires that it include at least three architects, one historian qualified in the field, one city planner or landscape architect, one realtor, and at least one resident of each of the city's five boroughs. N.Y.C. Charter § 534 (1976). In addition to the ordinance's requirements concerning the composition of the Commission, there is, according to a former chairman, a "prudent tradition" that the Commission include one or two lawyers, preferably with experience in municipal government, and several laymen with no specialized qualifications other than concern for the good of the city. Goldstone, Aesthetics in Historic Districts, 36 Law & Contemp.Prob. 379, 384–385 (1971).

Final designation as a landmark results in restrictions upon the property owner's options concerning use of the landmark site. First, the law imposes a duty upon the owner to keep the exterior features of the building "in good repair" to assure that the law's objectives not be defeated by the landmark's falling into a state of irremediable disrepair. See § 207–10.0(a). Second, the Commission must approve in advance any proposal to alter the exterior architectural features of the landmark or to construct any exterior improvement on the landmark site, thus ensuring that decisions concerning construction on the landmark site are made with due consideration of both the public interest in the maintenance of the structure and the landowner's interest in use of the property. See §§ 207–4.0 to 207–9.0.

In the event an owner wishes to alter a landmark site, three separate procedures are available through which administrative approval may be obtained. First, the owner may apply to the Commission for a "certificate of no effect on protected architectural features": that is, for an order approving the improvement or alteration on the ground that it will not change or affect any architectural feature of the landmark and will be in harmony therewith. See § 207–5.0. Denial of the certificate is subject to judicial review.

Second, the owner may apply to the Commission for a certificate of "appropriateness." See § 207–6.0. Such certificates will be granted if the Commission concludes—focusing upon aesthetic, historical, and architectural values—that the proposed construction on the landmark site would not unduly hinder the protection, enhancement, perpetuation, and use of the landmark. Again, denial of the certificate is subject to judicial review. Moreover, the owner who is denied either a certificate of no exterior effect or a certificate of appropriateness may submit an alternative or modified plan for approval. The final procedure—seeking a certificate of appropriateness on the ground of "insufficient return," see § 207–8.0— provides special mechanisms, which vary depending on whether or not the landmark enjoys a tax exemption, to ensure that designation does not cause economic hardship.

Although the designation of a landmark and landmark site restricts the owner's control over the parcel, designation also enhances the economic position of the landmark owner in one significant respect. Under New York City's zoning laws, owners of real property who have not developed their property to the full extent permitted by the applicable zoning laws are allowed to transfer development rights to contiguous parcels on the same city block. See New York City, Zoning Resolution Art. I, ch. 2, § 12–10 (1978) (definition of "zoning lot"). A 1968 ordinance gave the owners of landmark sites additional opportunities to transfer development rights to other parcels. Subject to a restriction that the floor area of the transferee lot may not be increased by more than 20% above its authorized level, the ordinance permitted transfers from a landmark parcel to property across the street or across a street intersection. In 1969, the law governing the conditions under which transfers from landmark parcels could occur was liberalized, see New York City

Zoning Resolutions 74–79 to 74–793, apparently to ensure that the Landmarks Law would not unduly restrict the development options of the owners of Grand Central Terminal. See Marcus, Air Rights Transfers in New York City, 36 Law & Contemp.Prob. 372, 375 (1971). The class of recipient lots was expanded to include lots "across a street and opposite to another lot or lots which except for the intervention of streets or street intersections f[or]m a series extending to the lot occupied by the landmark building[, provided that] all lots [are] in the same ownership." New York City Zoning Resolution 74–79 (emphasis deleted).[20] In addition, the 1969 amendment permits, in highly commercialized areas like midtown Manhattan, the transfer of all unused development rights to a single parcel. *Ibid.*

B

This case involves the application of New York City's Landmarks Preservation Law to Grand Central Terminal (Terminal). The Terminal, which is owned by the Penn Central Transportation Co. and its affiliates (Penn Central), is one of New York City's most famous buildings. Opened in 1913, it is regarded not only as providing an ingenious engineering solution to the problems presented by urban railroad stations, but also as a magnificent example of the French beaux-arts style.

* * * The Terminal itself is an eight-story structure which Penn Central uses as a railroad station and in which it rents space not needed for railroad purposes to a variety of commercial interests. The Terminal is one of a number of properties owned by appellant Penn Central in this area of midtown Manhattan. * * * At least eight of these are eligible to be recipients of development rights afforded the Terminal by virtue of landmark designation.

On August 2, 1967, following a public hearing, the Commission designated the Terminal a "landmark" and designated the "city tax block" it occupies a "landmark site." The Board of Estimate confirmed this action on September 21, 1967. Although appellant Penn Central had opposed the designation before the Commission, it did not seek judicial review of the final designation decision.

On January 22, 1968, appellant Penn Central, to increase its income, entered into a renewable 50–year lease and sublease agreement with appellant UGP Properties, Inc. (UGP), a wholly owned subsidiary of Union General Properties, Ltd., a United Kingdom corporation. Under the terms of the agreement, UGP was to construct a multistory office building above the Terminal. UGP promised to pay Penn Central $1

20. To obtain approval for a proposed transfer, the landmark owner must follow the following procedure. First, he must obtain the permission of the Commission which will examine the plans for the development of the transferee lot to determine whether the planned construction would be compatible with the landmark. Second, he must obtain the approbation of New York City's Planning Commission which will focus on the effects of the transfer on occupants of the buildings in the vicinity of the transferee lot and whether the landmark owner will preserve the landmark. Finally, the matter goes to the Board of Estimate, which has final authority to grant or deny the application. [ ]

million annually during construction and at least $3 million annually thereafter. The rentals would be offset in part by a loss of some $700,000 to $1 million in net rentals presently received from concessionaires displaced by the new building.

Appellants UGP and Penn Central then applied to the Commission for permission to construct an office building atop the Terminal. Two separate plans, both designed by architect Marcel Breuer and both apparently satisfying the terms of the applicable zoning ordinance, were submitted to the Commission for approval. The first, Breuer I, provided for the construction of a 55–story office building, to be cantilevered above the existing facade and to rest on the roof of the Terminal. The second, Breuer II Revised, called for tearing down a portion of the Terminal that included the 42d Street facade, stripping off some of the remaining features of the Terminal's facade, and constructing a 53–story office building. The Commission denied a certificate of no exterior effect on September 20, 1968. Appellants then applied for a certificate of "appropriateness" as to both proposals. After four days of hearings at which over 80 witnesses testified, the Commission denied this application as to both proposals.

* * *

Appellants did not seek judicial review of the denial of either certificate. Because the Terminal site enjoyed a tax exemption, remained suitable for its present and future uses, and was not the subject of a contract of sale, there were no further administrative remedies available to appellants. Further, appellants did not avail themselves of the opportunity to develop and submit other plans for the Commission's consideration and approval. Instead, appellants filed suit in New York Supreme Court, Trial Term, claiming, *inter alia,* that the application of the Landmarks Preservation Law had "taken" their property without just compensation in violation of the Fifth and Fourteenth Amendments and arbitrarily deprived them of their property without due process of law in violation of the Fourteenth Amendment. Appellants sought a declaratory judgment, injunctive relief barring the city from using the Landmarks Law to impede the construction of any structure that might otherwise lawfully be constructed on the Terminal site, and damages for the "temporary taking" that occurred between August 2, 1967, the designation date, and the date when the restrictions arising from the Landmarks Law would be lifted. The trial court granted the injunctive and declaratory relief, but severed the question of damages for a "temporary taking."[21]

21. Although that court suggested that any regulation of private property to protect landmark values was unconstitutional if "just compensation" were not afforded, it also appeared to rely upon its findings: first, that the cost to Penn Central of operating the Terminal building itself, exclusive of purely railroad operations, exceeded the revenues received from concessionaires and tenants in the Terminal; and second, that the special transferable development rights afforded Penn Central as an owner of a landmark site did not "provide compensation to plaintiffs or minimize the harm suffered by plaintiffs due to the designation of the Terminal as a landmark."

Appellees appealed, and the New York Supreme Court, Appellate Division, reversed. 50 A.D.2d 265, 377 N.Y.S.2d 20 (1975). The Appellate Division held that the restrictions on the development of the Terminal site were necessary to promote the legitimate public purpose of protecting landmarks and therefore that appellants could sustain their constitutional claims only by proof that the regulation deprived them of all reasonable beneficial use of the property. * * *

The New York Court of Appeals affirmed. 42 N.Y.2d 324, 397 N.Y.S.2d 914, 366 N.E.2d 1271 (1977). That court summarily rejected any claim that the Landmarks Law had "taken" property without "just compensation," *id.*, at 329, 397 N.Y.S.2d, at 917, 366 N.E.2d, at 1274, indicating that there could be no "taking" since the law had not transferred control of the property to the city, but only restricted appellants' exploitation of it. In that circumstance, the Court of Appeals held that appellants' attack on the law could prevail only if the law deprived appellants of their property in violation of the Due Process Clause of the Fourteenth Amendment. Whether or not there was a denial of substantive due process turned on whether the restrictions deprived Penn Central of a "reasonable return" on the "privately created and privately managed ingredient" of the Terminal. *Id.*, at 328, 397 N.Y.S.2d, at 916, 366 N.E.2d, at 1273.[22] The Court of Appeals concluded that the Landmarks Law had not effected a denial of due process because: (1) the landmark regulation permitted the same use as had been made of the Terminal for more than half a century; (2) the appellants had failed to show that they could not earn a reasonable return on their investment in the Terminal itself; (3) even if the Terminal proper could never operate at a reasonable profit some of the income from Penn Central's extensive real estate holdings in the area, which include hotels and office buildings, must realistically be imputed to the Terminal; and (4) the development rights above the Terminal, which had been made transferable to numerous sites in the vicinity of the Terminal, one or two of which were suitable for the construction of office buildings, were valuable to appellants and provided "significant, perhaps 'fair,' compensation for the loss of rights above the terminal itself." *Id.*, at 333–336, 397 N.Y.S.2d, at 922, 366 N.E.2d, at 1276–1278.

Observing that its affirmance was "[o]n the present record," and that its analysis had not been fully developed by counsel at any level of the New York judicial system, the Court of Appeals directed that counsel

---

22. The Court of Appeals suggested that in calculating the value of the property upon which appellants were entitled to earn a reasonable return, the "publicly created" components of the value of the property— *i.e.*, those elements of its value attributable to the "efforts of organized society" or to the "social complex" in which the Terminal is located—had to be excluded. However, since the record upon which the Court of Appeals decided the case did not, as that court recognized, contain a basis for segre- gating the privately created from the publicly created elements of the value of the Terminal site and since the judgment of the Court of Appeals in any event rests upon bases that support our affirmance see *infra*, this page, we have no occasion to address the question whether it is permissible or feasible to separate out the "social increments" of the value of property. See Costonis, The Disparity Issue: A Context for the *Grand Central Terminal* Decision, 91 Harv.L.Rev. 402, 416–417 (1977).

"should be entitled to present . . . any additional submissions which, in the light of [the court's] opinion, may usefully develop further the factors discussed." *Id.*, at 337, 397 N.Y.S.2d, at 922, 366 N.E.2d, at 1279. Appellants chose not to avail themselves of this opportunity and filed a notice of appeal in this Court. We noted probable jurisdiction. 434 U.S. 983 (1977). We affirm.

II

* * *

* * * The question of what constitutes a "taking" for purposes of the Fifth Amendment has proved to be a problem of considerable difficulty. While this Court has recognized that the "Fifth Amendment's guarantee * * * [is] designed to bar Government from forcing some people alone to bear public burdens which, in all fairness and justice, should be borne by the public as a whole," *Armstrong v. United States,* 364 U.S. 40, 49, 80 S.Ct. 1563, 1569, 4 L.Ed.2d 1554 (1960), this Court, quite simply, has been unable to develop any "set formula" for determining when "justice and fairness" require that economic injuries caused by public action be compensated by the government, rather than remain disproportionately concentrated on a few persons. * * *

In engaging in these essentially ad hoc, factual inquiries, the Court's decisions have identified several factors that have particular significance. The economic impact of the regulation on the claimant and, particularly the extent to which the regulation has interfered with distinct investment-backed expectations are, of course, relevant considerations. See *Goldblatt v. Hempstead, supra,* at 594. So, too, is the character of the governmental action. A "taking" may more readily be found when the interference with property can be characterized as a physical invasion by government, see, *e.g., United States v. Causby* 328 U.S. 256 (1946), than when interference arises from some public program adjusting the benefits and burdens of economic life to promote the common good. * * *

More importantly for the present case, in instances in which a state tribunal reasonably concluded that "the health, safety, morals, or general welfare" would be promoted by prohibiting particular contemplated uses of land, this Court has upheld land-use regulations that destroyed or adversely affected recognized real property interests. See *Nectow v. Cambridge,* 277 U.S. 183, 188, 48 S.Ct. 447, 448, 72 L.Ed. 842 (1928). Zoning laws are, of course, the classic example, see *Euclid v. Ambler Realty Co.,* 272 U.S. 365, 47 S.Ct. 114, 71 L.Ed. 303 (1926). * * *

* * *

Pennsylvania Coal Co. v. Mahon, 260 U.S. 393, 43 S.Ct. 158, 67 L.Ed. 322 (1922), is the leading case for the proposition that a state statute that substantially furthers important public policies may so frustrate distinct investment-backed expectations as to amount to a "taking." There the claimant had sold the surface rights to particular parcels of property, but expressly reserved the right to remove the coal thereunder. A Pennsylvania statute, enacted after the transactions, forbade any mining of coal that caused the subsidence of any house, unless the house was the property of the owner of the underlying coal and was more than 150 feet from the improved property of another. Because the statute made it commercially impracticable to mine the coal, and thus had nearly the same effect as the complete destruction of rights claimant had reserved from the owners of the surface land, the Court held that the statute was invalid as effecting a "taking" without just compensation. [   ]

* * *

In contending that the New York City law has "taken" their property in violation of the Fifth and Fourteenth Amendments, appellants make a series of arguments, which, while tailored to the facts of this case, essentially urge that any substantial restriction imposed pursuant to a landmark law must be accompanied by just compensation if it is to be constitutional. Before considering these, we emphasize what is not in dispute. Because this Court has recognized, in a number of settings, that States and cities may enact land-use restrictions or controls to enhance the quality of life by preserving the character and desirable aesthetic features of a city, appellants do not contest that New York City's objective of preserving structures and areas with special historic, architectural, or cultural significance is an entirely permissible governmental goal. They also do not dispute that the restrictions imposed on its parcel are appropriate means of securing the purposes of the New York City law. Finally, appellants do not challenge any of the specific factual premises of the decision below. They accept for present purposes both that the parcel of land occupied by Grand Central Terminal must, in its present state, be regarded as capable of earning a reasonable return, and that the transferable development rights afforded appellants by virtue of the Terminal's designation as a landmark are valuable, even if not as valuable as the rights to construct above the Terminal. In appellants' view none of these factors derogate from their claim that New York City's law has effected a "taking."

They first observe that the airspace above the Terminal is a valuable property interest. They urge that the Landmarks Law has deprived them of any gainful use of their "air rights" above the Terminal and that, irrespective of the value of the remainder of their parcel, the city has "taken" their right to this superadjacent airspace, thus entitling them to "just compensation" measured by the fair market value of these air rights.

* * * "Taking" jurisprudence does not divide a single parcel into discrete segments and attempt to determine whether rights in a particular segment have been entirely abrogated. In deciding whether a particular governmental action has effected a taking, this Court focuses rather both on the character of the action and on the nature and extent of the interference with rights in the parcel as a whole—here, the city tax block designated as the "landmark site."

Secondly, appellants, focusing on the character and impact of the New York City law, argue that it effects a "taking" because its operation has significantly diminished the value of the Terminal site. Appellants concede that the decisions sustaining other land-use regulations, which, like the New York City law, are reasonably related to the promotion of the general welfare, uniformly reject the proposition that diminution in property value, standing alone, can establish a "taking," see *Euclid v. Ambler Realty Co.*, 272 U.S. 365, 47 S.Ct. 114, 71 L.Ed. 303 (1926) (75% diminution in value caused by zoning law); *Hadacheck v. Sebastian,* 239 U.S. 394, 36 S.Ct. 143, 60 L.Ed. 348 (1915) (87½% diminution in value); and that the "taking" issue in these contexts is resolved by focusing on the uses the regulations permit. * * *

Stated baldly, appellants' position appears to be that the only means of ensuring that selected owners are not singled out to endure financial hardship for no reason is to hold that any restriction imposed on individual landmarks pursuant to the New York City scheme is a "taking" requiring the payment of "just compensation." Agreement with this argument would, of course, invalidate not just New York City's law, but all comparable landmark legislation in the Nation. We find no merit in it.

* * *

* * * It is, of course, true that the Landmarks Law has a more severe impact on some landowners than on others, but that in itself does not mean that the law effects a "taking." Legislation designed to promote the general welfare commonly burdens some more than others. The owners of the brickyard in *Hadacheck,* of the cedar trees in *Miller v. Schoene,* and of the gravel and sand mine in *Goldblatt v. Hempstead,* were uniquely burdened by the legislation sustained in those cases.[23] * * *

In any event, appellants' repeated suggestions that they are solely burdened and unbenefited is factually inaccurate. This contention overlooks the fact that the New York City law applies to vast numbers of structures in the city in addition to the Terminal—all the structures

---

23. Appellants attempt to distinguish these cases on the ground that, in each, government was prohibiting a "noxious" use of land and that in the present case, in contrast, appellants' proposed construction above the Terminal would be beneficial. We observe that the uses in issue in *Hadacheck, Miller,* and *Goldblatt* were perfectly lawful in themselves. They involved no "blameworthiness, ... moral wrongdoing or conscious act of dangerous risk-taking which induce[d society] to shift the cost to a pa[rt]icular individual." Sax, Takings and the Police Power, 74 Yale L.J. 36, 50 (1964). These cases are better understood as resting not on any supposed "noxious" quality of the prohibited uses but rather on the

ground that the restrictions were reasonably related to the implementation of a policy—not unlike historic preservation—expected to produce a widespread public benefit and applicable to all similarly situated property.

Nor, correlatively, can it be asserted that the destruction or fundamental alteration of a historic landmark is not harmful. The suggestion that the beneficial quality of appellants' proposed construction is established by the fact that the construction would have been consistent with applicable zoning laws ignores the development in sensibilities and ideals reflected in landmark legislation like New York City's.

contained in the 31 historic districts and over 400 individual landmarks, many of which are close to the Terminal. Unless we are to reject the judgment of the New York City Council that the preservation of landmarks benefits all New York citizens and all structures, both economically and by improving the quality of life in the city as a whole—which we are unwilling to do—we cannot conclude that the owners of the Terminal have in no sense been benefited by the Landmarks Law. Doubtless appellants believe they are more burdened than benefited by the law, but that must have been true, too, of the property owners in *Miller, Hadacheck, Euclid,* and *Goldblatt.*

Appellants' final broad-based attack would have us treat the law as an instance, like that in *United States v. Causby,* in which government, acting in an enterprise capacity, has appropriated part of their property for some strictly governmental purpose. Apart from the fact that *Causby* was a case of invasion of airspace that destroyed the use of the farm beneath and this New York City law has in nowise impaired the present use of the Terminal, the Landmarks Law neither exploits appellants' parcel for city purposes nor facilitates nor arises from any entrepreneurial operations of the city. The situation is not remotely like that in *Causby* where the airspace above the property was in the flight pattern for military aircraft. The Landmarks Law's effect is simply to prohibit appellants or anyone else from occupying portions of the airspace above the Terminal, while permitting appellants to use the remainder of the parcel in a gainful fashion. * * *

Rejection of appellants' broad arguments is not, however, the end of our inquiry, for all we thus far have established is that the New York City law is not rendered invalid by its failure to provide "just compensation" whenever a landmark owner is restricted in the exploitation of property interests, such as air rights, to a greater extent than provided for under applicable zoning laws. We now must consider whether the interference with appellants' property is of such a magnitude that "there must be an exercise of eminent domain and compensation to sustain [it]." *Pennsylvania Coal Co. v. Mahon,* 260 U.S., at 413, 43 S.Ct., at 159. That inquiry may be narrowed to the question of the severity of the impact of the law on appellants' parcel, and its resolution in turn requires a careful assessment of the impact of the regulation on the Terminal site.

Unlike the governmental acts in *Goldblatt, Miller, Causby, Griggs,* and *Hadacheck,* the New York City law does not interfere in any way with the present uses of the Terminal. Its designation as a landmark not only permits but contemplates that appellants may continue to use the property precisely as it has been used for the past 65 years: as a railroad terminal containing office space and concessions. So the law does not interfere with what must be regarded as Penn Central's primary expectation concerning the use of the parcel. More importantly, on this record, we must regard the New York City law as permitting Penn Central not only to profit from the Terminal but also to obtain a "reasonable return" on its investment.

* * *

On this record, we conclude that the application of New York City's Landmarks Law has not effected a "taking" of appellants' property. The restrictions imposed are substantially related to the promotion of the general welfare and not only permit reasonable beneficial use of the landmark site but also afford appellants opportunities further to enhance not only the Terminal site proper but also other properties.

Affirmed.

Mr. Justice Rehnquist, with whom The Chief Justice and Mr. Justice Stevens join, dissenting.

* * *

Only in the most superficial sense of the word can this case be said to involve "zoning." Typical zoning restrictions may, it is true, so limit the prospective uses of a piece of property as to diminish the value of that property in the abstract because it may not be used for the forbidden purposes. But any such abstract decrease in value will more than likely be at least partially offset by an increase in value which flows from similar restrictions as to use on neighboring properties. All property owners in a designated area are placed under the same restrictions, not only for the benefit of the municipality as a whole but also for the common benefit of one another. In the words of Mr. Justice Holmes, speaking for the Court in *Pennsylvania Coal Co. v. Mahon,* 260 U.S. 393, 415, 43 S.Ct. 158, 160, 67 L.Ed. 322 (1922), there is "an average reciprocity of advantage."

Where a relatively few individual buildings, all separated from one another, are singled out and treated differently from surrounding buildings, no such reciprocity exists. The cost to the property owner which results from the imposition of restrictions applicable only to his property and not that of his neighbors may be substantial—in this case, several million dollars—with no comparable reciprocal benefits. * * *

* * * In a very literal sense, the actions of appellees violated this constitutional prohibition. Before the city of New York declared Grand Central Terminal to be a landmark, Penn Central could have used its "air rights" over the Terminal to build a multistory office building, at an apparent value of several million dollars per year. Today, the Terminal cannot be modified in *any* form, including the erection of additional stories, without the permission of the Landmark Preservation Commission, a permission which appellants, despite good-faith attempts, have so far been unable to obtain. Because the Taking Clause of the Fifth Amendment has not always been read literally, however, the constitutionality of appellees' actions requires a closer scrutiny of this Court's interpretation of the three key words in the Taking Clause—"property," "taken," and "just compensation."

A

Appellees do not dispute that valuable property rights have been destroyed. * * *

While neighboring landowners are free to use their land and "air rights" in any way consistent with the broad boundaries of New York zoning, Penn Central, absent the permission of appellees, must forever maintain its property in its present state. The property has been thus subjected to a nonconsensual servitude not borne by any neighboring or similar properties.[24]

B

Appellees have thus destroyed—in a literal sense, "taken"—substantial property rights of Penn Central. While the term "taken" might have been narrowly interpreted to include only physical seizures of property rights, "the construction of the phrase has not been so narrow." * * * [A]n examination of the two exceptions where the destruction of property does *not* constitute a taking demonstrates that a compensable taking has occurred here.

1

As early as 1887, the Court recognized that the government can prevent a property owner from using his property to injure others without having to compensate the owner for the value of the forbidden use. * * *

Thus, there is no "taking" where a city prohibits the operation of a brickyard within a residential area, see *Hadacheck v. Sebastian,* 239 U.S. 394, 36 S.Ct. 143, 60 L.Ed. 348 (1915), or forbids excavation for sand and gravel below the water line, see *Goldblatt v. Hempstead,* 369 U.S. 590, 82 S.Ct. 987, 8 L.Ed.2d 130 (1962). Nor is it relevant, where the government is merely prohibiting a noxious use of property, that the government would seem to be singling out a particular property owner. *Hadacheck, supra,* at 413.[25]

The nuisance exception to the taking guarantee is not coterminous with the police power itself. The question is whether the forbidden use is dangerous to the safety, health, or welfare of others. * * *

Appellees are not prohibiting a nuisance. The record is clear that the proposed addition to the Grand Central Terminal would be in full compliance with zoning, height limitations, and other health and safety requirements. Instead, appellees are seeking to preserve what they believe to be an outstanding example of beaux-arts architecture. Penn Central is prevented from further developing its property basically because *too good* a job was done in designing and building it. The city of

24. It is, of course, irrelevant that appellees interfered with or destroyed property rights that Penn Central had not yet physically used. The Fifth Amendment must be applied with "reference to the uses for which the property is suitable, having regard to the existing business or wants of the community, *or such as may be reasonably expected in the immediate future.*" *Mississippi & Rum River Boom Co. v. Patterson,* 98 U.S. 403, 408, 25 L.Ed. 206 (1878) (emphasis added).

25. Each of the cases cited by the Court for the proposition that legislation which severely affects some landowners but not others does not effect a "taking" involved noxious uses of property. See *Hadacheck; Miller v. Schoene,* 276 U.S. 272, 48 S.Ct. 246, 72 L.Ed. 568 (1928); *Goldblatt.* See *ante,* at 2660–2661, 2664.

New York, because of its unadorned admiration for the design, has decided that the owners of the building must preserve it unchanged for the benefit of sightseeing New Yorkers and tourists.

Unlike land-use regulations, appellees' actions do not merely *prohibit* Penn Central from using its property in a narrow set of noxious ways. Instead, appellees have placed an *affirmative* duty on Penn Central to maintain the Terminal in its present state and in "good repair." Appellants are not free to use their property as they see fit within broad outer boundaries but must strictly adhere to their past use except where appellees conclude that alternative uses would not detract from the landmark. * * *

2

Even where the government prohibits a noninjurious use, the Court has ruled that a taking does not take place if the prohibition applies over a broad cross section of land and thereby "secure[s] an average reciprocity of advantage." *Pennsylvania Coal Co. v. Mahon*, 260 U.S., at 415, 43 S.Ct., at 160. It is for this reason that zoning does not constitute a "taking." While zoning at times reduces *individual* property values, the burden is shared relatively evenly and it is reasonable to conclude that on the whole an individual who is harmed by one aspect of the zoning will be benefited by another.

Here, however, a multimillion dollar loss has been imposed on appellants; it is uniquely felt and is not offset by any benefits flowing from the preservation of some 400 other "landmarks" in New York City. Appellees have imposed a substantial cost on less than one one-tenth of one percent of the buildings in New York City for the general benefit of all its people. It is exactly this imposition of general costs on a few individuals at which the "taking" protection is directed. The Fifth Amendment

> "prevents the public from loading upon one individual more than his just share of the burdens of government, and says that when he surrenders to the public something more and different from that which is exacted from other members of the public, a full and just equivalent shall be returned to him." *Monongahela Navigation Co. v. United States*, 148 U.S. 312, 325, 13 S.Ct. 622, 626, 37 L.Ed. 463 (1893).

* * *

As Mr. Justice Holmes pointed out in *Pennsylvania Coal Co. v. Mahon,* "the question at bottom" in an eminent domain case "is upon whom the loss of the changes desired should fall." 260 U.S., at 416, 43 S.Ct., at 160. The benefits that appellees believe will flow from preservation of the Grand Central Terminal will accrue to all the citizens of New York City. There is no reason to believe that appellants will enjoy a substantially greater share of these benefits. If the cost of preserving Grand Central Terminal were spread evenly across the entire population of the city of New York, the burden per person would be in cents per year—a minor cost appellees would surely concede for the benefit accrued. Instead, however, appellees would impose the entire cost of several million dollars per year on Penn Central. But it is precisely this sort of discrimination that the Fifth Amendment prohibits.

Appellees in response would argue that a taking only occurs where a property owner is denied *all* reasonable value of his property. The Court has frequently held that, even where a destruction of property rights would not *otherwise* constitute a taking, the inability of the owner to make a reasonable return on his property requires compensation under the Fifth Amendment. See, *e.g., United States v. Lynah,* 188 U.S., at 470, 23 S.Ct., at 357. But the converse is not true. A taking does not become a noncompensable exercise of police power simply because the government in its grace allows the owner to make some "reasonable" use of his property. "[I]t is the character of the invasion, not the amount of damage resulting from it, so long as the damage is substantial, that determines the question whether it is a taking."

* * *

Over 50 years ago, Mr. Justice Holmes, speaking for the Court, warned that the courts were "in danger of forgetting that a strong public desire to improve the public condition is not enough to warrant achieving the desire by a shorter cut than the constitutional way of paying for the change." *Pennsylvania Coal Co. v. Mahon,* 260 U.S., at 416, 43 S.Ct., at 160. The Court's opinion in this case demonstrates that the danger thus foreseen has not abated. The city of New York is in a precarious financial state, and some may believe that the costs of landmark preservation will be more easily borne by corporations such as Penn Central than the overburdened individual taxpayers of New York. But these concerns do not allow us to ignore past precedents construing the Eminent Domain Clause to the end that the desire to improve the public condition is, indeed, achieved by a shorter cut than the constitutional way of paying for the change.

Notes and Questions

1. Who better understood Holmes' tests—the majority or the dissenters in *Penn Central?* Would Penn Central have been victorious if Holmes had been on the bench for this case? Does it matter? Should takings analysis change over time as the public view of the appropriate role of government and the nature of private property rights changes? Or should takings analysis be the firewall between the vagaries of public opinion and the security of private property?

2. *Penn Central* added another test—the "reasonable investment backed expectation." What does this add? Does it simply expand protection for wealth? Is this the same as protecting property?

3. PER SE TAKINGS REVISITED

LUCAS v. SOUTH CAROLINA COASTAL COUNCIL

Supreme Court of the United States, 1992.
505 U.S. 1003, 112 S.Ct. 2886, 120 L.Ed.2d 798.

JUSTICE SCALIA delivered the opinion of the Court.

In 1986, petitioner David H. Lucas paid $975,000 for two residential lots on the Isle of Palms in Charleston County, South Carolina, on which he intended to build single-family homes. In 1988, however, the South Carolina Legislature enacted the Beachfront Management Act, S.C. Code Ann. § 48–39–250 *et seq.* (Supp.1990), which had the direct effect of barring petitioner from erecting any permanent habitable structures on his two parcels. [ ]A state trial court found that this prohibition rendered Lucas's parcels "valueless." [ ]This case requires us to decide whether the Act's dramatic effect on the economic value of Lucas's lots accomplished a taking of private property under the Fifth and Fourteenth Amendments requiring the payment of "just compensation." U.S. Const., Amdt. 5.

I

A

South Carolina's expressed interest in intensively managing development activities in the so-called "coastal zone" dates from 1977 when, in the aftermath of Congress's passage of the federal Coastal Zone Management Act of 1972, 86 Stat. 1280, as amended, 16 U.S.C. § 1451 *et seq.*, the legislature enacted a Coastal Zone Management Act of its own. See S.C. Code Ann. § 84–39–10 *et seq.* (1987). In its original form, the South Carolina Act required owners of coastal zone land that qualified as a "critical area" (defined in the legislation to include beaches and immediately adjacent sand dunes, § 48–39–10(J)) to obtain a permit from the newly created South Carolina Coastal Council (Council) (respondent here) prior to committing the land to a "use other than the use the critical area was devoted to on [September 28, 1977]" § 48–39–130(A).

In the late 1970's, Lucas and others began extensive residential development of the Isle of Palms, a barrier island situated eastward of the city of Charleston. Toward the close of the development cycle for one residential subdivision known as "Beachwood East," Lucas in 1986 purchased the two lots at issue in this litigation for his own account. No portion of the lots, which were located approximately 300 feet from the beach, qualified as a "critical area" under the 1977 Act; accordingly, at the time Lucas acquired these parcels, he was not legally obliged to obtain a permit from the Council in advance of any development activity. His intention with respect to the lots was to do what the owners of the immediately adjacent parcels had already done: erect single-family residences. He commissioned architectural drawing for this purpose.

The Beachfront Management Act brought Lucas's plans to an abrupt end. Under that 1988 legislation, the Council was directed to establish a "baseline" connecting the landward-most "point[s] of erosion . . . during the past forty years" in the region of the Isle of Psalms that includes Lucas's lots. S.C. Code Ann.§ 48–39–280(A)(2) (Supp.1988). In action not challenged here, the Council fixed this baseline landward of Lucas's parcels. That was significant, for under the Act construction of occupable improvements[26] was flatly prohibited seaward of a line drawn 20 feet landward of, and parallel to, the baseline. § 48–39–290(A).

The Act provided no exceptions.

B

Lucas promptly filed suit in the South Carolina Court of Common Pleas, contending that the Beachfront Management Act's construction bar effected a taking of his property without just compensation. Lucas did not take issue with the validity of the Act as a lawful exercise of South Carolina's police power, but contended that the Act's complete extinguishment of his property's value entitled him to compensation regardless of whether the legislature had acted in furtherance of legitimate police power objectives. Following a bench trial, the court agreed. Among its factual determinations was the finding that "at the time Lucas purchased the two lots, both were zoned for single-family residential construction and . . . there were no restrictions imposed upon such use of the property by either the State of South Carolina, the County of Charleston, or the Town of the Isle of Palms." [   ] The trial court finder found that the Beachfront Management Act decreed a permanent ban on construction insofar as Lucas's lots were concerned, and that this prohibition "deprive[d] Lucas of any reasonable economic use of the lots, . . . eliminated the unrestricted right of use, and render[ed] them valueless." [   ] The court thus concluded that Lucas's properties had been "taken" by operation of the Act, and it ordered respondent to pay "just compensation" in the amount of $1,232,387.50.[   ]

The Supreme Court of South Carolina reversed. It found dispositive what it described as Lucas's concession "that the Beachfront Management Act [was] properly and validly designed to preserve . . . South Carolina's beaches." [   ] Failing an attack on the validity of the statute as such, the court believed itself bound to accept the "uncontested . . . findings" of the South Carolina Legislature that new construction in the coastal zone—such as petitioner intended—threatened this public resource. [   ] The court ruled that when a regulation respecting the use of property is designed "to prevent serious public harm," [   ] no compensation is owing under the Takings Clause regardless of the regulation's effect on the property's value. . . .

We granted certiorari. [   ]

---

26. The Act did allow the construction of certain nonhabitable improvements, e.g., "wooden walkways no larger in width than six feet," and "small wooden decks no larger than one hundred forty-four square feet." §§ 48–39–290(A)(1) and (2).

* * *

III

A

Prior to Justice Holmes's exposition in *Pennsylvania Coal Co. v. Mahon,* 260 U.S. 393 (1922), it was generally thought that the Takings Clause reached only a "direct appropriation" of property, [ ] or the functional equivalent of a "practical ouster of [the owner's] possession," [ ] See also *Gibson v. United States,* 166 U.S. 269, 275–276 (1897). Justice Holmes recognized in Mahon, however, that if the protection against physical appropriations of private was to be meaningfully enforced, the government's power to redefine the range of interests included in the ownership of property was necessarily constrained by constitutional limits. [ ] If, instead, the uses of private property were subject to unbridled, uncompensated qualification under the police power, "the natural tendency of human nature [would be] to extend the qualification more and more until at last private property disappear[ed]." [ ] These considerations gave birth in that case to the oft-cited maxim that, "while property may be regulated to a certain extent, if regulation goes too far it will be recognized as a taking." [ ]

Nevertheless, our decision in Mahon offered little insight into when, and under what circumstances, a given regulation would be seen as going "too far" for purposes of the Fifth Amendment. In 70–odd years of succeeding "regulatory takings" jurisprudence, we have generally eschewed any " 'set formula' " for determining how far is too far, preferring to "engage[e] in ... essentially ad hoc, factual inquiries." [ ] We have, however, described at least two discrete categories of regulatory action as compensable without case-specific inquiry into the public interest advanced in support of the restraint. The first encompasses regulations that compel the property owner to suffer a physical "invasion" of his property. In general (at least with regard to permanent invasions), no matter how minute the intrusion, and no matter how weighty the public purpose behind it, we have required compensation. For example, in Loretto v. Teleprompter Manhattan CATV Corp., 458 U.S. 419 (1982), we determined that New York's law requiring landlords to allow television cable companies to emplace cable facilities in their apartment buildings constituted a taking, [ ]even though the facilities occupied at most only 1½ cubic feet of the landlords' property, [ ]

The second situation in which we have found categorical treatment appropriate is where regulation denies all economically beneficial or productive use of land. [ ]As we have said on numerous occasions, the Fifth Amendment is violated when land-use regulation "does not substantially advance legitimate state interests *or denies an owner economically viable use of his land.*" [ ].[27]

---

27. Regrettably, the rhetorical force of our "deprivation of all economically feasible use" rule is greater than its precision, since the rule does not make clear the "property interest" against which the loss of value is to be measured. When, for example, a regu-

We have never set forth the justification for this rule. Perhaps it is simply, as Justice Brennan suggested, that total deprivation of beneficial use is, from the landowner's point of view, the equivalent of a physical appropriation. See *San Diego Gas & Electric Co. v. San Diego*, 450 U.S., at 652 (dissenting opinion). "[F]or what is the land but the profits thereof[?]" 1 E. Coke, Institutes, ch. 1, § 1 (1st Am. ed. 1812). Surely, at least, in the extraordinary circumstance when *no* productive or economically beneficial use of land is permitted, it is less realistic to indulge our usual assumption that the legislature is simply "adjusting the benefits and burdens of economic life," [   ]in a manner that secures an "average reciprocity of advantage" to everyone concerned, [   ]And the *functional* basis for permitting the government, by regulation, to affect property values without compensation—that "Government hardly could go on if to some extent values incident to property could not be diminished without paying for every such change in the general law," [   ]does not apply to the relatively rare situations where the government has deprived a landowner of all economically beneficial uses.

On the other side of the balance, affirmatively supporting a compensation requirement, is the fact that regulations that leave the owner of land without economically beneficial or productive options for its use—typically, as here, by requiring land to be left substantially in its natural state—carry with them a heightened risk that private property is being pressed into some form of public service under the guise of mitigating serious public harm. [   ] As Justice Brennan explained: "From the government's point of view, the benefits flowing to the public from preservation of open space through regulation may be equally great as from creating a wildlife refuge through formal condemnation or increasing electricity production through a dam project that floods private property." *San Diego Gas & Elec. Co., supra*, at 652 (dissenting opinion).

lation requires a developer to leave 90% of a rural tract in its natural state, it is unclear whether we would analyze the situation as one in which the owner has been deprived of all economically beneficial use of the burdened portion of the tract, or as one in which the owner has suffered a mere diminution in value of the tract as a whole. (For an extreme—and, we think, unsupportable—view of the relevant calculus, see *Penn Central Transportation Co. v. New York City*, 42 N.Y.2d 324, 333–334, 366 N.E.2d 1271, 1276–1277 (1977), *aff'd*, 438 U.S. 104 (1978), where the state court examined the diminution in a particular parcel's value produced by a municipal ordinance in light of total value of the takings claimant's other holdings in the vicinity.) Unsurprisingly, this uncertainty regarding the composition of the denominator in our "deprivation" fraction has produced inconsistent pronouncements by the Court. Compare *Pennsylvania Coal Co. v. Mahon*, 260 U.S. 393, 414 (1922) (law restricting subsurface extraction of coal held to effect a taking), with *Keystone Bituminous Coal Assn. v. DeBenedictis*, 480 U.S. 470, 497–502 (1987) (nearly identical law held not to effect a taking); see also *id.*, at 515–520 (REHNQUIST, C.J., dissenting); Rose, *Mahon* Reconstructed: Why the Takings Issue is Still a Muddle, 57 S. Cal. L. Rev. 561, 566–569 (1984). The answer to this difficult question may lie in how the owner's reasonable expectations have been shaped by the State's law of property—*i.e.*, whether and to what degree the State's law has accorded legal recognition and protection to the particular interest in land with respect to which the takings claimant alleges a diminution in (or elimination of) value. In any event, we avoid this difficulty in the present case, since the "interest in land" that Lucas has pleaded (a fee simple interest) is an estate with a rich tradition of protection at common law, and since the South Carolina Court of Common Pleas found that the Beachfront Management Act left each of Lucas's beachfront lots without economic value.

The many statutes on the books, both state and federal, that provide for the use of eminent domain to impose servitudes on private scenic lands preventing developmental uses, or to acquire such lands altogether, suggest the practical equivalence in this setting of negative regulation and appropriation. [   ]

We think, in short, that there are good reasons for our frequently expressed belief that when the owner of real property has been called upon to sacrifice *all* economically beneficial uses in the name of the common good, that is, to leave his property economically idle, he has suffered a taking.[28]

B

The trial court found Lucas's two beachfront lots to have been rendered valueless by respondent's enforcement of the coastal-zone construction ban. Under Lucas's theory of the case, which rested upon our "no economically viable use" statements, that finding entitled him to compensation. Lucas believed it unnecessary to take issue with either the purposes behind the Beachfront Management Act, or the means chosen by the South Carolina Legislature to effectuate those purposes. The South Carolina Supreme Court, however, thought otherwise. In its view, the Beachfront Management Act was no ordinary enactment, but involved an exercise of South Carolina's "police powers" to mitigate the harm to the public interest that petitioner's use of his land might occasion. By neglecting to dispute the findings enumerated in the Act or otherwise to challenge the legislature's purposes, petitioner "concede[d] that the beach/dune area of South Carolina's shores is an extremely valuable public resource; that the erection of new construction, *inter alia*, contributes to the erosion and destruction of this public resource; and that discouraging new construction in close proximity to the beach/dune area is necessary to prevent a great public harm." [   ] In the

---

28. Justice Stevens criticizes the "deprivation of all economically beneficial use" rule as "wholly arbitrary," in that "[the] landowner whose property is diminished in value 95% recovers nothing," while the landowner who suffers a complete elimination of value "recovers the land's full value." *Post*, at 1064. This analysis errs in its assumption that the landowner whose deprivation is one step short of complete is not entitled to compensation. Such an owner might not be able to claim the benefit of our categorical formulation, but, as we have acknowledged time and again, "[t]he economic impact of the regulation on the claimant and ... the extent to which the regulation has interfered with distinct investment-backed expectations" are keenly relevant to takings analysis generally. *Penn Central Transportation Co. v. New York City*, 438 U.S. 104, 124 (1978). It is true that in at least *some* cases the landowner with 95% loss will get nothing, while the

landowner with total loss will recover in full. But that occasional result is no more strange than the gross disparity between the landowner whose premises are taken for a highway (who recovers in full) and the landowner whose property is reduced to 5% of its former value by the highway (who recovers nothing). Takings law is full of these "all-or-nothing" situations.

Justice Stevens similarly misinterprets our focus on "developmental" uses of property (the uses proscribed by the Beachfront Management Act) as betraying an "assumption that the only uses of property cognizable under the Constitution are *developmental* uses." *Post*, at 1065, n. 3. We make no such assumption. Though our prior takings cases evince an abiding concern for the productive use of, and economic investment in, land, there are plainly a number of noneconomic interests in land whose impairment will invite exceedingly close scrutiny under the Takings Clause. [   ]

court's view, these concessions brought petitioner's challenge within a long line of this Court's cases sustaining against Due Process and Takings Clause challenges the State's use of its "police powers" to enjoin a property owner from activities akin to public nuisances. [   ]

It is correct that many of our prior opinions have suggested that "harmful or noxious uses" of property may be proscribed by government regulation without the requirement of compensation. For a number of reasons, however, we think the South Carolina Supreme Court was too quick to conclude that that principle decides the present case.... [   ] [The Court's discussion of the harm/benefit test is omitted.—Eds.]

Where the State seeks to sustain regulation that deprives land of all economically beneficial use, we think it may resist compensation only if the logically antecedent inquiry into the nature of the owner's estate shows that the proscribed use interests were not part of his title to begin with. This accords, we think, with our "takings" jurisprudence, which has traditionally been guided by the understandings of our citizens regarding the content of, and the State's power over, the "bundle of rights" that they acquire when they obtain title to property. It seems to us that the property owner necessarily expects the uses of his property to be restricted, from time to time, by various measures newly enacted by the State in legitimate exercise of its police powers; "[a]s long recognized, some values are enjoyed under an implied limitation and must yield to the police power." *Pennsylvania Coal Co. v. Mahon*, 260 U.S., at 413. And in the case of personal property, by reason of the State's traditionally high degree of control over commercial dealings, he ought to be aware of the possibility that new regulation might even render his property economically worthless (at least if the property's only economically productive use is sale or manufacture for sale). See *Andrus v. Allard*, 444 U.S. 51, 66–67 (1979) (prohibition on sale of eagle feathers). In the case of land, however, we think the notion pressed by the Council that title is somehow held subject to the "implied limitation" that the State may subsequently eliminate all economically valuable use is inconsistent with the historical compact recorded in the Takings Clause that has become part of our constitutional culture.

Where "permanent physical occupation" of land is concerned, we have refused to allow the government to decree it anew (without compensation), no matter how weighty the asserted "public interests" involved, [   ] though we assuredly *would* permit the government to assert a permanent easement that was a pre-existing limitation upon the landowner's title. [   ] We believe similar treatment must be accorded confiscatory regulations, *i.e.*, regulations that prohibit all economically beneficial use of land: Any limitation so severe cannot be newly legislated or decreed (without compensation), but must inhere in the title itself, in the restrictions that background principles of the State's law of property and nuisance already place upon land ownership. A law or decree with such an effect must, in other words, do no more than duplicate the result that could have been achieved in the courts—by adjacent landowners (or other uniquely affected persons) under the

State's law of private nuisance, or by the State under its complementary power to abate nuisances that affect the public generally, or otherwise.[29]

On this analysis, the owner of a lake-bed, for example, would not be entitled to compensation when he is denied the requisite permit to engage in a landfilling operation that would have the effect of flooding others' land. Nor the corporate owner of a nuclear generating plant, when it is directed to remove all improvements from its land upon discovery that the plant sits astride an earthquake fault. Such regulatory action may well have the effect of eliminating the land's only economically productive use, but it does not proscribe a productive use that was previously permissible under relevant property and nuisance principles. The use of these properties for what are now expressly prohibited purposes was *always* unlawful, and (subject to other constitutional limitations) it was open to the State at any point to make the implication of those background principles of nuisance and property law explicit. See Michelman, Property, Utility, and Fairness, Comments on the Ethical Foundations of "Just Compensation" Law, 80 Harv. L. Rev. 1165, 1239–1241 (1967). In light of our traditional resort to "existing rules or understandings that stem from an independent source such as state law" to define the range of interests that qualify for protection as "property" under the Fifth and Fourteenth Amendments, [ ] this recognition that the Takings Clause does not require compensation when an owner is barred from putting land to a use that is proscribed by those "existing rules or understandings" is surely unexceptional. When, however, a regulation that declares "off-limits" all economically productive or beneficial uses of land goes beyond what the relevant background principles would dictate, compensation must be paid to sustain it.[30]

The "total taking" inquiry we require today will ordinarily entail (as the application of state nuisance law ordinarily entails) analysis of, among other things, the degree of harm to public lands and resources, or adjacent private property, posed by the claimant's proposed activities, see, e.g., Restatement (Second) of Torts §§ 826, 827, the social value of the claimant's activities and their suitability to the locality in question, see, *e.g., id.*, §§ 828(a) and (b), 831, and the relative ease with which the alleged harm can be avoided through measures taken by the claimant and the government (or adjacent private landowners) alike, see, *e.g., id.*, §§ 827(e), 828(c), 830. The fact that a particular use has long been engaged in by similarly situated owners ordinarily imports a lack of any common-law prohibition (though changed circumstances or new knowl-

---

29. The principal "otherwise" that we have in mind is litigation absolving the State (or private parties) of liability for the destruction of "real and personal property, in cases of actual necessity, to prevent the spreading of a fire" or to forestall other grave threats to the lives and property of others. *Bowditch v. Boston*, 101 U.S. 16, 18–19 (1880); see *United States v. Pacific R., Co.*, 120 U.S. 227, 238–239 (1887).

30. Of course, the State may elect to rescind its regulation and thereby avoid having to pay compensation for a permanent deprivation. See *First English Evangelical Lutheran Church*, 482 U.S., at 321. But "where the [regulation has] already worked a taking of all use of property, no subsequent action by the government can relieve it of the duty to provide compensation for the period during which the taking was effective." *Ibid.*

edge may make what was previously permissible no longer so, see *id.*,§ 827, Comment *g*. So also does the fact that other landowners, similarly situated, are permitted to continue the use denied to the claimant.

It seems unlikely that common-law principles would have prevented the erection of any habitable or productive improvements on petitioner's land; they rarely support prohibition of the "essential use" of land. [ ] The question, however, is one of state law to be dealt with on remand. We emphasize that to win its case South Carolina must do more than proffer the legislature's declaration that the uses Lucas desires are inconsistent with the public interest, or the conclusory assertion that they violate a common-law maxim such as *sic utere tuo ut alienum non laedas*. As we have said, a "State, by *ipse dixit*, may not transform private property into public property without compensation...." *Webb's Fabulous Pharmacies, Inc. v. Beckwith*, 449 U.S. 155, 164 (1980). Instead, as it would be required to do if it sought to restrain Lucas in a common-law action for public nuisance, South Carolina must identify background principles of nuisance and property law that prohibit the uses he now intends in the circumstances in which the property is presently found. Only on this showing can the State fairly claim that, in proscribing all such beneficial uses, the Beachfront Management Act is taking nothing.

* * *

The judgment is reversed, and the case is remanded for proceedings not inconsistent with this opinion.

So ordered.

JUSTICE KENNEDY, concurring in the judgment. (Omitted).

JUSTICE BLACKMUN, dissenting. (Omitted).

Notes and Questions

1. *Lucas* adds another category of *per se* takings—regulations that deprive landowners of "all economically beneficial use" of their land. But note that this rule is qualified by the requirement that the prohibited activity must be part of the landowner's property rights in the first place. How is this determination to be made? Does the application of tort law principles of nuisance help answer the question, or add to the confusion?

2. Suppose a city council enacts ordinances providing a mechanism, similar to that approved in *Kelo*, for converting leasehold interest in condominium units to fee interests, through the use of the city's condemnation power, and applies rent control provisions to limit increases in ground rent the owner of land under the condominium units can charge? See *Richardson v. City and County of Honolulu*, 124 F.3d 1150 (9th Cir.1997) (lease hold conversion mechanism upheld, applying *Midkiff* and refusing to apply heightened scrutiny under *Dolan, Lucas,* and *Nollan*, discussed *infra,* but rent control ordinance effects a regulatory taking under *Nollan* because it

lacks a mechanism for fulfilling it goal of creating affordable owner-occupied housing.)

3. As the Court has made clear in its takings opinions, the Court has struggled without much success to establish "bright-line" rules for determining when a government regulation causes a compensable taking of property or an unconstitutional deprivation of property. Commentators have written extensively about the Court's efforts. What do you think of the following suggestion by Professor Douglas Kmiec?

As noted, some courts already have perceived the value of the takings solution articulated by the United States Supreme Court in *Lucas*, *Nollan*, and *Dolan*, and have applied the proof burdens and heightened scrutiny from these cases to land-use takings claims generally. This trend should continue. It would be facilitated were *Agins* and *Penn Central* formally superseded and a clearly stated methodology of review outlined by the Court. What would such an outline look like or entail? By way of summary, the following is a sketch of the procedure for takings litigation (whether or not styled as a takings, substantive due process, or vested rights claim). To begin, the landowner would have the burden of producing evidence establishing: (1) a prima facie case of investment-based expectation (ownership if referring to the acquisition investment alone and/or improvement expenditure if referring to development expenditure) either with regard to a segment of the property if that segment is separately identifiable under state property law or if not, with regard to the property in its entirety; (2) that such an investment-based expectation was reasonable in light of the totality of state property law in existence at the time of investment; and (3) that a change in law or other regulatory action (e.g., denial of permit) has frustrated this reasonable expectation.

Upon making this prima facie showing, the regulating entity would then have the burden of proof to establish that the regulation is justified by antecedent inquiry into "background principles of [state] nuisance and property law," including as an element thereof the landowner's actual or constructive notice of law existing (though not pending) at the time of investment. Ordinarily, this showing would succeed if (1) the regulatory prohibition was not categorically off-limits to the state (e.g., uncompensated physical occupation) and (2) the state could demonstrate that the prohibition of the intended use was necessary to avoid substantial harm to public or private lands and resources, which harm outweighs the social value of the intended use and cannot be avoided responsibly by other means. Showing the lack of available "other means" would mean satisfied by reliance upon the causation principle, aptly incorporated in the essential nexus and rough proportionality aspects of *Nollan* and *Dolan*. . . .

The Supreme court has done its work by supplying a resolution of the takings puzzle that respects both private right and public need. . . . The Supreme Court can promote the realization of its well-considered reattachment of takings jurisprudence to the natural or common law reality of property and the reciprocal definition of property and the police power by forthrightly extending the *Lucas, Nollan,* and *Dolan* methodology to all land-use takings disputes.

Nothing the Court can do, however, will illuminate fully the inherently indeterminate nature of property and police power concepts. Natural law can do only so much. The rest depends upon prudential judgment exercised against an unknown future. The genius of a Takings Clause applied largely or presumptively by reference to state property law, especially state common law, developments is that it neither treats particular specifications of private property as absolute rights nor as licenses revocable by unsupervised police power. Rather, the natural law respects the character of a local community as it has defined itself chiefly within state judge-made precedent, rather than solely and deferentially in the too often acquisitive or exclusionary immediacy of legislative enactment. The building of any community takes time, and the incremental nature of common law adjudication reasonably supplies this opportunity and, with it, the promise of fairness called for by the Fifth Amendment. Douglas W. Kmiec, Inserting the Last Remaining Pieces into the Takings Puzzle, 38 Wm. & Mary L. Rev. 995, 1044–1046 (1997).

As the case that follows reveals, one of the most difficult tasks facing the courts is to decide whether the *per se* rule of *Lucas* or the *Ad Hoc* rule of *Penn Central* applies. Do you think the U.S. Supreme Court would have decided *R.T.G.* the way that the Ohio Supreme Court did? In *Tahoe-Sierra Preservation Council, Inc. v. Tahoe Regional Planning Agency,* 535 U.S. 302, 122 S.Ct. 1465, 152 L.Ed.2d 517 (2002), the Supreme Court applied *Penn Central* rather than *Lucas* in upholding a 32–month development moratorium.

STATE EX REL. R.T.G., INC. v. OHIO

Supreme Court of Ohio, 2002.
98 Ohio St.3d 1, 780 N.E.2d 998.

Lundberg Stratton J.

I. Introduction

This is a regulatory-takings case. Regulatory-takings issues are complex and difficult and have defied attempts to provide a simple solution. Even the United States Supreme Court "quite simply, has been unable to develop any 'set formula' for determining when 'justice and fairness' require that economic injuries caused by public action be compensated by the government, rather than remain disproportionately concentrated on a few persons." *Penn Cent. Transp. Co. v. New York City* (1978), 438 U.S. 104, 124, 98 S.Ct. 2646, 57 L.Ed.2d 631

R.T.G., Inc. ("RTG") is a coal-mining company that began surface-mining land located in eastern Ohio in the 1980s. This property consisted of tracts of land that RTG owned in fee and tracts of land in which RIG owned or leased coal rights only. Ultimately, the state of Ohio determined that RTG's surface mining of this property could adversely affect the aquifer that supplied water wells for the village of Pleasant City. Therefore, pursuant to R.C. 1513.073 the state designated 833 acres of property in Guernsey County as unsuitable for mining ("UFM"), including a substantial portion of RIG's property.

RIG filed a complaint seeking a writ of mandamus to compel the state to appropriate the coal that the state's UFM designation prevented RTG from mining. The appellate court held that imposition of the UFM regulation resulted in a taking of the coal that lies under the tracts of land that are located within the UFM-designated area and in which RTG owned coal rights only. However, the court held that the UFM designation did not result in a taking of the coal that lies under the tracts of land that RIG owned in fee. We reverse the judgment of the court of appeals in part and hold that the UFM regulation resulted in a taking of RIG's coal that lies under the tracts of land in which RTG owned only coal rights and that are located within the UFM-designated area, as well as the coal rights that lie under the tracts of land that RIG owned in fee and that are located in the UFM-designated area.

In a separate entry, the court of appeals denied RTG's motion for attorney fees and costs. We also reverse this judgment and hold that RIG is due reasonable attorney fees and costs.

II.   RTG's Efforts to Mine Its Property

James Rossiter is the president, CEO, and controlling shareholder of RIG. RIG is a coal-mining company. In 1982, RTG began investigating the viability of surface-mining coal in Valley Township, Guernsey County, just to the northwest of the village. RTG conducted extensive test drilling, which indicated the presence of high quality coal in this area. Consequently, RTG began acquiring property in this area for the purpose of mining coal. In all, RTG acquired approximately 500 acres of property through purchases in fee or purchases or leases of coal rights in sections 5, 7, and 8 of Valley Township. Approximately 200 acres of this property consisted of several tracts of property that RTG owned in fee (surface and coal rights). Approximately 300 acres consisted of several tracts of property in which RTG leased or owned coal rights only. Rossiter testified that RTG spent over $250,000 to acquire these property rights, to test-drill, and to prepare the mine permit applications.

In 1984, RIG filed an application to mine 21.8 acres of the property that it had acquired. Because the area subject to the permit application was within three-quarters of a mile of a well field that provided water to the village, the Ohio Department of Natural Resources, Division of Reclamation ("DOR"), required RTG to install monitoring wells between the area to be mined and the village's water wells to determine whether that mining would interfere with the village's water supply. A pump test indicated that the monitoring wells were in a different aquifer from the village's wells. Accordingly, on May 20, 1986, the state issued permit D–578, which allowed RIG to begin mining the 21.8 acres.

After receiving the D–578 permit, Rossiter testified, RTG paid $100,000 to prepare the land for mining, including building a sediment pond, establishing drainage controls, removing and segregating topsoil, and building roads and ramps into the excavation.

On June 5, 1987, pursuant to permit D–578–l, the permit area was revised to include an additional 77.2 acres adjacent to the original permit area. The DOR found that "[g]round water supplies monitored up to the date of this written finding have not displayed any significant changes in the quality and quality [sic] to the Village of Pleasant City's well field."

On September 10, 1987, the aquifer that served the village's water supply was designated a sole-source aquifer by the United States Environmental Protection Agency.

On September 21, 1988, pursuant to R.C. 15 13.073 the village filed a petition with the DOR that sought to designate 833 acres in Valley Township that lie below 820 feet in elevation as UFM because mining in this area would adversely affect the aquifer that supplies the village's wells.

On October 6, 1989, the chief of the DOR designated approximately 275 of the requested 833 acres as UFM. The chief determined that mining in this area could reduce the long-term productivity of the village's water wells. The UFM designation affected property that RTG sought to mine. RTG and the village appealed from the chiefs decision to the Ohio Reclamation Board of Review ("board").

Before the appeal was decided, the area subject to the permit was increased by

8.4 acres. The board found that "on the monitoring data collected by the Division of Water it is not anticipated that the quantity of water to the Village of Pleasant City's well field will be jeopardized by the proposed mining operation, application #D–0578–2."

Ultimately, however, on June 16, 1994, the board issued an order that designated as UFM the entire 833 acres, which consisted of all lands in Sections 7 and 8 of Valley Township that lie below 820 feet. The UFM designation prevented RTG from mining much of its property.

III.   RTG's Mandamus Proceedings

[The discussion of the mandamus proceeding is omitted.—Eds.]

* * *

V.   Regulatory-Takings Law

Both the United States and the Ohio Constitutions provide that private property shall not be taken for public use without just compensation. Fifth and Fourteenth Amendments to the United States Constitution; Section 19, Article I, Ohio Constitution see, also, R.C. Chapter 163. The purpose of the Takings Clause is to prevent government from "forcing some people alone to bear public burdens which, in all fairness and justice, should be borne by the public as a whole." *Armstrong v. United States*, 364 U.S. 40, 49, 80 S.Ct. 1563, 4 L.Ed.2d 1554.

It was Justice Holmes who first recognized that "while property may be regulated to a certain extent, if regulation goes too far it will be recognized as a taking." *Pennsylvania Coal Co. v. Mahon* (1922), 260 U.S. 393, 43 S.Ct. 158, 67 L.Ed. 322. However, it was not until 1978 that the United States Supreme Court formulated a test to help define when a regulation "goes too far" and results in a compensable taking. See *Penn Cent. Transp. Co. v. New York City* (1978), 438 U.S. 104, 98 S.Ct. 2646, 57 L.Ed.2d 631. "Penn Central does not supply mathematically precise variables, but instead provides important guideposts that lead to the ultimate determination whether just compensation is required." *Palazzolo v. Rhode Island*, 533 U.S. 606, 634, 121 S.Ct. 2448, 150 L.Ed.2d 592 (O'Connor, J., concurring). The three criteria that *Penn Cent.* identified to be examined in regard to a regulatory taking are (1) the nature of the governmental regulation, (2) the economic impact of the regulation on the claimant, and (3) the extent to which the regulation interfered with distinct investment-backed expectations. *Penn Cent.* at 124, 98 S.Ct. 2646, 57 L.Ed.2d 631.

Penn Cent. provides the proper taking test when the regulation deprives the property of less than 100 percent of its economically beneficial use. *Tahoe-Sierra Preservation Council, Inc. v. Tahoe Regional Planning Agency* (2002), 535 U.S. 302, 330, 122 S.Ct. 1465, 1483, 152 L.Ed.2d 517, 545.

In 1992, the Supreme Court again visited the regulatory-takings law in *Lucas*. The court acknowledged the *Penn Cent.* ad hoc balancing test, but recognized two situations in which a regulation results in a taking "without case-specific inquiry into the public interest advanced in support of the restraint." *Lucas*, 505 U.S. at 1015, 112 S.Ct. 2886, 120 L.Ed.2d 798. The first is where a regulation requires a physical invasion of property.... The second is "where regulation denies all economically beneficial or productive use of the land." *Lucas* at 1015, 112 S.Ct. 2886, 120 L.Ed.2d 798. However, even if a regulation results in categorical taking, no compensation is due if the claimant's use of the land violates "restrictions that background principles of the State's law of property and nuisance already place upon land ownership." *Lucas*, 505 U.S. at 1029, 112 S.Ct. 2886, 120 L.Ed.2d 798.

The rule in *Lucas*, recognizing these categorical takings, applies only "when a regulation deprives an owner of 'all economically beneficial uses' of his land." (Emphasis in Lucas.) *Tahoe-Sierra Preservation Council*, 535 U.S. 302, 330, 122 S.Ct. 1465, 1483, 152 L.Ed.2d 517, 545 quoting *Lucas*, 505 U.S. at 1019, 112 S.Ct. 2886, 120 L.Ed.2d 798

Thus, under *Lucas*, if a regulation deprives the property of all of its economic value, there is no need to examine the policy behind the regulation, and a compensable taking results, unless the regulation merely prevents use of the property in a manner that creates a nuisance under state law.

Accordingly, the United States Supreme Court has created a dichotomy in regulatory takings. *Lucas* applies where the regulation has deprived the property of all economic value, and *Penn Cent.* applies where the regulation deprives the property of less than all economic value.

A. Defining the Relevant Parcel, or The Denominator Problem

The regulatory-takings analysis requires a court to compare the value of the property that has been taken by the regulation against the value of the property that remains. *Keystone Bituminous Coal Assn. v. DeBenedictis* (1987), 480 U.S. 470, 497, 107 S.Ct. 1232, 94 L.Ed.2d 472 "[O]ne of the critical questions is determining how to define the unit of property 'whose value is to furnish the denominator of the fraction.'" *Id.*, quoting Michelman, *Property, Utility, and Fairness: Comments on the Ethical Foundations of "Just Compensation" Law* (1967), 80 Harv. L.Rev. 1165, 1192. The denominator, or the "relevant parcel," is the property interest that is subject to the regulation. See The Relevant Parcel Issue (1993), C872 AL1–ABA 167. The numerator of this fraction is the value of the property that has been taken due to the regulation. Fee, *Unearthing the Denominator in Regulatory Takings Claims* (1994), 61 U.Chi.L.Rev. 1535, 1536. If this fraction equals one (i.e., the value of the property taken equals the value of the relevant parcel), then there has been a categorical taking as defined in *Lucas* and compensation is due unless the use of the property conflicts with background principles of the state's law of property and nuisance. *Lucas*, 505 U.S. at 1027, 1029, 112 S.Ct. 2886, 120 L.Ed.2d 798. But if the fraction equals anything less than one, then there has been no categorical taking, and the *Penn Cent.* ad hoc balancing test applies to determine whether a compensable taking has occurred.

Determining the relevant parcel of the takings fraction is critical because it usually determines the applicable takings test. In other words, determining how broadly or narrowly the relevant parcel is defined will determine whether there has been a complete deprivation of the economic value of the property, or whether a taking of something less has occurred. The more broadly the relevant parcel is defined, the less likely that a regulation will result in a complete economic deprivation and that the *Penn Cent.* test will apply; conversely, the more narrowly the relevant parcel is defined, the more likely that a regulation will result in a complete economic deprivation and that the *Lucas* test will apply.

Determination of the denominator of the takings fraction has been a persistent and difficult issue. *Palazzolo*, 533 U.S. at 631, 121 S.Ct. 2448, 150 L.Ed.2d 592. The determination of the relevant parcel can include consideration of the vertical divisions of property (e.g., surface rights, air rights, and mineral rights) and horizontal divisions of property (e.g., surface divisions of property, such as can be shown on a map). Fee, *Unearthing the Denominator in Regulatory Takings Claims*, 61 U.Chi. L.Rev. at 1537, fn. 7 and 8.

1. The Appellate Court Erred in Defining the Relevant Parcel

In defining the relevant parcel, "effort should be to identify the parcel as realistically and fairly as possible, given the entire factual and regulatory environment." *Ciampitti v. United States* (1991), 22 Cl. of Ct. 310, 319. The appellate court determined that RTG's property consisted of two relevant parcels for purposes of the takings analysis, one being all the tracts of land in which RTG owned only coal rights, and the other being the tracts of land that it owned in fee. There is no analysis in the court's decision as to how the court arrived at this conclusion. For reasons made clear in our analysis below, we reject the appellate court's determination that there are two relevant parcels in this case.

2. The Relevant Parcel in the Vertical Context

RTG argues that we should define the relevant parcel in the vertical context as including only the coal rights that lie under RTG's property to the exclusion of any surface rights. The state asserts that coal rights cannot be severed from surface rights for purposes of this analysis and thus the relevant parcel must include both surface and coal rights. In this case, we agree with RTG.

In *Penn Cent.*, the court specifically declined to sever property rights in the vertical context for purposes of a takings analysis. In *Penn Cent.*, a regulation prevented Penn Central from building a 55-story addition onto Grand Central Station. *Penn Central* argued that the regulation deprived it of its use of the air rights over Grand Central Station. The court declined to consider *Penn Central's* air rights above Grand Central Station as a separate estate from the remainder of the property pursuant to the parcel-as-a-whole rule. *Penn Cent.*, 438 U.S. at 130. 98 S.Ct. 2646, 57 L.Ed.2d 631.

Penn Central's nonseverability rule was reaffirmed in *Keystone Bituminous Coal Assn.*, 480 U.S. 470, 107 S.Ct. 1232, 94 L.Ed.2d 472. In *Keystone*, the Bituminous Mine Subsidence and Land Conservation Act, Pa. Stat. Ann., Title 52, Section 1406.1 et seq., required coal companies during subsurface mining to leave certain amounts of coal in place to prevent subsidence of the surface estate. *Keystone* alleged that the statute resulted in a regulatory taking of the coal that was required to be left in place. Applying the parcel-as-a-whole rule, the court held that the coal required to be left in place by the Subsidence Act did "not constitute a separate segment of property." *Id.* at 498, 107 S.Ct. 1232, 94 L.Ed.2d 472.

However, subsequent to *Penn Cent.* and *Keystone*, some members of the court have expressed misgivings about the parcel-as-a-whole rule. In *Lucas*, the court discussed the uncertainty in determining the denominator and the resulting inconsistent pronouncements by the court in that regard. *Lucas*, 505 U.S. at 1019, 112 S.Ct. 2886, 120 L.Ed.2d 798, fn. 8; see, also, *Palazzolo*, 533 U.S. at 631, 121 S.Ct. 2448, 150 L.Ed.2d 592 (recognizing the discomfort of some justices with the parcel-as-a-whole rule). The majority in *Lucas* suggested that the solution to the difficult issue of determining the denominator "may lie in how the owner's reasonable expectations have been shaped by the State's law of property—i.e., whether and to what degree the State's law has accorded legal recognition and protection to the particular interest in land with respect to which the takings claimant alleges a diminution in (or elimination of) value." *Lucas*, 505 U.S. 1003, 112 S.Ct. 2886, 120 L.Ed.2d 798, fn. 7.

That discussion in *Lucas* was merely dicta. However, property rights are defined by state law. *Webb's Fabulous Pharmacies, Inc. v. Beckwith* (1980), 449 U.S. 155, 161, 101 S.Ct. 446, 66 L.Ed.2d 358, citing *Bd. of Regents of State Colleges v. Roth* (1972), 408 U.S. 564, 577, 92 S.Ct. 2701, 33 L.Ed.2d 548. Furthermore, states are free to interpret their constitutions independently of the United States Constitution so long as that interpretation affords, as a minimum, the same protection as its federal counterpart. *Arnold v. Cleveland,* 67 Ohio St.3d 35, 616 N.E.2d 163 at paragraph one of the syllabus.

We find that the criticism in *Lucas* regarding how to define the relevant parcel for the takings analysis is particularly relevant to coal rights in Ohio. Unlike other individual rights within the bundle of rights that make up a complete property estate, mineral rights are recognized by Ohio law as separate property rights. *Moore v. Indian Camp Coal Co.* (1907), 75 Ohio St. 493, 80 N.E. 6. Therefore, because the ownership of the coal is "both severable and of value in its own right, it is appropriate to consider the effect of regulation on that particular property interest." *Keystone*, 480 U.S. at 520, 107 S.Ct. 1232, 94 L.Ed.2d 472 (Rehnquist, C.J., dissenting). Accordingly, in determining the relevant parcel in a takings analysis pursuant to the Takings Clause of the Ohio Constitution, Section 19, Article I, coal rights are severable and may be considered as a separate property interest if the property owner's intent was to purchase the property solely for the purpose of mining the coal.

It is undisputed that RIG is a company that surface-mines coal. It is also undisputed that RIG acquired all the property at issue herein, whether in fee or through coal leases or purchases, for the sole purpose of surface-mining the coal from these properties. The surface rights served as nothing more than an impediment to acquiring the coal. Thus, the right to mine coal "is what, and only what, this suit is all about." *Whitney Benefits, Inc. v. United States* (C.A.Fed.1991), 926 F.2d 1169, 1174 Therefore, we hold that the relevant parcel for the takings analysis in the vertical context is the coal rights.

3.   The Relevant Parcel in the Horizontal Context

RTG urges us to define the relevant parcel in the horizontal context as the property that is located within the UFM-designated area. The state urges the court to find that the relevant parcel is all 500 acres of RTG's property pursuant to the parcel-as-a-whole rule. See *Penn Cent.* For the following reasons, we find that the relevant parcel in the horizontal context is limited to RTG's property that is within the UFM designated area.

Although contiguous tracts of property are typically considered as a single relevant parcel for purposes of a takings analysis, factual nuances may dictate a more flexible approach. *Loveladies Harbor, Inc. v. United*

States (C.A.Fed.1994), 28 F.3d 1171, 1181. These factual nuances may include the claimant's investment-backed expectations. *Machpongo Land & Coal Co. v. Pennsylvania* (Pa.2002), 569 Pa. 3, 799 A.2d 751, 768–769.

Of the approximately 500 acres of contiguous property at issue herein, approximately 100 of these acres are located outside the UFM-designated area. The state contends that these 100 acres of property are part of the relevant parcel because this property includes coal rights.

RIG has submitted evidence that of the approximately 500 acres at issue herein, the state's UFM designation prevented it from mining approximately 218 "coal acres, or 1.3 million tons of coal. RTG has admitted that fringe amounts of coal exist outside the regulated area. However, RIG's mining of the coal was dependent upon economies of scale. Therefore, when the UFM designation prevented RTG from mining a majority of its coal reserves within the regulated area, it made mining those minimal reserves outside the UFM-designated area economically impracticable.

Because there is no evidence that the coal outside the regulated area can be economically mined independent of the reserves in the regulated area, we hold that the relevant parcel in the horizontal context is limited on these facts to RTG's coal that is located within the UFM-designated area.

4. The Relevant Parcel

Merging our analyses regarding the relevant parcel in vertical and horizontal contexts, we hold that the relevant parcel in this case is the remaining coal located within the UFM-designated area.

B. The UFM Designation Destroyed RTG's Coal Rights

"What makes the right to mine coal valuable is that it can be exercised with profit." *Pennsylvania Coal*, 260 U.S. at 414, 43 S.Ct. 158, 67 L.Ed. 322. The UFM designation makes it impossible for RTG to mine coal, thereby depriving RTG from exercising its coal rights for profit. Thus, imposition of the UFM designation deprived RTG's coal rights of all economic value. Accordingly, applying *Lucas*, we hold that the UFM designation resulted in a categorical taking of RTG's coal rights.

VII. CONCLUSION

We hold that the state's UFM designation resulted in a categorical taking of all of RTG's coal rights pursuant to *Lucas*. Therefore, we reverse the judgment of the court of appeals and issue a writ of mandamus to compel the state of Ohio to appropriate the coal located within the UFM-designated area. In the appropriations proceedings, the value of RTG's coal within the UFM-designated area will be the sole issue to be determined.

We also reverse the judgment of the court of appeals that denied RTG attorney fees and costs, and remand the cause for the appellate court to determine RTG's reasonable attorney fees and costs.

Judgments affirmed in part, reversed in part, writ issued and cause remanded.

Note and Questions

Would the U.S. Supreme Court in *Penn Central* have decided *R.T.G.* the same way the Ohio Supreme Court did? What position do you think Justice Holmes or Brandeis would have taken in this case?

C. EXACTIONS

NOLLAN v. CALIFORNIA COASTAL COMMISSION

Supreme Court of the United States, 1987.
483 U.S. 825, 107 S.Ct. 3141, 97 L.Ed.2d 677.

JUSTICE SCALIA delivered the opinion of the Court.

The Nollans own a beachfront lot in Ventura County, California. A quarter-mile north of their property is Faria County Park, an oceanside public park with a public beach and recreation area. Another public beach area, known locally as "the Cove," lies 1,800 feet south of their lot. A concrete seawall approximately eight feet high separates the beach portion of the Nollans' property from the rest of the lot. The historic mean high tide line determines the lot's oceanside boundary.

The Nollans originally leased their property with an option to buy. The building on the lot was a small bungalow, totaling 504 square feet, which for a time they rented to summer vacationers. After years of rental use, however, the building had fallen into disrepair, and could no longer be rented out.

The Nollans' option to purchase was conditioned on their promise to demolish the bungalow and replace it. In order to do so, under California Public Resources Code §§ 30106, 30212, and 30600 (West 1986), they were required to obtain a coastal development permit from the California Coastal Commission. On February 25, 1982, they submitted a permit application to the Commission in which they proposed to demolish the existing structure and replace it with a three-bedroom house in keeping with the rest of the neighborhood.

The Nollans were informed that their application had been placed on the administrative calendar, and that the Commission staff had recommended that the permit be granted subject to the condition that they allow the public an easement to pass across a portion of their property bounded by the mean high tide line on one side, and their seawall on the other side. This would make it easier for the public to get to Faria County Park and the Cove. The Nollans protested imposition of the condition, but the Commission overruled their objections and granted the permit subject to their recordation of a deed restriction granting the easement.

On June 3, 1982, the Nollans filed a petition for writ of administrative mandamus asking the Ventura County Superior Court to invalidate the access condition. They argued that the condition could not be imposed absent evidence that their proposed development would have a direct adverse impact on public access to the beach. The court agreed, and remanded the case to the Commission for a full evidentiary hearing on that issue.

On remand, the Commission held a public hearing, after which it made further factual findings and reaffirmed its imposition of the condition. It found that the new house would increase blockage of the view of the ocean, thus contributing to the development of "a 'wall' of residential structures" that would prevent the public "psychologically . . . from realizing a stretch of coastline exists nearby that they have every right to visit." The new house would also increase private use of the shorefront. These effects of construction of the house, along with other area development, would cumulatively "burden the public's ability to traverse to and along the shorefront." Therefore the Commission could properly require the Nollans to offset that burden by providing additional lateral access to the public beaches in the form of an easement across their property. The Commission also noted that it had similarly conditioned 43 out of 60 coastal development permits along the same tract of land, and that of the 17 not so conditioned, 14 had been approved when the Commission did not have administrative regulations in place allowing imposition of the condition, and the remaining 3 had not involved shorefront property.

* * *

Had California simply required the Nollans to make an easement across their beachfront available to the public on a permanent basis in order to increase public access to the beach, rather than conditioning their permit to rebuild their house on their agreeing to do so, we have no doubt there would have been a taking. To say that the appropriation of a public easement across a landowner's premises does not constitute the taking of a property interest but rather, "a mere restriction on its use," is to use words in a manner that deprives them of all their ordinary meaning.

* * * We have repeatedly held that, as to property reserved by its owner for private use, "the right to exclude [others is] 'one of the most essential sticks in the bundle of rights that are commonly characterized as property.' "

* * * We think a "permanent physical occupation" has occurred, for purposes of that rule, where individuals are given a permanent and continuous right to pass to and fro, so that the real property may continuously be traversed, even though no particular individual is permitted to station himself permanently upon the premises.

* * *

Given, then, that requiring uncompensated conveyance of the easement outright would violate the Fourteenth Amendment, the question becomes whether requiring it to be conveyed as a condition for issuing a land use permit alters the outcome. We have long recognized that land use regulation does not effect a taking if it "substantially advance[s] legitimate state interests" and does not "den[y] an owner economically viable use of his land." [ ] Our cases have not elaborated on the standards for determining what constitutes a "legitimate state interest" or what type of connection between the regulation and the state interest satisfies the requirement that the former "substantially advance" the latter. They have made clear, however, that a broad range of governmental purposes and regulations satisfies these requirements. The Commission argues that among these permissible purposes are protecting the public's ability to see the beach, assisting the public in overcoming the "psychological barrier" to using the beach created by a developed shorefront, and preventing congestion on the public beaches. We assume, without deciding, that this is so—in which case the Commission unquestionably would be able to deny the Nollans their permit outright if their new house (alone, or by reason of the cumulative impact produced in conjunction with other construction) would substantially impede these purposes, unless the denial would interfere so drastically with the Nollans' use of their property as to constitute a taking.

The Commission argues that a permit condition that serves the same legitimate police-power purpose as a refusal to issue the permit should not be found to be a taking if the refusal to issue the permit would not constitute a taking. We agree. Thus, if the Commission attached to the permit some condition that would have protected the public's ability to see the beach notwithstanding construction of the new house—for example, a height limitation, a width restriction, or a ban on fences—so long as the Commission could have exercised its police power (as we have assumed it could) to forbid construction of the house altogether, imposition of the condition would also be constitutional. Moreover (and here we come closer to the facts of the present case), the condition would be constitutional even if it consisted of the requirement that the Nollans provide a viewing spot on their property for passersby with whose sighting of the ocean their new house would interfere. Although such a requirement, constituting a permanent grant of continuous access to the property, would have to be considered a taking if it were not attached to a development permit, the Commission's assumed power to forbid construction of the house in order to protect the public's view of the beach must surely include the power to condition construction upon some concession by the owner, even a concession of property rights, that serves the same end. If a prohibition designed to accomplish that purpose would be a legitimate exercise of the police power rather than a taking, it would be strange to conclude that providing the owner an alternative to that prohibition which accomplishes the same purpose is not.

The evident constitutional propriety disappears, however, if the condition substituted for the prohibition utterly fails to further the end advanced as the justification for the prohibition. When that essential nexus is eliminated, the situation becomes the same as if California law forbade shouting fire in a crowded theater, but granted dispensations to those willing to contribute $100 to the state treasury. While a ban on shouting fire can be a core exercise of the State's police power to protect the public safety, and can thus meet even our stringent standards for regulation of speech, adding the unrelated condition alters the purpose to one which, while it may be legitimate, is inadequate to sustain the ban. Therefore, even though, in a sense, requiring a $100 tax contribution in order to shout fire is a lesser restriction on speech than an outright ban, it would not pass constitutional muster. Similarly here, the lack of nexus between the condition and the original purpose of the building restriction converts that purpose to something other than what it was. The purpose then becomes, quite simply, the obtaining of an easement to serve some valid governmental purpose, but without payment of compensation. Whatever may be the outer limits of "legitimate state interests" in the takings and land use context, this is not one of them. In short, unless the permit condition serves the same governmental purpose as the development ban, the building restriction is not a valid regulation of land use but "an out-and-out plan of extortion." [   ]

* * *

* * * The Commission may well be right that [access to the beach] is a good idea, but that does not establish that the Nollans (and other coastal residents) alone can be compelled to contribute to its realization. Rather, California is free to advance its "comprehensive program," if it wishes, by using its power of eminent domain for this "public purpose;" but if it wants an easement across the Nollans' property, it must pay for it.

Reversed.

Justice Brennan, with whom Justice Marshall joins, dissenting.

There can be no dispute that the police power of the States encompasses the authority to impose conditions on private development. It is also by now commonplace that this Court's review of the rationality of a State's exercise of its police power demands only that the State "could rationally have decided" that the measure adopted might achieve the State's objective. In this case, California has employed its police power in order to condition development upon preservation of public access to the ocean and tidelands. The Coastal Commission, if it had so chosen, could have denied the Nollans' request for a development permit, since the property would have remained economically viable without the requested new development. Instead, the State sought to accommodate the Nollans' desire for new development, on the condition that the development not diminish the overall amount of public access to the coastline.

* * *

The Court's demand for this precise fit is based on the assumption that private landowners in this case possess a reasonable expectation regarding the use of their land that the public has attempted to disrupt. In fact, the situation is precisely the reverse: it is private landowners who are the interlopers. The public's expectation of access considerably antedates any private development on the coast. Article X, Section 4 of the California Constitution, adopted in 1879, declares:

> "No individual, partnership, or corporation, claiming or possessing the frontage or tidal lands of a harbor, bay, inlet, estuary, or other navigable water in this State, shall be permitted to exclude the right of way to any such water whenever it is required for any public purpose, nor to destroy or obstruct the free navigation of such water; and the Legislature shall enact such laws as will give the most liberal construction to this provision, so that access to the navigable waters of this State shall always be attainable for the people thereof."

It is therefore private landowners who threaten the disruption of settled public expectations. Where a private landowner has had a reasonable expectation that his or her property will be used for exclusively private purposes, the disruption of this expectation dictates that the government pay if it wishes the property to be used for a public purpose. In this case, however, the State has sought to protect *public* expectations of access from disruption by private land use. The State's exercise of its police power for this purpose deserves no less deference than any other measure designed to further the welfare of state citizens.

Even if we accept the Court's unusual demand for a precise match between the condition imposed and the specific type of burden on access created by the appellants, the State's action easily satisfies this requirement. First, the lateral access condition serves to dissipate the impression that the beach that lies behind the wall of homes along the shore is for private use only. It requires no exceptional imaginative powers to find plausible the Commission's point that the average person passing along the road in front of a phalanx of imposing permanent residences, including the appellants' new home, is likely to conclude that this particular portion of the shore is not open to the public. If, however, that person can see that numerous people are passing and repassing along the dry sand, this conveys the message that the beach is in fact open for use by the public. Furthermore, those persons who go down to the public beach a quarter-mile away will be able to look down the coastline and see that persons have continuous access to the tidelands, and will observe signs that proclaim the public's right of access over the dry sand. The burden produced by the diminution in visual access—the impression that the beach is not open to the public—is thus directly alleviated by the provision for public access over the dry sand. The Court therefore has an unrealistically limited conception of what measures could reasonably be chosen to mitigate the burden produced by a diminution of visual access.

The second flaw in the Court's analysis of the fit between burden and exaction is more fundamental. The Court assumes that the only burden with which the Coastal Commission was concerned was blockage of visual access to the beach. This is incorrect. The Commission specifically stated in its report in support of the permit condition that "[t]he Commission finds that the applicants' proposed development would present an increase in view blockage, *an increase in private use of the shorefront,* and that this impact would burden the public's ability to traverse to and along the shorefront." It declared that the possibility that "the public may get the impression that the beachfront is no longer available for public use" would be "due to *the encroaching nature of private use immediately adjacent to the public use, as well as* the visual 'block' of increased residential build-out impacting the visual quality of the beachfront."

* * *

The fact that the Commission's action is a legitimate exercise of the police power does not, of course, insulate it from a takings challenge, for when "regulation goes too far it will be recognized as a taking." *Pennsylvania Coal Co. v. Mahon,* 260 U.S. 393, 415, 43 S.Ct. 158, 160, 67 L.Ed. 322 (1922). Conventional takings analysis underscores the implausibility of the Court's holding, for it demonstrates that this exercise of California's police power implicates none of the concerns that underlie our takings jurisprudence.

In reviewing a Takings Clause claim, we have regarded as particularly significant the nature of the governmental action and the economic impact of regulation, especially the extent to which regulation interferes with investment-backed expectations. *Penn Central,* 438 U.S., at 124, 98 S.Ct., at 2659. The character of the government action in this case is the imposition of a condition on permit approval, which allows the public to continue to have access to the coast. The physical intrusion permitted by the deed restriction is minimal. The public is permitted the right to pass and re-pass along the coast in an area from the seawall to the mean high tide mark. This area is at its *widest* 10 feet, which means that *even without the permit condition,* the public's right of access permits it to pass on average within a few feet of the seawall.

* * *

Examination of the economic impact of the Commission's action reinforces the conclusion that no taking has occurred. Allowing appellants to intensify development along the coast in exchange for ensuring public access to the ocean is a classic instance of government action that produces a "reciprocity of advantage." *Pennsylvania Coal, supra,* 260 U.S., at 415, 43 S.Ct., at 160. Appellants have been allowed to replace a one-story 521–square–foot beach home with a two-story 1,674–square–foot residence and an attached two-car garage, resulting in development covering 2,464 square feet of the lot. Such development obviously significantly increases the value of appellants' property; appellants make no contention that this increase is offset by any diminution in value resulting from the deed restriction, much less that the restriction made the property less valuable than it would have been without the new construction. Furthermore, appellants gain an additional benefit from the Commission's permit condition program. They are able to walk along the beach beyond the confines of their own property only because the Commission has required deed restrictions as a condition of approving other new beach developments. Thus, appellants benefit both as private landowners and as members of the public from the fact that new development permit requests are conditioned on preservation of public access.

Ultimately, appellants' claim of economic injury is flawed because it rests on the assumption of entitlement to the full value of their new development. Appellants submitted a proposal for more intensive development of the coast, which the Commission was under no obligation to approve, and now argue that a regulation designed to ameliorate the impact of that development deprives them of the full value of their improvements. Even if this novel claim were somehow cognizable, it is not significant. "[T]he interest in anticipated gains has traditionally been viewed as less compelling than other property-related interests." *Andrus v. Allard,* 444 U.S. 51, 66, 100 S.Ct. 318, 327, 62 L.Ed.2d 210 (1979).

With respect to appellants' investment-backed expectations, appellants can make no reasonable claim to any expectation of being able to exclude members of the public from crossing the edge of their property to gain access to the ocean. It is axiomatic, of course, that state law is the source of those strands that constitute a property owner's bundle of property rights. "[A]s a general proposition[,] the law of real property is, under our Constitution, left to the individual States to develop and administer."

* * *

The foregoing analysis makes clear that the State has taken no property from appellants. Imposition of the permit condition in this case represents the State's reasonable exercise of its police power. The Coastal Commission has drawn on its expertise to preserve the balance between private development and public access, by requiring that any project that intensifies development on the increasingly crowded California coast must be offset by gains in public access. Under the normal standard for review of the police power, this provision is eminently reasonable. Even accepting the Court's novel insistence on a precise *quid pro quo* of burdens and benefits, there is a reasonable relationship between the public benefit and the burden created by appellants' development. The movement of development closer to the ocean creates the prospect of encroachment on public tidelands, because of fluctuation in the mean high tide line. The deed restriction ensures that disputes about the boundary between private and public property will not deter the public from exercising its right to have access to the sea.

Furthermore, consideration of the Commission's action under traditional takings analysis underscores the absence of any viable takings claim. The deed restriction permits the public only to pass and repass along a narrow strip of beach, a few feet closer to a seawall at the periphery of appellants' property. Appellants almost surely have enjoyed an increase in the value of their property even with the restriction, because they have been allowed to build a significantly larger new home with garage on their lot. Finally, appellants can claim the disruption of no expectation interest, both because they have no right to exclude the public under state law, and because, even if they did, they had full advance notice that new development along the coast is conditioned on provisions for continued public access to the ocean.

* * *

JUSTICE STEVENS, with whom JUSTICE BLACKMUN joins, dissenting.

The debate between the Court and JUSTICE BRENNAN illustrates an extremely important point concerning government regulation of the use of privately owned real estate. Intelligent, well-informed public officials may in good faith disagree about the validity of specific types of land use regulation. Even the wisest lawyers would have to acknowledge great uncertainty about the scope of this Court's takings jurisprudence.

* * *

Notes and Questions

1. Does the requirement of a public easement in *Nollan* represent a permanent physical invasion? Was the Nollans' proposed residence a nuisance? Does Justice Scalia hold that the public purpose requirement described in *Midkiff* is not met, or does he apply a form of Holmes' balancing test? Does he hold that California takes a segment of property, known as an easement? Or, do you conclude, along with dissenting Justice Stevens, that "even the wisest lawyers would have to acknowledge great uncertainty about the scope of this Court's taking jurisprudence"?

2. What must a municipality do in order to meet the *Nollan* nexus test? In *Dolan v. City of Tigard,* 512 U.S. 374, 114 S.Ct. 2309, 129 L.Ed.2d 304 (1994) the Supreme Court struck down biketrail and flood plain easement conditions attached to a permit for expansion of a commercial development. Although the Court was satisfied that the easement dedication conditions met the *Nollan* requirement that the regulation be rationally related to the purpose for which it was enacted, the Court held that the City had not evaluated sufficiently the impact of the landowner's proposed use of her property. Not only must the easement requirements be related to a proper public purpose, it also must be roughly proportional to the impact of the proposed use. The "rough proportionality" standard must be met by an "individualized determination" that the easement requirement was related "both in nature and extent" to the impact of the proposed expansion in use. The test now is called the *Nollan-Dolan* test. *Dolan* refined *Nollan* by emphasizing that an analysis must be made of the regulations both in

relation to the public purpose being served and the impact of the proposed use.

3. *Nollan* was one of the 1987 "trilogy" of Supreme Court takings cases. *Keystone,* described earlier, was another of this trio. The third, First English Evangelical Lutheran Church v. Los Angeles, 482 U.S. 304, 107 S.Ct. 2378, 96 L.Ed.2d 250 (1987), increased the risk to government of a wrong guess concerning the constitutionality of a land use statute or ordinance. In *First English,* the Court held that a property owner who is ultimately successful in arguing that the government action acted as a taking of property is entitled to compensation for recognized losses suffered for the "temporary taking" occurring during the period in which the law was in effect. Prior to *First English,* a court ruling that a taking existed allowed the government the choice of paying compensation or rescinding the offending act. *First English* would seem to require a more cautious approach on the part of government to land use control. One proposal suggests that "[I]t would be unfortunate if the only persons who benefit from [*First English*] are the lawyers and experts retained to argue the fine points of regulatory takings and compensation. The costs and uncertainties of the *First English* approach are so great that reason suggests that both land users and regulators seek an alternative * * * ". Salsich, Keystone Bituminous Coal, First English and Nollan: A Framework for Accommodation?, 34 J. of Urb. and Contemp.L. 173 (1988). Salsich suggests that local government develop an "early-warning administrative review process" to alert regulators to problems and to encourage the affected parties to identify common interests and effect compromise through mediation or accommodation.

Salsich also argues that the 1987 trilogy effectively establishes a hierarchy of property interests that relates to the argument that property and personhood are closely intertwined, as has been argued by Radin in Property and Personhood, 34 Stan.L.Rev. 957 (1982). Salsich concludes:

> Those property interests in land that may be said to vindicate important personal rights, such as the right to privacy and the right to choose how to dispose of one's property, have received greater protection from the Court than have the interests associated with the accumulation of wealth through land development. Substantial impairment of a property interest that protects personal liberties, such as the power to exclude others, may constitute a taking, even though the impairment occurs to only part of the property parcel. Substantial diminution in value that affects the profit potential of the property however, is not likely to be classified as a taking unless the regulation also impairs the use that can be made of the parcel as a whole.

> Increased public concern with environmental and natural resource issues is likely to sharpen the distinction between property interests that protect personal liberties and property interests that permit the accumulation of wealth. The next question may be whether the pursuit of profit through land development should be recognized as a personal liberty entitled to the constitutional protection of property. Salsich, Life After the Takings Trilogy—A Hierarchy of Property Interests? 19 Stetson L.Rev. 795, 811 (1990).

Is a wetlands protection statute that prohibits a property owner from changing the character of an identified wetlands area a question of property serving personal liberties or property serving the accumulation of wealth?

For further views on the "temporary taking" issue, see Williams, Smith, Siemon, Mandelker & Babcock, The White Junction Manifesto, 9 Vt.L.Rev. 193 (1984).

4. Of the thousands of pages of commentary on the question of takings, there is one article that always emerges from the pack. Frank Michelman's article "Property, Utility, and Fairness: Comments on the Ethical Foundations of 'Just Compensation' Law," 80 Harv.L.Rev. 1165 (1967) is one of the most frequently cited law review articles in history and is clearly the most frequently cited by the courts in takings cases. In this article, Michelman argues that the constitutional requirements of just compensation are the "visible, formal expression of society's commitment to fairness as a constraint on its pursuit of efficiency." He examines the most common "takings rules" in terms of their service to fairness. Although Michelman recognizes that the "psychological shock" produced by "the stark spectacle of an alien, uninvited presence in one's territory" supports compensation for physical invasion, he criticizes the rule: "A physical invasion test * * * can never be more than a convenience for identifying *clearly compensable* occasions. It cannot justify dismissal of any occasion as *clearly non-compensable*." Even as a rule limited to identifying compensable events, the rule of compensation for physical invasion is arbitrary and unfair, Michelman argues, because "the relevant comparison is between large losses and small losses—not between those which are and are not accompanied by total evictions." What, then, would be Michelman's opinion of *Loretto*? Of *Nollan*? Michelman goes on to identify the limitations of each of the theories used by the courts to identify takings requiring compensation.

Michelman concludes that courts are simply inherently limited in their ability to meet a fairness standard in such cases and that reliance on the court as the source of fairness causes other, perhaps more productive, methods of deciding compensation to be ignored. Michelman specifically argues that settlement or negotiation of claims can reduce the "demoralization costs" experienced by property holders losing their property to the government and can compensate persons for real losses (such as tenants for relocation costs) not otherwise recognized as losing "property." Michelman places the responsibility on the legislature to identify, "cost out," and compensate for real losses, even if not required to do so by the Constitution. Should the California legislature have provided compensation to the Nollans? You might consider Michelman's argument on this point when you study the cases on just compensation in the next section.

5. If you are not persuaded by attempts to reconcile the Supreme Court cases on whether property has been taken, you are not alone. Commenting on these cases, Laura Underkuffler writes: "The * * * incoherence [in these cases] is profound. An easement, conceptually severed from the underlying land, is property and compensable if taken; twenty-seven million tons of coal are not. The right to occupy land, or to pass land to one's heirs, is property compensable if taken; the right to modify a building that one owns, or to prevent physical invasion, is not."

Underkuffler offers instead a "comprehensive approach to property," which "incorporates the historical tension between the individual and the collective," in contrast to the "absolute approach," which "advances a clear case for the supremacy of individual interests." According to Underkuffler, the reclamation of a collective approach would change takings jurisprudence:

> The Supreme Court's ostensible use of an absolute approach to property results in a kind of patent dishonesty; property is portrayed as a matter of technical understanding or definition, while the conception is artificially manipulated to reach a result that is compatible with social goals. * * * Explicit acknowledgement of the mediating function of property, and the involvement of the collective in determining the nature and scope of individual rights, makes explicit the real policy issues.

How would "explicit acknowledgement of the mediating function of property" change the result or analysis in *Loretto, Pennsylvania Coal,* and *Nollan?* (Underkuffler cites *Penn Central* as an exception to the rule, one in which the court did explicitly engage in balancing individual and collective interests.) Underkuffler, On Property, 100 Yale L.J. 127, 130–131, 143 (1990). For a different view of property, see Epstein, Takings: Private Property and Eminent Domain (1985).

6. How much of the confusion or lack of predictability in takings jurisprudence is due to changes in generally held views on the role of property and the role of government? For example, is a heightened environmental awareness relevant to cases challenging the constitutionality of environmental protection regulations? Should it be relevant? See Michelman, Takings 1987, 88 Colum.L.Rev. 1600 (1988).

SALSICH, KEYSTONE BITUMINOUS COAL, FIRST ENGLISH AND NOLLAN: A FRAMEWORK FOR ACCOMMODATION?

34 J. Urb & Contemp L. 173, 187–190 (1988).

Although land use litigation is often framed as a contest between a developer and a land use regulator, scholars and practitioners have recognized a third party in most land use conflicts. An owner's proposed use of a particular tract often has an impact on two different groups of people. Adjacent landowners and residents experience the physical and aesthetic impacts of the size, shape, and density of the specific land use. A larger group of people, including residents and nonresidents of the governmental entity in which the land is located, may also experience a direct or indirect financial impact in the form of increased or decreased taxes. The degree of the impact on taxes depends on whether the particular land development increases the need for public services without a corresponding increase in the tax base, or whether the project increases the tax base without a corresponding increase in the demand for public services. It is also possible for this larger group to experience variations in choice of housing or employment, depending upon the nature of the particular development. These groups will also experience the environmental effects of the development.

These groups and the owner/developer may expect the governmental entity responsible for regulating land use to represent their best interests when making land use regulatory decisions. When subgroups emerge both to support and to oppose a land development project, the land use regulator may find itself caught in the middle of a struggle over competing values. The resulting relationship resembles a triangle with the owner/developer on one side, the neighbors on another, and the community at-large on the third. All three groups are locked into this relationship because of the external effects of a land development project, which varies with the nature and size of the development.

As with other relationships in which competing and common interests exist, owner/developers, neighbors, and the community at-large need to support one another for land use relationships to succeed. Although land does not depreciate in the sense that a building does, it is a finite resource that can be wasted by unnecessary or harmful development. When poorly executed development plans waste land, it may be lost for the current generation because of the enormous cost and difficulty of reclaiming such land. Although landowners and developers make the decisions that produce land waste, they are also members of the community at-large. As such, they too will benefit from land use regulations which effectively prevent land waste, and thus the community should urge developers to support such regulations.

Likewise, land use regulators need property users and developers. With the exception of land set aside in public parks and wilderness areas, legislators generally aim their regulations at balancing desirable and undesirable uses of privately owned land to benefit society. If regulations are so onerous that they discourage even desirable development, they do not benefit the community. Thus, the reaction of developers to land regulation provides important feedback to legislators concerning the utility of their regulations.

The availability of compensation as a remedy in taking cases is a significant addition to land use law. The compensation remedy supports those traditional arguments that accepted no difference in principle between "takings by dispossession" and "takings by excessive regulation." In addition, compensation can serve as a necessary check on government and as a means of retaining (or perhaps restoring) the consent of the people in their governments. Finally, compensation can be viewed as the price for public willingness to accept the "innovative," "flexible," and "comprehensive" land use regulations that today's legislators believe necessary.

The American system of property law, with its emphasis on private ownership of land, has two basic goals: to maximize and protect individual freedoms and to effectively utilize land. To achieve these goals, the chief actors in the American property law system—landowners, developers, users, neighbors, and regulators—must respect one another's interests. Additionally, state and local governments must provide the community with appropriate vehicles for asserting these competing interests.

Ideally, these interests should exist in equilibrium. If one is perceived to have an unfair advantage, the cooperation necessary for the system's functioning breaks down

* * *

D. JUST COMPENSATION

Whenever property is taken by the government, the Constitution requires that "just compensation" be paid for the property. In most cases the amount of compensation to be paid is resolved and settled between the government agency acquiring the property and the owner. In cases where these parties fail to settle on a price, the amount is set by the court. State and federal statutes may establish compensation goals or requirements that exceed constitutional standards. Absent such statutes, however, the Constitution establishes the minimum standards for payment.

ALMOTA FARMERS ELEVATOR & WAREHOUSE CO. v. UNITED STATES

Supreme Court of the United States, 1973.
409 U.S. 470, 93 S.Ct. 791, 35 L.Ed.2d 1.

Mr. Justice Stewart delivered the opinion of the Court.

Since 1919 the petitioner, Almota Farmers Elevator & Warehouse Co., has conducted grain elevator operations on land adjacent to the tracks of the Oregon–Washington Railroad & Navigation Co. in the State of Washington. It has occupied the land under a series of successive leases from the railroad. In 1967, the Government instituted this eminent domain proceeding to acquire the petitioner's property interest by condemnation. At that time there were extensive buildings and other improvements that had been erected on the land by the petitioner, and the then-current lease had 7 ½ years to run.

In the District Court the Government contended that just compensation for the leasehold interest, including the structures, should be "the fair market value of the legal rights possessed by the defendant by virtue of the lease as of the date of taking," and that no consideration should be given to any additional value based on the expectation that the lease might be renewed. The petitioner urged that, rather than this technical "legal rights theory," just compensation should be measured by what a willing buyer would pay in an open market for the petitioner's leasehold. . . .

In a pretrial ruling, the District Court accepted the petitioner's theory. . . .

On appeal, the Court of Appeals for the Ninth Circuit reversed, 450 F.2d 125; it accepted the Government's theory that a tenant's expectancy in a lease renewal was not a compensable legal interest and could not be included in the valuation of structures that the tenant had built on the property.... We * * * reverse the judgment before us and reinstate the judgment of the District Court.

The Fifth Amendment provides that private property shall not be taken for public use without "just compensation." "And 'just compensation' means the full monetary equivalent of the property taken. The owner is to be put in the same position monetarily as he would have occupied if his property had not been taken." [ ] To determine such monetary equivalence, the Court early established the concept of "market value": the owner is entitled to the fair market value of his property at the time of the taking. [ ] And this value is normally to be ascertained from "what a willing buyer would pay in cash to a willing seller." [ ]

By failing to value the improvements in place over their useful life—taking into account the possibility that the lease might be renewed as well as the possibility that it might not—the Court of Appeals in this case failed to recognize what a willing buyer would have paid for the improvements. If there had been no condemnation, Almota would have continued to use the improvements during a renewed lease term, or if it sold the improvements to the fee owner or to a new lessee at the end of the lease term, it would have been compensated for the buyer's ability to use the improvements in place over their useful life....

It seems particularly likely in this case that Almota could have sold the leasehold at a price that would have reflected the continued ability of the buyer to use the improvements over their useful life. Almota had an unbroken succession of leases since 1919, and it was in the interest of the railroad, as fee owner, to continue leasing the property, with its grain elevator facilities, in order to promote grain shipments over its lines. In a free market, Almota would hardly have sold the leasehold to a purchaser who paid only for the use of the facilities over the remainder of the lease term, with Almota retaining the right thereafter to remove the facilities—in effect, the right of salvage....

United States v. Petty Motor Co., 327 U.S. 372, 66 S.Ct. 596, 90 L.Ed. 729 (1946), upon which the Government primarily relies, does not lead to a contrary result. The Court did indicate that the measure of damages for the condemnation of a leasehold is to be measured in terms of the value of its use and occupancy for the remainder of the lease term, and the Court refused to elevate an expectation of renewal into a compensable legal interest. But the Court was not dealing there with the fair market value of improvements. Unlike *Petty Motor,* there is no question here of creating a legally cognizable value where none existed, or of compensating a mere incorporeal expectation.[31] The petitioner here has constructed the improvements and seeks only their fair market value.

---

31. Hence, this is not a case where the petitioner is seeking compensation for lost opportunities, see *United States ex rel. TVA v. Powelson,* 319 U.S. 266, 281–282, 63 S.Ct. 1047, 1055–1056, 87 L.Ed. 1390 (1943); *Omnia Commercial Co. v. United States,* 261 U.S. 502, 43 S.Ct. 437, 67 L.Ed. 773 (1923). The petitioner seeks only the fair value of the property taken by the Government. * * *

Petty Motor should not be read to allow the Government to escape paying what a willing buyer would pay for the same property.

The Government argues that it would be unreasonable to compensate Almota for the value of the improvements measured over their useful life, since the Government could purchase the fee and wait until the expiration of the lease term to take possession of the land. Once it has purchased the fee, the argument goes, there is no further expectancy that the improvements will be used during their useful life since the Government will assuredly require their removal at the end of the term. But the taking for the dam was one act requiring proceedings against owners of two interests.[32] At the time of that "taking" Almota had an expectancy of continued occupancy of its grain elevator facilities. The Government must pay just compensation for those interests "probably within the scope of the project from the time the Government was committed to it." [ ] It may not take advantage of any depreciation in the property taken that is attributable to the project itself. [ ] At the time of the taking in this case, there was an expectancy that the improvements would be used beyond the lease term. But the Government has sought to pay compensation on the theory that at that time there was no possibility that the lease would be renewed and the improvements used beyond the lease term. It has asked that the improvements be valued as though there were no possibility of continued use. That is not how the market would have valued such improvements; it is not what a private buyer would have paid Almota.

"The constitutional requirement of just compensation derives as much content from the basic equitable principles of fairness, [ ] as it does from technical concepts of property law." [ ] It is, of course, true that Almota should be in no better position than if it had sold its leasehold to a private buyer. But its position should surely be no worse.

The judgment before us is reversed and the judgment of the District Court reinstated.

MR. JUSTICE REHNQUIST, with whom THE CHIEF JUSTICE, MR. JUSTICE WHITE, and MR. JUSTICE BLACKMUN join, dissenting.

Petitioner is entitled to compensation for so much of its private "property" as was taken for public use. The parties concede that petitioner's property interest here taken was the unexpired portion of a 20-year lease on land owned by the Oregon-Washington Railroad &

---

32. "It frequently happens in the case of a lease for a long term of years that the tenant erects buildings or puts fixtures into the buildings for his own use. Even if the buildings or fixtures are attached to the real estate and would pass with a conveyance of the land, as between landlord and tenant they remain personal property. In the absence of a special agreement to the contrary, such buildings or fixtures may be removed by the tenant at any time during the continuation of the lease, provided such removal may be made without injury to the freehold. This rule, however, exists entirely for the protection of the tenant, and cannot be invoked by the condemnor. If the buildings or fixtures are attached to the real estate, they must be treated as real estate in determining the total award. But in apportioning the award, they are treated as personal property and credited to the tenant." 4 P. Nichols, Eminent Domain § 13.121[2] (3d rev. ed. 1971) (footnotes omitted).

Navigation Co. near Colfax, Washington. The Court recognizes the limited nature of petitioner's interest in the real property taken, but concludes that it was entitled to have its leasehold and improvements valued in such a way as to include the probability that petitioner's 20–year lease would have been renewed by the railroad at its expiration.

There is a plausibility about the Court's resounding endorsement of the concept of "fair market value" as the touchstone for valuation, but the result reached by the Court seems to me to be quite at odds with our prior cases. Even in its sharply limited reading of *United States v. Petty Motor Co.,* 327 U.S. 372, 66 S.Ct. 596, 90 L.Ed. 729 (1946), the Court concedes that the petitioner's expectation of having its lease renewed upon expiration is not itself an interest in property for which it may be compensated. But the Court permits the same practical result to be reached by saying that, at least in the case of improvements, the fair market value may be computed in terms of a willing buyer's expectation that the lease would be renewed.

In *United States v. Petty Motor Co., supra,* the Government acquired by condemnation the use of a structure occupied by tenants in possession under leases for various unexpired terms. The Court held that the measure of damages for condemnation of a leasehold is the value of the tenant's use of the leasehold for the remainder of the agreed term, less the agreed rent. The Court considered the argument, essentially the same raised by petitioner here, that a history of past renewal of the leases to existing tenants creates a compensable expectancy, but held that the right to compensation should be measured solely on the basis of the remainder of the tenant's term under the lease itself. * * *

The holding in *Petty* was consistent with a long line of cases to the effect that the Fifth Amendment does not require, on a taking of a property interest, compensation for mere expectancies of profit, or for the frustration of licenses or contractual rights that pertain to the land, but that are not specifically taken and that are not vested property interests. [ ]

While the inquiry as to what property interest is taken by the condemnor and the inquiry as to how that property interest shall be valued are not identical ones, they cannot be divorced without seriously undermining a number of rules dealing with the law of eminent domain that this Court has evolved in a series of decisions through the years. The landowner, after all, is interested, not in the legal terminology used to describe the property taken from him by the condemnor, but in the amount of money he is to be paid for that property. It will cause him little remorse to learn that his hope for a renewal of a lease for a term of years is not a property interest for which the Government must pay, if in the same breath he is told that the lesser legal interest that he owns may be valued to include the hoped-for renewal.

The notion of "fair market value" is not a universal formula for determining just compensation under the Fifth Amendment. * * *

It is quite apparent that the property on which the owner operates a prosperous retail establishment would command more in an open market sale than the fair value of so much of the enterprise as was "private property" within the meaning of the Fifth Amendment. Yet *Mitchell v. United States,* 267 U.S. 341, 45 S.Ct. 293, 69 L.Ed. 644 (1925), stands squarely for the proposition that the value added to the property taken by the existence of a going business is no part of the just compensation for which the Government must pay for taking the property. . . .

* * *

UNITED STATES v. 50 ACRES OF LAND ET AL.

Supreme Court of the United States, 1984.
469 U.S. 24, 105 S.Ct. 451, 83 L.Ed.2d 376.

JUSTICE STEVENS delivered the [unanimous] opinion of the Court.

The Fifth Amendment requires that the United States pay "just compensation"—normally measured by fair market value—whenever it takes private property for public use. This case involves the condemnation of property owned by a municipality. The question is whether a public condemnee is entitled to compensation measured by the cost of acquiring a substitute facility if it has a duty to replace the condemned facility. We hold that this measure of compensation is not required when the market value of the condemned property is ascertainable.

I

In 1978, as part of a flood control project, the United States condemned approximately 50 acres of land owned by the city of Duncanville, Texas.[33] The site had been used since 1969 as a sanitary landfill. In order to replace the condemned landfill, the city acquired a 113.7–acre site and developed it into a larger and better facility. In the condemnation proceedings, the city claimed that it was entitled to recover all of the costs incurred in acquiring the substitute site and developing it as a landfill, an amount in excess of $1,276,000. The United States, however, contended that just compensation should be determined by the fair market value of the condemned facility and deposited $199,950 in the registry of the court as its estimation of the amount due.

Responding to special interrogatories, the jury found that the fair market value of the condemned property was $225,000, and that the reasonable cost of a substitute facility was $723,624.01. The District

33. The United States initiated the condemnation proceedings by filing a declaration of taking under 40 U.S.C. § 258a. Under that procedure the Government deposits the estimated value of the land in the registry of the court. "Title and right to possession thereupon vest immediately in the United States. In subsequent judicial proceedings, the exact value of the land (on the date the declaration of taking was filed) is determined, and the owner is awarded the difference (if any) between the adjudicated value of the land and the amount already received by the owner, plus interest on that difference." *Kirby Forest Industries, Inc. v. United States,* 467 U.S. 1, 5, 104 S.Ct. 2187, 2191, 81 L.Ed.2d 1 (1984).

Court entered judgment for the lower amount plus interest on the difference between that amount and the sum already paid. . . .

The Court of Appeals reversed and remanded for further proceedings. . . . We granted the Government's petition for certiorari, and we now reverse with instructions to direct the District Court to enter judgment based on the jury's finding of fair market value.

II

The Court has repeatedly held that just compensation normally is to be measured by "the market value of the property at the time of the taking contemporaneously paid in money". . . .

This case is not one in which an exception to the normal measure of just compensation is required because fair market value is not ascertainable. Such cases, for the most part, involve properties that are seldom, if ever, sold in the open market. . . . In this case, however, the testimony at trial established a fairly robust market for sanitary landfill properties, and the jury's determination of the fair market value of the condemned landfill facility is adequately supported by expert testimony concerning the sale prices of comparable property. . . .

III

* * *

When the United States condemns a local public facility, the loss to the public entity, to the persons served by it, and to the local taxpayers may be no less acute than the loss in a taking of private property. Therefore, it is most reasonable to construe the reference to "private property" in the Takings Clause of the Fifth Amendment as encompassing the property of state and local governments when it is condemned by the United States. Under this construction, the same principles of just compensation presumptively apply to both private and public condemnees.

* * *

V

* * *

The city argues that its responsibility for municipal garbage disposal justifies a departure from the market value measure in this case. This responsibility compelled the city to arrange for a suitable replacement facility or substitute garbage disposal services. This obligation to replace a condemned facility, however, is no more compelling than the obligations assumed by private citizens. Even though most private condemnees are not legally obligated to replace property taken by the Government, economic circumstances often force them to do so. When a home is condemned, for example, its owner must find another place to live. The city's legal obligation to maintain public services that are interrupted by a federal condemnation does not justify a distinction between public and private condemnees for the purpose of measuring "just compensation."

... [T]he substitute-facilities doctrine, as applied in this case, diverges from the principle that just compensation must be measured by an objective standard that disregards subjective values which are only of significance to an individual owner. As the Court wrote in *Kimball Laundry Co. v. United States,* 338 U.S. 1, 5, (1949):

> "The value of property springs from subjective needs and attitudes; its value to the owner may therefore differ widely from its value to the taker. Most things, however, have a general demand which gives them a value transferable from one owner to another. As opposed to such personal and variant standards as value to the particular owner whose property has been taken, this transferable value has an external validity which makes it a fair measure of public obligation to compensate the loss incurred by an owner as a result of the taking of his property for public use. In view, however, of the liability of all property to condemnation for the common good, loss to the owner of nontransferable values deriving from his unique need for property or idiosyncratic attachment to it, like loss due to an exercise of the police power, is properly treated as part of the burden of common citizenship."

The subjective elements in the formula for determining the cost of reasonable substitute facilities would enhance the risk of error and prejudice. Since the condemnation contest is between the local community and a National Government that may be thought to have unlimited resources, the open-ended character of the substitute-facilities standard increases the likelihood that the city would actually derive the windfall that concerned both the District Court and the Court of Appeals....

The judgment of the Court of Appeals is reversed.

It is so ordered.

Notes and Questions

1. What costs or damages does this interpretation of "just compensation" in *Almota Farmers* and *50 Acres of Land* leave uncompensated? Does it require payment for pain and suffering? Sentimental value? Assume that the condemned land is the site of a house that has been occupied by the same family for a half-century. Does the family receive compensation for this history? What if the family was the Reagan family, most recently of California? Are these values "property"?

2. Federal and state statutes can require broader compensation. An example of such statutes is the federal Uniform Relocation Assistance and Real Property Acquisition Policies Act of 1970, 84 Stat. 1894, 42 U.S.C.A. § 4601 *et seq.* (requiring the payments of relocation assistance to specified persons and businesses displaced as a result of federal and federally assisted programs). Under what circumstances should a legislature mandate or

undertake a broader compensation duty than that required by the Constitution?

3. The Court in *50 Acres of Land* addressed a question left open by a previous case, *United States v. 564.54 Acres of Land, More or Less*, 441 U.S. 506, 99 S.Ct. 1854, 60 L.Ed.2d 435 (1979). In this earlier case, the U.S. government condemned a summer camp owned by the Lutheran Church. The government offered $485,400 and the church claimed $5.8 million, the cost claimed for replacing the camp. The church claimed that the large difference was due to the fact that the condemned property enjoyed the benefit of exemption, by grandfathering from "financially burdensome" regulations applicable to any other property the church would acquire. The Court refused to depart from the fair market value measure of compensation, acknowledging that "just compensation" does not require that the property owner receive all value attached to the property.

II. ZONING—THE MOST POPULAR FORM OF PUBLIC LAND USE REGULATION

Public regulation of the use and development of land comes in a variety of forms which generally focus on four aspects of land use: 1) the type of use, such as whether it will be used for agricultural, commercial, industrial, or residential purposes; 2) the density of use, manifested in concerns over the height, width, bulk, or environmental impact of the physical structures on the land; 3) the aesthetic impact of the use, which may include the design and placement of structures on the land; and 4) the effect of the particular use of the land on the cultural and social values of the community, illustrated by community conflicts over adult entertainment, housing for service-dependent groups such as low-income families and developmentally disabled persons, and whether the term "family" should be defined in land use regulations to include persons who are not related by blood or marriage.

The basic forms of modern land use regulation were established in the 1920's when the Supreme Court approved the comprehensive zoning concept, in which land in cities and counties is divided into zones or districts, and uniform regulations for land use, building height and area, as well as building setbacks, are imposed within those districts. Earlier, the Court had approved land use regulations prohibiting specific uses from particular areas when those uses were deemed to be harmful to people and land in the immediate vicinity.

A. THE CONCEPT OF ZONING

AMBLER REALTY CO. v. VILLAGE OF EUCLID, OHIO

District Court, N.D. Ohio, E.D., 1924.
297 Fed. 307.

[On November 13, 1922, the village council of Euclid adopted an ordinance establishing a comprehensive zoning plan that regulated and restricted the location of trades, industries, apartment houses, two-family houses, single family houses, the lot area to be built upon, and the size and heights of buildings in Euclid. The comprehensive ordinance divided the area of the village into six classes of use districts, U–1 to U–6 inclusive; three classes of height districts, H–1 to H–3 inclusive; and four classes of area districts, A–1 to A–4 inclusive. Use restrictions were cumulative, meaning that permitted uses in the U–2 district included those permitted in the U–1 district and so on. U–1, the most restricted district, was limited to single family homes, farms, parks and related uses. U–6, the least restricted district, included industrial and manufacturing activities as well as uses permitted in U–1, U–2, U–3, U–4 and U–5 districts. A seventh category included uses prohibited altogether. A similar plan for cumulative restriction on the height of buildings and size of lots was imposed by the height and area district regulations. Ambler Realty Company owned 68 acres of vacant land in the western end of the village. It sought to sell and develop the land for industrial purposes. Portions of the land were zoned U–2 and limited to single-family and two-family dwellings, while other portions were zoned U–3, multi-family housing, and U–6, industrial—Eds.]

WESTENHAVER, DISTRICT JUDGE. This suit is brought to have declared null and void and enforcement enjoined of Ordinance No. 2812, enacted by the municipal council of the village of Euclid, November 13, 1922, and amended by Ordinances Nos. 3367 and 3368, enacted June 11, 1923. This ordinance is what is popularly called a "zoning ordinance," i.e., one imposing a variety of restrictions upon the use of land within the village limits. After issue joined, the evidence was taken and submitted in deposition form.

This case is obviously destined to go higher. On appeal in equity cases, a reviewing court weighs the evidence, and when taken in deposition form it can do so as well as the trial court; hence it is unnecessary to make special findings of fact. Much of the evidence is immaterial; still more of it is without weight. Upon the facts the case really comes down to the provisions of the ordinance, certain physical facts characterizing the situation as it affects plaintiff's land, and the nature and extent of the impairment of its value by the ordinance restrictions. None of the important or controlling facts are in dispute, with the single exception of the extent of that damage; but even here there is no substantial denial that this damage is not only in excess of the jurisdictional amount but is substantial. As an instance of immaterial testimony may be noted the large volume relating to the inadequacy of the present water supply of the village of Euclid. Manifestly, the police power of the village to legislate in the interests of the public health or public safety cannot be enlarged by its failure or refusal to perform its fundamental duty of providing an adequate water supply. Upon the whole case, it is sufficient to say that the material and substantial allegations of plaintiff's bill are sufficiently proved.

* * *

The argument supporting this ordinance proceeds, it seems to me, both on a mistaken view of what is property and of what is police power. Property, generally speaking, defendant's counsel concede, is protected against a taking without compensation, by the guaranties of the Ohio and United States Constitutions. But their view seems to be that so long as the owner remains clothed with the legal title thereto and is not ousted from the physical possession thereof, his property is not taken, no matter to what extent his right to use it is invaded or destroyed or its present or prospective value is depreciated. This is an erroneous view. The right to property, as used in the Constitution, has no such limited meaning. * * *

A similar misconception or confusion of thought appears to exist touching the nature and extent of the police power. In one brief it is said:

"As is well known, the police power is the whole reserved power of the community to legislate concerning persons and things in the interests of the promotion of the public health, the public morals, the public safety, the public convenience, the public order, the public prosperity, and the general welfare."

It is from this broad generalization that counsel deduce the conclusion that since the ordinance in question does not take away plaintiff's title or oust it from physical possession, the power of eminent domain has not been exercised, but that the police power has been. This conception recognizes no distinction between police power and sovereign power. The power asserted is not merely sovereign, but is power unshackled by any constitutional limitation protecting life, liberty, and property from its despotic exercise. In defendants' view, the only difference between the police power and eminent domain is that the taking under the former may be done without compensation and under the latter a taking must be paid for. It seems to be the further view that whether one power or the other is exercised depends wholly on what the legislative department may see fit to recite on that subject. Such, however, is not the law. If police power meant what is claimed, all private property is now held subject to temporary and passing phases of public opinion, dominant for a day, in legislative or municipal assemblies.

* * *

Obviously, police power is not susceptible of exact definition. It would be difficult, even if it were not unwise, to attempt a more exact definition than has been given. And yet there is a wide difference between the power of eminent domain and the police power; and it is not true that the public welfare is a justification for the taking of private property for the general good. The broad language found in the books must be considered always in view of the facts, and when this is done, the difficulty disappears. A law or ordinance passed under the guise of the police power which invades private property as above defined can be sustained only when it has a real and substantial relation to the maintenance and preservation of the public peace, public order, public morals, or public safety. The courts never hesitate to look through the false pretense to the substance. * * *

Nor can the ordinances here be sustained by invoking the average reciprocity of advantage rule. * * * It is a futile suggestion that plaintiff's present and obvious loss from being deprived of the normal and legitimate use of its property would be compensated indirectly by benefits accruing to that land from the restrictions imposed by the ordinance on other land. It is equally futile to suppose that other property in the village will reap the benefit of the damage to plaintiff's property and that of others similarly situated. The only reasonable probability is that the property values taken from plaintiff and other owners similarly situated will simply disappear, or at best be transferred to other unrestricted sections of the Cleveland industrial area, or at the worst, to some other and far distant industrial area. So far as plaintiff is concerned, it is a pure loss. In the average reciprocity of advantage there is a measureless difference between adjoining property owners as regards a party wall or a boundary pillar, and the owners of property restricted as in this case. In the former there may be some reciprocity of advantage, even though unequal in individual cases. In the present case, the property values are either dissipated or transferred to unknown and more or less distant owners.

The plain truth is that the true object of the ordinance in question is to place all the property in an undeveloped area of 16 square miles in a strait-jacket. The purpose to be accomplished is really to regulate the mode of living of persons who may hereafter inhabit it. In the last analysis, the result to be accomplished is to classify the population and segregate them according to their income or situation in life. The true reason why some persons live in a mansion and others in a shack, why some live in a single-family dwelling and others in a double-family dwelling, why some live in a two-family dwelling and others in an apartment, or why some live in a well-kept apartment and others in a tenement, is primarily economic. It is a matter of income and wealth, plus the labor and difficulty of procuring adequate domestic service. Aside from contributing to these results and furthering such class tendencies, the ordinance has also an esthetic purpose; that is to say, to make this village develop into a city along lines now conceived by the village council to be attractive and beautiful. The assertion that this ordinance may tend to prevent congestion, and thereby contribute to the health and safety, would be more substantial if provision had been or could be made for adequate east and west and north and south street highways. Whether these purposes and objects would justify the taking of plaintiff's property as and for a public use need not be considered. It is sufficient to say that, in our opinion, and as applied to plaintiff's property, it may not be done without compensation under the guise of exercising the police power.

* * *

My conclusion is that the ordinance involved, as applied to plaintiff's property, is unconstitutional and void; that it takes plaintiff's property, if not for private, at least for public, use, without just compensation; that it is in no just sense a reasonable or legitimate exercise of police power. * * *

VILLAGE OF EUCLID v. AMBLER REALTY CO.

Supreme Court of the United States, 1926.
272 U.S. 365, 47 S.Ct. 114, 71 L.Ed. 303.

MR. JUSTICE SUTHERLAND delivered the opinion of the Court.

* * *

The ordinance is assailed on the grounds that it is in derogation of § 1 of the Fourteenth Amendment to the Federal Constitution in that it deprives appellee of liberty and property without due process of law and denies it the equal protection of the law, and that it offends against certain provisions of the Constitution of the State of Ohio. The prayer of the bill is for an injunction restraining the enforcement of the ordinance and all attempts to impose or maintain as to appellee's property any of the restrictions, limitations or conditions. * * *

Before proceeding to a consideration of the case, it is necessary to determine the scope of the inquiry. The bill alleges that the tract of land in question is vacant and has been held for years for the purpose of selling and developing it for industrial uses, for which it is especially adapted, being immediately in the path of progressive industrial development; that for such uses it has a market value of about $10,000 per acre, but if the use be limited to residential purposes the market value is not in excess of $2,500 per acre; that the first 200 feet of the parcel back from Euclid Avenue, if unrestricted in respect of use, has a value of $150 per front foot, but if limited to residential uses, and ordinary mercantile business be excluded therefrom, its value is not in excess of $50 per front foot.

It is specifically averred that the ordinance attempts to restrict and control the lawful uses of appellee's land so as to confiscate and destroy a great part of its value; that it is being enforced in accordance with its terms; that prospective buyers of land for industrial, commercial and residential uses in the metropolitan district of Cleveland are deterred from buying any part of this land because of the existence of the ordinance and the necessity thereby entailed of conducting burdensome and expensive litigation in order to vindicate the right to use the land for lawful and legitimate purposes; that the ordinance constitutes a cloud upon the land, reduces and destroys its value, and has the effect of diverting the normal industrial, commercial and residential development thereof to other and less favorable locations.

The record goes no farther than to show, as the lower court found, that the normal, and reasonably to be expected, use and development of that part of appellee's land adjoining Euclid Avenue is for general trade and commercial purposes, particularly retail stores and like establishments, and that the normal, and reasonably to be expected, use and development of the residue of the land is for industrial and trade purposes. Whatever injury is inflicted by the mere existence and threatened enforcement of the ordinance is due to restrictions in respect of these and similar uses; to which perhaps should be added—if not included in the foregoing—restrictions in respect of apartment houses. Specifically, there is nothing in the record to suggest that any damage results from the presence in the ordinance of those restrictions relating to churches, schools, libraries and other public and semi-public buildings. It is neither alleged nor proved that there is, or may be, a demand for any part of appellee's land for any of the last named uses; and we cannot assume the existence of facts which would justify an injunction upon this record in respect of this class of restrictions. For present purposes the provisions of the ordinance in respect of these uses may, therefore, be put aside as unnecessary to be considered. It is also unnecessary to consider the effect of the restrictions in respect of U–1 districts, since none of appellee's land falls within that class.

We proceed, then, to a consideration of those provisions of the ordinance to which the case as it is made relates, first disposing of a preliminary matter.

A motion was made in the court below to dismiss the bill on the ground that, because complainant [appellee] had made no effort to obtain a building permit or apply to the zoning board of appeals for relief as it might have done under the terms of the ordinance, the suit was premature. The motion was properly overruled. The effect of the allegations of the bill is that the ordinance of its own force operates greatly to reduce the value of appellee's lands and destroy their marketability for industrial, commercial and residential uses; and the attack is directed, not against any specific provision or provisions, but against the ordinance as an entirety. Assuming the premises, the existence and maintenance of the ordinance, in effect, constitutes a present invasion of appellee's property rights and a threat to continue it. Under these circumstances, the equitable jurisdiction is clear. [   ]

It is not necessary to set forth the provisions of the Ohio Constitution which are thought to be infringed. The question is the same under both Constitutions, namely, as stated by appellee: Is the ordinance invalid in that it violates the constitutional protection "to the right of property in the appellee by attempted regulations under the guise of the police power, which are unreasonable and confiscatory?"

Building zone laws are of modern origin. They began in this country about twenty-five years ago. Until recent years, urban life was comparatively simple; but with the great increase and concentration of population, problems have developed, and constantly are developing, which require, and will continue to require, additional restrictions in respect of the use and occupation of private lands in urban communities. Regulations, the wisdom, necessity and validity of which, as applied to existing conditions, are so apparent that they are now uniformly sustained, a century ago, or even half a century ago, probably would have been rejected as arbitrary and oppressive. Such regulations are sustained, under the complex conditions of our day, for reasons analogous to those which justify traffic regulations, which, before the advent of automobiles and rapid transit street railways, would have been condemned as fatally arbitrary and unreasonable. And in this there is no inconsistency, for while the meaning of constitutional guaranties never varies, the scope of their application must expand or contract to meet the new and different conditions which are constantly coming within the field of their operation. In a changing world, it is impossible that it should be otherwise. But although a degree of elasticity is thus imparted, not to the *meaning,* but to the *application* of constitutional principles, statutes and ordinances, which, after giving due weight to the new conditions, are found clearly not to conform to the Constitution, of course, must fall.

The ordinance now under review, and all similar laws and regulations, must find their justification in some aspect of the police power, asserted for the public welfare. The line which in this field separates the legitimate from the illegitimate assumption of power is not capable of precise delimitation. It varies with circumstances and conditions. A regulatory zoning ordinance, which would be clearly valid as applied to the great cities, might be clearly invalid as applied to rural communities. In solving doubts, the maxim *sic utere tuo ut alienum non laedas,* which lies at the foundation of so much of the common law of nuisances, ordinarily will furnish a fairly helpful clew. And the law of nuisances, likewise, may be consulted, not for the purpose of controlling, but for the helpful aid of its analogies in the process of ascertaining the scope of, the power. Thus the question whether the power exists to forbid the erection of a building of a particular kind or for a particular use, like the question whether a particular thing is a nuisance, is to be determined, not by an abstract consideration of the building or of the thing considered apart, but by considering it in connection with the circumstances and the locality. [   ] A nuisance may be merely a right thing in the wrong place,—like a pig in the parlor instead of the barnyard. If the validity of the legislative classification for zoning purposes be fairly debatable, the legislative judgment must be allowed to control. [   ]

There is no serious difference of opinion in respect of the validity of laws and regulations fixing the height of buildings within reasonable limits, the character of materials and methods of construction, and the adjoining area which must be left open, in order to minimize the danger of fire or collapse, the evils of over-crowding, and the like, and excluding from residential sections offensive trades, industries and structures likely to create nuisances. [   ]

Here, however, the exclusion is in general terms of all industrial establishments, and it may thereby happen that not only offensive or dangerous industries will be excluded, but those which are neither offensive nor dangerous will share the same fate. But this is no more than happens in respect of many practice-forbidding laws which this Court has upheld although drawn in general terms so as to include individual cases that may turn out to be innocuous in themselves. [   ] The inclusion of a reasonable margin to insure effective enforcement, will not put upon a law, otherwise valid, the stamp of invalidity. Such laws may also find their justification in the fact that, in some fields, the bad fades into the good by such insensible degrees that the two are not capable of being readily distinguished and separated in terms of legislation. In the light of these considerations, we are not prepared to say that the end in view was not sufficient to justify the general rule of the ordinance, although some industries of an innocent character might fall within the proscribed class. * * *

It is said that the Village of Euclid is a mere suburb of the City of Cleveland; that the industrial development of that city has now reached and in some degree extended into the village and, in the obvious course of things, will soon absorb the entire area for industrial enterprises; that the effect of the ordinance is to divert this natural development elsewhere with the consequent loss of increased values to the owners of the lands within the village borders. But the village, though physically a suburb of Cleveland, is politically a separate municipality, with powers of its own and authority to govern itself as it sees fit within the limits of the organic law of its creation and the State and Federal Constitutions. Its governing authorities, presumably representing a majority of its inhabitants and voicing their will, have determined, not that industrial development shall cease at its boundaries, but that the course of such development shall proceed within definitely fixed lines. If it be a proper exercise of the police power to relegate industrial establishments to localities separated from residential sections, it is not easy to find a sufficient reason for denying the power because the effect of its exercise is to divert an industrial flow from the course which it would follow, to the injury of the residential public if left alone, to another course where such injury will be obviated. It is not meant by this, however, to exclude the possibility of cases where the general public interest would so far outweigh the interest of the municipality that the municipality would not be allowed to stand in the way.

We find no difficulty in sustaining restrictions of the kind thus far reviewed. The serious question in the case arises over the provisions of the ordinance excluding from residential districts, apartment houses, business houses, retail stores and shops, and other like establishments. This question involves the validity of what is really the crux of the more recent zoning legislation, namely, the creation and maintenance of residential districts, from which business and trade of every sort, including hotels and apartment houses, are excluded. Upon that question this Court has not thus far spoken. The decisions of the state courts are numerous and conflicting; but those which broadly sustain the power greatly outnumber those which deny altogether or narrowly limit it; and it is very apparent that there is a constantly increasing tendency in the direction of the broader view.

* * *

The decisions enumerated * * * agree that the exclusion of buildings devoted to business, trade, etc., from residential districts, bears a rational relation to the health and safety of the community. Some of the grounds for this conclusion are—promotion of the health and security from injury of children and others by separating dwelling houses from territory devoted to trade and industry; suppression and prevention of disorder; facilitating the extinguishment of fires, and the enforcement of street traffic regulations and other general welfare ordinances; aiding the health and safety of the community by excluding from residential areas the confusion and danger of fire, contagion and disorder which in greater or less degree attach to the location of stores, shops and factories. Another ground is that the construction and repair of streets may be rendered easier and less expensive by confining the greater part of the heavy traffic to the streets where business is carried on.

* * *

The matter of zoning has received much attention at the hands of commissions and experts, and the results of their investigations have been set forth in comprehensive reports. These reports, which bear every evidence of painstaking consideration, concur in the view that the segregation of residential, business, and industrial buildings will make it easier to provide fire apparatus suitable for the character and intensity of the development in each section; that it will increase the safety and security of home life; greatly tend to prevent street accidents, especially to children, by reducing the traffic and resulting confusion in residential sections; decrease noise and other conditions which produce or intensify nervous disorders; preserve a more favorable environment in which to rear children, etc. With particular reference to apartment houses, it is pointed out that the development of detached house sections is greatly retarded by the coming of apartment houses, which has sometimes resulted in destroying the entire section for private house purposes; that in such sections very often the apartment house is a mere parasite, constructed in order to take advantage of the open spaces and attractive surroundings created by the residential character of the district. Moreover, the coming of one apartment house is followed by others, interfering by their height and bulk with the free circulation of air and monopolizing the rays of the sun which otherwise would fall upon the smaller homes, and bringing, as their necessary accompaniments, the disturbing noises incident to increased traffic and business, and the occupation, by means of moving and parked automobiles, of larger portions of the streets, thus detracting from their safety and depriving children of the privilege of quiet and open spaces for play, enjoyed by those in more favored localities,—until, finally, the residential character of the neighborhood and its desirability as a place of detached residences are utterly destroyed. Under these circumstances, apartment houses, which in a different environment would be not only entirely unobjectionable but highly desirable, come very near to being nuisances.

If these reasons, thus summarized, do not demonstrate the wisdom or sound policy in all respects of those restrictions which we have indicated as pertinent to the inquiry, at least, the reasons are sufficiently cogent to preclude us from saying, as it must be said before the ordinance can be declared unconstitutional, that such provisions are clearly arbitrary and unreasonable, having no substantial relation to the public health, safety, morals, or general welfare. [   ]

It is true that when, if ever, the provisions set forth in the ordinance in tedious and minute detail, come to be concretely applied to particular premises, including those of the appellee, or to particular conditions, or to be considered in connection with specific complaints, some of them, or even many of them, may be found to be clearly arbitrary and unreasonable. But where the equitable remedy of injunction is sought, as it is here, not upon the ground of a present infringement or denial of a specific right, or of a particular injury in process of actual execution, but upon the broad ground that the mere existence and threatened enforcement of the ordinance, by materially and adversely affecting values and curtailing the opportunities of the market, constitute a present and irreparable injury, the court will not scrutinize its provisions, sentence by sentence, to ascertain by a process of piecemeal dissection whether there may be, here and there, provisions of a minor character, or relating to matters of administration, or not shown to contribute to the injury complained of, which, if attacked separately, might not withstand the test of constitutionality. In respect of such provisions, of which specific complaint is not made, it cannot be said that the land owner has suffered or is threatened with an injury which entitles him to challenge their constitutionality. * * *

* * *

Decree reversed.

Mr. Justice Van Devanter, Mr. Justice McReynolds and Mr. Justice Butler, dissent.

Notes and Questions

1.　The *Euclid* case, which gave the stamp of approval to the technique which was to become the bedrock of the American law of public land use control, was decided by the narrowest of margins. Justice Sutherland, the authority of the majority opinion, was reported by a former law clerk of Chief Justice Stone to have been leaning in the other direction until "talks with his dissenting brethren * * * shook his convictions and led him to request a reargument" of the case, after which he changed his mind and voted with the majority to uphold the ordinance. McCormack, Law Clerk's Recollection, 46 Colum.L.Rev. 710, 712 (1946). The person generally given credit for turning the case around was Alfred Bettman, a well-known land use attorney in Cincinnati who filed an amicus curiae brief on behalf of a number of national and state organizations who were promoting comprehensive planning and zoning as necessary tools to enable municipalities to guide and control their growth. For histories of the case, see Brooks, The Office File Box—Emanations from the Battlefield, in Zoning and the American Dream at 3, (C. Haar & J. Kayden eds. 1989); Tarlock, Euclid Revisited, 34 Land Use L. & Zoning Dig. 4 (1982); A. Bettman, City and Regional Planning Papers (1946). An insightful debate on the legacy of *Euclid* is presented in Harr & Wolf, Euclid Lives: The Survival of Progressive Jurisprudence, 115 Harv. L. Rev. 2158 (2002) and Claeys, Euclid Lives? The Uneasy Legacy of Progressivism in Zoning, 73 Fordham L. Rev. 731 (2004).

See generally Rathkopf's The Law of Zoning and Planning 1–10 to 1–26 (E. Ziegler ed. 2005); D. Mandelker, Land Use Law 5.02–5.27 (5th Ed., 2003); J. Juergensmeyer & T. Roberts, Land Use Planning and Land Development Regulation Law 42–63 (2003); 1 N. Williams & J. Taylor, American Land Planning Law 461–477 (2003 Rev. Ed.). D. Kmiec, Zoning and Planning Deskbook 2–14 to 2–38 (2d Ed 2002); W. Stoebuck & D. Whitman, The Law of Property 3d Ed 568–583 (2000).

2. The first comprehensive zoning ordinance in America was enacted by New York City in 1916. Supporters were greatly influenced by the use of zoning in German cities in the late nineteenth century. As Justice Sutherland noted in *Euclid,* building regulations in the United States began around the turn of the century to combat the deleterious effects of the Industrial Revolution: squalor, filth, disease, and fire, particularly in the inner cities populated by immigrants. A second force, which District Judge Westenhaver protested, sought to protect personal sensibilities and property values from encroachment by activities and individuals deemed to be undesirable. The two movements came together in the New York City zoning ordinance of 1916. From that ordinance, and a similar one in St. Louis a few years later, came a series of "standard" state planning and zoning enabling acts and corresponding local ordinances promulgated by the United States Department of Commerce under the leadership of then—Secretary of Commerce Herbert Hoover. Following the Supreme Court's decision in *Euclid,* comprehensive zoning swept the country. For a readable and thorough history of the enactment of the New York City ordinance and its influence on the development of zoning as a political process, see S. Toll, Zoned American (1969).

3. Zoning as a concept was tied to the notion of comprehensive planning. In theory, communities were supposed to prepare a comprehensive plan that was to be the basis for land use regulation. Zoning was then to become the device for implementing the plan that had previously been adopted by the community. In practice, many communities dispensed with the formal planning process, at least in written form, and went straight to a zoning ordinance. The courts acceded to this approach by concluding that adoption of a formal plan was not a condition precedent to a valid zoning scheme so long as the zoning ordinance itself contained evidence that the community had engaged in a rational process of deliberation about the future of the community. See, e.g., Borsuk v. Town of St. John, 820 N.E.2d 118, 122 (Ind. 2005) (Indiana code requires local legislators to "pay reasonable regard" to comprehensive plan as well as other enumerated factors); AvalonBay Communities, Inc. v. Town of Orange, 256 Conn. 557, 575, 775

A.2d 284, 298 (2001) town (comprehensive) plan "is merely advisory.") Town of Bedford v. Village of Mt. Kisco, 33 N.Y.2d 178, 351 N.Y.S.2d 129, 306 N.E.2d 155 (1973). The seminal article discussing the relationship of zoning to planning is Haar, In Accordance With a Comprehensive Plan, 68 Harv. L. Rev. 1154 (1955).

4. The comprehensive zoning approach tended to impose a grid pattern of development, partly because of the uniformity of treatment within districts requirement, which was based on the premise that homogeneity of use was desirable and that different types of land use should be segregated from one another. Comprehensive zoning was prospective in nature and thus was best suited for the regulation of new uses of previously undeveloped land. When it was imposed on the built-up areas of major cities, an extensive "non-conforming use" component had to be added to recognize the reality of the heterogeneous use, market-focused type of development that already was in place in the cities. See, e.g., State ex rel. Manhein v. Harrison, 164 La. 564, 114 So. 159 (1927) (upholding Shreveport ordinance which contained non-conforming use regulations); City of Aurora v. Burns, 319 Ill. 84, 149 N.E. 784 (1925) (upholding Illinois zoning enabling act containing non-conforming use regulations); Building Inspector of Lowell v. Stoklosa, 250 Mass. 52, 145 N.E. 262 (1924) and In re Opinion of the Justices, 234 Mass. 597, 127 N.E. 525 (1920) (upholding Massachusetts zoning enabling act and Middlesex ordinance containing non-conforming use regulations).

5. Note that the ordinance approved in *Euclid* was cumulative in nature, U–1 uses were permitted in the U–2 district and so on. This produced a "hierarchy" of uses, based on exclusivity, which placed single-family residences and the persons who occupied them, at the top of a status pyramid. Note that the highest status use did not necessarily comport with the highest economic use. Ambler Realty Company claimed that industrial use of its property would make it four times as valuable as residential use. Was Ambler deprived of a property interest because of its loss of an expected increase in value of its property? Is expectation of profit a stick in the property bundle? Recall *Pennsylvania Coal v. Mahon, Penn Central Transportation Co. v. City of New York,* and *Lucas v. South Carolina Coastal Council* supra.

Although the *Euclid* ordinance also regulated the height and area of structures to be placed on land, the controlling variable in the ordinance was the use to which the land could be put. While alternative approaches to land development regulation based on the design of a structure (form-based zoning (FBZ)) and the effects of particular activities on the surrounding environment (performance zoning) have been popular, the main emphasis of land development regulation continues to be focused on the particular use or uses to which a parcel or building can be put. See, e.g., S.M. White, Classifying and Defining Uses and Building Forms: Land–Use Coding for Zoning Regulations, APA Zoning Practice, v. 22, n. 9 (September 2005).

6. On what basis is the segregation inherent in zoning justified by the *Euclid* Court? Is it that incompatible uses, if not segregated, would become harmful to the public? Or is it that the quality of life for the people favored by the segregation will be improved? Is it sufficient to say, as the Supreme Court did in Mugler v. Kansas, 123 U.S. 623, 665, 8 S.Ct. 273, 299, 31 L.Ed.

205 (1887), that property owners hold their property subject to "the implied obligation that the owner's use of it shall not be injurious to the community"? Did Justice Douglas provide the answer in Berman v. Parker, 348 U.S. 26, 33, 75 S.Ct. 98, 102, 99 L.Ed. 27 (1954), when he declared: "The concept of the public welfare is broad and inclusive. The values it represents are spiritual as well as physical, aesthetic as well as monetary. It is within the power of the legislature to determine that the community should be beautiful as well as healthy, spacious as well as clean, well-balanced as well as carefully patrolled." Is the true test of zoning the impact that it has on property rights or its impact on personal relationships? Recall *State v. Shack,* supra, Chapter One.

7. Considering the history of the development of American cities and suburbs since the 1920s, who was more perceptive, District Judge Westenhaver or Justice Sutherland? Dr. Robert B. Reich, a political economist, has lamented the "secession" of the "top fifth of working Americans" from the rest of the populace, driven in part by a "near obsessive concern with maintaining or upgrading property values." Reich, Secession of the Successful, New York Times Magazine, January 20, 1991, at p. 17.

Professor Eric Claeys, in his essay on *Euclid* cited supra, argues that zoning is an application of "Progressive political theory" developed in the 1910s and 1920s.

As they apply to zoning, the main features of Progressive political theory run as follows. First, in the Progressive understanding, "the general welfare" tends to elevate what the Progressives called "organic" goods and what we would now call collective, communitarian goods. It elevates order, community, homogeneity, financial security, and beauty, and subordinates more self-centered goods like freedom and individual expression in the use of land. Second, and conversely, Progressive theory reshapes how law and regulation conceive of property. Property is directed away from allocating to each owner a zone of noninterference within which to use her own property actively for her own peculiar purposes; instead, owners are transformed into stakeholders in the common civic, aesthetic, and property-value interests that unify everyone in the locality. Third, zoning expects that local majorities should be given free rein to express their own communal visions of community, security, and aesthetics. Last, zoning expects that these majority-driven community visions can be implemented by local planning experts, who bring them to life by promulgating a legislative pattern of use districts, by enforcing the districts, and by granting exceptions to them. Claeys, 73 Fordham L. Rev. 731, 735 (2004).

Professor Claeys expresses doubts about zoning, primarily because of his reservations about the viability of the Progressive political theory on which it is based and which Professors Haar and Wolf celebrate in their essay noted supra. He argues that two current theories of normative legal scholarship, law and economics and what he terms "law and society" (how people tend to use law to create status groups) "tend to be skeptical [of zoning] because they doubt that people are as oriented toward communitarian goals as Progressives and communitarians have assumed." *Id.*, at 765–766.

8. Two years after the *Euclid* decision, the Supreme Court sustained a due process challenge to the application of a zoning ordinance to a particular piece of property, in Nectow v. City of Cambridge, 277 U.S. 183, 48 S.Ct. 447, 72 L.Ed. 842 (1928). The zoning ordinance changed a 100–foot–wide strip of land from commercial to residential use, although the strip was surrounded by commercial and industrial development. The landowner argued that no practical use of the land could be made as it was rezoned. The Supreme Court upheld an injunction against implementation of the zoning amendment, based on the finding that the " * * * districting of the plaintiff's land in a residence district would not promote the health, safety, convenience and general welfare of the inhabitants of that part of the Defendant city, taking into account the natural development thereof and the character of the district and the resulting benefit * * * " Id. at 187.

Despite the Supreme Court's apparent signal in *Nectow* that it was prepared to supervise the application of zoning laws, it did not make another important zoning decision until upholding a restrictive definition of "family" in Belle Terre v. Boraas, 416 U.S. 1, 94 S.Ct. 1536, 39 L.Ed.2d 797 (1974), almost 50 years later.

9. One legacy of the *Nectow* decision and the Court's subsequent half-century abdication from the zoning field was an uncertainty about the appropriate relief to be awarded in zoning cases. For example, the Supreme Court of Michigan in Schwartz v. City of Flint, 426 Mich. 295, 395 N.W.2d 678, 686 (1986), quoted Professor Ellickson that *Nectow*:

"has been construed to mean that a landowner's standard remedy against overly restrictive zoning should be some form of injunctive relief and not damages. [Also,] by failing to specify what type of injunctive relief the landowner was to receive, *Nectow* reinforced the judicial tendency toward sloppiness in the specification of remedies in zoning cases." Ellickson, Suburban Growth Controls: An Economic and Legal Analysis, 86 Yale L.J. 385, 490 (1977).

The Court in *Schwartz* declined to award damages, described as an "intriguing" concept, and settled for a declaration of invalidity when a zoning ordinance is applied unconstitutionally, along with a permissible judicial finding that the plaintiff's proposed use is reasonable when the plaintiff has met that burden, and an injunction against interference with that use. 395 N.W.2d at 692–693. The Court was particularly concerned about not invading the legislative prerogative of local governments. Do you think it succeeded?

Relief in the form of a "builder's remedy"—a judicial order that a building permit be issued so long as the developer complies with other valid local regulations—has been granted by some courts. See, e.g., Britton v. Town of Chester, 134 N.H. 434, 595 A.2d 492 (1991); Southern Burlington County N.A.A.C.P. v. Township of Mount Laurel, 92 N.J. 158, 456 A.2d 390 (1983) (Mount Laurel II) discussed infra.

As we learn in contracts, torts and civil procedure courses, the traditional common-law remedy for injury is an award of monetary damages. Injunctive relief is an extraordinary remedy available only when damages would be inadequate. However, for a variety of reasons, including remnants of the tort doctrine of sovereign immunity, concern about potential budget-busting damages awards, and the delegation of taxing and spending decisions to the legislative branch of government by the separation of powers doctrine, the normal order of remedies is reversed in zoning cases: injunctive relief is ordinary and a damages award is extraordinary. See, e.g., Agins v. Tiburon, 24 Cal.3d 266, 157 Cal.Rptr. 372, 598 P.2d 25 (1979), aff'd on other grounds, 447 U.S. 255, 100 S.Ct. 2138, 65 L.Ed.2d 106 (1980).

Did the Supreme Court in *First English,* supra, reverse the normal remedy sequence in zoning cases? After *First English,* can a municipality be required to pay damages for invalid application of the zoning power? See Pheasant Bridge Corp. v. Township of Warren, 169 N.J. 282, 777 A.2d 334, 343 (2001) (no compensable temporary taking occurred "merely by having been subjected to an invalid ordinance during the time it took to challenge successfully the ordinance's application"); Bello v. Walker, 840 F.2d 1124 (3d Cir.1988), overruled on other grounds, United Artists Theatre Circuit, Inc. v. Township of Warrington, 316 F.3d 392 (3d Cir. 2003) (unlawful denial of building permit not a taking when other permissible uses were possible); City of Virginia Beach v. Virginia Land Investment Ass'n No. 1, 239 Va. 412, 389 S.E.2d 312 (1990) (invalid piecemeal downzoning did not deprive owner of all economically viable uses of property).

B. MANAGING CHANGE THROUGH ZONING ADMINISTRATION

Zoning was initially thought to be a technique for preserving the status quo, as that status was articulated by the planning and legislative process leading to enactment of a comprehensive zoning ordinance. However, communities constantly change, either by growth or decline, and it soon became apparent that a major function of zoning would be the management of change. The following case explores the use of traditional zoning techniques to manage change.

BELL v. CITY OF ELKHORN

Supreme Court of Wisconsin, 1985.
122 Wis.2d 558, 364 N.W.2d 144.

CALLOW, JUSTICE.

This is an appeal from a judgment of the circuit court for Walworth county denying plaintiffs' request for a declaratory judgment and upholding a city of Elkhorn (City) amendatory zoning ordinance. The appeal was certified by the court of appeals and accepted by this court. * * * We affirm the circuit court.

The issues presented on appeal are whether the existence of a formal comprehensive plan is a condition precedent to the adoption of a valid zoning ordinance; whether Elkhorn's rezoning of certain property constituted illegal spot zoning; and whether the commercial-shopping district portion of Elkhorn's zoning ordinance is unconstitutional for failure to limit the City's legislative discretion.

This action arises out of the city of Elkhorn's approval of an application to rezone two parcels of land from multiple family use to commercial-shopping use. The subject property is located at the southeast corner of the intersection of East Geneva and South Lincoln Streets in Elkhorn. In 1972, Elkhorn enacted zoning ordinance No. 426, which divided the city into districts and provided certain regulations with regard to the use of property in those districts. Prior to the rezoning amendment which is the subject of this action, three corners of the intersection of East Geneva and South Lincoln Streets were zoned B–3, commercial-shopping district. The southeast corner, where the subject property is located, was zoned R–4, multi-family residential district. At the time this action was commenced, a gas station, muffler shop, and pizza parlor were located on the corners which were zoned B–3. Two residences were located on the subject property.

In October, 1982, the defendant, Hardees C & S Foods, Inc., applied to the Elkhorn common council to have the property at the southeast corner of the East Geneva and South Lincoln Street intersection rezoned from R–4 to B–3. Hardees intended to build a restaurant on the site. The city clerk-treasurer gave notice of a public hearing to be held before a joint meeting of the common council and the city plan commission on the proposed amendment to Elkhorn's zoning law, pursuant to sec. 62.23(7)(d)2, Stats. The plaintiffs, who are owners of more than twenty percent of the property located within 100 feet of the subject premises, filed a protest petition in opposition to the proposed rezone. The effect of the protest petition was that a three-fourths vote of the city council was required to pass the amendatory zoning ordinance.

A public hearing was held on November 1, 1982, and the city plan commission recommended to the common council that the petition to rezone be approved. On November 15, 1982, the council passed the amendment to the zoning ordinance, which changed the zoning of the subject property from R–4 to B–3, by a five to one vote. The amendatory zoning ordinance was published and became effective on December 23, 1982. A building permit was issued to Hardees on December 27, 1982, and the restaurant opened on April 19, 1983.

On December 13, 1982, the plaintiffs filed a declaratory judgment action challenging the City's passage of the amendatory zoning ordinance. An amended summons and complaint were filed on April 26, 1983. The plaintiffs' attack on the City's action was threefold. First, plaintiffs contended that Elkhorn's zoning ordinances were invalid because Elkhorn has not adopted a comprehensive plan. Second, plaintiffs charged that the rezone amendment amounted to spot zoning. Finally, plaintiffs contended that the portion of Elkhorn's original zoning ordinance establishing B–3 commercial-shopping districts was unconstitutional because it lacked proper standards.

The matter was tried to the court in July, 1983. On December 20, 1983, the court issued its memorandum decision denying plaintiffs' request for a declaratory judgment. The court found that a formal comprehensive plan is not a condition precedent to the enactment of a valid zoning ordinance. The court also found that the rezone of the property did not constitute spot zoning. Finally, the court upheld the constitutionality of Elkhorn's original zoning ordinance and rejected plaintiffs' argument that the portion of the ordinance establishing B–3 districts lacked proper standards. * * *

The first issue we decide is whether the existence of a formal comprehensive plan is a condition precedent to the adoption of a valid zoning ordinance. To resolve this issue, we must turn to sec. 62.23, Stats., which sets forth Wisconsin's statutory scheme for city planning. Section 62.23(1) provides that a city may create a city plan commission. Section 62.23(2), Stats. states:

> "It shall be the function and duty of the commission to make and adopt a master plan for the physical development of the municipality * * *. The master plan, with the accompanying maps, plats, charts and descriptive and explanatory matter, shall show the commission's recommendations for such physical development, *and may include* * * * *a comprehensive zoning plan.*" (Emphasis added.)

Section 62.23(7)(a) gives the city council the power to enact zoning ordinances "[f]or the purpose of promoting health, safety, morals or the general welfare of the community." Section 62.23(7)(c) requires that "[s]uch (zoning) regulations shall be made in accordance with a comprehensive plan. * * * "The statutes do not define the term "comprehensive plan," and the parties hold conflicting views as to its meaning. The defendants argue that the requirement of a "comprehensive plan" can be met by the enactment of a comprehensive zoning ordinance itself and that the statute does not require a comprehensive plan to be a separate document. The plaintiffs contend that a zoning ordinance does not qualify as a comprehensive plan and that a separate document must be prepared and adopted before a city may enact a zoning ordinance.

The question of whether a zoning ordinance may constitute a comprehensive plan is a matter of first impression in Wisconsin. * * *

Commentators have defined a comprehensive plan as a guide to community development. * * * The objectives sought to be achieved through the development of a comprehensive plan include: (1) improving the physical environment of the community; (2) promoting the public interest; (3) facilitating the implementation of community policies on physical development; (4) effecting political and technical coordination in community development; (5) injecting long-range considerations into the determination of short-range actions; and (6) bringing professional and technical knowledge to bear on the making of political decisions concerning the physical development of the community. [   ]

* * *

The majority view held by courts and commentators that have considered the issue is that a zoning ordinance itself may satisfy the requirement that zoning be in accordance with a comprehensive plan. In *Lanphear v. Antwerp Township,* 50 Mich.App. 641, 646, 214 N.W.2d 66

(Mich.Ct.App.1973), the court rejected the view that the plan must be embodied in a separate document.

> " * * * [T]here is no requirement in (the statute) that the 'plan' be written or be anything beyond 'a generalized conception by the members of the board as to how the districts in the township shall be * * * used'. This 'generalized conception' is exhibited in the zoning ordinance itself, since the document zones districts, prescribes variances, land uses, etc., for the entire township, and thus plans the township's future development."

* * *

Several courts have held that planning legislation requires the preparation and adoption of a separate comprehensive plan document and that the adoption of a formal comprehensive plan is a condition precedent to the enactment of a zoning ordinance. [ ]. However, none of those cases involved the interpretation of a statute containing the language that ordinances must be "in accordance with a comprehensive plan."

We find the majority view to be persuasive on this issue. * * * The purpose of a comprehensive plan is to provide an orderly method of land use regulation for the community. That purpose can be accomplished by the zoning ordinance itself without the need of a separate document labeled "Comprehensive Plan." The clear intent of the legislature in enacting sec. 62.23, Stats., was to have cities design a general plan to control the use of property in the community. This can be accomplished with or without the advice of a plan commission because the creation of a plan commission is at the discretion of the governing body of the community. [ ] The power to zone is exclusively vested in the city council. [ ]

Elkhorn's zoning ordinance divided the city into eleven districts and provided certain restrictions for the use of property in each district. It set forth regulations regarding nonconforming and conditional uses. It provided a procedure for changes and amendments to the ordinance. It established a board of appeals and specified its powers. Elkhorn's zoning ordinance serves as a general plan to control and direct the use and development of property in the city and serves as a guide to future community development. As such, we hold that the ordinance itself is a comprehensive plan * * *. No separate comprehensive plan document need be adopted by a city as a condition precedent to enacting a zoning ordinance.

The next issue we decide is whether Elkhorn's adoption of the amendatory zoning ordinance constituted spot zoning. Spot zoning has been defined as "the practice whereby a single lot or area is granted privileges which are not granted or extended to other land in the vicinity in the same use district." *Howard v. Village of Elm Grove,* 80 Wis.2d 33, 41, 257 N.W.2d 850 (1977); *Cushman v. Racine,* 39 Wis.2d 303, 306–07, 159 N.W.2d 67 (1968). This court has previously held that such zoning is not illegal per se because it is not necessarily inconsistent with the purposes for which zoning ordinances can be passed * * *. However, rezoning should be consistent with long-range planning and be based upon considerations which affect the whole community. [ ] Spot zoning "should only be indulged in where it is in the public interest and not solely for the benefit of the property owner who requests rezoning." [*Cushman v. Racine,* 39 Wis.2d 303,] 309, 159 N.W.2d 67 (1968), citing *Buhler v. Racine,* 33 Wis.2d 137, 150–51, 146 N.W.2d 403 (1966).

We do not believe the facts of this case support a finding that the amendatory zoning ordinance constituted spot zoning. Three corners of the intersection where the subject property was located were zoned commercial at the time Hardees applied for rezoning. Those lots which were already zoned commercial contained a gas station, pizza parlor, and muffler shop. This was not a case of a single commercial use encroaching on a strictly residential area. Testimony was presented at trial that single family residential use in the area was deteriorating. The amendatory zoning ordinance did not grant special privileges to a single parcel inconsistent with the use of property in the general area. Thus, we hold that the rezoning of Hardees' property was not spot zoning.

* * *

The judgment of the circuit court is affirmed.

Notes and Questions

1.   In Schubach v. Silver, 461 Pa. 366, 336 A.2d 328 (1975), landowners sought to have a zoning amendment declared invalid as spot zoning. The change allowed construction of a nursing home on land located between residential and commercial areas. The Supreme Court of Pennsylvania characterized the spot zoning question as "whether the rezoned land is being treated unjustifiably different from similar surrounding land." Id. at 336. The court quoted 8 McQuillin on Municipal Corporations: "It is well-settled that an ordinance cannot create an 'island' of more or less restricted use within a district zoned for a different use or uses, where there are no differentiating factors between the 'island' and the district * * * thus, singling out one lot or a small area for different treatment from that accorded to similar surrounding land indistinguishable from it in character * * * " Id. at 336. The court upheld the rezoning, noting that the rezoned use was different from that of the surrounding area, but that by its location the land could actually only be used effectively as a "natural extension" of the already existing commercial use. Furthermore, the court took into consideration the fact that the area had been a problem spot because of its location between residential and commercial zoning areas. Construction of a nursing home would create a transition zone that would buffer the two zones, and thus could be seen as the best possible use of this land, the court concluded.

2.   Note the *Bell* court's definition of spot zoning—the practice of granting special privileges to a single lot or area. As the court noted, this is

not *per se* invalid. Spot zoning becomes invalid when it arbitrarily and unreasonably permits a use "inconsistent with ... the rest of the district ... and made for the sole benefit of the private interest of the owner." Treme v. St. Louis County, 609 S.W.2d 706 (Mo. App. 1980). Occasionally a statute or a regulation will provide a different definition of spot zoning and, in the tradition of viewing legislation as permissible modification or supplementation of the common law, courts will apply such legislative definitions. See, e.g., Redpath v. Missouri Highway and Transportation Commission, 14 S.W.3d 34 (Mo. App. 1999) (Highway Commission not required to consider public benefit of proposed billboard authorized by city's re-zoning of private property in denying application for a billboard permit under statute prohibiting spot zoning for the "sole purpose of accommodating a billboard").

3. Cases such as *Bell* and *Schubach* illustrate the traditional way that courts have approached rezoning decisions challenged by neighbors as illegal "spot" zoning—such decisions are clothed with a presumption of validity as legislative decisions, challengers have the difficult burden of overcoming the presumption, and "fairly debatable" decisions will not be second-guessed.

An alternative way of looking at rezoning decisions was advocated by the Supreme Court of Oregon in Fasano v. Board of County Commissioners of Washington County, 264 Or. 574, 507 P.2d 23 (1973). In *Fasano* the petitioners were a group of homeowners in Washington County who opposed a zoning change. The change anchored a previously-approved planned residential district (known as a floating zone because it does not receive a location designation on the zoning map when first approved) on 32 acres of land zoned residential to permit construction of a mobile home park. The court disallowed the change because "Once a [zoning scheme] is adopted, changes in it should be made only when such changes are consistent with the overall objectives of the plan and in keeping with changes in the character of the area or neighborhood to be covered thereby." Id. at 28.

The Court broke from the rigid pattern of characterizing all zoning decisions as legislative in character.

> At this juncture we feel we would be ignoring reality to rigidly view all zoning decisions by local governing bodies as legislative acts to be accorded a full presumption of validity and shielded from less than constitutional scrutiny by the theory of separation of powers. Local and small decision groups are simply not the equivalent in all respects of state and national legislatures. * * *

> Ordinances laying down general policies without regard to a specific piece of property are usually an exercise of legislative authority, are subject to limited review, and may only be attacked upon constitutional grounds for an arbitrary abuse of authority. On the other hand, a determination whether the permissible use of a specific piece of property should be changed is usually an exercise of judicial authority and its propriety is subject to an altogether different test. An illustration of an exercise of legislative authority is the passage of the ordinance by the Washington County Commission in 1962 which provided for the formation of a planned residential classification to be located in or adjacent to any residential zone. An exercise of judicial authority is the county commissioners' determination in this particular matter to change the

classification of A.G.S. Development Company's specific piece of property. Id. at 26.

As a quasi-judicial decision, the rezoning was not entitled to a presumption of legislative validity, the burden of proof was on the party seeking the change (the landowner), and the decision to change the zoning had to be justified by evidence of consistency with the adopted general plan or overriding public need, a test not met by a "conclusory and superficial" planning staff report, the Court held. 507 P.2d at 30.

Is the *Fasano* distinction between legislative policy-making zoning decisions and administrative, quasi-judicial, policy-implementing zoning decisions persuasive? Or does it permit courts to intrude too greatly into an inherently political process? See, e.g., Arnel Development Co. v. City of Costa Mesa, 28 Cal.3d 511, 169 Cal.Rptr. 904, 911–912, 620 P.2d 565, 572–73 (1980) (rejecting case-by-case adjudication of what is legislative or quasi-judicial, and approving use of generic classifications, e.g., zoning ordinances as legislative, and variances, special use permits, and subdivision map approvals as quasi-judicial). For a history of developments in Oregon after the *Fasano* decision, see Sullivan, Land Use in the Oregon Supreme Court: A Recent Retrospective, 25 Will.L.Rev. 259 (1989) (author was counsel for Washington County in *Fasano*). See also Board of County Commissioners of Brevard County v. Snyder, 627 So.2d 469 (Fla.1993) (comprehensive rezonings affecting a large portion of the public are legislative in nature, but rezoning actions impacting a limited number of persons in which the decision is contingent on facts derived from "distinct alternatives presented at the hearing" and the decision "can be functionally viewed as policy application" are quasi judicial in nature).

4. In addition to zoning amendments, municipalities traditionally have used special use permits and variances in the administration of comprehensive zoning programs. Uses that require special permits are legislatively-authorized uses identified in the zoning ordinance that are regulated by a administrative agency "because of special problems the use * * * presents from a zoning standpoint. * * * " Tullo v. Millburn Tp., 54 N.J.Super. 483, 149 A.2d 620, 625 (App.Div.1959). Typical examples include day care centers, fast food stores and gas stations.

Decisions regarding special use permits generally are considered to be administrative rather than legislative in character, Arnel Development Co. v. City of Costa Mesa, 28 Cal.3d 511, 169 Cal.Rptr. 904, 911, 620 P.2d 565, 572 (1980), although some courts hold otherwise. See, e.g., Board of Supervisors of Fairfax County v. Southland Corp., 224 Va. 514, 297 S.E.2d 718 (1982) (special use permit is legislative act). Disputes over special use permits usually center on whether proper standards have been articulated for the delegation of authority, whether the standards have been met, and whether special permit requirements create unconstitutional classifications. See, e.g., City of Cleburne v. Cleburne Living Center, 473 U.S. 432, 105 S.Ct. 3249, 87 L.Ed.2d 313 (1985) (disapproving special permit requirement for group home in multi-family district). See generally P. Salsich & T. Tryniecki, Land Use Regulation 225–229 (2d Ed. 2003); D. Mandelker, Land Use Law 6.53–6.59 (5th Ed. 2003); W. Stoebuck & D. Whitman, The Law of Property 643–648 (3d Ed 2000).

5. Variances are departures from the zoning regulations granted by an administrative body such as a board of zoning appeals in order to avoid overly harsh results from application of a zoning regulation. They originally were authorized by zoning enabling acts to avoid constitutional challenges to zoning ordinances that created "unnecessary hardship or practical difficulties." Strict application of the hardship standard ordinarily would limit variances to height and area restrictions, such as encroachment of a building into a required front, side or rear yard. In recent years, however, courts have been willing to approve the granting of variances to change permitted uses. The principal vice of the variance is that zoning map designations do not change when variances are granted, thus permitting municipalities to hide the "real" rules of the game by excessive use of variances to administer a zoning program. Like special use permits, variances are administrative rather than legislative acts. See generally P. Salsich & T. Tryniecki, Land Use Regulation 229–231 (2d Ed. 2003); D. Mandelker, Land Use Law 6.39–6.52 (5th Ed 2003); W. Stoebuck & D. Whitman, The Law of Property 649–656 (3d Ed 2000).

PROBLEM

We have three clients in the office—representatives of three farming families who have come in together to talk to us: Mrs. Schmidt, Mr. Sanchez, and Mr. and Mrs. Ippolito. Among the three families they own 2,000 acres of good farm land, all within a ten-mile radius of the city limits, the closest part of which is four miles from town.

What brings them in is alarmed agreement. This is the first time in years they have ever agreed on anything. Their history of dealing with one another is a history of squabbles over boundaries, water rights, fences and drifting pesticides.

But today they are in agreement. They are alarmed at the way the town is growing out toward their farms, and they want a lawyer to tell them how to stop it.

— Last year a furniture dealer bought ten acres one mile from Mr. Sanchez's gate and built a warehouse on the tract.

— There are already three fast food places between their farms and the city limits.

— They love being farmers. Their many children want to be farmers after they are dead. They even have grandchildren who already want to be farmers.

— And, although they have never agreed on political candidates, they agree that farming is a good way of life, something that benefits everybody—that even city people benefit from having wide open spaces at the edge of town.

Assume that the lowest category of zoning under the county zoning ordinance provides for an industrial-agricultural category, that includes all of the higher categories, which means that, at present, any land use is permitted on this farm land.

1. What zoning strategies are available to you? In planning your approach, would you expect to function in an adjudicative or a negotiating mode? Is there a role for a mediator here?

2. Can a lawyer represent all three families in seeking to obtain zoning restrictions all three families want to have imposed? Their differing interests in boundaries, water rights, fences, and pesticides will not disappear while they agree on save-the-farms zoning; the question—partly as a matter of the rules on legal ethics—is whether their commonality makes representation by a single lawyer or law firm possible. With regard to regulation, consider Model Rule 2.2, which the American Bar Association recommended in 1983, and most states adopted before the American Bar Association, in 2002, recommended that the rule be abolished and that such joint representation be analyzed under amended rule 1.7. (Some states kept 2.2.) (See the discussion of these changes in Chapter Two.)

- It would require that this lawyer consult each family (separately perhaps), advise each family on "the implications of the common representation"—including the fact that representing all three families will significantly dilute the attorney-client privilege—and obtain each family's consent to proceed.

- It may require that the lawyer herself determine "that the matter can be resolved on terms compatible with the clients' best interests." (Note the plural *clients'*.)

- Each of the three families must be consulted at each significant step in the representation and must renew its consent to proceed.

- And, upon the request of *any one* family, or when any of these conditions is no longer met, the lawyer must withdraw and may not then represent any of the families.

In terms of ethical theory, such rules assume that common interests are episodic, entirely contractual (not, to use the contrasting moral word, covenantal), and unusual. They assume that, for the most part, each human being is all alone. They therefore turn, as in old R.P.C. 2.2, on informed consent, rather than on any tradition, or assumption or perception of community. The fact that "clients' interests" is rendered in the plural, and the fact that, here, the rule would be applied to (in) a community of communities (families) is perhaps ironic.

Note that the formalities of consent would be changed somewhat by proposed new R.P.C. 1.0 which would probably require that the consent be "confirmed in writing" and which elaborates a bit on what "informed consent" is.

C. ADDING FLEXIBILITY TO THE PROCESS

Rezonings often are extremely controversial and municipalities may seek compromises between landowners and objecting neighbors. One way to do this is to place conditions on the use of the land being rezoned. For example, neighbors may drop their opposition to a rezoning if they are assured that only small markets and restaurants may be built, but not taverns, gas stations, or fast food stores. Other conditions may address environmental issues, such as requiring landscaping or appropriate drainage. While the process may take on the appearance of a negotiated agreement among the landowner, neighbors, and the municipality, serious legal questions are raised by such efforts, as the following case illustrates.

COLLARD v. INCORPORATED VILLAGE OF FLOWER HILL

Court of Appeals of New York, 1981.
52 N.Y.2d 594, 439 N.Y.S.2d 326, 421 N.E.2d 818.

JONES, JUDGE.

Where a local municipality conditions an amendment of its zoning ordinance on the execution of a declaration of covenants providing, in part, that no construction may occur on the property so rezoned without the consent of the municipality, absent a provision that such consent may not be unreasonably withheld the municipality may not be compelled to issue such consent or give an acceptable reason for failing to do so.

Appellants now own improved property in the Village of Flower Hill. In 1976, the then owners of the subject premises and appellants' predecessors in title, applied to the village board of trustees to rezone the property from a General Municipal and Public Purposes District to a Business District. On October 4 of that year the village board granted the rezoning application by the following resolution:

"RESOLVED that the application of Ray R. Beck Company for a change of Zone * * * is granted upon the following conditions:

"(a) The Subject Premises and any buildings, structures and improvements situated or to be situated thereon, will be erected, altered, renovated, remodelled, used, occupied and maintained for the following purposes and no other;

"(i) Offices for the practice of the professions of medicine, dentistry, law, engineering, architecture or accountancy;

"(ii) Executive offices to be used solely for the management of business concerns and associations and excluding therefrom, but without limitation, retail or wholesale sales offices or agencies, brokerage offices of all types and kinds, collection or employment agencies or offices, computer programming centres or offices, counseling centres or offices and training offices or business or trade schools.

* * *

"(d) No building or structure situated on the Subject Premises on the date of this Declaration of Covenants will be altered, extended, rebuilt, renovated or enlarged without the prior consent of the Board of Trustees of the Village.

* * *

Subsequently, appellants' predecessors in title entered into the contemplated declaration of covenants which was recorded in the office of the Clerk of Nassau County on November 29, 1976. Consistent with paragraph (d) of the board's resolution, that declaration provided that "[n]o building or structure situated on the Subject Premises on the date of this Declaration of Covenants will be altered, extended, rebuilt, renovated or enlarged without the prior consent of the Board of Trustees of the Village."

Appellants, after acquiring title, made application in late 1978 to the village board for approval to enlarge and extend the existing structure on the premises. Without any reason being given that application was denied. Appellants then commenced this action to have the board's determination declared arbitrary, capricious, unreasonable, and unconstitutional and sought by way of ultimate relief an order directing the board to issue the necessary building permits.

Asserting that the board's denial of the application was beyond review as to reasonableness, respondent moved to dismiss the complaint for failure to state a cause of action. Special Term denied the motion, equating appellants' allegation that the board's action was arbitrary and capricious with an allegation that such action was lacking in good faith and fair dealing—an allegation which it found raised triable issues of fact. The Appellate Division, 75 A.D.2d 631, 427 N.Y.S.2d 301, reversed and dismissed the complaint, holding that the allegation of arbitrary and capricious action by the board was not the equivalent of an allegation that the board breached an implied covenant of fair dealing and good faith. We now affirm.

At the outset this case involves the question of the permissibility of municipal rezoning conditioned on the execution of a private declaration of covenants restricting the use to which the parcel sought to be rezoned may be put. Prior to our decision in *Church v. Town of Islip,* 8 N.Y.2d 254, 203 N.Y.S.2d 866, 168 N.E.2d 680 in which we upheld rezoning of property subject to reasonable conditions, conditional rezoning had been almost uniformly condemned by courts of all jurisdictions—a position to which a majority of States appear to continue to adhere. Since *Church,* however, the practice of conditional zoning has become increasingly widespread in this State, as well as having gained popularity in other jurisdictions. [ ]

Because much criticism has been mounted against the practice, both by commentators and the courts of some of our sister States, further exposition is in order.

Probably the principal objection to conditional rezoning is that it constitutes illegal spot zoning, thus violating the legislative mandate requiring that there be a comprehensive plan for, and that all conditions be uniform within, a given zoning district. When courts have considered the issue [   ], the assumptions have been made that conditional zoning benefits particular landowners rather than the community as a whole and that it undermines the foundation upon which comprehensive zoning depends by destroying uniformity within use districts. Such unexamined assumptions are questionable. First, it is a downward change to a less restrictive zoning classification that benefits the property rezoned and not the opposite imposition of greater restrictions on land use. Indeed, imposing limiting conditions, while benefiting surrounding properties, normally adversely affects the premises on which the conditions are imposed. Second, zoning is not invalid per se merely because only a single parcel is involved or benefited [   ]; the real test for spot zoning is whether the change is other than part of a well-considered and comprehensive plan calculated to serve the general welfare of the community [   ]. Such a determination, in turn, depends on the reasonableness of the rezoning in relation to neighboring uses—an inquiry required regardless of whether the change in zone is conditional in form. Third, if it is initially proper to change a zoning classification without the imposition of restrictive conditions notwithstanding that such change may depart from uniformity, then no reason exists why accomplishing that change subject to condition should automatically be classified as impermissible spot zoning.

Both conditional and unconditional rezoning involve essentially the same legislative act—an amendment of the zoning ordinance. The standards for judging the validity of conditional rezoning are no different from the standards used to judge whether unconditional rezoning is illegal. If modification to a less restrictive zoning classification is warranted, then a fortiori conditions imposed by a local legislature to minimize conflicts among districts should not in and of themselves violate any prohibition against spot zoning.

Another fault commonly voiced in disapproval of conditional zoning is that it constitutes an illegal bargaining away of a local government's police power [   ]. Because no municipal government has the power to make contracts that control or limit it in the exercise of its legislative powers and duties, restrictive agreements made by a municipality in conjunction with a rezoning are sometimes said to violate public policy. While permitting citizens to be governed by the best bargain they can strike with a local legislature would not be consonant with notions of good government, absent proof of a contract purporting to bind the local legislature in advance to exercise its zoning authority in a bargained-for manner, a rule which would have the effect of forbidding a municipality from trying to protect landowners in the vicinity of a zoning change by imposing protective conditions based on the assertion that that body is bargaining away its discretion, would not be in the best interests of the public. The imposition of conditions on property sought to be rezoned may not be classified as a prospective commitment on the part of the municipality to zone as requested if the conditions are met; nor would the municipality necessarily be precluded on this account from later reversing or altering its decision [   ].

Yet another criticism leveled at conditional zoning is that the State enabling legislation does not confer on local authorities authorization to enact conditional zoning amendments [   ]. On this view any such ordinance would be *ultra vires*. While it is accurate to say there exists no explicit authorization that a legislative body may attach conditions to zoning amendments (see, e.g., Village Law, § 7–700 *et seq.*), neither is there any language which expressly forbids a local legislature to do so. Statutory silence is not necessarily a denial of the authority to engage in such a practice. Where in the face of nonaddress in the enabling legislation there exists independent justification for the practice as an appropriate exercise of municipal power, that power will be implied. Conditional rezoning is a means of achieving some degree of flexibility in land-use control by minimizing the potentially deleterious effect of a zoning change on neighboring properties; reasonably conceived conditions harmonize the landowner's need for rezoning with the public interest and certainly fall within the spirit of the enabling legislation [   ].

One final concern of those reluctant to uphold the practice is that resort to conditional rezoning carries with it no inherent restrictions apart from the restrictive agreement itself. This fear, however, is justifiable only if conditional rezoning is considered a contractual relationship between municipality and private party, outside the scope of the zoning power—a view to which we do not subscribe. When conditions are incorporated in an amending ordinance, the result is as much a "zoning regulation" as an ordinance, adopted without conditions. Just as the scope of all zoning regulation is limited by the police power, and thus local legislative bodies must act reasonably and in the best interests of public safety, welfare and convenience [   ], the scope of permissible conditions must of necessity be similarly limited. If, upon proper proof, the conditions imposed are found unreasonable, the rezoning amendment as well as the required conditions would have to be nullified, with the affected property reverting to the preamendment zoning classification.

Against this backdrop we proceed to consideration of the contentions advanced by appellants in the appeal now before us. * * *

The focus of appellants' assault is the provision of the declaration of covenants that no structure may be extended or enlarged "without the prior consent of the Board of Trustees of the Village". Appellants would have us import the added substantive prescription—"which consent may not be unreasonably withheld". Their argument proceeds along two paths: first, that as a matter of construction the added prescription should be read into the provision; second, that because of limitations associated with the exercise of municipal zoning power the village board would have been required to include such a prescription.

Appellants' construction argument must fail. The terminology employed in the declaration is explicit. The concept that appellants would invoke is not obscure and language to give it effect was readily available had it been the intention of the parties to include this added stipulation. Appellants point to no canon of construction in the law of real property or of contracts which would call for judicial insertion of the missing clause. * * *

The second path either leads nowhere or else goes too far. If it is appellants' assertion that the village board was legally required to insist on inclusion of the desired prescription, there is no authority in the court to reform the zoning enactment of 1976 retroactively to impose the omitted clause. Whether the village board at that time would have enacted a different resolution in the form now desired by appellants is open only to speculation; the certainty is that they did not then take such legislative action. On the other hand, acceptance of appellants' proposition would produce as the other possible consequence the conclusion that the 1976 enactment was illegal, throwing appellants unhappily back to the pre–1976 zoning of their premises, a destination which they assuredly wish to sidestep.

Finally, we agree with the Appellate Division that the allegation of the complaint that the village board in denying appellants' application acted in an arbitrary and capricious manner is not an allegation that the board acted in bad faith or its equivalent.

For the reasons stated the Board of Trustees of the Incorporated Village of Flower Hill may not now be compelled to issue its consent to the proposed enlargement and extension of the existing structure on the premises or in the alternative give an acceptable reason for failing to do so. Accordingly, the order of the Appellate Division should be affirmed, with costs.

Notes and Questions

1. Is the court being realistic when it concludes that there is no bargaining process in conditional zoning? Why would a restrictive covenant, such as the one in dispute in *Collard,* be placed on the property except in expectation of, or in return for, a favorable zoning decision?

2. Why should "bargaining away of the police power" be a concern? Is it a means for reaching acceptable compromises in neighborhood land use disputes, or an invitation to corruption of the parties involved?

3. Developers seeking approval for large, complex projects often have to obtain permits and submit to a series of reviews under flexible "wait and see" techniques described infra. Because of the uncertainties created by the permit review process, developers often seek "Developers Agreements," authorized in a number of states, to set the "rules of the game" for the continued review of their project. For a superb analysis of the use of negotiated agreements as a basis for land use regulation, see Wegner, Moving Toward the Bargaining Table: Contract Zoning, Development Agree-

ments, and the Theoretical Foundations of Government Land Use Deals, 65 N.C.L. Rev. 957 (1987). See also David L. Callies, Daniel J. Curtin, Jr. and Julie A. Tappendorf, Bargaining for Development: A Handbook on Development Agreements, Annexation Agreements, Land Development Conditions, Vested Rights and the Provision of Public Services (2003).

NOTE ON PLANNED UNIT DEVELOPMENTS AND OTHER TECHNIQUES FOR INCREASING FLEXIBILITY

Planned Unit Developments (Cluster Zoning)

The planned unit development (PUD) technique, popularized in the 1950s as part of a second generation of zoning, provides an opportunity for more flexible design and location of buildings and more creative use of open space than does the original Euclidean version of zoning. PUD zoning, also known as cluster zoning, permits developers to deviate from rigid lot size and building set-back requirements and, in some cases, to mix uses within a development.

The conceptual advance of the PUD concept was a shift in focus from individual lots in a development to the entire tract that comprises the development. For example, instead of requiring all houses in a 100–unit subdivision to be placed in the same spots on one-acre lots, with the same-sized front, rear and side yards, which often was the case under traditional zoning, a cluster zone provision permitting PUDs enables a developer to rearrange the houses in more attractive clusters around open spaces such as small ponds and parks, golf courses, village squares and woodlands. In effect, "[m]ore cluster here is traded for less cluster over there." Colao v. Maryland—National Capital Park and Planning Comm'n, 167 Md.App. 194, 892 A.2d 579, (2005).

PUDs have been praised for allowing more variety in appearance and for enabling developers to work with topographical features and terrain rather than against them. PUDs have been criticized for requiring more costly infrastructure such as roads and sewers and for contributing to a sense of isolation that residents of suburbia have sometimes experienced.

Cluster zoning usually is limited to relatively large tracts of land of at least 10 to 20 acres. Specific PUD proposals must be harmonious with the immediate environs and consistent with the municipality's land use plans.

Courts have been generally receptive to the cluster zone/PUD concept, including the extra scrutiny local officials may give a PUD proposal because of the contemplated relaxation of local land use regulations, but have required municipalities to deal fairly with developers by refraining from arbitrary denials or excessive requirements. See, e.g., Central Motors Corp. v. City of Pepper Pike, 73 Ohio St.3d 581, 653 N.E.2d 639, 643 (1995) ("By zoning the property for a higher density of units and clustering of those units, Pepper Pike provided the necessary flexibility for development of the property, addressed the impact of the outside influences on the property, and maintained the residential character of the neighborhood and community"); Kenart & Associates v. Skagit County, 37 Wash.App. 295, 680 P.2d 439 (1984), rev. den., 101 Wash.2d 1021 (1984) (denial of PUD application reversed because planning commission findings failed to "provide guidance to the developer [or] permit meaningful appellate review").

Floating Zones

A close companion of the cluster zone/PUD concept is the floating zone, designed to add flexibility to the way that PUDs and other similar techniques are administered. Under the original Euclidean system of comprehensive zoning, all land in the municipality is divided into districts containing fixed boundaries that are identified on a zoning district map. If a zoning amendment is approved, a corresponding change is made on the zoning map.

Floating zones differ from traditional Euclidean zones in that they "have no such defined boundaries [but] 'float' over the entire area * * * where [they] may eventually be established." Bigenho v. Montgomery County Council, 248 Md. 386, 237 A.2d 53, 56 (1968). Creating a floating zone is a two-step process. First the municipality enacts an ordinance authorizing a particular range of activities such as planned unit development, commercial office parks, multi-family residential projects and mixed use developments, without specifying specific areas in the municipality where these activities can take place. A second ordinance is enacted that "anchors" the floating zone to a particular tract of land in response to specific development proposals. In effect, the anchoring ordinance "carves a new zone out of an existing one." Heithaus v. Planning and Zoning Comm'n of Greenwich, 258 Conn. 205, 779 A.2d 750, 759 (2001).

After early doubts about the validity of the floating zone technique under traditional zoning enabling statutes, most courts have accepted the floating zone "as a recognition that municipal legislative bodies need a certain flexibility" in administering their zoning programs. Treme v. St. Louis County, 609 S.W.2d 706, 712 (Mo.App.1980), reviewing cases; Campion v. Board of Alderman of City of New Haven, 85 Conn.App. 820, 859 A.2d 586 (2004) (finding authority for floating zone in 1925 zoning ordinance). See also Richmarr Holly Hills, Inc. v. American PCS, L.P., 117 Md.App. 607, 701 A.2d 879 (1997) (floating zone cases are judged by "the same 'substantial evidence' and 'fairly debatable' standards as are applied in zoning cases generally).

Overlay Zones

For a variety of reasons, municipalities may desire to impose different regulations on certain permitted uses in part of an existing zoning district. To accomplish this goal, the new regulations are "laid over" the existing zoning map. Existing regulations that do not conflict with the overlay district provisions remain in effect, but conflicting ones are preempted. See, e.g., Franchise Developers, Inc. v. City of Cincinnati, 30 Ohio St.3d 28, 505 N.E.2d 966, 968 (1987) (upholding as reasonable an environmental quality district that prevented development of a fast food restaurant on a particular site in Cincinnati even though the proposed use was permitted by the commercial zoning district in which the site was located); Callison v. Land Conservation and Development Commission, 145 Or.App. 277, 929 P.2d 1061, 1063 (1996) (overlay zone "modifies some of the regulations ... while leaving the underlying zoning otherwise intact").

Overlay zones can be used for a variety of purposes, particularly in the environmental area. They permit land use regulations "to be tailored more specifically to [a] particular resource," such as an old growth forest, an area with significant biodiversity, or the top of a mountain. Sierra Club v. Commissioner of Dept. of Environmental Management, 439 Mass. 738, 791 N.E.2d 325, 338 (2003) (upholding use of four "significance" overlay zones in the management of a 2000 acre public land reservation).

Performance Standards

An alternative to the territorial division of zoning is the application of regulatory standards to control harmful effects of development, such as noise, pollution, and traffic, while permitting more heterogenous mixes of uses. The focus of regulation under a performance standard approach shifts from the type of use permitted to the impact of the use. Performance standard regulation requires municipalities to articulate meaningful and understandable standards and apply them in an even-handed manner. Most environmental regulation legislation has adopted the performance standard approach. For an excellent discussion of performance standards and other flexible techniques, see D. Porter, P. Phillips & T. Lassar, Flexible Zoning: How It Works (ULI, 1988). See generally, P. Salsich & T. Tryniecki, Land Use Regulation 180–182 (2003).

NOTE ON OREGON'S STATEWIDE LAND USE REGULATION SYSTEM

The State of Oregon has long been a leader in aggressive land use regulation. The state's landmark growth management statute enacted in 1973 established a comprehensive system of state, regional and local land use planning based on planning goals established at the state level. SB 100, 1973 Or. Laws 127, codified generally in Oregon Revised Statutes Chapter 197. A state administrative agency, the Land Use Board of Appeals (LUBA) has exclusive jurisdiction to review local land use decisions with appeals to the Oregon courts. ORS § 197.810(1).

Any city, county, or regional agency with planning authority is required to draft, adopt, and enforce comprehensive land use plans. ORS § 197.175. The comprehensive plans are required to conform with the statewide planning goals, currently numbering nineteen including, protection of farm lands and a diversified economy, provision of affordable housing and separation of rurual and urban land by an urban growth boundary. ORS § 197.250. The goals are described and evaluated in Sullivan, Remarks to University of Oregon Symposium Marking the Twenty–Fifth Anniversary of S.B. 100, 77 Or. L. Rev 813, 824–840 (1998). The comprehensive plans also have to include a land use map and a policy statement, and they have to address, at a minimum "sewer and water systems, transportation systems, educational facilities, recreational facilities, and natural resources and air and water quality management programs." ORS § 197.015(5). The Land Conservation and Development Commission (LCDC), a seven member body appointed by the governor, supervises the land use planning system by adopting the statewide planning goals, ORS § 197.015(8) and certifying that local plans and regulations comply with the goals through a process called acknowledgment. ORS §§ 197.175(2)(a), 251; Sullivan, *Id.*, at 818.

The LCDC has the power to take enforcement action against local governments that do not follow their approved comprehensive plans, or fail to update them as needed (usually every 5–10 years). See, e.g., Callison v. Land Conservation and Development Commission, 145 Or. App. 277, 929 P.2d 1061 (1996) (upholding LCDC periodic review of city of Portland's comprehensive plan.

Following acknowledgment by the LCDC that a local comprehensive plan and its implementing land use regulations comply with the statewide planning goals, all proposed amendments to the plan or its implementing regulations must be submitted to the Department of Land Conservation and Development. The Department notifies persons who have requested such notice of the proposed amendment and may participate in the local government hearing to express any concerns it may have and to make recommendations for addressing its concerns. ORS § 197.610. Interested persons, including the Director of the Department, may appeal local land use regulatory decisions to LUBA. ORS §§ 197.620, 830; Sullivan, *Id.*

LUBA relies on evidence presented at local government hearings and comments by the Department. ORS § 197.835(2)(b). Persons must have appeared orally or in writing before the local government at the evidentiary hearing in order to appeal a land use decision, and this standing requirement has stopped many landowners from appealing. ORS § 197.830(2)(b). Sullivan, *Id.*, at 838. See also Comment, Gone Too Far: Oregon's Measure 37 and the Perils of Over–Regulating Land use, 23 Yale L. & Pol'y Rev. 587, 592 (2005). LUBA may also award the government attorney's fees against frivolous appeals. ORS § 197.830(15). For summaries of the Oregon program, see Symposium on Oregon Land Use, 77 Oregon Law Review 807–1004 (1998); R. Liberty, Planned Growth: The Oregon Model, 13–SUM Nat. Resources & Env't 315.

While the Oregon program has a loyal following among state and national planning and environmental enthusiasts, it has become increasingly controversial over the years, particularly with private property advocates. In November 2004, Measure 37, a citizen-sponsored initiative proposal directing the state and local governments to compensate landowners for, or exempt them from, land use regulations that cause property values to decline was approved by the voters. Comment, Gone Too Far: Oregon's Measure 37 and the Perils of Over–Regulating Land Use, 23 Yale L. & Pol'y Rev. 587 (2005) (arguing that Measure 37 reflects voters' beliefs that Oregon's land use regulatory system had "gone too far," echoing Justice Holmes in *Pennsylvania Coal v. Mahon*). Measure 37 was challenged immediately in court and, on October 15, 2005, a trial judge held that it violated both the Oregon and federal constitutions, primarily because it intrudes too much on legislative authority. Measure 37 requires a government to "pay to govern," the court asserted. M. Stromberg, Measure 37 is Unconstitutional, Oregon Circuit Court Says, Planning, v. 71, n.11 (Dec. 2005), at p. 50. Four months later, the Oregon Supreme Court reversed the lower court's ruling and reinstated Measure 37, commenting in the process that "whether Measure 37 as a policy choice is wise or foolish, farsighted or blind, is beyond this court's purview." MacPherson v. Dep't of Administrative Services, 340 Or. 117, 130 P.3d 308, 322 (2006).

D. SEGREGATION OF UNDESIRED USES

STATE EX REL. STOYANOFF v. BERKELEY

Supreme Court of Missouri, 1970.
458 S.W.2d 305.

PRITCHARD, COMMISSIONER.

Upon summary judgment the trial court issued a peremptory writ of mandamus to compel appellant to issue a residential building permit to respondents. The trial court's judgment is that the below-mentioned ordinances are violative of Section 10, Article I of the Constitution of Missouri, 1945, V.A.M.S., in that restrictions placed by the ordinances on the use of property deprive the owners of their property without due process of law. Relators' petition pleads that they applied to appellant Building Commissioner for a building permit to allow them to construct a single family residence in the City of Ladue, and that plans and specifications were submitted for the proposed residence, which was unusual in design, "but complied with all existing building and zoning regulations and ordinances of the City of Ladue, Missouri."

It is further pleaded that relators were refused a building permit for the construction of their proposed residence upon the ground that the permit was not approved by the Architectural Board of the City of Ladue. Ordinance 131, as amended by Ordinance 281 of that city, purports to set up an Architectural Board to approve plans and specifications for buildings and structures erected within the city and in a preamble to "conform to certain minimum architectural standards of appearance and conformity with surrounding structures, and that unsightly, grotesque and unsuitable structures, detrimental to the stability of value and the welfare of surrounding property, structures and residents, and to the general welfare and happiness of the community, be avoided, and that appropriate standards of beauty and conformity be fostered and encouraged." It is asserted in the petition that the ordinances are invalid, illegal and void, "are unconstitutional in that they are vague and provide no standard nor uniform rule by which to guide the architectural board," that the city acted in excess of statutory powers (§ 89.020, RSMo 1959, V.A.M.S.) in enacting the ordinances, which "attempt to allow respondent to impose aesthetic standards for buildings in the City of Ladue, and are in excess of the powers granted the City of Ladue by said statute."

Relators filed a motion for summary judgment and affidavits were filed in opposition thereto. Richard D. Shelton, Mayor of the City of Ladue, deponed that the facts in appellant's answer were true and correct, as here pertinent: that the City of Ladue constitutes one of the finer suburban residential areas of Metropolitan St. Louis, the homes therein are considerably more expensive than in cities of comparable size, being homes on lots from three fourths of an acre to three or more acres each; that a zoning ordinance was enacted by the city regulating the height, number of stories, size of buildings, percentage of lot occupancy, yard sizes, and the location and use of buildings and land for trade, industry, residence and other purposes; that the zoning regulations were made in accordance with a comprehensive plan "designed to promote the health and general welfare of the residents of the City of Ladue," which in furtherance of said objectives duly enacted said Ordinances numbered 131 and 281. Appellant also asserted in his answer that these ordinances were a reasonable exercise of the city's governmental, legislative and police powers, as determined by its legislative body, and as stated in the above-quoted preamble to the ordinances. It is then pleaded that relators' description of their proposed residence as " 'unusual in design' is the understatement of the year. It is in fact a monstrosity of grotesque design, which would seriously impair the value of property in the neighborhood."

The affidavit of Harold C. Simon, a developer of residential subdivisions in St. Louis County, is that he is familiar with relators' lot upon which they seek to build a house, and with the surrounding houses in the neighborhood; that the houses therein existent are virtually all two-story houses of conventional architectural design, such as Colonial, French Provincial or English; and that the house which relators propose to construct is of ultra-modern design which would clash with and not be in conformity with any other house in the entire neighborhood. It is Mr. Simon's opinion that the design and appearance of relators' proposed residence would have a substantial adverse effect upon the market values of other residential property in the neighborhood, such average market value ranging from $60,000 to $85,000 each.

As a part of the affidavit of Russell H. Riley, consultant for the city planning and engineering firm of Harland Bartholomew & Associates, photographic exhibits of homes surrounding relators' lot were attached. * * * According to Mr. Riley the standards of Ordinance 131, as amended by Ordinance 281, are usually and customarily applied in city planning work and are: "(1) whether the proposed house meets the customary architectural requirements in appearance and design for a house of the particular type which is proposed (whether it be Colonial, Tudor English, French Provincial, or Modern), (2) whether the proposed house is in general conformity with the style and design of surrounding structures, and (3) whether the proposed house lends itself to the proper architectural development of the City; and that in applying said standards the Architectural Board and its Chairman are to determine whether the proposed house will have an adverse effect on the stability of values in the surrounding area."

Photographic exhibits of relators' proposed residence were also attached to Mr. Riley's affidavit. They show the residence to be of a pyramid shape, with a flat top, and with triangular shaped windows or doors at one or more corners.

Although appellant has briefed the point that it is a constitutional exercise of the police power for the Legislature to authorize cities to enact zoning ordinances, it is apparent that relators do not contest that issue. Rather, relators' position is that "the creation by the City of Ladue of an architectural board for the purpose of promoting and maintaining 'general conformity with the style and design of surrounding structures' is totally unauthorized by our Enabling Statute." (§§ 89.020, 89.040, RSMo 1959, V.A.M.S.) It is further contended by relators that Ordinances 131 and 281 are invalid and unconstitutional as being an unreasonable and arbitrary exercise of the police power (as based entirely on aesthetic values); and that the same are invalid as an unlawful delegation of legislative powers (to the Architectural Board).

Section 89.020 provides: "For the purpose of promoting health, safety, morals or the general welfare of the community, the legislative body of all cities, towns, and villages is hereby empowered to regulate and restrict the height, number of stories, and size of buildings and other structures, the percentage of lot that may be occupied, the size of yards, courts, and other open spaces, the density of population, the preservation of features of historical significance, and the location and use of buildings, structures and land for trade, industry, residence or other purposes." Section 89.040 provides: "Such regulations shall be made in accordance with a comprehensive plan and designed to lessen congestion in the streets; to secure safety from fire, panic and other dangers; to promote health *and the general welfare;* to provide adequate light and air; to prevent the overcrowding of land; to avoid undue concentration of population; to preserve features of historical significance; to facilitate the adequate provision of transportation, water, sewerage, schools, parks, and other public requirements. *Such regulations shall be made with reasonable consideration, among other things, to the character of the district and its peculiar suitability for particular uses, and with a view to conserving the values of buildings and encouraging the most appropriate use of land throughout such municipality.*" (Italics added.)

Relators say that "Neither Sections 89.020 or 89.040 nor any other provision of Chapter 89 mentions or gives a city the authority to regulate architectural design and appearance. There exists no provision providing for an architectural board and no entity even remotely resembling such a board is mentioned under the enabling legislation." Relators conclude that the City of Ladue lacked any power to adopt Ordinance 131 as amended by Ordinance 281 "and its intrusion into this area is wholly unwarranted and without sanction in the law." * * *

As is clear from the affidavits and attached exhibits, the City of Ladue is an area composed principally of residences of the general types of Colonial, French Provincial and English Tudor. The city has a comprehensive plan of zoning to maintain the general character of buildings therein. * * * [T]he character of the district, its suitability for particular uses, and the conservation of the values of buildings therein. * * * are directly related to the general welfare of the community. That proposition has support in a number of cases cited by appellant. [ ] The preamble to Ordinance 131, quoted above in part, demonstrates that its purpose is to conform to the dictates of § 89.040, with reference to preserving values of property by zoning procedure and restrictions on the use of property. This is an illustration of what was referred to in Deimeke v. State Highway Commission, Mo., 444 S.W.2d 480, 484, as a growing number of cases recognizing a change in the scope of the term "general welfare." In the Deimeke case on the same page it is said, "Property use which offends sensibilities and debases property values affects not only the adjoining property owners in that vicinity but the general public as well because when such property values are destroyed or seriously impaired, the tax base of the community is affected and the public suffers economically as a result."

Relators say further that Ordinances 131 and 281 are invalid and unconstitutional as being an unreasonable and arbitrary exercise of the police power. It is argued that a mere reading of these ordinances shows that they are based entirely on aesthetic factors in that the stated purpose of the Architectural Board is to maintain "conformity with surrounding structures" and to assure that structures "conform to certain minimum architectural standards of appearance." The argument ignores the further provisos in the ordinance: " * * * and that unsightly, grotesque and unsuitable structures, *detrimental to the stability of value and the welfare of surrounding property, structures, and residents, and to the general welfare and happiness of the community,* be avoided, and that appropriate standards of beauty and conformity be fostered and encouraged." (Italics added.) Relators' proposed residence does not descend to the " 'patently offensive character of vehicle graveyards in close proximity to such highways' " referred to in the Deimeke case, supra (444 S.W.2d 484). Nevertheless, the aesthetic factor to be taken into account by the Architectural Board is not to be considered alone. Along with that inherent factor is the effect that the proposed residence would have upon the property values in the area. In this time of burgeoning urban areas, congested with people and structures, it is certainly in keeping with the ultimate ideal of general welfare that the Architectural Board, in its function, preserve and protect existing areas in which structures of a general conformity of architecture have been erected. The area under consideration is clearly, from the record, a fashionable one. In State ex rel. Civello v. City of New Orleans, 154 La. 271, 97 So. 440, 444, the court said, "If by the term 'aesthetic considerations' is meant a regard merely for outward appearances, for good taste in the matter of the beauty of the neighborhood itself, we do not observe any substantial reason for saying that such a consideration is not a matter of general welfare. The beauty of a fashionable residence neighborhood in a city is for the comfort and happiness of the residents, and it sustains in a general way the value of property in the neighborhood." * * *

In the matter of enacting zoning ordinances and the procedures for determining whether any certain proposed structure or use is in compliance with or offends the basic ordinance, it is well settled that courts will not substitute their judgments for the city's legislative body, if the result is not oppressive, arbitrary or unreasonable and does not infringe upon a valid preexisting nonconforming use. [ ] The denial by appellant of a building permit for relators' highly modernistic residence in this area where traditional Colonial, French Provincial and English Tudor styles of architecture are erected does not appear to be arbitrary and unreasonable when the basic purpose to be served is that of the general welfare of persons in the entire community.

* * *

Relators claim that the * * * provisions of the ordinance amount to an unconstitutional delegation of power by the city to the Architectural Board. It is argued that the Board cannot be given the power to determine what is unsightly and grotesque and that the standards, "whether the proposed structure will conform to proper architectural standards in appearance and design, and will be in general conformity with the style and design of surrounding structures and conducive to the proper architectural development of the City * * *" and "the Board shall disapprove the application if it determines that the proposed structure will constitute an unsightly, grotesque or unsuitable structure in appearance, detrimental to the welfare of surrounding property or residents * * *," are inadequate. * * * Here, * * * the procedures are for public hearings with notice to the applicant, not only by the Architectural Board but also by the City Council on appeal on the factual issues to be determined under the ordinance. An applicant's rights are safeguarded in this respect * * *. Ordinances 131 and 281 are sufficient in their general standards calling for a factual determination of the suitability of any proposed structure with reference to the character of the surrounding neighborhood and to the determination of any adverse effect on the general welfare and preservation of property values of the community. * * *

The judgment is reversed.

Notes and Questions

1. *Stoyanoff* is an example of what has been called aesthetic zoning, the practice of discriminating against activities that depart from the norm, such as radical designs of buildings, unusual types of building materials (e.g., a plastic house), and the use of signs to convey messages. On what basis did the *Stoyanoff* court sustain the challenged zoning regulations? Was the offensive design threatening harm to the community? If so, what type of harm? Was the community's attack directed at the design of the building, or at the type of people who would live in such a house? Why were they perceived as threatening?

2. What defenses can a landowner raise to attacks against a proposed building design? Is there an unconstitutional "taking" of property? An arbitrary exercise of the police power? Must the offensive design or type of building materials constitute a nuisance in order for a ban to be sustained?

3. Signs raise particularly difficult First Amendment free speech issues, as well as property regulation issues. The Supreme Court has upheld the regulation, and in some cases the prohibition, of signs as a reasonable means of attacking "visual blight," but it has drawn the line against sign regulations that infringe on "political" speech or unreasonably restrict "commercial" speech. Members of City Council v. Taxpayers for Vincent, 466 U.S. 789, 104 S.Ct. 2118, 80 L.Ed.2d 772 (1984).

Regulation of political speech is off limits except for compelling governmental reasons, usually not found in a land use context. Metromedia, Inc. v. City of San Diego, 453 U.S. 490, 101 S.Ct. 2882, 69 L.Ed.2d 800 (1981). Commercial speech, such as billboard advertisements of commercial products, can be subjected to reasonable "time, place and manner" regulations so long as the regulations do not affect the "content" of the speech. Central Hudson Gas & Elec. Corp. v. Public Service Com'n, 447 U.S. 557, 100 S.Ct. 2343, 65 L.Ed.2d 341 (1980).

How would you advise a city wishing to preserve the ambience of its well-to-do residential areas and considering a ban on all yard signs in those areas? Would it have to allow "For Sale" signs? Could it restrict the size or number of such signs on a lot? In a block? See Linmark Associates, Inc. v. Township of Willingboro, 431 U.S. 85, 97 S.Ct. 1614, 52 L.Ed.2d 155 (1977) (prohibition of For Sale and Sold signs invalidated).

What about signs advertising private garage or estate sales? Signs supporting political candidates? Could your client community ban a sign advocating peaceful negotiations rather than war as a means of resolving an international dispute? Would it be relevant that a neighbor attorney stated that he did not wish to be confronted with that message when he arrived home after a hard day at the office? See City of Ladue v. Gilleo, 512 U.S. 43, 114 S.Ct. 2038, 129 L.Ed.2d 36 (1994) (Ordinance banning sign advocating no war in Persian Gulf invalidated as violation of land owner's right to free speech). Could landowners accomplish the same purpose by restrictive sign regulations in private covenants? See Chapter Six *supra*.

4.   First Amendment issues also are raised when municipalities attempt to regulate the locations and operation of adult entertainment through zoning ordinances. The increased scrutiny that courts give to regulations affecting commercial speech is applicable to efforts to control adult businesses. Again, the key question is whether a regulation affecting adult businesses, such as a requirement that such businesses be concentrated in one area, or dispersed away from residential areas and other adult businesses, is a reasonable time, place and manner regulation or an impermissible regulation of the content of constitutionally—protected commercial speech. See City of Renton v. Playtime Theatres, Inc., 475 U.S. 41, 106 S.Ct. 925, 89 L.Ed.2d 29 (1986) (City may regulate the secondary effects of adult entertainment businesses through a dispersal strategy based on review of experiences in other cities so long as the result is not a complete ban of such businesses). See also City of Los Angeles v. Alameda Books, Inc., 535 U.S. 425, 122 S.Ct. 1728, 152 L.Ed.2d 670 (2002) (city may rely on police department study linking concentrations of adult businesses to higher rates of crime in surrounding areas in regulating location of adult businesses). Enforceability of private covenants raising similar questions is discussed in Chapter Six, *supra*.

5.   The segregative aspect of zoning has occasionally led to challenges under federal antitrust statutes from persons who are disappointed by decisions to deny zoning permission for commercial or industrial development proposals. The Supreme Court laid to rest most questions about potential antitrust liability for zoning decisions in City of Columbia v. Omni Outdoor Advertising, Inc., 499 U.S. 365, 111 S.Ct. 1344, 113 L.Ed.2d 382 (1991), a case in which major revisions to a municipal sign ordinance were challenged as illegally favoring one company that had erected billboards before the sign ordinance was enacted and hindering the ability of a competitor by restricting the number of additional billboards that could be installed.

In concluding that zoning ordinances come within a long-standing "state action" exemption to federal antitrust states, the Court stated

> The very purpose of zoning regulation is to displace unfettered business freedom in a manner that regularly has the effect of preventing normal acts of competition, particularly on the part of new entrants. A municipal ordinance restricting the size, location, and spacing of billboards (surely a common form of zoning) necessarily protects existing billboards against some competition from newcomers.

111 S.Ct. at 1350.

E. EXCLUSIONARY ZONING—IMPERMISSIBLE SEGREGATION OF UNDESIRED PEOPLE

1. *State Responses*

SOUTHERN BURLINGTON COUNTY N.A.A.C.P. v. TOWNSHIP OF MOUNT LAUREL

Supreme Court of New Jersey, 1975.
67 N.J. 151, 336 A.2d 713, appeal dismissed, 423
U.S. 808, 96 S.Ct. 18, 46 L.Ed.2d 28.

HALL, J.

This case attacks the system of land use regulation by defendant Township of Mount Laurel on the ground that low and moderate income families are thereby unlawfully excluded from the municipality. The trial court so found, [   ] and declared the township zoning ordinance totally invalid. Its judgment went on, in line with the requests for affirmative relief, to order the municipality to make studies of the housing needs of low and moderate income persons presently or formerly residing in the community in substandard housing, as well as those in such income classifications presently employed in the township and living elsewhere or reasonably expected to be employed therein in the future, and to present a plan of affirmative public action designed "to enable and encourage the satisfaction of the indicated needs." Jurisdiction was retained for judicial consideration and approval of such a plan and for the entry of a final order requiring its implementation.

* * *

The implications of the issue presented are indeed broad and far-reaching, extending much beyond these particular plaintiffs and the boundaries of this particular municipality.

There is not the slightest doubt that New Jersey has been, and continues to be, faced with a desperate need for housing, especially of decent living accommodations economically suitable for low and moderate income families. The situation was characterized as a "crisis" and fully explored and documented by Governor Cahill in two special messages to the Legislature—*A Blueprint for Housing in New Jersey* (1970) and *New Horizons in Housing* (1972).

Plaintiffs represent the minority group poor (black and Hispanic) seeking such quarters. But they are not the only category of persons barred from so many municipalities by reason of restrictive land use regulations. We have reference to young and elderly couples, single persons and large, growing families not in the poverty class, but who still cannot afford the only kinds of housing realistically permitted in most places—relatively high-priced, single-family detached dwellings on sizeable lots and, in some municipalities, expensive apartments. We will, therefore, consider the case from the wider viewpoint that the effect of Mount Laurel's land use regulation has been to prevent various categories of persons from living in the township because of the limited extent of their income and resources. In this connection, we accept the representation of the municipality's counsel at oral argument that the regulatory scheme was not adopted with any desire or intent to exclude prospective residents on the obviously illegal bases of race, origin or believed social incompatibility.

* * *

I

THE FACTS

[The Court described in detail Mount Laurel Township, a unit of local government smaller than a county but containing small cities within its boundaries, that was about 10 miles northeast of Philadelphia. Mount Laurel's zoning ordinance designated 29.2% of the township land for industry, although less than 4% of the land was occupied by industries, a minuscule 1.2% of the land for retail business use, and the balance, about 70% of the total, for detached single family residential use. Two thirds of the land zoned residential was further restricted by the requirement that individual lots be at least one half acre in size. Apartments and mobile homes were not allowed under the general ordinance.—Eds.]

* * *

The record thoroughly substantiates the findings of the trial court that over the years Mount Laurel "has acted affirmatively to control development and to attract a selective type of growth" (119 N.J.Super. at 168, 290 A.2d at 467) and that "through its zoning ordinances has exhibited economic discrimination in that the poor have been deprived of adequate housing and the opportunity to secure the construction of subsidized housing, and has used federal, state, county and local finances and resources solely for the betterment of middle and upper-income persons." (119 N.J.Super. at 178, 290 A.2d at 473).

There cannot be the slightest doubt that the reason for this course of conduct has been to keep down local taxes on *property* (Mount Laurel is not a high tax municipality) and that the policy was carried out without regard for non-fiscal considerations with respect to *people*, either within or without its boundaries. This conclusion is demonstrated not only by what was done and what happened, as we have related, but also by innumerable direct statements of municipal officials at public meetings over the years which are found in the exhibits. The trial court referred to a number of them. [ ]

This policy of land use regulation for a fiscal end derives from New Jersey's tax structure, which has imposed on local real estate most of the cost of municipal and county government and of the primary and secondary education of the municipality's children. The latter expense is much the largest, so, basically, the fewer the school children, the lower the tax rate. Sizeable industrial and commercial ratables are eagerly sought and homes and the lots on which they are situate are required to be large enough, through minimum lot sizes and minimum floor areas, to have substantial value in order to produce greater tax revenues to meet school costs. Large families who cannot afford to buy large houses and must live in cheaper rental accommodations are definitely not wanted, so we find drastic bedroom restrictions for, or complete prohibition of, multi-family or other feasible housing for those of lesser income.

This pattern of land use regulation has been adopted for the same purpose in developing municipality after developing municipality. Almost every one acts solely in its own selfish and parochial interest and in effect builds a wall around itself to keep out those people or entities not adding favorably to the tax base, despite the location of the municipality or the demand for varied kinds of housing. There has been no effective intermunicipal or area planning or land use regulation. All of this is amply demonstrated by the evidence in this case as to Camden, Burlington and Gloucester counties. As to the similar situation generally in the state, see New Jersey Department of Community Affairs, Division of State and Regional Planning, *Land Use Regulation, The Residential Land Supply* (April 1972) (a study assembling and examining the nature and extent of municipal zoning practices in 16 counties as affecting residential land available for low and moderate income housing) and Williams and Norman, Exclusionary Land Use Controls: The Case of North–Eastern New Jersey, 22 Syracuse L.Rev. 475, 486–487 (1971). One incongruous result is the picture of developing municipalities rendering it impossible for lower paid employees of industries they have eagerly sought and welcomed with open arms (and, in Mount Laurel's case, even some of its own lower paid municipal employees) to live in the community where they work.

The other end of the spectrum should also be mentioned because it shows the source of some of the demand for cheaper housing than the developing municipalities have permitted. Core cities were originally the location of most commerce and industry. Many of those facilities furnished employment for the unskilled and semi-skilled. These employees lived relatively near their work, so sections of cities always have housed the majority of people of low and moderate income, generally in old and deteriorating housing. Despite the municipally confined tax structure, commercial and industrial ratables generally used to supply enough revenue to provide and maintain municipal services equal or superior to those furnished in most suburban and rural areas.

The situation has become exactly the opposite since the end of World War II. Much industry and retail business, and even the professions, have left the cities. Camden is a typical example. The testimonial and documentary evidence in this case as to what has happened to that city is depressing indeed. For various reasons, it lost thousands of jobs between 1950 and 1970, including more than half of its manufacturing jobs (a reduction from 43,267 to 20,671, while all jobs in the entire area labor market increased from 94,507 to 197,037). A large segment of retail business faded away with the erection of large suburban shopping centers. The economically better situated city residents helped fill up the miles of sprawling new housing developments, not fully served by public transit. In a society which came to depend more and more on expensive individual motor vehicle transportation for all purposes, low income employees very frequently could not afford to reach outlying places of suitable employment and they certainly could not afford the permissible housing near such locations. These people have great difficulty in obtaining work and have been forced to remain in housing which is overcrowded, and has become more and more substandard and less and less tax productive. There has been a consequent critical erosion of the city tax base and inability to provide the amount and quality of those governmental services—education, health, police, fire, housing and the like—so necessary to the very existence of safe and decent city life. This category of city dwellers desperately needs much better housing and living conditions than is available to them now, both in a rehabilitated city and in outlying municipalities. They make up, along with the other classes of persons earlier mentioned who also cannot afford the only generally permitted housing in the developing municipalities, the acknowledged great demand for low and moderate income housing.

II

THE LEGAL ISSUE

The legal question before us, as earlier indicated, is whether a developing municipality like Mount Laurel may validly, by a system of land use regulation, make it physically and economically impossible to provide low and moderate income housing in the municipality for the various categories of persons who need and want it and thereby, as Mount Laurel has, exclude such people from living within its confines because of the limited extent of their income and resources. Necessarily implicated are the broader questions of the right of such municipalities to limit the kinds of available housing and of any obligation to make possible a variety and choice of types of living accommodations.

We conclude that every such municipality must, by its land use regulations, presumptively make realistically possible an appropriate variety and choice of housing. More specifically, presumptively it cannot foreclose the opportunity of the classes of people mentioned for low and moderate income housing and in its regulations must affirmatively afford that opportunity, at least to the extent of the municipality's fair share of the present and prospective regional need therefor. These obligations must be met unless the particular municipality can sustain the heavy burden of demonstrating peculiar circumstances which dictate that it should not be required so to do.

We reach this conclusion under state law and so do not find it necessary to consider federal constitutional grounds urged by plaintiffs. We begin with some fundamental principles as applied to the scene before us.

Land use regulation is encompassed within the state's police power. Our constitutions have expressly so provided since an amendment in 1927. That amendment, now Art. IV, sec. VI, par. 2 of the 1947 Constitution, authorized legislative delegation of the power to municipalities (other than counties), but reserved the legislative right to repeal or alter the delegation (which we take it means repeal or alteration in whole or in part). The legislative delegation of the zoning power followed in 1928, by adoption of the standard zoning enabling act. * * *

It is elementary theory that all police power enactments, no matter at what level of government, must conform to the basic state constitutional requirements of substantive due process and equal protection of the laws. These are inherent in Art. I, par. 1 of our Constitution,[16] the requirements of which may be more demanding than those of the federal Constitution. [   ] It is required that, affirmatively, a zoning regulation, like any police power enactment, must promote public health, safety, morals or the general welfare. (The last term seems broad enough to encompass the others.) Conversely, a zoning enactment which is contrary to the general welfare is invalid. [   ] Indeed these considerations are specifically set forth in the zoning enabling act as among the various purposes of zoning for which regulations must be designed. [   ] Their inclusion therein really adds little; the same requirement would exist even if they were omitted. If a zoning regulation violates the enabling act in this respect, it is also theoretically invalid under the state constitution. We say "theoretically" because, as a matter of policy, we do not treat the validity of most land use ordinance provisions as involving matters of constitutional dimension; that classification is confined to major questions of fundamental import. [   ] We consider the basic importance of housing and local regulations restricting its availability to substantial segments of the population to fall within the latter category.

* * *

This brings us to the relation of housing to the concept of general welfare * * * and the result in terms of land use regulation which that relationship mandates. There cannot be the slightest doubt that shelter, along with food, are the most basic-human needs. * * *

It is plain beyond dispute that proper provision for adequate housing of all categories of people is certainly an absolute essential in promotion of the general welfare required in all local land use regulation. Further the universal and constant need for such housing is so important and of such broad public interest that the general welfare which developing municipalities like Mount Laurel must consider extends beyond their boundaries and cannot be parochially confined to the claimed good of the particular municipality. It has to follow that, broadly speaking, the presumptive obligation arises for each such municipality affirmatively to

---

16. The paragraph reads:

All persons are by nature free and independent, and have certain natural and unalienable rights, among which are those of enjoying and defending life and liberty, of acquiring, possessing, and protecting property, and of pursuing and obtaining safety and happiness.

plan and provide, by its land use regulations, the reasonable opportunity for an appropriate variety and choice of housing, including, of course, low and moderate cost housing, to meet the needs, desires and resources of all categories of people who may desire to live within its boundaries. Negatively, it may not adopt regulations or policies which thwart or preclude that opportunity.

It is also entirely clear, as we pointed out earlier, that most developing municipalities, including Mount Laurel, have not met their affirmative or negative obligations, primarily for local fiscal reasons. * * *

In sum, we are satisfied beyond any doubt that, by reason of the basic importance of appropriate housing and the long-standing pressing need for it, especially in the low and moderate cost category, and of the exclusionary zoning practices of so many municipalities, * * * judicial attitudes must be altered from that espoused in that and other cases cited earlier, to require, as we have just said, a broader view of the general welfare and the presumptive obligation on the part of developing municipalities at least to afford the opportunity by land use regulations for appropriate housing for all.

We have spoken of this obligation of such municipalities as "presumptive." The term has two aspects, procedural and substantive. Procedurally, we think the basic importance of appropriate housing for all dictates that, when it is shown that a developing municipality in its land use regulations has not made realistically possible a variety and choice of housing, including adequate provision to afford the opportunity for low and moderate income housing or has expressly prescribed requirements or restrictions which preclude or substantially hinder it, a facial showing of violation of substantive due process or equal protection under the state constitution has been made out and the burden, and it is a heavy one, shifts to the municipality to establish a valid basis for its action or non-action. [ ] The substantive aspect of "presumptive" relates to the specifics, on the one hand, of what municipal land use regulation provisions, or the absence thereof, will evidence invalidity and shift the burden of proof and, on the other hand, of what bases and considerations will carry the municipality's burden and sustain what it has done or failed to do. Both kinds of specifics may well vary between municipalities according to peculiar circumstances.

* * *

III

The Remedy

As outlined at the outset of this opinion, the trial court invalidated the zoning ordinance in toto and ordered the township to make certain studies and investigations and to present to the court a plan of affirmative public action designed "to enable and encourage the satisfaction of the indicated needs" for township related low and moderate income housing. Jurisdiction was retained for judicial consideration and approval of such a plan and for the entry of a final order requiring its implementation.

We are of the view that the trial court's judgment should be modified in certain respects. We see no reason why the entire zoning ordinance should be nullified. Therefore we declare it to be invalid only to the extent and in the particulars set forth in this opinion. The township is granted 90 days from the date hereof, or such additional time as the trial court may find it reasonable and necessary to allow, to adopt amendments to correct the deficiencies herein specified. It is the local function and responsibility, in the first instance at least, rather than the court's, to decide on the details of the same within the guidelines we have laid down. If plaintiffs desire to attack such amendments, they may do so by supplemental complaint filed in this cause within 30 days of the final adoption of the amendments.

We are not at all sure what the trial judge had in mind as ultimate action with reference to the approval of a plan for affirmative public action concerning the satisfaction of indicated housing needs and the entry of a final order requiring implementation thereof. Courts do not build housing nor do municipalities. That function is performed by private builders, various kinds of associations, or, for public housing, by special agencies created for that purpose at various levels of government. The municipal function is initially to provide the opportunity through appropriate land use regulations and we have spelled out what Mount Laurel must do in that regard. It is not appropriate at this time, particularly in view of the advanced view of zoning law as applied to housing laid down by this opinion, to deal with the matter of the further extent of judicial power in the field or to exercise any such power. * * *

The judgment of the Law Division is modified as set forth herein. No costs.

SOUTHERN BURLINGTON COUNTY N.A.A.C.P. v. TOWNSHIP OF MOUNT LAUREL

Supreme Court of New Jersey, 1983.
92 N.J. 158, 456 A.2d 390.

Wilentz, C.J.

This is the return, eight years later, of *Southern Burlington County N.A.A.C.P. v. Township of Mount Laurel*, 67 *N.J.* 151, 336 A.2d 713 (1975) (*Mount Laurel I*). We set forth in that case, for the first time, the doctrine requiring that municipalities' land use regulations provide a realistic opportunity for low and moderate income housing. The doctrine has become famous. The *Mount Laurel* case itself threatens to become infamous. After all this time, ten years after the trial court's initial order invalidating its zoning ordinance, Mount Laurel remains afflicted with a blatantly exclusionary ordinance. Papered over with studies, rationalized by hired experts, the ordinance at its core is true to nothing but Mount Laurel's determination to exclude the poor. Mount Laurel is not alone;

we believe that there is widespread non-compliance with the constitutional mandate of our original opinion in this case.

To the best of our ability, we shall not allow it to continue. This Court is more firmly committed to the original *Mount Laurel* doctrine than ever, and we are determined, within appropriate judicial bounds, to make it work. The obligation is to provide a realistic opportunity for housing, not litigation. We have learned from experience, however, that unless a strong judicial hand is used, *Mount Laurel* will not result in housing, but in paper, process, witnesses, trials and appeals. We intend by this decision to strengthen it, clarify it, and make it easier for public officials, including judges, to apply it. * * *

A brief statement of the cases may be helpful at this point. *Mount Laurel II* results from the remand by this Court of the original *Mount Laurel* case. The municipality rezoned, purportedly pursuant to our instructions, a plenary trial was held, and the trial court found that the rezoning constituted a bona fide attempt by Mount Laurel to provide a realistic opportunity for the construction of its fair share of the regional lower income housing need. Reading our cases at that time (1978) as requiring no more, the trial court dismissed the complaint of the N.A.A.C.P. and other plaintiffs but granted relief in the form of a builder's remedy, to a developer-intervenor who had attacked the total prohibition against mobile homes. Plaintiffs' appeal of the trial court's ruling sustaining the ordinance in all other respects was directly certified by this Court, as ultimately was defendant's appeal from the grant of a builder's remedy allowing construction of mobile homes. We reverse and remand to determine Mount Laurel's fair share of the regional need and for further proceedings to revise its ordinance; we affirm the grant of the builder's remedy.

* * *

[The Court reviewed the history of, and constitutional basis for, the *Mount Laurel* doctrine and summarized its rulings: every municipality has an obligation to provide housing opportunities for at least some of its residents as well as nonresidents desiring to move in; the fair share obligation extends to all municipalities in state-designated "growth areas," not just "developing" municipalities; results, not merely good faith attempts, are required; affirmative action may be necessary; providing least cost housing is acceptable only if all other alternatives have been unsuccessful; builder's remedies will be afforded on a case-by-case basis, and future Mount Laurel litigation will be assigned only to a panel of judges selected by the Court.—Eds.]

II.

RESOLUTION OF THE ISSUES

A. *Defining the Mount Laurel Obligation*

* * *

The Constitution of the State of New Jersey does not require bad planning. * * * There is nothing in our Constitution that says that we cannot satisfy our constitutional obligation to provide lower income housing and, at the same time, plan the future of the state intelligently.

Sound planning requires that municipalities containing "growth areas" have a *Mount Laurel* obligation and that, together, all of those municipalities affirmatively provide a realistic opportunity for the construction of sufficient lower income housing to meet the needs of New Jersey's lower income population. * * *

* * *

As noted before, *all* municipalities' land use regulations will be required to provide a realistic opportunity for the construction of their fair share of the region's present lower income housing need generated by present dilapidated or overcrowded lower income units, including their own. Municipalities located in "growth areas" may, of course, have an obligation to meet the present need of the region that goes far beyond that generated in the municipality itself; there may be some municipalities, however, in growth areas where the portion of the region's present need generated by that municipality far exceeds the municipality's fair share. The portion of the region's present need that must be addressed by municipalities in growth areas will depend, then, on conventional fair share analysis, some municipality's fair share being more than the present need generated within the municipality and in some cases less. In non-growth areas, however (limited growth, conservation, and agricultural), no municipality will have to provide for more than the present need generated within the municipality, for to require more than that would be to induce growth in that municipality in conflict with the SDGP.

* * *

C. *Calculating Fair Share*

The most troublesome issue in *Mount Laurel* litigation is the determination of fair share. It takes the most time, produces the greatest variety of opinions, and engenders doubt as to the meaning and wisdom of *Mount Laurel*. Determination of fair share has required resolution of three separate issues: identifying the relevant region, determining its present and prospective housing needs, and allocating those needs to the municipality or municipalities involved. Each of these issues produces a morass of facts, statistics, projections, theories and opinions sufficient to discourage even the staunchest supporters of *Mount Laurel*. The problem is capable of monopolizing counsel's time for years, overwhelming trial courts and inundating reviewing courts with a record on review of superhuman dimensions.

We have had enough experience with *Mount Laurel* litigation to warrant procedural modifications designed, over a period of time, to simplify these determinations. The procedural modification provided in this opinion (confining all *Mount Laurel* litigation to a limited number of judges) is well within conventional judicial techniques.

* * *

As for fair share, however, we offer some suggestions. Formulas that accord substantial weight to employment opportunities in the municipality, especially new employment accompanied by substantial ratables, shall be favored; formulas that have the effect of tying prospective lower income housing needs to the present proportion of lower income residents to the total population of a municipality shall be disfavored; formulas that have the effect of unreasonably diminishing the share because of a municipality's successful exclusion of lower income housing in the past shall be disfavored.

In determining fair share, the court should decide the proportion between low and moderate income housing unless there are substantial reasons not to do so. The provisions and devices needed to produce moderate income housing may fall short of those needed for lower. Since there are two fairly distinct lower income housing needs, an effort must be made to meet both.

* * *

D. Meeting the Mount Laurel Obligation

1. Removing Excessive Restrictions and Exactions

In order to meet their Mount Laurel obligations, municipalities, at the very least, must remove all municipally created barriers to the construction of their fair share of lower income housing. Thus, to the extent necessary to meet their prospective fair share and provide for their indigenous poor (and, in some cases, a portion of the region's poor), municipalities must remove zoning and subdivision restrictions and exactions that are not necessary to protect health and safety.

* * *

2. Using Affirmative Measures

Despite the emphasis in *Mount Laurel I* on the *affirmative* nature of the fair share obligation, [ ] the obligation has been sometimes construed * * * as requiring in effect no more than a theoretical, rather than realistic, opportunity. As noted later, the alleged realistic opportunity for lower income housing in *Mount Laurel II* is provided through three zones owned entirely by three individuals. There is absolutely no assurance that there is anything realistic in this "opportunity": the individuals may, for many different reasons, simply not desire to build lower income housing. They may not want to build any housing at all, they may want to use the land for industry, for business, or just leave it vacant. It was never intended in *Mount Laurel I* that this awesome constitutional obligation, designed to give the poor a fair chance for housing, be satisfied by meaningless amendments to zoning or other ordinances. "Affirmative," in the *Mount Laurel* rule, suggests that the *municipality* is going to do something, and "realistic opportunity" suggests that what it is going to do will make it *realistically* possible for lower income housing to be built. Satisfaction of the *Mount Laurel* doctrine cannot depend on the inclination of developers to help the poor. It has to depend on affirmative inducements to make the opportunity real.

* * *

There are two basic types of affirmative measures that a municipality can use to make the opportunity for lower income housing realistic: (1) encouraging or requiring the use of available state or federal housing subsidies, and (2) providing incentives for or requiring private developers to set aside a portion of their developments for lower income housing. Which, if either, of these devices will be necessary in any particular municipality to assure compliance with the constitutional mandate will be initially up to the municipality itself. Where necessary, the trial court overseeing compliance may require their use. We note again that least-cost housing will not ordinarily satisfy a municipality's fair share obligation to provide low and moderate income housing unless and until it has attempted the inclusionary devices outlined below or otherwise has proven the futility of the attempt.

* * *

E.   Judicial Remedies

If a trial court determines that a municipality has not met its *Mount Laurel* obligation, it shall order the municipality to revise its zoning ordinance within a set time period to comply with the constitutional mandate; if the municipality fails adequately to revise its ordinance within that time, the court shall implement the remedies for noncompliance outlined below; and if plaintiff is a developer, the court shall determine whether a builder's remedy should be granted.

1.   Builder's Remedy

Builder's remedies have been one of many controversial aspects of the *Mount Laurel* doctrine. Plaintiffs, particularly plaintiff-developers, maintain that these remedies are (i) essential to maintain a significant level of *Mount Laurel* litigation, and the only effective method to date of enforcing compliance; (ii) required by principles of fairness to compensate developers who have invested substantial time and resources in pursuing such litigation; and (iii) the most likely means of ensuring that lower income housing is actually built. Defendant municipalities contend that even if a plaintiff-developer obtains a judgment that a particular municipality has not complied with *Mount Laurel*, that municipality, and not the developer, should be allowed to determine how and where its fair share obligation will be met.

In [Oakwood at Madison, Inc. v. Township of] *Madison*, this Court, while granting a builder's remedy to the plaintiff appeared to discourage such remedies in the future by stating that "such relief will ordinarily be rare." 72 *N.J.* at 551–52 n. 50, 371 *A.2d* 1192. Experience since *Madison*, however, has demonstrated to us that builder's remedies must be made more readily available to achieve compliance with *Mount Laurel*. We hold that where a developer succeeds in *Mount Laurel* litigation and proposes a project providing a substantial amount of lower income housing, a builder's remedy should be granted unless the municipality establishes that because of environmental or other substantial planning concerns, the plaintiff's proposed project is clearly contrary to sound land use planning. We emphasize that the builder's remedy should not be denied solely because the municipality prefers some other location for lower income housing, even if it is in fact a better site. Nor is it essential that considerable funds be invested or that the litigation be intensive.

Other problems concerning builder's remedies require discussion. Care must be taken to make certain that *Mount Laurel* is not used as an unintended bargaining chip in a builder's negotiations with the municipality, and that the courts not be used as the enforcer for the builder's threat to bring *Mount Laurel* litigation if municipal approvals for projects containing no lower income housing are not forthcoming. Proof of such threats shall be sufficient to defeat *Mount Laurel* litigation by that developer.

* * *

Notes and Questions

1. The *Mount Laurel* litigation became famous as the most vigorous judicial response to the phenomenon of "fiscal zoning"—zoning to attract activities such as commercial and light industrial uses that would increase the tax base, and to keep out people who would drain the tax base through increased pressure on public schools, local welfare agencies, public transit systems and the like. This practice also has been called "exclusionary zoning" because its effect is to increase the cost of housing, thereby reducing the ability of low-and moderate income persons to live in the community. See generally, C. Haar, Suburbs Under Siege: Race, Space, and Audacious Judges (1996); D. Kirp et al., Our Town: Race, Housing and the Soul of Suburbia (1995) (social history of *Mt. Laurel* cases); K. Jackson, Crabgrass Frontier: The Surbanization of the United States (1985); V. Been, Residential Segregation: Vouchers and Local Government Monopolists, 23 Yale L. & Pol'y Rev. 33 (2005) (reviewing housing chapter in P. Schuck, Diversity in America: Keeping Government at a Safe Distance 203–60 (2003); B. Katz and M. Turner, Rethinking Local Affordable Housing Strategies: Lessons from 70 years of Policy and Practice (2003) (Brookings Institution discussion paper); Williams and Norman, Exclusionary Land Use Controls: The Case of North–Eastern New Jersey, 22 Syracuse L.Rev. 475 (1971); Sager, Tight Little Islands: Exclusionary Zoning, Equal Protection and the Indigent, 21 Stanford L.Rev. 767 (1969).

An amicus curiae brief of the American Planning Association argued that:

"Exclusionary zoning is particularly pernicious because lower income individuals are unable to find affordable housing near suburban places of work, necessitating lengthy commuting trips. As these areas typically have limited, if any, mass transit, the journey to work must be by automobile, creating additional economic hardship for lower income individuals.''

Brief of American Planning Association, Wayne Britton v. Town of Chester, 134 N.H. 434, 595 A.2d 492 (1991), citing R. Babcock and F. Bosselman, Exclusionary Zoning: Land Use Regulation and Housing in the 1970s, 114–115 (1973).

2. Does the jurisprudence of *Mount Laurel* strike you as unusual, with its use of the state constitution and the "general welfare" principle? In cases we have studied, "general welfare" was used as a basis to keep out activities and people deemed harmful or undesirable. Here, is "general welfare" being used to allow people in? How can this be accomplished? Is general welfare being read not only as a limit on what government can do when it wants to act, but also as a substantive requirement for what it must do when it acts? When government decides to regulate the development of residential property, must it do so in a way that everyone in the community shares in the good in the same way—everyone in the community has an opportunity to obtain affordable and decent housing? Does this approach not assume a definition of what the community is? Does the court define the community? Should it, or should that be left to the legislative process? In the court's view, is the group to be considered limited to persons who own property in the jurisdiction, or does the group include all those who might choose to live there if regulatory barriers to affordable housing were removed?

3. Is it necessary to be concerned about standing to sue under the *Mount Laurel* court's approach? Persons challenging zoning decisions must be able to show that they have been affected by the zoning decision in some special way different from the general impact all zoning decisions may have on residents and taxpayers. This usually has been held to mean that the challenger must own property and be able to show that the zoning decision at issue harmed that property interest. One of the reasons that *Mount Laurel* was litigated in state courts is that federal courts have taken a very narrow view of the standing required to raise exclusionary zoning issues under the federal Constitution, refusing to consider complaints of persons who did not live or own property in the community whose regulations were being challenged. Warth v. Seldin, 422 U.S. 490, 95 S.Ct. 2197, 45 L.Ed.2d 343 (1975). See Housing for All Under Law 98–104 (R. Fishman ed. 1977) (Report of the American Bar Ass'n Advisory Comm'n on Housing and Urban Growth). See also D. Mandelker, Land Use Law § 7.02 (5th Ed.2003).

Some state courts have taken a more relaxed view of standing issues in exclusionary zoning cases, primarily because of the fact that zoning is a delegation of the state's police power to be used to promote the general welfare of the citizens of the state. See, e.g., Britton v. Town of Chester, 134 N.H. 434, 595 A.2d 492 (1991) (low income residents who did not own property, along with nonprofit housing corporation, resident taxpayers and person who claimed he had to leave town to find housing had standing to challenge zoning as exclusionary), quoting the Supreme Court's recognition in *Euclid* of "the possibility of cases where the general public interest would so far outweigh the interest of the municipality that the municipality would not be allowed to stand in the way." 272 U.S. at 390. See also Home Builders

League v. Township of Berlin, 81 N.J. 127, 405 A.2d 381 (1979) ("inherently fluid" standing rules in cases involving a "substantial public interest," along with state statute granting standing in zoning cases to nonresidents, held sufficient to grant standing to builders trade associations, nonprofit housing organizations and the "public" through the New Jersey Public Advocate). See generally D. Mandelker, Land Use Law § 806 (5th Ed.2003).

4.   Why does the *Mount Laurel* court require a local government to look beyond its borders when implementing land use regulations? Is it because the police power is a state power, with the local authority acting only as a delegate of that power and being restricted in the same manner as is the state? Thus when a regulation has a substantial external effect, the welfare of the state's citizens beyond the borders of the particular municipality must be recognized and served? Are there any limits to this view? Must Mount Laurel, New Jersey consider the interests of residents of Philadelphia? Kansas City, Kansas the interests of Kansas City, Missouri? The governmental doctrine of home rule and the moral principal of subsidiary assume that the most effective use of governmental authority is at the level closest to the people directly affected. Is *Mount Laurel* consistent or inconsistent with this assumption? Planners and economists often talk of achieving "economies of scale" that come from operating on a larger rather than a smaller scale. Does *Mount Laurel* push in this direction?

5.   What happens under the *Mount Laurel* doctrine when concerns about protecting the tax base or the environment clash with affordable housing needs? Does *Mount Laurel* favor affordable housing over the environment? Over lower tax rates? Or does it hold merely that environmental and tax-base arguments cannot be used to disguise efforts to exclude lower-income persons?

6.   Suppose a municipality adopts an affordable housing plan in which it permits higher density, lower cost housing in certain areas of the community. May it adopt higher floor area and lot size requirements in the remaining residential areas, thereby increasing the cost of housing and keeping the rich and the poor separate? Does the "general welfare" require different economic classes to live together, as is the effect of federal law on segregation according to race, religion, sex, age, and family status?

In Builders Service Corp. Inc. v. Planning & Zoning Com'n., 208 Conn. 267, 545 A.2d 530 (1988), the Supreme Court of Connecticut held that local governments had authority to impose minimum floor-area requirements for dwelling units, but invalidated a 1300–square foot requirement that was higher than floor-area requirements in other residential districts in the municipality. The effect of the higher floor-area requirement was to increase the construction cost of a proposed three-bedroom ranch-style modular home with 1026 square feet of living space from $59,000 to $70,000 (over 18 percent). Experts agreed that minimum floor-area requirements that are not linked to the number of occupants can not be justified as promoting public health. Occupancy-based floor-area requirements assume each person needs about 150 square feet, so a three-bedroom house serving a family of six could be as small as 900 square feet before health questions would be raised. The municipality raised two main points in defense of the 1300–square foot requirement: 1) it has the beneficial effect of conserving property values; and

2) an affordable housing plan was in effect in other parts of the municipality. In rejecting the arguments, the Court said:

> We recognize that an essential purpose of zoning regulation is to stabilize property uses. Nevertheless, "[t]he justification for zoning. * * * in any municipality is that it serves to promote the public health, safety, welfare and prosperity of the community." Devaney v. Board of Zoning Appeals, 132 Conn. 537, 539, 45 A.2d 828, 829 (1946). Conserving the value of buildings is only one facet of this archetypical justification for zoning * * *.
>
> * * * The trial court has already, in effect, conceded that this minimum floor area regulation without reference to occupancy cannot pass rational relation muster on the ground of the promotion of public health, but suggests that what is bigger and costlier is compatible under the circumstances with conserving the value of buildings in this district. That, in turn, implicitly suggests two justifications for this regulation, both of which are questionable. First, most expensive single-family houses are more desirable and, second, more such houses generate more taxes from persons better able to pay more taxes with perhaps less demand upon municipal services.

> * * *

> Under all the circumstances, the trial court's determination in this case that the challenged "varying minima" regulation without reference to occupancy promotes a legitimate purpose of zoning in that it conserves the value of buildings cannot stand. That determination cannot be supported even giving the commission that deference to which it is due on such matters, which includes our obligation not to substitute our judgment for that of the local zoning authority. The absence of satisfying a proper objective of zoning raises serious concerns that the only possible justification for such varying minima is an intent to discriminate against those with moderate and lower incomes in that district. This form of denial of access to certain residential districts is unequivocally not a purpose authorized by § 8–2....545 A.2d at 540, 543, 546.

7. While the *Mount Laurel* cases have generated an enormous amount of discussion and have influenced courts and legislatures in a number of other states, particularly with respect to consideration of the extraterritorial effect of zoning decisions, the fact that the decisions were based on the New Jersey Constitution has limited the transferability of the doctrine to other states. See, e.g. Berenson v. Town of New Castle, 38 N.Y.2d 102, 378 N.Y.S.2d 672, 341 N.E.2d 236 (1975); Township of Willistown v. Chesterdale Farms, 462 Pa. 445, 341 A.2d 466 (1975); Associated Home Builders v. City of Livermore, 18 Cal.3d 582, 135 Cal.Rptr. 41, 557 P.2d 473 (1976). Developments in New York and Pennsylvania, as well as other states are discussed in W. Stoebuck & D. Whitman, The Law of Property Law 630–637 (3d Ed., 2000). See also D. Mandelker, Land Use Law §§ 7.14–7.25 (5th Ed.2003).

In a case with potential national impact, the Supreme Court of New Hampshire applied the *Mount Laurel* principles to the state's zoning enabling act and concluded that the zoning ordinance of a small suburban "bedroom" municipality which effectively limited residential development to single family homes on two-acre lots or duplexes on three acre lots exceeded the municipality's authority under the zoning enabling statute. Britton v. Town of Chester, 134 N.H. 434, 595 A.2d 492 (1991). The statute, based on the Standard State Zoning Enabling Act discussed in *Euclid* from which virtually all state enabling acts initially were drawn, authorized municipalities to zone property "to promote the health, safety, and general welfare of the community." The court's key decision was its conclusion that the term "community" was not equated with the territorial boundaries of the town.

RSA 674:16 authorizes the local legislative body of any city or town to adopt or amend a zoning ordinance "[f]or the purpose of promoting the health, safety, or the general welfare of the community." (Emphasis added.) The defendant asserts that the term "community" as used in the statute refers only to the municipality itself and not to some broader region in which the municipality is situated. We disagree.

The possibility that a municipality might be obligated to consider the needs of the region outside its boundaries was addressed early on in our land use jurisprudence by the United States Supreme Court, paving the way for the term "community" to be used in the broader sense. In Village of Euclid v. Ambler Realty Co., 272 U.S. 365, 47 S.Ct. 114, 71 L.Ed. 303 (1926), the Court recognized "the possibility of cases where the general public interest would so far outweigh the interest of the municipality that the municipality would not be allowed to stand in the way." Id. at 390. When an ordinance will have an impact beyond the boundaries of the municipality, the welfare of the entire affected region must be considered in determining the ordinance's validity. * * *

Municipalities are not isolated enclaves, far removed from the concerns of the area in which they are situated. As subdivisions of the State, they do not exist solely to serve their own residents, and their regulations should promote the general welfare, both within and without their boundaries. Therefore, we interpret the general welfare provision of the zoning enabling statute [ ] to include the welfare of the "community", as defined in this case, in which a municipality is located and of which it forms a part. Britton v. Town of Chester, 134 N.H. 434, 595 A.2d 492, 495–496 (N.H.1991).

Finding the exclusionary aspects of the town's land use regulations to be incompatible with the housing needs of low and moderate income persons in the "community" affected by the town's decisions, the court invalidated the town's zoning ordinance "in that it flies in the face of the general welfare provision" of the statute and "is, therefore, at odds with the statute upon which it is grounded." 595 A.2d at 496. The Court did not reach constitutional questions raised by the plaintiffs.

8. As noted earlier, important remedy questions are raised in exclusionary zoning cases. What should a court do if it concludes that a zoning ordinance is invalid as exclusionary? Would an award of monetary damages be sufficient? How would it be calculated? To whom would it be paid? If persons who were excluded by the zoning ordinance do not own property in the community, what have they lost for which they can receive compensation? If the court invalidates the ordinance, does that mean the municipality becomes "unzoned" and loses its ability to regulate land? If not, can the

municipality simply amend its ordinance in a minor way, say by reducing a two acre lot minimum to a one acre minimum and still effectively keep out affordable housing?

Courts generally do not order specific changes in a zoning ordinance because of concerns that such action would constitute judicial legislation in violation of constitutional separation of powers principles. See, e.g., Britton v. Town of Chester, 134 N.H. 434, 595 A.2d 492 (1991) "[I]t is not * * * within the power of this court to act as a super zoning board"). However, as discussed in *Mount Laurel II,* courts have been willing to grant a "builder's remedy" to enable a particular development plan to go forward so long as it complies with other valid local regulations. In Britton v. Town of Chester, 134 N.H. 434, 595 A.2d 492 (1991), the court concluded that the "builder's remedy" was "appropriate in this case, both to compensate the developer who has invested substantial time and resources in pursuing the litigation, and as the most likely means of insuring that low and moderate-income housing is actually built." In awarding the "builder's remedy," the court rejected the *Mount Laurel* approach that it characterized as requiring "the calculation of arbitrary mathematical quotes" in favor of an approach developed by the Illinois courts and adopted in Michigan, Ohio, Pennsylvania and Virginia. Under the Illinois approach, relief is awarded

> if development is found to be reasonable, i.e., providing a realistic opportunity for the construction of low and moderate-income housing and consistent with sound zoning concepts and environmental concerns. Once an existing zoning ordinance is found invalid in whole or in part, whether on constitutional grounds or, as here, on grounds of statutory construction and application, the court may provide relief in the form of a declaration that the plaintiff builder's proposed use is reasonable, and the municipality may not interfere with it. [　] The plaintiff must bear the burden of proving reasonable use by a preponderance of the evidence. [　] Once the plaintiff's burden has been met, he will be permitted to proceed with the proposed development, provided he complies with all other applicable regulations. [　]

Britton v. Town of Chester, 134 N.H. 434, 595 A.2d 492, 497–498 (1991). For additional discussion of remedies, see D. Mandelker, Land Use Law §§ 8.08–8.22 (5th Ed. 2003).

9. Despite the New Jersey Supreme Court's efforts and the extensive public discussion of the *Mount Laurel* doctrine, affordable housing remained a problem in New Jersey communities more than 25 years after the first *Mount Laurel* decision and 15 years after enactment of a state statute implementing the *Mount Laurel* doctrine, the New Jersey Fair Housing Act, L. 1985, c. 222, N.J.S.A. §§ 52:27D–301 to–329, upheld in Hills Development Company v. Bernards Township, 103 N.J. 1, 510 A.2d 621 (1986). See Fair Share Housing Center v. Township of Cherry Hill, 173 N.J. 393, 802 A.2d 512 (2002) (development fees approved by state Council on Affordable Housing may be imposed on developers as mechanism for funding affordable housing but cannot be imposed as a device to remove land permanently from consideration as a site for affordable housing).

2. Fair Housing Statutes

As we discussed in the chapter on landlord-tenant relations, federal, state, and local statutes now prohibit the denial of housing opportunities on the basis of race, sex, religion, age, family status, or disability. These statutes have been held to apply to local land-use regulations. Metropolitan Housing Development Corp. v. Village of Arlington Heights, 558 F.2d 1283, 1288 (7th Cir.1977), cert. denied, 434 U.S. 1025, 98 S.Ct. 752, 54 L.Ed.2d 772 (1978) (discriminatory effect can in some instances establish Fair Housing Act violation); Huntington Branch, NAACP v. Town of Huntington, 844 F.2d 926 (2d Cir.1988), cert. den. and appeal dism'd, 488 U.S. 15, 109 S.Ct. 276, 102 L.Ed.2d 180 (1988) (refusal to rezone to enable multi-family housing to be constructed outside of largely minority "urban renewal area" held violative of Fair Housing Act). Similar limitations on the enforceability of racially-restrictive covenants are discussed in Chapter Six supra.

As is often the case with regulatory schemes, legitimate policy objectives may clash in the implementation phase. These clashes usually are first detectable in the law office, at least when a lawyer is contacted to help plan a proposed course of action.

Consider, for example, a family that wishes to build an addition on their house to create an accessory apartment for an elderly parent. The apartment would have a separate entrance, as well as separate kitchen and bath facilities. The zoning code prohibits two-family units (duplexes) in the single-family district where the family lives. Assuming the addition will comply with all applicable building and fire codes, can the city deny a building permit to the family? Suppose the family wishes to rent it to any elderly or disabled person, whether related to them or not? See, e.g., 42 U.S.C.A. § 3607(b)(1) (Fair Housing Act does not limit the applicability of reasonable local regulations regarding maximum number of occupants permitted to occupy a dwelling).

Suppose a non-profit agency plans to acquire a house and convert it into a group home for six developmentally disabled students. The applicable zoning regulation requires special use permits for group homes, and prohibits group homes from being closer than 1000 feet from another group home. If another group home is operating on the same block, less than 1000 feet away, can the special use permit be denied? See Familystyle of St. Paul, Inc. v. City of St. Paul, 923 F.2d 91 (8th Cir.1991) (zoning ordinance requiring group homes for mentally impaired to be located at least a quarter of a mile apart upheld as reasonable accommodation of Federal goal of non-discrimination, and state goal of deinstitutionalization).

Suppose the city's zoning ordinance, through its definition of "family," allows only four unrelated persons to occupy single family houses, but places no such limitations on related persons. If the non-profit agency finds a house on another block that is more than 1000 feet from other group homes, can a permit still be denied, this time under the Fair Housing Act's exemptions for reasonable occupancy limitations? See City of Edmonds v. Oxford House, Inc., 514 U.S. 725, 735, 115 S.Ct. 1776, 1782, 131 L.Ed.2d 801 (1995) ("rules designed to preserve the family character of a neighborhood, fastening on the composition of households rather than on the total number of occupants living quarters can contain" are not protected by the reasonable occupancy limitation exemption); Fair Housing Advocates Association, Inc. v. City of Richmond Heights, Ohio, 209 F.3d 626 (6th Cir. 2000) (minimum habitable floor area requirements per occupant upheld as reasonable under *Edmonds* standard).

The statutory requirements that local governments make "reasonable" accommodations in local land use rules when "necessary" to give handicapped persons "equal opportunity to use and enjoy a dwelling" (42 U.S.C.A. § 3604 (f)(3)(B)) has been the subject of controversy. See e.g., Howard v. City of Beavercreek, 276 F.3d 802, 806 (6th Cir. 2002) (upholding denial of a variance for construction of a six-foot privacy fence by the owner of a single family home who suffered from post traumatic stress disorder and a heart condition). Does a city fail to make reasonable accommodations when it denies a parking requirement variance that prevents a licensed group home from expanding to fifteen residents from its permitted eight residents? Courts have approached the answer to such a question in two ways. The Second, Third, Seventh, Eighth, Ninth and Tenth Circuits apply a burden-shifting approach, "requir[ing] a plaintiff to make an initial showing that an accommodation is reasonable, but then plac[ing] the burden on the defendant [city] to show that the accommodation is unreasonable." Oconomowoc Residential Programs, Inc. v. City of Milwaukee, 300 F.3d 775, 783–784 (7th Cir. 2002) (citing cases). The Fourth and Fifth Circuits place the full burden of proof concerning the reasonable accommodation issue on plaintiffs. Bryant Woods Inn, Inc. v. Howard County, Md., 124 F.3d 597 (4th Cir.1997) (petitioner failed to prove by preponderance of the evidence that variance request met three-part statutory test of being 1) reasonable, 2) necessary, and 3) affording equal opportunity); Elderhaven v. City of Lubbock, Texas, 98 F.3d 175, 178 (5th Cir. 1996).

F. NON ADVERSARIAL RESOLUTION OF LAND USE DISPUTES

In recent years, a number of states and local governments have experimented with the use of mediation and other alternatives to litigation for the resolution of zoning disputes. For example, the Massachusetts Mediation Services, a state agency, offers mediation services to parties appealing adverse zoning decisions concerning affordable housing development proposals to a state housing appeals committee established as part of a state statutory procedure to encourage affordable housing development. Mass. Gen. Laws ch. 40B, §§ 20–23 (Law. Co-op 1993 & 2005 Supp.) See generally Krefetz, The Impact and Evolution of the Massachusetts Comprehensive Permit and Zoning Appeals Act: Thirty Years Experience with a State Legislative Effort to Overcome Exclusionary Zoning, 22 W. New Eng. L. Rev. 381 (2001); Resnick, Mediating

Affordable Housing Disputes in Massachusetts: Optimal Intervention Points, 45 Arb. J. No. 2, 15, 20 (June 1990) (noting that about 25 percent of cases appealed to the state housing appeals committee were resolved through mediation).

P. SALSICH & T. TRYNIECKI, LAND USE REGULATION: A LEGAL ANALYSIS AND PRACTICAL APPLICATION OF LAND USE LAW, 2D ED.

266–268 (2003).

Several jurisdictions are experimenting with various "early warning" techniques to resolve zoning disputes before they escalate into major litigation over whether a particular regulatory decision has "taken" property in a constitutional sense. Examples of such techniques include the use of negotiation between landowners and landmarks preservation boards to seek agreement on appropriate "controls and incentives" to preserve property receiving landmark designation while allowing the owner a reasonable return on investment, and the use of a two-step mediation/arbitration process to resolve disputes regarding appropriate rental increases under rent control ordinances. Pennsylvania, for example, has enacted legislation permitting mediation as a "wholly voluntary" supplement to zoning appeal procedures.

The New Jersey Fair Housing Act, enacted in response to the *Mount Laurel* cases, establishes a mediation process for the resolution of disputes regarding certain decisions of the Council on Affordable Housing, a state agency established to determine housing regions, estimate housing need, and establish criteria for determining municipal fair share requirements under the *Mount Laurel* principles. The council is required to engage in mediation in the following situations:

(1) when timely objections are filed to a municipality's proposed substantive certification that its fair share plan and housing element meet the requirements of the Act; or

(2) whenever exclusionary zoning litigation has been instituted against a municipality that has filed a fair share plan and housing element, or has filed a timely resolution of intent to participate in the fair share determination process. NJ Stat Ann § 52:27D–315 (West 1991).

In the latter case, the statute treats the mediation process as an administrative remedy that must be exhausted before a trial on the complaint may be obtained. If objections cannot be resolved through the mediation process, the case is referred to an administrative law judge, who hears it in an expedited manner as a contested matter. The administrative law judge makes an initial decision and forwards that initial decision to the council, which make the final administrative decision on the matter. If the review and mediation process is not completed within six months of receipt of a request for mediation from a party who has instituted litigation, the party may be relieved of the obligation to exhaust administrative remedies upon motion to a court of competent jurisdiction.

The Supreme Court of New Jersey upheld the constitutionality of the Act in *Hills Development Co. v. Bernards Township,* 103 N.J. 1, 510 A.2d 621 (1986) (*Mount Laurel III*). With respect to the use of mediation prior to litigation when cities have filed fair share plans, the Court made the following observation:

> In any lawsuit attacking a municipality's ordinances that have received substantive certification as not in compliance with the Mount Laurel constitutional obligation, the plaintiff will be required to prove such noncompliance by clear and convincing evidence, and the Council shall be made a party to any such lawsuit. § 17a. The difficulties facing any plaintiff attempting to meet such a burden of proof are best understood by noting the variety of methodologies that can be used legitimately to determine regional need and fair share as well as the many different ways in which a realistic opportunity to achieve that fair share may be provided. If the Council conscientiously performs its duties, including determining regional need and evaluating whether the proposed adjustments and ordinances provide the requisite fair share opportunity, a successful Mount Laurel lawsuit should be a rarity. There is therefore a broad range of municipal action that will withstand challenge, given this burden of proof. 510 A.2d 621, 639 (1986).

Mediation as an approach to resolution of zoning disputes has been suggested as part of a governmental "accommodation power" which can serve as a "middle ground" between use of eminent domain (taking with compensation) and police power regulation (no compensation). The accommodation power would be triggered whenever governmental control denied a landowner "reasonable beneficial use" or "adequate return," giving rise to options such as a variance, payment for the difference in value between the controlled value and the reasonable beneficial use value, or payment in non-dollar values such as transfer of development rights. Mediation and the accommodation power may offer "a flexibility [to some forms of land use dispute] which can ease the conflict between the public and the private owner." Proponents of accommodation argue that it has potential in cases involving particular buildings, such as landmarks preservation, but doubt its ability to achieve much in disputes over environmental protection or resource preservation. They stress that the essential balancing process of "public benefit versus private detriment" cannot be reduced to "metric measure," but argue that the public can expect that "the process be open, that it be fair, that whenever possible it seek to accommodate." Berger, *The Accommodation Power in Land Use: A Reply to Professor Costonis,* 76 Colum.L.Rev. 799, 800–01, 817, 821–23 (1976) (commenting on Costonis, *"Fair" Compensation and the Accommodation Power: Antidotes for the Takings Impasse in Land Use Controversies,* 75 Colum.L.Rev. 1021 (1975)).

* * *

PROBLEM

Northfield Partnership announced plans to develop a 15–acre tract near the intersection of two thoroughfares in a rapidly growing suburban community into a 200–unit apartment complex for moderate and middle-income persons. The apartments were expected to appeal to young married couples with small children, "empty nesters" and "on the go" persons and couples between the ages of 50 and 65. Rents were to be in the $450—$600/month range, which require incomes of about $15–20,000. Approximately fifteen percent of the units, scattered throughout the development, would be leased to Supportive Housing Partnership (SHP), a consortium of local churches engaged in providing housing and social services to families facing the loss of welfare benefits under federal welfare reform legislation. SHP plans to sublease these units to families who qualify for federal housing assistance. The average income of families that SHP has helped in the past is between $7,000–10,000.

Northfield filed an application to rezone the acreage to multi-family use. A group of homeowners who live adjacent to the site in $150,000–200,000 homes have filed petitions opposing the rezoning. The homeowners are concerned about the size of the development, its impact on badly overcrowded streets in the area, the obvious difference in economic status between the homeowners and the expected apartment residents, the project plans which called for rows of "boxy" townhouses encircling a common area, and the lack of effective buffers between the existing houses and the proposed development.

The controversy has begun to heat up in the press. A resident who has not signed the petition but who is concerned about the proposal has consulted you for advice "before the controversy gets out of hand." What advice can you give her?

Is the following selection helpful?

T. SHAFFER & R. COCHRAN, LAWYERS, CLIENTS, AND MORAL RESPONSIBILITY
113–134 (West 1994).

A FRAMEWORK FOR MORAL DISCOURSE

Lawyers resolve many of the moral issues that arise in legal representation as a matter of habit, sometimes for good, sometimes for ill. Some lawyers will join in a motion for a continuance for the convenience of the other lawyer as a matter of habit; some will answer questions honestly and fully (without the necessity of formal interrogatories) as a matter of habit. Some lawyers have bad moral habits. (Classical ethics calls these vices.) Some will oppose any motion made by the other lawyer, irrespective of the interest of the client. Lawyers generally learn these habits, good and bad, by observing and imitating other lawyers. . . .

When we face new issues, or when something causes us to doubt our habitual reaction, we engage in moral reasoning. When lawyer and client together resolve issues in legal representation (as we believe they should), lawyer and client engage in moral discourse; they engage in moral reasoning together. Lawyers and clients reason together best when four elements are present:

> (1) *Client involvement:* Lawyer and client should be partners in resolving moral issues. The difficulty here may be getting the client involved. The client must overcome what may be a tendency to defer to the lawyer, and for that the client may need the lawyer's help.

> (2) *Moral sensitivity:* Recognition of the moral issues. During legal representation this generally consists of recognizing how others may be affected and may be harmed by each possible course of action.

> (3) *Moral judgment:* Applying moral values to problems and determining what is the right thing to do.

> (4) *Moral motivation:* Despite the existence of competing values (often lawyer or client selfishness), deciding to do what the client perceives to be the right thing.

* * *

Making clients feel comfortable (especially when talking about difficult moral issues) is largely a matter of letting them know that the lawyer cares about them as people, not just as a source of income or a bundle of rights. Following Martin Buber, lawyers should show that they view the client as a "thou" and not an "it." If clients do not sense that their lawyer cares for them, they may find it difficult to say what they really want in the representation, much less to trust the lawyer in a discussion about moral values.

* * *

We can see how a lawyer might lay the groundwork for client involvement in decision-making as we examine the first meeting between the lawyer and her client in our story:

* * *

Albert: We've all wondered what would happen to the Sheldon place. It was once a great place, but it's really run down now. It's not like any of the other houses in the neighborhood. We've all got new three-and four-bedroom homes, and it's old and run-down, and it's huge. It must have eight bedrooms. They've had it for sale over a year but I don't think there's been much interest.

Ann: Sort of a white elephant.

Albert: Yes, it has been. Then last week, we got this notice. Mrs. Sheldon's estate is trying to get the zoning on the Sheldon property changed.

Ann: You're upset. I can see that.

Albert: Yes! I sure am!

Ann: The prospect of having your neighborhood change is really troubling.

Albert: Yea. We like our neighborhood just the way it is.

* * *

Following the first interview, Ann talks to the lawyer for the Sheldon estate and arranges to have Albert come back to the office.

Ann: Good to see you again, Albert.

Albert: Thank you. What did you learn?

Ann: I called the lawyer whose name is listed on the notice, and he said that they want to sell the house to a group called the "Seventh Day Adventist Home for Men." The Home was founded in 1952 by the Seventh Day Adventists. It was created for men who have below normal intelligence and emotional development and have difficulty functioning on their own. It was originally called the Home for Subnormal Men, but the name was changed in the mid–60s. Their lawyer says that residents are limited to men who do not have any history of violent activities.

Albert: I was afraid of something like that. I don't want a bunch of weird old men right across the street from us. Can you imagine what would happen to the value of our house? It's a family neighborhood.

Ann: And having these men in the neighborhood would trouble you.

Albert: Well–yes.

* * *

Ann: One of the residents of the Home was hit and seriously injured by a car a little over a year ago. It was probably the resident's own fault for failing to keep a lookout as he crossed a street; but part of the problem is that traffic is usually quite heavy in the area.

Albert: Yes, I see.

Ann: Reardon has been asking to find a location for the men that will be more pleasant and not so dangerous. They think that the Sheldon mansion would be an ideal location for the home and the Seventh Day Adventist Church has agreed to help with the expenses that would be created by the move.

* * *

Albert: Great! Sheldon's family is getting out and destroying the neighborhood. What should we do?

Ann: Well, we have to make some decisions. I would like to describe what I think would be the best way to make those decisions. First, we can identify the alternatives that you have and the impact that each alternative will have on you and others. Then we can decide what would be the best thing to do. How does that sound to you?

* * *

One way to think about [moral sensitivity] is to notice that in legal representation, moral sensitivity generally means recognizing the *cost* the various alternatives will create for others. At the time the lawyer and client discuss alternative courses of action, they can identify the effects that each alternative is likely to have on others (as well as the effects on the client). For example:

Ann: A third possibility is that we could negotiate with the people from the Home. If we can think of limitations on the use of the property that would make the Home more acceptable to you, we might be able to get the director to agree to the limitations in exchange for our not opposing the zoning change. What options do you see, Albert?

* * *

Note that Ann does not assume-or let her client assume-that they are going to oppose the zoning change. She lists that possibility as one of the options they have. She does not attempt to steer the client toward one option by emphasizing it more than the other. She also keeps Albert from jumping too quickly to one option. Ann mentions not doing anything as an option—an option lawyers often overlook. We continue with the discussion.

* * *

Albert: I guess I don't see any other options.

Ann: Which option would you like to discuss first?

Albert: Well, I don't want a bunch of crazy people living in my neighborhood. Let's talk about stopping them.

Ann: Okay. In my experience, the Commission tries to balance the interest of all of the parties. Here, that would include the men at the Home, the Sheldon family, the neighbors-such as you and your family, and others in your community. What other people might be affected by the zoning decision?

Albert: I suppose that's right. Otherwise they would have sold it by now.

Ann: However, the use of the house as a home for men is different than the use of other homes in the neighborhood, and the Commission might hesitate to approve the zoning change if someone opposes. . . . You mention your concern about the safety of your children. The Home's lawyer told me that the Home does not take residents who have a history of violent behavior.

* * *

Ann: So you've thought about the expense. Any other disadvantages that you see to opposing the zoning change?

Albert: Not that I can see. Do you see any?

Ann: Let's see: If the Sheldon house isn't purchased by the Home for Men, what do you think will happen to it?

* * *

. . . The alternatives to fighting the zoning change are to do nothing, which might allow the change to take place, and to try and seek some kind of compromise. But it seems to me that one of the problems that we have in evaluating the alternatives is that we don't really know what these men are like and how your family or the Higgins family would react to them.

Albert: Well, that's true. I have never known a person like that.

Ann: So, it's kind off hard to determine how concerned you should be about the men in the Home when you have never met them. I would guess that they have visitors at the Home from time to time. Would you be willing to take your family to the home for a visit if I can arrange it? Maybe bring the Higginses along? it might give you some basis for determining how concerned you should be about them living in your neighborhood. . . .

Ann: How did it go?

Albert: It went well—maybe too well. A few days ago, I was sure that I wanted to keep that group out of the neighborhood. Now I'm not so sure. You've complicated my life.

Ann: Tell me what happened.

Albert: We didn't tell the kids anything about the zoning controversy. We just told them that we were going to take a basket of fruit to a home for mental difficulties. When we first got there, it was awkward, at least for me and my wife. We gave them the fruit and they thanked us. . . . Our awkwardness didn't seem to bother the kids. Pretty interesting. . . .

Albert: I'm not so concerned with any danger to the kids from the guys that are at the Home now, but I do wonder what kind of people might live there in the future. That's also what Consuelo Higgins says, and I think Jerry agrees. We wouldn't want it changed to a home for juvenile delinquents. And, I guess, I'm a little more sensitive to the plight of the men in the Home—they live in a pretty rough neighborhood.

* * *

Moral judgment can be painful in any context, but the lawyer-client relationship adds special complications. We believe lawyers should help the client make moral judgments without imposing their moral values on the client. We do not believe that lawyers should merely exercise their own moral judgment (as when the lawyer is a guru), nor do we believe that the lawyer should merely follow the client's initial impulse (as when the lawyer is a hired gun).

But if both lawyer and client are to participate in a shared moral life during legal representation, they must develop a way of talking about and making moral judgments. Lawyers can stimulate such judgment in at least two ways. First, when clients indulge in the natural tendency to see the situation solely from their own perspective (which generally will leave them feeling that they are being treated unfairly by other people or by a court). . . .

During the course of decision-making, the lawyer can introduce moral judgment as a legitimate objective. It is likely that clients will look to lawyers to structure the conversation. We believe that lawyers must develop a way of bringing moral considerations into the discussion, but without controlling the result. . . .

The lawyer might raise a concern with justice by wondering, "What would be a fair resolution of this dispute?" The lawyer might then draw the client out with further questions such as, "Would that be fair to X?" or, "I wonder what the effect of that settlement would be on Y." Such questions invite the client to see the dispute through the eyes of other people.

* * *

The lawyer can invite the client to consider an ethic of mercy by discussing the harsh outcomes that some alternatives might have on those other than the client. In an appropriate case, the lawyer might even ask whether the client's religious values help to resolve the issue that they face.

* * *

Maybe one of the sources of the dispute in our zoning case was the fact that the lawyer for the Sheldons allowed Albert to learn of the proposed zoning change from a formal notice that was served on him by a police officer. The lawyer for the Sheldons did not, as he might have, put a human face on his own clients; he hid his clients and himself from the human faces of his clients' neighbors. The problem might have been worked out if the Sheldons had talked to Albert and his neighbors about the problem they were having in selling their house.

Maybe lawyers and clients should look for settings in which the opposing parties can talk to one another. This might be risky: If the parties are angry, contact in the wrong setting can increase hostility. (We are reminded of the case in which a mother attempted to run a father over with her car when bringing the children for visitation.) But we do not claim that moral courses of action are without risk. We do claim that stories, human experience, observation, and the modern literature of mediation all suggest that the hostility that may accompany a face-to-face encounter is likely to be followed by person-to-person communication and understanding.

* * *

In our story, Ann acted as friend; she and Albert wrestled with the moral issue. (1) Ann kept Albert involved in the decision-making process (client involvement); (2) they identified the costs that his alternatives would have, not only to himself, but to others (moral sensitivity); (3) they tried to determine what would be fair and caring (moral judgment); and (4) Albert met with the men at the home and developed an empathy for them that led him to a concern with what would happen to them (moral motivation).

We ended the story with Albert wrestling with what he should do and Ann's affirmation that she was with him either way. We could include Albert's decision to seek some sort of settlement or his decision to fight the zoning change. But our story is not the story of Albert's decision; it is the story of the way that he and Ann wrestled with it. We think that what he decides is important—important for Albert, his family, his neighbors, and for the men in the Home. But we feel that as important as the decision that is ultimately made is the way that it is made. If Albert has wrestled with this decision honestly, and it appears that he has, it will be an occasion for moral growth, an opportunity for him to become a better person.

A NOTE ON FURTHER READING

The case is discussed critically in Jack L. Sammons, "Rank Strangers to Me: Shaffer and Cochran's Friendship Model of Moral Counseling in the Law Office," and Shaffer and Cochran, "Lawyers as Strangers and Friends: A Reply to Professor Sammons," 18 U. Ark. Little Rock L.J. 1, 69 (1995). For a discussion of facilitation techniques and their potential for achieving moral transformations while helping people resolve environmental disputes, see Chris Maser, Resolving Environmental Conflict (St. Lucie Press 1996).

G. DOES ZONING SERVE A USEFUL PURPOSE?

From the beginning, zoning has had its share of critics. One of the most vocal has been Professor Bernard Siegan:

"I submit that zoning is not entitled to constitutional protection. It is not necessary; it is not desirable, it is detrimental. It has no relationship to public health, safety, and welfare, except, on the whole, an adverse one. * * *" Siegan, Land Use Without Zoning 221 (1972), quoted in Wolf, The Prescience and Centrality of Euclid v. Ambler, Zoning and the American Dream 267 (C. Haar & J. Kayden eds. 1989).

The American Planning Association, believing that local zoning does serve a useful purpose but that it should be linked more directly to comprehensive state and local planning programs, has published a two volume *Legislative Guidebook* containing detailed recommendations for modernizing local land use regulations as well as state, regional and local planning activities. The *Legislative Guidebook* offers numerous alternatives that can be adopted to particular state and local needs. American Planning Association, Growing Smartsm Legislative Guidebook (S. Meck, ed., 2002).

What do you think your community would be like today without zoning? Houston, the last big-city holdout against zoning, succumbed in January, 1991 to a ground-swell of dissatisfaction with a private, market-based regulatory system and enacted an ordinance changing the name of the Houston Planning Commission to the Houston Planning and Zoning Commission, and directing the Commission to prepare a zoning plan for consideration by the City Council "to undo, or at least freeze, the effects of decades of laissez-faire building." Belkin, Now That City's Grown, They Plan, New York Times, February 10, 1991, at p. 14, col. 6.

However, in November, 1993, Houston voters rejected, for the third time since World War II, a proposed zoning ordinance. Low voter turnout (only 21 percent of registered voters) was blamed for the defeat. Houston Voters Again Reject Zoning; City Still Only Major U.S. Municipality Without Land–Use Rules, The Washington Post, November 6, 1993, at p. 71.

Relatively affluent residential areas in Houston are regulated by private land use covenants and deed restrictions of the type discussed in Chapter Six supra. In other areas, though, single-family homes, garden apartments, high-rise condominiums, office towers and manufacturing plans exist side-by-side or in relative proximity. In an interesting land use regulatory wrinkle, Houston has followed the unusual practice of publicly enforcing private restrictions. The practice was upheld as serving a proper public purpose in Young v. City of Houston, 756 S.W.2d 813, 814 (Tex.App.1988).

Most local governments with comprehensive zoning and public subdivision regulation ordinances have not been willing to spend public money to enforce private residential covenants and deed restrictions, although zoning administrators often are requested to do so. Should they? Would a system of public enforcement of privately negotiated covenants and restrictions likely be more or less efficient, and more or less susceptible to political pressure, than the separate public and private systems?

Index

References are to Pages

†